LOUISIANA SUCCESSIONS, DONATIONS, AND TRUSTS:
Cases and Materials

Kathryn Venturatos Lorio
Monica Hof Wallace

Casebook Series

Baton Rouge
CLAITOR'S PUBLISHING DIVISION
2015

ISBN NUMBER:

Paper: 1-59804-788-4
Hardcover: 1-59804-789-2

Published and for sale by:
CLAITOR'S PUBLISHING DIVISION
P.O. Box 261333, Baton Rouge, LA 70826-1333
800-274-1403 (In LA 225-344-0476)
Fax: 225-344-0480
Internet address:
e mail: claitors@claitors.com
World Wide Web: http://www.claitors.com

Dedication

To our families with love.

Acknowledgements

First Edition

I am indebted to many people who were of aid in the preparation of this casebook and I wish to extend my thanks to them.

To my teacher, mentor, and colleague Fred Swaim for collaborating with me for so many years and for offering his all-too-frank commentary and criticism. To the Alfred J. Bonomo, Sr. and Rosaria Sarah LaNasa Families for the scholarship assistance afforded to my research assistants through their generous contribution to Loyola Law School.

To my outstanding student research assistants - Justine Cotsoradis for her meticulous and thoughtful aid in the preparation of the donations and trusts portions, and to Kelly Grieshaber Dunn and Amanda Bray for their fine work in continuing with the successions section and for aid in the final editing. To Diana Sandigo-Cabrera for her assistance in editing the text and to Jackie Williams for her secretarial aid in preparing the manuscript.

To Loyola, New Orleans School of Law for its assistance in the form of sabbatical leave and summer research grant funding. To the gracious and supportive donor who financed the Leon Sarpy Professorship and to the state of Louisiana for its partial matching of funds. To the Dean and Faculty of Loyola, New Orleans School of Law who have been supportive of my work.

To the many students who have used this casebook and to those who will do so in the future, for being the inspiration for this entire effort.

To my family - my husband, Philip and our two children, Elisabeth and Philip, and who have sacrificed time and attention so that this work could be completed, and to my mother Dita, whose understanding and advice continues to guide me.

Second Edition

In addition to those who helped me prepare the first edition of this casebook, I thank those who helped me to update it. To Professor Dian Tooley-Knoblett and Professor Monica Hof Wallace, who have adopted this casebook and inspired improvements for this new edition.

To the Alfred J. Bonomo, Sr. and Rosaria Sarah LaNasa Families for their scholarship assistance afforded to my research assistant through their generous contribution to Loyola College of Law.

To my student research assistants – Molly Stanga for the collection of new cases and materials, Tyler Rench for the aid in editing the manuscript, and Nicole Stillwell for her many hours of research, editing, and final preparation of the draft of the manuscript.

To Dean Brian Bromberger who was encouraging of my work and who approved the necessary support to complete it. To Dawn Harvey for her professional, conscientious and dedicated assistance in preparation of the final manuscript.

To my students who are the reason for doing this.

To my family for making it all worth doing.

Third Edition
(with Monica Hof Wallace)

To Professor Monica Hof Wallace – A wonderful colleague in whose capable hands, the future teaching of Louisiana Successions and Donations will flourish. (Kathryn Venturatos Lorio) To Professor Kathryn Venturatos Lorio – it has been an absolute pleasure working on this project with my teacher, mentor, and friend. (Monica Hof Wallace) To the Alfred J. Bonomo, Sr. and Rosaria Sarah LaNasa Families for their scholarship assistance afforded to our research assistants through their generous contribution to Loyola College of Law.

To our outstanding research assistants, Kristen Frick and Meagan Impastato for their suggestions, collections of new cases, drafting of new hypotheticals, and editing the manuscript. You are both gems!

To all of the students we have taught and those who we will teach – you challenge us, give us great joy, and make it all worthwhile.

To our wonderful families who provide us with the love and support to make projects like this possible. For those not yet mentioned, Monica's husband Todd and her two kids, Jack and Grace and for Kathy's new additions – her first grandchild, Carter and soon-to-be arriving, Caitlyn.

Preface

This casebook has been prepared to aid students in learning the fascinating subject of successions, donations and trusts in Louisiana. Laced with legal history of the state and with its unique politics, the subject is intriguing, as well as essential to one about to embark on the practice of law in Louisiana.

The text has been organized to facilitate the learning process. Notes, problems, and hypotheticals accompany the caselaw to encourage practical application of the concepts.

Additional assistance has been provided in places as references to law review commentary follow case citations where applicable. Also, the authors have included references to current code numbers in cases, which make reference to substantive provisions that have been renumbered, reenacted, and/or amended in later legislative revision.

The appendix contains a set of hypothetical problems on which to practice a student's understanding of intestate succession principles and two experiences for students to learn the practice of will drafting and other estate planning documents.

TABLE OF CASES

TABLE OF CONTENTS

PART I: SUCCESSIONS

CHAPTER 1: OVERVIEW OF THE LAW OF SUCCESSION

CHAPTER 2: INTESTATE SUCCESSION
La. C.C. 880-901

CHAPTER 3: CHILDREN BORN OUT OF WEDLOCK
La. C.C. 184-198

CHAPTER 4: ABSENT PERSONS
La. C.C. 47-59

CHAPTER 5: COMMENCEMENT OF SUCCESSION
La. C.C. 944-938

CHAPTER 6: LOSS OF SUCCESSION RIGHTS
(INCAPACITY AND UNWORTHINESS)
La. C.C. 939-946 *& ren few*

CHAPTER 7: ACCEPTANCE AND RENUNCIATION
La. C.C. 947-967, 1415-29

CHAPTER 8: COLLATION
La. C.C. 1227-1288

PART II: DONATIONS

CHAPTER 9: OVERVIEW OF THE LAW OF DONATIONS

CHAPTER 10: CAPACITY
La. C.C. 1470-1483

CHAPTER 11: THE DISPOSABLE PORTION, THE *LEGITIME*,
AND REDUCTION
La. C.C. 1493-1514

CHAPTER 12: DONATIONS *OMNIUM BONORUM* AND DISPOSITIONS REPROBATED BY LAW
La. C.C. 1498, 1519-1522, 1527, 1769

CHAPTER 13: DONATIONS *INTER VIVOS* AND OTHER DONATIVE DEVICES
La. C.C. 1467-1469, 1526-1567.1

CHAPTER 14: DISPOSITIONS *MORTIS CAUSA* AND THE MARITAL PORTION
La. C.C. 1570-1616, 2432-2437

PART III: TRUSTS

CHAPTER 15: TRUSTS IN LOUISIANA
La. R.S. 9:1721-2252, La. C.C. 1520

Appendices

Biographies

CHAPTER 1:
OVERVIEW OF THE LAW OF SUCCESSION

The law of succession in Louisiana applies in default of the valid expression in a testament by a decedent of his or her wishes as to the devolution of the property left by the decedent at the time of death. Thus, the law of intestate succession applies in cases in which the decedent (1) dies without a will (intestate), (2) dies without a valid will, (3) dies with a will which disposes of only part of the decedent's property, or (4) dies with a will attempting to dispose of all the decedent's property, but which is only partly valid. In such cases, the law tries to carry out what societal values indicate would most likely be the intent of the decedent, since the decedent's intent has not been validly manifested.

Devolution of Property by Intestate Succession

A decedent may die possessed of both separate and community property. Different rules apply to the devolution of each. Thus, the first step in determining who inherits the property is to determine the nature of the property.

Once the determination is made as to whether the property to be distributed is separate or community in nature, the separate property of the decedent is distributed in accord with La. C.C. articles 888, 891-896 and the community property in accord with La. C.C. 888-890. In order to make the distribution, one must find the nearest relation to the decedent in the priming class. *deceased*

Classes of heirs as to separate property are categorized, in a hierarchy, as (1) descendants, *kids* (2) parents and siblings or descendants of siblings, (3) surviving spouse, (4) more remote ascendants than parents, and (5) more remote collaterals than siblings or their descendants. One must first determine if there are any relations in the first class. If so, the closest such relation will inherit. The nearness of the relationship is established by the number of generations between the decedent and the relation, each generation being a degree. The series of degrees form a line-either direct or collateral. The direct line is composed of those who descend from one another and is divided into the ascending and descending lines. There are as many degrees as there are generations. The collateral line is composed of those who share a common ancestor, but do not descend from one another. If there are no relations in the first class, one moves on to the next class, looking for the closest relation in that class. *Meme is our common ancestor*

Classes that inherit community property are (1) descendants and (2) the surviving spouse in default of descendants. When descendants inherit the community property of the decedent, the surviving spouse enjoys a usufruct over that community property, until his or her death or remarriage. By testament, the decedent may expand that usufruct beyond remarriage, grant it over separate property, and also grant the survivor the right to consume nonconsumables.

There are three ways one can inherit – (1) in one's own right, being the nearest relation to the decedent in the priming class, as mentioned above, La. C.C. 899, (2) by representation, an exception to the rule that the nearest relation in the priming class takes, allowing a representative to inherit in place of a higher ranking heir who has predeceased the decedent, La. C.C. 881, and

(3) through transmission, by succeeding to the rights and obligations of an heir who dies after the decedent but who has not accepted or renounced the decedent's succession, La. C.C. 937.

Filiated Children

A child may be filiated by proof of maternity or paternity or by adoption. La. C.C. 179. Maternity is generally established by a preponderance of the evidence that the child was born of a particular woman. La. C.C. 184.

Paternity is established through the use of presumptions or court actions in which the biological father is proven. Paternity of the husband of the mother is presumed when a child is born during a marriage or within 300 days from the marriage's termination. La. C.C. 185. The mother of a child may establish that the man to whom she was married at the time of her child's birth or conception is not the father of the child and that her present husband is the father of the child if the latter has acknowledged the child by authentic act or by signing the birth certificate. La. C.C. 191. Additionally, a man who marries the mother of a child who is not filiated to another man, and who, with the mother's concurrence acknowledges the child by authentic act or by signing the child's birth certificate, may be presumed to be the father of that child. La. C.C. 195. A presumption of paternity may also be invoked on behalf of a child who is not filiated to another man, if acknowledged by a man declaring in an authentic act or by signing the child's birth certificate. La. C.C. 196.

Additionally, a child may also bring an action to prove paternity even if the child is presumed to be the child of another man; although for succession purposes, this must be brought within a one year peremptive period, commencing at the time of the death of the alleged father. La. C.C. 197. A man may also bring an action to prove his paternity to a child even if the child is presumed to be the child of another man. If the child is already filiated to another man, the action must be brought within one year of the child's birth unless the mother in bad faith deceived the man about his paternity. In such a case, the man has one year from actual or constructive knowledge of his paternity but the action must be raised before the child reaches ten years of age. La. C.C. 198.

Absent Persons

An "absent person" is "one who has no representative in this state and whose whereabouts are not known and cannot be ascertained by diligent effort." La. C.C. 47. The law of absent persons provides a means to deal with the property owned by such person at the time of his disappearance, as well as the property acquired by that person after that time.

When an absent person owns property in Louisiana and upon a showing of necessity, an interested person can be appointed curator to manage the property of the absent person until his return. La. C.C. 47. Curators have the ability to manage and dispose of the property of the absent person, and those rights will terminate when the absent person reappears, dies, or appoints a person to represent his interests. La. C.C. 48, 50. If an absent person is absent for a period of five years, the curator must petition a court to have the absent person judicially declared dead, at which time the succession of the absent person can be opened. La. C.C. 51, 54, 55.

Upon his return, an absent person can recover his property and any inheritance in the condition in which he finds it from his successors or their gratuitous transferees. La. C.C. 57-59.

If the property is still under the control of the curator, the curator will render an accounting and turn over the property to the absent person. La. C.C. 52.

Commencement of Succession

The succession process begins at the moment of the decedent's death. La. C.C. 934. In order for one to succeed to a decedent, the person must "exist." La. C.C. 939. Determining existence, particularly in cases in which the order of death of reciprocal heirs is involved, is often a difficult task. Previous presumptions as to the order of death of reciprocal intestate heirs who died in a common disaster (termed commorientes) were eliminated, and now a person who claims a right through another must prove that the person existed when the right accrued. La. C.C. 31.

Related to the opening of the succession is the oft-confused concept of seizin, which is defined as a constructive right of possession bestowed upon a successor, granting that successor the legal personality of the decedent. Although distinct from ownership, seizin is often mistaken for it, resulting in more confusion. After revisions in the law, the concept of seizin has been modernized and is important for two reasons. First, at the death of the decedent until the time when successors are placed in possession of the property, one must continue the rights of the decedent. Until the appointment of a succession representative, certain successors must be "seized" with the right to act on behalf of the decedent's estate. La. C.C. 935. Second, in the event the deceased was merely a possessor of property (as compared to the owner), his successors may continue the possession for purposes of acquisitive prescription. La. C.C. 936.

Loss of Succession Rights (Incapacity and Unworthiness)

As noted above, a successor must exist at the death of the decedent to have capacity to inherit. La. C.C. 939. For an unborn child, the child must be conceived at the death of the decedent and later be born alive to have the right to inherit. La. C.C. 940.

An heir who had capacity to succeed at the time of the decedent's death may lose that right if he is judicially divested of the right due to his behavior toward the decedent. An heir "shall be declared unworthy if he is convicted of a crime involving the intentional killing, or attempted killing, of the decedent or is judicially determined to have participated in the intentional, unjustified killing, or attempted killing, of the decedent." La. C.C. 941. Such an action to declare a successor unworthy is properly brought in the succession proceeding by a person who would succeed in place of, or in concurrence with the person to be declared unworthy, or by one who claims through the alleged unworthy. The action may be defeated if the successor is able to prove reconciliation or forgiveness by the decedent. La. C.C. 943.

Acceptance and Renunciation

A successor may selectively accept or renounce his rights to succeed. La. C.C. 947. Although a minor is deemed to accept the right to succeed, his legal representative may renounce, with court approval, on behalf of the minor. La. C.C. 948. In any event, a successor may not accept or renounce prior to the death of the decedent, La. C.C. 949, and the successor must have knowledge of the death and realize he has rights to succeed. La. C.C. 950.

The acceptance may be "formal," manifested in an express writing, or in the assumption of rights in a judicial proceeding, or it may be "informal." La. C.C. 957. The revision equates to the latter with an implied intention to accept. Regardless of the form taken, an acceptance no longer results in personal liability of the successor for the acts or omission of the decedent. Since a successor who accepts is now protected from personal liability, it is presumed that an heir has accepted a succession, unless he specifically renounces. La. C.C. 962.

A renunciation must be express and in writing. La. C.C. 963. The question of who acquires the rights renounced by the successor raises the question of accretion. In an intestate succession, those rights accrete to those who would have taken if the successor had predeceased the decedent. La. C. C. 964.

Collation

Collation is the "supposed or real return to the mass of the succession which an heir makes of property which he received in advance of his share or otherwise, in order that such property may be divided together with the other effects of the succession." La. C.C. 1227. The concept of collation was originally part of the intricate balance relating to the institution of forced heirship. The basic idea was that parents generally wish to treat all their children equally, and thus, any gift given to one but not all, of the children during life, would be presumed to be an advance of the portion that the child would later receive.

Collation was based on two presumptions, that the ancestor intended equality among his children, and that any favoring of one child over another was merely temporary and would be remedied at the death of the ancestor. The concept originally applied to forced heirs. However, when some children were eliminated as forced heirs (by virtue of being twenty-four or older and healthy), limiting collation to forced heirs would actually result in inequality, rather than the desired equality. Thus, collation was redefined and its application was limited to gifts given during the last three years of the donor's life. La. C.C. 1235. Because of the conceptual incongruity of this new definition, the law of collation has become inconsistent at best.

CHAPTER 2:
INTESTATE SUCCESSION
La. C.C. 880-902

Devolution of Separate Property: La. C.C. 880, 888, 891-896

La. C.C. 888, 891-896 provide for the devolution of the deceased separate property. Seven basic classes of heirs are established by these articles, a higher class excluding all lower classes. Under La. C.C. 899, the nearest relation in each class primes the more remote relations in that class.

nearest relation > more remote relations
children, parents, siblings > Grandparents, Aunts, cousins.

The seven classes of heirs are the following:

1. Descendants (La. C.C. 888)
2. Brothers and sisters and parents (Brothers and sisters take naked ownership and parents take usufruct.) (La. C.C. 891)
3. Parents in the absence of brothers and sisters (La. C.C. 892) *} Added!*
4. Brothers and sisters in the absence of parents (La. C.C. 892)
5. Surviving Spouse (La. C.C. 894)
6. Ascendants (more remote than parents) (La. C.C. 895)
7. Collaterals (more remote than brothers and sisters) (La. C.C. 896)

Rockfeller
Dad — JR. — JR's kid
then, as the kid, Dad he primes succeed b/c he over JR & JR's kid. One closest to deceased.

La. C.C. 899 provides that among the successors in a class, the nearest relation will succeed. Thus, if a decedent's children are living and he leaves behind children, grandchildren and great-grandchildren (all of whom are members of the highest class, that is, descendants) the children prime the others and succeed to the decedent's estate because the children are the closest relations. However, when determining the nearness of relationship is not as simple as the example above, La. C.C. 900 provides a guide for determining the "propinquity of consanguinity" (another name for "nearness of blood relationship").

According to La. C.C. 900, nearness of relationship is established by the number of generations, each generation being a degree. The number of degrees between the relation and the deceased determines the closeness to the decedent and thus who is entitled to inherit within each class. La. C.C. 901 provides the methods for counting degrees in direct and collateral lines. Degrees are counted as follows:

Powerpoint slide; brackett?

Direct line – Count down from the ancestor or up from the descendant, excluding the starting point.

Collateral line – Count up to the common ancestor and back down, excluding the starting point.

*"Bequest" → Request? * Relates to Rule #3 of intestate!*

"Testimitarian of the intent" → The intent of the testator

Relates to Rule 4 of intestate!

For example:

A
|
B
|
C
|
D

B is A's first degree descendant, C is A's second degree descendant, and D is A's third degree descendant. C is D's first degree ascendant, B is D's second degree ascendant and A is D's third degree ascendant.

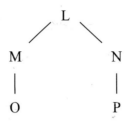

L
M   N
| |
O   P

N is related to M in the second degree (the nearest collateral degree). P is related to M in the third degree and to O in the fourth degree.

Note that the heirs referred to in the articles dealing with separate and community property include children born of a marriage and children born outside of a marriage. Children born outside of a marriage are included in a family tree as long as the requisite formalities necessary to filiate them, either by blood or by adoption, have been satisfied. *See* La. C.C. 184-214.

Applies when sibling is the deceased.

La. C.C. 893 provides for the devolution in the collateral line of property to brothers and sisters when half-blood siblings are taking with whole-blood siblings. When brothers and sisters are born from the same marriage, they take equally. If the brothers or sisters are born from different unions, the property is divided equally between maternal and paternal lines of the deceased. Within each line, the property is divided among the children of that line. Therefore, full brothers and sisters of the deceased take from both lines while half brothers and sisters take from only one line. If brothers and sisters are only in one line, they take all, regardless of whether there are any other relations in the other line.

If X died intestate survived only by his five siblings –
A, his half sister born during his mother M's first marriage to H;
B and C, his full brothers, the issue of the marriage of his mother M's first marriage to H;
B and C, his full brothers, the issue of the marriage of his mother M and his father F, and

1/2 ÷ 9/5 = 1/10

Comm. — Seperate count by head / by # of descendant

D and E, his half sister and brother, born of his father F's first marriage to W, the following calculation should be made.

# of kids b4 X Death

split ÷ by 2 of amount of heir

3 Kids from MOM: 1/6   4 kids from dad

Not Add

Siblings related to X on his maternal side take one-half	Siblings related to X on his paternal side take one-half	Total fraction due each sibling
A 1/6	The 4th comes from	1/6
B 1/6	B 1/8 adding	7/24
C 1/6	C 1/8 D & E	7/24
	D 1/8	3/24
	E 1/8	3/24

H → Father   MOM's kids [M] W   H & F
F → Stat
Total of heads
H — M = F   12
A BC

1/6 + 1/8 = 2·1 / 14 ; 2 : 1 / 2 ; 7

La. C.C. 895 deals with the inheritance rights of more remote ascendants, such as grandparents and great grandparents. The nearest ascendant has a right to the entire estate, excluding all other ascendants. However, if ascendants of the same degree exist, the succession is, on paper, divided into two lines: the maternal and paternal lines. When heirs of the same degree exist in both lines, the succession property is equally divided between the maternal and paternal lines, regardless of the number of ascendants in each line. For instance, if the deceased is survived by his maternal grandmother and has a paternal great grandfather, the grandmother takes 100% and the great grandfather gets nothing. But, if the deceased is survived by his maternal grandmother and his paternal grandmother and grandfather, then the maternal grandmother takes one-half, one-fourth going to each.

(paternal Grandma 1/2; Paternal Grandpa 1/2)

Representation: La. C.C. 881-887

The fundamental purpose of representation is to neutralize the effects of an heir's death prior to that of the decedent and thus avoid cutting off the predeceased heir's line. Because the heir predeceased the decedent, the heir does not exist when the succession is opened and the heir, himself, is incapable of taking. Representation allows the descendants of *certain* predeceased heirs to step into the shoes of the predeceased. So if A was survived by one child, B, and by two grandchildren, both the children of A's predeceased child C, representation would allow the grandchildren to participate in A's succession in place of their late parent, C. Without representation, C's line would be completely cut off, contrary to the basic policy of distribution reflected in the Civil Code.

Representation takes place in both the descending direct line and the collateral line. Representation does not take place in favor of ascendants. (A mother may not represent her son in a succession.) La. C.C. 883. Furthermore, in the collateral line representation takes place *only* in favor of the descendants of the decedent's *brothers and sisters*. La. C.C. 884. In all cases, when representation applies, it takes place *ad infinitum*, meaning that even very remote descendants of the represented could potentially participate in the succession. La. C.C. 882.

The representative has the same place, degree, and rights in relation to the succession as the person represented. La. C.C. 881. Therefore, the children (or other descendants) of the predeceased take no more collectively than the one who is represented would have taken had he survived.

Although La. C.C. 886 provides that, "only deceased persons may be represented," this rule is somewhat qualified by La. C.C. 946 and 964 as enacted by Act 421 of 1997, effective July 1, 1999, which provide that in an intestate succession, the succession rights that would have devolved on an heir who is declared unworthy or on an heir who renounces devolve as if the unworthy or renouncing heir has predeceased.

Renouncing the right to succeed in one person's succession will not prevent that heir from representing that person in another's succession. La. C.C. 887. In other words, if a child, C, renounced the right to take in his mother, M's succession, C would still be able to represent M in his grandmother's succession, even though he had already renounced the rights to M's estate.

Collation is a concept that was initially intended to insure that all children shared equally in their parent's property, unless the parent specified otherwise. At the time of these opinions, as a result of collation, any child had a right to compel his sibling to subtract from his portion the value of gifts he received during the parent's life. Collation and the many changes in collation are covered more thoroughly in Chapter 8.

SUCCESSION OF THE MISSES MORGAN
23 La. Ann. 290 (1871)
[23 Tul. L. Rev. 312 (1949); 10 Tul. L. Rev. 621 (1936)]

The Misses Morgan, four sisters, perished in a common calamity on the twenty-eighth November, 1867. Dying intestate, and leaving neither ascendants nor descendants, their succession was claimed by a sister, Mrs. Mary Harrod, and a brother, William H. Morgan, to the former of whom letters of administration were granted. Thomas A. Morgan, a brother of the half blood of decedents, died in 1858, leaving seven children, his heirs, whose claim to one-sixth of this succession, by representation, is the subject of controversy before us. The succession is valued at about $52,000.

It is admitted that Thomas A. Morgan died insolvent, that he was indebted at the time of his death to the Misses Morgan in the sum of $12,850, an amount largely exceeding what would have been his distributive share in their succession had he survived his half-sisters; that no part of this sum has been paid; and that the claimants by representation, his children, long since renounced his successions.

The judge below decided in favor of the claims by representation of the children of Thomas A. Morgan, and decreed them to be heirs for one-sixth of the succession of the Misses Morgan, that is to say in the proposition of one forty-second part to each. From this judgment Mrs. Harrod, individually and officially, and William H. Morgan have appealed.

The appellees contend that as representation of their father, T.A. Morgan, they are collectively entitled to one-sixth of the estate of their aunts without regard to the larger debt he owed those aunts; because, having renounced the succession of T.A. Morgan and their rights of inheritance not being acquired by transmission through him, but conferred by the law in the form of a representation of him, they can not be compelled to discharge his obligations or collate his debts.

The appellants, on the other hand, contend that, as the children of T.A. Morgan do not, and indeed can not, claim a share in the estate of their aunts in their own right, but only by representation of their father, they can have no greater rights than he himself if still alive could exercise; that is to say, the right to one-sixth of the estate, less the sum of $12,850; and that as this admitted debt is larger than the distributive share the claim of his representatives must be dismissed.

Representation is a fiction of law, the effect of which is to put the representative in place, degree and rights of the person represented.

*   *   *

A dead man can neither get nor give; he can neither inherit nor transmit. The representative of the deceased person does not receive by transmission from that person and jure alieno; he receives by designation of law and jure suo. It follows therefore that the representative is not by the fact of representation merely rendered personally liable for the debts of the person whom he represents. He is endowed by the law with the rights of the latter in a certain succession, but is not laden with the obligations of that latter to the rest of the world. He is not an accepting heir, but a designated representative. This doctrine is elementary, and we do not understand that its correctness is questioned by the appellants.

But to reach the exact question in this case we have to go one step further, and inquire, not merely if the appellees are liable for the debts of T.A. Morgan to the outside world (if we may use the expression), but if their share in the succession of the Misses Morgan must be reduced by the amount of debts due by their pre-deceased parent to the Misses Morgan. The question is not free from doubt; much may be said on principle for each side, and either view may be copiously illustrated by analogies drawn from the jurisprudence of France. But after a careful examination, both of our own books and the French authorities, we have decided to follow the rule indicated in the case of *Destrehan*, 4 N.S. 557. That case was hotly contested. The court (Judge Matthews delivering the opinion) held that the share of a grandchild, coming by representation to the succession of his grandfather, should not be reduced by the amount of a debt due by the pre-deceased father to that grandfather. The eminent counsel against whom the decision was pronounced made an earnest application for a rehearing, in which they urged the same views substantially as those now pressed upon us by the appellants. The rehearing was granted, and after argument the opinion of the court, adhering to its former decision, was delivered by Judge Porter, who gave the subject an elaborate review. He admitted that if the article of the Code above quoted, which defines representation to be a fiction which places the representative in the place, degree and rights of the person represented, stood alone, it would go the whole length for which the appellants at bar contend; but he proceeded to show that it did not stand alone, and that there were several cases in which, in a certain sense, the representative had greater rights than the person to be represented.

*   *   *

jure alieno → in one's own right

jure suo → in his own right

Now, the case at bar is rather stronger than that of *Destrehan* in favor of appellees. In that case it was admitted that the share of the grandchild must be reduced by any gift made to the father, the thing given being collated. C.C. 1318. But in this case the appellees, collateral relatives, are not bound to collate either gifts or debts. C.C. 1313 *[current La. C.C. art 1240]**

It is urged by appellants that the effect of the judgment of the court below is inequitable. It must be remembered, however, that there is no question of natural right in the case. The right of property terminates with the death of the proprietor. We brought nothing into this world, and it is certain that we can take nothing out. The right of succession is not a natural but a civil and a social right. Succession is a civil institution, by which the law transmits to a new proprietor, designated in advance, the thing that the preceding proprietor had just lost. Especially is this true of the succession of collaterals, ab intestato, under the provisions of law which create and control the fiction of representation. The parties to this controversy are all collaterals, the succession is intestate, its distribution is regulated by rules that are purely artificial, and the question in controversy is one purely of law.

It is therefore ordered that the judgment appealed from be affirmed with costs of appeal.

Rehearing refused.

NOTES

Morgan cites *Destrehan*, 4 Mart. (N.S.) 557 (1827), in support of its opinion, noting that "the case at bar is rather stronger than that of *Destrehan* in favor of appellees." What did the court mean? In *Destrehan*, although the children did not have to pay the debts their pre-deceased father owed to their grandfather, they did have to collate the gifts their grandfather made to their father during his life. Because the heirs in *Morgan* were collateral relations rather than descendants, collation did not apply to them; they neither had to pay debts, nor collate gifts.

So, can the representative have greater rights than the represented? Because the person represented is dead, he has no rights. Therefore, the answer is certainly "yes." However, can the representative have greater rights than the one represented in the succession of the deceased? *Morgan* and *Destrehan* indicate that the representative is not responsible for the represented person's debt but will be expected to collate gifts made to the represented. *See also McKenzie v. Bacon*, 40 La. Ann. 157, 4 So. 65 (1888) (concluding that children representing their predeceased father in the succession of their uncle were permitted to prosecute an action derived from their uncle's estate, although the father himself may have been estopped from prosecuting the action had he been succeeding to his brother's estate). Therefore, a representative may have greater rights than the one represented in the succession of the deceased. According to La. C.C. 881, the representative has the rights of the person represented. What does this mean?

In *Succession of Meyer*, 44 La. Ann. 871, 11 So. 2d 532 (1892), it was argued that the obligation to collate by taking less imposed in the act of donation amounted to a debt which the grandchildren coming to the succession by representation did not have to collate under *Destrehan* and *Morgan*. The court held that it was a gift, and not a debt, and had to be collated. What is the significance of the distinction between a debt and a gift? *See* La. C.C. 1238-41 which codify the rules as to which gifts to the represented should be collated.

---

* Bracketed material in italics added by author.

In *Succession of Jacobs*, 129 La. 432, 56 So. 2d 358 (1911), the court held that the word "descendants" in article 897 [La. C.C. 884] means that representation takes place ad infintum in the collateral line with predeceased brothers and sisters just as in the descending line.

The law prior to July 1, 1999 provided that representation did not apply in a testate succession. *See Succession of Kern*, 252 So. 2d 507 (La. App. 4th Cir. 1971). Effective July 1, 1999, any descendants by root of a predeceased legatee who is a child or sibling of the decedent or a descendant of a child or sibling of the decedent, may take by accretion the portion that the legatee would have taken had he survived the decedent. La. C.C. 1593. Absent a contrary intention by the testator, representation is permitted in a testament.

Transmission: La. C.C. 937

La. C.C. 937 allows for the transmission of rights that a decedent has in the succession of another. Therefore, should a person die with a right to accept or reject a succession that right will be transmitted to his own heirs? The deceased need not know he has the right to accept or reject a succession before the right is transmitted to his heirs at his death.

SUCCESSION OF DUBOS
508 So. 2d 920 (La. App. 4th Cir. 1987)

KLEES, Judge.

Appellants challenge the judgment of the district court declaring appellees to be the sole rightful heirs of the decedent, Regina Dubos. We affirm.

Regina Dubos died on March 5, 1980 survived by collateral relations only. Her will, probated on March 27, 1980, was attacked for lack of testamentary capacity and was declared valid by the district court on January 15, 1981. On September 30, 1983, we affirmed that judgment on devolutive appeal and the Supreme Court later denied writs. Because the will only revoked a prior will and did not make any disposition of the decedent's estate, the succession is to be distributed according to the laws of intestacy.

On March 5, 1980, when Regina Dubos died, Rene Girot, her half-uncle, was related to decedent in the nearest degree – the third. He was the son of decedent's maternal grandfather from his second marriage. Rene Girot passed away on September 21, 1981. Appellees are his universal legatees, who claim to take in his stead. Appellants are decedent's first cousins (the children of the siblings of decedent's father) and are related to the decedent in the fourth degree.

Appellees filed a petition for declaratory judgment seeking a declaration that Rene Girot was related to Regina Dubos in the nearest degree, excluding all others, and that the rights of Rene Girot to decedent's succession were transmitted upon his death to appellees, entitling them to be called to the Succession of Regina Dubos to the exclusion of appellants and all other collateral relatives. Appellants contend that they, not appellees were the rightful heirs of decedent. After a trial consisting solely of arguments by counsel and the introduction of documentary evidence, the district court held that because Rene Girot was related to decedent in the nearest degree at the time of her death, his legatees, appellees herein, are entitled to her estate to the exclusion of all others. This judgment has been appealed devolutively.

We find the trial court's judgment to be a correct application of Louisiana law, as all of decedent's survivors belong to the same class, that of collateral relations, the person or persons nearest in degree takes the succession to the exclusion of the others. LA.CIV.CODE arts. 899, 900, 901. This person, who is called the legal heir, succeeds immediately upon the decedent's death, even before having accepted the succession or having been put in possession. LA.CIV.CODE arts. 940, 941. Civil Code article 944 [current La. C.C. 937] states:

> The heir being considered as having succeeded to the deceased from the instant of his death, the first effect of this right is that the heir transmits the succession to his own heirs, with the right of accepting or renouncing, although he himself have not accepted it, and even in case he was ignorant that the succession was opened in his favor.

Thus, under the Code, it is unquestionable that Rene Girot, who was related to decedent in the nearest degree at the time of her death, became her sole heir and immediately transmitted his rights of inheritance to his own heirs, the appellees.

Appellants make three arguments as to why they should share in the succession, none of which have any merit. First, appellants contend that they are whole blood relations of the fourth degree, whereas appellees are only half-blood relations of the same degree. This argument is fallacious because appellees, although actually related to the decedent in the fourth degree, are considered as being related in the third degree, because they stand in the shoes of Rene Girot, from whom their rights were transmitted. Whether appellees' connection to the decedent is of whole or half blood is completely irrelevant. *Pearson v. Grice*, 6 La. Ann. 232 (1851).

Appellee's second argument is that the legal heir could not have been called to the succession until the time that the Supreme Court denied writs in the appeal of the judgment upholding decedent's will, at which time Rene Girot was dead. This argument flies in the face of article 944's [current La. C.C. 937] blanket statement that the legal heir succeeds at the instant of decedent's death. Moreover, even if it were necessary to wait for the validity of the will to be determined, in this case that fact was determined in February of 1981, when the trial court's judgment upholding the will became final, at which time Rene Girot was still alive. That judgment was appealed devolutively, which did not suspend its effect.

Appellees' final argument is that Rene Girot was not a legal relative of decedent because the marriage of Rene Girot's parents was bigamous. Rene's father, Leopold Girot, was married to Francoise Remy in France prior to his marriage to Rene's mother, Marie Claverie. The marriage to Francoise Remy was dissolved in 1883 by means of a divorce decree rendered by a Louisiana Court. Leopold Girot married Marie Calverie in 1884 in Louisiana. Appellees claim that the 1883 divorce was invalid because the court lacked jurisdiction, thereby rendering the marriage of Rene's parents invalid and making Rene illegitimate. We do not have to consider the merits of this contention because we find that even if the marriage of Leopold and Marie was bigamous, their son Rene would be legitimate by virtue of the Civil Code articles regarding putative marriages. LA.CIV.CODE arts. 117, 118 [current La. C.C. 96]. There is no evidence in the record of bad faith on the part of both spouses, which would be required to erase the legitimacy of their children.

Accordingly, for the reasons herein stated, we affirm the judgment of the trial court declaring appellees to be the sole heirs of Regina Dubos.

AFFIRMED.

NOTES

Destrehan, noted in *Morgan* above, is also noteworthy for explaining why heirs may have different rights when coming to a succession by representation versus transmission:

> The latter arises from a right vested in one person being transferred to another. In such case, he who receives it can have no other, or greater rights, than the person from whom it has passed. As, if the father should die after the succession was opened, and his children came forward to represent him in the partition of their grandfather's estate; in such case they could take neither more nor less than he did. But when the father dies before the grandfather, the grandchildren do not take their right from their father; they receive it from the law, independent of his acts or his will; and even when he should have manifested a contrary intention. This distinction, which is obvious enough, does not originate with this court; it is taken from the jurists and tribunals of France, who have commented on those articles of the Napoleon Code, from which ours are copies; and they deduce from it the necessary consequence, that the grandchild, when he comes in by representation, is not obliged to pay the debts of his father.

Destrehan, 4 Mart. (N.S.) 557 (1827) (citations omitted).

Complete for Mond.

PROBLEMS

1. The decedent Peter dies leaving three children Ann, Bill, and Carol, and eight grandchildren. Four of his grandchildren are the children of a predeceased son, David. Ann has two children, Laura and Michael; Bill has two children, Nora and Olga; and Carol has no children. What fraction of Peter's estate will each child get? Each grandchild? What right enables each person to take?

2. If the decedent above left only grandchildren, all his children had predeceased him, how would his estate devolve? *Thru re presentation*

3. Arthur marries and has three daughters Ashley, Brenda, and Cynthia. His wife Frieda dies, and he later marries Susan. Darlene and Eve are born of the second union. If Brenda dies, who has a right to her succession? What rights does each person have? Would your answer change if her father predeceased her?

4. Phyllis dies survived only by her grandmother, Samantha, her great-grandmother, Teresa on her mother's side, her grandmother, Marta, and her grandfather Herbert on her father's side. What rights doe they have to her property? Would your answer change if Phyllis also left a sister, Gail? *More remote ascendant rule / Grandparents (1/2) each. If she left a sister rule of sibling applied (full ownership)*

5. The deceased, Marlena, died leaving a nephew, Timothy, and her father, Albert. What rights does each have in her separate property? Would your answer change if she had also left a husband, John? *If no descendant, parents, siblings or descendants of them (2-9) may inherit the deceased separate property. No, my answer would not change b/cuz surviving spouse comes later in the classification.*

6. Nancy and her daughter, Christine, were in a car accident. Nancy died instantly and Christine died a few hours later. Nancy was survived by her father, Martin, the daughter's grandfather, and by her two sisters, Sarah and Katherine, the daughter's aunts. Christine left a husband, Philip. What rights do the survivors have to Nancy and/or Christine's property? Would your answer change if Christine died before Nancy?

Right of Reversion: La. C.C. 897-898

La. C.C. 897 and 898 are exceptions to the devolution of property upon death. These articles provide for the right of reversion in favor of ascendants who have given immovables to their descendants. La. C.C. 897 provides that ascendants who have donated immovable property to their descendants will inherit that immovable property, "to the exclusion of all others," at the death of the donee if the donee dies without posterity and the object is "found in the succession" of the donee. This unique rule, which deviates from the ordinary rules of succession, is sometimes referred to as the "anomalous succession" rule. For the rule to apply, all four prerequisites must be satisfied: 1) the donation must be from an ascendant to a descendant, 2) the donation must be of immovable property, 3) the donee must die without posterity, and 4) the property must be "found in the succession" of the donee.

In *Succession of Christensen*, 248 So. 2d 45 (La. App. 1st Cir. 1971), *writ denied* 259 La. 748, 252 So. 2d 451 (1971), a grandmother donated a house to her granddaughter by authentic act. The granddaughter subsequently died with no descendants. Her will named her father universal legatee and executor. The grandmother argued that the house reverted to her. However, the court held that immediate ownership vested in her father, the universal legatee, upon the granddaughter's death. Therefore, the house did not revert to the grandmother as it would have had she died intestate.

Devolution of Community Property: La. C.C. 888-890

La. C.C. 889 provides that if the decedent is not survived by descendants, his share of the community property devolves in favor of his surviving spouse. Should the deceased leave descendants, according to La. C.C. 888, his descendants succeed to his property. The child of the deceased spouse does not also have to be the child of the surviving spouse in order to inherit community property under La. C.C. 888, but can be a child of a prior marriage of the deceased spouse. *See Succession of Pavelka*, 161 La. 728, 100 So. 403 (1926). Unless the deceased provides otherwise by testament, the surviving spouse will have a usufruct over the deceased's share of the community property that is inherited by the descendants. This usufruct terminates on remarriage of the surviving spouse. La. C.C. 890.

PALINE v. HEROMAN
211 La. 64, 29 So. 2d 473 (1946)

KENNON, Justice.

The judgment appealed from rests on an interpretation on Article 1022 of the REVISED CIVIL CODE.

Joseph Paline died intestate, leaving his widow and their two sons, Paul and Emile, and certain community property, title to part of which is at issue in the present suit. By authentic act, both sons renounced the succession and their mother was placed in possession of the entire estate—one half in her own right and one half by virtue of the children's renunciation. Upon the widow's death, she bequeathed to her two children (the ones who had renounced in her favor) the real property owned by the community. Emile Paline, plaintiff in this suit, through a partition with his brother, Paul Paline, acquired title to a 2.83 acre tract out of this property and on December 5, 1945, he entered into an agreement with Fred I. Heroman, Jr., the defendant to sell him this tract of land. This suit was filed for specific performance when Heroman refused to accept plaintiff's title to the property as merchantable. Mrs. Virginia Paline Sherill, one of the five children of the plaintiff's brother, Paul Paline, intervened, in the suit, claiming as heir of Joseph Paline, her grandfather, an undivided one tenth interest in the property. The lower court rendered judgment in favor of defendant, Heroman, rejecting plaintiff's demand for specific performance and recognizing intervener, Mrs. Virginia Paline Sherill, as owner of an undivided one tenth interest in the property. Emile Paline appealed.

The question presented is whether the husband's portion of the community property, after the renunciations of his children, passed to the surviving spouse in community or to the five children of the renouncing heir, Paul Paline. (Mrs. Sherill, intervener, is one of these children.)

Plaintiff argues that when the two heirs of Joseph Paline renounced his succession, which consisted entirely of community property, title to his undivided one half interest in the property vested in his surviving widow in community under the provisions of Articles 915 and 1022 of the REVISED CIVIL CODE. Article 915 provides: "When either husband or wife shall die, leaving neither a father nor mother nor descendants, and without having disposed by last will and testament of his or her share of the community property, such undisposed of share shall be inherited by the surviving spouse in full ownership. In the event the deceased leaves descendants, his or her share in the community estate shall be inherited by such descendants in the manner provided by law. Should the deceased leave no descendants, but a father and mother, or either, then the share of the deceased in the community estate shall be divided in two equal portions, one of which shall go to the father and mother or the survivor of them, and the other portion shall go to the surviving spouse, who, together with father or mother inheriting in the absence of descendants, as provided above, shall inherit as a legal heir by operation of law, and without the necessity of compliance with the forms of law provided in this chapter for the placing of the regular heirs in possession of the succession to which they are called." [*This has been significantly changed. See La. C.C. 889-890.*]*

Under Article 915 quoted above, the sons inherited (subject to their acceptance) all of their father's portion of the community.

Section 2 of Chapter 6 of the REVISED CIVIL CODE deals with the manner in which successions are accepted, and renounced. The articles of this chapter dealing with the rights of creditors and heirs who benefit by the renunciation are numbers 1021, to 1928, inclusive. Article 1022 reads:

---

* Bracketed material in italics added by author.

The portion of the heir renouncing the succession, goes to his coheirs of the same degree; if he has no coheirs of the same degree, it goes to those in the next degree.

This right of accretion only takes place in legal or intestate successions. In testamentary successions, it is only exercised in relation to legacies, and in certain cases.

[*This has been significantly revised and reenacted.*]*

Mrs. Sherill, the intervener, contends that since Paul Paline and Emile Paline, who were all of the coheirs of the same degree, renounced, the succession under the above-quoted article "goes to those in the next degree" and, therefore, she and her sisters and brothers, five in all, being all the grandchildren of the deceased, are "those in the next degree" and inherit in their own right. The contention is based upon the theory that the phrase in Article 1022, R.C.C., "next degree" refers to persons who are related by blood in the next degree to the renouncing heir.

At this time the Civil Code was adopted, only those who were kinsmen of the deceased were called to his succession, and hence, the word "degree" was generally conceded to be limited to people having blood relationship to the decedent. Article 915 was later amended to include the wife and amended again in 1938 it provided that she " . . . shall inherit as a legal heir by operation of law, and without the necessity of compliance with the forms of law provided in this chapter for the placing of irregular heirs in possession of the successions to which they are called." Thus, a study of Article 915 (as amended), the other articles in the chapter relating to renunciation of successions, and a careful analysis of Article 1022 leads to the conclusion that the expression in Article 1022 "those (coheirs) in the next degree" refers to the heirs of the de cujus who are next in rank or right to inherit in the succession which the heir was renounced, By this amendment, the wife was virtually—for succession purposes as set forth in Article 888—placed in the same category as a blood relation to the deceased.

*   *   *

The interpretation that the beneficiary of a renunciation under Article 1022, is when all the coheirs entitled to the succession in the first instance renounce, the heir next called to the succession by operation of law rather than the kinsman next in kin is indicated by a sentence under the discussion of "Seizin of Heirs," page 199 of the Alfred Bonomo Edition of Saunder's Lectures on the Civil Code: "[N]ow if the heir who is called to accept, renounces then the seizin goes to the heir in the next order of right."

This interpretation of Article 1022 gives meaning to the provisions of the preceding Article (1021) which sets forth the rights of creditors of a renouncing heir. The third paragraph of that article reads:

If, therefore, after the payment of the creditors, any balance remain, it belongs to his coheirs who may have accepted it, or if heir who has renounced be the only one of his degree, it goes to the heirs who come after him.

---

* Bracketed material in italics added by author.

The article does not mention "those in the next degree of blood relationship." The expression "the heirs who come after him" is consistent with the interpretation of Article 1022 that "those in the next degree" refers to "those in the next category or rank" (as heirs of the decedent).

Article 946 declares that if an heir rejects (renounces) the succession, he is considered as never having received it, and it follows that the rights of other heirs become the same as if the renouncing heir had never been an heir, in fact, as if had never existed. Nor can the grandchildren inherit by representation the portion renounced by the living sons, as there can be no representation of a living person. Article 899, R.C.C.

The case of *Jacob v. Falgoust*, 150 La. 21, 90 So. 426, which involved the renunciation of the community by the descendants of the deceased (the wife) is to some extent applicable here. The plaintiffs were the nieces and nephews of the deceased, who, as in the present case, claimed their right of inheritance by accretion under the provisions of Article 1022. The fact in that case that the heirs renounced the community and not the succession makes no difference in the present case as the Paline succession and entire estate consisted only of community property and there were not debts. The Court held that the renunciation of the children gave the nieces and nephews no interest in the community property; that the portion which the heirs of the wife renounced belonged to the surviving partner in community. It was also held that the renunciation of a community by the heir of the wife, has, like that of a succession, a retrospective effect; the heir of the wife who renounces the community is considered as never having had any interest in it.

Reading and considering together the provisions of Article 915 which deals with the rights of heirs to inheritance of community property and sets forth as recipients, first descendants and secondly, ascendants and surviving spouse as coheirs, and Article 1022, which states that the portion of renouncing heirs goes "to those in the next degree," we conclude that since all the children of the deceased spouse renounced the succession, the surviving widow (in the absence of parents) became recipient of the accretion as she is the heir in the next rank or degree, under the provisions of Article 915, R.C.C.

For the reasons assigned, the judgment appealed from is reversed, and it is now ordered that there be judgment in favor of plaintiff, Emile Paline, and against the defendant, Fred I. Heroman, Jr., ordering the specific performance of the contract aforesaid and ordering defendant to accept title to the property involved in accordance with the agreement entered into by him and plaintiff on December 5, 1945.

*   *   *

HAWTHORNE, Justice (dissenting).

*   *   *

Under the facts in this case, the sole question involved is whether the renunciation of the succession of the husband, Joseph Paline, by his two children, Emile and Paul Paline, vested title in the surviving wife, Mrs. Denise Granier Paline, when there were descendants of one of the children, one of whom is the intervener, Mrs. Virginia Paline Sherill.

Plaintiff contends that, as the only property owned by Joseph Paline at his death was community property, when his two sons, Paul and Emile, renounced his succession, his undivided one-half of the community property was inherited, under the provisions of Article 915 of the REVISED CIVIL CODE, by the widow in community, from whom plaintiff contends that he acquired title to the 2.83 acres involved in this suit. In support of his contention he cites and relies on the case of *Jacob et al. v. Falgoust* et al., 150 La. 21, 90 So. 426, which the majority opinion finds to be to some extent applicable.

I am of the opinion that the position taken by plaintiff-appellant herein is not well founded and that the Jacob case is not authority for his contention. In that case it is to be noted that the heirs of the wife renounced the community that existed between their mother and father, as they plainly had a right to do under the provisions of Articles 2410, 2411, and 2423 of the REVISED CIVIL CODE, as follows:

* * *

In the case here under consideration, the two children and forced heirs of Joseph Paline renounced the succession of their father, and not the community that existed between him and their mother. In truth and in fact, I know of no authority which would permit the husband, much less his heirs, to renounce the community.

* * *

In this case it so happens, as contended by appellant, that all the property left by the decedent, Joseph Paline, was community property. But, in my opinion, this fact makes no difference whatsoever, for the reason that his two children renounced his succession, and succession is defined as the transmission of the rights and obligations of the deceased to the heirs and signifies also the estates, rights, and charges which a person leaves after his death. REVISED CIVIL CODE, Articles 871, 872. His interest in the community property in this case constituted the estate of the deceased and the succession which his heirs renounced.

Article 915 of the Civil Code, in dealing with the inheritance and disposition of community property, states: "When either husband or wife shall die, leaving neither a father nor mother nor descendants, and without having disposed by last will and testament of his or her share of the community property, such undisposed of his share shall be inherited by the surviving spouse in full ownership. In the event that deceased leave descendants, his or her share in the community estate shall be inherited by such descendants in the manner provided by law. . ."

Under the provisions of this article, in the absence of the renunciation of the share of the community property belonging to the decedent, Joseph Paline, would have been inherited by his two sons who were his descendants and forced heirs.

I agree with the court in its majority opinion that Mrs. Virginia Paline Sherill, intervener, a daughter of Paul Paline and a granddaughter of the deceased Joseph Paline could not inherit or be called to the succession of her grandfather by representation inasmuch as her father was alive on the date of the death of her grandfather, as Article 899 of the Code specifically provides: "Persons deceased only can be represented; persons alive cannot."

However, I cannot agree that "Since all the children of the deceased spouse renounced the succession, the surviving widow (in the absence of parents) became recipient of the accretion as she is the heir in the next rank or degree, under the provisions of Article 915, R.C.C."; for, in my opinion, the intervener, Mrs. Virginia Paline Sherrill, granddaughter of the deceased, could be called to the succession of her grandfather and could acquire an interest in the property by inheritance under other provisions of our law.

Articles 948, 979, and 1022 of the REVISED CIVIL CODE provide:

When all the heirs in the nearest degree renounce the succession, which is accepted by those in the next degree, these last are considered as having succeeded directly and immediately to the rights and effects of the succession from the moment of death of the deceased. . . . (Article 948).

"A person can not accept a succession before it has fallen to him."

Thus, a relation to the deceased in the second degree can neither accept nor renounce the succession, until he who is related in the first degree, has expressed his intention on the subject. . . (Article 979)

The portion of the heir renouncing the succession, goes to his coheirs of the same degree; if he has no coheirs of the same degree, it goes to those in the next degree.

This right of accretion only takes place in legal or intestate successions. In testamentary successions, it is only exercised in relation to legacies, and in certain cases. (Article 1022)

Under the plain provisions of the articles quoted above, upon the death of the grandfather, Joseph Paline, and upon the renunciation of his succession by his two sons, Paul and Emile Paline, the grandchildren, children of his son Paul, the heirs of the deceased in the next degree, inherited, not by representation, but in their own right, all the rights and effects of his succession from the moment of his death; and his surviving spouse, Mrs. Denise Granier Paline, did not inherit the property which belonged to his succession.

To say that the surviving spouse inherited the property in this case does violence to the plain provisions of the REVISED CIVIL CODE and to the cardinal principle of succession law that the nearest relation in the descending line is called to the succession of the deceased.

Article 877 of the Code provides:

Legal succession is that which the law has established in favor of the nearest relation of the deceased.

Article 888 provides:

The nearest relation in the descending, ascending or collateral line, conformable to the rules hereafter established, is called to the legal succession.

In conformity with the rules set out in that part of Article 915 hereinabove quoted, and Articles 948, 979, and 1022 of the REVISED CIVIL CODE, the nearest relations to the deceased, after the renunciation of the succession by his children, are his grandchildren. In my opinion there is nothing in the majority opinion to rebut this conclusion. The result reached by the majority opinion, as I appreciate it, is based on the interpretation placed in Act 408 of 1938 which amended Article 915, and by such interpretation the court finds a rule which makes the spouse the nearest relation or the heir in the next degree under Article 1022 after the sons of the deceased have renounced. The 1938 amendment provides that the surviving spouse shall inherit "as a legal heir by operation of law, and without the necessity of compliance with the forms of law provided in this chapter for the placing of irregular heirs in possession of the successions to which they are called." The court finds that "By this amendment, the wife was virtually—for succession purposes as set forth in Article 888—placed in the same category as a blood relation to the deceased." I agree that by the 1938 amendment the wife was made a legal heir, or a regular heir, but I cannot agree that "The effect of the 1938 amendment is to include the wife in the definition of 'those in the next degree' after the sons of the deceased have renounced under Article 1022"; however, I concede that the surviving wife would inherit community property to the exclusion of collaterals when all of the descendants renounce, because under the plain provisions of Article 915 she is made an heir when there are no descendants.

The 1938 amendment, Act 408 of 1938, and the 1942 amendment, Act 82 of 1942, were enacted to facilitate the administration of community property when the wife is an heir, to obviate the necessity of the proceedings of an irregular succession in such case, and to eliminate the discrimination against a surviving spouse who comes to the succession concurrently with other legal heirs.

This was pointed out by Messrs. Paul M. Hebert and Carlos E. Lazarus in *The Louisiana Legislation of 1938*, 1 La.L.Rev. 80, 96, and by Mrs. Harriet S. Daggett, *Matters Pertaining to the Civil Code*, 5 La.L.Rev.83. The purpose was to eliminate discrimination as to the spouse, but it was never the intention, in my opinion, to place the spouse in a higher position in the succession line, or to accelerate the time when the spouse is called to the succession, and certainly it was never the intention to cause her to come to the succession to the prejudice of the descendants. The 1938 amendment has nothing whatever to do with the solution of the problem in this case. The grandchildren and the spouse are all legal heirs when called to the succession, but the problem here is which should be called to the succession of the deceased when all of the children renounce. In my opinion, under the plain language of Article 1022, the grandchildren are the heirs in the next degree to the deceased after the renunciation by the sons who are in the first degree, and the succession goes to them.

Article 891 provides: "In the direct line there are as many degrees as there are generations. Thus the son is with regard to the father, in the first degree, the grandson the second, and vice versa with regard to the father and the grandfather toward the sons and grandsons." Certainly under the provisions of this article the spouse could not be in the "next degree" unless there were no descendants capable of inheriting from the deceased.

I know of no provision of the Code or any law of this state which makes the grandchildren, who are in the "next degree" in this case, incapable of inheriting from the deceased. The most effective argument against their being capable of inheriting is that their father is still alive. But the fact that the father is alive makes no difference unless the grandchildren must inherit by representation. They do not inherit by representation in this case because there is no reason to employ this fiction which makes an exception to the rule that the nearest relation to the deceased inherits. In other words, these stand in line with those who are the nearest relatives. The grandchildren are the nearest relatives to the deceased in their own degree after the renunciation by all of those of the first degree, and come to the succession in their own right and not by representation.

* * *

It cannot be seriously argued that grandchildren are not next of kin to a deceased after his own children, under the codal provisions, and therefore, if all the children renounce the succession, the grandchildren will be called to the succession as nearest relatives in the descending line under the cardinal rule of succession law. The question is how are they called to the succession. They are not called by representation because they are not exercising the right of a person who was dead at the opening of the succession; they are not called by transmission because they are not exercising the right of a person who died after the succession was opened. The grandchildren, therefore, are called to the succession in their own right.

So far as I have been able to find, the writers who have discussed this problem have been of the opinion that this result is the correct one.

CROSS ON SUCCESSIONS, page 509, says: "…We have seen that the grandchild inherits in his own right when he is nearest in degree; as in case of a son whose father has renounced and who comes to the succession, if he is nearest in degree, . . . The grandchild who thus comes de son chef or in his own right inherits without assuming any obligations derived from the father, who has never been heir; while he who comes by representation takes it as if his father were alive and had accepted the grandfather's succession. . . ."

The problem presented in this case was anticipated by Mr. Fontaine Martin, Jr., in his comment in 10 Tulane Law Review 614, 621, *Inheritance by Grandchildren in Their Own Right and by Representation*, wherein it is stated:

The presumptive heir loses his right to inherit in three cases: when he has been disinherited; when he has been excluded from the succession for unworthiness; and when he has renounced the succession.

* * *

The French commentator, Toullier, discussed the situation wherein the presumptive heir was renounced or has been declared unworthy, and reached this same conclusion. 4 Toullier, *Droit Civil Français* (5° éd. 1839) n° 201, 202, 203, page 198 et seq. We summarize his conclusion as set out in those sections thus:

The law calls in first order, to the exclusion of all other relatives, ascendant or collateral, the descendants of the deceased person. This calling of the descendants of the deceased to the exclusion of all other classes or lines is independent of the nearness of degree. They exclude all other relatives, ascendant or collateral, of an equal degree, or even those more nearly related to the deceased. For example:

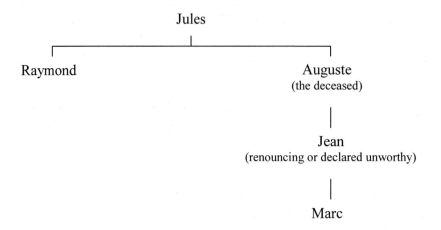

Marc, not being able to represent Jean, his father, who renounces or has been declared unworthy, remains a relative of Auguste, his grandfather, in the second degree. Nevertheless he excludes from the succession both Jules, father of Auguste, who is in the first degree, and Raymond, brother of Auguste, who is in the second degree, because relatives of the ascendant line and those of the collateral line, even brothers, are not called to the succession except in a case where the deceased does not leave descendants.

But, if Auguste had left other children and grandchildren, the extent of the right of each of them, in relation to the others, would be governed by the nearness of the degree. They succeed in equal portions and by heads when they are in the first degree and are called of their own right; they succeed by roots when all or part of them come by representation. For example:

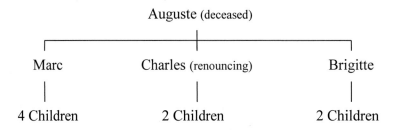

Marc and Brigitte, his sister, would succeed their father in equal portions because they are of the same degree and called of their own right. If Brigitte were dead, her children, being put in their mother's place by the effect of representation, would succeed concurrently with Marc, their uncle; but they would succeed by roots; they would receive only the portion which their mother would have had, that is to say, half of the estate, which they would share equally between them. Thus each of them would have only a fourth of the succession, while Marc would have a half. The children of Charles would not be able to succeed because of not being able to represent their father; they remain placed in the second degree.

If Marc and Brigitte were both dead, their children would come to the succession together and would partake by roots. The first would receive the half which Marc would have had, to share equally among them; the others, the share which Brigitte would have had, to share also equally between them. Thus the children of Marc would each have an eighth, those of Brigitte each a quarter.

If Marc and Brigitte were declared unworthy, their children, not being able to represent them, would find themselves in the same degree as those of Charles. All would succeed in their own right and would share the succession equally and by heads. Each would have an eighth.

*   *   *

In my opinion, the district court was correct in recognizing Mrs. Virginia Paline Sherill, intervener, to be the owner of an undivided one-tenth interest in the property involved in this lawsuit, in rejecting plaintiff's demands for specific performance, and in awarding to defendant judgment against the plaintiff in the sum of $1,400.

I respectfully dissent.

NOTES

Paline interprets former La. C.C. 915 (now La. C.C. 888 and 889), dealing with community property, thus limiting its application to former community property cases.

Also, for years, the *Paline* rationale afforded estate tax relief to the surviving spouse when the children renounced. If the surviving spouse were deemed the next in line after the children, the renunciations by the children qualified to disclaim under Section 2518 (a) of the Internal Revenue Code, entitling the estate to a marital deduction under Section 2056(a) of the Code. *See* Private Letter Ruling 9113008 of the Internal Revenue Service.

Under the successions revision of 1997, effectively July 1, 1999, (Act 1421 of 1997) the results of *Paline* are in question. According to present La. C.C. 964, when an intestate heir renounces, his portion accretes to those who would have taken had he predeceased. Because under current law if a child predeceases a parent, his children—the grandchildren—may represent him, the grandchildren and **not** the surviving spouse are the recipients of either their predeceased or renouncing parent's share. (*See* La. C.C. 964 cmt. b.)

If grandchildren come to the estate of their grandparent by accretion when their parent renounces, what obligations do they have? Must they answer for debts that their parent owed his parent? Are they obligated to collate for gifts that their father received? Consider the terminology in La. C.C. 946 as compared to La. C.C. 964.

What happens to community property if there are no descendants and the surviving spouse (who must survive or there would be no community property because the community would have been previously dissolved by that spouse's death) renounces? Does the Civil Code directly answer this question? If La. C.C. 888 and 889 cannot apply because no descendants survived and the surviving spouse has renounced, what other articles should be applied through civilian analogy? Should the articles dealing with the devolution of separate property apply, or should the property go to the state? The problem with applying the separate property articles to the devolution of community property is that those articles (La. C.C. 891-896) expressly state that they deal with separate property. Contrast this situation to one where the spouse survives but dies before accepting or renouncing. In such a case, the right to take would be transmitted to the spouse's heirs as "separate property" and would be available as such property to her ascendants and collaterals.

Putative Marriage: La. C.C. 96

By Acts 1987, No. 886, § 1, effective January 1, 1988, Title IV ("Of Husband and Wife") of Book I of the LOUISIANA CIVIL CODE OF 1870 was revised, amended, and re-enacted. The substance of previous articles 117 and 118 is now contained in La. C.C. 96. One substantive change was made. When the cause of the nullity is one party's prior undissolved marriage, the other party may continue to enjoy the civil effects of marriage until the putative marriage is pronounced null or until the party still enjoying those civil effects contracts a valid marriage. This change, however, does not affect the essence of the principles illustrated in the following case dealing with the division of community assets acquired during the existence of both the legal and the putative marriages.

PRINCE v. HOPSON
230 La. 575, 89 So. 2d 128 (1956)
[37 Tul. L. Rev. 764 (1963); 31 Tul. L. Rev. 551 (1957); 17 La. L. Rev. 303 (1957); 17 La. L. Rev. 489 (1957)]
(Footnotes omitted)

HAWTHORNE, Justice.

Plaintiff-appellee, Clementine Prince, instituted this proceeding seeking to be declared the owner of a lot of ground purchased by her during the existence of her marriage with James Brough, deceased. The defendants are Victoria H. Albert, surviving legal wife of James Brough, and Irita B. Hopson, sole issue of the marriage between Brough and Victoria H. Albert and the only living child of Brough. The defendants claim the ownership of, or an interest in, this property.

The facts giving rise to this litigation are as follows: James Brough, the deceased, married Victoria H. Albert on December 31, 1907, and of this marriage one child was born, Irita Elizabeth Brough, now wife of Willie Ray Hopson. In January 1919, James Brough filed a suit against his wife for an absolute divorce on the grounds of seven years separation. A preliminary default was entered in that case but final judgment was never rendered. Clementine Prince, relying upon the statement of James Brough that he was divorced from his first wife, was by a minister of the gospel married to Brough on May 19, 1919, after a marriage license to perform such ceremony had been duly obtained. After this marriage Clementine Prince and James Brough lived together as man and wife until his death on May 18, 1940, for a period of approximately 21 years, and in fact Clementine Prince did not know that Brough had not been divorced until she attempted to borrow money on the property here involved in 1955, some 15 years after his death. Moreover, his first wife, Victoria Albert, believed that she and the deceased were divorced, and she had contracted a marriage with Elijah Albert.

The property here involved, which is a lot of ground in the City of New Orleans, was sold according to the deed by Elizabeth McCluskey to Clementine Brough on March 4, 1939, during the time she and James Brough were living together as husband and wife. Although this deed names the vendee as Clementine Prince, wife of James Brough, it contains no recitation of paraphernality. The consideration named is $215 in cash.

After trial on the merits the district judge concluded that the marriage of James Brough and Clementine Prince was an absolute nullity, and that James Brough was in bad faith, and rendered judgment recognizing Clementine Prince Brough to be the owner of the property in question. From this judgment defendants have appealed.

There is no doubt that Clementine Prince contracted her marriage with James Brough in good faith; in fact, this is not even an issue in the case and is conceded by all parties. Moreover, in spite the trial judge's ruling to the contrary, there is no allegation, no evidence, and no contention that James Brough himself was in bad faith in contracting the second marriage with Clementine Prince. Victoria Albert in her answer states that both she and James Brough believed that they had been legally divorced, and there is no evidence to the contrary. The law is well settled in this state that where a man and a woman marry and live together as husband and wife, as James Brough and Clementine Prince did for 21 years, there is a presumption that they have been validly married, and that the marriage though null was nevertheless contracted in good faith. *Succession of Braud*, 170 La. 411, 127 So. 885; *Succession of Chavis*, 211 La. 313, 29 So. 2d 860; *Succession of Verrett*, 224 La. 461, 70 So. 2d 89, citing *Succession of Fields*, 222 La. 310, 62 So. 2d 495.

Under these circumstances there is only one conclusion that can be reached, and that is that both Clementine Prince and James Brough were in good faith at the time their marriage was contracted although this marriage was a nullity.

Since the marriage of Clementine Prince and James Brough was contracted in good faith, under Article 117 of the Civil Code this marriage produced its civil effects, and the existence of a community of acquets and gains between them is such a civil effect.

*   *   *

Since Clementine Prince and James Brough both contracted their null marriage in good faith, the question then arises: How should we divide this property acquired during the coexistence of both the first and the second marriage, or during the existence of the putative community? The claimants are Victoria H. Albert, the legal wife; Irita B. Hopson, legitimate child of the first marriage, and Clementine Prince, putative wife of James Brough.

*   *   *

In *Succession of Fields, supra*, this court quoted with approval from *Ray v. Knox, supra*, as follows:

And the rule was correctly laid down in *Patton v. [Cities of] Philadelphia [and New Orleans]*, 1 La.Ann. 98, an *[and]** has since been followed, that where a man marries, and afterwards contracts a second marriage without the first having been dissolved, the community property acquired during the coexistence of said two marriages belongs exclusively and in equal shares to said two wives as long as the second wife is in good faith, i.e. as long as she has no certain knowledge of the

---
* Bracketed material in italics added by author.

existence of the first marriage, and the bigamous husband has no share whatever in said property. *Cf.* [LSA] R.C.C. Art. 117 *supra*.

The famous case of *Patton v. Cities of Philadelphia and New Orleans, supra*, is the source from which this rule of property springs. In that case Abraham Morehouse was married to Abigail Young, by whom he had children and whom he abandoned in the State of New York. He came to Louisiana and here in bad faith as clearly shown by the facts contracted a second marriage with Eleonore Hook, untruthfully representing himself as a widower. Children were also born of the putative marriage. In disposing of the property left by Morehouse at his death, this court applied the Spanish law, and concluded that the property should go one-half to the legal wife and one-half to the putative wife, the forced heirs getting nothing, on the theory that Morehouse had wronged the second wife by creating a bigamous marriage and for his wrong the second wife had a claim in damages against the husband equal to his share in the community. The court applied the Spanish law because Morehouse's death in 1813 gave rise to the cause of action before the incorporation in our Civil Code of Articles 117 and 118 (Articles 119 and 120 of the Code of 1825). Articles 117 and 118 *[La. C.C. 96]* * read as follows:

> Art. 117. The marriage, which has been declared null, produced nevertheless its civil effects as it relates to the parties and their children, if it has been contracted in good faith.

> Art. 118. If only one of the parties acted in good faith, the marriage produces its civil effects only in his or her favor, and in favor of the children born of the marriage.

The holding in the *Patton* case has been followed ever since by this court, even though, as pointed out in *Hubbell v. Inkstein, supra*, decided in 1852, the decision in the *Patton* case was under the former laws of the country (Spanish) which had been repealed at the time of the decision of this court in the *Hubbell* case. The court in the *Hubbell* case deduced that the reasoning of the *Patton* case had equal force under both the Spanish law and the system of law existing at the time of that decision. We note, however, that in the *Hubbell* case the court did not mention Articles 119 and 120 of the Code of 1825 (now Articles 117 and 118).

Be that as it may, in none of the cases cited above which rely on the *Patton* case and apply the rule of law there announced, was the good faith of both parties to the second marriage considered or discussed in connection with Article 117 of the Civil Code. Moreover, in these cases the good faith of both parties to the second marriage was not a factor. Again, where the property acquired during the putative marriage was divided between the two wives, the facts in most of those cases clearly show that the husband in contracting a second marriage was in bad faith. Such is not a fact in the case which we now have under consideration, as both parties to the second marriage here were in good faith, and the rule of law announced in the *Patton* case cannot be reconciled with the express provisions of Article 117 of our Civil Code in regard to a situation where both parties are in good faith. To follow the *Patton* rule in the instant case and to give to the putative wife the husband's one-half of the property acquired during the existence of the putative community would be to deny to him and his heirs the civil effects of the second marriage, in the teeth of the provisions of Article 117.

---

* Bracketed material in italics added by author.

James Brough being in good faith in his second marriage, this marriage also produced its civil effects to him, and accordingly he became the owner of an undivided one-half of all property acquired during the existence of the putative community, for under the provisions of Article 2402 of the Code community property consists, among other things, of the estate which the parties to the marriage may acquire during such marriage by purchase, even though the purchase be only in the name of one of the spouses and not of both. Thus, although the property in the instant case was purchased in the name of the second wife, it fell into the putative community. Accordingly when James Brough died one-half of this property belonged to his succession. He was survived by one child, Irita B. Hopson, who therefore inherited his share of the community property under Article 915 of the Civil Code which provides: ". . . In the event the deceased leave descendants, his or her share in the community estate shall be inherited by such descendants in the manner provided by law."

We have disposed of James Brough's one-half of the community property acquired during the putative marriage, but the serious question remains: What division shall we make of the remaining one-half of this property?

As we have heretofore pointed out, James Brough's second wife, Clementine Prince, was also in good faith when the marriage was contracted and remained in good faith until after his death. Under the provisions of Article 117 she would therefore be entitled to one-half of all property acquired during the existence of the putative community although the marriage was a nullity. However, during this entire time the legal community was also in existence, and it likewise was not dissolved until James Brough's death, and during the coexistence of both these communities the property was acquired. Under Article 2406 of the Civil Code the effects which compose the community of acquets and gains are divided into two equal portions between the husband and the wife or between their heirs at the dissolution of the marriage. Consequently under the provisions of this article Victoria Albert, the legal wife, is also entitled to the remaining one-half of such property. The provisions of our law which give to each of these wives one-half of the property are of equal dignity and rank. However, it is impossible to give each wife under these laws one-half of the entire property as there remains to be divided between them only one-half of the property because James Brough's one-half is inherited by his daughter. The question then presented is: How should the remaining one-half of the property be divided between the legal wife and the putative wife?

Articles 117 and 118 of the LOUISIANA CIVIL CODE are literal translations of Articles 201 and 202 of the FRENCH CIVIL CODE, and as heretofore pointed out, their provisions first appeared in our Code as Articles 119 and 120 of the Code of 1825. For a solution of this problem, then, we think it is proper to look at the French commentators who have had occasion to discuss it.

Under the views of Aubry and Rau; Baudry-Lacantinerie; Colin and Capitant; and Ripert and Boulanger, where both parties to a putative marriage are in good faith the husband is entitled to his share of all property acquired during the existence of both the legal and the putative marriage under Article 201 of the French Code, and accordingly he or his heirs take as civil effects one-half of the entire property acquired from the date of the legal marriage to its dissolution. *See Colin et Captitant, 1 Traité de Droit Civil (1953) 375, no 623; Ripert et Boulanger, 1 Traité Élementaire de Droit Civil de Planiol (5 ed. 1950) 384, no 1050; Baudry-Lacantinerie, 3 Traité de droit civil (3e ed. 1908) 505, nos 1912-1924; Aubry et Rau, 7 Cours de Droit Civil Français (5 ed. 1913) 68-71.* These commentators then point out that, as to the remaining half, the putative wife can have no claim to any portion of the property acquired during the legal marriage, for this would be outside her community, whereas the legal wife certainly is entitled to one-half of all property acquired during the legal marriage. As to the property acquired during the putative marriage, the legal wife under the provisions of the law is entitled to one-half thereof since her marriage was in existence at that time and the community was not dissolved until the husband's death. However, under the provisions of Article 202 of the French Code the putative wife because of her good faith is also entitled to this same one-half of the property. The commentators then say that since these claims are equal in nature on the same object, the only division that can be effected is to split the property acquired during the putative community and give each wife one-half. *See Aubry et Rau, 7 Cours de droit civil Français* (5e ed. 1913) 75, 76, n. 24; *Baudry-Lacantinerie, 3 Traité de droit civil* (3e ed 1908) 516-518, nos 1930-1932. *See Comment, The Civil Effects of a Putative Marriage*, 1 Loy.L. Rev. 54 (1941).

Under the view which these commentators deem to be the most equitable, in the instant case the legal wife, Victoria H. Albert, and the putative wife, Clementine Prince, would each be entitled to an undivided one-fourth interest in the property in question.

The French commentators also allow the children to inherit community property from a father who contracted a second marriage in bad faith, which seems to us to be correct under Article 118 of our Code. *See Colin et Capitant, 1 Traité de droit civil* (1953) 376, no 624; Comment, *The Civil Effects of a Putative Marriage*, 1 Loy.L.Rev. 54, 67 (1941). Of course we are not here called upon to, nor do we think we should, go that far because of our decision in *Patton v. Philadelphia* and the cases which followed the ruling announced there—holding, in effect, as we have pointed out above, that children do not inherit community property acquired by their father during a second marriage contracted in fad faith. However, we see no reason why we should not accept such a solution when both parties to the marriage are shown to be in good faith, and by adopting this solution we certainly are following the provisions of Article 117 by allowing to the husband who is in good faith the civil effects of his second marriage, and we are also following the provisions of the article as to the putative wife's share as far as we can possibly do so by recognizing her to be entitled to the civil effects of her marriage, which she also contracted in good faith.

Although the lot here in question was purchased for $215, the record shows that after it was bought certain improvements were built on it, and it was stipulated during the trial that the total amount spent for these purposes was approximately $4,800, the greater portion of which was spent by Clementine Prince after her husband's death. Consequently there is reserved to her the right to claim from these two defendants in a proper proceeding the proportionate share of the enhanced value of the property resulting from improvements placed upon it after the death of James Brough.

For the reasons assigned the judgment of the district court is annulled and set aside, and it is now ordered, adjudged, and decreed that there be judgment declaring the property here involved together with the improvements thereon to be owned in indivision in the proportion of one-half to Irita B. Hopson, one-fourth to Victoria H. Albert, and one-fourth to Clementine Prince, said property being more particularly described as "Lot 19, in Square 578, bounded by N. Villere, Andry, Flood and N. Robertson Streets, and measures 32 feet front on N. Villere Street, by a depth between parallel lines of 170 feet, 9 inches and 6 lines, and starts at a distance of 120 feet from the corner of N. Villere and Andry Streets." There is reserved to plaintiff, Clementine Prince, the right to claim from the defendants the proportionate share of the enhanced value of the property resulting from the improvements placed upon it after death of James Brought. All costs in these proceedings are to be paid by litigants in the proportion of one-fourth by plaintiff-appellee and three-fourths by defendants-appellants.

*   *   *

NOTES

Is the result in *Prince* equitable to the putative spouse? Should we distinguish between good and bad faith cases? Who suffers the effects of the good or bad faith of the deceased? Throughout her marriage to James, Clementine was unaware of the existence of a previous wife and child. Then, she was forced to share property she reasonably believed to be hers with those who were strangers to her, and ultimately, her share of the property was to be only one-fourth. This seems to be carrying the technicalities of community property and succession law to the extreme without serving any useful policies of those laws whatsoever.

One has to wonder, in light of Justice Hawthorne's criticism of the *Patton v. Cities of Philadelphia and New Orleans*, 1 La. Ann. 98 (1846), the case cited in *Prince*, whether the case of the deceased spouse being in bad faith would be decided the same way today. *Patton* gave the property to the putative spouse using a tort theory, thereby effectively cutting out the child to whom civil effects were supposed to flow under previous La. C.C. 117 and 118. The putative spouse's claim against the deceased's estate, measured by the community half of which his bad faith had deprived her, makes theoretical sense. Civil effects, according to La. C.C. 888, flow to the child. However, when the child comes to the succession, no community property is in it, having already been paid out in satisfaction of the putative spouse's delictual claim. But is this allowing the child to pay for the sin of the father?

The question of who has a right to the usufruct of the surviving spouse in these putative marriage cases is also problematic. Apparently the legal spouse should enjoy the usufruct pursuant to La. C.C. 890, and simultaneously, enjoyment of the usufruct is a civil effect flowing from the putative marriage in favor of the putative spouse. When the usufruct extended only over property inherited by the "issue of the marriage" (as was the case under prior La. C.C. 916) it could be said that the legal spouse would have the usufruct over what was inherited by the legal child, and the putative spouse would have the usufruct over what was inherited by the child of the putative marriage. Now that La. C.C. 890 refers simply to descendants, however, the surviving spouse is no longer required to be the mother or father of the child descendant. So which spouse gets the usufruct? Do they split it as they did the community property in *Prince*? And what about the property acquired by the legal spouse and his/her putative spouse?

Does it make sense to distinguish between good and bad faith cases? After all, the survivors are in good faith or it would not be a putative marriage in the first place and the questions would never have arisen. Only the dead spouse was potentially in bad faith, and why should this control? Should not the only relevant consideration be that the survivors are in good faith?

Prince could be viewed as a grand example of a fine civilian jurist invoking previous La. C.C. 21 (La. C.C. 21 was repealed by Acts 1987, No. 124 § 1, effective January 1, 1988. La. C.C. 4 has replaced it). Both spouses had a right to all of the surviving spouse's community share and the Civil Code simply did not foresee the case of two surviving spouses. Perhaps a more equitable solution, however, would result from amending the definition of community property to exclude property such as that in *Prince* from the legal spouse's community. Or, Louisiana could enact a putative divorce to more appropriately divide property at the death of a common spouse. Courts have continued to recognize one continuous community, resulting in

2-25

inequities to the putative spouse. *See Succession of Jones*, 6 So. 3d 331 (La. App. 3d Cir. 2009); *In re Succession of Gordon,* 461 So. 2d 357 (La. App. 2 Cir.1984), *writ denied,* 464 So. 2d 319 (La.1985).

Monica Hof Wallace, *The Pitfalls of a Putative Marriage and the Call for a Putative Divorce*,
64 La. L. Rev. 71 (2003)
[Reprinted and edited with permission;
bracketed information inserted by casebook author]

V. Curing the Pitfalls: A Suggestion for Revision

To cure the pitfalls present in Louisiana law, the time has come for Louisiana to adopt a mechanism-a putative divorce-that puts an end to the legal community and allows the putative community to begin.[196] Like a putative marriage, a putative divorce would separate the communities and allow the spouses who contribute to each community to reap the benefits of that community at the other's death.[197] One French scholar reached the same conclusion by suggesting successive and separate liquidation of each community regime to achieve equal treatment of the putative spouse.[198]

To adopt the concept of putative divorce, Louisiana need not stray from the classic civilian doctrine of putative marriage.[199] Putative spouses should be entitled to the same community property rights as the legal spouse. The idea that, like the legal spouse, the putative spouse is entitled to a share of the community has been parlayed into the principle that both the legal and the putative spouse must take from the same community.[200] That need not be the case. With the aid of the putative divorce, the legal community could end and the putative community could begin. Each community would consist only of two spouses contributing and withdrawing from their community, and the legal spouse would be entitled to a share of the putative community in certain limited circumstances.[201]

When dividing property between the legal and putative spouses who equally have a claim

---

[196]

[197] Blakesley, supra note 8, at 38-39; Pascal, supra note 107, at 303; Godwin, supra note 99, at 491. Each of these authors suggest that two separate communities can exist.

[198] See supra notes 49-51 and accompanying text. Interestingly, Aubry and Rau considered the legal community, from the legal marriage until contraction of the putative marriage, to be "fictitiously liquidated" in favor of the legal spouse at the time the putative marriage was created. Aubry et Rau, supra note 37, at 76. Use of the putative divorce would likewise result in fictitious liquidation of the legal community, but contrary to Aubry and Rau's views, the legal spouse generally would have no share in the second community.

[199] See Blakesley, supra note 8, at 40 (noting that Louisiana is the only state that follows the classic civil law putative marriage rule).

[200] See id. at 38 (recognizing the theory that a legal spouse has an interest in the community property acquired by the putative spouse during the simultaneous existence of the legal and putative marriages); Prince, 89 So. 2d at 132-33 (concluding that the property entered the putative community but allowing the legal wife to enjoy a share of it); see also Pascal, supra note 107, at 303.

[201] By separating the communities, each would then meet the Civil Code's definition of a matrimonial regime, which consists of two, not three, spouses. See La. Civ. Code art. 2325; see also Godwin, supra note 99, at 491 ("A concept of two communities is entirely consistent with the Code articles on community property."); supra notes 106-107 and accompanying text.

to the same share, it is nearly impossible to ensure that neither spouse suffers any prejudice. Each is legally entitled to one-half of the putative community. In Louisiana today, however, the legal spouse is entitled to one-fourth of the putative community, due to her technical relationship and regardless of her actual relationship with the common spouse.[202] Use of the putative divorce would prevent the status of the legal spouse from being elevated over the innocent, intimate working-relationship with the putative spouse.[203] Although separating the two communities by a putative divorce may, in some cases, benefit the putative spouse, such benefit is appropriate in light of the relative ease at which the legal spouse can terminate the community and the makeup of today's family.[204]

A. The Putative Divorce

Logistically, how would the putative divorce function? The putative divorce would function the same as any divorce-the community property regime would terminate at the time the putative divorce became effective.[205] The putative divorce would take effect at the earlier of 1) filing suit for divorce even if the divorce was legally invalid or 2) contracting the putative marriage.[206] The bad faith of the common spouse would not prevent his heirs from succeeding to his estate. Indeed, his heirs would be entitled to inherit the community share of assets that the bad faith spouse would not be entitled to if he were alive.[207] Additionally, equity would enter the analysis when no divorce was attempted and the legal spouse could demonstrate, based on a number of factors, an entitlement to a share of the property acquired during the putative community.

1. Filing suit for divorce even if the divorce was legally invalid

Take again for example, A (the legal spouse), B (the putative spouse), and C (the common spouse) as presented above. If C left A in the good faith belief that the marriage had legally terminated by divorce and he married B, the putative divorce would take place at the moment C or A filed the legally invalid divorce. C and A would share equally in the legal community and C and B in the putative community. C's heirs would receive his share of the community property from both marriages. B's rights as the putative spouse would be preserved and A, even though technically a legal wife, would take only from the community to which she

---

[202] Patton, 1 La. Ann. at 106; see also supra note 75.

[203] See Homes, supra note 7, at 119 (submitting that there are strong considerations for favoring the putative wife over the legal wife in most community property situations).

[204] See infra Section V(A)(3).

[205] Currently, the legal regime terminates "by the death or judgment of declaration of death of a spouse, declaration of the nullity of the marriage, judgment of divorce or separation of property, or matrimonial agreement that terminates the community." La. Civ. Code art. 2356. A putative divorce likewise would terminate the regime. The author recognizes, but leaves unanswered, the effect that a putative divorce could have on other incidents to divorce, such as an award of alimony or reimbursement claims between spouses.

[206] It is the author's preference that putative divorce should be adopted into Book I of the Civil Code after article 96 to ensure a statutory foundation and proper integration into the Code.

[207] The bad faith of either putative spouse will prevent the civil effects from flowing to that spouse during the spouse's lifetime. La. Civ. Code art. 96. At the time of death, however, the bad faith of the common spouse would not affect his or her heirs.

contributed.

In this situation, the parties intended to end the community property regime. A, therefore, should not be granted a share of property acquired during the putative community. Whether or not C or A remarried, both spouses believed that their marriage had ended and all rights to property acquired by their ex-spouse had ceased. Causing the putative divorce to take place at the time the parties believed that the community terminated realizes the parties' expectations and assures that the legal spouse does not receive an unearned, unexpected gratuity.

2. Contracting the putative marriage

A more difficult question arises when no divorce was attempted, but the spouses separate. In that case, if C left A and married B knowing that he was legally married to A, the putative divorce would take place at the moment he contracted the putative marriage with B. The legal community would begin at the moment of the valid marriage and would end when the putative marriage was contracted.[208] The putative community would begin at the putative marriage and end at C's death. Any property acquired by C or A during the legal marriage would enter the legal community and would be shared equally by them and any property acquired by C or B during the putative marriage would enter the putative community and would be shared equally by them. Again, C's heirs would receive his share of the community property from both marriages.

Not raised by this example is the potential harm to the legal spouse by causing a putative divorce without her knowledge or consent. For example, a common spouse could leave his legal spouse and enter into a putative marriage, while his legal spouse, having no desire to remarry, awaits his return. Even more egregious, a deceitful common spouse could carry on separate lives, one with the legal spouse and the other with a putative spouse. In either situation, because the legal community ends when the putative marriage begins, the legal spouse is no longer entitled to property acquired by the common spouse after he enters the putative marriage.[209] To ameliorate any harm to the legal spouse, property from the putative community would be available to the legal spouse in certain circumstances.[210]

To explain, some have suggested that property acquired during the existence of a putative marriage should be divided among the legal and putative spouses based on which party acquired the property.[211] Under this theory, the legal and the putative communities coexist. If the legal spouse or the putative spouse acquired property during the putative marriage, that property would remain in their respective communities. Consequently, the legal spouse would not be entitled to a share of the property acquired by the putative spouse. If, however, the common spouse acquired property during the putative marriage, that property would enter both communities.[212] In this author's opinion, property acquired during the putative marriage-by either the common or the putative spouse-should remain in the putative community. Just as the

---

[208] If C did not remarry, the legal community would end at his death.

[209] The reverse is also true. If the legal spouse acquires property at the time when the common spouse has entered the putative marriage, the common spouse will have no claim to that property.

[210] See infra Section V(A)(3).

[211] Pascal, supra note 107, at 303-04; Blakesley, supra note 8, at 39.

[212] Pascal, supra note 107, at 303-04 (noting that the value of property entering each community would be governed by equity); Blakesley, supra note 8, at 39 (concluding that reliance on equity would be necessary to divide the property into both communities).

putative spouse has no right to property in the legal community, the legal spouse should have no right to the property in the putative community unless the legal spouse can demonstrate, based on several factors, the requisite entitlement to such property.[213]

3. Entitlement to property in the putative community by the legal spouse

The legal spouse, in certain circumstances, should have a claim to a portion of the putative community.[214] To determine whether the legal spouse can demonstrate an entitlement to certain property, certain factors should be considered: a) the contact between the legal and the common spouse, b) the legal spouse's understanding of the marital status of the common spouse, and c) whether the legal spouse received any benefit or enjoyment from property in the putative community.[215] These factors should be weighed against each other to award the legal spouse a share of property from the putative marriage when equity so dictates.

For example, in the case of the bigamous spouse leading two separate lives, the legal spouse may be able to demonstrate an entitlement to property in the putative community through her continued contact with the common spouse and her ignorance of the putative marriage. It seems equitable that if two wives coexist in relationships with the common spouse, ignorant of the other's marriage, neither should receive a greater benefit in property than the other. In the case of a common spouse who abandoned his legal wife, however, the legal spouse may have to demonstrate that she received a benefit or enjoyment from property acquired during the putative community to establish her entitlement. For example, if the legal spouse, who had little interaction with the common spouse and was unaware of his second marriage, was given a car to use by the common spouse, she may be entitled to a share of that property at his death even if it was acquired during the putative community.[216] Again, it seems equitable that if the legal spouse, believing that she is married, uses property that she thinks entered her patrimony, she should be entitled to a share of the property notwithstanding the putative marriage.

By focusing on the actual relationship between the legal and the common spouse, the status of the legal spouse is appropriately elevated when her marriage with the common spouse is

---

[213] Although some scholars have suggested that the legal spouse should only be able to recover property acquired by the common spouse, see Pascal, supra note 107, at 303, Blakesley, supra note 8, at 39, the legal spouse may be disadvantaged if the common spouse places assets in the name of the putative spouse. If, for example, the putative spouse purchased property in her name with community funds, but the common spouse allowed the legal spouse to use the property (most likely without knowledge of the putative spouse). The legal spouse should not be prevented from collecting a share of the property because the property was acquired in the name of the putative spouse. Based on community property principles, whether it was purchased by either spouse, it presumptively enters the community between them. La. Civ. Code art. 2340 (the presumption is rebuttable). Consequently, if the legal spouse could demonstrate an entitlement to the property based on her relationship with the common spouse, even if the property was acquired by the putative spouse, the legal spouse should be protected.

[214] Two other authors have also recognized the potential harm to a legal spouse if she is denied any right to claim property in the putative community. See Blakesley, supra note 8, at 39; Homes, supra note 7, at 125. Mr. Homes argues that a legal spouse should have a claim against the community only where she has been "truly wronged" and suggesting that positive economic need ought to be shown to constitute a wrong. Homes, supra note 7, at 125.

[215] If the legal spouse is aware of the putative marriage, it seems implausible that she would be able to demonstrate an entitlement to property. See Pascal, supra note 107, at 304 (noting that it would be an abuse of the law to allow the legal spouse to collect property acquired by the common spouse during the putative community if the legal spouse has knowledge of the putative marriage and does nothing to prevent or terminate it).

[216] If the legal spouse demonstrates an entitlement to property, its division among the legal and putative spouse should be left to the discretion of the court.

more than a mere formality. Otherwise, the putative spouse, who shares the responsibilities of a conventional marriage-working together, mutually assuming responsibilities, and enjoying benefits-should be protected against claims of a spouse who had no involvement in the putative community.

During the putative marriage, in most circumstances, the legal wife neither contributes to nor withdraws from the putative community. When one spouse leaves the other, even if the other spouse did not want a divorce or separation, the other spouse (i.e. the legal spouse) has limited involvement in building the putative community.[217] Although technically the legal community does not end until the marriage is terminated,[218] the institution of marriage and the contributions into and withdrawals from the community by the legal spouse generally terminate before the putative marriage begins. The putative spouse, rather than the legal spouse, should be entitled to her full one-half share of the assets acquired during the community in which she contributed as an equal partner in the marriage.

Fairness dictates that the parties enjoying and contributing to the community property regime ultimately take pleasure in its benefits. The law should not elevate the formal tie between the legal and common spouse over the mutual participation and productivity of the putative spouses.[219] The innocent, putative spouse lives the life of a legal spouse in all respects except technical validity. Indeed, the putative spouse is recognized in the community as the actual spouse, lives with the common spouse, and enjoys the benefits and detriments of a conventional marriage-devoid only of the formality of legal marriage.[220]

The putative spouse deserves protection from the claims of the legal spouse who reaps the benefit of the putative spouse's work.[221] All of the community property states that have considered the issue consistently protect the innocent spouse.[222] In addition, the children of the decedent, as the priming class of successors, should benefit from the fruits of their parent's labor. Even though one Texas court recognized what this writer believes is the correct separation of communities, that court allowed the legal spouse to enjoy property to the detriment of the decedent's children based on her technical status alone.[223]

With the advent of a putative divorce, the legal spouse is not forgotten. The legal spouse remains protected if her level of interaction with the common spouse or property acquired during the putative marriage elevates her above a technical, non-participating spouse. Additionally, because the putative divorce takes effect at the earlier of contracting the putative marriage or

---

[217] It is possible that the legal spouse's share of the legal community could be used to build the putative community. At all times, though, the legal spouse is entitled to property acquired during the legal community.

[218] See La. Civ. Code art. 2356.

[219] See Homes, supra note 7, at 122 (noting that the concept of community property is dependent on the active participation of two partners joined in a vital relationship, not the formality of marriage between two partners); Pascal, supra note 107, at 305 (suggesting that effects of marriage should be withheld if the parties, although technically married, do not believe themselves to be married).

[220] See Chavis, 29 So. 2d at 864; Homes, supra note 7, at 122-23.

[221] Homes, supra note 7, at 122 ("[T]o allow the legal wife to participate in the putative community in that situation would usually work an injustice to the parties in the putative relationship who have worked together to acquire the property, and at the same time would constitute a pure gratuity to the legal wife who, although legally united to one of the parties to the putative relationship, has in no way participated in the very relationship which is the foundation of the community property theory.").

[222] See supra Section IV.

[223] Parker, 222 F. at 194; see supra notes 142-47 and accompanying text.

filing the invalid divorce, the legal spouse would be entitled to one-half of the property acquired while the other spouse lived alone-even when separated from the legal spouse.[224] If the common spouse never remarried or filed for divorce, the legal regime would persist until the common spouse's death.[225]

The legal spouse in today's society needs less protection than the legal spouse of years past. In the lines of cases stemming from Patton and Prince, legal wives were left behind by their husbands, often faced with a difficult and lengthy process to obtain a divorce.[226] The husbands were the heads of the households, and the wives, who did not work outside of the home, were left behind with either promises of divorce or promises for a return. Today, the makeup of the family has changed. Wives are not only wage-earners in the family, but can obtain a divorce more quickly[227] and can unilaterally obtain a separation of property.[228]

If the legal spouse learns of the putative marriage or is abandoned by the common spouse, she can terminate the community. In fact, the putative divorce would protect any assets acquired by the legal spouse from claims of the common spouse. If the community is not terminated, both spouses are entitled to a share of the other's acquisitions. After the putative divorce, all acquisitions made in the name of the legal spouse would be the legal spouse's separate property and all those made by the common spouse would enter the putative community.[229]

Without so stating, one Louisiana court has applied the concept of putative divorce by awarding the putative spouse and the heirs of the common spouse property acquired during the putative community. In Succession of Chavis,[229] the common spouse married his second, putative wife having obtained only a separation from bed and board from his first wife but not a judgment of divorce.[230] Prior to his death but during his putative marriage, the common spouse acquired two pieces of property, to which the legal wife asserted a claim. Failing to cite its own decision in Patton, the Chavis court awarded the putative spouse one-half of the property and the children of the common spouse, both from the legal and the putative marriage, the other one-half of the property.[231] The legal spouse received no portion of the property acquired during the putative community because "she [did] not appear to have contributed a penny to the acquisition or improvement of the property involved in [the] suit" and "[the property] was acquired entirely

---

[224] The community is not terminated by mere separation. See La. Civ. Code art. 2356 for the causes of termination of the community regime. By giving the legal spouse one-half of the community property acquired while the other spouse is separated but has failed to file a divorce, there is an incentive for the other spouse to properly terminate the regime through a judgment of divorce or separation of property.

[225] See id. (providing that death terminates the community property regime).

[226] See Katherine Shaw Spaht, Louisiana Practice Series: Family law in Louisiana §§ 7.1-7.7 (3d ed. 2000) for a discussion of the progression of development of the law of divorce from 1808 to the present.

[227] See La. Civ. Code arts. 102, 103(1) (1999) (providing that a divorce can be granted after living separate and apart continuously for one hundred and eighty days).

[228] See La. Civ. Code art. 2374 (1999) (providing that "[w]hen the interest of a spouse in a community property regime is threatened to be diminished by the fraud, fault, neglect or incompetence of the other spouse, or by the disorder of affairs of the other spouse, he may obtain a judgment decreeing separation of property," and "[w]hen a spouse is an absent person, the other spouse is entitled to a judgment decreeing separation of property.").

[229] 29 So. 2d 860 (La. 1947).

[230] Id. at 861.

[231] Id. at 864. See also Jones v. Squire, 69 So. 733, 737 (La. 1915) in which the Louisiana Supreme Court, without any reference to its decision in Patton, awarded one-half of the putative community to the putative spouse and the other half to the child of the common spouse from the legal marriage, even though the legal spouse was alive.

through the union of the labors of [the putative spouses].”[232] Even though there was no mention of a putative divorce, the court allowed the putative spouses to contribute to a separate community to which the legal spouse had no claim-the practical effect of a putative divorce.[233]

Many formulas can be advocated to legally divide the putative community and, with any of these formulas, one if not all of the parties' legal rights will be compromised.[234] When considering the reality of putative marriage, one solution captures the balance of equality and fairness, and that solution is accomplished by recognizing two communities separated by the putative divorce. To achieve the appropriate balance between the legal and putative spouses, Louisiana courts should not only consider the analysis of other states[235] but, as instructed by the Civil Code, should rely on principles of equity.[236]

B. Effect on Patton and Prince

A putative divorce solves the problems presented in Patton and Prince. First, the Patton line of cases, which awards the legal and putative spouses the entirety of the common spouse's community at his death, is outmoded and outdated. While the goal of the Patton case was to punish bigamous spouses, the only persons punished on his death are the bad faith spouse's testate and intestate heirs. Second, the Prince line of cases, in attempting to protect the heirs of the common spouse, unduly prejudices the innocent, putative spouse. The putative divorce not only protects the heirs of the common spouse, even if the common spouse is in bad faith, but strikes the appropriate balance between the legal and putative spouses.

1. Patton inappropriately punishes the heirs of the common spouse

Reliance on the Patton case is fraught with problems, most notably the application of Spanish law, which is no longer a part of positive law in Louisiana.[237] Under the Spanish regime, bigamous spouses were punished for their infidelity by being denied any share in the community property earned during the invalid marriage.[238] Rather than punish the bigamist, the division of property unfairly punished the heirs of the bigamous spouse, who were denied any inheritance

---

[232] Chavis, 29 So. 2d at 864. The court did not consider whether the common spouse was in bad faith.

[233] See Homes, supra note 7, at 126-27 (citing Chavis as the correct application of the putative marriage rule when the common spouse dies leaving both legal and putative wives).

[234] See id. at 122-23 (taking the position that the solutions in the Patton and Prince cases are unfair to the putative spouse); Pascal, supra note 107, at 304 (suggesting two solutions: one in which the common spouse receives one-half and the legal and putative spouses split the other one-half and the second giving all three parties an equal one-third share).

[235] A California appeals court considered the case of Estate of Vargas, 111 Cal. Rptr. 779 (Cal. Ct. App. 1974), in which the decedent had lived a double life for twenty-four years as a husband and father to two separate families. The court recognized that its laws are not designed to cope with the extraordinary circumstance of purposeful bigamy and therefore resorting to equitable principles was mandatory. Id. at 781. Using equitable principles, the court divided the estate one-half to each spouse. Id.

[236] The Civil Code provides that “[w]hen no rule for a particular situation can be derived from legislation or custom, the court is bound to proceed according to equity.” La. Civ. Code art. 4; see also Pascal, supra note 107, at 303.

[237] See Hubbell, 7 La. Ann. at 252 (recognizing that Spanish law was no longer in force in Louisiana but still applying its principles as background for interpretation); see also Henderson, supra note 31, at 58; and Homes, supra note 7, at 121.

[238] See supra notes 31-34 and accompanying text.

from their ascendant.[239]

Admittedly, there is some appeal in punishing spouses who knowingly lure another into a marriage knowing it to be a sham. Prior to the death of the bigamous spouse, Louisiana law provides such a punishment. Article 96 of the Civil Code allows civil effects of a putative marriage to flow only to the party in good faith.[240] If the bigamous spouse is not in good faith at the inception of the putative marriage, civil effects will never flow to him.[241] The Louisiana Third Circuit in Price v. Price[242] denied civil effects to a common spouse when the legal and putative spouses were still living. In Price, the putative wife sought a declaration of nullity after learning of her husband's prior undissolved marriage. Because she was in good faith, she sought one-half of a piece of property acquired by her husband during the putative marriage.[243] The court awarded one-half of the property to the good faith putative spouse and the other half to the legal spouse based on Patton, thereby denying the common spouse any share in the property.[244]

Based on Price, the rule articulated by the Patton court makes sense when the putative marriage is discovered while the bigamous husband is still alive.[245] Because the bad faith, bigamous spouse is not entitled to civil effects of the putative marriage, one-half of the community belongs to his putative spouse and the other half belongs to his legal wife, under the principle that the legal spouse has a legal entitlement to one-half of all the property acquired during the marriage.[246]

The appeal to punish bigamous spouses, however, loses its luster once the bigamous spouse dies. The heirs of the bigamous spouse suffer, rather than the one who committed the wrong.[247] French scholars failed to embrace this punishment rationale and recognized the right of the bigamist to property that he earned during the marriage.[248] In fact, the interpretation in Patton contradicts the spirit of article 96, which specifically grants civil effects to the children of a putative marriage when one spouse is in good faith.[249] Applying Patton, the children are denied

---

[239] See Prince, 89 So. 2d at 133; Homes, supra note 7, at 124; Godwin, supra note 99, at 490 n.6.

[240] Article 96 also contains an exception for spouses who are putative as a result of the other spouse's prior undissolved marriage. La. Civ. Code art. 96. Civil effects will continue, despite the putative spouse's knowledge of the prior undissolved marriage. Id. Because that exception applies to the putative spouse, and not the common spouse, it is inapplicable in this context.

[241] Id.

[242] 326 So. 2d 545 (La. App. 3d Cir. 1976).

[243] Id. at 549.

[244] Id. Because the Price case dealt with division of one piece of property, it is not known whether a court would deny a bad faith common spouse any share of his earnings during the putative marriage.

[245] See id. (La. App. 3d Cir. 1976) (applying Patton in a divorce when both putative spouses were still alive); Pascal, supra note 107, at 304 (noting that generally the rule in Patton and depriving the common spouse of any community property is equitable when the common spouse is in bad faith).

[246] See Price, 326 So. 2d at 549.

[247] See Harriet S. Daggett, Work of the Supreme Court: Successions, Donations and Community Property, 14 La. L. Rev. 152, 162 (1953) (noting that to punish a dead bigamist by preventing his children from inheriting was illogical).

[248] Aubry et Rau, supra note 37, at 72 n.18; see also Vazeille, supra note 37, § 285.

[249] See Prince, 89 So. 2d at 132 ("To follow the Patton rule in the instant case and to give to the putative wife the husband's one-half of the property acquired during the existence of the putative community would be to deny to him and his heirs the civil effects of the second marriage, in the teeth of the provisions of Article 117."). For an interesting discussion of why the Patton case violates the principles of the Civil Code, see Henderson, supra note 31, at 61-62.

inheritance from their parent (the bad faith spouse) even though the other parent is in good faith. Even if the right of inheritance persists, there is nothing to inherit because the community property has been forfeited to the putative spouse.[250] Inheritance becomes meaningless to the child, thus violating the spirit of article 96.

The Patton case has been applied in a number of cases since its decision in 1846.[251] In Succession of Choyce,[252] the five children of a man who had entered into a putative marriage were denied any inheritance in favor of a legal wife who had lived with the decedent for two years and believed that she had been divorced from decedent.[253] Initially, the trial court awarded the putative wife one-half of the property and the five children as his legal heirs the other half.[254] The appellate court reversed, focusing solely on the common husband who, the court concluded, was in bad faith.[255] Because the husband entered a fifteen year marriage in bad faith, his children did not inherit his share of the community property and the legal and putative spouses were awarded equal proportions.[256]

The result in this case highlights the windfall to the legal spouse, who, due to a technical relationship, will enjoy property to the detriment of decedent's children. Courts have recognized that the rationale in Patton is no longer appropriate or applicable in Louisiana.[257] Creation and application of a putative divorce would ameliorate the consequences present in Patton.

2. The result in Prince unduly prejudices the innocent spouse

The result in Prince allowed an absent, legal wife to prevent the putative spouse from realizing her full share of property earned during her putative marriage. With the use of the putative divorce, the putative spouse in Prince would have been able to retain her full one-half interest in property of the putative community. Essentially, the putative divorce serves the exact same function as the putative marriage. The parties intend for the community property regime to end and simply need a legal device-the putative divorce-to give them the legal effect of a divorce and terminate the regime. In Prince, because the legal spouses attempted to get a divorce, which was later discovered to be invalid, the putative divorce would have become effective at the time the divorce petition was filed.

Even if the legal spouses had simply parted ways, without attempting the divorce, the result would be the same. Because the property was acquired after the putative marriage, the

---

[250] For a discussion of the anomalous results when applying the forfeiture theory, see Homes, supra note 7, at 121-22.

[251] See supra note 75.

[252] 183 So. 2d 457 (La. App. 2d Cir. 1966).

[253] Id. at 458-59. Indeed, the legal wife had entered into another marriage. Id. at 458.

[254] Id. at 457.

[255] Id. at 458-59. The court's conclusion was based on scant evidence. The common husband in his marriage license to his putative wife stated that he had not been married, but in statements made to his putative and legal wives, he acknowledged the marriage and said that he had been divorced. Id. at 459.

[256] Id. at 459.

[257] See Prince, 89 So. 2d at 132 (noting that the Patton case, which prevents children from inheriting community property from a father who contracted a marriage in bad faith, is an incorrect interpretation of Article 118 of the Civil Code). In fact, as early as 1892, the Louisiana Supreme Court realized the impending problems of Patton. See Jermann v. Tenneas, 11 So. 80 (La. 1892) (hinting that children of the common spouse should inherit from him under the French system, regardless of the spouse's bad faith).

property would remain in the putative community. The facts in Prince do not suggest that the legal spouse could demonstrate an entitlement to the property based on any ongoing relationship with the common spouse. In fact, she married someone else.

Similar to the inequitable results caused by application of Patton, the Prince interpretation has produced unfortunate consequences for the putative spouse. In the Succession of Gordon,[258] the common spouse had been married to his legal spouse for approximately five years and then married his putative spouse, with whom he remained married for thirty-eight years.[259] At issue was the common spouse's succession, which contained one piece of property purchased during the putative community.[260] Because the court concluded that the common and putative spouses entered the marriage in good faith, the heirs were awarded one-half of the property and the putative spouse had to relinquish one-half of her share to the legal spouse.[261]

Using the putative divorce, the putative spouse would have been entitled to keep her share of the putative community. The property was purchased during the putative community and absent any evidence of the legal spouse's entitlement to a share of the property, the property would have been shared by the putative spouse and the heirs of the common spouse. The legal spouse in Gordon lived out of state for many years after the separation and claimed to have no knowledge of the putative marriage.[262] Further, she testified that she had been in contact with the common spouse, who purportedly told her that he would never divorce her.[264] If the testimony of the legal spouse was deemed credible, the trial court could have awarded a certain share of the property to the legal spouse.

Usufruct of the Surviving Spouse: La. C.C. 573, 890, 1499, 1514

The usufruct of the surviving spouse over community property inherited by the decedent's children was first introduced by Act 152 of 1844. With the adoption of the *until* LOUISIANA CIVIL CODE of 1870, § 2 of Act 152 of 1844 became article 916. Article 916 *death* provided that the surviving spouse would enjoy a usufruct over community property inherited by *or remarr-* "issue of the marriage" between the decedent and the survivor. The original article contemplated *iage*. the application of this usufruct in cases in which the decedent "shall not have disposed by last will and testament, of his or her share in the community property." The article also provided that the usufruct would terminate on the surviving spouse's remarriage. The usufruct was designed basically to allow the parent of the decedent's children to enjoy the use of the property inherited by the children. Because the interest of the spouse was mostly involved with the property shared in community with the decedent, the usufruct extended only over that property. In the event that the spouse were to remarry and have another spouse to provide support and assistance, the usufruct would terminate. Also, since the usufruct was not originally contemplated as a *legitime* or forced right of inheritance, the decedent could provide otherwise by will. The article was carefully structured to protect the well-respected position of the forced heir children.

---

[258] 461 So. 2d 357 (La. App. 2d Cir. 1984).

[259] Id. at 359-61.

[260] Id. at 358.

[261] Id. at 365.

[262] Id.

Gradually, through case law and legislative amendment, the balance afforded by the original article 916 was modified to favor the surviving spouse. Protection for the forced heir has been limited to a qualified right to request security to protect the naked ownership inherited by a forced heir. *See* La. C.C. 573 (A)(2) and La. C.C. 1514. Pursuant to La. C.C. 890 today, when a spouse dies intestate, survived by descendants, his surviving spouse will enjoy a usufruct of the decedent's share of the community property inherited by the descendants. The usufruct terminates upon the remarriage of the surviving spouse. However, one may provide by testament that the usufruct is to extend over both separate and community property or any combination thereof. If no time for this usufruct is provided, it will be presumed for life. La. C.C. 1499. In the limited instance in which the usufruct affects the *legitime* of a child who is not the child of the surviving spouse, he may request security to protect his interest. If the forced heir is a child of the survivor, he may only request such security to the extent that the usufruct over his *legitime* affects separate property. La. C.C. 1514.

Usufruct of the Surviving Spouse: Pre 1996 Revisions

Prior to 1996 and the adoption of special articles dealing with the spousal usufruct in a testament, the courts allowed testate successors to grant their surviving spouses a spousal usufruct even when the decedent had made no specific mention of the usufruct in the will. The legal usufruct was deemed "confirmed" if no disposition contrary thereto appeared in the will. In such case, since it was a mere confirmation of the codal intestate usufruct, it terminated on the remarriage of the survivor. The law, as a result, began to conflate legal and conventional usufructs for purposes of protecting the surviving spouse. The following four cases provide the background and the progression of the changing usufruct to help one understand the status of the concept today.

For a thorough discussion of the cases and the history of the spousal usufruct, see A.N. Yiannopoulos, *Of Legal Usufruct, the Surviving Spouse, and Article 890 of the LOUISIANA CIVIL CODE: Heyday for Estate Planning*, 29 La. L. Rev. 803 (1989).

WINSBERG v. WINSBERG
233 La. 67, 96 So. 2d 44 (1957)
[37 Tul. L. Rev. 118 (1962); 32 Tul. L. Rev. 328 (1958); 33 Tul. L. Rev. 47 (1958);
9 Loy L. Rev. 108 (1958-59); 18 La. L. Rev. 574 (1958)]
(Footnotes omitted)

FOURNET, Chief Justice

This suit was filed on behalf of the minor, Kathleen Hilda Winsberg, by her mother, as her tutrix, and as administratrix of the succession of the minor's late father, Hermand W. Winsberg, against her paternal grandmother and her uncle and aunts, heirs of Jacob Winsberg, the deceased father of Hermand W. Winsberg, for an accounting of her grandfather's estate; and is now before us on a writ of certiorari to review the judgment of the Court of Appeal affirming the judgment of the District Court awarding to plaintiff the sum of $1,460. *See* 87 So. 2d 362.

Jacob Winsberg died testate on May 8, 1937, leaving all he died possessed of, consisting wholly of community property, to his wife, Mrs. Sarah Silverman Winsberg. Surviving him also were two daughters, Mrs. Stella Winsberg Levy and Mrs. Jessie Winsberg Bluhm, and two sons, Winfred J. Winsberg and Hermand Woodward Winsberg, all born of the union. His estate consisted of certain movable property and immovable property, the latter bearing municipal numbers 4304—06 Magazine Street in New Orleans, where Winsberg's Store was conducted – a small enterprise engaged in the sale of shoes. The legacy to the widow having been reduced to the disposable one-third, the heirs were placed in possession of the estate by judgment of court, the widow being recognized, as surviving spouse in community, to be the owner of an undivided half and, as legatee, to be entitled to ownership of an undivided two-twelfths of all property left by the decedent; and the four children being recognized as his sole heirs at law and entitled as such to the ownership each of an undivided 1/12th of the said property. No mention was made of a usufruct in favor of the widow either in the will or in the judgment of possession. There was no actual division of the assets which, aside from the real estate, consisted mainly of the stock of shoes, fixtures, etc., contained in the store, and the business was continued by the son of Winfred, assisted by his mother and sisters. Hermand took no part in the business; after completing law school he had moved to North Carolina where he was employed by a judge, and later as a salesman traveling the Carolinas for a shoe manufacturer. He was so engaged at the time of his father's death and for a period thereafter, and on June 20, 1937, addressed a letter to his brother expressing the feeling that the business should be turned over to him (Winfred) by October 1st and offering to transfer his own one-twelfth interest without compensation therefore, acknowledging that he had already received from his father more than would be due him.

*   *   *

In the summery *[summer]** of 1945 Hermand was released from service in the Army and Winfred, wishing to get out of the store and go into the business of wholesale selling of shoes, encouraged Hermand to take over the store.

*   *   *

On June 24, 1947, Hermand married the plaintiff herein; their child was born on May 5, 1948, a few months after his death which had occurred in February of that year. This suit followed on June 9, 1948, for an accounting of the estate of Jacob Winsberg for the period from May 8, 1937 (the date of his death) through December 31, 1945, the allegation being that Hermand never received his proportionate share "of the incomes, emoluments, salaries and other perquisites" of the said estate "and more particularly his share from Winsberg's Store."

*   *   *

The sole question posed for our determination in reviewing the Court of Appeal decision is whether or not the share of the community real estate inherited by Hermand Winsberg is subject to a usufruct in favor of his mother.

The plaintiff contends that under Article 916 of the Civil Code, as interpreted by this Court in the case of *Forstall v. Forstall*, 28 La. Ann. 197, the property passed to the children in full ownership; and in any event the defendants, who accepted purely and unconditionally the

---

* Bracketed material in italics added by author.

succession of Jacob Winsberg, are concluded by the judgment therein decreeing the widow to be owner of an undivided two-twelfths of the property left by the deceased in addition to her interest as surviving spouse in community, and the children to an undivided one-twelfth each, there being no mention of usufruct anywhere in their pleadings or the judgment; and since the widow was instrumental in obtaining the judgment on the basis alleged in her petition, she renounced all rights in conflict with the judgment for which she prayed and is estopped from attacking that judgment, citing Civil Code Article 2291 and jurisprudence of this Court. The defendants, on the other hand, admitting that the *Forstall* decision is squarely against the proposition for which they contend, i.e., that the widow did acquire the usufruct of the children's share, say that in effect the *Forstall* case was overruled by the later case of *Succession of Moore*, 40 La.Ann. 531, 4 So. 460.

It is apt to observe that the facts of the case under consideration here, for all intents and purposes, are identical with those in the case of *Forstall v. Forstall, cited supra*. There, as in the case at bar, the deceased husband had been disposed in favor of his surviving widow by last will and testament of his share of the community property; the heirs at law (more than three surviving children born of the union) contended they were entitled to have the legacy reduced to one-third and to receive the other two-thirds in full ownership, while the widow contended that she was entitled to the usufruct of the two-thirds reserved by law to the issue; and this Court held that the surviving widow was not entitled to the usufruct reasoning: "Article 916 must be construed with article 1493. Taken together, the meaning is: Where there has been no testamentary disposition of the disposable share of the predeceased husband or wife in the community property, the survivor shall be entitled to a usufruct during his or her natural life of so much of the share of the deceased in such community property as may be inherited by such issue. The condition upon which the survivor shall have a usufruct is, that the predeceased husband or wife shall not have disposed of his or her share, that is the share that he or she was permitted by law to dispose of. In the case at bar the disposable quantum was one-third of the property of the deceased, and the surviving widow has acquired this in full ownership by testamentary disposition. If the usufruct of the share of the deceased was more desirable than the full ownership of one-third thereof, the surviving widow could have renounced the legacy. As she prefers the rights acquired by the will to those accorded to her by law, she has no cause to complain. She cannot hold both."

But this Court in the case of *Succession of Moore, supra*, refused to follow the rationale in the *Forstall* decision, and while stating that the rule there announced could not be invoked as a precedent because of the different facts of the *Moore* case (where, by will, the wife was given the usufruct of all the husband's property, and, by codicil thereto, was bequeathed the disposable portion), nevertheless embarked on an exhaustive reexamination and reconsideration of the pertinent articles of the Code as well as all the prior jurisprudence, and in a very carefully considered opinion gave an interpretation to those articles that had the effect of overruling the *Forstall* case, squarely holding, "that a spouse in community can legally bequeath to the survivor the disposable portion of his or her estate, as it always was known, and may confirm in his or her favor, the usufruct provided by law, either by remaining silent or by expressing himself clearly on the subject, the language used, whether a bequest or a ratification being immaterial." In the course of the opinion the Court branded as "untenable" the proposition, affirmed in the *Forstall* case, that where there is a will which diverts from the issue the disposable part of the community property, so that the issue do not inherit the whole, the usufruct does not attach – observing that while a burden may not be placed on the share of the minors by will, the usufruct was created not by the will but by the law itself, *i.e.*, Article 916 of the Civil Code.

We think that the decision in the *Moore* case shows a well reasoned, exhaustive study and analysis of the subject, and is basically sound. It is perfectly clear that Jacob Winsberg did not in any manner dispose by testamentary disposition adversely to the usufruct created by law in favor of his surviving wife; in fact, he intended that she should have even more than the law allows.

*   *   *

NOTES

Thus, the magic phrase in *Winsberg* is "adverse disposition." The question after *Winsberg* was no longer intestate versus testate, but the nature of the testate disposition. Intestate versus testate is certainly much easier. However, the nature of the disposition, whether or not it is adverse to the spousal usufruct is much more difficult as it depends on the intention of the decedent and he is not available to explain his intention.

The rationale supporting the simpler approach represented by *Forstall v. Forstall*, 28 La. Ann. 197 (1876), has some appeal. When the decedent dies testate, he possibly has diverted some of his property away from the descendant heir. In that case, after the usufruct ends, the heir will not receive all of the decedent's half of the community property. Perhaps, in such a case, it is not as fair to the heir to make him suffer the burden of the usufruct as it would be in the intestate situation where he will receive the full property at the expiration of the usufruct. Perhaps this was the distinction being recognized by the original La. C.C. 916. Thus, if the spouse is given the disposable portion, the equities switch in favor of the descendant heir, gaining his legacy immediately without encumbrance. After all, in such a situation, the heir would never receive any part of the disposable portion; whereas, in the intestate context, he would have received the naked ownership of the disposable portion, something that the deceased spouse could have willed elsewhere. Thus, it is something of a condition on the receipt of the whole of the decedent's interest that the heir suffer the burden on his share in order to ultimately receive full ownership of the decedent's entire interest, of which he could have deprived through the will of the decedent. (Additionally, since under the original scheme the heir was always a forced heir, the *legitime* unencumbered was protected.) Note Justice Dixon's dissent in *Succession of Waldron*, 323 So. 2d 434 (La. 1975).

PROBLEM

Decedent was survived by his wife and two young children, both forced heirs. A valid olographic will was found in his desk drawer. The will contained only the following legacy: "I want my brother, Billy Joe to get Dad's army watch and my sister, Ellie Mae, to get my account at First Bank."

Decedent died possessed of an army watch he inherited from his father. In addition, he died possessed of community property including his half interest in a bank account at First Bank.

How would the decedent's estate be distributed before the revision to articles 890 and 1499? Will there be a usufruct in favor of his wife? If so, how long will it continue? How would you answer these questions in applying today's law?

SUCCESSION OF CHAUVIN
260 La. 828, 257 So. 2d 422 (1972)
[47 Tul. L. Rev. 218 (1972); 48 Tul. L. Rev. 1209 (1974); 35 La. L. Rev. 276 (1975); 22 Loy. L. Rev. 611 (1976)]
(Footnotes omitted.)

DIXON, Justice.

Writs were granted in this case to consider the effect of the remarriage of the surviving widow upon the usufruct of the surviving spouse.

B.J. Chauvin, Sr., was married once, and was survived by his widow and son. By last will and testament, olographic in form, he had provided: "I leave all I die possessed of to my son Bernard J. Chauvin, Jr., subject to the usufruct thereon which I leave to my loving wife, Bernice." The will did not mention that the usufruct was to be for life. All the property involved in the succession of B.J. Chauvin, Sr., was community property. There was a judgment of possession on April 8, 1969 recognizing the widow's ownership in her one-half of the community, recognizing Bernard J. Chauvin, Jr., as the only child and sole heir and the owner of the other undivided one-half of the community property "subject to the usufruct in favor of his mother, Mrs. Bernice Buwe, widow of B.J. Chauvin, Sr."

On June 12, 1969, Mrs. Bernice Chauvin remarried. Her son subsequently sought to have her usufruct terminated because of the remarriage. Mrs. Chauvin filed an exception of no cause of action to her son's rule; the district court maintained the exception and dismissed the rule.

On appeal, the ruling of the district court was reversed and the case was remanded in part and affirmed in part. The Court of Appeal, relying on *Smith v. Nelson*, 121 La. 170, 46 So. 200 (1908) and *Succession of Carbajal*, 154 La. 1060, 98 So. 666 (1924), held that the surviving spouse was allowed to retain the usufruct after her remarriage, saying:

> Thus our jurisprudence holds that a donation mortis causa of the usufruct of community property to the surviving spouse confers a lifetime usufruct which is not terminated by a subsequent marriage. This is true even if the testament grants the same usufruct the survivor would have acquired by operation of law under LSA-C.C. Art. 916 in an intestate succession. (*Succession of Chauvin*, La.App., 242 So. 2d 340, 342).

After reaching the conclusion that testamentary confirmation of the legal usufruct does not terminate on remarriage, the Court of Appeal went on to hold that C.C. art. 916 [footnote omitted] is a statutory exception to the general rule of C.C. art. 1493, which restricts the testator to all the provisions of C.C. art. 916 and requires termination of the usufruct over the *legitime* when the usufructuary remarries.

Civil Code Article 540 provides the manner in which the usufruct may be established:

> Usufruct may be established by all sorts of titles; by a deed of sale, by a marriage contract, by donation, compromise, exchange, last will and even by operation of law. Thus the usufruct to which a father is entitled on the estate of his children during the marriage is a legal usufruct.

Both the relator and respondent before us take the position in their briefs that the usufruct created by Chauvin's will was merely a confirmation of the legal usufruct created by C.C. art. 916. Although there is no statutory basis for the doctrine of confirmation of a legal usufruct, the idea is firmly embedded in our jurisprudence.

For convenience, the usufruct of the surviving spouse provided for in C.C. art. 916 is called the "legal usufruct." (*See also* C.C. art. 560). Usufructs created by a will are, naturally, called testamentary usufructs.

The relator relies on *Winsberg v. Winsberg*, 233 La. 67, 96 So. 2d 44 (1957), which overruled *Forstall v. Forstall*, 28 La.Ann. 197 (1876) and reaffirmed *Succession of Moore*, 40 La.Ann. 531, 4 So. 460 (1888). *Forstall* held that where the decedent bequeathed his share of the community to his widow, C.C. art. 916 did not apply, and the widow was not entitled to the usufruct over the *legitime*, because the deceased disposed by last will and testament of his share of the community property. In the *Succession of Moore, supra*, it was held that Article 916 applied to a testamentary disposition of the "disposable portion" of all the property to the surviving spouse, and the wife thus obtained the usufruct over the *legitime*, in addition to the disposable portion.

In *Winsberg*, the husband's will left all his property (community) to his wife. The heirs were placed in possession of the *legitime* and the wife was placed in possession of the balance. There was no mention of usufruct in the judgment of possession. In a suit for an accounting by a grandchild, it was held that the terms of the will indicated an intention of the testator to leave his wife more than the law allowed, and that since there was no testamentary disposition adverse to the usufruct created by law, the widow would receive the disposable portion in addition to the usufruct over the *legitime*. The *Winsberg* case squarely decided that the *legitime* is subject to the usufruct of the surviving spouse when it is a legal usufruct confirmed by a testamentary disposition.

Relator argues that neither the legal usufruct confirmed by testament nor a purely testamentary usufruct terminates on remarriage, relying on *Smith v. Nelson, supra*, and the *Succession of Carbajal, supra*. The respondent argues that the confirmation of the legal usufruct by testament subjects the legal usufruct to all the provisions of C.C. art. 916. In the alternative, the respondent argues that if we find the usufruct to be purely testamentary rather than the testamentary confirmation of a legal usufruct, then he is entitled to his *legitime* in full ownership.

In *Smith v. Nelson, supra*, the widow of Michael Smith married the defendant Nelson. She died testate in 1897, leaving three children by the first marriage. The will left to her children the property acquired during the first community, and to the surviving spouse, Nelson, the property acquired during the second community, with this further disposition: "Should my children claim the *legitime*, then I give and bequeath to my said husband the usufruct of all the property, movable and immovable, that was acquired during out [*our*]* marriage."

The Smith children were sent into possession of the first community in full ownership and were sent into possession of the second community, subject to the usufruct in favor of Nelson. In 1906 the heirs and their issue sought a partition, alleging that their stepfather had remarried, and had thus "lost the usufruct by operation of law."

The trial court dismissed the suit and the Supreme Court affirmed, noting that the trial court had held: "that as the usufruct enjoyed by Nelson was established by the will of his deceased wife, and by the judgment ordering its execution and putting him in possession, it is not

---

* Bracketed material in italics added by author.

affected by his remarriage." The opinion then states: "Adhering to the conclusions stated, we deem it unnecessary to cite additional authority in their support." 121 La. at 173-174, 46 So. at 200-201. The opinion then proceeds to discuss the problems involved in the demands for a partition between the naked owners and the usufructuary.

It is easy to understand how *Smith v. Nelson* is subject to misinterpretation. It has been cited to support the proposition that the part of C.C. art. 916 providing for the termination of the legal usufruct upon the remarriage of the usufructuary will not be enforced when the legal usufruct is confirmed by testament. *Smith v. Nelson* cannot stand for such a proposition. C.C. art. 916 is in no way involved, although it was listed in the authorities cited by the trial court. C.C. art. 916 is applicable "when the predeceased husband or wife shall have left issue of the marriage with the survivor . . ." In *Smith v. Nelson* the predeceased wife left no children who were the issue of the marriage with the survivor. The widow's children were the issue of the marriage with her first husband, who had predeceased her.

The only other Louisiana case located involving the termination of the usufruct upon the remarriage of the surviving spouse is the *Succession of Carbajal, supra*. For two reasons the *Carbajal* case is inapplicable. (it was only in a Per curiam on the application for rehearing that the Supreme Court considered the contention that the remarriage of the widow terminated the usufruct.) First, the court referred to C.C. art. 1753 (repealed in 1918), which dealt with property inherited by the surviving spouse from the decedent, and gave the naked ownership, upon the second marriage of the surviving spouse, to the children of the first marriage, the remarrying spouse retaining only the usufruct of the property. The court noted that the "right to the usufruct thereof remained, under the very terms of the Code. . ."

Second, an examination of the record in the *Carbajal* case reveals that the testamentary disposition involved was: "I give and bequeath unto my said wife, Rosa Lopez Carbajal, the usufruct of all the remainder of my estate wherever situated, *during the term of her natural life..."* (Emphasis added). Therefore, the *Carbajal* case involved a testamentary disposition of a usufruct which was clearly intended, by the terms of the testament, to exist for the life of the usufructuary, as well as the usufruct formerly provided for in C.C. art. 1753 before its repeal.

Therefore, the question before us is res nova. A Louisiana case has not been found which had to decide whether a testamentary disposition of the usufruct of the surviving spouse which merely confirmed the legal usufruct granted by C.C. art. 916 terminated upon the remarriage of the surviving spouse.

Louisiana courts have frequently considered the effects of the classification of the usufruct of the surviving spouse as either legal or testamentary. The surviving spouse as a testamentary usufructuary owes taxes. *Succession of Baker*, 129 La. 75, 55 So. 714 (1911). The *Succession of Brown*, La.App. 94, So. 2d 317 (1957), held that the usufruct of the community home left to the husband in a will was a confirmation of a legal usufruct and therefore not taxable. A testamentary usufructuary must give security, in the absence of a testamentary provision dispensing with security. *Succession of Carlisi*, 217 La. 675, 47 So. 2d 42 (1950); C.C. art. 558. The legal usufructuary is not required to give bond. C.C. art. 560. One of the principal issues in the *Succession of Moore, supra*, was whether the legal usufruct, confirmed by testament, would attach to the *legitime*. The court held that it would, saying at 40 La Ann. 542, 4 So. At 466:

Next, Mrs. Moore will be entitled to the usufruct of the remaining share of the deceased in the community during her widowhood, under the law, as confirmed by the will.

Finally, the portion of the estate of the deceased as shall be thus subjected to the usufruct of Mrs. Moore shall be deemed as the *legitime*, accruing in naked ownership to the nine children, as forced heirs of the deceased, share alike, . . .

The only reason suggested for departing from the practice of consistently treating the legal usufruct according to the terms of C.C. art. 916 has been the contention that *Smith v. Nelson* and *Succession of Carbajal* stand as authority for the proposition that the legal usufruct confirmed by testament is not terminated by the marriage of the surviving spouse. The two cases do not support this conclusion. On the other hand, the language of the codal article (916) is clear and unequivocal: "This usufruct shall cease, however, whenever the survivor shall enter into a second marriage." And the words "This usufruct" refer to the usufruct over "so much of the share of the deceased in such community property as may be inherited by such issue."

In the case before us, the will bequeathed the naked ownership of all the community property (both the disposable and forced portions) to the issue of the marriage, Bernard J. Chauvin, Jr. This second sentence of C.C. art. 916 became applicable. The usufruct ceased when the survivor, Bernice Buwe, remarried. Consequently, the Court of Appeal was in error when it concluded that the usufruct terminated only over the child's forced portion when the wife remarried under the will confirmative of the dispositions of the statutory law, the usufruct terminated over all the community property which was bequeathed to the son. Mr. Chauvin, Sr. failed to indicate in his will that he intended to bequeath a life usufruct to his wife. If he had, we would be presented with different questions.

We therefore conclude that the mere confirmation, in a last will and testament, of the legal usufruct conferred by C.C. art. 916 does not free the usufruct from the limitations of that article and it terminates "whenever the survivor shall enter into a second marriage."

Both parties have applied to this court for writs to review the judgment of the Court of Appeal. The application of Bernard J. Chauvin., was denied, and that of Mrs. Bernice Buwe, widow of B.J. Chauvin, Sr., was granted.

The trial court sustained an exception of no cause of action and dismissed the rule filed by Bernard J. Chauvin, Jr., to terminate the usufruct. When Bernard J. Chauvin, Jr., appealed from this ruling, the Court of Appeal affirmed in part, reversed in part and remanded. One question decided by the Court of Appeal is not before us: the court affirmed a judgment of the district court holding that a certain homestead savings account was the subject of an imperfect usufruct. The Court of Appeal then held that "a donation mortis causa of the usufruct of community property to the surviving spouse confers a lifetime usufruct which is not terminated by a subsequent marriage," a holding with which we disagree. Further, the Court of Appeal held that the usufruct over the forced portion, inherited by the son, terminated by remarriage, because of the provisions of C.C. art. 916. (We do not reach this problem). The Court of Appeal remanded the case to the district court not for trial on the merits, but to determine whether the usufruct infringed on the *legitime*, and to what extent it might need be reduced. The demand of Bernard J. Chauvin, Jr., in his rule to terminate the usufruct did not require the introduction of evidence.

We now believe we erred in denying the application of Bernard J. Chauvin, Jr., for writs. His application should have been granted, as well as the other. Nevertheless, the rejection is final, and operates as a final determination of the issues presented in the application of Bernard J. Chauvin, Jr. The part of the judgment of the Court of Appeal unfavorable to him and favorable to the widow of B.J. Chauvin, Sr., will not be disturbed. *Jordan v. Travelers Insurance Company*, 257 La. 995, 245 So. 2d 151. In spite of the fact that we differ with the Court of Appeal on the applicable law, and would have disposed of the case differently, we must affirm.

For these reasons, the judgment of the Court of Appeal is affirmed, at the cost of the relator.

*   *   *

TATE, Justice (concurring).

The writer concurs in the majority's scholarly analysis of the prior law on the subject, in its finding that the questions before us is actually res nova, and in its decree affirming the court of appeal. The writer, however, disagrees with the majority's conclusion that, where one spouse confers a usufruct by will over that spouse's share of the community property (the naked title to which is in the issue of the marriage), such usufruct in *[is]** nothing more than a confirmation of the similar legal usufruct provided by Civil Code Article 916. From this, the majority concludes that such usufruct, confirmed or (in my opinion) granted, terminates upon the surviving spouse's re-marriage – just as would the legal usufruct of Article 916, had there been no will.

I agree, instead, with the court of appeal that, upon re-marriage, the usufruct (until then merely confirming the legal usufruct) now is subject to reduction if it infringes upon the forced portion due to the heir.

The majority's conclusion is not unreasonable. It has the merit of logical consistency in holding that such a usufruct, contained in (confirmed by) a will, is for all purposes no more and no less than the legal usufruct provided by Article 916. To grant the survivor a lifetime usufruct, the bequeathing spouse must specify that the usufruct is granted for the duration of the surviving spouse's life. Then, if I read the rationale of the majority right, the usufruct is a testamentary usufruct.

However, this rationale will open up further issues for decision, such as whether in that case the usufruct is for all purposes a testamentary usufruct. If it is, the rationale in my opinion involves unfortunate results, such as (even though the [w]idow never remarries in fact) estate tax consequences (since the widow receives the usufruct by will, not by law) and the necessity for the widow to give security, Civil Code Article 558, since the parent is dispensed with bond only as to the legal usufruct over their children's estate, Article 560. Also, since only the legal usufruct of Article 916 does not impinge on the *legitime*, presumably such a merely testamentary usufruct is subject to reduction even before the re-marriage of the widow.

I therefore prefer the rationale of the court of appeal that the usufruct given to a surviving spouse by the decedent's will is merely the confirmation of the legal usufruct insofar as it gives her no further rights than that conferred by law (i.e. by Article 916). However, it becomes a testamentary usufruct to the extent and when it confers upon the surviving spouse greater rights—pertinently, here, when by virtue of the lifetime nature (i.e., despite re-marriage) of the usufruct granted by the will, such usufruct attempts to grant the widow a usufruct over the child's property which impinges on the *legitime*, and which is therefore subject to reduction—the

---

* Bracketed material in italics added by author.

legal usufruct does not infringe on the *legitime*, by operation of law (Article 916), but this usufruct terminates upon re-marriage; a testamentary usufruct may infringe and may therefore be reduced, if the value of the usufruct exceeds the disposable portion. *See:* Article 1499; Yiannopoulos, PERSONAL SERVITUDES, Section 16, pp. 55—58 (1968); Yiannopoulos, *Testamentary Dispositions in Favor of the Surviving Spouse and the Legitime of Descendants*, 28 La.L.Rev. 509 (1968).

Thus, as the court of appeal noted, the usual interpretation of the prior jurisprudence (which the majority here reasonably corrects as based on erroneous dicta) was that a "donation mortis causa of the usufruct of community property to the surviving spouse confers a lifetime usufruct which is not terminated by marriage . . ., even if the testament grants the same usufruct the survivor would be acquired by operation of law under LSA-C.C. Art. 916 in the intestate succession." 242 So. 2d 342. The court of appeal further held, correctly in my opinion, that "While we find the usufruct left by testament in the instant case was not terminated in its entirety by the second marriage of the usufructuary, nonetheless we are of the opinion it cannot burden the one-third *legitime* due the forced heir." 242 So. 2d 343.

The court of appeal's interpretation—that the usufruct mentioned by the testament is legal insofar as "confirming" the legal usufruct of Article 916, but testamentary insofar as [e]ncumbering the *legitime* with a burden not there authorized (i.e., insofar as surviving beyond remarriage)—is not as intellectually attractive as that adopted by the majority, by which the usufruct is either legal or testamentary but not a blurred composition of both. However, this interpretation is one sanctioned by a logical extension of interpretation. It is beneficial, insofar as in accord with the probable intent of the testator to grant a usufruct (at least until re-marriage) without the unfortunate tax or reduction-as-in-excess-of-the-*legitime* problems, whether or not the testament mentions that the usufruct is to be for the survivor's lifetime. And such interpretation is further in accord with the usual interpretation that a usufruct created by a will is for the usufructuary lifetime, unless a shorter duration is expressed.

For what help it may be in any reconsideration of this issue, I would like, at the risk of unduly lengthening this concurrence, to incorporate the following analysis of the problems here involved. The analysis is taken almost verbatim from the galley proof of an article by Professor Yiannapoulos to be published in the forthcoming number (2) of Volume Thirty-Two of the Louisiana Law Review, *The Work of the Louisiana Appellate Court for the 1970-1971*, 32 La.L.Rev. 164, et seq.

The analysis (*see* paragraphs 1 through 5 below) proceeds as follows:

1.   In Louisiana, a usufruct may be either testamentary or legal. It is testamentary when created by mortis causa juridical act; it is legal when created by operation of law. Classification of a usufruct as legal or testamentary carries significant consequences concerning the usufructuary's duty to give security, liability for inheritance taxes, termination of the usufruct upon remarriage, and impingement on the *legitime* of forced heirs. *See* Yiannopoulos, PERSONAL SERVITUDES § 105 (1968). If the usufruct is legal, it terminates upon remarriage, according to Article 916 of the Civil Code; the usufructuary is relieved of the obligation to give security by application of Article 560 of the same Code; the usufructuary is not liable for the payment of inheritance taxes according to fiscal legislation, as interpreted by Louisiana courts; *Succession of Marsal*, 118 La. 212, 42 So. 778 (1907); and the usufruct does not violate the *legitime* of forced heirs:

Succession of Moore, 40 La.Ann. 531, 4 So. 460 (1888). If, on the other hand, the usufruct is Testamentary the opposite results follow. Thus, a testamentary usufruct does not terminate upon remarriage: *Smith v. Nelson,* 1212 La. 170, 46 So. 200 (1908). The usufructuary owes taxes: *Succession of Eisemann,* 170 So. 2d 913 (La.App.4th Cir., 1965), *writ refused* 247 La. 489, 172 So. 2d 294. The usufructuary, in the absence of testamentary dispensation, must furnish security: *Succession of Carlisi,* 217 La. 675, 47 So. 2d 42 (1950). And it ought to follow clearly that a testamentary usufruct may impinge on the *legitime* of forced heirs: LA. CIVIL CODE art. 1499; Yiannopoulos, PERSONAL SERVITUDES § 16 (1968).

2. The distinction between testamentary and legal usufruct has been blurred by the judicial doctrine of "confirmation" of a legal usufruct by will. Article 916 of the Civil Code establishes the legal usufruct in favor of the surviving spouse in community "when the predeceased husband or wife . . . *Shall not have disposed* by last will and testament, of his or her share in the community property." (Emphasis added.) Early Louisiana decisions hold that any disposition by will defeats the legal usufruct under Article 916, *Succession of Schiller,* 33 La.Ann. 1 (1881); *Forstall v. Forstall,* 28 La.Ann. 197 (1876); *Grayson v. Sanford,* 12 La.Ann. 646 (1957). These cases have been long overruled by a long line of decision establishing the proposition that the legal usufruct under Article 916 may be defeated only by a disposition that is "adverse" to the interest of the surviving spouse a dispensation that is not adverse to the in excess of the surviving spouse merely "confirms" the legal usufruct. *Succession of Maloney,* 127 La. 913, 54 So. 146 (1911); *Fricke v. Stafford,* 159 So. 2d 52 (La.App.1st Cir. 1963); Yiannopoulos, PERSONAL SERVITUDES § 103 (1968).

3. The doctrine of confirmation of a legal usufruct by will has no statutory foundation; Article 916 of the Civil Code does not contain the word "adverse" and its obvious interpretation is that any testamentary disposition excludes the legal usufruct. Moreover, the doctrine of confirmation is an anomalous theoretic construction that has complicated unduly the Louisiana law of successions, as it gives rise to the troublesome question whether a legal usufruct confirmed by will is "legal" or "testamentary." It might be indeed simpler to accept the view that any testamentary disposition excludes the legal usufruct under Article 916. Nevertheless, the doctrine of confirmation is deeply imbedded in Louisiana jurisprudence and favors strongly the interests of the surviving spouse. In practical terms, this doctrine allows the surviving spouse to cumulate rights under Article 916 of the Civil Code and under the will of the deceased spouse. See Yiannopoulos, PERSONAL SERVITUDES § 104 (1968).

4. Assuming that the doctrine of confirmation is here to stay, the basic question is whether a confirmed legal usufruct ought to be classified as "legal" or "testamentary." In this respect there are conflicting determinations. For purposes of taxation, Louisiana courts have reached the conclusion that the mere confirmation of the legal usufruct does not change the nature of the usufruct into a testamentary one. It remains "legal" and inheritance taxes are avoided. See *Succession of Baker,* 129 La. 74, 55 So. 714 (1911); *Succession of Brown,* 94 So. 2d 317 (La.App.Orl.Cir.1957); *Succession of Lynch,* 145 So. 42 (La.App.Orl.Cir.1932); Yiannopoulos, PERSONAL SERVITUDES § 17 (1968).

Insofar as the usufructuary's obligation to give security is concerned, the usufruct that has been confirmed by will presumably is regarded as "legal," and the survivor is dispensed from the duty to give security. Cf. *Winsberg v. Winsberg*, 233 La. 67, 96 So. 2d 44 (1957); *Succession of Moore*, 40 La.Ann. 531, 4 So. 460 (1888); Yiannopoulos, PERSONAL SERVITUDES § 61 (1968). In cases involving the question of infringement of the *legitime*, Louisiana courts have likewise reached the conclusion that the mere confirmation of the legal usufruct does not change its nature. It remains legal; hence, *legitime* of issue of the marriage is not violated. This was one of the main issues in *Succession of Moore*, 40 La.Ann. 531, 4 So. 460 (1888). But in cases involving the question whether a confirmed legal usufruct terminates upon the remarriage of the usufructuary, lower courts and commentators have reached the conclusion that the usufruct is "testamentary" in order to exclude its termination upon the remarriage of the usufructuary. As the majority correctly holds, there is no controlling authority for this inconsistency.

5. Consistent and even-handed administration of justice might treat a confirmed usufruct as legal or testamentary for all purposes. The question whether a confirmed usufruct is legal or testamentary might be resolved by application of the following tests: "If the testator intended to give to the survivor the same rights that the law would have accorded him in the absence of a will, the survivor's usufruct is legal . . . If, on the other hand, the intention of the testator was to alter the scheme of intestate succession and to give to the survivor additional rights, the usufruct ought to be classified as testamentary."

Yiannopoulos, PERSONAL SERVITUDES § 105, page 350 (1968).

With regard to the above analysis, the majority has in effect concluded that it will be presumed that a testator intended merely to confirm the legal usufruct, for all purposes, and subject to all the limitations thereof, when such usufruct of the will includes property of the community which is also subject to the legal usufruct provided by Article 916.

As noted, this may not be an unreasonable conclusion. However, I do not think it to be unrealistic to conclude that the ordinary testator with issue of the marriage (and the ordinary notary or practitioner, using language sanctioned by a century of use as having contrary meanings) will necessarily realize (a) that when his will grants (confirms) the usufruct over property to his wife, such usufruct is not for life insofar as (only) Community assets are concerned and (b) that when his will does specify that such usufruct is for life, such language may constitute the usufruct a testamentary one (not a legal one), with unforeseen tax consequences and also subject to immediate reduction at the testator's death if it infringes on the *legitime*, whether or not the widow ever remarries in fact.

For the reasons assigned, I would adhere to what many until now felt was the proper resolution of the conflicting interests of the widow-protection afforded by Article 916 and the demands of forced heirship-that the usufruct mentioned in the will may indeed be for life (the ordinary meaning of the language when no other duration is specified), but that it does not infringe on the *legitime* insofar (but Only insofar) as not burdening the *legitime* in excess of the legal usufruct provided by Article 916. Conversely, to the extent (and Only to the extent) that the usufruct mentioned by the will is identical with the legal usufruct of Article 916, the will merely "confirms" the latter; if, however, the *legitime* is (becomes) burdened by the usufruct to any greater extent than it would be burdened by the legal usufruct, to such greater extent the usufruct is Created rather than merely confirmed by the will.

I respectfully concur.

NOTES

Apparently Justice Tate viewed the "confirmed" legal usufruct as a hybrid creature carrying features of both the legal and the testamentary usufruct. Thus, a usufruct could be legal, testamentary, or confirmatory. Justice Dixon, for the majority, seems to limit the usufructs to two types: legal and testamentary, with the confirmatory being merely a kind of legal usufruct.

In *Chauvin*, the question was not whether the testator had intended his spouse to have a usufruct, but whether or not the usufruct granted to her was confirmation of the intestate (legal) usufruct, or rather was a testamentary usufruct. As you may have gleaned from the case, the question at the time of *Chauvin* was significant because a legal usufruct was not subject to Louisiana inheritance tax or to security provisions, and was not considered an impingement on the *legitime* of forced heirs; whereas, a testamentary usufruct was subject to inheritance taxes and to the giving of security, and was considered an impingement on the *legitime*.

Under current La. C.C. 1499, a testator may grant a usufruct to a surviving spouse over all or part of his community or separate property and such a usufruct would not impinge upon the *legitime*. Also, a testator may grant his surviving spouse a usufruct with the power to dispose of nonconsumables without the usufruct being considered an impingement on the *legitime*. (La. C.C. 1499, Comment b). Professor A.N. Yiannopoulos, in his editorial note to article 1499 in the Civil Code Special Millennium Edition (2000), cautions that the law of usufruct as expressed in La. C.C. 568, requires that such a power to dispose of nonconsumables must be granted *expressly*.

Although Revision Comment (d) states that *Chauvin* has been legislatively overruled, Professor Yiannopoulos warns that one must be careful with the wording of the granting of a usufruct by will, as he notes

> If a testator gave by will to the surviving spouse "a usufruct under Article 890," question would arise whether this usufruct is a legal usufruct or a testamentary usufruct. According to the [comments] accompanying Article 1499, such a usufruct should be "for life" because the possibility of confirmation by will no longer exists. However, naked owners, and especially the descendants of the testator, may plausibly argue that the testator clearly intended to create a usufruct that should terminate on the remarriage of the usufructuary.

Could one avoid the conflict between the comments and editorial notes by pointing out that if a testator leaves or confirms "an 890 usufruct" in favor of a surviving spouse, the testator did in fact designate a time, i.e. the time period in article 890, thus terminating the usufruct upon the spouse's remarriage? What about the statement in article 1499 that a shorter period must be "*expressly* designated"? Are there other ways that a testator might still confirm the 890 usufruct?

SUCCESSION OF WALDRON

323 So. 2d 434 (La. 1975)

(Footnotes omitted.)

MARCUS, Justice.

Gilbert Spence Waldron died testate on February 23, 1973, survived by his widow, Mrs. Katherine L. Waldron, and their only child, Mrs. Thelma Waldron Denn. The decedent's estate consisted solely of community property. The dispositive portion of his olographic will, valid in form, provided as follows:

> Second, I will and bequeath unto my wife, Katherine L. Waldron, the usufruct of my entire estate for life, in addition to the naked title to all other property that I own at my death, subject to and less that portion that under the law my daughter Thelma is entitled to inherit as her *legitime* or forced portion.
>
> In case my wife predeceases me, in that event, I will and bequeath unto my grandchild Phillip Anthony Parrino, Jr. Five Hundred (500.00) Dollars, Cash, and unto my daughter, Thelma Alice Parrino, only that portion of my estate that under the law she is entitled to inherit as a forced portion, it being my intention to limit her inheritance to only her *legitime*. The balance of my estate, in case my wife predeceases me, I will and bequeath unto my grandchildren, George Frederick Denn and Thomas James Denn, in equal proportion, share and share alike.

After the will was probated, the testator's daughter filed suit to reduce the usufruct in favor of her mother, alleging that it impinged upon the forced portion. The trial court rendered judgment in favor of defendant, and the court of appeal reversed. 308 So. 2d 364 (La.App.1st Cir. 1975). Upon defendant's application, we granted certiorari. 313 So. 2d 245 (La.1975).

In the portion of the will set forth above, the testator bequeathed to defendant the usufruct of his entire estate for life, as well as the naked ownership of the disposable portion, which was two-thirds of the estate. LA.CIVIL CODE art. 1493 (1870). He left to plaintiff, his only child, the naked ownership of the forced portion. These dispositions, in addition to his twice-repeated desire that his daughter's inheritance be restricted to her *legitime*, make quite evident his intention to leave to his wife the maximum amount allowed under Louisiana law.

Our law generally mandates that the forced heir inherit the *legitime* in full ownership. LA.CIVIL CODE arts. 1493, 1494, 1710 (1870). To this general rule there is an exception in article 916 of the Civil Code, which, prior to its amendment in 1975, provided as follows:

> In all cases, when the predeceased husband or wife shall have left issue of the marriage with the survivor, and shall not have disposed by last will and testament, of his or her share in the community property, the survivor shall hold a (in) usufruct, during his or her natural life, so much of the share of the deceased in such community property as may be inherited by such issue. This usufruct shall cease, however, whenever the survivor shall enter into a second marriage.

We have held that the legal usufruct authorized by article 916 does not apply only in intestate successions. The testator may confirm in his will the usufruct that the surviving spouse

2-49

inherits by operation of law under article 916. *Succession of Chauvin*, 26 La. 828, 257 So. 2d 422 (1972). Additionally, he may donate mortis causa the disposable portion of his estate to her in full ownership. *Succession of Moore*, 40 La.Ann. 531, 4 So. 460 (1888). In practical effect, the surviving spouse is permitted to cumulate the legal usufruct in her favor with donations mortis causa that do not exceed the disposable portion. The testator is not permitted, however, to burden the *legitime* with a usufruct beyond the period authorized by Civil Code article 916. LA.CIVIL CODE art. 1710 (1870); *Chauvin, supra*. Hence, the legal usufruct, even when confirmed in the testament, terminates by operation of law upon the surviving spouse's remarriage.

In the case Sub judice, defendant has not remarried, plaintiff was issue of her marriage with the decedent, and the decedent's entire estate consists solely of community property. Clearly, then, if Mr. Waldron had died intestate a legal usufruct in defendant's favor would have attached to his entire estate. Or, if he had left the disposable portion in full ownership to his widow and had merely confirmed the article 916 usufruct, a legal usufruct would have attached to the forced portion. The testator, however, did not merely confirm the legal usufruct, which, as stated above, ends upon remarriage; he provided that the usufruct should last for life. The question for determination is whether the testator, in attempting to give defendant greater rights than the law permits, has deprived her of the legal usufruct.

The court of appeal held that he did. The court stated that a usufruct that "departs from the provision of Article 916" must be characterized as wholly testamentary, rather than legal, and thus must be reduced to the extent that it impinges on the forced portion. It therefore held that plaintiff was presently entitled to the forced portion in full ownership.

We disagree. In *Succession of Moore*, 40 La.Ann. 531, 4 So. 460 (1888), this court, rejecting prior cases to the contrary, held that the surviving spouse is entitled to the article 916 usufruct unless a testamentary disposition is adverse to the legal usufruct. The testator can exclude the operation of article 916 if he exhausts, by means of donations mortis causa to persons other than his spouse, the portion of his estate that under article 916 is subject to the legal usufruct. He may also defeat the legal usufruct simply by stating his intention that his share of the community property inherited by issue of the marriage shall not be subject to it. Absent such an adverse testamentary disposition, the surviving spouse inherits, by operation of law, a usufruct of the estate to the extent permitted by Civil Code article 916.

Accordingly, our task is to examine the testament in this case in order to determine whether the decedent disposed of his estate adversely to the legal usufruct. He provided that his widow should enjoy a usufruct of the forced portion of his estate for life. As we stated in *Winsberg v. Winsberg*, 233 La. 67, 96 So. 2d 44 (1957), a bequest to one's spouse of More than the law allows is not an adverse disposition that defeats the legal usufruct. Since the disposition Sub judice is obviously not adverse, the legal usufruct is not defeated.

We reaffirm *Moore* and *Winsberg*, believing that these decisions are consonant with the Civil Code. Article 1712 of the Civil Code [footnote omitted] directs us to interpret a testament in a way that furthers, rather than frustrates, the testator's lawful intent. In addition, article 1502 provides that excessive donations are not null, but merely reducible to the disposable portion. The court of appeal reached a result that was contrary to the mandate of article 1712 and to the spirit of article 1502. For, if the testator in this case had left his widow the disposable portion in full ownership, and had either been silent as to the devolution of the *legitime* or had provided that the forced portion was only "subject to" a usufruct, the surviving spouse could have inherited both the disposable portion in full ownership and a usufruct of the *legitime* until her remarriage.

The result reached by the court below makes the testator's widow, who has not remarried, the victim of his liberality. Furthermore, it frustrates the intention of the testator, who sought to leave his wife the maximum amount that was legally permissible.

It must be remembered that the surviving spouse's usufruct of the *legitime* is created by virtue of the law, not by the will. *Moore, supra.* Hence, the usufruct is legal, and does not impinge on the *legitime*, to the extent that it gives the surviving spouse the same rights that she inherits by operation of law under article 916. Only to the extent that, and at such time as, allowance of the usufruct would give the surviving spouse greater rights than those she inherits by operation of law must it be considered testamentary, and must it be examined to determine whether it impinges on the *legitime*.

This result is totally consistent with *Moore* itself, the seminal case in this area. Indeed, the facts in *Moore*, are indistinguishable from those in the present case. In *Moore*, the testator bequeathed his wife the disposable portion in full ownership, and further provided that she should have a usufruct of the forced portion "during her natural life." We held that the forced portion would be subject to a usufruct during her widowhood. Implicit in this holding was a recognition by this court that the usufruct would not be regarded as testamentary ab initio, but only upon such time as the spouse should remarry.

*   *   *

We hold, therefore, that defendant is entitled to inherit, in addition to the disposable portion in full ownership, a usufruct of the forced portion until remarriage. If she remarries, article 916 will cease to have application, and the usufruct of the forced portion will be extinguished by operation of law. Defendant thus receives no more than the testator could lawfully have bequeathed her, and no less.

Decree

For the reasons assigned, the judgment of the court of appeal is reversed, and the judgment of the trial court is reinstated; all costs of this proceeding are to be assessed against plaintiff.

DIXON, J., dissents and assigns reasons.

DIXON, Justice (dissenting).

I respectfully dissent.

It seems to me that the court does little today except perpetuate the confusion that naturally follows the "adverse disposition" doctrine-a doctrine which effectively erases one of the important conditions precedent to the operation of C.C. 916: ". . . when the predeceased . . . shall not have disposed by last will and testament, of his or her share in the community property . . ." 25 La.L.Rev. 873, 877ff.; 18 Tul.L.Rev. 181, 199ff.; Yiannopoulos, PERSONAL SERVITUDES, §§ 103, 104 (West, 1968).

We also continue to approve an erosion of one provision of C.C. 1710: ". . . no charges or conditions can be imposed by the testator on the legitimate portion of forced heirs . . ." *See also* C.C. 1493-1495.

True, C.C. 916 is a "charge" upon the *legitime*, necessarily recognized because it is imposed by the same kind of statute that protects the *legitime*. But its history indicates its application should not be extended beyond its terms.

C.C. 916 appeared in the Code for the first time in 1870. Its source was Act 152, § 2 of 1844. There was no corresponding article in the Code Napoleon, perhaps the result of a drafting mistake (*see Planiol, The Civil Law*, Vol. 3-Part 1, § 1868, La. State Law Institute, 1959), a mistake perpetuated in part because of a continental preference for devolution to blood kin, rather than to those presumed closest in affection to the decedent. Reform in France establishing a widow's usufruct came much later than in Louisiana. (*Planiol, supra*, § 1869ff.).

Our Civil Code has contained a prohibition against "charges" upon the *legitime* since 1808. Article 1703 of the 1825 Code (art. 1710, Civil Code of 1870) was held to prohibit the bequest to the surviving spouse of a life usufruct on the entire estate. *Clarkson v. Clarkson*, 13 La.Ann. 422 (1858). In *Succession of Turnell*, 32 La.Ann. 1218 (1880), C.C. 1710 was held to prevent a testamentary requirement that the property be administered for five years and held under administration until each minor heir reached majority. Until Act 152 of 1844, not even the widow's usufruct would burden the *legitime*; the widow was protected, as in France, by her right to one-half of the community, the needy spouse's marital fourth, and the privileged claim to $1000 from an insolvent estate. (Dainow, *Forced Heirship*, 4 La.L.Rev. 42, 63).

Although the *Succession of Chauvin*, 260 La. 828, 257 So. 2d 422 (1972), involved the "confirmation" doctrine, it should not be interpreted as favoring the perpetuation of the "adverse disposition" notion-a doctrine which seems to produce result-oriented decisions rather than decisions predictably based upon clear statutory provisions.

The *Succession of Chauvin, supra*, held that, when a will left "all I die possessed of to my son . . . subject to the usufruct thereon which I leave to my loving wife . . .," there was a "confirmation" of the C.C. 916 widow's usufruct which terminated upon remarriage, according to the provisions of C.C. 916. The only reason (that can be gleaned from the *Chauvin* opinion) for deciding that C.C. 916 required that remarriage ended the widow's usufruct is that the will purported to make no disposition of property that would not have been made in the absence of a will by operation of law. Although we had the opportunity to abandon the "confirmation" concept, we declined and chose instead to follow the "deeply imbedded" jurisprudential doctrine of "confirmation." Yiannopoulos, *Property*, 32 La.L.Rev. 172, 197. If the will in *Chauvin* had done other than "confirm," we could not have enforced the last sentence of C.C. 916, because, by its terms, if the forced heir had not inherited the disposable portion, C.C. 916 would not have been applicable.

We now have in our jurisprudence enough cases to evaluate the judicial gloss on C.C. 916, and it seems to me that it is time to return to the codal provision, and hold that, if the testator disposed (to anyone) of his share in the community, C.C. 916 should not apply, and there should be no legal usufruct over the portion of the community inherited by the children. We should overrule the *Succession of Moore*, 40 La.Ann. 531, 4 So. 460 (1888) and *Winsberg v. Winsberg*, 233 La. 67, 96 So. 2d 44 (1957), and reinstate the rule of *Forstall v. Forstall*, 28 La.Ann. 197 (1876).

If the *legitime*, then, is thought by the forced heirs to be burdened by a testamentary usufruct, C.C. 1499, is available, the heirs are protected in their right to an unfettered *legitime*, and the erstwhile usufructuary is compensated by becoming the owner of the disposable portion.

NOTE

In *Benoit v. Benoit*, 379 So. 2d 270 (La. App. 3d Cir. 1979), the plaintiff argued that his mother's usufruct should terminate because she was living in concubinage. The court rejected the argument, explaining that the article dealing with the spousal usufruct expresses that termination occurs upon remarriage.

PROBLEM

How would *Waldron* be decided today, assuming that Waldron's daughter, Thelma, is a minor?

DARBY v. ROZAS
580 So. 2d 984 (La. App. 3d Cir. 1991), *writ granted*, 585 So. 2d 554 (La. 1991)
[Footnotes omitted]

LABORDE, Judge.

Dr. Sidney J. Rozas died testate on April 6, 1986. In his last will and testament dated August 13, 1982, Dr. Rozas made the following bequests:

*   *   *

I give and bequeath to my beloved wife, Dorothy Prejean Rozas, our home property located at 1115 Dietlein Boulevard, Opelousas, Louisiana, together with the vacant lot located to the south of such residence, including all furnishings, furniture and contents.

I also will and bequeath to my wife, Dorothy Prejean Rozas, the personal automobile which she may be using at the time of my death.

Subject to the above, I will and bequeath to my wife, Dorothy Prejean Rozas, the usufruct of all properties owned by me, movable and immovable, separate and community, including the usufruct of all royalties and minerals.

Subject to the above, I further will and bequeath to my wife, Dorothy Prejean Rozas, such additional bonds, stock and cash in order that she would receive, including the above bequest, one-half of the net value of my estate.

Subject to the foregoing and to the payment of all debts and claims, including estate taxes, I bequeath all of the remainder of my properties, movable and immovable, that I may own at my death to my two daughters, Alice Augusta Rozas Bienvenu and Mary Ann Rozas Nicholson, share and share alike, or per stirpes, to the descendants of any of them who predecease me.

*   *   *

Dr. Rozas' will was duly probated and the legatees were placed into possession of the assets of the estate by Judgment of Possession rendered January 8, 1987, under Probate No. P86-117-C of the 27th Judicial District Court, St. Landry Parish, Louisiana.

On June 8, 1988, defendant, Dorothy Prejean Rozas, the surviving spouse of Dr. Rozas, contracted another marriage. Plaintiffs, Mary Ann Rozas Darby and Alice Augusta Rozas Bienvenu, Dr. Rozas' children from a prior marriage, brought suit to terminate defendant's usufruct. Plaintiffs also sought to recover all sums paid to defendant as usufructuary since the date of her remarriage. The trial court ruled that the usufruct did not terminate upon defendant's remarriage. Plaintiffs have now perfected this appeal. We reverse and remand.

The sole issue raised by this appeal is whether the usufruct granted to defendant terminates upon the remarriage or the death of the usufructuary. Resolving this issue necessarily involves determining whether the usufruct granted to defendant is a legal or testamentary usufruct.

Under Civil Code Article 544, a usufruct may be established by a juridical act either inter vivos or mortis causa, or by operation of law. The usufruct created by a juridical act is referred to as a conventional usufruct, and the usufruct created by operation of law is referred to as a legal usufruct. Conventional usufructs are of two kinds: contractual (created by an inter vivos juridical act) or testamentary (created by a mortis causa juridical act). There are various kinds of legal usufructs in Louisiana; the one we are concerned with is the legal usufruct of the surviving spouse over the deceased spouse's share in the community that has been inherited by descendants.

For well over one hundred years, Louisiana has adopted some form of usufruct in favor of the surviving spouse "to secure means of sustenance for the surviving spouse and to prevent partition or liquidation of the community to the prejudice of that spouse." Yiannopoulos, 3 Louisiana Civil Law Treatise: Personal Servitudes, at 381 (1989). In the Civil Code of 1870, the usufruct of the surviving spouse was contained in Article 916. By Act 919, which acquired the force of law on January 1, 1982, Civil Code Article 916 was repealed and replaced by Article 890. Article 890 provides:

> If the deceased spouse is survived by descendants and shall not have disposed by testament of his share in the community property, the surviving spouse shall have a legal usufruct over so much of that share as may be inherited by the descendants. This usufruct terminates when the surviving spouse contracts another marriage, unless confirmed by testament for life or for a shorter period.

> The deceased may by testament grant a usufruct for life or for a shorter period to the surviving spouse over all or part of his separate property.

> A usufruct authorized by this Article is to be treated as a legal usufruct and is not an impingement upon legitime.

> If the usufruct authorized by this Article affects the rights of heirs other than children of the marriage between the deceased and the surviving spouse or affects separate property, security may be requested by the naked owner.

It is important to point out that a usufruct granted in favor of a surviving spouse can be legal or testamentary. When a usufruct is created by operation of law under Article 890, the following consequences attach: (1) the usufruct terminates upon remarriage; (2) the surviving spouse is not liable for the payment of Louisiana inheritance taxes; (3) the surviving spouse is relieved of giving security when the naked owners are children of the marriage; and (4) the usufruct does not impinge on the legitime. If the usufruct is testamentary: (1) in the absence of contrary testamentary disposition, the usufruct is for life; (2) the surviving spouse owes taxes; (3) in the absence of contrary testamentary disposition, the surviving spouse must provide security; and (4) the usufruct can potentially impinge on the legitime.

As Professor Yiannopoulos notes in his treatise, "[t]he distinction between legal usufruct and testamentary usufruct has been blurred in Louisiana by the doctrine of *confirmation* of the legal usufruct by will." Yiannopoulos, Personal Servitudes, at 392. Several early decisions interpreted Article 916 (the predecessor to Article 890) very narrowly, holding that any disposition by will defeated the legal usufruct in favor of the surviving spouse. See e.g. *Succession of Schiller,* 33 La.Ann. 1 (1881); *Forstall v. Forstall,* 28 La.Ann. 197 (1876). However, later, a line of jurisprudence overruled these cases and determined that a testamentary disposition that was not adverse to the interests of the surviving spouse did not defeat the usufruct. See e.g. *Succession of Waldron,* 323 So. 2d 434 (La.1975); *Succession of Chauvin,* 260 La. 828, 257 So. 2d 422 (1972). In other words, the surviving spouse is entitled to the legal usufruct under Article 890 unless a testamentary disposition is adverse to the legal usufruct. The Louisiana Supreme Court in *Succession of Waldron,* supra, observed that such an adverse disposition may occur when the testator makes an excessive disposition to persons other than the surviving spouse of the portion of the estate which is subject to the legal usufruct, or, very simply, if the testator expressly states his intention that the legal usufruct does not apply.

Under Article 890, a testator may confirm by testament the legal usufruct of the surviving spouse over the share of the community inherited by descendants "for life or for a shorter period." A testator may also grant to the surviving spouse "for life or a shorter period" a usufruct over all or a portion of his separate property. Professor Yiannopoulos points out that whenever a testator grants the surviving spouse a usufruct, the question that naturally arises is whether that usufruct is testamentary or legal. He writes:

> In all cases in which a predeceased spouse bequeaths to the surviving spouse a right of usufruct, the right may qualify as a legal usufruct, even if the usufruct is over separate property. However, it would be absurd to suggest that because the application of Article 890 ordinarily favors the interests of the surviving spouse a testator necessarily establishes a legal usufruct when he grants a usufruct to his surviving spouse. A testator enjoys testamentary freedom *not* to confirm the legal usufruct under Article 890, and he may by will enlarge or diminish the rights that the surviving spouse has under Article 890 in the absence of a will. As in the past, the question of the nature of the usufruct that the testator intended to create is a matter of testamentary interpretation.

> In the absence of express language qualifying the usufruct as legal or testamentary, the intent of the testator must be gathered from the provisions of the will. When a testator grants to the surviving spouse as usufructuary rights that are

incompatible with the notion of legal usufruct, he intends to grant a testamentary usufruct.

Yiannopoulos, Personal Servitudes, at 394. As examples of "rights that are incompatible with the notion of legal usufruct" Professor Yiannopoulos uses the hypothetical of a testator authorizing the usufructuary to grant a mineral lease without the consent of the naked owner, in contravention of Louisiana Mineral Code Article 190(B), and the hypothetical of the testator granting the usufructuary free reign to dispose of at his discretion corporeals and incorporeals, movables and immovables, contrary to Article 568 of the Civil Code.

In the case at bar, we can find nothing in Dr. Rozas' testament which would indicate that his intent was to create a testamentary and not a legal usufruct. Essentially, defendant received the disposable portion of the estate in full ownership and a usufruct over the community and separate property bequeathed to plaintiffs. We determine that such a bequest is not "incompatible with the notion of legal usufruct" and in no way constitutes an adverse disposition.

*   *   *

Defendant also argues that the usufruct granted over separate property is an exclusive characteristic of testamentary usufruct. This is simply just not the case under Civil Code Article 890 and the jurisprudence construing it. Article 890 allows the testator to grant a usufruct over all or part of his separate property. Paragraph three of Article 890 states that "[a] usufruct authorized by this Article is to be treated as a legal usufruct and is not an impingement upon legitime." In *Succession of Steen,* 499 So. 2d 1338 (La.App.3d Cir.1986), *rev'd on other grounds,* 508 So. 2d 1377 (La.1987), the decedent died possessing both community and separate property. By testament the deceased spouse gave his descendants the forced portion of his community and separate property and bequeathed to his spouse the disposable portion of his estate. The testament further confirmed the legal usufruct over all of his community property and granted his surviving spouse a usufruct over all of his separate property. This court observed in that case: "It is clear from the literal provisions of Article 890 of the Louisiana Civil Code that a decedent may by testament grant a usufruct for life to his surviving spouse over all or a part of his separate property.... Such a testamentary usufruct is a legal usufruct by operation of law." *Succession of Steen,* at 1342; see also *Succession of Daly v. McNamara,* 515 So. 2d 661 (La.App.3d Cir.1987), *writ denied,* 519 So. 2d 119 (La.1988). The Supreme Court granted writs in that case and in its review stated, "By testament, a spouse may grant a usufruct over all or part of his separate property.... any usufruct granted by a testator to a spouse is to be treated as a legal usufruct." *Succession of Steen,* 508 So. 2d 1377, 1379 (La. 1987). Additionally, Professor Yiannopoulos notes: "Normally, a usufruct created by a testament ought to be qualified as a testamentary usufruct; however, according to Article 890(2) and (3), the usufruct that a spouse establishes by a testament over his separate property in favor of the surviving spouse qualifies as a legal usufruct." Yiannopoulos, Personal Servitudes, at 409. Accordingly, we find that the usufruct granted by Dr. Rozas over both his community and separate property qualifies as a legal usufruct.

In his testament, Dr. Rozas neglected to set out the duration of the usufruct over his community property and his separate property. It is clear that under Article 890 (paragraph one), if no period is designated for the confirmed legal usufruct over community property, it terminates on the surviving spouse's remarriage. See *Succession of Chauvin,* supra; *Succession of Vallette,* 538 So. 2d 707 (La.App.4th Cir.), *writ denied,* 543 So. 2d 20 (La.1989). Regarding the usufruct over separate property, Article 890 (second paragraph) states that the testator may grant it for life or shorter period, but nothing is stated concerning what happens when the testator neglects to set out the duration of the usufruct. Professor Yiannopoulos squarely addresses this point: "It is preferable ... to read Article 890(2) and (3) in the light of the first paragraph of the same article and to conclude that the usufruct should terminate upon the remarriage of the surviving spouse. The alternative would be to qualify the usufruct as testamentary, which, in certain cases at least, would be contrary to the intent of the testator." Yiannopoulos, Personal Servitudes, at 409. Professor Yiannopoulos' view makes good sense and we agree with it. Therefore, the usufruct granted over Dr. Rozas' community and separate property terminated on defendant's remarriage occurring June 8, 1988.

Plaintiffs would have this court remand this matter to the trial court for an accounting for all sums which may have been paid to defendant as usufructuary after her remarriage, as the trial court did not allow any evidence with regard to values. This court grants the remand for such purpose.

For the foregoing reasons, the judgment of the trial court is reversed. The case is remanded for further proceedings not inconsistent with this opinion. All costs are to be borne by defendant, Dorothy Prejean Rozas.

REVERSED AND REMANDED.

FORET, J., dissents with reasons.

FORET, Judge, dissenting.

I respectfully dissent from the majority opinion. I would affirm the result of the trial court judgment, although not necessarily the reasoning.

The uncertainty of the law in this area is exemplified by the fact that the majority, as I did as the original author, relied a great deal on Professor Yiannopoulos' treatise. In this dissent, as I did in my review, I will refer to the page numbers in 49 LLR 803 rather than the treatise as cited by the majority opinion. This is purely for my convenience and I apologize therefor. The articles are identical.

With all due respect to the majority opinion, and to Professor Yiannopoulos, I make mention of the fact that Professor Yiannopoulos' article and the majority reviewer vacillate a great deal in discussing the Louisiana jurisprudence and statutory law.

The fiction of the legal usufruct relied on by the majority is just that, a fiction. The "legal" usufruct evolved *in this context* as an inheritance tax avoidance device and to pronounce, in Article 890 (third paragraph), that such a usufruct "is not an impingement on the legitime."

A usufruct is either legal or testamentary. It is a legal usufruct where it comes into being by *operation of law, ... period.* If a usufruct does not come into effect by operation of law, then it is a conventional or testamentary usufruct. There is no other way. You can call it a flop-eared dog if you wish, but you are still dealing with a testamentary usufruct.

Testamentary usufructs terminate as specified by the testator, either specifically, or as gleaned from his intent. It appears to me that it is just as logical, if not more so, to hold that if a testator does not designate a term for the testamentary usufruct, that his intention can be presumed to be that it will terminate at the death of the usufructuary. To surmise, as does the majority, that the testator's intent was that it would terminate upon remarriage of the usufructuary, is rank speculation.

As for the majority's relying on Professor Yiannopoulos' observation that it is "preferable" that the usufruct terminate at remarriage, I would simply note here that some folks like their eggs scrambled; others hate broccoli.

One observation by Professor Yiannopoulos in an Epilogue to his article, that the majority fails to mention, is that in 1983 Senator Casey introduced Senate Bill 137. At 49 LLR, 803, page 839, Professor Yiannopoulos points out that, among other things, Senator Casey proposed to amend the third paragraph of C.C. art. 890 as follows: "A usufruct authorized by this article terminates when the surviving spouse contracts another marriage, unless confirmed by testament for life or for a shorter period. A usufruct authorized by this article is to be treated as a legal usufruct and is not an impingement on the legitime…."

Yiannopoulos goes on to say, at page 840, that: "The third paragraph of the proposed amendment would clarify the ambiguity of the present law concerning the termination of a usufruct granted to the surviving spouse over separate property without indication as to its duration. Under the proposed amendment, a usufruct over separate property would terminate, like a usufruct over community property, upon the remarriage of the surviving spouse, unless confirmed by testament for life or for a shorter period. *These modest amendments met resistance from professors and attorneys and were advisedly deferred."* (emphasis provided.)

The "modest amendments" are still "deferred" by the Louisiana Legislature. The majority opinion, it seems to me, is indulging in judicial legislation by reading into the third paragraph of Article 890 an interpretation thereof that was declined by the Louisiana Legislature and advised against by professors and attorneys as being better left to triers of fact to determine the intent of the testator. To use the term "legal usufruct" as a tool to possibly thwart the intent of the testator and substitute the court's own sense of equity to dispose of the testator's will is injudicious. If the testator, a medical doctor, had intended the usufruct of his separate property to be for a shorter period, he would have said so. If he had intended the usufruct to terminate at the marriage of the usufructuary, he would have said so.

The term "legal" in the context of Article 890 is ambiguous when it is considered in the context of the other provisions of conventional, legal, and testamentary usufructs. As such, the legislative intent is determinative. The failure of the attempted amendment to Article 890 by Senator Casey loudly attests to the fact that the legislative intent is contrary to the majority opinion herein.

I respectfully dissent.

Usufruct of the Surviving Spouse: Post 1996 Revision

By Act 77 of 1996, effective June 18, 1996, the law was amended to provide that a surviving spouse usufruct, whether granted by operation of law or in a testament, does not create an impingement on a forced heir's *legitime*. C.C. 890 gives the surviving spouse a usufruct over all of the decedent's share of the community property inherited by his descendants to the extent that the decedent does not dispose of it through a testament. The usufruct terminates on the remarriage of the surviving spouse. For a usufruct granted under C.C. 890, the surviving spouse need not post security to the naked owner descendant, unless the naked owner is not a child of the usufructuary (i.e., stepparent) or if the naked owner is a child of the usufructuary, only if the child is a forced heir and only to the extent of his *legitime*. C.C. 573(A)(2).

C.C. 1499 permits a decedent to leave a surviving spouse usufruct in a testament over both community and separate property, which may include the power to dispose of the nonconsumables. The power to dispose of nonconsumables must be given expressly to the surviving spouse. See C.C. 1499, editor's note. The duration of the usufruct shall be for the life of the surviving spouse unless the testator provides a shorter period in the testament. When the usufruct is left in a testament, the right of children to request security is limited to forced heirs only, and when the forced heir children are the children of the usufructuary, security is available only to the extent the usufruct affects separate property in the legitime. C.C. 1514.

Why is it important to understand the legal fiction of "confirming" a legal usufruct that existed pre-1996? Because testaments written prior to the revision will be probated today. As a result, in Act 77 of 1996, the legislature included La. R.S. § 9:2441, which provides:

§ 2441. Duration of usufruct in previously executed testament
When a testament executed prior to June 18, 1996 leaves a usufruct to the surviving spouse without specifying its duration, the law in effect at the time the testament was executed shall govern the duration of the usufruct.

After the revision, "confirmation" of a legal usufruct is no longer necessary to protect the surviving spouse. While issues may still arise, usufructs left in a testament will be governed by C.C. 1499, and usufructs granted by law will be governed by C.C. 890.

SUCCESSION OF RICHAUD
835 So. 2d 653 (La. App. 1 Cir. 2002)

Foil, J.

This succession matter involves a dispute between the decedent's surviving spouse and her three children from a previous marriage. For the reasons that follow, we reverse in part, affirm in part and render.

Leah Heitkamp Richaud died testate on May 16, 1999, survived by her husband, Ronald J. Richaud, and three daughters from a previous marriage, Rana DaSilva, Devon DaSilva Roberts, and Arlissa DaSilva Ferrara. At the time of her death, Mrs. Richaud's children were each competent and over the age of 23 years. In her last will and testament dated June 25, 1998, Mrs. Richaud bequeathed the entirety of her estate and the residuary estate to her three daughters. The will named her daughter Rana DaSilva as executrix with full seizin and without bond. Mrs. Richaud's surviving spouse was not mentioned in the will.

Thereafter, Rana DaSilva was confirmed as testatrix. She filed a petition for probate and the will was ordered probated. The surviving spouse, however, refused to turn over the property of the decedent, claiming he had a usufruct over the community property of his deceased wife. As such, a petition for declaratory judgment, a temporary restraining order, and a preliminary and permanent injunction was filed on behalf of the succession, seeking to protect the succession property and to require the surviving spouse to turn over the property to the executrix. Following a hearing on the request for a preliminary injunction, the trial court denied the same, finding that the legal effect of the will was that the surviving spouse was entitled to a statutory legal usufruct.

The surviving spouse subsequently filed a reconventional demand, asking the court to declare that he is entitled to a legal usufruct over the decedent's share of the community property. The heirs then filed a motion for security, asking the court to require the surviving spouse to post security to protect their interests.

Following a trial on the merits, the trial court rendered judgment recognizing that the surviving spouse has a legal usufruct over the decedent's share of the community property until his death or remarriage. The court dismissed the request for permanent injunction. On the motion for security, the court ordered the surviving spouse to provide security and further imposed several restrictions and prohibitions. Both the heirs and the surviving spouse appealed.

On appeal, the heirs contend that, where the express language of a statutory will explicitly leaves the entire estate and residuary estate to the decedent's three children and makes no mention whatsoever of the surviving spouse, it is manifest error to hold there is a "legal" usufruct in favor of the surviving spouse. They further assert that the trial court erred in failing to grant a declaratory judgment and permanent injunction against the surviving spouse, who is illegally attempting to assert an intestate usufruct in a testate succession and usurp control of the decedent's estate.

In response, the surviving spouse argues that under Louisiana jurisprudence, he is entitled to a legal usufruct where the decedent leaves a statutory will leaving all of her property to her children, but not expressly granting or denying a usufruct to her surviving spouse.

We agree with the heirs that the surviving spouse is not entitled to a usufruct under the facts of this case. La. Civ.Code art. 890 establishes a usufruct in favor of a surviving spouse, which is recognized by our courts as a legal usufruct. Under the clear wording of that article, however, it only establishes a usufruct to the extent that the decedent has not disposed of her share of the community property by testament. This case involves a testate succession and, thus, is governed under the Civil Code Title "Of donations inter vivos and mortis causa." La. Civ.Code art. 1499, which is found in that title, provides that "the decedent *may* grant a usufruct to the surviving spouse over all or part of his property." [Emphasis added.] Here, the decedent apparently chose not to do so. Rather, she left her entire estate to her three daughters. In her will, the testatrix dispensed with collation and explicitly named her daughter, Rana DaSilva, as executrix with full seizin and without the necessity of posting a bond.

The surviving spouse argues that "the adverse disposition rule" applies in testate successions. In other words, a testator must specifically state "there is no usufruct" in the will. Otherwise, he asserts, the legal usufruct is confirmed by a testator's silence. We disagree, but in any event, we believe that leaving one's entire estate to three daughters certainly constitutes an "adverse disposition." In conclusion, we find that the surviving spouse is not entitled to a usufruct over the decedent's share of the community property in this case and the heirs are entitled to a declaratory judgment to that effect.

*   *   *

Accordingly, we reverse that portion of the trial court's judgment declaring that Ronald J. Richaud is entitled to a legal usufruct over the decedent's portion of the community property. Judgment is hereby rendered in favor of Rana DaSilva, Devon DaSilva Roberts, and Arlissa DaSilva Ferrara, declaring that Ronald J. Richaud is not entitled to a legal usufruct over the decedent's portion of the community property, and Mr. Richaud is ordered to turn over that property to the executrix. That portion of the trial court's judgment ordering that Ronald

J. Richaud provide security and imposing restrictions and prohibitions upon Ronald J. Richaud is hereby affirmed and ordered to remain in full force and effect until the judgment of this court becomes executory. Costs of this appeal are assessed to Ronald J. Richaud.

REVERSED IN PART; AFFIRMED IN PART AND RENDERED.

IN RE SUCCESSION OF FEINGERTS

162 So. 3d 1215, 1217-24 (La. App. 4th Cir. 2015) *writ denied,* 2015-0754 (La. 6/1/15)

EDWIN A. LOMBARD, Judge.

The Appellant, Bruce Feingerts, seeks review of the district court's October 31, 2013 judgment denying his Motion to Traverse the Second and Amended Usufructuary Accounting, Motion to Traverse the Amended Estimative and Descriptive List of Assets and Liabilities, and Motion to Annul Judgment of Partial Possession and Return of Particular Legacies. Finding that the judgment of the district court was not manifestly erroneous or clearly wrong, we affirm.

The late Maurice and Doris Feingerts (collectively referred to as "the Feingerts") had three children born of their union: Susan Hackmeier ("Susan"), Bruce Feingerts ("Mr. Feingerts") and Jane Rushing ("the Executrix"). During their marriage, the Feingerts owned a home ("the Property") located on Bellaire Dr. in Orleans Parish. The Feingerts also owned a 50% interest in a food brokerage company, Specialty Food Sales Co., Inc. ("Specialty Foods"). The remaining half of the company was owned by Simon Pailet, who was the uncle of Maurice Feingerts. Maurice Feingerts died testate in 1967.

Pursuant to the will of Maurice Feingerts, he left Susan, the Executrix and Mr. Feingerts all of his separate and community property to be divided equally among them. Said legacies were placed in three separate trusts, subject to a lifetime usufruct granted to Doris Feingerts ("the Decedent"), who was also named as the trustee of all three trusts. Pursuant to the Judgment of Possession in the succession of Maurice Feingerts, the assets of his estate, consisted of: 1) his one-half share of the community property, i.e., the Property; 2) an undivided one-half interest in four lots located in Jefferson Parish; and 3) "[a]ny and all property remaining in the name of Maurice P. Feingerts, including, but not limited to, bank accounts, stock, United States Savings Bond [sic], accounts receivable, automobiles, jewelry, and all other movable property of any nature or kind whatsoever."

The Decedent later sold the Feingerts' interest in Specialty Foods to Mr. Pailet. She subsequently made a series of personal loans to Mr. Feingerts and, on occasion, his law firm, following an accident wherein he sustained serious injuries. While the total amount of the loans made to Mr. Feingerts by the Decedent is in dispute, it is undisputed that Mr. Feingerts never paid off the entirety of his debt to his mother.

The Decedent, in July 2009, sold the Property, which was flooded in Hurricane Katrina, for $127,000. She sold the Property individually and in her capacity as trustee. During the same month, the Decedent also executed a will leaving Susan and the Executrix a particular legacy of $250,000 each. The Decedent further expressly stated within her 2009 will that she intentionally left no part of her estate to Mr. Feingerts because of "numerous gifts", "donations" and "loans" she made to him "over the years". The Decedent also forgave all debts, owed to her by Mr. Feingerts, but conditioned her forgiveness upon Mr. Feingerts not making any claims against her

Succession, such as challenging the validity of her testament or asserting naked ownership claims against her estate or her in her capacity as usufructuary.

On February 23, 2011, the Decedent executed a codicil to her 2009 testament wherein she left Susan and the Executrix a third of the residue of her estate each, with the remaining third being left to Mr. Feingerts' children. She additionally increased the particular legacies to Susan and the Executrix from $250,000 to $300,000 each. The last significant change made by the Decedent in her 2011 codicil was an acknowledgement that although her estate would owe a usufructuary debt to Mr. Feingerts for his naked ownership interest in the sale proceeds from the Property, she was applying the amount due to him toward his indebtedness to her. She concludes by stating that Mr. Feingerts is not due anything from her because his indebtedness to her exceeded her usufructuary debt to him.

The Decedent contemporaneously executed an Authentic Act with the aforementioned codicil. Principal statements, relevant to the instant matter, within the Authentic Act include:

1. She sold the Property for $127,000 and that the one-sixth interest of her three children in the proceeds from the sale is $21,166 each;
2. She made numerous loans to Mr. Feingerts between September 1994 and April 2005, totaling $352,300, with the "express condition, understanding, and promise" that he would repay her over time; and
3. She further states that she considers that his indebtedness to her to be reduced by $30,000 he repaid and the $21,166 due to him as his naked ownership interest; thus, his indebtedness remained at just over $300,000.

The Decedent passed away in September 2011, and her succession was subsequently opened. In 2012, Mr. Feingerts filed a Proof of Claim principally asserting a claim against the succession of the Decedent in the amount of $103,313.01, which he calculated as the value of his naked ownership interest in the Succession of Maurice Feingerts.

Mr. Feingerts later filed three motions in the succession proceeding: (1) Motion to Traverse the Second and Amended Usufructuary Accounting; (2) Motion to Traverse the Amended Estimative Descriptive List of Assets and Liabilities; and (3) Motion to Annul Judgment of Partial Possession and Return of Particular Legacies. After holding a two-day hearing in the summer of 2013, the district court denied all three motions on October 18, 2013. The district court further granted the Executrix's Petition to Homologate the Second Amended Usufructuary Accounting and Petition for Partial Possession. The instant suspensive appeal followed the denial of Mr. Feingerts' motion for new trial.

Mr. Feingerts [argues that] . . . the district court erred in failing to find that Mr. Feingerts' debts to the Decedent were not prescribed.

*   *   *

Lastly, Mr. Feingerts argues that the district court erred in denying his motions because the alleged $322,300 debt owed to the Decedent has prescribed. He maintains that because the debt prescribed it cannot be used to offset his inheritance, particularly from his father's estate.

The objective of usufructuary accounting is to determine the amount of the debt due to the naked owner by the usufructuary at the termination of the usufruct. 2 La. Prac. Est. Plan. § 8:18 (2014–2015 ed.). Furthermore, with regard to descriptive lists, La. Code Civ. Proc. art. 3137 provides that a sworn descriptive list of the property of a succession is deemed prima facie correct, but it may be traversed if an interested party believes it is in error. The burden is on the party filing a motion to traverse to show that the descriptive list is in error. *In re Succession of Feitel,* 05–1482, p. 4 (La. App. 4 Cir. 4/18/07), 958 So. 2d 58, 60, *writ denied,* 07–1046 (La.8/31/07), 962 So. 2d 436. Thus, it was Mr. Feingerts' burden to demonstrate that the alleged debt was not due to his mother's estate.

The district court explained in its Reasons for Judgment that it was "incumbent upon Mr. Feingerts to prove the inaccuracy of the amended lists." It further reasoned that he failed to produce credible evidence or testimony that his debt to the Decedent could not be offset against any sums due to him from her succession or from the succession of his father. The court also noted that under the terms of the Decedent's 2009 will and 2011 codicil, and the evidence adduced by the Executrix, these debts "subsisted until the death of [the] Decedent and are sufficiently related to his claims to be offset against any sums that [the] Decedent or her succession might owe to Mr. Feingerts." We agree.

Citing *Oilbelt Motor Co. v. George T. Bishop, Inc.,* 167 La. 183, 185, 118 So. 881, 882 (1928), *Wolff v. Warden,* 141 So. 821, 822 (La.App. 2 Cir.1932), and *McElroy Metal Mill, Inc. v. Hughes,* 322 So. 2d 822, 824 (La.App. 2 Cir.1975), Mr. Feingerts argues that it is well settled law that there is no offset if one set of debts is prescribed. None of the above cases, however, pertains to successions and/or usufructuaries.

Additionally, both Mr. Feingerts and the Appellees assert that the holding of the Fifth Circuit in *Succession of Dittmar,* 493 So. 2d 221 (La.App. 5 Cir.1986) bears examining. In *Dittmar,* Ms. Dittmar had a usufruct over the estate of her deceased husband, which included consumables and non-consumables. During her lifetime, she and her children sold some of the non-consumables, immovable property. Additionally, her son, Mr. Quinn, borrowed $75,000 from her as evidenced by a promissory note, which he never repaid. *Id.* at 223.

After Ms. Dittmar's death, her succession filed a petition proposing the distribution of funds to heirs and including collation due by each heir. The executor of Ms. Dittmar's estate, who was one of her children, sought to offset Mr. Quinn's legitime—owed from his father's succession—against the debt he owed to Ms. Dittmar. Over the objection of Mr. Quinn, the district court ordered homologation as calculated by the executor. *Id.* at 224.

The Fifth Circuit affirmed the judgment of the district court holding that Ms. Dittmar's succession could offset the payment owed to Mr. Quinn against what he owed to his mother. The appellate court reasoned that the ultimate issue was whether the executor of a succession of one spouse, which has funds belonging to the other's spouse's succession, can raise "compensation" as a defense to an action by a forced heir for his legitime from the pre-deceased spouse. *Id.* at 224–25. "Compensation takes place by operation of law when two persons owe to each other sums of money or quantities of fungible things identical in kind, and these sums or quantities are liquidated and presently due." La. Civ. Code art. 1893.

Additionally, the appellate court applied La. Code Civ. Proc. art. 424 in holding that the parties' obligations could be offset. *Dittmar,* 493 So. 2d at 227. "Except as otherwise provided herein, a prescribed obligation arising under Louisiana law may be used as a defense if it is incidental to, or connected with, the obligation sought to be enforced by the plaintiff." La. Code Civ. Proc. art. 424. The Court explained that Mr. Quinn's obligation to collate was closely connected to the succession's obligation to pay him his legitime. *Dittmar,* 493 So. 2d. at 227. Thus, it held that the parties' obligations to pay each other could be offset. The Fifth Circuit additionally explained that the succession's obligation to deliver to Mr. Quinn any immovable property over which Ms. Dittmar had usufruct could not be offset by Mr. Quinn's obligation to pay because the debts are not identical in kind. *Id.*

In the matter *sub judice,* Mr. Feingerts avers that there is no offset here because the debts—the obligation to pay and the obligation to deliver—are not identical in kind. He argues that because he did not consent to the sale of the Property, the Decedent still owes him the obligation to deliver the Property. Additionally, he points out that in the instant matter there is not a promissory note evidencing his indebtedness.

The Decedent, by selling the Property, converted her usufruct over a nonconsumable to a usufruct over a consumable, the proceeds of the sale. Thus, her succession has no obligation to deliver the Property to Mr. Feingerts, but her obligation to pay him his naked ownership interest remained. Pursuant to *Dittmar,* we find that the parties' obligations to pay each other can be offset because even if Mr. Feingerts's obligation to pay the Decedent has prescribed it is at least incidental to the obligation he seeks to enforce in this succession. Moreover, because Mr. Feingerts admits he still owed his mother money and did not present evidence contesting the amount of his alleged indebtedness, the lack of a promissory note or other instrument reflecting his indebtedness is of no moment. Furthermore, his argument that the succession has to deliver his interest in the Property because its sale was invalid is not properly before us. That issue is being litigated in a separate district court proceeding.

Moreover, we note that the inheritance of the Executrix and Jane would be diminished if Mr. Feingerts' debt was deemed prescribed and he could still claim a usufructuary debt was due. Mr. Feingerts' position in essence is that he is entitled to receive his naked ownership interest where he has: 1) loaned funds from a usufructuary parent; 2) failed to repay the total loan amount despite agreeing to do so; and 3) waited until the debt prescribed to avoid repayment to the Decedent or her succession. However, it was clearly the Decedent's intention to leave legacies to her daughters to equal what she had already loaned Mr. Feingerts. We further note that it is unclear whether the Decedent was loaning money to Mr. Feingerts from her own funds or those over which she had usufruct. Regardless, as a debtor and naked owner, he cannot be allowed to deplete the estate of the Decedent or his father. Therefore, based upon the foregoing, we do not find that the judgment of the district court is manifestly erroneous or clearly wrong.

*   *   *

Forced Heirs Qualified Right to Request Security

IN RE SUCCESSION OF BEARD
147 So. 3d 753 (La. App. 1st Cir. 2014)

CRAIN, J.

In this succession proceeding, a legatee filed a petition seeking to terminate a testamentary usufruct or, alternatively, requesting that the usufructuary post security. The trial court granted a partial summary judgment finding that the usufructuary had the right to sell the property subject to the usufruct; and, after a trial, the court entered a judgment that denied any relief to the petitioner. We amend the summary judgment and affirm the judgment as amended; and we reverse, in part, the judgment on the merits and remand.

FACTS AND PROCEDURAL HISTORY

Carole Bagwell Beard died testate on November 5, 1993. Her surviving husband, Julius Beard, Jr., instituted this proceeding shortly after her death and obtained an order probating Carole's last will and testament. Carole's will bequeathed to Julius a life-time usufruct over her community property and separate property, except for certain property bequeathed to Julius in full ownership. The usufruct was created in Article IV of the will, which provides, in pertinent part:

> 4.2 Except for the property which is used in satisfaction of the forced portion of my estate, my spouse shall have the right, power and authority to sell or otherwise dispose of any property subject to my spouse's usufruct without having to obtain the consent of the naked owners thereof. Should any property subject to the usufruct granted herein to my spouse be sold or exchanged at any time, or from time to time, the usufruct to which said property was subjected shall apply to the proceeds of the sale or exchange of such property and to any property in which such proceeds may from time to time be reinvested.

After probating the will, Julius obtained a judgment of possession on June 29, 1994, that, in pertinent part, placed him in possession of the "usufruct for his lifetime of all [of Carole's] share in the community property and of any separate property" owned by Carole at the time of her death, less and except the property bequeathed to Julius in full ownership. The judgment of possession further provided:

> That Julius Beard, Jr., be recognized as the surviving spouse in community, and as such entitled to the ownership and sent into possession of an undivided one-half (1/2) interest in the property belonging to the community of acquets and gains which existed between the deceased and her husband, *together with usufruct for his lifetime of the remaining undivided one-half (1/2) as provided in the decedent's Last Will and Testament* ... which property is described as follows.... (Emphasis added.)

The ensuing list of property consists of both immovable and movable property, including 295.51 acres of immovable property located in East Feliciana Parish (referred to herein as "the farm") and a parcel of property located in the Virgin Islands, which Julius subsequently sold. The judgment of possession also vested each of Carole's four children, two by a prior marriage and two from her marriage with Julius, with an undivided one-eighth (1/8th) interest in the property subject to the usufruct.

In September of 2008, approximately 14 years after the entry of the judgment of possession, one of Carole's children from her first marriage, Christopher D. Shows, filed a petition in the succession proceeding seeking to terminate the usufruct based upon allegations that Julius had sold movable and immovable property subject to the usufruct without authorization from the naked owners and that he intended to sell more in the future. The petition further alleged that Julius had allowed fraud, waste, and abuse to impinge and devalue the property, that he failed to prevent encroachments, and that he failed to properly manage the property by diverting, converting, and dissipating the assets. Shows also recorded a notice of lis pendens in the mortgage records for East Feliciana Parish and East Baton Rouge Parish. He subsequently amended the petition to request that Julius be enjoined from selling or otherwise alienating or encumbering the property.

Julius answered and asserted a reconventional demand alleging that he was entitled to sell the property in accordance with the judgment of possession and Carole's will. Julius contended that the judgment of possession provided him with all rights and privileges of a usufructuary as provided in Carole's will, including, without limitation, paragraph 4.2, which set forth the right of the usufructuary to sell the property. He requested that the court declare his authority to sell or exchange the property subject to the usufruct, order the cancellation of the notice of lis pendens, and award him all damages caused by the filing of the notice of lis pendens. The reconventional demand was subsequently amended to include an alternative claim requesting that the court amend or reform the judgment of possession to include the right to sell the property if the court found that the judgment of possession did not already incorporate the pertinent terms of Carole's will by reference. In response to the reconventional demand, Shows filed a peremptory exception raising the objection of res judicata contending that the judgment of possession could not be modified because it was a final judgment and had the effect of res judicata.

While the exception was pending, Julius moved for a partial summary judgment seeking, among other relief, a judgment: ... declaring that Julius is authorized to sell the property subject to the usufruct without the consent of Shows, with the proceeds thereof to become part of the usufruct. . .

In addition to his argument that the judgment of possession expressly incorporated the terms of the usufruct contained in Carole's will, Julius also contended that the judgment statutorily incorporated those terms pursuant to Louisiana Code of Civil Procedure article 3061C, which provides:

> A judgment sending one or more petitioners into possession under a testamentary usufruct or trust automatically incorporates all the terms of the testamentary usufruct or trust without the necessity of stating the terms in the judgment.

This provision was added to Article 3061 by Louisiana Acts 2010, No. 226, § 1, which became effective on August 15, 2010; however, Julius maintained that the amendment was either procedural or curative and, therefore, applied retroactively to the judgment of possession rendered in 1993.

The trial court granted the motion for partial summary judgment and overruled the peremptory exception raising the objection of res judicata, finding that Carole's will unequivocally gave Julius the authority to sell the property and that the language of the will should be binding. The court further found that the 2010 amendment to Article 3061 applied retroactively but noted that "the court's ruling would be the same without the legislative enactment" of that amendment.

The partial summary judgment, however, did not adjudicate the merits of the principal claim by Shows seeking to terminate the usufruct or, alternatively requesting that Julius post security, nor Julius' claim seeking damages and attorney's fees caused by the filing of the notices of lis pendens. Those claims proceeded to trial where the trial court heard testimony from numerous witnesses that primarily addressed the condition of the farm before and during the existence of the usufruct and Julius's intention to sell that property.

The evidence established that Carole and Julius purchased the farm during their marriage, and Shows and his children used the property for recreational purposes. Shows testified that as his mom was dying in the hospital, the family had a meeting at her bedside and agreed that the farm would "stay in the family, and the kids and grandkids would play on it and enjoy it, and it rocked along like that just fine for [the next] 15 years." At some point thereafter, Julius contacted Shows and advised that he was going to sell the farm and offered Shows the option to purchase it for appraised value. When the parties were unable to reach an agreement, Julius informed Shows that he was going to sell the property on a specified date; and, according to Shows, Julius informed him that he "would never see a penny" of the proceeds. Shows, who is an attorney, believed that any sale of the property required his consent as a naked owner, and he cited the fact that Julius had obtained their consent in connection with the sale of some stock in a privately held corporation that was subject to the usufruct. Shortly before the identified sale date, Shows filed the petition seeking to terminate the usufruct and, as amended, to enjoin any sale of the property subject to the usufruct.

In support of his allegations of abuse and waste, Shows relied on Julius' sale of the property in the Virgin Islands without the consent of the naked owners and his stated intent to sell the farm without their consent. Shows also testified that he and his immediate family have been banned from the farm since he filed the petition. As to Julius' maintenance of the property, Shows described Julius' efforts with the farm as "up or down over the years," but Shows cited only one instance of any purported damage or deterioration, which he described as some "drainage problems" on one end of the property resulting from development on adjacent property that was "not a giant problem." Shows confirmed that Julius "nearly always" bore the financial expense of the maintenance of the farm and that Julius purchased tractors and related equipment for that purpose. Shows conceded that Julius had the property logged and re-planted after the existing timber sustained damage from beetles, and that he paid for other improvements, including a water well and the construction of a pond.

Brian Hodges, a forester accepted by the trial court as an expert in timber assessment and management, testified that he supervised the replanting of pine trees on the farm several years ago and did a follow-up assessment of the property during the year prior to the trial. In his opinion, the growth of the trees was in accordance with his expectations, and he did not see any signs that Julius had abused the timber operation or had not followed Hodges's instructions in connection therewith. He also did not see any signs of significant erosion or damage to the property. Leonard Kilcrease, an adjacent property owner, testified that he sometimes accesses the farm with permission, and he has never seen any erosion on the property caused by Julius.

Julius testified that when he and Carole purchased the property in the early 1990s, it was in "pretty bad shape" and "everything was in disrepair." There was "junk all over the place [and] the house was infested with rats." They remodeled the house and cleaned up the property. The property had been clear-cut prior to their acquisition, and Julius had any remaining timber cut and replanted. He also paid for several improvements, including a barn for the equipment, a pond, and a new water well. His usual maintenance consisted of cutting the grass, "bush hogging," grading the access road, maintaining the equipment, and repairing the house.

He decided to sell the farm because he and his present wife intend to move to Washington, and he no longer has any use for the property and has grown tired of maintaining it. He denied any knowledge of the family meeting at Carole's bedside where the family agreed not to sell the property, and he intended to use the proceeds from the sale to invest in an annuity that would be payable to all four children. Julius obtained an appraisal and contacted Shows to determine if he was interested in purchasing the farm because Shows had previously said he wanted to buy the property if it was ever offered for sale. During this time, an interested buyer approached Julius and offered to purchase the farm for $1,100,000.00. When Shows failed to produce a promised purchase agreement after several months, Julius informed Shows that he was going to sell the property to the other party. He gave Shows a definite deadline, and Shows then filed the petition and recorded the notices of lis pendens shortly before that deadline.

As to the property in the Virgin Islands, Julius testified that he and Carole had listed the property for sale before her death, and a buyer signed and forwarded a purchase agreement two days after Carole's death. Julius contacted the closing attorney in the Virgin Islands and was informed that Carole's death certificate would be sufficient to allow Julius to sign the act of sale and complete the transaction. He eventually used the proceeds from the sale to purchase a house in Baton Rouge, which is occupied by a son from his marriage to Carole. As to the movable property subject to the usufruct, it consists primarily of accounts at several financial institutions, and Julius confirmed that he has a financial advisor who manages the investment of those funds.

After taking the matter under advisement, the trial court denied Shows' claim to terminate the usufruct or to require Julius to post security, finding that Julius has acted as a prudent administrator of the property and that Shows failed to prove that Julius had "placed the property itself or the rights of the naked owners in peril." The court also denied Julius' claim for damages asserted in his reconventional demand.

A judgment was signed that set forth the court's earlier rulings granting partial summary judgment and overruling the exception of res judicata, and the court's ruling after the trial on the merits. More specifically, the summary judgment (1) declared that the provisions of Carole's will related to the usufruct are incorporated in the judgment of possession by the terms of the judgment and/or amended the judgment of possession to include the provision of Article IV of the will; (2) declared that Julius was granted and has the power to sell all property of the succession subject to the usufruct, with all of the sale proceeds being subject to the same usufruct, including the farm property; and (3) ordered the cancellation of the notices of lis pendens. For the trial on the merits, the judgment denied any relief requested by Shows in his petition, as amended, to terminate the usufruct or to post security and denied any relief requested by Julius in his reconventional demand.

Shows appealed and assigns as error the trial court's denial of the exception of res judicata and the concurrent granting of summary judgment to Julius, "i.e. in allowing the modification of the existing 'Judgment of Possession' by judicially including the right to sell in favor of Julius Beard, Jr., the usufructuary." Shows also assigns as error the trial court's failure to impose upon Julius the obligation to post bond.

LAW AND ANALYSIS

In support of the summary judgment, Julius argues that the authority to sell the property subject to the servitude was incorporated by reference into the judgment of possession by the language appearing therein that vested him with a usufruct "as provided in the decedent's Last Will and Testament." Shows counters that this language was merely a reference to the source of the usufruct rather than an incorporation of the terms of the usufruct. Shows also argues that permitting the terms of the usufruct to be incorporated into the judgment of possession would violate the Louisiana Public Records Doctrine.

The pleadings and other matters of record in this succession proceeding include Carole's will and an order probating that will. Pursuant to the terms and conditions of Article IV of the will, Carole granted Julius the authority to sell property that is subject to the usufruct. Shows has never disputed that the will granted that authority to Julius. Based upon the clear intent of the testator reflected in the will probated with the court, we construe the language in the judgment of possession vesting Julius with a usufruct "as provided in the decedent's Last Will and Testament" as including, by reference, the terms and conditions of the usufruct set forth in Carole's will. This interpretation of the judgment of possession is entirely consistent with the undisputed facts and law presented to the court when the judgment was rendered.

* * *

Accordingly, the trial court did not err in granting partial summary judgment and declaring that the judgment of possession incorporated by reference the terms and conditions of Carole's will relating to the testamentary usufruct granted to Julius....

* * *

B. Denial of Request for Security

In his second assignment of error, Shows contends that the trial court erred in failing to impose upon the usufructuary the obligation to post bond. Consideration of this assignment of error first requires a determination of the applicable law, as the provisions governing a usufructuary's obligation to post bond have undergone numerous amendments since the date of Carole's death in 1993.

Julius specifically seeks to invoke an amendment to Louisiana Civil Code article 1499, added by Louisiana Acts 2003, No. 548, § 1 ("2003 Act"), which relieves a surviving spouse of the obligation to post security for the usufruct "except as expressly declared by the decedent or as permitted when the legitime is affected." However, the 2003 Act provides that the "provisions of this Act are interpretive, procedural, and remedial *and shall apply to testaments executed on or after June 18, 1996.*" La. Acts 2003, No. 548, § 2 (emphasis added). We construe this statement as an expression of intent by the legislature that the amendment *does not apply* to wills executed *before* June 18, 1996. Otherwise, the statement would be superfluous. Carole's will was executed in 1993, so the 2003 Act does not apply to this case. *See* La. Civ. Code art. 6; *Keith v. United States Fidelity & Guaranty Company,* 96–2075 (La.5/9/97), 694 So. 2d 180, 183 (recognizing that if a legislative enactment expresses legislative intent regarding retrospective or prospective application, no further inquiry is warranted unless the enactment impairs contractual obligations or vested rights).

Furthermore, it is well settled that the law in effect at the time of the decedent's death controls the substantive rights of inheritance in and to the succession property. *See In re Succession of Buck,* 02–0401 (La.App. 1 Cir. 11/8/02), 834 So. 2d 475, 477; *Succession of Landry,* 460 So. 2d 29, 30 (La.App. 1 Cir.1984), *writ denied,* 462 So. 2d 1249 (La.1985); *see also* La. Civ.Code art. 870 (providing, in pertinent part, that testate and intestate succession rights, including the right to claim as a forced heir, are governed by the law in effect on the date of the decedent's death). The alleged obligation to provide security for the usufruct pertains to substantive rights of inheritance for both Julius, as the usufructuary of the designated property, and Shows, as a naked owner of that property. Accordingly, the law in effect at the time of Carole's death in 1993 governs whether Julius is required to post security for the usufruct. Louisiana Civil Code article 571 provided as follows in 1993:

> The usufructuary *shall give security* that he will use the property subject to the usufruct as a prudent administrator and that he will faithfully fulfill all the obligations imposed on him by law or by the act that established the usufruct *unless security is dispensed with.* (Emphasis added.)

The circumstances under which "security is dispensed with" are the subject of Louisiana Civil Code article 573, which at the time of Carole's death provided:

> Security may be dispensed with by the grantor of the usufruct or by operation of law. Legal usufructuaries, and sellers or donors of property under reservation of usufruct, are not required to give security.

Thus, under these provisions, legal usufructuaries were exempted from the obligation to post security. The usufruct granted in favor of a surviving spouse, whether testate or intestate, is a legal usufruct under the former version of Louisiana Civil Code article 890. *See* La. Civ.Code art. 890 (repealed by La. Acts. 1996, No. 77, § 1); *Succession of McCarthy*, 583 So. 2d 140, 142 (La.App. 1 Cir.1991). Therefore, Julius, as a legal usufructuary, was generally exempted from the obligation to post security. However, Article 890 carved out the following exception from the exemption applicable to legal usufructuaries:

> If the usufruct authorized by this Article affects the rights of heirs *other than children of the marriage* between the deceased and the surviving spouse or affects separate property, *security may be requested* by the naked owner. (Emphasis added.)

Similarly, Louisiana Code of Civil Procedure article 3154.1 (repealed by La. Acts. 2004, No. 158, § 2) provided:

> If the former community or separate property of a decedent is burdened with a usufruct in favor of his surviving spouse, successors to that property, other than children of the decedent's marriage with the survivor, may request security ... in an amount determined by the court as adequate to protect the petitioner's interest.

In reliance upon these articles, this court has repeatedly held that a surviving spouse who receives a legal usufruct over estate property is required to post security if the naked owners are children of a previous marriage of the decedent. *See Succession of Weidig*, 96–1214 (La. App. 1 Cir. 2/14/97), 690 So. 2d 134, 137 (reversing trial court's order permitting a delay for surviving spouse to post security until she was placed in possession where naked owners were children of the decedent's prior marriage); *Morgan v. Leach*, 96–0173 (La. App. 1 Cir. 9/27/96), 680 So. 2d 1381, 1385 (holding that "plaintiffs herein, being children of a previous marriage, are clearly entitled to security"). Accordingly, although the record supports the trial court's finding that Julius has acted as a prudent administrator of the property, his obligation to post security is mandatory under the law in effect at the time of Carole's death because Shows is a child of Carole's prior marriage. *See* La. Civ. Code arts. 571, 573, 890, and 3154.1; *Succession of Weidig,* 690 So. 2d at 137; *Morgan,* 680 So. 2d at 1385. The trial court erred in failing to order Julius to post security.

However, the trial court does have discretion concerning the amount and form of the security. As to the amount of the security, Louisiana Civil Code article 572 sets forth that the security "shall be in the amount of the total value of the property subject to the usufruct," but the article authorizes the court to "increase or reduce the amount of the security, on proper showing, but the amount shall not be less than the value of the movables subject to the usufruct."

The form of the security is governed by Louisiana Civil Code article 1514 and Louisiana Revised Statute 9:1202, both of which authorize the court to "order the execution of notes, mortgages, or other documents as it deems necessary" or "impose a mortgage or lien" on the property as security. Comment (d) to Article 1514 further explains:

> And the very word "security" itself is susceptible of several different meanings. There are many forms of security, such as a surety bond, a legal or conventional mortgage, and perhaps, in a more colloquial sense, a designation of the nature of an investment. An example of that latter kind of provision is found in Civil Code Article 618, which applies when, for example, a usufruct of a nonconsumable is transformed into a usufruct of a consumable and the naked owner and the usufructuary are unable to agree on the investment of the proceeds within one year of the transformation of the property. In that case, Civil Code Article 618 authorizes the court to determine the nature of the investment. It is hoped that courts will not inflexibly apply the rule of this Article to require a usufructuary to post bond every time a naked owner requests security, but will consider all of the circumstances of the situation, such as the nature of the property that comprises the legitime, and whether the property is movable or immovable, consumable or nonconsumable, and what practical controls exist or may be used to protect the right of the naked owner without infringing on the rights of the usufructuary, or if so, by infringing in the least restrictive manner possible.

The trial court's discretion is further guided by the purpose of the security as set forth in Article 571, providing that the usufructuary "shall give security that he will use the property subject to the usufruct as a prudent administrator and that he will faithfully fulfill all the obligations imposed on him by law or by the act that established the usufruct...." In that regard, we note that Julius' expressed intention to exercise his right to sell the farm is not a breach of those obligations, nor is it otherwise relevant to the determination of the amount and form of the security appropriate under Articles 571 and 572. Rather, in the event of a sale of any property, Louisiana Civil Code article 618 may be invoked in a timely manner by the naked owners to permit the court to impose appropriate security at that time for that specific purpose. *See* La. Civ. Code arts. 616, 618.

In accordance with the foregoing, we remand the matter to the trial court for a determination of the amount and form of security to be provided by Julius. *See Succession of Weidig,* 690 So. 2d at 137 (remanding to trial court for determination of appropriate security); *Morgan,* 680 So. 2d at 1385 (remanding to trial court for determination of appropriate security).

PROBLEMS

1. If the decedent died today with a will he wrote shortly before his death, proper in form, leaving all of his property to his wife, and he died with one forced heir, would the wife receive a usufruct over the forced portion and if so, how long would it last? Would you answer change if the decedent died without a valid will?

2. How would *Beard* be decided today, applying the revised articles on security? *See* La. C.C. 571-573.

3. Louise wrote a valid will in 2007, leaving her entire estate to her husband George. Several months after Louise wrote the will, her thirty-year-old son Lionel was in a serious accident, rendering him incapable of taking care of his person or administering his estate. Louise was concerned about providing for Lionel, but was assured by her attorney, that, due to the accident, Lionel was rendered, a forced heir and would be guaranteed a forced portion of her estate and that it was unnecessary to rewrite her will.

On May 1, 2010, Louise died. George married Florence in July of the same year. Subsequent to the marriage of George and Florence, Lionel asked for his portion of his mother's estate. George informed him that although Lionel was entitled to his *legitime*, the *legitime* was burdened with a usufruct in favor of George. George informed Lionel that he planned to sell the family dry-cleaning business, as well as the mansion on St. Charles Avenue that was Louise's separate property. George told Lionel that he and Florence were planning to cruise around the world in first-class accommodations. Lionel is fearful that there will be no inheritance left and demands full ownership of his forced portion immediately. At the very least, he wants to prevent George from selling any of the immovable property that is part of his *legitime*.

Is Lionel entitled to any relief? On what theories?

Provision for Usufruct over Pensions: La. R.S. 9:1426

A.   (1) If a recurring payment is being made from a public or private pension or retirement plan, an annuity policy or plan, an individual retirement account, a Keogh plan, a simplified employee plan, or any other similar retirement plan, to one partner or to both partners of a marriage, and the payment constitutes community property, and one spouse dies, the surviving spouse shall enjoy a legal usufruct over any portion of the continuing recurring payment which was the deceased spouse's share of their community property, provided the source of the benefit is due to payments made by or on behalf of the survivor.

(2) This usufruct shall exist despite any provision to the contrary contained in a testament of the deceased spouse.

B.   The usufruct granted by this Section shall be treated as a legal usufruct and is not an impingement upon the *legitime* and a naked owner shall not have a right to demand security.

NOTE

Does this statute provide a form of forced heirship for a surviving spouse? Compare *Boggs v. Boggs*, 520 U.S. 833 (1977) *infra* Chapter 10. Does this limit the application of La. R.S. 9:1426? How?

HYPOTHETICAL

Jose was married to Mirta. They had three children – Tomas, Alexandro and Maria. Jose and Mirta divorced and Jose married Teresa three years later. Jose and Teresa had one child, Antonio. Jose bought each of his children an acre of land in St. Helena Parish. Tomas and Alexandro unfortunately were killed in an automobile accident. Both died intestate. At the time of his death, Tomas was married with two children, Philip and Magdelena. Alexandro was never married.

After the deaths of his two sons, Jose died intestate possessed of both separate and community property. Who has a right to his separate property? His community property? Explain.

Suppose, unbeknownst to them, the divorce of Jose and Mirta was invalid. What is the effect on the devolution of community and separate property? Would your answer differ if Jose knew that his first marriage was undissolved but he failed to tell Teresa?

Who has an interest in Tomas's property upon his death?   Separate property? Community property? Should the property in St. Helena Parish be treated any differently?

Who has an interest in the property of Alexandro upon his death? In what proportions?

[handwritten margin note: Not on Bar/ Final]

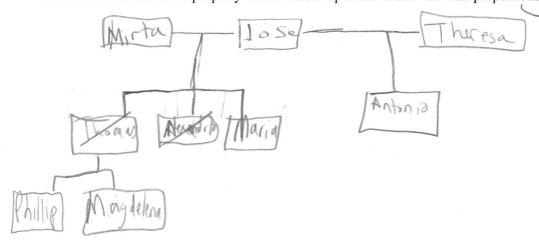

CHAPTER 3:
CHILDREN BORN OUT OF WEDLOCK
AND FILIATION
La. C.C. 184-198

Introduction

Several factors contributed to the need for the legislative revision of 1981, which effectively eliminated the legal distinction between legitimate children, and properly acknowledged or filiated illegitimate children, with regard to inheritance rights. Litigants in the 1970's and early 1980's challenged the constitutionality of codal articles that preferred legitimate relations in the succession hierarchy over illegitimates, thus chipping away at the codal scheme regarding irregular heirs. A case of major significance which helped to provoke the legislative revision was *Succession of Brown*, 388 So. 2d 1151 (La. 1980).

In *Succession of Brown*, the decedent died intestate with four acknowledged illegitimate children and one adopted child, who had been illegitimate but the adoption gave her status as a legitimate child. The trial court recognized the adopted child as the sole heir based on article 919 of the Civil Code, which excluded acknowledged illegitimate children from participating in the succession of their father when he is survived by legitimate descendants, ascendants, collaterals or a surviving spouse. The illegitimate children appealed, arguing that article 919 violated their rights under the Equal Protection Clause of the United States and Louisiana Constitutions. *Id.* at 1152.

To survive constitutional scrutiny, the Louisiana Supreme Court considered whether the classification was substantially related to a permissible state interest. The state advanced three interests: (1) the promotion of legitimate family relationships; (2) the possibilities available to the father to ensure that the illegitimates would take in the succession; and (3) the orderly disposition of property. The Court rejected all three interests and found the classification in article 919 to be unconstitutional. The Court explained that even though Louisiana could not flatly deny an illegitimate rights simply because other relatives exist, it could solve its problem by passing a statute that would allow an illegitimate to establish his or her rights of filiation. *Id.* at 1153-54. Ultimately, this is exactly what the Louisiana legislature did.

Even before the *Brown* decision was released, the legislature passed Civil Code article 209, which allowed a child to prove filiation to an alleged parent within one year of the death of the alleged parent or within nineteen years of the child's birth. La. C.C. 209 (repealed by Act 192 of 2005). The issue then arose of the retroactive application of the Succession of Brown case. In other words, could illegitimate children assert rights to a parent's estate when the parent died before the date of the decision? *Succession of Clivens* provided the answer.

Succession of Clivens, 426 So. 2d 585 (La. 1983) concluded that the *Succession of Brown* holding, which found article 919 to be unconstitutional, must be applied retroactively to all successions, from January 1, 1975, the effective date of the Louisiana Constitution of 1974, from which the illegitimate children derived their rights.

The law of filiation developed slowly after the *Brown* and *Clivens* holdings, and underwent a complete revision in 2005. The following section will explain the filiation laws prior to the 2005 revisions and the law review article will explain the law as revised.

Law Prior to 2005 Revisions

In order to qualify as an heir to his parent prior to the 2005 revisions, a child had to either be legitimate, formally acknowledged, or filiated. In any of those instances, the child had all rights of heirship, including the potential right to take as a forced heir.

A child was defined as legitimate if he or she was born or conceived during marriage. La. C.C. 179. A child who was not legitimate could have become legitimated by the subsequent marriage of his father and mother, if the parents had formally or informally acknowledged the child, either before or after the marriage. La. C.C. 198, as amended by La. Acts 76 § 607. A parent could also have legitimated his illegitimate child by making a formal declaration to that effect before a notary and two witnesses. La. C.C. 200, as amended by 1983 La. Acts 7 § 1.

Formal acknowledgment required the initiative of the parent declaring before a notary and two witnesses that he was the parent or the parent registering as such in the birth or baptismal records of the child. La. C.C. 203. In the *Succession of Robinson*, 654 So. 2d 682 (La. 1995) the Louisiana Supreme Court held that such acknowledgments were void, absent a biological relationship and authorized the trial court in *Robinson* to order blood tests if a prima facie showing of reasonable possibility that no blood relationship existed.

Filiation to an alleged parent could have been proved by an illegitimate child when the parent had not legitimated or formally acknowledged the child. La. C.C. 209, as amended by 1984 La. Acts no. 810, § 1. In the case of *Griffin v. Succession of Branch*, 479 So. 2d 3224 (La. 1985), the Louisiana Supreme Court held that, although former La. C.C. 209 stated that a child "not entitled to legitimate filiation" could bring the action for filiation, the words were not meant to preclude a child who was legitimate as to one man (the husband of his mother), from bringing a filiation action to establish his relationship to another man (his biological father). Agreeing with the earlier decision of the First Circuit in *Succession of Levy*, the court interpreted the words "entitled to legitimate filiation" to mean legitimate filiation to the parent to whom the child was attempting to filiate. In other words, Louisiana would permit "dual paternity," filiation to a presumed father through a presumption and filiation to the biological father.

In a filiation proceeding, if the alleged parent were living, the child had to prove the relationship by a "preponderance of the evidence"; whereas, if the alleged parent was deceased, the level of proof rose to "clear and convincing." The Louisiana Supreme Court had held that the amendment to former Article 209 making the distinction as to the levels of proof required was procedural in nature, and thus was to be applied retroactively. *Sudwicher v. Estate of Hoffpauir*, 705 So. 2d 24 (La. 1997).

The action for filiation prior to the 2005 revision had to be brought within one year of death of the alleged parent or within nineteen years from the child's birth, whichever first occurred. La. C.C. 209, as amended by 1984 La. Acts no. 810, § 1. The nineteen years from birth prescription was held to be constitutionally permissible in *Succession of Grice*, 462 So. 2d 131 (La. 1985). Note, however, that the time period for filiation for purposes of recovery in La. C.C. 2315 was, as is currently, one year from the death of the alleged parent. This time period was held to be peremptive in *Matherne v. Broussard*, 959 So. 2d 975 (La. App 1st Cir. 2007).

2005 Changes to the Law of Filiation

In 2005, the Louisiana legislature passed an act that comprehensively revised the law of filiation. 2005 La. Acts No. 192, § 1. The following article explains these changes and suggests areas that still need to be considered.

NO CHILD LEFT BEHIND, EXCEPT FOR YOU, YOU, AND YOU: AN ANALYSIS OF THE 2005 REVISIONS TO THE LOUISIANA LAWS ON FILIATION
by Elisabeth Lorio Baer
[Edited and reprinted with permission;
bracketed information inserted by casebook author]

*   *   *

I. INTRODUCTION

The 2005 revision of Title VII (Parent and Child) of the LOUISIANA CIVIL CODE represents significant and much needed progress for the legal status of the Louisiana family. The new filiation articles, effective June 29, 2005, culminate fourteen years of preparation and analysis by the Marriage/Persons Committee of the Louisiana State Law Institute.[1] The new articles not only update Louisiana filiation laws to more accurately reflect the current status of the modern family,[2] but also respond to United States and Louisiana Supreme Court decisions that significantly alter determinations of parenthood by eliminating the distinctions between legitimate and illegitimate children.[3]

In revising the articles, the Marriage/Persons Committee's (hereafter referred to as the Committee) main objectives were to determine if Louisiana's unique jurisprudence on dual paternity should be codified; to clarify existing and newly created paternity and maternity presumptions; to determine prescriptive and peremptive periods for avowal and disavowal actions; and to update the laws to respond to new reproductive technologies that challenge

---

[1] The Louisiana Law Institute is an organization formed in 1938 "to promote and encourage the clarification and simplification of the law of Louisiana and its better adaptation to present social needs; to secure the better administration of justice and to carry on scholarly legal research and scientific legal work." See, LA. REV. STAT. ANN. § 24:204 (2007). The statute begins with this general purpose and continues to explain the multiple duties of the Louisiana Law Institute. Of particular importance to this comment, one of the roles of the Institute is "to recommend from time to time such changes in the law as it deems necessary to modify or eliminate antiquated and inequitable rules of law, and to bring the law of the state, both civil and criminal, into harmony with modern conditions." Id. The legislature places great confidence in the recommendations of the Institute, but is not bound to adopt all of the Institute's proposed laws.

[2] See, LA. CIV. CODE ANN. arts. 184-198 (2007); Katherine Shaw Spaht, Who's Your Momma, Who Are Your Daddies? Louisiana's New Law of Filiation, 67 LA. L. REV. 307 (2007).

[3] See, Levy v. Louisiana, 391 U.S. 68, 72 (1968); Trimble v. Gordon, 430 U.S. 763 (1977); Succession of Brown, 388 So. 2d 1151 (La. 1980); Successions of Clivens, 426 So. 2d 585 (La. 1983) (collectively contributing to the elimination of the distinction between legitimate and illegitimate children). See infra Part II for a discussion on the elimination of the terms legitimate and illegitimate.

traditional notions of parenthood.[4] The fundamental purpose of the revisions was to protect the best interests of the children of Louisiana.[5] The Committee presented recommendations to the Louisiana State Law Institute Council which, then, discussed the revisions and voted on the final proposed articles that were presented to the legislature for enactment.[6]

The Committee's fourteen years of preparation reflect careful consideration and offer a comprehensive series of articles that greatly improve the laws on filiation. Unfortunately, not all of the Committee's recommendations were accepted by the legislature, and many of the Committee's progressive ideas, were revised by the Legislature to incorporate more traditional concepts of family into the law.[7] Additionally, while the Committee consistently referred to a chapter of the revision dedicated to alternative means of reproduction in their Committee Reports, this section never came to fruition.[8] Therefore, children conceived by assisted reproductive technologies and same-sex couples are left with virtually no legislation protecting them.

The 2005 revisions to the filiation articles of the Code significantly update the parentage laws of Louisiana. However, it is evident that both the Committee and the Legislature see-sawed between the desire to promote the ideals of a traditional nuclear family and the desire to adequately address the realities of today's families, many consisting of same-sex and unwed couples, children of remarriage, and children born of assisted reproductive technologies. Unfortunately, the see-saw fell to the conservative end in sections of the revision, hindering the promotion of the best interests of children born of certain situations.

*   *   *

III. LOUISIANA'S RESPONSE TO THE EVER-WIDENING GAP BETWEEN THE TRADITIONAL AND THE MODERN FAMILY: The 2005 Revisions to the Louisiana Civil Code's Laws of Filiation

A.   Establishing Maternity

Chapter 1 of Title VII, labeled "proof of maternity," is comprised of one article that establishes maternity. This revision is the first time the legislature has dedicated an article to

---

[4] Louisiana State Law Institute, Marriage/Persons Committee Report, March 1996 (manuscript at 1, on file with author).

[5] In one of the first Committee Reports the question was posed: "Is it best for society to protect and preserve the marital unit, to provide for the individual child's needs or to recognize biological fact?" Through analyzing the final recommendations by the Committee and speaking with various Committee members, the author concludes that the majority of the articles were written with the best interests of the child as the primary focus of the revision. Louisiana State Law Institute, Marriage/Persons Committee Report, October 1994 (manuscript at 5, on file with the author).

[6] *Id.* at 1.

[7] *See infra* Part III.B.1.b (comparing LA. CIV. CODE ANN. art. 186 (2007) with proposed art. 186 found in Louisiana State Law Institute, Marriage/Persons Committee Report, Articles for Reconsideration, December 2001 (manuscript at 4, on file with the author)).

[8] *See infra* Part IV.A; Louisiana State Law Institute, Marriage/Persons Committee Report, March 1996 (manuscript at 1, on file with author).

[handwritten at top: LA does not recognize surrogacy unless surrogate is related to the mother + the father!]

identifying motherhood.[9] Article 184 states "maternity may be established by a preponderance of the evidence that a child was born of a particular woman, except as otherwise provided by law."[10] In most circumstances, the woman who gave birth to the child is the genetic mother because Louisiana law deems traditional paid contracts for gestational or genetic surrogacy unenforceable[11] and only recognizes gestational surrogacy in the limited case of a surrogate who is a blood relative of either the husband or wife.[12]

Initially, the Committee wrote a very basic article declaring that "maternity should be established by a preponderance of the evidence."[13] There were no qualifications that a child had to be born of a particular woman. By the time the Committee met in 1996, the Committee had revised the article to read as it does currently, provided that the presumption would be limited by exceptions to be included in a future third chapter of the Parent and Child section of the Code. The third chapter was intended to address assisted means of reproduction and would have clarified potential problems determining maternity when surrogacy contracts are involved.[14] Unfortunately, chapter three has not been written to date, and the exceptions to the maternity presumption are limited to the gestational surrogate mother who is a blood relative to one of the donors.[15]

The Uniform Parentage Act (UPA) was first written in 1973 to provide guidance in writing legislation concerning the parent-child relationship.[16] Elements of the UPA have been adopted by many states legislatures and serve as an important tool to analyze Louisiana's revised parentage laws. The UPA offers a broader definition of maternity. It provides that the mother-child relationship is established by:

[handwritten: Mother-Child Elements!]

> "1) the woman having given birth to the child (except as otherwise provided in [the surrogacy section]; 2) an adjudication of the woman's maternity; 3) adoption of the child by the woman; 4) an adjudication confirming that the woman is a parent of the child born to a gestational mother if the agreement was validated under article eight or is enforceable under another law."[17]

The UPA's definition of maternity would have coincided with the Committee's intended chapter three because the chapter would have offered exceptions to article 184.

---

[9] Spaht, *supra* note 3, at 309.

[10] LA. CIV. CODE ANN. art. 184 (2007).

[11] LA. REV. STAT. ANN. §9:2713 (2007).

[12] LA. REV. STAT. ANN. §40:32 (2007).

[13] Louisiana State Law Institute, Marriage/Persons Committee Report, October 1996 (manuscript at 2, on file with author) (defining mother and father as the providers of sperm and egg for in vitro fertilization with a relative surrogate), LA. REV. STAT. ANN. §40:34 (2007) (declaring that the birth certificate will reflect the mother and father of the child through in vitro fertilization in the prior situation).

[14] *Id.*; *see infra* Part IV.A.2.

[15] LA. CIV. CODE ANN. art. 184 (c) (2007).

[16] The Uniform Parentage Act was first written in 1973 but has since been revised in 2000 and amended in 2002. UNIF. PARENTAGE ACT (2000).

[17] UNIF. PARENTAGE ACT § 201(a) (2000).

As a general rule, the maternity presumption in article 184 will bestow motherhood on the correct woman, but surrogacy contracts may produce undesirable results. While the Code specifically states that compensated genetic[18] surrogacy contracts will be found unenforceable,[19] there is no legislation that addresses gratuitous surrogate contracts or gestational surrogacy.[20] Therefore, a couple could enter into a surrogacy contract, and under the presumption in article 184, the surrogate would be the mother of the child. The legislature needs to address this issue by including a surrogacy exception to the article, which would presume that the contracting mother is the mother of the child in all circumstances.[21]… If a couple so desperately wants a child that they will contract with another woman to carry the child, the contracting mother, and not the surrogate should be the presumed mother.[22] The addition of this exception would better protect the best interests of the child because his presumed mother would be the woman who intended to have a child and not the one who contracts to relinquish the child.[23]

[handwritten in margin: Parental to contracting Mother > Surrogate Mother]

B.   Establishing Paternity

While the 2005 revision addresses the determination of motherhood for the first time in the history of the Code, the Code has always dedicated various articles to establishing paternity. Because of the nature of childbirth, maternity has traditionally been easy to determine. Fatherhood, however, has been more difficult to prove due to the less obvious connection between it and childbirth. The Code, therefore, offers a variety of methods to establish paternity. This section will first address the various presumptions that a man can use to align himself with a child. It will, then, discuss the ways to rebut these presumptions and analyze the new option of a mother's contestation and establishment action. Finally, the section will discuss dual paternity through both a man's, and a child's action to establish paternity.

1.   The Presumptions

a. Presumption of Paternity of the Husband

---

[18] *See,* Christine L. Kerian, *Surrogacy: A Last Resort Alternative for Infertile Women or a Commodification of Women's Bodies and Children?*, 12 WIS. WOMEN'S L. J. 113, 114 (1997) (defining gestational surrogacy as a contract in which the surrogate provides a uterus to carry the contracting couple's gametes and genetic surrogacy as a contract in which the surrogate provides both the uterus and the egg to be inseminated by the contracting husband's sperm).

[19] LA. REV. STAT. ANN. § 9:2713 (2007) ("a contract for surrogate motherhood as defined herein shall be absolutely null and shall be void and unenforceable as contrary to public policy" (the statute defines surrogacy as genetic surrogacy). *See infra* Part.A.2.

[20] A court may, by analogy, find these contracts null as contrary to public policy. However, no statute specifically declares them unenforceable.

[21] Revised Statute §9:2713 would not have to be repealed because paid surrogacy contracts could still be considered unenforceable, while gratuitous contracts could be recognized under the law.

[22] *See e.g.,* Sandi Varnado, *Who's Your Daddy? A Legitimate Question Given Louisiana's Lack of Legislation Governing Assisted Reproductive Technology*, 66 LA. L. REV. 609 (2006); Archer, *supra* note 22 (supporting legislation for surrogacy contracts).

[23] *Id.*

Article 185 of the Louisiana Civil Code provides the first legal presumption of paternity. It states "the husband of the mother is presumed to be the father of a child born during the marriage or within three hundred days from the date of the termination of the marriage."[24] This article does not change the law, but merely combines former articles 184 and 185.[25] The presumption that the husband of the mother is the father of the child has been considered one of the strongest presumption in the law.[26] The presumption is reasonably safe because, most likely, a child born within a marriage will be the biological child of the couple. If the child is born of the infidelity of the wife, the presumption may be refuted by the husband through a timely filed disavowal action or by a timely filed contestation and establishment action, both of which are discussed in more detail below.[27]

b. Presumption if Child is Born After Divorce or After Death of Husband

The second presumption provides guidance for determining paternity after the death or divorce of the first husband when the mother remarries. Article 186 of the Louisiana Civil Code determines that if a child is born within three hundred days of the dissolution of a marriage and the mother remarries again before his birth, the child is presumed to be the child of the first husband.[28] If the first husband obtains a judgment of disavowal, the second husband is presumed the father.[29] The second husband or his successor has a peremptive period of one year from the day of the first husband's judgment of disavowal to institute his disavowal action.[30] Before the 2005 revision, former articles 185 and 186 combined to have the same effect of current article 186 with much less clarity.[31] Former article 186 stated that a husband of the mother is not the presumed father of the child if another man is presumed to be the father.[32]

Both the former and the current legislation have illogical consequences for couples who obtain a divorce. If a couple gets a divorce, then within three hundred days of the first marriage the woman gets married to another man and has a child, there is a likelihood that the child is not the biological child of the first husband. If a couple is on the verge of a divorce, and a woman remarries soon after the termination of the first marriage, the stronger presumption is that the second husband is the true father of the child. The article produces even greater illogical results

---

[24] LA. CIV. CODE ANN. art. 185 (2007).

[25] *See*, LA. CIV. CODE ANN. art. 184 (2005) (the husband of the mother is presumed to be the father of the child born during marriage); LA. CIV. CODE ANN. art. 185 (2005) (a child born within three hundred days of the marriage is presumed to have been conceived during the marriage, after three hundred days this presumption does not apply).

[26] *See, e.g.*, Tannehill v. Tannehill, 261 So. 2d 619, 624 (La. 1972) (holding that a husband could not disavow a child born during his marriage despite his sterility); LA. CIV. CODE ANN. art. 187 (2007).

[27] LA. CIV. CODE ANN. arts. 187, 191 (2007); *see infra* III.B.2.a,e.

[28] LA. CIV. CODE ANN. art. 186 (2007).

[29] *Id.* If the missing husband lived separate and apart from the mother continuously during the three hundred days immediately preceding the birth of the child, prescription for disavowal does not begin to run until the husband is notified in writing by an interested party that he is claimed to be the father. LA. CIV. CODE ANN. art. 189 (2007).

[30] *Id.*

[31] *See* Dupre v. Dupre, 02-0902, (La. App. 3 Cir. 12/30/02); 834 So. 2d 1272, 1282 (highlighting the ambiguous results of paternity analysis using former articles 185 and 186).

[32] LA. CIV. CODE ANN. art. 186 (2005).

when the reason for the divorce is the wife's infidelity, a case when it is much more likely that the child is that of the second husband's.[33]

The presumption has the most irrational results when a husband has been absent for more than five years and is presumed dead.[34] A child born within three hundred days from this declaration of death is presumed the child of a dead and missing man when the mother is married to her new husband, who is most probably the child's biological father. Presuming that a child belongs to a missing and declared dead man over a man who is married to the child's mother serves as a detriment to the child. *Succession of Mitchell* presented the Louisiana Supreme Court with a situation where the husband disappeared shortly after the marriage.[35] The marriage was never dissolved, but the wife began a relationship with her brother-in-law and had a child.[36] Although the husband never reappeared, he was the presumed father despite the obvious fact that his brother was the father of the child.[37] The Court would be forced to arrive at the same illogical conclusion under the revised article.

While a disavowal action is available to the first husband[38], there is no reason for the parents and the child to endure litigation. The psychological effects of a disavowal for both the parents and the child can easily be avoided by presuming that the second husband is the father in the case of a divorce when the mother remarries before the child's birth.

The enacted article 186 differs greatly from the version recommended by the Committee. The Committee's version provided that if a child was born within three hundred days after the termination of a marriage, and the mother remarried, the child was presumed to be the child of the second husband if the marriage terminated by a judgment of divorce, declaration of nullity, or declaration of death under article 54.[39] The first husband was presumed to be the father of the child if the marriage terminated by the death of the first husband.[40] The presumed father could disavow the child, making the other husband the presumed husband. The action for disavowal by the second husband is subject to a one hundred and eighty day peremptive period that begins from the day of disavowal by the first.[41] This presumption is much more logical than the enacted legislation because it more accurately reflects modern society.

Arguably, a presumption that assumes infidelity is contrary to public policy. The legislature may feel that making a law that presumes infidelity is against public policy because it could be seen as condoning the behavior. However, the purpose of the Code is not to preach morality in hopes that the people will listen. The legislature must provide laws for the reality in

---

[33] Kerry Triche, Family Law Handbook (2006).

[34] LA CIV. CODE ANN. art. 54 (2007).

[35] 323 So. 2d 451 (La. 1975).

[36] *Id.*

[37] *Id.*

[38] LA. CIV. CODE ANN. art. 186 (2007).

[39] Louisiana State Law Institute, Marriage/Persons Committee Report, October 1996 (manuscript at 4, on file with author) (If a child is born within three hundred days after the termination of a marriage, and his mother has married before his birth: 1) the second husband is presumed to be the father if the previous marriage was terminated by judgment of divorce, declaration of nullity, or declaration of death under article 54; 2) the first husband is presumed to be the father if the previous marriage was terminated by death.).

[40] *Id.*

[41] *Id.*

which we live, whether it agrees with current trends or not. The fundamental goal of the filiation articles is to protect the best interests of the child.[42] A child, whose mother recently divorced a man and is now happily married to another man, would benefit more from being in the loving environment of the intact family. If the mother married so soon after the divorce, reality tends to suggest that the child is not the biological child of the first husband. In circumstances where the first husband is the biological father, he has the option to institute an action to establish his paternity.[43] In that case, the child would enjoy the benefits of dual paternity.[44]

Instead of entirely rejecting the Committee's proposed article, the legislature could have compromised by adopting the majority of the proposed article without presuming infidelity. The legislature could have enacted a law that presumes that the first husband is the father of the child when the marriage terminates by the death of the first husband or through divorce when the divorce is *not due to infidelity*. The second husband would be the presumed father of the child when the first marriage terminated by a declaration of nullity, declaration of death under article 54, or divorce based on adultery. While there are benefits to both the first and the second husband presumption of fatherhood, this article would best conform to both the legislature's and the Committee's proposals.

c. Presumption by Marriage and Acknowledgment When the Child is not Filiated to Another Man

The third presumption provided by law concerns a man's voluntary acknowledgment of a child. Article 195 states that a man, who marries a mother of a child that is not filiated to another man and who, with the concurrence of the mother, acknowledges the child by authentic act or by signing the birth certificate is presumed the father of the child.[45] If, after the man filiates with the child, he decides to disavow he may do so under the provisions in article 187 (clear and convincing; corroborated evidence) within a peremptive period of one hundred and eighty days from the day of the marriage or the acknowledgement, which ever occurs later.[46] This article updates former article 198 by eliminating the outdated and unconstitutional classifications of legitimate and illegitimate.[47] It establishes a paternal presumption arising from a subsequent marriage after the birth of a child coupled with acknowledgement by authentic act or by signing of the birth certificate, as distinguished from the former article which recognized legitimation of a child whose parents later married if the father formally or informally acknowledged the child before or after the marriage.[48] The informal method through a non authentic act or conversation is not sufficient to prove the desire of the father to filiate with the child under this article.[49] The

---

[42] *See supra* note 6.

[43] LA. CIV. CODE ANN. art. 198 (2007).

[44] *Id.*

[45] LA. CIV. CODE ANN. art. 195 (2007).

[46] *Id.*

[47] *See supra* Part II on legitimate/illegitimate distinction.

[48] *Id.*; LA. CIV. CODE ANN. art. 198 (2005).

[49] LA. CIV. CODE ANN. art 193 (2005) (proof of filiation may be established through registry of birth or baptism); LA. CIV. CODE ANN. art. 194 (2005) (proof of filiation may be established through reputation by showing that the

revised article does not specifically addresses whether a false acknowledgement is recognized. However, jurisprudence interpreting the old law found that a false acknowledgement resulted in an absolute nullity because acknowledging something means to admit that it is true.[50] Since the new article refers to acknowledgement as well, it can be concluded that only the biological father can formally acknowledge the child through this presumption.[51]

The article provides a one hundred and eighty day peremptive time period for a husband who, with the mother's consent and formal acknowledgement, decides to later disavow the child.[52] The peremptive period begins to run from the day of the marriage or the acknowledgement, whichever occurs later.[53] The Committee made the disavowal time period short and peremptive because it would be detrimental for the child to experience a see-saw of avowal and disavowal with a father. Article 195 also outlines formal requirements for acknowledgement. A husband simply giving the child his last name is not sufficient.[54] A husband giving the mother money to pay for baby food is not sufficient.[55] The man, with the mother's consent, must sign the birth certificate or formally acknowledge the child through an authentic act.[56] Such formality gives the husband adequate time to carefully consider whether he wants to be filiated to the child. If he, then, determines that filiation was a mistake he must act quickly or be responsible for the child. The short peremptive period protects the child by ensuring that a man does not filiate and then years later decide he made a mistake and disavow the child.

d. Presumption After Formal Acknowledgement

The fourth, and final, presumption allows a man not married to his child's mother to acknowledge the child. Article 196 allows a man, by authentic act or by signing the birth certificate, to acknowledge a child not filiated to another man, creating a presumption of paternity.[57] The presumption is only on behalf of the child and only favors the man for purposes of custody, visitation, and child support.[58] The presumption in favor only of the child means that the child enjoys the benefits of being able to inherit from the father and file a wrongful death action if the father should die.[59] Conversely, the father acknowledges the child for the benefit of

---

child has constantly be considered as a child born during the marriage); LA. CIV. CODE ANN. art. 196 (2005) (if no other proof exists, proof of his legitimate filiation may be made by written or oral evidence).

[50] *See,* Trahan, J.R., *Glossae on the New Law of Filiation,* 67 LA. L. REV. 387, 426, 435 (2006) (citing Succession of Robinson, 654 So. 2d 682, 684 (La. 1995)).

[51] *Id.*

[52] LA. CIV. CODE ANN. art. 195 (2007).

[53] *Id.*

[54] LA. CIV. CODE ANN. art. 195 (2005) (material facts to prove filiation by reputation are calling the child by the father's surname; the husband treating him as a child by financing education, maintenance, and settlement in life; or the child be acknowledged as the husband's or part of the husband's family).

[55] *Id.*

[56] LA. CIV. CODE ANN. art. 195 (2007).

[57] LA. CIV. CODE ANN. art. 196 (2007).

[58] *Id.*

[59] Spaht, *supra* note 3, at 319.

the child and can seek visitation or custody and must pay child support.[60] Unlike the previously mentioned presumptions, there is no limitation of who can bring the action to rebut the presumption, nor is there a prescriptive or peremptive time period to challenge the presumption.[61]

This article resembles former article 203.[62] Former article 203 created a presumption of paternity by a man acknowledging a child by signing the registry of birth or baptism which was rebuttable by a preponderance of the evidence.[63] The former article created a reciprocal legal finding of paternity for both parties, meaning that the father as well as the child enjoyed the benefits of paternity.[64] The former article allowed for the man to inherit from the child under the presumption where as the current article does not.

This article is a positive addition to the filiation articles in that it gives a child the benefits of being filiated to a father without the possibility that a man will be filiated with a child simply for financial reasons. For example, suppose a child gets into a horrific accident with his mother and the mother dies instantly. The child, however, is in a coma and it is uncertain if the child will live. Upon the mother's death, the child succeeded to all of his mother's estate. Any man could institute an authentic act or sign the child's birth certificate, acknowledging the child, and, if the child dies, inherit the entirety of the mother's estate. A simple formal acknowledgment of a child would not be sufficient alone to create a bilateral presumption of paternity under the new law. However, if a man desires to protect and support and child, there is no reason that the law should prohibit him from it.

Arguably, the restricted paternal presumption creates more fathers who have to file paternity actions instead of reciprocally benefiting from the presumption. This, however, was probably intended by the legislature. While the father may have to go through the costly litigation of a paternity action to enjoy the benefits of paternity, the child benefits outright from the presumption. The one-sided benefits related to inheritance and wrongful death actions ensure that the child is protected, while not putting the child in financial jeopardy. If a man desires the reciprocal benefits of paternity, he has the option of filing a paternity action.

2. Rebutting the Presumptions

While the Civil Code provides presumptions for a parent to more easily align himself with a child, it also offers methods for disproving the presumptions. The disavowal action allows a presumed father (or heir) to prove that he is not the father.[65] The contestation action and establishment action gives the mother, for the first time, the ability to disprove a father's paternity.[66] The following sections will describe these actions.

---

[60] *Id.*

[61] La. Civ. Code Ann. art. 196 (d) (2007).

[62] *See*, LA. CIV. CODE ANN. art. 203 (2005).

[63] *Id.* (the preponderance of the evidence standard was the same as that used in former Civil Code article 187 (2005)).

[64] *Id.*

[65] *See, infra* Part III.2.a.

[66] *See, infra* Part III.2.e.

a. The Disavowal Action

Article 187 provides that "a husband may disavow paternity of a child by clear and convincing evidence that he is not the father."[67] The husband's testimony must be corroborated by other evidence.[68] This article differs from former article 187 by imposing the higher standard of proof of clear and convincing over preponderance of the evidence.[69] This higher burden of proof protects a child from being disavowed without sufficient evidence. While the present article heightens the burden of proof, it also eliminates the need for proof of "facts susceptible of independent verification or of corroboration by physical data or evidence, such as scientific tests and verifiable physical circumstances of remoteness."[70] The former article listed different scientific tests that would provide sufficient corroborating proof such as negative blood tests, unmatched DNA prints and sterility.[71] While this physical evidence is still acceptable to meet the burden of proof, other non-physical evidence such as testimony of other witnesses is sufficient to corroborate the husband's testimony.[72]

In *Mock v. Mock*, the Louisiana Supreme Court analyzed the then-existing language of article 187 requiring the husband to prove *facts* reflecting his non-paternity to mean that only facts susceptible of outside verification would meet the preponderance of the evidence standard.[73] The Court's analysis clarified that corroboration by testimony of other witnesses was not sufficient to meet the burden.[74] Contrary to the decision in *Mock*, the comments of the revised article allow testimony of other witnesses to corroborate the presumed father's testimony in order to meet the heighten burden of clear and convincing evidence.[75]

Louisiana Revised Statute 9:396 authorizes the courts to order blood samples in any civil action in which paternity is a relevant issue to compare blood samples.[76] Although DNA testing has been found to be the most reliable source for determining paternity, there is a possibility that a chance match in DNA pattern can exist.[77] In paternity cases, where half of a person's DNA is

---

[67] LA. CIV. CODE ANN. art. 187 (2007).

[68] *Id.*

[69] LA. CIV. CODE ANN. art 187 (2005).

[70] *Id.*

[71] *Id.*

[72] LA. CIV. CODE ANN. art. 187 (b) (2007). It can be argued that the law is essentially the same since, although the specific independent facts were eliminated from the article, the higher standard of proof necessitates the use of such facts. However, if there is sufficient non-physical proof, such as parol evidence, to meet the clear and convincing standard, a man can prevail in a disavowal action.

[73] 411 So. 2d 1063, 1064 (La. 1982).

[74] *Id.* at 1067.

[75] LA. CIV. CODE ANN. art. 187 (b) (2007) ("other evidence includes…tangible evidence and testimony of lay witnesses").

[76] LA. REV. STAT. ANN. § 9:396 (2007).

[77] The press has often quoted a probability of one in a thirty billion chance for two individuals to randomly display the same pattern of DNA bands, but critics express concern because the testing sample was provided by a small, homogenous population. Dan L. Burk, *DNA Fingerprinting: Possibilities and Pitfalls of a New Technique*, 28 JURISMETRICS J. 455, 466 (1988); Dee O'Neil Andrews, *DNA and Dads: Considerations For Louisiana In Using DNA Blood Tests To Determine Paternity*, 38 LOY. L. REV. 425, 441 (1992).

inherited from each parent, the possibility of a chance match increases because only half of the bands are used for identification.[78] Regardless of the minute possibility of randomly matched bands, Louisiana relies on DNA as one of the methods to corroborate a husband's testimony to meet his clear and convincing standard of proof for disavowal.

The revised article better protects a child from disavowal by heightening the burden of proof from preponderance of the evidence to clear and convincing evidence and by requiring corroboration of the husband's testimony. Accepting testimony by other witnesses is a positive addition because there may not be enough physical evidence to meet the burden of proof.

The only potential downside to the revised article is the omission of specific examples of what constitutes clear and convincing evidence. The lack of specificity could potentially give the courts too much discretion in determining what meets the burden of proof. Some husbands could be allowed to disavow paternity, while others, with the same amount of proof, could be denied the right. To maintain consistency, it would be beneficial for the legislature to return to the listed methods in the former article 187 in order to give the courts guidance. The list need not be exclusive but merely give a variety of examples that would constitute sufficient evidence.

b. Disavowal Precluded in Case of Assisted Conception

Not possible

Article 188 of the Louisiana Civil Code prohibits a husband from disavowing a child born to his wife as a result of an assisted conception to which he consented.[79] The former article's preclusion of disavowal by the husband after artificial insemination was extended to all methods of assisted conception, such as in vitro fertilization and embryo transfer, by the current article.[80] This is a positive revision as the varying methods of assisted conception have multiplied and become more accessible and utilized.[81] The article does not mandate how consent should be manifested. The Committee suggested that consent should be in writing as provided in the future chapter three of the Parent and Child Title.[82] Since chapter three was never written, the method of consent remains unanswered.

While the article does not outline a method of consent, other statutes that mandate consent to establish paternity can be used as an indication of the intentions of the legislature. Louisiana Revised Statute § 9:391.1 requires that the consent for a surviving spouse to use the gametes of a decedent within three years from the death of the decedent must be authorized in writing.[83] Both the Committee and the legislature likely intended consent to be in writing

---

[78] *Id.* Because there are fewer DNA bands solely from the father (only half the bands as opposed to all of the child's bands of DNA) there is a greater chance that a false match could exist.

[79] La. Civ. Code Ann. art. 188 (2007).

[80] La. Civ. Code Ann. art. 188 (2005).

[81] Varnado, *supra* note 49 at 611 (citing, Anna Mulrine, *Making Babies*, U.S. News and World Rep., Sept. 27, 2004, at 61, one in every one hundred children are born from assisted means of reproduction in the United States today).

[82] Louisiana State Law Institute, Marriage/Persons Committee Report, October 1996 (manuscript at 8, on file with author).

[83] La. Rev. Stat. Ann. § 9:391.1 (2007) provides:

"Notwithstanding the provisions of any law to the contrary, any child conceived after the death of a decedent, who specifically authorized in writing his surviving spouse to use his gametes, shall be deemed the child of such decedent with all rights, including the capacity to inherit from the decedent, as the child would have had if the child

without the need for an authentic act. Requiring highly formal means such as an authentic act could result in a child being left with no protection simply because his parents failed to follow the right procedure.

The present Code article also eliminates the provision that denied a husband the right to disavow a child if he married a pregnant woman knowing that she was pregnant.[84] The former article had an exception that allowed disavowal when the husband had been deceived into marrying a woman thinking that a child was his.[85] This disavowal exception usually failed because it was often a mother's testimony against a father's, negating his right to disavow.[86] Furthermore, since the revised articles make it easier for a child to establish paternity through his own action, he no longer needs protection from disavowal by the man who marries his pregnant mother.[87]

c. Time Limit for Disavowal by the Husband

Under article 189, a husband may institute an action for disavowal of paternity within a liberative prescriptive period of one year.[88] Prescription begins to run from the day the husband learns or should have learned about the child's birth.[89] The article makes an exception that if the husband lived separate and apart from the mother continuously during the three hundred days preceding the birth, the prescription does not begin to run until the husband is notified in writing that an interested party has claimed that the husband is the father.[90] This article modifies the time period for initiating a disavowal action, changing the peremptive period established by former article 189 to a prescriptive period.[91] Former article 189 allowed the father a special suspension period for reasons beyond the husband's control.[92] This suspension is no longer necessary because the time period is now prescriptive which by definition allows interruption and suspensions.[93]

There was much debate among the members of the Committee concerning whether the time period for disavowal by the husband should be a prescriptive or a peremptive period and if

---

had been in existence at the time of the death of the deceased parent, provided the child was born to the surviving spouse, using the gametes of the decedent, within three years of the death of the decedent."

[84] *See*, LA. CIV. CODE ANN. art. 188 (2005).

[85] Louisiana State Law Institute, Marriage/Persons Committee Report, October 1996 (manuscript at 9, on file with author).

[86] *Id.*

[87] *Id.*

[88] LA. CIV. CODE ANN. art. 189 (2007).

[89] *Id.*

[90] *Id.*

[91] LA. CIV. CODE ANN. art. 189 (2005).

[92] *Id.* at com (a).

[93] The new article overrules Pounds v. Schori, 377 So. 2d 1195 (La.1979) (concluding that the disavowal action is limited by a peremptive period).

peremptive, what suspensions would exist.[94] The original recommendation of the Committee referred to the period as a peremptive period of one hundred and eighty days, which was then extended to a one year peremptive period unless the husband was mentally or physically incapable of instituting an action in which case the period would be extended to five years.[95] Certain members of the Council expressed concern over referring to the period as a peremptive one when it was subject to suspension, yet the Council continued to stress the importance of a time limit for the action to protect a child from being disavowed years after his birth.[96] Nevertheless, the Council had strong concerns about automatically precluding a father from disavowal in all cases in which the peremptive period expired.[97] One Council member offered an example that unfairly precluded a father from bringing a disavowal action. The Council member hypothesized a situation in which a man separated from the mother, never obtained a divorce, and then the mom had children with another man with whom she was living, leaving the husband liable for support for children that were not his.[98]

Another Council member warned against tampering with presumptions in the Code.[99] He stressed that the purpose of the law was not to "forment imprudence that leads people into unhappy situations [but] try to prevent it."[100] If a husband's wife leaves him, he needs to protect himself by either obtaining a divorce or remaining diligent over the wife's condition to promptly disavow the child.[101] There is no reason to protect an inattentive husband over a child who is left with no parent to support him.[102]

The Council's debate infers that circumstances may arise in which a presumed father needs exceptions to the strict time limit for disavowal to account for circumstances out of his control. Juxtaposed against the father's right is a strong need to protect the child from disavowal years after his birth. The current article continues to protect the child by giving the husband a short period of one year to act, but also safeguards the husband from circumstances outside of his control that may suspend the period.

The suspension of prescription when the father lived separate and apart from the mother during the three hundred days preceding the child's birth was an especially important amendment to the article because a husband could be completely unaware that his wife gave birth to a child. The Council added the exception in response to the decision in *State v.*

---

[94] Louisiana State Law Institute, Marriage/Persons Committee Report, March 1996 (manuscript at 12, on file with author). The author wishes to note that by definition a peremptive period would not allow any exceptions in which the period could be interrupted or suspended.

[95] *Id.* at 9; Louisiana State Law Institute, Marriage/Persons Committee Report, October 1996 (manuscript at 10, on file with author).

[96] Louisiana State Law Institute, Council Meeting on Filiation Revision, March 1996 (manuscript at 12, on file with author).

[97] *Id.*

[98] *Id.* at 13.

[99] *Id.* at 18.

[100] *Id.*

[101] *Id.*

[102] Louisiana State Law Institute, Council Meeting on Filiation Revision, March 1996 (manuscript at 16, on file with author).

Walker.[103] In that case, a husband and wife separated in 1977 but did not divorce. She gave birth to a child of another man in 1979 which the husband failed to disavow.[104] When the wife died in 1994, her sister became the child's custodian and she demanded support from the husband.[105] The trial court allowed the husband to disavow after the results from a blood test revealed he was not the father.[106] The Court of Appeal affirmed but the Supreme Court of Louisiana reversed claiming that "disavowal is now barred by prescription and the presumption of paternity is irrebutable."[107] Despite scientific proof that the husband was not the biological father, the pre-revision articles forced the Supreme Court to come to that decision. The Council added the exception to prevent forcing a man to remain the father of a child who is not biologically related to him if he lived separate and apart from the mother and was never notified of the birth of the child.[108]

d. Time Limit for Disavowal by Heir or Legatee

Article 190 provides that if prescription has commenced to run and the husband dies before he can disavow, his successor whose interest is adversely affected may institute the action subject to a liberative prescription of one year that begins from the day of the death of the husband.[109] If the husband's prescription has not begun to run, the successor is subject to a liberative prescriptive period of one year from the day the successor is notified in writing that a party in interest has asserted that the husband is the father of the child.[110] This article clarifies former article 190, by specifying exactly when prescriptive periods begin to run depending on the circumstances.[111] The Committee considered only giving the successor related by consanguinity, adoption, or affinity the right to disavow to protect the child of the decedent from losing his inheritance to unrelated legatees.[112] During the March 1996 Council meeting, a motion was made to omit the limitation of related legatees due to the potential injustice that could result to non-related legatees.[113] For example, consider a man whose girlfriend cared for him as he died of cancer. In his will, the decedent left his entire estate to his girlfriend that remained by his side throughout his entire illness. Upon hearing of his death and his fortune, an alleged daughter, who never came forward during his life, instituted an action to establish

---

[103] 700 So. 2d 496 (La. 1997).

[104] *Id.* at 497.

[105] *Id.*

[106] *Id.*

[107] *Id.* at 498.

[108] LA. CIV. CODE ANN. art. 189 (2007).

[109] LA. CIV. CODE ANN. art. 190 (2007).

[110] *Id.*

[111] *See*, LA. CIV. CODE ANN. art 190 (2005) (stating similar time limits for a successor of a presumed father to disavow).

[112] Louisiana State Law Institute, Marriage/Persons Committee Report, March 1996 (manuscript at 9, on file with author).

[113] Louisiana State Law Institute, Council Meeting on Filiation Revision, March 1996 (manuscript at 19, on file with author).

paternity.[114] The girlfriend has the right to institute a disavowal action to protect her succession. The amended article now applies to all successors of the decedent, giving them each a liberative prescriptive period of one year from the death of the husband.

e. Contestation and Establishment of Paternity by Mother

The mother's contestation and establishment action is a new addition to Louisiana law and, for the first time, allows a mother to contest the paternity of her child.[115] Article 191 of the revised filiation articles gives a mother the ability to institute an action to establish both that her former husband is not the father of her child and that her current husband is the father.[116] This action can only take place if the present husband has acknowledged the child by authentic act or by signing the birth certificate.[117] The contestation action breaks from Louisiana jurisprudence that has long upheld that a mother is not permitted to "bastardize" her child.[118]

While the article is revolutionary for Louisiana in that it extends a mother's rights concerning her child, the right is limited to protect the best interests of the child.[119] The objective of the revision is to more closely align biological and legal paternity, and in doing so, it also strives to keep the child in an intact family.[120] Therefore there is an obligatory joinder of the two actions, one to contest the mother's former husband's paternity and one to establish the paternity of the child's biological father, her current husband.[121] This ensures that a mother cannot leave her child without a legal father and conforms to the notion that a child is better protected with two parents. The mother's right to contest is a personal one, but it hinges on her current husband's acknowledgment of the child by authentic act or by signing the birth certificate.[122]

To further protect the child, Article 192 provides that a mother must prove by clear and convincing evidence both that her former husband is not the father and that her present husband is the father.[123] Her testimony must be corroborated by other evidence.[124] Article 193 states that a mother has a peremptive period of one-hundred and eighty days from the marriage to her present husband and within two years from the birth of the child to bring a contestation action.[125]

---

[114] *See*, LA. CIV. CODE ANN. art. 197 (2007).

[115] *Id.* cmt. (a).

[116] LA. CIV. CODE ANN. art. 191 (2007).

[117] *Id.*

[118] *See, e.g.*, Feazel v. Feazel, 62 So. 2d 119 (1952) (holding that a mother's testimony that contradicts the presumption that her husband is the father of her child was non-admissible because it bastardized her child).

[119] Spaht, *supra* note 3, at 313-14.

[120] LA. CIV. CODE ANN. art. 191 (b) (2007); Louisiana State Law Institute, Marriage/Persons Committee Report, March 1996 (manuscript at 11, art. 190 (b), on file with author).

[121] Lucie R. Kantrow, *Presumption Junction: Honey, You Weren't Part of the Function—A Louisiana Mother's New Right to Contest Her Husband's Paternity*, 67 LA. L. REV. 633, 650 (2007).

[122] *Id.*

[123] LA. CIV. CODE ANN. art. 192 (2007).

[124] *Id.*

[125] LA. CIV. CODE ANN. art. 193 (2007).

The short peremptive period requires a mother to bring an action quickly to best protect all interested parties, especially the child.[126] The Committee created a short time period so that a child could establish a relationship with his biological father early in life and so that the child would not suffer psychological and emotional damage from severing an attachment with a person whom he believed was his father.[127] In extraordinary circumstances, however, a former husband may be granted visitation rights if the court deems it is in the child's best interests.[128] Article 194 concludes the section on the mother's contestation action and states that "a judgment shall not be rendered decreeing that the former husband is not the father of the child unless the judgment also decrees that the present husband is the father of the child."[129]

The mother's contestation action has its origins in the laws of many foreign jurisdictions as well as the 1973 Uniform Parentage Act (UPA).[130] Article 318 of the French Civil Code states, "even in the absence of disavowal, the mother can contest the paternity of the husband, but only for the purposes of legitimation, when after dissolution of the marriage, she has remarried with the true father of the child."[131] Article 318.1 establishes that the contestation action must be initiated by the mother and her new husband within six months of their marriage and before the child is seven years old.[132] The Committee adopted the French Code's six month period but altered the age the child could attain before peremption runs to two years as opposed to seven. If the child is conceived from the mother's relationship with her current husband, and not her former husband who is the presumed husband, any evidence that she would have to prove this would exist within two years from the birth of the child. Waiting seven years only increases the chances that a child will suffer psychological and emotional damage from severing a relationship with his presumed father. It also saves a presumed father who is not the biological father from paying child support to a child that is not his. After the two year period has passed, a presumed father is not precluded from bringing a disavowal action on his own; he is simply protected from the mother instituting a contestation action.

The Belgian and German Civil Codes give the husband, the mother, and the child the ability to contest the presumption of paternity.[133] In Italy, a mother (and a major child) has the

---

[126] *Id.* cmt. (a).

[127] Spaht, *supra* note 3, at 316.

[128] "A judgment rendered in favor of the mother terminates existing child custody and visitation orders. However, the former husband in extraordinary circumstances may be granted reasonable visitation if the court finds it is in the best interest of the child in accordance with the Civil Code." LA. REV. STAT. ANN. § 9:403(C) (1) (2007) (as added by 2006 La. Acts 344 § 4).

[129] LA. CIV. CODE ANN. art. 194 (2007).

[130] Kantrow, *supra* note 148 at 644-649 (noting that the comments to article 191 reference the 1973 version of the UPA and not the revised 2000 or amended 2002 version because UPA § 6(a) no longer exists in the current revisions- this comment compares the current version of the UPA to the Louisiana law); *See*, LA. CIV. CODE ANN. art. 191 (a) (2007).

[131] C. CIV. art. 318 (Fr.).

[132] Louisiana State Law Institute, Marriage/Persons Committee Report, October 1996 (manuscript at 11, on file with author); C. CIV. art. 318.1 (Fr.).

[133] *See*, CIV. CODE art. 332, ¶ 1 (Belg.); Burgerliches Gesetzbuch [BGB] [Civil Code] § 1600 (F.R.G.).

right to bring any action of "disrecognition" which a father can bring.[134] Quebec, having the most liberal legislation, allows "any interested party" to bring a contestation action.[135]

Oddly, the legislature cited the 1973 version of the UPA in the comments to article 191 as opposed to the revised 2000 and 2002 version of the UPA. [136] Section 6(a)(2) of the 1973 UPA allowed a presumed father, a mother, or a child to bring an action to dissolve the paternity presumption.[137] The current version of the UPA allows a mother to rebut a paternal presumption no later than two years after a child's birth.[138] The time period may be extended if the presumed father lived apart from the mother and did not have sexual relations with her during the probable time of conception.[139] He also must not have openly acknowledged the child as his own.[140] Louisiana's law is more restrictive than the UPA in that it provides no exceptions to the time limit of the mother's contestation action.[141]

The most important difference between the UPA and article 191 is that under article 191 a mother must file an establishment of paternity action with her contestation action.[142] This must be done by clear and convincing evidence and she must be married to the child's true biological father.[143] The Law Institute Committee intentionally rejected the one-sided action because it was against the Committee's objective to leave a child with no legal father.[144]

It could be argued that the UPA's contestation act would produce better results in some situations. For example, consider a situation in which a mother divorces an abusive husband, the mother has relations with another man, and a child is born within three hundred days of the termination of the marriage. The child would be presumed the child of the mother's ex-husband and she could be forced to share custody or give him visitation rights.[145] Under the UPA the mother would be able to contest the ex-husband's paternity, while Louisiana law would provide her with no personal remedies, since she is not married to the biological father. Yet, the child is still protected because Louisiana law provides other remedies such as the biological father could institute a paternity action under article 198 or the mother could argue the detriments of the prior husband's visitation or custody in a custody hearing.[146] The child could also file a paternity action under article 197. A possible scenario that provides no remedy for the mother under

---

[134] C.C. art. 235, ¶ 6 (Italy).

[135] CIV. CODE art. 531, ¶ 1 (Quebec).

[136] LA. CIV CODE ANN. art. 191 (a) (2007).

[137] UNIF. PARENTAGE ACT § 9, 9(b) U.L.A. 435 (1973).

[138] UNIF. PARENTAGE ACT § 607(a) (amended 2002).

[139] Id. § 607(b).

[140] Id.

[141] Kantrow, supra note 148 at 648.

[142] Id.

[143] Id.

[144] LA. CIV. CODE ANN. art. 191 (b) (2007).

[145] While maintaining paternity would be beneficial to get child support from him, the detriment of potentially exposing the child to an abusive father would far outweigh the financial benefit.

[146] LA. CIV. CODE ANN. art. 198 (2007); LA. CIV. CODE ANN. art. 133 (2007) (if custody would result in substantial harm to the child, the court will award custody to another person who can provide a wholesome and stable environment).

Louisiana law would be if she divorced her ex-husband for his infidelity, but he had no characteristics that would warrant the denial of custody. In that case, she would have to cope with him being the presumed father. While there are conceivable situations where it would be beneficial for a mother to contest her husband's paternity without joining it to a paternity action by her current husband, the legislature, with just cause, limited this right so as not to allow a mother to disavow her child's father, leaving a child fatherless.

Proponents of the UPA could also argue that, under Louisiana law, requiring a mother to join disavowal with avowal in her contestation action creates unequal treatment between the man and the woman in filiation actions.[147] While a presumed father can disavow a child under article 187 by clear and convincing corroborated evidence, he is not precluded from disavowing the child if another man is not avowing the child.[148] This inequality could lead to questions of constitutionality, based on gender equality.[149] However, protecting the best interests of children serves as a legitimate governmental interest. Therefore, any inequality created by the different requirements of mothers and fathers is justifiable for the best interests of the child.

The mother's contestation/establishment action is a positive addition to the Louisiana filiation laws. It gives a mother, who arguably is the most knowledgeable person concerning her child's paternity, the ability to place her child with its biological father in an intact family.[150] The legislature correctly placed limits on the UPA's liberal approach to the contestation action that would allow a mother to contest the paternity of one father without filiating the child with another father. As aligning the biological and legal paternity of a child and keeping the child in an intact family are the legislature's ultimate goals, the contestation and establishment action affords the mother some rights as to her child's paternity without striping the child of a father.

3. Other Methods for Establishing Paternity/ Dual Paternity

The final two articles of the revision, article 197 and article 198 provide the legislation for Louisiana's principle of dual paternity. Louisiana's codification of dual paternity is significant because Louisiana is the only state that recognizes that a child may be filiated to more than one man.[151] Therefore, a child can have two legal fathers; the first being his legally presumed father who is married to his mother at the time of the child's birth, and, the second, his biological father if the child can prove his paternity by a preponderance of the evidence.

---

[147] Kantrow, *supra* note 148, at 659-660.

[148] *Id.*

[149] *See*, Craig v. Boren, 429 U.S. 190 (1976) (finding that Equal Protection claims based on gender are to be tested by the middle level of scrutiny in that sex-based discrimination is unconstitutional unless it serves a legitimate state interest).

[150] Empirical data tends to show that on average a child reared in an intact family comprised of his married biological parents prospers in ways that children in other family structures do not, such as lower high school drop out rates, alcohol and drug problems, criminal behavior, and teen pregnancy. Spaht, *supra* note 3, at 315; *See* Maggie Gallagher & Joshua Baker, *Do Mothers and Fathers Matter? The Social Science Evidence on Marriage and Child Well Being*, iMAPP Policy Brief (Feb. 27, 2004), available at http://www.marriagedebate.com/pdf/MothersFathersMatter.pdf (last visited March 30, 2007); William Bradford Wilcox, WHY MARRIAGE MATTERS: TWENTY-SIX CONCLUSIONS FROM THE SOCIAL SCIENCES (2d ed. 2005).

[151] LA. CIV. CODE ANN. art 197 (b) (2007).

The revised articles codify, for the first time, Louisiana jurisprudence that interpreted former Civil Code article 209.[152] As early as 1974 with *Warren v. Richard*, Louisiana courts have recognized the concept of dual paternity.[153] Although dual paternity has become accepted law, there was no legislation codifying the principle until the 2005 revision of the filiation articles.[154] While *Smith v. Cole* upheld the established notion that a child can have two legal fathers, the Louisiana Supreme Court did not address whether the legally presumed father and the biological father would possess the same rights and obligations in relation to the child.[155] The jurisprudence left many unanswered questions to determinations of dual paternity.

Dual paternity was the impetus that fueled the entire filiation article revision process.[156] It sparked the most debate among the Council of the Louisiana Law Institute, as the Council struggled with whether dual paternity should exist in the first place, and if so, under what circumstances.[157] The United States Supreme Court's decision in *Michael H. v. Gerald H.* further provoked the Council to determine whether it would codify or abolish the jurisprudence of dual paternity.[158] The decision established that it was constitutional to deny a biological father the right to filiate with a child if the child was already the presumed child of another man; therefore, the Council had a full range of possible legislative options in regard to dual paternity.[159]

The Council first discusses dual paternity at the October 1994 meeting of the Council of the Louisiana Law Institute.[160] The Council concluded that dual paternity should exist but should be limited.[161] The members decided that a biological father should be able to filiate with a child already filiated to another man in at least two scenarios: 1) when two people engage in a non-adulterous relationship, conceive a child, and then the mother marries another man and does not tell the father about the marriage; 2) when two people engage in a non-adulterous relationship, a child is conceived, and the mother marries another man after the biological father proposes to her and she rejects the proposal.[162]

---

[152] *Id.* at com. (a); *See also*, LA. CIV. CODE ANN. art 209 (2005).

[153] 296 So. 2d 813 (La. 1974) (holding that a child could recover for her biological father's wrongful death even though she was the legal child of another man). *See*, Smith v. Cole, 553 So. 2d 847, 849-55 (La. 1989) (summarizing the history of dual paternity jurisprudence in Louisiana).

[154] *See, e.g.*, Smith v. Cole, 553 So. 2d 847 (La. 1989); Griffin v. Succession of Branch, 479 So. 2d 324 (La. 1985); Succession of Mitchell, 323 So. 2d 451 (La. 1975) (all holding that a child can have more than one legal father).

[155] *Smith*, 553 So. 2d at 855.

[156] The Council met six separate times to discuss dual paternity, each time coming to a different conclusion. Spaht, *supra* note 3, at 321.

[157] *Id.*

[158] 491 U.S. 110 (1989) (finding that the California statute creating a presumption that a child born to a married woman living with her husband is the child of the marriage did not violate the putative natural father's procedural due process rights). This decision establishes that a state has a Constitutional right to only recognize one father.

[159] Spaht, *supra* note 3, at 321-22.

[160] Louisiana State Law Institute, Marriage/Persons Committee Report, October 1994 (manuscript at 1-5, on file with author).

[161] Louisiana State Law Institute, Marriage/Persons Committee Report, September 2002 (manuscript at 5, on file with author).

[162] *Id.*

During the November 1996 meeting, the Council had second thoughts about codifying the dual paternity principle and requested the reporter to gather additional materials for reconsideration.[163] At the September 1997 Council meeting, the Council instructed the Committee to refrain from codifying dual paternity, but to create a narrow exception where a child could bring a paternity action to establish rights only in favor of himself.[164] Furthermore, the biological father should not be called "father" but be given another name and his rights and obligations would be covered in another chapter of the Code.[165] The meeting ended with the Council suggesting that the Committee explore all options of abolishing dual paternity.[166]

Dual paternity was discussed once again during the November 2001 Council meeting.[167] At this meeting, each of the previous conclusions was brought to the table- from abolition of the principle to codifying it.[168] The Council finally decided to codify the principle, but did not come to a conclusion on whether each father had equal rights and obligations.[169] During the May 2002 meeting, the Council finally decided that dual paternity would be codified with the civil effects of paternity being enjoyed by both fathers and the child.[170]

Arguably, the principle of dual paternity upholds the principal goal of the revision: protecting the best interests of the child. Both men owe child support and both can inherit equally from the child. There is no reason that a child should not enjoy the parenting and financial support of two fathers.[171] Many children are fortunate to have only one set of parents, however if there are multiple parents that desire to participate in the support of a child, why should the law deny them that right?

Alternatively, having multiple fathers perpetuates confusion and unjust results, particularly when a child with two fathers would inherit from both of them. Yet, the benefits associated with dual paternity far outweigh the potential unfairness. While some children may receive "double protection," others may not get full support from one father and can, thus, benefit from the combined support of two fathers. Double inheritance fails as an argument for its abolition because adopted children also enjoy the benefit of inheriting from two sets of parents without any adverse consequences.[172] The codification of this principle does bring to the surface interesting questions of equality between men and women. Does the existence of dual paternity mean that, with the advancements in reproductive technology, there can also be dual maternity?[173] Eventually the courts will be faced with this decision. Regardless, the revised

---

[163] *Id.* at 6.

[164] *Id.* (this is akin to the parent/child relationship established in revised article 196).

[165] *Id.*

[166] *Id.*

[167] Louisiana State Law Institute, Marriage/Persons Committee Report, November 2001 (manuscript at 6-7, on file with author).

[168] *Id.*

[169] *Id.*

[170] *Id.* at 7.

[171] *See, e.g.,* Smith v. Cole, 553 So. 2d 847 (La. 1989); State in interest of Poche v. Poche, 368 So. 2d 175 (La. 4 Cir. 1979).

[172] LA. CIV. CODE ANN. art. 214 (2007) (providing that an adopted child can inherited from both his biological and adopted parents) [In 2009, the substance of Article 214 was moved to Civil Code article 199].

[173] *See infra* IV.A.2 and IV.B.

articles create legislation on a principle that has been supported by Louisiana courts for decades.[174] Since there have been few difficulties with the jurisprudence, it is likely that the legislation will only serve to protect children.

a. Child's Action to Establish Paternity

Article 197 of the revised filiation laws gives a child the ability to institute an action to prove paternity even if he is presumed to be the child of another man.[175] If the alleged father is alive, the child need only prove his paternity by a preponderance of the evidence.[176] If the alleged father has died, the child must prove paternity by clear and convincing evidence.[177] For succession purposes, the child has a peremptive period of one year from the death of the alleged father to institute an action.[178] Additionally, the child can institute this action at any time if the father is alive.[179] Once the child succeeds in the action, all of the civil effects of filiation flow from the relationship. This includes the right to inherit intestate, to sue for wrongful death, and for support.[180]

Former article 209 had similar burdens of proof depending on if the parent was alive.[181] However, under former article 209(c), a child had one year from the death of the alleged parent or within nineteen years of the child's birth, whichever occurred first to file a paternity action.[182] Louisiana courts have found that the more liberal prescriptive period of article 197 can not be applied retroactively.[183]

b. Father's Action to Establish Paternity

Article 198 concludes the revision of Title VII, Parent and Child, of the Louisiana Civil Code. The article provides that a man may institute an action to establish paternity of a child at any time according to the exceptions laid out in this article.[184] This action is strictly personal meaning that only the father can institute the action.[185] If the child has a presumed father, the

---

[174] *See,* Warren v. Richard, 296 So. 2d 813 (La. 1974) (holding that a child could recover for her biological father's wrongful death even though she was the legal child of another man).

[175] LA. CIV. CODE ANN. art. 197 (2007).

[176] This can be inferred from the statute since it specified the heightened standard of clear and convincing evidence if the father has died.

[177] LA CIV. CODE ANN. art. 197 (2007).

[178] *Id.*

[179] *Id.*

[180] *Id.* cmt. (a).

[181] LA. CIV. CODE ANN. art. 209 (c) (2005).

[182] *Id.*

[183] *See,* Succession of McKay, 05-0603 (La. 3 Cir. 2/1/06), 921 So. 2d 1219 (holding that even though the paternity action of the over nineteen year-old alleged children of the decedent had not prescribed under the revised law, the law could not be applied retroactively); Jeanmarie v. Butler, 05-1439 (La. 4 Cir. 10/11/06), 942 So. 2d 578 (affirming that article 197 could not be applied retroactively).

[184] LA. CIV. CODE ANN. art. 198 (2007).

[185] *Id.*; LA. CIV. CODE ANN. art. 1766 (2007).

man has one year from the birth of the child to institute an action unless the mother deceived the father regarding the paternity of the child; in that case the man has one year from constructive knowledge of the birth, but regardless within a peremptive period of ten years from the birth of the child and no later than one year from the death of the child.[186] If the child is not filiated to another man, the action can be brought at any time, but no later than one year from the death of the child.[187] This article replaces former Code article 191 which allowed a man to establish his paternity to a child that is presumed to be the child of another man within two years from the birth of the child.[188]

This article further defines and limits dual paternity. While a man can filiate with a child that has a presumed father, the Code applies a short time period of one year from the birth of the child.[189] Only in cases of fraud by the mother, does the time period extend to the father's acquisition of constructive knowledge and under no circumstances can the action be brought after the child's tenth birthday.[190] The time periods are peremptive and, therefore, cannot be extended.[191] These limitations are present to protect the child from upheaval from an intact family and the stresses of litigation. It is best for a father to filiate with his child early in life to fully establish the father/child relationship.

IV. THE CHILDREN LEFT BEHIND

The 2005 revisions to the Louisiana filiation laws significantly modernize the conception of the family under Louisiana law. The laws prior to the revision were archaic, outdated, and did not clearly reflect today's society.[192] Most of the new laws reflect extensive and considerate research by the experts on the Marriage/Persons Advisory Committee and show an understanding of the current status of the Louisiana family. Elements of the revision, such as the codification of the jurisprudence on dual paternity, place Louisiana above other states that fail to offer such benefits to a child. The Committee's fundamental goals of both protecting the best interests of a child and keeping him in an intact family were, for the most part, realized in the 2005 revision.[193] However, certain aspects of the law remain outmoded because they fail to recognize that not all modern families fit into the mold of the traditional family.

* * *

The first shortcoming of the current revision is that the legislature failed to adopt the Committee's recommendation concerning the presumption of a child's paternity born within three hundred days of the dissolution of a marriage.[194] This problem is discussed thoroughly above in Section III.B.1.b. Article 186 of the Louisiana Civil Code determines that if a child is

---

[186] LA. CIV. CODE ANN. art. 198 (2007).

[187] *Id.*

[188] LA. CIV CODE ANN. art 191 (2005).

[189] LA. CIV. CODE ANN. art. 198 (2007).

[190] *Id.*

[191] *Id.*

[192] Many of the articles had not been revised since 1976. *See,* LA CIV. CODE ANN., Title VII, (2005).

[193] *See supra* note 6.

[194] *See supra* III.B.1.b.

born within three hundred days of the dissolution of a marriage and the mother remarries again before his birth, the child is presumed to be the child of the first husband.[195] As discussed earlier, the presumption has illogical consequences for coupes who divorce because of adultery.[196] A child born within three hundred days from the termination of his parents marriage because of his mother's adultery is presumed the child of the first husband.[197] Similarly illogical, a mother's husband could be absent and declared dead and, if a child is born within three hundred days from the declaration of death, he is presumed to be the child of a missing and dead man.[198] The legislature adhered too strongly to a traditional view and failed to see the irrational results of their legislation.

Second, and the most detrimental omission of the revision articles, is that the Committee's promised third chapter of the Parent Child Title, concerning artificial means of reproduction, never came to fruition. The number of children born in the United States through artificial insemination, in vitro fertilization, surrogacy, and egg donation has grown significantly in the past twenty-five years.[199] The dearth of legislation protecting children born by assisted means of reproduction leaves an entire class of children unprotected.

*　　*　　*

A. Children Born of Assisted Means of Reproductive Technology

The initial intention of the Committee was to have a third chapter of the revised filiation articles that pertained exclusively to children born of assisted means of reproductive technology.[200] An early Committee report speaks of a third chapter that would contain articles addressing parentage in circumstances where artificial means of reproduction are used- such as artificial insemination, in vitro fertilization, embryo transfer, egg donation, and surrogacy.[201]

*　　*　　*

1. Artificial Insemination

Artificial insemination[202] was officially recognized by the Civil Code in 1989 when article 188 was amended to prohibit a husband from disavow a child born of his wife through

---

[195] LA. CIV. CODE ANN. art. 186 (2007).

[196] *See supra* section III.B.1.b.

[197] *Id.*

[198] *Id.*

[199] The number of children born of assisted means of reproduction has quadrupled from 1994 to 2001. Varnado, *supra* note 49, at 610; *See also, Assisted Reproductive Technology Success Rates, National Summary and Fertility Clinic Reports*, compiled by U.S. Department of Health and Services, 2004, available at http://ftp.cdc.gov/pub/Publications/art/2004ART508.pdf (last visited March 30, 2007).

[200] Louisiana State Law Institute, Marriage/Persons Committee Report, March 1996 (manuscript at 1, on file with author).

[201] Louisiana State Law Institute, Marriage/Persons Committee Report, October 1996 and September 1997 (manuscript at 24 and 3, respectively, on file with author).

[202] A process for achieving conception, whereby semen is inserted into a woman's vagina by some means other than intercourse. BLACK'S LAW DICTIONARY (8th ed. 2004).

artificial insemination to which he consented.[203] Article 188 has now been expanded to prohibit a husband from disavowing a child born of any type of consensual methods of assisted reproduction.[204] While artificial insemination has proved to be a helpful means of conceiving a child, significant problems may arise with the codification of dual paternity. Consider a married couple in which the husband is infertile and the wife (with the consent of the husband) undergoes artificial insemination. Under article 185 the husband of the mother is the presumed father of the child and under article 188 the husband who consents to assisted conception is precluded from disavowing the child.[205] Yet, with the 2005 revision codifying the principle of dual paternity, the child or the sperm donor could institute an avowal action under article 197 or 198, respectively, because the sperm donor is the biological father of the child.[206] Filiation with the sperm donor, in the majority of circumstances, is not the intent of either the receiving couple or the donor.

While the donor would only have a one year time limit to institute an action, his intrusion into the couple's family would likely cause great turmoil for the couple because their intention was to create a child, and not to bring a stranger into their family.[207] If the couple was not married at the time, the child would not have a presumed father. The donor could, therefore, acknowledge the child through an authentic act and become his legal father, precluding the intended father from filiating with the child.[208]

On the other hand, a child could institute a filiation action to align himself with his biological father, the sperm donor, at any time. This would create a financial obligation of the donor to provide child support until the child reaches eighteen years old.[209] Additionally, if the donor dies, his family could be forced to share his estate with the result of his sperm deposit to which he had no desire to be filiated.[210] The donor's children could be completely unaware of his sperm donation, and, if the child brings the action within a year from the father's death, the donor's children would be bound to share his estate.[211] Filiation between the donor and the conceived child is not the intention of any of the parties involved in the artificial insemination.

*   *   *

---

[203] 1989 La. Act 790 § 1.

[204] LA. CIV. CODE ANN. art. 188 (2007).

[205] LA. CIV. CODE ANN. art, 185, 188 (2007).

[206] LA. CIV. CODE ANN. art. 197, 198 (2007).

[207] Varnado, *supra* note 49, at 632.

[208] LA. CIV. CODE ANN. art. 196 (2007).

[209] Varnado, *supra* note 49, at 632; This age is raised to nineteen for an emancipated child who is a full-time student in good standing at a secondary school or its equivalent, and is dependent upon either parent. The age is raised to twenty-two if the child has a developmental disability (defined in LA. REV. STAT. ANN. § 28:451.2 (2007)) and is a full-time student at a secondary school. *See* LA. REV. STAT. ANN. § 9:315.22 (2007). *See also*, LA. CIV. CODE ANN. art. 229 (2007) (stating that there is a reciprocal alimentary duty to support among ascendants and descendants). [La. Rev. Stat. 9:315.22 was amended by acts 2015, No. 379, eff. Aug 1, 2016, to add: "An award of child support continues or shall be set with respect to any unmarried child who, whether institutionalized or not, is incapable of self-support and requires substantial care and personal supervision because of an intellectual or physical disability that is manifested before the child attains the age of majority. A disability under this Subsection shall not include substance abuse or addiction."]

[210] Varnado, *supra* note 49, at 632.

[211] LA. CIV. CODE ANN. art. 197 (2007).

2. Surrogacy

When drafting article 184 and providing the presumption of maternity to the woman who gave birth to the child, the Committee intended on making the definition subject to exceptions provided in chapter three of the Parent Child Title.[212] Since the chapter was never written, multiple questions concerning the determination of maternity are left open. The possibility of surrogacy and egg donation make legislation on maternity in these situations imperative because two different women may provide genetic material and give birth to the child. If legislation does not clarify who is presumed the mother of the child, undesirable consequences may occur.

As currently written, the comments of article 184 discuss the limited circumstance in which 184's presumption of maternity does not apply.[213] The only time 184's presumption does not apply is when a husband and wife provide gametes to be implanted in a surrogate blood relative of either the husband or the wife.[214] At present, the only type of surrogacy contracts that are legislatively declared null by the Civil Code are compensated genetic surrogacy contracts.[215] Gratuitous genetic and gestational surrogacy contracts are not specifically addressed, and therefore, not specifically prohibited in the Civil Code. Therefore, since surrogacy contracts are not legislatively declared illegal, people are using them in Louisiana.[216] The legislature cannot turn a blind eye to the children conceived from these situations and must consider legislation that places the presumption of maternity on the correct woman.

*   *   *

A few scenarios will demonstrate the importance of a surrogacy exception to article 184. Imagine a couple in which the woman cannot get pregnant or produce eggs.[217] The couple locates a (non-related) surrogate who is willing to get artificially inseminated by the man and contract to give the baby to them after the child is born.[218] During the nine months of pregnancy the surrogate becomes attached to the child growing inside of her and decides she wants to keep the baby. Because the only legislation that currently exists is article 184, which presumes that the woman who gave birth is the mother of the child, the surrogate is the presumed mother.[219] The only remedy available to the couple is to sue for breach of contract, but since a Court will find the contract null and void as against public policy, the infertile couple is left with no child.[220] The adoption of the surrogacy exception would guarantee that the contracting couple would be the legal parents of the child.

---

[212] Louisiana State Law Institute, Marriage/Persons Committee Report, October 1996 (manuscript at 2, on file with author).

[213] *See*, LA. CIV. CODE ANN. art. 184 (2007).

[214] LA. REV. STAT. ANN. 40:34 (2007).

[215] LA. REV. STAT. ANN. § 9:2713 (2007).

[216] The Fertility Institute of New Orleans offers fertility treatment using both hosts uteruses and egg donation. *See*, Fertility Institute of New Orleans website, available at http://www.fertilityinstitute.com/html/technologies.html (last visited March 30, 2007). [The facility no longer offers fertility treatment using host uteruses, but still offers egg donation. See http://fertilityinstitute.com/treatments/other-treatments/]

[217] Varnado, *supra* note 49, at 633-34 (providing similar scenarios).

[218] This contract would be a genetic surrogacy contract because the egg is provided by the surrogate.

[219] LA. CIV. CODE ANN. art. 184 (2007).

[220] LA. REV. STAT. ANN. § 9:2713 (2007).

To make matters even more complicated, the contracting husband is the biological father, so the child, or the surrogate on his behalf, can file a filiation action under article 197, making the couple pay child support for the baby that another woman has taken from them![221] Furthermore, if the surrogate is married, because article 185 provides the presumption that the husband of the mother is the father of the child, the surrogate's husband, who had nothing to do with the contract, is the presumed father of the child. If the contracting husband wanted to filiate with the child as his biological father, he would have to share paternity with the surrogate's husband. The birth mother relinquishing all rights and obligations would prevent this scenario from coming to fruition.

Placing a different spin on the situation, what happens if, after entering into the surrogacy contract, the couple no longer wants the child? The surrogate, who never had any intention of raising a child, is now the presumed mother of the child. Like the couple in the scenario above, she probably will not even be able to sue for breach of contract, because a Louisiana court would find the surrogacy contract null and void as against public policy.[222]

The surrogacy exception would place the baby with the contracting couple. Since they are the couple that instigated the contract, they should be the legal parents. Just like a couple who has a child through traditional conception and birth, if the couple no longer wants the child, they can put the child up for adoption. If the surrogate mother wants the child, she could adopt the child from them.

What if the couple could produce gametes, but the wife could simply not carry the baby?[223] The genetic material would belong to the couple, making them the biological parents. The surrogate would have only provided a "home" for the baby for the nine months of pregnancy. However, under current law, she would still be the presumed mother of the child. Since the revised filiation articles only address avowal actions in favor of fathers, the wife would have no legal remedy to align herself with her child.[224] The surrogacy exception would, again, provide protection for the couple, the child, and the surrogate.

One foreseeable problem with the proposed surrogacy exception occurs if, after entering into the contract, the couple dies. Because the surrogacy contract would most likely be found to be a strictly personal obligation, the contract would end at the death of the couple.[225] Therefore, the surrogate would be left with the child. In this case, if she did not want the child, she would have to put it up for adoption. This rare scenario, while not ideal for the surrogate, still provides better protection for the child, because the child is not left an orphan.

Some may argue that surrogacy is unnatural and that the Code should not provide relief for people that are manipulating natural childbirth. Some refer to surrogacy as "baby selling"

---

[221] In this scenario the biological father could institute a paternity action under LA. CIV. CODE ANN. art. 198 (2007) and the couple may be able to sue for custody and succeed if the court find that their custody would be in the best interests of the child. LA. CIV. CODE ANN. art. 133 (2007).

[222] *Id.*

[223] This is a gestational contract because the genetic material belongs to the contracting couple. It is the contract that Senate Bill 1052 would have protected.

[224] *See*, LA. CIV. CODE ANN. art. 198 (2007) (a *man* may institute an action to establish paternity…(emphasis added by author)).

[225] LA. CIV. CODE ANN. art. 1766 (2007) (an obligation is strictly personal when its performance can be enforced only by the obligee or only against the obligor. When the performance requires the special skill or qualification of the obligor, the obligation is presumed to be strictly personal on the part of the obligor).

and stress the importance of the relationship formed between a woman and the child growing in her womb. While these are valid concerns, a couple who is desperate to have a child will go to great lengths to do so. Regardless of the Code's recognition of surrogacy contracts, people will continue to use them. The legislature's main goal should be to protect children that are born from them. If a couple who cannot have children resorts to contracting with a surrogate, are these not the people that should be the presumed parents of the child? There is no reason that the surrogate, who never intended to have a child and who contracted away her child, should be presumed the mother, over the infertile mother.

Additionally, it is only a matter of time before a woman brings an avowal action before a Louisiana court.[226] Although the articles currently only provide remedies for a man, the question remains if the court will allow a woman to filiate with a child under article 198. If not, will the woman succeed in filing an Equal Protection claim?[227] Louisiana must provide legislation for children born of assisted means of reproduction because it is inevitable that the future holds many filiation issues relating to these children, many of which are yet unimaginable.

*   *   *

V. CONCLUSION

The revisions to the Louisiana Civil Code's, Title VII, Parent and Child, reflect thoughtful and knowledgeable consideration for today's children. Much progress was made for the children born into today's modern family. While the new laws as a whole can be seen as a success, the best interests of all of Louisiana's children have yet to be achieved. The task is a large one because filiation legislation rests, in large part, on other areas of law such as the legality of certain assisted reproductive techniques and same-sex marriage. The children born of these more modern concepts will not be adequately protected until these other areas are addressed. While it is understandable that the legislature is fearful of venturing into the uncharted territory established by methods of assisted reproduction and parentage by non-married and same-sex couples, it is imperative that they take the plunge before too many children are left to drown.

IN RE SUCCESSION OF HARRISON
129 So. 3d 681 (La. App. 2d Cir. 2013), writ denied, 135 So. 3d 1185 (La. 2014)

WILLIAMS, J.

In this action against defendant to compel the return of succession property, plaintiff, Henry L. Himes, appeals a district court's sustention of exceptions of no right of action and prescription/peremption filed by defendant, Susan Speed. For the following reasons, we reverse and remand for further proceedings.

---

[226] Varnado, *supra* note 49, at 635.

[227] *Id.*

Plaintiff, Henry L. Himes, was born on October 31, 1941, to Sallie Himes; no father was named on his birth certificate. On June 21, 1950, the decedent, Thomas A. Harrison, signed an affidavit which stated:

> Before, me, the undersigned authority, personally came and appeared Thomas A. Harrison, who upon oath deposes and says: That he is the father of the minor child Henry Lavelle Himes, whose mother is Sallie Himes, residing at 916 Palestine Street, Shreveport, Louisiana, which said child was born on the 31st day of October, 1941 and I have supported said child since its birth.

The document was notarized by C.H. Messer; however, it was not signed by two witnesses.

On January 1, 2011, the decedent died intestate. At the time of the decedent's death, Himes was 69 years old. On April 11, 2011, Himes filed a petition for possession, alleging, *inter alia,* "[The decedent] had one (1) child born out of wedlock, namely Henry Himes, petitioner herein." The petition also alleged that the estate was "relatively free from debt," administration was unnecessary and Himes "desire[d] to accept this succession purely, simply and unconditionally."

On April 26, 2011, the district court signed an *ex parte* judgment of possession, declaring Himes to be "the sole heir of the decedent" and as such, the sole owner of the decedent's property, including two parcels of immovable property and two vehicles. The judgment also provided:

> IT IS FURTHER ADJUDGED AND DECREED that all banks, trust companies, and other persons, partnerships, corporations or depositories, having on deposit or in their possession or under their control any monies, credits, stocks, dividends, bonds or other things of value, depending upon or belonging to the succession of the [decedent] are hereby required to deliver them unto HENRY HIMES.

Himes was placed in possession of the decedent's estate.

Subsequently, Himes discovered that prior to the decedent's death, defendant, Susan Speed (the decedent's great niece), had removed approximately $85,000 from the decedent's Capital One Bank account. He further discovered that Speed had also taken possession of other items owned by the decedent, including a cash box (which contained an unspecified amount of cash, documents and an antique handgun), funds which had been issued to the decedent by the Veterans Administration, a battery-powered wheelchair, a riding lawnmower and the two automobiles described in the judgment of possession (a 1996 Chevrolet Lumina and a 1998 Ford LTD).

On June 21, 2011, Himes filed a "Motion to Compel Turnover of Succession Property," alleging that he was the sole surviving heir of the decedent. Himes requested a temporary restraining order to enjoin Speed, Capital One Bank, and all financial institutions with accounts in Speed's name, from "dispensing funds or removing funds from any account without further order from th[e] court." A hearing was conducted on July 6, 2011, during which counsel for Speed argued that the decedent donated the $85,000 to Speed approximately one year before he died.

The following day, the court issued an interim order, directing Speed to immediately deposit a cashier's check in the amount of $85,000 into the registry of the court. The court also ordered Speed to turn over to Himes specific items in her possession, including the cash box and its contents, the riding lawnmower and the 1996 Chevrolet Lumina.

On January 5, 2012, Speed filed peremptory exceptions of no right of action and prescription/peremption, arguing that Himes was born out of wedlock and the decedent never formally acknowledged him, by authentic act, as his son. Consequently, according to Speed, Himes was required by law to prove filiation. Additionally, she argued that Himes failed to prove filiation within one year of the decedent's death; therefore, his claims were barred by prescription/peremption.

Following a hearing, the district court sustained the exceptions of no right of action and prescription. Himes now appeals.

Himes contends the district court erred in sustaining Speed's exceptions. He argues that he presented clear and convincing evidence that the decedent informally acknowledged him as his son prior to his death.

*　　*　　*

A man may, by authentic act or by signing the birth certificate, acknowledge a child not filiated to another man. The acknowledgment creates a presumption that the man who acknowledges the child is the father. LSA–C.C. art. 196. An authentic act is a writing executed before a notary public or other officer authorized to perform that function, in the presence of two witnesses, and signed by each party who executed it, by each witness, and by each notary public before whom it was executed. LSA–C.C. art. 1833(A).

LSA–C.C. art. 197 provides: A child may institute an action to prove paternity even though he is presumed to be the child of another man. If the action is instituted after the death of the alleged father, a child shall prove paternity by clear and convincing evidence.

For purposes of succession only, this action is subject to a peremptive period of one year. This peremptive period commences to run from the day of the death of the alleged father.

Peremption is a period of time fixed by law for the existence of a right, and unless timely exercised, the right is extinguished upon the expiration of the peremptive period. LSA–C.C. art. 3458; *Borel v. Young,* 2007–0419 (La.11/27/07), 989 So. 2d 42; *Thomas v. Roberts,* 47,411 (La.App.2d Cir.9/26/12), 106 So. 3d 557. Where a statute creates a right of action and fixes the time in which to commence the action, the time so fixed is an integral part of the right created and is peremptive or substantive, as opposed to prescriptive or procedural. Upon expiration of the peremptive period, the right is extinguished. *Thomas v. Roberts, supra; Houston Industries, Inc. v. Fitch,* 32,654 (La.App.2d Cir.2/1/00), 752 So. 2d 974, *writ denied,* 2000–0643 (La.4/20/00), 760 So. 2d 351.

From 1980 until 2005, Louisiana law permitted the "informal acknowledgment" of an illegitimate child. For example, former LSA–C.C. art. 209 provided that proof of "paternal descent" could be made "[b]y all kinds of private writings, in which the father may have acknowledged the 'bastard' as his child, or may have called him so;" or "[w]hen the father, either in public or in private, has acknowledged him as his child, or has called him so in conversation, or has caused him to be educated as such[.]"

However, the passage of Acts 2005, No. 192, resulted in the enactment of the current LSA–C.C. art. 197, which became effective on June 29, 2005, and replaced former LSA–C.C. art. 209. Thus, pursuant to the law as it exists today (and at the time of the decedent's death), there are two ways for a child born outside of marriage to prove the existence of a parent-child relationship: (1) formal acknowledgment by the father, either by authentic act or by signing the child's birth certificate; and (2) the institution of a legal proceeding to prove filiation. *See* LSA–C.C. arts. 196 and 197. During the proceedings to prove filiation, the child is permitted to introduce evidence, such as blood tests and evidence of informal acknowledgment.

In the instant case, Himes did not file any pleadings specifically captioned as a petition to establish filiation. As stated above, the decedent died on January 1, 2011; Himes filed the judgment of possession on April 11, 2011, alleging that he was the "surviving sole heir of the decedent, Thomas A. Harrison"; he was judicially declared to be the decedent's sole heir and was placed in possession of the decedent's property on April 26, 2011.

Subsequently, Himes instituted proceedings to compel the turnover of succession property, during which he introduced multiple documents into evidence to prove that he was informally acknowledged by the decedent. The evidence included the above referenced affidavit, in which the decedent attested that he was Himes' father. Himes also introduced other documents, including correspondence from the Social Security Administration and the Department of Veterans Affairs, which established that Himes received a portion of the decedent's disability benefits. Additionally, the documents from the Department of Veterans Affairs show that the decedent listed Himes as the beneficiary of his disability benefits and that Himes, in fact, received those benefits dating from 1950 until he graduated from high school in 1960.

As stated above, on June 21, 2011, Himes filed a motion to compel turnover of succession property, alleging that he was the decedent's sole heir. During these proceedings, Himes introduced evidence to establish filiation. Although the exceptions were filed January 5, 2012, days after the peremptive period for proving filiation had expired, the proceedings were initiated when Himes filed the motion to compel—June 21, 2011.

Thus, within a year of his father's death, Himes filed a civil demand by filing the motion to compel, which initiated the proof of filiation. It is well settled in Louisiana that courts look beyond the caption, style and form of pleadings to determine from the substance of the pleadings the nature of the proceeding. *Smith v. Cajun Insulation, Inc.,* 392 So. 2d 398 (La.1980); *Murrell v. Murrell,* 42,070 (La.App.2d Cir.4/25/07), 956 So. 2d 697.

Accordingly, we find that Himes instituted a civil proceeding within one year of his father's death, during which he presented clear and convincing evidence to establish filiation. Thus, under the facts of this case, we find that the district court erred in sustaining defendant's exceptions of no right of action and prescription/peremption.

For the foregoing reasons, the district court's judgment, sustaining the exceptions of no right of action and prescription/peremption, is reversed; we remand this matter to the district court for further proceedings. Costs of this appeal are assessed to defendant, Susan Speed.

REVERSED; REMANDED FOR FURTHER PROCEEDINGS.

SUCCESSION OF JAMES
994 So. 2d 120 (La. App. 1 Cir. 2008)

McCLENDON, J.

In this succession proceeding, the plaintiff-in-intervention, Mona Lisa Tyler Thibodeaux, filed a "PETITION TO ESTABLISH FILIATION" and sought to have the deceased, Mr. Haywood Lee James, declared to be her biological father. Finding that the matter has prescribed, we affirm the judgment.

FACTS AND PROCEDURAL BACKGROUND

Barbara James Collins, the sister of the deceased Mr. James, initiated his succession proceeding by filing a petition for administration. The petition alleged that Mr. James died on May 24, 2007 and that he had no children.

On June 15, 2007, Ms. Thibodeaux filed the intervention in the succession proceeding. Her petition to establish filiation alleged that she was born on January 16, 1966, and that Mr. James was her biological father. Individually, and on behalf of the succession as its administrator, Ms. Collins answered the petition and generally denied the intervenor's allegations.

Subsequently, Ms. Collins filed a peremptory exception raising the objection of prescription. Ms. Collins argued that Ms. Thibodeaux failed to file her petition to establish filiation within nineteen years of her birth, and thus, under former LSA–C.C. art. 209 in effect at the time of Ms. Thibodeaux's nineteenth birthday, the matter had prescribed before Mr. James died in 2007. Because the matter had prescribed years before article 209 was replaced by LSA–C.C. art. 197, which contains a more beneficial prescriptive period, Ms. Collins argued that article 197 was not applicable to the filiation action and the prescribed claim could not be revived. After a hearing, the trial court granted the exception of prescription and dismissed the intervention seeking filiation.

Ms. Thibodeaux appealed. On appeal, Ms. Thibodeaux notes that Mr. James did not die until 2007, and the change in the prescriptive period was made applicable to actions filed after article 197's effective date of June 29, 2005. Thus, she argues that LSA–C.C. art. 197 controlled her cause of action, not LSA–C.C. art. 209.

APPLICABLE LEGAL PRECEPTS
PEREMPTION OF FILIATION ACTIONS

Former LSA–C.C. article 209 contained the following pertinent provisions:

B. A child not entitled to legitimate filiation nor filiated by the initiative of the parent by legitimation or by acknowledgment under Article 203 must prove filiation as to an alleged deceased parent by clear and convincing evidence in a civil proceeding instituted by the child or on his behalf within the time limit provided in this article.

C. The proceeding required by this article must be brought within one year of the death of the alleged parent or within nineteen years of the child's birth,

whichever first occurs. This time limitation shall run against all persons, including minors and interdicts. If the proceeding is not timely instituted, the child may not thereafter establish his filiation, except for the sole purpose of establishing the right to recover damages under Article 2315. A proceeding for that purpose may be brought within one year of the death of the alleged parent and may be cumulated with the action to recover damages. (Emphasis added.)

In *Matherne v. Broussard,* 2006–0838, p. 8 (La.App. 1 Cir. 2/14/07), 959 So. 2d 975, 980, this court held that the time limitation in article 209 was peremptive.

The passage of Acts 2005, No. 192, resulted in the enactment of the current LSA–C.C. art. 197, which became effective on June 29, 2005, and replaced former LSA–C.C. art. 209. Article 197 provides as follows:

A child may institute an action to prove paternity even though he is presumed to be the child of another man. If the action is instituted after the death of the alleged father, a child shall prove paternity by clear and convincing evidence.

For purposes of succession only, this action is subject to a peremptive period of one year. This peremptive period commences to run from the day of the death of the alleged father.

Thus, article 197, which was deemed peremptive by the legislature, changed the time period for bringing an action to establish filiation or paternity, in a succession proceeding, to one year from the day of the death of the alleged father. *See* LSA–C.C. art. 197 & Revision Comments–2005(e). Section 3 of Act 192 stated that the new time provision was applicable to "all claims existing or actions pending on its effective date and all claims arising or actions filed on and after its effective date."

Peremption "is a period of time, fixed by law, within which a right must be exercised or be forever lost." *Borel v. Young,* 2007–0419, p. 8 (La.11/27/07), 989 So. 2d 42, 48; *see* LSA–C.C. art. 3458. "Peremption may not be renounced, interrupted, or suspended." LSA–C.C. art. 3461. In addition, exceptions to prescription, such as *contra non valentem,* do not apply to a peremptive period. *Borel,* 2007–0419 at pp. 8–9, 989 So. 2d at 49.

RETROACTIVE REVIVAL OF CAUSES OF ACTION

When faced with the issue of whether a change in a prescriptive period can be applied retroactively to revive an action or right that prescribed before a change in the law, the Louisiana Supreme Court, in the products liability case of *Chance v. American Honda Motor Company, Inc.,* 93–2582 (La.4/11/94), 635 So. 2d 177, 177–78, employed the following analysis:

Although prescriptive statutes are generally procedural in nature, the revival of an already prescribed claim presents additional concerns. For while the defendant does not acquire anything during the running of the prescriptive period, once the time period has elapsed, the legislature grants the defendant the right to plead the exception of prescription in order to defeat the plaintiffs claim. La.Code Civ.P. arts. 927 & 934. Because the defendant acquires the right to plead the exception of prescription, a change in that right constitutes a substantive change in the law as applied to the defendant. *See St. Paul Fire & Marine Ins. Co. v. Smith,* 609 So. 2d 809,

817 (La.1992) ("Substantive laws either establish new rules, rights, and duties or change existing ones."); *Thomassie v. Savoie,* 581 So. 2d 1031, 1034 (La.App. 1st Cir.1991) ("[I]f a statute which is remedial or procedural also has the effect of making a change in the substantive law, it must be construed to operate prospectively only."). Thus, were we to interpret the amendment at issue to allow the revival of prescribed causes of action, the substantive rights of the defendant would be materially changed because he would be stripped of this acquired defense. Guided by the principles established in [La.Civ.Code] article 6 [which provides that substantive laws apply prospectively only], we require, at the very least, a clear and unequivocal expression of intent by the legislature for such an "extreme exercise of legislative power." (Footnote omitted.)

Based on its analysis and a finding that the legislature had not provided a clear expression of any intent to make the change in a prescriptive article retroactive, *Chance* held that the barred action could not be revived.

In *Cameron Parish School Board v. Acands, Inc.,* 96–0895 (La.1/14/97), 687 So. 2d 84, our supreme court again considered the issue of the revival of a previously prescribed claim and employed the *Chance* analysis. Although the supreme court noted that the legislature directed that the statute in question was to apply to "any action," the court found:

> Liberal use by the legislature of the word or phrases "action," "any action," "all actions," and "any and all actions" in these prescriptive statutes supportive of our determination that the legislature, in using such wording in the statute at issue herein, has not clearly and unequivocally expressed an intent to revive an already prescribed cause of action....
>
> . . .
>
> [T]he language used in the statute does not contain *any* reference to revival of prescribed claims. Moreover, the legislative history of this statute gives no indication of any intent on the part of the legislature that this statute should apply to revive causes of action which had already prescribed under the law existing prior to the statute's enactment.

Cameron Parish School Board, 96–0895, pp. 10–11, 687 So. 2d at 91.

To decide cases involving the change in the law effected by the adoption of Civil Code article 197, the *Chance* analysis was adopted by the third circuit in *Succession of McKay,* 2005–603, pp. 4–6 (La.App. 3 Cir. 2/1/06), 921 So. 2d 1219, 1222–23, *writs denied,* 2006–0504 (La.6/2/06), 929 So. 2d 1252 & 2006–0631 (La.6/2/06), 929 So. 2d 1253; and subsequently by this court in the similar case of *Succession of Faget,* 2005–1434, 2005–1435 (La.App. 1 Cir. 6/9/06), 938 So. 2d 1003, *writ denied,* 2006–1719 (La.11/9/06), 941 So. 2d 40, *See also Jeanmarie v. Butler,* 2005–1439 p. 3 (La.App. 4 Cir. 10/11/06), 942 So. 2d 578, 579 (followed holding in *Succession of McKay*).

Specifically, *Succession of McKay,* 2005–603 at p. 1, 921 So. 2d at 1221, involved an alleged father who died before the effective date of article 197. In its review, the third circuit analyzed the issue of retroactivity of article 197 under *Chance* and *Cameron Parish School Board,* and came to the following conclusion:

> Similarly, ... 2005 La.Acts No. 192 § 3, provides that "[t]he provisions of this Act shall be applicable to all claims existing or actions pending on its effective date and all claims arising or actions filed on and after its effective date." We find no

"clear and unequivocal" expression by the legislature that Article 197 revives filiation claims which have already prescribed. It is clear that the intent of the legislature was to ensure that the provisions of the Act applied to causes of action that had not prescribed but were existing or already in litigation on June 29, 2005, the effective date of the Act. We, therefore, find that Article 197 is not applicable to these already-prescribed claims.

Succession of McKay, 2005–603 at pp. 5–6, 921 So. 2d at 1223.

In *Succession of Faget,* 2005–1434 at pp. 3 & 6–7, 938 So. 2d at 1005 & 1007, which also involved an alleged father who died before the effective date of the change in the law, this court cited *Succession of McKay* and employed the *Chance* and *Cameron Parish School Board* analysis. After a review of the new legislation, we found that Act 192 did not clearly and unequivocally express an intent to have LSA–C.C. art. 197 apply retroactively to revive a claim or create new rights. *Succession of Faget,* 2005–1434 at pp. 6–7, 938 So. 2d at 1006–1007.

ANALYSIS

To distinguish this case from previously cited appellate opinions holding that LSA–C.C. art. 197 cannot be applied retroactively to revive an action, including this court's holding in *Succession of Faget,* Ms. Thibodeaux points out that the alleged parent in those cases died before the enactment of LSA–C.C. art. 197. In contrast, her alleged father died after the effective date of the article. Thus, she argues, article 197, the law in effect on her alleged father's date of death, should apply. Ms. Thibodeaux's primary support for her argument appears to stem from the language of section 3 of Act 192, providing that the new law, article 197, applied to "claims existing or actions pending on its effective date" and "actions filed on and after its effective date." Further, she argues that her cause of action herein is one to determine her status as an heir in a succession, and is not a true action for filiation that would have prescribed under LSA–C.C. art. 209.

We disagree. Firstly, though filed in a succession proceeding, the cause of action here is one to establish paternity or filiation; a prerequisite action necessary before Ms. Thibodeaux can qualify as an heir. For such actions to establish heirship in succession proceedings, former 209 and current 197 were and are the specifically applicable articles. We also note that, while the caption of a pleading is not always definitive, Ms. Thibodeaux's action is not only entitled "FILIATION," the facts alleged assert a claim for filiation.

Secondly, despite the death of the alleged father in this case after the effective date of article 197, a close reading of the appellate courts' analysis of the article 197 retroactivity issue, relying on the principles developed by our supreme court, expose the flaw in Ms. Thibodeaux's argument. Although we agree that section 3 of Act 192 makes article 197 applicable to "existing claims" and "actions" filed after the effective date, it is clear from the language of *Cameron Parish School Board* that the legislature's use of the terms "claims" or "actions" refers to existing or viable causes of action and does not denote a matter that has prescribed or been preempted. *See Cameron Parish School Board,* 96–0895, p. 10, 687 So. 2d at 91. Referencing the language from *Cameron Parish School Board,* this court, in *Succession of Faget,* 2005–1434 & 1435 at p. 7, 938 So. 2d at 1007, and the third circuit in *Succession of McKay,* 2005–603 at pp. 5–6, 921 So. 2d at 1223, also held that such wording referred to still existing and pending claims, not actions that had prescribed or been preempted. Thus, it is clear from the applicable jurisprudence that the analysis applied, to determine whether article 209 or 197 controlled, did not rest on whether the alleged father died before or after the effective date of article 197. Rather, the focus was on the date that the time limit for filing her viable action for filiation ended.

Under article 209, which was in effect on Ms. Thibodeaux's nineteenth birthday, her action for filiation was perempted when Ms. Thibodeaux, born in 1966, failed to file her action before said nineteenth birthday, many years before the death of her alleged father. Her cause of action or right was not merely barred and rendered inchoate, but was extinguished and ceased to exist more than twenty years before she filed her filiation claim.

The *Chance* jurisprudential analysis, followed by this court and other circuits, determined that, in the case of a prescribed or perempted action, a retroactive application would deprive a defendant of a right to plead prescription or peremption. However, before deciding if such a substantive right may ever be impaired, the threshold inquiry is whether the legislature clearly and unequivocally expressed an intent to apply retroactively a change in the time limitation. Thus, the inquiry here is the same as in *Succession of Faget*: whether article 197 was clearly intended by the legislature to apply retroactively to Ms. Thibodeaux's filiation action that had already been perempted before the effective date of the change.

The legislature did not clearly and unequivocally express, in either the act, the new law, or revision comments, an intent to have new article LSA–C.C. art. 197 apply retroactively to revive the right, claim, or cause of action at issue here. In the absence of retroactive application, article 209 controlled. *See Succession of Faget,* 2005–1434, 2005–1435 at p. 7, 938 So. 2d at 1007. Thus, Ms. Thibodeaux's action was no longer pending or viable at the time of the filing of the petition to establish filiation, and the trial court was correct in dismissing the intervention.

CONCLUSION

For these reasons, we affirm the judgment of the trial court. The costs of the appeal are assessed to appellant, Ms. Mona Lisa Tyler Thibodeaux.

AFFIRMED.

NOTE

How does one reconcile the *Harrison* and *James* cases? In *Harrison*, the court applied article 197, the law in effect on the date of the decedent's death, to permit a descendant to file a paternity action within one year of the decedent's death. To the contrary, in *James*, even though the decedent died after the effective date of article 197, the court denied the descendant the right to file a paternity action within one year of the decedent's death, finding that the right of filiation was preempted when the descendant turned nineteen, as provided under repealed article 209.

How was the right of the heir perempted when that right did not come into fruition until the death of the decedent? Rights transmit at the moment of death and not before. La. C.C. 924, 937. La. C.C. 870 instructs that the law in effect at the time of the decedent's death applies, but yet the James court applied the law in effect at the time of the descendant's nineteen birthday?

Other courts have found the descendant's right to filiate preempted because the descendant had reached the age of nineteen at the date of the decedent's death, but in many of those cases, the decedent had died **before** the effective date of article 197. Because old article

209 applied to those proceedings (the law in effect on the decedent's death), the courts correctly denied the descendant the right to participate in the succession. *See Succession of Hebert*, 153 So. 3d 1101 (La. App. 3d Cir. 2014). (the decedent died on June 27, 2003 and the court concluded that his daughter's action to filiate was preempted because she had reached nineteen before the decedent's death without filing an action of paternity); *Succession of Faget*, 938 So. 2d 1003 (La. App. 1 Cir. 2008) (decedent also died before the effective date of article 197); *Succession of McKay*, 921 So. 2d 1219 (La. App. 3d Cir. 2006) (decedent died before the effective date of article 197).

The *James* court makes much of the distinction that the action is one for "filiation" and not to qualify as an heir in a succession. However, whether a descendant is or is not properly filiated to a decedent, his rights do not exist until the death of the decedent. His quality as an heir to the succession occurs only upon the death of the decedent. A successor cannot accept or renounce prior to the death of the decedent. A descendant who had not properly filiated would not do so until some event or condition that would impact his rights, such as the death of his father. The Second Circuit in *Harrison* applied the proper analysis but failed to mention the First Circuit decision or the other circuits that found to the contrary. *See In re Succession of Smith*, 29 So. 3d 723 (La. App. 3d Cir. 2010) *writ denied*, 38 So. 3d 325 (La. 2010) (following *James*, denying descendants action to filiate); *see also Thomas v. Roberts*, 106 So. 3d 557 (La. App. 2d Cir. 2012). (applying *James* to deny the right of a descendant to filiate when the alleged father was still living).

HYPOTHETICAL

Delia had a son Mendez who was a crooked corrections officer at a women's prison and had several inappropriate relationships with the inmates.

Mendez's friend and fellow corrections officer, Bennett met inmate Daya in the prison and fell madly in love. When Daya discovered that she and Bennett were pregnant, she became very upset. The warden suspected that Bennett and Daya were too close and this baby would be the proof. He could fire Bennett and he would go to jail. But, Daya and her mother were both incarcerated, so no one would be able to raise the baby. Daya's mother came up with a brilliant plan: Everyone knew that Mendez engaged in inappropriate relations with the inmates, so Daya should have sex with Mendez, they should be discovered, and Mendez would believe he was the father. The plan worked. Ultimately, Mendez was fired and charged with raping an inmate and sent to prison. Before he left, he professed his undying love for Daya, his excitement about being a father, and the two were validly married in the prison chapel.

Upon hearing the news that "her grandchild" was on the way, Delia wrote to Daya and offered to raise the baby. Daya wrote back, telling her the truth. Delia then decided to tell Mendez the truth. When she told him that the baby was not his, he denied it and said that marrying Daya was the best thing he'd ever done. He begged his mother to raise the baby until he or Daya got out. Delia decided to raise the baby as her own granddaughter.

Six months after the baby was born, Mendez was killed in a prison riot. Unbeknownst to his family, Mendez's estate was worth $30 million. His two brothers came into town for the funeral and met their new niece. Delia told them the truth and of her intentions to raise the little girl. The brothers were infuriated. As the intestate heirs of Mendez, they want to know whether they can prevent the baby from inheriting from their brother's estate. Mendez has no other known descendants.

a)   Do the brothers have a claim? If so, when must the claim be brought, what must they prove? Does Delia have a right to bring a claim as well?

b)   While Mendez was still a corrections officer, he had an affair with another inmate named Leanne in exchange for drugs. Leanne got pregnant while in prison and the baby, a son, was born shortly after Daya's daughter. Just before Mendez was killed, Leanne was able to get a DNA sample from Mendez. Leanne believes that Mendez is the father of her baby. Is an action available for the son to be able to take from Mendez's estate? If so, when must the claim be brought and what must be proven?

complete

CHAPTER 4:
ABSENT PERSONS
La. C.C. 47-59

Overview of the Law of Absent Persons

By Act 989 of 1990, effective January 1, 1991, major changes were made in the law regarding absent persons. Title III of Book I, previously articles 47 through 85 of the LOUISIANA CIVIL CODE, was replaced by new articles 47 through 59. The procedure to be followed for the curatorship of absent persons is contained in Part II of Chapter 13 of Title 13 of the LOUISIANA REVISED STATUTES, entitled "Curatorship of the Property of Absent Persons," and includes La. R.S. 13:3421-3445.

Chapter I of the new Title III remains the institution of curatorship for absent persons, although changes in the manner of administration have been made. The concept of provisional possession, previously provided for in Chapter II of Title II (articles 57 through 69), has been rejected in favor of a presumption of death after five years' absence and a subsequent judicial declaration or death. Since a person who is absent for at least five years is then presumed or declared dead, he is not considered a successor in any succession that would have opened in his favor after such time. This change, and the ramifications should such a person reappear, are contained in new articles 58 and 59, replacing the old Chapter 3, composed of articles 76 through 79.

An "absent person" is defined as "one who has no representative in this state and whose whereabouts are not known and cannot be ascertained by diligent effort." La. C.C. 47. If such a person owns property, either movable or immovable, in this state, the court upon petition of any interested party and upon a showing of necessity, may appoint a curator to manage such property. La. C.C. 47. In contrast to the previous law, which granted the curator only the power of administration (La. C.C. 50 of 1870), the curator under the new scheme has both the power to administer and the power to alienate the property in accordance with the new procedural rules contained in La. R.S. 13:3431-3440. La. C.C. 48. However, if the absent person is a spouse in community, the powers of the curator affect only the separate property. La. C.C. 48. As to most community property, the present spouse could merely continue the management pursuant to La. C.C. 2346. However, as to property which was exclusively controlled by the absent spouse, La. C.C. 2355.1 permits the spouse of such absent person to bring a summary proceeding showing that the other spouse is "absent" and is not merely "temporarily absent," *see* Comment c to La. C.C. 2355.1, and that it is in the best interest of the family to authorize the petitioning spouse to "manage, alienate, encumber or lease" the community property that was exclusively within the control of the absent spouse. The community property regime terminates if the absent person dies or a judgment of declaration of death is obtained. La. C.C. 2356.

Even during curatorship, the absent person retains his full legal capacity, although any acts disposing of immovable property would be ineffective toward third persons unless registered in the parish of the immovable property. La. C.C. 49. For movables, an act would be ineffective toward third persons unless the property were delivered.

How To terminate curatorship!

The curatorship may terminate either "of right" without the need of a judgment, by the appointment by the absent person of a representative in the state, by the absent person reappearing, or by death of the absent person, La. C.C. 50, or it may terminate by a rendering of a judgment of declaration of death when the absent person has no known heirs and is presumed dead. La. C.C. 51. Upon learning of the termination of the curatorship, the curator must file notice in the curatorship proceeding that his authority as curator has ceased. La. C.C. 53. He must also render an accounting and return the formerly absent person's property either to the person himself or to the formerly absent person's successor. La. C.C. 52.

The changes allow for the property of the absent person to remain in commerce, by granting the curator the right to alienate or mortgage the absent person's property. The interests of the absent person are protected by providing that a curatorship would be established only upon a showing of necessity. However, by allowing the possibility of both the curator and the absent person to potentially be acting simultaneously with regard to the same property, potential conflicts could arise. *See* J. Carriere, *The Rights of the Living Dead: Absent Persons in the Civil Law*, 50 La. L. Rev. 901 (1990), in which these points are made and which provides a thorough analysis of the subject of absent persons, tracing the historical treatment, the previous statutory scheme in Louisiana, and the recent changes.

Perhaps the most significant change in the new provisions is the elimination of the concept of provisional possession, which allowed presumptive heirs of the absent person to enjoy the limited powers of possession and administration of the absent person's property after five years' absence. At that point, any interested party could petition the court requesting a declaration of death of the absent person. La. C.C. 54. However, no provision requires an attempt to notify the absent person that the absent person is about to be declared dead. Therefore, this system suggests a due process problem. J. Carriere, *The Rights of the Living Dead: Absent Persons in the Civil Law*, 50 La. L. Rev. 901, 935 (1990). Perhaps a mailing to the absent person's last known address could be added to alleviate this problem.

According to comment b relating to Article 54, such a presumption is "applicable to all matters, including the opening of the succession of the absent person and the recovery of the proceeds of his life insurance." The absent person's succession is then opened with the date of death established in the judgment. La. C.C. 55. Should new "clear and convincing evidence" later surface which would indicate a different date of death, then the judgment of declaration of death could be amended accordingly. La. C.C. 56. If the new date of death results in different successors than those originally placed in possession of the absent person's property, then the previous successors would be required to return the property they possessed to the new successors, but could retain any fruits gathered in the interim. (La. C.C. 56). The comment to article 56 indicates that should the property have been sold by the first possessors, then those possessors would be bound to restore the value of the property "at the time of the restoration," there being no recourse against any third parties.

In the event that the person declared dead should reappear, he would have the opportunity to retrieve his property, either from the successors or their transferees under gratuitous title, in the condition in which it existed at the time of the absent person's reappearance. If the property had been sold, the absent person could recover from the successors the net proceeds of such an alienation. The articles do not indicate what would happen if the successors had alienated the property and had also consumed the proceeds. Also, by not making the successors personal debtors to the absent person, problems of tracing funds exist. J. Carriere, *The Rights of the*

Living Dead: Absent Persons in the Civil Law, 50 La. L. Rev. 901 (1990). If the property had been encumbered, the absent person would be entitled to recover for the diminution of value of things due to the encumbrance. La. C.C. 57. However, no recourse is available against third parties.

As to any fruits accruing since the absent person's disappearance, Comment c to article 57 refers back to C.C. article 486, which permits the good faith possessor to keep such fruits, subject to the possessor's claim for reimbursement of expenses. As to improvements made by the possessors to any immovables, this comment refers back to C.C. articles 496 and 497, the general articles dealing with the rights of possessors. Article 496 grants the good faith possessor the right to demand payment for improvements made on the property, and the owner may not demand their demolition or removal. At the absent person's option, he may pay to the possessor either the cost of the improvements, their current value, or their enhanced value. If the improvements were made by a bad faith possessor, the absent persons may either keep them or demand their removal at the absent person's expense, while holding the possessor liable for any injury sustained by the absent person. If the absent person chooses to keep the improvements, he would be bound to pay, at his option, either the current value of the improvements, or the enhanced value of the immovable. La. C.C. 497. Reference to the property articles has elicited some criticism. Since no act translative of ownership, necessary for good faith possession, has been rendered, it may be argued that the possession would by definition be in bad faith in any absent person situation. *See* J. Carriere, *The Rights of the Living Dead: Absent Persons in the Civil Law*, 50 La. L. Rev. 901 (1990).

The new law clarifies an issue that had caused much confusion under the old system. Replacing previous article 77 which dealt with successions opening in favor of an absent person, new article 58 states that the person who is presumed or declared dead at the time a succession would have opened in his favor, is considered as not existing at the time such a succession is opened. If the absent person happened to be the only heir of the person whose succession was opened, then the property that would have gone to the absent person would devolve on persons who would have taken in his default. If, however, the absent person would have concurred with others had he been in existence at the time of the opening of such a succession, then the declared dead could be represented by his descendants. Should the person declared dead reappear, he would have the right to his inheritance, either from those taking in his default or from their transferees under gratuitous title, only in the condition in which such property existed at the time of the person's reappearance. If the property had been alienated, he would have an action against those persons for the net proceeds of the sale. If it had been encumbered, recovery for the dimunition of value due to the encumbrance would be available against those who took in his default or their gratuitous transferees. Again, third parties purchasing under onerous title from those taking in default of the absent person would be protected. La. C.C. 59. Comment c to article 59 refers back to C.C. articles 486, 496, and 497 for determining rights to fruits and improvements. Comment d to article 59 indicates that an absent person who reappears within two years of the judgment of possession should have the same rights as omitted heirs under R.S. 9:5630, i.e. the right to assert an interest against a third person acquiring onerous title from a recognized heir or legatee, for a period of two years from the date of the finality of the judgment of possession.

La. R.S. 9:1441-1443, which were added to by Acts 1960, No. 31, provide special presumptions regarding absent military personnel.

4-3

La. C.C. 30 provides a general presumption of death in instances where a person has disappeared under circumstances that make his death appear to be certain. This presumption applies even though no body is found. Consider the tragedy of September 11, 2001, and Louisiana's law of absent persons.

IN RE BOYD
723 So. 2d 1107 (La. App. 1st Cir. 1998)

REMY CHIASSION, Judge Pro Tem.

In this action, petitioner seeks to have his sister, an absentee, declared legally dead based upon a showing that no member of petitioner's family has had any communication or correspondence with said absentee since 1983. Following the trial court's denial of judgment, petitioner now appeals.

Facts

In a Petition For Declaration Of Death filed on his behalf in East Baton Rouge Parish on January 23, 1996, petitioner, Ralph E. Pitzel (hereafter, "Mr. Pitzel"), asserts that he is the sole sibling of Penelope Elizabeth Pitzel Boyd (hereafter, "Penelope"), an absentee. Based upon the facts as set forth by Mr. Pitzel, it appears that his sister Penelope was born in October of 1937, and last resided in East Baton Rouge Parish in 1983. According to Mr. Pitzel, Penelope left Baton Rouge in the spring of 1983 after becoming angry with her mother, the late Thelma Harriet Johnson Pitzel (hereafter, "Thelma Pitzel") and her brother, Mr. Pitzel, and "ran away to Dallas, Texas". She is reputed to have been 46-years old at the time.

It is further alleged that Penelope was last employed by the Callier School for the Deaf in Dallas, Texas, and was last known to be living with one Urban Rodgers or Urban Rogers in that same city. According to the allegations of Mr. Pitzel, no member of the Pitzel family has had any contact with Penelope since her disappearance. Mr. Pitzel alleges that his mother, the late Thelma Pitzel, attempted to contact Penelope in June of 1986; however, the letter was subsequently returned. Thelma Pitzel is reputed to have died on January 14, 1990, without having any further correspondence from her daughter, Penelope.

At trial, Mr. Pitzel testified that following his mother's death, the Prudential Insurance Company tried unsuccessfully to contact Penelope or the last person she lived with in Dallas, but the pleadings allege that, "no listing of her name or the name of Urban Rodgers or Urban Rogers remains in Dallas, TX." According to the testimony of Mr. Pitzel, Prudential Insurance Company also attempted to contact Penelope through her last known employment with the county school for the deaf. Mr. Pitzel alleges in his pleadings that the Callier School for the Deaf purportedly has no existing record regarding Penelope's employment at that institution. Mr. Pitzel testified that he personally had not made any other effort to contact his sister.

The record reflects that upon motion of Mr. Pitzel, an attorney ad hoc was appointed by the court on January 26, 1996, to represent Penelope and accept service on her behalf in accordance with LA.CODE CIV. P. art. 5091, et seq. Following a hearing on March 12, 1997, the trial judge took this matter under advisement and thereafter rendered judgment denying Mr. Pitzel's request to have his sister, Penelope, declared dead. Mr. Pitzel now appeals.

Issue

The sole issue raised by Mr. Pitzel in his appeal of this matter is whether LOUISIANA CIVIL CODE art. 54 sets forth a "mandatory statutory presumption" of death based upon proof by an interested party that an absentee has been missing for a period of five (5) years.

Analysis and Law

LOUISIANA CIVIL CODE art. 54 provides as follows:

One who has been an absent person for five years is presumed to be dead. Upon petition by an interested party, the court shall render judgment declaring the death of the absent person and shall determine the date on which the absence commenced and the date of death.

LA. CIV.CODE art. 54 was enacted in 1990, as part of a revision of Title III of Book I of the LOUISIANA CIVIL CODE OF 1870. Former Title III, entitled, "Of Absentees", consisted of articles 47 to 85; however, pursuant to Acts 1990, No. 989, § 1, which became effective on January 1, 1991, this section, was revised, amended and re-enacted under a new heading entitled "Absent Persons", and consists of articles 47 to 59.

In his brief to this court, Mr. Pitzel directs our attention to *Ledet v. State, Department of Health & Human Resources*, 465 So. 2d 98 (La.App. 4th Cir.), *writ denied*, 468 So. 2d 1211 (La.1985), for a discussion of Louisiana law regarding absentees prior to the revisions of 1990. As the fourth circuit observed in *Ledet*, former Civil Code art. 57 provided that the heirs of a person who was not at his usual place of domicile or habitual residence, and who had not been heard of for five years, could be placed into provisional possession of the estate which belonged to said absentee. The court in *Ledet* went on to note that former Civil Code art. 60 authorized provisional possession of an absentee's property prior to the elapse of five years "when it shall be shown that there are strong presumptions that the person absent has perished." *Ledet*, 465 So. 2d at 100 (quoting former LA. CIV.CODE art. 60). Thus, under the prior law, if there existed additional circumstances to suggest that the absentee had perished, then, the case would be governed by former art. 60 rather than by former art. 57. *Id.*

In *Ledet*, the plaintiff-appellant relied upon former Civil Code art. 70 to prove that his mother, an absentee, was presumed to be dead inasmuch as she had abandoned her family and had not been heard from in over twenty-five years. The court in *Ledet* held that the presumption of the mother's death following ten years absence as provided by former art. 70 was applicable in deciding whether the plaintiff's deceased half-brother had "left no ... parent surviving", and further, that the plaintiff was entitled to bring a wrongful death and survivorship action under former Civil Code art. 2315(3).

In the instant case, Mr. Pitzel points out that unlike *Succession of Haydel*, 96-0528 (La.App. 4th Cir.12/27/96), 685 So. 701, *writ denied*, 97-0395 (La.3/2/97), 692 So. 2d 395, the most recent case interpreting the revised civil code articles, the constitutional requirements designed to protect the absentee from deprivation of his property without due process of law have been complied with through the appointment of an attorney ad hoc. In *Haydel*, the fourth circuit annulled an earlier declaration of death on the grounds that in violation of LA.CODE CIV. P. art. 5091, an attorney or curator had not been appointed to represent the absentee whose death had been declared.

Following a review of both the law and the record in this matter, we agree with Mr. Pitzel that LA.CODE CIV. P. art. 5094 requires only that an attorney ad hoc appointed to represent an absentee use "reasonable diligence" to locate and inform him of the pendency of the action against him. The appointed attorney testified that he tried to locate Penelope through the telephone book in Dallas, Texas, the city of her last known residence. The attorney further testified that he also placed a missing person ad in The Dallas Morning News on June 19, 20 and 21, 1996, as well as The Advocate in Baton Rouge on June 23, 24 and 25, 1996. Copies of these ads were introduced as exhibits at trial.

In light of the foregoing, we conclude that the trial judge erred in denying Mr. Pitzel's petition for a declaration of death based upon the showing made. While we concede that the trial judge was correct in his belief that an effort to locate Penelope in cities other than Dallas might have been more successful, and that the assistance of a private investigator would be helpful, it is our belief that such lengths exceed the "reasonable diligence" mandated under LA.CODE CIV. P. art. 5094 and while desirable, are not required. Should Penelope subsequently reappear and wish to assert her rights, the codal scheme provides that she may attempt to recover her property or the net proceeds.

Accordingly, we reverse the judgment of the trial court which dismissed Mr. Pitzel's suit, and hereby declare the absentee, Penelope Elizabeth Pitzel Boyd to be legally dead based upon the showing made by Mr. Pitzel. Inasmuch as LA. CIV.CODE art. 54 requires that we also determine the date her absence commenced as well as the date of her death, we conclude that based upon the record before us, Penelope's absence commenced when she left Baton Rouge, her last known domicile no later than June 1, 1983. We further conclude that her legal death occurred five years thereafter on June 1, 1988.

Inasmuch as there is no other party in this matter, all costs associated with this appeal are assessed against petitioner-appellant, Ralph E. Pitzel.

REVERSED AND RENDERED.

NOTES

Other courts have concluded that sending certified letters to the last known address and to property owned by the absent person to be enough to meet the standard of "reasonable diligence" *See, e.g., Wright v. Waguespack*, 836 So. 2d 436 (La. App. 1 Cir. 2002); *Leidig v. Leidig,* 187 So. 2d 201 (La. App. 3d Cir. 1966).

HYPOTHETICAL

In the summer of 2005, Henry decided to seek out his lifelong dream to become an actor. He sold his house and arranged for his brother to keep his boat while he was away. He moved to L.A. and kept up with his family until 2007, when the correspondence from Henry mysteriously stopped. Henry's mother and his brother hired a private investigator to find Henry, but his investigations proved unsuccessful. Henry has not been heard from again.

a) Assume it is 2010, and Henry's brother has moved to a condominium. He can no longer keep the boat and wants to sell it. Can he? Under what process must he proceed? What, if any, showing must be made?

b) In 2013, Henry's half sister died intestate without descendants and her estate is being distributed to her sisters and brothers. Is Henry entitled to his share of the estate?

c) Assume Henry's mother visits your office today and wants to seek a declaration of death? Can she?

d) Assume that Henry is declared dead and his brother never sold the boat. Henry suddenly reappears. Is he entitled to any property? If so, which property and in what condition?

CHAPTER 5:
COMMENCEMENT OF SUCCESSION
La. C.C. 934-938

Commencement of Succession

Chap 4 Commencement of succession
Civil Code p. 301

La. C.C. 934 as enacted by Act 1421 of 1997, effective July 1, 1999, provides that succession occurs at the death of a person. The LOUISIANA CIVIL CODE of 1870 used the term "open" to describe that instant at which the succession process begins. It is at that exact moment of death that the rights of succession become fixed.

"Death" as used in article 934 includes both physical death and death established by presumption under La. C.C. 54 which deals with the legal declaration of death of an absent person. *See* Comment (a) accompanying La. C.C. 934. Physical "death" is further clarified in La. R.S. 9:111 which provides:

A. A person will be considered dead if in the announced opinion of a physician, duly licensed in the state of Louisiana based on ordinary standards of approved medical practice, the person has experienced an irreversible cessation of spontaneous respiratory and circulatory functions. In the event that artificial means of support preclude a determination that these functions have ceased, a person will be considered dead if in the announced opinion of a physician, duly licensed in the state of Louisiana based upon ordinary standards of approved medical practice, the person has experienced an irreversible total cessation of brain function. Death will have occurred at the time when the relevant functions ceased. In any case when organs are to be used in a transplant, then an additional physician, duly licensed in the state of Louisiana not a member of the transplant team, must make the pronouncement of death.

B. The medical pronouncement of death by a coroner may also be based on personal observation, information, or statements obtained from coroner investigators or emergency medical technicians at the scene who are reporting from firsthand observation of the physical condition of the deceased. The time of death shall be reported as the time that the death was reported or discovered. The name of the personnel that the coroner is relying on shall be noted on the coroner's day record or protocol.

In order to succeed to a decedent, a person must "exist" at the moment of the decedent's death. La. C.C. 939. What result, then, if two people, each of whom would succeed the other, are killed in the same accident, and it cannot be determined who died first? Assume, for example, that two sisters, Mary and Jane are reciprocal intestate heirs and both are killed in an airplane crash in which it is impossible to establish the order of death. Thus, it cannot be ascertained if Mary "existed" at the time of Jane's death, permitting Mary to inherit from Jane, or whether the reverse is true, allowing Jane to inherit from Mary.

One way, used prior to the revision of the Code Act 1421 of 1997, to deal with this problem, was for the law to indulge certain presumptions that determined the order of death of reciprocal intestate heirs who died in a common disaster. Thus, it could be determined which of the reciprocal heirs, termed "commorientes," should inherit. To qualify as a common disaster triggering the effect of the presumptions, the event had to be one such as "a wreck, a battle, or a conflagration." La. C.C. 936 (1870) (repealed). Today, we might include explosions and airline crashes in which there is no possibility of ascertaining the order of death from the circumstances of fact. *See* La. C.C. 937 (1870) (repealed). Guided by probabilities of survival based on age, the presumptions provided that if:

(1) All who died together were under the age of fifteen, the oldest survived.
(2) All who died together were older than sixty, then the youngest survived.
(3) Some who died together were younger than sixty and some were sixty or older, then those under sixty survived.
(4) Some who died together were under fifteen and some were fifteen or older but younger than sixty, then the latter were presumed to have survived.
(5) Some who died together were fifteen or older and younger than sixty, the younger were presumed to survive.

The sometimes inequitable and/or illogical result of indulging these presumptions is illustrated in the following case.

SUCCESSION OF LANGLES
105 La. 39, 29 So. 739, 750 (1901)
(50 Tul. L. Rev. 443 (1976); 41 Tul. L. Rev. 44 (1966))

[Pauline Costa Langles and her daughter, Angèle Marie, executed reciprocal wills prior to their untimely deaths as passengers on the ill-fated *La Bourgongne*, a steamer which sank and resulted in the death of over five-hundred passengers. The mother Pauline was a "robust widow of fifty-two" whose will left all her property to her daughter, and in case of her daughter's prior death, made several personal and charitable legacies leaving the remainder to build a memorial hospital for women and children. The will also provided that two thousand dollars be spent for her tomb. The daughter Angèle, thirty-five, was "slight, frail, and delicate." Angèle's will left all her property to her mother and in case of the mother's prior death, made several personal and charitable legacies, stipulating that the remainder of her estate, after payment the sum of debts should go to the support of the memorial hospital built by her mother. The sum of three thousand dollars was also directed to be apportioned for Angèle's tomb.]

On Application for Rehearing.

MONROE, J.

The city of New Orleans and Mrs. Emile Kuntz have applied for a rehearing, mainly upon the ground that the presumptions of survivorship established by the REVISED CIVIL CODE are inapplicable to testamentary successions, and from this point the arguments of the counsel representing the two opponents mentioned, as also those of counsel representing other parties in interest, diverge in support of different theories as to the law which should govern the case. It is not now contended by any one that the "circumstances of the fact" which are disclosed are such as to justify the court in holding that either of the decedents survived the other, or that they died simultaneously; the counsel who have presented arguments in support of the application for rehearing, although disagreeing as to the disposition which should ultimately be made of the successions, concurring in the opinion that neither decedent has been affirmatively shown to have survived the other, that neither can, therefore, be held to have inherited from the other, and hence that neither succession passes through the other, but that each is transmitted directly to those entitled to it, as though the other succession had never existed. The question, then, is does the law of Louisiana, as applied to the case presented, so read or intend?

* * *

Applying the rules thus prescribed to the case at bar, it would be presumed that Miss Angèle Langles survived her mother, since they were "above the age of fifteen years and under sixty," and she was the younger. But it is said that this rule is inapplicable to testamentary successions, and an earnest effort has been made to sustain this proposition by appeals to reason and authority, and by the argument "ab inconvenienti." Considering this last-mentioned argument first, we find that the learned counsel who represent Mrs. Emile Kuntz have this to say concerning the effect, in this case, of the application of the doctrine of the opinion which has been handed down, to wit: "By the operation of law, in the absence of proof as to the happening of the conditions under which alone the succession of the mother could have passed to the daughter, the estate of Pauline Langles would have been transmitted to the nearest of kin, to whom, by every tie of affection, as well as the policy of the law, it should have passed. By giving effect to the legal presumptions, one-half of the inheritance is conferred upon persons to whom she neither declared nor designed that it should revert. The order of nature, instead of being pursued, is inverted, and the property which she had accumulated passes to persons having claims neither upon her affection nor upon her gratitude. If the present judgment is to stand, no portion of the estate will be transmitted in accordance with the express desire of the testatrix. None of the relatives mentioned in its legacies are to obtain the veriest mite; none of the charitable bequests provided for are to be made efficacious. Her estate is to be transmitted, not to her heirs, not to her legatees, not to her beneficiaries, but to the heirs, beneficiaries, and legatees of her *daughter*. (Italics by the counsel.) Her affection for her kindred is evidenced by the dispositions of *her* testament. . . . She had every reason to believe that, unless her daughter survived, with the exception of the legacies conferred in the will, all the residue of her estate would pass to her heirs at law, should it happen from any cause that the projected memorial hospital for women and children could not be established, pursuant to the directions of her testament." The opponent on whose behalf this argument is presented is a niece of the late Mrs. Pauline Langles. But she is not mentioned in her aunt's will nor in that of her cousin, Miss Angèle Langles. Hence she will get nothing from either succession, unless it is held that Mrs. Langles survived, and inherited from her daughter, or else that neither survived, and that the two successions are to be disposed of independently of each other (in which case she will inherit, by representation, from her aunt's succession), and unless, in any event, the principal bequest in her aunt's will-i.e. the bequest in favor of the memorial hospital for women and children-is set aside and annulled. This opponent alleges, and has undertaken to prove, that her cousin, Angèle Langles, was not likely to have survived her mother, and she prays in her opposition that Mrs. Langles be held to have survived, and thereby to have become the sole heir of, her daughter, and that the legacies in the will of Miss Angèle Langles be held, therefore, to be of no effect; or that it be held that the deaths were simultaneous, and that both wills are inoperative; or, in any event, that the dispositions in favor of the memorial hospital be decreed null, etc. Under these circumstances, and in view of the fact that the opponent's sole object in coming into court is to prevent the declared wishes of her aunt and cousin concerning the disposition of their respective estates from being carried into effect, the solicitude which is expressed in her behalf lest that result should be accomplished otherwise than in accordance with the prayer of her deposition may be readily understood. But although the hardship, if there be any, may fall upon different persons, it will be no greater, and hence the general consequences will be no more disastrous, that the estate of Mrs. Langles does not go to her heirs or to her legatees, etc., but goes to those of her daughter, under the judgment as rendered, than it would be if the estate of the daughter should go, not to her heirs or to her legatees, etc., but to those of her mother, as the opponent would have it. In the latter case it is true that the opponent would participate in the distribution; but it is difficult to perceive what precise principle of law or equity would thereby be subserved, since Mrs. Langles seems to have done her best to exclude the opponent from such participation, and it can hardly be denied that she had that right. The proposition that because she made a will disposing of the whole of her estate to the exclusion of the opponent she thereby intended to show her affection for the latter, and to secure to her a portion of the estate from which she was excluded, involves, as it seems to us, a paradox, the clue to which we have been unable to discover, possibly because of our inability to follow the learned counsel in the attempt to show that we shall be conforming to the wishes of the two testatrices by decreeing, according to the prayer of the opposition, that none of those wishes, as expressed in the testaments before us, shall be carried into effect, but that the opponent, who, by the terms of both testaments, is entirely excluded from both successions, shall nevertheless participate in the distribution of one or both. We pass on, then, to the opponent's appeal to reason and authority.

It is said that our law, like that of France, and unlike the law of Rome, favors the transmission of property, not by testament, but by what is called "natural descent," to the nearest of kin. "Legal succession," say the learned counsel for Mrs. Kuntz, "Is the intent of the law. It favors legal succession; it permits testamentary disposition. In so far as its policy can be indicated by legislative enactment, it endeavors to mark the distinction. While reserving to the individual the right of disposing of his property (and this with the limitations marked by the legitime), it has required that he shall make his dispositions subject to these conditions, and every condition, imposed by law. With respect to legal successions, which it favors, it attempts by every possible means to encourage the order of nature which it designs to perpetuate. . . . Pursuant to this disposition in our law to favor the order of nature, and to so direct, when it replaces the intestate, that a man's posterity, or his ascendants, or his nearest of kin in the collateral line, shall enjoy the fruits of his accumulations,-in its zealous endeavor to secure this end, it has provided means that are denied to those whose claims to a gratuity conferred is founded merely upon the desire of the testator. . . . The law has no desire, except with regard to natural heirs, to see that any property shall go to the persons to whom it may please the fancy of the testator to transmit it. Its object is to protect its own policy as to the doctrine of transmission, to keep the property within the family, to follow the order of nature, and to see that children, and, in the absence of children, ascendants, and, in the absence of both, the nearest collaterals, shall enjoy the inheritance. Therefore, in relation to these two classes of successions, the law has decreed certain evidentiary requirements as to both, but a special presumption as to the one of them. As to the commorientes, he who claims by testament is obliged to establish, affirmatively and by evidence, the survivorship of the person from whom it is pretended that the property was transmitted to the claimant; and if he fail to establish the existence of his author, under the article of the Code which is written under the title of 'Donations and Testaments,' the testamentary disposition is ineffective,-there is caducity. But if his right is derived from the operation of law; if his claim be in harmony with the design of favoring the order of nature; if there has been no will, and his title is of the kind which it is the settled policy of the state to encourage, out of the very necessity which arises that there should be no vacancy, no lapse, no suspension, no moment at which there shall cease to be actual ownership,-a contingency possible solely in the case of successions ab intestato, and only under the very circumstances provided against in article 936, and one which can never occur where there has been a testamentary disposition, there is established a presumption of ownership." When we consider the facilities which are afforded for the making of testaments in this state, and the solicitude which the courts have always exhibited to maintain testaments when made, the idea suggests itself that the learned counsel may perhaps be pressing their argument as to the policy be the law beyond the support upon which it rests. But let us accept it as sound, and apply it to the instant case. Miss Angèle Langles was the daughter of Mrs. Pauline Langles. She and her mother were, respectively, entitled by law to inherit from one another. She was over 15 years of age, and her mother was under 60, and they perished in the same "Wreck, . . . without any possibility of ascertaining which died first." Under these circumstances, there can be no doubt, for the purpose of the question whether the mother should inherit from the daughter, or the daughter from the mother, or whether neither should inherit from the other, that it is the policy of the law that the daughter should have inherited from the mother, since the law provides that, the daughter surviving the mother shall inherit from her, and declares in terms that in the precise case stated, "The younger must be presumed to have survived the elder." And the policy of the law, as thus indicated and declared, has been carried out in the judgment of which the learned counsel complain, and which holds that the daughter survived the mother, and therefore inherited her estate, and that the natural and legal order of succession was thereby established. But the argument to which we have referred holds that by reason of the fact that this mother and daughter, who, by law, were respectively entitled to inherit from one another, made wills, each in favor of the other, and in strict conformity, therefore, to the supposed policy of the law, they thereby took themselves beyond the reach and effect of that policy, and should be denied the presumptions established in favor of those who conform thereto; and the counsel concludes as follows: "The only method by which it is possible, even approximately, to carry out the intention of the two commorientes, is to pursue the usual and accepted practice, and the orderly course of law; to adopt that theory of the law which is consonant with the truth of the fact, and to declare that it is impossible to determine which of the two perishing in a common event survived the other." It seems to us that this conclusion is a complete non sequitur, with respect to all that has been heretofore stated concerning the law, and the policy of the law which it purports to express. If the law favors the transmission of estates to the nearest relative of the deceased, it would be unreasonable to hold that it disapproves of measures taken to secure that result. And when, as we find in this case, it establishes, under particular circumstances, a presumption of survivorship between persons respectively entitled to inherit from one another, no good reason has been suggested why such persons should be held to forfeit the benefit of such presumptions, because by their wills, respectively and reciprocally, they undertake to dispose of their estates in favor of each other, and thus to conform to that policy to subserve the purposes of which the presumption in question is established. If, therefore, it is true that, upon construing the provisions of the Code upon the subject of successions, with those which relate to donations mortis causa, it necessarily results that the presumptions established in order to secure the transmission of property according to the policy of the law are destroyed in all cases where testaments are made transmitting property according to such policy, it must be admitted that such a result is equally illogical and unfortunate, and ought not, therefore, to be accepted if the law to be construed is susceptible of any other interpretation.

It is said, however, that article 936 et seq. of the REVISED CIVIL CODE are found under the title "Legal Successions," the provisions of which are intended to apply exclusively to successions ab intestato, and hence that, by reason of their position, it must be held that these articles are inapplicable to testamentary successions. The proposition is thus stated in the argument of the counsel: "Therefore . . . the provisions embraced under the title 'Legal Successions' are restricted, exclusively, to successions by the operation of the law, unless, by the positive declaration of a given article, its operation is extended to dispositions inter vivos and mortis causa." This observation is applied to articles 936-939, which establish the presumption of survivorship, as we have seen, with respect to certain persons under certain circumstances, and without specific reference to whether they die testate or intestate. Now, the preceding article under the same title (article 935) reads: "The place of the opening of the succession is fixed as follows," etc.; and the article goes on to prescribe where successions shall be opened, also without specific reference to whether they are testamentary or ab intestato. Yet it will hardly be contended that this article is inapplicable to testamentary successions; so that it follows that the proposition of the learned counsel is too broadly stated when applied to the Civil Code of Louisiana, and an examination of the different commentaries upon the Code Napoleon, to which we have been referred, leads to the conclusion that, as stated, it is not sustained by those authorities. It is, no doubt, true that a majority of the French writers are of the opinion that article 720 et seq. of the Code Napoleon, which correspond with article 936 et seq. of our Code, do not apply to cases where the persons who perish together are entitled to inherit from each other only by reason of reciprocal testaments, and not otherwise. And it is also true that, unless the particular case of commorientes who are at once the heirs at law and the instituted heirs of each other is specially mentioned, the opinion referred to is enunciated in such general terms as perhaps, prima facie, to warrant the inference that it relates as well to the case stated as to the case of commorientes who are entitled to inherit from one another by virtue of testaments alone. But where the fact is at all recognized that the commorientes may be the heirs ab intestato as well as the testamentary heirs of each other, so far as we have been able to discover, the further fact is also recognized that such a case constitutes an exception to the rule of the inapplicability of the presumption of survivorship to testamentary successions, and we have been referred to no author, and have found none, who holds, specifically and affirmatively, that the heir at law in whose favor the presumption of survivorship is established is deprived of the benefit of that presumption because the person from whom he is entitled to inherit has chosen to make a will in his favor. Nor does the reason of the law sustain such a conclusion; quite the contrary. Troplong, in dealing with this particular question, says: "Then, the son being at the same time instituted heir and heir ab intestato, the survivorship must be established by the law of legal successions, because the two rights are fused together, and what the law decides in behalf of the heir ab intestato cannot be destroyed by the disposition of man, making him a testamentary heir. Is there anything which can prevent this son from being the legal heir or his father? No, indeed; and certainly the testament made to benefit him cannot impair this imperishable quality. It is therefore clear that he will preserve the benefit of the presumptions which the law has intended to attach to it, and that he will preserve this even if he unites to the right of heir ab intestato the right of testamentary heir, which fortifies it." 3 Troplong, DONATIONS, pp. 635-646.

Applying these observations to the case at bar, Mrs. Langles and her only daughter, an unmarried woman, were not only the legal heirs, but, for a certain portion of their respective estates, were the forced heirs, of each other. To them the law said: "If you perish in the same wreck, without any possibility of ascertaining which died first, that question will be determined by a presumption which is established in the interest of the natural order of succession, and agreeably to which, in your case, it will be held that the daughter survived the mother." No one denies that this was the law before the making of the two wills which have been submitted for our consideration, and before the makers of those wills sailed upon their last voyage, and no one denies that it then applied to those two ladies. But it is said that this law was abrogated and annulled by the making of the wills; and the inquiry is thus suggested, if the law, in unqualified terms, established a presumption, as a result of which, in the event of their perishing in the same wreck, Miss Langles was to have been held to have survived, and to have inherited from, her mother, which presumption the heirs, legatees, and creditors of Miss Langles were authorized to invoke in the contingency provided for, upon what theory of law could Mrs. Langles, by any act of hers, deprive her daughter and her daughter's heirs, legatees, and creditors of the benefit of the presumption thus established by law in their behalf? And upon what theory of reason, assuming that she had the power to accomplish such a result, must she be held to have done so, when it is manifest that she had no intention of interfering with such presumption, but that she was doing the best she could to transmit her estate in accordance with the policy of the law, in support of which the presumption in question was established? If these two ladies had not been entitled by law to inherit one from the other, it might have been said (and that is what we understand the majority, though by no means all, of the French writers to say) that they could not, by conferring such right, each upon the other, by means of their respective testaments, also confer, each upon the other, the benefit of the presumption of survivorship, since that presumption is established by law in favor of persons who are entitled to inherit each from the other, irrespective of their testaments, and is not a benefit or advantage which is to be considered as lying about at large, and which any two persons can confer upon each other, at their option, by making wills in each other's favor. But, being as they were, the question was not whether Mrs. Langles and her daughter, by their joint action, could acquire the benefit of the presumption of survivorship, but whether, being already, and by operation of the law, entitled to the full benefit of that presumption, the one of them could be deprived of it by the other, and, if so, whether she must be held to have been so deprived, not only without any indication that that other intended to deprive her, but in the face of an act affirmatively indicating a contrary intention. And these questions, we think, for the reasons which have been given, should be answered in the negative.

The learned counsel for the city of New Orleans argues that article 936 et seq. of the Code establish a presumption of survivorship only in cases where (as we understand the argument) the fact of survivorship is otherwise established or rendered probable. They say, referring to the articles in question, "They were never to control cases in which the supposition of survivorship is repelled by the known facts or made highly improbable." It is, however, conceded that the commorientes in this case perished in the same wreck, "without any possibility of ascertaining which died first"; and we are unable to say that the supposition of survivorship is repelled by the known facts. On the contrary, the case is within the letter and spirit of the law establishing the presumptions upon that subject. If persons perish in the same event, "such as a wreck, a battle, or a conflagration," it is not to be supposed that either has survived for any great length of time, since such events do not, ordinarily, last for any great length of time. As a fact, Miss Langles may not have survived her mother at all, or she may have survived her during the smallest conceivable subdivision of time. But we have nothing to do with those matters. The fact with which we have to deal are those which the law requires as the basis, not of the fact or the duration of the survivorship, but of the presumption of survivorship, i.e. that the persons who perished were entitled to inherit from each other, that they perished by the same event; and that, being of the same sex, they were over 15 years of age and under 60, respectively. These facts being established, the presumption follows, with the consequence, that the person who is presumed to have survived inherits from the other, exactly as though such survival has been established as a fact. The learned counsel asks the question: "Did the testatrix in each will mean to say, 'I endow a hospital, but if we are killed in a wreck, and I die thirty seconds before you, I withdraw the endowment from the hospital, and give all I possess, not to my heirs, but to your heirs, whether I know them or not,-whether their relations with me have been friendly or otherwise'?" And from this it is argued that, conceding that Angèle Langles survived her mother, and conceding that, by the terms of the will, she inherited her mother's estate, nevertheless, as the survival was not long enough to enable her to use or enjoy the inheritance, it ought to be decided in this case that she never inherited at all. Probably, if it had been proved as a fact that Miss Langles survived her mother, this argument would not have been presented. If she had survived, say, for five minutes, and had devoted that time to the writing of another will, and the will had been here presented, it is reasonably certain that the argument would not have been presented. And yet the results, so far so Mrs. Langles' wishes are concerned, would have been the same. Her endowment of the hospital would have been withdrawn, and her estate would have gone to the heirs of her daughter, and not to her heirs. It is to be regretted, no doubt, that the pious and benevolent intentions of the two ladies whose estates are here in controversy cannot be carried into effect; but the law which regulates the transmission and distribution of estates, whether ab intestato or by means of testamentary dispositions, is a rule of property which concerns the living as well as the dead, and as to the duty of applying which the courts have no discretion. Rehearing refused.

*   *   *

NOTES

The basic objection to the application of the commorientes articles in the testate context of *Langles* is that each party, mother and daughter, had clearly expressed the intention that, if her estate could not go to the other because of the other's prior death, it was the desire of the respective testatrix that the estate could go instead to expressly-designated alternate legatees. Thus both mother and daughter had an alterative plan if the other did not live to enjoy the legacy. Did either intend a "millisecond" of life to be sufficient enjoyment? Surely not. Therefore, did the use of the commorientes presumptions render a "just" result?

The outrage of *Langles* is that the court knew perfectly well what the deceased persons desired as to the disposition of their property. It is one thing not to be able to carry out the ambiguously-expressed wishes of someone because the deceased's true wishes are unclear; it is quite another thing to refuse to carry out clearly expressed desires as in *Langles*.

Is it reasonable to apply the presumptions in a purely intestate situation, where alternative legatees have obviously not been designated? If the law of intestacy is based on the premise that it carries out the presumed intentions of the decedent, is there any reason to indulge the presumptions in that case either? Consider again the situation of the two sisters, Mary and Jane, each dying possessed of separate property. If Mary were married to Tom and Jane were married to John, who do you suppose Mary would want to inherit her separate property if Jane did not survive her? Would Mary want her own husband Tom to inherit? Or would she prefer instead that the law presume that Jane survived for a millisecond, having the effect of depositing Mary's property into Jane's estate and thus, ultimately allowing John, Jane's husband to inherit both Jane's other property as well as that which Jane supposedly inherited for that one millisecond from Mary?

Consider the approach taken by the insurance law as provided in La. R.S 22:645.

Payments of proceeds; simultaneous deaths

Where the individual insured and the beneficiary designated in a life insurance policy or policy insuring against accidental death have died and there is not sufficient evidence that they have died otherwise than simultaneously, the proceeds of the policy shall be distributed as if the insured had survived the beneficiary, unless expressly provided in the policy.

Is this also a reasonable way to distribute intestate property in the case of simultaneous deaths of reciprocal heirs?

Now that the commorientes presumptions have been repealed, the controlling code articles for determination of distribution of property are La. C.C. 939, providing that "a successor must exist at the death of the decedent," and La. C.C. 31, stating that "one claiming a right that has accrued to another person is bound to prove that such person existed at the time when the right accrued." Thus in our hypothetical situation involving Mary and Jane, in order for Jane to inherit from Mary, Jane (or her heirs) would have the burden of proving Jane's existence at the moment Mary died. Absent such proof, Jane would not inherit from Mary, and thus, the next class heir, Tom in this case, would inherit Mary's separate property. Is that not the more logical resolution?

When the commorientes presumptions were viable, the issue often arose as to whether the presumptions would be applicable to tort-related issues. Confusion abounded as cases were inconsistent in answering the question, leading one scholar to conclude:

> It thus appears that in answer to the question whether the presumption of survivorship provisions apply to actions under Article 2315, one can only say the issue is undecided. In one case, the provisions were applied to defeat any recovery; in another, they were applied to permit recovery; and in the third, their applicability was denied, thus permitting one recovery and defeating another.

Johnson, *Death on the Callias Coach: The Mystery of Louisiana Wrongful Death and Survival Actions*, 37 La. L. Rev. 1, 26 (1976).

With the repeal of presumptions, the applicability to tort law apparently becomes moot.

Note that in a testate succession, it is permissible for the testator to provide that, in order for his legatee to receive a legacy, the legatee must survive for a certain period of time, up to six months. Thus, the legatee would perhaps be afforded a more meaningful opportunity to enjoy the property. Such a suspensive condition has been sanctioned by La. C.C. 1521.

Seizin

Seizin may be defined as a constructive right of possession bestowed on a successor which grants that successor the legal personality of the decedent, thus authorizing the successor to institute all actions which the decedent had a right to institute and to continue any actions already begun by the decedent. It is a right that is transmitted to the successor even if the successor is unaware of the death of the decedent.

The Codal concept of seizin has been confused and misunderstood throughout the years. It has been mistakenly equated to the concept of ownership, weakened by the granting of seizin to the succession representative by the CODE OF CIVIL PROCEDURE, qualified by the requirement that no inheritance be delivered until inheritance taxes have been paid, and generally interpreted inconsistently by the courts.

To add to the confusion, the revision provided by Act 1421 of 1997, effective July 1, 1999, does not even mention the term "seizin," yet indicates in the Comments that the concept has been retained but modernized. Comment (b) to La. C.C. 935.

Ownership v. Seizin

Much of the confusion regarding the concept of seizin stems from its equation by many courts with the maxim *le mort saisit le vif*, **the dead seize the living**. Actually the latter is broader in that it expresses what the dead pass to the living, including both rights of ownership and possessory rights of seizin. However, as illustrated in the following cases, one person may be seized of the decedent's property, while another enjoys the ownership.

TULANE UNIVERSITY v. BOARD OF ASSESSORS
115 La. 1025, 40 So. 445 (1905)
[41 La. L. Rev. 270 (1980)]

PROVOSTY, J.

The Tulane University enjoins the revenue officers from proceeding to enforce the collection of state and city taxes assessed against the succession of A. C. Hutchinson, deceased. The ground of the injunction is that plaintiff is the universal legatee of the succession, and as such is owner of the property assessed, and that its property is exempt from taxation under the Constitution.

*   *   *

There were particular legacies of money, and also one of specific property. The plaintiff university was universal legatee. Owing to litigation the settlement of the succession was delayed, and the executors still had possession of the entire estate when the assessment of 1903 was made, and of the entire estate less to particular legacies when the assessment of 1904 was made. The entire estate was assessed to the succession in 1903, and the entire estate less the particular legacies in 1904. For that part of the estate embraced in the legacy of specific property the taxes have been paid; for the remainder of the estate the taxes are enjoined. There is no denial that the property of Tulane University is exempt from taxation under the Constitution.

The case resolves itself into the question of how far, at the time these assessments were made, the property of the succession belonged to Tulane. In so far as it did so belong it was exempt. On the part of defendant it is contended that at the time these assessments were made the entire estate was vested in the succession, and none of it in Tulane; on the part of plaintiff it is contended that all of it was vested in Tulane subject to the charge of the particular legacies, which were nothing more than mere debts of the universal legatee. The lower court correctly held that the part represented by the particular legacies did not belong to the universal legatee, but that the remainder did, and rendered judgment accordingly, maintaining the assessment of 1903 up to the amount of the particular legacies $219,601.88, and annulling it for the remainder, and annulling in toto the assessment of 1904. . . .

Our Code leaves no room whatever for doubt or surmise as to the fact of the property of a deceased person being transmitted directly and immediately to the legal heir, or, in the absence of forced heirs, to the universal legatee, without any intermediate stage when it would be vested in the succession representative, or in the legal abstract called "succession." . . . Therefore the property forming the subject-matter of the universal legacy became at once the property of Tulane, and as such exempt from taxation.

Not so with that part of the estate covered by the particular legacies. It became, in a sense, the property of the particular legatees, "from the day of the testator's death." Civ. Code, art. 1626. It stood in the hands of the executors to be delivered, not to Tulane, but to the particular legatees. Civ. Code, art. 1630. It had to be deducted from the estate before Tulane could take anything under the will. Civ. Code, art. 1634. Indeed, not only did the ownership not pass to Tulane, but even the possession did not. The will did not provide that it should; and the law expressly provided that in case the executors were divested of the seisin by the universal legatee there should be left in their hands "a sum sufficient to pay the movable legacies." Civ. Code, art. 1671. Therefore this fund formed no part of the property of Tulane, and was not exempt from taxation.

The learned counsel for defendants contend that, pending the administration of the succession, the ownership of the property is vested in the succession; and in support of that contention they cite the cases of *City v. Stewart's Estate*, 28 La. Ann. 180; *State v. Brown*, 32 La. Ann. 1020; *Carter v. City*, 33 La. Ann. 816; and *Succession of Levy* (La.) 39 South. 37.

If these decisions went counter to the doctrine expressed by the maxim, "Le mort saisit le vif," whereby the ownership of the property is transmitted directly and immediately from the testator to the heir, or to the universal legatee, as the case may be, they would be in the teeth of the Code, and would simply have to be brushed aside. Far from it, they are to the contrary effect. Thus, in the case cited from 32 La. Ann. 1020 (*State v. Brown*), the court expressly says:

> The maxim, "Le mort saisit le vif," is expressly embodied in our Civil Code, and excludes the interposition of any temporary and qualified ownership, such as that of administrators, between the deceased and his heirs. Civ. Code, art. 940 et seq.

These decisions do not mean to hold, and do not hold, that the abstract being called "succession" is owner of the property in the sense of excluding, or affecting in the slightest degree, the ownership vested in the heir or in the universal legatee. When these decisions speak of the succession being owner, they mean, as a matter of course, that it is holding for the true owner, and merely for the purposes of administration. Nothing that is said in them is intended to detract in the slightest degree from the recognized ownership of the heir, or of the universal legatee, as the case may be, and from the substantial rights (such as that of exemption from taxation) flowing from such ownership. This is very clearly expressed in CROSS ON SUCCESSIONS, § 35, as follows:

> The seisin of the succession representative operates merely to protect his title as detainer of the property for the purpose of his administration; while the seisin of the heir, conflicting in no respect with the other, operates as the sign of his title as owner of the estate, subject to its liquidation under administration. The former has actual control of the estate under the legal conditions prescribed; but it is the heir or universal legatee, as the case may be, who reaps all the proprietary advantages of possession, such as accretion, prescription, perception of fruits, etc. So, Toullier (IV, 582) says: "The seisin of the executor does not interfere with that of the heir of blood, or of the universal legatee, in the case where the latter has seisin. It is always the heir who has the veritable possession; he is alone seised as proprietor. The executor possesses only as depositary in the name of the heir, or universal legatee, who can put an end to the seisin by offering to turn over to the executor a sufficient amount to pay the movable legacies, or by giving security for their payment, and that, even when the testator had charged the executor to sell all his property."

*   *   *

. . . [T]he learned counsel for Tulane University argues that the ownership and the seisin of the entire estate, including the amount required to pay the particular legacies, passed to the universal legatee under the maxim "Le mort saisit le vif"; that the particular legacies were but charges upon this ownership and seisin-mere debts of the universal legatee.

*   *   *

True, under the maxim "Le mort saisit le vif," the universal legatee becomes invested with the legal seisin from the moment of the death of the testator; but the taxability, vel non, of the property does not depend upon the seisin, but upon the ownership-upon the substantial rights of the parties. The seisin may very well be in the universal legatee and the ownership in the particular legatee. Marcadé, in his commentary upon article 724, Code Napoleon, explains this with his usual felicity of exposition:

> The seisin is not always accompanied by the ownership of the property. Thus, where the deceased leaves a legitimate child and also a natural child, the latter, without having the seisin, in other words, the possession, of any part of the property, is nevertheless owner of a part of the succession; so that, although the legitimate heir has the seisin, that is to say, the possession, of the entire succession, he has nevertheless the ownership only of a part. The same thing would happen if this legitimate heir found himself confronted by one or more legatees who took away from him a part of the succession; it would still be the heir who would be seised of the property, which would remain under his administration until the legatees should demand the delivery of the part coming to them. In fact, such a thing might be as that the heir thus having the seisin should be owner of no part of the estate, as where the entire succession was absorbed by particular legacies.

BATEN v. TAYLOR
386 So. 2d 333 (La. 1979)
[57 Tul. L. Rev. 145 (1982); 41 La. L. Rev. 262 (1980);
42 La. L. Rev. 462 (1982); 27 Loy. L. Rev. 259 (1981)]

DENNIS, Justice.

This case presents the question of whether a testator can make a valid will bequeathing his property to his wife, upon the condition that she survive him for thirty days, or, if the condition is not fulfilled, to his nephews.

The testator's sister unsuccessfully attacked the will in the district court and appealed. The court of appeal reversed, holding that the disposition is null because it conflicts with Civil Code Article 1520, which prohibits any disposition constituting a substitution as defined by that article, and Article 1609, which gives the universal legatee seizin of the succession immediately at the testator's death. Accordingly, the intermediate court decreed that the deceased's estate, which was his separate property, must be transferred as an intestate succession, effectively depriving the widow of her husband's property even though she had survived him for thirty days. We reverse, upholding the will, because the double conditional legacy is not a prohibited substitution as defined by the code and does not prevent seizin of the succession immediately at the testator's death.

Decedent, Gordon D. Baten, died testate on February 2, 1974 at his domicile in Beaumont, Texas, leaving separate immovable property situated in Louisiana. He was survived by his widow, Floy Taylor Baten, and his sister, Ruby Mae Baten Taylor. He left no ascendants or descendants.

The testament, valid in form, contains the following dispositive provisions:

2.

I give, devise and bequeath all of my property, real, personal or mixed, wheresoever located to my beloved wife, Floy Baten, should she be living at my death.

3.

In the event my said wife shall have predeceased me, or should my said wife and I die under circumstances that there is not sufficient evidence to determine the order of our deaths or if she shall die within a period of thirty (30) days after the date of my death, then all bequests, devises and provisions made herein to or for her benefit shall be void; and my estate shall be administered and distributed in all respects as though my said wife, Floy Taylor Baten, had predeceased me.

* * *

Mrs. Baten survived her husband for thirty days, fulfilling the condition of survivorship. She instituted ancillary probate proceedings resulting in a judgment of possession on January 19, 1977, which recognized her as the surviving spouse of the decedent and, as legatee under his will, entitled to the ownership of all Louisiana property belonging to him.

On October 14, 1977, the decedent's sister, Ruby Mae Baten Taylor, filed a petition of intervention in the ancillary probate proceedings, seeking to annul the will and to have that portion of the judgment of possession recognizing Mrs. Baten's legacy set aside. Mrs. Taylor alleged that, as the decedent's sole intestate heir, she should be placed in possession of all of his Louisiana property, because the legacy to his widow contained a prohibited substitution and was therefore null.

* * *

The court of appeal, holding that the conditional bequest was prohibited by law, concluded:

At the outset, we find that the first difficulty encountered in the legacy involves our concept of seizin and le mort saisit le vif. By his very terms, the testator attempted to keep title to his property in abeyance for an indefinite period following his death. Under a literal interpretation of the will, no one would get title to the property until either one of the two things occurred: (1) The expiration of thirty days, or (2) (t)he death of the wife. This does not conform to our law on successions.

* * *

Preliminarily, we must decide whether the condition attached to the wife's bequest is suspensive or resolutory. The condition of survivorship for thirty days is suspensive under a common sense interpretation, considering the nature and purpose of the clause. The brief period stipulated and the other provisions of the will indicate the testator's intention was to avoid multiple taxes and a transfer of the succession to his wife's heirs if she died closely following him. Thus, the survivorship clause is very similar to standard suspensive conditions employed for these purposes by practitioners in Louisiana and other states. . . . Although the testator's language is ambiguous, we do not think he intended to create the possibility of a vesting of full ownership in his wife for a period of less than thirty days and a subsequent transfer to his nephews.

The issues presented are: (1) whether a double conditional legacy, whereby the first legatee's bequest is subject to a suspensive condition that he survive the testator for thirty days and the second legatee's bequest is conditioned upon the lapse of the first legacy, is a substitution prohibited by Civil Code Article 1520 and (2) whether a universal legacy dependent upon a suspensive condition is in conflict with the rules of seizin.

* * *

2. Seizin

The Civil Code articles pertaining to seizin do not prevent a testator from making a universal legacy subject to a suspensive condition. Immediately after the death of the deceased person, one of three classes of heirs is seized of the succession under the civil code scheme. Seizin is given first to the forced heirs of the deceased. In default of a forced heir, it is given to the universal legatee. Finally, in the absence of a member of the first two classes, the legitimate heirs are seized of the deceased's property. LA. CIVIL CODE arts. 887, 915, 940, 1607, 1609, and 1613. Consequently, when there are no forced heirs and the universal legatee has been installed under a suspensive condition, as in the present case, the legitimate heirs acquire seizin, under the codal order of priority, and remain provisionally seized of the succession until the condition is fulfilled.

* * *

The Civil Code does not expressly or impliedly prohibit a universal legacy subject to a suspensive condition. The Code permits a testator to impose any conditions he pleases, whether suspensive or resolutory, provided they contain nothing contrary to law or good morals. LA.CIV.CODE arts. 1519, 1527, 1698, and 1699; 3 Aubry & Rau, *supra*, § 715. It makes no exception in the case of a universal legacy subject to a suspensive condition. To infer from the Code such an exception so as to maintain an immutable hierarchy of seizin would attribute to the lawmakers a bizarre sense of values. Under this interpretation of the law, the Courts would be required to thwart the testator's will by declaring a universal legacy under a suspensive condition null whenever there were no forced heirs, rather than allow seizin to pass to the legitimate heirs. We therefore reject the contention that the redactors of the Code intended to create such an arbitrary restriction on the testator's authority. Congruously, nothing we have found in the French jurisprudence or doctrine suggests that the concept of seizin either restricts or conflicts with the testator's authority to make conditional legacies of all kinds. . . .

Furthermore, since the enactment of the CODE OF CIVIL PROCEDURE in 1961, the question of whether an heir has seizin is of less practical consequence. Article 3211 of the CODE OF CIVIL PROCEDURE provides that the succession representative is deemed to have possession of all property of the succession and shall enforce all obligations in its favor. LA.CODE CIV.P. art. 3211; Cf. LA.CODE CIV.P. art. 685. According to the redactors, this provision is a deliberate departure from the former law relating to seizin and, as a practical matter, gives the succession representative full seizin of all the property of the deceased. LA.CODE CIV.P. art. 3211, Official Revision Comment (a). *See generally*, Nathan, *supra*, at 51; Comment, 49 Tul.L.Rev. 1110, 1122 (1975). Consequently, seizin is not suspended by the enforcement of the testator's disposition of his property.

The court of appeal saw the concept of seizin as an obstacle to the enforcement of the will because it mistakenly equated seizin with ownership. Seizin is not ownership, however, but the legal investiture of one class of heirs with possession of the succession upon the death of the deceased, enabling the heirs who acquire seizin, from the instant of death, to bring all the actions which the deceased could have brought. Lazarus, *The Work of the Louisiana Appellate Courts for the 1971-72 Term*, 33 La.L.Rev. 199, 201-02 (1973); 3 Marcade, *Explication Du Code Civil no. 47*, at 33 (7th ed. 1873) as cited in Lazarus, *supra*, at 202 n. 12. Ownership, on the other hand, is transmitted by operation of law at the moment of death to heirs and legatees designated by the Code, regardless of whether they have seizin of a particular succession or whether they can ever have seizin.[1] For example, although a legatee under a particular title cannot acquire seizin, he has ownership of the thing bequeathed to him from the day of the testator's death. LA.CIV.CODE art. 1626. In order to be eligible for seizin, an heir must be either a forced heir, universal legatee or legitimate heir; and the latter two classes acquire seizin only in default of those preferred to them. Whether an heir acquires seizin depends, therefore, not on his ownership of succession property, but on whether he is a member of the class of heirs entitled to seizin of a particular succession according to the codal order of priority.

The redactors of the Code of 1825 made the distinction between ownership and seizin clear when they adopted the French system of succession, which embodies two different concepts: (1) Ownership rights of the heir are vested from the moment of the death, and (2) seizin, the faculty of claiming and exercising possession, is acquired by either the forced heirs, the universal legatee or the legitimate heirs at the moment of death. Lazarus, *supra*, at 201;

---

[1] *See* Lazarus, *supra*, at 202 where he states:

> Although not as clearly formulated as they might have been, the pertinent articles of the LOUISIANA CIVIL CODE do in effect make this distinction between the actual transmission of the inheritance to the heir, and the possession thereof which is rightfully deemed to be in the legitimate heir, although not actually so. Thus, article 940 speaks of the acquisition of the inheritance by the heir immediately upon the death of the deceased, whereas articles 942 and 943 speak of the possession thereof which is continued in the person of the heir "with all its defects as well as all its advantages, the change of proprietor producing no alteration in the nature of the possession." (footnotes omitted).

See also La. Civ. Code arts 870, 871, 1626 and cf. art. 949.

Comment, 49 Tul.L.Rev. 1110, 1111 (1975); 1 Louisiana Legal Archives, Projet of the Civil Code of 1825 at 115. In other words, as Planiol observes:

> Seizin has nothing to do with the transfer of property, which takes place immediately, whether it is in favor of heirs who have seizin, or who are deprived of it. It affects only the taking of possession of the estate, which takes place in two forms, one for the property in kind, the other for the rights of action. 3 Planiol, *supra* § 1938, pp. 604-05.

Accordingly, we conclude that there is no conflict between a suspensively conditional universal legacy and the civil code's seizin provisions. In the present case, the universal legatee *(wife)* having been installed under a suspensive condition, the legitimate heirs acquired seizin at the *sister* moment of death under the civil code scheme and remained provisionally seized until the legacy's suspensive condition was fulfilled. Furthermore, the succession representative is given full seizin of the deceased's property, as a practical matter, by Article 3211 of the CODE OF CIVIL PROCEDURE. The survivorship clause in the present will, therefore, does not suspend seizin of the succession, but is a valid disposition of ownership subject to suspensive conditions.

*   *   *

Dorothy Singer Jacobs, *Comment, A Reasoned Seizin and Prohibited Substitutions*
56 Tul. L. Rev., 350-369 (1981)
(Footnotes omitted.)

Recently, a long overdue decision interpreting fundamental inheritance rights brought Louisiana citizens economic advantages enjoyed by citizens in other states. Survivorship provisions, valid and enforceable in common law jurisdictions, had consistently been found invalid in Louisiana. Louisiana has steadfastly maintained the civilian tradition regarding the transmission of property at death. This means that Louisianians have not had the same freedom to determine the subsequent ownership of their property after death as have other American citizens. These civilian principles evolved at a time when wealth was determined by ownership of land; and these principles were a means by which wealthy families protected their holdings. Now, the increasing importance of securities and movable wealth has diminished the significance of landed estates. It therefore becomes appropriate to examine the relevance of property concepts developed for an agrarian society in light of the needs of a highly technological one.

In *Baten v. Taylor*, decided by the Louisiana Supreme Court in October, 1979, the court for the first time upheld a survivorship clause, an event of extreme importance in the evolution of Louisiana law. In the process, the court clarified two ancient doctrines of the civil law, seizin and prohibited substitutions. The focus of this comment will be to appraise the history and rationale of both doctrines, and to explore the course civil law in Louisiana may follow in the wake of this landmark decision.

*   *   *

Seizin

Seizin is a word that has been given many definitions and which is conceptually so amorphous that "no other expression in French law . . . is more often used and less understood." Scholars disagree as to the origin of this ancient institution, finding both Germanic and Romanic influence on it.

Both the common and the civil law developed concepts of seizin in order to insure that the title to property would at all times be vested in an identifiable owner, that the right to possession would be continuous, and that the person who had this right would be readily ascertainable. Seizin in common law connoted not just actual possession but, because it developed out of feudal investiture of title by actual possession, it also implied seignorial acceptance. The feudal system required the fulfillment of duties and obligations to the over-lord by one who had possession or seizin of the land. If the one who had possession died and no one succeeded him, there was no one to fulfill these duties, hence seizin or "vesting of the estate" was developed at common law and used as a method to prevent a gap in possession. The definition of seizin evolved to mean possession under legal title or some right to hold, and in modern common law statutes, the word "seizin" is usually treated as synonymous with ownership.

Similarly, in civil law, seizin performs the function of preventing a gap in possession. However, civil law never reached the conclusion that seizin is synonymous with ownership. There have been misinterpretations of the civil law concept of seizin because of the influence on Louisiana law of the common law and its definition of seizin. While the doctrines of seizin in both common and civil law are rooted in the same past, great differences grew in the theoretical application of the concept.

Civil law expresses the doctrine by the term *le mort saisit le vif* (the dead gives seizin to the living) and Civil Code article 940 incorporates it into the LOUISIANA CIVIL CODE. In essence, through seizin the legal personality of the deceased descends immediately and instantaneously upon the heirs without any act on their part. This has a double effect. The first is that an heir with seizin can take possession of the decedent's estate without any formalities. The second effect is that the seized heir may bring any action which the decedent had a right to bring, or defend any action which third persons had against the decedent. This capacity both to bring and defend actions is noteworthy with regard to possessory actions because the heir might not ever have been in possession of the property in dispute. The double effect of seizin is expressed in the saying "the seized heirs have a possession by law, [a constructive possession] and . . . it is left to them to add to it a possession in fact." That there is a distinction between the right of possession and possession in fact is clearly stated in article 942, which provides: "The heir being considered seized of the succession from the moment of its being opened, the right of possession, which the deceased had, continues in the person of the heir, as if there had been no interruption, and *independent of the fact of possession*." Seizin, therefore, is not the acquisition of ownership; it is the legal investiture of possession. Louisiana courts, however, have confused ownership and seizin. The ownership of property inherited by the deceased's heirs or legatees is transmitted by law to all successors with or without seizin. The law provides that natural children and the surviving spouse of the deceased do not have seizin, nor do particular legatees. However, they have a right of action to be put in possession of the succession, and this right can be transmitted to their heirs. They do not have a right of possession without any action on their part, but they do have a right of action to seek possession. On the other hand, legal and testamentary heirs or universal legatees do acquire seizin and succeed to all rights the deceased had which can be transmitted.

The maxim *le mort saisit le vif* was not operative under the Code of 1808. With respect to successions, Louisiana law was formerly based on Spanish law which was profoundly affected by Roman rule. At Roman law, a succession was regarded as a fictitious entity representing the deceased until the succession could be delivered to the heir. The heir had to request and judicially be put into possession of the inheritance.

The Code of 1825 suppressed the Roman-Spanish rule and substituted the French system in which the legatee is the owner at the moment of decedent's death and the legitimate heir is "seized" from the moment of decedent's death. The redactors observed that they thought it best to have a rule which dispensed with the necessity of the heirs having to apply to the court to be put into possession. They found this to be in accord with other property dispositions prescribed by the Code.

Under this codal principle of seizin, the heir represents the succession from the moment of its opening, and as such, he may sue and be sued in its behalf. In *Tulane University v. Board of Assessors*, the court recognized the distinction between ownership and the right to possession. Here, the deceased left a will which made Tulane University the universal legatee but also bequeathed particular legacies. Counsel for the University argued that the entire estate should be exempt from taxation because under article 940, and according to the maxim *le mort saisit le vif*, the universal legatee, Tulane University, became invested with legal seizin (i.e., the right of possession) from the moment of the death of the testator. Revenue officers wanted to enforce the collection of state and city taxes against the entire succession of the deceased. The issue was to determine at what point the ownership of the property was acquired by Tulane University, a tax exempt organization. The court held that taxability does not depend upon seizin, but rather upon ownership. Seizin may well be in the universal legatee and ownership in the particular legatee. Therefore, Tulane's tax exemption would not apply to the particular bequests and while the property acquired by Tulane from the deceased was exempt from the tax, the particular bequests were taxable. The court cited the noted French commentator Marcade as authority.

The seisin is not always accompanied by the ownership of the property. Thus, where the deceased leaves a legitimate child and also a natural child, the latter, without having the seisin, in other words, the possession, of any part of the property, is nevertheless owner of a part of the succession; so that, although the legitimate heir has the seisin, that is to say, the possession, of the entire succession, he has nevertheless the ownership only of a part.

Serious doubts have been raised regarding the continuing vitality of the doctrine of the right of possession, otherwise referred to as constructive possession, because of significant exceptions to *le mort saisit le vif*. Over the years, statutes have eroded the application of seizin, one being the inheritance tax statute which was first enacted in 1906. Today the inheritance tax law clearly limits the right of an heir to possess and still maintain his right of renunciation of the succession. If he exercises any rights of possession before he has obtained the authority of the court, he becomes personally liable for any inheritance tax due. Contrary to this, but of equal importance, article 942 establishes that seizin does include the right of possession. The supreme court has reconciled the conflict between the inheritance tax statute and article 942 through its interpretation of the tax law, finding that a violation of the inheritance tax statute would not invalidate a transfer of property made by the heir, but only make him personally liable for the payment of the taxes. The tax is interpreted to be on the transmission of the property by inheritance and not a tax on the property itself. In this way the court mitigated the barrier to the right of possession created by the inheritance tax statute. Even so, the concept of the heir having all the rights in the property which the decedent had has been modified by the tax law and the principle of seizin thereby eroded.

Articles 3211 and 685 of the CODE OF CIVIL PROCEDURE have also eroded the doctrine of seizin. Article 3211 states: "A succession representative shall be deemed to have possession of all property of the succession and shall enforce all obligations in its favor." Article 685 provides that a succession representative appointed by the court has the right of actions of the deceased while the succession is under the administration of the appointee. The official comments to article 3211 state explicitly that this is a departure from the law relating to seizin. Because the succession representative now has full seizin of all property of the deceased, the utility of the concept of seizin in Louisiana law has been questioned by legal scholars.

Noted commentators have disagreed as to seizin's continuing viability. Oppenheim claims that the doctrine still has a function, but Lazarus says article 3211 abolished seizin and placed the regular heir in the same position as the irregular heir who never had any seizin. The latter maintains that the regular heir acquires ownership of his hereditary share by operation of law, but he may not have constructive possession of the succession. Oppenheim does not share this view and states in a footnote in Volume 10 of his Louisiana Civil Law Treatise that the comment to article 3211 concerning seizin is "too strong a statement."

While these code articles could be read as abrogating seizin and bringing Louisiana closer to the common law concept of the succession as a fictitious entity, seizin still has effects. One such effect is the transmission of the succession by the heir to his heirs whether or not the former has accepted. Article 944 of the LOUISIANA CIVIL CODE provides:

> The heir being considered as having succeeded to the deceased from the instant of his death, the first effect of this right is that the heir transmits the succession to his own heirs, with the right of accepting or renouncing, although he himself have not accepted it, and even in case he was ignorant that the succession was opened in his favor.

Another area affected is in property law where the concept of seizin is the basis for the tacking of adverse possession of ancestor to heir or testator to universal legatee in order to meet the requirements of acquisitive prescription.

Additionally, there are non-statutory exceptions to the doctrine of *le mort saisit le vif*. These stem from the Civil Code and relate to the suspension of seizin until a condition has been achieved. Suspensive conditions are allowed by the Code as long as they are not contrary to law or good morals. Recognition of the legality of holding seizin in abeyance until the fulfillment of a condition is apparent in article 985 which provides: "The heir who is instituted under a condition can not accept nor renounce the succession, before the condition has happened, or while he remains in ignorance of the condition having happened." Articles 954 through 963 provide that a child born alive has a right to inherit if he can prove he had been conceived at the time of his father's death, that is, "at the moment of the opening of the succession." Therefore, if a man dies during his wife's pregnancy, until it is determined whether the child will be born alive, seizin will be in suspense. Seizin may also be suspended until the heir has accepted or renounced the succession according to article 946. If the heir accepts the succession, he is considered as receiving it, not at the time of acceptance but retroactively at the death of the deceased. If the succession is renounced, the heirs of the next nearest degree to the deceased "are considered as having succeeded directly and immediately to the rights and effects of the succession from the moment of death of the deceased."

This recognition of the legality of the suspension of seizin allowed the court in *Baten v. Taylor* to determine that there is no conflict between a suspensively conditional universal legacy and the Civil Code's seizin provisions. For the first time in Louisiana, judicial sanction has been accorded to survivorship clauses in a will, giving testators greater freedom in tax and estate planning. However, the court based its finding that the condition was suspensive on the fact that the survivorship period was brief, only thirty days. This leaves open the question of how long a survival stipulation may be before it will be considered invalid. The court does not identify what duration of time will be considered a charge to preserve and perhaps thereby result in the finding of a prohibited substitution. Nevertheless, a large step has been taken to provide the estate planning flexibility long sought by Louisiana practitioners for the benefit of their clients.

*   *   *

NOTES

Who had seizin in the *Tulane* case? In *Baten*? What was the significance of having seizin in each case?

Note that at the time of the *Baten* decision, there was no provision in the Civil Code sanctioning a waiting period which could suspend the period of ownership of a legatee. Obviously, a short period would meet the decedent's objective of ensuring that his property would be enjoyed by the intended legatee, or absent that, by an alternative legatee of the decedent's choice. But how long should that period be before it is too long and compromises the public policy of keeping property in commerce? In 1981, an act was presented to the Louisiana legislature which permitted a thirty-day waiting period. This would have validated the *Baten* case, and yet at the same time, legislatively limited the period to this short time span. The Louisiana legislature initially failed to enact the provision into law. Did this have any effect on *Baten*? What were the reasons for the legislative rejection? Was the negative vote against the waiting period or against so short a period? In 1984, the legislature reconsidered the matter and enacted the thirty-day period into law. (La. C.C. 1521, as amended by 1984 La. Acts, No. 957) In 1987, the period was extended to ninety day (La. C.C. 1521, as amended by 1987 La. Acts No. 680) and extended again to six months. (La. C.C. 1521, as amended by 2001 La. Acts No. 825.) What result if the testator provides for a waiting period of nine months?

Succession Representative v. Successor

SUCCESSION OF DEAL
129 So. 3d 686 (La. App. 3d Cir. 2013)

KEATY, Judge.

Carolyn D. Deal (Carolyn) appeals from a judgment of eviction. For the following reasons, we reverse.

Carolyn is a surviving half-sibling of Sandra Jean Deal (Sandra or the Decedent), who died intestate on February 13, 2011. The Decedent was also survived by her parents, Clarence Davis and Anna Belle Deal (Anna); however, she was never married, and she had no descendants.

On April 7, 2011, Anna was confirmed as administratrix of the Succession of Sandra Jean Deal (the Succession). In that capacity, Anna filed a detailed descriptive list in September of 2011. Among the assets listed was the immovable property located at 2104 Cherry Palm Circle in New Iberia, Louisiana (the home), upon which sat the home where Sandra resided at the time of her death. Anna also filed a petition for authority to execute a real estate listing agreement for the home wherein she alleged that it was necessary to sell the home in order to pay the debts and expenses of the Succession....

On April 4, 2012, Anna, in her capacity as Succession administratrix, filed a rule to evict Carolyn from the home. She alleged therein that Carolyn had refused to vacate and surrender the premises despite having been provided with a letter dated September 15, 2011, terminating her continued occupancy of the home and ordering her to surrender its possession by September 30, 2011. The letter also indicated that her failure to vacate would result in the filing of an eviction proceeding against her. Anna also alleged that the Succession lacked sufficient funds necessitating sale of the home. The rule for eviction was set for April 16, 2012. . . .the trial court granted the rule for eviction in open court. . .

Carolyn ... asserts that the trial court erred in finding that the Succession was the owner of the home and that the administratrix had authority to evict her. . .

DISCUSSION

[Louisiana Code of Civil Procedure Article] 3191 ... provides, in part, that a succession representative is "a fiduciary with respect *to the succession* " and "shall have the duty of collecting, preserving, and managing the property of the succession in accordance with law." (Emphasis added.) Further, the succession representative "shall act at all times as a prudent administrator, and shall be personally responsible for all damages resulting from his failure so to act." LSA–C.C.P. art. 3191. Since "the succession" is "the *transmission of the estate* of the deceased to his successors," as defined in LSA–C.C. art. 871, then, logically, it follows that part of the succession representative's fiduciary duty is to transmit property contained in the deceased's estate to his heirs. (Emphasis added.)

Matthews v. Horrell, 06–1973, p. 18 (La.App. 1 Cir. 11/7/07), 977 So. 2d 62, 75 (footnote omitted).

In *Coon v. Miller,* 175 So. 2d 385 (La.App. 2 Cir.1965), the second circuit set aside and reversed a judgment ordering the defendant, surviving spouse of the decedent, to vacate the family home in which she had been living prior to decedent's death, in conjunction with an action for eviction filed by the administrator of the decedent's succession. Prior to filing the eviction, the administrator obtained a default judgment against the defendant in the amount of $1,920 for rent of the home accruing since the decedent's death. After noting that defendant, "as surviving widow in community with the deceased," was the owner of an undivided one-half interest in the home, the court concluded that "a co-owner cannot be divested of possession by an action of eviction." *Id.* at 386–87. The court reiterated that "the rights of co-owners to possession of property [are] equal and coextensive," and that "[a] co-owner deprived of the possession and benefit of property has a remedy by a suit for partition." *Id.* (citing *Juneau v. Laborde,* 228 La.

410, 82 So. 2d 693 (1955); *Moreira v. Schwan,* 113 La. 643, 37 So. 542 (1904); and *Arcemont v. Arcemont,* 162 So. 2d 813 (La.App. 4 Cir.1964)). Upon the administrator's application for certiorari or writ of review in *Coon,* the supreme court refused the writ, stating: "On the facts found by the Court of Appeal the result is correct." *Coon v. Miller,* 247 La. 1089, 176 So. 2d 145 (1965).

More recently, in *Matthews,* the provisional administratrix of the succession of Edward Horrell, Sr. (the succession) filed a rule to evict against Walter Horrell and his wife, Edna, (collectively referred to as Walter) alleging that they were occupying a house in Covington, Louisiana (the property) that was owned by the succession. Walter was one of five of Edward Horrell's (the decedent's) adult children. According to a detailed descriptive list filed shortly after decedent's death, he died owning certain separate immovable properties, including the property located in Covington. Walter, who happens to be an attorney, responded to the rule to evict by filing exceptions and an answer, wherein he denied that he was an occupant of the property, instead asserting that he was a legal possessor with an ownership interest in the property. He asserted that because he had a real right in the property "that could only be resolved through an ordinary proceeding and not a summary ... proceeding such as the action for eviction." *Id.* at 71.

Walter also contended that the rule for eviction was premature. Following a hearing, the trial court granted the rule and signed a judgment of eviction. According to the oral reasons for judgment, the trial court determined that good cause to evict Walter existed because of his failure to cooperate in the appraisal of the property and the movable property thereon, coupled with the "extremely protractive nature" of the litigation. *Id.*

Walter appealed, and the first circuit reversed, holding that because the provisional administratrix failed to prove that the purpose of Walter's occupancy of the property as an owner thereof had ceased, he was not subject to being evicted. In so doing, the court found that the provisional administratrix was mistaken in her claim that the succession owned the property. *Matthews,* 977 So. 2d 62. To the contrary, the court reasoned that, despite "the succession representative's fiduciary duty is to transmit property contained in the deceased's estate to his heirs," the succession representative in that case "seeks to do the opposite; i.e., to divest succession property from the decedent's heir who has a one-fifth ownership interest therein." *Id.* at 75. Relying on *Coon,* the court affirmed the notion that "a co-owner cannot be divested of possession by an action of eviction." *Id.* at 76 (quoting *Coon,* 175 So. 2d at 387). Finally, the *Matthews* court concluded that the Louisiana Code of Civil Procedure dictated that "questions regarding the ownership of immovable property or the right to possession of immovable property were not intended by the legislature to be litigated in eviction proceedings." *Matthews,* 977 So. 2d at 77. As a result, the first circuit reversed the judgment ordering Walter's eviction and remanded the matter to the trial court with instructions that the suit be dismissed.

In the instant case, the administratrix concedes that Carolyn is a naked owner of the home. Because Carolyn possesses the home as an owner, we conclude that the trial court erred in granting the administratrix's motion to evict her in a summary proceeding because she has a real right in the property that must be challenged via an ordinary proceeding. Accordingly, the judgment of eviction is reversed, and we need not address Carolyn's claim that the eviction was rendered prematurely.

For the forgoing reasons, the judgment of the trial court ordering that Carolyn Deal be evicted from the immovable property located at 2104 Cherry Palm Circle in New Iberia,

Louisiana is reversed. All costs of this proceeding are assessed against the Succession administratrix personally. *See* La.Code Civ.P. art. 3191.

REVERSED.

AMY, J., dissents and assigns reasons.
AMY, J., dissenting.

I respectfully disagree that a reversal is required in this case. Rather, I find the jurisprudence on this point fact specific and dependent upon circumstances not present here. In my opinion, this matter must be resolved by application of La.Civ.Code art. 938(B), which states that: "If a successor exercises his rights of ownership after the qualification of a succession representative, the effect of that exercise is subordinate to the administration of the estate." The record indicates that the administratrix in this case demonstrated to the trial court's satisfaction that the liabilities of the succession exceeded its assets. Thus, it seems to me that a motion for eviction, within the confines of the succession, was within the administratrix's authority.

NOTE

Do you agree with the majority in *Deal* or the dissent? Why?

Judge Amy references La. C.C. article 938, which permits a successor to exercise ownership rights prior the qualification of a succession representative, but once the succession representative has qualified, those rights are subordinate to the administration of the estate. In other words, a person may acquire an interest in a succession from a successor, but the interest acquired only comprises what the successor would eventually acquire, which could be affected by the rights of a creditor. The successor does not warrant title, but only his rights as an heir. La. C.C. 938, comment (a).

The Modernizing of Seizin

The LOUISIANA CIVIL CODE, as revised by act 1421 of 1997, effective July 1, 1999, makes no specific mention of "seizin" although the concept is referenced in the title to La. C.C. 935 and is also discussed in the accompanying revision comment. La. C.C. 935 provides that at the moment of the decedent's death, the universal successors acquire the ownership of the estate and the particular successors acquire ownership of the things that were bequeathed to them. Thus, part of the concept of *le mort saisit le vif* is contained in this article as it recognizes ownership interests of the successors. The second paragraph, in dealing with the exercising of the rights of the decedent, is more directly relating to the concepts of seizin, or the right to legal possession. That paragraph states that before the qualification of a succession representative, only a universal successor has the right to exercise the rights of the decedent. Thus, although all successors, including particular successors may **own** the decedent's property, it is only the universal successor who is **seized** of that property. It is he who thus has the rights associated with being a seized heir, those rights to represent the decedent. However, those rights cease at the moment a succession representative is qualified pursuant to the provisions of La. C.C.P. 3211.

The revision also provides for a continuation of possession in La. C.C. 935, recognizing that the decedent's possession is transferred to all his successors, testate or intestate, and likewise, particular, general, or universal. The possession that the universal successor attains is the same as the decedents, whereas the particular successor is afforded the opportunity, at his option, of commencing a new possession for purpose of acquisitive prescription.

While the concept of seizin has been modernized, two important aspects have remained: (1) exercising the rights of the decedent until a succession representative is appointed, and (2) continuing the possession of the decedent. The following article explains both.

Dian Tooley Arruebarrena, PROPERTY CHANGES IN THE PROPOSED SUCCESSIONS REVISION
57 La. L. Rev. 149 (1996)

[Reprinted and edited with permission; footnotes omitted;
bracketed information inserted by casebook author]

*　　*　　*

I. Seizin

Seizin, a term used in both the common and the civil law, has had a fairly long history in each system. Although the meaning and importance of the concept has changed significantly over time in each system, this paper will focus only upon its place in Louisiana today, ...

What Exactly Is Seizin?

Under the current successions articles, designated classes of successors are automatically invested with seizin immediately at the moment of the predecessor's death. Exactly what these seized heirs are automatically vested with has been the subject of both dispute and misunderstanding. According to Planiol, even the celebrated French jurist Pothier was confused about seizin. In Louisiana, one vocal critic of seizin called it a concept whose "chief justification . . . is its pedagogical value in exercising the minds of law students in metaphysical gymnastics." Scholars cannot even seem to agree on how to spell the word.

The meaning of the word "seizin" can be determined by examining two sources-- one historical and the other jurisprudential. The historical source is the fundamental change effected by the 1825 Civil Code. Prior to this Code, a juridical person (i.e., the succession) came into existence at the death of a natural person, and continued to exist until all of the debts of the decedent had been paid and the remaining property distributed to his successors. Under the pre-1825 regime, the decedent's patrimony was transmitted at his death to "the succession," and then subsequently transmitted to his successors. [FN 9: The Digest of 1808 provided: Until the acceptance or renunciation, the inheritance is considered as a fictitious being, representing in every respect, the deceased who was the owner of the estate. La. Digest of 1808, Book III, title 1, ch. 6, S 1, art. 74.]

*　　*　　*

Under [the post-1825] regime, the decedent's patrimony is transmitted to his seized heirs immediately at his death without the interposition of a juridical person. Being seized of the decedent's patrimony, the seized heirs stand in his shoes. Article 945 explains: The second effect of (seizin) is to authorize the heir to institute all the actions, even possessory ones, which the deceased had a right to institute, and to prosecute those already commenced. For the heir, in every thing, represents the deceased, and is of full right in his place as well for his rights as his obligations. [Article 945 was eliminated in the 1997 revision, even though it's theory was maintained, see La. C.C. 935, comment b.]

The second source providing insight into the meaning of the concept of seizin is the Louisiana Supreme Court decision in Baten v. Taylor. The testator in that case had written a will instituting his wife as universal legatee upon the condition that she survive him for thirty days. His sister attacked the will alleging inter alia that the condition prevented the universal legatee from receiving seizin immediately at the testator's death. Justice Dennis, in a characteristically scholarly opinion, found that the survivorship clause created no gap in seizin.

The court first classified the survivorship clause as a suspensive condition, which, while permissible, did prevent the wife as universal legatee from acquiring seizin at her husband's death. Nonetheless, until fulfillment of the condition, the testator's legitimate heir (his sister) was invested with seizin. The court then explained how the testator's sister could be seized of her brother's succession yet ultimately receive no ownership of his property:

> Seizin is not ownership, however, but the legal investiture of one class of heirs with possession of the succession upon the death of the deceased, enabling the heirs who acquire seizin, from the instant of death, to bring all the actions which the deceased could have brought. . . . Whether an heir acquires seizin depends, therefore, not on his ownership of succession property, but on whether he is a member of the class of heirs entitled to seizin of a particular succession according to the codal order of priority.

It is clear from these two sources that the transmission of a decedent's patrimony occurs immediately at his death in favor of his seized heirs who then stand in his place. However, since seizin is not ownership, the seized heirs are the mere custodians of the decedent's patrimony. [FN 12: In this sense the seized heirs can be compared to the trustee of a trust, who is invested with ownership of the trust property for the benefit of the beneficiaries. See Reynolds v. Reynolds, 388 So. 2d 1135 (La. 1981).] Ownership devolves in accordance with the decedent's will or the laws of intestacy subject of course to the superior rights of the decedent's creditors.

What Is Seizin's Present Significance in Louisiana Successions Law?

Perhaps the most important significance of seizin is its role in providing logic and consistency in the law of successions. The Civil Code's property rules are very explicit: only persons can own property. Persons can be either natural or juridical. When the decedent dies, he loses his status as a person. Of course, since *le mort seizit le vif,* the successor's ownership is retroactive to the instant of the decedent's death. Nonetheless, the successor may never get ownership since his rights are subject to the claims of the decedent's creditors. Furthermore, the successor has the option to renounce the succession, and has thirty years within which to choose. Moreover, the testator himself may impose suspensive conditions upon the legacy.

In the case of the legacy subject to a suspensive condition, the legatee's ownership is clearly retroactive to the instant of death once the condition has been satisfied. But until that occurs, what is the status of the property? Since the decedent can no longer own any property, the doctrine of seizin provides the theoretical bridge to explain the status of the decedent's patrimony until the successor's rights have been determined.

The second role served by seizin is more practical. Until the successor's rights have been determined, someone needs to act as the decedent's representative, both for the purpose of asserting claims that the decedent may have against others, as well as for the purpose of defending claims asserted by the decedent's creditors.

*   *   *

Assuming That Seizin Has Been Eliminated by the Revision, What Are the Ramifications of Its Suppression?

Until the successor's rights have been determined, the decedent's patrimony must vest in a person, either natural or juridical. It is true of course that in many cases there will be an administration and that the succession representative will administer the decedent's estate. However, suppose the case where there are no debts, yet none of the successors has either accepted or renounced the succession. Who has the legal authority to assert rights on behalf of the decedent? Unless the decedent's legal personality is carried on by someone, confusion results.

It does not help to say that the ownership of the successors is retroactive. Although the situation is clear once the successor's rights have been determined, there needs to be someone designated as the custodian of the decedent's patrimony until that occurs. Without seizin, there is a void, both theoretically and practically.

Of course, there is the real possibility that the concept of seizin will subsist even if the revision does eliminate all references to it. We certainly have experienced the phenomenon of a term being suppressed yet continuing to exist in the jurisprudence. And, who can forget Article 3467, which states in its text that legislation alone can establish causes of suspension, yet suggests (correctly) in comment (d) that the jurisprudentially created doctrine of *contra non valentem* "continues to be relevant." If seizin is eliminated as a concept expressly acknowledged in the Code, then this writer predicts that it will continue to live on, not just in the ivory tower of legal academia where abusively logical law professors reside, but in the halls of justice, to be reflected in the jurisprudence.

II. The Transfer and Tacking of Possession

*   *   *

What Is Existing Law on the Transfer and Tacking of Possession?

As explained by Professor A.N. Yiannopoulos, the term possession refers to "the factual authority that a person exercises over a corporeal thing with the intent to own it or the corresponding authority by which a person exercises a real right with the intent to have it as his own." In Louisiana, rights resulting from possession fall into three categories. The first category, acquisition of the status of possessor, is the least protected under property law. One attains this status by complying with the dual requirements set forth in Article 3424, which provides: "To acquire possession, one must intend to possess as owner and must take corporeal possession of the thing." The second category, acquisition of the right to possess, requires that the possessor continue his status as possessor for one year. The third category is the acquisition of ownership through acquisitive prescription.

The transfer of possession is expressly provided for in Article 3441, which states: "Possession is transferable by universal title or by particular title." While this article permits the transfer of possession for both types of successors, there is of course a fundamental difference.

5-27

The successor by universal title "represents the person of the deceased, and succeeds to all his rights and charges," while the successor by particular title "succeeds only to the rights appertaining to the thing which is sold, ceded or bequeathed to him." In other words, the universal successor stands in the shoes of the ancestor, and is substituted in his place for both rights and duties. By contrast, the particular successor acquires the ancestor's rights relative to the specific property that has been transferred. Universal succession occurs mortis causa, either through operation of law or in accordance with a will. Particular succession occurs either mortis causa (through particular legacy) or inter vivos (through onerous or gratuitous transfer).

Tacking of possession is described in Article 3442, which provides: "The possession of the transferor is tacked to that of the transferee if there has been no interruption of possession." When tacking occurs, the possession of the ancestor is cumulated with the possession of the successor. Universal successors clearly have the right to add the period of their ancestor's possession onto their own, since they stand in the shoes of the decedent. Technically, this is not tacking but the universal successor's continuation of the possession begun by the ancestor.

By contrast, since the particular successor begins a new possession, tacking is the vehicle through which he can cumulate his ancestor's possession with his own. Under Louisiana jurisprudence, tacking requires a juridical link between the parties, meaning an act sufficient to transfer ownership (or possession).

Does Proposed Article 936 Change the Law as Its Comment (b) States?

The first sentence of proposed Article 936 says that the decedent's possession is transferred to his successors. This sentence is certainly accurate as applied to the universal successor, but is not accurate under present law as applied to the particular successor, who must demand delivery of his legacy from the person or persons with seizin.[31] This is not valid basis for criticism of the article, however, since Article 3441 permits the transfer of possession, but does not provide for the transfer of possession at the possessor's death.

* * *

The [third] sentence provides: "A particular successor may commence a new possession for purposes of acquisitive prescription." . . . . [Neither the article nor the comments] expressly mention Bartlett v. Calhoun, but the intent behind the change in the law must be the overruling of Bartlett, a decision that created a major roadblock for particular successors seeking to tack possession for purposes of ten year acquisitive prescription. Article 3482, at issue in Bartlett, then provided: It is sufficient if the possession has commenced in good faith; and if the possession should afterwards be held in bad faith, that shall not prevent the prescription.

It is clear from Article 3482 that a possessor's loss of good faith will not prevent him from attaining ownership through ten year acquisitive prescription, since the good faith requirement is satisfied for that possessor so long as his possession commences in good faith and continues for ten years.

Until 1982, the Louisiana courts allowed any particular successor whose transferor had commenced his own possession in good faith to tack that transferor's possession, even where the transferee had never been in good faith. According to the seminal case of Devall v. Choppin and its progeny, the transferor's good faith satisfies the requirement of good faith for ten year acquisitive prescription. Bartlett overruled this long line of cases and held that Article 3482 envisions a single possession, and is thus inapplicable to the particular successor, since he commences a new possession separate from his ancestor's. Under Bartlett, the particular successor and the ancestor must both have begun their possession in good faith in order for the

"against the law"

particular successor to tack for purposes of ten year acquisitive prescription.

Bartlett overruled 142 years of jurisprudence constante in the area of property, where rules tend to be more "crystalline" than "muddy." Of course, in a civil law jurisdiction, where legislation is the source of law, Louisiana courts have the duty to disregard judicial opinions that are contra legem. If Devall had erroneously interpreted Article 3482, then the Bartlett court was correct in overruling it. While the writer agrees with those commentators who have already stated their disagreement with Bartlett, the present discussion is limited to the issue of whether that decision is affected by proposed Article 936.

The [third] sentence of proposed Article 936 is apparently intended to bypass Bartlett by allowing the particular successor to choose whether he wants to continue the decedent's possession or whether he wants to commence a new possession. If he decides to continue the possession of the decedent, then there would exist only one possession which would satisfy Article 3482 and enable the possessor to claim ownership through ten year acquisitive prescription.

It must be remembered that Bartlett imposes no limitations upon tacking by particular successors in contexts other than ten year acquisitive prescription. Thus, for purposes of thirty year acquisitive prescription, where good faith is not an ingredient, particular successors can tack even though they technically begin a new possession. The following hypothetical is illustrative: Assume that Y, a good faith possessor, commences his possession of Greenacre in 1965. In 1973, Y conveys Greenacre to Z, who is in bad faith. Under Bartlett, Z, as a particular successor of Y, is precluded from tacking Y's possession since Z has begun a new possession. However, for purposes of thirty year acquisitive prescription, where good faith is not an ingredient, Z is permitted to tack Y's possession. Thus, despite the fact that Z's possession is considered a new possession, he has the right to tack Y's possession for purposes of thirty year acquisitive prescription. Of course, under the above facts, it is in Z's interest to do so, since he could acquire ownership of Greenacre in 1995 through thirty year acquisitive prescription.

The Code already allows the particular successor to choose whether to forego tacking in order to take advantage of the technical fact that his possession is a new possession, or whether to take advantage of tacking, thereby foregoing whatever advantage he might have otherwise obtained because his possession is a new possession. Bartlett denies the particular successor that choice if he is a particular successor who commenced his own possession in bad faith, and who relies on tacking to acquire ownership through ten year acquisitive prescription.

The principal problem with the [third] sentence of the proposed article is that it misses the mark: it fails to focus upon tacking, which is the key concept. The [third] sentence of proposed Article 936 would be much clearer if it addressed the tacking issue head on, ideally through an affirmative statement that the particular successor need not be in good faith to tack for purposes of ten year acquisitive prescription.

To find that the [third] sentence has overruled Bartlett, one must first conclude that the [third] sentence is intended to overrule a famous Louisiana Supreme Court decision not cited in the comment, but referred to obliquely as "law." Referring to a judicial opinion as law seems uncivilian, since the very first article of the Civil Code declares that "(t)he sources of law are legislation and custom." Furthermore, even if one accepts the proposition that proposed Article 936 intends to overrule Bartlett, there remains the question of whether the [third] sentence will accomplish that result, since it does not refer specifically to tacking.

Finally, the Bartlett decision was concerned with particular successions in the general sense, and was not limited to mortis causa transmission. The underlying facts of that case involved a typical inter vivos particular succession--a sale. Proposed Article 936 clearly is limited to mortis causa transfers. Even if the article is successful in overruling Bartlett, it applies only to mortis causa particular successors, who probably represent only a handful of possessors affected by the Bartlett decision. Most people attempting to prove ownership through ten year acquisitive prescription are buyers whose titles were defective, but who were aware of the risk of eviction and bought the property nonetheless. The combined weight of these factors convinces this writer that Bartlett needs to be addressed directly in the acquisitive prescription articles, not in the succession articles, where the focus is more limited.

Continuation of Possession

Consider the following articles and scenarios on possession and its application in practice.

ARTICLES
Art. 936. Continuation of the Possession of decedent
The possession of the decedent is transferred to his successors, whether testate or intestate, and if testate, whether particular, general, or universal legatees.

A universal successor continues the possession of the decedent with all its advantages and defects, and with no alteration in the nature of the possession.

A particular successor may commence a new possession for purposes of acquisitive prescription.

Other relevant articles--
Art. 3506. General definitions of terms
Successor.— Successor is, generally speaking, the person who takes the place of another.
There are in law two sorts of successors: the universal successor, such as the heir, the universal legatee, and the general legatee; and the successor by particular title, such as the buyer, donee or legatee of particular things, the transferee.
The universal successor represents the person of the deceased, and succeeds to all his rights and charges.
The particular successor succeeds only to the rights appertaining to the thing which is sold, ceded or bequeathed to him.

Art. 3473. Prescription of ten years
Ownership and other real rights in immovables may be acquired by the prescription of ten years.

Art. 3475. Requisites
The requisites for the acquisitive prescription of ten years are: possession of ten years, good faith, just title, and a thing susceptible of acquisition by prescription.

Art. 3480. Good faith
For purposes of acquisitive prescription, a possessor is in good faith when he reasonably believes, in light of objective considerations, that he is owner of the thing he possesses.

Art. 3981 Presumption of good faith

Good faith is presumed. Neither error of fact nor error of law defeats this presumption. This *[handwritten: partiala]* presumption is rebutted on proof that the possessor knows, or should know, that he is not owner of the thing he possesses.

[handwritten at top: If Not in the code, it Falls under]

Art. 3482 Good faith at commencement of prescription
It is sufficient that possession has commenced in good faith; subsequent bad faith does not prevent the accrual of prescription of ten years. *[handwritten: More explanation needed!]*

Art. 3483. Just title
A just title is a juridical act, such as a sale, exchange, or donation, sufficient to transfer ownership or another real right. The act must be written, valid in form, and filed for registry in the conveyance records of the parish in which the immovable is situated.

Art. 3486. Immovables: prescription of thirty years
Ownership and other real rights in immovables may be acquired by the prescription of thirty years without the need of just title or possession in good faith.

SCENARIOS
The universal successor continues the ancestor's possession, not really tacking, but rather continuing, the possession begun by the ancestor. The universal successor "stands in the shoes" of the ancestor taking on the character ("good" or "bad" faith) of the ancestor.

The particular successor begins a new possession, separate and distinct from that of the ancestor. He, therefore, establishes his own character ("good" or "bad" faith). He thus starts a new possession. He does, however, have the right to tack on the time of his ancestor, but not the character.

For purposes of acquisitive prescription, the important point in time for determining the character of possession is the time when the possession begins.

Scenario I
X begins possession of an immovable, believing in good faith that he has a right to possess. He possesses for eight years before he dies.

When X dies, he leaves all his property to Y.

Y is X's universal legatee and "steps into the shoes" of X. Y acquires the character of X. Since X began his possession in good faith, Y is deemed in good faith, regardless of what he objectively knows about the possession. Stepping into X's shoes, Y takes on X's time as well. Thus, Y has only to wait two more years and acquire the immovable by ten years good faith possession.

Scenario II
X begins possession of an immovable in bad faith, knowing his possession is questionable. He possesses for eight years before he dies.

When X dies, he leaves all his property to Y.

Y is X's universal legatee and "steps into the shoes" of X. Since X began his possession in bad faith, Y is deemed in bad faith. Stepping into X's shoes, Y takes on X's time as well. Thus, Y has to wait another twenty-two years to acquire the land through thirty years bad faith prescription.

Scenario III

X begins possession of an immovable, believing in good faith that he has a right to possess. He possesses for eight years before he dies.

When X dies, he leaves a will, bequeathing that immovable to Y as a particular legatee.

Y, as a particular legatee, begins his own possession, with its own character. If he chooses to use X's time, it is a matter of tacking. Since X was on the land for eight years in good faith, and Y was also in good faith, Y could use X's eight years and tack on two of his own, thus acquiring the property by ten years good faith possession. Since X had begun possession in good faith, the beginning of X's possession may begin start the clock for purposes of acquisitive prescription and Y may avail himself of the eight years already accumulated by X.

Scenario IV

X begins possession of an immovable, believing in good faith that he has a right to possess. He possesses for two years before he dies.

When X dies, he leaves a will, bequeathing that immovable to Y as a particular legatee.

Y, as a particular legatee, begins his own possession with its own character. If he chooses to use X's time, it is a matter of tacking. If Y is in bad faith, his possession begins with that bad faith character. Thus, Y is relegated to acquiring the property through thirty years bad faith acquisitive prescription. Y may avail himself, however, of the two years time that X had accumulated and wait another twenty-eight years to acquire the property.

Scenario V

X begins possession of an immovable in bad faith, knowing his possession is questionable. He possesses for eight years before he dies.

When X dies, he leaves a will, bequeathing that immovable to Y as a particular legatee.

Y, as a particular legatee, begins his own possession, with its own character. If he chooses to use X's time, it is a matter of tacking. Y might not know of X's bad faith and Y could independently be of good faith. Thus, Y could acquire the property by ten years good faith acquisitive prescription. However, the time clock for this prescription starts ticking at the time there is a good faith possessor. Thus, Y cannot tack on the eight years that X possessed in bad faith. Thus, Y should opt to commence his own good faith prescription and he can acquire the property in ten years from the time his good faith possession began.

Scenario VI

X begins possession of an immovable in bad faith, knowing his possession is questionable. He possesses for eight years before he dies.

When X dies, he leaves a will, bequeathing that immovable to Y as a particular legatee.

Y, as a particular legatee, begins his own possession, with its own character. If he chooses to use X's time, it is a matter of tacking. If Y is in bad faith, having knowledge of some potential problem, he can only acquire the property on the basis of thirty years acquisitive prescription. Y may use X's prior eight years and tack on twenty-two of his own, thus acquiring the property.

Scenario VII

X begins possession of an immovable in bad faith, knowing his possession is questionable. He possesses for twenty-seven years before he dies.

When X dies, he leaves a will, bequeathing that immovable to Y as a particular legatee.

Y, as a particular legatee, begins his own possession, with its own character. He may, opt, however, to continue the possession of X, with its advantages (twenty-two years already accumulated) and its disadvantages (possession begun in bad faith). If Y were in good faith, he could acquire the property through ten years acquisitive prescription. The time starts from the point of having a good faith possessor. Since Y was the one beginning the good faith possession, in order to acquire through good faith possession, ten years must pass from the beginning of Y's possession. Yet, Y still has the option to use X's bad faith time, coupled with the bad faith character of possession. In this scenario, since X had already been on the property for twenty-seven years, only three years remain for Y to acquire the property through thirty years acquisitive prescription.

Problem

Assume that John possesses an immovable in bad faith for a period of eight years and then John dies, bequeathing that immovable to his friend Mitch, and the rest of his property to Ann. If Mitch is unaware of John's bad faith, and is himself in good faith, how long will Mitch have to wait in order to acquire the immovable by acquisitive prescription? Would it matter if Mitch were also in bad faith? What if Mitch were a universal successor, rather than a particular successor?

HYPOTHETICAL

Alice dies and leaves a 1971 green convertible MG to Barbara and the rest of her estate, which includes a lot on the Northshore, to Clay. Hurricane Lili hit land the day before Alice died and during the storm, a neighbor's tree hit Alice's MG, breaking the front windshield. Once Alice died, it is discovered that, in bad faith, she was merely a possessor of the MG and the lot on the Northshore for the past 2 years.

a)   Who, if anyone, can assert a claim against Alice's neighbor for the damage to the MG?

b)   How long must Barbara wait to acquire ownership of the MG?

c)   How long must Clay wait in order to acquire ownership of the lot on the Northshore?

clarify!?

Bad faith does not bar a person from acquiring a property for the sake of acquisition, + would push back the year/time person in bad faith may acquire the property!

5-33

CHAPTER 6:
LOSS OF SUCCESSION RIGHTS
(INCAPACITY AND UNWORTHINESS)
La. C.C. 939-946

Incapacity: La. C.C. 939-940, La. R.S. 9:391.1

Act 1421 of 1997, effective July 1, 1999, revised Chapter 5 of Book III of Title I of the Civil Code which was previously entitled "Of the Incapacity and Unworthiness of Heirs," replacing it with a new Chapter 5 entitled "Loss of Succession Rights." The first two articles of the new chapter deal with the capacity of an heir to succeed at the death of a decedent. La. C.C. 939 provides that "a successor must exist at the death of the decedent," as did its source article 953 in the Civil Code of 1870. La. C.C. 940 explains that an unborn child that is conceived at the time of the decedent's death and later born alive is considered as existing at the death of the decedent. The comment to the article indicates that the article reproduces the substance of prior article 954 of the Civil Code of 1870 which provided that a child *in utero* at the time of the decedent's death, who was later born alive, was considered as born and thus capable of succeeding to the decedent. Actually, the new La. C.C. 940 merely requires, as did the previous article 956 of the Civil Code of 1879, that the child would be conceived and later born alive. Certainly a child *in utero* that is later born alive would qualify, but what about an *in vitro* fertilized ovum that was conceived, but not yet implanted into his mother's womb, at the time of the decedent's death? If that child is later born alive, may he take in a succession opened prior to his implantation, but after his conception? Certainly, the redactors of the Civil Code of 1870 could not have considered the possibility of children born of these assisted means of reproduction. Compare La. C.C. 1474 which requires that a child be *in utero* at the time a donation is made in order to have capacity to receive the donation. Is there a difference in capacity depending on whether the decedent dies testate or intestate? Should there be?

What about a child that is not even conceived at the time of the decedent's death, but is the genetic child of the decedent? Consider the following case from the state of New Jersey. How would it be resolved in Louisiana?

ESTATE OF KOLACY
332 N. J. Super. 593, 753 A. 2d 1257 (2000)

STANTON, A.J.S.C.

On March 31, 2000, I delivered an oral opinion declaring that Amanda Kolacy and Elyse Kolacy, three year old girls who are residents of New Jersey, are the heirs of their father William Kolacy, even though they were born eighteen months after his death. This opinion supersedes my earlier oral opinion.

The plaintiff in this action is Mariantonia Kolacy. She has brought this action to obtain a declaration that her two children, Amanda and Elyse, have the status of intestate heirs of her late husband, William J. Kolacy. Because this action involves a claim that one or more statutes of the State of New Jersey are unconstitutional, the Attorney General of New Jersey was notified of the action and has appeared through a Deputy Attorney General to defend the constitutionality of the state statutes involved.

On February 7, 1994, William J. Kolacy and Mariantonia Kolacy were a young married couple living in Rockaway, New Jersey. On that date, William Kolacy was diagnosed as having leukemia and he was advised to start chemotherapy as quickly as possible. He feared that he would be rendered infertile by the disease or by the treatment for the disease, so he decided to place his sperm in the Sperm and Embryo Bank of NJ. On the morning of February 8, 1994, William Kolacy and Mariantonia Kolacy harvested his sperm and Mariantonia Kolacy delivered it to the sperm bank. Later that day, the chemotherapy began. After the chemotherapy had been in progress for one month, a second harvesting of sperm occurred and was placed in the sperm bank.

Unfortunately, William Kolacy's leukemia led to his death at the age of 26 on April 15, 1995. He died domiciled in New Jersey. On April 3, 1996, almost a year after the death of William Kolacy, plaintiff Mariantonia Kolacy authorized the release of his sperm from the Sperm and Embryo Bank of NJ to the Center for Reproductive Medicine and Infertility at Cornell University Medical College in New York City. An IVF fertilization procedure uniting the sperm of William Kolacy and eggs taken from Mariantonia Kolacy was performed at the Center. The procedure was successful and the embryos which resulted were transferred into the womb of Mariantonia Kolacy. Twin girls, Amanda and Elyse, were born to Mariantonia Kolacy on November 3, 1996. The births occurred slightly more than eighteen months after the death of William Kolacy.

I find that the certifications submitted by Mariantonia Kolacy and Dr. Isaac Kligman of the Center for Reproductive Medicine and Infertility are fully credible and that they firmly establish the facts set forth above. Accordingly, it is clear that Amanda and Elyse Kolacy are genetically and biologically the children of William Kolacy.

In Paragraphs 7 through 9 of the verified complaint in this action, the plaintiff states her reasons for bringing this action as follows:

> 7. The Social Security Administration has denied dependent benefits to Amanda and Elyse Kolacy contending they are not children of a deceased worker. On November 16, 1999 Administrative Law Judge Richard L. De Steno upheld the denial of benefits in a written decision.
>
> 8. Section 216 of the Social Security Act provides, inter alia, that "[c]hild's insurance benefits can be paid to a child who could inherit under the State's intestate laws."
>
> 9. Plaintiff seeks a declaration that her daughters, posthumously conceived utilizing the late William J. Kolacy's stored sperm, are among the class of persons who are his intestate heirs so as to pursue her claim for child's insurance benefits on behalf of the decedent's children under the Social Security Act.

Plaintiff is currently pursuing her claims and those of the children through appellate process within the Social Security Administration, and, if necessary, will eventually litigate them in the federal courts. In bringing this action in the Superior Court, the plaintiff is attempting to obtain a state court ruling which will be helpful to her in pursuing her federal claims before a federal administrative agency and before the federal courts.

The State of New Jersey, speaking through the Deputy Attorney General appearing in this action, has urged me not to adjudicate this case. The State argues that the plaintiff's claim really is not justiciable in this court. The argument is that plaintiff is basically seeking to assert federal rights before federal tribunals and that she should be restricted to presenting her case before federal tribunals. Those tribunals, of course, are capable of looking at New Jersey law and of making perfectly intelligent judgments with respect to it. The State, in effect, argues that it would be an inappropriate intrusion on federal adjudicatory processes for me to become involved in determining the status of Amanda and Elyse Kolacy.

* * *

I also note that, entirely aside from claims being asserted with respect to Social Security benefits, Amanda and Elyse are entitled to have their status as heirs of their father determined for a variety of state law purposes. The State argues that, because William Kolacy left no assets and thus had no estate at the time of his death, there is really no point in determining who are his heirs under New Jersey law. William Kolacy died without a will, but he did not leave any assets which would pass under the intestate laws of New Jersey. His assets were modest because of his young age and because of the difficult economic stresses that were placed upon him and his wife by his illness. Such assets as he had passed to his wife because of the joint ownership of property. Therefore, a determination that Amanda and Elyse were his heirs would not presently entitle them to any property under intestate law.

However, a present determination of their status as heirs is appropriate because of the effect it has on their general legal and social status and because of the impact which it may have upon property rights as they evolve over a period of time. For one thing, it is conceivable, though not very likely, that William Kolacy might have an estate because of assets passing to him at a future date. More realistically, a determination that the children are the heirs of William Kolacy could be significant in terms of their rights to take from his parents or from his collateral relatives in the event that one or more of those persons were to die intestate. Their status as his heirs could also be significant in determining their rights under the wills of their father's relatives. Thus, for a variety of estate law purposes, there is a present real utility to a declaration of the inheritance status of Amanda and Elyse. I will therefore entertain this action and I will make a ruling with respect to whether Amanda and Elyse legally qualify as the heirs of William Kolacy.

There are no New Jersey decisions dealing with the central issue presented in this case-whether Amanda and Elyse Kolacy, conceived after the death of their biological father and born more than eighteen months after his death, qualify as his heirs under state intestate law. I have not been able to find any American appellate court decisions dealing with that central issue.

Counsel have discussed at some length N.J.S.A. 3B:5-8, which is the New Jersey statute dealing with after born heirs. That statute provides as follows: "Relatives of the decedent conceived before his death but born thereafter inherit as if they had been born in the lifetime of the decedent." Counsel for plaintiff argues that this statute, as applied to children such as Amanda and Elyse Kolacy, is unconstitutional because "the effect of the statute as to posthumously conceived children is to both invidiously and irrationally discriminate against them." My view is that the constitutional argument against this statute is fundamentally misplaced and that it really is not necessary to reach the issue of whether this statute is constitutional.

A brief discussion of elementary estate law concepts is appropriate at this point. When a person dies, whether he dies leaving a will or whether he dies intestate, there is a real life need and a legal need to determine which persons are entitled to take his estate, and when that determination is made the general policy is to deliver to those persons rather promptly the property to which they are entitled. Thus, the identity of people who will take property from a decedent has traditionally been determined as of the date of the decedent's death.

However, there have long been exceptions to the rule that the identity of takers from a decedent's estate is determined as of the date of death. Those exceptions are based on human experience going back to time immemorial. We have always been aware that men sometimes cause a woman to become pregnant and then die before the pregnancy comes to term and a child is born. It has always been routine human experience that men sometimes have children after they die. To deal fairly with this reality, decisional law and statutory law have long recognized that it is appropriate to hold the process of identifying takers from a decedent's estate open long enough to allow after born children to receive property from and through their father. *See Byerly v. Tolbert*, 250 N.C. 27, 108 S.E.2d 29 (1959); *Baugh v. Baugh*, 25 Kan.App.2d 871, 973 P.2d 202 (1999).

Aside from the fact that a man sometimes dies before his child is born, there is the fact that when any person dies, a woman related to that decedent may be pregnant with a child who upon birth will qualify as a member of a class of persons entitled to take property from the decedent. The law has traditionally held the class of persons entitled to take from the decedent open long enough to allow a child who was being carried in his or her mother's womb at the time of the decedent's death to receive a share of the property. *See Estate of Wolyniec v. Moe*, 94 N.J.Super. 43, 226 A. 2d 743 (Ch.Div.1967); *Chemical Bank & Trust Company v. Godfrey*, 29 N.J.Super. 226, 102 A. 2d 108 (Ch.Div.1953).

N.J.S.A. 3B:5-8 is part of that traditional recognition of exceptions to the rule that takers from a decedent's estate should be determined as of the date of the decedent's death. N.J.S.A. 3B:5-8 was enacted in 1981 as part of a fairly broad reorganization of statutory law dealing with decedents' estates. In 1981, reproductive technology had advanced to the point that it is conceivable that the legislature might have been aware of the kind of problem posed by our present case. However, the relevant legislative history indicates that the current statute was simply a carryover of earlier statutes going back to at least 1877. The simple fact is that when the legislature adopted N.J.S.A. 3B:5-8 it was not giving any thought whatever to the kind of problem we have in this case. To the extent that there was a conscious legislative intent about reproductive processes involved, the intent was undoubtedly to deal fairly and sensibly with children resulting from traditional sexual activity in which a man directly deposits sperm into the body of a woman. With one exception mentioned hereafter, the New Jersey Legislature has never addressed the problems posed in estate law by current human reproductive technology.

The ability to remove sperm and eggs from human beings and to preserve their viability by storing them for long periods of time at low temperatures makes it possible for children to come into existence as the genetic and biological offspring of a father or of a mother who has long since been dead. My impression is that it is now possible to preserve the viability of human genetic material for as long as ten years. It is likely that the time will be extended in the future. The evolving human productive technology opens up some wonderful possibilities, but it also creates difficult issues and potential problems in many areas. It would undoubtedly be useful for the Legislature to deal consciously and in a well informed way with at least some of the issues presented by reproductive technology.

The State has urged that courts should not entertain actions such as the present one, but should wait until the Legislature has dealt with the kinds of issues presented by this case. As indicated above, I think it would be helpful for the Legislature to deal with these kinds of issues. In the meanwhile, life goes on, and people come into the courts seeking redress for present problems. We judges cannot simply put those problems on hold in the hope that some day (which may never come) the Legislature will deal with the problem in question. Simple justice requires us to do the best we can with the statutory law which is presently available. As I look at N.J.S.A. 3B:5-8 and other statutory provisions dealing with intestate succession, I discern a basic legislative intent to enable children to take property from their parents and through their parents from parental relatives. Although the Legislature has not dealt with the kind of issue presented by children such as Amanda and Elyse, it has manifested a general intent that the children of a decedent should be amply provided for with respect to property passing from him or through him as the result of a death. It is my view that the general intent should prevail over a restrictive, literal reading of statutes which did not consciously purport to deal with the kind of problem before us.

Given that general legislative intent, it seems to me that once we establish, as we have in this case, that a child is indeed the offspring of a decedent, we should routinely grant that child the legal status of being an heir of the decedent, unless doing so would unfairly intrude on the rights of other persons or would cause serious problems in terms of the orderly administration of estates.

I note that after born children who come into existence because of modern reproductive techniques pose special challenges to society and to our legal system. Historically, after born children were conceived and in their mother's womb at the time of a decedent's death and they could be counted on to appear no later than approximately nine months after that death. Now they can appear after the death of either a mother or a father and they can appear a number of years after that death. Estates cannot be held open for years simply to allow for the possibility that after born children may come into existence. People alive at the time of a decedent's death who are entitled to receive property from the decedent's estate are entitled to receive it reasonably promptly. It would undoubtedly be both fair and constitutional for a Legislature to impose time limits and other situationally described limits on the ability of after born children to take from or through a parent. In the absence of legislative provision in that regard, it would undoubtedly be fair and constitutional for courts to impose limits on the ability of after born children to take in particular cases.

In our present case, there are no estate administration problems involved and there are no competing interests of other persons who were alive at the time of William Kolacy's death which would be unfairly frustrated by recognizing Amanda and Elyse as his heirs. Even in situations where competing interests such as other children born during the lifetime of the decedent are in existence at the time of his death, it might be possible to accommodate those interests with the interests of after born children. For example, by statutory provision or decisional rule, payments made in the course of routine estate administration before the advent of after born children could be treated as vested and left undisturbed, while distributions made following the birth of after born children could be made to both categories of children.

There has been some discussion in this case of the possible impact of the New Jersey Parentage Act, N.J.S.A. 9:17-38 to -59. That act is very important in dealing with problems posed by fathers seeking to avoid their responsibility for the support of children, and it also deals with a number of other parentage issues. But most of its provisions are not even remotely relevant to the kind of issues posed by our present case.

One provision of the Parentage Act which is facially somewhat relevant to our case is N.J.S.A. 9:17-43a(1) which reads: "A man is presumed to be the biological father of a child if: He and the child's biological mother are or have been married to each other and the child is born during the marriage, or within 300 days after the marriage is terminated by death, annulment or divorce." This provision might arguably be interpreted as creating the reverse presumption that a child born more than 300 days after the death of a man shall be presumed not to be the biological child of the deceased man. I think that treating the cited provision as creating such a reverse presumption of non-parentage would be somewhat strained because it is counterproductive to the purposes of the act, but even if such a reverse presumption is read into the act, it is subject to being rebutted by clear and convincing factual evidence. In our present case, there is clear and convincing evidence that Amanda and Elyse are the biological children of William Kolacy.

It is interesting to note that there is one section of the Parentage Act in which the Legislature does deal explicitly with parentage issues (and derivative estate law issues) posed by new reproductive technology. That section is N.J.S.A. 9:17-44, which reads in pertinent part:

> a. If under the supervision of a licensed physician and with the consent of her husband, a wife is inseminated artificially with semen donated by a man not her husband, the husband is treated in law as if he were the natural father of a child thereby conceived. The husband's consent shall be in writing and signed by him and his wife....
>
> b. Unless the donor of semen and the woman have entered into a written contract to the contrary, the donor of semen provided to a licensed physician for use in the artificial insemination of a woman other than the donor's wife is treated in law as if he were not the father of a child thereby conceived and shall have no rights or duties stemming from the conception of a child.

This legislative treatment of certain issues arising out of reproductive technology is interesting and sensible. But it does not deal expressly with posthumous conception, and, more importantly, it does not deal with sperm contributed by the husband of the woman giving birth to a child. It is not relevant to the facts of our present case.

The ability to cause children to come into existence long after the death of a parent is a recently acquired ability for human society. There are probably wise and wonderful ways in which that ability can be used. There are also undoubtedly some special problems that the exercise of that ability might pose. There are, I think, ethical problems, social policy problems and legal problems which are presented when a child is brought into existence under circumstances where a traditionally normal parenting situation is not available. One would hope that a prospective parent thinking about causing a child to come into existence after the death of a genetic and biological parent would think very carefully about the potential consequences of doing that. The law should certainly be cautious about encouraging parents to move precipitously in this area.

I accept as true Mariantonia Kolacy's statement that her husband unequivocally expressed his desire that she use his stored sperm after his death to bear his children. She did, in fact, use his sperm to bear his children. Some may question the wisdom of such a course of action, but one can certainly understand why a loving and caring couple in the Kolacys' position might choose it. Be all that as it may, once a child has come into existence, she is a full-fledged human being and is entitled to all of the love, respect, dignity and legal protection which that status requires. It seems to me that a fundamental policy of the law should be to enhance and enlarge the rights of each human being to the maximum extent possible, consistent with the duty not to intrude unfairly upon the interests of other persons. Given that viewpoint, and given the facts of this case, including particularly the fact that William Kolacy by his intentional conduct created the possibility of having long-delayed after born children, I believe it is entirely fitting to recognize that Amanda and Elyse Kolacy are the legal heirs of William Kolacy under the intestate laws of New Jersey.

NOTE

After the Kolacy case and in response to other posthumously conceived children seeking social security benefits, Louisiana passed Act 479, § 1 of 2001, which added La. R.S. 9:391.1 to the ancillaries of the Civil Code. The statute was amended by Act 495, § of 2003 and reads:

§ 391.1. Child conceived after death of parent
A. Notwithstanding the provisions of any law to the contrary, any child conceived after the death of a decedent, who specifically authorized in writing his surviving spouse to use his gametes, shall be deemed the child of such decedent with all rights, including the capacity to inherit from the decedent, as the child would have had if the child had been in existence at the time of the death of the deceased parent, provided the child was born to the surviving spouse, using the gametes of the decedent, within three years of the death of the decedent.

B. Any heir or legatee of the decedent whose interest in the succession of the decedent will be reduced by the birth of a child conceived as provided in Subsection A of this Section shall have one year from the birth of such child within which to bring an action to disavow paternity.

How are the posthumously conceived children protected by this statute? What about other potential heirs? Creditors? What if an unmarried couple use the procedure to create a child? Is the child still protected? *See* Kathryn Venturatos Lorio, *Conceiving the Inconceivable: Legal Recognition of the Posthumously Conceived Child*, 34 ACTEC J. 154 (2008).

In 2012, the United States Supreme Court had the occasion to consider the issue of a posthumously conceived child in a case involving Florida law. *Astrue v. Capato ex rel. B.N.C.,* 132 S. Ct. 2021 (2012). The Court held that the posthumously conceived children could not inherit from the decedent under Florida's intestacy laws so they were not entitled to Social Security survivor benefits. Florida law permitted posthumously born children to inherit only if they were *conceived* during the decedent's lifetime, *unless* they were provided for in the decedent's will. The Court referenced other state laws that permitted posthumously conceived children to inherit under state intestate laws:

[T]he statutes of several States accord inheritance rights to posthumously conceived children. See Cal. Prob.Code Ann. § 249.5(c) (allowing inheritance if child is in utero within two years of parent's death); Colo.Rev.Stat. Ann. § 15–11–120(11) (2011) (child in utero within three years or born within 45 months); Iowa Code Ann. § 633.220A(1) (child born within two years); La.Rev.Stat. Ann. § 9:391.1(A) (child born within three years); N.D. Cent.Code Ann. § 30.1–04–19(11) (child in utero within three years or born within 45 months). See also Uniform Probate Code § 2–120(k), 8 U.L.A. 58 (treating a posthumously conceived child as "in gestation at the individual's death," but only if specified time limits are met).

Unworthiness: La. C.C. 941-946

Is not automatic; person must file petition

The remaining articles of Chapter 5 on "Loss of Succession Rights" deal with the concept of unworthiness. Essentially, an heir who had capacity to succeed may lose that right if he is judicially divested of the right due to his behavior toward the decedent. La. C.C. 941 provides that a successor "shall be declared unworthy if he is convicted of a crime involving the intentional killing, or attempted killing, of the decedent, or was judicially determined to have participated in the intentional, unjustified killing, of the decedent." References in the pre-revision articles to bringing a serious accusation against the decedent or not taking measures to bring the decedent's murderer to justice have been deleted as "archaic." Revision Comment (a) to La. C.C. 941. *old-fashioned,*

The action to declare a successor unworthy is to be brought in the succession proceeding itself, rather than in a separate proceeding, La. C.C. 941, and may be brought by a person who would succeed in place of, or in concurrence with, the person to be declared unworthy, or by one who claims through the alleged unworthy. La. C.C. 942.

To defeat the action of unworthiness, a successor must prove either reconciliation or forgiveness by the decedent. La. C.C. 943. An executive pardon or pardon by operation of law is insufficient. La. C.C. 941. Additionally, forgiveness by a decedent parent is no longer presumed from the parent's failure to disinherit an unworthy child. La. C.C. 975 (1870) (repealed).

In a sense the unworthy person is repr. Another major change in the law is that the revision provides that, in an intestate succession, an unworthy successor's rights devolve as if he predeceased the decedent, thus establishing a type of exception to the rule of representation that only deceased persons may be represented. Thus, the children of an unworthy successor may succeed to the unworthy successor's rights, rather than allowing a first degree descendant of the decedent to exclude the grandchildren. However, neither the unworthy successor nor the other parent of the unworthy's child may enjoy a legal usufruct over the property inherited by their child. La. C.C. 946. Thus, if X dies with three children, A, B, and C, and A is declared unworthy, no longer will B and C split all of X's estate, excluding any children of A. Rather, if A had two children, D and E, the revision provides that D and E take the 1/3 that would have been inherited by A had he been worthy and B and C take 1/3 a piece. In any event, neither A nor the other parent of D and E would have the legal usufruct over the property inherited by D and E. The revision also provides that if the decedent dies testate, the succession rights devolve according to the provisions on accretion, La. C.C. 946, which would treat the legacy to the unworthy as a lapsed legacy. La. C.C. 1589.

In addition to being deprived of his right to succeed, the unworthy is also precluded from serving as an executor, trustee, attorney or other fiduciary with regard to the succession. La. C.C. 945. If the unworthy has possession of the decedent's property, he must return it, as well as all fruits and products derived therefrom, and must account for any impairment of value due to his encumbering or failing to properly preserve the property. If he no longer has possession of the property due to his own fault, he must account for the value of the loss of possession at the time of transfer, as well as for all fruits and products he derived from it. If the alienation, encumbrance, or leasing of the property was by onerous title, the third party is protected; however, if the property was donated and the donee or his successors have possession of the property, the donation is annulled. La. C.C. 945.

CALIFORNIA-WESTERN STATES LIFE INSURANCE v. SANFORD
515 F. Supp. 524 (E.D. 1981)
[Footnotes omitted.]

SEAR, District Judge

On the evening of February 16, 1979, on a street in New Orleans, Edward Sanford, Jr. shot and killed his estranged wife, Jennifer, while the couple's three children watched from the backseat of a car. Sanford then shot himself, but survived the injury. He was arrested and prosecuted for his wife's murder in the Criminal District Court for the Parish of Orleans. After stipulating to the shooting, Sanford presented the testimony of a psychiatrist that he was insane during the commission of the crime. The prosecution did not present any witnesses. The court acquitted Sanford on grounds of insanity and committed him to the custody of a mental institution. *State of Louisiana v. Sanford*, No. 269-061-H (September 6, 1979).

By virtue of her employment with the Ralph M. Parsons Co., Mrs. Sanford held a policy of life insurance with California-Western States Life Insurance Co. ("Cal-Western"), No. G-3848, in the principal amount of $17,500 and for an additional $17,500 in accidental death and dismemberment benefits. Mrs. Sanford named her husband as the beneficiary of the policy.

Faced with potentially conflicting claims to the $35,000 in policy proceeds by Sanford and the three Sanford children, Cal-Western commenced this interpleader action pursuant to FED.R.CIV.P. 22 and 28 U.S.C. § 1332(a)(1) (1976) to adjudicate the claimants' legal rights to the money. Cal-Western deposited the proceeds in the registry of the Court, and was subsequently granted summary judgment. Sanford has now moved for judgment on the pleadings pursuant to FED.R.CIV.P. 12(c).

Sanford relies on LA.REV.STAT.ANN. § 22:613(D) (West Supp.1981) which states:

No beneficiary, assignee, or other payee under any personal insurance contract shall receive from the insurer any benefits thereunder accruing upon the death, disablement, or injury of the individual insured when said beneficiary, assignee, or other payee who (sic) is held by a final judgment of a court of competent jurisdiction to be criminally responsible for the death, disablement or injury of the individual insured. Where such a disqualification exists, the policy proceeds shall be payable to the secondary or contingent beneficiary, unless similarly disqualified, or, if no secondary or contingent beneficiary exists, to the estate of the insured.

Since under Louisiana law, one who commits a crime but is unable to distinguish right from wrong because of mental disease or defect may not be held criminally responsible for the offense, Sanford argues that the acquittal of his wife's murder on grounds of insanity conclusively establishes his eligibility to receive the insurance proceeds under § 22:613(D). Sanford's children respond that while under the statute a criminal conviction bars a beneficiary from receiving insurance proceeds, an acquittal is not afforded the same conclusive effect, and argue that they are entitled to litigate the issue of Sanford's sanity in this proceeding.

Perhaps because § 22:613(D) was enacted only recently by the Louisiana legislature, *see* Acts 1979, No. 246, no reported decision has yet construed the statute. Furthermore, there are no Louisiana cases dealing with the right of a beneficiary to insurance proceeds after he is acquitted of the murder of the insured. Therefore, this motion presents a novel question of Louisiana law. Unlike federal appellate courts, this Court may not certify a question of Louisiana law to the state supreme court for its authoritative determination. I must therefore derive the proper meaning of § 22:613(D) from the plain language of the statute, from existing Louisiana jurisprudence in this area, meager though it is, and from precedents of other American jurisdictions.

*   *   *

Sanford has cited no case, and my own research has revealed none, in which a beneficiary was permitted to invoke an acquittal to secure his right to insurance proceeds on the affirmative ground that he had been found not guilty, rather than simply because of the absence of a conviction. To the contrary, there have been several cases in which courts have disregarded acquittals of beneficiaries. . . . Although Louisiana uses a civil standard of proof for criminal insanity defenses . . . the disparate consequences of a criminal adjudication and a civil proceeding, as well as the constitutional limitations on procedure and evidence in a criminal trial which do not exist in a civil action, make it unlikely that the Louisiana legislature intended that an acquittal have any effect on the civil question of a beneficiary's right to property.

Accordingly, because § 22:613(D) does not require that a beneficiary be convicted of the felonious and intentional homicide of the insured before he is disqualified to receive the policy proceeds, nor make an acquittal conclusive on the issue of guilt, the children must be permitted to litigate the issue of Sanford's sanity. Sanford's motion for judgment on the pleadings, therefore, is DENIED.

NOTE

How is the insurance statute different from La. C.C. 941? Which standard is stricter? Compare La. C.C. 941 to Uniform Probate Code § 2-803:

> **(b) [Forfeiture of Statutory Benefits.]** An individual who feloniously and intentionally kills the decedent forfeits all benefits under this Article with respect to the decedent's estate, including an intestate share, an elective share, an omitted spouse's or child's share, a homestead allowance, exempt property, and a

family allowance. If the decedent died intestate, the decedent's intestate estate passes as if the killer disclaimed his [or her] intestate share.

(G) [Felonious and Intentional Killing; How Determined.] After all right to appeal has been exhausted, a judgment of conviction establishing criminal accountability for the felonious and intentional killing of the decedent conclusively establishes the convicted individual as the decedent's killer for purposes of this section. In the absence of a conviction, the court, upon the petition of an interested person, must determine whether, under the preponderance of evidence standard, the individual would be found criminally accountable for the felonious and intentional killing of the decedent. If the court determines that, under that standard, the individual would be found criminally accountable for the felonious and intentional killing of the decedent, the determination conclusively establishes that individual as the decedent's killer for purposes of this section.

Might clear and convincing be a preferable standard?

CRAIN v. CRAIN
754 So. 2d 261 (La. App. 1st Cir. 1999)
[Footnotes omitted.]

The issue in this appeal is whether the three minor children of Shanda Spears Crain have the legal right to succeed to the estates of their grandparents (Shanda's parents), in light of the fact that Shanda was convicted of murdering her parents and can thereby be declared unworthy as an heir, and also in light of renunciations allegedly executed by Shanda, which, if valid, left her two brothers as the remaining heirs in the first degree with respect to the decedents' estates.

Shanda Spears Crain was convicted of the first degree murder of her parents, George Lander Spears, Sr. and Bobbie Jean Toney Spears, and is incarcerated at the Louisiana State Prison for Women in St. Gabriel, Louisiana. The three minor children on whose behalf this action has been filed are the children of Shanda Spears and the grandchildren of the decedents. In addition to Shanda, the decedents had two other children, George Lander Spears, Jr. and Landon Scott Spears. Although absent from the record before us, it appears that subsequent to the murders, Shanda executed two acts of renunciation of her parents' successions.

This action, filed by Yancy Brett Crain, Shanda's former husband and the tutor of the three minor children, is an attempt to secure the portion of the decedents' estates that would have devolved to Shanda, absent her renunciations and unworthiness, for her three minor children. The petition seeks to have the renunciations declared null and a declaration of Shanda's unworthiness. According to the petition, once these two declarations are made, the children "should be called to the successions by representation of their mother."

The defendants, which include the two successions and the two remaining heirs in the first degree, Shanda's brothers, filed a motion for summary judgment, claiming that the children have no legal right to inherit through their mother, who is still alive, by representation whether she is declared unworthy or renounces the successions or both. Defendants maintain that in either scenario, the children would succeed in their own right, and therefore, inherit only if they are

6-11

nearest in degree. Because Shanda, the renouncing/unworthy heir has two siblings who are in the first degree, the children, who are in the second degree, have no rights of inheritance.

The trial court granted the motion for summary judgment, finding no genuine issues of material fact and that the children have no legal right to any portion of their grandparents' successions. The petition was dismissed; plaintiffs appeal.

Plaintiffs' claim that the children may represent Shanda in the successions after a declaration of unworthiness is based on La. C.C. art. 973, which provides as follows:

> The children of the person declared unworthy to succeed, being admitted to the succession ab intestato in their own name and without the aid of representation, are not excluded by the fault of their father; but the father cannot claim, in any case, upon the property of that succession, the usufruct which the law grants him in certain cases.

The trial court, in the absence of any jurisprudence interpreting the article, relied on the comments of Professors Frederick Swaim and Kathryn Lorio in 10 *Louisiana Civil Law Treatise, Successions and Donations* § 6.3, at 127-128 (1995) interpreting the phrase "in their own name" to mean inheriting "in their own right," as opposed to inheriting through representation, which is allowed only when the legal heir is deceased. Thus, according to this interpretation, the children of an unworthy heir can inherit only if the unworthy heir had no siblings.

Not only do we agree with the interpretation cited above, and the trial court's reliance thereon, but we also find great support for this interpretation in the comments to the revised civil code articles on successions enacted by Acts 1997, No. 1421, § 1, eff. July 1, 1999. Revised Art. 946 now governs the devolution of succession rights of a successor declared unworthy, as follows:

> If the decedent died intestate, when a successor is declared unworthy, his succession rights devolve *as if he had predeceased the decedent* .... (Emphasis added.)

The comments to the revised article provide:

> (a) This Article is new and definitely changes the law. In an intestate succession, the Article protects the innocent descendants of a successor whose rights are judicially divested for unworthiness. It changes the law by permitting the descendants of a person whose rights have been divested to inherit even when their degree of relationship would not otherwise permit them to do so. It establishes an exception to the normal rule of representation, which is that only deceased persons may be represented (*see* Civil Code Article 886 (1870)). It permits the children who could have represented the successor now judicially divested of his rights to succeed despite the cause for which their ancestor's rights are divested and despite his having survived the decedent. *Civil Code Article 973 (1870) permits such children to take only in their own right. Thus they would be excluded by a first-degree descendent in the absence of this Article.* (Emphasis added.)
>
> An example of the application of this Article is as follows: The decedent is survived by two sons, A and B. A has participated in the intentional murder of the decedent, but A has a son, C, who is totally innocent and blameless in the affair.

In the absence of the provisions contained in this Article, when A is declared unworthy, his one-half interest in the estate is inherited entirely and exclusively by his surviving brother, B, and the innocent grandchild C inherits nothing. Under the provisions of this Article, C would inherit ahead of A's co-heirs of the same degree. (Emphasis added.)

The clear and expressed changes in the new law lend further support for the interpretation given to the old law by Professors Swaim and Lorio and adopted by the trial court. We are sympathetic to the plaintiffs, because although the new law has been changed to remedy the unfortunate application of the old law, the old law is nevertheless applicable to their claim and we are constrained to follow it. Based on that application, there is no genuine issue of material fact and defendants are entitled to judgment as a matter of law, based on the unworthiness of Shanda Crain.

In light of the foregoing, it is unnecessary to address plaintiffs' arguments that the trial court erred in finding the renunciations are valid and in refusing to declare them null. Whether the renunciations are valid or invalid, the children may not inherit via representation through their mother, a living heir, albeit unworthy, since there are other heirs in the first degree.

Accordingly, for the reasons assigned, we find no error in the judgment of the trial court, and that judgment is hereby affirmed. Costs of this appeal are assessed to the plaintiffs.

AFFIRMED.

* * *

HYPOTHETICAL

COMplete, This Hypo!

Adam and his six cousins, David, Eric, Frank, Harry, Ivan, and Jack, all gathered at their Uncle Charles' home in order to draft players for their family fantasy football league. David, Eric, and Frank are Charles' children. Harry, Ivan and Jack are the children of Adam's predeceased Uncle Greg. Adam's parents are also deceased.

Over the course of the draft, Adam and his Uncle Charles got into a heated argument, which ultimately culminated in an altercation. At one point during the altercation, Uncle Charles said to his nephew the following, "I WILL END YOU BOY." The two men ultimately beat each other to a pulp, and Adam died as a result of his wounds.

The children, shocked at what they just witnessed, reported Charles to the relevant authorities and the District Attorney hastily filed a bill of information for murder in the 2nd degree. Charles was indicted, but is vigorously defending his actions on the basis of self-defense.

Upon Adam's death, his cousins learned that he owned 50 shares of stock in a corporation formed by several of his classmates when he was an engineering student. The corporation created a design for a concussion-reducing helmet for football players and had been purchased by the National Football League. As a result, Adam's estate is worth $100,000.

Adam died intestate and Charles has opened his succession.

a)   Harry, Ivan, and Jack have brought an action to have Charles declared unworthy to succeed to Adam. What must they prove to be successful? What is the standard of proof? What if Charles can prove he acted in self-defense? How will Adam's estate be distributed?

b)   During the course of the succession proceedings, Layla, Adam's long-time girlfriend, claims that she is pregnant with Adam's child and is due in six months. She had not even told Adam before his death. Can the child take in Adam's succession? Will your answer to part a) change?

Bring a filiation claim to have the unborn child take in Adam's succession.

CHAPTER 7:
ACCEPTANCE AND RENUNCIATION
La. C.C. 947-967, 1415-29

Introduction

The revision of succession and donations law provided by Act 1421 of 1997, effective July 1, 1999, includes a revision of the articles addressing the acceptance and renunciation of successions. Chapter 6 of Title I of Book III contains the new articles. Some of the articles are mere restatements of the previous law, others use different terminology for similar concepts, and some significantly alter the law relating to the acceptance and renunciation of successions.

La. C.C. 947 provides that "a successor is not obligated to accept rights to succeed. He may accept some of those rights and renounce others." However, a minor is deemed to accept rights to succeed although his legal representative may renounce on behalf of the minor if expressly authorized to do so by the court. La. C.C. 948. There are two prerequisites to the acceptance or renunciation of a succession. First, a successor may not accept or renounce rights to succeed prior to the death of the decedent. La. C.C. 949. Second, the successor must know of the death of the decedent and know he has rights to succeed; Although, he need not know the extent of those rights or even the nature of his relationship to the decedent. La. C.C. 950.

Any act of acceptance or renunciation that is premature is null. La. C.C. 951. Also null is an acceptance or renunciation under the laws of intestacy if a testament is subsequently probated, or under a testament if the testament is later annulled or the rights are altered by a subsequent testament or codicil. La. C.C. 952.

Acceptance: La. C.C. 957-962

Under the law as provided in the Civil Code of 1870, a successor could accept simply and unconditionally, rendering him personally liable for his pro-rata share of the decedent's debts La. C.C. 988, 1013 (1870) (repealed), or he could accept under benefit of inventory, shielding him from personal liability to the decedent's creditors and thus risking only the value of the assets in the estate. La. C.C. 1032 (1870) (repealed). The simple acceptance could be either express or tacit. La. C.C. 988 (1870) (repealed). Due to the relatively informal nature of the latter, heirs often found themselves in the dangerous position of having unintentionally rendered themselves personally liable to the creditors of the decedent. To protect heirs from this harsh result, the Louisiana legislature passed Act 602 of 1986, adding La. R.S. 9:1421 to the Civil Code ancillaries, providing for an extension of the security of benefit of inventory "where an inventory or descriptive list" had been executed. This protection has been continued in the revision of 1997 and been placed in the Civil Code articles.

The revision by Act 1421 of 1997, effective July 1, 1999, replaces the terms "express" and "tacit" with "formal" and "informal," La. C.C. 957, although the Revision Comment to article 957 represents that the change is purely a "change of terminology," not intended to change the law. *See* Cynthia Samuel, *The 1997 Successions and Donations Revision – a Critique in Honor of A.N. Yiannopolous*, 73 Tul. L. Rev. 1041 (1999), partially reproduced below.

La. C.C. 957 defines a formal acceptance as one where "the successor expressly accepts in writing or assumes the quality of successor in a judicial proceeding" and an informal acceptance as one where "the successor does some act that clearly implies his intention to accept."

The following cases illustrate the interpretation rendered by the courts with regard to "tacit" acceptance. As the intention in the revision was to merely rename this form of acceptance as "informal," some of the analysis could be used today.

BRADLEY v. UNION NATIONAL LIFE INSURANCE COMPANY
359 So. 2d 663 (La. App. 1st Cir. 1978)

LANDRY, Judge.

* * *

Decedent died possessed of movable property and possibly a one-half interest in a house. The movable property consisted of household effects totaling about three rooms of furniture, personal effects and clothing and some inexpensive jewelry.

Following her mother's death, Appellant took possession and control of decedent's movable effects. Appellant gave decedent's clothing to the decedent's sisters and kept the furniture for herself. At the time of trial, Appellant was using the furniture and claimed it as her own. No succession proceedings were instituted concerning decedent's estate.

* * *

In determining whether a succession has been tacitly accepted, the intent of the person must be considered along with his actions. We have no hesitancy in concluding that Appellant has tacitly accepted his mother's succession. Appellant herein took possession of decedent's movable assets and exercised undisputed acts of ownership with respect thereto. Appellant disposed of decedent's clothing as though it were Appellant's own. Appellant has appropriated to her own use decedent's furniture which Appellant frankly stated she considered as Appellant's property. Appellant has never opened decedent's succession.

* * *

REED v. TAYLOR
522 So. 2d 1262 (La. App. 4th Cir. 1988)

PLOTKIN, Judge.

The issue in this case is whether a creditor can secure a personal judgment for reimbursement of a decedent's debts against the sole heir of an unopened solvent succession.

Plaintiffs, Mr. and Mrs. Lloyd Reed, seek recovery of monies allegedly expended on behalf of Albert James Taylor Jr. (Mr. Taylor, Jr.), father of defendant Albert James Taylor III, for funeral expenses, medical expenses, food and mortgage payments.

Defendant's grandmother, Mrs. Mary Jackson Taylor Herron (Mrs. Herron), died intestate on November 15, 1983, leaving only a residence located on North Robertson Street, where she had lived for several years with her son, Mr. Taylor Jr. Following her death, Mr. Taylor, Jr., Mrs. Herron's sole heir, continued to occupy the house until he died on February 15, 1986. He never opened or renounced his mother's succession.

On July 15, 1986, the defendant formally opened and was placed into legal possession of his grandmother's succession. At that time, he paid off the mortgage on the immovable property. Defendant has not opened his father's succession, but occupies the property on North Robertson Street.

* * *

The defendant admitted at trial that he had had little to do with his father during the last years of his life. He said they didn't get along, so he avoided him. He also stated that he had nothing to do with the funeral arrangements and admitted that he had not attended the funeral.

The trial judge awarded plaintiffs $4,336.58--$2,076.35 for mortgage payments, $1,468.49 for burial expenses, $291.74 for medical expenses and $500 for the cost of food and maintenance. In his reasons for judgment, he stated that the defendant obligated himself to pay the debts of his late father when he accepted and occupied the house, which was the only asset of the successions of both Mrs. Herron and Mr. Taylor Jr. He held that the defendant was responsible for his father's obligations, even though he had not opened his father succession, because under Louisiana law, succession property passes to regular heirs at the moment of death. La.C.C.art. 940.

* * *

Obviously, the defendant attempted to avoid liability for his father's debts by "skipping" Mr. Taylor Jr.'s succession and accepting only his grandmother's succession. However, the applicable Civil Code articles state that when the defendant formally opened his grandmother's succession and had himself legally placed in possession of his grandmother's house, he tacitly accepted his father's succession as well.

La.C.C. art. 934 provides that all successions become open by death or presumption of death caused by long absence. Therefore, even though Mr. Taylor Jr. never formally opened his mother's succession, it became open by operation of law at the moment of her death. At that point, under the provisions of La.C.C. art. 940, Mr. Taylor Jr. acquired the assets of his mother's succession. La.C.C. art. 940 states that "[a] succession is acquired by the legal heir, who is called by law to the inheritance, immediately after the death of the deceased person to whom he succeeds."

Under the Civil Code articles, simple acceptance of a succession may be either express or tacit. La.C.C. art. 988. Tacit acceptance occurs when the heir performs some act which necessarily supposes his intention to accept, and which he would have no right to do but in his capacity as heir. *Id.* Any act of ownership, which can be legally performed by a person only in his capacity as heir, "supposes necessarily his acceptance, for to act as owner is to make himself heir." La.C.C. art. 994. Therefore, when Mr. Taylor Jr. acted as owner of his mother's property after her death, he accepted her succession tacitly and made himself her heir. Likewise, when the defendant had himself put in legal possession of the only asset of his father's succession, he expressly and/or tacitly accepted his father's succession, and made himself his father's heir. The fact that he tried to "skip" his father's succession, and thus avoid his father's debts, does not change this result.

*   *   *

SUCCESSION OF MENENDEZ
248 La. 488, 115 So. 2d 829 (1959)

SIMON, Justice.

On February 3, 1957, Mrs. Marie Louise Menendez died leaving as her sole heirs her children, Dr. Anthony M. Menendez, Mrs. Pauline Menendez Salzer, Dr. Joseph C. Menendez, Louis R. Menendez, Mrs. Anita Menendez Sierra, Mrs. Velma Menendez Haydel and Miss Alice Mary Menendez. On February 12, 1957, Dr. Anthony M. Menendez, one of the appellees herein, filed a petition and obtained an authorization to search for a will and to make an inventory of the effects of his mother's estate. On February 20, 1957, his sisters, hereinabove named, obtained the probate of the decedent's will in olographic form therein appointing Miss Alice Mary Menendez as testamentary executrix and bequeathing to her an extra portion. In due course an inventory of the effects of the decedent was completed and filed for homologation. At the insistence of Dr. Anthony M. Menendez and his brother, Louis R. Menendez, the co-appellee herein, the Notary preparing the inventory included therein certain described real property and jewelry which had previously been conveyed by the decedent to the testamentary executrix, Mrs. Anita Menendez Sierra and a grandchild, Edwin Salzer, Jr., the son of Mrs. Pauline Menendez Salzer.

*   *   *

Article 988 of the Civil Code-LSA provides that the acceptance of a succession may be expressed or tacit. "It is tacit, when some act is done by the heir, which necessarily supposes his intention to accept, and which he would have no right to do but in his quality of heir." The only acts which appellees performed were:

1. Dr. Anthony M. Menendez instituted these proceedings by petitioning the District Court to search for a last will and testament and to inventory the effects left by the decedent.
2. Dr. Anthony M. Menendez and his brother, Louis R. Menendez, executed the inventory.
3. They also appeared and opposed a rule to show cause filed by the Testamentary Executrix why certain properties should not be removed from the inventory.
4. They opposed all of the final account with the exception of the payment of notarial and appraisal fees.

In *Succession of Hart*, 52 La.Ann. 364, 27 So. 69, this Court held (quoting from Syllabus No. 3 by the Court) that: "The mere reference to themselves as 'children and heirs' of a deceased person, made in a petition by his children asking for the probate of his will, and the placing of his succession under administration of executors selected by him, is not an unconditional acceptance of his succession." The petition by appellees to search for a will and the execution of the inventory, therefore, were not a tacit acceptance of the succession. The other two actions of appellees not only were not a tacit acceptance of the succession but an indication that they had no intention of accepting until the question of simulation or collation was finally judicially determined.

*   *   *

McCLELLAND v. CLAY
444 So. 2d 639 (La. App. 5th Cir. 1984)

CHEHARDY, Judge.

This is a suit on a note for $5,266.06 executed by the late Isaac Clay in favor of his concubine Gloria Landry McClelland. Mrs. McClelland instituted this suit against decedent's brother Joseph Bobby Clay, claiming he unconditionally accepted his brother's succession, and therefore is liable on the note.

Following trial, judgment was granted in favor of plaintiff. Defendant has appealed.

The record reflects the following facts:

After the death of his brother Isaac, defendant signed an agreement with the undertaker to pay the funeral expenses.

Defendant paid these expenses by withdrawing funds from a bank account belonging to his late parents which was used as a fund whereby various family members would withdraw funds as needed and repay the money at a later date. The fund operated as an interest-free loan for the family when necessary.

Several days after the death defendant found out that his brother had a $20,000 life insurance policy at his place of employment and that defendant was the named beneficiary. He collected the proceeds of the policy and repaid the family fund for the money he had withdrawn to pay the funeral expenses.

Mrs. McClelland had anticipated that she would be named beneficiary. When defendant failed to give her any of the proceeds she instituted this suit on the note.

In finding for the plaintiff the trial judge held that acceptance of the proceeds of the life insurance policy and payment of the funeral expenses out of a fund which belonged partially to the decedent constituted unconditional acceptance of the succession.

The trial judge recognized his error, and plaintiff now concedes that the proceeds of a life insurance policy form no part of the estate when the policy is made payable to a designated beneficiary. LSA-R.S. 22:647, 648, 649; *Succession of Dumestre*, 174 La. 482, 141 So. 35 (1932).

Neither are such proceeds liable for decedent's debts, subject to community rights or to reduction or collation. *Ticker v. Metropolitan Life Insurance Co.*, 11 Orl.App. 59 (1914).

However, the trial court refused to grant a new trial because of payment of the funeral expenses from the family fund, which he found constituted unconditional acceptance of the succession.

The acceptance of a succession is a question of fact, as clearly disclosed by Article 988 of the revised Civil Code:

The simple acceptance may be either express or tacit.

It is express, when the heir assumes the quality of heir in an unqualified manner, in some authentic or private instrument, or in some judicial proceeding.

It is tacit, when some act is done by the heir, which necessarily supposes his intention to accept, and which he would have no right to do but in his quality of heir.

There must be an intention to accept. LSA-C.C. art. 989. And Article 990 recites, "It is necessary that the intention should be united to the fact, or rather manifested by the fact, in order that the acceptance be inferred."

The acceptance of a succession by heirs must appear in terms so clear as to leave no doubt regarding intention to accept under full responsibilities attaching to acceptance. *Vuillemont v. Gonsulin*, 134 So. 419 (La.App. 1st Cir.1931).

While the acceptance of a succession may be established against an heir by proof of payment of its debts by him, the payment of funeral expenses does not constitute acceptance.

C.C. art. 1001 provides:

An act of piety or humanity towards one's relations is not considered an acceptance; it is not therefore an acceptance to take care of the burial of the decease [deceased], or to pay the funeral expenses, even without protestation.

The fact that defendant paid for the funeral expenses with money used by all of the family for emergencies does not imply to us a tacit acceptance of the succession. The funds belonged to the deceased parents and apparently no succession had ever been opened. It is also possible decedent himself may have used the fund and actually owed it money.

There is insufficient evidence in the record to indicate that defendant's actions constituted an unconditional acceptance of his brother's succession.

For the reasons assigned the judgment appealed from is reversed, and it is now ordered that there be judgment in favor of defendant Joseph Bobby Clay and against plaintiff Gloria Landry McClelland dismissing her suit.

Cost in this court is to be paid by appellee.

REVERSED.

BREUX v. COZY COTTAGES, LLC
151 So. 3d 183, 187-89 (La. App. 3d Cir. 2014)

SAUNDERS, Judge.

This is a case involving a dispute over title to immovable property located in Cameron Parish, Louisiana. Two parties claim title to the same tract of land from two separate chains of title. Samuel R. Breaux, II (hereafter "Plaintiff") filed suit for declaratory judgment against Cozy Cottages, LLC (hereafter "Cozy Cottages"), seeking recognition of his right of ownership.

This case revolves around a title dispute over Lot 8, located in the Edmond Doiron Subdivision in Cameron Parish (hereafter "the property"). Lot 8 of the Edmond Doiron Subdivision in Cameron Parish came into being in 1883 when Edmond Doiron's children partitioned his property. His son, Edward Doiron, received Lot 8. Edward Doiron had ten children. One of them was Antoine Doiron. Antoine Doiron had no children, but was married to Mary Viola Doiron, who had a son, Lawrence Marsh.

Antoine Doiron died testate in 1952. His testament, executed on March 31, 1949, provided that his wife, Mary Viola Doiron, be given "use, enjoyment, rents, royalties, and income of and from all lands owned by me, or in which I may have an interest, in Cameron Parish, Louisiana, to have and to hold the same for her and during her natural life." The next paragraph of the testament provided that the "reversion and remainder of my lands above mentioned, from and after the decease [sic] of my said wife, to my brothers and sisters, in fee simple, share and share alike." A judgment of possession was signed on November 15, 1952, which decreed that Antoine Doiron's wife, Mary Viola Doiron, be "sent into possession, as owner, of the use and usufruct, and all emoluments, issuing and emanating from the rent, royalties, and incomes from that certain property, left by the deceased in Cameron Parish, Louisiana." Then, the property is described. Finally, the next paragraph orders that Antoine Doiron's widow "be sent into possession, as owner, of the above estate, free and clear of any inheritance tax."

Antoine Doiron's wife, Mary Viola Doiron, died in 1983. In 1988 and 1989, the Cameron Parish Tax Assessor's office sent notices of a tax sale in the name of the Viola Doiron Estate. It is undisputed that the notices were sent through Lawrence Marsh, the son of Mary Viola Doiron, who was the tax sale purchaser.

Lawrence Marsh was married to Mabel Marsh, and their son is Robert Marsh. Lawrence Marsh's testament willed his entire estate to his wife, Mabel. After Lawrence Marsh died, Mabel Marsh and Robert Marsh sold their interest in the property to Plaintiff.

Cozy Cottages claims title to the property at issue from a completely different chain of title, beginning with persons named Clarville Doiron and Isaac Doiron. Clarville Doiron sold part of the property to Clarence Turner on October 18, 1949. Isaac Doiron sold part of the property to Clarence Turner on March 22, 1958. The record contains no information as to who these persons may be or the source of their title. From the sales to Clarence Turner, the property changed hands multiple times, eventually leading to the purchase by Cozy Cottages from Richard, Jessica, and Marion Abshire, and the Abshire's company, Richcore Enterprises, in 2008. It is from this complicated set of facts that this dispute arises.

Plaintiff filed suit for declaratory judgment, claiming title to the property at issue following his purchase in 2005. Cozy Cottages claims an interest in the same property, following its purchase in 2008 from the Abshires and Richcore Enterprises. Cozy Cottages purchased title insurance from Chicago Title Insurance Company (hereafter "Chicago Title") in conjunction with its 2008 purchase of the property. Through the course of several supplemental and amended third-party petitions, Cozy Cottages filed third-party demands against Chicago Title, seeking defense of Plaintiff's claims against it or damages, and damages for failing to cure additional defects in the title. All parties filed separate motions for summary judgment.

In its motion for summary judgment, Chicago Title sought dismissal of Cozy Cottages' claims against it, asserting: Plaintiff has no claims against Cozy Cottages because the tax sales were absolute nullities for failure to give all owners notice of the tax sale, thus, Cozy Cottages has no claims against Chicago Title.

*   *   *

Cozy Cottages also filed a motion for summary judgment seeking dismissal of Plaintiff's claims against it, asserting that Plaintiff has no interest in the property because the tax sales were absolute nullities for failure to provide all owners with notice of the tax sale. All parties' motions for summary judgment were denied.

Chicago Title and Cozy Cottages filed separate writ applications, both requesting review of the trial court's denial of their respective motions for summary judgment seeking to have the other ones claims against their respective Title's dismissed. Because there is an issue common to both writ applications [whether the tax sales were absolute nullity's for failure to give all owners notice] we consolidate the two writs and address them in a single opinion. We find the trial court did not err in failing to grant either motion for summary judgment and, thus, deny these writs.

Nullity of the tax sales

Chicago Title and Cozy Cottages maintain summary judgment dismissing the claims of Plaintiff is appropriate because notice of the tax sale was not given to the siblings of Antoine Doiron, the alleged naked owners of the property. Although there is no dispute that the siblings of Antoine Doiron or the heirs of the siblings of Antoine Doiron were not notified of the pending tax sale, we find summary judgment inappropriate on this issue.

Notice of a tax sale to the property owner is a prerequisite to the validity of the tax sale. Failure to give the requisite notice is a violation of Due Process and the subsequent tax sale is an absolute nullity. *Quantum Res. Mgmt.,* 112 So. 3d 209. However, the notice requirement announced in *Mennonite Board of Missions v. Adams,* 462 U.S. 791, 103 S.Ct. 2706, 77 L.Ed.2d 180 (1983), will not serve to retroactively undo prescription that has already accrued. *Quantum Res. Mgmt.,* 112 So. 3d 209.

Antoine Doiron died in 1952. All succession rights are "governed by the law in effect on the date of the decedent's death." La. Civ. Code art. 870(B). At the time of his death, former La. Civ. Code art. 1030 (1870), provided a prescriptive period of thirty years for acceptance or renunciation of a succession. Prescription began to run at the death of the testator. *Sun Oil Co. v. Tarver,* 219 La. 103, 52 So. 2d 437 (1951). The heir that failed to accept or renounce within the thirty-year period "bec[ame] a stranger to the succession," 10 La. Civ. L. Treatise, *Successions and Donations* § 7.11 (1995), and "[could] neither accept nor renounce." *Id.* at n. 21 (citing *Sun Oil Co.,* 52 So. 2d 437). Former La. Civ. Code art. 1030 was still in effect in 1982, when the prescriptive period accrued.

Under the prior law, an heir was able to expressly or tacitly accept a succession. *See* La. Civ. Code art. 988 (1870). Express acceptance occurred "when the heir assume[d] the quality of heir in an unqualified manner, in some authentic or private instrument, or in some judicial proceeding." *Id.*; *See also Succession of Blanchard,* 243 So. 2d 329, 332–33 (La. App. 4 Cir.1971). Tacit acceptance occurred "when some act [was] done by the heir, which necessarily supposes his intention to accept, and which he would have no right to do but in his quality of heir." La. Civ. Code art. 988 (1870); *Blanchard,* 243 So. 2d at 333. "Not only the person who is entitled to an inheritance may accept it, but if he dies before having expressly or tacitly accepted or rejected it, **his heir shall have a right to accept it under him.** La. C.C. art. 1007 [(1870)]." *In re Succession of Moore,* 97–1668, 97–1669, p. 16 (La. App. 4 Cir. 4/1/98), 737 So. 2d 749, 758, *writ denied,* 99–0781 (La.4/30/99), 743 So. 2d 207. Intent to accept was required. La. Civ. Code arts. 990 and 991(1870). Under the prior law, renunciation of a succession was not presumed. La. Civ. Code art. 1017 (1870). Renunciation must have been expressly made in authentic form. *Id.* Renunciation may have also occurred by pleading it in a judicial proceeding or by failing to accept or renounce within thirty years of the death of the ancestor. 10 La. Civ. L. Treatise, *Successions and Donations* § 7.8 (1995).

Under the current law, an heir may still expressly or tacitly accept a succession, although the terminology has changed to formal or informal acceptance. La. Civ. Code art. 957. Formal acceptance occurs when the successor "expressly accepts in writing or assumes the quality of successor in a judicial proceeding." *Id.* Informal acceptance occurs when the successor takes an action which implies the intention to accept. *Id.* Intent to accept is still required. *See* La. Civ. Code arts. 957 and 958. Currently, acceptance is presumed, La. Civ. Code art. 962, and renunciation must be express and in writing, although it is no longer required to be in authentic form, La. Civ. Code art. 963. *Compare* La. Civ. Code art. 1017 (1870).

Whether or not the tax sales were null turns on whether Antoine Doiron's siblings were entitled to notice. Under the former law, this depends on whether they were actually naked owners of the property, which turns on whether they, or their heirs, accepted, renounced, or renounced by failing to accept or renounce the succession within thirty years. Under the current law, it also turns on whether the heirs accepted or renounced the succession. Under both the prior and current law, if the siblings of Antoine Doiron accepted the succession, then they were naked owners and entitled to notice of the tax sale. Since they did not receive notice, then the tax sales would be absolute nullities, and Plaintiff's claims fail. However, if they renounced, under both the prior and current law, or failed to accept or renounce within the thirty-year prescriptive period, under the prior law, then they were not naked owners and, therefore, not entitled to notice of the pending tax sale. If they were not entitled to notice, then Plaintiff may indeed have an interest in the property.

Although the record indicates that the siblings of Antoine Doiron did not participate in the succession proceeding of their deceased brother, they were not required to do so in order to accept or renounce the succession. Under both the former and current law, acts of ownership may suffice to constitute acceptance. La. Civ. Code art. 994 (1870); La. Civ. Code art. 959. Leasing or occupying the succession property, execution of a deed, and donation, sale, or assignment of succession rights have been held to constitute tacit acceptance. 10 La.Civ. L. Treatise, *Successions and Donations* § 7.7 (1995). Even granting another co-heir permission to occupy the property has been held to constitute tacit acceptance. *Id.* at n. 9 (citing *Succession of Blanchard,* 243 So. 2d 329 (La. App. 4 Cir.1971)). From the record before us, we cannot determine whether the siblings of Antoine Doiron, or their heirs, accepted or renounced the succession of Antoine Doiron. There is no evidence in the record concerning either. All that is known is that it is undisputed the siblings of Antoine Doiron did not formally participate in the succession proceedings.

Finally, "issues pertaining to subjective facts such as intent, knowledge, motive, malice, or good faith are usually not appropriate to a summary judgment determination." *Murphy's Lease & Welding Serv., Inc. v. Bayou Concessions Salvage, Inc.,* 00–978, 00–979, p. 6 (La.App. 3 Cir. 3/8/01), 780 So. 2d 1284, 1289, *writ denied,* 01–1005 (La.6/1/01), 793 So. 2d 195. Thus, even if Cozy Cottages and Chicago Title could point to some evidence in the record of an act that might indicate Antoine Doiron's siblings accepted the succession, summary judgment would nonetheless be inappropriate as the intent of the act must be explored at trial. Therefore, we conclude that a genuine issue of material fact exists on this issue, precluding a finding that Plaintiff has no ownership interest in the property at issue. Thus, the trial court's denial of Chicago Title's and Cozy Cottages' motions for summary judgment seeking a determination that the tax sales were absolute nullities was not in error.

*   *   *

For the reasons above, we conclude the trial court did not err in denying Chicago Title's and Cozy Cottages' motions for summary judgment and, therefore, deny these writs.

WRITS DENIED.

NOTE

As mentioned above, heirs who have filed an inventory or descriptive list have been shielded from personal liability for a decedent's debts since the effective date of La. R.S. 9:1421 as enacted by Act No. 602 of 1986. Found to be substantive in nature, the statute has been held to apply prospectively only. *Genusa v. Dominique,* 708 So. 2d 784 (La. App. 1st Cir. 1998).

After the 1997 revision, effective July 1, 1999, La. C.C. 961 now provides that acceptance obligates a successor to pay estate debts in accordance with Title II of Book I of the Civil Code and other applicable laws. La. C.C. 1416, found in Title II, protects universal successors by limiting their liability to creditors of the estate for payment of estate debts "in proportion to the part which each [successor] has in the succession only to the extent of the property received by him, valued as of the time of receipt." Since all successors are protected from personal liability, it is presumed that they have accepted succession rights, unless they specifically renounce. La. C.C. 962.

La. R.S. 9:1421 therefore became unnecessary and was repealed as part of the initial revision. Due to an apparent oversight, however, La. R.S. 9:1421 was not actually repealed as part of the initial revision, but was repealed by Act 572 of 2001.

Attempted Renunciation Deemed Acceptance: La. C.C. 960

The following cases deal with an attempted renunciation of a succession, which can be deemed to be an acceptance. Today, this principle is found in La. C.C. 960, which provides that a renunciation is deemed to be an acceptance "to the extent if causes the renounced rights to devolve in a manner other than that provided by law or by the testament if the decedent died testate." The law disfavors parties altering the natural or expressed order of succession. While a successor may accept and donate to whomever he wishes, he cannot renounce with direction on who should succeed unless the law would naturally so provide.

AURIENNE v. MT. OLIVET
135 La. 451, 96 So. 29 (1923)
[23 Tul. L. Rev. 254 (1948); 7 Loy. L. Rev. 35 (1953)]

O'NEILL, J.

The question presented in this case is whether a certain instrument, purporting to be a renunciation of an inheritance, is, in reality, an act of donation. The plaintiffs are the sons and daughters, forced heirs, of Peter Aurienne, deceased. The prayer of the petition is for a reduction of the so-called donation, to what is alleged to have been the disposable portion of the estate. The suit was dismissed on an exception of no cause of action; and the plaintiffs have appealed.

We reproduce the document in question, which was produced by the plaintiffs in response to a prayer for oyer, viz.:

No. 250. June 14, 1902.

Renunciation of Rights in the Succession of Adele Aurianne by Edward and Peter Aurianne in Favor of Their Sister, Marie Aurianne.

State of Louisiana, Parish of Orleans, City of New Orleans.

Be it known that, on the fourteenth day of June, in the year one thousand nine hundred and two, before me, William B. Barnett, a notary public, in and for the city and parish of Orleans, state of Louisiana, aforesaid, duly commissioned and qualified, and in the presence of the witnesses hereinafter named and undersigned, personally appeared Edward Aurianne and Peter Aurianne, both residents of this city, who severally declared that, for and in consideration of the love and affection and kind treatment they bear towards their sister, Miss Marie Aurianne, and relative to the same, that they hereby renounce, relinquish, assign, transfer and set over in favor of their sister, Miss Marie Aurianne, All the right, title, claim, interest and ownership whatsoever, in and to the succession of their late sister, Adele Aurianne, deceased; Intending and understanding that our sister, Marie Aurianne, shall have full authority, right and power to dispose of our rights, titles and interest in and to the above and herein described succession, as she, the said Marie Aurianne, may think proper. For the notification of these presents, to whom it may concern, full power and authority is hereby given unto our said sister, Marie Aurianne, bearer of this, hereby consenting that this present renunciation shall have its full force and effect. To have and to hold our said rights, title and interest in and to the above herein described and named succession unto our said sister, Marie Aurianne, her heirs and assigns, forever. And the said Marie Aurianne, also a resident of this city, being present, hereby acknowledges due delivery and possession of the above and herein named

7-11

succession. Thus done and passed in the city of New Orleans, in the presence of Jean Moulou and John P. Montamat, competent witnesses, residing in this city, who hereunto sign their names, with said appearers and me, notary, on the day and date set forth in the caption hereof.

It is admitted in plaintiffs' petition that Edward, Peter and Marie Aurienne (or Aurianne, as the name is spelled in the instrument) were the only heirs at law of their deceased sister, Adele Aurienne. The effect, therefore, of the renunciation-if it was a renunciation-was to make Marie Aurienne the sole heir of her sister.

It is virtually conceded by the learned counsel for appellant-in fact it must be conceded-that the petition in this case does not disclose a cause of action if the instrument in question was a renunciation, not a donation. Plaintiffs do not claim that they have the right, which is given by article 1021 of the Civil Code to creditors of a person who has renounced an inheritance, to accept it to the extent of their claims; and we express no opinion as to whether plaintiffs, as forced heirs, ever had any such right. By the prayer of their petition, they affirm the act of their father, except in so far as it may have disposed of their alleged legitime. It is sufficient to say that a renunciation of an inheritance, unlike a donation, is not subject to reduction at the instance of the forced heirs of the heir who has renounced. The Civil Code (article 977) declares that no one can be compelled to accept a succession, whether acquired by testament or by operation of law.

The doubt as to whether the instrument in question was intended to be a renunciation or a donation arises only from the redundancy in the instrument-which, by the way, seems to be a characteristic of notarial acts-in containing after the word "renounce," the words "relinquish, assign, transfer and set over." In its caption, the instrument is styled a "renunciation;" and that is what we believe, quite firmly, it was intended to be. No reason could be given for supposing that the two heirs who made the renunciation intended to accept the succession and thereby to make themselves liable for the obligations of the deceased, without any compensating advantage whatever to themselves. Aside from the presumption which we refer to, the case comes clearly within the rules established by the Civil Code. Article 1002 declares that a donation or sale or assignment made by an heir, of his right of inheritance, whether made to a stranger or to a coheir, or to coheirs, is to be considered an acceptance of the inheritance, on the part of the donor, seller, or assignor. And article 1003 declares that the same may be said of a renunciation-meaning, of course, that a pretended renunciation may also be said to be an acceptance on the part of the heir who pretends to renounce-if the so-styled renunciation be made in favor of one or more of the coheirs, even though it be made gratuitously, or if it be made for a price or consideration, even though it be made to all of the coheirs indiscriminately. The reason for those provisions of the Code is that the law itself has said what shall become of an inheritance which an heir has renounced. Article 1022 declares that it shall go to the coheirs of the same degree, or, if there be none, to those next in rank. And article 994 declares that, if an heir exercises any act of ownership of an inheritance, which he has no right to exercise except in his capacity of heir, he is supposed to have accepted the inheritance, and thereby to have acknowledged himself an heir of the deceased. Carrying out those general provisions of the law, and making them more specific, article 1003 merely forbids an heir to divert the established destiny of an inheritance which he renounces. If the heir exercises his right to say what disposition shall be made of his inheritance-which right can be exercised only in his capacity as an heir-he thereby accepts the inheritance and declares himself an heir; or, if he sells his inheritance to his coheirs indiscriminately, and receives from them a price in lieu of his inheritance-which, of course, he cannot do except in his capacity as an heir-he thereby accepts the inheritance and declares himself an heir. The first clause in article 1003, mentioning a gratuitous renunciation made by an heir "in favor of one or more of his coheirs," means, of course, in favor of any number less than all of the coheirs, because the next clause in the same article makes provision for a renunciation made "in favor of all his coheirs indistinctly," (meaning indiscriminately, the French word, in the Code of 1825, being indistinctement). Articles 1002 and 1003 were translated literally from article 780 of the Code Napoleon, viz.:

> Art. 1002. The donation, sale or assignment, which one of the coheirs makes or rights of inheritance, either to a stranger or to his coheirs, is considered to be, on his part, an acceptance of the inheritance.

> Art. 1003. The same may be said, 1st, of the renunciation, even if gratuitous, which is made by one of the heirs in favor of one or more of his coheirs; and, 2d, of the renunciation which he makes in favor of all his coheirs indistinctly, when he receives the price of this renunciation.

The French writers saw no doubt about the meaning of article 780 of their Code. Laurent, vol. 9, p. 375, says that, if a renunciation be made in favor of all of the coheirs of the heir renouncing, the naming of the beneficiaries in the act of renunciation does not make the act an acceptance and donation of the inheritance; because, in such case, the heir who renounces merely declares the effect to be what the law itself declares it shall be. And the author adds: "Such is the unanimous opinion of the authors, ancient and modern." Baudry-Lancantinerie, vol. 2, p. 103, says that, when an heir renounces the inheritance in favor of all his coheirs, he may name them in the act of renunciation, without thereby making his renunciation an acceptance and donation of the inheritance, because, by naming the beneficiaries of the renunciation, the heir who renounces merely declares that his renunciation shall have the effect which the law itself gives it. And the author says that that is true, "even if the act of renunciation be declared to be dictated by an intention of good will towards the person called to benefit by the renunciation." That statement is pertinent to the argument of the learned counsel for appellants, that the act now under consideration was a donation because it was declared to have been made "for and in consideration of the love and affection and kind treatment," which the renouncers bore towards their sister, the beneficiary of the renunciation. The reason why such a consideration does not, of itself, make the so-called renunciation a donation is that such a consideration is not regarded as a price; and article 1003, in terms, declares that it is only "when he receives the price of this renunciation,' that an heir's renunciation in favor of all of his coheirs shall be 'considered to be, on his part, an acceptance of the inheritance." In other words, a renunciation made in consideration only of love and affection for the beneficiary or beneficiaries, or as a matter of gratitude, is not to be considered as made for a price, or for value received.

The controlling feature of this case is that the renunciation was made in favor of the only remaining coheir. If there had been other coheirs, or one other coheir, not named as a beneficiary of the renunciation, the renunciation would not have been made to all of the coheirs indiscriminately, and, therefore, according to the precise language of article 1003 of the Code, the so-called renunciation would have been an acceptance of the succession and, in turn, a donation of it.

It is argued on behalf of appellants that their father could not make a valid renunciation at the time when he signed the act in question, because the succession of Adele Aurienne, although she was dead, had not been formally opened by any judicial mortuary proceedings. The learned counsel for appellants cites and relies upon articles 978, 979, 984 and 1887 of the Civil Code, and the ruling in *Succession of Jacobs*, 104 La. 447, 29 South. 241. The ruling in the case cited was that the mother of the deceased Jacobs could not have renounced during his lifetime her right of inheritance as his forced heir. The articles of the Code, referred to, declare merely that a person cannot accept or renounce the succession of a living person. Article 978 says that, for an heir to be able to accept a succession, it is necessary that the succession should be open by the death of the person who is to be succeeded. Article 979 repeats that a person cannot accept a succession before it has fallen to him. Article 984 says that an acceptance or rejection made by an heir, before the succession is opened or left, is absolutely null and can produce no effect, but that it does not prevent the heir who has thus accepted from accepting or rejecting validly when his right so to do is complete. In the expression, "opened or left," the words "opened" and "left" are synonymous. That is made certain by reference to article 934, which declares that a succession, whether testamentary or legal, or irregular, becomes "open" by death, or by the presumption of death in the cases in which long absence establishes such presumption. Article 1887, under the title of Conventional Obligations, declares "future things may be the object of an obligation," and immediately makes the exception, "one cannot, however, renounce the succession of an estate not yet devolved, nor can any stipulation be made with regard to such a succession, even with the consent of him whose succession is in question." We are not aware of any authority, either in the Code or in the jurisprudence, for the statement that an heir cannot renounce an inheritance until the succession has been opened by a judicial proceeding.

*   *   *

UNITED STATES v. BRUMFIELD
CIV. A.96-7508-B-M1, 1998 WL 834999 (M.D. La. 1998)
[Footnotes omitted.]

POLOZOLA, Chief J.

This case requires the Court to resolve important issues involving the rights of the Internal Revenue Service ("IRS") against a taxpayer's interest in the estate of his mother.

*   *   *

Background

Noel A. Brumfield owed income taxes for 1983 and 1984. The IRS assessed these taxes on December 2, 1985 and February 6, 1993, respectively. Noel A. Brumfield, his brother William Brumfield, his son Vincent Brumfield, and the succession of his mother, Bernice Addison Brumfield, were named as defendants in the federal foreclosure action filed by the United States in 1996. Later, the succession suit was removed from the Nineteenth Judicial District Court for the Parish of East Baton Rouge and consolidated with the federal suit.

$$* \quad * \quad *$$

There is little dispute in the underlying facts except for the validity of the renunciation allegedly made by Noel A. Brumfield of his interest in his mother's estate.

As previously stated, the IRS assessed income taxes for 1983 and 1984 against Noel A. Brumfield on December 2, 1985 and on February 6, 1993. The United States filed a Notice of Federal Tax Lien with respect to Noel A. Brumfield's unpaid tax liabilities in East Baton Rouge Parish, Louisiana on July 19, 1993.

Despite notice of the assessments and demand for payment, Noel A. Brumfield has refused to pay the full amount of the assessments described above. As of July 19, 1993, Noel A. Brumfield remained indebted to the United States in an amount exceeding $2.4 million, plus statutory additions according to law. Additional unassessed interest and all statutory additions thereon as provided by law continue to accrue on this liability, which exceeds $3.5 million.

Bernice Addison Brumfield died testate on November 8, 1995. On November 14, 1995, the state court ordered the olographic will of Bernice Addison Brumfield to be executed according to law. The will of Bernice Addison Brumfield granted to her son, William Louis Brumfield, everything which she possessed "except the following two properties; the six and one-half acres with improvements located at 11136 Julia Aubin Lane, Baton Rouge, La. and the house and lot located at 10590 Toledo Bend, Baton Rouge, La. which I leave and bequeath to my grandson Noel Vincent Brumfield II with Noel Addison Brumfield usufruct."

Despite this specific bequest and his right to a "forced portion" in the assets of his mother's succession under Louisiana law, Noel A. Brumfield executed a document on July 15, 1996 which purported to renounce his usufruct interest in the two subject properties. On July 28, 1996, Noel A. Brumfield executed another document which purported to renounce both his usufruct interest in the two subject properties and his "forced portion" in the succession's assets.

The state court had previously granted a judgment of possession to the legatees for all of the succession property except for the two parcels which are the subject of the petition by the United States to foreclose, thus leaving the disposition of these two properties as the only matter pending in the succession. The United States then intervened in the state court succession case as a creditor of Noel A. Brumfield. Thereafter, the United States filed a petition in state court to foreclose the tax liens on the usufruct interest of Noel A. Brumfield in the Aubin Lane and Toledo Bend properties. The succession action was removed to federal court. Thereafter, this Court denied defendant's motion to remand. The case is now before the Court on the pending motions.

In its motion for summary judgment and motion for default judgement, the United States seeks an order "determining that the tax liens of the United States encumbered, as of November 8, 1995, Noel Brumfield's interests in the assets of the Succession and specifically in the two parcels of property bequeathed to him under his mother's will." The United States also seeks an order allowing it to foreclose its tax liens on Noel A. Brumfield's interest in the succession through a judicial sale.

$$* \quad * \quad *$$

The resolution of this issue requires an analysis of both Louisiana succession law and federal law. It is the ownership of the succession property which the Court is concerned with on these motions. Ownership is transmitted at the moment of death to the heirs and legatees. Thus, Noel A. Brumfield acquired the forced portion and the two usufructs on November 8, 1995, the date of Bernice Brumfield's death.

The United States' tax lien, which was filed against Noel A. Brumfield pursuant to 26 U.S.C. § 6321, arose at the time of its assessments of Noel A. Brumfield's deficiencies on December 2, 1985 and February 6, 1993. This tax lien attached to "all property and rights to property" belonging to Noel A. Brumfield, whether owned at the time of the assessments or subsequently acquired. The Court must look to state law to determine whether and when Noel owned "property" or "rights to property."

As noted above, it is clear that Noel A. Brumfield acquired the right to his forced portion and to the usufructs at the moment Bernice Brumfield died on November 8, 1995. Since Noel acquired "rights to property" on November 8, 1995, the conclusion would seem to be that the United States' tax lien attached to the property on the same date and is effective as of the date of the assessments.

However, LOUISIANA CIVIL CODE article 946, which was cited by the Brumfields in their prior memoranda, complicates the Court's resolution of the issue and is at the crux of the dispute between the parties. Article 946 provides that while Noel A. Brumfield is said to acquire the right to his forced portion and to the usufructs at the time of Bernice Brumfield's death, such right is "in suspense" until he decides whether to accept or renounce the part of the succession that has fallen to him.

The article further provides that if Noel A. Brumfield accepts his part of the succession, he is deemed to have succeeded to such part from the moment of Bernice Brumfield's death. However, if he renounces such part, he is considered as never having received it. The Court cannot overlook the retroactive nature of this code article. Louisiana law provides that no one may be compelled to accept a succession and that one may accept or renounce a succession.

The Brumfields, relying on this retroactive language and on the Fifth Circuit's recent decision in *Leggett v. United States*, argue that the July 28, 1996 renunciation by Noel A. Brumfield of his rights to the property was valid. Thus, the Brumfields argue that under article 946, it must be that Noel A. Brumfield never succeeded to the property. Accordingly, the Brumfields argue that since Noel is deemed to never have had any rights in the property, the government's tax liens could not attach to the property.

In *Leggett*, the Fifth Circuit was confronted with a similar fact scenario in which a delinquent taxpayer renounced her succession rights in an alleged attempt to prevent the government's tax lien from attaching to her rights. Applying Texas succession law containing a retroactivity provision similar to Louisiana's article 946 and an immediate vesting provision similar to Louisiana articles 940 and 1626, the Fifth Circuit attempted to determine whether the taxpayer ever had a property interest in the succession property to which the government's lien could attach. The court noted the contradiction between the two provisions of Texas law which on the one hand provided that the heir was vested with a property right from the moment of death, while on the other hand provided that the renouncing heir never had a property interest at all. There is a similar contradiction between article 946 and articles 940 and 1626 of the LOUISIANA CIVIL CODE.

The Fifth Circuit noted two ways to resolve this apparent contradiction: the "transfer theory" and the "acceptance-rejection theory". The court then examined Texas succession law and noted that under Texas law, like Louisiana law, the heir had the right to accept or reject the succession. The court then concluded that the Texas courts have followed the "acceptance-rejection theory". Based on this analysis, the Fifth Circuit concluded that the taxpayer had not accepted the bequest but rather had executed a valid renunciation and, accordingly, the taxpayer never had a property right to which the tax lien could attach.

The United States argues, based on the language of article 946, that its tax lien against Noel A. Brumfield attached at the time of Bernice Brumfield's death and, thus, federal law controls thereafter. It further argues that since federal law controls once the lien attached to the property, state law (namely, Noel's renunciation and the retroactivity provision under article 946) could not defeat the attachment of the lien. The United States relies on *United States v. Comparato*, which cites the Supreme Court's decisions in *United States v. Rodgers* and *United States v. Bess*. The New York successions provisions noted in the *Comparato* opinion are also similar to Louisiana's provisions.

The Fifth Circuit in *Leggett* distinguished *Comparato*, noting that New York law was at issue and that the New York courts had held heirs to have a property interest in the right to accept or reject the inheritance to which the federal tax lien attached. Therefore, New York law follows the so-called "transfer theory". Thus, the delinquent taxpayers in *Comparato* could not destroy the property right by renouncing the underlying succession.

The Court's research reveals that the Louisiana courts have not decided whether Louisiana follows the "transfer theory" or the "acceptance-rejection theory". In fact, there are very few cases applying or interpreting the above-cited code articles. Thus, the Court must rely on the language of the code articles and the Fifth Circuit's guidance in *Leggett*.

The situation this Court is now faced with is similar to the situation the Ninth Circuit was faced with in *Mapes v. United States*. In *Mapes*, the court was applying Arizona law which had not been interpreted by the Arizona courts. Thus, the Ninth Circuit assumed that Arizona's statutory scheme followed the so-called "acceptance-rejection theory." The Fifth Circuit in *Leggett* noted that the "acceptance-rejection theory" is the majority rule. Because (a) the "acceptance-rejection theory" is the majority rule; (b) there is a substantial similarity between the Texas statutes cited in *Leggett* and the Louisiana provisions; and (c) the language of LOUISIANA CIVIL CODE article 946 states that the heir's right is in suspense until the heir decides whether to accept or reject the succession, it is reasonable to conclude that the Louisiana Supreme Court would follow the "acceptance-rejection theory" and that the Fifth Circuit would so hold.

Therefore, this Court finds that it is bound by the Fifth Circuit's holding in *Leggett*. Thus, the validity of the United States' tax lien on Noel A. Brumfield's interest in the succession property is dependent on the Court's resolution of three issues:

A. Was Noel A. Brumfield's July 28, 1996 Renunciation a Valid Renunciation?

If Noel A. Brumfield's renunciation of July 28, 1996 was a valid renunciation, *Leggett* dictates that he never had an interest in the property to which the tax lien could attach. Thus, the property would pass unencumbered by the lien. In its prior memoranda, the United States contests the validity of the renunciation. On its face, the renunciation appears valid because it meets all of the codal requirements. The renunciation was, on its face, executed by notarial act before a notary and two witnesses. Noel A. Brumfield had the requisite capacity to make the renunciation. Further, his right to renounce had not prescribed.

The court believes that what the government is really asserting when it claims the renunciation was invalid is that the renunciation should be annulled because of its allegedly fraudulent purpose.

Thus, in the absence of a separate petition filed by the United States seeking to set aside the renunciation on one of the above grounds, Noel A. Brumfield's renunciation appears to be a valid renunciation.

B. Did Noel A. Brumfield Actually Accept the Succession?

The Court must now determine whether Noel A. Brumfield, by his actions, actually accepted the succession, thus making his right to the property, under LOUISIANA CIVIL CODE article 946, effective as of the date of Bernice Brumfield's death. If Noel A. Brumfield actually accepted the succession, the United States' tax lien, under *Leggett*, attached to the property at the same time. An acceptance of the succession by an heir is irrevocable. An acceptance can be either express or tacit. There was clearly no express acceptance by Noel A. Brumfield under the facts of this case.

However, the United States contends that Noel A. Brumfield tacitly accepted the succession by residing in and on one of the properties, in the capacity of an heir, from 1994 until the time he was incarcerated in 1996. While the United States did not cite a code article, the Court presumes it is relying on article 993 and/or article 994 of the LOUISIANA CIVIL CODE. Considering that Noel resided in and on the property before Bernice Brumfield's death in 1995, the Court does not believe it would be proper to conclude that he was occupying the property after his mother's death in the capacity of an heir. Thus, the Court concludes that there was no tacit acceptance of the succession by Noel A. Brumfield on this basis.

However, the Court finds that Noel A. Brumfield, via his renunciation and the "receipt and full release" agreement of July 28, 1996, accepted the succession under article 1003 of the LOUISIANA CIVIL CODE. Article 1003 provides that a renunciation in favor of a coheir is an acceptance when the renouncing party receives a "price" for the renunciation. Noel's renunciation was in favor of his co-heir and brother William Brumfield as the civil code provides that Noel's portion of the succession, once renounced, falls to William as the instituted universal legatee. Although the United States contends several times in its memoranda that the renunciation was in favor of the son, Vincent Brumfield, the Court can find no support for this in the language of the renunciation or in the civil code.

The Court finds that Noel A. Brumfield did receive a "price" for his renunciation. A careful reading of the "receipt and full release" agreement reveals that Noel received valuable consideration in exchange for his renunciation, including a release from William for any and all liability for inheritance taxes pertaining to his part of the succession and a release from any and all claims that William had against Noel, including the claims pertaining to the Livingston suit debt and to Noel's alleged wrongful taking of items from Bernice Brumfield's home after her death. While the Court could not locate any cases interpreting the meaning of the term "price" as used in the article, it is reasonable to conclude that the valuable consideration set forth above clearly satisfies this requirement.

Therefore, the Court concludes that under the clear terms of article 1003 of the LOUISIANA CIVIL CODE and *Leggett*, Noel A. Brumfield accepted his mother's succession. Thus, the Court finds, under the facts of this case and as a matter of law, that the United States' tax lien attached to the property at the time of Bernice Brumfield's death.

The Court also finds as a matter of law that Noel A. Brumfield accepted the succession under article 1002 of the LOUISIANA CIVIL CODE. This article provides that a donation, sale, or assignment by a coheir of his/her rights of inheritance to a fellow coheir is considered to be an acceptance of the succession. Since Noel A. Brumfield executed the renunciation in exchange for the valuable consideration mentioned above, it follows that such a transaction was a sale or assignment of Noel's rights in the succession.

C. Does Louisiana's Succession Law Follow the "Acceptance-Rejection Theory" or the "Transfer Theory" as Termed and Defined by the Fifth Circuit in *Leggett*?

For reasons noted above, the Court concludes that Louisiana follows the "acceptance-rejection theory" and thus the Court is bound by the *Leggett* holding.

IV. Summary and Conclusion

For reasons set forth above, the Court finds that the renunciation was valid in form and that Louisiana follows the "acceptance-rejection theory." However, because Noel A. Brumfield accepted the succession under articles 1002 and 1003 of the LOUISIANA CIVIL CODE, the Court finds that, pursuant to article 946 of the Louisiana Civil Code, Noel had rights in the succession as of the moment of Bernice Brumfield's death at which time the United States' tax liens attached.

Therefore, the Court concludes that the United States' tax liens are valid and that the United States is entitled to foreclose on the property. The United States is also entitled to a lien for its share of the proceeds from the judicial sale of the property.

The parties shall have until October 16, 1998 to submit a prepared judgment which shall include a provision for the disposition of the funds in the registry of the Court.

*   *   *

Cynthia Samuel, *The 1997 Successions and Donations Revision – A Critique in Honor of A.N. Yiannopoulos*, 73 Tul. L. Rev. 1041-1086 (1999)

[Reprinted in part with permission; footnotes omitted;
bracketed information added by author]

*   *   *

II. Transfer of the Decedent's Assets, Rights, and Liabilities--Acceptance with Limited Liability

Since 1825 the Civil Code's foundational concepts of succession have provided Louisiana with a simple, efficient system for the transfer of the decedent's patrimony to the heirs. The concepts relevant to the acquisition by the heirs of the decedent's property, rights, and liabilities and to the exercise of those rights are universal succession, succession to the person, and le mort saisit le vif or seizin. These concepts, especially the last, allow the heirs to acquire and even to exercise the decedent's rights and wind up his affairs without any court involvement except to establish the authenticity of a will. They are also the basis in the substantive law for Louisiana's simple procedure by which a judge sends the heirs into possession of a succession of any size without a court-supervised administration or with only an incomplete administration. Louisiana's procedure contrasts favorably with the costly and time-consuming common-law probate system where, as a general rule except for small successions, an administration is required if the decedent died owning property titled in his name. The common-law system has caused people in those states increasingly to try to avoid probate by the use of numerous substitutes for wills, which entail new problems in themselves. Indeed, Louisiana's system is envied by reformers in other states for its simplicity and efficiency in transferring the property of the decedent to his heirs or legatees. One leading common-law textbook says: "A system of universal succession [i.e., the European system such as Louisiana's] can have enormous advantages where the heirs or the residuary devisees are all adults."

The only drawback to Louisiana's system, the exposure of the heirs who accepted the decedent's succession without an administration to unlimited personal liability for the decedent's debts, was eliminated by the legislature in 1986. Section 9:1421 of the LOUISIANA REVISED STATUTES, as interpreted by the Louisiana Supreme Court, requires only that the heirs make an inventory or descriptive list (the statute does not say when the inventory or descriptive list must be made) in order to limit their personal liability to the value of the inheritance, each heir's liability being in proportion to his share of the succession. Ever since this change, Louisiana's system has continued to function well. Creditors have not complained, for despite the limitation on the heirs' liability, the creditors still possessed effective means under Louisiana law of collecting the debts of the deceased. Louisiana does not have a nonclaim statute barring the creditor's claim against the heirs that is typical of common-law probate systems; the creditor of the deceased may assert his claim against the heirs until the debt itself has prescribed. Louisiana law, unlike the common law, also protects the creditors of an heir who renounces an inheritance to avoid paying his debts.

Thus, no wholesale reconceptualization or reworking of Louisiana's system was called for. On the contrary, the soundness of the present law, to say nothing of its convenience to the nonspecialist practitioner accustomed to this system, warranted a revision that would improve the law more by clarifying than by changing it. The version of Act 1421 that was introduced in the legislature on the Law Institute's recommendation in 1995, however, contained radical change in the fundamental concepts. It contained no rule like present Civil Code article 945, which states that "the heir, in every thing, represents the deceased, and is of full right in his place as well for his rights as his obligations." Nor did it include a rule like that of the present code, which states that if the heir accepts, he is considered to have succeeded from the moment of the decedent's death by operation of law alone without taking steps to obtain possession. Instead, it spoke of an heir as accepting "rights to succeed," language that might imply that after acceptance of the rights another step, such as court intervention, was required in order for the right to be realized. Compare this requirement with the language of present law, whereby the heir accepts "the succession," implying an immediate acquisition of the decedent's patrimony. One commentator who studied the 1995 Law Institute successions bill thought the concept of seizin had probably been eliminated; another commentator could not tell from the bill's provisions whether the concept of seizin had been preserved or scrapped. Fortunately, the 1995 version was deferred by the legislature, and subsequently it underwent revision by both the Law Institute and

House Civil Law and Procedure Committee to emerge as Act 1421 of 1997. Act 1421 contains new article 935 that says "a universal successor may represent the decedent with respect to the heritable rights and obligations of the decedent" and contains an assurance in the official comment that the theory of seizin has been retained, but modernized. The language of "rights to succeed" was not revised as it should have been, but, in light of new article 935 and its comment, such language, though it does not fit the theory of seizin as well as the old language, ought not to cause a problem.

The revision incorporates the limited liability of the accepting heir of Revised Statute 9:1421 into the Civil Code by creating only one kind of acceptance, called "acceptance." "Simple or unconditional acceptance" and "acceptance with benefit of inventory" are eliminated. Because the accepting heir's liability is limited, the new law creates a presumption of acceptance. This presumption may either be confirmed by an actual acceptance or rebutted by a renunciation. The new law replaces the terms "express" and "tacit" acceptance with "formal" and "informal" acceptance; no change in the substance is intended, but the examples of tacit acceptance in the present code are eliminated as unnecessary. The new terms are not synonymous with the old, however, nor are the new terms more precise. "Informal" does not mean "implied" and thus does not denote the crucial characteristic of acceptance by an act of the heir, that is, that the act be one that implies acceptance. "Tacit," on the other hand, does mean "implied." Nor is the new terminology the same as that used in modern civil codes. On the contrary, the QUEBEC CIVIL CODE of 1993 uses express and tacit acceptance. So does the 1988 project for the revision of the French Code civil articles on succession. The discarding of civil-law legal terminology that is accurate, familiar, and modern is simply perverse tinkering.

The heirs' liability under the new acceptance will be limited and proportional as under section 9:1421 of the LOUISIANA REVISED STATUTES and the present code. In other respects, however, the new acceptance goes beyond the terms of section 9:1421. A universal successor accepting under the new law will obtain limited liability without making the inventory or descriptive list that section 9:1421 requires. Sensibly, the new law does not create a requirement of an administration as a prerequisite to limited liability; however, the removal of the requirement of an inventory or descriptive list means that the heirs are not required to make any demarcation of the patrimony of the decedent to separate it from their own patrimonies. Yet, despite mixing the patrimonies of decedent and heirs, the new law also specifies that the accepting heir may assert any right he has as creditor of the decedent. In other words, the debt owing between the heir and the decedent is not extinguished by confusion upon acceptance. It is difficult conceptually to see how the debt cannot be extinguished by confusion if the two patrimonies are not separated upon acceptance; the qualities of obligor and obligee would seem to be united in the same person. In practice, the new rule may give the heir-creditor an unfair advantage over the other creditors of the decedent. The rule allows the heir-creditor of an insolvent decedent to pay himself as creditor without receiving anything as heir that would render him liable to the other creditors of the decedent. The issue of confusion should have been resolved consistently with the decision not to require the heirs to demarcate the decedent's patrimony from their own.

Furthermore, the new law increases the liability of the accepting heir beyond that imposed by section 9:1421 by changing the measure of the liability. The measure of the heir's personal liability as stated in section 9:1421 was "the extent and value or amount of his inheritance." It was unclear whether this meant that (1) the heir's liability was limited to the inherited assets themselves and the proceeds of the sale of these assets or (2) the heir was liable out of his own assets for the value of the inherited assets established by the inventory or descriptive list, even if those assets declined in value after the decedent's death. Under the new law the measure of the heir's personal liability is "the value of the property and its fruits and products received by him, valued as of the time of receipt." By focusing on the value that the heir received, rather than on the value of the inheritance, the new law appears to have adopted the first measure. This measure would have been consistent with doctrinal interpretation of Louisiana's measure of liability for acceptance under benefit of inventory. The new law goes further, however, by including in the measure of the heir's limited personal liability the value of the fruits and products of the property received by the heir. The fruits and products included are not just those that have accrued by the time the heir receives the property that generated them, but also those that have accrued at any time thereafter. The fruits and products that accrue after the heir received the property that generated them are the heir's property, yet they subject the heir to increased personal liability for the decedent's debts. In this respect the new rule partakes of simple acceptance under which the heir's liability is not limited to the value of the decedent's property. If the heir has sold the property and reinvested the proceeds, will his liability be increased by the fruits and products of the new investment? Did the redactors of the new law intend such tracing despite its practical difficulty? Creditors had not complained about the limitation of the heir's personal liability in section 9:1421. There was thus no reason to increase the heir's liability by changing the measure of limitation; all that was called for was a choice between the two measures mentioned above. [La. C.C. 1416 was amended by Act No. 710, 824, § 1 in 2001 to eliminate the reference to the fruits and products].

New article 1419 makes clear that when there is an administration, a late-appearing creditor may nevertheless collect his debt from the successors to whom distribution has been made, subject, of course, to the limitation of liability. This is the doctrinal interpretation of the present law concerning acceptance with benefit of inventory, but the present code is actually silent on this point. The new article eliminates the three-year prescription of present article 1068 on the late-appearing creditor's claim against creditors and legatees who were paid during the course of the administration pursuant to an acceptance with benefit of inventory. Thus, creditors under the new law have slightly less incentive to make a timely presentation of their debts during an administration.

Estate Debts: La. C.C. 1415-1429

Bar question

La. C.C. 961 provides that acceptance obligates a successor to pay estate debts in accordance with Title II of Book I of the Civil Code and other applicable laws. Chapter 13 provides more specifics regarding estate debts and the rights of creditors. Estate debts are defined as the debts of the decedent and administration expenses. The debts of the decedent include the obligations of the decedent incurred during his lifetime, as well as expenses arising as a result of his death, such as funeral and burial. Administration expenses are those incurred in preserving and operating the estate until final distribution. La. C.C. 1415.

As noted above, limited liability is continued in the revision, making each universal successor liable to creditors only to the extent of the value of the property received by the successor, valued at the time of the receipt. A creditor has no action against a successor who receives no property from the estate. La. C.C. 1416.

→ Loophole: can't succeed what's theirs.

Unless a testator provides otherwise or the successors reach agreement, estate debts are paid from the property of the estate and its fruits and products. La. C.C. 1421. No agreement by the successors, however, can prejudice the rights of creditors. La. C.C. 1420. And, any successor who is also a creditor is paid in the same order of preference as the other creditors. La. C.C. 1418.

If there is an estate debt that is identifiable to a certain piece of property, the debt will be charged against that property. For example, if a debt that was incurred to make improvements on the decedent's home, the debt will be charged against the home. If however, the decedent used his home to secure a debt that was not related to the property, a successor can prove that the secured debt was not attributable to the encumbered property. La. C.C. 1422.

If a debt is not attributable to an identifiable or encumbered piece of property, then it is charged ratably to the property that devolves by intestacy, the property of universal or general legatees, or the fruits and products of each, depending on the type of expense. Debts of the decedent are charged first to the property and second to its fruits and products, while administrative expenses are charged first to fruits and products and second to the property. Only after any universal or general legacies are exhausted are particular legacies and their fruits and products charged. La. C.C. 1423-24.

When a succession is under administration and a creditor establishes a claim after payments have been made to other creditors or successors pursuant to a court order, the creditor can claim his debt first from the assets remaining under administration in the estate, second from successors wow home distribution was already made, and third from unsecured creditors who received payments in proportion of the amount received by the unsecured creditor. La. C.C. 1419. No successor will be liable for contribution or reimbursement in an amount greater that the value of the property or the fruits and products received by him, valued at the date of the receipt. La. C.C. 1425.

PROBLEM

Christian died with the following will, valid in form: "I leave my house and furnishings to my long time girlfriend Jana, my antique jukebox to my sister Sarah and the remainder of my estate to my brother Ryan." Christian's estate consists of the house and furnishings worth $250,000, the antique jukebox worth $50,000, and 1,000 shares of Disney stock worth $120,000.

At the time of his death, Christian had a mortgage on the house for $50,000, a homeowner's insurance bill for $2,500, and a home equity loan with a balance of $20,000. Additionally, funeral expenses were $10,000 and attorney's fees were $5,000. You learned that Christian used his home equity loan to purchase the antique jukebox from a local antique dealer just last year.

How are the debts allocated and why?

Renunciation: La. C.C. 963-967

A renunciation of succession rights must be express and in writing, La. C.C. 963, although it no longer need be by authentic act as was previously required by C.C. 1017 of the Civil Code of 1870.

Accretion of Rights upon Renunciation: La. C.C. 964-966

Act 1421 of 1997, effective July 1, 1999, made a significant change in the law regarding accretion of rights upon the occasion of a successor's renunciation. Under the law of the revision, in an intestate succession, the rights of a successor who renounces now accrete to those who would have succeeded to them if the successor had predeceased the decedent. La. C.C. 964. Pursuant to an amendment to La. C.C. 965 by Act 824 of 2001, the same rule applies when a testate successor renounces, absent a governing testamentary disposition.

When succession rights accrete to a person, he may accept or renounce all or part of the accretion. Also, a successor who has renounced his original inheritance may accept succession rights that accrete to him thereafter. Conversely, one who has accepted the original inheritance, may renounce a part later falling to him by accretion. La. C.C. 966. Thus, for example, if X dies survived by his two children, A and B, and A renounces his succession rights to X's estate, allowing them to accrete to B, B may accept the half of X's estate falling to him originally, and renounce the half which accretes to him through A's renunciation.

Consider the following case that was decided prior to the revision of Act 1421 of 1997. How would that case be decided today? Which way seems more appropriate?

SUCCESSION OF WILLIAMS
418 So. 2d 1317 (La. 1982)
[Footnotes omitted.]

MARCUS, Justice.

Stella Lea Williams died intestate on March 7, 1978, leaving two children, Milton L. Williams and Rachel Beth Williams Kleinpeter. On April 18, 1978, Mr. Williams, desiring that his inheritance vest directly in his son and daughter, renounced his interest in his mother's succession. On April 25, 1978, pursuant to a joint petition stating that Mr. Williams had renounced the succession of his mother and that his children were representing him, a judgment of possession was signed recognizing Mrs. Kleinpeter and Mr. Williams' children as the sole heirs of decedent and as such they were placed into possession of all property left by the decedent in the proportions of one-half (1/2) to Mrs. Kleinpeter and one-fourth (1/4) each to Mr. Williams' son and daughter.

On May 8, 1978, Mrs. Kleinpeter filed a rule contradictorily with her niece and nephew to show cause why the judgment of possession signed on April 25, 1978 should not be corrected to reflect that Mrs. Kleinpeter was the sole heir of her mother by virtue of her brother's renunciation of his interest in the succession. The Williams children answered alleging that Mrs. Kleinpeter was estopped to deny her judicial confession made in the joint petition upon which the judgment of possession was based. Mr. Williams intervened alleging that his renunciation was conditioned upon the execution by his sister of the joint petition judicially confessing the interest belonging to his children.

After a hearing, the trial judge, finding that Mrs. Kleinpeter was estopped from seeking nullity of the judgment of possession, rendered judgment in favor of defendants-in-rule and intervenor and against plaintiff-in-rule rejecting her demands at her cost. The court of appeal, on original hearing, found that the judgment of possession was contrary to law and therefore null and void but that Mrs. Kleinpeter was "equitably estopped" to accept the succession until Mr. Williams had a reasonable opportunity (fifteen days from finality of the judgment) to revoke his renunciation. On rehearing, the court found that Mrs. Kleinpeter by her participation in the petition for possession, "solemnly acknowledged in a judicial proceeding" that she was the co-heir with the Williams children and accordingly was only entitled to one-half of the succession property. On Mrs. Kleinpeter's application, we granted certiorari to review the correctness of that decision. The primary issue presented for our determination is whether Mrs. Kleinpeter is precluded from asserting that she is the sole heir of her mother's succession.

LA. CIV. CODE art. 2291 provides:

The judicial confession is the declaration which the party, or his special attorney in fact, makes in a judicial proceeding.
It amounts to full proof against him who has made it.
It can not be divided against him.
It can not be revoked, unless it be proved to have been made through an error in fact.
It can not be revoked on a pretense of an error in law.

Where one makes a judicial declaration and judgment is rendered in accordance therewith, he cannot ordinarily revoke the declaration and attack the judgment under the pretense of having made an error of law. LA. CIV. CODE art. 2291. Nor does it seem to make any difference that the proceeding in which the declaration was made and the judgment rendered was a consent proceeding. *Doll v. Doll*, 206 La. 550, 19 So. 2d 249 (1944); *Succession of Williams*, 168 La. 1, 121 So. 171 (1929); *Succession of Carter*, 149 La. 189, 88 So. 788 (1921); *Succession of Rufin*, 143 La. 828, 79 So. 421 (1918).

In the instant case, the judgment of possession was rendered in accordance with the declarations of the parties that Mrs. Kleinpeter and her niece and nephew should be recognized as the "sole heirs" of decedent and as such placed in possession of all property left by decedent in the proportions of one-half to Mrs. Kleinpeter and one-fourth each to her niece and nephew. Although Mr. Williams and Mrs. Kleinpeter were the sole heirs of their mother at the time of her death, Mr. Williams renounced his interest in the succession. By operation of law, his portion devolved to Mrs. Kleinpeter as his only co-heir of the same degree. LA. CIV. CODE art. 1022. Under art. 1024, Mrs. Kleinpeter could not refuse the portion of her brother and keep that part which had fallen to her in her own right because she was bound to accept or renounce for the whole. *[See La. C.C. 966, as enacted by 1997 La. Acts no. 1421, § 1]**. In the joint petition for possession, however, Mrs. Kleinpeter accepted only that part of the estate that had fallen to her in her own right, impliedly refusing the portion of her brother. That portion went to her brother's children who took by representation of their father. Under art. 886, however, only deceased persons may be represented. Hence, the judgment of possession was based on erroneous legal conclusions that Mrs. Kleinpeter could refuse her brother's portion and that Williams' children could represent him in the succession.

Nonetheless, we consider that Mrs. Kleinpeter is precluded from asserting that she is the sole heir of her mother's succession since she joined in the pleadings on which the judgment of possession was based. On April 17, 1978, the attorney for the succession mailed to Mrs. Kleinpeter the following documents:

---

* Bracketed material in italics added by author.

1. A detailed descriptive list, the preamble to which stated that Mrs. Kleinpeter, her niece and nephew were the joint petitioners for possession, that the factual allegations of the joint petition were correct, and that they accepted the succession unconditionally.

2. A state inheritance tax return, showing the heirs as Mrs. Kleinpeter, her niece and nephew, with the taxes computed on the basis that Mrs. Kleinpeter was receiving 1/2 of the estate and the Williams children 1/4 each.

3. A cash deed under the terms of which immovable property belonging to the estate was conveyed to Alan G. Pierce. Named as vendors were Mrs. Kleinpeter, the Williams children and Mr. Williams (who with his sister already owned an interest in this property by inheritance from their deceased father).

Mrs. Kleinpeter received these documents on returning from a trip on April 22, 1978. It is disputed whether she also received a copy of the joint petition and the judgment of possession. On April 24, 1978, Mrs. Kleinpeter signed the detailed descriptive list, the state inheritance tax return and the cash deed. Mrs. Kleinpeter's husband, an attorney of thirty years experience, notarized his wife's signature where required. Since the loan closing for the transaction involving the property described in the cash deed was scheduled for April 25, 1978, the Kleinpeters brought the signed documents to the office of the succession attorney on that morning. At that time, it is undisputed that the Kleinpeters received copies of all the succession pleadings including the act of renunciation executed by Mr. Williams. The Kleinpeters then went to Mr. Williams' office where Mr. Kleinpeter expressed concern over title complications that he believed would result from the manner in which the succession was being handled. These concerns were also discussed over the telephone with the succession attorney. The succession attorney explained to Mr. Kleinpeter that all of the parties were competent and free to stipulate to whatever they wanted and thus any title lawyer would approve the title on the basis of the joint petition. He also pointed out that the deed was being executed by all the parties who had or could have had any possible interest in the property. (The detailed descriptive list reflects that the property described in the cash deed was the only piece of real estate in the succession.) After this conversation, the succession attorney proceeded to file the joint petition, with the supporting documents, and to procure the signing of the judgment of possession. That afternoon, the Kleinpeters, Mr. Williams and his daughter (who had a power of attorney for her brother) met with the vendee of the succession property for the loan closing. All necessary papers were signed. At no time during this meeting did the Kleinpeters express any reservations over the manner in which the succession was handled. The attorney handling the loan closing explained to the vendors that the loan proceeds would be distributed later. However, by letter dated April 26, 1978, Mr. Kleinpeter advised the attorney that his wife would not accept any of the proceeds from the sale and the check remitted to her was later returned.

Although Mrs. Kleinpeter claims that she knew nothing of her brother's renunciation until April 25, 1978, as early as April 22, 1978, Mrs. Kleinpeter was fully aware of the manner in which the estate was to be distributed. On April 24, 1978, she signed the detailed descriptive list stating that she and her niece and nephew were the joint petitioners in the petition and that all the allegations of fact contained therein were true and correct. By signing the succession pleadings, Mrs. Kleinpeter gave the attorney for the succession her implied, if not express, consent to procure the signing of the judgment of possession. Moreover, Mrs. Kleinpeter's representations in the succession pleadings that she and her niece and nephew were the sole heirs of the decedent were instrumental in obtaining judgment on that basis and had the effect of a renunciation of all rights in conflict with the judgment obtained. *Succession of Kranz*, 162 La. 546, 110 So. 750 (1926). In all cases in which it is not expressly or impliedly prohibited, parties can renounce what the law has established in their favor, when the renunciation does not affect the rights of others and is not contrary to the public good. LA. CIV. CODE art. 11. Mrs. Kleinpeter's renunciation of her right to her brother's portion did not affect the rights of others since all parties who had an interest in the succession participated in obtaining the judgment of possession. Moreover, there is nothing contrary to public order in the manner in which the estate was distributed. Since Mrs. Kleinpeter judicially declared that she was only entitled to one-half of the succession property and judgment was rendered in accordance therewith, she cannot now revoke her declarations and complain that the judgment of possession is erroneous as a matter of law. Accordingly, the judgment of the court of appeal is affirmed.

* * *

NOTE

Recall *Paline v. Heroman*, 29 So. 2d 473 (La. 1946). Would the result be the same after the revision of the law by Act 1421 of 1997? How? Why?

C. Samuel, *The 1997 Successions and Donations Revision – A Critique in Honor of A.N. Yiannopoulos,* 73 Tul. L. Rev. 1041-1086 (1999).
[Footnotes Omitted]
[Reprinted with permission]

* * *

IV. Postmortem Estate Planning and the New Rules on Renunciation

Act 1421's changes in the law of renunciation will facilitate postmortem estate planning for large estates or wealthy heirs and legatees for whom transfer taxes are a concern, but some of the changes may not be well suited to the average testator, heir, or legatee. New article 964 changes the rule for the accretion of a share that is renounced in an intestate succession: The renouncing heir's rights will accrete not to his co-heir, as under present article 1022, but to the person who would have succeeded to those rights if the renouncing heir had predeceased the decedent. In a class of heirs where representation is permitted, that is, the decedent's descendants or brothers and sisters and their descendants, the renouncing heir's share will go to his descendants because they would have taken his share by representation if he had predeceased. The new rule allows the renouncing heir to pass on the decedent's property to a lower generation without having to accept the inheritance and then make a gift of it to his descendants. The property will pass directly from the decedent to the generation below that of the renouncing heir. The renouncing heir will avoid incurring a gift tax or using up any of the amount that he is allowed to donate free of federal transfer tax. Under present law the same objective can be accomplished, but only if the co-heir cooperates and renounces the accretion. The new rule overrules *Paline v. Heroman*, however, a notoriously wrong decision that nevertheless afforded an opportunity to obtain the marital deduction in an intestate succession. *Paline* passed the decedent's community property in full ownership to the surviving spouse upon the renunciation of the decedent's children even though the grandchildren did not also renounce. Under the new law the grandchildren must also renounce in order for the surviving spouse to receive the decedent's community property in full ownership. If the grandchildren are minors, the new law provides that their tutors can renounce for them with court authorization. Thus far, the new rule appears suitable for all decedents and estates.

Difficulty for average estates may be encountered, however, under the new rule that allows an heir who has renounced to accept an accretion from another heir who later renounces. New article 966 says that "[t]he acceptance or renunciation of the accretion need not be consistent with [the heir's] acceptance or renunciation of other succession rights." Since 1986, an heir who has accepted has been allowed to renounce an accretion from a co-heir who renounced. But present law only allows an heir who has accepted to receive an accretion; an heir who has renounced cannot receive an accretion from another heir who later renounces. Thus, under present law an heir who renounced his original share becomes a stranger to the succession. Under the new law, however, an heir who has renounced his original share is still entitled to accept an accretion from a co-heir who renounces. For example, where the decedent's sons (who have no descendants) renounce one after the other so that the surviving spouse will get the decedent's community property in full ownership à la *Paline*, the first son to renounce may unwittingly end up with the share that accretes to him from the renunciation of the second son. A title problem will thereby arise when the surviving spouse tries to sell any of the former community property. Everyone is so accustomed to a renunciation meaning a final separation of the heir from the estate that even a conscientious lawyer, unless he specializes in estate planning, might inadvertently allow his clients to fall into this trap. Estate planners will avoid the trap by changing their renunciation forms to say "I renounce the succession and any future accretions." But the average family may not consult such a specialist. Furthermore, the new law does not require the formality of an authentic act for a renunciation, just a private writing. Thus, renunciations can take place without the supervision of any legally trained person at all, increasing the danger for the unwary renouncing heir.

* * *

PROBLEMS

1. Assume Mary died intestate, survived by her brother Charles, her sister Ann, and Ann's three children, William, George, and Thomas. If Ann renounced her interest in Mary's succession, who would take it? Why?

2. Assume that instead of dying intestate, Mary, in the question above, left a will, leaving her property to Charles and Ann and further specified in the will that if Charles or Ann did not take the property, then it should got to Mary's friend Beth. If Ann survived Mary and renounced her interest, who would take it? Why? Would it make any difference if the provision in Mary's will was that she wanted Beth to receive the property if Charles or Ann predeceased her? Why? Consider *Succession of Jouet*, 17 So. 3d 501 (La. App. 2d Cir. 2001).

3. Assume Arnold wrote a will bequeathing his golf clubs to his friend Brandon, with whom Arnold played golf every Saturday. Brandon had a son Chip whom Arnold detests. Just prior to Arnold's death, Brandon fell ill and was told he could never play golf again. When Arnold died, Brandon and Chip survived him and Brandon renounced the legacy of the golf clubs. Who would get the clubs? Why? What if Brandon had predeceased Arnold?

Creditor's Acceptance of Succession: La. C.C. 967

La. C.C. 967 provides for the possibility of a creditor of a successor, with judicial authorization, to accept succession rights that the successor has renounced to the prejudice of the creditor's rights. In that case, the renunciation of the successor is annulled in favor of the creditor, but only to the extent of the creditor's claim against the successor. The renunciation would remain effective against the successor.

SUCCESSION OF NEUHAUSER
579 So. 2d 437 (La. 1991)
[Footnotes omitted.]

DENNIS, Justice.

In this case a creditor seeks to reopen a succession in order to have a debtor's renunciation of a legacy revoked so that the creditor may accept the legacy in the debtor's stead. After a trial-type hearing, the district court concluded that proper cause to reopen the succession had not been shown. On appeal, the creditor argued that the renunciation of the legacy and the closing of the succession without prior notice to the creditor deprived it of a right or interest without due process of law in violation of the federal and state constitutions, but the Court of Appeal rejected this argument and affirmed. *Succession of Neuhauser*, 561 So. 2d 956 (La.App. 4th Cir.1990). We affirm, concluding that the creditor failed to show that it had the right or interest under state law for which it claims constitutional protection. Before a creditor may be authorized by a court to annul a renunciation and accept an inheritance in the debtor's stead pursuant to Civil Code articles 1021, 1071 and 1072 (1870), the creditor must prove that the debtor acted fraudulently and that the renunciation caused injury to the creditor. In the present case, the creditor failed, in a full evidentiary hearing, to establish either required element. Therefore, on the showing made, the creditor did not have a right to be authorized to annul the debtor's renunciation and accept the debtor's inheritance. By the same token, under the circumstances of this case, the creditor did not actually have the right or property interest for which it claims constitutional protection. Consequently, it is unnecessary for us to reach the constitutional issue. Considering all of these factors, the trial court exercised sound discretion in concluding that proper cause had not been shown to reopen the succession and the court of appeal correctly affirmed its judgment. *See* LA.CODE CIV.P. art. 3393.

Facts and Procedural History

The decedent, Clare Fogarty Neuhauser, widow of David A. Neuhauser, died testate on February 10, 1986. In her will she bequeathed her estate, in equal shares, to her three children, Janet Neuhauser Zeringer, Catherine Neuhauser Bell, and David A. Neuhauser, Jr. Catherine Neuhauser Bell predeceased the decedent, Clare Fogarty Neuhauser, leaving seven children. The will was probated on February 10, 1986. Janet Neuhauser Zeringer renounced her legacy on September 21, 1987. The district court rendered judgment on October 6, 1987 sending David A. Neuhauser, Jr. and the seven children of Catherine Neuhauser Bell into possession and closing the succession. The total gross estate consisted of property valued at $176,419.24. Therefore, the legacy of one-third of the estate renounced by Janet Neuhauser Zeringer was worth no more than $58,806.

On October 4, 1988, Janet Neuhauser Zeringer's creditor, the Federal Savings & Loan Insurance Corporation Resolution Fund as receiver for Alliance Federal Savings & Loan Association petitioned the court to reopen the succession of Clare Fogarty Neuhauser alleging that the creditor was a judgment creditor of Janet Neuhauser Zeringer pursuant to a judgment rendered by the United States District Court for the Eastern District of Louisiana on May 9, 1988 in the amount of $2,389,718.49 plus interest and costs, that Mrs. Zeringer's renunciation of her legacy prevented the creditor from subjecting to execution the property she would have received, and that the creditor desires to exercise its right under Civil Code article 1072 to accept the renounced legacy. At a hearing conducted on the petition on March 3, 1989, the district court concluded that proper cause to reopen the succession had not been shown and signed a judgment denying the petition on March 6, 1989.

*   *   *

On appeal, the creditor, maintaining that it was a reasonably ascertainable creditor under the rulings of *Tulsa Professional Collection Services, Inc. v. Pope*, 485 U.S. 478, 108 S.Ct. 1340, 99 L.Ed.2d 565 (1988) and *Mennonite Board of Missions v. Adams*, 462 U.S. 791, 103 S.Ct. 2706, 77 L.Ed.2d 180 (1983), asserted that it did not receive actual notice of the debtor's renunciation, and that such a deficiency amounts to a deprivation and taking of their property rights afforded under Civil Code articles 1071 and 1072. Consequently, the creditor argued that since the debtor's actions amount to a deprivation of due process under both the Louisiana and United States Constitutions, the district court abused its discretion by refusing to reopen the succession. The court of appeal disagreed, finding that the district court did not abuse its discretion in refusing to reopen the succession because the "balance of equities" favored the heirs. *Succession of Neuhauser*, 561 So. 2d at 958.

This court granted certiorari to decide whether the creditor had a right to be authorized to annul the debtor's renunciation and accept the debtor's legacy, and, if so, whether the creditor had been unconstitutionally deprived of this right. *Succession of Neuhauser*, 567 So. 2d 86 (La.1990). After a full review, we conclude that the creditor failed to show that it actually had such a right or property interest under state law, that the trial court correctly refused to reopen the succession, and that it is unnecessary for us to reach the constitutional issue the creditor seeks to raise.

Application of Legal Precepts

Before a creditor may have his debtor's renunciation of an inheritance set aside by a revocatory action and accept it in place of the heir, the creditor must prove that the party renouncing acted fraudulently and that the renunciation caused injury to the creditors. This substantive right of a creditor is established by Civil Code article 1021, the first paragraph of which provides: "The creditors of the heir who refuses to accept or who renounces an inheritance to the prejudice of their rights, can be authorized by the judge to accept it, in the name of the debtor and in his stead, according to the forms prescribed on this subject in the following section." Although a literal interpretation of article 1021 in isolation would seem to indicate that only injury to the creditors need be proven, construction of the article within the context of legislative history, doctrinal interpretations and the civil code system, requires that fraudulent renunciation be shown before a creditor can be subrogated to his debtor's inheritance.

The first paragraph of Civil Code article 1021 (1870) substantially reproduces that of article 788 of the FRENCH CIVIL CODE of 1804. Article 1021, par. 1, essentially was enacted by the codification of 1808 (C.C. 1808, pp. 164-165, Art. 92) and reenacted in its present text as article 1014, par. 1, of the Civil Code of 1825. The wording of the first paragraphs of the French versions of the 1808 and 1825 enactments were identical to that of FRENCH CIVIL CODE article 788, except for punctuation and phrases that were added to both the French and English versions of the 1825 enactment. ["... refuse d'accepter une succession, ou qui la repudie ... suivant les formes qui sont prescrites a cet egard dans la section suivante."] ["... who refuses to accept or ... according to the forms prescribed on this subject in the following section."] One phrase pertains to the creditor's right in cases in which the debtor refuses to accept, rather than renounces, and the other refers to the procedural rules contained in a subsequent section of chapter 6 of TITLE I- OF SUCCESSIONS, BOOK III OF THE CIVIL CODE. *See* article 1021, La.C.C.Comp.Ed., in 16 West's L.S.A.-C.C., p. 595 (1972).

French commentators report that, while there was initially a difference of opinion, the prevailing view was that the action to annul a renunciation provided by article 788, par. 1 of the FRENCH CIVIL CODE was in the nature of a revocatory action and therefore required that the creditor prove fraud as well as prejudice in order to succeed. Planiol observed:

> The wording of Art. 1167, which gives an action to creditors damaged by fraudulent behavior of their debtor, is general. So it applies also to the election of the eligible heir, if it is in fraud against them. Creditors can, and always could, sue, for instance, for the annulment of an acceptance of an insolvent succession.
>
> On the other hand, Art. 788 expressly provides for an action in revocation in case of a fraudulent renunciation of the succession. This article was drafted to sanction a difference between Roman and French laws. Roman law gave no action against a debtor who simply neglected to acquire some assets; ....
>
> Doubts have arisen as to the burden of proof under Art. 788. Do the creditors have to prove fraud of the renouncing heir, that means his intention to damage them, or does it suffice that they prove prejudicial results of the renunciation? Art. 788 speaks of "prejudice," whereas the general rule of Art. 1167 requires a "fraud." Actually, the question is broader and applies to all cases of renunciation of any right (cf. Arts. 622, 1053, 1464, 2225). Today it is generally admitted that fraud must be proved (cf. Vol. II, No. 313). Arts. 622 and 788 were drafted before the principal Art. 1167 was; Art 1464, drafted after it,

speaks of fraud and not of prejudice, in situations quite similar to Arts. 622 and 788.

Planiol, *Traité Élémentaire De Droit Civil*. Vol. 3, Part 1, §§ 1990-91 (11th ed. 1938)

Aubry & Rau, further explained:

> The general principles set forth in § 313 on the revocatory action as well as those set forth in § 312 on the creditors' exercise of the rights and actions of their debtor, are generally applicable in the cases contemplated by Article 788. In these cases, the revocatory action may be brought by the creditors of the renouncing heir only upon proving that the renunciation was fraudulent on the part of the latter.

Aubry & Rau, *Droit Civil Français,* Vol IX, § 613(5)(b)(6th ed. 1954) (footnotes omitted).

Under the LOUISIANA CIVIL CODES of 1808, 1825 and 1870, as well as under the FRENCH CIVIL CODE of 1804, the basic requirement of a successful revocatory action of any kind was proof of the debtor's fraud, i.e., the debtor's intent to deprive the creditor of his eventual right upon the debtor's property. LA.CIV.CODE art. 1969 (1870); LA.CIV.CODE art. 1964 (1825); LA.CIV.CODE art. 67 (1808); C.Civ. art. 1167 (1804). Consequently, when Civil Code article 1021 (1870), or any of its antecedents, is read in light of this basic principle underlying all revocatory actions, it is clear that a creditor must prove that an heir renounced his inheritance fraudulently or with an intent to wrongfully deprive the creditor of his claim on the debtor's property in order for the creditor to have a right to have the renunciation annulled and to accept the inheritance in the heir's stead. Moreover, other provisions of the 1825 and 1870 civil codes corroborate that fraud was a generic ingredient of the revocatory action. *E.g.,* LA.CIV.CODE arts. 1970, 1978, 1988 (1870); LA.CIV.CODE arts. 1965, 1073, 1983 (1825); *See* Comment, *The Revocatory Action*, 9 Tul.L.Rev. 422, 423 (1934-35); *Cf.,* Note, *Fraudulent Conveyances-Dation en Paiement to Creditor-Rights of other Creditors-Article 2658*, LA.CIVIL CODE of 1870, 8 Tul.L.Rev. 277, 278 (1933-34).

In the 1984 revision of Title IV on CONVENTIONAL OBLIGATIONS OR CONTRACTS, BOOK III, of the Civil Code, the legislature dispensed with fraud as the principal criterion for revocatory actions under that title and adopted instead as a test whether the debtor's act or omission caused or increased his insolvency. LA.CIV.CODE arts. 2036-2044 (effective Jan. 1, 1985). The obligations articles revision did not purport to amend art. 1021 or any other rule of Title I, Book III pertaining to successions. The rules of Title IV may apply to non-contractual obligations when compatible with their nature. LA.CIV.CODE art. 1917. In our opinion, however, it would create disharmony with the history, settled interpretation and underlying policies of article 1021 of the Civil Code (1870) to allow creditors to attack any renunciation solely on the ground that it increased the debtor's insolvency.

First, the obligations which arise under article 1021 in the event of a fraudulent renunciation are not innominate or newly discovered obligations. They are based on article 1021 which has a venerable source in French law and a long-lived, distinguished doctrinal interpretation. When the legislature intends to change such a well established principle of law it normally does so expressly and precisely after careful consideration of the impact of alteration on related provisions, e.g., in this case, the system of successions rules related to article 1021. Second, there is nothing in the obligations articles revision that suggests an intent to upset established principles of law outside the ambit of the obligations articles reform. Further, the creditor in this case does not seek to rely upon an obligation arising in contract; the present action is not based on any provision in the title on conventional obligations.

Finally, there are serious policy considerations that weigh against permitting a creditor to assail the renunciation of a legacy or an inheritance merely because it has increased the debtor's insolvency. If creditors could prevent disclaimers by heirs merely because they are insolvent, these creditors would receive more than they bargained for. Evidence indicates that creditors in evaluating risks ordinarily show little interest in their debtors' expectancies. Consumer credit is largely extended on dossiers reporting only credit history, income, assets, debts and obligations. Creditors making larger loans usually protect themselves by demanding a security interest in collateral and consequently can disregard the debtor's other resources. A. Hirsch, *The Problems of the Insolvent Heir*, 74 Cornell L.Rev. 587, 614 (1989) (and authorities cited therein); *See also*, Hersbergen, *The Improvident Extension of Credit as an Unconscionable Contract*, 23 Drake L.Rev. 225, 267-69 (1974); Countryman, *The Diminishing Right of Privacy: The Personal Dossier and the Computer*, 49 Tex. L. Rev. 837, 839-42 (1971). Further, the legitimate motives of familial devotion and estate planning that may underlie renunciations arguably should not be threatened or frustrated, and therefore they should not be vulnerable to attack unless there are grounds to claim that the renouncing party's intent was fraudulent. By the same token, the tradition of our law favoring personal autonomy is a reason against permitting creditors to compel debtors to accept successions against their wills merely because doing so would diminish their insolvency.

Not only does article 1021 require proof of fraud on the heir's part to set aside his disclaimer, but subsequent articles of the code place the burden of this proof squarely on the creditor. As article 1021 points out, the procedural forms by which a creditor may seek court authority to accept a debtor's inheritance are set forth in the following section of the Civil Code. Article 1071 of that section provides:

When the creditors wish to be authorized to accept a succession, which their debtor refuses to accept, or which he has renounced to their prejudice, they must present a petition to the judge of the place where the succession is opened, to obtain the authorization necessary for that purpose, after the debtor or his representative has been duly cited, or a counsel appointed to him, if he is absent, by the judge.

Article 1072 provides:

If, on this demand, it is proved to the judge that the debtor refuses to accept the succession, or has renounced it to the prejudice of his creditors, he is bound to authorize the creditors to accept it in his stead; and it is the duty of the judge to cause immediately to be made an inventory of the effects of the succession, to appoint an administrator to manage them, sell them and pay the creditors, on his giving good and sufficient security for the fidelity of his administration, as in the case of acceptance with the benefit of inventory.

Article 1072 is particularly important in the present case because it allocates to the creditor the burden of proving that proper grounds exist for the court to authorize the creditor to accept the succession in the debtor's stead. In other words, article 1072 requires the creditor to prove the substantive elements of his right of action, i.e., fraud on the part of the debtor and resulting injury to the creditor, before he may receive judicial approval to accept the debtor's inheritance. Article 1073 governs the distribution of succession assets, and article 1074 provides that creditors accepting in the name of their debtor do so under the benefit of inventory.

Applying the foregoing precepts to the present case, we conclude that the creditor failed to plead or prove that Mrs. Zeringer fraudulently renounced her legacy or that her renunciation injured her creditors by rendering her insolvent. The creditor herein assumed in pleading, proof and argument that its right to become subrogated to her legacy accrued upon proof that she renounced her legacy after becoming indebted to the creditor. If this were the law, a creditor's revocatory action would always lie to annul the heir's renunciation or failure to accept even when the debtor was clearly solvent and in complete good faith. But this has never been the law. Under Civil Code article 1021 and its antecedents, including article 788 of the FRENCH CIVIL CODE of 1804, creditors have been required to prove that the renouncing heir acted fraudulently to the prejudice of the creditors; in order to prove prejudice or injury, the creditor must prove that the act rendered the heir insolvent or augmented her pre-existing insolvency. Comment, *The Revocatory Action, supra* at 424.

In the present case, the evidence adduced by the creditor fails to demonstrate either Mrs. Zeringer's insolvency or her fraudulent intent. The record contains absolutely no evidence as to Mrs. Zeringer's assets and liabilities, other than the judgment obtained against her by the creditor herein. Of course, there is a substantial possibility that anyone who becomes a debtor under a $2.3 million judgment may have been rendered insolvent. But without concrete, particular evidence as to Mrs. Zeringer's actual financial condition, a conclusion that she was in fact insolvent would be little more than a speculation or assumption. There is even less support for the proposition that Mrs. Zeringer acted fraudulently in renouncing her legacy in favor of her brother and nephews. The record contains absolutely no evidence of her knowledge with respect to the judgment or its effect upon her financial condition and no information regarding her intention with respect to the effect, if any, of her renunciation upon the judgment creditor's rights.

The right of a creditor to attack and overturn a debtor's renunciation of an inheritance or a legacy is purely a creature of state statutory law. Nevertheless, the right may be a constitutionally cognizable property interest for the protection of which the state is required to provide an adequate procedure. In the present case, however, it is not necessary that we consider whether the interest is protected or whether the state's procedure is adequate, for, under the circumstances herein, the creditor has failed to establish the grounds necessary to give rise to the right under statutory law for which it claims constitutional protection.

Decree

For the reasons assigned, the judgments of the court of appeal and the trial court are affirmed.

AFFIRMED.

SUCCESSION OF WAGNER

746 So. 2d 696 (La. App. 5th Cir. 2000)

[Footnotes omitted.]

CANELLA, J.

The Succession of Claude Joseph Wagner (the succession) appeals from a trial court judgment finding that Andre Wagner (Andree) is a creditor of Gerald F. Wagner (Gerald), who renounced his father's, Claude Wagner's, succession and authorizing her to accept the succession to the extent of Gerald's past due child support and his portion of the minor children's medical expenses. For the reasons which follow, we affirm.

On June 22, 1990, Claude Joseph Wagner died intestate. He was married to Edith Massa Wagner (Edith), who survived him. There were three children born of this marriage: Gerald F. Wagner, Claude L. Wagner and Darlene Wagner Catania. Gerald F. Wagner was married to Andre Maduell Wagner. They had three children: Cheri Wagner, Richard Wagner and Nicole Wagner Perniciaro (the children). The marriage between Gerald and Andre ended in divorce on June 10, 1976. By judgment, Gerald was ordered to pay $300 per month in child support and one-half of the children's medical bills. He did not make the payments as required by law.

Following his father's death, Gerald became increasingly ill. On September 14, 1992, Gerald, with the assistance of counsel, executed a Last Will and Testament and an Act of Renunciation of his father's, Claude's, succession. In the will, with the exception of a clock that he left to his daughter Nicole, Gerald left his children none of his estate.

Thereafter, on March 13, 1996, Edith was appointed administratrix of the succession. Andree, on July 23, 1998, and her children, on May 30, 1996, both filed petitions to annul Gerald's renunciation of his father's succession. The children claimed that the renunciation was invalid due to a lack of mental capacity. Andree asserted that she was a creditor of Gerald's for past due child support and one half of the medical expenses for the minor children that he was ordered to pay pursuant to their divorce.

Following the completion of trial, delayed by disputes regarding the admissibility of certain hearsay evidence, the trial court made the following rulings: (1) Andree's motion to annul the renunciation by Gerald of Claude's succession was granted in part so as to allow Andree to assert her claim as a creditor, thereby accepting the succession, to the extent of the past due child support and medical expenses that Gerald owed her; (2) Andree's claims regarding partition of the community between her and Gerald were dismissed without prejudice; (3) the petition of the children to annul the renunciation by Gerald of Claude's succession was dismissed; and (4) costs were assessed against the administratrix of the succession. It is from this judgment that the succession has appealed.

On appeal the succession contends that the trial court erred in allowing Andree to assert her claim as Gerald's creditor for the past due child support and medical expenses. The succession supports its contention on two grounds. First, it argues that Andree did not prove the elements of her claim as a creditor, by showing fraudulent intent in the renunciation and detriment to the creditor, which would entitle her to accept the succession in the amount of the debts. Second, the succession argues that any claims Andree might have had for past due child support and medical expenses have prescribed.

Andree responds that the claims have not prescribed because she was incapable of asserting them previously because of threats to her life by Gerald. Further, she argues that she has met her burden of proof as a creditor by showing that Gerald was otherwise insolvent, therefore she could not recover any amount from him, absent acceptance of Claude's succession. He renounced the succession to prevent her from recovering these past due child support obligations that he refused to pay during his lifetime.

It is well settled that, on appellate review of a factual determination, the reviewing court may not set aside the factfinder's findings of fact in the absence of manifest error or unless they are clearly wrong. Also, where there is a conflict in the testimony, reasonable evaluations of credibility and reasonable inferences of fact should not be disturbed upon review, even though the appellate court may feel that its own evaluations and inferences are as reasonable. *Rosell v. ESCO*, 549 So. 2d 840 (La.1989); *Arceneaux v. Domingue*, 365 So. 2d 1330 (La.1978); *Canter v. Koehring*, 283 So. 2d 716 (La.1973).

The issue to be resolved by the reviewing court is not whether the trier of fact was right or wrong, but whether the factfinder's conclusion was a reasonable one. *Stobart v. State through DOTD*, 617 So. 2d 880 (La.1993). Thus, where two permissible views of the evidence exist, the factfinder's choice between them cannot be manifestly erroneous or clearly wrong. *Stobart, supra*.

When findings are based on determinations regarding the credibility of witnesses, the manifest error or clearly wrong standard demands great deference to the trier of fact's findings, because, only the factfinder can be aware of the variations in demeanor and tone of voice that bear so heavily on the listener's understanding and belief in what is said. *Canter, supra* at 724; *Virgil v. American Guarantee & Liability Ins. Co.*, 507 So. 2d 825, 826 (La.1987); *Boulos v. Morrison*, 503 So. 2d 1, 3 (La.1987); *Williams v. Keystone General Contractors, Inc.*, 488 So. 2d 999, 1001 (La.1986); *Johnson v. Insurance Co. of North America*, 454 So. 2d 1113, 1117 (La.1984); *Berry v. Livingston Roofing Co.*, 403 So. 2d 1247, 1249 (La.1981); *Crump v. Hartford Accident & Indemnity Co.*, 367 So. 2d 300, 301 (La.1979).

After viewing the witnesses and considering the testimony, the trial court made a credibility call, finding that prescription had been interrupted by Gerald's acknowledgment of the debt. The court also found that, due to Andree's ongoing attempts to collect the past due child support and medical expenses, the renunciation was done with intent to defraud. Gerald's attorney testified that Gerald's debts exceeded his assets, supporting Andree's claim that she was prejudiced by the renunciation. Further, supporting the trial court determination that prescription had been interrupted, we note that Andree's contention that she was prevented from asserting her claims against Gerald for the support payments and medical expenses for their minor children by threats of violence were not rebutted.

Therefore, based on the forgoing, we cannot find that the trial court was manifestly erroneous or clearly wrong in ruling that Andree established the elements of her claim as a creditor of Gerald, entitling her to accept the succession which Gerald had renounced, to the extent of the debt which Gerald owed her.

Accordingly, the judgment of the trial court is affirmed. Cost of appeal are assessed to the succession.

AFFIRMED.

HYPOTHETICAL

Jay had three children and one step-son. Mitchell and Claire were born of his first marriage, Joe a newborn was born of his current marriage to Gloria, and Manny was Gloria's son from a prior relationship. Jay never adopted Manny.

Mitchell married Cameron and they adopted a daughter, Lily from Vietnam. Claire married Phil, and they had three children, Haley, Alex, and Luke. Haley and Alex are over the age of majority.

Jay, Mitchell, and Phil were grilling burgers at a family BBQ. Jay and Phil were arguing about how long to let the meat cook, while Mitchell feigned interest. Both Phil and Mitchell desperately wanted to impress Jay, to the aggravation of the rest of the family. Tired of the endless fighting, Haley stormed off shouting, "Dad, when you die I want nothing from you or this family!" Alex was moving out and thought she would be far more successful than her family. She went inside and wrote the following: "I hereby renounce any rights that come from my father, my mother, or my siblings' successions." She signed it and put it in her desk drawer. Seconds later, an explosion erupted at the grill. All three men were killed.

Later that evening, in her concern over Manny, Gloria wrote the following: "I renounce Jay's succession in favor of my son Manny." Gloria had the document witnessed and notarized.

After the accident, Haley flunked out of college again. Claire let Haley move into Jay's old bachelor pad, a condo on the golf course that he had purchased between marriages. Soon after, creditors came knocking on Claire's door. Against her better judgment, she had let Phil handle all of the finances, and there was extraordinary credit card debt for tight ropes, magic tricks, and other toys. The credit card company was threatening to file suit. Jay, Phil, and Mitchell died intestate. Please answer the following questions.

a) Did Haley validly renounce Phil's succession?

b) Did Alex validly renounce Phil's succession?

c) Did Gloria validly renounce Jay's succession?

d) Claire would like to renounce her share of Jay's succession to prevent the condo from being seized. Advise her.

e) If Mitchell dies possessed of separate and community property, who inherits his estate?

f) If Phil dies possessed of only community property and Alex validly renounced, who inherits his estate?

CHAPTER 8:
COLLATION
La. C.C. 1227-1288

Introduction

Collation is defined in the Civil Code as "the supposed or real return to the mass of the succession which an heir makes of property which he received in advance of his share or otherwise, in order that such property may be divided together with the other effects of the succession." La. C.C. 1227. The concept of collation requires that an heir return to the mass estate, property given to him by the decedent during the lifetime of the decedent. The gifts given by a decedent to his descendant heirs can be returned in kind or in value so that these gifts can be considered in the division of the property of the succession. La. C.C. 1227.

Collation is based on two rebuttable presumptions. First, Louisiana law presumes that an ancestor intends to treat all of his children alike in the final distribution of his estate. Second, the law presumes that when an ancestor makes an *inter vivos* donation to one of his forced heirs and not the other, he only intended to temporarily favor one heir over the other heir. Such *inter vivos* donation is considered an advance on the forced heir's right to his ancestor's estate.

Ronald J. Scalise, *The Chaos and Confusion of Modern Collation:*
A Critical Look Into an Institution of Louisiana Succession Law
75 Tul. L. Rev.411 (2000)
[Reprinted with permission]

*   *   *

I.   INTRODUCTION

Collation is the process by which gifts given by a decedent to his descendant heirs are returned in kind or in value so that those gifts can be considered in the division of the property of the succession.[1] The underlying rationale for this procedure of collation is based on two presumptions. First, collation presumes that parents intend any gifts to be an advancement on what a child will ultimately receive from the succession (advancement d'hoirie). Secondly, collation presumes that parents intend all their children to share equally in their succession-not in what they receive from the remaining succession property but in what the children will receive from the parent over the course of the parent's life.

---

[1] *See* LA. CIV. CODE ANN. art. 1227 (West 2000). By way of an oversimplified example, if a parent dies possessed of assets valued at $90,000, and made a gift of $10,000 during his life to one of his minor children, upon the death of the parent, the other child can demand that the gift of $10,000 given to the first child be returned in calculating the division of the succession property. That is, the first child, having received the $10,000 gift, would receive only $40,000 from the property remaining after the death of the parent, while the second child, having not received a similar gift, would receive $50,000.

While the roots of collation stretch far back into history, its current application in Louisiana law is in need of serious examination and reconsideration. Scholars have noted that "[t]he present doctrine of collation is at sea with neither compass nor rudder."[2] This current crisis in collation law is due to several factors. First, the last significant revision to the collation articles occurred in 1870.[3] In fact, many of the articles in this area date further back.[4] Because the articles on collation are written in language now over 130 years old, their application becomes increasingly difficult as society progresses into the twenty-first century. Moreover, due to the age of the current collation articles, very few of the articles include comments to aid in interpretation, application, and historical comprehension. Within recent history only ten of the articles have been amended, with many of those amendments creating new ambiguities and problems of their own. Judicial interpretation of the collation articles has also resulted in confusion between codal language and codal application.

*　　*　　*

III.　A LOOK AT THE LEGISLATIVE BACKGROUND

Until the 1990s the concept of collation had remained fairly static in Louisiana for over one hundred years.[39] In 1990, however, a significant change in Louisiana succession law occurred. At that time, the forced heirship laws were revised to limit the concept of forced heirship to those under twenty-four and those permanently disabled.[40] Because collation in Louisiana had been limited to forced heirs since at least 1808, reexamination of this corollary principle was necessary in light of the new definition of forced heirship.[41] "Otherwise, older children who were not forced heirs, but who had received major gifts, could avoid the very equality contemplated by the concept of collation."[42] That is, without revision of the collation articles, the change in forced heirship would result in only those under twenty-four or permanently disabled being required to collate gifts, while those (even within the same family)

---

[2] Frederick William Swaim, Jr. & Kathryn Venturatos Lorio, SUCCESSIONS AND DONATIONS § 8.3, at 26 (10 LOUISIANA CIVIL LAW TREATISE, 1995 & Supp. 1999).

[3] Interestingly enough, while the Code of 1825 relied on the French structure in placing the articles on partition before the articles on collation, the Code of 1870 rejected that order and reversed the position of the articles. See Leonard Oppenheim, An Introduction to the Louisiana Law of Successions 7 n.20 in LA. STAT. ANN. (West 1987).

[4] See COMPILED EDITION OF THE LOUISIANA CIVIL CODE, (Joseph Dainow ed. 1972), codified at LA. STAT. ANN. (West 1972) [hereinafter COMPILED EDITION].

[39] Although as early as the 1970s, there were calls to abolish forced heirship (a change, as will be seen, that would have substantially altered the application of the collation rules), no serious alteration of forced heirship was made until later. See Gerald Le Van, Alternatives to Forced Heirship, 52 TUL. L. REV. 29, 29-30 (1977-78). See also Max Nathan, Jr., An Assault on the Citadel; A Rejection of Forced Heirship, 52 TUL. L. REV. 6 (1977-78).

[40] See 1990 La. Acts No. 147. Note that the 1990 bill was a revision of an earlier bill that had limited forced heirship to those under twenty-three and those who are "interdicted or subject to being interdicted." See 1989 La. Acts No. 788. For an interesting discussion of the events leading up to this change in the law, see Cynthia Samuel, Letter from Louisiana: An Obituary for Forced Heirship and a Birth Announcement for Covenant Marriage, 12 TUL. EUR. & CIV. L. FORUM 183, 185-86 (1997).

[41] See LA. CIV. CODE ANN. art. 1236 (1870) (stating that "[s]uch children or descendants only are obligated to collate who have a right to a legitimate portion in the succession of their fathers, mothers, or other ascendants").

[42] Swaim & Lorio, supra note 2, at 170.

who did not qualify as forced heirs would be exempt from collation. Consequently, the collation law was similarly revised. The main approach to solving the confusion, also contained in the same act, was the repeal of Article 1236, which defined those obligated to and those who could benefit from collation.[43]

Viewing this solution as inadequate, the Succession Law Review Committee of the Louisiana State Law Institute considered three possible approaches to remedy the situation.[44] The first approach favored an update to the rules governing collation (e.g., shortening the time in which gifts are subject to collation) but a wholesale preservation of the concept of collation.[45] The second approach also retained the concept of collation but reversed the presumption from one viewing the gifts as advancements to the presumption that gifts were intended as extra portions.[46] This reversal still allowed for collation if the donor expressed an intention for equality among the heirs.[47] Finally, the third approach outrightly abolished the concept and institution of collation in Louisiana.[48] The Law Institute opted for the third approach and recommended the abolition of collation.

Before action could be taken on the Law Institute's proposal, the Louisiana Supreme Court preempted further discussion of the issue when it decided Succession of Lauga.[49] In Lauga, the court held the entire act altering forced heirship to be unconstitutional.[50] Thus, the corresponding amendments to collation contained in the same act were also repealed. Given the constitutional mandate for and the long-standing definition of forced heirship,[51] the court saw this legislative attempt at altering the definition of forced heirship to be tantamount to legislative repeal of a constitutionally required institution.[52]

As a result of the Supreme Court's decision in Lauga, (sic) a constitutional amendment was proposed and passed by the voters of Louisiana that, in essence, implemented the earlier legislative attempt to redefine forced heirship.[53] Consequently, it again became necessary to repeal Article 1236 to avoid the same problems that were feared earlier. Thus, the legislature, in the very act that implemented the constitutional amendment to forced heirship, repealed Article 1236.[54]

---

[43] See 1990 Acts No. 147.

[44] See Supplement to Report to Council– Louisiana State Law Institute Report and Recommendations with Regard to Collation, Max Nathan, Reporter, and Julio Romanach, Staff Attorney (La. Law. Inst. doc., rev. May 21, 1993)) [hereinafter Supplement to Report].

[45] See id. at 7.

[46] See id. at 6-7.

[47] See id.

[48] See id. at 6.

[49] See 624 So. 2d 1156 (La. 1993).

[50] See id. at 1172.

[51] See id. at 1171 (discussing LA. CONST. art. XII, § 5).

[52] See id.

[53] For more detailed discussion of forced heirship and the changes introduced by the 1995 amendment, see Swaim & Lorio, supra note 2, at 264-67 and 32-36 (Supp. 1999).

[54] See 1995 Acts No. 1180.

angry; Bitter

Viewing the time for action as ripe, the House of Representatives, on recommendation of the Law Institute, voted to "repeal [the] articles defining collation and by whom it is due."[55] In the Committee's view, collation resulted in "acrimonious results and expensive litigation."[56] The Senate, however, rejected the House's approach and sought to preserve the institution of collation.[57] In a Conference Committee between the two houses of legislature, a compromise was struck. The institution of collation was preserved but an amendment to article 1235 was adopted, delineating who is entitle to demand collation.[58]

In the aftermath of this flurry of activity regarding collation, commentators have roundly criticized the compromise embodied in article 1235 as "incoherent,"[59] an "inconsistent and confusing article,"[60] and as "not mak[ing] any policy sense."[61] Whether for good or ill, the legislative compromise of preserving collation but adopting article 1235 has changed the institution of collation. It has divorced the historically reciprocal concepts of the obligation to collate and the right to demand collation. The ambiguity that now exists as a result of this compromise and the institution that remains must now be examined in light of its historical foundation and comparative application.

* * *

Katherine Shaw Spaht, *Forced Heirship Changes: The Regrettable "Revolution" Completed*
57 La. L. Rev. 55 (1996)
[Footnotes Omitted]
[Reprinted with permission]

* * *

E. Collation Among Descendants, Not Confined to Forced Heirs

In Act No. 1180 as in the 1990 legislation, Article 1236 of the Civil Code, restricting collation to forced heirs, was repealed. The consequence of repealing the article is to extend collation to all "descendants succeeding to their fathers and mothers or other ascendants, whether ab intestato or by virtue of a testament." Thus, rather than determining if a descendant is a forced heir, the relevant inquiry is whether the descendant, forced heir or not, is coming to the succession as an heir or a legatee. *Testate* *intestate*

---

[55] H.R. 55, First Extraordinary Sess. (1996).

[56] Supplement to Report, *supra* note 44, at 8.

[57] *See* Swaim & Lorio, *supra* note 2, at 25 (Supp. 1999).

[58] See 1996 Acts No. 77 § 1.

[59] Samuel, *supra* note 40, at 187.

[60] Kerry J. Miller, Comment, *The New Forced Heirship Law, Its Implementing Legislation, and Major Substantive Policy Changes of the Louisiana State Law Institute's Comprehensive Revision of the Successions and Donations Law*, 71 TUL. L. REV. 223, 246 (1996).

[61] Swaim & Lorio, *supra* note 2, at 24 (Supp. 1999). For a critical discussion of article 1235, *see* Katherine Shaw Spaht, *Forced Heirship Changes: The Regrettable "Revolution" Completed*, 57 LA. L. REV. 55, 128-33 (1996).

Collation, a concept independent of impingement of the *legitime*, is "founded on the equality which must be naturally observed between children and other lawful descendants, who divide among them the succession of their father, mother and other ascendants; and also on the presumption that what was given or bequeathed to children by their ascendants was so disposed of in advance of what they might one day expect from their succession." The difference between reduction and collation has been succinctly explained elsewhere: "Reduction is the protection of certain heirs from disinherison without cause, but collation is simply the evening up between co-heirs who have inherited." Extending the obligation of collation to descendants other than forced heirs, assures that younger children, even though forced heirs, are not treated unfavorably when compared to their older siblings. Consider the following compelling illustration which when written assumed that collation would remain an obligation owed only by forced heirs:

> (A)ssume a parent has three children, one of whom is under twenty-three when the parent dies. The parent has made *inter vivos* gifts totaling at least three quarters of the succession but that were not designated extra portions to his two children who were over twenty-three when the gifts were made. The children over twenty-three are not obliged to collate those gifts because they are not forced heirs. The same result may follow when the donees were under twenty-three when the gifts were made, but are over twenty-three when the parent dies. Thus even though the parent did not manifest an intention to treat his children unequally, the child under twenty-three cannot demand collation of his older siblings and thus is relegated to his forced share of one-fourth, instead of an equal one-third share of all property donated to the children.

Despite the important social purpose achieved by a concept that assures equality among children, there were unforeseen and unanticipated problems with "a descendant coming to the succession" in cases where he was only a legatee. Collation among descendant heirs who all received a share of the estate of the deceased under intestate succession law involved little complexity or subversion of one of the principal reasons for the concept--the gift represented a presumed advance on what the heir would one day receive. However, the collation among descendants when one or more are only legatees, needs reconsideration. Under French law, only intestate successors, including those who were not descendants, owed the obligation to collate; legatees did not. A sensible reform of collation would restrict its application to intestate succession but extend the obligation unambiguously to all descendants, not just forced heirs. The policy of treating children equally and solidifying the family after the death of the parents, as even the majority of letters received by Ann Landers would support, outweigh any arguments that implementing the policy is too difficult and requires too complex a scheme. As the authors of the book BEYOND THE GRAVE: THE RIGHT WAY AND WRONG WAY OF LEAVING MONEY TO YOUR CHILDREN (AND OTHERS) expressed the sentiment:

> If you care about maintaining family harmony after your death, leave your money and property to your children equally, regardless of their economic circumstances or their beau geste declarations.

*   *   *

Failing to equalize lifetime gifts is one of the most significant sources of dispute between my clients' children. Why such emotional upheaval? One child explained it to me this way: "My parents must not have loved me as much as my sister. While they were alive, they gave more to my sister than to me."

Intent of Donor to Dispense with Collation: La. C.C. 1230-1233

Collation is presumed, but may be expressly rebutted. La. C.C. 1230. A declaration to exclude collation must be unequivocal and indicate the will of the donor to favor an heir with an extra portion. La. C.C. 1231. Article 1233 provides that no magic words are required to dispense with collation; however there must be an indication by "other equivalent terms" that the gift was intended as an advantage or extra portion.

JORDAN v. FILMORE
167 La. 725, 120 So. 275 (1929)
[25 La. L. Rev. 984 (1965); 34 La. L. Rev. 219 (1974); 11 Loy. L. J. 35 (1930)]

O'NIELL, C. J.

Mrs. Julia B. Miles died in Los Angeles, Cal., on the 5th of December, 1925, leaving an estate in Louisiana, consisting of a plantation in Morehouse parish, worth $50,000, cash on deposit in a bank there, amounting to $2,300, a credit for $125, and property in Sabine parish, the value of which is not shown by the record. There are two heirs to the succession, namely, Mrs. Pearl Miles Reilly, known professionally as Charlotte Shelby, who is the daughter of the deceased, and Mrs. Hazel Minter Jordan, who is the granddaughter, being the only child of a predeceased daughter, of Mrs. Miles. The two heirs are therefore forced heirs of Mrs. Miles, and would have inherited her estate equally if she had died intestate.

On the 13th of November, 1925, Mrs. Miles attempted to donate the plantation in Morehouse parish to Mrs. Margaret Shelby Filmore, a daughter of Mrs. Reilly, by an instrument in the form of a sale for $10. Mrs. Jordan brought suit against Mrs. Filmore to annul the donation on the ground that it was not valid in form, the instrument being not an authentic act, and there being no acceptance by authentic act. Mrs. Shelby intervened in the suit, and claimed the whole estate of her mother, under the latter's will, which is as follows:

Los Angeles, Cal.

Saturday, 21st Feb. 1925.

This my last will and testament. This is to certify that my beloved daughter Pearl Miles Reilly, known as Charlotte Shelby, is to have and to hold and fall heir to all my belongings whatsoever, real estate, moneys, personal property, wherever located, and I further name and appoint her my Executrix.

[Signed] Julia B. Miles.

Witness: Chauncy T. Eaton.

...In her petition, praying for annulment of the will and opposing its probate, Mrs. Jordan prayed that she and Mrs. Reilly should be recognized as the forced heirs of Mrs. Miles, and that her estate should be divided equally between them. Mrs. Jordan's suit against Mrs. Filmore and Mrs. Jordan's opposition to the probate of the will of Mrs. Miles were, by mutual consent, consolidated and tried together; and, after hearing the evidence, the court rendered judgment, annulling the donation which Mrs. Miles had made to Mrs. Filmore, of the plantation in Morehouse parish, and at the same time the court gave judgment declaring the will of Mrs. Miles valid, but reduced the legacy of Mrs. Reilly to a half of the estate, on the theory that, as there were two forced heirs, the disposable portion was only a half of the estate, and, as the testatrix did not declare in her will that she intended the legacy of the whole estate to be an extra portion, Mrs. Reilly could take only a half of the estate--either as heir or as legatee. The court, therefore, in its judgment, decreed that Mrs. Jordan was entitled to a half of the estate....

The effect of the judgment, declaring Mrs. Jordan to be entitled to half of the estate, was the same as if the court had declared the will null--except that Mrs. Reilly was allowed to perform the duties of executrix. She and Mrs. Filmore appealed from the decision. As Mrs. Jordan did not appeal, or file an answer to the appeal taken by Mrs. Reilly and Mrs. Filmore, the judgment is final in so far as it decrees the will to be valid. It is conceded by the appellants, Mrs. Reilly and Mrs. Filmore, that the judgment is correct in so far as it decrees the nullity of the donation to Mrs. Filmore of the plantation in Morehouse parish, and in fact that the judgment is correct in every respect except in so far as it reduces the legacy of Mrs. Reilly of the whole estate to only a half of the estate. It is conceded also by the appellants that Mrs. Jordan is entitled to a fourth of the estate as a forced heir, and, therefore, that the legacy of the whole estate to Mrs. Reilly should be reduced to three-fourths. The only question to be decided is whether Mrs. Jordan is entitled to only a fourth of the estate, as a forced heir, or is entitled to a half of the estate on the theory that the testatrix did not declare in unequivocal terms in her will that her intention was to leave the estate to Mrs. Reilly "as an advantage or extra portion." The issue in the case is stated in the brief filed on behalf of Mrs. Jordan, thus:

> The question in this case is not, as stated by counsel for appellant, whether, under the circumstances, your honors can conclude that the donor intended her daughter [Mrs. Reilly] to be privileged over her granddaughter [Mrs. Jordan], but is, whether or not, under the wording of the will which was executed by the testatrix and duly proved, the testatrix expressed in terms of unequivocal meaning, or in express terms, an intention to give her daughter, Pearl Miles Reilly, all of the disposable portion of her estate as an extra portion; and we believe that your honors will search the will in vain for any language showing any such intention or inference; and, as stated before, the apparent intention of the testatrix was to disregard the law of Louisiana in reference to inheritance and give all of her property to one forced heir to the entire exclusion of the other heir.

*   *   *

There is some confusion in the jurisprudence on this subject, due to the failure of the court in some cases to observe the distinction between "collation," which a descendant heir may demand of his coheir, and the reduction of an excessive donation or legacy to the disposable portion, which reduction the forced heirs may demand of any donee or legatee. The difference between the right to demand collation and the right to demand a reduction of an excessive donation or legacy to the disposable portion is that collation can be demanded only from a coheir, but does not depend upon the extent of the inequality in the disposition of the ancestor's estate; whereas the right to demand a reduction of an excessive donation or legacy to the disposable portion may be demanded from any donee or legatee--whether he be an heir or a stranger--but it can be demanded only when--and to the extent that--the donation or legacy exceeds the disposable portion. The right to claim collation, strictly speaking, arises only from a donation made or an advantage given to a prospective heir by his ancestor during the latter's lifetime, and not from a legacy given by last will. That is rendered certain by the theory or presumption on which the obligation of an heir to collate is founded, as explained in articles 1228 and 1229 of the Code; that is, that what is given by ancestors to their offspring is presumed to be given "in advance of what they might one day expect from their succession." It would be absurd to say that what is given by last will and testament, by an ancestor to his offspring, is presumed to be given in advance of what the legatee might one day expect from his ancestor's succession. The absurdity seems to have been overlooked in the writing into articles 1228, 1229, 1231, 1232 and 1233 such expressions as "donations and legacies" and "given or bequeathed."

The same confusion of terms appeared in article 843 of the Code Napoleon, from which article 1228 of the REVISED CIVIL CODE of Louisiana--article 1306 of the Code of 1825--was translated; but the confusion in article 843 of the FRENCH CODE, which made it seem that collation was applicable to testamentary dispositions, as well as to donations *inter vivos*, was removed by legislation, by the Act of March 24, 1898. The article, originally, declared:

> Every heir, even beneficiary, coming to a succession, must bring to his co-heirs all that he has received from the deceased, by donation *inter vivos*, directly or indirectly; he cannot retain the gifts or claim the legacies given to him by the deceased, unless the gifts and legacies had been made to him expressly as an advantage over his coheirs and besides his portion, or with dispensation from collation.

The first part of the article would leave no doubt that collation is applicable only to donations *inter vivos*, and not to testamentary dispositions, but for the use of the word "legacies," along with the word "gifts," in the last part of the article. The purpose and effect of the amendment of the article, by the Act of March 24, 1898, was to make it plain that the obligation of an heir to collate, in the absence of an express exemption from collation, is applicable only to donations *inter vivos*, and is not applicable to legacies given by testament unless the testator has declared that the legacy is not given as an advantage or extra portion. As amended by the Act of March 24, 1898, article 843 of the FRENCH CODE now reads:

> Every heir, even beneficiary, coming to a succession, must bring to his co- heirs all that he has received from the deceased by donations *inter vivos*, directly or indirectly; he cannot retain the gifts made to him by the deceased unless they were made to him expressly as an advantage over his co-heirs and besides his portion, or with exemption from collation.
>
> The legacies made to an heir are reputed (held to be) made as an advantage over other heirs, and as an extra portion, unless the testator has expressed a contrary intention, in which case the legatee cannot claim his legacy except by taking less.

Article 1501 of the REVISED CIVIL CODE of Louisiana, which was article 1488 of the Code of 1825, was taken, though not literally, from article 919 of the FRENCH CODE, which provides:

> The disposable portion may be given in whole or in part, be it by act between living person or by testament, to the children or other heirs [successibles] of the donor, without being subject to collation by the donee or legatee coming to the succession, provided that as to the gifts the disposition was made expressly as an advantage over other heirs and as an extra portion.
>
> The declaration that the gift is made as an advantage over other heirs and as an extra portion may be made either by the act which contains the disposition, or subsequently according to the forms of donations *inter vivos* or testaments.

Article 1501 of the Louisiana Code indicates, more plainly than article 919 of the FRENCH CODE, that it is only when the disposable portion is given to a prospective heir by donation *inter vivos*, and not when it is given to an heir by testament, that it must be expressly declared to be given as an advantage or an extra portion, in order to exempt the donee from the obligation of collation, strictly so called; for article 1501 provides that such a declaration must be made by the donor, to avoid the obligation of the donee to collate. There is no indication in article 1501--for there would be no sense in the requirement--that a testator who bequeaths more of the disposable portion of his estate to one of his descendant heirs than to another must express, any more plainly than his favoritism itself expresses, his intention that the legacy bequeathed to the favored heir is intended as an advantage over the other heir, or as an extra portion--in order to avoid the obligation of collation, strictly so called. All that the testator has to do in the distribution of his estate among his heirs as he sees fit, to be sure that his will shall be carried out, is to avoid impinging upon the *legitime* which the law reserves to each of his forced heirs.

Another significant difference between the provisions of the FRENCH CODE and those of the Louisiana Code on this subject is that, in the second paragraph of article 919 of the FRENCH CODE, it is required that the declaration that a donation is given as an advantage over other heirs, or as an extra portion, must be made according to the form either of a donation *inter vivos* or of a testament, if the declaration is made subsequent to the making of the donation itself; whereas, in article 1232 and in the second paragraph of article 1501 of the Louisiana Code, it is only required that the declaration shall be made by an act executed before a notary public and two witnesses, if it is made by an act subsequent to the making of the donation itself. Surely, if such a declaration had to be made in order to give effect to a testamentary disposition, as well as to give effect to a donation *inter vivos*, of an extra portion of an estate, it would have to be made in one of the forms prescribed for the making of testaments when made for the purpose of giving effect to a testamentary disposition of an extra portion of an estate.

What we have said, however, is perhaps not so much to the point as is the fact that there is no such article in the FRENCH CODE as article 1233 of the Louisiana Code, which provides that the declaration that a donation "is made as an advantage or extra portion" need not be expressed in those words, but "may be made in other equivalent terms, provided they indicate, in an unequivocal manner, that such was the will of the donor."

Notwithstanding the differences which we have pointed out, between the provisions of the FRENCH CODE and those of the Louisiana Code, on the subject of collation, the jurisprudence in France--and the opinions of some of the commentators--maintained, before article 843 of the

FRENCH CODE was amended by the Act of March 24, 1898, that an exemption from collation was not required to be expressed in any sacramental terms, but might be inferred from the language of the instrument, and was necessarily inferred in the case of an universal or a residuary legacy. In Dalloz's Annotated Codes, we find the following notes to article 843, viz.:

No. 75.   Incontestably, it is not necessary that the exemption or dispensation from collation be formulated in sacramental termas.

No. 76.   And dispensation or exemption [from collation] may be formulated in any manner whatever, provided the term used does not leave any doubt about the disposer's intention.

No. 77.   But, does the necessity of an express exemption imply the necessity of a formal declaration and ad hoc, inserted in the act by which the disposer manifested his intention or will?

No. 78.   Following many writers, all tacit dispensation, that is, resulting from circumstances and the merely presumed intention of the donor, is ineffectual.

No. 79.   Following the jurisprudence and certain authors, the exemption from collation may result not only from a literal and special declaration but also from comparing and reconciling the different clauses of the act, *from the nature and character of the disposition*, etc. (The italics are ours.)

No. 118.   The exemption from collation may result, not only from the whole of the different and several clauses, but from the very nature of the disposition.

No. 119.   Following the unanimous opinion, the heir was virtually discharged from collation (in the legislation anterior to the law of March 24, 1898) when the disposition made in his favor was an universal legacy.

No. 120.   Consequently, the universal disposition made in favor of one heir imputed itself in full right upon the disposable portion.

*   *   *

It is conceded in this case--for there could be no dispute about it-- that Mrs. Jordan would be entitled to claim a reduction of only a fourth of this estate, if the legacy which was given to Mrs. Reilly had been given to a stranger. It would be an anomalous doctrine, therefore, if Mrs. Jordan could virtually annul the will, by claiming all of the *legitime*, whereas, if the estate had been bequeathed to a stranger, instead of being bequeathed to the coheir, Mrs. Jordan could claim only a fourth of the estate as her *legitime*.

The judgment appealed from is amended, in that it is now ordered, adjudged and decreed that the interest of Mrs. Hazel Minter Jordan in the estate of Mrs. Julia B. Miles, deceased, is one-fourth of the estate, and that the interest of Mrs. Pearl Miles Reilly is three-fourths of the estate, and, as thus amended, the judgment is affirmed. The costs of these proceedings art to be paid by the estate of Mrs. Julia B. Miles.

*   *   *

NOTES

In *Jordan,* Justice O'Niell judicially amended various articles of the civil code. What do you think of this judicial revision? Should he have waited for the legislature to amend the Code?

What is the holding of *Jordan v. Filmore*? Are all legacies exempt from collation unless the obligation is imposed? Is it a La. C.C. 1233 case? If so, what "other equivalent terms" are used? What words or terms are the equivalents? Is it the mere fact that gifts are made by way of the testament? Would this mean that *Jordan* recognizes a "tacit" dispensation from collation? Or would the dispensation still be "express?"

SUCCESSION OF HIGGINS
275 So. 2d 447 (La. App. 4th Cir. 1973)

STOULIG, Judge.

This appeal involves the disposition of a legacy lapsed by the death of the co-legatee, William D. English, who predeceased his testator mother. The court is called upon to decide the rights of the surviving co-legatee, James D. English, Jr., in the lapsed legacy vis-a-vis those of the children of the deceased legatee, who are now forced heirs by representation in the succession of the testator.

The decedent, Mrs. Lena Wallace Higgins, by olographic will, left her estate, "share and share alike," to James and William English, her only children born of a former marriage. William predeceased her, leaving seven children who are called to this succession by representation of their father. These heirs opposed the distribution of the estate, proposed by the dative testamentary executor, which allocated three-quarters of the estate to James and one-quarter to them.

The trial court maintained the opposition and ordered the executor to "... refile said account in accordance with law, i.e. one half of the estate to each of the legatees or the heirs as mentioned in the olographic will under the terms and condition of 'share and share alike.'" From this judgment James D. English, Jr., the surviving co-legatee, has devolutively appealed.

The appellant does not pursue accretion under LSA-C.C. arts. 1707 and 1708, it being undisputed by all parties that the legacy of the estate to James and William to "share and share alike" is not a conjoint legacy, but rather a distributive legacy of halves. This determination of the character of the legacy is in accordance with the jurisprudence expressed in the cases of *Succession of McCarron*, 247 La. 419, 172 So. 2d 63 (1965), and *Succession of Lambert*, 210 La. 636, 28 So. 2d 1 (1946).

Appellant also relies on the results of these cases in maintaining the efficacy of his legacy and the distribution of the lapsed legacy of his deceased brother in accordance with the laws of intestacy. On this basis James English, Jr., submits that the proposed distribution of the dative testamentary executor is correct and that he is entitled to three-quarters of the entire estate by virtue of a one-half interest under his own legacy and an additional one-quarter interest from the intestate part of the estate (being one-half of the half share of his deceased brother's lapsed legacy); and further that the forced heirs of the decedent William English are entitled to the remaining undivided one-half of his share, being one-quarter of the estate.

Appellees argue that they are entitled to one-half of the entire estate as successors of their father to his legacy. They contend that this distribution accomplishes the testator's "intention" and that their particular case is distinguishable from *McCarron, supra*, because they are forced heirs, not collaterals.

It is our impression that the issue presented is res nova, for if there is any jurisprudence apposite to the facts of the instant case it has escaped our research. We are of the opinion that Civil Code Articles 1697, 1709, 1501, 1231, 1228, 1230, 1237, 1235 and 1236 are the controlling laws governing the distribution of this estate.

The death of William, nine years prior to that of this mother, caused the lapse of her legacy to him (LSA-C.C. art. 1697). This lapsed legacy now forms an intestate part of the succession of the decedent and shall devolve upon her legitimate heirs (LSA-C.C. art. 1709). It follows that the decedent's estate, being partially testate and partially intestate, is subject to the laws governing dispositions *mortis causa* and legal successions, respectively.

Article 1501 permits the donor to favor one or more forced heirs with the disposable portion of the estate, to the exclusion of other forced heirs, without being subject to collation, "provided it be expressly declared by the donor that this disposition is intended to be over and above the legitimate portion." The requirement that the extra advantage be formally expressed is also exacted by Article 1231.

By the very terms of her will, wherein she bequeathed her net estate to her sons "share and share alike," Mrs. Higgins obviously expressed her intention not to favor either of her sons to the prejudice of the other. Accordingly, the surviving son is precluded from maintaining that his legacy is not subject to collation because it was bequeathed as an extra portion. Since the testator did not intend either of her forced heirs to receive an extra advantage, the legacy to James must be collated as required by Articles 1228, 1230 and 1231.

As we have previously noted the succession of the decedent has a dual nature: testate as to the legacy of James and intestate as to the lapsed legacy of William. In this circumstance Article 1237 of the Civil Code affords the surviving son, James, the right to elect to either accept the legacy and renounce the legal succession or to collate the legacy and share as a forced heir in the legal succession.

The rationale of this article is that if James accepts the legacy and renounces the legal succession his status changes from that of a forced heir to that of a legatee with no greater rights than those of a stranger. As such, he could not then be forced to collate since the obligation of collation is restricted to descendants who have a right to a legitimate portion in the succession, as recognized in LSA-C.C. arts. 1235 and 1236. These articles do not affect the right of a forced heir to demand a reduction in the legacy where it impinges on the *legitime* (LSA-C.C. art. 1237).

Should the legatee fail to renounce his rights in the succession then he must bring his legacy back into the succession (collate) and share therein in the capacity of a forced heir.

Applying this reasoning to the facts in the instant case, in either event, whether James occupies the status of a legatee or forced heir, his share in the estate of his mother is an undivided one-half interest and the heirs of his deceased brother William inherit the remaining one-half interest. This result obtains by virtue of the fact that his legacy under the testament was an undivided one-half interest and as a forced heir he would inherit the same proportion, being one of the two children born to the testator.

*   *   *

The Court in *Jordan v. Filmore*, 167 La. 725, 120 So. 275 (1929), after discussing the development of the right to collation in the FRENCH CODE and declaring that collation does not apply to legacies, rendered its discussion dicta by deciding the case on the basis that the testamentary disposition clearly evidenced the legacy was intended as an extra advantage.

While my colleagues are not in accord, I agree in principle with the dicta expressed by Chief Justice O'Niell in *Jordan v. Filmore, supra*, and *Doll v. Doll, supra*, that legacies should not be subject to collation. Admittedly certain of our Civil Code articles governing collation do specifically make reference to legacies, thereby creating the incongruous situation of being in conflict with the meaning of the term "collation" as defined by Article 1227. In my opinion the phrase "or otherwise" in said article was not intended to apply to legacies (but to methods by which an advance may be accomplished during the life of the testator other than by donations *inter vivos*) since there was no reluctance on the part of the redactors of the Code to make specific use of the term "legacy" in the succeeding articles in the collation section. As contemplated by Article 1227, collation encompasses the return of advances whereas dispositions *mortis causa* are intended as the ultimate distribution of property. However, the resolution of this problem addresses itself to the legislative rather than the judicial process.

For the foregoing reasons the judgment of the trial court is affirmed. All costs of these proceedings are assessed to the succession of Mrs. Lena Wallace Higgins.

Affirmed.

NOTES

See In the Matter of Kendrick, 361 So. 2d 309 (La. App. 1st Cir. 1978). It might seem absurd that a testator would want to impose the obligation to collate in his testament (in light of the advance theory.) But the problem usually arises in contexts such as *Higgins* where circumstances have materially changed since the will was written, perhaps years before. We must look to the words in the testament to determine what the testator would have intended had he thought about the changes.

The lawyer for the heir of the predeceased son in *Higgins* found a rather frightening challenge, did he not? On first glance, it seemed that *Jordan* was squarely against him; after all, he was arguing in favor of the collation of a donation *mortis causa*. But, instead of giving up, he went back to the books and carefully reread *Jordan*. This set him on a search for words in the testament which would have the effect of imposing the obligation to collate - words authorized by *Jordan* itself: "share and share alike." This means share equally; more perfect words of equality could not be found short of expressly using the terms "equality" or "advance." *Jordan* had indicated that "other equivalent terms" under La. C.C. 1233 could be read broadly. If this could be done in *Jordan* for dispensation from collation, why not do it in *Higgins* for imposition of collation? Instead of treating *Jordan* as an enemy, as an obstacle to surpass, the lawyer relied on it and used it. He did not ask the circuit court to overrule the Supreme Court precedent, but rather asked the court to apply it.

Can a testator dispense with collation by so stating in an olographic will? In the *Succession of Hendrick*, 430 So. 2d 734 (La. App. 2d Cir. 1983), the court, relying on Civil Code article 1232, as it read at that time, held that collation could not be dispensed with in an olographic will because such a will is not an authentic act. *Hendrick* was legislatively overruled by Act 246 in 1986 which amended Civil Code articles 1232 and 1501. A declaration dispensing with collation may now be made in the instrument of donation, by a subsequent notarial act, or in the donor's last will and testament.

SUCCESSION OF ODUM
760 So. 2d 435 (La. App. 1st Cir. 2000)

FOIL, Judge.

This is an appeal from a judgment of the Nineteenth Judicial District Court granting a motion for partial summary judgment in favor of appellee, the Succession of Marilyn Lee Odum Titus Haubert, and against appellants, the Executor of the Succession of Earnest Stanley Odum; the Trustees of the Earnest Stanley Odum Trust; and Deborah Sue Odum, Kathy Jane Odum, Stanley Karl Odum and Bobbie Jean Odum. The trial court held that Marilyn Titus Haubert and her successors are entitled to receive one-fifth of the assets of the Earnest Stanley Odum *inter vivos* trust by application of the collation articles of the LOUISIANA CIVIL CODE. For the reasons that follow, we reverse.

FACTS

Earnest Stanley Odum established the Earnest Stanley Odum Trust on June 8, 1988, and, by the time of his death on November 10, 1993, had transferred more than 90% in value of his assets to the Trust. Mr. Odum was the sole beneficiary of the Trust during his lifetime; upon his death, the secondary beneficiaries were "the class composed of all Settlor's children, namely, Deborah Sue Odum, Kathy Jane Odum, Stanley Karl Odum and Bobbie Jean Odum."

At the same time that the Trust was created, Mr. Odum also executed his Last Will and Testament, in which he confirmed the Trust and stated that he left all of his remaining property to the four named children.

Unbeknownst to his current family, as well as his long-time friend and the executor of his will, Harding J. Alleman, Mr. Odum had another child from a short-lived first marriage. After Mr. Odum's death, the executor learned that there might be another child. He employed the services of a research company to search for the missing child, who was eventually found residing in the State of Pennsylvania. Her name was Marilyn Lee Odum Titus Haubert. Mrs. Haubert was born in 1935 to the decedent and his first wife, who were subsequently divorced in Ohio in 1938. Mrs. Haubert thereafter passed out of Mr. Odum's life. She was adopted by her stepfather, E. James Titus, and her surname was changed from Odum to Titus. Mrs. Haubert was not mentioned in the Odum Trust or in Mr. Odum's will.

Having located Mrs. Haubert, the executor informed her that she could have rights in the Odum succession as a forced heir. The executor and the four named children were prepared to recognize that Mrs. Haubert was entitled to a forced portion of the estate under Louisiana law in effect at the time of the decedent's death. The forced portion for one of five children is 1/5th of one-half, or 1/10th, of the mass of the estate. Mrs. Haubert, however, brought this action in Louisiana claiming not just 1/10th of the mass of the estate, but a full 1/5th of the assets of the Trust. Mrs. Haubert died after being notified of her forced heirship rights, and her executor has pursued the action on behalf of her estate.

The Haubert estate filed a motion for partial summary judgment asserting that, under the Civil Code Articles dealing with collation, Mrs. Haubert was entitled to receive an amount equal to 1/5th of the assets of the Trust, if greater than her forced portion. The executor and the four named children filed cross- motions for partial summary judgment denying that Mrs. Haubert was entitled to any assets greater than her forced portion.

ACTIONS OF TRIAL COURT

In their initial answer, appellants raised numerous defenses. The trial court appointed a special master to make recommendations on those issues. The special master analyzed all of the defenses and was of the view that none of them sufficed to defeat Mrs. Haubert's claim that gifts in trust by Mr. Odum should be collated. The trial court followed the special master's recommendations in that regard and granted the motion for partial summary judgment in favor of the Haubert estate, thereby denying appellants' motions for partial summary judgment. The court decreed that Mrs. Haubert was entitled to 1/5th of the assets of the Trust, and that such rights passed to the Haubert estate.

DISCUSSION

Appellants challenge the trial court's finding that Mrs. Haubert is entitled to more than her forced portion by application of the law of collation. Specifically, they seek review of the court's findings that: (1) the decedent did not sufficiently demonstrate his intent to favor the four named children over Mrs. Haubert; and (2) Mrs. Haubert would benefit from collation as requested.

Under Louisiana law in effect at the time of Mr. Odum's death, a child of any age was a forced heir. Because Mr. Odum had five children, the forced portion of his estate was one-half of the "mass" of his estate. The forced portion for each child was 1/5 of one-half, or 1/10th, of the mass. The mass consisted of probate assets and property donated during life, including the property donated to the Trust. The record shows that the executor is not aware of any other gifts made by Mr. Odum during his life.

The executor, having located Mrs. Haubert and determined that she was Mr. Odum's daughter, expected to deliver to her 1/10th of the mass. Mrs. Haubert, however, proceeded to assert a right to more than her forced portion. Her estate now claims that the law of collation awards her a full 1/5th of the Trust assets. We hold that the record does not support this claim.

*   *   *

Article 1229 is the real starting point for the analysis of this case. It makes it clear that collation is based on two presumptions: (1) that a decedent intends for all his property to be divided equally among his children; and (2) that a particular gift made to one of them during life is an advance on that child's equal share. *See Succession of Gomez*, 223 La. 859, 869-870, 67 So. 2d 156, 159-160 (1953).

Collation under Civil Code articles 1227, et seq., is often confused with reduction. Reduction, sometimes referred to as "fictitious" collation, is the means by which an omitted forced heir collects his forced portion, and is set forth in Civil Code articles 1493, et seq. Collation, sometimes referred to as "actual" or "real" collation, is the means by which a forced heir gives effect to the decedent's intent that he share equally in the estate. Thus, reduction defeats a decedent's intention to leave out a forced heir, while collation gives effect to a decedent's intention.

In *Jordan v. Filmore*, 167 La. 725, 120 So. 275 (1929), the decedent left her entire estate to only one of her two children. The excluded child claimed not just her forced portion, but a full half of the estate, on the grounds that the decedent's will did not specifically exempt the legacy from collation. The Supreme Court rejected this claim, explaining that the legacy of all the estate to one child was itself a sufficient expression of the decedent's intention to dispense with collation. In this regard, the court stated:

> [T]here would be no sense in the requirement--that a testator who bequeaths more of the disposable portion of his estate to one of his descendant heirs than to another must express, any more plainly than his favoritism itself expresses, his intention that the legacy bequeathed to the favored heir is intended as an advantage over the other heir, or as an extra portion--in order to avoid the obligation of collation....

Jordan, 120 So. at 278.

A similar action to compel collation was brought in *Succession of Degelos*, 446 So. 2d 412 (La. App. 4th Cir.1984). In that case, the decedent left his estate to his surviving spouse and the three children of his second marriage. Another daughter who was left out of her father's will filed suit seeking entitlement to an equal fourth with the other children, on the grounds that the will did not expressly state that the legacy to the other three children was intended as an extra portion. *Degelos*, 446 So. 2d at 413. The court followed *Jordan*, which it identified as "a time honored case", and added the following reasons for rejecting the claim to compel collation:

> The testator's intention to favor the three children of his second marriage over his oldest daughter Inez is expressed in his bequest to the former as universal legatees and his failure to mention Inez. There is no legal requirement that he expressly state or declare the bequests to be an advantage or extra portion....
>
> To uphold Inez' claim for an undivided 1/4 interest in the entire estate would effectively ignore the testator's intent and cause the property to pass as if by intestacy. It is well settled that when a testator disposes of his entire estate to the prejudice of a forced heir, such a bequest does not make the will null and void but merely subjects it to an action for reduction by the forced heir for the recovery of his *legitime*.

Degelos, 446 So. 2d at 414.

The foregoing cases concerned the operation of collation in the absence of lifetime donations, but, if one forced heir is favored over another in the will, it makes no difference whether the donations to the favored heir occurred during life or at death. Whenever a decedent by his will shows that he did not intend for a forced heir to share in the disposable portion, that heir cannot claim collation of any advantages. The decedent's actual intention overrides the presumed intention to benefit all the heirs equally.

The first issue before the court is whether or not, under the Civil Code and the jurisprudence, Mr. Odum sufficiently indicated that he intended to favor the four named children over Mrs. Haubert both in his will and in the Trust. The record shows that Mr. Odum did dispense with collation, and that the trial court erred in ruling otherwise on this issue.

In this case, it is clear that Mr. Odum: (1) did not intend for his property to benefit his five forced heirs equally; and (2) intended instead to benefit the four named children only. Further, it can be presumed that he intended to leave nothing to Mrs. Haubert. This intent is shown both by Mr. Odum's decision to exclude Mrs. Haubert from the Trust and by his express intention to leave the remainder of his estate to the four named children with nothing to Mrs. Haubert under his will.

The evidence of his intent is the language Mr. Odum used in his will: "I leave the rest and remainder of my property to my four beloved children, Deborah Sue Odum, Kathy Jane Odum, Stanley Karl Odum, and Bobbie Jean Odum, to share and share alike." The Louisiana Supreme Court has specifically stated that, in order for a testator to dispense with collation in his last will and testament, "it is not necessary for the language of the will to include a direct reference to collation." *Succession of Fakier*, 541 So. 2d 1372, 1380 (La.1988). All that is necessary is that the intent to give an advantage to some heirs over others be set forth "in an unequivocal manner." Id. (citing Article 1233). Thus, the presumption that Mr. Odum intended Mrs. Haubert to share equally in the succession is overcome, and Mrs. Haubert cannot compel collation. It is clear from the record that Mr. Odum sufficiently evidenced his intent. Thus, Mrs. Haubert is limited to her forced portion.

We conclude that the language of Mr. Odum's will had the effect of excluding collation of the Trust property because the will clearly expresses his intent to give the maximum amount allowable by law to his four named children.

CONCLUSION

The law of forced heirship allows an omitted forced heir to partially defeat a testator's intentions where the heir has been denied his forced portion. On the other hand, the law of collation is designed to give effect to a testator's intentions to the fullest extent possible. It is presumed that the testator intends all his children to benefit equally, and that gifts made to one or more of them during life are advances on their equal shares. This presumption, however, is defeated when the testator in his will favors some forced heirs over others. When the presumption of equality no longer exists, the omitted forced heir cannot make a claim of collation. The testator's unequivocal desire to limit the forced heir to his forced portion cannot be defeated by collation.

Here, Mr. Odum transferred most of his property to a trust whose beneficiaries after his death are his four named children, and further made a will confirming the trust and leaving the remainder of his estate to the same four named children. Clearly, Mr. Odum's intent was to leave everything to those four named children. Here, the omitted heir can claim reduction to satisfy her forced portion, but she cannot compel collation. It is our opinion that since the law of collation is designed to give effect to the decedent's intent, it cannot be applied to defeat the clear evidence of actual intent as exists in this case.

DECREE

For the foregoing reasons, that portion of the trial court's judgment that grants collation is reversed. Judgment is rendered in favor of appellants, decreeing that the Succession of Marilyn Lee Odum Titus Haubert is not entitled to collation. In all other respects, the judgment is affirmed. Costs of this appeal are assessed against appellee, the Succession of Marilyn Lee Odum Titus Haubert.

AFFIRMED IN PART, REVERSED IN PART, AND RENDERED.

GONZALES, J., dissents.

GUIDRY, J., dissents and assigns reasons.

GUIDRY, J. dissenting.

I disagree with the majority opinion in this matter because I do not find that Mr. Odum ever expressly or unequivocally dispensed with collation in his will or in the trust in a manner sanctioned by the Civil Code. The presumption in favor of collation was not rebutted. I would affirm the judgment of the trial court. Therefore, I respectfully dissent.

SUCCESSION OF FAKIER
541 So. 2d 1372 (La. 1988)
[63 Tul. L. Rev. 942 (1989)]

CALOGERO, Justice.

The issue in this case is whether certain property transferred by the testatrix to her daughters is subject to collation. The property in question includes a diamond ring which the decedent gave to one of her daughters, and five annuity policies purchased by the decedent which named both of her daughters as beneficiaries in the event of her death.

The parties seeking collation of the subject property are grandchildren, the children of testatrix's predeceased son. Under the terms of the will, the grandchildren received only the share of the forced portion reserved for them by law, whereas the daughters were jointly bequeathed their respective shares of the forced portion and the entire disposable portion of the estate.

The trial judge rejected the grandchildren's demand for collation, finding that the diamond ring is not collatable for two reasons: (1) the decedent's *inter vivos* transfer constituted a manual gift, and (2) the will dispensed with the necessity of collation because it reflected the decedent's intent to favor her daughters to the maximum extent allowed by law. The trial judge also concluded that the annuities are similar to life insurance policies and are not subject to collation because the proceeds of life insurance policies are legally protected from the claims of forced heirs under LA. REV. STAT. ANN. §22:647 (West 1978 & 1988 Supp.) and LA. CIV. CODE ANN. art. 1505 (West 1987). Relying on similar reasoning, the court of appeal affirmed. *Succession of Fakier*, 509 So. 2d 33 (La. App. 1st Cir.1987). We granted a writ to review the judgment of the court of appeal. 513 So. 2d 1198 (La.1987).

We now reverse that portion of the court of appeal's judgment which held that the ring is not to be collated. The ring is not exempt from collation simply because it was a manual gift. Nor did the decedent dispense with the necessity of collating the ring in her will, or in any other manner sanctioned by the LOUISIANA CIVIL CODE. Therefore, the ring is subject to actual collation under the provisions of LSA-C.C. art. 1227, et seq.

The annuities, on the other hand, are not subject to actual collation for the reason that they were not transferred by *inter vivos* donation. For this reason alone, we affirm the portion of the court of appeal's judgment which held that the annuity proceeds are not collatable.

In so holding, we expressly note that we do not pass upon the issue of whether the value of the annuities should be fictitiously collated for the purpose of calculating the active mass of the succession and the corresponding amount of the *legitime* under LSA-C.C. art. 1505. Although raised in brief by the grandchildren, that issue was neither presented by the motion filed by them nor directly addressed by the lower courts. Nothing in our opinion today prevents the parties from seeking to adjudicate that issue in the future.

(I) FACTS AND DISPOSITION BY THE COURTS BELOW

Flossie Fakier died on January 7, 1983. She was predeceased by her husband, George Fakier, Sr., as well as by her son, George Fakier, Jr. She was survived by two daughters, Patricia and Mary, and her son's four children.

In 1981, after the death of her husband, Mrs. Fakier executed a statutory will. The will appointed Patricia as executrix of her estate, made certain specific bequests to her granddaughters and left the entire disposable portion of the estate to the two daughters. The testament contained the following explanation of the dispositions made therein:

> In explanation of my bequests hereinafter made, I provide the following. It was always my intention and the intention of George C. Fakier, Sr., that our three children would share equally at the time of our deaths, in the estate that we had acquired together during our marriage. George C. Fakier, Sr., had sincerely desired that our son, George C. Fakier, Jr., should have a business in order to support his family. Following the death of George C. Fakier, Sr., and at a time when George C. Fakier, Jr., was terminally ill, my daughters and I executed various documents, wherein George C. Fakier, Jr., and his heirs, were enabled to obtain, in full ownership, the entirety of our family business, George C. Fakier & Son, Inc. At the time of the disposition of the stock held by myself and by my daughters to George C. Fakier, Jr., and to his children, I and my daughters were not fully informed or made aware of the valuations, exact details, consequences and divestitures resulting from the transfer agreements. Accordingly, a significantly less dollar value was received by each of my daughters than they were apparently entitled to. As the direct result, the heirs of my son, George C. Fakier, Jr., have been greatly favored over my daughters by their sole ownership of a business corporation, owning real estate, improvements, and merchandise of great value, both then and now.

As a direct consequence of the lesser and unequal monetary sums received by my daughters in my husband's estate in comparison to the value of the monetary sums and benefits received by my son, George C. Fakier, Jr., and his heirs, as stated in the last preceding paragraph, it is my desire to provide my two daughters with as much property, of whatever nature, movable and immovable, community and separate, including all rights and credits that I may own at the time of my death, to the fullest extent and as may be authorized by law.

More particularly, it is my desire that my two daughters, Patsy Ann and Mary Jude, shall receive, along with the heirs of my son, George C. Fakier, Jr., their respective forced portions. Additionally, it is my express desire that my two daughters, Patsy Ann and Mary Jude, shall receive, in equal parts and share and share alike, the entirety of the disposable portion of my estate which remains after the computation of the forced portion to which each of my daughters and the heirs of George C. Fakier, Jr., shall each legally receive.

After the succession was opened and the will was entered into probate, the executrix filed a detailed descriptive list of the property owned by the decedent at the time of her death. The children of the testatrix's predeceased son (the grandchildren) then filed a "Motion to Traverse Detailed Descriptive List; To Require Collation of Gifts; And to Require Appraisal of Gifts."

In the motion, the grandchildren alleged that the detailed descriptive list omitted "certain collatable gifts of annuity contracts" made by Mrs. Fakier to Patricia and Mary, the total value of said annuities being $301,800. The motion further alleged that the descriptive list omitted another "collatable gift," that being a $10,000 ring that Mrs. Fakier had given to Patricia. Finally, the motion described certain immovable property donated by Flossie to her daughters in 1980.

The motion requested the following relief:

(1) appraisal of the immovable property "so that the disposable portion might be calculated in accordance with C.C. Article 1505";
(2) supplementation of the detailed descriptive list to include the ring and the annuities;
(3) the issuance of an order directing the daughters to "show cause why the items of property (the ring and the annuities) should not be collated."

At the hearing on the motion, testimony was presented only with respect to the annuity contracts. Patricia Fakier testified that after her father died, Mrs. Fakier attempted to purchase life insurance but was unable to do so because of a health problem. As an alternative, she purchased two of the annuity policies in question, naming her daughters as beneficiaries in the event of her death. In addition to these two policies, Mr. Fakier had purchased three policies of life insurance which named Mrs. Fakier as the beneficiary. After her husband's death, Mrs. Fakier exercised her option as beneficiary of the latter policies to convert them into supplemental annuity contracts. These three annuity contracts provided that the proceeds would be received by the two daughters in the event of her death.

The trial judge ruled that neither the ring nor the annuities would be collated. He held that the ring was exempt from collation because it was a manual gift and because the explanatory statement in the decedent's will evidenced her intent to have any *inter vivos* gift which was made to either of her daughters considered as "an extra portion." Citing La. R.S. 22:647 and LSA-C.C. art. 1505 for the proposition that life insurance policies are exempt from "collation," the trial judge further concluded that under the "distinctive facts" of this case, the annuities have "the same legal status as life insurance policies" and therefore are not collatable.

The court of appeal affirmed. It agreed that the ring was exempt from collation because it was a manual gift. It also reasoned that in light of the fact that Mrs. Fakier's son and her son's heirs had apparently received more than an equal share of her estate by virtue of the earlier transfer of the business, collation of the ring would "defeat the equality among heirs which the rules of collation are designed to protect." 509 So. 2d at 34. The court of appeal also agreed with the trial court that Mrs. Fakier intended for the annuities to operate as death benefits, thus giving them "the same practical effect as life insurance." Id. at 35. Emphasizing the importance of the fact that Mrs. Fakier intended to bequeath to her daughters the maximum amount allowable by law, the appellate court concluded that the annuities would not be subject to collation.

*   *   *

(IV) RESOLUTION OF ISSUES PRESENTED FOR REVIEW

(A) Actual Collation of the Ring

The grandchildren's motion alleges that the decedent made to her daughter Patricia an *inter vivos* donation of a ring valued at $10,000. At the hearing on the motion, counsel for the grandchildren acknowledged, or stated, that his request for collation of the ring was premature. As a consequence no testimony was taken on that subject. For reasons not clear from the record, the trial court ruled on the issue anyway, holding that the ring is not subject to collation. The court of appeal also addressed the donation of the ring, and affirmed the trial court's finding that the ring is not collatable. Because neither party has ever objected to the fact that the trial court and the court of appeal ruled on this issue, we conclude that they have implicitly consented to its adjudication.

The grandchildren contend that because the decedent executed no instrument dispensing with the requirement that the ring be collated, actual collation must occur. The executrix disagrees, contending that decedent's will is the instrument which dispenses with the requirement of collating the ring.

LSA-Art. 1232 provides that the act which dispenses with collation may be the donor's last will and testament. In order to effectuate a dispensation, it is not necessary for the language of the will to include a direct reference to collation. Article 1231 states that a declaration that the donation was "made as an advantage or extra part" is sufficient. The declaration that the donation was so intended may be made "in other equivalent terms," as long as that intention is set forth "in an unequivocal manner." LSA-C.C. art. 1233.

However, Mrs. Fakier's will does not refer to the transfer of the ring, or to any other *inter vivos* donations that she may have made to one or more of her children. In order to relieve Patricia from the obligation of collating the ring, in a manner required by the civil code, the testatrix could have (1) made a reference in her will to the transfer of the ring, and indicated by appropriate language that she gave the ring to Patricia as part of the latter's extra portion, or (2) stated generally that all *inter vivos* gifts to her daughters, or to her children, were intended as

8-21

advantages. The testatrix chose neither option, and the civil code requirements for dispensation from collation were not met.

The executrix would have us assume that because Mrs. Fakier left the entire disposable portion of her estate to her daughters (minus certain particular legacies), and stated in her testament that she desired to favor her daughters in order to equalize the effect of past advantages to her son, she did not intend for the daughters to collate any *inter vivos* donations. The trial court and the court of appeal accepted this assumption, reasoning that collation of the ring was contrary to the testatrix's intention.

We reject this assumption for two reasons. First and foremost, the Civil Code sets forth with precision the method by which a donor may dispense with collation, and absent a dispensation sanctioned by the Code, courts are not free to decline to order collation based upon their assumptions about the donor's intentions. To the contrary, "collation is always presumed, where it has not been expressly forbidden," according to C.C. article 1230.

Secondly, the will cannot be considered as a reflection of the testatrix's intentions regarding any *inter vivos* donations that she made to her daughters, for the simple reason that the will does not mention such donations. The fact that Mrs. Fakier's will expresses the desire for her daughters to inherit the disposable portion does not speak to whether she intended that Patricia would or would not have to collate the value of the ring by taking that amount less when succession assets are distributed. Further, if the testatrix gave the ring to Patricia as an advantage, that advantage would exist not only over the grandchildren, but also over Patricia's sister, Mary. There is no indication in the will that Mrs. Fakier intended to favor Patricia in this fashion.

Nor does the testatrix's expressed desire to have her three children "share equally" in the amount ultimately received from her and her husband, *inter vivos* and *mortis causa*, constitute a dispensation from collation. There is no indication in the will that Mrs. Fakier thought that collation of *inter vivos* gifts would defeat this equal sharing or the "evening up" that she hoped to achieve by bequeathing her daughters the disposable portion.

This case is readily distinguishable from *Darby v. Darby*, 118 La. 328, 42 So. 953 (1907), where the act of donation specified that the property was donated in order to place the donee on equal footing with other descendants who had received previous advances. We concluded that the language in that act of donation reflected the donor's intention that the donee receive the property described in the act of transfer as an extra portion. In this case, however, there is no document, be it the will or otherwise, which refers at all to the gift of the ring, or which generically exempts from collation *inter vivos* donations to Patricia. Thus we do not know what the testatrix's intentions were regarding the donation of the ring, and, in light of the presumption in favor of collation required by article 1230, we decline to guess.

*   *   *

NOTES

The sole question addressed by the court in *Darby v. Darby*, 118 La. 328, 42 So. 953 (1907), was whether or not the son of the decedent should have been required to collate the value of land donated to him by the decedent through a valid donation *inter vivo*.

The language of the act was as follows:

. . . and given to each [child] money or property amounting in each case to more than two thousand five hundred dollars, and having given nothing to her son, Octave Darby, it is her wish and intention to place him upon footing equal to her other children, and to equalize the advance in money and otherwise which she has made to her other children as named and for that purpose, to place the said donee upon a footing equal with said other children, it was her intention to make, and she does make, a donation *inter vivos* unto her son, Octave Darby, who is here present accepting for himself and his heirs and assigns, the following described property. . .

The court found it unnecessary to consider whether or not the other children had actually received any money from the decedent. What was important, according to the court, was that the decedent believed that she had granted advantages to her other children and that she clearly intended that the son should have the property over and above his share in her succession.

If the donor exerts the effort to disguise his donation as a sale, doesn't that effort display an intention to dispense with collation? Couldn't we characterize that as "other equivalent terms"? *See Montgomery v. Chaney*, 13 La. Ann. 207 (1858). Review La. C.C. 1248, 2444, and 2025-2028. Is an "advantage" as used in La. C.C. 1248 equivalent to a gift, or is it merely another thing to be collated. If the latter, is it subject to the three-year provision of La. C.C. 1235?

Leslie J. Clement, Comment, *Some Aspects of Collation*
34 La. L. Rev. 782 (1974)
[Reprinted with permission]

*   *   *

Collation of Donations Mortis Causa

Although the Civil Code requires the collation of both *inter vivos* and *mortis causa* donations, since the 1929 case of *Jordan v. Filmore* the jurisprudence has indicated that the obligation to collate does not apply to legacies. Jordan arose when a decedent left a will in which one of two forced heirs was named as universal legatee. When the excluded heir sued to annul a donation by the decedent to a third person, the universal legatee intervened and claimed the entire estate under the will. The lower court annulled the donation and declared the decedent's will to be valid, but reduced the intervenor's legacy to one-half of the decedent's succession on the theory that since the de cujus had not declared an intent to bestow an advantage on either of her heirs, the universal legatee could take only half the succession--either as heir or as legatee. On appeal to the Louisiana supreme court, the only issue was whether the universal legatee was entitled to one-half or three-fourths of the succession, the latter being composed of the *legitime* of one-fourth plus the entire one-half disposable portion in the event that collation was not required. Chief Justice O'Niell, speaking for the majority, asserted   that the right to demand collation arises only from donations *inter vivos* and not from legacies since "it would be absurd to say that what is given by last will and testament, by an ancestor to his offspring, is presumed to be given in advance of what the legatee might one day expect from his ancestor's succession."

However, the basis of the court's award of three-fourths of the succession to the universal legatee was apparently the decedent's intent since the Chief Justice added:

> there is no indication . . . .that a testator who bequeaths more of the disposable portion of his estate to one of his descendant heirs than to another must state, any more plainly than his favoritism itself expresses, his intention that the legacy bequeathed to the favored heir is intended as an advantage, or as an extra portion-in order to avoid the obligation of collation, strictly so called.

Thus, the assertion that donations *mortis causa* need never be collated was clearly dicta; nevertheless it has frequently been repeated in subsequent cases.

Several Civil Code articles indicate that a forced heir who claims a share of his ancestor's succession must collate all   donations *inter vivos* and *mortis causa* which were not declared by the donor to be an extra portion. However, the declaration that the gift or legacy is intended as an extra portion need not be made in sacramental terms so long as it is indicated "in an unequivocal manner" that such was the will of the donor. Although an unequivocal intent to bestow an extra portion may be evident in some testamentary donations to forced heirs, the non-collation of all donations *mortis causa* cannot be justified on the same basis. Thus, if the de cujus bequeaths all or a large portion of his property to a forced heir, it may be presumed to be an extra portion. The testator's intent is likewise apparent if the legacy is specifically from the disposable portion. In other cases, the testator's intent is not so obvious, and there may be an express indication that a legacy is not intended as an extra portion. In such cases, there is no justification for exempting advantages from collation merely because they were received by donation *mortis causa*.

Although the non-collation of donations *mortis causa* appears to be a settled jurisprudential rule since *Jordan*, the result in every case in which this rule has been cited was determined by other considerations. In *Winbarg v. Winbarg*, the decedent's testament expressly indicated that there should be no collation. The terms of the will under attack in *Succession of Meyer* were contradictory, possibly indicating the testator's intent to dispense with collation. In any event, that suit was based upon a claim for the reduction of an excessive donation rather than for collation. What was said about the collation of *mortis causa* donations in *Doll v. Doll* was clearly extraneous since the issue there was whether a judgment of possession barred a demand for collation. In *Succession of Fertel*, the testatrix had bequeathed her entire estate, less $100 per month to her son, to her two daughters. The daughters were not required to collate their legacies, allegedly because of the prohibition against collating donations *mortis causa*, yet the son was required to collate his legacy because the court interpreted the intent of the testatrix to so require. The testatrix in *Roach v. Roach* bequeathed all her property to certain of her eight surviving children; collation was not required because of her intent to favor the named legatees.

The most recent discussion of the collation of donations *mortis causa* occurred in *Succession of Higgins*. There the de cujus had willed her entire estate, "share and share alike," to James and William English, her only children. William had predeceased the testatrix, leaving seven children who claimed their father's share *ab intestado* by representation. When the testamentary executor proposed to distribute three-quarters of the succession to their uncle, the children filed an opposition. The trial court maintained the opposition and ordered the executor to distribute the succession equally between James and the children of William. On appeal to the Fourth Circuit Court of Appeal, James claimed that he should be entitled to receive three-quarters of the succession by virtue of a one-half interest under his own legacy and an additional one-quarter interest from the intestate part of the succession (being one-half of the half share of his deceased brother's legacy). The court decided that since the succession was partially testate and partially intestate, it was subject to the laws governing dispositions *mortis causa* and legal successions. The court then found that by the terms of her testament, the decedent had expressed no intention to favor either of her sons, and it therefore concluded that James would either have to accept his legacy and renounce the legal succession, or collate his legacy and share as a forced heir in the legal succession. In either event, the court held that James could recover only one-half of his mother's succession. However, the author of the opinion then proceeded to contradict the court's holding by stating that he personally felt that the right to demand collation should not extend to legacies, even though he acknowledged that statements to that effect in earlier cases were dicta.

Although the holding in *Higgins* was correctly based upon the testator's intent, the dicta concerning the collation of legacies evidences a continuing problem in this area of the law. Henceforth, questions relating to the collation of donations *mortis causa* should be settled by application of the rules of the Civil Code which state that forced-heir legatees cannot claim their legacies in addition to their hereditary shares unless the legacies are unequivocally declared to have been made as an advantage or extra portion. Otherwise, the Civil Code provisions on collation, as well as the rule that the fundamental goal in the probate of testaments is the ascertainment and execution of the testator's true intent, may be circumvented.

* * *

Who May Demand Collation and from Whom: La. C.C. 1235, La. C.C. 1228, 1238

SUCCESSION OF HURD
489 So. 2d 1029 (La. App.1st Cir. 1986)

WATKINS, Judge.

Anita Vincent Hurd died intestate on May 26, 1981, and was survived by three children, Roy Edward Hurd, Jr., Gayle Hurd Swords, and Royanne Hurd Blossman. Her succession was opened in the 22nd Judicial District Court for the Parish of St. Tammany, Louisiana, and remains open with no judgment of possession having been rendered.

Roy Edward Hurd, Jr., filed a Petition for Relief under Chapter 11 of the Bankruptcy Code on March 12, 1982. Subsequently, on July 7, 1983, that proceeding was converted to a liquidation under Chapter 7 of Title 11 of the Bankruptcy Code. Robert L. Marrero was appointed trustee in bankruptcy.

On October 17, 1984, Robert L. Marrero, as Trustee in Bankruptcy of Roy Edward Hurd, Jr., filed a petition against the two sisters of Roy Edward Hurd, Jr., viz. Gayle Hurd Swords and Royanne Hurd Blossman, seeking collation of all gifts made by Anita Vincent Hurd to Mr. Hurd's two sisters, alleging that certain purported sales to them from their mother were donations in disguise.

To this petition for collation, Gayle Hurd Swords and Royanne Hurd Blossman filed an exception of no right of action contending that the right to demand collation is limited to forced heirs in the descending line under La. C.C. art. 1235. The trial court sustained the exception of no right of action. We reverse and remand.

La. C.C. art. 1235 reads as follows:

> The obligation of collating is confined to children or descendants succeeding to their fathers and mothers or other ascendants, whether *ab intestato* or by virtue of a testament.
>
> Therefore this collation can not be demanded by any other heir, nor even by the legatees or creditors of the succession to which the collation is due.

Thus, the right to demand collation may not be exercised by creditors of the succession. It was held by analogy in *Succession of Henican*, 248 So. 2d 385 (La.App. 4th Cir.1971), *writ refused*, 259 La. 756, 252 So. 2d 454 (1971), that the creditors of a forced heir could not demand reduction to the forced portion; the right to demand collation or reduction being personal to the forced heir. *See also*, Yiannopoulos, Vol. 2, CIVIL LAW TREATISE, PROPERTY, West 2d Ed. § 128, Note 107. It should be noted that the present La.C.C. art. 2044 provides that an obligee of a debtor who is insolvent may exercise a right of the debtor by the oblique action unless the right is strictly personal to the debtor.

It is thus clear that a creditor of a bankrupt cannot demand collation from the bankrupt's co-forced heirs, as that right is personal to the bankrupt debtor. But the question we must now answer is may a trustee in bankruptcy demand collation from the co-forced heirs of the bankrupt?

Under Section 541(a)(1) of the Bankruptcy Code, all legal or equitable interests of the bankrupt form part of the bankruptcy estate. COLLIER ON BANKRUPTCY, Vol. 4, § 541.09 interprets the quoted section of the Bankruptcy Code to include as property of the bankruptcy estate property rights that are personal to the debtor, regardless of whether or not they would be transferable or whether or not the creditor could levy upon those property rights. Although the trustee in bankruptcy has all the rights of a judgment lien creditor as was held in *Angeles Real Estate Co. v. Kerxton*, 737 F.2d 416 (4th Cir.1984), his rights, as *Angeles* indicates, are somewhat broader than the rights enjoyed by a judgment lien creditor. A trustee in bankruptcy, as the cited section of Collier indicates, may collect as part of the bankruptcy estate, property which the creditors of the bankrupt could not levy upon because they are personal to the bankrupt.

The Bankruptcy Code was obviously formulated with the common law in mind under which collation is unknown (although a device somewhat similar, "putting in hotchpot", is found). We are constrained under the Supremacy Clause of the UNITED STATES CONSTITUTION (Article VI) to apply laws enacted thereunder as the Supreme Law of the Land. Although the Bankruptcy Code, which the UNITED STATES CONSTITUTION empowered Congress to enact under Article I, Section 8, was enacted without mention (or probably specific consideration) of the civilian concept of collation, we must conclude by virtue of 11 U.S.C. § 541(a)(1) that the trustee in bankruptcy of a forced heir has the right to demand collation from the co-forced heirs, any state policy in the LOUISIANA CIVIL CODE or Louisiana jurisprudence to the contrary notwithstanding.

Accordingly, the judgment of the trial court is reversed, and the case remanded for further proceedings, with all costs to await final disposition of the matter.

REVERSED AND REMANDED.

Kerry J. Miller, *The New Forced Heirship Law, Its' Implementing Legislation, and Major Substantive Policy Changes of the Louisiana State Law Institute's Proposed Comprehensive Revision of the Successions and Donations Laws*
71 Tul. L. Rev. 223 (1996)
[Reprinted with permission]

*   *   *

Traditionally, collation meant that descendants coming to the succession of a parent or other ascendant must return either directly or indirectly the *inter vivos* donations they received from the decedent which were not declared as extra portions.[118] In the absence of an unequivocal declaration[119] by the decedent that an *inter vivos* donation is an extra portion, or unless one of the automatic exemptions from collation apply,[120] collation must take place.[121] Collation is based on two policies. The first is the policy of equality among the heirs.[122] The second policy is that an *inter vivos* donation should be treated as an advance on the decedent's inheritance, unless the decedent intended otherwise.[123] In the original house bill of the 1996 First Extraordinary Session, House Bill 55 (Act 77 is the final enrolled form of House Bill 55), collation was to be repealed in its entirety.[124] However, collation was included in the final enrolled house bill,

---

[118] *See* LA. CIV. CODE ANN. arts. 1227-1228 (West 1987).

[119] Such declarations may be made in the act of donation itself, in a subsequent authentic act, or in a testament. *See* LA. CIV. CODE ANN. art. 1232 (West 1987).

[120] Automatic exemptions from collation are: expenses for board, support, education or apprenticeship; wedding presents that do not exceed the disposable portion; usual and customary manual gifts; profits derived from onerous contracts with the decedent; and immovables donated by the decedent that were destroyed in the hands of the donee due to no fault of the donee. *See* LA. CIV. CODE ANN. arts. 1244-1246, 1250 (West 1987). In addition, a donee may avoid the obligation to collate by renouncing the succession. *See id.* art. 1237. However, the *inter vivos* donation that has not been collated must not exceed the disposable portion. *See id.*

[121] *See* LA. CIV. CODE ANN. art. 1228 (West 1994).

[122] *See id.* art. 1229.

[123] *See id.* art. 1227.

[124] *See* La. H.R. 55, 22d Leg., 1st Ex. Sess. (1996) (original). This bill was recommended by the Louisiana State Law Institute. The Law Institute's recommendation to repeal collation in the original bill may have been influenced by the forced heirship constitutional amendment. However, the policies of forced heirship and collation are not identical. As noted in the text, the policies of collation are equality among the heirs and the notion that any *inter vivos* donation is merely an advance on the donee's inheritance. Collation is not mandatory; it is a rebuttable presumption. *See* LA. CIV. CODE ANN. art. 1230 (West 1987). The donor may expressly exempt *inter vivos* donations from collation by declaring them to be extra portions. Forced heirship, on the other hand, is grounded on the ancient policies of preventing concentrations of wealth and maintaining family property and the more contemporary (and only relevant) policy today in Louisiana of protecting children. *See* 3 Planiol & Ripert, TREATISE ON THE CIVIL LAW, pt. 2, ch. 4, no. 3049, at 490 (La. St. L. Inst. trans., 11th ed. 1959); Harriet Spiller Daggett, *General Principles of Succession on Death in Civil Law*, 11 Tul. L. Rev. 399, 401-02 (1937); Dainow, *supra* note

which became Act 77, but is now ostensibly limited by the Act. For the purposes of contrast, new and old Article 1235 are reproduced below. Article 1235 of Act 77 provides:

> The right to demand collation is confined to descendants of the first degree who qualify as forced heirs, and only applies with respect to gifts made within the three years prior to the decedent's death, and valued as of the date of the gift. Any provision of the Civil Code to the contrary is hereby repealed.[125]

Former Article 1235 provided:

> The obligation of collating is confined to children or descendants succeeding to their fathers and mothers or other ascendants, whether *ab intestato* or by virtue of a testament. Therefore this collation can not be demanded by any other heir, nor even by the legatees or creditors of the succession to which the collation is due.[126]

Article 1235 of Act 77 restricts those who can demand collation to children of the decedent who qualify as forced heirs under new Article 1493. However, what is unclear from Article 1235 of Act 77 is who is obligated to collate. Literally, it appears that a descendant of the first degree who qualifies as a forced heir may demand collation from any other descendant

---

16, at 43, Joseph Dainow, *Limitations on Testamentary Freedom in England,* 25 Cornell L.Q. 337, 340 (1940); Joseph Dainow, *Restricted Testation in New Zealand, Australia and Canada*, 36 Mich. L. Rev. 1107, 1130 (1938); Le Van, *supra* note 11, at 30. Forced heirship is not a default rule; it is mandatory. The only ways to defeat forced heirship are disinherison, renunciation, or an action for unworthiness. *See* Act No. 77, 77 West La. Sess. Law Serv. No. 2, at 151, 154, 157 (1996). Another possible explanation for the Law Institute's recommendation that collation be repealed is jurisprudence that has made the application of collation unworkable. For example, in *Succession of Fakier*, the decedent was survived by two daughters and four grandchildren, children of a predeceased son. 541 So. 2d 1372, 1374 (La. 1988). The grandchildren brought an action for collation of a $10,000 ring donated by the decedent during her lifetime to one of her daughters. *See id.* at 1375. The donee argued that by being left the disposable portion in her mother's will plus her share of the *legitime*, the ring was exempt from collation. *See id.* The will also stated that because her son had "been greatly favored over [her] daughters" by being given a business, the decedent desired that her daughters be provided with "as much property, of whatever nature, movable and immovable, community and separate, including all rights and credits that I may own at the time of my death, to the fullest extent and as may be authorized by law." *Id.* The basis for the donee's argument was Article 1233, which states that collation may be dispensed with as long as the dispensation is made in an unequivocal manner so that the will of the donor is clear. *See id.* at 1380; LA. CIV. CODE ANN. art. 1233 (West 1987). Astonishingly, the Louisiana Supreme Court held that the decedent had not dispensed with collation. *See Fakier*, 541 So. 2d at 1380. The court reasoned that the will was too vague to dispense with collation of the ring. *See id.* The court further noted that in order for the ring to have been exempt from collation, the will would have had to specifically state that the ring at issue was intended to be an extra portion or that all *inter vivos* donations made to her daughters were exempt from collation. *See id.* The *Fakier* decision is simple and straightforward compared to the Louisiana Third Circuit Court of Appeals' decision in *Succession of Pierson*, 339 So. 2d 1337 (La. Ct. App. 3d Cir. 1976). In a mess of litigious fervor, four descendants demanded collation for what seemed like every gift delivered or check written from the decedent to each forced heir. *See id.* at 1340. The court examined every gift and check written to determine if it was subject to collation. After this examination, the court assessed to each descendant either a net amount due to or from the succession. *See id.* at 1353. As two commentators have pointed out, the only ones profiting from such litigation were the lawyers. *See* Swaim & Lorio, *supra* note 15, § 8.16, at 204.

[125] Act No. 77, 77 West La. Sess. Law Serv. No. 2, at 151, 152 (1996).

[126] LA. CIV. CODE ANN. art. 1235 (West 1987), repealed by Act No. 77, 77 West La. Sess. Law Serv. No. 2, at 151, 152 (1996).

regardless of whether that descendant qualifies as a forced heir.[127]   Under old Article 1235, it was clear that descendants coming to their parents' succession could both demand collation and were obligated to collate upon demand.[128]   As written, Article 1235 undermines both the policy of equality among the heirs and the notion that an *inter vivos* donation to one child is merely an advance on his inheritance. Furthermore, it creates an inequity in the law by allowing forced heirs to demand collation from nonforced-heir siblings, but does not allow a nonforced-heir sibling to demand collation from forced heir siblings or nonforced-heir siblings. A few simple illustrations point out this inequity.

Suppose a parent has two children, one of whom is a forced heir. *Inter vivos* donations are made to the nonforced-heir sibling without any declaration that they are extra portions. Under new Article 1235, the forced heir sibling could demand that the nonforced-heir sibling collate these *inter vivos* donations.   However, if the forced heir sibling had received *inter vivos* donations that exceeded his *legitime*, and the nonforced-heir sibling had not received any *inter vivos* donations, then under the literal terms of Article 1235, the nonforced-heir sibling could not demand collation of the excess amount from the forced heir sibling. In a third example, if both the forced heir sibling and the nonforced-heir sibling had both received *inter vivos* donations that were not declared extra portions, the forced heir sibling could demand collation from the nonforced-heir sibling, but the nonforced-heir sibling could not demand collation in return when the value of the *inter vivos* donations exceeded the *legitime*. In effect, Article 1235 of Act 77 creates an automatic extra portion to the extent that a forced heir is not required to collate *inter vivos* donations made to him that exceed his *legitime* when the other descendants are nonforced-heir siblings.

Another interesting problem that Article 1235 creates is the question whether nonforced-heir siblings can benefit from an action for collation brought by a forced heir sibling against another nonforced-heir sibling. A hypothetical illuminates this problem. Assume that decedent, D, is survived by four children, W, X, Y, and Z; W qualifies as a forced heir. During the decedent's lifetime he made one *inter vivos* donation of $10,000 cash to Z, which was not declared an extra portion. Upon the death of D, pursuant to Article 1235, W may bring an action against Z to collate the donation. Technically, when a gift is subject to collation, the gift is returned to the succession mass and then distributed equally to those descendants entitled to bring an action for collation.[129] Prior to the enactment of Article 1235 of Act 77, in the above hypothetical, Z would return the $10,000 donation to the succession mass which would then be distributed equally to W, X, Y, and Z, that is, each would receive $2,500. Under Article 1235 of Act 77 it is unclear whether this result would be the same or whether Z would receive a $5,000 windfall because his nonforced-heir siblings, X and Y, are not entitled to bring an action for collation, and thus are unable to benefit. If, however, a collation action pursuant to Article 1235 of Act 77 allows X and Y to receive an equal share of the *inter vivos* donation that has been collated, X and Y will receive indirectly through W's collation action what they could not receive directly through their own action for collation.

One possible way to rectify this inconsistent and confusing article would be to simply reverse the presumption in favor of collation. This would make all *inter vivos* donations

---

[127] *See* Act No. 77, 77 West La. Sess. Law Serv. No. 2, at 151, 152 (1996).

[128] *See* LA. CIV. CODE ANN. art. 1235 (West 1987), repealed by Act No. 77, 77 West La. Sess. Law Serv. No. 2, at 151, 152 (1996).

[129] LA. CIV. CODE ANN. art. 1227 (West 1987).

automatic extra portions. In order for collation to apply, the decedent would have to expressly declare that the particular donation is subject to collation or is merely an advance on the donee's inheritance.

Article 1235 of Act 77 establishes the principle that only gifts made within three years of the donor's death are collatable.[130] Lastly, Article 1235 of Act 77 sets forth a blanket rule that all donations subject to collation are valued as of the date of the donation.[131] To this extent, Article 1235 of Act 77 overrules Article 1269 which states that, for immovable property, if the donee elects to take less, the immovable is valued as of the date of death.[132]

PROBLEMS

1. Suppose Herbert was survived by his three children, Elisabeth, Trudy, and Marta, ages 27, 24, and 22 respectively. Within three years prior to his death, Herbert donated sums of money to each of the children. Elisabeth received $5000, Trudy received $8000, and Marta received $12,000. Which of the children may bring an action for collation? After collation what property will each receive? Have the children been treated equally? Justly?

2. Maurice gave his grandson, Thomas, $10,000 in cash. Maurice died intestate and his daughter, Lucy (age 22), demands collation from Thomas. Must Thomas collate? Suppose Maurice had given the $10,000 to Bert, Thomas's father, and Bert had died before Maurice. Would collation be due? What if Maurice had made the gift to Thomas, but while Bert was still living? Explain.

---

[130] *See* Act No. 77, 77 West La. Sess. Law Serv. No. 2, at 151, 152 (1996). Prior to January 1, 1996, all *inter vivos* donations that were not declared extra portions were subject to collation regardless of when they were made. *See* LA. CIV. CODE ANN. art. 1235 (West 1987), repealed by Act No. 77, 77 West La. Sess. Law Serv. No. 2, at 151, 152 (1996). However, as of January 1, 1996, it was unclear whether only *inter vivos* donations made within three years of the donor's death were collatable. *See* LA. CIV. CODE ANN. art. 1235 (West Supp. 1996), repealed by Act No. 77, 77 West La. Sess. La Serv. No. 2, at 151, 152 (1996). Part IV, chapter 3, title 9 of the Revised Statutes was titled "Calculation of mass, reduction and collation." Under part IV in section 2372, however, the provision only stated that donations made more than three years prior to the donor's death were free from reduction. *See* LA. REV. STAT. ANN. 9:2372 (West 1991). Despite the title, the text of Revised Statutes section 9:2372 did not mention collation. *See id.*

[131] *See* Act No. 77, 77 West La. Sess. Law Serv. No. 2, at 151, 152 (1996).

[132] *See* La. Civ. Code Ann. art. 1269 (West 1987), repealed by Act No. 77, 77 West La. Sess. Law Serv. No. 2, at 151, 152 (1996).

SUCCESSION OF SIMMS
371 So. 2d 272 (La. App. 3d Cir. 1979)
[26 La. L. Rev. 487 (1966); 26 La. L. Rev. 546 (1966); 27 Loy. L. Rev. 262 (1967)]

SWIFT, Judge.

*   *   *

2. Collation by Harold A. Simms, III et al. of the "Annex".

Willard Simms contends that the trial judge erred in not requiring Harold Simms, III et al. to collate the donation *inter vivos* of the 55.48 arpent tract designated by Mrs. Florence Simms as the "Annex" that was donated by her to their father, Harold A. Simms, Jr., on September 22, 1955. The basis for the ruling was LSA-C.C. Art. 1240 which reads as follows:

> In like manner, the grandchild, *when inheriting in his own right* from the grandfather or grandmother, is not obliged to refund the gifts made to his father, even though he should have accepted the succession; but if the grandchild comes in only by right of representation, he must collate what had been given to his father, even though he should have renounced his inheritance. (Emphasis added).

In the trial judge's opinion Harold Simms, III, et al inherited from their grandmother in their own right as legatees under her will and did not come into the succession through representation of their deceased father. Consequently, collation was not required. We agree.

The term "inheriting in his own right" is not defined in our civil code and the articles thereof in regard to collation are ambiguous in a number of respects. We have not been cited nor has our own research disclosed a case wherein the particular point with which we are concerned has been decided. However, in *Miller v. Miller*, 105 La. 257, 29 So. 802 (La.App.1901), a grandfather bequeathed $20,000.00 to the daughter of a predeceased son and left the balance of his estate to his four children, share and share alike. When the grandchild elected to claim her *legitime*, the court held that she had to collate an $8,000.00 donation *inter vivos* previously given by the grandfather to this legatee's father and include the $20,000.00 legacy as a part of her *legitime*. Thereafter in *Jordan v. Filmore*, 167 La. 725, 120 So. 275 (La.1929), in referring to *Miller* our Supreme Court said:

> The court held that if the grandchild had not demanded a reduction of the residuary legacy to the disposable portion, and had accepted the legacy of $20,000, the grandchild could not be compelled to collate the $8,000 given to the grandchild's father by the testator during his lifetime, but that by claiming her *legitime*, the grandchild was obliged to collate the $8,000 and that the grandchild could not claim the legacy of $20,000 without deducting it from her *legitime*.

We take it from this that the Supreme Court interpreted Article 1240 of our civil code to mean that if the grandchild had chosen to take the legacy rather than claiming her *legitime*, she inherited the legacy in her own right under the will and would not have had to collate. However, when she took the other course she came into the succession through representation of her predeceased father and was required to collate under that codal article.

Although it was actually dictum, this same interpretation of Article 1240 was expressed by Chief Justice O'Niell in the *Succession of Schneidau,* 182 La. 613, 162 So. 196 (1935) as follows:

> It is true that Mrs. Le Breton, as a testamentary heir, or an instituted heir, came into her grandmother's succession *In her own right*, and *Not by representation.* As a legal heir of her grandmother, Mrs. Le Breton would have inherited only by representation of her father; but she is not being called upon to collate in the succession of her grandmother for gifts or advances made by the grandmother. (Emphasis added).

We believe this to be the most logical and reasonable interpretation of Article 1240 and the other codal articles on the subject of collation in regard to the circumstances presently before this court. Consequently, the judgment of the lower court in this respect will be affirmed.

*   *   *

4. Collation by Mrs. Hough.

The appellants contend that Mrs. Hough should be required to collate the cost of board, support and education expended by the decedent on Mrs. Hough while she lived with her grandparents as a child.

The trial judge concluded from his study of LSA-C.C. Articles 1242, 1243, 1244 and 1245 and their history as related in *Succession of Gomez,* 223 La. 859, 67 So. 2d 156 (1953), that she was not obligated to do so. We are inclined to agree with his interpretation of these codal articles even though Article 1244, which specifically exempts such donations from collation, seems to be confined to expenditures and gifts by parents to their children. Our view in this respect is buttressed by Civil Code Article 3556(8) which defines the word "children" as including grandchildren and all other descendant in the direct line and Article 229 which provides that ascendants are bound to maintain their needy descendants and vice versa. Be that as it may, we note that there is no evidence in the record to prove just when and in what amounts such donations were made and conclude that appellants have failed to carry the burden of proof required of them in this instance.

*   *   *

PROBLEMS

1. Felix dies, survived by his children, Curly(32), Larry(28), and Moe(22). Under article 1235, only Moe has the "right" to demand collation. Must Moe collate? If he demands collation, must he also collate his gifts even though neither Curly nor Larry have the right to demand collation?

2. Maureen dies, survived by her children, Matthew(25), Mark(22), and a predeceased son John(21). John leaves behind a child Peter(1). Who can demand collation?

GRANDCHAMPS v. DELPEUCH
7 Rob. 429 (La. 1844)

Morphy, J.

This is an action brought by Emile Grandchamps to obtain from his sisters and co-heirs, Louise M. C. Delpeuch, M. E. Foulon, and M. M. Conseil, the collation to the successions of his father and mother, of certain sums of money they have respectively received in advance of their hereditary shares in such successions. The statement of facts shows, that his sisters, Delpeuch and Foulon, received by marriage-contract, as a dowry jointly settled upon them by their father and mother, the sum of $3000 each, and that Madame Conseil received, as a part of her hereditary rights in the succession of her mother, $1500, when she married, and some time after, a further sum of $150 in advance of her portion in the future succession of her father. The defendants, Delpeuch and Foulon, renounced the estate of Francois Grandchamps, which is admitted to be insolvent; the two other heirs accepted it with the benefit of inventory. There was a judgment below decreeing the collation to be so made, as to distribute equally among the four heirs, the sums advanced to three of them by their parents. The defendants, Delpeuch and Foulon, have appealed.

There is no dispute with regard to the succession of Louise Marie Grandchamps, to which the appellants admit their obligation to collate the sums they have received from her, the donation to them not being made as an advantage or extra-portion; but their counsel contends that, as they have renounced the succession of their father, they have a right to retain the $3000 received from him, without being subject to any collation. It is true, that article 1315 of our Code authorizes the heir who renounces, to keep the property he has received in advance of his hereditary rights, and releases him from the obligation of collating; but the same article provides also that, "if the remaining amount of the inheritance should not be sufficient for the legitimate portion of the other children, including in the estate of the deceased the property which the person renouncing would have collated had he become heir, he shall then be obliged to collate up to the sum necessary to complete such legitimate portion." *[See La. C.C. 1237]**.

In the present case, all the property belonging to the late F. Grandchamps at the time of his death, being admitted to be insufficient to pay his debts, his estate, so far as his forced heirs are concerned, may be said to consist, and really consists only, of the donations *inter vivos* he formerly made to his children. These donations must then form the amount on which the disposable portion is to be calculated. 5 Toullier, No. 144. Rogron, on articles 845 and 922 of the Nap. Code. The deceased having left four children, the disposable portion is one-third of the sums to be collated. This proportion the defendants are authorized to retain in the same manner as if the donation had been made to them as an advantage or extra-portion; but they cannot surely derive from their renunciation the unjust privilege of keeping for themselves alone the whole of what they have received, when their father left nothing at his death out of which his other children can receive their legitimate portion. The obligation of collating is founded on that

---

* Bracketed material in italics added by author.

equality which should reign among heirs who are called upon to divide the inheritance of their father, mother, or other ascendants, and also on the presumption, that whatever is given to some of them is so disposed of, in advance of what they might one day expect from their succession. ...The circumstances of the succession of his father being insolvent, and of his having accepted it with the benefit of an inventory, presents, in our opinion, no obstacle to the plaintiff's right to call upon the appellants to collate. The donations made by the deceased to his children, when he was in more affluent circumstances, constitute a fund which the creditors have no right to look to, as it did not belong to their debtor at the time of his death. He had made these donations long before, and, for aught that appears in the record, had a perfect right to make them. In order to exercise his claim for collation against the defendants, the plaintiff was under no obligation to accept unconditionally a succession over burthened with debts, and thus endanger his own property. Had he taken such a step, he would have become personally liable to the creditors of the estate, to whose advantage alone the collation would then have enured; whereas, by accepting with the benefit of an inventory, the plaintiff has, without danger to himself, preserved his quality of heir, without which he could not have called upon the defendants to collate. But it is next argued, that if the appellants are not entitled to the whole sum of $3000, they should, at least, have and retain, in addition to the disposable portion, a share equal to that of the other heirs in the balance remaining. This pretension is entirely inadmissible. Having absolutely renounced the succession of their father, the appellants have become strangers to it, and can claim no share in the legitimate portion reserved to the heirs alone. Were it otherwise, they would, by renouncing the estate, have secured to themselves that which they could not have obtained by accepting it, unless the donation had been made to them as an advantage or extra-portion, which is not the case here. They are clearly then entitled to no more than the disposable portion. This would give to each of the appellants only one-sixth part of the $3000 to be collated, while the judgment below allows them a portion equal to that of the two other heirs, to wit, one-fourth of that amount; but of this, the latter do not complain, as it was so decreed on their own demand, that their sisters should be placed upon a footing of perfect equality with themselves.

Judgment affirmed.

NOTE

When is it in an heir's best interest to renounce his right to succeed? How does the enactment of La. C.C. 1500 by Acts No. 77 of 1996 affect the resolution of a case such as *Grandchamps*?

Property Subject to Collation: La. C.C. 1243-1250

SUCCESSION OF PIERSON
339 So. 2d 1337 (La. App. 3d Cir. 1976

PAVY, Judge.

*   *   *

The claims for collation cover a period from shortly after Dr. Pierson's death in 1934 until Mrs. Pierson's death in 1971. In many instances the evidence as to a particular transaction is incomplete although it is apparent that, in most instances, the parties did place in the record everything of probative value which was available. There are a total of twenty claims for collation urged between all the parties. Some are easily disposed of as obviously either meritorious or without merit. Others present serious questions of fact or law. We will now proceed to consider these individually.

*   *   *

[Clarence's funeral bill]*

Another claim for collation is that of $1,184.80 by Mrs. Whaley representing the amount of the funeral bill of her father, Clarence Pierson, Jr., which was paid by decedent. The trial judge recognized it. The widow has acknowledged the payment and the records of the funeral home verify it.

The check for payment of the funeral bill was not in evidence. Most of Mrs. Pierson's checks during this period were not available. Counsel for Mrs. Whaley argues the proof was insufficient that the payment by decedent was from her own funds and suggests that it may have come from monies of Dr. Pierson's estate or monies of Clarence, Jr. that were under the control of decedent.

Clarence, Jr. died in 1951. In the late thirties, a final account was rendered in Dr. Pierson's estate showing each heir was due the sum of $319.12. These sums were receipted for by all the children long prior to Clarence's death. We are unable to understand how there could have been funds from the father's estate still available in 1951. Although some property of the estate was sold nonjudicially after the final account, the evidence generally shows that these funds were distributed to the heirs upon the occasion of each sale.

In 1947 Clarence, Jr. was seriously injured and recuperated at his mother's home. She handled some of his financial affairs during this time. In 1948, he issued a check to her for $5,000. Counsel suggests the funeral bill payment may have come from that source. The evidence shows that Clarence had considerable expenses in connection with his injury. He recovered and lived until late 1951. It is difficult to imagine how decedent still had some of this money after that length of time. The burden of proof does not require negation of a mere theoretical possibility.

---

* Sub-headings added by author of casebook.

Argument is further made that collation is not due on this item because there could have been no donation *inter vivos* in favor of a deceased person. Collation is due regardless of the form or manner by which the advantage to the descendant occurs. The law expressly states that it need not be in the form of a donation. See Civil Code Article 1248. Many collations arise from transactions or situations not involving a donation between living persons. We think the payment of this funeral expense was an advantage to Clarence's estate or his daughter, Mrs. Whaley, and she should be made to collate the amount of it.

*   *   *

[Insurance Policy on David's life]

The record reveals decedent paid the Veterans Administration a considerable sum as premiums on David's National Service Life Insurance policy which he had obtained as a serviceman in World War II. This was a term policy with no cash value. In rejecting the claim for collation of these sums by David, the court stated:

> David had dropped the policy and Mrs. Pierson commenced paying the premiums and she was the beneficiary. Mrs. Pierson was the only one that stood to benefit under this life insurance policy. David by no stretch of the imagination could ever have benefitted by this insurance policy. In actuality, Mrs. Pierson never benefitted by this policy as she predeceased David. These monies were not paid to David but were paid to the Veterans Administration and Mrs. Pierson paid those because she stood to profit by these premium payments. This was a speculative investment that did not bear fruit.

After decedent's death, the policy was dropped permanently. David was indifferent to its continuance and gained nothing from the payments. Although decedent's estate was depleted by the payments, there was no "advantage" to David. We hold that under the particular facts of this case no collation is due. What might be the proper ruling with regard to premium payments on other types of insurance and in other fact situations is not before us now.

*   *   *

[Monies to David]

Further claims are made against David for collation of monies received from his mother. The trial judge disallowed them for the reason that the mere issuance of checks to David did not constitute proof of donations and that if they represented loans it was the duty of the succession representative to collect those debts. We have previously pointed out that unpaid debts of an heir are subject to collation.

When David returned to Alexandria in 1956, he lived in a small garage apartment on his mother's home premises until approximately a year and a half prior to her death at which time he moved into the home. They were apparently very close, shared grocery expenses and obviously had many minor financial transactions between them.

In order to prove these collatable items, there were filed in evidence two batches of cancelled checks issued by Mrs. Pierson during the period from the late thirties to her death in '71 except for the period from 1949 to 1960. None of her cancelled checks issued between 1949 to 1960 were available.

Of the two groups of checks for which collation claims are made, one is made up of 113 checks totaling $804.73, all issued by Mrs. Pierson in favor of David and only one of these has any indication of its purpose. The other group is made up of 76 checks totaling $2,203.61, all issued by Mrs. Pierson to other parties with notations on the checks to the effect that the check was to be applied to David's account or that it was otherwise for his benefit.

David admitted that his mother helped him with his delinquent accounts on many occasions and that he had received gifts from her from time to time. He contends that the gifts were offset by services he rendered and that he repaid loans. In his deposition, he stated that he had cancelled checks for several years back but produced none of these at trial and claimed that his mother had urged him to destroy all his old records. We realize that it would have been unusual for David to have retained his cancelled checks for as long as thirty years back and feel a certain inadequacy in dealing with this issue. However, we cannot ignore the consistent pattern of transfers of money from Mrs. Pierson to her son. Those that were gifts must be collated. Those that were loans must be collated unless repaid. We have previously held that unpaid loans are collatable items.

However, because of the closeness of David and his mother and the fact that they shared the grocery bill there must have been many small monetary transactions between them represented by some of the checks. For instance, we note one of the checks to David is for $6.71 and was secondly endorsed by a seafood market. We cannot imagine how this could have constituted a loan to David or a payment by him of his sole account at such an establishment. We think these type checks represent transactions between him and his mother of a type other than loans or gifts. Additionally, in the group of checks payable to third parties, are notations indicating that they were not loans or collatable gifts. One of these is for Community Concert tickets for both Mrs. Pierson and David. As to David's ticket, this would be a gift for his own pleasure and use as provided by Civil Code Article 1245. Another check has a notation not that it is for David's account at the particular store but it is for "David's suit". This was in January. We do not think gifts on such rare occasions are collatable. They are also for the use and pleasure of the donee as per Civil Code Article 1245. It is impossible to discuss each of these individual checks which we have decided should or should not be collated. Of the group of checks representing payments directly to David, we have considered that a total of $734 must be collated. Of the group of checks representing payments to third parties, we have determined that a total of $1,010 must be collated. With the $700 previously decreed to be subject to collation, the total for cash items (gifts or unpaid loans) would amount to $2,534. This collation must be reduced to $2,000, the amount claimed in the petition.

*   *   *

[1958 Ford to Hunter]

Another claim for collation by Hunter's estate is the value of a 1958 Ford automobile. Hunter admitted this donation. Trial judge disallowed it because of lack of evidence of the value. There is nothing in the record to show the value of the automobile at the time in question. A suggestion is made by counsel that we assign a figure of $2,000 for the value. We think the holding below was correct. The party asserting collation must show the value of the item to be collated. This is not a situation where an exact amount cannot be shown and the court must determine some fair minimum in the interest of justice. The exact value of the automobile could have been easily proved. We must disallow this claim.

* * *

[Rental value of properties occupied by Hunter and David]

Claims for collation against both Hunter and David were made for the rental value of the properties (the garage apartment and the Marye Street residence) occupied by them for a number of years. Additionally, a collation claim was made against David for board for the same period. We think the evidence preponderates that David and his mother shared board expenses and that claim will be disallowed. The trial judge rejected the claims for rental values as a matter of law. His reasoning was that the value of occupancy was equivalent to the revenue that would have been derived from the properties and that revenue, as distinguished from capital, is not collatable as it would have been used by the decedent anyway and hence there was no depletion of his estate. He further stated that if the properties had been donated, the donees would not have had to collate the revenue (rental) of these items.

LOUISIANA CIVIL CODE Articles 1243 through 1248 deal with what things are subject to collation. Article 1243 specifies those types of benefits subject to collation. Articles 1244 through 1247 deal with various types of benefits to an heir which are not subject to collation. Article 1248 is a sort of catchall provision mandating collation generally. Articles 851 through 856 of the Code Napoleon deal with what matters are collatable and contain substantially the same language as Articles 1243 through 1247 except that there is no counterpart to Civil Code Article 1248 in the Code Napoleon and there is contained in the Code Napoleon an article (856) which provides that the revenue of the thing subject to collation is not due until the opening of the succession. From this codal scheme, the Louisiana Jurisprudence has approached the question of what is collatable by starting with the general rule that collation is due for any benefit or advantage and that any exemption or dispensation from it is the exception.

This approach was used in the scholarly opinion in *Succession of Gomez, supra.* That case dealt with manual gifts of money. Although it dealt with the manner in which the benefit or advantage was conferred and not with the nature of the benefit conferred, we think the *Gomez* rationale is pertinent here.

The court stated:

> Finally, then, the law contemplates a perfect equality among heirs and presumes that the ascendant intends equality among his heirs. Our rules of collation have come into existence to maintain and effectuate this equality, and they permit collation to be dispensed with only when the intention of the ascendant to dispense has been manifested expressly and in the manner provided by law. *Benoit v. Benoit's Heirs*, 8 La. 228; *Grandchamps v. Delpeuch*, 7 Rob. 429; *Berthelot v. Fitch*, 44 La.Ann. 503, 10 So. 867; *King v. King*, 107 La. 437, 31 So. 894; *Champagne v. Champagne*, 125 La. 408, 51 So. 440; *Jung v. Stewart*, 190 La. 91, 181 So. 867. The law exempts, however, in Articles 1244 and 1245 of the

Code of 1870 certain things from collation. By virtue of this legal exemption an express intention on the part of the donor to dispense with collation of these things is not required. Because this legal exemption may operate to destroy the equality among the heirs, *nothing* should be exempt from collation unless it falls squarely within the provisions of these articles. (Emphasis herein). We have concluded, therefore, that it was never the intention and purpose of the redactors of the Code of 1825 to make a drastic change from the provisions of the 1808 Code relating to exemptions or, for that matter, a radical departure from our fundamental concept of collation. Any other conclusion would be inconsistent with the emphasis on equality in the general provisions relating to the nature of collation and the strict rules for maintaining that equality. Legal exemptions from collation have always been based on the soundest grounds--the things exempt were by their nature not really advancements because they were obligations of the parent, or they were things given under such circumstances as to overcome the presumption that they were advancements.

Determinative here are the court's two observations: (1) That only exemptions squarely within the terms of the pertinent articles are to be recognized and (2) that those exemptions either pertain to obligations of the decedent to the child or result from benefits conferred under circumstances naturally indicative of an intent to confer an advantage or extra portion.

We realize that, as pointed out by the learned trial judge, respectable authority among the French commentators holds that a gift of revenues is not collatable. This view of the learned French scholars is based on Code Napoleon Article 856 which provides that revenues from a collatable item are only due from the opening of the succession. But our code does not contain any counterpart to Code Napoleon Article 856 in the section dealing with collation. In CROSS ON SUCCESSIONS, at page 523, is found the following observation:

C.N. 856 provides that "the fruits and interest of the things subject to collation are due only from the day of the opening of the succession." This rule is the consequence of the principle, that the property donated as an advancement d'hoirie is supposed to be immediately reunited to the succession at the death of the deceased. The object of its insertion in that Code seems however, to be, to protect the donee from a claim for the revenues accruing before the opening of the succession. "We have already seen, under Article 852," (LOUISIANA CIVIL CODE Article 1244) says *Marcade* (III, 343) "that the gift of simple revenues not encroaching on the capital are not subject to collation. The law considers that the deceased would have spent it some other way, and in living with less economy the periodical revenues with which he has gratified his successible would have been used, and that consequently the donation has not diminished the quantity of property he has left. This principle has been recognized in our article. When the deceased has given a farm, a house, or other property, the heir should collate this property, but not the revenues which he has derived from it; the property is, in fact, a capital, the absence of which would diminish the patrimony; but its fruits on the contrary are only revenues that the deceased would probably have spent otherwise." This article has not been reproduced in our Code, and it is held in

LeBlanc vs. Bertant (16 A. 298) that, where it is presumed from circumstances that the mother intended to make a remission of interest to her sons on a loan of money to them, the interest remitted should be considered an advance on their portion of the succession and should be collated.

However, the contention of Cross was not accepted as law. In *Clark v. Hedden*, 109 La. 147, 33 So. 116 (1902) the Supreme Court held that collation is not due for revenues of property, the full ownership of which had been donated. The court relied on Civil Code Article 1515 which by its terms applies only to revenues from donated property subject to reduction. No mention was made of the limited applicability of that article nor of the fact that Code Napoleon Article 856 which exempted from collation revenues of collatable items was in the 1808 code but omitted from the 1825 and 1870 codes. While the rule in *Clark* may be dispositive on the precise question of whether revenues from collatable items are exempt, it does not follow that the rule is by analogy obligatory on this court in dealing with the question of whether collation is due for the value of donated use, occupancy or habitation which themselves constitute the benefit or advantage.

Here David and Hunter did not own the apartment or the house. They did not even have the usufruct of these. Theirs were only the rights of habitation or use. This produced no revenues. In a sense, what they had was the equivalent of revenue. But to make them collate the value of their occupancy and not compel an owner to collate the value of the revenues produced by the thing owned is not contradictory. In both cases the donee or beneficiary returns to the ancestor's estate the value equivalent of exactly what he got--in one case the basic ownership and in the other the occupancy.

Other considerations might warrant a difference in treatment between an heir given basic ownership and one who gets only a portion of the ownership. The hardship and problems of making the latter account for the revenues could justify the difference.

We cannot agree with the view that revenues should not be collated because the gift of such does not deplete the ancestor's estate. Depletion of the estate would be germane to a reduction situation. There, the ultimate value of the estate is the question. But, as to collation, benefit or advantage to the heir is the test regardless of whether the estate is depleted. Although there is no depletion of the estate, any benefit or advantage to an heir affects presumed equality.

Even if depletion of the ancestor's estate would be pertinent, to hold that a gift of revenue never depletes the donor's ultimate estate is unrealistic. Modern investment practices do not justify such a view. The question of depletion, vel non, should be resolved on the facts of each particular case.

If decedent had barely subsisted from month to month and left no assets of any consequence, it could be argued that she would have consumed the rental revenues of the properties occupied by her children and the free occupancy would have had no effect on her estate's ultimate value. The record herein clearly shows the contrary. Mrs. Pierson lived to the full extent of her wishes during the years of free occupancy. Her estate was considerable. If she had rented out the properties instead of allowing their free use by her children, the estate would have been increased pro tanto.

Accordingly, we hold that a gift of use or habitation is not exempt from collation solely because of its nature as the equivalent of revenue or because revenues from collatable items are deemed exempt from collation. By this ruling, we do not intend to require collation of every use or occupancy permitted by a parent to a child. Many of these will be so trifling, temporary, intermittent, on such occasions and under such circumstances that they would clearly fall within the language of the *Gomez* case as ". . . things usual for parents of this country to give to a child without thought or regard to his having to account for them to his co-heirs."

We think that the permitted occupancy of the garage apartment by David should be exempt from collation. David was never married; he and his mother were very close. He assisted her in many ways. Originally, he occupied a room in the family residence. After a maid who occupied the garage apartment left, he moved into it. The apartment was very meagre; its rental value was estimated at $25 per month. In winter, David was forced to move into the family residence with his mother. He actually lived in the family home with her for several months prior to her death. The arrangement was to a large extent for Mrs. Pierson's convenience and requirements. Considering all these circumstances, we conclude that the permitted occupancy "… was without thought or regard to his (David's) having to account for them (it) to his co-heirs."

Hunter moved into the residence around 1950 and paid rental for two years. He then added onto the house and thereafter paid only the taxes and insurance. A realtor fixed the rental value from 1952 to 1960 at $100 per month and thereafter at $120 per month. This would amount to $24,000. We cannot say that the whole rental value should be collated because it was not completely free. Hunter paid about $2,000 for the addition which inured to the value of the property and consequently the estate. Additionally, he paid insurance and taxes for the 18 years involved. The payments for the addition, insurance and taxes were part of the overall arrangement between him and his mother and should be calculated into the amount due. From the record available, we calculate the taxes and insurance paid for the 18 years at $2,880. We will allow this total of $4,880 for the addition, insurance and taxes as a credit against the gross rental of $24,000 leaving a net collatable figure of $19,120.

*   *   *

SUCCESSION OF HOFFPAUIR
446 So. 2d 931 (La. App. 3d Cir. 1984)
[Footnotes Omitted]

DOMENGEAUX, Judge.

In this succession proceeding, five of the decedent's children, namely, Juanita Verna, Willie Mae, Helen Lee, Velma Lurline, and Wilmer Ray filed a petition for collation, for an accounting, and a return of assets held in usufruct against their brother, Wilfred. The petitioners allege that Wilfred received an advantage (as a forced heir) of his succession share through the sales of immovable property. The petitioners claim that the sales of some Acadia and Vermilion Parish tracts (and the surviving spouse usufruct on the Vermilion tract) by Mrs. Hoffpauir to Wilfred were, in fact, disguised donations *inter vivos*; additionally, petitioners claim that Wilfred also received an advantage from the interest-free credit sales made to him by his mother.

After a bench trial, the district court determined that the sales were made for a fair and valid price which did not constitute disguised donations; nor were the interest-free credit sales an advantage. Therefore, no collation was required of the property (or the value thereof), or of the interest on the credit sales.

Three of the plaintiffs in the original proceedings withdrew their claim after the trial court rendered judgment in favor of the defendant. However, two of the plaintiffs, Willie Mae and Helen Lee, have suspensively appealed the adverse judgment. The defendant brother answered the appeal seeking payment of deposition fees.

ISSUES

Appellants contend that the trial court erred in its findings. They argue: (a) that the price paid for the sale of the Vermilion Parish property and usufruct was so low as to require collation; (b) that the no-interest credit sale was an advantage; (c) that the price paid for the sale of the Acadia Parish property was so low as to require collation; and (d) that the no- interest credit sale for that purchase was an advantage.

FACTS

In December 1962, defendant Wilfred Wayne Hoffpauir and his father Rollie Hoffpauir purchased as co-owners a 160 acre tract of farmland in Acadia Parish for $48,000.00 ($300.00 per acre). After Rollie Hoffpauir died in December 1963, Wilfred Hoffpauir wanted to purchase the tract of land to continue farming rice. On September 30, 1964, Allie Hoffpauir conveyed 40 acres, her ½ undivided interest in the Acadia Parish property, to her son, Wilfred, for $12,000.00, i.e., $300.00 per acre (the same price per acre that Rollie and Wilfred Hoffpauir had paid). The deed was an authentic act properly recorded. The terms of the sale consisted of $1,000.00 cash paid and an $11,000.00 note payable in annual installments (with 2% interest to accrue from maturity). Mrs. Hoffpauir held a mortgage on that property. Wilfred Hoffpauir testified at trial that he paid his mother the remaining amount due the following year. He produced the check and the note marked "Paid," both of which were admitted into evidence.

On January 10, 1967, Mrs. Allie Hoffpauir sold her ½ undivided interest plus her surviving spouse usufruct over the other undivided ½ interest in certain tracts of land in Vermilion Parish to Wilfred for $37,509.15. This act of sale was properly confected and recorded. Wilfred paid his mother $2,509.15 down and executed a note for $35,000.00 (with 4% interest to accrue from maturity). The note was payable in twenty equal annual installments of $1,750.00, with the first installment due January 10, 1967. All payments have been timely made. Wilfred Hoffpauir testified at trial that he still owed some money on this last note, but had not paid it because both the property and loan were currently in dispute.

Two appraisers testified at trial as to the valuation of the land at the time the sales were made. Both appraisers' reports were submitted into evidence. Richard Pease qualified as an expert real estate appraiser and broker on behalf of the plaintiffs. Mr. Pease, on direct examination, valued the Acadia farm property in question, i.e. 40 acres, which constituted Allie Hoffpauir's half of the community property in full ownership at $350.00 per acre at the time of the sale. The total value amounted to $14,346.50. On cross-examination, Mr. Pease admitted that the estimated value is actually a median value and that $300.00 per acre paid in 1964 was not a very low price.

Mr. Pease also rendered an opinion as to the value of the Vermilion farm property at the time of the sale in 1967. He stated that the ½ undivided full ownership interest was worth $81,750.00 and that Mrs. Hoffpauir's usufruct over the other ½ undivided naked ownership interest was valued at $34,649.57 (Mr. Pease relied upon Department of Revenue actuarial tables used for inheritance tax purposes); for a total value of $116,399.57 in 1967.

Mr. Pease also testified that he was unable to locate any comparable sales transacted for property in Vermilion Parish during 1967, so he inspected the property and used LSU Agri-Business publications; he also used local savings and loan estimates, and Federal Land Bank records to determine the price. However, defendant's expert witness, Cecil Gremillion, who qualified as an expert real estate appraiser testified that the Vermilion farm acreage was worth between $190 and $200 per acre (for an average total value of $34,515.00). Mr. Gremillion was able to discover from the Vermilion Parish vendor-vendee indices two transactions within a year of the sale at issue involving similar farmlands; one which was adjacent to the Hoffpauir tracts and another which was in close proximity. Mr. Gremillion used these comparables, as well as interviews with local property owners, and an inspection of the farm, to formulate an estimate. Mr. Gremillion also testified that he took cognizance of the surviving spouse usufruct over the Vermilion Parish property but did not ascribe any value to it.

In written reasons for judgment, the trial court found that the plaintiffs failed to sustain their burden of proving that the credit sales, and no-interest loans made incident thereto, constituted an advantage which required collation.

COLLATION AND VALUATION

La. C.C. Art. 2444 allows forced heirs to demand collation if the transfer of immovable property has been a disguised donation.

> The sales of immovable property made by parents to their children, may be attacked by the forced heirs, as containing a donation in disguise, if the latter can prove that no price has been paid, or that the price was below one- fourth of the real value of the immovable sold, at the time of the sale.

La. C.C. Art. 2444; Roy *v. Roy*, 382 So. 2d 253 (La. App. 3rd Cir.1980). The transfer could also be subject to collation if the price paid was greater than 1/4th (the standard provided in La. C.C. Art. 2444) but less than fair market value based upon the provisions of La. C.C. Art. 1248.

> The advantage which a father bestows upon his son, though in any other manner than by donation or legacy, is likewise subject to collation. Thus, when a father has sold a thing to his son at a very low price, or has paid for him the price of some purchase, for [or] has spent money to improve his son's estate, all that is subject to collation.

La. C.C. Art. 1248.

In each instance, the forced heir alleging that an advantage or extra portion has been made must prove that it has violated the equality among forced heirs in order to require collation with the resulting real or supposed return to the mass of the succession. La. C.C. Arts. 1227 and 1229. Collation is required on the basis of the value at the time of the transfer. *Johnston v. Bearden*, 127 So. 2d 319 (La. App. 2nd Cir.1961).

The trial judge concluded that Mrs. Hoffpauir sold land to Wilfred on credit bearing no interest. This was not a situation where there was a debt due by interest, then later remitted. *Rican v. Rican*, 139 La. 364, 71 So. 581 (1916). The trial court declined to find that an interest-free credit sale automatically becomes a disguised donation subject to collation. When the court finds that consideration exceeding one-fourth of the real property of the property at the time of sale was actually paid, it is unnecessary for the court to consider the claim for collation on the theory that the transfer was a donation in disguise. *Cannon v. Cannon*, 244 So. 2d 64 (La.App. 1st Cir.1971).

Further, the trial judge found that plaintiffs' own expert witness only confirmed that defendant paid fair market value for the Acadia Parish farm. Therefore, plaintiffs failed to establish that collation was required. As to the Vermilion Parish property, the trial judge found that Mr. Gremillion, expert appraiser on behalf of the defendant, offered a credible opinion as to the value of the Vermilion Parish property and on that basis found that the property was not under-valued in the credit sale. The trial judge further held that this finding is supported by the fact that defendant was buying an undivided interest. Therefore, since the price paid for each sale of immovable property was well within the fair market value as estimated by the court, plaintiffs' suit was dismissed with court costs (including expert witness fees) assessed against them.

The trial court is granted a great deal of discretion in determining the value of land; this discretion applies to any case involving the value of real estate. *Successions of Mack*, 413 So. 2d 642 (La.App. 1st Cir.1982). We find no manifest error in the court's handling of the property valuation.

Plaintiffs claim that the price paid for the Vermilion tract included remuneration for the surviving spouse usufruct, thereby reducing the actual price paid for the immovable property.

Defendant urges that the valuation standard for a disguised donation cannot be applied in this instance because the value of the usufruct sold (which was subject to termination upon death or remarriage of the vendor-usufructuary) is too speculative and conjectural; and that a certain value of the interest sold cannot be ascertained.

The trial court, in considering the issue of the purchase of the usufruct, found that there was no active market for such a commodity; and consequently he concluded that the usufruct did not have a value which would necessitate collation.

Regardless of the trial judge's finding on this issue, we conclude that the price paid by defendant was sufficient, irrespective of the value of the usufruct. *See Parker v. Rhodes*, 260 So. 2d 706, 714-715 (La.App. 2nd Cir.1971), *on rehearing*, 260 So. 2d 716, 718-719 (La.App. 2nd Cir.1972); A. Yiannopoulos, PERSONAL SERVITUDES note 333, § 17 (LA.CIV.L. TREATISE Vol. 3, 2d ed. 1978).

We find that there was no disguised donation, based on an evaluation of the property from the evidence presented at trial. Therefore, we find that no collation is required.

Defendant thus paid more than 1/4th the market value of the land, i.e., approximately the exact fair market value, rendering the claim under La.C.C. Arts. 2444 and 1248 invalid.

DECREE

For the above and foregoing reasons, the judgment of the trial court is affirmed. All costs are assessed against appellants.

AFFIRMED.

GUIDRY, J., concurs and assigns reasons.

GUIDRY, Judge, concurring.

I cannot agree with the trial court's conclusion that the sale of a usufruct has no value which would necessitate collation. Quite to the contrary, although a surviving spouse's usufruct may be of unknown duration, subject to termination on death or re-marriage, it has some value and a transfer thereof, without consideration, is, in my view, subject to collation. In the instant case, however, considering the valuation of the Vermilion Parish property in the year 1967, as ascribed by Mr. Gremillion, who I likewise consider to be the most credible of the experts, the price paid by defendant clearly exceeded one-fourth of the real value of the land together with the usufruct and was not a "very low price". Under such circumstances, defendant, as a result of such sale, received no advantage over his co-heirs which requires collation. For these reasons, I respectfully concur.

SUCCESSION OF MOORE v. MOORE
387 So. 2d 1231 (La. App. 1st Cir. 1980)

LOTTINGER, Judge.

This is a rule for collation filed by a nephew against his aunt. The trial court found that the plaintiff-in-rule failed to prove by a preponderance of the evidence the fair market value at the time of transfer of the four groups of immovable property involved in this suit. The plaintiff has appealed.

* * *

We agree with the trial court's determination as to the St. Tammany, Allard Street and Tulane Street properties. The plaintiff-in-rule has simply failed to bear the burden imposed upon him by law. To determine whether the forced heir from whom collation is sought paid such a "very low price" for immovable property so as to require the collation, the claimant must prove the fair market value of the property at the time of the transaction. La.C.C. art. 1248; *Estate of Schwegmann v. Schwegmann*, 298 So. 2d 795 (La.1974). The fair market value of immovable property at the date of death is important and relevant only after a determination has been made that collation is due. Fair market value at date of death then becomes important to show how much must be collated. *[Altered by the Amendment of La. C.C. 1235 by Act 77 of 1996.]*[*]

Given the propinquity of the dates of transfer and the date of death in this case, we are willing to concede that the testimony of the petitioner's appraiser bears some probative value. But even conceding arguendo that the value of the three groups of property remained fairly constant from the date of transfer until the date of death, the plaintiff has still failed to prove the

---

[*] Bracketed material in italics added by author.

fair market property value at the date of death. We agree with the trial court's reservations as to the testimony of the appraiser and find that collation is not due on the three groups of property.

The Caddo property, however-the one discussed first in the facts above- presents a more difficult question. Even considering the preinflation value of the dollar in the mid-1950s, the sale of 29 acres and three lots of land for $200.00 in 1955 appears to be on the low side. But the inadequacy vel non of the $200.00 consideration never ripened into an issue in this case, because the plaintiff failed to show by a preponderance of the evidence the fair market value of the property at the time of transfer. No comparable sales were introduced into evidence and the appraiser based his judgment solely on conversations with area residents and on his own inspection of the property. The probative value of the plaintiff's appraisal was further weakened by Gladys' testimony that there was a squatter on the land and that the property was sold some 13 years later for only $2,000.00. As indicated earlier, the testimony as to the sale of the property by Gladys in 1968 is confusing and meager. But it is also unrebutted. The defendant's testimony and other evidence was sufficient to convince the trial court that the appraiser's valuation was less than credible, and we must agree.

* * *

NOTE

In *Succession of Hoover*, 517 So. 2d 471, the price paid by a daughter to her mother for property, was found to exceed 1/4 of the value of the property, since the cash transferred was deemed augmented by the services rendered by the daughter to care for her aging mother.

SUCCESSION OF GOMEZ
223 La. 859, 67 So. 2d 156 (1953)
[14 La. L. Rev. 295 (1953); 16 La. L. Rev. 230 (1956));
27 La. L. Rev. 452 (1967)]
(Footnotes Omitted)

HAWTHORNE, Justice.

This is a suit by three grandchildren of the deceased Mrs. William Gomez, children of a predeceased son, against the only surviving child, Mrs. Amelie Gomez Salatich, and against the testamentary executrix for collation of certain sums given by Mrs. Gomez during her lifetime to her daughter Mrs. Salatich.

The facts disclose that Mrs. Salatich received from her mother from 1930 through 1946 sums of money which were alleged to total $19,200. This money was given to her in installments on or about the first day of each month through that period of time. The defense is that the monthly sums were for services rendered to the mother by the daughter, the defendant, or, in the alternative, that, if not for services, they were manual gifts and for that reason exempt from collation under the provisions of Article 1245 of the Civil Code.

* * *

We agree with the district judge's conclusion that the defendant did not prove that the sums given were for services rendered, but we cannot agree that manual gifts, as such, are exempt from collation.

*   *   *

The law exempts, however, in Articles 1244 and 1245 of the Code of 1870 certain things from collation. By virtue of this legal exemption an express intention on the part of the donor to dispense with collation of these things is not required. Because this legal exemption may operate to destroy the equality among the heirs, nothing should be exempt from collation unless it falls squarely within the provisions of these articles.

In the instant case there is no doubt that the donation of a large sum of money to one of the heirs destroyed the equality among them. The question presented then is whether this gift of money is clearly exempt by law from collation by virtue of the sole fact that it was a manual gift.

*   *   *

Certain things were exempt from collation by Article 852 of the Code Napoleon, which read as follows:

> The expenses of board, support, education, and apprenticeship, the ordinary expenses of accountrement, those of marriage and customary presents, are not subject to collation.

Under this article of the FRENCH CODE, the exemptions from collation may be divided into two classes: (1) Those resulting from the obligation of the parent, and (2) those resulting from social customs or usage. Those things exempt in the first class could not even be considered donations as they were by their very nature obligations of the parent, such as support, maintenance, and education of the children. Those things exempt in the second class were things given because of the customs and usage of the time, on special occasions, and under special circumstances which would refute completely that the donor gave them as an advancement of a hereditary share. The basis for the exemption of those things in the first class is made clear by *Domat*: "The children, or other descendants, succeeding to the inheritance of their father, or mother, or other ascendant, do not bring in that which has been laid out upon their studies, or in other expenses which their education may have required. For these sorts of expenses are what parents are bound to lay out upon their children, and are as it were a debt which they ought to acquit." *Domat,* op. cit. *supra*, n° 2963, p. 251. Those of the second class, customary presents, were given on special occasions, such as marriage, New Year's, first communion, and baptism. See Baudry-Lacantinerie et Wahl, TRAITÉ THEORIQUE ET PRATIQUE DE DROIT CIVIL, VIII (2e ed. 1899), DES SUCCESSIONS III, n° 2811, p. 273. The French have required that such gifts be in proportion to the wealth of the donor to be exempt from collation.

The things exempt from collation in our Code of 1808 were substantially the same as those in the FRENCH CODE, though our Code was somewhat more liberal in its view of what were usual gifts and was more detailed in its language, thus:

> Art. 207. There exists however one sort of advantage made by ascendants to their children or lawful descendants, which by their privileged nature, are not subject to

collation, though it cannot be said they were not taken out of the mass of the donor's estate.

Thus pensions, aliments and maintenance supplied to children, and books and other expenses laid out for their education, are not liable to collation, though a library is.

No collation is due to the wedding clothes and wedding expenses; but the trousseau of the daughter is liable to it.

New year's gifts and small presents, money given to the minor and by him spent and even money given to the son of age, for play and for his pleasures, are not subject to collation.

Art. 208. But the child is obliged to collate what has been spent to provide him a living or instruct him in some trade or profession or to give him a dowry or marriage portion.

The redactors of the Code of 1808 evidently recognized that American parents were more generous and liberal with their children, did not confine their giving of presents to special occasions, and often gave money to children for their play and pleasure. The fourth paragraph of our Article 207 contained a deliberate departure from the French view that even a sum of money given to the heir for his small pleasures was subject to collation, because there was nothing habitual about it in France and it was not imposed by usage. *See* Baudry-Lacantinerie et Wahl, loc. cit. *supra*.

The Code of 1808 did not expressly exempt manual gifts from collation, and the language of the articles in that Code does not permit even by implication the interpretation that manual gifts were exempt because of the one fact that they were manual gifts.

Articles 1322 and 1323 of the Code of 1825 contained the exemption provisions of that Code. Since those articles are identical with Articles 1244 and 1245 of our present Civil Code, what we hereafter say as to the provisions of the 1825 Code is pertinent and applicable to the present provisions.

The redactors of the Code of 1825 considered that the articles of the Code of 1808 were too wordy and detailed, and they explained in their project that they "suppressed these articles to place them in a different order from that which they occupy in the Code [of 1808], and to abridge some dispositions which are too much overloaded with details. Here follow the articles which we have substituted for them [Articles 1322 and 1323 of the Code of 1825]." 1 LOUISIANA LEGAL ARCHIVES, PROJÉT OF THE CODE of 1825, p. 182.

The redactors themselves, then, did not indicate that they had changed in any way the law relating to things exempt from collation in the Code of 1808. The redactors of the Code of 1825 were men learned in the law, and they were familiar with the term "manual gift", for they mentioned it expressly when they defined it in Article 1526 of that Code. If they had intended to exempt manual gifts as such from collation, they could very easily have made that intention clear. After providing that the expenses of board, etc., are not subject to collation, they undoubtedly would have said simply, in Article 1323, "The same rule is established with respect to manual gifts" instead of saying "The same rule is established with respect to things given by a father, mother or other ascendant, by their own hands, to one of their children for his pleasure of other use." Their express purpose for abridging these dispositions was to improve those overloaded with detail. If such was their purpose, and they intended to exempt manual gifts, why did they overload this disposition by the use of the limiting phrase 'for his pleasure or other use'?

What possible difference would the purpose of the giving make if manual gifts as such were exempt?

When the redactors used the expression "by their own hands, to one of their children for his pleasure or other use," they were contemplating those things usual for parents of this country to give to a child without thought or regard to his having to account for them to his co-heirs. The word "pleasure" has special significance in this respect because it best describes the motive that usually prompts the giving of such things. The language the redactors chose to describe this kind of giving was broad and elastic enough to keep space of changes in our social development.

We have concluded, therefore, that it was never the intention and purpose of the redactors of the Code of 1825 to make a drastic change from the provisions of the 1808 Code relating to exemptions or, for that matter, a radical departure from our fundamental concept of collation. Any other conclusion would be inconsistent with the emphasis on equality in the general provisions relating to the nature of collation and the strict rules for maintaining that equality. Legal exemptions from collation have always been based on the soundest grounds--the things exempt were by their nature not really advancements because they were obligations of the parent, or they were things given under such circumstances as to overcome the presumption that they were advancements. The exemption of manual gifts as such cannot be justified under either of these theories, and no consideration comes to our minds which would have prompted the redactors to foster inequality by providing a means-- the manual gift--whereby a large portion of an estate could be given to a descendant free of the obligation of collation by virtue of the law.

We want to make it clear that our holding here in respect to exemption of manual gifts cannot affect these things that are exempt in Article 1244 because they are obligations. The expenditures for board, support, education, etc., are exempt whether they are made in the form of a manual gift or not.

Under our interpretation of Article 1245, the money given to the defendant in this case, under an arrangement for a monthly stipend which lasted over 15 years, is not one of those things contemplated by Article 1245, and is therefore not exempt from collation under that article.

The exemptions from collation which we have been discussing are provided by law. The donor, however, may provide for dispensation from collation of gifts made to his children, although they are not things legally exempt, if his intention so to dispense is clearly expressed in the manner and form provided in the Code. We shall now consider how that intention must be manifested as to a manual gift, and whether the donor in the instant case so manifested her intention.

Under Article 1538 of our Civil Code a donation *inter vivos*, even of movable effects, will not be valid unless passed before a notary public and two witnesses. A corresponding provision was found in Article 948 of the Code Napoleon, which provided that "No act of donation of movable effects shall be valid, for any other effects than those of which an estimate, signed by the donor and donee, or by those who accept for him, is annexed to the record of the donation." Thus, under the provisions of both of these articles a donation of movable effects must be in writing and with certain formalities.

Under Article 1232 of our Civil Code it is provided that the declaration that the gift or legacy is made as an advantage or extra portion may be made not only in the instrument where such disposition is contained, but even afterwards by an act passed before a notary and two witnesses. There was a comparable provision in the Code Napoleon, Article 919, as follows: "The declaration that the gift or legacy is made as a preference or extra portion, may be made, either in the instrument where such disposition is contained, or afterwards in the form prescribed for dispositions *inter vivos* or testamentary."

These provisions present the question: Must the dispensation from collation of a manual gift, which is subject to no formality, be made expressly and by the formality of a notarial act, under Article 1232 of the Civil Code? No provision defining the manual gift was in our Code of 1808. It was first defined in the Code of 1825 in Article 1526 (Article 1539 of our present Code). Therefore, we can safely conclude that the formality required by the Code of 1808 for making the declaration that the gift was made as an advantage or extra portion applied only to donations of movable effects made *inter vivos* under Article 48, Book III, Title II, of that Code, and not to manual gifts, which were not even recognized in the Code.

Did the redactors of the 1825 Code, who made provisions for the manual gift, intend that a manual gift could be dispensed from collation only by a notarial act under the provisions of Article 1310 (now Article 1232), or did they simply overlook the incongruity that would result from such a requirement of formality when the gift itself was subject to no formality, and omit a necessary provision from our Code?

In an effort to find a solution to this very perplexing problem, we have examined the authorities and commentators of France, where the same problem has arisen. There was no provision for the manual gift in the FRENCH CODE, but that form of giving was nevertheless recognized in France, and the manual gift was subject to collation.

Baudry-Lacantinerie and Wahl, who consider the problem in the light of the provisions of the FRENCH CODE, take the view: Dispensation from collation, insofar as it concerns manual gifts, can be tacit, and the judge can infer it from the circumstances of the case. It is difficult to conceive that a donation which can validly be made without an act can be dispensed from collation only by virtue of a declaration inserted in an act. Manual donations are a simple fact; it is the province of the judge to appreciate it and to determine its import. However, the word expressly which Article 843 employs necessarily infers a written clause; one ought therefore to think that Article 843 has envisaged the sole case of a donation made by act; this idea is corroborated by Article 919, according to which the declaration of extra portion must be made by the act which contains the disposition. It must be noted, however, that manual gifts have been omitted by the Code; this lack of regulation is a new argument that Article 843 must be disregarded in the question which is under discussion. But it is false that manual gifts are of themselves dispensed from collation. It is the judge who in his sovereign power decides whether the manual gift has been dispensed from collation in the intention of the donor. The proof of the dispensation from collation can result even from witnesses and judicial presumptions. The reason which justifies this solution is that same one on which is founded the doctrine which authorizes here the tacit dispensation from collation--the donee could not procure a writing authorizing the dispensation from collation. Baudry- Lacantinerie et Wahl, op. cit. *supra*, n° 2789, p. 258.

Others accept this view but at the same time recognize that there are authors who maintain that the manual gift can be excepted from collation only by express declaration. *See* Planiol et Ripert, TRAITÉ ÉLÉMENTAIRE DE DROIT CIVIL, III (11e ed. 1937), LA SUCCESSION, CHAPITRE 1, DES RAPPORTS, DONATIONS SOUMISES AU RAPPORT, n° 2251, p. 567; Cass. 19 October 1903, Sirey 1904. L. 40 n.l. The answer to this question for us should be clearly expressed in the Code, but it is not. The solution of the problem may address itself to the Louisiana Law Institute. That body can recommend appropriate action so that our Code will be explicit and clear on the subject.

In this case we could solve the problem in one of two ways. First, we could hold that, since the manual gift (for which no form is required) is not exempt by law from collation, its dispensation from collation must be established in the manner and form provided by Article 1232 of our Civil Code, that is, by a declaration that the donation is an advantage or extra portion made in a written act before a notary and two witnesses. Second, we could hold that the donor's intent to dispense collation of a manual gift could be established by the facts and circumstances of the case. Under this latter holding the donee would have the burden of establishing the intent to dispense by strong and convincing proof so as to overcome the presumption of collation, for under our law, where the donor has remained silent, collation is always presumed. Art. 1230, Civil Code.

Under either solution appellee cannot prevail, and collation will have to be ordered. There is no declaration by the donor, made in the manner and form provided by law, that the money (manual gift) was given as an advantage or extra portion, nor do the facts and circumstances of the case constitute proof sufficient to overcome the presumption of collation.

Mrs. Gomez, the donor, died testate, leaving a large estate. This action for collation was brought by children of a predeceased son. At the time the monthly payments were begun to Mrs. Salatich, she had left her mother's home, where she had been living with her children since her first husband's death, to reside elsewhere. The donor gave a like sum to her other daughter, Mrs. Barba, but made no such arrangement as to the surviving children of the predeceased son. Upon Mrs. Barba's death no payments were made to her surviving children, grandchildren of the donor, but the payments to Mrs. Salatich were continued. These payments to her began in 1930 and continued through 1946 and were alleged to have amounted to the sum of $19,200. According to one of the briefs, Mrs. Gomez, the deceased, left the disposable portion of her estate to three of her grandchildren, children of the defendant Mrs. Salatich, plus a particular legacy to one of them. From the fact that the will is not in the record we conclude that there was no provision therein indicating an intent on the part of the deceased to dispense from collation the manual gift to Mrs. Salatich. These facts are not sufficient to show that the donor intended to give the monthly sums to defendant as an extra portion.

*   *   *

SUCCESSION OF SKYE
417 So. 2d 1221 (La. App. 3d Cir. 1982)

FORET, Judge.

*   *   *

Decedent's $10,000 Gift to Plaintiff

Plaintiff contends that the trial court committed manifest error in finding that she must collate $10,000 given to her by decedent in the form of a check. Plaintiff argues that this check was given to her as a birthday gift and can in no way be considered an advance on that which she would later inherit from decedent. Plaintiff relies on the provisions of LSA-C.C. Articles 1244 and 1245 in support of her argument.

LSA-C.C. Article 1244 provides:

Art. 1244. Expenditures not subject to collation
Art. 1244. Neither the expenses of board, support, education and apprenticeship are subject to collation, nor are marriage presents which do not exceed the disposable portion.

LSA-C.C. Article 1245 provides:

Art. 1245. Manual gifts
Art. 1245. The same rule is established with respect to things given by a father, mother or other ascendant, by their own hands, to one of their children for his pleasure or other use.

It would seem that LSA-C.C. Article 1245 exempts manual gifts from the rules regarding collation. However, *Succession of Gomez*, 223 La. 859, 67 So. 2d 156 (1953), decided otherwise. *Gomez* noted, on page 157, that:

The question of whether manual gifts are exempt from collation has never, so far as we can ascertain, been adjudicated directly by this court.

Gomez conceded that, "The problem before us in this case is extremely difficult . . .", and then provided a brief review of the history surrounding the concept of collation. . . .

*   *   *

Plaintiff introduced in evidence a birthday card sent to her by decedent, in which decedent informed her that she had planned to send the $10,000 check to plaintiff for her birthday, but decided to hold on to the money for a while to collect extra interest. Decedent sent the check to plaintiff some five months after plaintiff's birthday. Plaintiff also introduced in evidence certain letters written by decedent in which she stated, among other things, that she was giving plaintiff the $10,000 to make up for the fact that plaintiff had failed to receive any portion of her brother's property after his death. There were other letters written by decedent, in which decedent clearly and unequivocally expressed that plaintiff was being given the $10,000 because decedent had given many gifts and done many things for her other children.

*   *   *

It is our opinion that, under the facts and circumstances of this case, plaintiff (the donee) has proven by clear and convincing evidence that decedent (the donor) intended to dispense from collation, the $10,000 she gave plaintiff in the form of a manual gift. The trial court's finding to the contrary is clearly wrong.

*   *   *

Berrigan, Comment, *Collation of the Manual Gift*
7 Loy. L. Rev. 24 (1953)
[Reprinted with permission; footnotes omitted]

These articles [1244, 45; 1538, 39; 1232, 85] comprise the rules set forth for the collation of the manual gift in Louisiana. Instead of treating each article individually, they will be considered collectively in connection with the recent case of *Succession of Gomez* which very thoroughly examined the problems concerning the collation of manual gifts.

In that case plaintiffs, children of deceased's predeceased son, brought suit against deceased's only surviving child to have her collate $19,200 which the deceased during her life time had given to her in monthly checks over a period of years. In the lower court the defendant contended that the monthly sums were for service rendered or if not for services, that they were manual gifts and for that reason exempt from collation under the provisions of Article 1245 of the Civil Code. Defendant failed to establish that the sums were for services rendered but the lower court nevertheless dismissed the plaintiff's suit on the theory that the money given to the defendant was a manual gift and for that reason exempt from collation under the provisions of Article 1245. On appeal the Supreme Court of Louisiana held that Article 1245 does not exempt all manual gifts as such from collation but only those manual gifts which it is usual or customary for a parent of this country to give to his child for his pleasure or use without thought or regard to his having to account for them to his co-heirs.

There are really two issues involved in the case which, when fully discussed, cover all of the problems involving the collation of manual gifts. The first is whether manual gifts as such are exempt from collation under Article 1245. The second is whether the deceased clearly expressed an intention to dispense with collation in a manner provided by law. As to the first issue the court traced the development of collation from its inception in Roman law to its present status in Louisiana law. The source of Roman law was ancient custom which excluded the children that were emancipated from the succession of their fathers, when there were children that were not emancipated. Afterwards when emancipated children were permitted to share in their father's succession in common with their brothers who had remained under their father's authority, they were obliged to bring back to the inheritance that which they had received since their emancipation. Soon the distinction between emancipated and unemancipated children ceased and both had to collate that which they had received to be shared alike by the children who did not receive a similar donation from their ascendant. Thus it can be seen that the purpose of the law was to ensure equality among the heirs without any regard to the father's wishes. This type of collation was also in the early French law but was later modified so that collation could be dispensed with by the express will of the donor. However, the strong presumption of equality still existed and could be overcome only by the positive expressed intention of the donor.

Article 842 of the Code Napoleon states that "Every heir, even a beneficiary one, coming to a succession, must collate to his co-heirs, what he has received from the deceased, by donation *inter vivos*, directly or indirectly; and he cannot retain the donation or claim the legacy made to him by the deceased, unless the donation and the legacies have been expressly made to him as a preference over his co-heirs and besides his portion, or as exempt from collation." When the LOUISIANA CIVIL CODE was drafted in 1808 the collation articles were taken from the French and accordingly were based on the equality which should exist among the heirs. It was provided that a donor could exempt a gift from collation by formally expressing his will either in the act of donation itself or in a separate instrument provided that the separate instrument be executed before a notary public and two witnesses.

In the Revision of 1825 the rule was relaxed as to the content of the declaration dispensing with collation and Article 1311 was adopted which provided that the declaration that the gift or legacy is intended as an advantage or extra portion may be made in other equivalent terms, provided that they indicate in an unequivocal manner that such was the will of the donor. To the same effect is Article 1233. It has often been held that there is a strong presumption of equality and the intention of the donor to dispense with collation has to be clearly shown in the manner provided by law.

Under Article 1244 and 1245 certain things are exempt from collation by law and there need be no express intention on the part of the donor to dispense therewith, but since this legal exemption can destroy the equality among the heirs their provisions must be met exactly before they are applicable. Article 1244 reads, "Neither the expenses of board, support education and apprenticeship are subject to collation nor are marriage presents which do not exceed the disposable portion." Article 1245 reads, "The same rule is established with respect to things given by a father, mother or other ascendant, by their own hands, to one of their children for his pleasure or other use." It is by virtue of this latter article that the defendant in the *Succession of Gomez* contended that all manual gifts are exempt from collation. The court pointed out that certain things were exempted from collation by Article 852 of the Code Napoleon, which reads as follows: "The expenses of board, support, education and apprenticeship, the ordinary expenses of accoutrement, those of marriage and customary presents, are not subject to collation." As was noted, this article divided donations that were exempted from collation into two classes; (1) Those resulting from the obligation of the parent, and (2) Those resulting from social custom or usage. When the LOUISIANA CIVIL CODE was drafted in 1808, the things exempted from collation were essentially the same as those in the FRENCH CODE but more liberal in its views as to what were usual gifts and more detailed as to those gifts. This can be noted in the Code of 1808: "There exists however one sort of advantage made by ascendants to their lawful children or descendants, which by their privileged nature, are not subject to collation, though it cannot be said they were not taken out of the mass of the donor's estate. Thus pensions, aliments and maintenance supplied to children, and books and other expenses laid out for their education, are not liable to collation, though a library is. No collation is due to the wedding clothes and wedding expenses; but the trousseau of the daughter is liable to it. New Years gifts and small presents, money given to the minor and by him spent and even money given to the son of age, for play and for his pleasure, are not subject to collation." The court pointed out that it seemed apparent that the redactors of the code realized that American parents were not only more liberal in their gifts merely given on special occasions but also exempted money given to the child for his play or pleasure. It is evident that the Code of 1808 did not exempt all manual gifts from collation simply because they were manual gifts. When the code was revised in 1825, the redactors cut down the language of this article and compiled it into Article 1322 and 1323 of the Code of 1825 which are the same as Article 1244 and 1245 of the Code of 1870. The redactors of the 1825 Code tell why they changed the wording of this article; "...to abridge some dispositions which are too much overloaded with details." It does not seem that the redactors intended to change the law in respect to what was exempt from collation but merely to do away with excess verbiage. The redactors knew what a manual gift was, for they defined it in article 1526 of the Code of 1825, and if they wanted to exempt all manual gifts from collation they could have simply stated that the same rule is established with respect to manual gifts instead of stating "The same rule is established with respect to things given by a father, mother or other ascendant, by their own hands, to one of their children for his pleasure or other use." Why would they have added the limiting prepositional phrase "for his pleasure or other use" if they intended to exempt all manual gifts from collation? The court noted that when they adopted this phrase (for his pleasure or other use) they were probably contemplating those things usual for parents of this country to give to a child without thought or regard to his having to account for them to his co-heirs. This language is broad enough to meet the changes in our social development. Thus by following the development of Article 1244 and 1245, it seems that all manual gifts are not exempt from collation simply by virtue of the fact that they are manual gifts; only those manual gifts which it is usual for a parent of this country to give to his child for his pleasure or other use are exempt. The court's opinion in the *Succession of Gomez* does not affect those things exempted under Article 1244 because they are based on obligations of the parents and are not donations strictly speaking. The court found that the donations made to the defendant in this case were not those manual gifts which it was usual for a parent to give to a child for his pleasure or other use and therefore not exempt from collation under the provisions of Article 1245.

The exemptions under Article 1244 and 1245 are provided by law, but the donor may dispense with the collation of gifts which are not automatically exempted by law if his intention to so dispense is clearly expressed in the manner provided by law. This takes us to the second issue of the *Gomez* case, which is somewhat involved. Article 1538 provides that a donation *inter vivos*, even of movable effects, will not be valid unless made by an act passed before a notary and two witnesses. Article 1539 provides that the manual gift, that is, the giving of corporeal movable effects, accompanied by a real delivery, is not subject to any formality. Article 1232 states that the declaration that the gift or legacy is made as an advantage or extra portion, may be made, not only in the instrument where such disposition is contained, but even afterwards by an act passed before a notary and two witnesses. Both Article 1538, as to the formality of donations *inter vivos*, and Article 1232, as to the formality of exempting such donations from collation, had identical provisions in the Code of 1808, but Article 1539 which dispenses manual gifts from the requirement of formality found its inception in the Code of 1825. In the language of the court, "Did the redactors of the 1825 Code, who made provisions for the manual gift, intend that a manual gift should be dispensed from collation only by a notarial act under the provisions of Article 1310 (now Article 1232), or did they simply overlook the incongruity that would result from such a requirement of formality, and omit a necessary provision from our Code." In seeking a solution the court went to the French commentators where the same problem exists. There was no provision for the manual gift in France but the jurisprudence recognized that method of donation and subjected it to collation. In France there are two conflicting views as to whether there must be a formal dispensation from collation of a manual gift, the donation of which requires no form. One view is that since the gift itself requires no form, there need be no formality in excepting it from collation. This view maintains that the intent of the donor to dispense with collation can be tacit and is to be determined from the circumstances of the case. However, the advocates of this theory also maintain that the donations which must be made before a notary can be exempted from collation only by an act of similar strength. Other commentators maintain, however, that the manual gift can be exempted from collation only by express declaration. In the instant case, the court did not have to resolve the issue, for it found that under either interpretation of our Codal Articles the donations to the defendant were not exempt from collation. The court concluded, "There is no declaration by the donor, made in the manner and form required by law, that the money (manual gift) was given as an advantage or extra portion, nor do the facts and circumstances of the case constitute proof sufficient to overcome the presumption of collation."

The defendant also argued that the money was for her support and therefore should be exempted from collation under the provisions of Article 1244. The court found that the defendant was not in necessitous circumstances and had sufficient funds to provide for her own support. The court noted that there have been many cases in which collation was demanded of gifts that were in fact manual. However in all of these cases it was argued that gifts were remunerative donations and therefore not subject to collation. In these cases the court considered the problem only in respect to whether or not the manual gifts were remunerative donations and never addressed itself to the manual gift problem. In the *Succession of Gomez*, therefore, this matter was res novo before the Supreme Court; however, there has been an earlier Court of Appeal case, *LeBlanc v. Voelker*, which presented the identical problem. In that case it was sought to have collated 12 shares of Homestead stock which had been gratuitously donated to the defendant in accordance with the provisions of the Uniform Stock Transfer Act. Defendant contended that in the absence of proof of consideration, the transfer was valid as a manual gift and was not subject to collation. The court cited Article 1244 and 1245 and then made this statement, "A manual gift is not subject to collation. Can Homestead stock be the subject of a manual gift within the contemplation of the Code?" The court then quoted Article 1536 which declares that the donation of an immovable or an incorporeal thing, such as rents, credits and rights of action, must be made before a notary and two witnesses, and Article 1539 which states that the manual gift, the giving of corporeal movable effects, accompanied by a real delivery, is not subject to any formality. The court concluded that the transfer of the Homestead stock was, in view of the provisions of the Uniform Stock Transfer Act, a valid donation *inter vivos*, but nevertheless the subject of collation since it was an incorporeal and therefore under the provisions of Article 1539 could not be the subject of a manual gift. The court decided that the manual gift exempted from collation under Article 1245 has to be a corporeal movable as provided in Article 1539. In the case under discussion it could have been argued that the checks donated by the deceased to her daughter were validly transferred by endorsement but were incorporeals and therefore not the subject of a manual gift so as to be exempted from collation. The reasoning of the *Succession of Gomez* seems to be in conflict with *LeBlanc v. Voelker* for apparently the court deciding the *Gomez* case would not entertain the distinction between corporeals and incorporeals for purposes of collation under Article 1245. Also, the decision in the *Succession of Gomez* does not apply Article 1539 to collation problems. Nevertheless the same conclusion reached by the Orleans Court of Appeals in the *LeBlanc* case may result from an application of the legal analysis of the *Succession of Gomez* to the facts of that case if it were found that the donation of the Homestead stock was not customary for the pleasure of the donee considering the social and economic status of the donor.

Also, the court could have justified its decision that all manual gifts as such are not exempt from collation by referring to Article 1285 which subjects donations of money to collation. It is well settled that checks and money can be the subject of manual gifts. However, Article 1285 provides the method in which money is to be collated. This Article was substantially the same in the Civil Codes of 1808 and 1825. Since money and checks can be the object of manual gifts and since Article 1285 declares how money is to be collated, then clearly not all manual gifts are exempt from collation.

Exactly what manual gifts are exempt from collation under Article 1245? The Article speaks of things given by a parent with his own hands to his child for his pleasure or other use. By tracing the history of its development, the court concluded that this Article referred not only to those manual presents which it was the custom for parents to give to their children on special occasions, such as Christmas and Birthday presents, but also to those manual gifts which under the circumstances of each case it is usual for certain parents to make to their children. In the latter instance many factors will have to be taken into consideration, for example: What is the economic and social status of the donating parents? Do parents of the same financial and social status make similar donations to their children without any thought of collation? In other words, is it the usual practice for parents of the same classification as the donor to make manual donations to their children similar to the donation which is sought to be collated? If the answer is in the affirmative, then the specific manual gift is exempt from collation. Under this interpretation of Article 1245, the same manual gift might be exempt from collation in one instance while not in another. For example, it might be customary for parents of a certain status to give an automobile to their children without any thought as to collation in which case the gift would be exempt from collation. The same gift might be made by a parent of a different status in which such donations are not customary and in such a case collation would be ordered. This is apparently the test the court had in mind in the *Succession of Gomez* when it stated, "Under our interpretation of Article 1245, the money given to the defendant in this case, under an arrangement for a monthly stipend which lasted for over fifteen years, is not one of those things contemplated by Article 1245, and therefore is not exempt from collation under that Article." The Court pointed out that its decision has no effect whatsoever on Article 1244 because the things that are exempt under that Article are in reality obligations of the parents and are not donations strictly speaking.

The problem which remains unsolved in the *Succession of Gomez* and which the court did not have to answer is--does the manual gift which needs no form have to be formally exempted from collation if it is not exempted under Articles 1244 and 1245? The Court addressed this problem to the manual gift which is valid by mere delivery to the donee. In order to exempt this type of gift from collation must there be a formal declaration or can it be dispensed tacitly from the circumstances of the case? As has been noted, the French Commentators are in conflict as to what is necessary. However, all of them agree that the donation which must be made formally must also be exempted from collation formally. As to the method of exempting from collation the manual gift which needs no form, they are in conflict. One view is that the gift does not need to be formally exempted from collation; the other is that it does. The purpose of requiring collation is to secure equality among the heirs. This presumption of equality can be overcome only by the clear intention of the donor to dispense with collation. Because of this strong presumption of equality and because the present law is silent on this subject, it seems that the safest thing to do as of now would be to follow Article 1232 and expressly exempt the manual gift from collation, either in the instrument of donation (if such is required) or in a subsequent act before a notary and two witnesses. This procedure, however, could prove cumbersome and inconvenient. There is however, another more practical method of exempting such a gift from collation. When the donor draws his final will, he could ratify all his previous donations and expressly exempt them from collation. The decision in *Barrow v. Barrow* is the only one in the jurisprudence on the subject. In that case it was sought, among other things, to have *inter vivos* donations collated. In the third clause of his will the deceased made particular legacies to certain of his children, "to equalize them with all my other children that have left me heretofore." The court said, ... its terms are sufficient to cut off any claim for any collation of advantages previously received by heirs; for the third clause of the will shows conclusively that the legacies therein made to certain heirs were intended "to equalize them with my other children which, under Article 1233, C.C., is a sufficient indication of the testator's intention to exclude all question of collation of previous advantages."

It is clear that the LOUISIANA CIVIL CODE and jurisprudence provides for methods of formally exempting a donation from collation, but nowhere in Louisiana law can authority be found for allowing tacit dispensation from collation of manual gifts not otherwise exempted by law under Articles 1244 and 1245, as is recognized by some of the French Commentators. Because of this strong presumption of equality among the heirs, probably the reason for this omission is intentional rather than accidental. It would seem that any disturbance of the presumption of equality should be allowed only by the express will of the donor, with the exception, however, of Articles 1244 and 1245 which state the legal exemptions from collation.

A solution to this problem raised in the *Succession of Gomez* could be effected in a statute specifically providing for the conditions under which manual gifts are exempt from collation. Such a statute would clear up the doubt unresolved in this case and could read as follows:

An Act

To amend the Civil Code of Louisiana by adding a new Article to be designated as Article 1245.1, relative to the collation of manual gifts, and to repeal all conflicting laws.

Section 1. Be it enacted by the Legislature of Louisiana that the Civil Code of Louisiana is hereby amended by adding thereto a new Article designated as Article 1245.1:

Article 1245.1. The manual gift may be made as an advantage or extra portion only in an act passed before a notary and two witnesses or in the last will and testament of the donor. Those manual gifts which are exempted from collation because they are parental obligations of the donor, or because they are customary or usual gifts for a child's pleasure or other use made by parents of the same status of the donor, under the provisions of the two preceding Articles, are excepted from the provisions of this Article.

Section 2. All laws or parts of laws contrary to or in conflict with this Article, are hereby repealed.

NOTES

In actions for collation and reduction, revendication was the right of a forced heir descendant to reclaim immovable property from a third person who had onerously obtained the property from a donee who received it as an *inter vivos* gift from the decedent. This right, which was limited only to immovable property, was established in La. C.C. 1281, 1517, and 1518, but was repealed in 1981 by Act 739.

La. C.C. 1281, prior to its amendment, provided that if the coheir who owed the obligation to collate had disposed of the immovable property and could not satisfy his or her obligation from the other property by taking less, the other forced heirs had the right to seek and take the property from the transferee.

Similarly, La. C.C. 1517 and 1518 applied when the donee was someone other than a coheir. Under these articles, the forced heir's rights to claim the property from an onerous transferee was allowed only when necessary to satisfy the *legitime* and only after the forced heir had attempted to first satisfy the *legitime* from the assets of the donee. The rights of the forced heir were against the property only; therefore, if the transferee had himself disposed of the property, the heir had no right to satisfy the *legitime* from the transferee's remaining assets.

Today, the right of a forced heir to reclaim donated property from someone other than the donee is limited to situations where the transferee obtained the property gratuitously from the original donee. *See* La. C.C. 1281, 1517, and 1518, as amended in 1981.

When Collation May Occur

SUCCESSION OF DELESDERNIER
184 So. 2d 37 (La. App. 4th Cir. 1966)
[27 La. L. Rev. 452 (1967)]

BARNETTE, Judge.

*　　*　　*

II The Pleas of Judgments of Possession as a Bar to Demands for Collation

It is firmly established in the jurisprudence of this State that collation cannot be demanded after a succession has been closed by a judgment sending the heirs in possession. *Succession of McGeary*, 220 La. 391, 56 So. 2d 727 (1951); *Doll v. Doll*, 206 La. 550, 19 So. 2d 249 (1944). If, however, there are nullities in the succession proceedings and the judgment therein is attacked and set aside because of those nullities, the right to demand collation would not be precluded by the former judgment. Obviously, if the judgment of possession is a nullity, legal effects would not flow from it.

Plaintiff here has alleged many nullities, not in the Succession proceedings attacked, but in acts of purported transfer of certain property, the formation of the family corporation, and her tutorship proceedings. These alleged acts of nullity might be reasons or causes of action upon which to demand collation if there had been no judgment of possession, but they do not strike at the validity of the succession proceedings themselves. We find no allegation in any of the numerous pleadings in these consolidated cases setting forth a cause or right of action to set aside or annul the judgments sending the heirs in possession in either succession. We must hold, therefore, that the plaintiff has no cause or right of action to demand collation in either succession.

Plaintiff has alleged, however, that certain property rightfully belonging to the succession of her grandfather George W. Delesdernier was omitted, not included in the inventory, and to this extent the succession should be reopened in order that the omitted property might be distributed among his heirs in their just proportion. This does not imply a nullity, but rather an incompleteness in the succession proceedings and an amendment to the judgment of possession would be in order. Express authority for this procedure is found in LSA-C.C.P. art. 3393. Therefore, plaintiff should have an opportunity to point out such omissions on remand and petition for a supplemental or amending judgment of possession.

* * *

SUCCESSION OF WEBRE
247 La. 461, 172 So. 2d 285 (1965)
[25 La. L. Rev. 986, 988 (1965)]
(Footnotes Omitted)

SANDERS, Justice.

This is a succession proceeding. Certain children and grandchildren of Louis Robert Webre and Mrs. Ulyssia Landry Webre, the decedents, seek an inventory and administration of the estates. They also seek to annul as simulations separate conveyances of land by the decedents to two other children, Septime Raymond Webre and Ada Webre Boudreaux. Alternatively, the petitioners pray for collation of the property.

The assailed conveyances were executed on February 15, 1938. Louis Robert Webre died on September 25, 1940; his wife, Ulyssia Landry Webre, died on November 10, 1947. The petitioners brought this proceeding on November 6, 1950, more than ten years after the death of Louis Robert Webre.

In the answer filed, the defendants asserted the validity of the conveyances and resisted collation. They also pleaded the prescription of five years under LSA-C.C. Article 3542 and of ten years under LSA-C.C. Article 3544 as to the conveyance made by Louis Robert Webre.

On September 26, 1962, the petitioners sought to file a supplemental and amended petition alleging alternatively that if it should be found that the defendants had paid any consideration for the land, then the price was very low, being an advantage to be collated by the defendants under LSA-C.C. Article 1248. The defendants objected to the supplemental petition, and the Court maintained the objection.

The district court sustained the plea of prescription of five years for the reduction of excessive donations under LSA-C.C. Article 3542 as to the conveyance made by Louis Robert Webre. The plaintiffs appealed. The defendants answered the appeal, praying that the judgment of the district court sustaining the prescription of five years be affirmed and, alternatively, that the prescription of ten years under LSA-C.C. Article 3544 be maintained.

The Court of Appeal sustained the prescription of ten years under LSA-C.C. Article 3544 and affirmed the judgment of the district court, as thus amended. La.App., 164 So. 2d 49. Upon application of the plaintiffs, we granted a writ of certiorari to review the judgment of the Court of Appeal. 246 La. 728, 167 So. 2d 304.

In this Court, the defendants have filed a plea of prescription of ten years under LSA-C.C. Article 2221.

We have before us, therefore, three pleas of prescription directed at the attack upon the conveyance of Louis Robert Webre: five years under LSA-C.C. Article 3542, relating to reduction of excessive donations and nullity or rescission of contracts; ten years under LSA-C.C.

Article 2221, relating to actions of nullity or rescission of agreements; and ten years under LSA-C.C. Article 3544, relating to personal actions. These pleas of prescription must be considered in the light of the allegations of the petition.

The petition and attached documents disclose the following facts: Louis Robert Webre and Ulyssia Landry were married on July 3, 1886. Seven children were born of the marriage.

On February 15, 1938, Louis Robert Webre executed in authentic form an act of sale of a tract of land in St. John the Baptist Parish to two of his children, Septime Raymond Webre and Ada Webre Boudreaux, who executed the act with him. The act of sale recited a price of $1200.00, of which $600 was payable in cash and the balance of $600 was represented by a promissory note due in one year, and secured by a mortgage and vendor's lien. The act recited that Louis Robert Webre had acquired the property by purchase on December 31, 1896.

Likewise on February 15, 1938, Mrs. Ulyssia Landry Webre executed an act of sale of another tract of land to the same children. Although this conveyance has been attacked in this proceeding, no issue concerning it is now before this Court.

Louis Robert Webre died intestate on September 25, 1940, and his wife died intestate on November 10, 1947.

The petition further alleged that the land was worth more than $20,000.00 on the date of the act of sale from Louis Robert Webre. The named transferees gave "no consideration whatsoever" for it, and the sale was a "pure simulation and in fraud of the rights of your petitioners."

In Article 11, the petition further alleged:

That subsequent to the aforesaid purported acts of sale, and particularly during the month of August, 1941, it was freely admitted by the defendants and the decedent, Mrs. Ulyssia Landry, widow of Louis Robert Webre, that the said sales were "fake" sales and that they were made purely for the purposes of convenience and were not bona fide sales.

Plaintiffs prayed that the acts of sale be declared null, void, and of no effect. In the alternative only, they prayed that the defendants be ordered to collate the property to the successions of the decedents.

After an analysis of the pleadings, the Court of Appeal concluded that the plaintiffs had alleged no ground for the primary demand of nullity but only a basis for collation. The Court held that the demand for collation had prescribed under the ten year prescription of Article 3544, LSA-C.C. since the suit had been filed more than ten years after the death of Louis Robert Webre.

We do not agree with this construction of the petition. Although the petition is inartistically drawn, the allegations are sufficient to admit proof that the act of sale was a sham or that the sale was at a very low price or that it was a donation in disguise.

*   *   *

The following articles of the LOUISIANA CIVIL CODE control the relief sought in this proceeding:

Article 2239. "Counter letters can have no effect against creditors or bona fide purchasers; they are valid as to all others; but forced heirs shall have the same right to annul absolutely and by parol evidence the simulated contracts of those from whom they inherit, and shall not be restricted to the legitimate (*legitime*)."

Article 1248. "The advantage which a father bestows upon his son, though in any other manner than by donation or legacy, is likewise subject to collation. Thus, when a father has sold a thing to his son at a very low price, or has paid for him the price of some purchase, for (or) has spent money to improve his son's estate, all that is subject to collation."

Article 2444. "The sales of immovable property made by parents to their children, may be attacked by the forced heirs, as containing a donation in disguise, if the latter can prove that no price has been paid, or that the price was below one-fourth of the real value of the immovable sold, at the time of the sale."

* * *

The petition therefore presents two demands: a demand in declaration of a simulation and a demand for collation. To the demands, as previously noted, the defendants have pleaded the prescriptions of five and ten years.

To dispose of the pleas of prescription, we must consider the two demands separately.

* * *

We said in *Spiers v. Davidson*, 233 La. 239, 96 So. 2d 502:

...(A) simulated contract is one which has no substance at all, or is purely fictitious and a sham, an act of mere pretense without reality. Such a contract, although clothed in concrete form, is entirely without effect and may be declared a sham at any time at the demand of any person in interest.

An action to annul a simulated contract under Article 2239, LSA-C.C. is imprescriptible.

Hence, the pleas of prescription must be overruled as to the demand in declaration of simulation.

More difficult are the pleas of prescription to the demand for collation.

It is now well settled that the five year prescription of LSA-C.C. Article 3542 does not apply to collation. This Court, however, has not as yet determined which, if any, of the several prescriptions does apply to collation. The identification of the prescription was reserved in *Himel v. Connely*, 195 La. 769, 197 So. 424, holding the five year prescription inapplicable. The prescriptive period has been ably treated in the law journals. *See* 3 Louisiana Law Review 284, 460; 27 Tulane Law Review 241; and 9 Loyola Law Review 912.

After a thorough analysis, the Court of Appeal applied the prescription of ten years under LSA-C.C. Article 3544. We agree that this prescription applies to collation.

Article 3544 provides:

In general, all personal actions, except those before enumerated, are prescribed by ten years.

Collation, or the return of property to a succession, is the means by which the law seeks to assure the equal distribution of the ancestor's property among the direct descendants. It arises from an obligation, or duty, imposed upon the heir by law. The heir may release himself from this duty by renouncing the succession. Despite a renunciation, however, the law protects the *legitime* of the heirs.

Collation can be demanded only by the heirs designated by law. It is accomplished in two ways: in kind or by taking less. Collation is made in kind when the property is returned to the succession; it is made by taking less when the heir reduces his inheritance in proportion to the value of the property he has received. Generally, the collation of immovables may be made either in kind or by taking less. The collation of movables must be made by taking less.

Basic to collation, as we view it, is the duty of the heir. The right to enforce the duty is restricted to the designated co-heirs. Although the demand has unique features, we think that it must be classified as a personal action under LSA-C.C. Article 3544 for purposes of prescription. We hold that the ten year prescription of that article applies to a demand for collation.

* * *

Having concluded that the ten year prescription applies, we reach the question of when the prescription begins to run. The plaintiffs assert that it runs only from the date they acquired knowledge of the conveyance. Alternatively, they assert that it runs only from the filing of the formal succession proceedings. We find no merit in either contention.

A succession is opened upon the death, and all rights vest as of that time. From that moment, an heir may file formal succession proceedings and demand collation.

Activating the prescription only from the filing of formal succession proceeding would severely limit its effect. Collation is barred in any event after the heirs unconditionally accept a succession and obtain judgment putting them in possession of the property.

We conclude that prescription runs from the death of the person to whose succession collation is to be made.

* * *

Leslie J. Clement, Comment, *Some Aspects of Collation*
34 La. L. Rev. 782 (1974)
[Reprinted with permission; footnotes omitted]

* * *

The Proper Time for Collation

No legislation specifically indicates the proper time for a forced heir to demand collation from a co heir, consequently, rules governing this matter have evolved jurisprudentially. It is settled that a demand for collation during the life of the de cujus is premature. Ostensibly likewise settled is a rule barring the demand for collation after a judgment of possession in favor of the forced heirs. Whereas the prohibition against a demand for collation prior to the death of the de cujus seems correct, the notion that a judgment of possession forecloses the right to demand collation appears questionable.

Those cases which indicate that a judgment of possession vitiates the right to demand collation are based on the proposition that by the judgment of possession co-heirs become co-owners, thereby extinguishing the succession, and with it, the right to demand collation. While there is no doubt that collation can only be made to a succession, there appears to be no justification for the conclusion that a judgment of possession changes the character of ownership and results in an extinguishment of the succession.

A judgment of possession merely constitutes judicial recognition of rights which come into existence by operation of law at the moment of an ancestor's death. This conclusion is supported by several articles of the Civil Code. For example, article 944 provides that the heir succeeds to rights of the deceased from the moment of his death; article 946 indicates that a succession is acquired by an heir from the moment of the death of the deceased; and article 1292 states that heirs become undivided "proprietors upon the death of the person from whom they inherit." Furthermore, the comments of the redactors in the Projét of the Code of 1825 expressly indicate that the Roman and Spanish law, by which the transmission of the succession did not take effect until the acceptance by the heir, was rejected in favor of a rule by which the heir's rights vest at the moment of death.

A succession is not a fictitious entity subject to extinguishment by the judgment of possession. Although such a theory may have been valid under a provision of the Digest of 1808, it is no longer appropriate since that article was deleted by the redactors of the Civil Code of 1825 in accord with their announced intention to abandon the fictitious entity concept. Moreover, article 872 of the present Civil Code states that, in addition to signifying the transmission of rights and obligations of the deceased, and the right of the heir to the possession thereof, "succession signifies also the estates (estate), rights and charges which a person leaves after his death...." It therefore seems illogical to describe a succession as "extinguished" so long as its effects continue to remain in existence.

The barring of collation by a judgment of possession can have harsh practical effects. It is not unusual for forced heirs to hold a succession in common for many years after the death of either of their parents, especially if any of the heirs are unmarried and continue to live in the family home. Formerly, heirs often possessed this property without first having obtained a judgment of possession, but the present inheritance tax law makes this practice ill-advised since it prohibits such heirs from later renouncing their inheritance and subjects them to personal liability for the tax. The result is that heirs usually obtain a judgment of possession soon after their ancestor's death but may not make a demand for collation at that time since the succession may not be immediately partitioned. Later, when the property is partitioned, collation is unavailable because of the previous judgment of possession, which may have been obtained solely for inheritance tax purposes, and the principle of equality among forced heirs is thereby frustrated.

The scheme of the Civil Code indicates that collation is an incident of the judicial partition of a succession. This view, advocated by most French commentators, is supported in several Louisiana cases. Although collation claims have been advanced and adjudicated independently of partition proceedings, in only one instance does a court appear to have been aware of the inconsistency of an attempt to equalize the distribution of a succession which is to remain intact. It is no statutory coincidence that the same section of the Civil Code which provides for the manner in which judicial partitions are to be accomplished also regulates the procedure for collation. If the partition is to be made among forced heirs, and collation is necessary, the decree of partition is exhibited to the heir bound to collate who then decides whether the collation is to be made in kind or by taking less. The active mass of the succession, when formed by the officer appointed to effect the partition, includes all the objects collated in kind, as well as a credit for the appraised value of all property collated by taking less. When the effects of the succession are divided among the heirs, allowances are made for collation in order to equalize the share of each heir. Other Civil Code articles indicate even more explicitly that collation is an incident to the partition of a succession. Article 1227 declares that the purpose of collation is "in order that such property may be divided together with the other effects of the succession"; article 1229 indicates that collation is founded on the equality of descendant heirs "who divide among them (selves)" the succession of their ascendants; and articles 1283 and 1255 respectively allow movables and immovables to be collated by taking less.

Since it clearly appears that collation is an incident to the partition of a succession, the proper time for a forced heir to demand collation must arise concurrently. It follows that a forced heir may either institute a suit for partition coupled with a demand for collation or may simply demand collation during partition proceedings instituted by a co-heir. In either case, a previous judgment of possession should have no effect so long as the succession was never previously partitioned. However, if no demand for collation is raised prior to the homologation of the partition, all claims for collation should thereafter be barred.

PRESCRIPTION OF THE RIGHT TO DEMAND COLLATION

Initial judicial attempts to establish a prescriptive period for the right to demand collation culminated inconclusively in *In re Andrus*. There the supreme court expressly overruled an earlier case which had held that the prescription of five years in Civil Code article 3542 applied to collation. But since it was superfluous to the facts presented in Andrus, the question of whether the prescription of ten or thirty years might apply to collation was left unanswered.

The issue of a prescriptive period for the right to demand collation was ostensibly resolved in *Succession of Webre*. In that case, certain children and grandchildren of the de cujus sought to have annulled as simulations separate conveyances of land which had been made to other forced heirs. Alternatively, the petitioners prayed for collation of the allegedly simulated conveyances. Since more than ten years had elapsed since their father's death, the defendant heirs raised pleas of prescription of five and ten years. The court of appeal refused to annul the conveyances but instead found them to be disguised donations, normally subject to collation. However, the court concluded that collation is a "personal action" governed by Civil Code article 3544, and it therefore upheld the exception of ten years prescription. On certiorari, the supreme court determined that the transfers to the defendants were simulated conveyances which should have been annulled by the lower court. Since a reversal and remand thereby became necessary, the court need have said no more. Nevertheless, the majority proceeded to affirm the court of appeal's opinion that collation is a personal action which prescribes ten years after the death of an ancestor.

The ten-year prescription embodied in article 3544 can be applied to collation only if it can be classified as a "personal action." Yet, the Civil Code speaks of collation as an obligation of forced heirs, enforcement of which is a right of any co-heir; and the CODE OF CIVIL PROCEDURE defines a personal action as "one brought to enforce an obligation against the obligor, personally and independently of the property which he may own, claim, or possess." It is therefore disputable whether the right to demand collation can be categorized as a personal action. In any event, the right to demand collation should not prescribe ten years after the death of the de cujus, principally because of the inseparable nexus between collation and the action of partition. Since the right to compel the partition of a succession held in common is imprescriptable, the right to demand collation should not be independently subject to prescription. Otherwise, the illogical consequence is that the right to demand a partition may be partially extinguished by prescription, insofar as it relates to collation, while simultaneously remaining in full force and effect indefinitely, insofar as it relates to the distribution of the effects of the succession. Moreover, there are some circumstances under which collation within ten years of an ancestor's death may be impractical or impossible.

Even if it be conceded that ten years prescription under article 3544 should apply to collation, the practical effect seems negligible. The running of prescription should commence only when partition proceedings are instituted since prior to that time there is no effective opportunity to demand collation. The fact that the prescriptive period for the action to reduce excessive donations begins upon the death of the de cujus does not justify a similar rule for the right to demand collation, since the reduction of an excessive donation, unlike collation, is independent of the action of partition. As noted previously, demands for collation made after a partition should be barred unless the partition is later rescinded. Since the action to rescind a partition prescribes in five years, a ten-year prescriptive period for collation would usually be irrelevant.

The adverse effects of the present jurisprudential rule of prescription are readily apparent. Forced heirs who take no action regarding an ancestor's succession for ten years after his death may be deprived of an opportunity to obtain their rightful inheritance. Apparently the only argument in favor of the current rule is that it may promote the alienability of gifts and legacies which forced heirs have received from an ancestor. However, this is an illusory contention since a forced heir who wishes to alienate such property need not wait ten years before doing so. Both movables and immovables can be collated by taking less; thus, a forced heir can always alienate or mortgage the property which he holds up to the value of his *legitime*. Moreover, any heir who desires to clarify his rights need only demand a partition of the succession. Third party purchasers and mortgagees are already protected by other provisions of law.

*   *   *

NOTE

In *Trouard v. Heimback,* 281 So. 2d 863 (La. 3d Cir. 1973), the plaintiffs sought to annul a judgment of possession solely on the ground that at the time of the judgment, the heirs were unaware of a will that provided for collation of a sum of money given to one of the heirs as an advance to his inheritance. The Louisiana Third Circuit Court of Appeal refused to annul the judgment of possession solely to enable some of the heirs to demand collation.

How Collations are Made: La. C.C. art. 1251-1288

BAILLIO v. BAILLIO
5 MART. (N.S.) 228 (La. 1826)

Mathews, J. delivered the opinion of the court.

*   *   *

In the present case, advances were made by donations from the father to some of his children, out of the property of the community, or common stock of acquets and gains belonging to him and their mother, who is still living. In bringing back these donations, a question arises as to the manner in which they ought to be collated.

The law requires property given in advances to heirs, to be collated to the succession of the donor; and as the husband is master of the community of acquets subsisting between him and his wife during his lifetime, and may sell, or in any other manner dispose of the effects belonging to such community, it would seem that a gift made by him to one of his children, which should, after his death, be subject to collation, ought to be returned in toto to his succession. But, according to the most celebrated commentator on the FRENCH CODE, which is very similar in its provisions to our own, on the subjects of community of goods between husband and wife, succession, and collation, a contrary doctrine is maintained; which requires that, when the donation is of common property, collation takes place by moiety, although the husband should have been sole agent in the gift or advance to the children; and this appears to us to be equitable. See 4 Toullier, p. 460, no. 464. Collation, however, cannot be required, until the opening of the succession to which it belongs. Admitting that the advances made by P. Baillio to his heirs, must be collated by halves, one moiety to be returned to his succession, and the other to that of his wife, the latter return cannot take place until her succession be opened; this part of the donation must remain undisturbed in the possession of the donees until that event happens. The judge of probates erred in collating the advances made to P. Baillio as to the whole mass of the community, and giving to the widow one-half of the aggregate thus formed. The common property, as it was at the time of the death of one of the partners, should have been divided between the survivor and the heirs of the former; and to the half thus allotted to said heirs, should be added one-half of the advances made to them, as subject to collation in the succession of their father; as the other half cannot legally be disturbed until the opening of the succession of the mother, it should not have been acted on.

*   *   *

PROBLEM

Doris had two children, Audrey and Carlotta. During her lifetime, Doris gave Audrey a parcel of land worth $30,000 when given. It was worth $60,000 at the time of Doris's death. If Carlotta was able to demand collation of Audrey, what options would be available to her?

SUCCESSION OF DOLL v. DOLL

593 So. 2d 1239 (La. 1992)

[footnotes selectively omitted]

COLE, Justice.

The issues in this collation action are, first, whether the fruits of an immovable collated in kind are themselves subject to actual collation; and second, if the fruits are subject to actual collation, whether such collation is due from the date of acquisition, the date of the donor's death, or from the date of judicial demand. A threshold question is whether mineral lease bonuses and the revenues derived from the sale of timber constitute "fruits" of an immovable within the meaning of Louisiana Civil Code article 551.

* * *

Having clarified the classification of the proceeds, we now turn our attention to collation. The Civil Code defines collation as the supposed or real return to the mass of the succession which an heir makes of property which he received in advance of his share or otherwise, in order that such property may be divided together with the other effects of the succession. LA. CIV. CODE ANN. art. 1227 (West 1987). The obligation of collating is founded on the equality between direct descendants in dividing among them the succession of their ancestor and on the presumption what was given was in the nature of an advance to the donee of his hereditary portion. LA. CIV. CODE ANN. art. 1229 (West 1987). To assure this equality, collation is always presumed. LA. CIV. CODE ANN. art. 1230 (West 1987). Thus, unless the donor has expressly dispensed the donation from collation, LA. CIV. CODE ANN. art. 1231 (West 1987), or a statutory exception is applicable, see LA. CIV. CODE ANN. arts. 1244-1247, 1250 (West 1987), the descendants coming to the succession must collate what they have received from their ascendant by donations *inter vivos*, directly or indirectly.[21] LA. CIV. CODE ANN. art. 1228 (West 1987). Absent a dispensation sanctioned by the Code, courts are not free to decline to order collation based upon their assumptions about the donor's intentions. *Succession of Fakier*, 541 So. 2d 1372, 1380 (La.1988). Indeed, the mere fact the donation was made under the guise of a contract is insufficient to indicate the intent of the ascendant to bestow an extra portion and thus dispense with collation. *Champagne v. Champagne*, 125 La. 408, 51 So. 440 (1910); *Clark v. Hedden,* 109 La. 147, 33 So. 116 (1902); *Montgomery v. Chaney*, 13 La. Ann. 207 (1858). In the absence of another ground for nullity, the appropriate relief for a disguised donation under article 2444 is collation. *Succession of Webre*, 247 La. 461, 172 So. 2d 285 (1965); *Clark, supra*; *Montgomery, supra*. The advantage bestowed by the transfer is also subject to collation where the price paid is greater than one fourth but less than fair market value. *See* LA. CIV. CODE ANN. art. 1248 (West 1987). *See also, Succession of Guerin*, 542 So. 2d 1102 (La. App. 1st Cir.1989).

---

[21] At the time of Charlie Doll's death, only forced heirs had the right to demand collation and the obligation to collate. *See* LA. CIV. CODE ANN. art. 1236 (repealed by 1990 La. Acts, No. 147, § 3, effective July 1, 1990).

Generally, collation of immovable property is made in kind or by taking less. See LA. CIV. CODE ANN. arts. 1251-1255 (West 1987). Collation in kind is made when the thing which has been given is delivered up by the donee to be united to the mass of the succession. LA. CIV. CODE ANN. art. 1252 (West 1987). The donee collating in kind is entitled to reimbursement for improvements resulting in an increase in the value of the property as well as the costs of preserving the estate. LA. CIV. CODE ANN. arts. 1256, 1257 (West 1987).

A distinction must be drawn between two oft-confused doctrines: the fictitious collation ordered by article 1505 and the right to demand actual or real collation. *See Jordan v. Filmore*, 167 La. 725, 732, 120 So. 275, 277 (1929). Fictitious collation, a simple paper return, is the method of calculating the *legitime* and disposable portion. *Succession of Fakier, supra*; L. Oppenheim, SUCCESSIONS AND DONATIONS § 35, at 112. Fictitious collation's remedy of reduction, predicated on the impingement of the *legitime*, may be demanded by forced heirs against any recipient of an excessive donation. Actual collation depends upon the existence of inequality in the disposition of the ancestor's estate and may be demanded by, and from, descendants coming to the succession. Hence, the right to demand collation and the duty to collate is reciprocal. *See* 3 M. Planiol, *Traité Élémentaire De Droit Civil* No. 2235 (11th ed. La.St.L.Inst. trans. 1959). And, whereas the test for reduction is the ultimate value of the estate, the crucial consideration in actual collation is the benefit or advantage to the heir, regardless of the depletion of the estate. *Succession of Pierson*, 339 So. 2d 1337, 1352 (La.App. 3d Cir.1976), *writ denied* 342 So. 2d 216 (1977). *See also Succession of Fakier, supra*.

Dr. Doll maintains the Civil Code does not expressly nor impliedly authorize the actual collation of the fruit of immovable property collated in kind.[22] Indeed, Dr. Doll argues her obligation to collate was satisfied by the collation in kind of the "thing which has been given" or the immovable itself. See LA.CIV.CODE ANN. art. 1252. She thus contends she is only obligated to restore the fruits received subsequent to the judicial demand for collation, a total of $7,810. In light of the $120,000 interlocutory consent judgment in her favor, Dr. Doll seeks judgment in her favor in the amount of $112,190.

The jurisprudence on this issue is conflicting and vague. Counsel have not pointed out, nor have we found, any cases which mandate the actual collation of the fruits of an immovable collated in kind other than *Ellis v. Benedict*, 408 So. 2d 987 (La.App. 2d Cir.1981). Moreover, the cases discussed in brief pertaining to the "return" or restoration of the fruits of collatable property are devoid of all but analogous codal authority, and conflict regarding the date on which the obligation to return accrues.

In *Clark* this Court applied Civil Code article 1515 in a collation case, affirming a judgment ordering the collation of immovable property deemed a donation in disguise and the return of revenues derived therefrom from the date of judicial demand. Although article 1515 applies only to revenues from donated property subject to reduction, *Clark* was thereafter authority for the proposition no collation is due for revenues of property, the full ownership of

---

[22] Dr. Doll contends the only codal provisions defining the type of distributions which must be collated are articles 1243 and 1248. The former mandates collation of "what has been expended by the father and mother to procure an establishment of their legitimate descendant coming to their succession, or for the payment of his debts." LA.CIV.CODE ANN. art. 1243 (West 1987). The latter orders collation of "the advantage which a father bestows upon his son, though in any other manner than by donation or legacy." LA.CIV.CODE ANN. art. 1248. Both articles are contained in Section 2 of Chapter 11 of Title I of Book III of the Code, entitled "To Whom the Collation is Due, and What Things are Subject to It." The remaining definitional articles in the section define what distributions are not subject to collation.

which had been donated. *See Osterland v. Gates,* 400 So. 2d 653, 658 (La.1981); *Succession of Pierson, supra; LeBlanc v. Volker*, 198 So. 398 (La.App.Orl.1940).

To the contrary are *Carroll v. Succession of Carroll*, 48 La.Ann. 956, 20 So. 210 (1896) and *Succession of Weber*, 110 La. 674, 34 So. 731 (1901). In *Carroll* interest was due on amounts received and to be collated by heirs from the donor's date of death. Following the reasoning in *Carroll, Weber* ruled the parties owed legal interest from the opening of the succession. Further, the donee owed the rents derived from the collatable property from the date of the donor's death, allowing a credit for expenses. Both *Carroll* and *Weber* were conclusory, employing neither reasoning nor codal authority. *See Succession of Schonekas*, 155 La. 401, 414, 99 So. 345, 349 (1924).

Moreover, to the extent *Carroll* and *Weber* held interest was due from the date of the opening of the succession, these cases were overruled by *Succession of Schonekas, supra*. In *Schonekas* we announced the proposition no interest can be claimed on cash collation until the heir, called upon to make the partition, has declined to do so. It was there stated:

> The money was given as advanced portions. It was not contemplated, therefore, that it should be returned until the partition was had. It may be said that the obligation to collate it did not mature until the partition was had. It was then only that the money could be collated. In the absence of an agreement to the contrary, debts do not bear interest, except from maturity.

155 La. at 414, 99 So. at 349. *See King v. King*, 107 La. 437, 31 So. 894 (1902) (Unless the heir bound himself to pay interest, interest is not due on amounts brought to the mass by collating heirs.).

As stated, however, these cases are not helpful in resolving the precise problem before us. *Clark, supra*, is premised on reference to the distinctly dissimilar reduction action, an action entirely apart in origin and purpose from collation, and thus the decision rests upon a frail foundation. *See* criticism of *Clark* in *Succession of Pierson, supra. Osterland, supra*, despite reference to *Clark*, was concerned with legal interest on the amounts to be collated rather than with the proceeds derived from management of immovable property. Indeed, as can be readily observed from the above discussion, the supreme court jurisprudence cited by Dr. Doll, other than *Clark* and *Weber*, is concerned with judicial interest on sums to be collated or with sums due for the restitution of fruits rather than to collation of fruits of immovable property collated in kind. *See Osterland, supra; Schonekas, supra; Carroll, supra; King, supra; LeBlanc, supra*.

The remaining case, *Ellis, supra*, cited with approval by the second circuit in the instant case, specifically holds the donee is obligated to collate rental income derived from the immovable collated in kind. There the court rejected the donee's contention she must only restore rent received after demand for collation was made, and ruled the income received from the date of death must be collated.[23] The holding is premised upon the presumption in favor of collation, as well as what the court perceived as an equitable link between the right to reimbursement of expenses under Civil Code articles 1256 and 1257 and the duty to collate fruits from the date of death. *See Ellis*, 408 So. 2d at 992 (citing *Succession of Weber, supra*, as authority for that proposition).

We disagree with the reasoning of *Ellis*. The right to reimbursement and the duty to collate fruits of an immovable collated in kind are not reciprocal. Rather, the right to

---

[23] In *Ellis* no revenues were received by the donee prior to the donor's death.

reimbursement, limited as it is to expenses which preserve or improve the value of the immovable, simply serves to place the donee in a position of parity with respect to her co-heirs.

Cognizant of the dearth of jurisprudence on this issue and ever mindful of our civilian heritage, we turn now to a codal analysis and an historical excursus.

Article 856 of the Code Napoleon provides, "The fruits and revenues of things subject to collation are due only from the day on which the succession is opened." LA.CIV.CODE Comp. ed. in 17 LSA-CC at 756 (West 1972). The article thus exempts from collation the fruits and revenues of collatable items on the principle the donation is immediately united to the succession at the death of the donor. K.A. Cross, A TREATISE ON SUCCESSIONS (1891) at 523. The heir, however, is required to account for fruits from the opening of the succession. According to Aubry and Rau, Article 856 is premised upon the presumed intention of the donor, "whose pretended liberality would turn to the detriment of the donee, if the latter were obliged to collate, not only the thing given, but also all the fruits and income thereof." 4 Aubry & Rau, DROIT CIVIL FRANCAIS § 631, at 389 n. 43 (La.St.L.Inst. trans. 1971) (citing Demolombe, XVI, 437). See Id., § 631 at 390 n. 46 ("[T]he ... fruits paid are destined to be consumed"); 3 M. Planiol, TRAITÉ ÉLÉMENTAIRE DE DROIT CIVIL No. 2259 at 97. ("It would often be ruinous for [the donee] if he had to return both the land and the harvest.") Indeed, Planiol posits collation was not intended to deprive the heir retroactively of at least his temporary usufruct over the collatable property. 3 Planiol, TRAITÉ ÉLÉMENTAIRE DE DROIT CIVIL No. 2259.

Article 856 appeared as article 222 in the Civil Code of 1808. See Concordance for Code Napoleon in 17 LSA Civil Code Comp. ed. at Table 3, p. 890 (West 1972). However, article 222 was suppressed on recommendation of the redactors of the Projet of the Civil Code of 1825 with the following comment, "With regard to art. 222, relating to the fruits and revenues of things subject to collation, it has been before provided for."[24] Project of the Civil Code of 1825 (1823) at 190, contained in Louisiana Legal Archives, Vol. I (1936).

Dr. Doll contends the final phrase of the redactors' comment regarding suppression of article 222 is more properly translated as "it has already been provided for herein."[25] She then points out the amendment of what is now article 1559, expanding the causes for revocation of donations *inter vivos* to include the "legal or conventional return" in paragraph (4), and the adoption of present article 1569, making the donee of the revoked donation accountable for fruits from the date of judicial demand, and the suppression of article 222 occurred simultaneously. *See* PROJET OF THE CIVIL CODE of 1825 at 190, 211; CONCORDANCE FOR CIVIL CODE in 17 LSA Civil Code Comp. ed. at Table 3, p. 848. Lastly, Dr. Doll contends the redactors wrought additional changes to effectuate a harmonious revendication system in which the obligation to restore the fruits of revendicated immovables returned by either a donee, vendee, or good faith possessor accrues as of the date of judicial demand.[26] Hence, Dr. Doll suggests the redactors

---

[24] "A l'egard de l' article 222, relatif aux fruits et interets des choses sujettes au rapport, il y a deja ete pourvu ci-dessus."

[25] While we agree that the translation of the redactors' comment is imprecise, we find the final phrase should read, "has already been provided for above."

[26] Dr. Doll directs the Court to LA.CIV.CODE art. 486 (possessor's rights to fruits); arts. 1408, 1409 (termination of succession partition); art. 1515 (reduction of excessive donations, where demand is made more than one year from donor's death); art. 1563 (revocation of donations for ingratitude); art. 1569 (revocation of donations *inter vivos*); arts. 2506, 2517, 2518 (warranty for eviction); art. 2575 (redemption); and art. 2592 (lesion). In contrast, the unworthy heir must return fruits from the date of death. LA.CIV.CODE ANN. art. 969 (West 1975).

intended to encompass within article 1559(4) circumstances wherein the donation is revoked by collation in kind.

The court of appeal summarily concluded 1559(4) does not encompass collation, and further found application of Civil Code article 1569 confined to those causes enumerated in 1559. We find the court of appeal erred in failing to define 1559(4), one of the grounds for revocation of donations *inter vivos*, so as to embrace collation of an immovable collated in kind. Accordingly, we find the court of appeal also erred in failing to apply article 1569.

A donation *inter vivos* is defined by article 1468 as an act by which the donor divests himself, at present and irrevocably, of the thing given, in favor of the donee who accepts it. LA.CIV.CODE ANN. art. 1468 (West 1987). The Civil Code treats donations *inter vivos* in three sections, the first and second addressing general dispositions and form, respectively, and the third setting forth the exceptions to the rules respecting the irrevocability of donations *inter vivos*. *See* LA.CIV.CODE ANN. arts. 1523-1569 (West 1987 & Supp.1991). The causes for which donations *inter vivos* may be revoked are set forth in article 1559 and the donee's liability for fruits is articulated in article 1569.[27] The "legal or conventional return" enumerated as 1559(4) is the sole cause conceivably relevant to this case. To apply 1559(4), we must first determine if collation in kind is a revocation, and second, if collation in kind constitutes a legal or conventional return.

Webster defines revocation as an act of recalling or calling back. Although the donation retains its effect during the life of the donor, we find the demand for collation and the resultant return of the property in kind to be united to the mass of the succession constitutes a revocation. This conclusion is supported by the Civil Code and doctrinal materials.

It was observed by the redactors of the PROJET OF THE CIVIL CODE of 1825, "The donee, to whom a real estate has been given, has in it only a defeasible property, it being subject to collation." PROJET OF THE CIVIL CODE of 1825 at 189, concerning collation of an immovable. *See* 4 Aubry & Rau, DROIT CIVIL FRANCAIS § 634 at 403 (When the donor stipulates the collation must take place in kind, the heir has only a right of revocable ownership.). Accordingly, under the Code Napoleon, ownership is retroactively resolved from the date of the opening of the succession. 4 Aubry & Rau, DROIT CIVIL FRANCAIS § 634 at 403; 3 M. Planiol, TRAITÉ ÉLÉMENTAIRE DE DROIT CIVIL Nos. 2276, 2277 (construing Code Napoleon art. 865).

The concept of revocation is embraced by the Civil Code articles pertaining to collation in kind. *See* LA.CIV.CODE ANN. art. 1227 (collation is the real return to the mass of the succession); art. 1252 (the property is united to the mass of the succession); art. 1332 (property collated in kind in an action of partition becomes united to the other effects of the successions from the moment of the donee's election to collate in kind). *See also Berthelot v. Fitch*, 44

---

[27] Article 1559 provides:

"Donation [Donations] *inter vivos* are liable to be revoked or dissolved on account of the following causes:
  1. The ingratitude of the donee;
  2. The non-fulfillment of the eventual conditions, which suspend their consummation;
  3. The non-performance of the conditions imposed on the donee;
  4. The legal or conventional return."

Additionally, donations *inter vivos* may be revoked by the mutual consent of the parties. *See, e.g., Quirk v. Smith*, 124 La. 11, 49 So. 728 (1909).

Article 1569 states, in pertinent part:

"In all cases, in which the donation is revoked or dissolved, the donee is not bound to restore the fruits by him gathered previous to the demand for the revocation or rescission."

LA.ANN. 503, 10 So. 867 (1892). Thus, collation in kind, abolishing the right and title of the donee by the return of the property to the succession, is a revocation of a donation *inter vivos*.[28]

We now direct our attention to the phrase "legal or conventional return." The conventional return refers to the right of return specially reserved or stipulated in favor of the donor in the act of donation itself. *See* LA.CIV.CODE ANN. arts. 1534, 1535 (West 1987); *Quirk v. Smith*, 124 La. 11, 49 So. 728 (1909). Thus, the conventional return envisions a rescission of the donation by mutual consent of the donor and donee. *See Liquidators of Prudential Sav. and Homestead Soc'y v. Langermann*, 156 La. 76, 100 So. 55 (1924), overruled on other grounds by *Bartlett v. Calhoun*, 412 So. 2d 597 (La.1982). Clearly, collation in kind does not manifest a conventional return.

In contrast to the conventional return, arising by agreement of act of the parties, the legal return arises by operation of law. *See Atkins v. Johnston*, 213 La. 458, 468, 35 So. 2d 16, 20 (1948) (McCaleb, J., dissenting). Generally, the Civil Code employs the word "legal" to indicate arising or imposed by operation of law. *See, e.g.*, LA.CIV.CODE ANN. art. 544 (West 1980) (legal usufruct); art. 654 (West 1980) (legal servitudes); art. 1825 (West 1987) (legal subrogation); art. 3286 et seq. (West 1973) (legal mortgage). The "legal return" articulated by article 1559(4) unquestionably includes the ascendant's right of reversion as contained in Civil Code articles 897 and 898. We are also cognizant of the fact the ascendant's right of reversion was added in the 1823 Projét, simultaneously with the adoption of articles 1559(4) and 1569.[29] However, we are not thereby compelled to confine the applicability of the "legal return" in 1559(4) to articles 897 and 898. *See, e.g. Vaughn v. Coco*, 409 So. 2d 282 (La.App. 1st Cir.1981) (construing 1559(4) to include revocation of donations caused by separation pursuant to former LA.CIV.CODE art. 156 (repealed)). We also are not persuaded collation, defined in article 1227 as the supposed or real return, can not thereby also be a legal return. The supposed or real return refers simply to the manner in which the collation is made, i.e., by taking less or in kind, respectively, and does not negate the conclusion collation in kind is a legal return imposed by operation of law. See K.A. Cross, A TREATISE ON SUCCESSIONS (1891) at 505 (The definition of collation does not even describe the thing analyzed). Accordingly, we find a uniform rule for the return of fruits in all cases of revocation is best effectuated by defining legal return so as to encompass collation in kind.

A succession is opened upon the death, and all rights vest at that time. LA.CIV.CODE ANN. arts. 934, 940 (West 1975); *Succession of Webre*, 247 La. at 475, 172 So. 2d at 290. From that moment, an heir may file formal succession proceedings and demand collation. *Id.* Collation arises from an obligation, or duty, imposed upon the heir by law. *Id.* at 473, 172 So. 2d at 289 (citing 3 M. Planiol, *Traité Élémentaire De Droit Civil* Nos. 2211, 2214). Accordingly, the right and the duty of collation arise by operation of law, and collation in kind is a legal return.

---

[28] Of course, the conveyance to Dr. Doll, while a disguised donation, was in proper form and thus merely a relative simulation. *See* La.Civ.Code Ann. art. 2027 (West 1987). *See also Owen v. Owen*, 336 So. 2d 782, 786 (La.1976); *Succession of Daste*, 254 La. 403, 223 So. 2d 848 (1969). As a relative simulation, the transfer was susceptible to annulment pursuant to art. 2444.

[29] Present articles 897 and 898 were added in the 1823 projet and appeared in the Civil Code of 1825 as articles 904 and 906. See Projet of Civil Code of 1825 at 110 and 111; Concorde for Civil Codes in 17 LSA Civ.Code Comp. ed. at Table 3, p. 837. Article 1559(4) and 1569 were added in the 1823 projet without comment and adopted in the Civil Code of 1825 as articles 1546 and 1562, respectively. *See* Projet of the Civil Code of 1825 at 211; Concorde for Civil Codes in 17 LSA Civ.Code Comp. ed. at Table 3, p. 848.

Mrs. Sullivan contends 1569 is applicable only to those cases of revocation enumerated in 1559, pointing to the placement of the article for support. Because we find actual collation in kind is a "legal return," we need not reach this issue. However, even if we were to assume the "legal return" does not encompass collation in kind, we would be hesitant to construe the language of 1569, viz., "In all cases, in which the donation is revoked or dissolved," so narrowly. *See e.g., Clarke v. Brecheen*, 387 So. 2d 1297 (La.App. 1st Cir.), *writ denied* 394 So. 2d 606, 607 (1980) (applying by analogy art. 1569 to a donation *inter vivos* subject to annulment under pre-amendment art. 1533 for inclusion of a reservation of usufruct); *Whited v. United States*, 219 F.Supp. 947 (W.D.La.1963) (revocation of interspousal donations).

In conclusion, we find Dr. Doll's obligation to collate was satisfied by the collation in kind of the Blanchard property. She is required to collate only the Blanchard property itself and not the fruits emanating therefrom. Further, her obligation to restore the fruits derived from the Blanchard property accrues at the date of judicial demand pursuant to Civil Code articles 1559(4) and 1569, not from an obligation to collate imposed by Civil Code articles 1227, et seq.

Hence, we distinguish the donee's obligation to restore the fruits derived from an immovable previously collated in kind from the donee's obligation to collate the fruits. The distinction is crucial. The fruits emanating from a donation of an immovable which has been revoked by collation in kind must be restored only from the date of judicial demand. In contrast, not only are the fruits emanating from the immovable previously collated in kind not subject to actual collation, but actual collation of the immovable itself is due from the date of the opening of the succession.

Argument is made allowing one to restore the fruits only from the date of judicial demand thwarts collation's goal of equality among the heirs called to the succession and is unfair to deserving heirs. We also face the contention collation is the general rule and a release from collation the exception.

We observe, however, collation is not based on "deservedness" but on the ascendant's presumed intent to treat descendants equally as regards the eventual distribution of his property. *See* LA.CIV.CODE ANN. art. 1229. Thus, the remedy of collation is the means by which the civil law seeks to enforce a relatively equal distribution of the ancestor's property among descendant heirs coming to the succession. *See Arsht v. Davis*, 561 So. 2d 58, 61 (La.1990); *Estate of Schwegmann v. Schwegmann*, 298 So. 2d 795, 797 (La.1974).

Dr. Doll has returned to the donor's estate precisely what she received, i.e., the basic ownership of the property. *See* LA.CIV.CODE ANN. arts. 1251, 1252; Succession *of Pierson*, 339 So. 2d at 1352. The benefits which may possibly be derived from the donation were not intended to be subject to a collation demand. *See* 4 Aubry & Rau, *Droit Civil Francais* § 631; 3 M. Planiol, *Traité Élémentaire De Droit Civil* No. 2259. Nor is collation punitive in nature. *See* 4 Aubry & Rau, *Droit Civil Francais* § 631. Moreover, this is not an instance where the coheir was ignorant of her right to demand collation. Indeed, collation is an inchoate right which must be invoked by the heirs prior to judgment of possession; otherwise, the right to demand collation is lost. LA.CIV.CODE ANN. art. 1242 (West 1987); *Succession of Webre, supra*; *Doll v. Doll*, 206 La. 550, 19 So. 2d 249 (1944).

By this ruling we do not propose to exempt collation of every fruit in every case. In this case, neither the mineral leases nor the timber contracts were in force at the time of the donation. However, in certain circumstances the fruits themselves may constitute an advantage, as where the ascendant "bestows" the fruits or gift of revenues, rather than the immovable itself, upon the donee. In such an instance the advantage may be subject to collation. *See* LA.CIV.CODE ANN. art. 1248. Such was not the case here, and we reserve discussion for another day.

*   *   *

HYPOTHETICAL

[handwritten: No forced heirs.]

[handwritten top right: Grandkids are not forced heirs]

Robert and Kris were married and had four children: Kourtney (36), Kim (35), Klohe (31) and Rob (28). After 12 years, Robert and Kris divorced. All community property issues were resolved. A year later Kris married Bruce. Together they had Kendall (20) and Kylie (18). *[handwritten: → Forced heir]* Kourtney married Scott and they have three children: Mason (6), Penelope (3), and Reign (1). Kim married West and they have a daughter, North (2), and a son on the way. Khloe married Lamar. They have no children. Rob, Kendall, and Kylie never married and have no children.

Four years ago, Kris suffered a massive heart attack. She recovered but remained in poor health. Fearing that her time was short, Kris made several transactions within the past three years:

1. Kris gave Bruce $6,000 to pay off credit card debt incurred by Bruce before they were married. *[handwritten: Reduction against another, not a 3rd person]*
2. Kris paid $10,000 directly to USC Law School for Rob to attend school in fall of last year. He went for 2 weeks, dropped out, and came home. The tuition was not refunded. *[handwritten: ed. purp.]*
3. Kris gave $12,000 to Mason for his birthday for a motorized Humvee. *[handwritten: → no collation]*
4. Kris sold Kylie 10 acres in The Hills for $15,000. It was worth $50,000 at that time. *[handwritten: → other advantage]*
5. Kris donated a condominium in Calabasas to Khloe worth $75,000. Khloe lived there with Lamar until it was completely destroyed during wildfires in September of last year. *[handwritten: Not liable for damages that are not of donee's fault]*

[handwritten: Permanent disability - Forced heir??]

Last year Mason contracted bacterial meningitis and sustained a permanent cognitive impairment preventing him from caring for himself for the rest of his life. Kourtney died six months ago and her children went to live with Kim. Kris died last month without a will. All transactions before her death were valid in form. *[handwritten: intestate]*

a) Who is entitled to demand collation in Kris's succession and why?
[handwritten: 1rst degree forced heir against his siblings.]

b) For each of the five transactions listed above, which if any are subject to collation? Why or why not? For any items subject to collation, consider the value and how the collation would be made.

[handwritten:]
1. NO, subject to reduction
2. yes, used it for ed. purposes, tuition was not refunded
3. NO, given directly to grandchild while parent was alive is exempt.
4. Yes, other advantage, such as very low payment on the sale of property is subject to collation.
5. NO, because the thing accidentally loss w/out the fault of the donee may not obdige donee to reimbursed the value to be collated.

[handwritten: On the Bar (x3Times)]

[handwritten: X Mason does not qualify as an forced, because Kourtney died @ the age of 36yrs.]

CHAPTER 9:
OVERVIEW OF THE LAW OF DONATIONS

Introduction

The law of donations deals with gratuitous dispositions, both *inter vivos* (made during life) and *mortis causa* (made in contemplation of death). Different from intestate successions, donations manifest an expressed will of the donor to give to a certain donee. Since the donor selects the recipient and the gift, the participation of the state is not as evident. The role of the law is limited to two basic functions:

(a) substantiating that the gift was in fact intended; and

(b) protecting some basic policies of the state.

Corresponding to these two functions are the modes of accomplishing them:

(a) rules as to form; and

(b) rules as to substance.

To assure that the disposition was in fact intended as a gift, the Louisiana law of donations establishes specific requirements as to acceptable forms of giving. The basic idea is that if the specifics of form are present, it is fairly safe to assume that the donor consciously intended the gift.

The Louisiana Civil Code requires that donations *inter vivos* of immovables and incorporeals be made by notarial act. Non-codal exceptions will be examined in the materials to follow. In addition to the notarial act form, corporeal movables may also be validly donated by manual gift accompanied by delivery of the object.

Donations *mortis causa* must be in one of the forms for testaments designated in the Civil Code. Revisions, effective on July 1, 1999, provide for two will forms - olographic and notarial. Prior to the revisions, the Civil Code provided for four will forms - nuncupative by public act, nuncupative under private signature, mystic, and olographic. A fifth form, the statutory will was prescribed in the ancillaries to the Civil Code. Although only two forms remain for wills written after July 1, 1999, wills that were previously written, and valid as to form, will be recognized.

State and federal statutes have also added methods of transfer for such property as life insurance proceeds, annuities, United States Savings Bonds, and certain pension plans. Also, there are particular rules pertaining to negotiable instruments.

The substantive rules of donations reflect societal norms. In essence, the donor is restricted from making certain donations because some interests of society conflict with the intent of the donor. The societal interest may be familial, as in assuring that the donor's minor and disabled children are provided for, as illustrated by the rules of forced heirship. Also, the protection may be focused on the donor himself, such as assuring the donor's mental capacity at the time of donation. Other substantive rules relate to keeping property in commerce, rather than passing it from generation to generation through multiple substitute donees.

Capacity

Louisiana law is concerned both with the capacity to give and to receive. As in intestate succession, the donee must exist in order to be capable of receiving. For donations *inter vivos*, the donee must exist when the gift is made, and for donations *mortis causa*, at the time of the donor's death. The donee who is a natural person must either be alive at that time, or conceived and later born alive. Other entities, such as corporations, must also prove existence at the important moments of receipt. Requiring existence fulfills the interest of the state in having property in commerce by preventing property from being suspended indefinitely, awaiting the appearance of a donee. Special provisions are made for the unborn child and an exception is made by statute for posthumously conceived children.

For donations, the capacity to give, as well as the capacity to receive, is essential. The donor must possess a state of mind that can comprehend generally the nature and consequences of his disposition and be capable of manifesting his true intent. Because the act of donation is so personal, it is not ruled by the same laws as the act of onerous contracting. No curator can be substituted to write one's will. Thus, the law contains a strong presumption of capacity.

Donations that are the product of fraud or duress are null, as well as those that are the product of such influence that impairs the volition of the donor.

(See Chapter 10, *infra*.)

Forced Heirship

The concept of forced heirship has changed dramatically since it was first introduced to Louisiana. Originally, the concept provided that a decedent with children or other descendants was required to leave a portion of his estate, whether separate or community, to his children or other descendants. After much controversy and the passage of an amendment to the Constitution of Louisiana, the concept of forced heirship today relates more to support for the young and disabled, than a general concept of familial obligation. Only those children of the decedent who are under the age of twenty-four at the time of the decedent's death, or children incapable of administering their person or their estate, and grandchildren in some cases, are forced heirs. If the decedent has one such heir, one-fourth of the decedent's estate is reserved for that heir. For two or more, the amount is one-half.

To determine the forced portion, a calculation of the mass estate must be made. First, liabilities at death are subtracted from assets. Following that, donations made within three years of the decedent's death are added in, valued at the time of the gift. Then, the percentages are calculated, counting all forced heirs at the time of the parent's death, excluding any that are disqualified.

If the forced heir's portion cannot be satisfied from assets remaining at death, the procedure of reduction may be followed. However, after the changes in the 1990's, the concept of forced heirship has become so diluted that reduction will rarely be necessary.

(*See* Chapter 11, *infra*.)

Omnium Bonorum

Another substantive restriction, *omnium bonorum*, prohibits a donor from giving away all of his property. Presumably meant to prevent the creation of wards of the state, the action may only be brought by a donor during his life and by his forced heirs after his death.
(*See* Chapter 12, *infra*.)

Conditions Reprobated by Law

The law of donations restricts the placing of certain conditions on donations. If a gift is given, only upon the condition that an immoral, illegal, or impossible condition be fulfilled, the condition is deleted, while the gift remains. If, however, the condition was the moving force behind the gift, the entire donation is null.

A very complicated area of donations law is that dealing with prohibited substitutions. Described in more detail in the materials to follow, the prohibited substitution is the (a) double disposition in full ownership (b) with a charge on the donee to preserve and render the property to another in (c) successive order. Such a disposition is entirely invalid.

However, even dispositions meeting the above description may be upheld if they are in a form sanctioned by the Trust Code. The Trust Code, one of Louisiana's most significant accommodations to the common law, does not sanction all prohibited substitutions, but only a few.

The Trust Code itself must be examined by any serious Louisiana estate planner. The difficulties of integrating this common law entity into Louisiana with its civilian property basis are discussed in the following materials.

Finally, one must distinguish the prohibited substitution from allowable donations which resemble the prohibited substitution. These include the *fidei commissum* (which does not include a duty to preserve), the vulgar substitution (where a third person is called to take a gift in default of the original donee), and the permissible donation of usufruct and naked ownership.
(*See* Chapter 12, *infra*.)

Donations *Inter Vivos*

A donation *inter vivos*, between living persons, is a present and irrevocable divestiture of property. There are three types of such donations: purely gratuitous, onerous, and remunerative. The gratuitous donation is the one with which this course is mostly concerned. The other two types are studied only to determine if the law governing gratuitous donations will apply to a particular donation.

Certain formal requisites must necessarily be complied with to ensure that a donation *inter vivos* is valid. Strict compliance with the prescribed forms is required because a donation is a transfer of property without consideration. These formal requirements serve to protect the donor from error and coercion in making the donation. The basic rule is that the donation *inter vivos* must be perfected by an authentic act to be valid. The codal exception to this is that the

manual gift of a corporeal movable requires no particular form (other than delivery) for its effectiveness. The question as to what may constitute the subject of a manual gift will be discussed in the following materials. A discussion of the status of the proper transfer of checks, stocks, bonds, savings accounts, etc., will also follow.
(*See* Chapter 13, *infra*.)

Donations *Mortis Causa*

Proponents of a donation *mortis causa* must truly demonstrate that the donation was intended as such. Accordingly, even documents meeting certain specific formalities must be proven to be intended as solemn declarations of the donor's last will. A casual note referring to someone as an heir or legatee will not a will make, even if entirely written, dated, and signed by the writer in true olographic form. Words of giving, such as "I leave," or "I bequeath" are clues of intent. The specificity of property given is also important. The two sanctioned forms of wills, as provided by the revisions effective July 1, 1999, are described in the materials to follow with examples to illustrate.

It is also essential to determine the type of legacy bequeathed. The revisions provide for three types of legacies: universal, general, and particular. The type of legacy is important in determining certain responsibilities and benefits, including who will ultimately receive a lapsed legacy.
(*See* Chapter 14, *infra*).

Trusts

Estate planners in Louisiana need to have a working knowledge of trusts. This versatile common-law addition to our tools initially elicited much controversy in Louisiana, but has been adapted to accommodate for many of the unique characteristics of our law such as forced heirship. (*See* Chapter 15, *infra*).

Characterizing the Type of Donation

SUCCESSION OF SINNOTT v. HIBERNIA NATIONAL BANK
105 La. 705, 30 So. 233 (1901)

NICHOLLS, C. J.

*　　　*　　　*

Mrs. C. Otto Weber, as the testamentary executrix and residuary legatee of Miss Emily C. Sinnott, claims that the ownership of certain 12 shares of stock of the Hibernia National Bank is in the succession of Miss Sinnott, and that the certificates for said shares are in the possession of Mrs. Langtry, who asserts ownership of the shares themselves. She brings this suit to have said ownership decreed to be in said succession, and to have Mrs. Langtry directed to deliver the certificates to her in her said capacity. Mrs. Langtry claims ownership of the shares under alleged gift to her from Miss Sinnott prior to her death. Mrs. Langtry, as a witness on the stand, testified: That she was the owner of the shares of stock claimed, covered by certificates Nos. 50 and 128. That she had been in possession of the certificates since July, 1896, uninterruptedly. That they were handed and given to her by Miss Sinnott, and she had them in her possession from that time up to the time of testifying. That she and Miss Sinnott had a conversation with reference to the certificates. Miss Sinnott told witness she should keep them, and she gave them to her, saying: "They are yours. At least, after my death they are yours." During Miss Sinnott's lifetime witness did not consider she had anything to do with them. She said, "After my death I want you to have them," and she gave them to witness. That was in 1896. The ownership of this stock was to become absolute in witness at the time of Miss Sinnott's death, but before that she had nothing to do with same. Witness collected no dividends paid upon the stock. Mrs. Weber was aware that the certificates were in witness' possession before she became executrix. She became aware of that fact about a year before Miss Sinnott's death, in 1897 or 1898. She saw them in witness' possession. She knew that she had them. Miss Sinnott was between 82 and 84 years of age when she died. She was delicate, and had been so for many years. Miss Sinnott lived with witness from 1878 up to six months of the time of her death. She boarded with witness, and paid her board. She died on December 6, 1897. Witness was not related to her, nor was Mrs. Weber. She was an old friend of witness, and had known witness since childhood. Witness paid her every attention when she lived with her. There was scarcely a day that she was out of her sight. She was with her all the time. She was very fond of witness, and went to live with her by preference. In addition to this property, Miss Sinnott gave her a bedroom set and some table silver, which she said should be witness' after her death. That also was in witness' possession. She had possession of it during Miss Sinnott's life. A part of it was taken during Miss Sinnott's life, but, no matter what she asked for, witness would have given it to her during her lifetime. Mrs. Weber knew witness also had the movables and silver. On cross-examination witness produced the certificates and handed them to counsel of the executrix. They were in the same condition all the time. There were several dividends declared on these certificates while they were in witness' possession. She made no effort to collect any of them. Witness recognized them as belonging to Miss Sinnott. After her death they belonged to witness. Before her death, of course, they did not. Miss Sinnott, or somebody else for her, collected the dividends, because it was understood they were not witnesses until after Miss Sinnott's death, just as the bedroom set and the silver. She (Miss Sinnott) said to witness, "I will give them to you after my death." Naturally, she was at liberty to take them at any time. It was understood between witness and Miss Sinnott that the title of the stock remained with her until she died, and that witness' right arrived at the moment of her death. There was no mistake about that. Nobody was present when this conversation took place. She went into witness' room and said: "Anna, I want to do something for you when I die. I want you to keep these, and when I die this bedroom set and silver, and anything else that is in your possession when I die, you can keep." They spoke about it several times, witness said. "I want you to keep them," Miss Sinnott said. This was given to witness sometime after Miss Sinnott had made her will. She went into witness' room some six or seven months after the will was made, and she said, "I want you to keep them after I am dead." Witness knew nothing of the will then. Witness did not expect Miss Sinnott would have a clause in her will to carry out this intention. She gave them to witness just as she did the silver and the bedroom set. Being asked whether the certificates were given to her only in the contingency that they should be witnesses after her (Miss Sinnott's) death, she answered, "That is right." Witness did not know who they belonged to if witness had died first. That was not discussed. This happened about two years before Miss Sinnott died. During these two years Miss Sinnott collect the dividends. She acted with complete dominion and control over them, and she was free to come and get the certificates from her at any time. Witness did not tell anyone about this happening between Miss Sinnott and herself. She made no more remarks about this than anything else given to her. It was a matter between witness and Miss Sinnott, just as it was about the other things she gave her. Witness was the only witness who knew anything about that conversation. On re-examination witness stated that Mrs. Weber knew that she had possession of these certificates about two or three years before Miss Sinnott died,--before Miss Sinnott gave them to witness. Mrs. Weber had never made any demand of witness for possession of the certificates, either as the representative of Miss Sinnott before her death, or as her executrix, except by advertising for them in the newspapers. She had made no demand, either by letter or in person, for either the stock or the silver or immovables. She had knowledge witness had them. Miss Sinnott up to the time of her death could have got them, simply for the reason that she said that after her death they would be witnesses; and during her lifetime, if she had demanded the silver or the furniture, she could have taken it. Witness claimed no interest in the stock or furniture or silver until after Miss Sinnott's death.

*   *   *

Counsel further say: "It may be well to note here that the donation causa mortis of the common law is not the donation *mortis causa* of our law,--the civil law. With us the donation *mortis causa* can be made only by last will and testament. Under the common law, however, three kinds of donations are made known: (1) The donation *inter vivos*; (2) the donation causa mortis; (3) that by last will and testament. The second is a gift during life, but in expectation of death, and not to take effect until after the death of the donor."

It will thus appear that the donation *mortis causa* of the common law is but the donation *inter vivos* established by our Code with this exception: that the first was not complete until the death of the donor, while the second becomes effective at once. There is nothing, however, in our law which prevents a donor from imposing upon his donation *inter vivos* the condition that it should not be effective until after the death, as was perhaps done in the present case; and we therefore have a case before us in which all the doctrines of the cited cases as to whether a certificate of stock is such a chattel as may be the subject of a donation *inter vivos* without other formality than the mere giving, accompanied by delivery, apply with full force. Counsel contends that the words used by Mrs. Sinnott, referring to the certificates, "After my death they are yours," giving them the greatest weight, have simply the effect of imposing upon a donation *inter vivos* what might be termed a suspensive condition. Our Code divides things into "corporeal" and "incorporeal," "movables" and "immovables." It declares: That "corporeal things" are such as are made manifest to the senses, which we may touch or take, which have a body, whether animate or inanimate. Of this kind are fruits, corn, gold, silver, clothes, furniture, lands, meadows, woods, and houses. That "incorporeal things" are such as are not manifest to the senses, and which are conceived only to the understanding, such as the rights of inheritance, servitudes, and obligations. REV. CIV. CODE, art. 460. Referring to the division of things into "movables and immovables," the Code says: "Incorporeal things consisting only of a right are not of themselves strictly susceptible of the quality of movables or immovables, nevertheless they are placed in one of these classes according to the object to which they apply, and the rules hereafter established." Civ. Code, art. 470. Referring to the subject of delivery, where delivery is necessary for the completion of a title, article 2478 declares that tradition or delivery of movable effects takes place either by their real tradition, or by the delivery of the buildings in which they are kept, or even by the bare consent of the parties, if the things cannot be transported at the time of sale, or if the purchaser had them already under another title; that the tradition of incorporeal rights is to be made either by the delivery of the titles and of the act of transfer, or by the use made by the purchaser with the consent of the seller. REV. CIV. CODE, arts. 2478- 2481. Article 743 of the Code, referring to servitudes, declares that "servitudes are established by all acts by which property can be transferred, and as they are not susceptible of real delivery the use which the owner of the estate to whom the servitude is granted makes of this right supplies the place of delivery." Article 2247 refers to delivery as being of two kinds, -- one as actual, the other as constructive, delivery. Under the heading of "Donations *Inter vivos* (between Living Persons)" and "*Mortis causa* (in Prospect of Death)," the Code declares in article 1467 that property can neither be acquired nor disposed of gratuitously, unless by donations *inter vivos* or *mortis causa*, made in the forms hereafter established. It then declares (article 1468) that a donation *inter vivos* (between living persons) is an act by which the donor divests himself at present and irrevocably of the thing given, in favor of the donee who accepts it; that a donation *mortis causa* (in prospect of death) is an act to take effect when the donor shall no longer exist, by which he disposes of the whole or a part of his property, and which is revocable. Article 1469. Article 1570 declares that "no disposition *mortis causa* shall henceforth be made otherwise than by last will and testament. Every other form is abrogated." And article 1576, that the custom of making verbal testaments (that is to say, resulting from the mere deposition of witnesses who were present when the testator made known to them his will, without having committed it or caused it to be committed to writing) is abrogated. Article 1536 provides that an act shall be passed before a notary public and two witnesses, of every donation *inter vivos* of immovable property or incorporeal things, such as rents, credits, rights, or actions, under the penalty of nullity; and article 1538 provides that a donation *inter vivos*, even of movables, will not be valid unless an act be passed of the same as is before prescribed. Such an act ought to contain a detailed estimate of the effects given. But article 1539 declares that the manual gift (that is, the giving of corporeal movable effects, accompanied by a real delivery) is not subject to any formality.

The French writers inform us that formerly the French law, in addition to donations *inter vivos* and *mortis causa*, authorized another form of gratuitous disposition of property,--the donation causa mortis,--but that this character of donation had been abrogated. . . .

A verbal donation causa mortis of a movable, whether it be a corporeal movable or an incorporeal movable, is invalid under our laws. According to the version given by Mrs. Langtry herself, this was the character of the donation made to her by Miss Sinnott. Appellee claims that the donation was a manual donation *inter vivos*, but it cannot be at one and the same time a donation *inter vivos* and a donation causa mortis. In order to have been a manual gift *inter vivos*, it was essentially necessary that the donor should have "devested herself at once and irrevocably of the thing given, in favor of the donee who accepted it." The moment the effect of the donation was to be postponed to the death of the donor, it became an unauthorized donation causa mortis. It is a mistake to suppose that, because an understanding should have been reached between two living persons that the ownership of the property of the one should vest at her death in the other, the agreement evidenced a donation *inter vivos*. It is the thing done by the living persons, and not the fact that what was done should have been transacted between living persons which gives character to the act. Independently, however, of this view of the situation, the appellee's claims could not be sustained. It is true that shares of stock in corporations are movables. Article 474 of the Code expressly declares them to be movables, but they are not corporeal movables. Stockholders in a bank are not the owners of any portion of the bank's property, though they are interested in its affairs, and indirectly and consequentially in its property. Article 436 of the Code declares that the estate and rights of a corporation belong so completely to the body that none of the individuals who compose it can dispose of any part of them. In this respect the thing belonging to the body is very different from a thing which is common to several individuals, as respects the share which everyone has in the partnership which exists between them, and, according to the above rule, what is due to a corporation is not due to any of the individuals who compose it. Article 437. The stockholders are neither owners of the property of the corporation, nor are they creditors of the corporation. The certificate of stock which they may hold does not represent any portion of its property, nor do they evidence any debt due to them by the bank. Article 1763 of the Code says that the contract must not be confounded with the instrument in writing by which it is witnessed, and so rights must not be confounded with writings which evidence them. The certificates involved in this case are mere admissions of the Hibernia Bank that the party named therein is interested in the bank to the extent therein named. *Board v. Campbell*, 48 La. Ann. 1549, 21 South. 184. The rights of the holders of the shares in the bank are back of and beyond the certificates. The certificates could be lost or destroyed, and the rights of the owners of the stock would remain intact. They are not orders of the owners on the bank to pay money to any one, as counsel claim. Parties having the mere possession of these certificates would have no shadow of right from that single fact to demand payment of any money from it, or to be recognized by it as shareholders. They are not negotiable, in the commercial sense of that word, though by proper assignment and transfer thereof the legal title of the shares of stock referred to therein may be shifted. Until assigned or transferred, possession of the certificates and title to the shares do not go together. The right of a stockholder in a bank is an incorporeal right. It is not, when not transferred, susceptible of a real and actual delivery to the transferee or donee. It is susceptible only of a constructive delivery, and this constructive delivery is not simply by the delivery of the titles, but by accompanying the delivery of the titles with the act of transfer of the same. REV. CIV. CODE, art. 2481. The certificates, of themselves, and without such act of transfer, would not pass from hand to hand by simple delivery. Something else would have to appear upon them to make them pass in that way. They are not substantive and completed things, in commerce, without a transfer of some kind. We have no reason to doubt the absolute correctness of the testimony of Mrs. Langtry as to what took place between Miss Sinnott and herself. Her testimony gives evidence of candor and sincerity, but where the law, to support certain acts, requires evidence of a particular kind and sufficiency, the courts are powerless to receive other or less as proof. We are constrained to recognize that the ownership of the shares of stock here involved has never passed from Miss Emily C. Sinnott, and that the same is now in the succession of Miss Sinnott...

NOTES

If the court was accurate in observing that the donor could condition her donation *inter vivos* to take effect at the donor's death, *see* La. C.C. 1528, why was the donation of the stock invalid? Was it truly because of the time of the effectiveness of the donation, or was it perhaps because of the form of the donation? *See* La. C.C. 1541. Could the donation of the furniture be salvaged as a valid manual gift, subject to the resolutory condition that Miss Sinnott predecease Mrs. Langtry? *See* La. C.C. 1543.

Compare the case of *Mitchell v. Clark*, 448 So. 2d 681 (La. 1984). In *Mitchell*, an aunt paid cash for a piece of immovable property in 1958, placing it in the name of her nephew and recording the sale in the conveyance records. It was the aunt's intention to live on the property until her death and then for the property to pass to her nephew upon her death "without the expense and bother of succession proceedings." In 1981, when the nephew learned of the property being placed in his name, he demanded to be allowed to live on the property, but his demand was rejected by the aunt. When the aunt petitioned to have the deed altered to reflect her as owner, the nephew objected to the use of parol evidence to support the aunt's position. The aunt placed title in the name of the nephew in an effort to effect a donation *causa mortis*, a donation not recognized under Louisiana law; nevertheless, parol evidence was inadmissible to alter the authentic act conveying title to the nephew.

Would the result have been different if the property in question were movable instead? What if the aunt had purchased an expensive oriental rug, wrote the nephew's name across the back, and told him that it would be his when she died? If she kept it in her home, what result? What if she allowed the nephew to keep it in his home?

CHAPTER 10:
CAPACITY
La. C.C. 1470-1483

Introduction

The LOUISIANA CIVIL CODE presumes that all persons are capable of giving or receiving donations, except those expressly precluded. La. C.C. 1470.

Incapacity must be examined in light of timing. The capacity to give must exist at the time the donation is made, La. C.C. 1471, whereas the capacity to receive must exist at the time of acceptance of a donation *inter vivos*, or, in the case of a donation *mortis causa*, at the time of the opening of the testator's succession, i.e., at the testator's death. La. C.C. 1472.

Previous Incapacities

The LOUISIANA CIVIL CODE of 1870, after giving the general rule that all persons were capable of giving and receiving donations *inter vivos* or *mortis causa*, unless expressly declared incapable, La. C.C. 1470 (1870), categorized the express incapacities as either *absolute*, preventing the giving or receiving as to *all* persons, or *relative*, preventing the giving or receiving as to only *certain* persons. La. C.C. 1471 (1870).

Absolute incapacities included certain restrictions on giving by minors, La. C.C. 1476-1477 (1870), requirements that a married woman obtain the consent of her husband or court approval to make a donations *inter vivos*, La. C.C. 1480 (1870), prohibition of one receiving a donation unless he was "in existence," and a constraint on foreigners receiving donations unless their state afforded reciprocity of receipt by Louisiana citizens. La. C.C. 1490 (1870).

Relative incapacities under previous law dealt with the inability of a minor to give to his tutor, La. C.C. 1478-1479 (1870), constraints on donations between persons who had lived together in "open concubinage," La. C.C. 1481 (1870), certain prohibitions of receipt of donations by illegitimate children, La. C.C. 1483-1488 (1870), and constraints on doctors and ministers receiving donations from those whom they had served in an official capacity. La. C.C. 1489 (1870).

The above-mentioned incapacities have either been altered or eliminated and thus, when the law was revised in 1991, the categorization of incapacities as "absolute" or "relative" was eliminated. Those restrictions which remain are discussed below.

Capacity to Receive

To be capable of receiving a donation, one must be in existence. Thus, from the moment of live birth, a natural person may receive. La. C.C. 25. Likewise, a juridical person such as a corporation may receive from the time of its incorporation.

Even some unborn are capable of receiving a donation. For example, if a child is conceived and is being carried in his mother's womb at the time of his father's death, that child may receive a donation, provided the child is later born alive. This has traditionally been accepted and allowable. However, new reproductive techniques have raised some questions as to whether all unborn children who are conceived at the time a donation is made and subsequently born alive should be permitted to receive donations. Consider the child conceived through the process of *in vitro fertilization*. Suppose a fertilized ovum has not yet been implanted in the mother's womb at the time of the death of the father. Perhaps the fertilized ovum is frozen and is not implanted into the mother's womb until years after the father's death. Should the child who is later born alive be permitted to receive a donation left to him by the deceased father? How long should the estate of the father be kept open in order to determine if all previously conceived children have been implanted and born alive? Perhaps due to the difficulty of resolving such a dilemma, the Louisiana legislature reached a policy decision in 1991 to limit the capacity of receiving to unborn children who are *in utero* at the time the donation is made. La. C.C. 1474. What if the father has contemplated the possible existence of such a child and wishes to leave him a legacy? How does this compare with the ability to inherit under the rules of intestacy? *See* La. C.C. 940. Which is the better rule? Is there some room for compromise? *See* La. R.S. 9:391.1.

CARR v. HART
220 La. 883, 57 So. 2d 739 (1952)

MOISE, Justice.

This litigation involves an attack upon two dispositions contained in the will of Mrs. Eva Hart, who died in the Parish of Natchitoches, on June 3, 1949, without forced heirs. The will which was admitted to probate on June 16, 1949, is an olographic one, and is valid as to form, being entirely written by the testatrix and properly dated and signed; it contains a list of particular legacies to various relatives and to certain religious bodies, and appoints decedent's daughter-in-law, defendant herein, her executor (executrix).

Plaintiff, a sister and collateral heir of decedent, attacks the following provisions of the will:

> For cemetery fund to keep cemetery clean and repairs $2500.00 and
> If there is any money left, after bequest (sic) have been paid, I want it to
> go to cemetery fund.

*   *   *

Plaintiff seeks to have both the legacy of the residuum and the particular legacy of $2,500, quoted above, declared null and void, on the ground that there is no one to receive either bequest, nor any trust, person, corporation, congregation, or legal entity capable of receiving delivery and administering the same.

*   *   *

[P]rior to the institution of these proceedings attacking said bequests to the "cemetery fund", Mrs. Virginia G. Hart, acting pursuant to authority of court, entered into an agreement with the City Bank and Trust Company of Natchitoches whereby the latter agreed to accept the $2,500 legacy, invest it, and use the proceeds realized from the investment for the purpose of keeping up the "cemetery." The agreement was executed under date of December 31, 1949.

* * *

There is no doubt as to the cemetery which the testatrix had in mind. It is a small Protestant burying ground located just west of the Village of Campti (her domicile), on the Grappes Bluff Road, in which her husband, her only child, and now she herself, are all buried. The attorney for the succession testified that the testatrix's son, Robert Hart, Jr., who had predeceased her, had discussed with him the matter of creating a trust fund for the purpose of keeping up said cemetery, that it had been his (Hart's) desire to do this in view of the fact that it has already been neglected and he (Hart) felt that after his death and after the death of his immediate family there would be no one left in Campti who had enough interest in the cemetery to see to its upkeep. However, neither Robert Hart, Jr., nor his mother, Mrs. Eva Hart, ever set up such a fund; and there was not in existence at the date of the testatrix's death any person, political entity or body corporate charged with the administration of either fund or cemetery.

While it is true that the law favours testacy, the capacity to take, or receive, must exist at the opening of the succession of the testatrix, i.e., at the time of her death. Art. 1473, R.C.C. The status of the cemetery in the instant case is even less favourable legally than that of the unincorporated church involved in the *Succession of Hardesty*, 22 La.Ann. 332. There a particular legacy to the Baptist Church of Clinton was held null and void, despite the incorporation thereof subsequent to the testatrix's death; we held:

> A number of individuals had associated themselves together, under the name of the Baptist Church of Clinton; and they had a house in which they worshipped, in the town of Clinton, but they were not incorporated until after the death of the testatrix. It is clear the association had not the legal capacity to receive on the opening of the succession...
>
> Did the subsequent incorporation of the association give it the capacity to receive the legacy? We believe it did not. The legacy was made in praesenti. If the legatee had not the capacity to take when the succession was opened, the property by law was transmitted to the heirs; and the subsequent incorporation of the society could not divest their rights. 22 La.Ann. 333.

It being our conclusion that both bequests to the "Cemetery fund" must fall for lack of a recipient to take, it is unnecessary to consider the other questions raised by this appeal.

For the reasons assigned, the judgment appealed from is reversed, annulled and set aside, insofar as it decrees that the particular bequest of $2,500 to the "Cemetery fun" is valid; and, in all other respects, as thus amended, the judgment of the district court is affirmed.

MILNE'S HEIRS v. MILNE'S EXECUTORS
17 La. 46 (1841)
[15 Tul. L. Rev. 186 (1941)]

Morphy, J.,

The question presented for our decision in this case arises out of a clause in the last will and testament of Alexander Milne; it is in the following words, to wit:

> It is my positive will and intention that an asylum for destitute orphan boys, and another asylum for the relief of destitute orphan girls, shall be established in Milneburg, in this parish, under the name of the Milne Asylum for destitute orphan boys, and Milne Asylum for destitute orphan girls, and that my executors shall cause the same to be duly incorporated by the proper authorities of this state; and to the same two contemplated institutions and to the present institution of the Society for the relief of destitute orphan boys in the City of LaFaytte and parish of Jefferson, in this state; and to the Poydras female asylum in this City, I give and bequeath in equal shares or interests, of one-fourth to each, all my lands on the bayou St. John, and on the lake Pontchartrain; including the unsold lands of Milneburg.
>
> I institute for my universal heirs and legatees in equal shares or portions the said four institutions, that is to say: the two intended institutions at Milneburg, and the two asylums aforesaid in this City, and in the City of LaFaytte, to whom I give and bequeath the residue of all the property and estate, moveable and immoveable, I may possess at the time of my decease, to be equally divided and apportioned among them.

The testator died in October, 1838, and in February following the general assembly of this state wishing to enable the executors to carry into full effect his beneficent intentions, incorporated the two asylums mentioned in the will. When the executors filed their account, the absent heirs of the deceased, through the attorney appointed to represent them, opposed all such disbursements as had been made for establishing or maintaining the two institutions at Milneburg, on the ground that said disbursements were made by the executors without authority, and in their own wrong. They averred that the two incorporated asylums had acquired no right, title or interest, in or to said succession, or any part of it; that at the death of the late A. Milne they were not *in esse*, and had no capacity to take under the will; that at the opening of the succession, the heirs at law and the next of kin of the deceased, acquired a vested right to all such parts or portions of said estate, as had lapsed or fallen, for want of capacity to take in any or all of the particular legatees or legatees under a universal title, or from any other cause; and that the executors had full notice of the incapacity of these institutions to take because an application made by them to be recognized as universal legatees, and put in possession of their respective positions, had been proposed on the same grounds. The court below dismissed the opposition so far as it contested the capacity of the Milne asylums to receive their bequests. The heirs at law appealed.

They rest their objections to the validity of these bequests, on all these articles of the Louisiana Code which declare a legacy to be void if the legatee be not in existence, or be incapable of receiving it, at the opening of a succession. La. Code art. 944, 947, 948, 949, 1459, 1469, 1478, 1598, 1690, 1696. They contend that as these two institutions had no legal existence at the time of the death of the testator, they could not take under his will; that the nearest legitimate heirs became immediately entitled by law to these legacies, and that their title to the same being thus vested, could not be destroyed by the subsequent acts of incorporation obtained from the general assembly. This question does not present itself to us surrounded by those difficulties which would attend its solution in those states whose statutes of wills exclude corporations as competent devisees. The statutes of mortmain and the reasons which produced them do not exist among us; and corporations are placed by our laws on the same footing as natural persons, as to their capacity to take by devise.

Two things must concur to enable a legatee to take under our laws; 1st. He must be in existence at the time of the opening of the estate; 2d. He must have capacity to receive at that time, if the legacy be absolute; if it be conditional, it is sufficient if the capacity to receive exists at the time of the fulfilment of the condition. La. Code art. 1460. 5 Toulier, p.99, No. 91. [Pothier des donations testamentaires p. 361m abd traute des oblig. Nos. 203, 208 & 222.]

It is in general true that the person of a legatee must be designated in terms not to be mistaken; if the designation is so vague and indefinite that the intention of the testator cannot be ascertained the legacy falls, for want of sufficient certainty. But this precision is required only as to individuals in regard to whom the will cannot be executed if their identity cannot be established; when a legacy is made to a certain class or collection of persons and is not dictated by caprice but by charitable and meritorious motives, although the individuals are unknown to the testator, such a legacy will not under our laws be considered void for uncertainty. Pothier des testamens chap. 1, art.5.–Domat, Lois Civiles, Book 4, c. 11, sect. 6, § 4 & 5. Our Code art 1536 provides that:

> Donations made for the benefit of a hospital, the poor of a community or of establishments of public utility, shall be accepted by the administrators of such community or establishments.

In the Napoleon Code which contains provisions similar to ours as to the necessity of a legatee being in existence at the death of the testator, we find an enactment recognizing the validity of such donations but providing that they shall not be carried into effect unless approved of by the government, N.C. art. 910. Such donations are there made conditional; the capacity to receive is made to depend on the fulfilment of a condition, to wit: the sanction of the sovereign; until that is obtained, the poor or other class of persons intended to be benefitted are without capacity to receive. Had the deceased made a legacy to the destitute orphans of this parish without providing that they should be incorporated, the question would have presented itself whether under article 1536, above quoted, the police jury of the parish would not have been competent to accept it on behalf of the intended objects of his benevolence. There appearing to be some doubt on this subject, we have seen, on former occasions of this kind, the general assembly of the state acting as the parens patriae in the carrying into effect charitable dispositions in the wills of public benefactors. 2 Moreau's Dig. P. 208; laws of 1837, p. 24. They authorized the acceptance by the police juries of Pointe Coupee and West Baton Rouge of three legacies by the late Julien Poydras, two of $30,000 to each parish, to be appropriated as dowries to the young ladies of the parishes to encourage their marriages, and one of $20,000 to be appropriated to the maintenance of an academy in the parish of Pointe Coupee. In the will of

Poydras the legacies were absolute and the difficulty laid in the absence of capacity in the legatees to take at the moment of the opening of the succession. In the case under consideration, the testator appears to have been aware that unless incorporated the two asylums had no capacity to receive, and to have intended that his dispositions in their behalf should not be carried into effect until after their incorporation. This intention is not expressed in positive terms but can and must, we think, be fairly inferred from the wording of the will. The Roman law informs us that one who is incapable may be instituted as heir, for the time when his incapacity shall cease.

*   *   *

Dispositions of this kind are conditional in their nature and the condition is fulfilled by the creation of the capacities to receive: thus in this case, it was intended, we think, that the legacies should be delivered to these institutions upon their becoming incorporated; the implied condition was that they should be rendered capable of receiving and that condition was fulfilled by the subsequent acts of incorporation. Somewhat analogous are the cases of a legacy to a femme sole upon her marriage, or to an infant *in ventre sa mere*, the marriage or the birth which fulfils the condition creates the capacity to receive which did not exist at the time of the opening of the succession.

But to take a less limited view of this matter, must not every disposition in a man's will not reprobated by law, be carried into effect? [S]uch is the rule universally laid down for the construction of wills. Here a testator who has acquired his wealth in this country and has no forced heirs wishes to create with the aid of the Legislature two institutions of manifest public utility; as soon as this desire of the deceased is made known to the general assembly, they grant the necessary acts of incorporation and the executors discharge the trust committed to them. We can see nothing in the law to prevent this being done. After the strong and positive declaration of Milne with respect to the disposition of his property, shall a technical objection drawn from provisions of law, not perhaps applicable to cases of this kind, defeat his purpose? [N]othing short of an express prohibition in the law should, we think, have such an effect.

*   *   *

NOTES

On the surface, it appears difficult to distinguish *Carr* from *Milne*. If *Milne's* characterization of its legacy as conditional is taken to its logical limits, why not allow the *Carr* disposition to stand when the creation of the "cemetery fund" was arranged? Is the fact that the testator in *Milne* contemplated the incorporation of the institutions "by the proper authorities of this state" significant? Is formal incorporation necessary? Compare the sanctioned receipt of a legacy by an unincorporated entity that was characterized as "a formal organization with a definable membership operating under a written constitution" with "a governing body, the Executive Board, and established procedures for the election of members to the Board." *Lord v. District VIII Baptist Convention,* 391 So. 2d 942 (La. App. 2nd Cir. 1980). In contrast, the Fourth Circuit had earlier held in *In re Shepard's Succession,* 156 So. 2d 287 (La. App. 4th Cir. 1963), that the United States Government was not capable of disposing or receiving donations since it is not a "natural person." Note the criticism of the *Shepard* case at 24 La. L. Rev. 919 (1964). How would you redraft the *Carr* will to preserve the legacy?

What about the social utility of the contemplated institutions?

Compare *Fink v. Fink's Executor*, 12 La. Ann. 301 (1857), in which the legacy to "be applied to the erection and maintenance and support of a suitable asylum in this city, to be used solely as an asylum for Protestant widows and orphans" was upheld, characterizing "the Protestant widows and orphans in the city of New Orleans as the true residuary legatees." *Fink* was later distinguished in the case of *City of New Orleans v. Hardie,* 43 La. Ann. 251, 9 So. 12 (1891), where a legacy "to the support of asylums in the faith of the Protestant religion specially devoted to the care of aged persons. . . to be located in the city of New Orleans," fell since no such asylum was in existence. If the widows and orphans of New Orleans were truly the recipients of the legacy in *Fink,* what result on the occasion of the death of one of those widows or orphans?

What vehicle might be used today to accomplish the objectives contemplated by the preceding cases? Consider La. R.S. 9:2271.

La. R.S. 9:2271

Charitable purpose; beneficiary; conditions

A charitable trust is created when a person makes a donation *inter vivos* or *mortis causa* in trust for the relief of poverty, the advancement of education or religion, the promotion of health, governmental or municipal purposes, or other purposes the achievement of which is beneficial to society. The trust instrument may be specific or general in the statement of its purposes and may include any conditions that are not contrary to law or good morals. The charitable trust may have as its purpose to benefit one or more institutional beneficiaries. An "institutional beneficiary" is a trust, corporation, or other entity that has any of the foregoing purposes and is a current mandatory or discretionary beneficiary. Otherwise, the beneficiaries of the trust shall be selected by the trustee or any other person, pursuant to the terms of the trust instrument.
Acts 2008, No. 637, § 1, eff. Jan. 1, 2009.

Capacity to Give

Restrictions Based on Age

A person under the age of sixteen is incapable of making donations. Upon reaching the age of sixteen, a minor has capacity to make any donation *mortis causa* and to make donations *inter vivos* to his spouse or children. La. C.C. 1476.

Mental Condition

In 1991, the law governing the capacity to give was revised by the Louisiana Legislature at the behest of the Louisiana State Law Institute. Act 363 of 1991. In contrast to the old concept, formerly contained in the now-repealed article 1475, which stated simply that a person must be of "sound mind" in order to give, the revision provides a greater specificity requiring the donor be able to "comprehend generally the nature and consequences of the disposition that he is making." La. C.C. 1477. Revision comment (b) to the article states that the test of mental capacity in this article "[i]n many respects... is derived from the common-law test for testamentary (donative) capacity" that originated in the old English case of *Banks v. Goodfellow*,

L.R. 5 Q.G. 549 (1870), and which required that a person understand the nature and extent of his property, his relationship to those persons considered to be the natural objects of his bounty, and the consequences of the disposition being made. The Law Institute deleted the provision concerning the natural objects of a person's bounty, to prevent a court from substituting its own conceptions about who this should be for the testator and perhaps too readily find incapacity on that basis.

Although the revision comments state that article 1477 is meant to change the law, it may be questioned, in light of the case of *Succession of Lyons*, 452 So. 2d 1161 (La. 1984), whether this is in fact the case. In determining that the testator in *Lyons* was "of sound mind," the Louisiana Supreme Court reduced the question to "whether the testator understood the nature of the testamentary act and appreciated its effects." *Id.* at 1164. This test is quoted approvingly in the later case of *Succession of Hamiter*, 519 So. 2d 341, 344 (La. App. 2nd Cir. 1988), *cert. denied*, 521 So. 2d 1170 (1988). If the test was basically the same under the old law and also under the revision, what jurisprudence will be important in interpreting Article 1477 – common law cases under the *Banks* test or Louisiana cases on "sound mind"? Does it matter?

The comments to article 1477, in addition to telling us that the article changes the law, add that the focus of the article, "like the common-law formulation," is upon the donor's ability to comprehend, rather than on his actual comprehension of the donation. La. C.C. 1477, comment (c). Under the test of capacity as contained in article 1477, it is not necessary that the particular testator, for instance, understand technical tax formulae or highly complex legal language. He is capable if he understands generally what he is doing. He must understand he is writing a testament; he need not understand the terms of the specific testament being executed. The test is not that he understand, but that he be "able" to understand.

Under the law interpreting the former article 1475 dealing with "sound mind," there was developed a strong presumption of capacity, of sanity. This presumption still exists under Article 1477. It is a strong presumption, but rebuttable. *Chandler v. Barnett*, 21 La. Ann. 58 (1869). To attack the presumption, one must establish a pattern of habitual insanity. The burden then switches to the proponents of the donation to show (1) that the insanity is not the type that would preclude the occurrence of a lucid interval, and (2) that the disposition was made during such an interval.

In *Aubert v. Aubert*, 6 La. Ann. 104 (1851), the lucid interval was defined.

A lucid interval, under the civil law, is not an apparent tranquility or a seeming repose. It is not a simple diminution or a remission of the disease, but a temporary cure: an intermission so clearly marked that it perfectly resembles the return of health; and as the nature of the interval cannot be ascertained in an instant, it must continue during a length of time sufficient to give the certainty of the temporary restoration of reason. That time must, in all cases, be considerable.

Additionally, in *Lyons*, the Supreme Court established that an opponent of a testament would have to prove the testator's incapacity by clear and convincing evidence. Stating that "strong policy considerations" were involved, the court quoted from the earlier case of *Kingsbury v. Whitaker,* 32 La. Ann. 1055 (1880), which explained,

To wrest a man's property from the person to whom he has given it, and to divert it to others from whom he has desired to withhold it, is a most violent injustice, amounting to nothing less that postmortem robbery, which no court should sanction, unless thoroughly satisfied. . . that the testator was legally incapable of making a will. 32 La. Ann. 1055 at 1062-1063.

The 1991 revisions codified the clear and convincing standard for a challenger to prove mental incapacity. A revision of La. C.C. 1482 provides, however, that a full interdict lacks capacity to make or revoke both donations *inter vivos* and *mortis causa*. A limited interdict lacks capacity to make or revoke donations *inter vivos* and is presumed to lack capacity to make or revoke donations *mortis causa*, with respect to property on which has been placed under the authority of a curator. For other property, a limited interdict is presumed to have capacity to make or revoke donations. These presumptions may be rebutted by a preponderance of the evidence. La. C.C. 1482.

Fraud, Duress, and Undue Influence

LOUISIANA CIVIL CODE article 1478, as added by the revisions of 1991, clearly declares that a donation that is the product of fraud or duress shall be declared null. Although the Revision Comment to the article indicates that this is not a change in the law, and indeed the Civil Code contains articles on fraud and duress in Book III, Title IV, in its Chapter 4, Vices of Consent, courts in the past were reluctant to admit evidence showing fraud or duress unless the behavior in question occurred at the actual time that the donation was made. *See* Katherine Shaw Spaht, Kathryn Venturatos Lorio, Cynthia Picou, Cynthia Samuel, Frederick W. Swaim, Jr., *The New Forced Heirship Legislation: A Regrettable "Revolution,"* 50 La. L. Rev. 409 (1990).

Prior to its repeal, article 1492 of the Louisiana Code of 1870 provided that "[P]roof is not admitted of the dispositions having been made through hatred, anger, suggestion, or captation." This provision was successful in avoiding the plethora of undue influence suits so prevalent in common law states, by not allowing proof of such influence and also provided a rationale for courts which did not allow evidence of fraud or duress unless actually exercised at the time of the making of the donation. One explanation offered for Louisiana not needing a concept of "undue influence" was that certain classes of persons, specifically forced heirs, already had protection against an unscrupulous individual's influence resulting in the total disinheritance of the aggrieved party. With the virtual attempted elimination of most forced heirs by Act 147 of 1990 amending La. C.C. 1493, there was a desire to provide some way for those important classes, previously forced heirs, to protect against disinheritance resulting from someone unduly influencing the testator to eliminate his children from inheritance. One proposal was to repeal the provisions of La. C.C. 1492 only as they might apply to those heirs. Thus, only those who were previously defined as forced heirs, but no longer included in that definition, would be permitted to introduce evidence showing that a disposition may have been the product of hatred, anger, suggestion, or captation. Another approach, the one that ultimately prevailed, was to repeal La. C.C. 1492 in its entirety and open the door to such evidence for all.

La. C.C. article 1479 in the 1991 revisions clearly declares null any donation that is proved to be "the product of influence by the donee or another person that so impaired the volition of the donor as to substitute the volition of the donee or other person for the volition of the donor."

The standard of proof for fraud, duress, or undue influence is the same, "clear and convincing evidence." This standard is relaxed to a mere preponderance of the evidence when a relationship of confidence exists between the donor and the party exercising the influence unless the latter is related to the donor by affinity, consanguinity, or adoption. La. C.C. 1483.

The link between mental capacity and undue influence is obvious. Indeed, it may be easier to influence the behavior of a person with diminished capacity.

NOTE

What constitutes a relationship by "affinity"? Would a second cousin of the testator's wife be included? *See Cupples v. Pruitt*, 754 So. 2d 328 (La. 2nd Cir. 2000).

As you read the following cases, think about whether the resolution is based on capacity, or rather on fraud, duress, or undue influence, or some combination thereof. Ask yourself what remedy this dictates. What considerations should be considered in determining the theory propounded by a litigant?

SUCCESSION OF COLE
618 So. 2d 554 (La. 4th Cir. 1993)

ARMSTRONG, Judge.

Appellant, Louis Cole, appeals from a judgment confirming the validity of the olographic will of his father, Ellard Leroy Cole (Cole). The issues for review are whether the trial court erred in assigning the burden of proof and in upholding the will against challenges of lack of donative capacity and undue influence.

On June 15, 1990, Cole executed an olographic will in favor of his sister-in- law, Thelma Cole (hereinafter "Donee"). It is undisputed that the will is entirely written, dated, and signed in the testator's hand, and is therefore valid in form as an olographic will. *See* La.C.C. Art. 1588. The will states in its entirety:

> This is my will and testament.
> I Ellard L. Cole have decided to leave all my possessions personal and real to my sister-in-law Mrs. Thelma Cole excep my house. I want to leave my house to my son Louis Cole at 100i Lamar St. Abbeville. Since my brother died Thelma never changed she has treated me the same. I could not have been treated any different. They were the only family to take me in their home. I cant thank her enough. please see that she get everything I promised.

The will is signed by Ellard L. Cole and three "witnesses," all of whom were present at the party.

Cole died in New Orleans on December 11, 1991, leaving property in Orleans and Vermillion Parishes. He was predeceased by his wife, and his only living issue was his son Louis, the appellant in this matter. For the last nineteen years of his life, Cole had resided in New Orleans under the care and custody of Donee.

A veteran of World War II, Cole returned to the United States with a mental infirmity known as "shellshocked syndrome." From 1946 until 1972 he resided at V.A. Hospitals under the custody of the Veterans Administration. On April 21, 1970, Cole was judged incompetent by a Louisiana Court. In 1972, he was placed under the custody of his brother, Robert Cole, husband of Donee. He resided in their home in New Orleans from 1972 until 1978, and then lived on his own in a nearby apartment. In 1984, Robert Cole died. For the next seven years, Donee assumed sole responsibility for Cole, continuing to feed him daily, wash his clothing and bedding, and to disburse his monthly veterans benefits in satisfaction of his living expenses. Cole was in the care of Donee at the time of his death.

Following Cole's death, Appellant filed a Petition for Confirmation as Administrator in Vermillion Parish on March 2, 1992. On March 23, 1992, Donee filed a Petition for Probate of Olographic Testament in Orleans Parish. By order dated the same day, Cole's olographic will was recorded for execution in Orleans Parish. Appellant subsequently filed a Petition to Annul Testament, and the parties proceeded to trial.

Trial was held August 17, 1992. Sitting as trier of fact, the trial judge heard testimony from Appellant, Donee, one of Cole's brothers, and the three witnesses who signed Cole's olographic testament. On September 3, 1992, the trial court rendered judgment finding the will valid and dismissing Appellant's petition to annul. No reasons for judgment were assigned.

The first issue for review is whether the trial court erred in assigning the burden of proof. In his appellate brief, Appellant alleges that "the trial court declared during pre-trial discussions that the burden of proof would rest with the appellant to first prove that the deceased was mentally infirm before any presumption of invalidity would be imposed upon the testament." There is nothing in the record which indicates that this was the exact pre-trial ruling of the trial court. Furthermore, review of the trial transcript reveals that Appellant correctly assumed the burden of proving undue influence, pursuant to La.C.C. Art. 1479, and that Donee correctly assumed the burden of proving donative capacity, pursuant to La.C.C. Art. 1482.

La.C.C. Art. 1479, nullity of donation procured by undue influence, provides:

A donation *inter vivos* or *mortis causa* shall be declared null upon proof that it is the product of influence by the donee or another person that so impaired the volition of the donor as to substitute the volition of the donee or other person for the volition of the donor.

La.C.C. Art. 1482, proof of capacity to donate, provides:

A person who challenges the capacity of a donor must prove by clear and convincing evidence that the donor lacked capacity at the time the donor made the donation *inter vivos* or executed the testament. However, if the donor made the donation or executed the testament when he was judicially declared to be mentally infirm, then the proponent of the challenged donation or testament must prove the capacity of the donor by clear and convincing evidence.

[Compare La. C.C. 1482, as amended by Act 1008, § 1 in 2003.][*]

Under the plain wording of La.C.C. Art. 1479, the party challenging a will on the basis of undue influence must provide "proof that it is the product of influence by the donee."

---

[*] Bracketed material in italics added by author.

ngly, Appellant proceeded as plaintiff at the trial on this matter, attempting to show that :xercised undue influence. As part of his case, Appellant introduced exhibits showing le had been judicially declared mentally incompetent. Under La.C.C. Art. 1482, this showing shifted the burden of proof to Donee to prove that Cole had the capacity to make a donation *mortis causa*. However, nothing in La.C.C. Art. 1479 indicates that a showing of mental infirmity shifts the burden of proof on the issue of undue influence; in fact, the comments to La.C.C. Art. 1477 draw a clear distinction between the two issues: "This Article ... presumes a donor who has capacity. Obviously, if a donor lacks capacity, then the entire donation or will is invalid for that reason alone, and issues of ... undue influence are irrelevant." *Id.*, comment (b). Accordingly, when counsel for Appellant rested at the conclusion of Appellant's case, counsel for Donee stated: "Inasmuch as the jurisprudence is certainly clear that the capacity to make a will is tested at the time the will is made, I want to call the witnesses who were there at the time this document was confected." This statement, together with the testimony which followed, shows that Donee assumed the burden of proving capacity.

The record reveals no error in the trial court's assignment of the burden of proof. We therefore confine the remainder of our opinion to the issue of whether the trial court erred in determining whether the parties met their respective burdens of proof.

Donee's showing as to capacity:

La.C.C. Art. 1477, capacity to donate, provides:

> To have capacity to make a donation *inter vivos* or *mortis causa*, a person must also be able to comprehend generally the nature and consequences of the disposition that he is making.

La.C.C. Art. 1477 was enacted in 1991 and is intended to change the law. *Id.*, comment (a). Comment (c) to La.C.C. Art. 1477 sets forth the following criteria for determining donative capacity: "The donor who is capable of understanding has donative capacity even though he may not actually understand the exact instrument that he executes. . . . The focus under this new test in Louisiana is thus not on the accuracy of the understanding but the ability to understand."

In attempting to prove donative capacity, Donee had to meet the difficult "clear and convincing" standard of proof. La.C.C. Art. 1482. To prove a matter by clear and convincing evidence means to demonstrate that the existence of a disputed fact is highly probable, that is, much more probable than its nonexistence. *Louisiana State Bar Association v. Edwins*, 329 So. 2d 437 (La.1976). In the instant case, the testimony shows that it is highly probable that Cole understood exactly what he was doing at the time he executed his olographic will

Donee and the three witnesses to the will all testified as to the following scenario surrounding the drafting of the will: On June 15, 1990, Donee threw a birthday party for her daughter. A few of her daughter's friends showed up. While they gathered in Donee's dining room for cake and ice cream, Cole sat in Donee's kitchen, eating the supper which Donee prepared for him each day. When he finished eating, Cole joined the party in the dining room. After sitting with them for awhile, Cole made a statement to the effect of, "Now would be a good time to make a will, while there are people here to witness it." Paper was produced, and Cole completed a draft in pencil in which he left everything to Donee. Donee told Cole to rewrite the will in ink, and stated that she wanted Cole to leave his house in Abbeville to Appellant. Following Donee's instructions, Cole completed a second draft in ink in which he left everything to Donee except for his house in Abbeville. Donee then suggested that he rewrite the will one more time to eliminate misspellings. Cole subsequently completed a third draft of his will, which was then signed by the three witnesses, all of whom were present throughout the birthday party. The third draft is the version which was probated.

Based on the testimony summarized above, Cole understood exactly what he was doing at the time he executed his will. He drafted the will entirely on his own initiative, and modified it twice in accordance with suggestions from donee. According to witness Lucille Poole, it was Cole himself who suggested that witnesses were needed.

In addition, the testimony overwhelmingly indicates that Cole was in most respects a normal individual. Testifying as to Cole's condition, Donee stated, "He wasn't really normal, but he was close to it. You would never detect anything wrong with him had you not known." Donee explained Cole's general competence in day-to-day living: "He did everything. The only thing I did for him was to prepare his meals, wash his--kept his clothing clean, his bedding, and that's all." Donee also testified that Cole had taken his medication on his own from the time he came to live with she and her husband. The three witnesses to the will reiterated Donee's testimony that Cole appeared to be a normal individual. Witness Lucille Poole, who had known Cole for twenty years, testified that she talked to Cole "all the time," and that "[h]e talked normal to me."

Appellant offered nothing to rebut Donee's showing as to Cole's donative capacity. In fact, some of Appellant's testimony suggests that Cole was capable of quite reasoned thought. Discussing a situation in which he asked his father to come live with him in Abbeville, Appellant summarized Cole's response as follows:

He said, "Son, I'd like that, but--I'd like to do that, but I like that my work, the center that I go to"--He called it his work, his work. He said he didn't know if it (sic) they had a place around Abbeville that was like that, and I said maybe I could call the V.A. in LaFaytte and see if I could find out. And, he said, "Oh, son that would be too much trouble for you." And, I said, "It wouldn't be no trouble." He said, "I'm happy. Don't worry about it. I'm happy." [tr. 39-40]

Although Cole was declared judicially incompetent by a Louisiana court in 1970, it is clear from the record that he understood exactly what he was doing at the time he drafted his will. Cole had donative capacity within the meaning of La.C.C. Art. 1477 because the evidence shows, clearly and convincingly, that he was "able to comprehend generally the nature and consequences of the disposition that he [was] making."

In a related argument, Appellant asserts that Cole could not have had the requisite donative intent to leave all of his assets to Donee because he was unaware of the extent of his assets. Although Appellant asserts in brief that "[i]n the world of Ellard Cole, his possessions consisted of his household furnishings," there is nothing in the record which indicates that Cole was unaware of the extent of his assets. Furthermore, this argument appears to have been disposed of by the comments to La.C.C. Art. 1477, which outline the following standards for determining donative capacity:

In many respects it [*i.e.* the new test for donative capacity] is derived from the common-law test for testamentary (donative) capacity that requires a person to be able to understand in a general way the nature and extent of his property. . . . In other words, at common law to be competent to make a will, a person must have a general and approximate understanding of the nature and extent of his assets to be disposed of . . . .

Id., comments (b) and (c) (emphasis added). *See also* comment (e). Thus, even if Cole did not know the exact extent of his holdings, such knowledge was not requisite for donative capacity. Cole's will expresses his intention to leave all but his house to Donee, and we see no reason to disturb this expression through a technical finding of "lack of donative intent."

Appellant's showing as to undue influence:

As set forth above, La.C.C. Art. 1479 provides that a donation *mortis causa* will be declared null if it is "the product of influence by the donee . . . . that so impaired the volition of the donor as to substitute the volition of the donee . . . .for the volition of the donor." Comment (b) to La.C.C. Art. 1479 explains the subjective nature of a determination of undue influence, and concludes: "Mere advice, or persuasion, or kindness and assistance, should not constitute influence that would destroy the free agency of the donor and substitute someone else's volition for his own." Appellant has offered nothing to show that Donee exercised anything more grievous than advice and persuasion, together with kindness and assistance, in influencing Cole to execute his will.

Appellant visited Cole only once during the nineteen years Cole lived in New Orleans. Accordingly, his testimony as to Donee's undue influence is highly conjectural, being based largely on impressions Appellant received during Cole's visits to his family in Abbeville, and on the difficulty Appellant experienced in attempting to contact his father in New Orleans.

Up until 1984, when Donee's husband died, Cole visited his family in Abbeville almost every summer. On one such visit, Appellant alleges that his father "told me my aunt wanted him to make a will, and he didn't want to." Appellant did not elaborate on this statement, but later explained his impressions as to the general influence Donee had over Cole: "It sort of like--She had, how would you say, the power to get him to do what she wanted him to do. . . . the way she talked to him, sort of stern, and something she wanted him to do, she'd tell him to do it, and the way she told him." When asked whether Cole complained about Donee telling him what to do, Appellant stated, "He just told me that [Donee] was sort of--He didn't use this exact word--expletive--but that's what he meant in so many words." Appellant also alleged that Donee had threatened to send Cole back to the hospital as a means of getting him to do things. When asked why Donee had done this, Appellant replied: "Say, for instance, if he didn't want to take his medicine or something like that, you know. I imagine it was nothing really specific."

Although Appellant visited his father only once in New Orleans, he testified that he asked Donee to put a telephone in his father's apartment. This was never done, and Appellant alleges that numerous attempts to contact his father by calling Donee's home failed because Appellant never returned his calls.

While Donee may have exercised some influence over Cole, Appellant's highly conjectural showing was insufficient to prove that Donee's influence rose to the level contemplated by La.C.C. Art. 1479--i.e. that she substituted her own volition for that of Cole.

Appellant's showing as to Donee's undue influence is largely contradicted by Donee's testimony. Furthermore, the testimony of Cole's brother, Wilbert Cole (Wilbert), tends to show that the making of a will remained largely in Cole's discretion.

Wilbert testified that shortly before Donee's husband died in 1984, Cole told him that "[Donee] had asked him [Cole] about making a will, but he didn't know too much about making a will because of his son." When Wilbert spoke to Donee about the will, "She said that, 'I spoke to [Cole] concerning about a will, but I don't know whether he wants to make a will or not after I been taking care of him.'" These statements tend to show that as of 1984, the making of a will was still very much under Cole's discretion. The fact that Cole did not write a will until seven years later is further indication that Cole was acting under his own volition.

In addition to the above arguments, Appellant has challenged the credibility of Donee and her witnesses, alleging in his appellate brief that "this entire event was staged and orchestrated by the [Donee], at best." Determinations of credibility fall largely within the discretion of the trier of fact, and are reviewed under the manifest error/clearly wrong standard. *Rosell v. ESCO*, 549 So. 2d 840 (La.1989). Donee and the three witnesses to Cole's will have presented a consistent and plausible description of Cole's actions and behavior in drafting the will. Based on our review of the trial transcript, the trial court was neither manifestly erroneous nor clearly wrong in crediting their testimony.

For the foregoing reasons, the judgment of the trial court is affirmed.

AFFIRMED.

NOTE

Consider what law the court applied to resolve this case. When did that law become effective? When did the decedent in *Cole* die? When did he write his will? Compare the result in *Succession of Reynaud*, 619 So. 2d 628 (La. 3rd Cir. 1993). How would the resolution of this case be different under La. C.C. art. 1482, as amended by Act 1008, § 1 in 2003? Consider the wisdom of the amendment.

SUCCESSION OF HORRELL
680 So. 2d 725 (La. App. 4th Cir. 1996)

LANDRIEU, Judge.

Edward A. Horrell, Sr. died July 9, 1993, at age 84, leaving his wife of more than fifty years, Clare Younger Horrell (Mrs. Horrell), and five adult children, Walter (born in 1939), Gaye[1] (born 1940), Michael (born 1942), Edward, Jr. (born in 1946), and Marie Elise a/k/a "Liz" (born in 1948). Shortly after his death, Mrs. Horrell filed a petition and order for appointment of administratrix with a sworn descriptive list, stating that Mr. Horrell died intestate.

---

[1] Throughout the record Ms. Horrell's name is inconsistently spelled as Gay, Gaye, and Gayle.

The detailed descriptive list indicates that at the time of his death Mr. Horrell owned the following separate immoveable property: The family home at 505 Florida Avenue (valued at $125,000) and industrial property at 2020 LaFaytte Street (valued at $150,000), both in New Orleans, as well as an entire city block[2] located at 19th and Tyler Streets in downtown Covington (valued at $300,000).

Mr. Horrell owned, as community property with his wife, a camp located in Lake Catherine, Louisiana (valued at $50,000), and the industrial property at 4821 Earhart Boulevard in New Orleans where his company (Horrell and Company, Inc.) business office and warehouse were located (valued at $200,000). In addition, Mr. and Mrs. Horrell owned as joint tenants with a right of survivorship a house in Bay St. Louis, Mississippi(valued at $125,000) and two lots in Diamondhead, Mississippi (valued at $24,000).

Several days prior to the filing of Mrs. Horrell's petition and descriptive list, however, the Horrell's oldest son, Walter, sought to have his father's statutory will (executed on April 13, 1993) probated. It provided the following:

> I, Edward A. Horrell, make this my last will and testament. I hereby revoke any prior wills or codicils that I may have made.
>
> I give, grant, donate and bequeath the usufruct of all shares that I own in companies listed on the New York Stock Exchange and the usufruct of my home located at 505 Florida Boulevard, New Orleans, Louisiana, to my spouse, Clare Younger Horrell, for the rest of her life.
>
> Subject to the usufruct of the premises at 505 Florida Boulevard, New Orleans, Louisiana, granted to my spouse, I give, grant, donate and bequeath all the immovable property (real estate) that I own in the Parish of Orleans, State of Louisiana, to four of my five children, namely Marie Elise Horrell, wife of Paul LeCour, Edward A. Horrell, Jr., Michael J. Horrell, and Gay Ann Horrell, divorced wife of John B. Coffer.
>
> I give, grant, and bequeath all the immovable property (real estate) that I own in the Parish of St. Tammany, State of Louisiana, to my fifth child, Walter J. Horrell.
>
> I give, grant, donate, and bequeath all the remainder of my property to my five children, Walter J. Horrell, Gay Ann Horrell, divorced wife of John B. Coffer, Michael J. Horrell, Edward A. Horrell, Jr., and Marie Elise Horrell, wife of Paul LeCour. I make them my universal legatees.
>
> I name and appoint Walter J. Horrell as executor of my succession with full seizin and without bond or security.

The will, which had been prepared by Walter's daughter, Mary F. Horrell, a notary public, was signed in Mr. Horrell's hospital room at Mercy Hospital and witnessed by Edna a/k/a "Betty" Horrell (Walter's wife) and Allen E. Horrell (Walter's son) with Walter present. On the

---

[2] The record indicates that at least two houses were located on the property and there is some indication that it was subdivided into 10 lots.

same day that Mr. Horrell signed the will, he also signed an Act of Donation prepared by Walter (who was an attorney) giving Walter the property in Covington.[3]

On July 23, 1993, Mrs. Horrell was appointed administratrix. On August 31, 1993, she and four of her children (Gaye, Michael, Edward, and Marie Elise) petitioned to have the will declared invalid, alleging lack of testamentary capacity, undue influence, lack of sufficient number of witnesses, and conflict of interest. The two proceedings (the intestate succession filed by Mrs. Horrell and the testate succession filed by Walter) were consolidated on December 22, 1993.

On Jan. 10, 1994, Walter sought to remove his mother as administratrix and to have all the succession property delivered to him as executor. He alleged that his mother (1) failed to include two vehicles (a 1980 truck and a car) in the descriptive list; (2) used only rough estimates in valuing the succession property; (3) commingled funds and continued to write checks for her own purposes; (4) paid succession debts without authorization of the court; (5) had taken steps to continue the business without complying with codal requirements and failed to operate it for the benefit of the succession. The trial court granted Walter's motion, removing Mrs. Horrell as administratrix and ordering her to deliver all succession property to Walter.

On March 23, 1994, an accountant completed a list of deposits and disbursements in the Horrells' four bank accounts. In April, Walter filed a rule for contempt because his mother had failed to deliver the succession property to him. On April 7th, Mrs. Horrell petitioned for an interim allowance because Walter was receiving the stock dividends which Mr. Horrell had transferred to her prior to his death giving her an annual income of approximately $21,140 in monthly payments of $700 and quarterly payments of $3000. Walter opposed the petition, arguing that his mother received social security payments of $750 per month and that the house in Mississippi (where his sister Gaye lived) "should be producing income in the approximate amount of $600 per month."[4]

On Sept. 28, 29, and October 3, 1994, a hearing was held on the petition to nullify the will and the rule to remove Walter as executor. On November 17, 1994, the trial court denied both, stating that Walter's siblings failed to prove by clear and convincing evidence that Mr. Horrell lacked testamentary capacity when he executed the April 13th testament. The trial judge found that the testimony of Walter, his wife, and children as to what occurred on the evening of April 13 was consistent in all material respects and "made it clear that Mr. Horrell had total control and use of his faculties, that he was aware of his surroundings and that he knew exactly what he was doing." The trial judge dismissed the testimony of Dr. Harvey Rifkin, stating that his psychiatric examination of Mr. Horrell shortly after the will was executed was based on inadequate facts and contradicted by the testimony of Dr. Robert Jeanfreau, Mr. Horrell's treating physician.

Appellants challenge that judgment, arguing that Mr. Horrell lacked capacity to execute the will or that the will was a product of fraud and/or undue influence exerted by Walter and his daughter Mary.

---

[3] Six weeks later, after discovery of this Act of Donation filed in the St. Tammany public records, Mr. Horrell signed a Revocation of Donation prepared by an attorney hired by Mr. Horrell's other children.

[4] Nothing in the record indicates that Walter, who has lived rent-free on the Covington property his entire life and whose son likewise lives rent-free in a separate house on the property, began paying rent to the succession.

DISCUSSION

"To have capacity to make a donation *inter vivos* or *mortis causa*, a person must also be able to comprehend generally the nature and consequences of the disposition that he is making." LA.CIV.CODE ANN. art. 1477 (West Supp.1996). In determining testamentary capacity the question is whether the testator understood the nature of the testamentary act and appreciated its effects. *Succession of Dowling*, 93-1902 (La.App. 4 Cir. 2/25/94), 633 So. 2d 846, 855 (citation omitted). "As used in this Article the reference to the 'nature' of the disposition means that the donor must be capable of understanding that he is making a gratuitous transfer of property that he owns to someone else who will become the owner of it, without recompense...." LA.CIV.CODE ANN. art. 1477, comment (d). "A person who challenges the capacity of a donor must prove by clear and convincing evidence that the donor lacked capacity at the time the donor made the *inter vivos* donation or executed the testament...." LA.CIV.CODE ANN. art. 1482 (West Supp.1996).

The trial judge's finding that Walter and his family were consistent in their testimony as to the events of the evening of April 13 is not dispositive as to the issue of whether Mr. Horrell understood the nature of the testamentary act or appreciated its effects. Clearly, Walter's wife, Edna, and his children, Mary and Allen, who both lived on the Covington property rent-free[5] and who, in the natural course of events might stand to eventually inherit the property from their father have an interest in upholding the will.

Seven months prior to the testator's death, he slipped and fell in a grocery store, fracturing his hip. He underwent surgery at Mercy Hospital in New Orleans in January 1993 to repair the fractured hip and was released in mid- February. In March, Mr. Horrell was readmitted for pressure sores on his heel. He remained in Mercy Hospital through May and it was during this second hospitalization that the disputed will was signed. Mr. Horrell then went to a nursing home in Mississippi for a short stay, was readmitted to Mercy Hospital for a short period and then sent to a long-term care facility. While there, he suffered respiratory arrest for which he returned to Mercy Hospital where he died. At the hearing, his treating physician and a psychiatrist testified as to Mr. Horrell's mental status during his periods of hospitalization.

Dr. Robert Jeanfreau, his treating physician, testified that he began treating Mr. Horrell shortly before the surgery and continued to treat him daily because of Mr. Horrell's atrial fibrillation. He noted that during his first hospitalization Mr. Horrell was physically debilitated and exhibited poor memory. At the time of his discharge, Mr. Horrell continued to exhibit poor memory. Upon readmittance to the hospital for heel sores, Mr. Horrell appeared more debilitated, his overall nutritional status appeared worse, and he still had poor memory. Dr. Jeanfreau stated that Mr. Horrell was frequently confused,[6] particularly during the second hospitalization, and that he often did not know where he was. When questioned as to whether Mr. Horrell was competent to execute a will during his second hospitalization, Dr. Jeanfreau asserted that he did not feel that Mr. Horrell was competent and that the confusion exhibited by Mr. Horrell interfered with his ability to fully understand and comprehend the implications of

---

[5] Mary (who prepared the will giving the property to her father) lived rent-free with her parents while her brother (who had, along with his mother, witnessed the signing of the will which gave the property to his father) lived rent-free in a separate residence on the property.

[6] Dr. Jeanfreau noted that this frequently occurs when elderly people are put in the hospital, although they often return to their normal level of functioning when they return to their home environment.

legal documents like the will and the Act of Donation which he executed. Dr. Jeanfreau testified that he did not remember if he had explicitly ordered the psychiatric consultation, but that he thought that it was appropriate in light of the execution of the will.

Dr. Harvey Rifkin, the psychiatrist who examined Mr. Horrell on April 27th, stated that Mr. Horrell was very disoriented, answering "January" in response to a question as to the date. Mr. Horrell became very agitated, refused to answer any further questions and told Dr. Rifkin to "get the hell out of my room."

The doctors' testimony as to Mr. Horrell's mental status is corroborated by the testimony of Mr. Horrell's son-in law, Paul LeCour. LeCour testified that when he visited Mr. Horrell during the week of April 5th he looked "glassy- eyed." Further, Paul related an incident where his father-in-law asked him if he had brought a diesel engine starter for him which he had, in fact, worked on and returned 18 years before.

In addition, several provisions of the will itself are indicative of Mr. Horrell's lack of comprehension as to the document and its consequences. He left the house in Mississippi, which he owned jointly with a right of survivorship with his wife, to four of his children subject to the usufruct of his wife. However, Mrs. Horrell became the sole owner of the house in Mississippi upon Mr. Horrell's death. Accordingly, it was not within Mr. Horrell's power to give that property to his children.

Furthermore, since the witnesses agree that the Act of Donation was signed first, Mr. Horrell no longer owned the Covington property at the time he signed the will and, thus, it was not within his power to give that property by will. Even if the Act of Donation was signed after the will and Mr. Horrell maintained ownership of the property at the time the will was signed, the fact that the two documents were signed at the same time indicate Mr. Horrell did not understand the nature or consequences of the documents.

In essence, by the terms of the purported will, one child received an unencumbered piece of property valued at $300,000, while his four siblings received shared ownership of property (subject to their mother's usufruct) valued at approximately $375,000. There is no apparent reason why Mr. Horrell would so favor one child over the others, although it was suggested in oral argument that Walter was given the Covington property because he had always lived on it. We note that Mr. Horrell's other children and wife were similarly situated (Gaye lived in her parents' house in Mississippi, Michael[7] lived in his parents' camp on Lake Catherine, Edward worked with his father in the business on Earhart Boulevard, and Mrs. Horrell had lived in the Florida Avenue residence for over fifty years), but inexplicably did not receive similar treatment.

Moreover, the testimony of Elwin J. Bostwick (Mr. Horrell's accountant since 1956 and a disinterested witness), refutes the suggestion that Mr. Horrell would favor one child to the detriment of the others. Mr. Bostwick testified that a few months prior to Mr. Horrell's hospitalization, in the course of a conversation pertaining to the taxes and insurance which Mr. Horrell paid on the Covington property, he suggested "why don't you just give the property to Walter?" Mr. Horrell replied "I can't do that. I have other children I have to worry about."[8]

---

[7] Michael Horrell, a career merchant marine, keeps some of his belongings at his parents' home on Florida Avenue, as well as at the camp on Lake Catherine, and used his parents' car when he was in the country.

[8] In addition, Gaye Horrell Coffer testified that, when she questioned her father on April 23, 1993, as to whether he had given Walter the Covington property, her father told her "I only gave him an option to buy that property." This is consistent with Mr. Bostwick's testimony indicating that Mr. Horrell did not consider giving Walter the property to the detriment of his other children. In addition, Ms. Coffer testified that Mr. Horrell executed a handwritten note

Based on the objective evidence, as well as the medical testimony, it is clear that Mr. Horrell lacked the requisite understanding of the nature of the testamentary act and its effects. Accordingly, we do not reach the issues of undue influence and fraud.

For the foregoing reasons, we find that the trial judge was manifestly erroneous in denying the petition to nullify the will. Accordingly, the judgment of the trial court is reversed. The Petition for Declaration of Invalidity of Alleged Testament and the Motion to Remove Executor are granted, and the matter is remanded for further proceedings.

REVERSED.

SUCCESSION OF DESHOTELS
735 So. 2d 826 (La. App. 3rd Cir., 1999)

SULLIVAN, Judge.

Jacqueline Deshotels Cashen appeals the dismissal on summary judgment of her opposition to the probate of her mother's will. For the following reasons, we affirm.

Facts and Procedural History

Hilda Tate Deshotels died on August 16, 1997 at the age of eighty-four. Mrs. Deshotels was survived by her adopted daughter, Jacqueline, and her biological daughter, Loretta A. Deshotels. On January 9, 1997, Mrs. Deshotels executed a statutory will in which she bequeathed her entire estate, less several items of furniture, to Loretta.

Jacqueline opposed the probate of the will, alleging that Mrs. Deshotels lacked testamentary capacity or, in the alternative, was subjected to undue influence from Loretta. Loretta then filed a motion for summary judgment, attaching as exhibits the depositions of the attorney who prepared the will, the witnesses to the will, and the sitters who cared for Mrs. Deshotels before her death. Jacqueline's opposition to the summary judgment included the depositions of Mrs. Deshotels' doctor and Loretta's roommate, who drove Mrs. Deshotels to her attorney's office for an appointment about the will. Near the close of business on the day before the summary judgment hearing, Jacqueline also filed into the record and faxed to opposing counsel the affidavits of three of Mrs. Deshotels' relatives.

The trial court refused to consider the affidavits filed by Jacqueline, finding that they were served on opposing counsel without proper notice to respond. After reviewing the depositions, the trial court concluded there was no genuine issue of material fact that Jacqueline would not be able to produce the clear and convincing evidence required to invalidate the will. On appeal, Jacqueline assigns as error (1) the trial court's failure to consider the affidavits; (2) the trial court's conclusion that Mrs. Deshotels' doctor's opinion as to her mental capacity had no factual foundation; (3) the trial court's failure to recognize that the deposition evidence revealed a genuine issue of material fact; and (4) the trial court's failure to recognize that the affidavits, together with the depositions, created a genuine issue of material fact.

---

dated 4/29/93 stating that "The Masons have my will only at the consistory only" and that "as of this day, there is no will except with the consistory."

Opinion

*   *   *

Deposition Testimony

The testament in question was prepared by Thomas Fuselier, an attorney practicing in Mamou, Louisiana. In his deposition, Mr. Fuselier stated that he had known Mrs. Deshotels all of his life. He had also performed legal work for Mrs. Deshotels and her late husband, Darby, including a donation of their principal residence to Loretta before Mr. Deshotels' death. At the time of that donation, both Mr. and Mrs. Deshotels told Mr. Fuselier of their desire to provide more for their natural daughter, Loretta, than for Jacqueline, whom "they felt they had given a lot to." On other occasions (unrelated to either the donation or the will), Mrs. Deshotels discussed with Mr. Fuselier her desire to favor Loretta over Jacqueline. Mrs. Deshotels explained that she and her husband had taken in Jacqueline, who was the child of Mr. Deshotels' brother, when Jacqueline's mother abandoned her. Mrs. Deshotels believed that they had provided Jacqueline with a good life and home, but that Jacqueline was unappreciative and caused disturbances in the family. Mr. Fuselier recalled Mrs. Deshotels stating that she felt she had done enough for Jacqueline and it was time to take care of Loretta. Mr. Fuselier was aware that Jacqueline and Loretta had received cash gifts from their parents, including a gift of $30,000 to each daughter in one year.

Mr. Fuselier met with Mrs. Deshotels twice about her will. At the first visit, Mrs. Deshotels was accompanied by Mary Ayo, Loretta's roommate. Ms. Ayo, who appeared to be friendly with Mrs. Deshotels, attended the meeting, but did not participate when they discussed the substance of the will. After Mrs. Deshotels told Mr. Fuselier that she wanted to leave her entire estate to Loretta, except the specific bequests, Mr. Fuselier suggested that Jacqueline might challenge the will. Mrs. Deshotels replied that she "wouldn't be around then," "that's where she wanted it to go," and "so be it." Even though he anticipated that the will might be challenged, Mr. Fuselier saw no need for a medical opinion about Mrs. Deshotels' capacity.

Mrs. Deshotels returned to Mr. Fuselier's office a few days later to sign the will. Mr. Fuselier first questioned Mrs. Deshotels about where she was, what she was doing, and whether she understood the consequences of her actions. He asked her to repeat her instructions about the will and whether she had changed her mind. Again, she replied that she wanted everything to go to Loretta. Mr. Fuselier was not surprised about the contents of the will because Mrs. Deshotels had previously related the same intentions to him. Mr. Fuselier admitted that Mrs. Deshotels was not as sharp as she once was, but he, nonetheless, believed her to be competent and in full control of her faculties. When asked whether anyone suggested that either Loretta or Ms. Ayo tried to influence Mrs. Deshotels, he responded that the will appeared to be Mrs. Deshotels' decision.

The will was witnessed by two legal secretaries, Leisa Deshotel and Marla Yeager, and by the sitter who drove Mrs. Deshotels to the law office that day, Veniter Joyce Duplechain. Both secretaries agreed that Mrs. Deshotels responded appropriately when asked about whether she knew what day it was and why she was at the office. According to Leisa Deshotel, Mrs. Deshotels appeared insulted that Mr. Fuselier asked her those questions.

Ms. Duplechain testified that Mr. Fuselier read the will aloud as Mrs. Deshotels followed with a copy. He then asked if this was what she wanted, and she answered that it was and that no changes would be necessary. Upon leaving Mr. Fuselier's office, Ms. Duplechain took Mrs. Deshotels to her sister's home. There, Mrs. Deshotels remarked about the will, "I know Jackie won't be happy." She also commented that Jacqueline had a husband who could give her "the good life," but that Loretta was not married and would have to work for everything until she retired. Ms. Duplechain believed that Mrs. Deshotels understood what she was doing that day.

Dr. Wayne LaHaye was Mrs. Deshotels' family physician as well as her nephew. Dr. LaHaye had diagnosed his aunt with moderate Alzheimer's disease in February of 1996, but he observed its symptoms as early as 1994. He also treated her for generalized arteriosclerotic vascular disease. Dr. LaHaye described Alzheimer's as an incurable disease with a gradual but progressive worsening of symptoms. Its classic symptoms are confusion, forgetfulness, and the development of a placid personality. He believed that even patients in the moderate stage of Alzheimer's would suffer from judgment problems, notwithstanding their ability to appear lucid for short periods of time. Based upon his diagnosis and his observation of Mrs. Deshotels' mental capacity over the years, he did not believe that she would have had the capacity to execute a will in January of 1997. Dr. LaHaye recalled speaking with Loretta about her mother's mental capacity on the telephone, but he did not note this conversation in the medical records. Dr. LaHaye's last visit with his aunt before she signed her will was in October of 1996.

In the last year of Mrs. Deshotels' life, sitters attended to her around the clock. The sitters' testimony painted a picture of someone who functioned well, but only in an environment totally planned by others. They agreed that Mrs. Deshotels required twenty-four hour care, mainly because of her inability to prepare her own food, but that she could dress, bathe, and clothe herself without assistance and could engage in intelligent conversation. They all described instances of forgetfulness, but in varying degrees.

Ms. Duplechain stated that between July of 1996 and April of 1997 she did not observe any confusion or memory loss other than Mrs. Deshotels frequently misplacing her purse. According to Ms. Duplechain, Mrs. Deshotels did not decline mentally until Easter of 1997, after which she lost interest in her handiwork, began stuttering, and experienced more memory problems. Rita Shillow, Mrs. Deshotels' housekeeper for thirty-three years, said that Mrs. Deshotels needed someone to prepare her meals and often got confused as to "who was who," but that she carried on normal conversations with visitors and "seemed mentally okay." Rose Guillory said Mrs. Deshotels always knew where she was and who she was talking to, but that she could not make long range plans.

Anna Tate testified that Mrs. Deshotels had trouble following instructions, could not remember her schedule from day to day, and often repeated conversations. Ms. Tate did state that Mrs. Deshotels never confused her sitters, could answer her telephone, and could carry on a conversation, at least in 1996. Bertie Guillory testified that Mrs. Deshotels was always aware of her surroundings, but that she had short term memory problems, such as forgetting what she had for lunch or who had visited that day, misplacing money and jewelry, and being unable to follow her favorite television programs. Jacqueline testified that her mother could not remember recent events such as who had visited her, what she had for lunch, and where she was told she was being driven.

Bertie Guillory also believed that Mrs. Deshotels was controlled by Loretta, Ms. Ayo, and Mrs. Deshotels' sister, Hazel. She testified that she heard Loretta "say bad things" about Jacqueline and that Mrs. Deshotels would "put Jackie down" after Loretta had visited for the weekend. Bertie Guillory also heard Mrs. Deshotels complain that Jacqueline had not visited on several occasions when Jacqueline had. However, Bertie Guillory was not working for Mrs. Deshotels in January of 1997, having left in August of 1996 to undergo major surgery.

Loretta, who works as the social services director for a nursing home, testified that her mother was forgetful, but that she did not have the typical dementia of other Alzheimer's patients. She denied disparaging Jacqueline to Mrs. Deshotels, but she admitted that her Aunt Hazel does favor her over Jacqueline. Ms. Ayo, Loretta's roommate, drove Mrs. Deshotels to an appointment about the will at Loretta's request. At Mr. Fuselier's office, Ms. Ayo heard Mrs. Deshotels say that she had done a lot for Jacqueline, but that Jacqueline had turned her back on her. From Mr. Fuselier's responses, she assumed that Mrs. Deshotels had expressed these sentiments to him on other occasions. Ms. Ayo described Loretta as her best friend and companion. They purchased a home, a vehicle, and a camper together, and Loretta is the beneficiary on Ms. Ayo's life insurance policy.

Affidavits

Jacqueline also proffered the affidavits of three of Mrs. Deshotels' relatives. Millard, Flo, and Lear Deshotels, who regularly visited with the testator, stated that their aunt could not recall recent activities, confused family members, and repeated conversations. Millard recalled that his aunt discussed selling some property with him without remembering that she had already donated that land to Loretta. Flo once observed Mrs. Deshotels crying because she was supposed to have signed a paper that caused her daughters to fight, but she did not remember signing anything. Lear stated that in January of 1997 he observed his aunt near tears because she had to "go to the lawyer's office" and "sign some papers" and that "[w]hen Jackie finds out, she won't be happy." Lear had the impression that his aunt was being pressured to sign whatever the lawyer had prepared.

We agree with Jacqueline that the trial court should have considered these affidavits.... Although we find that the affidavits were timely, for the following reasons, we disagree with Jacqueline's argument that they create a genuine issue of material fact.

Testamentary Capacity

To have the capacity to donate *inter vivos* or *mortis causa*, a person must be able "to comprehend generally the nature and consequences" of his action. LA.CIV.CODE art. 1477. "Capacity to donate *mortis causa* must exist at the time the testator executes the testament." LA.CIV.CODE art. 1471. A person challenging the capacity of a testator must prove lack of capacity at the time of the testament by clear and convincing evidence. LA.CIV.CODE art. 1482. *[Rule]*

Jacqueline argues that the trial court erred in concluding that Dr. LaHaye's opinion had no factual basis and that the depositions and affidavits created a genuine issue of material fact as to Mrs. Deshotels' mental capacity. Although we disagree with the trial court's characterization of Dr. LaHaye's testimony, we, nonetheless, find Dr. LaHaye's opinion and the affidavits insufficient to defeat summary judgment, given the testimony of those present when the will was signed.

Concerning the role of medical testimony in a challenge to a will, the court in *Succession of Braud*, 94-668, p. 5 (La.App. 4 Cir. 11/17/94); 646 So. 2d 1168, 1171, *writ denied*, 95-383 (La.3/30/95); 651 So. 2d 841 (emphasis added), stated:

The only witnesses present when the will was actually executed all testified unequivocally that [the testator] did have the necessary mental capacity to execute the will *on the day the will was actually prepared.* None of [the opponent's] evidence rebuts this testimony. *The caselaw [sic] is clear that proof of the presence of a mentally-debilitating condition at the approximate time that the will was executed is insufficient to prove lack of testamentary capacity at the time the will was executed by clear and convincing evidence, especially in light of conflicting evidence of the decedent's capacity at the actual time the will was executed.* Even the fact that the decedent had previously been interdicted was insufficient to prove lack of testamentary capacity in [*Succession of Cole,* 618 So. 2d 554 (La. App. 4 Cir.1993)] *[See La. 1482, as amended by Act 1008, § 1 in 1997]*[*].

Succession of Christensen, 94-263 (La.App. 1 Cir. 12/22/94); 649 So. 2d 23, *writ denied sub nom. Succession of McGhee,* 95-234 (La.4/7/95); 652 So. 2d 1346, is remarkably similar to the instant case in that (1) the testator suffered from moderate Alzheimer's disease, (2) several sitters offered conflicting testimony about her capacity, but (3) the witnesses who had contact with the testator on the day she wrote her will indicated that she understood and appreciated the consequences of what she was doing. Under those circumstances, the court in Christensen found the opponents to the will failed to meet the clear and convincing standard, given the presumption in favor of capacity.

* * *

...At trial, Jacqueline will have to prove that Mrs. Deshotels lacked capacity when the will was executed by clear and convincing evidence. Although she has presented evidence that Mrs. Deshotels suffered a moderate form of Alzheimer's disease, she has not come forward with evidence that this condition prevented her mother from understanding the "nature and consequences" of her action. The affidavits of the Deshotels relatives only confirm the sitters' testimony that Mrs. Deshotels was forgetful and repeated conversations; they do not conflict with the testimony that Mrs. Deshotels understood what she was doing when she executed her will. Indeed, her statement that "[Jackie] won't be happy" indicates that she understood the consequences of her decision. On this record, we find that summary judgment was properly granted as to Mrs. Deshotels' capacity to make her will.

Undue Influence

A donation *inter vivos* or *mortis causa* shall be declared null upon proof that it was the product of influence by the donee or another person "that so impaired the volition of the donor as to substitute the volition of the donee or other person for the volition of the donor." La.Civ.Code art. 1479. The burden of proof for one challenging a donation based on "undue influence" is found in La.Civ.Code art. 1483:

---

[*] Bracketed material in italics added by author.

A person who challenges a donation because of fraud, duress, or undue influence, must prove it by clear and convincing evidence. However, if, at the time the donation was made or the testament executed, a relationship of confidence existed between the donor and the wrongdoer and the wrongdoer was not then related to the donor by affinity, consanguinity or adoption, the person who challenges the donation need only prove the fraud, duress, or undue influence by a preponderance of the evidence.

Prior to the adoption of the above articles, evidence of undue influence was admissible only to show testamentary incapacity or mental weakness. *Succession of Hamiter*, 519 So. 2d 341 (La.App. 2 Cir.), *writ denied*, 521 So. 2d 1170 (La.1988). "[T]he addition of Civil Code article 1479 in 1991 created a new cause of action .... By adopting that article the legislature has specifically recognized the cause of undue influence, *in addition to incapacity, as a separate basis for nullifying a testamentary disposition.*" *Succession of Dowling*, 93-1902, p. 15 (La. App. 4 Cir. 2/25/94); 633 So. 2d 846, 855 (emphasis added).

Comment (b) to Article 1479 provides in part:

[E]veryone is more or less swayed by associations with other persons, so this Article attempts to describe the kind of influence that would cause the invalidity of a gift or disposition. Physical coercion and duress clearly fall within the proscription of the previous Article. The more subtle influences, such as creating resentment toward a natural object of a testator's bounty by false statements, may constitute the kind of influence that is reprobated by this Article, but will still call for evaluation by the trier of fact. Since the ways of influencing another person are infinite, the definition given in this Article is used in an attempt to place a limit on the kind of influence that is deemed offensive. Mere advice, or persuasion, or kindness and assistance, should not constitute influence that would destroy the free agency of a donor and substitute someone else's volition for his own.

Comment (d) of the same article addresses when the influence must be present: "It is implicit in this Article that *the influence must be operative at the time of the execution of the inter vivos donation or testament.* Obviously, it should not be necessary that the acts themselves be done at that time, or that the person exercising the pressure be present then." (Emphasis added.)

The record established that Mrs. Deshotels lived alone but with the help of sitters at the time of her will, with Loretta and Ms. Ayo visiting every other weekend. The only evidence suggesting that Mrs. Deshotels was influenced by Loretta or Ms. Ayo was found in the deposition of Bertie Guillory, who had stopped working for Mrs. Deshotels approximately five months before the will was executed. Although Ms. Ayo was present at a meeting about the will, Mr. Fuselier testified that she did not participate in discussing it and that the substance of the will appeared to be Mrs. Deshotels' decision. Mr. Fuselier saw no reason to question the will, in part because *Mrs. Deshotels had told him in previous conversations that she intended to favor Loretta over Jacqueline.* Mrs. Deshotels had also expressed the same intentions to others. Again, we find no genuine issue of material fact that Jacqueline will not be able to produce the clear and convincing evidence necessary to invalidate the will.

Decree

For the above reasons, the judgment of the trial court is affirmed at appellant's cost.

AFFIRMED.

SUCCESSION OF CULOTTA
900 So. 2d 137 (La. App. 5th Cir. 2005)

MARION F. EDWARDS, J.

Appellant Anthony Culotta ("Anthony") appeals a judgment of the district court granting a Rule to Annul Probate of Testament, Vacate Appointment of Executor and Probate Previous Will in favor of appellees Judy Culotta Sudo, Frances Culotta Blanchard, Michelle Sudo, Renee Sudo Galey, and Cherie Sudo Lara (hereinafter referred to in the singular as "Judy Sudo"). The judgment further appointed Judy Sudo administratrix of the Succession of Salvadore Culotta Jr.

In August, 2001, Anthony filed a Petition for Probate of Notarial Testament and Appointment of Executor. The petition alleged that Anthony's father, Salvadore, died on April 27, 2001, and left a will in notarial form, dated February 16, 2001, naming him (Anthony) testamentary executor, without the necessity of posting bond. Attached to the petition was a copy of the will and Oath of Office. In the will, Salvadore stated that he had a visual impairment which prevented him from reading the testament, which was executed under the provisions of LOUISIANA CIVIL CODE Article 1579. Salvadore left all of his property to Anthony, making him the executor without bond. The will bore the signature of Salvadore and two witnesses, and was duly notarized. On August 6, 2001, the court signed the Order of Probate, permitting the appointment of Anthony as Executor.

On September 14, 2001, Judy Sudo filed a Petition to Annul Probate of Testament. The group alleged that they are the children and grandchildren of Salvadore, and were the heirs to his estate under a will dated April 21, 1989. They further alleged that the earlier will itself had been improperly destroyed by Anthony, and that the court should accept a copy of that will that was attached to the petition. They urged that Anthony was not in control of his mental faculties in February 2001, and that Anthony had exercised undue influence such that he substituted his own volition for that of Salvadore, and therefore, the will should be declared null and void.

Trial was held on June 24, 2004. At trial, Anthony testified that his relationship with his sister is strained, and many times he was not allowed to see his father. A worker from Elderly Protective Services suggested he visit his father at Judy's home accompanied by a friend, Mr. Johnny Williams.

Anthony and his wife had come to live with Salvadore, at Salvadore's home, on February 4, 2001. Anthony commenced living with him after Salvadore insisted at dinner one evening that he would not go back to stay with his daughter, Judy, in Slidell. To reassure Salvadore, Anthony took his father to the police, who told him he could live wherever he wanted to, and thereafter Anthony and his wife went to stay at Salvadore's home with him. Salvadore did suffer from dementia at times, when he became agitated. Anthony knew that Salvadore took a lot of medication, but could not remember the names or the conditions for which he was treated. Salvadore was also on oxygen most of the time.

Some time after Anthony and his father came to live together, Anthony had an attorney, Mr. James Maguire, draw up a power-of-attorney for his father. Later, at the request of his father, he brought Salvadore to see Mr. Maguire again, at which time Salvadore made a will. Anthony was not in the room when the terms of the will were discussed and signed, and had not talked with Mr. Maguire about the document.

Salvadore had been married twice, and had one child, Frances, from a previous marriage, with whom Salvadore was not close. Anthony did not know why the will in question stated that Salvadore had been married only once. Anthony never suggested his father write a new will, or suggest the terms, but he was certain that Salvadore was lucid at that time. Investigators from protective services sent by Judy had inspected the living situation and verified that Anthony was caring for Salvadore.

James Maguire testified that he had been practicing for over thirty years, and had executed many wills. Anthony brought Salvadore into his office, at which time Salvadore discussed the power-of-attorney with him; Anthony was not present when the power-of-attorney was executed. Approximately ten days later, Anthony brought his father back to execute the will. Anthony told Maguire that his father was not incompetent. Maguire was not aware that Salvadore had been married twice, and had not seen any previous will of Salvadore's until after his death. Maguire and Salvadore discussed the will privately, at which time the attorney ascertained that Salvadore wished to leave his entire estate to Anthony and make him executor. Maguire was aware that Salvadore could not read, but did not know the extent or type of any visual impairment. He did not know that Salvadore had a diagnosis of dementia, and was not aware of any other medical condition. Salvadore seemed a little confused and a little disoriented, but this is fairly common among older people. However, Maguire believed Salvadore knew why he was there and what he wanted to do, and there was no question but that Salvadore understood the nature of what he was doing. It was his impression that Salvadore believed the other children would inherit from their mother, and that he wished to leave his portion of the estate to Anthony. Maguire based his decision to make the will on his own evaluation of Salvadore's mental status and his ability to express his wishes.

There were disputes between Anthony and Judy over the care of their father, as well as over the management of his assets. Maguire had the impression that Judy had total control over Salvadore, and that Anthony was concerned about his medical treatment as well as his finances. Maguire knew there would be some controversy over this new will, but was convinced that Salvadore understood what he was doing with the property. Salvadore had some money, ten or fifteen thousand dollars, and a house on Thirba Street as well as some property in Plaquemines Parish that pays royalties.

Judy Sudo testified that Salvadore first came to live with her in September, 1999 while her mother was sick, then he went home for a time until her mother died. He came back to stay with her in December, 1999. Salvadore could not be left alone and did not remember how to take care of himself. After his wife's death, Salvadore was devastated and got worse. He took medication for blood pressure and dementia, and had heart and lung problems for which he had to take oxygen. When not taking oxygen, Salvadore would become sluggish and sometimes not remember where he was or what he was doing. During the time that he lived with Judy, Salvadore was often confused and didn't know the time or date, and this confusion progressed.

He sometimes called Judy by his wife's name and had other delusions. However, at other times he knew family members and knew what was going on, and there were days when he did not suffer delirium.

Salvadore never expressed unhappiness in her home, but did want to live in his own place. Judy could not move there with him, and Salvadore could not live alone. Anthony visited Salvadore every four to six weeks, but did not provide support or care for him. After he went to live with Anthony, it appeared his mental status got worse. When asked why she contested the will in question, Judy replied that she did not think Salvadore remembered what he was doing at the time, and that he always said he would take care of all the children.

Judy Sudo's daughter, Michelle, testified that she assisted her grandfather in taking his medications when he lived in Judy's home. Salvadore's mental status was bad, and got worse as time went on. On the day that Anthony went to live with Salvadore, a policeman came to the house to collect Salvadore's things and told her that her grandfather was going to live in his home with Anthony. She did not speak to Salvadore at that time. She saw him again some time later at a restaurant, where he looked deplorable and did not eat anything. Salvadore stated that he regretted going home, and that Anthony and his wife slept in his bedroom. On that day, Michelle tried to use the telephone at Salvadore's home, and Anthony tried to hit her with it because she did not ask his permission.

In her opinion, her grandfather died because Anthony did not take good care of him. On one occasion, she visited Salvadore at home and he was not wearing his oxygen. She had no evidence, other than what she believed, regarding Salvadore changing his will.

Johnnie Williams, a longtime friend of Salvadore's, testified that he went to visit Salvadore after he moved in with Judy. At the suggestion of a worker from Elderly Protection, he accompanied Anthony and took notes on the visits. There was a lot of tension between Judy and Anthony, and they argued in front of Salvadore. This upset Salvadore very much. On February 4th, Mr. Williams was with Anthony when they picked him up from Judy's. Mr. Sam, as Williams called him, said: "Thank God you're here. I'm not coming back. There's no way I will come back to this home. Things have just become too bad. I can't take it anymore ... I'd rather be in the penitentiary then come back to this house." Salvadore was upset because he was questioned after Anthony would take him out, and called Michelle a "bitch" and said the family was evil. Salvadore said he was afraid of Judy's husband Michael, because Michael would go through his things. When Williams tried to reassure him, Salvadore said: "You don't know this family." When Salvadore said these things, Anthony did not egg him on.

"Mr. Sam" had dementia, and there were times when he was confused. On the date he said he wanted to leave, he was not in a confused state. When he first moved back to his home, he was no longer terrified as he had been on the visits to Judy's, but he did continue to have episodes of dementia. Williams accompanied Salvadore on the day he signed the will. Salvadore asked for Williams' opinion on what he should do, but Williams refused to comment. Salvadore was still angry about Michael, and had told Williams more than once that he didn't want his daughters and granddaughters "to get a damn thing." On February 16, 2001, Salvadore was not in a demented state. Williams accompanied Anthony and Salvadore to the attorney's office, and sat in the waiting room. At that time, Salvadore had his oxygen. Williams did not see Salvadore discuss the will with his attorney or sign it.

Admitted into evidence was a letter from Dr. Said Ahmed, dated February 20, 2001, in which he stated that Salvadore had been his patient for over ten years, that he had examined Salvadore that day, and that Salvadore was totally coherent with no dementia. The doctor concluded that Salvadore was of sound mind and able to handle any and all of his own affairs.

Other medical records were introduced. Dr. Pedro Serrant, an internist who treated Salvadore, stated that Salvadore took numerous medications, among them Exelon for dementia, which helps maintain the current level of brain functioning. The physician testified that Salvadore needed oxygen for his lung problems, and it also helped his brain functioning. Salvadore could have improved at times, and regressed at others. Dr. Serrant last saw Salvadore in January 2001 after he had fallen, at which time he was also having a flare-up of this lung disease and suffered deteriorating general health. He was a little less coherent, according to the family, with periods of disorientation. The Exelon was increased to improve his mental status. Dr. Serrant testified that in his best state, Salvadore was cooperative and able to communicate, but his mental status changed frequently.

Dr. Ratnakar Pernenkil, a cardiologist, testified that in addition to Exelon, Salvadore took numerous medications, including Haldol, which is also prescribed for agitation, Ambien, a sleeping aid, Valium, and Celexa, which is given for depression. Dr. Pernenkil was aware that Salvadore had progressive dementia, and at times he was very lucid while at other times he was totally confused.

Following presentation of the evidence, the case was taken under advisement, and subsequently, the trial court granted judgment in favor of Judy Culotta Sudo and the other appellees, granting the Rule to Annul Probate of Testament, Vacate Appointment of Executor and Probate Previous Will. The court also appointed Judy Sudo as executrix of Salvadore's succession. No reasons for judgment were given.

On appeal, Anthony urges that the court failed to apply the proper legal presumption in favor of capacity, and failed to apply the correct standard of proof to the claims of lack of capacity and undue influence.

The following Civil Code articles control our disposition in this case. Capacity to donate mortis causa must exist at the time the testator executes the testament. La. C.C. art. 1471. To have capacity to make a donation *inter vivos* or *mortis causa*, a person must also be able to comprehend generally the nature and consequences of the disposition that he is making. C.C. art. 1477. A donation *inter vivos* or *mortis causa* shall be declared null upon proof that it is the product of influence by the donee or another person that so impaired the volition of the donor as to substitute the volition of the donee or other person for the volition of the donor. C.C. art. 1479. A person who challenges the capacity of a donor must prove by clear and convincing evidence that the donor lacked capacity at the time the donor made the donation *inter vivos* or executed the testament. C.C. art. 1482. A person who challenges a donation because of fraud, duress, or undue influence, must prove it by clear and convincing evidence. However, if, at the time the donation was made or the testament executed, a relationship of confidence existed between the donor and the wrongdoer and the wrongdoer was not then related to the donor by affinity, consanguinity or adoption, the person who challenges the donation need only prove the fraud, duress, or undue influence by a preponderance of the evidence. C.C. art. 1483.

The intent of the testator controls the interpretation of his testament. If the language of the testament is clear, its letter is not to be disregarded under the pretext of pursuing its spirit. C.C. art. 1611. Revocation of a legacy or other testamentary provision occurs when the testator makes a subsequent incompatible testamentary disposition or provision. C.C. art. 1608.

Because the trial court did not give reasons for judgment, we do not know the basis of its apparent determination that the 2001 will was invalid. Here, the testament executed by Salvadore on February 16, 2001, is proper in form under La. C.C. art. 1579. Although Salvadore's declaration that he had been married only once and had only two children of that marriage is incorrect, we do not find that clause invalidates the will. The applicable codal articles require the courts to ascertain the intent of the testator and give it effect.

> The … code articles direct us to interpret a testament in a way that furthers, rather than frustrates, the testator's lawful intent.... The cardinal principle of the interpretation of acts of last will is to ascertain and honor the intent of the testator ascribing meaning to a disposition so that it can have effect …
>
> In interpreting these articles, the courts endeavor to ascertain the testator's intention, and all other rules of construction are only means to that end. The Supreme Court has indicated that the function of the courts is to carry out the intention of the testator and effect should be given to all language contained in the will if possible.

By the time the will was written in 2001, forced heirship had been abolished for some years, and thus Salvadore could lawfully leave his entire estate to Anthony if he chose to do so. The language in Salvadore's will leaves no doubt that such was his intention. Therefore, we find that his failure to include Frances' name in the will as his legal child is of no effect in these circumstances and does not operate to invalidate this testament.

Regarding the issue of Salvadore's capacity, there is a presumption in favor of testamentary capacity. This presumption can only be overcome by clear and convincing evidence. The clear and convincing standard requires a party to prove the existence of a contested fact is highly probable, or much more probable than its non-existence.

In the present case, the experienced attorney who prepared the will testified that although Salvadore seemed a little confused and a little disoriented as older people often are, Maguire believed Salvadore knew why he was there and what he wanted to do, and there was no question but that Salvadore understood the nature of what he was doing. Johnnie Williams, who frequently saw Salvadore both when he was confused and when he was not, testified that on February 16, Salvadore was not in a confused state and specifically told him what he was going to do.

As far as the medical evidence is concerned, Dr. Pernenkil agreed that although Salvadore had dementia and took numerous medications, at times, he was very lucid. Dr. Serrant testified that Salvadore's mental status changed frequently, but that in his best state, he was cooperative and able to communicate, and there were times when he was a lot more aware then others. Dr. Ahmed opined that Salvadore was of sound mind; however, this report was not obtained on the date in question, and under C.C. Art. 1482, the essential question before this court is Salvadore's state of mind at the time the will was confected. The appellees failed to introduce any evidence that Salvadore was incapable of understanding the nature and consequences of his actions on the day he made the will.

The case law is clear that proof, by clear and convincing evidence, of the presence of a mentally-debilitating condition at the approximate time that the will was executed is insufficient to prove lack of testamentary capacity at the time the will was executed, especially in light of conflicting evidence of the decedent's capacity at the actual time the will was executed.

Our courts have determined that given the presumption in favor of capacity, opponents to a will failed to meet the clear and convincing standard, where a testator suffered from moderate Alzheimer's disease and there was conflicting testimony about her capacity. In that case, the witnesses who had contact with the testator on the day she wrote her will indicated that she understood and appreciated the consequences of what she was doing. Similarly, testimony that a testator had been released from a geriatric psychiatric ward just days before she revoked her will was insufficient to establish incapacity where numerous witnesses testified that the testator understood the nature and consequences of her actions upon her release from the hospital and particularly on the day she executed the revocation.

In another instance, hospital records showing that a testator had been diagnosed as suffering from anxiety, depression, dementia, organic brain involvement, brain atrophy, and metastatic brain disease, and was taking antidepressants, anti-anxiety drugs, tranquilizers, hypnotic drugs, and pain medication did not overcome the presumption of testamentary capacity.

*   *   *

As in the above cases, appellees' evidence is insufficient to meet their burden of proving lack of testamentary capacity at the time the will was created. The fact that Salvadore suffered from dementia does not prove that he lacked the mental capacity to understand his actions, especially in light of the testimony of the only witnesses present with Salvadore on February 16th.

The issue of undue influence presents a more complicated question, one that often involves nuances that are difficult for the courts to interpret.

The concept of undue influence in our case law has been inexact. As a subjective standard, it is difficult to define, and thus prove. Article 1479 states that undue influence requires a showing that the "volition" or free will of the donor was replaced by the will of someone else.

The Official Comments to C.C. art. 1479 read in part as follows:

> Physical coercion and duress clearly fall within the proscription of the previous Article. The more subtle influences, such as creating resentment toward a natural object of a testator's bounty by false statements, may constitute the kind of influence that is reprobated by this Article, but will still call for evaluation by the trier of fact. Since the ways of influencing another person are infinite, the definition given in this Article is used in an attempt to place a limit on the kind of influence that is deemed offensive. Mere advice, or persuasion, or kindness and assistance, should not constitute influence that would destroy the free agency of a donor and substitute someone else's volition for his own.

In attempting to interpret the term, the courts have noted that aside from the statutory definition, undue influence is generally understood to mean "the exercise of psychological domination over a person to the extent that the person cannot help but do what the dominating party wishes."

In a case arising out of the Third Circuit, two sons filed suit to invalidate their father's will, alleging undue influence by the third son, Michael, who became sole beneficiary. In finding that undue influence existed, the trial court had given extensive oral reasons, citing certain incidents which it found to have "served no useful purpose, other than exacerbating and creating resentment in that regard." The court could not accept these actions as in any way facilitating an improvement in the father's emotional condition. There was medical testimony that Michael reinforced his father's delusions about his brothers:

Although the trial court's reasons do not specifically refer to Dr. Ware or his testimony, the reasons for ruling reflect acceptance of the evidence presented by the plaintiffs insofar as they describe Sidney's "delicate emotional state" and facilitation of resentment existing toward Ronald and Errol. Only in the context of this background, can the actions at issue then be considered.

Here, although Anthony did take his father to the Police Department on February 4th and alleged abuse, Salvadore's comments quoted by Mr. Williams indicate that Salvadore had already determined to leave Judy's home. Further, when Salvadore would complain about Judy, Anthony would not encourage him. Salvadore told Williams more than once that he did not want his daughters and granddaughters to get anything. The only rebuttal offered by Judy was what she and Michelle believed to be Salvadore's desires. When the evidence shows that the execution of a testament was well within the discretion of the testator, the court should find that the testator's volition has not been substituted by the volition of any donee. The evidence here falls far short of the necessary proof that Salvadore did not act of his own volition.

The trial court's finding of, or failure to find, undue influence is fact intensive, and such a finding cannot be disturbed on appeal in the absence of manifest error. Reversal is warranted only if the appellate court finds that no reasonable factual basis for the trial court's finding exists in the record, and that the finding is clearly wrong.

Without the benefit of reasons for judgment in the present matter, we cannot determine the evidence upon which the trial court relied. Nevertheless, our review of the record compels us to conclude that the trial court was manifestly erroneous, as there are no facts evidencing physical or emotional coercion on the part of Anthony within the meaning of C.C. art. 1479. Judy Sudo failed to carry her burden of proving, by clear and convincing evidence, that Salvadore lacked the necessary testamentary capacity or that the will was null because of undue influence.

For the foregoing reasons, the judgment of the trial court is reversed. The Order of Probate dated August 6, 2001 is reinstated. Appellees are taxed with all costs of this appeal.

REVERSED AND RENDERED.

NOTE

Consider that the three previous cases dealt with donations made by a parent, favoring one child over another. Are there special considerations that might affect a court's conclusion in such cases?

The *Horrell* case is somewhat aberrational in that the court held that lack of capacity was established. Compare the resolution in *Horrell* with that in the *Succession of Deshotels and Culotta*. What facts in each case help to distinguish one from the other? How can you explain the difference?

How would the following provision help in determining the true intent of the testator and his/her capacity?

La. C.C. P. art. 2904

Admissibility of videotape of execution of testament

A. In a contradictory trial to probate a testament under Article 2901 or an action to annul a probated testament under Article 2931, and provided the testator is sworn by a person authorized to take oaths and the oath is recorded on the videotape, the videotape of the execution and reading of the testament by the testator may be admissible as evidence of any of the following:

(1) The proper execution of the testament.

(2) The intentions of the testator.

(3) The mental state or capacity of the testator.

(4) The authenticity of the testament.

(5) Matters that are determined by a court to be relevant to the probate of the testament.

B. For purposes of this Article, "videotape" means the visual recording on a magnetic tape, film, videotape, compact disc, digital versatile disc, digital video disc, or by other electronic means together with the associated oral record.

Added by Acts 2005, No. 79, § 1.

SUCCESSION OF REEVES
704 So. 2d 252 (La. App. 3rd Cir. 1998)

SAUNDERS, Judge.

Robert Roger Reeves, Jr., died in 1992, leaving a statutory will in which he left certain bequests to his second wife, Jarrett Ganey Reeves, with whom he had been married more than eleven years. This appeal arises from the allegation that the bequests to Jarrett Reeves resulted from her undue influence over Reeves before his death. The trial court found that Jarrett Reeves had indeed exerted undue influence and nullified all bequests to her. The trial court further dismissed Ms. Reeves as executrix of the Roger Reeves estate. For the following reasons, we reverse and remand.

DISCUSSION OF THE RECORD

Before the couple's 1980 divorce, decedent Robert Roger Reeves, Jr., an attorney and prominent member of the community of Harrisonburg, Louisiana, had ten children by his first wife, Dorothy Dale: Dorothy Ann Reeves Faillace (Ann), Joan Reeves Lossin, Robert Roger Reeves (Bob), Mary Rebecca Reeves (Becky), John Cotton Reeves, Michael Reddick Reeves, Joseph McCleary Reeves, Sophie Sarita Reeves Holland (Sarita), Noah Blackstone Reeves, and Alma Roger Reeves Moss.

Not long after his divorce, Reeves met and began dating Jarrett Ganey Young, an acquaintance of decedent's daughter, Ann, who had recently separated from her husband. Roger and Jarrett were married on July 18, 1981, when Roger was sixty years of age, and Jarrett was thirty-eight.

After being married for approximately nine years, Roger Reeves was diagnosed with prostate cancer in 1990 from which he died on December 10, 1992, at age seventy-two. His statutory will dated September 16, 1992, left approximately one-half of his estate to Jarrett, including a lifetime usufruct over the children's ownership interest in Elmly Plantation. The remaining one-half of his estate was left to nine of his ten children. The will further named Jarrett as executrix and Lawrence Sandoz as the attorney for the succession.

One of the Reeves' children, Bob, was excluded from his father's will, leading him to file the instant suit to annul his father's will on March 15, 1993, alleging alternatively that the will was not properly executed and was a product of Jarrett Reeves' undue influence. A five day trial concerning the alleged undue influence was held in July 1995. Based on the evidence, the trial judge found that Jarrett Reeves had indeed exerted undue influence and rendered judgment nullifying the bequests to his widow. Jarrett appeals this determination of the trial court.

Jarrett Reeves' appeal assigns the following errors:

1. The trial judge erred and committed manifest error in admitting the testimony, over timely objection, of a psychiatrist who had never seen the testator that undue influence existed at the execution of the testament which invalidated the bequest to wife since his opinion was not a psychiatric diagnosis.

2. The trial judge was clearly wrong in relying on the testimony of a psychiatrist who had never examined testator, who based his opinion on subjective information received from two daughters that the personality of their father changed during eleven years of second marriage, which invalidated bequest to wife based on undue influence.

3. The trial judge was clearly wrong and committed manifest error in ignoring the consistent pattern of five wills and a codicil prepared and executed by Testator over a period of eleven years that established a plan to divide assets between wife and children.

4. The trial judge committed manifest error in ignoring the testimony of long-time business associates of Testator, who testified concerning the relationship between Testator and wife, including no change in the personality of Testator as opposed to relying on post-mortem psychological autopsy of psychiatrist who never saw Testator.

5. The trial judge was clearly wrong in concluding that the evidence of the psychiatrist and two daughters of Testator established "clear and convincing" evidence of undue influence as required by Article 1483 of the Civil Code.

6. The trial judge committed manifest error in declaring the bequests to wife invalid due to undue influence when the record contains no evidence from doctors who attended testator that he suffered from mental problems that rendered him susceptible to undue influence.

Jarrett Reeves' maintains that the trial court erred in finding that undue influence was proven by clear and convincing evidence. In particular, Jarrett Reeves points to testimony indicating that, at the time of the execution of the will, Roger Reeves appeared to be acting of his own volition and was able to properly execute a will. Appellant argues that in rendering an adverse judgment, the trial court incorrectly discounted the testimony of friends and business associates who had known the decedent both before and after his marriage to her, all of whom offered testimony in support of the testator's capacity.

In response to these charges, appellees remind us of the great deference to be accorded the trial court's findings of fact, which they suggest were adequately supported by the testimony of some of the children that their father had become increasingly isolated from them in latter years, and by a psychiatric autopsy performed by their retained expert, whose profile of decedent led him to conclude that decedent had indeed become vulnerable.

LAW

Present

Wills in Louisiana today may be voided on the authority of LOUISIANA CIVIL CODE Articles 1478 or 1479. Article 1478 provides for the nullification of wills upon grounds of fraud or duress.

> A donation *inter vivos* or *mortis causa* shall be declared null upon proof that it is the product of fraud or duress.

LA.CIV.CODE art. 1479, on the other hand, provides for the annulment of a donation *mortis causa* on the more subtle grounds of undue influence.

> A donation *inter vivos* or *mortis causa* shall be declared null upon proof that it is the product of influence by the donee or another person that so impaired the volition of the donor *as to substitute the volition of the donee or other person for the volition of the donor*. (Emphasis ours).

[handwritten margin note: Fraud, Duress Rule of will.]

There is precious little Louisiana jurisprudence on the topic of undue influence, as prior to the 1991 enactment Article 1479, such donations could not be annulled on this basis. Moreover, applying Article 1479 in pari materia with Article 1478 restated above is not without difficulty. Nonetheless, some insight may be drawn from the official Comment to LA.CIV.CODE art. 1479 and the experience of common law jurisdictions, who have long recognized the principle.

> (b) This Article, like the preceding Article, presumes a donor who has capacity. Obviously, if a donor lacks capacity, then the entire donation or will is invalid for that reason alone, and issues of fraud and undue influence are irrelevant. This Article intentionally does not use the word "undue" to describe the influence (although the word is intentionally used in the title of the Article and in two later Articles that refer to this Article), but instead defines the influence as being of such a nature that it destroys the free agency of the donor. No single definition of "undue influence" has been found acceptable in all of the relevant legal writings. The common-law rules concerning "undue influence", fraud, and duress are derived almost entirely from case law rather than statutes. Any number of definitions exist in court opinions and in instructions to juries, but the law clearly deals largely with subjective elements, making the term "undue influence" therefore very difficult to define. In the case law, the objective aspects of undue influence are generally veiled in secrecy, and the proof of undue influence is either largely or entirely circumstantial. By referring to "influence" that impaired the volition of the donor, this Article attempts to indicate that the character of the gift or testamentary disposition itself is not determinative of the issue, although it

may nonetheless be evidence on the issue. Moreover, everyone is more or less swayed by associations with other persons, so this Article attempts to describe the kind of influence that would cause the invalidity of a gift or disposition. Physical coercion and duress clearly fall within the proscription of the previous Article. The more subtle influences, such as creating resentment toward a natural object of a testator's bounty by false statements, may constitute the kind of influence that is reprobated by this Article, but will still call for evaluation by the trier of fact. Since the ways of influencing another person are infinite, the definition given in this Article is used in an attempt to place a limit on the kind of influence that is deemed offensive. Mere advice, or persuasion, or kindness and assistance, should not constitute influence that would destroy the free agency of a donor and substitute someone else's volition for his own.

(c) The Article intentionally defines the influence as being that of the donee or some other person in order to avoid a challenge based solely on the workings of the donor's own mind without pressure from someone else. It seems obvious that the influence has to be exercised with the object of procuring a particular gift or bequest. While the influence may be exerted by the donee himself, the Article covers the situation where the donee takes no part in the activities (and may even be ignorant of them), so long as some person does exercise control over the donor, presumably one who is interested in the fortunes of the donee.

(d) *It is implicit in this Article that the influence must be operative at the time of the execution of the inter vivos donation or testament.* Obviously, it should not be necessary that the acts themselves be done at that time, or that the person exercising the pressure be present then.

LA.CIV.CODE art. 1479 (Revision Comments b-d)(emphasis added).

History

Prior to the 1991 amendment, article 1492 was controlling with respect to allegations of undue influence. *Succession of Dowling*, 93-1902 (La.App. 4 Cir. 2/25/94); 633 So. 2d 846. That provision provided that "[p]roof is not admitted of the dispositions having been made through hatred, anger, suggestion or caption."

Giving deference to this language, this circuit had adopted the view that evidence of undue influence could only be presented to show testamentary incapacity, but not as an independent basis for nullifying a will. *Succession of Dowling*, 633 So. 2d 846, citing *inter alia*, *Guidry v. Hardy*, 254 So. 2d 675 (La.App. 3 Cir.1971), *writ denied*, 260 La. 454, 256 So. 2d 441 (1972). This view was not universally accepted, however, as other tribunals construed former Article 1492 to permit such evidence of undue influence to void wills, provided that it "must have been exercised upon the testator at the moment the will was executed, not before nor afterwards." *Texada v. Spence*, 166 La. 1020, 118 So. 120, 121 (1928). In accord, *Succession of Hamiter*, 519 So. 2d 341, 344 (La. App. 2 Cir.), *writ denied*, 521 So. 2d 1170 (La.1988).

Thus when Article 1492 was repealed by Act 788 of 1989 and later, Act 147 of 1990 it was well established that evidence of undue influence was admissible to prove testamentary incapacity, and at least some jurisprudence recognized it as grounds for nullifying a disposition if the influence occurred at the moment of making the disposition. *Succession of Dowling*, 633 So. 2d at 855.

However, this schism was effectively laid to rest by the addition of Article 1479, which is recognized to have created a new cause of action for nullifying a donation. *Succession of Dowling*, 633 So. 2d 846. "By adopting that article the legislature has specifically recognized the cause of undue influence, in addition to incapacity, as a separate basis for nullifying a testamentary disposition." *Succession of Dowling*, 633 So. 2d at 855.

Policy

Applying such an amorphous concept as "undue influence" is not made any easier by the high stakes involved, the absence of the testator, and society's heartfelt intent to care for the wishes of the fallen.

> Strong policy considerations are ... involved when testamentary capacity is disputed. As the court stated in *Kingsbury v. Whitaker*, 32 La.Ann. 1055, 36 Am.Rep. 278 (1880):

>> To wrest a man's property from the person to whom he has given it, and to divert it to others from whom he has desired to withhold it, is a most violent injustice, amounting to nothing less than post-mortem robbery, which no court should sanction, unless thoroughly satisfied ... that the testator was legally incapable of making a will." 32 La.Ann. 1055 at 1062-1063.

Succession of Lyons, 452 So. 2d 1161, 1165 (La.1984).

Thus, a will is strongly presumed to have intended the effects of its stated intentions when it complies with the legal formalities imposed by the law. "A party is presumed to have testamentary capacity, and the opponent bears the burden of defeating this presumption by putting forth clear and convincing evidence to the contrary. *Succession of Lyons*, 452 So. 2d 1161, 1166 (La.1984)." *Succession of Fletcher*, 94-1426 (La. App. 3 Cir. 4/5/95); 653 So. 2d 119, 121, *writ denied*, 95-1105 (La.6/16/95); 655 So. 2d 338. In accord, *Succession of Franz*, 232 La. 310, 94 So. 2d 270 (1957). To placate its unease, our legal regime imposes procedural safeguards to ensure that a testament indeed is enforced to reflect a testator's last will. For instance, those intending to have a will's terms disregarded for alleged want of capacity or "undue influence" are required to come forward not only with proof by a preponderance, but with clear and convincing evidence. LA.CIV.CODE art. 1483.

> Proof by "clear and convincing" evidence requires more than "preponderance of the evidence," the traditional measure of persuasion, but less than "beyond a reasonable doubt," the stringent criminal standard. To prove a matter by "clear and convincing" evidence means to demonstrate that the existence of a disputed fact is highly probable, that is, much more probable than its nonexistence. [Citations omitted].

Succession of Dowling, 633 So. 2d at 855. In accord, *Succession of Bartie*, 472 So. 2d 578 (La.1985); *Succession of Fletcher*, 653 So. 2d 119.

The strong policy considerations reiterated above in *Succession of Lyons*, 452 So. 2d 1161, remain applicable today, notwithstanding that at the time it was rendered, parties seeking to have a will voided were required to prove their case beyond a reasonable doubt, the same burden required to overcome the presumption of innocence in a criminal proceeding, whereas the law today only requires satisfaction of the lesser clear and convincing standard.

No one doubts testator Reeves' compliance with the formal requirements of will drafting. More importantly, though, there is an absence of evidence to suggest that decedent Reeves was anything but a fully capable man who loved both his surviving spouse and his children and who freely chose to whom and in what proportions he would leave his estate. Consequently, we hold that the trial court erred in concluding that the testator was adequately susceptible to being inordinately susceptible to manipulation by his wife of eleven years.

Trial Court Ruling

In its written reasons, the trial court concluded that the record contained clear and convincing evidence that the testator's will was the product of Jarrett Reeves' volition rather than his own. Observing that LA.CIV.CODE art. 1479 offers little instruction as to what factors suggest the presence or absence of "undue influence," the trial court relied upon the following expression of common law jurisprudence in its analysis:

> The elements that are set for in these common law cases have provided the court with substantial guidance in construing Article 1479 in the instant case.
> Most courts have listed four (4) elements as establishing a prima facie case of undue influence:
> **(1) Susceptibility**--a person who is susceptible of being unduly influenced by the person charged with exercising undue influence.
> **(2) Opportunity**--The opportunity of the alleged influencer to exercise such influence on the testator.
> **(3) Disposition**--a disposition--a disposition on the part of the alleged influencer to influence the testator for the purpose of procuring an improper favor either for himself or another.
> **(4) Coveted Result**--a result caused by, or the effect of, such undue influence.

After listing these four factors, the trial court concluded that Ms. Jarrett Reeves had exerted undue influence which voided the decedent's most recent will. Its finding was based almost exclusively on the opinion of psychiatrist, Dr. George Seiden, a forensic psychiatrist presented as an expert by the Reeves children. In particular, the trial court found that Dr. Seiden's psychiatric testimony supported a finding that decedent was susceptible to undue influence due to his sexual dependency upon Jarrett Reeves and his fear of abandonment. Dr. Seiden opined that Roger Reeves was susceptible to influence due to his extreme need for love and sexual intercourse and, additionally, his need for companionship and his fear of being alone.

To support his conclusion, Dr. Seiden alluded to Roger's self-proclaimed need for intimacy with a woman, as testified to by family and friends, suggested that Roger was particularly vulnerable to the presence of a woman, particularly the type of woman Dr. Seiden characterized as "a rescuing, supportive woman who [would] pretty much [give Roger] what he wanted" because, although Roger offered "an appearance of confidence and assertiveness, but underneath [he had] ... a sense of emptiness and dependency."

Dr. Seiden suggested that decedent's relationship with Jarrett fit the description:

Q: Was he dependent upon Jarrett Reeves for love and sex?

A: Yes, he was.

Q: Would you tell the Court, please, what was the level of Roger Reeves' dependence?

A: It was extreme, to the point that--that he at times felt that he could not live without it.

To support his conclusion, Dr. Seiden alluded to Roger's reaction on a few occasions when he and Jarrett had disagreements (i.e. distraught, closed off from others, exhibited suicidal tendencies, etc.).

OPINION

The weight of the evidence and the public policies articulated above in *Succession of Lyons*, 452 So. 2d 1161, compels us to reverse the judgment of the trial court.

I.

Initially, we observe that Ms. Jarrett Reeves was the testator's wife of eleven years, and while we are unable to categorically state that the charge of undue influence can never be leveled against a surviving spouse who is the main beneficiary of a testament by her spouse of eleven years, we do believe that a surviving spouse is not the intended target of Article 1479. *Compare, e.g., Estate of Larsen*, 7 Wis.2d 263, 96 N.W.2d 489 (1959) (Wisconsin Supreme Court: elderly widow showing signs of senility induced to transfer shares of stock to guardians, who later failed to contact her family in regards to her death and misstated size of estate in order to gain control of it). This is a classic case of undue influence in which the deceased, affectionately referred to as "Aunt Minnie," was prevailed upon to disinherit the "natural object of her bounty" in favor of more distant relatives.

The two closest relationships that exist between persons are the relationship of parent to child and that of husband and wife. Either a spouse or a child is clearly a "natural object of a testator's bounty." Both the comments to LA.CIV.CODE art. 1479 and the jurisprudence which we have reviewed suggests that the purpose of legislation such as Article 1479 is to protect the "natural object of a testator's bounty" from being cheated out of an inheritance by a person who, in the normal course of events, would have little or no expectation of inheritance but who, by use of devious means, manages to convince the testator to do that which in his heart of hearts he did not will or intend.

In a case such as *Estate of Larsen*, the elements relied upon by the trial court in the present case, i.e., susceptibility, opportunity, disposition, and coveted results are meaningful and relevant and lead to a reasonable and desired result.

In a case such as the present case, however, where a spouse is the recipient of the testator's bounty, these elements are almost totally meaningless in determining whether a person might have exerted undue influence.

> **(1) Susceptibility**--it is in the nature of a matrimonial relationship that the spouses are mutually bound to one another and should be responsive to the needs, desires and opinions of one another. A spouse is required by the nature of the relationship to be susceptible and sensitive to the desires of his or her mate. In a case such as *Larsen* where "Aunt Minnie" was staying with more distant relatives, susceptibility would be a meaningful concept. In a marital situation, the element of susceptibility is inherent in the relationship and has no bearing on the issue of use of undue influence.
>
> **(2) Opportunity**--people who live together as man and wife see each other daily, discuss all manner of business and personal relationships and have unlimited opportunity to influence one another. In a classic case such as *Larsen*, the opportunity of the outsider to influence the person becomes a very relevant inquiry when the person who inherits has little or no natural claim. In the case of a spouse, the existence of an opportunity to influence once again is inherent in the relationship, not contra bones mores, and is thus not relevant in determining undue influence.
>
> **(3) Disposition**--the element of disposition requires that the alleged influencer must have a disposition to procure "an improper favor" for himself or another. We would shake the bedrock of matrimonial law if we were to rule that the disposition of one's property to a spouse, to provide for the surviving spouse after the donor's death is in any way an "improper favor." Once again we note that such an inquiry would be meaningful in a classic case where the people who seem intent upon divesting the testatrix do not comprise the "natural object of a testator's bounty." But in the case of a spouse, this position would not be a meaningful inquiry as being cared for after the death of a spouse is not an "improper favor.
>
> **(4) Coveted result**--this, of course, begs the question as without the result there would be no inquiry in the first place.

A review of these elements suggests that they are meaningful in a case where property is left to a person when the natural object of a testator's bounty is passed over in favor of strangers or persons of much lower claims to consideration. What then would be the proper inquiry as to undue influence on the part of a spouse? Several come to mind: physical abuse, emotional abuse, fraud, deceit, or criminal conduct. Our review of the record suggests that none of these elements are present in this case.

We are told in the trial court's reasons for judgment that the undue influence of the spouse was that she was able to exploit the decedent's sexual dependency and fear of abandonment because of his extreme need for love and sexual intercourse and additionally, his need for companionship and his fear of being alone. A moment's reflection suggests that love, companionship and intimacy are the primary reasons that people marry, ergo, the marital imperatives.

The court would note that had Mrs. Reeves been a paramour rather than a wife of eleven years, the court below might have been correct in finding that the need of the testator for love, companionship and sexual intimacy might have formed a basis for undue influence which might have been a solid ground for invalidating the will. In the case of a spouse, this is not so. The need for love, companionship and intimacy are among the foremost reasons for marriage. Each spouse owes these things reciprocally to one another. Either may and should expect love, intimacy and companionship and either might well be expected to be generous in making donations, either *mortis causa* or *inter vivos*, to the other.

In the case before us, we are told that because of his need for love, companionship and sexual intimacy, the testator left his property to the person who gave these things to him--his wife of eleven years. We are told that if he had not been willing to include her in the will, she might have withheld the love, intimacy and companionship upon which he was so dependent. Thus, her desire to be included in the will, coupled with her ever-present ability to withhold intimacy, constituted a force strong enough to substitute her volition for his.

On public policy grounds, we decline to find these grounds adequate for reversing the stated will of the testator. Rather, we hold that the granting or withholding of love, companionship and intimacy are matters reserved to the good judgment of the member of the marriage unit; that either spouse is free at any time to ask for consideration on the part of the other, including the ability to ask for gifts, donations or inclusion in the will; and that ground rules for the granting or withholding of intimacy are best provided by the married couple rather than the civil courts. To be more specific, we hold that the granting or withholding of love, companionship and intimacy, i.e., the marriage imperatives, are matters reserved to the married couple and shall not, standing alone, serve to invalidate a will.

II.

Marital status is the primary reason that we feel compelled to reverse the judgment of the trial court. However, it is not the only reason.

Our review of the record shows that Dr. Seiden's opinions were based upon an incomplete picture of Mr. Reeves' personality, being derived not from his having conferred with the testator, but rather from the recollections of a few of his children. We find this evidence, while admissible, unequal to the task of dismantling the clear intent of the testator, particularly given the overwhelming weight of evidence, specifically the disinterested opinions of Mr. Reeves' personal physicians and the persons in whose presence the will was prepared. According to all of these persons who, unlike Dr. Seiden actually knew Mr. Reeves and not his caricature, Mr. Reeves retained his faculties to the very end of his life and prepared and signed the will in the absence of the accused meddler.

Ms. Muriel Davis, Mr. Reeves' counselor during his life, expressed her opinions that decedent did not feel as though he was overly susceptible to the domination of women and that the couple had an unexceptional second marriage. Moreover, when asked point-blank, Ms. Davis said she saw no undue influence. Similarly, Attorney Lloyd Love, a close friend of decedent's for some fifty years, saw nothing to suggest other than an "excellent" marital relationship, and with his own eyes saw that decedent, far from being vulnerable in his financial dealings, "handled his own business," even after his marriage to Jarrett. The disinterested and firsthand testimony of Davis and Love was buttressed by the testimony of Bob Alexander, the manager of the bank next to decedent's law office, who indicated that his fellow board member was always alert, active, and well-informed at Catahoula Bank board meetings, and by Barry Maxwell of another bank from whom decedent borrowed money in order to pay a debt to decedent's first wife. According to Maxwell, decedent very clearly laid out his financial status and, more importantly, left no question but that Jarrett would be in charge of his estate after his demise. Even by the deferential standards of appellate review, we conclude that this overwhelming evidence clearly overcame the weight of evidence presented by Bob and the other children.

In *Succession of Lyons*, 452 So. 2d 1161, the court of appeal reversed the trial court's finding a will invalid. It differed with the trial court "not on credibility, but on the sufficiency of the evidence" and concluded that the trial court incorrectly found that the will's opponents had overcome the presumption of statutory capacity by the requisite measure.

We do likewise today, thus giving force to the articulated wishes of the testator.

III.

Thus, we reverse the judgment of the trial court on grounds of both law and evidence.

DISPOSITION

Because of the trial court's ruling, it was not necessary for the trial court to consider the merits of Bob Reeves' alternate contention, that the will contained bequests to Jarrett that were either impossible, illegal or immoral. Bob Reeves had filed an amended petition in which he sought not only a reduction of any excessive donation above the forced portion due free and clear of any usufruct in favor of Jarrett Reeves, but also sought a judgment declaring that his father's will contained certain impossible, illegal, or immoral conditions pursuant to LA.CIV.CODE art. 1519.

In view of our reversal of the trial court on the issue of undue influence, a remand is in order so that the trial court may consider the alternate grounds of relief raised by Bob Reeves, after additional briefing by the parties, including Jarrett and the other heirs who have yet to address them.

DECREE

For the foregoing reasons, the judgment of the trial court is reversed and this case is remanded. Costs of these proceedings to be determined following trial on the merits.

REVERSED AND REMANDED.

DOUCET, C.J., concurs in the result.

WOODARD, J., concurs and assigns written reasons.

AMY and YELVERTON, JJ. dissent and assigns reasons.

*　　*　　*

AMY, Judge, dissenting.

I respectfully disagree with the majority decision. In my view, a spouse's manipulation of "the marital imperatives" in an effort to create "resentment toward a natural object of [the] testator's bounty" was contemplated by our legislature when enacting LA.CIV.CODE art. 1479. Our codal provisions recognize and respect the intimacy shared between a husband and wife. A person challenging a donation *mortis causa* because of undue influence is required to prove his or her claim by the higher burden of proof, proof by clear and convincing evidence, unless the wrongdoer shares a relationship of confidence with the testator and is not "related to the donor by affinity, consanguinity or adoption." LA.CIV.CODE art. 1483. As such, any further differential treatment on account of public policy considerations is unwarranted. I believe that the legislature's recognition of the differential burden of proof where the wrongdoer is "related to the donor by affinity, consanguinity or adoption" is a clear expression that the public policy considerations behind LA.CIV.CODE art. 1479 were intended to include claims such as that brought in the instant case.

The trial court, after hearing extensive testimony, found that Jarrett Reeves had exerted undue influence over her husband so that her volition was substituted for his own, making the bequests to her in his will nullities pursuant to LA.CIV.CODE 1479. In particular, the trial court found that Dr. Seiden's psychiatric testimony supported a finding that the decedent was susceptible to undue influence due to his sexual dependency upon Jarrett Reeves and his fear of abandonment. Next, the trial court found that there was opportunity to unduly influence the decedent as he and his second wife lived alone and, further, there was evidence indicating that she sought to isolate him by limiting contact with his children. With regard to Jarrett Reeves' disposition, the trial court once again turned to the testimony of Dr. Seiden who opined that "Jarrett Reeves was a strong and opinionated individual with a high and sometimes violent temper who used threats of abandonment to influence Roger Reeves' financial decision making." The trial court also considered Dr. Seiden's opinion that "Jarrett Reeves was clearly preoccupied with obtaining Roger Reeves' assets and that she took pains to exert control over the management of those assets by involving herself repeatedly in decisions about finance." The trial court stated that "[t]he evidence introduced at trial clearly shows that Dr. Seiden's opinions were true."

Additionally, the record reveals that Jarrett Reeves routinely kept a diary during the second half of her marriage to Leo Young and during the eleven years she was married to Roger Reeves. At trial there was much speculation as to what the eight to ten diaries that Jarrett Reeves burned only five days before the instant suit was filed would have revealed. Jarrett testified that she did not destroy the diaries to avoid their contents being revealed in court, but instead because she was "bringing a phase of [her] life to a closure." Jarrett further testified that she had no idea suit would be filed and it was a mere coincidence that she burned the diaries shortly before Bob Reeves filed suit to annul the will. However, the trial court was not convinced given the fact that two of the Reeves children contacted the attorney for the succession, to discuss their displeasure and possibility of a suit being filed, prior to the destruction of the diaries. Accordingly, the trial court applied the "theory of spoliation of evidence" which provides for the presumption that the destroyed evidence contained information detrimental to the party who destroyed the evidence unless such destruction is adequately explained. *Randolph v. General Motors* Corp., 93-1983 (La.App. 1 Cir. 11/10/94); 646 So. 2d 1019, *writ denied*, 95-0194 (La.3/17/95); 651 So. 2d 276;

Kammerer v. Sewerage & Water Bd. of New Orleans, 93-1232 (La.App. 4 Cir. 3/15/94); 633 So. 2d 1357, *writ denied*, 94-0948 (La.7/1/94); 639 So. 2d 1163.

Also of particular importance to the trial court were several excerpts from Jarrett Reeves' diary which had been misplaced by the Appellant and which the trial court found "disclosed Jarrett Reeves' intent to devise a plan to acquire Roger Reeves' assets, to keep John Reeves out of his father's law practice and to gain ownership of the Harrisonburg home." These excerpts, which were written in 1984, were found in a classroom at Northeastern University where Jarrett Reeves was attending college. These excerpts were found, turned over to Roger Reeves' son, Joe, and kept without the knowledge of Jarrett Reeves. They were entered into evidence and were read into the record by the Appellant.

The trial judge, in his written reasons, stated: "The contents of these fragmented entries that were accidentally left by Jarrett Reeves in a Northeast Louisiana University classroom and the destruction and refusal to produce the vast preponderance of the diaries is very detrimental to the contentions of Jarrett Reeves." It is abundantly clear that the trial judge placed great weight on these expressions of Jarrett's thoughts, and that he found Jarrett's version of the relationship she shared with her husband to be less credible than that presented by the plaintiff.

The majority opinion, citing *Succession of Lyons*, 452 So. 2d 1161 (La.1984), concludes that Bob Reeves did not overcome the presumption of statutory capacity by the requisite measure. However, testamentary capacity of Roger Reeves, a separate basis for nullifying a testamentary disposition, is not presently under review. While Roger Reeves' business associates testified that Jarrett was not present during negotiations for farm leases or bank loans, this does not necessitate a finding that Jarrett's influence was not present during these negotiations. As noted by Dr. Seiden, Jarrett's physical presence was not necessary. He testified that in areas that concerned the children or Roger's assets, Jarrett's influence was present throughout their eleven-year marriage. From the record, it appears that the witnesses in question did not have a familiarity with Roger Reeves on a personal basis, as did several other witnesses, whose testimony the trial judge accepted, who testified as to Roger and Jarrett's interaction at home, around the children, and any change in Roger's personality. Also, a large amount of evidence presented by the defense was directed toward Roger's mental capacity at the time the will was executed rather than the absence of any undue influence. As discussed previously, testamentary capacity is a separate and distinct issue. Furthermore, even with the heightened burden of proof, the official comments to LA.CIV.CODE 1479 recognize that "the objective aspects of undue influence are generally veiled in secrecy, and the proof of undue influence is either largely or entirely circumstantial."

The testimony of the Reeves' children, their spouses, and several longtime friends revealed that, after his marriage to Jarrett, they observed marked, and unexpected, changes in Roger's personality when interacting with his children. Some examples include: (1) the children had to call for permission before coming over to visit with their father; (2) Bob was required to visit his father at the law office, and was never allowed to visit when Jarrett was present; and, (3) the usual weekday family lunches at the "Granny House" were canceled, even at times Jarrett was away at work.

Also of note was the absolute omission of Bob Reeves from his father's will. It was undisputed at trial that Roger Reeves loved all of his ten children throughout the entire span of his life, and that Jarrett Reeves had problems with Bob and that she did not allow Bob to be around when she was present. There was testimony presented to illustrate Roger's disenchantment with Bob due to Bob's difficulty in farming Elmly and his alignment with his mother, Dorothy Dale, during litigation stemming from Roger Reeves' marriage to Dorothy. However, even accepting the above facts as true, throughout this same period of time, evidence was presented that indicated that Roger Reeves still loved his son and that his absence was because of Jarrett. Roger continued to seek ways to clandestinely preserve Bob's presence in his life. For example, Roger hired Bob to plant trees on sixty acres of Elmly Plantation in 1990, a year after Bob's farm lease was terminated and even longer after Bob was prohibited from visiting Elmly or being around Jarrett. More importantly, in hiring Bob to plant the trees, Roger was forced to do so without Jarrett's knowledge and required receipt and payment be made in the name of Roger Carter so that Jarrett would not find out. Sarita, Roger's daughter, testified that Roger admitted that this was necessary because Jarrett would not let him hire Bob. Additionally, before Bob's lease to farm Elmly was canceled, Dennis Dosher, Roger Reeves' son-in-law, testified that Roger Reeves approached him about farming Elmly with Bob in hopes that Jarrett would be pacified. Dennis testified that Roger told him that "Jarrett wanted to get rid of Bob and [he] was trying to figure out some way to keep Bob on Elmly."

Additionally, Dr. Seiden described Jarrett's behavioral pattern as "random intermittent punishment" with her goals being control of Roger's financial assets and interaction with his children, and, most importantly, Dr. Seiden noted Jarrett's pattern of alienating or isolating Roger from his children. Considering the evidence of the children and others close to the decedent, as well as the overwhelming testimony of the forensic psychiatrist, Dr. Seiden, I conclude that the trial court was not manifestly erroneous in finding that the evidence presented was sufficient to support the claim that the bequests to Jarrett resulted from her undue influence over Roger before his death.

Accordingly, I respectfully dissent.

YELVERTON, Judge, dissenting.

I dissent for the reasons expressed by Judge Amy. I write separately to emphasize my disagreement with the statement in the majority opinion that "a surviving spouse is not the intended target of Article 1479." I think the law does not exclude anyone as a potential undue influencer--certainly not second spouses, and particularly as in this case not a younger, second spouse with six children of her own.

Article 1479 was introduced by House Bill 882 of 1991. The minutes of the House Civil Law and Procedure Committee meeting on May 21, 1991, reveal that "Mr. Max Nathan, representing the Louisiana State Law Institute ... stated that this bill was in response to the change in the law on forced heirship last year." The relationship between this bill and the eventual nigh-abolition of forced heirship has been studied by scholars. I believe that one of the legislative concerns in creating Article 1479 was "the protection of the donor's family, the 'natural objects of his bounty,' from the harsh effects of disinheritance." *See* Comment, *Louisiana's New Law on Capacity to Make and Receive Donations: "Unduly Influenced" By The Common Law?* 67 Tul.L.Rev. 183, 184 (1992).

The virtual abolition of forced heirship was a statement of preference for the common law freedom of testation. With forced heirship gone, actions such as undue influence are essentially the only means left to protect the donor and his family. The legislature adopted a common law remedy in providing for undue influence. In an oral presentation made at Loyola University School of Law Forced Heirship Symposium on January 31, 1997, published in 43

Loy.L.Rev. 43, 48, Professor Katherine Spaht put it this way: "Once forced heirship was eliminated for most children, which is what we have, the legislature understood that to avoid the possibility of legalized theft, we would have to do as our opponents of forced heirship had long cried--that is, become like the other forty-nine states, permitting the litigation of undue influence." We should look to the common law for guidance in applying Article 1479. The trial judge did that in deciding this case.

The trial court conducted a five-day trial, heard 20 witnesses, evaluated the evidence and the credibility of witnesses, and found clear and convincing proof of undue influence. The trial court gave thoughtful and scholarly reasons for judgment. It is our duty to affirm this purely factual, reasonable determination.

NOTE

The *Reeves* case elicited a great deal of controversy within the legal community. Although the trial court, after review of the facts, concluded that the second wife of the decedent had exerted undue influence, resulting in the exclusion of testator's son from the will, the appellate court disagreed. It was not so much the conclusion which sparked the controversy, but the statement by the appellate court that "we do believe that a surviving spouse is not the intended target of Article 1470." *Reeves*, 704 So. 2d at 258. The dissent, in its review of legislative history, reflects the concern of many of the critics. If the legislature, in passing article 1479, was somewhat motivated by the fact that adult children were no longer protected as forced heirs against disinherison, would the exclusion of a second spouse, not the parent of those children, from the protection of article 1479 make sense? Should marriage to the testator insulate the surviving spouse from scrutiny? After there has been a remarriage, who do you suppose is the most likely candidate to profit when children of a prior marriage are excluded by a testator?

Although the Louisiana Supreme Court granted a writ in this case, the court never had an opportunity to render a decision as the case was settled prior thereto.

PROBLEM

Consider the following facts from the *Succession of Hamiter*, 519 So. 2d 341 (La. App. 2nd Cir. 1988). The *Hamiter* case was decided based on prior law, thus was not afforded the use of present article 1479. It was referred to numerous times in the discussion of adoption of the new articles and may have inspired some of the changes.

Joe B. Hamiter, former Chief Justice of the Louisiana Supreme Court, was born in 1899. He retired from the court in 1971. In 1972, he broke his hip and, from that time forward, had to use either a walker or a wheelchair. In addition to that problem, Justice Hamiter suffered from a restricted blood flow to the brain. In 1981, he became heartbroken when his wife, whom he dearly loved, and his brother, to whom he was very close, both died.

Between 1981 and his suicide in 1986, Hamiter wrote several wills. In the first will, written in 1982, he left several particular legacies, one to Sue Brown, his sister-in-law, and another to his two nieces, and also named the Boy Scouts of America as his residuary legatee.

His second will, written later in 1981, was the same, except he named as residuary legatee, a foundation he created to benefit the Boy Scouts.

In 1983, Hamiter met Roxanne Cox through his sister-in-law, Mrs. Sue Brown. Mrs. Cox helped manage Hamiter's financial affairs. Concerned about possible abuse of their uncle's affairs, Hamiter's two nieces instituted interdiction proceedings which culminated in an agreement to have Hamiter's accountant monitor his checking account and approve all expenditures over $350. Although Hamiter was upset by the interdiction attempt, he was not present at its settlement, but was represented by Mrs. Cox. A third will was written at this time. Mrs. Cox was left part of a tract of land previously left to another, $100,000 was left to the Boy Scouts in trust, and Mrs. Brown was named residuary legatee.

Testimony established that Mrs. Cox became the "dominant force" in the household, hiring and firing Hamiter's sitters and even instructing the sitters as to how much medicine Hamiter should receive. On one occasion, she was heard to say that the Boy Scouts were getting too much. On another occasion, Mrs. Cox told Hamiter that his nieces had stolen bonds from him, an allegation which was not substantiated. During her time with Hamiter, Mrs. Cox was given a credit card with her name on it, which was billed to Justice Hamiter. Mrs. Cox's son used the credit card on trips to Las Vegas and New York. Mrs. Cox also received a money order of $50,000 from Hamiter and another gift of $25,000.

Justice Hamiter's final will was written in 1985. Evidence indicated Mrs. Cox had made arrangements for its preparation by the attorney, and had knelt at the side of Hamiter at the time of its reading in the attorney's office. Although excluded from the room at the time of the signing of the will, Mrs. Cox waited outside. This last will excluded the two nieces, and the Boy Scouts. Mrs. Brown remained a particular legatee. Karin Adams, a friend of Mrs. Cox whom Hamiter had met only two months before executing the will, was left a legacy of twenty acres of land. Mrs. Cox was left a number of individual legacies and was named residuary legatee.

Medical evidence was admitted showing that Hamiter had a chronic organic brain syndrome, "secondary to impaired blood flow to his brain and several prior strokes," rendering him susceptible to "outside influences."

How might Hamiter's nieces attack the will or wills under present law? What about the Boy Scouts? Which wills would each prefer to see prevail? On what theory would each prevail?

For further reference, *see* Laurie Dearman Clark, Comment, *Louisiana's New Law on Capacity to Make and Receive Donations: "Unduly Influenced" by the Common Law*, 67 Tul. L. Rev. 183 (1992); James Dalferes, *Undue Influence, Interdiction and Other New Means to Annul Wills & Donations in Louisiana*, 40 La. B.J. 170 (1992); and Julia Cowan Spear, Comment, *Undue Influence in Louisiana: What It Was, What It Is, What It Might Be*, 43 Loy.L. Rev. 443 (1997).

Introduction

The concept of forced heirship provides that a portion of the patrimony of persons survived by forced heirs is reserved for those heirs. La. C.C. 1495 sets forth the reserved portion as one-fourth if one forced heir survives and one-half if more than one forced heir survives the decedent. The individual forced heir's amount is referred to as his *legitime*. The remainder, after reserving the forced portion, is disposable and may be freely alienated. La. C.C. 1495 clearly pronounces that no donation, whether *inter vivos* or *mortis causa*, may exceed the disposable portion. Gifts given during the last three years of the decedent's life, even to non-forced heirs, are included in calculating the mass estate, *see* La. C.C. 1505, upon which the percentages provided for in La. C.C. 1495 are applied.

The following article provides a background of the sources of the concept of forced heirship, its changes through the years, the current "rules," and the political arena that created them. Use it as guide as you explore the intricate web of forced heirship illustrated by the materials in this chapter.

THE CHANGING FACE OF FORCED HEIRSHIP:
A NEW LOUISIANA CREATION *
by
Kathryn Venturatos Lorio**
[Reprinted with permission]

Forced heirship, as contemplated by the drafters of the LOUISIANA CIVIL CODE of 1870, is no longer part of Louisiana law. It has been replaced by a unique creation, having some semblance to the maintenance laws prevalent in the British Commonwealth countries, yet resembling the succession laws of civilian jurisdictions in its retention of a fixed percentage for the minors and disabled children granted protection from disinheritance. Interestingly, and presumably unconsciously, the Louisiana legislature has now provided a system for Louisiana which resembles that of former Soviet law.[1] An examination of the history of forced heirship in

---

* This article was originally printed in LOUISIANA: MICROCOSM OF A MIXED JURISDICTION (Vernon Valentine Palmer ed.) Carolina Academic Press, 1999.

** Leon Sarpy Professor of Law, Loyola University School of Law, New Orleans. The author gratefully acknowledges the research assistance of Bernadine Lenahan, made possible by the support of the Alfred J. Bonomo, Sr. Family and the Rosaria Sarah LaNasa Memorial Scholarship fund and to Professor Cynthia Samuel, W.R. Irby Professor of Law, Tulane University for reviewing a preliminary draft of this manuscript.

[1] Civ. Code art. 532 (Soviet Civil Legislation, by Whitmore Gray ed. 1965) (Russia), provided in part:

Louisiana may help in understanding the evolution of this distinctive creation loosely referred to today in Louisiana as "forced heirship."

Sources of Forced Heirship

Forced heirship, as originally adopted in Louisiana, was basically a mixture of two previously-existing systems, Roman law and the customary German law of the tribes that later conquered Rome.[2]

Early Roman Law, as promulgated in the Twelve Tables, provided for unrestricted freedom of testation[3] by the father (*paterfamilias*) who was the absolute master of the family (*patria potestas*).[4] This absolute power of the father to donate was eventually tempered in an effort to protect two of the most important institutions of the Roman law - the family or *familia* as an organization and the continuity of the *sacra*, or worship of household gods.[5] So important were the *familia* and the *sacra* that rules began to develop to insure that an heir would be instituted for the purpose of carrying on both institutions.[6] Thus, the first wills were designed

---

In the case of statutory inheritance, the following are heirs with equal shares:

First: children (including adopted children), spouse and parents (adoptive parents) of the decedent, as well as a child of the decedent born after his death.

Second: brothers and sisters of the decedent, and his paternal and maternal grandfathers and grandmothers.

Heirs of the second class have a statutory right to inherit only in the absence of heirs of the first class, or if the heirs of the first class fail to accept or if all heirs of the first class have been deprived by will of the right to inherit.

Statutory heirs include persons unable to work who were dependent upon the decedent for not less than one year prior to his death. If there are other heirs, such persons inherit equally with heirs of the class which receives the inheritance.

Grandchildren and great-grandchildren of the decedent are statutory heirs if their parent who would have been an heir is no longer alive at the time of the opening of the succession; they take by equal portions the statutory share which would have been due their deceased parent.

Civ. Code art. 535 (Soviet Civil Legislation ed. by Whitmore Gray 1965) (Russia), provided in part:

Minor children (including adopted children) of the decedent inherit no less than 2/3 of their statutory share regardless of the contents of the decedent's will (compulsory share), as do any of the following who are unable to work: decedent's children, spouse, parents (adoptive parents) and those dependent on him.

[2] Michael P. Porter, *Forced Heirs, the Legitime, and Loss of the Legitime in Louisiana*, 37 Tul. L. Rev. 710, 710 (1963).

[3] No matter in what way the head of a household may dispose of his estate, and appoint heirs to the same, or guardians; it shall have the force and effect of law.

Id. at 711, *citing*, Twelve Tables, 5.1, *in* 1 Civil Law 66 (S.P. Scott trans., 1932); *See also* Aubry & Rau, 3 Civil Law Translations 187, § 678 (Carlos E. Lazarus trans., West 1969).

[4] Joseph Dainow, *The Early Sources of Forced Heirship: Its History in Texas and Louisiana*, 4 La. L. Rev. 42, 43 (1941).

[5] *Id.*

[6] Porter, *supra* note 2, at 711.

with the purpose of guaranteeing that the heirs be protected, rather than affording the *paterfamilias* a mechanism for excluding his children from inheriting.[7]

Near the end of the Roman Republic in approximately the second century B.C.,[8] the remedy of the *querela inofficiosi testamenti* arose, which allowed an heir who was not adequately provided for by will the opportunity to claim a legitimate portion or *legitime*.[9] The rationale for relief for the heir was that the testator must have been insane to have excluded the heir from receiving a reasonable portion of his estate.[10] Around 40 B.C., the *Lex Falcidia* set the amount which could be claimed at one-fourth of the intestate portion.[11] Justinian made some changes to the concept by increasing the portion to one-third if there were four or fewer children and to one-half if there were five or more children.[12] Additionally, Justinian provided the first complete compilation of the legal grounds of disinherison, allowing a testator to exclude a child from inheritance for certain specified causes.[13]

The main concern of the Roman system was that of duty of maintenance of family members,[14] rather than preservation of family property. Thus, the *legitime* of Roman law was levied against all property,[15] not just immovables. Consistent with the system which emphasized individual ownership,[16] the claimant asserted his right, not as an heir of the succession, but as an individual against the beneficiaries of the decedent's property,[17] rendering the *legitime* a right *pars bonorum*, rather than *pars heriditatis*.[18] In addition to the Roman influence, the tradition of the Germanic tribes which conquered Rome contributed to the original version of forced heirship in Louisiana. Among the Germanic tribes, ownership of land was a family matter in which that ownership was held by the association of the family, or *sib*.[19] In order to preserve family estates, the protection of a reserve for descendants, ascendants, and collaterals arose.[20] The only property included in this protection for relatives was that property gained through succession

---

[7] Dainow, *supra* note 4, at 44.

[8] *Id.*

[9] 3 Marcel Planiol, Civil Law Treatise § 3054 (La State Law Institution trans., 1959).

[10] William W. Buckland, A TEXTBOOK OF ROMAN LAW FROM AUGUSTUS TO JUSTINIAN 128, 327 (2d ed. 1932); *See* The Enactments of Justianian: The Digest or Pandects 5.2.2, *in* 3 Civil Law 2 (S.P. Scott trans., 1932).

[11] Porter, *supra* note 2, at 712; Andrew Borkowski, Textbook on Roman Law 123, § 8.6.3 (1994); William W. Buckland, A MANUAL OF ROMAN PRIVATE LAW 79, 312, § 80 (2d ed. 1981); *See also* Institutes of Gaius 2.227, *in* 1 Civil Law 142 (S.P. Scott trans., 1932); Ulpian 24.32, *in* 1 Civil Law 249 (S.P. Scott trans., 1932); The Digest of Pandects 35.2.1, Concerning the Falcidian Law, *in* 8 Civil Law 1-41 (S.P. Scott trans. 1932); Code of Our Lord the most Holy Emperor Justinian 3.28.31, *in* 12 Civil Law 299 (S.P. Scott trans., 1932).

[12] Dainow, *supra* note 4, at 49.

[13] Porter, *supra* note 2, at 713.

[14] Joseph Dainow, *Forced Heirship in French Law*, 2 La. L. Rev. 669, 671 (1940).

[15] Porter, *supra* note 2, at 714.

[16] Gerald LeVan, Alternatives to Forced Heirship, 52 Tul. L. Rev. 29, 31 (1977).

[17] Dainow, *supra* note 14, at 671.

[18] Planiol, *supra* note 9, § 3054.

[19] LeVan, *supra* note 16, at 31.

[20] Planiol, *supra* note 9, § 3055.

(*propres*).[21]   So strong was the concept of retaining family control of property that in cases in which there were no descendants to inherit, the collaterals inherited, although limited to the property in the estate which was derived from their branch of the family.[22]   Limited to testamentary dispositions, this protection did not extend to donations inter vivos made by the decedent.[23]   The fraction of the reserve was four-fifths (*reserve des quatre quint des propres*) and the claim for such a fraction could only be brought by those with the status of heir, thus rendering the right *pars heriditatis*.[24]

By the thirteenth century, the law of southern France, that of the Romans, or *les pays de droit ecrit*, became mixed with that of the north, or *les pays de droit coutumier*,[25] resulting in the Custom of Paris. The customary *legitime* or *legitime* coutumier carried with it the idea that a father should provide for his children and if the reserve did not provide an adequate amount to take care of the child's welfare, then the child was entitled to claim his *legitime coutumier*.[26]   Originally, the amount was set by a judge at what was deemed to be sufficient for the heir to live reasonably.[27]

The customary *legitime* took on some of the aspects of the Roman law but altered the Roman concept to the extent that the claim became available only to the decedent's descendants and was considered a right to which an heir to the succession was entitled, thus rendering it *pars hereditatis*.[28]   It came to be calculated at a fixed amount of one-half of the intestate part[29] which could be imposed on acquets and movables, as well as inherited immovables.[30] Additionally, the protection was afforded for donations inter vivos, as well as mortis causa.[31]   This combination, which became Article 298 of the Custom of Paris,[32] was referred to as the *légitime* of customary law and, as a supplement to the *réserve*,[33] could only be claimed if the *réserve* was inadequate.[34]

The influence of Spanish rule during the latter part of the eighteenth century also affected the Louisiana law of forced heirship.[35]   The Louisiana Digest of 1808 adopted the Spanish laws on the *legitime*, allowing for a disposable portion which did not exceed one-fifth of the

---

[21] *Id.*

[22] Porter, *supra* note 2, at 714.

[23] Planiol, *supra* note 9, § 3055.

[24] *Id.*

[25] Porter, *supra* note 2, at 715.

[26] *Id.*

[27] *Id.*; J. Brissaud, A History of French Private Law, 3 Continental Legal History Series 743, § 516 (1912).

[28] Planiol, *supra* note 9, § 3055.

[29] Porter, *supra* note 2, at 715; Planiol, *supra* note 9, § 3055.

[30] Aubry & Rau, *supra* note 3, at § 678; Porter, *supra* note 2, at 715.

[31] Porter, *supra* note 2, at 715; Aubry & Rau, *supra* note 3, at § 678; Planiol, *supra* note 9, § 3055; Brissaud, *supra* note 27, at 753.

[32] Porter, *supra* note 2, at 715.

[33] Dainow, *supra* note 14, at 674.

[34] Porter, *supra* note 2, at 715.

[35] Dainow, *supra* note 4, at 42.

decedent's estate if he had children.[36] If the decedent had no children surviving him, he could not dispose of more than one-third of his estate to the detriment of his parents.[37] The Spanish rules on disinherison were also adopted,[38] although the remainder of the laws dealing with the disposable portion are arguably of French origin.[39]

The LOUISIANA CIVIL CODE of 1825 graduated the disposable portion as the French had done,[40] but increased it to two-thirds if only one child survived, one-half if two survived, and one-third if three or more survived.[41] That Code also provided for a forced portion of one-third to parents, in the absence of surviving children.[42] The LOUISIANA CIVIL CODE of 1870 carried the same provisions.[43]

The LOUISIANA CIVIL CODE of 1870 also provided that the legitimate portion was set by the number of children living or represented at death and was not diminished by the renunciation of any one of them.[44] The mass estate was to include the decedent's donations inter vivos, valued at the decedent's death in the state in which they were at the time of donation.[45] Causes for disinherison were the same as those under Spanish law[46] and the burden of providing the facts supporting the cause was on the heirs who stood to gain by the heir's disinherison.[47]

A usufruct over the forced portion representing community property inherited by issue of the marriage with the surviving spouse was sanctioned and was to last until the latter's death or remarriage.[48]

Changes after 1870

The concept of forced heirship of the LOUISIANA CIVIL CODE of 1870 served Louisiana well and remained essentially unchanged for over a century.[49] Accompanying the constitutional

---

[36] Digest of the Civil Laws: Territory of Orleans 1808, La. Civ. Code art. 19, p.212, *amended by* La. Civ. Code Ann. art. 1495 (West Supp. 1998).

[37] Digest of the Civil Laws: Territory of Orleans, 1808, La. Civ. Code art. 20, p. 212, *repealed by* 1981 La. Acts No. 442 § 1. The source for these rules was presumably the *Nueva Recopilacion de Castile* (1567). Porter, *supra* note 2, at 717.

[38] Digest of the Civil Laws: Territory of Orleans, 1808, La. Civ. Code arts. 126-133, pp. 234-238, amended by La. Civ. Code Ann. arts. 1617-1624 (West 1973 & West Supp 1998).

[39] Porter, *supra* note 2, at 718.

[40] Dainow, *supra* note 4, at 59-60.

[41] La. Civ. Code art 1480 (1825), *amended by* La. Civ. Code Ann. art. 1495 (West Supp. 1998).

[42] La. Civ. Code art. 1481 (1825), *repealed by* 1981 La. Acts No. 442, § 1.

[43] La. Civ. Code art. 1493 & 1494 (1870), *repealed by* Acts 1981, No. 442 § 1. A subsequent amendment to article 1494 by Act 313 of 1956, following the rule of the *Succession of Greenlaw*, 86 So. 786 (La. 1920), clarified that the forced portion for a parent was not to be increased above the intestate fraction. La. Civ. Code art. 1493 & 1494 (1956), *repealed by* Acts 1981, No. 442 § 1.

[44] La. Civ. Code art. 1498 (1870), *amended by* La. Civ. Code Ann. art 1500 (West Supp. 1998).

[45] La. Civ. Code art. 1505 (1870), *amended by* La. Civ. Code Ann. art. 1505 (West Supp. 1998).

[46] La. Civ. Code arts. 1621-1622 (1870), *amended by* La. Civ. Code Ann. arts. 1621-1622 (West 1973 & West Supp. 1998); and La. Civ. Code arts. 1623 (1870), *repealed by* Acts 1990 No. 147, § 3 & Acts 1995, No. 1180 § 3.

[47] La. Civ. Code art. 1624 (1870), *amended by* La. Civ. Code Ann. art. 1624 (West Supp. 1998).

[48] La. Civ. Code art. 916 (1870), *amended by* La. Civ. Code Ann. art. 1499 (West Supp. 1998).

sanctioning by the 1921 Louisiana Constitution of trusts and of the placing of the *legitime* in trust was a protection against the abolition of forced heirship.[50] That protection was repeated in the 1974 Constitution with additional language to the effect that the legislature could determine who were forced heirs, the amount of the forced portion, and the grounds for disinherison.[51]

The period following the Constitutional Convention of the seventies was wrought with much discussion as to the value of forced heirship. In a debate held in September 1976 at the Louisiana State University Law Center, Max Nathan criticized forced heirship as a "primitive kind of socialism," "unsound in theory and . . . unsound in practice."[52] According to Mr. Nathan, ascendant forced heirship was "archaic and outmoded, and should be abolished no matter what happens to descendant forced heirship."[53] Additionally, forced heirship placed Louisianians at a disadvantage in that they could not fully utilize the marital deduction.[54] Thomas Lemann, in defense of forced heirship, reminded the audience that forced heirship was more than a law, it was an "institution," and he prophetically warned that "[w]e tinker with such institutions at our peril."[55] Yet, perhaps it is the more radical "alternatives" mentioned by Gerald LeVan that most closely resemble the new forced heirship of the nineties. Professor LeVan described the family maintenance system for needy children.[56] His more modest alternatives, such as excluding pension benefits from the calculation of the active mass and crediting both pension benefits and

---

[49] Article 1494, as it related to ascendant forced heirship, was amended by 1956 La. Acts No. 313, conforming to the holding in the *Succession of Greenlaw*, 86 So. 286 to provide that the forced portion for parents was never to exceed the legal portion. La. Civ. Code art 1494 (1956), *repealed by* 1981 La. Acts No. 442 § 1. Also, case law had recognized proceeds of life insurance policies made payable to named beneficiaries as sui generis and thus exempt from the calculation of the mass estate. *Vinson v. Vinson*, 29 So. 701 (La. 1901); *Ticker v. Metropolitan Life Ins. Co.* 11 Orl. App. 55 (1914); *Sizeler v. Sizeler,* 127 So. 388 (1930). *See also* 1948 La. Acts No. 195, § 14.37(1), *amended by* La. Rev. Stat. Ann. § 22:647 (West Supp. 1998) (provided that proceeds of life insurance were not subject to the rules of forced heirship).

[50] La. Const. art. 4, § 16 (1921), *amended by* Acts 1995, No. 1321 § 1.

> No law shall be passed abolishing forced heirship or authorizing the creation of substitutions, *fidei commissa* or trust estates; except that the Legislature may authorize the creation of trust estates for a period not exceeding 10 years after the death of the donor; provided, that where a natural person is the direct beneficiary said period may be made to extend until 10 years after his majority; and provided further, that this prohibition as to trust estates or *fidei commissa* shall not apply to donations strictly for educational, charitable or religious purposes.

[51] La. Const. art. 12, § 5 (1975), *amended by* Acts 1995, No. 1321, § 1. Before the amendment, article 12 of the 1974 Constitution provided:

> No law shall abolish forced heirship. The determination of forced heirs, the amount of the forced portion, and the grounds for disinherison shall be provided by law. Trusts may be authorized by law, and a forced portion may be placed in trust.

[52] Max Nathan, Jr., *An Assault on the Citadel: A Rejection of Forced Heirship*, 52 Tul. L. Rev. 5, 6 (1977).

[53] *Id.* at 16.

[54] *Id.* at 18 referring to I.R.C. § 2056 (West 1977), *amended by* I.R.C. § 2056 (West 1998). This particular criticism had been substantially accommodated by the expansion of the usufruct of the surviving spouse by the amendment of 1975. *See* La. Civ. Code art. 916 (as amended by 1975 La. Acts No. 680), *amended by* La. Civ. Code Ann. art. 1499 (West Supp. 1998), which permitted the confirmation of that usufruct for life. *See Shaw, Spaht, and Samuel, infra* note 86.

[55] Thomas B. Lemann, *In Defense of Forced Heirship*, 52 Tul. L. Rev. 20, 27-28. (1977).

[56] LeVan, *supra* note 16, at 48.

life insurance proceeds payable to a forced heir toward satisfaction of the heir's *legitime*,[57] were adopted even earlier than the sweeping changes to forced heirship in the eighties.[58]

As the debate over the merits of forced heirship continued, another major change in Louisiana succession law was becoming inevitable, the recognition of equal inheritance rights for illegitimate children. The United States Supreme Court in *Matthew v. Lucas*[59] recognized that state laws discriminating against illegitimate children should be subjected to a middle level of judicial scrutiny pursuant to equal protection analysis.[60] Later, in *Trimble v. Gordon*[61] the Court examined an Illinois statute, which did not provide for inheritance by the decedent father's illegitimate daughter,[62] "more critically" than it had previously viewed the parallel LOUISIANA CIVIL CODE article 919[63] in the earlier case of *Labine v. Vincent*.[64] In 1980, the Louisiana Supreme Court rendered its decision in the *Succession of Brown*,[65] finding LOUISIANA CIVIL CODE article 919, which provided that an illegitimate child would inherit only ahead of the state on the death of his intestate father,[66] was unconstitutional based on both the federal and state equal protection clauses. The corollary to the recognition of intestate inheritance rights for illegitimates was the recognition of illegitimate children as forced heirs. Accordingly in 1980, a legislative subcommittee dealing with succession rights of illegitimate children was fused with another subcommittee dealing with forced heirship.[67] As that joint subcommittee worked, the Successions Committee of the Louisiana Law Institute was studying the same issues, and the legislation of 1981 was the result of the work of both groups, as well as that of other legislators with independent bills.

The 1981 changes of the forced heirship laws were major. The complete elimination of parents as forced heirs was accomplished[68] just as legislation only two years prior had eliminated parents as forced heirs to community property.[69] The amount of the forced portion was decreased from one-third to one-fourth for one child.[70] The portion for two children remained at one-half, but for three or more, the fraction was reduced from the previous two-thirds to one-

---

[57] *Id.* at 48.

[58] *See infra.* nn. 66-77 and accompanying text; *infra.* nn. 100-118 and accompanying text.

[59] *Matthew v. Lucas*, 427 U.S. 495 (1976).

[60] *Id.* at 506.

[61] *Trimble v. Gordon*, 430 U.S. 762 (1977).

[62] *Id.* at 763-764.

[63] La. Civ. Code art. 919 (1870), *repealed by* Acts 1981, No. 919, § 1. Prior to repeal, art. 919 provided in part:

> Natural children are called to the inheritance of their natural father, who has duly acknowledged them, when he has left no descendants nor ascendants, nor collateral relations, nor surviving wife, and to the exclusion only of the State.

[64] *Labine v. Vincent*, 401 U.S. 532 (1971).

[65] *Succession of Brown*, 388 So. 2d 1151 (La. 1980), *cert. denied*, 450 U.S. 998 (1981).

[66] *Supra* note 63.

[67] The result was the Joint Legislative Subcommittee on Forced Heirship and Rights of Illegitimate Children.

[68] 1981 La. Acts No. 442. Parents were eliminated as forced heirs to separate property.

[69] 1979 La. Acts No. 778, § 1.

[70] La. Civ. Code art. 1493 (as amended by 1981 La. Acts No. 884, § 1), *amended by* La. Civ. Code Ann. art. 1495 (West Supp. 1998).

half.[71] The legitimate portion, although not diminished by renunciation, could be diminished by disinherison or declaration of unworthiness.[72]

The changes recognized new exclusions from the active mass upon which the forced portion was calculated. These included donations inter vivos from the donor to his descendants if each forced heir and the root represented by each forced heir received the same value of property by donations inter vivos during the same calendar year.[73] LeVan's recommendation that life insurance proceeds payable to a forced heir be credited in satisfaction of that heir's forced portion was accepted and incorporated into the new law,[74] as was the similar recommendation dealing with pension benefits. [75] Also excluded from the active mass were donations inter vivos to charitable, educational, or religious organizations made at least three years prior to the donor's death[76] and donations to a spouse of a previous marriage made during that marriage.[77] Additionally, the removal of revendication by the 1981 legislation[78] weakened the efficacy of remedy to the forced heirs.

The original article 916 of the LOUISIANA CIVIL CODE of 1870, granted the surviving spouse a usufruct over the community property inherited by issue of the marriage with the intestate spouse and lasted until the survivor's death or remarriage.[79] Case law recognized that the usufruct could apply even if the decedent did not die intestate.[80] In 1979, the legislature again extended the dimensions of the spousal usufruct by allowing a testator to grant such a usufruct over separate property inherited by issue of the marriage.[81]

The issue of the extension of the usufruct for a period beyond the remarriage of the spouse was raised by cases in the seventies. A mere confirmation of the usufruct in a will was not recognized as having the effect of extending the usufruct beyond remarriage of the survivor,[82] nor could the legal usufruct be extended by will beyond remarriage,[83] until the

---

[71] *Id.* Perhaps, more than coincidentally, as illegitimate children were recognized as forced heirs, the value of such recognition was diminished.

[72] La. Civ. Code art. 1498 (as amended by 1981 La. Acts No. 645, § 1), *amended by* La. Civ. Code Ann. art. 1500 (West Supp. 1998).

[73] 1981 La. Acts No. 765, § 1. This bill was introduced by Senator Brinkhaus individually and was **not** part of the packages of either the Law Institute or the Joint Subcommittee. *See also* La. Civ. Code Ann. art. 1505 (West Supp. 1998).

[74] 1981 La. Acts No. 646, § 1; *See also* La. Civ. Code Ann. art. 1505 (West Supp. 1998).

[75] 1981 La. Acts No. 909, § 1; *See also* La. Civ. Code Ann. art. 1505 (West Supp. 1998).

[76] La. Rev. Stat. Ann. § 9:2372 (as enacted by 1981 La. Acts No. 740, § 1), *amended by* La. Rev. Stat. Ann. § 9:2372 (West Supp. 1998).

[77] La. Rev. Stat. Ann. § 9:2354 (as enacted by 1981 La. Acts No. 881, § 1), *amended by* La. Rev. Stat. Ann. § 9:2373 (West Supp. 1998).

[78] 1981 La. Acts No. 739.

[79] La. Civ. Code art. 916 (1870), *amended by* La. Civ. Code Ann. art. 1499 (West Supp. 1998).

[80] The Louisiana Supreme Court used an "adversity test" in the *Succession of Moore*, 4 So. 460 (La. 1888) to justify the application of the spousal usufruct even though the decedent left a will. *Id.* Distinguishing the earlier case of *Forstall v. Forstall*, 28 La. Ann. 197 (La. 1876), the *Moore* case allowed the testator to grant the surviving spouse both the disposable portion of his estate and a usufruct over the forced portion. *Succession of Moore,* 4 So. 460 (La. 1888). *See also Winsberg v. Winsberg*, 96 So. 2d 44 (1957).

[81] 1979 La. Acts No. 678, §1.

[82] *Succession of Chauvin*, 257 So. 2d 422, 426 (La. 1972).

amendment of article 916 in 1975 which sanctioned such a confirmation for life.[84] It was the 1981 legislation that extended the application of the usufruct even over the forced portion of heirs who were not issue of the marriage with the surviving spouse.[85] Thus, even before the nineties, major changes in forced heirship had been made and even the most ardent supporters of the institution were confident that the changes were positive.[86] These changes had a variety of sources and had been integrated into the Code in such a way as to effectively remodel the concept into a more workable system for modern times.

Although some argued that the removal of ascendant forced heirship was an unconstitutional abolition of forced heirship,[87] others opined that the removal of parents as forced heirs was a mere acceptance by the legislature of the invitation extended to it by the 1974 Constitutional Convention permitting the legislature to determine who were forced heirs.[88] The criticism that had been voiced in the seventies against sending property back up the family line through ascendant forced heirship, resulting in multiple successions and additional estate taxes,[89]

---

[83] *Succession of Waldron*, 323 So. 2d 434, 436 (La. 1975).

[84] 1975 La. Acts No. 680.

[85] La. Civ. Code art. 890 (1981), *amended by* La. Civ. Code Ann. art. 890 (West Supp. 1998). The possibility of the forced heirs being able to request security was provided as a protection against abuse. The article, as enacted in 1981, provided as follows:

> If the usufruct authorized by this article affects the rights of heirs other than children of the marriage between the deceased and the surviving spouse or affects separate property, security may be requested by the naked owner.

La. Civ. Code Art. 890 no longer addresses the issue of when a usufructuary must post security. The exception is contained in La. Civ. Code Art. 1514.

[86] *See* Cynthia A. Samuel, William Shaw, and Katherine Shaw Spaht, *Successions and Donations: What Has Become of Forced Heirship?*, 45 La. L. Rev. 575, 575 in which the authors state:

> At one time forced heirship stood like a citadel among the institutions of Louisiana private law. Its impregnable walls offered limited egress to the testator and loomed as an inhospitable barrier to that outsider, the surviving spouse. The citadel contained draconian weapons with which to wrest property from the hands of unsuspecting third parties. Its menacing form intimidated the bravest of lawyers from foreign lands, and even a few title examiners and estate planners within the realm. Within its protection dwelt not only the innocent descendants but almost all manner of dissolute, disobedient, and greedy parent. No wonder the citadel was assaulted.
>
> The walls have not remained in tact. An informed and unemotional evaluation of forced heirship must not proceed with the old citadel in mind, for the image of the old citadel only inflames and distorts. In fact, the Louisiana Trust Code, the 1981 amendments to the Civil Code, and the 1981 amendments to the Internal Revenue Code have answered most of the criticisms of forced heirship. Present law gives testators much greater flexibility than they previously had in disposing of their property, while protecting descendants in a more just and less cumbersome fashion than before. Further reform is still necessary, but the rules of forced heirship today are much more closely tuned to modern society that were their antecedents.

[87] Professor Robert Pascal, Professor of Law Emeritus, Paul M. Hebert Law Center, Louisiana State University, On Forced Heirship: The Unconstitutionality of Senate Bill 264 (Mr. Nelson, et al) to "Amend" the Laws on Forced Heirship, Unpublished memorandum prepared for the House Civil Law and Procedure Committee (June 13, 1989), p. 6.

[88] La. Const. art. 12, § 5 (1975), *amended by* 1995 La. Acts No. 1231, § 1.

[89] *See* Nathan, *supra* note 52.

had apparently been heard. The decrease in amount of the forced portion was not something new, nor unanticipated. It is not surprising that, with the impetus of the marital portion provided [deduction] by the Internal Revenue Code,[90] the maximum forced portion would be reduced to one-half deduction.

The influence of tax considerations can also be seen in the exemptions from the active mass of donations evenly given to all roots in the same calendar year, as parents attempted to take advantage of the gift tax exemption afforded to them under the Internal Revenue Code.[91] The additional exemption of pension proceeds from the state law of forced heirship in a manner analogous to life insurance is consistent with the trend of federal regulation preempting the law regulating pensions.[92] It should also be noted that neighboring common law states had exempted both pensions and life insurance proceeds from the calculation of the spouse's elective share.[93] By exempting gifts to charitable, educational or religious organizations given more than three years prior to death, Louisiana law actually adopted a course of action similar to that of other civilian jurisdictions which limit the donations inter vivos that are added back in to calculate the mass estate, to those made within a specified time prior to death.[94] Ultimately, this treatment of charitable gifts served to pave the way for exempting all gifts made within three years, an exemption which was added in the legislation of the nineties.[95] Selecting a three-year cut-off may also have been suggested by the three year limit on gifts considered in contemplation of death under the Internal Revenue Code.[96]

In many ways, the changes in forced heirship over the years were revealed in the changing face of the spousal usufruct. The extension of the usufruct of the surviving spouse was a gradual process, working its way through the courts and ultimately into the Civil Code. That delicate balance between the rights of a decedent's children and the rights of the decedent's surviving spouse was slowly, but surely, tilted in favor of the spouse. In days where the spouse was also the parent of the children, this preference for the spouse would have been of limited significance. In instances in which the children are issue of the marriage, the children usually

---

[90] *See* Nathan, *supra* note 54 and accompanying text.

[91] I.R.C. § 2503 (West 1981) provided in part:

> In computing taxable gifts for the calendar quarter, in case of gifts . . . made to any person by the donor, . . . $3,000 of such gifts to such person less the aggregate of the amounts of such gifts to such person during all preceding calendar quarters of the calendar year shall not . . . be included in the total amount of gifts made during such quarter.

I.R.C. § 2503 (West 1981) has been amended by I.R.C. § 2503 (West 1998), which provides in part:

> In the case of gifts . . . made to any person by the donor during the calendar year, the first $10,000 of such gifts to such person shall not . . . be included in the total amount of [taxable] gifts made during such year.

[92] *See Boggs v. Boggs*, 520 U.S. 833 (1997).

[93] Sheldon F. Kurtz, *The Augmented Estate Concept under the Uniform Probate Code: In Search of an Equitable Elective Share*, 62 Iowa L. Rev. 981 (1977).

[94] *See* Civ. Code art. 2325(3) (Jan S. Forrester, Simon L. Goren, and Hans-Michael Iigen 1995) (Germany) (provides for a ten year cut-off); Civ. Code art. 527 (Ivy Williams, Sigfried Wyler, Barbara Wyler 1987) (Switz) (provides for a five year cut-off). *See also* Paul G. Haskell, *The Power of Disinheritance: Proposal for Reform*, 52 Geo. L.J. 499 (refers to the above provisions of Germany and Switzerland)

[95] La. Civ. Code Ann. art. 1505(A) (West Supp. 1998) (as enacted by 1996 La. Acts No. 77, § 1).

[96] I.R.C. § 2053 (West 1998).

receive the inheritance eventually, albeit indirectly. Such was the rationale behind the common law marital estates of dower and curtesy.[97] However, as our society is changing to one characterized by "successive polygamy,"[98] the expansion of the rights of the surviving spouse at the expense of the children is problematic.

To many, the changes of 1981 were warranted and sufficient, with the possible exception of a need to also examine critically the causes for disinherison.[99] The concept of forced heirship had been retained within the confines prescribed by the Louisiana Constitution. A set percentage, to be divided equally among them,[100] was reserved for all children except the disinherited. Although the link to family property had been somewhat weakened by the repeal of revendication and the acceptance of insurance and pension proceeds as satisfactory to satisfy the forced portion, the changes were basically in keeping with the more modern view that perpetuation of family wealth in the form of immovable property was no longer a desired goal of society.[101] Although an exception was made for charitable gifts given within three years of death, the basic concept of including donations inter vivos in the calculation of the mass estate preserved the protection against efforts to circumvent the concept of forced heirship.

Even with the changes of 1981, some were not satisfied. Many were still concerned about the fact that unworthy children would be forced heirs to a portion of a parent's estate. The grounds for disinherison had remained essentially unchanged since the time of the Civil Code of 1825 until 1981[102] and only the additional ground of conviction of a felony punishable by death or life imprisonment was added in 1983.[103] The courts interpreted reconciliation quite liberally.[104] Also, although the testator named the child to be disinherited, the cause, and expressed a desire in his will to disinherit,[105] the burden of proving disinherison was on the other surviving heirs. Thus, disinherison of an undeserving child was not a viable option in most

---

[97] *See* Ralph C. Brashier, *Disinheritance and the Modern Family*, 45 Case W. Res. L. Rev. 83, 115-116 (1994).

[98] Mary Ann Glendon, The Transformation of Family Law 54 (1989).

[99] Letter from Senator Casey to Professors Katherine Shaw Spaht, Cynthia A. Samuel, and Kathryn Venturatos Lorio, dated August 7, 1984 (on file with Professor Kathryn Venturatos Lorio). *See also* Samuel, Shaw, and Spaht, *supra* note 86.

[100] *Succession of Lauga*, 624 So. 2d 1156 (La. 1993). The importance of the equality among children as a definitional part of forced heirship which would discourage litigation, was emphasized by Justice Dennis in his majority opinion in the *Succession of Lauga*.

> . . . the safeguard of forced heirship embraced both the individual child's interest in dignity and equality of treatment within the family and his or her personal economic interest in inheriting a forced share of a fixed portion of the family estate. These concerns are inextricably related: a legally assured right to share equally in the *legitime* is an important cornerstone to an individual's relations of the most fundamental sort -- familial respect, dignity, love, and trust. *Id.* at 1169.

[101] *See* Mary Ann Glendon, *The New Family and the New Property*, 61 (1938). Glendon notes that a recommendation by the American Bar Foundation to revise existing intestate succession laws to make the surviving spouse the sole intestate heir was tempered by concerns for the children when the decedent left children of a previous marriage. *See Id.* at 7; Unif. Probate Code § 2-202 (1990).

[102] *See* La. Civ. Code art. 1621 (1870), *amended by* La. Civ. Code Ann. art. 1621 (West Supp. 1998).

[103] La. Civ. Code Ann. art. 1621 (West Supp. 1998). Conviction of a felony punishable by death or life imprisonment was added as a ground for disinherison by 1983 La. Acts No. 566.

[104] *See Succession of Lissa*, 196 So. 924 (La. 1940).

[105] La. Civ. Code art. 1624 (1870), *amended by* La. Civ. Code Ann. Art. 1624 (West Supp. 1998).

cases. Even the most ardent supporters of forced heirship recognized the need for reform in this area.[106] In 1984, five bills proposing to amend the code articles on disinherison were introduced into the Legislature, but none passed.[107] The only change in the law of disinherison accepted in that year was an amendment to Article 1622, allowing ascendants to disinherit descendants when the cause for disinherison had been committed either against the grandparents or against the parents.[108] The reformers continued however[109] and ultimately, in 1985, some significant changes were made. The additional ground of failure of a major child to communicate with a parent without just cause for a period of two years was added to the causes for disinherison[110] and the burden of proving that the cause for disinherison did not exist, or that reconciliation had taken place, was shifted to the forced heir.[111] After those changes, a number of disinherisons were successfully accomplished.[112]

Thus, by the mid eighties, many of the reformers were content that forced heirship had been sufficiently restructured to meet the needs of our changing society.[113] However, others wished to proceed further, even to the point of abolishing the concept of forced heirship entirely. A strong constituency in northern Louisiana, predominantly in the Bossier-Shreveport area, heavily influenced by residents at the Barksdale Airforce Base, convinced Senator Sydney Nelson to proceed on a mission of free testation in Louisiana. A movement for total abolition of forced heirship required the passing of an amendment to the 1974 Louisiana Constitution. The affirmative vote of two-thirds of the Louisiana legislature placing such an amendment on the state ballot for public approval was a prerequisite to success. Numerous attempts to pass such a resolution proposing a constitutional amendment failed.[114]

Thus, it was in the late eighties that the idea of "redefining" forced heirship was born. The new definition, proposed in Act 788 of 1989, included as forced heirs only those under the age of twenty-three or those of any age who had been interdicted or were subject to interdiction

---

[106] Samuel, Shaw, and Spaht, *supra* note 86, at 600.

[107] *See* Samuel, Shaw, and Spaht, *supra* note 86, *citing*, H.B. 503, 504, and 638, 184th Leg., Reg. Sess. (La. 184); and S.B. 12, and 13, 184th Leg., Reg. Sess. (La. 184).

[108] 1984 La. Acts No. 441, § 1.

[109] Letter from Senator Casey to Katherine Spaht, Cynthia Samuel and Kathryn Lorio, dated Aug. 7, 1984 (on file with Professor Kathryn Venturatos Lorio).

[110] 1985 La. Acts No. 456 amending La. Civ. Code art. 1621 (1985), *amended by* La. Civ. Code Ann. art. 1621 (West Supp. 1998). That general concept was first introduced in legislation the previous year. Samuel, Shaw, and Spaht, *supra* note 86, at n. 131, *citing*, La. H. B. 638, 503, and La. S. B. 12.

[111] 1985 La. Acts No. 456, § 1.

[112] *See Ambrose Succession v. Ambrose*, 548 So. 2d 37 (La. App. 2d Cir. 1989); *Succession of Vincent v. Vincent*, 527 So. 2d 23 (La. App. 3rd Cir. 1988); *Succession of Bertaut*, 572 So. 2d 142, *writ denied,* 573 So. 2d 1111 (1991*); Succession of Cure*, 633 So. 2d 590 (La. App. 1st Cir. 1991).

[113] Former Senator Tom Casey, who worked on the reform of forced heirship in the early eighties expressed his intent as being to arrive at a "reasonable liberalization of the concept to render it workable and less onerous." Telephone Interview with Senator Thomas Casey (March 6, 1998).

It was clear to Senator Nelson that his colleague, Senator Casey, in the reform movement of the eighties, was satisfied with the changes and "was not interested in going further." Interview with Senator Sydney Nelson (Feb. 2, 1998).

[114] *See* S.B. No. 100 (1980); S.B. 45 (1984) and H.B. No. 115 (1985).

because of mental incapacity or physical infirmity.[115] Some viewed this redefinition as innovative and perfectly constitutional.[116] After all, when the Louisiana Constitution was amended in 1974, it provided that the legislature could determine who were forced heirs, as well as the amount of the forced portion.[117] Restricting forced heirs to children under the age of twenty-three and to those of any age with a mental or physical disability[118] was rationalized as a mere redefinition within the parameters provided by the Constitution itself. Others strongly disagreed, outraged that the words of the Constitution would be used to defeat the very protection afforded by the document.[119] The opponents to this redefinition argued it was not a redefinition at all, but merely an abolition of the concept in a politically feasible way. It also seemed inappropriate that a central institution of the civil law of Louisiana would be rejected without the imprimatur of the Louisiana Law Institute,[120] the esteemed body commissioned by the Louisiana legislature to study and recommend amendments to the Civil Code.

Realizing that the changes in Act 788 were indeed significant and would affect other provisions of the Civil Code, the legislature deferred the effectiveness of the act, and further directed the Louisiana State Law Institute to prepare amendments to the Civil Code, Revised Statutes and to the CODE OF CIVIL PROCEDURE so as to "correlate" existing law with the provisions of Act 788. The result was Act 147 of 1990, which contained essentially the same definition of forced heirs as that in Act 788, but substituted, for the reference to interdiction, language to the effect that the disabled forced heirs be "incapable of taking care of their person or administering their estates . . . because of a mental incapacity or physical infirmity."[121] Despite warnings of possible challenge on constitutional grounds, the new law was followed in the administration of a number of estates[122] until the Supreme Court in its decision in the

---

[115] 1989 La. Acts No. 788.

[116] Memorandum on "Constitutional Issues Raised by Act 788 of 1989" prepared by Julio Romanach, Jr. to Max Nathan, Jr. Reporter of the Successions Revisions Committee, Louisiana State Law Institute on September 26, 1989; Affidavit of Max Nathan submitted as Exhibit B to Memorandum in Opposition to Motion for Summary Judgment filed on behalf William Ponder Terry in *Succession of Beatrice Asprion Terry*, No. 418-130 (24th Jud. D.Ct., La. July 30, 1992).

[117] La. Const. art. 12, § 5 (1975), *amended by* 1995 La. Acts No. 1321, § 1. Before the amendment, article 12 of the 1974 Constitution provided:

> No law shall abolish forced heirship. The determination of forced heirs, the amount of the forced portion, and the grounds for disinherison shall be provided by law. Trusts may be authorized by law, and a forced portion may be placed in trust.

[118] 1989 La. Acts No. 788. The original version of the bill submitted by Senator Nelson did not include the disabled of any age as forced heirs. Telephone interview with Senator Sydney Nelson (Feb. 2, 1998). However, Senator Nelson's bill was heard in Senate Judiciary a Committee immediately after a bill which had been introduced by Senator Chris Ullo proposing the elimination of disabled children as forced heirs (thus allowing them to qualify for other governmental benefits). *Id.* Senator Ullo's bill was soundly defeated in committee and the ultimate effect was the amendment of Senator Nelson's bill to specifically include the disabled, regardless of age, as forced heirs. *Id.*

[119] *See* Katherine Spaht, Kathryn Lorio, Cynthia Picou, Cynthia Samuel, & Frederick Swaim, *The New Forced Heirship Legislation: A Regrettable "Revolution"*, 50 La. L. Rev. 409 (1990).

[120] Act 788 was not the product of the Louisiana Law Institute. In fact, a positive vote recommending the abolition of forced heirship had never been passed by the Council of that body.

[121] La. Civ. Code art. 1493 (as amended by 1990 La. Acts 147), *amended by* La. Civ. Code Ann. art. 1493 (West Supp. 1998).

[122] *See Succession of Vilarrubia*, 680 So. 2d 1147 (La. 1996).

Succession of Lauga[123] declared both Act 788 of 1989 and Act 147 of 1990 void "in their entirety."[124] In rendering the Court's opinion, Justice Dennis noted three ways that the "new" definition of forced heirship violated the constitutional protection afforded in Article XII, §5 of the Louisiana Constitution of 1974. First, it purported to deprive each child "of his individual right as a child to an equal share of a forced portion of his decedent's estate."[125] Second, it purported "to abrogate the core principle of equality of heirship in the *legitime* among children of a family."[126] Third, it abolished or rendered "wholly ineffective the legal institution of forced heirship to serve the purposes intended by the constitutional limitation upon legislative power," those being "to guarantee the principle of treatment as equals in heirship in order to further important social and economic goals, viz., elimination of intra-family litigation; promotion of family harmony, strength, and solidarity; and prevention of excessive concentration of wealth."[127]

The *Succession of Lauga* was decided in September, 1993. In the first non-fiscal session of the legislature following that decision, after five years of adapting to the redefinition, the legislature, by two-thirds vote, passed Act No. 1321 in the Regular Session of 1995, placing a constitutional amendment on the ballot of the gubernatorial primary election which was held on October 21, 1995.[128] Accompanying the resolution for the constitutional amendment was an implementation act which was to take effect on January 1, 1996 in the event that the constitutional amendment were approved by a majority vote of the people of Louisiana.[129] The provisions of the implementation act contained a number of ambiguities[130] which required

---

[123] *Succession of Lauga*, 624 So. 2d 1156 (La. 1993).

[124] *Id.* at 1172. A separate act, Act 367 of 1989, requiring "clear and unequivocal evidence in writing and signed by the testator" to effect a reconciliation after an act constituting cause for disinherison, was unaffected by the decision in *Succession of Lauga*.

[125] *Id.* at 1169. Justice Dennis further elaborated:

> Thus, it was established under the former constitution that the safeguard of forced heirship embraced both the individual child's interest in dignity and equality of treatment within the family and his or her personal economic interest in inheriting a forced share of a fixed portion of the family estate. These concerns are inextricably related: a legally assured right to share equally in the *legitime* is an important cornerstone to an individual's relations of the most fundamental sort - familial respect, dignity, love, and trust.

[126] *Id.* at 1170.

[127] *Id.*

[128] The amendment to Article XII, § 5 of the Louisiana Constitution, which was passed on Oct. 21, 1995, provides:

> To abolish forced heirship, except to require forced heirship for children twenty-three years of age or younger and to authorize the legislature to classify as forced heirs children of any age who are incapable of taking care of their person or estate due to mental incapacity or physical infirmity.

[129] 1995 La. Act 1180.

[130] 1990 La. Acts No. 147. First degree descendants were included as forced heirs if they were **twenty-three years of age or younger**, whereas representation of a predeceased child by a grandchild required that the predeceased child **not have attained the age of twenty-three** at the time of the donor's death. *Id.* This inconsistency, as well as the broad provision allowing any disabled grandchild to claim a forced portion even if the parent of that grandchild survived and the vagueness of the requirement of disability, were addressed in Act 77. 1996 La. Acts No. 77. *See generally* Kathryn Venturatos Lorio, *Forced Heirship: The Citadel Has Fallen -- Or Has It?*, 44 La. Bar Journal 16 (1996).

further study, resulting in a review by the Louisiana Law Institute, culminating in the subsequent passage of yet another more extensive act at the Special Session of the Legislature in 1996.[131]

The New Forced Heirship of Act 77 of 1996

Act 77 of 1996 was more than a remedy for the confusing implementation act. It was in effect a comprehensive revision of the entire area of forced heirship. Pursuant to Act 77, forced heirs are now defined as children under the age of twenty-four, or those "of any age who, because of mental incapacity or physical infirmity, are permanently incapable of taking care of their persons or administering their estates at the time of the death of the decedent."[132] A grandchild may represent if the grandchild's parent predeceased the decedent and would have been younger than twenty-four at the time of the decedent's death had he survived[133] or if the grandchild had a permanent disability at the time of the decedent's death and the grandchild's parent predeceased the decedent.[134]

The amount of the forced portion remains at one-fourth for one forced heir and one-half for two or more. However, since not all children may be forced, the possibility of a forced portion larger than the legal portion by intestacy arose. Act 77 solves the dilemma by restricting the forced heir to the intestate fraction, albeit calculated on the mass estate including donations inter vivos.[135] The new rules provide, however, that renunciation by a forced heir of his *legitime* will result in a diminishment of the forced portion, just as with unworthiness or disinherison.[136]

The method of calculating the mass estate appears similar to the method introduced during the compromise era of the early eighties in that life insurance premiums and proceeds, as well as pension benefits, are excluded from the calculation, although they are credited to a forced heir in satisfaction of the forced heir's *legitime*. However, two significant changes in the method of calculation of the mass were introduced by Act 77. First, only those donations inter vivos which were made within three years of the decedent's death are added in to calculate the mass estate. Thus, the limitation that was inserted as a workable compromise in 1981 for charitable, educational, and religious organizations[137] has been extended to all donees.[138] The other change is that all donations that are added in, are valued at the time of the donation, rather than at the time of the donor's death.[139]

---

[131] 1996 La. Act No. 77.

[132] La. Civ. Code Ann. art. 1493 (West Supp. 1998), (as enacted by 1996 La. Act No. 77). The Law Institute had actually recommended that there be no provision for the disabled child over the age of twenty-four. However, that approach was rejected in favor of limiting the definition to those having a "permanent" disability. *Id.*

[133] La. Civ. Code art. 1493(B) (enacted by 1996 La. Acts No. 77), amended by La. Civ. Code Ann. art. 1493(B) (West Supp. 1998).

[134] La. Civ. Code Ann. art. 1493(C) (West Supp. 1998), (as enacted by 1996 La. Acts No. 77). Some have questioned whether the inclusion of grandchildren as forced heirs is even sanctioned in the wording of the constitutional amendment. *Supra* note 128.

[135] La. Civ. Code Ann. art. 1495 (West Supp. 1998), (as enacted by 1996 La. Acts No. 77).

[136] La. Civ. Code Ann. art. 1500 (West Supp. 1998), (as enacted by 1996 La. Acts No. 77).

[137] La. Rev. Stat. § 9:2372 (as enacted by 1981 La. Acts No. 740, § 1), *amended by* La. Rev. Stat. Ann. § 9:2372 (West Supp. 1998).

[138] La. Civ. Code Ann. art. 1505 (West Supp. 1998), (as enacted by 1996 La. Acts No. 77).

[139] *Id.*

As before, the *legitime* may not be satisfied by a usufruct of income interest in trust.[140] Burdens on the *legitime* are prohibited,[141] except for the possibility of placing the *legitime* in trust, making it subject to the usufruct of the surviving spouse, and placing a survivorship provision on the *legitime*.[142]

The provisions for the spousal usufruct have been appropriately divided into three articles, one dealing with intestacy,[143] another dealing with the testate possibilities,[144] and the third providing for the possibility of the forced heir requesting security to protect his *legitime*.[145] The intestate usufruct remains as it did prior to this revision in that it applies to community property inherited by the decedent's descendants and lasts until the surviving spouse dies or remarries.[146] The revisions allow for the decedent to grant a usufruct to the surviving spouse over all or part of his property, including the forced portion, as a permissible burden on the *legitime*. Two major expansions of this usufruct appear in this revision. First, the power to dispose of nonconsumables, as permitted in article 568, may be granted to the usufructuary and will not be considered an impingement on the *legitime*[147] and secondly, the duration of the usufruct shall be considered for life unless specified for a shorter period.[148] A change in the security provision for the forced heirs renders the heirs less secure under the new system. Previous to the revision, all children, both issue and non-issue of the marriage of the decedent and the surviving spouse, could request security to the extent the spousal usufruct extended over their inheritance of any separate property. Non-issue of the marriage could also request security to the extent the usufruct extended over their inheritance of community property.[149] Under the revision, the relief granted in the form of security is limited only to the portion of the heir's inheritance representing the *legitime* of the heir.[150]

Another major change in Act 77 is that the right to demand collation has now been restricted to "descendants of the first degree who qualify as forced heirs," although the request may be made against all those who come to the succession, but is limited to gifts given within three years of the donor's death, valued as of the date of death.[151]

---

[141] La. Civ. Code Ann. art 1496 (West Supp. 1998), (as enacted by 1996 La. Acts No. 77).

[142] *See* La. Civ. Code Ann. art. 1496, revision cmt. (West Supp. 1998).

[143] La. Civ. Code Ann. art. 890 (West Supp. 1998), (as enacted by 1996 La. Acts No. 77).

[144] La. Civ. Code Ann. art. 1499 (West Supp. 1998), (as enacted by 1996 La. Acts No. 77).

[145] La. Civ. Code Ann. art 1514 (West Supp. 1998), (as enacted by 1996 La. Acts No. 77).

[146] La. Civ. Code Ann. art. 890 (West Supp. 1998), (as enacted by 1996 La. Acts No. 77).

[147] *See* A.N. Yiannopoulos, *Of Legal Usufruct, the Surviving Spouse, and Article 890 of the Louisiana Civil Code: Heyday for Estate Planning*, 49 La L. Rev. 803 (1989) (discussion of the power of surviving spouse usufructuary to dispose of nonconsumables).

[148] Changing the rule of the *Succession of Chauvin*, 257 So. 2d 422 (La. 1972), this provision now allows for the unwary to benefit from the marital deduction for estate tax purposes in that such a usufruct will be considered a QTIP. I.R.C. § 2053 (West 1998).

[149] La. Civ. Code art. 890 (as amended by 1990 La. Acts No. 1075, § 1), *amended by* La. Civ. Code. Ann. art. 890 (West Supp. 1998).

[150] La. Civ. Code Ann. art. 1514 (West Supp. 1998). Thus, if the heir were granted **more** than his forced portion, but with the spousal usufruct over the entire amount, the request for security would only protect the part corresponding to the *legitime*. *Id.*

[151] La. Civ. Code Ann. art. 1235 (West Supp. 1998), (as enacted by 1996 La. Acts No. 77).

What Influenced the New Creation

After reviewing the history of this new creation, the question remains - What inspired it? Was it a product of the conscious melding of our civil law traditions with the customs of our common law neighbors that surrounded us? Or was it more of a political accident, albeit influenced by the debate surrounding it?

It might make a much more scholarly paper to propose that the new creation was a deliberate attempt to combine the best of our heritage exemplified by protecting the young and disabled with the common law concept of freedom of testation recognizing an individual's right to distribute his own property. However, such a conclusion, even if documented by the laws of other jurisdictions, would be ingenuous and would not accurately reflect what transpired in the late eighties and early nineties in Louisiana, culminating in the new forced heirship laws. For, in actuality the end product was the result of a "unique Louisiana political compromise."[152] Encouraged by his constituency to abolish the concept of forced heirship, Senator Sidney Nelson attempted to do so within the confines of the political system which existed. Acutely aware that there were insufficient votes in the Louisiana legislature to obtain the two-thirds vote needed to pass a resolution proposing a constitutional amendment to the people of Louisiana, the proponents of abolition conceived the "redefinition."[153]

One option may have been to define only the surviving spouse as a forced heir. Certainly, that would be consistent with the pattern followed by our common law neighbors.[154] However, excluding children completely would be too radical a concept for acceptance in the same political climate that consistently rejected proposals of a constitutional amendment. Without undertaking any organized survey of political opinion, the proponents of the changes came to a savvy conclusion which is supported by a number of previous surveys on public opinion in the United States, i.e. that most people wish to leave the bulk, if not all, of their estate, to their surviving spouse,[155] while recognizing a moral obligation to provide for minor children.[156] Conveniently, a proposal protecting only minor children would be perfectly acceptable to the retired and aging constituents who strongly supported the change, and also to many of the second spouses who donned "Freedom of Testation" buttons at the legislative hearings.[157] Linking the concept to the need of minor children would incorporate that balance

---

[152] Interview with Senator Sydney Nelson (Feb. 2, 1998). When asked what influenced the structure of the new law, Sen. Nelson replied, "I do remember reading Gerry LeVan. Need was a consideration and a factor but the final result was a unique Louisiana political compromise, reached when I ultimately concluded we could not get the two-thirds vote" to pass a resolution for a constitutional abolishing forced heirship. *Id.* The reference is to LeVan, *supra* note 16 (discussion of the maintenance systems prevalent in other nations). *See also* discussion of maintenance, *infra* at note 56 and accompanying text.

[153] *Infra* note 152 and accompanying text.

[154] *See* Helene Shapo, *"A Tale of Two Systems": Anglo-American Problems in Modernization of Inheritance Legislation*, 60 Tenn. L. Rev. 707, (1993); J. Thomas Oldham, *Should the Surviving Spouse's Forced Share Be Retained?*, 38 Case W. Res. L. Rev. 223 (1987-88).

[155] *See* Shapo, *supra* note 154, at n. 59.

[156] Deborah A. Batts, *I Didn't Ask to Be Born: The American Law of Disinheritance and a Proposal for Change to a System of Protected Inheritance*, 41 Hastings L. J. 1197, 1232-1236 (1990).

[157] Sen. Nelson found two of his strongest allies in redefining forced heirship to be Chalin Perez and his second wife, Lynn Perez. Sen. Nelson noted, "The Perezes were not in charge of this move in any way, but they became

which has been reflected in public opinion.[158] Indeed, the original version of the bill which ultimately became Act 788 of 1989 restricted forced heirs to those under the age of twenty-three, but related the relief much more closely to actual need of the child by providing that a **maximum** portion be set, one-quarter if only one child under twenty-three, and one-half, if two or more. The actual amount paid to the children would **not** be fixed, but rather dependent on "the amount necessary for the support, lodging, maintenance and education of each forced heir of the decedent, according to his station in life, until such forced heirs attains the age of twenty-three."[159] The age of twenty-three was based on a number of factors, including that many insurance policies provided coverage for dependents until the age of twenty-three[160] and that would generally cover sufficient time for a child to complete high school and four years of college.[161] Ultimately, the idea of a discretionary amount, dependent on the individual needs of the heirs, was rejected as "too complicated to administer."[162]

Thus, Louisiana was struggling with that recurring dilemma of achieving the proper balance between freedom of testation represented by its common law neighbors and protection of the family with a reserved portion exemplified by its civil law brethren. In fact, some scholars marveled that Louisiana actually withstood the political pressure to alter its forced heirship laws until the end of the twentieth century, recognizing that the law of succession, by not bearing on the immediate concerns of the legislative majority, is "particularly vulnerable to the pressures of political accommodation."[163]

Legal systems have been struggling for centuries at striking the proper balance between complete freedom of testation and protection of the family. Even in Britain, regarded as the center of free testation, the Roman law influence in the form of a *legitime* for the surviving wife and children was operative in the twelfth century.[164] Although the rule of primogeniture controlled the disposition of land, chattels were left to the authority of the ecclesiastical jurisdiction, which was influenced by the Roman law.[165] A tripartite principle controlled the distribution of property composed of the "wife's part," the "bairn's part" to be equally divided among the decedent's children, and the "dead's part," which could be distributed by the

---

very active." Telephone interview with Senator Sidney Nelson (Feb. 2, 1998). The support of the Chalin Perezes included the hiring of former speaker of the House E.L. "Bubba" Henry to lobby the legislature to vote for the bill. Cynthia Samuel, "Let's Rescue Forced Heirship", *Baton Rouge Advocate* 11B (Nov. 26, 1989).

[158] Realizing that compromise was the name of the game, Senator Nelson honestly stated:

> What we're talking about is how you determine what would be a fair amount to give the children, a right to claim against the parents' estate. . . . Well, of course, as opponents observed, my preference would be to repeal it outright, but it seems that twenty-three is a fair age under this concept. . . .

> Telephone interview with Senator Sydney Nelson (Feb. 2, 1998).

[159] Original version of Senate Bill 264 of 1989.

[160] Telephone interview with Senator Sydney Nelson (Feb. 2, 1998).

[161] Comments by Senator Sidney Nelson at the Civil and Procedure Committee Hearing (June 5, 1989).

[162] Telephone interview with Senator Sydney Nelson (Feb. 2, 1998).

[163] Joseph W. McKnight, S*panish Legitim in the United States - - Its Survival and Decline*, 44 Am. J. Comp. L. 75, 104 (1996).

[164] Batts, *supra* note 156, at 1205.

[165] Joseph Dainow, *Limitations on Testamentary Freedom in England*, 25 Cornell Law Quarterly 337, 340 (1940).

decedent.[166] By the fourteenth century, the tripartite principle was no longer generally used in England, although it continued by local custom until later abolished by statute, with London being the last vestige until 1724.[167] Thus, the forced portion for chattels was disappearing in England just as America was being colonized, and was virtually extinct by the time of the American Revolution.[168] However, the concepts of dower protecting a widow, and curtesy, for the widower, were generally adopted. These provided a life estate of a certain proportion of the lands of the decedent for the surviving spouse.[169] Additionally, at a time when divorce was the exception, these life estates for the surviving spouse indirectly protected most minor children from disinheritance by providing a source of income for their support and education.[170] However, dower and curtesy affected only real property, creating a cloud on title, and could often be circumvented by the creation of a corporation to hold the realty.[171] Additionally, in the twentieth century, wealth took the form of personality more and more, leading common law states to gradually discard dower and curtesy in favor of granting the surviving spouse a fixed share of the entire estate of the decedent.[172]

This elective share, often referred to as a forced share for the spouse, provided that a surviving spouse could elect to take a specified portion of the decedent's estate, generally one-third or one-half depending on the particular state law.[173] Being fixed by statute, the fraction was not dependent on the size of the decedent's estate; nor was it related to the needs or conduct of the survivor, or the length of the marriage with the decedent.[174] In order to ensure that a decedent did not jeopardize the survivor's forced share by making inter vivos transfers to her prejudice, the Uniform Probate Code, as published in 1970, calculated the fixed portion on an "augmented estate" which increased the net probate estate by including the value of inter vivos transfers.[175] Only those gifts given within two years of the donor's death and exceeding $3000 in any one calendar year to any single donor were included.[176] Gifts given to the survivor by will during the marriage, as well as life insurance and pension benefits granted to the surviving spouse, were credited in satisfaction of the survivor's elective share.[177] The revised Uniform Probate Code in 1990 further altered the calculation of the spouse's elective share by introducing

---

[166] *Id.* If only widow or children survived, the reserved portion for the survivor was one-half, leaving the other half disposable. *Id.* at 341.

[167] *Id.* at 342.

[168] Brashier, *supra* note 97, at 113.

[169] Oldham, *supra* note 154, at 225.

[170] Brashier, *supra* note 55, at 155-116.

[171] Oldham, *supra* note 154 at 225.

[172] *See* Brashier, *supra* note 97, at 92 and 99-102 (in-depth review of changes).

[173] Oldham, *supra* note 154, at 226.

[174] Brashier, *supra* note 55, at 102.

[175] Unif. Probate Code § 2-202 (1970), *amended by* Unif. Probate Code § 2-202 (1990).

[176] Unif. Probate Code § 2-202 (1970), *amended by* Unif. Probate Code § 2-202 (1990); *See* Sheldon F. Kurtz, *The Augmented Estate Concept under the Uniform Probate Code: In Search of an Equitable Elective Share*, 62 Iowa L. Rev. 981 (1977).

[177]Unif. Probate Code § 2-202(a) (1970), *amended by* Unif. Probate Code § 2-207 (a) (1990).

an "accrual system" whereby the fraction due to the spouse was graduated based on the number of years of marriage to the decedent.[178]

Yet in our common law sister states which provided these protections to the surviving spouse, the interests of the children were essentially not addressed.[179] Commentators lamenting this callous approach often cited Louisiana as exemplary and unique in the United States for her forced heirship system.[180] Yet, its critics pointed to the rigidity of forced heirship. Thus, it would be "only natural," as described by Professor Mary Ann Glendon in 1986 that some "well-intentioned persons would propose what appears to be an ideal compromise," a family maintenance system allowing a court to make an award of reasonable allowance for needy children.[181]

The model for such systems would be the discretionary maintenance systems as first adopted by New Zealand in 1900 with its Family Protection Act and later modified in 1939 to include intestate successions.[182] The basic idea is that maintenance be provided for a decedent's dependent spouse and children. If the decedent failed to so adequately provide, then the claimant could apply to the court which would determine the proper amount to be awarded, based on the claimant's needs.

In 1938, England passed its Inheritance (Family Provision) Act[183] which adopted the same principle as that of New Zealand.[184] It was followed in 1975 with the Inheritance (Provision for Family and Dependents) Act of 1975 which expanded the recipients to include not only the spouse and children of the decedent, but also the former spouse who had not remarried, and children, though not of the decedent, who were treated as children of the family, and to any person "who immediately before the death of the deceased was being maintained, either wholly or partly, by the deceased."[185] The judge was given the power to determine what was "reasonable in all circumstances,"[186] leading to the criticism that he could substantially fix a new

---

[178] Unif. Probate Code § 2-202(a) (1970), *amended by* Unif. Probate Code § 2-202(a) (1990).

[179] Mary Ann Glendon, *Fixed Rules and Discretion in Contemporary Family Law and Succession Law*, 60 Tul. L. Rev. 1165, 1185. Some limited relief was afforded in the form of the "family allowance," affording short term relief during the administration of the estate (Unif. Probate Code § 2-404 (1970), *amended by* Unif. Probate Code § 2-404 (1990)); the "homestead allowance" (Unif. Probate Code § 2-402 (1970), *amended by* Unif. Probate Code § 2-402 (1990)); and the "exempt property allowance" (Unif. Probate Code § 2-403 (1970), *amended by* Unif. Probate Code § 2-403 (1990)).

[180] Glendon, *supra* note 179, at 1185. Batts, *supra* note 156, at 1198; Ralph C. Brashier, *Protecting the Child From Disinheritance: Must Louisiana Stand Alone?*, 57 La. L. Rev. 1, 1-2 (1996).

[181] Glendon, *supra* note 179, at 1186.

[182] Batts, *supra* note 156, at 1214. It is interesting that Professor Dainow noted that in 1899 Henri Coulon in France, presumably unaware of the New Zealand legislative debates, proposed a similar system. Joseph Dainow, *Forced Heirship in French Law*, 2 La. L. Rev. 669, 690 (1940).

[183] *See* Dainow, *supra* note 165.

[184] For a discussion of family maintenance legislation, see Joseph Laufer, *Flexible Restraints on Testamentary Freedom - A Report on Decedents' Family Maintenance Legislation*, 69 Harv. L. Rev. 277 (1955).

[185] Inheritance (Provision for Family and Dependents) Act 1975, ch. 63, § 1 (Eng.) (Effective Apr. 1, 1976).

[186] *Id.* at § 2.

estate plan for the decedent.[187] Donees who received gifts from the donee within six years of his death were subject to providing contribution to the maintenance.[188]

Accepted in many areas of the British Commonwealth,[189] the system of family maintenance bears close resemblance to the concept of "alimentos," which has been adopted in Mexico, a civilian jurisdiction which repealed forced heirship in 1884.[190] The Mexican provision lists among its potential recipients minor descendants and descendants "who are incapable of gainful employment, regardless of age."[191] The award is based on need[192] and is discretionary with the judge, but may not be less than one-half of the recipient's intestate portion, nor more than the intestate portion.[193]

Despite its popularity in other jurisdictions, the family maintenance concept has not been accepted in the United States.[194] However, neither has there been an outcry to adopt the system of forced heirship as a means of providing some protection for the children of the decedent. Struggling with this problem of balance between freedom of testation and protection of the family, numerous scholars have proposed other forms of compromise. One proposal suggests a forced portion for all children, with the possibility of an additional amount to be held in trust for minor children.[195] Another scholar suggests a "protected inheritance plan" for all children. Under the plan, the needs of dependant and minor children would first be met, leaving the excess to be divided equally among all children.[196] Attempting to strike a balance between a fixed forced portion and the wide discretionary power inherent in the family maintenance plan, another proposal suggests posthumously awarding child support to a decedent's minor children. The amount of the support would be calculated using support schedules used in child support guidelines for living parents.[197]

Conclusion

Critics of the traditional forced heirship, as provided in the LOUISIANA CIVIL CODE of 1870, condemned the institution as an inflexible deprivation of free testation. The system forced a testator to leave a portion of his estate to persons who neither needed, nor deserved, to inherit. Ironically, the same criticism may be made of the "new" forced heirship adopted in Louisiana,

---

[187] Glendon, *supra* note 179, at 1185.

[188] *Supra* note 179, at § 10.

[189] *See* Laufer, *supra* note 184; Joseph Dainow, *Restricted Testation in New Zealand, Australia and Canada*, 36 Mich. L. Rev. 1107 (1938) (description of testation in Australia and Canada).

[190] Introduction to the Civil Code for the Federal District and Territories of Mexico, translated by Otto Schoenrch, 1950 as cited in Spaht, Lorio, Picou, Samuel and Swaim, *supra,* note 119, at 418.

[191] Civ. Code art. 1368 (Abraham Eckstein and Enrique Zepeda Tryillo 1996) (Mex.).

[192] Civ. Code art. 1370 (Abraham Eckstein and Enrique Zepeda Tryillo 1996) (Mex.).

[193] Civ. Code art. 1372 (Abraham Eckstein and Enrique Zepeda Tryillo 1996) (Mex.).

[194] Maine repealed its version of family maintenance, 18 Me. Rev. Stat. § 21, in 1979.

[195] Paul G. Haskell, *The Power of Disinheritance: Proposal for Reform*, 52 Geo. L.J. 499, 518. *See also*, author's general discussion of previous proposal. *Id.* at 511-518.

[196] Batts, *supra* note 156.

[197] Brashier, *supra* note 97, at 174.

with the added problem that both deserving and needy older children of the testator may now be excluded. The new system wreaks of inequality among siblings, an inequality that may be both unnecessary and contrary to the desires of the testator. Excluding a twenty-four year old child from protection, while providing a forced portion for his sister, only a year his junior, promotes disharmony[198] and supports an argument that the new forced heirship is subject to a challenge based on age discrimination.[199] Furthermore, in cases where a decedent has made a number of gifts during his last three years of life, and also happens to have more than four children, his inability to treat his children equally, even if he so desires, is problematic. Further exacerbating the inequality of the current system is the limiting of the claim for collation to this new limited group of forced heirs.[200]

Although the new system does not leave the determining of the amount of the forced portion to the discretion of the judge,[201] it still suffers from a lack of predictability. Even the most sophisticated estate planner cannot be assured that he will die after all his children become adults, or that, even if he lives to see his children reach adulthood, that those children will be healthy and competent at the time of his death.

The real impetus for change in Louisiana was not law reform,[202] but rather the personal desires of a group of people who wished to leave their property as they saw fit, completely free of government intervention. Provided the children of these people were able-bodied, competent adults, the new system of forced heirship offered no threat to their plan. The tragedy is that succession law of the state of Louisiana has suffered greatly as a result. Unconsciously borrowing from both civil and common law sources, this "unique Louisiana political compromise" we now refer to as forced heirship, has deprived most of the players in this drama of even a portion of what they wanted.

For Senator Nelson, a conscientious legislator, whose first choice was a system of completely free testation,[203] the new plan may have satisfied many of his constituents, but certainly was not the "reform" measure it purported to be. Also, many of the voters that approvingly voted for the constitutional amendment on October 21, 1995, were unaware that their vote would not result in a system of free testation, but would in fact create new legal problems, not even contemplated by the drafters of either the constitutional amendment, nor the implementation act.[204] Additionally, the Law Institute of Louisiana neither initiated the "reform," nor ever voted approvingly to abolish forced heirship.

---

[198] The inequality among grandchildren is even more acute. Consider the case of a testator survived by two sets of minor grandchildren, one set fathered by a predeceased child of the decedent who would have been twenty-four at the time of the decedent's death, and the other set having a predeceased mother who would have been only twenty-three at the time of the decedent's death.

[199] *See* Spaht, Lorio, Picou, Samuel, and Swaim, *supra* note 119; Lorio, *supra* note 130.

[200] *See* Cynthia Samuel, Letter From Louisiana: An Obituary for Forced Heirship and a Birth Announcement for Covenant Marriage (1998) (Unpublished manuscript on file at Tulane).

[201] *See* Glendon, *supra* note 179 (criticism of discretionary awards).

[202] *See infra* note 120, noting that the Louisiana State Law Institute did not initiate, nor vote approvingly, of a proposal abolishing forced heirship.

[203] *See infra* note 114 and accompanying text.

[204] The constitutional amendment mandated the abolition of forced heirship except for children twenty-three years of age or younger, while authorizing the legislature to include as forced heirs those with medical or physical incapacities. Some have argued that the inclusion of grandchildren as forced heirs may actually be an expansion by

Although the Louisiana Constitution refers to this new plan as "forced heirship" for children under the age of twenty-four, the new system hardly resembles the traditional civilian institution. While maintaining the part of the concept providing for maintenance of one's dependents,[205] the new system has completely abandoned the part of forced heirship dealing with the preservation of family property. Additionally, it no longer promotes equality of inheritance among children as to the part of the decedent's estate received for her children, a central precept of the traditional civilian forced heirship.[206]

Even the maintenance concept of this new system is not consistent with the duties imposed on individuals by the LOUISIANA CIVIL CODE. Article 229 of the Civil Code, while providing for an obligation of maintenance between parents and their descendants, imposes the duty of support reciprocally. If the legislature was concerned about support by a decedent to those dependents to whom the decedent owed a duty to support, then the analysis at death should be phrased in terms actually determining dependence on the decedent. Thus, if an aging parent was being supported by the decedent at the time of his death, a portion of the decedent's estate should be reserved to provide maintenance for that dependent parent after the decedent's death. Although the twenty-four year limit was obviously chosen as a shorthand for need, it often does not reflect true dependency of those one is obligated to support. Actually, the Civil Code imposes a duty during life to support a needy forty-year-old child, rather than a twenty-three year old who has completed his education and is adequately employed. A person could be in need although both physically and mentally competent. Also, this duty of support exists regardless of the actions of the dependent person. Thus, arguments to the effect that disinherison should play no part in a system of forced heirship based on maintenance alone are logically consistent.[207]

A frequently espoused criticism of the traditional forced heirship is that it affords little protection to minor children who might suffer at the hands of adult siblings with whom the minors would have to share a forced portion. In the case of a small estate, the criticism is well taken, since the entire estate might be inadequate to sufficiently provide for the support and education of these minors. In such a case, the new system has a great deal of appeal, although its underinclusiveness would need to be remedied. However, in the case of a larger estate, where there are adequate assets to both provide for the minor children and allow for a share for the older siblings, some accommodation is in order. The remedy proposed by Professor Ralph Brashier is to calculate the needs of the dependent children based on child support guidelines, reserving for the minors, from the decedent's estate, an amount reflecting what the decedent's contribution would have been had he survived.[208] Any insurance or pension benefits that the dependent would have received from the decedent could be credited to his reserve.[209] A forced

---

the legislature beyond the limits of the constitutional provision. *See* original Revision Comment(c) to La. Civ. art. 1493, as it appeared in the H.R. 55 of 1996.

[205] *See Succession of Lauga*, 624 So. 2d at 1184 (Kimball, K. dissenting).

[206] *See Succession of Lauga*, 624 So. 2d at 1169 (Dennis's discussion of equality as a fundamental part of forced heirship)

> . . . a legally assured right to share equally in the *legitime* is an important cornerstone to an individual's relations of the most fundamental sort -- familial respect, dignity, love, and trust.

[207] *See* Samuel, *supra* note 200.

[208] Brashier, *supra* note 97, at 173-180. A similar type of analysis could be applied for an aging parent, based on the parent's life expectancy.

[209] *Id.* at 175.

portion including all children could be determined. From that larger forced portion, the reserve for dependents would first be subtracted. Then the remaining amount of the forced portion could be equally divided among all the children. Undoubtedly, in small estates, the reserve for minors might exhaust the forced potion. However, in larger estates, all children would be granted a portion of the deceased parent's estate, thus promoting equality and family harmony, central goals of our civilian notion of forced heirship.

Obviously, a system such as that proposed above would not be acceptable to those who gained most from the revised forced heirship since the objective of those was to completely disinherit their adult children, regardless of the worthiness of the children. Thus, a blessing from those sectors of the population would not be forthcoming. However, such a revision to the current system would answer many of the criticisms raised by many who voted to "abolish" forced heirship due to its flaws. It would also result in a law that is more consistent with the objectives articulated by our Civil Code and its proud heritage of concern for the family.

NOTE

For more general information concerning the "new" forced heirship, *see* Kathryn Venturatos Lorio, *Forced Heirship: The Citadel Has Fallen - or Has It?*, 44 La. B. J. 16 (June 1996); Katherine Connell-Thouez, *The New Forced Heirship in Louisiana: Historical Perspectives, Comparative Law Analysis and Reflections Upon the Integration of New Structures into a Classical Civil Law System*, 43 Loy. L. Rev. 1 (1997); Katherine Shaw Spaht, *Forced Heirship Changes: The Regrettable "Revolution" Completed*, 57 La. L. Rev. 55 (1996); Kathryn Venturatos Lorio, LOUISIANA CIVIL LAW TREATISE ON SUCCESSIONS AND DONATIONS, Second Edition, Chapter 10, (2009).

Who are Forced Heirs

A. Age - La. C.C. 1493, La. Const. Art. XII, Sec. 5.

PROBLEMS

Read Civil Code article 1493 carefully and consider who among the following persons are forced heirs:

1. Testator's three children who are twenty-seven, twenty-four, and eighteen years old, respectively.

2. Testator's two grandchildren who are both healthy. One is fifteen and the other is ten. Testator leaves no other surviving descendants. His daughter, the children's mother predeceased the testator and was thirty-five years old at the time of her death. No, does not fall w/in range.

3. Testatrix's twenty-five year old son and two grandchildren, One grandchild is two years old and the other, six months old. Their twenty year old mother, testatrix's daughter, died in a car accident two months before the testator. Two minor grandchild bcuz their mother predeceased the decedent @ 20 yrs old decedent's death.

11-24

4. Same facts as number 3 above, except that at the time of her death, testatrix's daughter was thirty-three. Might the otherwise healthy grandchildren qualify as forced heirs by virtue of "mental incapacity" or "physical infirmity"? Are they "permanently incapable of taking care of their person or administering their estates," at the time of death? If the time of death is the critical time for analysis, how can their incapacity be deemed a "permanent" condition?

No, bcuz while minor children, they don't have an inherited, incurable condition that will render them unable to care for themselves or to administer their estates in the future.

B. Mental Incapacity or Physical Infirmity - La. C.C. 1493

SUCCESSION OF MARTINEZ
729 So. 2d 22 (La. 5th Cir. 1999)

CANNELLA, Judge.

Plaintiff, Floyd Martinez, appeals from a judgment dismissing his petition to reopen the Succession of Mary Margaret Loyola Martinez (Mary Margaret), his mother. We affirm.

In 1979, Mary Margaret executed a will in favor of Frederick Baldamar Martinez, Jr. (Frederick), her husband and the father of plaintiff. In 1993, Mary Margaret and Frederick were divorced. Mary Margaret died in 1997. *recognize will*

In August of 1997, Frederick filed petitions to probate the statutory will and for possession. On August 14, 1997, a judgment was rendered placing him in possession of his divorced wife's estate. On February 20, 1998, plaintiff filed a petition seeking to have the succession re-opened, contending that he is a forced heir under La. C.C. art. 1493. On July 8, 1998, the trial judge ruled against plaintiff and dismissed his petition.

On appeal, plaintiff argues that the trial judge erred in finding that plaintiff is not a forced heir and in dismissing plaintiff's case.

La.C.C. art. 1493 A. provides:

A. Forced heirs are descendants of the first degree who, at the time of the death of the decedent, are twenty-three years of age or younger or descendants of the first degree of any age who, because of *mental incapacity or physical infirmity, are permanently incapable of taking care of their persons or administering their estates at the time of the death of the decedent.* [Emphasis added]

The trial judge found that to be mentally incapable within the meaning of art. 1493, the person must be "severely handicapped." She cited the comments to the article in the third paragraph of Comments (c), relying on that part which states:

... Article 1493(A) clarifies the law in several respects and should help reduce unwarranted or inappropriate claims. For one thing, the Article specifies that the time at which the incapacity or infirmity is determined to be relevant is at the donor's death, which was always intended but may not have been fully clear in the earlier legislation. More important, the Legislature added the word "permanently" before the word "incapable" for the express purpose of emphasizing that a temporary incapacity or infirmity, even if severe, should not

11-25

apply. The legislature thereby expressly manifested its intent that the rule making disabled children of any age forced heirs should only apply to "seriously handicapped" individuals. The Legislature requested specifically that these Comments be written to explain that it is the purpose of adding the word "permanently" to more effectively express the public policy intended, namely, to protect children who are over the age of 23 as forced heirs if, and only if, they are severely disabled.

In this case, the evidence shows that plaintiff is 33 years old and mildly mentally handicapped. He receives Social Security disability income and is enrolled in the U.S. Navy's Incapacitated Dependant Program. Plaintiff has difficulty with money transactions, banking and he cannot perform more than one task at a time. His brother, aunts and uncles help him with banking tasks and make sure he gets to appointments. Plaintiff lived with his mother until her death. He now lives with his brother, Robert Martinez (Robert), who works offshore. Robert buys the groceries and gives money to one of plaintiff's uncles for plaintiff's use before he goes offshore. While Robert is offshore, plaintiff's family help him with purchasing other groceries or necessities. A friend stays with plaintiff during his brother's absence. Although plaintiff held a job for a short time some years in the past, he is unemployable.

Plaintiff does not consider himself severely handicapped and is socially active. Plaintiff is a float lieutenant in the Krewe of Choctaw. As such, he is responsible for the members getting on the float before the parade. Plaintiff is also a member of the Knights of Columbus. He volunteers with the Women's Auxiliary of the Fleet Reserve, at local church fairs, selling nacho chips. He gets along well with others and appears to be well-liked and likable. Plaintiff can take care of his home, his physical needs and is a good cook. When his mother was alive, he cleaned house and cooked for her and himself.

La.C.C. art. 1493 states that, in order to become a forced heir after the age of 23, the person must be permanently incapable of taking care of their persons or administering their estates. The comments indicate that the intent of the legislature was to provide this remedy only for "severely handicapped" persons. Based on the evidence, plaintiff is considered mildly mentally handicapped, even though he is incapable of taking care of certain aspects of his life without assistance. Consequently, since he is not "severely" handicapped, we find that the trial judge did not err in finding that plaintiff is not a forced heir under La.C.C. art. 1493.

*   *   *

AFFIRMED.

NOTES

At the 1998 1st Extraordinary Session of the Louisiana State Legislature, Concurrent Resolution No. 1 was passed. The resolution directed the Louisiana State Law Institute to edit the 1996 Revision Comment (c) of article 1493, deleting "all references describing incapable children in terms other than those used in that article, to-wit: Children who are 'permanently incapable of caring for their persons or administering their estates.'" West Publishing Company was instructed to reprint Comment (c). The edited version omits two sentences relied on by the court in *Martinez* in reaching its decision, specifically -

The Legislature thereby expressly manifested its intent that the rule making disabled children of any age forced heirs should only apply to "seriously handicapped" individuals. The Legislature requested specifically that the Comments be written to explain that it is the purpose of adding the word "permanently" to more effectively express the public policy intended, namely, to protect children who are over the age of 23 as forced heirs if, and only if, they are severely disabled.

IN RE SUCCESSION OF CARROLL
125 So. 3d 505 (La. App. 2d Cir. 2013) *writ denied*, 130 So. 3d 947 (La. 2014)

BROWN, Chief Judge.

Agnes Wylonda Carroll died testate on January 3, 2008. She was survived by three adult children. Her testament designated her daughter, Ethyl Joyce Cruse Hornsby, as executrix and as the universal legatee. The testament was probated on August 1, 2008. Plaintiffs, Donna Cruse Cagle and Thomas B. Cruse, Jr., who were decedent's other two children, petitioned to annul and declare the testament to be invalid. As relates to this appeal, plaintiffs filed a motion for partial summary judgment declaring them to be forced heirs of their mother. The trial court denied plaintiffs' motion for partial summary judgment. Specifically, the trial court determined that genuine issues of material fact existed as to whether either plaintiff was permanently incapable of caring for his/her person or administrating his/her estate at the time of decedent's death. The trial court certified this judgment as a final judgment for appeal. For the reasons stated herein, we now affirm.

Facts and Procedural Background

In their petition, filed on November 20, 2008, plaintiffs/appellants, Donna Cagle and Thomas Cruse, Jr., sought to nullify the Agnes Carroll will and certain real estate transactions based on the following grounds: 1) Agnes Carroll was of unsound mind; 2) Agnes Carroll was acting under fraud, duress or mistake; and/or 3) Agnes Carroll lacked testamentary capacity.

In an amended petition, plaintiffs subsequently raised, among other claims, the issue that is central to this appeal, forced heirship. On September 19, 2012, plaintiffs filed the instant motion for partial summary judgment asking the trial court to recognize both of them as forced heirs of Agnes Carroll. Each claimed that they were permanently physically disabled. The trial court denied plaintiffs' motion, finding that genuine issues of material fact exist regarding their claims of forced heirship.

Discussion

Article 12, § 5 of the Louisiana Constitution abolished forced heirship effective January 1, 1996, except that it provides in part that:

(B) The legislature shall provide for the classification of descendants, of the first degree, twenty-three years of age or younger as forced heirs. The legislature may also classify as forced heirs descendants of any age who, because of mental incapacity or physical infirmity, are incapable of taking care of their persons or administering their estates. The amount of the forced portion reserved to heirs and the grounds for disinherison shall also be provided by law. Trusts may be authorized by law and the forced portion may be placed in trust.

The legislature enacted La. C.C. art. 1493, which provides in part that:

(A) Forced heirs are descendants of the first degree who, at the time of the death of the decedent, are twenty-three years of age or younger or descendants of the first degree of any age who, because of mental incapacity or physical infirmity, are permanently incapable of taking care of their persons or administering their estates at the time of the death of the decedent.

...

(E) For purposes of this Article "permanently incapable of taking care of their persons or administering their estates at the time of the death of the decedent" shall include descendants who, at the time of death of the decedent, have, according to medical documentation, an inherited, incurable disease or condition that may render them incapable of caring for their persons or administering their estates in the future.

Article 1493(A) clarifies the law in several respects and should help reduce unwarranted or inappropriate claims. For one thing, art. 1493 specifies that the time at which the incapacity or infirmity is determined to be relevant is at the donor's death, which was always intended but may not have been fully clear in the earlier legislation. More importantly, the legislature added the word "permanently" before the word "incapable" for the express purpose of emphasizing that a temporary incapacity or infirmity, even if severe, should not apply. Although the jurisprudence on limited interdiction may be helpful, the new rule expressed in this article is intentionally different and more restrictive than the standard for interdiction because of the use of the word "permanently" to describe the nature of the incapacity or infirmity. La. C.C. art. 1493, Revision Comment (c).

FN 1: The adverb "permanently" in Civil Code article 1493 modifies incapable and refers to the duration, not extent of the incapacity, even though some of the original language of comment (c) drafted after legislative passage suggested to the contrary. In 1998 the legislature by resolution directed the Law Institute to change the comment because the comment "incorrectly characterizes permanently incapable children by terms not included within the article as enacted by the legislature, such as 'severely disabled' and 'seriously handicapped' and thereby purports to limit the category of incapable children as defined by the legislature." Katherine Spaht, *The Remnant of Forced Heirship: The Interrelationship of Undue Influence, What's Become of Disinherison, and the Unfinished Business of the Stepparent Usufruct,* 60 La L.R. 637, 643 (2000).

11-28

*　　*　　*

For plaintiffs to qualify as forced heirs, they must show that at the time of their mother's death they were permanently incapable of taking care of their persons or administering their estates due to either mental incapacity or physical infirmity. Permanent incapacity "shall include descendants who, at the time of death of the decedent, have, according to medical documentation, an inherited, incurable disease or condition that may render them incapable of caring for their persons or administering their estates in the future." La. C.C. art. 1493(E).

In support of their motion for summary judgment plaintiffs each submitted a personal affidavit, an affidavit of their respective treating physicians, and Social Security Administration ("SSA") documents showing that prior to their mother's death they had been declared disabled. It is on the latter two types of evidence that plaintiffs primarily rely in support of their motion for summary judgment.

Donna Cagle was born on January 11, 1947. She was diagnosed with a tumor known as a vestibular schwannoma or Acoustic Neuroma, which was surgically removed on June 6, 2005, due to the chronic imbalance it was causing her. Prior to her mother's death, Ms. Cagle was declared disabled by both her private insurer and the SSA, a classification that remains today.

Thomas Cruse, Jr., was born on March 13, 1943. He was diagnosed with prostate cancer in 2003, which returned after treatment and a temporary remission. Prior to his mother's death, Mr. Cruse was also declared disabled by the SSA. The SSA deemed Mr. Cruse's disability to have "onset" by at least March 4, 2004, and he remains classified as disabled. In addition, Mr. Cruse also suffers from an irregular heartbeat and postherpetic neuralgia.

The SSA document submitted by Donna Cagle was a determination and finding of disability by the SSA. Tommy Cruse submitted a SSA document showing current SSA benefits. Donna Cagle and Tommy Cruse also submitted affidavits from their treating physicians, Drs. Brian McKinnon and Robert Raulerson, respectively.

In opposition to the summary judgment motion, defendant submitted exhibits, including an affidavit from a private investigator that identified numerous physical activities that plaintiffs have performed. The exhibits showed that Donna Cagle, who lived in Georgia, had driven back and forth from Georgia to Louisiana and to New Jersey where she "pet" sat for her son. Meanwhile, the exhibits showed that Tommy Cruse drove his truck, refueled it, unloaded groceries and dry cleaning, made numerous visits to businesses, and even went deer hunting.
Dr. McKinnon's affidavit, dated September 13, 2012, states, in pertinent part:

> 4. I have treated Donna Cagle as a patient for approximately three (3) years.
> 8. Mrs. Cagle underwent resection of a right vestibular schwannoma via middle fossa approach on 6/7/05 at the House Ear Clinic.
> 9. She executed this procedure on account of her chronic imbalance caused by her condition.
> 10. My record show Mrs. Cagle has been declared physically disabled due to the above conditions by her disability insurance carrier, as well as, the Social Security Administration under its guidelines.
> 11. Mrs. Cagle's symptoms have remained persistent, and in view of the apparent recurrence of her acoustic neuroma on the right, she will likely need further intervention preventing Mrs. Cagle from effectively administering her affairs and/or taking care of her estate.

11-29

12. I anticipate her physical infirmity will remain unchanged, if not digress, in view of my current findings.

Considering that there is no mention of whether Ms. Cagle's physical infirmity is an inherited, incurable disease, we are left to determine whether she suffered a physical infirmity that rendered her "permanently incapable" of taking care of her person or estate at the time of her mother's death. Based upon a reading of the affidavit, Dr. McKinnon began treating Ms. Cagle after her mother's death; he was not the physician in 2005 when she underwent resection; and he fails to state at what point in time the apparent recurrence of her acoustic neuroma occurred. The affidavit merely states that "she will likely need further intervention preventing [her] from effectively administering her affairs and/or taking care of her estate." This appears to show that Ms. Cagle suffers from a physical infirmity that may render her incapable of caring for her person or estate at some point in the future, not that she was permanently incapable at the time of her mother's death. As noted above, the opposition affidavits show that she drove to Louisiana from Georgia on multiple occasions. Specifically, they showed that she drove to Louisiana after her mother's death to assist in making arrangements for her mother's funeral, she ran errands and went shopping without assistance. Considering the aforementioned, the trial court correctly determined that genuine issues of material fact exist as to whether Ms. Cagle was permanently incapable of caring for her person or estate at the time of her mother's death and/or whether the acoustic neuroma is an inherited, incurable disease.

Likewise, the affidavit of Dr. Raulerson, Mr. Cruse's treating physician, fails to state whether the prostate cancer and other ailments that Mr. Cruse suffers from are inherited, incurable diseases or conditions. Furthermore, the affidavit of Mr. Cruse's treating physician fails to establish that on the date of his mother's death he was "permanently incapable." In fact, Dr. Raulerson's affidavit states that Mr. Cruse's prostate cancer is "a disease which may render Mr. Cruse permanently incapable of taking care of his person or administering his estate at some point in the future." Again, the opposition showed that his activities put at issue whether he was permanently incapable caring for himself and administering his estate. As the trial court correctly found, this opinion, coupled with the opposition's affidavits, does not support a finding that he was "incapable" on January 3, 2008, the date of his mother's death.

Plaintiffs submit in their appellate brief that the SSA classification "is, at the very least, a factor to consider in determining whether a descendant qualifies as a forced heir under Louisiana law." We agree, it is a factor to consider. This is a motion for summary judgment, not a trial. A factor, without more, fails to meet plaintiffs' burden of showing that there is no genuine issue as to material facts. Just because a person qualifies for disability benefits does not mean that he or she is permanently incapable of taking care of his or her person or estate. In Ms. Cagle's case, we note that the adjudication of disability by the SSA concludes by stating that "Medical improvement is expected with appropriate treatment. Consequently, a continuing disability review is recommended in 18 months."

Further, considering defendant's offerings in opposition to plaintiffs' motion for summary judgment, it is clear that there were genuine issues of material fact regarding either plaintiff's status as a forced heir. Plaintiffs contend that since defendants failed to present an affidavit from a countervailing medical expert, their opposition to plaintiffs' motion for summary judgment is insufficient and the trial court erred in not decreeing each a forced heir. Louisiana law does not entitle a party to summary judgment solely on the grounds that the moving party offered medical testimony and the opposing party did not. The trial court must still examine the medical testimony to determine if it eliminates any genuine issue of material fact. Here, the trial court analyzed the affidavits of plaintiffs' treating physicians, as well as the exhibits offered in opposition, and correctly determined that there were genuine issues of material fact as to whether either plaintiff suffered from a physical incapacity at the time of their mother's death which rendered them permanently incapable of caring for their persons or estates.

Conclusion

Based on the foregoing, the trial court's denial of plaintiffs' motion for partial summary judgment is affirmed. Costs of this appeal are assessed to plaintiffs.

SUCCESSION OF ARDOIN
957 So. 2d 937 (La. App. 3rd Cir. 2007)

AMY, Judge.

In this succession proceeding, the trial court found that the decedent's daughter was not a forced heir under La.Civ.Code art. 1493. The daughter appeals, contending that the medical evidence showed that she has an inherited, incurable condition that may render her permanently incapable of caring for her person or administering her estate in the future. For the following reasons, we reverse and remand.

Factual and Procedural Background

The decedent, Jeanette Perron Ardoin, died on May 4, 2004. She was survived by her husband, Wayne Ardoin, and three adult children from a previous marriage. Mr. Ardoin filed a petition to file and execute Ms. Ardoin's olographic testament. Dated May 7, 2001, the testament purports to bequeath the entirety of Ms. Ardoin's estate to Mr. Ardoin.[1]

Ms. Ardoin's daughter, Mary Plonsky Sailors, filed a "Petition for Reduction of Excess Legacy," alleging that she is a forced heir as, at the time of Ms. Ardoin's death, an inherited, incurable disease or condition rendered her incapable of caring for herself and administering her estate in the future. She requested that the excess donation to Mr. Ardoin be reduced to satisfy her legitime, viz., the portion of the decedent's estate reserved to her by law.

At the August 2006 hearing on Ms. Sailors' petition, the trial court heard testimony regarding Ms. Sailors' diagnosis of bipolar disorder and the alleged incapacity associated with

---

[1] The olographic testament provides:

> I Jeanette Perron Ardoin wife of Wayne Ardoin, make this my last will and testament hereby revoking any and all prior wills that I have made.
>
> I give and bequeath to my husband Wayne Ardoin all properties, movable and immovable, that I may own at my death.
>
> I name and appoint my husband Wayne Ardoin, executor of my estate with full seizin and without bond.
>
> This my will was written dated and signed by me at Opelousas, Louisiana, this 7th day of May 2001.

the condition. In its reasons for ruling, the trial court found that Ms. Sailors was "not permanently incapable of taking care of her person or administering her estate as of the time of the death of the decedent nor does she have an inherited, incurable disease or condition that may render her permanently incapable of caring for her person or administering her estate in the future." The trial court's ruling reveals not only its consideration of LA.CIV.CODE art. 1493, but its reliance on *Succession of Martinez,* 98-962 (La.App. 5 Cir. 2/10/99), 729 So. 2d 22, wherein the fifth circuit affirmed a determination that the phrase "mentally incapable" within the meaning of Article 1493 required the heir to be severely handicapped.

Ms. Sailors appeals the trial court's determination that she is not a forced heir and asserts the following assignments of error in her brief to this court:

> 1. The trial court failed to follow the specific law of the State of Louisiana, in effect at the death of the decedent, specifically Article 1493 of the Louisiana [Civil Code] as amended by Act 1207 of 2003.
> 2. The trial court failed to utilize the clear medical evidence presented by the expert witnesses for both the Plaintiff and Defendant in finding that the plaintiff, Mary Plonsky Sailors, was [not] a forced heir of the decedent under the provisions of [LA.CIV.CODE art.] 1493.
> 3. The defendant did not present any medical evidence contrary to the testifying experts that contravened their testimon[ies] as to the inherited, incurable disease of Mary Plonsky Sailors and her probable future incapacity to care for her person or administer her estate.

Discussion

Ms. Sailors argues that the trial court's reliance on *Martinez,* 729 So. 2d 22 in rendering its judgment was misplaced. In particular, she points out that Article 1493 has been amended since the fifth circuit rendered *Martinez.* She asserts that the article now provides a "more comprehensive definition of when a person is to be considered a forced heir." In particular, she observes that a 2003 amendment added Paragraph E to Article 1493 and that it does not require that the person claiming forced heir status be "severely handicapped" at the time of decedent's death. She contends that she satisfied her burden of proving forced heir status under the dictates of Article 1493 as it presently exists.

LOUISIANA CIVIL CODE Article 1493 provides, in pertinent part:

> A. Forced heirs are descendants of the first degree who, at the time of the death of the decedent, are twenty-three years of age or younger or *descendants of the first degree of any age who, because of mental incapacity or physical infirmity, are permanently incapable of taking care of their persons or administering their estates at the time of the death of the decedent.*

> *   *   *

> E. For purposes of this Article "permanently incapable of taking care of their persons or administering their estates at the time of the death of the decedent" shall include descendants who, at the time of death of the decedent,

have, according to medical documentation, an inherited, incurable disease or condition that may render them incapable of caring for their persons or administering their estates in the future.

(Emphasis added.)

As referenced above, the trial court interpreted Article 1493 in light of *Martinez*, 729 So. 2d 22, a case rendered by the fifth circuit in 1999. Central to *Martinez* and to the trial court's reasoning in this case as well, is the concept that Article 1493(A) requires that a purported forced heir be "severely handicapped." However, such a requirement is not contained within the text of Article 1493. Furthermore, examination of *Martinez* reveals that this analysis can be traced to a version of Article 1493, comment (c) that has been edited by direction of the legislature and no longer appears in the commentary.

As reported by the fifth circuit, the plaintiff in *Martinez*, 729 So. 2d at 24, was "33 years old and mildly mentally handicapped." The trial court in that case determined that the plaintiff was not a forced heir under Article 1493 as he failed to prove that he was "severely handicapped." In doing so, it relied on a portion of Article 1493, comment (c) indicating that the legislature "expressly manifested its intent that the rule making disabled children of any age forced heirs should only apply to 'seriously handicapped' individuals."[2] *Id.* at 24. According to the comment, this intent was evident due to the use of the word "permanently" before the word "incapable."[3] *Id.* The fifth circuit considered the facts presented in *Martinez* in light of this commentary and affirmed the trial court's determination that the plaintiff was not a forced heir because he was not "severely handicapped."

The trial court in the present case discussed *Martinez* at length, applying the "severely handicapped" qualification to the evidence presented.[4] This reliance, however, was in error as

---

[2] The comments to Article 1493 are not "part of the law and not enacted into law by virtue of their inclusion in this Act." *See* 1996 La.Acts No. 77, § 4. However, we reference the comments insofar as they formed the basis for the ruling in *Martinez* and, in turn, were adopted by the trial court in the present case.

[3] *Martinez*, 729 So. 2d at 24 sets forth the comment relied upon in that case as follows:

> ... Article 1493(A) clarifies the law in several respects and should help reduce unwarranted or inappropriate claims. For one thing, the Article specifies that the time at which the incapacity or infirmity is determined to be relevant is at the donor's death, which was always intended but may not have been fully clear in the earlier legislation. More important, the Legislature added the word "permanently" before the word "incapable" for the express purpose of emphasizing that a temporary incapacity or infirmity, even if severe, should not apply. *The legislature thereby expressly manifested its intent that the rule making disabled children of any age forced heirs should only apply to "seriously handicapped" individuals. The Legislature requested specifically that these Comments be written to explain that it is the purpose of adding the word "permanently" to more effectively express the public policy intended, namely, to protect children who are over the age of 23 as forced heirs if, and only if, they are severely disabled.*

[4] With regard to *Martinez*, 729 So. 2d 22, the trial court's extensive reasons for ruling reveal, in part:

> The major holding of the *Martinez* case is that the legislature intended that "the rule making disabled children of any age forced heirs should only apply to 'seriously handicapped' individuals." *Id.* at 24. The *Martinez* court, in relying on the Revision Comments, went on to say, "The Legislature requested specifically that these comments be written to explain that it is the purpose of adding the word 'permanently' to more effectively express the public policy intended, namely, to protect children who are over the age of 23 as forced heirs if, and only if, they are severely disabled." *Id* at 25. In the *Martinez* case, a 33-year-old, mildly mentally handicapped man

was found *not* to qualify as a forced heir. Despite the fact that he was found to be unemployable and was receiving Social Security disability benefits, he was found to not qualify as a forced heir for reasons such as: his social activity, participation in volunteer groups, ability to take care of his home, and his ability to cook. Thus, he was not found to satisfy the "permanently incapable" language of Article 1493.

Therefore, under *Martinez* it would be required of Ms. Sailors to show that her disorder rises to the level of a "serious handicap" or "severe disability." However, it should be noted that the *Martinez* decision occurred prior to the addition of Section E to Article 1493. Ms. Sailors places heavy reliance upon Section E of Article 1493, claiming that it "totally changes the coverage of the law," and "provides to the court a completely different standard than that suggested by the *Martinez* case." *Pretrial Memorandum for Plaintiff.* This interpretation of Section E would force this Court to completely disregard the holding of *Martinez,* and to instead rely solely on the language of Section E.

Section E of Article 1493

Unlike Section A, there is a complete lack of Revision Comments concerning the addition of section E to Article 1493. There is no specification of legislative intent concerning its language. The lack of comments is despite a request to the Louisiana State Law Institute "to write comments to all changes made by this Act." 2003 La. Sess. Law Serv. Act 1207. However, the text of section E itself makes clear that its purpose is to clarify and broaden the meaning of "permanently incapable of taking care of their persons or administering their estates at the time of the death of the decedent." The Article now specifically provides that this language includes "descendants, who, at the time of death of the decedent, have, according to medical documentation, an inherited, incurable disease or condition that may render them incapable of caring for their persons or administering their estates in the future." However, it is not the opinion of this Court that the addition of Section E "totally changes the coverage of the law," nor does it appear to "provide to the court a completely different standard than that suggested by the *Martinez* case. What Section E does appear to do is to liberalize the "as of the time of death of the decedent" requirement of Article 1493(A). Thus, a claimant need not be permanently incapable of taking care of their person or administering their estate *at the time of death,* but may now still qualify as a forced heir if medical documentation can be produced to show that as of *the time of death* the claimant has an inherited, incurable disease or condition that may render them so incapable in the future. It is the opinion of this Court that whereas the language of Section E contributes to the *time* at which a person must have a condition or incapability, Section A and the *Martinez* decision contribute to the required level of severity and permanence of such condition. There is no statement, whether in the non-existent comments of Section E or the jurisprudence of this state, that suggests an intended overruling of *Martinez.*

Proof of Forced Heirship

Based upon the requirements of Article 1493, in order for Ms. Sailors to be considered a forced heir, it must be found that:

    1. Her bipolar condition existed at the time of Jeanette Ardoin's death and is medically documented;

    2. That the bipolar condition is an inherited, incurable disease;

    3. That the bipolar condition causes a "serious handicap" or "severe disability" that does, OR will, render her permanently incapable of taking care of her person AND/OR permanently incapable of administering her estate.

We further note that, after setting forth this standard, the trial court discussed the testimony and other evidence in the record and made numerous factual findings. Thereafter, the trial court referenced that portion of comment (c) to Article 1493 indicating that it was

the basis for the *Martinez* ruling has been eroded. By Concurrent Resolution No. 1 of the 1998 First Extraordinary Session,[5] the legislature directed the reprinting of "the Revision Comments

---

"contemplated that the guidelines that the courts would use in interpreting and enforcing the incapacity or infirmity provisions were the jurisprudence" concerning limited interdiction. In this regard, the trial court examined *Interdiction of Cornwell v. Cornwell*, 97-425 (La.App. 3 Cir. 10/15/97), 702 So. 2d 938, which discussed both full and limited interdiction. Ultimately, the trial court concluded that Ms. Sailors was not a forced heir, stating:

In summary, this Court finds that Ms. Sailors' condition does not rise to the level of a "serious handicap" or cause her to be "severely disabled" as stated in the *Martinez* decision. For the same reasons, this Court also finds that her condition does not render her "permanently incapable of taking care of her person," nor does it cause her to be "permanently incapable of administering her estate." This Court further finds that, based upon the facts, it has not been sufficiently shown that her condition may render her so incapable in the future.

[5] Concurrent Resolution No. 1 provides:

WHEREAS, the Louisiana Legislature revised the laws on forced heirship but continued the protection and status as forced heirs of those children who are "permanently incapable of taking care of their persons or administering their estates"; and

WHEREAS, the legislature rejected the Louisiana State Law Institute's recommendation to deny such children the protection and classification as forced heirs; and

WHEREAS, the legislature in Section 4 of Act No. 77 of the First Extraordinary Session of 1996 directed the Louisiana State Law Institute to draft comments regarding the meaning of such permanently incapacitated children "which are consistent with the provisions of the Act"; and

WHEREAS, the Revision Comments of 1996 to Civil Code Article 1493 (comment (c)) published by West Publishing Company incorrectly characterize permanently incapable children by terms not included within the article as enacted by the legislature, such as "severely disabled" and "seriously handicapped", and thereby purport to limit the category of incapable children as defined by the legislature; and

WHEREAS, the language of the Civil Code Article 1493 does not require that the child prove that he is either "severely disabled" or "seriously handicapped" but instead provides for a protection for a child who is "permanently incapable of caring for his person or administering his property"; and

WHEREAS, the term "permanently" as used in Civil Code Article 1493 relates to duration of the incapacity; and

WHEREAS, the phrase "incapable of caring for his person or administering his property" relates to the extent of his incapacity; and

WHEREAS, the terms "disabled" and "handicapped" are terms not adopted by the legislature and not necessarily coextensive with the standard "incapable of caring for his person or administering his property"; and

WHEREAS, as a consequence, portions of comment (c) to Civil Code Article 1493 are not consistent with the provisions of the article as enacted by the legislature; and

WHEREAS, pursuant to R.S. 24:256, West Publishing Company is authorized to print, publish, sell, and distribute any edition or supplement of the Louisiana Revised Statutes, including the Civil Code, prepared and certified by the Law Institute.

THEREFORE, BE IT RESOLVED that the Legislature of Louisiana hereby directs the Louisiana State Law Institute to instruct West Publishing Company to reprint the Revision Comments of 1996 to Civil Code Article 1493 (comment (c)) by deleting all references describing such incapable children in terms other than those used in the article, to wit: children who are "permanently incapable of caring for their persons or administering their estates".

BE IT FURTHER RESOLVED that copies of this Resolution shall be transmitted to the

of 1996 to Civil Code Article 1493 (comment (c)) by deleting all references describing such incapable children in terms other than used in the article, to wit: children who are "permanently incapable of caring for their persons or administering their estates."

We recognize that neither the trial court nor the parties were focused on the foundation of *Martinez* or the correctness of its requirements. Rather, the parties' focus below, and also before this court, was whether the addition of Paragraph E to Article 1493 legislatively overruled *Martinez*. Analysis of *Martinez* and its basis reveal that it was error to rely on the case as authority. Recall that the text of Article 1493 makes no reference to the "severely disabled" or "seriously handicapped" criteria. Instead, this criteria was utilized in *Martinez* due to a previous version of comment (c).[7] Although we recognize the complexities raised by the changing commentary, we conclude that the trial court erred in applying *Martinez* and the standard expressed therein. As this reversible error of law pervades the trial court's ruling, it is necessary for this court to perform a *de novo* review of the record and render a judgment on the merits. *See Thompson v. State*, 97-0293, 97-0302 (La.10/31/97), 701 So. 2d 952. We turn to consideration of the evidence presented in light of the requirements of Article 1493.

Ms. Sailors seeks forced heir's status as a descendant of the first degree who, because of mental incapacity or physical infirmity, is permanently incapable of taking care of her person or administering her estate at the time of the death of the decedent. LA.CIV.CODE art. 1493(A). Paragraph E of Article 1493 indicates that the "permanently incapable" requirement of Paragraph A includes "descendants who, at the time of death of the decedent, have, according to medical documentation, an inherited, incurable disease or condition that may render them incapable of caring for their persons or administering their estates in the future." Having examined this record, we conclude that Ms. Sailors has proven the criteria of Article 1493.

By the time of Ms. Ardoin's 2004 death, Ms. Sailors had been diagnosed with bipolar disorder and hospitalized several times for behaviors associated with her condition. Dr. Catherine McDonald, Ms. Sailors' treating psychiatrist, explained that she began treating Ms. Sailors in 2001 while Ms. Sailors was hospitalized on one such occasion. The records detailing the hospitalizations indicate that Ms. Sailors has suffered from auditory hallucinations, delusional thoughts, and, at times, demonstrated a complete inability to care for her person. Both Dr. McDonald and Dr. Philip Arnold Landry, a psychiatrist who conducted a psychiatric examination of Ms. Sailors prior to trial, opined that Ms. Sailors' disorder is likely an inherited, genetic disorder.

Successions Committee of the Louisiana State Law Institute and to West Publishing Company.

[7] The Editor's Note to La.Civ.Code art. 1493 (West, 2007 edition), provides, in part:

> Editor's note. Article 1493 was amended by Acts 1996, 1st Ex.Sess., No. 77, § 1 with revision comments. The original revision comments, however, were modified by the Louisiana State Law Institute *after* the amendment of Article 1493 and the publication of Act No. 77 in the Session Law Service. For the original comments, see West's Louisiana Session Law Service 1996, No. 2, p. 153.

> Revision Comment (c) under Article 1493 has been and reprinted in accordance with Concurrent Resolution No. 1 (1988 1st Ex.Sess.). The legislature directed the Louisiana State Law Institute to edit the 1996 Revision Comment (c) under Article 1493 by deleting all references describing incapable children in terms other than those used in that article, to-wit: children who are "permanently incapable of caring for their persons or administering their estates" and instructed West Publishing Company to reprint the Comment (c), as edited.

While Dr. McDonald testified that bipolar disorder is incurable, she explained that prescribed medications can help patients lead healthy and productive lives in that the frequency and severity of episodes may be reduced. Dr. McDonald noted that Ms. Sailors was hospitalized for two months "because she had refused to take medication." According to Dr. McDonald, the refusal to take medication is "part of any psychotic disorder.... [T]he patient be-comes paranoid that what you're doing is trying to hurt them, poison them or somehow or another alter the way they feel and they don't want you to do that." Dr. McDonald also explained that the efficacy of the medications may be affected by the use of alcohol and drugs. According to her estimate, "sixty to seventy percent of our bipolar patients self-medicate." The record contains evidence of Ms. Sailors' past use of marijuana and alcohol. Although Dr. McDonald discourages these behaviors, she explained that "if [her patients] drink, I would just as soon they go ahead and take their medication also because a psychotic person who's drinking is even worse than a non-psychotic person who's drinking."

Ms. Sailors' work history indicates that she has held various positions, including one requiring bookkeeping skills. However, both Dr. McDonald and Dr. Landry were of the opinion that Ms. Sailors' bipolar disorder will prevent her from being consistently employed. In fact, Ms. Sailors has not been regularly employed since 2003 and was deter-mined by the Social Security Administration to be eligible for monthly disability benefits beginning May 2004.[8] Ms. Sailors also denied at trial that she is able to work.

It is clear that Ms. Sailors typically has the ability to care for many facets of her everyday life, as Dr. McDonald opined that she can buy groceries, drive, apply for a loan, and balance a bank account. Ms. Sailors maintains a residence where she explained that she lives "alone with assistance." She stated that she also performs her shopping with assistance. However, this level of functioning is possible only when Ms. Sailors is not acutely ill. Dr. McDonald testified that, despite the appearance that Ms. Sailors can appear "okay," and able to care for her affairs, "the next day it may be totally different." Dr. McDonald explained that, during periods of illness, Ms. Sailors is "completely" incapable of taking care of her affairs. Dr. McDonald testified that during her hospitalization, "it's so severe she can't even function. At times she wasn't eating. You know, just taking a bath, she couldn't do that." Ms. Sailors' sister-in-law testified that she has assisted Ms. Sailors over the years with various issues, including obtaining health insurance coverage.

In short, this case presents a situation in which a person suffers from a permanent incapacity, but the extent of that incapacity varies.[9] Notwithstanding her inability to maintain employment, Ms. Sailors may function well much of the time. However, as reference to her past

---

[8] A letter from the Social Security Administration, dated April 19, 2005, is contained in the record and indicates that Ms. Sailors was determined to have become disabled on November 9, 2003 and entitled to begin receiving benefits in May 2004.

[9] We note that Article 1493, comment (c) appears to anticipate a situation in which a descendent may suffer from a permanent incapacity, but may experience periods in which the extent of that incapacity fluctuates. It provides, in part:

> The Legislature also requested that these Comments note that as a factual matter a person can be permanently incapable or infirm but on occasion have a temporary remission. It is not intended to be the policy of the Article that a mere temporary remission at the time of the decedent's death would disqualify an heir from being classified as "permanently" incapable or infirm within the new definition, provided that the condition is otherwise permanent.

history indicates, Ms. Sailors' inability to care for either her person or her estate has been absolute during times of acute illness.[10] Dr. McDonald testified as to the fluctuating nature of Ms. Sailors' condition, labeling it as unpredictable and recurrent, and opined that "the future could be the same as the past." Given these considerations, we find that Ms. Sailors' condition satisfies the criteria of La.Civ.Code art. 1493 and that she has proven herself to be a forced heir of Ms. Ardoin. We enter judgment reflecting this determination and remand for further proceedings.

DECREE

For the foregoing reasons, the judgment of the trial court is reversed. Judgment is entered finding the appellant, Mary Plonsky Sailors, to be a forced heir of the decedent Jeannette P. Ardoin. This matter is remanded for further proceedings consistent with this opinion. All costs of this proceeding are assigned to the Succession of Jeanette P. Ardoin.

REVERSED AND REMANDED.

NOTE

For other cases holding that children suffering from mental illness, including bipolar disorder, may be deemed forced heirs, *see Stewart v. Estate of Stewart*, 966 So. 2d 1241 (La. App. 3rd Cir. 2007) and *Succession of Forman*, 2010 WL 1780087 (La. App. 3rd Cir. 2010).

PROBLEMS

1. Would a twenty-five year old quadriplegic, in law school with a 4.0 GPA qualify as a forced heir? *Yes, she has a permanent physical infirmity that render it uncapable of taking care of of being in the future.*

2. What if the twenty-five year old was a paraplegic with an IQ of 80 who was able to work at "Good Will" forty hours per week sorting donated clothes? *No*

3. Testator's grandson was born deaf. His mother, testator's daughter died when she was thirty-two. At testator's death, his grandson was two years old. Would the grandson qualify as a forced heir? *No*

4. What if, at the time of testator's death, the grandson mentioned in problem 3 above, was twenty-five, had learned to read lips, and was working as a data entry clerk? *Still No*

---

[10] Portions of the testimony presented at the hearing relate to the standards of limited interdiction due to that portion of Article 1493, comment (c) which suggests that the incapacity provisions of the Article may be made in reference to the guidelines of limited interdiction. *See* La.Civ.Code art. 390. However, this reference is of little guidance in the present case as Ms. Sailors' capacity to function with the permanent condition of bipolar disorder varies.

C. The Transition: La. C.C. 870, 1611

In an effort to make the transition from the classic forced heirship structure in the Civil Code of 1870 to the new rules promulgated by the changes of Act 77 of 1996 easier, La. R.S. 9:2501 (Act No. 1421 of 1997), the transition act itself, created its own problems by imposing a restrictive structure for determining testamentary intent. *See In re Boyter*, 756 So. 2d 1122 (La. 2000) and K. Duna, *Comment, Forced Heirship Lives: The Effects of Louisiana Revised Statute Title 9, Section 2501*, 46 Loy. L. Rev. 619 (2000).

La. R.S. 9:2501 was repealed by Act 560 of 2001 and replaced by La. C.C. 870(B) and La. C.C. 1611(B). Thus, the approach to be taken in application of the new forced heirship provisions is (1) start with the general rule that the right to claim as a forced heir is governed by the law in effect at the time of the decedent's death; and (2) if the decedent's testament used a term such as "forced portion" or "*legitime*," the legal effect of which had changed after the testator executed his will, then the court **may** consider the law in effect at the time the testament was executed to ascertain the testator's intent in the interpretation of a legacy after testamentary provision. La. C.C. 1611. ✱

PROBLEMS → Ask for help

1. Testatrix executed her will **prior** to January 1, 1996. She died **after** July 15, 1997, survived by her husband and her only child, an able-bodied and sound-minded young man who was twenty-five at the time of his mother's death.

For each of the following phrases, consider which law applies and thus what the son would receive if the phrase appeared in the testatrix's will. What is your authority for your conclusion in each case?

testator's intent at testator's...

   a. I wish to disinherit my son. → Rule of disinherision
   b. I leave all my property to my sister. contradict - ?
   c. I leave my entire estate to my husband.
   d. I leave the usufruct of my estate to my husband. which is forever unless written otherwise
   e. I leave to my son a fractional interest in my property equal to the value of his *legitime* under Louisiana law as it may exist at the time of my death. → testator's intent; provisions contradict the law so its not applicable
   f. I leave the forced portion of all of the property of which I die possessed to my son.
   g. I leave to my son the minimum amount required by law at the time of my death. → La law has no provision that requires a decedent to leave anything in her will to a body & mind
   h. I leave one-fifth of all my property to my son. able adult over the age of 23
   i. I leave one-fourth of all my property to my son.
   j. I leave one-third of all my property to my son.
   k. I leave to my son his forced portion of one-fourth. → He is no longer a forced heir

2. Assume the testator died in 1998, survived only by his wife and his mother. If decedent left a will written in 1975, in which he left his mother her forced portion, and the remainder of his estate to his wife, who receives and what amount?

D. Conflict of Laws - La. C.C. 3532-3534   *Bar questions*

The general rule is that the succession of movables is governed by the law of the state in which the deceased was domiciled at the time of his death, La. C.C. 3532, and that the disposition of immovables is governed by the laws of the state in which the immovable is located. La. C.C. 3533-3534.

In the 1990's, certain exceptions were made to the law as applied to conflicts of law with respect to forced heirship. As to immovables situated in Louisiana, the forced heirship laws of Louisiana will not apply: (1) if the deceased was domiciled outside of Louisiana and (2) he also left no forced heirs domiciled in Louisiana at the time of his death. La. C.C. 3533. The rationale of this exception to the general conflict of laws rule is that the forced heirship rules are designed to protect domiciliaries of this state. Where neither the decedent nor the heirs are domiciled in Louisiana, the interest of the state is minimal. La. C.C. 3534, comment (c). Employing the same rationale, Louisiana may be concerned with immovables situated in another state as those immovables relate to the interests of Louisiana domiciliaries. Thus, another exception provides that as to immovables situated outside of Louisiana, Louisiana forced heirship laws will apply: 1) if the decedent died while domiciled in Louisiana and 2) if the decedent left at least one forced heir who, at the time of the decedent's death, was domiciled in this state. In such cases, the interest is limited to including the value of the immovables in the calculation of the forced portion for purposes of satisfying the *legitime*. La. C.C. 3534.

PROBLEMS

Consider the following hypothetical:

Decedent died as a Louisiana Domiciliary. At the time of his death, he owned a condominium in Florida valued at $200,000 and a home in Louisiana worth $250,000. He owned movables including jewelry, an automobile, and stock. His movables were valued collectively at $100,000. Decedent wrote a valid will leaving all his property to his surviving spouse, who was his second wife. He was survived by his wife and by his four-year old daughter Rebecca, born of his first marriage. Rebecca lives with her maternal grandmother.

1. If Rebecca and her grandmother are Louisiana domiciliaries, what assets of her father, if any, will be included in calculating her forced portion?
LA home ($250K) & the movables @ (100K)

2. What if Rebecca was domiciled in Kansas at the time of her father's death?
No, bcuz she was not domiciled in LA

3. Would it matter if Rebecca was domiciled in Kansas, but had a two-year old half-brother, decedent's son, who was living in Louisiana?
Yes, bcuz decedent died in LA & left a FH (2 yr old) @ time of his death. Her portion would be minimal.

4. If Rebecca lives in Louisiana, and all the facts are the same except that, at decedent's death, he is a domiciliary of Texas, is Rebecca entitled to a forced portion? What assets will be included in determining the forced portion? If Rebecca's father left her the condominium in Florida, does she still have a right to claim her *legitime* in Louisiana?

Protecting the Forced Portion

A. Unlawful impediments - La. C.C. 1496

SUCCESSION OF WILLIAMS
184 So. 2d 70 (La. App. 4th Cir. 1966)

HALL, Judge.

The decedent, Wilhelmina Johnson, divorced wife by first marriage of Booker T. Bolds and wife by second marriage of Daniel Williams, died in the City of New Orleans on March 1, 1962. She was survived by James Bolds, only child of her first marriage, and by her second husband Daniel Williams. She had no children by her second marriage.

Decedent left a last will and testament in typewritten form (See LSA-R.S. 9:2442 et seq.) reading as follows:

LAST WILL AND TESTAMENT OF WILHELMINA JOHNSON BOLDS
New Orleans, Louisiana
December 9, 1958

I, Wilhelmina Johnson Bolds, being of sound mind and knowing that life is precarious do hereby make this my last will and testament, revoking all prior wills or codicils thereto.

At my death I desire that all of my property of whatever nature or kind be inherited by all of the descendants of James Bolds, sometimes called Booker. I hereby encumber this inheritance with a usufruct for life in favor of James Bolds, sometimes called Booker; and I also encumber this bequest to James Bolds' children with a right of habitation for life in favor of Isaac Anderson, who is the son of a niece of mine, both of whom I raised.

I hereby appoint James Bolds, sometimes called Booker, as testamentary executor of this estate and grant him full seizin and dispense with the furnishing of bond or any other security.

I hereby appoint Louis C. Philips as attorney for my executor and for my estate to handle the affairs thereof in their entirety.

(s) Wilhema (sic) J. Bolds
WILHELMINA JOHNSON BOLDS

The will was probated on March 29, 1962 and on May 15, 1963 her son, James Bolds, who was named as testamentary executor therein, filed a petition to annul it....

*　　　*　　　*

In holding the will valid in all respects, and dismissing plaintiff's suit, the Trial Court in effect denied plaintiff's alternative prayer that he be declared to be entitled to his *legitime* as the only child and forced heir of decedent.

As we have seen, decedent's entire estate was left to plaintiff's children (decedent's grandchildren) subject: (a) to a usufruct for life in favor of plaintiff, and, (b) to a right of habitation for life in favor of Isaac Anderson. Plaintiff contends that, as the sole child and forced heir of decedent, he is entitled to receive his *legitime* of one-third (1/3) of the estate together with a usufruct over the balance of the estate as awarded him in the will.

Proponents of the will contend that according to a calculation made by them and accepted by the Trial Judge, the value of the usufruct bequeathed to plaintiff is far more than the value of his legitimate portion of 1/3, and therefore his *legitime* has been satisfied.

Article 1493 of the REVISED CIVIL CODE (LSA-C.C. Art. 1493) provides in part as follows:

> Art. 1493. Donations Inter vivos or Mortis causa cannot exceed two-thirds of the Property of the disposer, if he leaves at his decease, a legitimate child.... (Emphasis supplied)

which means that the child is entitled to one-third of the Property of the disposer (not one-third of the value of such property) as a forced portion of which he cannot be deprived, and we know of no law which declares, or jurisprudence which holds, that the child's forced portion or *legitime* may be defeated, satisfied or reduced by the bequest to him of the usufruct of the estate, regardless of the value of the usufruct as compared to the value of the *legitime*.

Actually no true value can be placed upon a usufruct since its value depends upon the uncertainty of life. Moreover since a usufruct ceases to exist upon the death of the usufructuary while an heir's forced portion of an estate is transferable at death to his heirs, no comparison of their values is possible.

*   *   *

In conclusion we are of the opinion that James Bolds is entitled by law to his *legitime* of one-third of the estate in full ownership plus a usufruct for life over the remaining two-thirds, and that his children are entitled to the said remaining two-thirds in naked ownership. The right of habitation bequeathed to Isaac Anderson must fall because Bolds' *legitime* cannot be subjected to a right of habitation (See LSA-C.C. Art. 1710; *Clarkson v. Clarkson*, 13 La.Ann. 422) and a right of habitation cannot exist in two-thirds of a house.

For the foregoing reasons the judgment dated November 23, 1964 herein appealed from is amended by providing that James Bolds be decreed to be entitled to one-third (1/3) of decedent's estate in full ownership together with a usufruct during his life over the remaining two-thirds (2/3), and that "all of the descendants of James Bolds" be decreed to be entitled to the ownership of the said remaining two-thirds (2/3) of the estate, subject however to the usufruct in favor of James Bolds. As so amended, and in all other respects said judgment is affirmed; and the mortuary proceedings are remanded to the District Court for further proceedings according to law consistent with the views herein expressed. Costs of this appeal are to be borne by the Succession.

Amended and affirmed.

NOTE

La. C.C. article 1496 was introduced by Act 77 of 1996, but the Revision Comment correctly points out that the article reproduces the substance of former La. C.C. 1710 which was relied upon by the *Williams* court.

B. Spousal Usufruct and Security - La. C.C. 890, 573(B), 1499, 1514

The usufruct of the surviving spouse has been recognized as a sanctioned burden on the *legitime*. In an intestate succession, the usufruct extends over the decedent's half of the community property and terminates when the surviving spouse dies or remarries. La. C.C. 890. By testament, the testator may grant the surviving spouse a usufruct over all or part of his separate or community property and may also grant the spouse the right to dispose of nonconsumables. Such a usufruct is deemed to be for life, unless expressly designated for a shorter period. Even to the extent that the usufruct affects the *legitime*, it is permissible. La. C.C. 1499.

A protection afforded to forced heirs is that, in certain circumstances, a forced heir may request that the surviving spouse post security to protect the heir's interest in the naked ownership.

With regard to a usufruct created pursuant to La. C.C. 1499, the rules regarding security are provided in La. C.C. 1514. If the forced heir is **not** a child of the surviving spouse, he may request such security but the protection is limited to a request for security **only to the extent that the usufruct affects the *legitime* of the forced heir**. If the forced heir **is** a child of the surviving spouse, the request is limited **to the extent that the spousal usufruct over the *legitime* affects separate property**. La. C.C. 1514.

With regard to the 890 usufruct, the rules regarding security are found in La. C.C. 573(B) and provide that a child **whether forced or not**, who is **not** a child of the usufructuary, may obtain security **to the full affect of his inheritance**; whereas a child who **is** a child of the usufructuary may obtain security **only if he is a forced heir** and **only to the effect of his *legitime*. La. C.C. 573(B).

PROBLEMS

In *Succession of Malbrough*, 685 So. 2d 631 (La. App. 1st Cir. 1997), a case decided under prior law, a forced heir challenged his father's will alleging that his mother's usufruct was an impermissible burden upon his *legitime*. After reviewing the testament left by the father, consider how the case might be decided today in light of La. C.C. 1499. Consider carefully the Editor's notes to articles 890, 1499, and 1514, by Professor A.N. Yiannopoulos in the LOUISIANA CIVIL CODE (Special Millennium Edition).

I have been married but once, and then unto, Mary F. Brister Malbrough, with whom I am presently living and residing. Of the union between myself and Mary F. Brister Malbrough only three (3) children were born, namely: Philip S. Malbrough, Mark D. Malbrough and Charles J. Malbrough, Jr. . .

I leave and bequeath unto my wife, Mary F. Brister Malbrough, the usufruct, for life, over all of the community and/or separate property of which I die possessed, including the use of the family home. . . .

I expressly grant to my wife, Mary F. Brister Malbrough, as lifetime usufructuary, the right to sell, mortgage, lease or otherwise dispose of all assets subject to the usufruct whether the assets are consumable or non-consumable things. Such disposition shall not require the consent of the naked owners. The usufruct shall not terminate upon such disposition and shall attach to the proceeds and any reinvestment thereof. My wife, Mary F. Brister Malbrough, shall have the power and authority to convert any and all property which is not productive of income into income producing property and to convert any or all non-consumable property into consumable property.

I leave and bequeath unto my children. . . the naked ownership of my entire estate, in equal portion of a one-third (1/3) interest each, subject to the usufruct, for life, granted in favor of my wife. . . .

1. If all three children are forced heirs, can they successfully contest the usufruct granted to their mother? Has the father granted excessive powers to his wife by allowing her "to sell, mortgage, lease or otherwise dispose" of the assets?

2. If the court finds that the *legitime* is not unduly burdened by the usufruct, do the forced heirs have a right to obtain security from their mother to protect their interests? Over which property? In conjunction with this question, read Civil Code article 1514 carefully. Consider the property over which the heirs are entitled to security and the extent of that security. Note as well, that under the article, forced heirs are permitted to "request security." Although Revision Comment (c) explains that "if one parses the sentence, it is apparent that the requirement of 'security' is not automatic," that same language appeared in former article La. C.C. 890 prior to its revision and also is the term used in former La. C.C.P. 3154.1 (repealed by Act 158, § 2, of 2004). Cases, in granting relief to forced heirs under the latter articles, spoke in terms of "entitlement." *See Morgan v. Leach*, 680 So. 2d 1381 (La. App. 1st Cir. 1996) and *Succession of Jones*, 537 So. 2d 825 (La. App. 5th Cir. 1989).

3. Would the right of decedent's sons to request security be different if the spouse was their father's second wife and they were children of his first marriage?

C. The *Legitime* in Trust

A testator may now leave the *legitime* in trust, provided the forced heir is named as both income and principal beneficiary of the same interest. La. C.C. 1502. Today, a parent or a grandparent could validly place the *legitime* of his or her child or grandchild in trust for the life of that child or for a shorter period and could also provide for investing the assets pursuant to his instructions. Until the revisions of 1999, the net interest accruing to the forced heir's *legitime* had to be paid to him not less than once a year. In 1999, La. R.S. 9:1841 was amended to require only that "[T]he trustee after taking into account all of the other income and support to be received by the forced heir during the year shall distribute to the forced heir, or to the legal guardian of the forced heir, funds from the net income in trust sufficient for the health, maintenance, support, and education of the forced heir."

SACHNOWITZ v. NELSON
357 So. 2d 894 (La. App. 1st Cir. 1978)

LOTTINGER, Judge.

This is a suit by Nancy J. Sachnowitz, natural tutrix of Nancy Katherine Nelson, Anne Schreiner Nelson and Strauder Goff Nelson, III, forced heirs of Strauder Goff Nelson, Jr., against the legatee, Carolyn Moffitt Henderson Nelson and the Fidelity National Bank of Baton Rouge (Fidelity), trustee, for the partial termination of a trust. From a judgment concluding that the trust was terminated to the extent of two-thirds as of July 15, 1974, and assessing Fidelity for all costs, Fidelity has appealed.

The record points out that Strauder G. Nelson, the father of Strauder Goff Nelson, Jr., died on July 26, 1972, domiciled in San Antonio, Texas, and leaving property in both Louisiana and Texas. He was survived by three children. That portion of his estate bequeath to Strauder Nelson, Jr. both in Texas and in Louisiana was left in trust, with Strauder Nelson, Jr. being the income beneficiary of the Texas trust of all income remaining after the payment of charges and expenses incurred in the administration of the trust as well as the establishment of a reserve payable quarterly or other convenient installments. Fidelity is the trustee of the Louisiana trust and was to hold the property for ten years and to cumulate the funds except for $300.00 to be distributed to Strauder Nelson, Jr.

Strauder Nelson, Jr. died on July 15, 1974, and plaintiff contends that pursuant to LSA-R.S. 9:1832 and 9:1841(3) the Louisiana trust of that portion of the property constituting the *legitime* of Strauder Nelson, Jr. terminated on his death and an undivided two-thirds of said trust property became free of all restrictions of the trust instrument creating such trust.

Fidelity argues that the *legitime* of Strauder Nelson, Jr. was satisfied by the bequest of an income interest in property outside of Louisiana held in trust for him for life.

The trial judge concluded that since the only interest acquired by Strauder Nelson, Jr. in the Texas trust was that of an income beneficiary, under LSA- R.S. 9:1845, his *legitime* was satisfied to the same extent as that of a usufruct, and thus an undivided two-thirds of the trust terminated and became free of all restrictions.

The question before the court is whether an income interest in a Texas trust can satisfy the rights of a nonresident forced heir under Louisiana law?

We hold it cannot.

The determination of Strauder G. Nelson, Jr.'s forced portion as an heir of his father is computed by the value of the property located in Louisiana only, however, the total bequest to Strauder Nelson, Jr., wherever located, can satisfy the amount of the forced portion. *Jarel v. Moon's Succession,* 190 So. 867 (La. App. 2nd Cir. 1939). Thus, if the *legitime* of Strauder Nelson, Jr. held in trust by Fidelity was not satisfied by any bequest outside of Louisiana, the trust must fall under the provisions of LSA-R.S. 9:1832 and 9:1841(3).

The only bequest to Strauder Nelson, Jr. outside of Louisiana was in a Texas trust, wherein he was only an income beneficiary.

LSA-R.S. 9:1845 provides that "an unconditional income interest in the trust, without an interest in principal, payable not less than annually for a term or for the life of the beneficiary satisfies the *legitime* to the same extent as would a usufruct of the same property for the same time period". Thus, we must conclude that by the adoption of this section, the legislature has determined that an income interest in trust is synonymous with a usufruct as far as the satisfaction of the *legitime* is concerned.

Since a usufruct cannot satisfy the *legitime, Succession of Williams,* 184 So. 2d 70 (La.App. 4th Cir. 1966) *writ refused,* 250 La. 748, 199 So. 2d 183 (1967), neither can an unconditional income interest in a trust, irrespective of where the trust may be located.

Fidelity further argues the trial judge erred in assessing it for all costs citing LSA-R.S. 9:2091.

LSA-C.C.P. art. 1920 allows the trial judge to assess costs against either party as he may consider equitable. We find no abuse of discretion.

Therefore, for the above and foregoing reasons the judgment of the trial court is affirmed at appellant's cost.

AFFIRMED.

Calculating and Satisfying the Forced Portion: The Mass Estate and Reduction - La. C.C. 1495, 1500, 1503-1513, La. R.S. 9:2373

A. The Mass Estate and the Forced Portion

After the determination is made as to the number of any existing forced heirs pursuant to La. C.C. 1493, the percentage reserved for those heirs is ascertained by reference to La. C.C. 1495 and La. C.C. 1500. The forced portion is one-fourth of the mass estate if the decedent leaves one forced heir and one-half if he leaves two or more. If, however, one of the forced heirs renounces his *legitime*, is disinherited, or declared unworthy, the forced portion is reduced accordingly, while not affecting the *legitime* of any remaining forced heirs. Also, the forced portion may be reduced below one-fourth if the fraction calculated is greater than the fraction of the decedent's estate that the heir would receive by intestacy. Thus, where a decedent has five surviving children, only one of which is a forced heir, the forced heir's *legitime* would be only one-fifth of the mass estate. The percentage thus determined is then applied to the mass estate. Together the disposable portion and the forced portion total the mass estate.

The mass estate is calculated according to the formula given in La. C.C. 1505. The value of all the property of which the decedent died possessed is added together and any debts are subtracted from this sum. Also "fictitiously" added to this calculation is the value of any donations *inter vivos* made within three years of the decedent's death, valued at the time the donation was made.

Not added into the calculation are life insurance premiums or proceeds on the life of the donor, La. C.C. 1505(C), employer and employee contributions, as well as benefits payable under the decedent's pension plan, La. C.C. 1505(D), donations made to the decedent's spouse of a previous marriage during that marriage, La. R.S. 9:2373, and non-gratuitous portions of onerous and remunerative donations, La. C.C. 1510-11. However, life insurance proceeds and pension plan benefits paid to a forced heir are credited to that forced heir's portion in satisfaction of his *legitime*.

B. Reduction - La. C.C. 1503-1513

SUCCESSION OF WILLIS
682 So. 2d 920 (La. App. 3rd Cir. 1996)

SULLIVAN, Judge.

This appeal involves an action for the reduction of testamentary donations made by Joseph Burton Willis, Sr. to Elizabeth Lee Willis Zimmerman, one of his six surviving children. The trial court rendered judgment which decreed that Elizabeth be allowed to pay $60,583.04 to Willis' succession in satisfaction of her obligation to reduce, to the disposable quantum, the donations mortis causa she received. The trial court also ordered that, after such payment is made to the succession, Elizabeth be placed in possession of the particular legacies bequeathed to her by Mr. Willis in his testament.

Elizabeth appealed, maintaining that the trial court erred in applying LA.CIV.CODE art. 1505(C) to reduce her testamentary legacies by the amount of life insurance proceeds that she received and in miscalculating the life insurance proceeds at $22,000.00 instead of $20,000.00, the proper amount. Mr. Willis' three sons, Phillip Willis, John Willis, and Joseph Burton Willis, Jr., and Mr. Willis' divorced wife, Celine Willis, answered Elizabeth's appeal. These four parties, hereafter referred to as the Willises, assert that the trial court erred in undervaluing a sixteen acre tract of land bequeathed by particular legacy to Elizabeth and in denying their motion for new trial to correct an inaccurate acreage measurement on a separate tract of land which was also bequeathed by particular legacy to Elizabeth. The Willises also contest the propriety of the trial court's assessment of costs to them.

For the following reasons, we reverse the trial court's judgment insofar as it required Elizabeth to pay to her deceased father's succession the amount of life insurance proceeds which she received upon his death. In all other respects, we affirm.

FACTS

Most of the facts which are pertinent to this opinion were concisely set forth by the trial judge in his reasons for judgment, which were rendered on January 24, 1995. From these reasons, we adopt the following factual recitation:

Joseph Burton Willis, Sr. died testate on March 28, 1993. Mr. Willis was survived by six of his seven children: Elizabeth Lee Willis Zimmerman, Joseph Burton Willis, Jr., Marilyn Faye Willis, John David Willis, Phillip Robert Willis, and Emily Anne Willis Bronfield.

In Mr. Willis' olographic will dated February 5, 1989, he bequeathed to Father Robert Willis Courville the usufruct for life of the 54 acres, more or less, located in the fifth ward. He bequeathed his home and grounds, free of debt, with all contents and his law office, including all contents, books and files, to Emily. He also bequeathed 15[sic] acres, more or less, located in the first ward and all of the property owned, approximately 150 acres, in the Kidderville Plantation to Elizabeth. He granted a lifetime usufruct of all property inherited from his parents to his sister, Hazel Willis Fruge. Finally, he left the balance of his property to all seven of his children, subject to the lifetime usufruct of his former wife, Celine Willis....

*   *   *

The property in question was inventoried by Randall P. Serrett, Attorney and Notary Public. Mr. Serrett filed the inventory list in the succession proceedings on February 18, 1994. Mr. Serrett determined that, as of the date of his death, Mr. Willis owned immovable property valued at $661,797.00 and movable property valued at $127,191.80. From this total asset value of $788,988.80, Mr. Serrett deducted the total estate debts of $231,067.30 to arrive at a net estate value of $557,921.50.

Using this net estate value, the law of forced heirship mandates that the forced portion of the estate is $278,960.75 and the disposable portion is the same amount. Each of the six children are therefore entitled to receive one- sixth of $278,960.75 or $46,493.46 as their respective forced portions.

After Elizabeth appealed and the Willises answered her appeal, the trial court rendered and signed a judgment of possession on August 31, 1995, which placed Elizabeth into possession of the sixteen acre tract located in the first ward and seven of the eight tracts owned by Mr. Willis in Kidderville Plantation. The trial court recognized and approved Elizabeth's renunciation of the easternmost 55.11 acres of the eighth Kidderville Plantation tract, which measured 89.78 acres. The trial court also ordered that the westernmost 34.67 acres of this tract remain in the succession until the happening of "a final resolution of the matters presently on appeal resulting from the order of this Court entered March 10, 1995." Additionally, the trial court recognized and approved Elizabeth's renunciation of her *legitime*.

LIFE INSURANCE PROCEEDS

Elizabeth asserts the trial court erred in requiring her to pay $22,000.00 in life insurance proceeds to the succession in addition to the $38,583.04 she was required to pay under her obligation to reduce. She maintains that the trial court erred by, in effect, including the life insurance proceeds in the calculation of the mass of Mr. Willis' succession, which she alleges is a misapplication of La.Civ.Code art. 1505(C). Elizabeth also contends that the trial court erred in setting the life insurance proceeds amount at $22,000.00 and not $20,000.00, the amount that she actually received.

We note initially that Elizabeth testified that she did in fact receive only $20,000.00 from two separate veterans life insurance policies on which she apparently was Mr. Willis' named beneficiary. No other evidence contradicted her testimony. The trial court erred in finding that she received $22,000.00.

La.Civ.Code art. 1505 provides, in pertinent part, as follows:

> A. To determine the reduction to which the donations, either *inter vivos* or *mortis causa*, are liable, an aggregate is formed of all the property belonging to the donor or testator at the time of his decease; to that is fictitiously added the property disposed of by donation *inter vivos*, according to its value at the time of the donor's decease, in the state in which it was at the period of the donation.
>
> B. The sums due by the estate are deducted from this aggregate amount and the disposable quantum is calculated on the balance, taking into consideration the number of forced heirs.
>
> C. Neither the premiums paid for insurance on the life of the donor nor the proceeds paid pursuant to such coverage shall be included in the above calculation. Moreover, the value of such proceeds at the donor's death payable to a forced heir, or for his benefit, shall be deemed applied and credited in satisfaction of his forced share.

Life insurance proceeds which are payable to a named beneficiary other than the insured's estate are not a part of the insured's estate. *Succession of Lane*, 95-0558 (La. App. 4 Cir. 9/28/95), 662 So. 2d 82, *writ denied*, 95-2510 (La.12/15/95), 664 So. 2d 440. These proceeds "do not come into existence during the life of the insured, never belong to him, and are passed by virtue of the contractual agreement between the insured and the insurer to the named beneficiary." *Kambur v. Kambur*, 94-775, p. 6 (La. App. 5 Cir. 3/1/95), 652 So. 2d 99, 103, citing *American Health & Life Ins. Co. v. Binford*, 511 So. 2d 1250, 1253 (La. App. 2 Cir.1987). The life insurance proceeds paid to a named beneficiary are not subject to the civil code articles on donations *inter vivos* or *mortis causa* or the constitutional principles of forced heirship. *Succession of Lane*, 662 So. 2d 82; *Kambur*, 652 So. 2d 99; *Binford*, 511 So. 2d 1250.

In his reasons for judgment, the trial judge applied the second sentence of La.Civ.Code art. 1505(C) in finding that the $22,000.00 life insurance proceeds Elizabeth received must be credited to her *legitime*. The trial judge then added this amount to the $38,583.04 and determined that her legacies must be reduced by $60,583.04. The trial court erred in doing so. By ordering Elizabeth to pay the life insurance proceeds to the succession, the trial court effected a redistribution of these proceeds from the intended and named beneficiary to the other forced heirs. This is not the purpose of the second sentence of Article 1505(C). If Elizabeth had claimed and did not intend to renounce her forced share, then the life insurance proceeds would have properly been "applied [to] and credited in satisfaction of [her] forced share." Id. However, Elizabeth opted to renounce her forced share and seek delivery of her particular legacies, subject to the reduction thereof to the disposable portion.

The life insurance proceeds are Elizabeth's and form no part of Mr. Willis' estate. They are not subject to being included in a reduction calculation. In the realm of forced heirship, life insurance proceeds, when payable to a forced heir, can only be used as a credit against that heir's forced portion. The trial court erred in requiring Elizabeth to pay this money to Mr. Willis' succession, a result which violated the intent of the contractual provisions of the life insurance policies.

*   *   *

DECREE

For the foregoing reasons, we reverse in part the trial court's judgment ordering Elizabeth to pay $60,583.04 to Mr. Willis' succession by $22,000.00, and order her to pay $38,583.04 to the succession in satisfaction of her obligation to reduce her excessive legacies.

Costs of this appeal are assessed to the Willises.

REVERSED IN PART; AFFIRMED IN PART; AND RENDERED.

NOTE

If Mr. Willis died today and all his children were healthy and twenty-four years of age or older, would it be necessary to calculate a forced portion? If he died today and only one of the six were under twenty-four, would this child be entitled to a forced portion? To what percentage of the mass estate would he be entitled as a forced heir?

Mechanics of Reducing Excessive Donations - La. C.C. 1503, 1507 -1513

A donation that impinges on the *legitime* is not null, but is subject to reduction to the extent necessary to eliminate the impingement. La. C.C. 1503. According to the Revision Comment (b) accompanying article 1503, if a husband leaves all to his wife and he is survived by a forced heir, the wife's legacy would be reduced to the disposable portion in full ownership with a usufruct for life that included the power to dispose of nonconsumables. However, Professor Yiannopoulos in his Editor's note to this article strongly disagrees, stating:

> The surviving spouse will be clearly entitled to the full ownership of the disposable portion, and, if the *Winsberg* decision has not been undermined by the revision, the surviving spouse will also receive a usufruct over the forced portion consisting of community property. There is absolutely no authority for the proposition that the surviving spouse will also receive a usufruct over the forced portion consisting of separate property of the deceased. A usufruct on separate property may be created by testament only. *See* La. Civil Code art. 1499. A usufruct by operation of law attaches to community property only. *See* La. Civil Code art. 890. Accordingly, in *Winsberg*, the surviving spouse received a usufruct over the share of the deceased in the community property.
>
> Further, there is absolutely no authority for the proposition that the surviving spouse will have power of disposition over non-consumables other than corporeal movables that are gradually and substantially impaired by use, wear, or

11-50

decay. *See* La. Civil Code art. 568. The right to dispose of non-consumables generally may only be granted by *express* disposition.

A request for reduction may only be made after the death of the donor. La. C.C. 1504. When reduction is necessary, donations *mortis causa* are the first to be reduced. A testator may specify in his will that a legacy is to "be paid in preference to others, in which case the preferred legacy shall not be reduced until the other legacies are exhausted." La. C.C. 1508. Prior to the 1996 revision of these articles, former article 1511 made it clear that, absent such a specification by the testator, the donations *mortis causa* were to be reduced proportionately. By repealing former article 1511, the revision is unclear as to whether the reduction should be pro rata or whether universal and general legacies are to be reduced prior to particular legacies. *See* Katherine Shaw Spaht, *Forced Heirship Changes: The Regrettable "Revolution" Completed*, 57 La. L. Rev. 55, 134 (1996).

Only if the donations *mortis causa* are insufficient to satisfy the forced portion will *inter vivos* donations be subject to reduction. La. C.C. 1507. When further funds are needed to satisfy the forced portion, *inter vivos* donations made within three years of the decedent's death are to be reduced "beginning with the most recent and proceeding successively to the most remote." La. C.C. 1508. If a donee is insolvent when reduction is demanded, he may be skipped over and the forced heir "may claim his *legitime* from the donee of the next preceding donation." La. C.C. 1509. When a forced heir requests reduction of an onerous or remunerative donation, he is only entitled to a reduction of that portion which is gratuitous. La. C.C. 1510-1511. If the donee no longer owns the donated property and it is not in the hands of a successor by gratuitous title, the forced heir will not have a right to take his reduction in kind; however, the donee and his successor by gratuitous title will be required to contribute to the payment of the *legitime* "to the extent of the value of the donated property at the time the donee received it." La. C.C. 1513.

Fruits and products of the donated property remain with the donee except for those that accrue after the donee receives a written demand for reduction. La. C.C. 1512.

The Right to Reduction

SUCCESSION OF HENICAN
248 So. 2d 385 (La. App. 4th Cir. 1971)

CHASEZ, Judge.

On August 12, 1968 Mrs. Alice Boning Henican departed this life, leaving an olographic testament. During the term of her marriage with her husband, Joseph P. Henican, the testator gave birth to two sons who are by virtue of law her forced heirs. One son, Joseph, Jr., predeceased his mother while the other son, C. Ellis Henican, is still alive, although not mentioned in the will of the deceased. Rather the testator bypassed C. Ellis Henican entirely in favor of his five children, her grandchildren. Pursuant to the terms of her will, one half of the property of the deceased was bequeathed to the children of Mrs. Henican's son, Joseph, Jr. The other one half was bequeathed to the children of her other son, C. Ellis Henican.

Ellis Henican is not contesting any portion of his mother's will. Although the testament deprives him of his forced portion, i.e., one quarter of his deceased mother's estate, he is making no attempt to have his reserved portion recognized. To the contrary, it is the National American Bank, hereinafter referred to as the Bank, that has so petitioned the court.

The Bank has alleged that it is the creditor of C. Ellis Henican and that its rights as a creditor are being prejudiced "by an obvious attempt to avoid the payment to C. Ellis Henican of the *legitime* due to him in said succession" and "by (the) failure of said C. Ellis Henican to assert his claim to the *legitime* due to him with referencc to said succession." The Bank therefore prays that it be authorized as a creditor of C. Ellis Henican to accept the succession of Mrs. Alice Boning Henican in the name of her son and forced heir, C. Ellis Henican, and that it be placed in possession of the *legitime* due C. Ellis Henican to the extent of his indebtedness.

Exceptions of no cause of action and/or no right of action were filed by C. Ellis Henican and C. Ellis Henican, Jr. executor of the estate of Mrs. Alice Boning Henican. The exceptions were maintained by the lower court and the suit of the National American Bank was dismissed at its costs. From this adverse judgment the Bank has appealed to this court.

The question thus squarely presented for our determination is whether or not a creditor of a forced heir may exercise the right of the forced heir to reduce a legacy which infringes on the forced portion of the debtor. We are of the opinion that the creditor has no such right.

LSA-C.C. art. 1504 enunciates the right of reduction and provides as follows:

> On the death of the donor or testator, the reduction of the donation, whether Inter vivos or Mortis causa, can be sued for only by forced heirs, or by their heirs or assigns; neither the donees, legatees, nor creditors of the deceased can require that reduction nor avail themselves of it.

As may be seen from the literal terms of the article the right to compel a reduction does not extend to the creditor of the forced heir. Furthermore, the Supreme Court has refused to interpret the article so as to bring creditors of the forced heir within its terms and scope.

In *Tompkins v. Prentice*, 12 La.Ann. 465 (1857), one Joseph Prentice died testate, survived by his mother and father, one brother and one sister. In his will, Joseph Prentice conveyed his entire estate to his mother, brother and sister to the complete exclusion of his father. Moreover, the father of the deceased executed a notarial act of renunciation of any interest which he might have had in his son's succession. The creditors of the father and forced heir of the deceased instituted suit to set aside the renunciation on the ground that it was in defraud of their rights and to have their debtor's share of the succession determined and pro rated among them to satisfy the indebtedness. In that case the court specifically held that the wording of codal article 1504 did not create a right in the creditor of the forced heir to assert the action to reduce a legacy. The court concluded that the term "assign" used in the article did not include creditors but only "those to whom rights have been transferred by particular title: such as sale, donation, legacy, transfer or cession." LSA-C.C. art. 3556.

* * *

. . . The right to bring an action to reduce a legacy like the right to force a co- heir to collate is a personal right which a creditor may not assert. As was stated in the *Tompkins* case:

> Possibly the law-giver may have preferred to give effect to the wishes of the testator and allow his estate to take the direction he had indicated, rather than

subject it to the seizure of creditors of an heir who did not feel himself aggrieved by the universal legacy to another.

After a careful review of the jurisprudence of the state, we find that the *Tompkins* case has not been modified by subsequent legislation or jurisprudence and that the principle of law enunciated therein is dispositive of the case at bar. This court is aware of the fact that under the French Code Napoleon the result of this matter would be different--that a creditor would have the right to assert the action to reduce a legacy if his debtor refused to do so. However, the law of the state of Louisiana on this matter differs from the French....

Accordingly, unless and until the legislature sees fit to make the appropriate changes, the creditor of a forced heir has no right to assert the right of reduction of a legacy absent a specific assignment from the debtor.

For the foregoing reasons the judgment of the lower court is affirmed. Costs of this proceedings to be borne by plaintiff-appellant.

Affirmed.

NOTE

Article 1504 would maintain the result reached by *Henican*, according to the Revision Comment, an attempt to avoid the application of the decision reached in *Succession of Hurd*, 489 So. 2d 1029 (La. App. 1st Cir. 1986), in which a trustee in bankruptcy was permitted to demand collation for a forced heir.

[handwritten: 20K − 10K = 10K Net]
[handwritten: 10 + 40K = 50K]

PROBLEMS

[handwritten: 1/4 × 50K = 12,500]

1) Decedent died leaving assets of $20,000, debts of $10,000 and he made one donation last year to the Boy Scouts of $40,000. He left a will, valid in form, leaving $5,000 to a friend. He has one forced heir. How much is the forced heir entitled to and from what sources? *[handwritten: F.h. may request it, after the death of his father, to be reduced from donation made to deceased friend]*

2) Decedent died leaving five healthy children – A(26), B(25), C(22), D(21), and E(20). *[handwritten: 73 F.h.]* He left a will, valid in form, stating: "I want all of my children to receive equal portions." He died leaving assets of $50,000 and debts of $30,000. Two and one half years ago, he donated $15,000 to X and one year ago, he donated $25,000 to Y. How much does each child receive and from what sources? *[handwritten: 30K.]*

3) Decedent died yesterday. He is survived by two children, A(19) and B(20) and one grandchild D(5), the son of decedent's predeceased child C, who would have been 23 when Decedent died. Decedent died leaving a will, valid in form, which stated, "I leave all of my estate to Cancer Crusaders." Decedent left $70,000 in assets and $55,000 in debt. Five years ago, he gave $30,000 to Cancer Crusaders; two years ago, he gave $25,000 to his brother, and last year he gave $7,000 to his friend and $13,000 to his mother. Decedent had purchased a life insurance policy on himself in the amount of $50,000 and he named D as the beneficiary.

a. How much are A, B, D, and Cancer Crusaders entitled to?

b. If Decedent's will was invalid and his property succeeded by intestacy, would your answer change? How and why?

Prescription for Reduction

The action for reduction of an excessive donation is subject to a liberative prescription of five years. La. C.C. art. 3497. Prescription begins to run for donations *inter vivos* from the date of the donor's death. For donations *mortis causa,* prescription begins to run from the date of the probate of the decedent's will. *In re Andrus*, 221 La. 96, 60 So. 2d 899 (1952).

IN RE SUCCESSION OF SCURLOCK
140 So. 3d 318 (La. App. 5th Cir. 2014)

HANS J. LILJEBERG, Judge.

Plaintiff, John T. Scurlock, Jr. ("Tom"), appeals the trial court judgment sustaining defendants' exceptions of prescription and dismissing his petition to reopen the succession of his mother, Frances Carr Scurlock. He also appeals the denial of his motion for new trial. For the following reasons, we affirm.

FACTS AND PROCEDURAL HISTORY

Frances Carr Scurlock ("Frances") died on September 7, 1990. She was survived by her husband, John T. Scurlock, Sr. ("John"), as well as her four children, Tom, Frank, Jeffrey, and Steven. Frances left a last will and testament, executed on August 21, 1990, in which she bequeathed 25 percent of her interest in some property in Kenner, Louisiana to Tom. The remainder of her estate was bequeathed to John and to her other three children, subject to a usufruct in favor of John.

A "Petition for Probate and for Possession," naming John, Tom, Frank, Jeffrey, and Steven as petitioners, was filed on December 6, 1991. That same day, the trial court signed a "Judgment of Possession" in accordance with the terms set forth in Frances' last will and testament. The judgment of possession was apparently amended thereafter on two occasions: May 12, 1994, and July 15, 2005.

On July 20, 2012, Tom filed a "Petition to Reopen Succession, for Amended Judgment of Possession and Delivery of Legitime." In his petition, Tom asserts that the bequests to him in Frances' will were less than the forced portion reserved to him under Louisiana law at the time of her death. Tom claims that he suffers from Bipolar Disorder I, which has caused him to be an absentee who has remained missing from his family for most of his life, including when his mother died, when her will was probated, and when the judgments of possession were rendered. He asserts that he was never given notice of the succession proceedings pertaining to Frances' estate. Tom contends that he did not learn of his potential rights as a forced heir in his mother's estate until he was contacted in 2011 by the attorney appointed for him in his father's succession proceedings. In his petition, Tom requests that Frances' succession be reopened, that the judgment of possession last rendered on July 15, 2005, be amended to recognize his rights as a forced heir entitled to one-eighth of her estate, and that his legitime be delivered.

On December 14, 2012, Patricia Scurlock ("Patricia"), in her capacity as the testamentary executrix of John T. Scurlock, Sr.'s succession, filed exceptions of prescription and no cause of action, seeking dismissal of Tom's petition to reopen Frances' succession. Patricia asserts that in Tom's petition, he is seeking reduction of an excessive donation, which is subject to liberative prescription of five years. She contends that because Tom did not bring his claim until 20 years after Frances' will was probated and a judgment of possession was rendered, his claim is clearly prescribed.

Patricia also asserts that Tom has no cause of action, because: 1) he was a petitioner in the original petition for probate and possession filed in Frances' succession proceeding; and 2) a claim for reduction of an excessive donation cannot be brought by a petition to reopen a succession under La. Code Civ. Proc. art. 3393.

*   *   *

Tom filed an [opposition] memorandum asserting that he has set forth proper cause for reopening Frances' succession, pursuant to La. Code Civ. Proc. art. 3393. He also contends that defendants' exceptions are premature and that prescription of Tom's claims was suspended under the doctrine of *contra non valentum,* because Tom was an absentee, incompetent, and disabled, which prevented him from discovering his rights as a forced heir. He further claims that although he was listed as a petitioner in the pleadings to initiate Frances' succession proceedings, he, in fact, had no knowledge of these proceedings or his rights as a forced heir.

The exceptions of prescription and no cause of action came for hearing before the trial court on April 30, 2013. At the conclusion of the hearing, the trial court granted the exceptions of prescription filed by defendants, dismissed the petition to reopen Frances' succession, and found the exceptions of no cause of action to be moot.

On May 9, 2013, Tom filed a motion for new trial, arguing that the trial court incorrectly applied the five-year prescriptive period in La. Civ. Code art. 3497 for reduction of an excessive donation to this case. He asserts that neither defendants nor the trial court has cited a prescriptive period for reopening a succession, and that he has set forth good and proper cause for reopening the succession in this case. After a hearing on July 2, 2013, the trial court denied Tom's motion for new trial. Tom appeals.

LAW AND DISCUSSION

On appeal, Tom asserts that the trial court erred in granting defendants' exceptions of prescription, dismissing Tom's petition to reopen Frances' succession, and denying Tom's motion for new trial, where any applicable prescriptive period had not run or was suspended under the doctrine of *contra non valentum.* He claims that prescription has not run against his cause of action to nullify the judgment of possession, because his petition was filed on July 20, 2012, which was less than one year after Tom's discovery of defendants' fraud or ill practices in obtaining the judgments of possession which impinge on his rights as a forced heir. He further contends that even if the five-year prescriptive period for an action for reduction of an excessive donation applies, prescription was suspended under the doctrine of *contra non valentum* because Tom was an absentee, incompetent, and defendants filed a petition for probate falsely stating that Tom was a petitioner, which prevented him from asserting his undisputed rights as a forced heir.

La. Civ. Code art. 1503 provides that a donation *mortis causa* that impinges on the legitime of a forced heir is not null but is merely reducible to the extent necessary to eliminate the impingement. When a testator disposes of her entire estate to the prejudice of a forced heir, the donation *mortis causa* is subject to an action by the forced heir for reduction of the donation and for recovery of the legitime. *Kilpatrick v. Kilpatrick*, 625 So. 2d 222, 225 (La. App. 2 Cir. 9/22/93), *writ denied*, 631 So. 2d 445 (La.1994). Where the plaintiff makes no attack on the validity of the will and seeks only to recover his legitime, such an action can only be construed as one for reduction of an excessive donation. *Id.*

In the present case, Tom's petition to reopen Frances' succession does not contain any language requesting annulment of the judgments of possession. Rather, in his petition, Tom requests that the succession be reopened for amendment of the judgments of possession to recognize his rights as a forced heir and for delivery of his legitime under the law. Because Tom has made no attack on the validity of Frances' will and seeks only to recover his legitime, this action must be construed as one for reduction of an excessive donation.

The five-year prescriptive period set forth in La. Civ. Code art. 3497 is applicable to claims for reduction of an excessive donation. A cause of action to reduce an excessive donation arises when the will is probated, and the five-year prescriptive period begins to run at that time. *West v. Gajdzik*, 425 So. 2d 263 (La. App. 3 Cir. 12/22/82), *writ denied*, 428 So. 2d 475 (La.1983). If the forced heir fails to bring a claim to reduce the donation and to claim his legitime within the five-year prescriptive period, ownership of the donation by the donee or legatee is maintained. *Kilpatrick*, 625 So. 2d at 226.

In the instant case, Frances' will was probated in December of 1991. Tom did not file his petition to reopen succession, seeking reduction of an excessive donation, until over 20 years later, in July of 2012. Clearly, the five-year prescriptive period expired. Nevertheless, Tom claims that his claim is not untimely, because prescription was suspended under the doctrine of *contra non valentum.* He asserts that defendants' petition for probate and possession in Frances' succession proceedings contains false statements that he was a petitioner in order to obtain a judgment of possession without notifying him, thereby preventing him from asserting his undisputed rights as a forced heir. He also claims that he was an absentee, disabled, incompetent, not served with any pleadings, and unable to recognize or assert his rights as a forced heir.

Prescription runs against absent persons and incompetents, unless an exception has been established by legislation. La. Civ. Code art. 3468. Louisiana has recognized a limited jurisprudential exception to the running of prescription, known as *contra non valentum,* where in fact and for good cause, a plaintiff is unable to assert a cause of action when it accrues. *In re: Succession of Ferguson*, 47,941 (La. App. 2 Cir. 5/29/13), 114 So. 3d 1260, 1263. *Contra non valentum* is based on the theory that when the claimant is not aware of the facts giving rise to his cause of action against a defendant, the running of prescription is suspended until the plaintiff discovers or should have discovered the facts on which the action is based. *Id.* It is not necessary to have actual knowledge as long as there is constructive knowledge. *Wells v. Zadeck*, 11–1232, p. 9 (La.3/30/12), 89 So. 3d 1145, 1151; *Kilpatrick*, 625 So. 2d at 227. For purposes of *contra non valentum,* a plaintiff will be deemed to know what he could have learned with reasonable diligence. *Caro v. Bradford White Corp.*, 96–120, p. 6 (La. App. 5 Cir. 7/30/96), 678 So. 2d 615, 618. The doctrine of *contra non valentum* may apply when: (1) there is some legal cause which prevented the court or its officers from taking cognizance of and acting on the plaintiff's actions; or (2) where there is some condition coupled with the contract or coupled with the proceedings which prevented the creditor from suing or acting; or (3) where the debtor has done some act effectually to prevent the creditor from availing himself of his cause of action; or (4) where the cause of action is not known or reasonably knowable by the plaintiff even though his ignorance is not induced by the defendant. *Kilpatrick,* 625 So. 2d at 226; *West v. Gajdzik,* 425 So. 2d at 266–267.

In the present case, Tom admits that he was informed of his mother's death in 1990. Tom assumed that his mother had left her assets to his father, who was living at the time, so he did not feel it was necessary to contact his father or siblings. While it may be true that Tom had no knowledge of Frances' succession proceedings and that he was not aware that he was listed as a petitioner in those proceedings, it is undisputed that he did not contact any family members or make any efforts to obtain information pertaining to his mother's succession or estate.

In 2012, Tom was evaluated by Dr. Brian Jordan, a clinical psychologist, who opined that due to Tom's bipolar disorder, he has generally been incapable in his lifetime of having passively acquiesced in the legal proceedings concerning the estates of his parents. However, Dr. Jordan also notes in his report that Tom has obtained two colleges degrees, including one in computer science. It is noted that while Tom's illness may have caused negative consequences in his life, he has never been interdicted, and the record does not establish that he was unable to obtain the necessary information to assert his claims of forced heirship in his mother's succession. Based on our review of the record before us, we find that the doctrine of *contra non valentum* does not apply in this case.

Tom failed to file his action seeking reduction of excessive donation within five years of the probate of his mother's will, and no exception to the running of prescription has been shown by the facts of this case. Accordingly, we find no error in the trial court's judgment granting the exceptions of prescription filed by defendants.

*   *   *

DECREE

For the foregoing reasons, we affirm the trial court judgment sustaining the exceptions of prescription filed by defendants and dismissing Tom's petition to reopen Frances' succession. We also affirm the denial of Tom's motion for new trial.

AFFIRMED.

Disinherison

Disinherison provides a mean for depriving an erring descendant of his legitime. The LOUISIANA CIVIL CODE of 1870 included a procedure for disinherison in articles 1617-1644. Inadvertently, the Louisiana legislature repealed those articles when it passed Act 1421 of 1997. The concept was reinstated, although revised by Act 573, § 1 of 2001, effective June 22, 2001.

The twelve causes for a parent to disinherit his child have been replaced with eight. La. C.C. 1621. Grandparents may also disinherit their grandchildren for seven of the enumerated causes. La. C.C. 1622.

To disinherit a child, a parent must expressly indicate the cause for disinherison and must identify the person to be disinherited, La. C.C. 1619, in one of the forms prescribed for testaments. La. C.C. 1618. Following such a procedure gives rise to a presumption of truth, which may be rebutted by a preponderance of evidence. La. C.C. 1624. The burden would then shift to the heir to prove that the cause did not exist or that he reconciled with the testator after the cause took place. Proof of reconciliation must be clear and convincing; a signed writing by the testator which "clearly and unequivocally" demonstrates reconciliation constitutes such evidence. La. C.C. 1625.

Since forced heirs are now limited to the young and disabled, the legislature added an article providing that proof that the heir was "not capable of understanding the impropriety of his behavior" due to age or mental incapacity or showing, by a preponderance of the evidence, that the behavior was unintentional or justified, constitutes a defense. La. C.C. 1626.

Although the following cases predate 2001, they illustrate many of the concepts of disinherison in current Louisiana law.

SUCCESSION OF VINCENT
527 So. 2d 23 (La. 1988)

GUIDRY, Judge.

This appeal questions the testamentary disinherison of a son by his father. The decedent, Joseph Manson Vincent, died testate on April 11, 1986, in Lake Charles, Louisiana. He was survived by his spouse, Viola Mae Vincent, and two children, Paul Roy Vincent and Beverly Ann Vincent Romero.

The decedent's last will, made pursuant to the provisions of La.R.S. 9:2442, is dated April 17, 1984, and contains the following, among other, provisions:

> I specifically disinherit my son, Paul Roy Vincent, under the authority of Civil Code Article 1621 due to the incident in the spring of 1978, in which my son struck me three (3) times and fired at me with a .22 caliber automatic rifle and as a result, an offense report was filed with the Cameron Parish Sheriff's Department with Deputy Dewey Hebert and witnessed by Mr. William Poole, who saved my life.

On August 1, 1986, the decedent's will was admitted to probate. Thereafter, Viola Vincent and Beverly Ann Romero, universal legatees of the decedent, petitioned the court for possession and, in addition, sought judicial recognition of the disinherison of Paul Roy Vincent. Paul Roy Vincent, answered denying the allegations of the petition for possession. A contradictory hearing was held following which the trial court, for oral reasons assigned, rendered judgment recognizing the decedent's disinherison of his son, Paul Roy Vincent, to be valid and in accordance with La.C.C. art. 1621. This judgment also placed Viola Mae Vincent and Beverly Ann Romero in possession of the estate of Joseph Manson Vincent in the proportions of one- half to each. Paul Roy Vincent appealed.

Mrs. Vincent, Mrs. Romero, William Poole, and Paul Roy Vincent testified at the hearing.

Mrs. Vincent stated that she did not know about the disinherison of Paul until after the making of the will. She was present at the lawyer's office on April 17, 1984, when her husband made his will, and was then made aware of the incident alleged to have occurred in 1978. Mrs. Vincent admitted that the deceased and her son argued quite often and did not get along with one another and agreed that their arguments were loud and violent.

Mrs. Romero's testimony was basically the same as her mother's, reiterating the bad relationship that existed between the deceased and his son.

Poole testified that he and the decedent were at the latter's camp working on the property when the 1978 incident took place. At that time, Paul Vincent was working at Consolidated Aluminum and living with his wife and two young children at the camp which the decedent owned. On the day in question, Paul had come off of the grave-yard shift, gone bass fishing, and returned home to get some sleep before returning to work at eleven o'clock that night. Upon Paul's return to the camp, the decedent asked Paul why he could not keep the place clean. An argument erupted and a physical struggle ensued. Paul's wife was sitting on the porch and evidently saw the entire episode but did not testify.

Poole testified that Paul Vincent did attempt to strike the deceased, but could not testify as to who threw the first punch or blow, because the two were grappling when he turned to view the altercation. Poole stated that the deceased did strike Paul with a stick after the struggle ensued.

Poole testified that at some point, Paul obtained a .22 caliber rifle from his truck. Poole stated that he yelled at Paul to put the rifle down and not to shoot his father. According to Poole, Paul then laid the rifle down. Poole testified that he heard no shots fired, but his hearing could have been impaired, as he was approximately 150 feet away from Paul standing next to a dump truck with its engine running. According to Poole, the truck was not equipped with a muffler.

Thereafter, the decedent went into the camp and evidently called the police, as a sheriff's deputy later arrived on the scene. Poole testified that Deputy Dewey Hebert handcuffed Paul and took Paul's rifle into his possession. Poole's testimony is somewhat vague as to how many times or at what point the deceased entered and exited the camp, before the argument and confrontation erupted in the front yard. However, his testimony is clear that there was a struggle between Paul and the deceased, that Paul raised his hand against his father, and that Paul pointed a rifle at his father.

The testimony of Poole and Paul Vincent is in serious conflict. Paul Vincent denied that Poole was ever present. Paul denied striking his father, stating that the decedent struck him from behind as he was walking into the camp when he told him he would clean up the yard after he got some sleep. Paul testified that he got the weapon, a .22 rifle, only in an effort to prevent his father from beating him. He testified that he did not try to shoot his father. He stated that Deputy Hebert did not arrest him and no charges were filed against him. Although decedent's will states that an offense report was filed in the sheriff's office, no evidence of such was presented at trial.

Appellant complains that the proponents of the will failed to carry their burden of proving the acts described in decedent's will as justifying disinherison.

La.C.C. art. 1621 was last amended by Act 456 of 1985 and, since the effective date of that act, reads in pertinent part as follows:

> The just causes for which parents may disinherit their children are twelve in number. There shall be a rebuttable presumption as to the facts set out in the act of disinherison to support these causes. These causes are, to-wit:
>
> 1. If the child has raised his or her hand to strike the parent, or if he or she has actually struck the parent; but a mere threat is not sufficient .... *[See La. C.C. 1621(1)]**

Prior to the 1985 amendment, the article contained no language relative to the burden of proof in cases involving disinherison for cause by parents of their children. The cases prior to the 1985 amendment placed the initial burden of proof on the succession or heirs to prove the acts described in the will justifying disinherison by a preponderance of the evidence. *See Succession of Chaney*, 413 So. 2d 936 (La.App. 1st Cir.1982), *writ denied* 420 So. 2d 449 (La.1982); Succession *of Lissa*, 198 La. 129, 3 So. 2d 534 (La.1941). The 1985 amendment establishes a rebuttable presumption as to the facts set forth in the will supporting the act of disinherison and the burden now rests with the party opposing the disinherison to rebut this presumption.

The trial court, at the close of evidence, found the appellant's testimony self-serving and incapable of belief. The trial court accepted William Poole's testimony as credible and concluded that cause for disinherison under La.C.C. art. 1621(1) was established. Although the trial court did not allude to the presumption accorded by the 1985 amendment to Article 1621, it is clear that, accepting the trial court's credibility determination, the evidence offered by appellant is totally insufficient to rebut the presumption accorded by Article 1621. We find no error in the trial court's conclusion.

Appellant argues that the presumption now accorded by Article 1621 should not be applied in this case because the will was written in 1984 and, at that time, the heirs enjoyed no such rebuttable presumption. We disagree. Rights in a succession do not vest until death. The testator in this case died on April 11, 1986, after the effective date of the amendment. *Henry v. Jean*, 238 La. 314, 115 So. 2d 363, 367 (1959).

For these reasons, the judgment of the trial court is affirmed. Appellant is cast with all costs of this appeal.

AFFIRMED.

SUCCESSION OF BERTAUT
572 So. 2d 142 (La. App. 1st Cir. 1990)

LANIER, Judge.

This action is a suit by a testamentary executrix seeking to enforce the provisions of a last will and testament which disinherited two forced heirs. A rule to show cause was filed by Etta Bertaut, the surviving spouse and testamentary executrix of Shelly Atkins Bertaut, against Shelly

---

* Bracketed material in italics added by author.

Morris Barto and Peter Joseph Barto (hereinafter collectively referred to as the Bartos), sons and forced heirs of Mr. Bertaut, seeking to have them disinherited for failure to communicate with him without just cause for a period in excess of six years. The Bartos filed a peremptory exception raising the objection of no cause of action which was overruled. After a contradictory hearing, the trial court found that the Bartos had failed to prove their failure to communicate with Mr. Bertaut was with just cause and rendered a judgment approving the disinherison. The Bartos took this suspensive appeal.

Facts

Mr. Bertaut was born on September 27, 1915. Prior to May of 1935, he married Antoinette Lalumia (Mrs. Barto). On May 17, 1935, Shelly M. Barto was born of this union. Two years later another son, Peter J. Barto, was born.

Shortly before the birth of Peter, Mr. Bertaut left his family for unknown reasons. He met and began seeing Etta Chemin in April of 1940. On June 7, 1940, at approximately 2:00 p.m., Mr. Bertaut and Mrs. Barto were divorced. At 5:00 p.m. on the same day, Mr. Bertaut and Etta Chemin (Mrs. Bertaut) were married. Mr. and Mrs. Bertaut resided in Baker, Louisiana, for most of their married years. They had two daughters during their marriage.

In the middle of 1942, Mr. Bertaut was arrested for failure to support his two sons. As a result of his arrest, Mr. Bertaut began paying $25 a month in child support. Prior to his arrest, Mr. Bertaut had not paid any support for his sons.

Shelly Barto saw his father twice during his father's lifetime. He saw Mr. Bertaut once for an hour when he was ten years old. This visit took place at Mrs. Barto's home in Slidell, Louisiana. He also saw Mr. Bertaut when he was eighteen years old and a freshman at Louisiana State University in Baton Rouge, Louisiana. This visit lasted about an hour.

Peter Barto saw his father approximately seven times during Mr. Bertaut's lifetime. He last saw his father in 1979 after his father had suffered a stroke.

Mr. Bertaut died on October 28, 1987, in Mandeville, St. Tammany Parish, Louisiana. He left a will dated April 3, 1986.

Objection of No Cause of Action
(Assignment of error number 1)

The Bartos contend the trial court erred in overruling their peremptory exception raising the objection of no cause of action. They contend the disinherison provision is defective because it states that Mr. Bertaut desires to disinherit them under the provisions of La.C.C. art. 1623 (12) which does not exist and it fails to state that their failure to communicate with Mr. Bertaut was without just cause.

The peremptory exception raising the objection of no cause of action tests the legal sufficiency of the petition and is triable on the face of the pleadings. For the purpose of determining the validity of the exception, all well-pleaded allegations of fact are accepted as true, and if the allegations set forth a cause of action as to any part of the demand, the exception must be overruled. *Ledet v. Hogue*, 540 So. 2d 422 (La.App. 1st Cir.1989). Doubts are resolved in favor of the sufficiency of the petition. *Reeder v. Laks Corporation*, 555 So. 2d 7 (La.App. 1st Cir.1989), *writs denied*, 559 So. 2d 142 (La.1990). These rules apply to the determination of whether a provision in a will states a cause for disinherison.

The disinherison provision of Mr. Bertaut's will reads as follows:

I specifically disinherit my two (2) sons, Shelly Morris Bertaut, and Peter Joseph Bertaut, under the provisions of Article 1623(12) inasmuch as they have failed to make any effort to communicate with me for a period in excess of six (6) years even though they have known of my whereabouts and they have not been in the military forces of any kind.

For a disinherison to be valid, it must be made in one of the forms prescribed for testaments. La.C.C. art. 1618. The disinherison must be made by name and expressly, and for just cause, otherwise it is null. La.C.C. art. 1619. There are no just causes for disinherison except those expressly recognized by law. La.C.C. art. 1620.

The causes for disinherison of a child by a parent are found in La.C.C. art. 1621. The causes for disinherison of a parent by a child are found in La.C.C. art. 1623. La.C.C. art. 1621(12) provides the following:

If the child has known how to contact the parent, but has failed *without just cause* to communicate with the parent for a period of two years after attaining the age of majority, except when the child is on active duty in any of the military forces of the United States. (Emphasis added). *[See La. C.C. 1621(8).]* *

It is apparent that the disinherison provision of Mr. Bertaut's will contains a typographical error when it refers to La.C.C. art. 1623, instead of La.C.C. art. 1621. This error does not make the provision defective because it clearly states the substance of a cause for disinherison under La.C.C. art. 1621(12). *See Ambrose Succession v. Ambrose*, 548 So. 2d 37 (La.App. 2nd Cir.1989).

The sufficiency of a disinherison provision to state a cause of action must be decided on a case by case basis. The disinherison provision is not defective because it fails to state that the Bartos' lack of communication for six years is without just cause. The facts recited in the disinherison provision adequately state the cause for which Mr. Bertaut is attempting to disinherit his sons. The requirement of expressly stating the cause of disinherison is fully accomplished when the statement is made that the child has failed to communicate with the parent for a period of two years when the child has known how to contact the parent. *See Stephens v. Duckett*, 111 La. 979, 36 So. 89 (1904).

The trial court found that the disinherison provision in Mr. Bertaut's will sufficiently stated a cause for disinherison against the Bartos and overruled their peremptory exception raising the objection of no cause of action. For the reasons stated above, we find that the trial court was correct.

This assignment of error is without merit.

Validity of the Cause for Disinherison
(Assignment of error number 2)

---

* Bracketed material in italics added by author.

The Bartos contend the trial court erred in finding that they failed to meet their burden of proving that the cause stated for disinherison was not sufficient to disinherit them. They contend that they sufficiently proved that their failure to communicate with Mr. Bertaut was with just cause.

La.C.C. art. 1624 requires the testator to express in his will the reasons for disinherison of a forced heir. La.C.C. art. 1621 provides for a rebuttable presumption that the facts set out in the act of disinherison are correct. Prior to 1985, the other heirs of the testator were obliged to prove the facts on which the disinherison was founded, otherwise the disinherison was null. In 1985, the legislature amended La.C.C. art. 1624 to shift to the disinherited forced heir the burden of proving that the cause stipulated for disinherison did not exist or that the forced heir was reconciled with the testator after the acts alleged to constitute the cause for disinherison. *Succession of Vidrine*, 562 So. 2d 52 (La.App. 3rd Cir.1990); *Ambrose Succession v. Ambrose*, 548 So. 2d at 39; K. Spaht, *Successions and Donations, Development in the Law*, 1984-1985, 46 La.L.Rev. 707 (1986).

In K. Spaht, *supra*, pp. 711-713, just cause is discussed as follows:

> The heir may also prove as a defense to disinherison that his failure to communicate was with "just cause." "Just cause" explicitly provided by the statute includes lack of knowledge concerning how to contact the parent and active military service. Other examples of "just cause" can be borrowed perhaps from the statute dispensing with the natural parent's consent to an adoption. A condition of the parent's failure to communicate with the child which makes his consent to the adoption unnecessary is that the failure to communicate be without just cause. A survey of the jurisprudence interpreting the adoption provision reveals that parents have urged the following circumstances as just cause: incarceration, drug addiction, and emotional state. Incarceration urged as just cause for failure to communicate with a child was rejected by the court: "We would think that a father situated such as this who had a real concern for his children would recognize that, in order to maintain a relationship under these circumstances, an extra effort is necessary." The same should be true if the child is incarcerated and fails to communicate with the parent. It is also obvious that the Legislature intended to place the burden of making the effort to communicate on the child, since failure, not refusal, to communicate is the ground for disinherison. In the two cases where drug addiction and the emotional state of the parent were offered as "just cause" for failure to communicate or pay support, the issue was avoided by the court.
>
> In deciding what constitutes just cause for failure to communicate by the child, the child's psychological state of mind presents the most difficulty. Drug addiction with its accompanying dependency and anxiety, other serious psychiatric problems that can be clinically identified, or psychological disturbances created by such events as an argument with the parent or a stepparent may be urged by the heir as "just cause." Consider, for example, the factual circumstances of *Succession of Landry* [463 So. 2d 681 (La.App. 4th Cir.1985)]. If the case had been decided under Civil Code article 1621 as amended, the heir would have been compelled to argue "just cause" for his failure to communicate with his mother from 1947 until her death in 1980. The "just cause" for his

failure to communicate was an acrimonious incident involving the removal of the heir's refrigerator from an apartment owned by his mother. In her will the mother wrote, "My son, Wilbert, never apologized for striking me or for the above referred to attack upon me and although he has always lived in the City of New Orleans or the Greater New Orleans Area, he has never come to see his mother even on many occasions (sic) when I was confined to the hospital because of a heart condition or other physical ills." The court suggested in its opinion that the mother was as much at fault as the child in failing to heal the breach: "Respect between parent and child is a mutual obligation."

However, in *Succession of Landry*, the executrix was seeking to prove that the disinherited heir had been guilty of cruelty to his mother. The court responded to the allegations of cruel treatment in the following manner: "An argument which results in prolonged indifference by both parties cannot be characterized as 'cruelty' by one of the parties." It then added gratuitously, "[d]isinherison cannot result from a child's failure to communicate with a parent."

The law has changed. Because the legislation now imposes a responsibility upon the child to communicate with a parent, an argument that creates strained relations with the parent should not constitute "just cause." The communication by the child need not apologize to the parent for an argument where both parties were at fault, but it should be respectful in tone, as was previously discussed. Furthermore, reliance upon the jurisprudence interpreting "just cause" under the adoption statute should proceed cautiously because the policies underlying adoption and disinherison differ substantially. Whereas the adoption statutes dispensing with the natural parent's consent must be strictly construed as in derogation of the natural parent's rights, *the disinherison legislation should be interpreted liberally to permit a parent greater freedom in disinheriting an unworthy child.* The motivation of the law regulating parent-child relations is to assure the natural parent the opportunity to establish strong emotional ties to the child. If the parent is dead, there is no reason to deny the disinherison to encourage such emotional relationship. Yet, balanced against the strict interpretation of the adoption statutes is a consideration also not present in the laws on disinherison--the critical need to provide a stable, warm, loving environment for the minor child. (Emphasis added; footnotes omitted)

The record reveals that Mr. Bertaut abandoned the Bartos when Shelly was two years old and Peter was still in utero. After he abandoned his two sons, Mr. Bertaut began a new life in Baker, Louisiana. He met Etta Chemin (Mrs. Bertaut) in Baker and after a six week courtship proposed to her. At this time, he informed her that he could not get married until he obtained a divorce from his first wife. Mrs. Bertaut found out at this time that Mr. Bertaut had two small children. About two weeks after his proposal, Mr. Bertaut obtained a divorce from his first wife. This occurred on June 7, 1940 at 2:00 p.m., and at 5:00 p.m. on the same day, he married Mrs. Bertaut. Mr. Bertaut at this time told Mrs. Bertaut that he did not have to pay support for the children. Mr. Bertaut did not pay child support for his sons until he was legally forced to pay.

The record shows that Mr. Bertaut had contact with Shelly twice in fifty years. These meetings occurred when Shelly was 10 and 18 years old. He last saw his father in 1953.

Mr. Bertaut saw Peter seven times in forty-eight years. He first met Peter when Peter was eight years old. He saw Peter again when Peter was about thirteen years old. On this occasion, Mrs. Bertaut wanted to meet Peter, so she picked him up from in front of his house. This meeting was the result of Mrs. Bertaut's efforts. Mr. Bertaut saw Peter again when Peter was in high school. Peter had gotten into trouble, and Mr. Bertaut went to Slidell to get the problem straightened out. Mr. Bertaut saw Peter twice in 1969 as a result of his daughter's efforts. Peter also visited Mr. Bertaut twice in 1979 after Mr. Bertaut had suffered a stroke. Peter did not see his father after 1979.

The record reveals that Mr. Bertaut did not seek to establish any type of meaningful relationship with his sons. The majority of his contacts with his sons were initiated by other people.

The trial court in its oral reasons for judgment stated the following:

THE COURT FINDS THAT THE HEIRS' FEELINGS ABOUT THEIR FATHER'S SEPARATION AND DIVORCE MAY BE THEIR REASON FOR LACK OF COMMUNICATION. HOWEVER, IT DOES NOT EQUATE TO JUST CAUSE. *THERE IS NO EVIDENCE WHATSOEVER IN THE RECORD TO THE EFFECT THAT THE FATHER DISCOURAGED OR PROHIBITED HIS SONS IN ANY WAY FROM COMMUNICATING WITH HIM.* IN FACT, THE LAST CONTACT WITH SHELLEY [sic], AS PREVIOUSLY STATED, WAS INITIATED BY THE FATHER, HIMSELF. THE COURT FINDS THAT THE PROOF IS CLEAR AND THAT THE HEIRS HAVE FAILED TO CARRY THEIR BURDEN OF ESTABLISHING THAT THEIR FAILURE TO COMMUNICATE, IN ACCORDANCE WITH CIVIL CODE ARTICLE 1621(12), WAS WITHOUT JUST CAUSE AND THE COURT THEREFORE WILL SIGN A JUDGMENT APPROVING THE DISINHERISON AND WILL ORDER THE WILL EXECUTED, AND WILL SIGN JUDGMENT ACCORDINGLY. (Emphasis added)

The purpose of La.C.C. art. 1621(12) is to require communications between children and parents so that strong family ties are maintained. This court is in accord with the trial court and legal scholars who feel that in ordinary situations La.C.C. art. 1621(12) places the burden of making the effort to communicate on the child. However, we do not think that a child must attempt to communicate with his parent when this attempt would be futile. If attempts by a child to communicate with his parent are futile, his failure thereafter to communicate with the parent is with just cause. A person should not be required by law to perform a vain and useless act.

In this case, the evidence shows that Mr. Bertaut did not want to establish a parental relationship with his sons. Most of his contacts with his sons were not a result of his efforts. The efforts by the Bartos to communicate with their father proved to be futile. The Bartos' failure to communicate with their father under the particular facts and circumstances in this case was with just cause. The trial court erred as a matter of fact and law in finding otherwise.

The Bartos have met their burden of establishing that their failure to communicate with Mr. Bertaut was with just cause and that the cause for disinherison stated in Mr. Bertaut's will is invalid. The disinherison provision in Mr. Bertaut's will will not be enforced against the Bartos.

This assignment of error has merit.

Decree

For the foregoing reasons, the judgment of the trial court disinheriting Shelly M. Barto and Peter J. Barto is reversed, and the rule to enforce the disinherison provisions of the testament is dismissed with prejudice. This case is remanded to the trial court for further proceedings in accordance with law. Etta Bertaut, as testamentary executrix of the estate of Shelly Atkins Bertaut, is cast for the cost of this appeal.

REVERSED, RENDERED AND REMANDED.

SUCCESSION OF GRAY
736 So. 2d 902 (La. App. 3rd Cir. 1999)

PICKETT, Judge.

Pamela Gray Williams and Michelle Gray, daughters of the decedent, appeal the trial court's judgment dismissing their opposition to the probate of Ernest Felton Gray's last will and testament. In the original opposition the appellants attacked the will on several grounds. However, in this appeal the only issue before this court concerns the provision of the will which disinherits Pamela Gray Williams and Michelle Gray for failing to communicate with the decedent for two years. For the following reasons, we affirm the trial court's judgment.

The last will and testament of Earnest Felton Gray was executed on May 23, 1994 and contained the following provision:

> I hereby disinherit my daughter, Pamela Gray Williams, who is an adult, as provided by Article 1617, 1618, 1619 and Article 1621, paragraph 12, because she has known how to contact me but has failed to do so without just cause and for a period of over two years.

The will contained an identical provision disinheriting Michelle Gray.

The testator then died on September 15, 1994. On October 10, 1994, Lamar Allen and Dorothy Elizabeth Allen, legatees of Earnest Felton Gray's estate, filed the petition for probate of the will. The trial court's ruling on Pamela and Michelle's opposition to that probate forms the cause of this appeal.

LA.CIV.CODE art. 1621 states in pertinent part:

> The just causes for which parents may disinherit their children are twelve in number. There shall be a rebuttable presumption as to the facts set out in the act of disinherison to support these causes. These causes are, to wit:

*   *   *

12. If the child has known how to contact the parent, but has failed without just cause to communicate with the parent for a period of two years after attaining the age of majority, except when the child is on active duty in any of the military forces of the United States.

LOUISIANA CIVIL CODE art. 1624 imposes the requirement on the testator to express in the will the reason for disinheriting the heir and it imposes the burden on the disinherited forced heir to prove that the cause stipulated for the disinherison did not exist. *Succession of Steckler*, 95-227 (La.App. 5 Cir.11/28/95); 665 So. 2d 561. Therefore, in order for the decedent's daughters to invalidate their disinheritance, they must rebut the presumption by a preponderance of the evidence that a two year period did not exist between their age of majority and the date of the will that they knew of their father's whereabouts and failed to communicate. *Succession of Gruce, Sr.,* 96-0238 (La.App. 1 Cir. 11/8/96); 683 So. 2d 362. In the alternative, they must show that such failure to communicate was with just cause. *Succession of Cure*, 633 So. 2d 590 (La.App. 1 Cir.1993).

The trial court found that the opponents of the will failed to rebut the presumption that the facts recited in the will as the reason for disinherison are true and failed to show just cause in doing so. It is a settled principle of law that when there is evidence presented to the trial court which, upon its reasonable evaluation of credibility, supplies a reasonable factual basis for its finding, on review the appellate court will not disturb this factual finding in the absence of manifest error.

The relationship between the decedent and his daughters became estranged in 1989 when Mr. Gray moved to Rogers, Louisiana. The trial testimony indicates that both daughters at one time or another since that time attempted to communicate with their father. Pamela testified to having stopped on the road when she saw her father and talked. She also saw her father at the post office located in Trout, Louisiana and the Belah grocery. All of these meetings were corroborated by witnesses. Both daughters visited Mr. Gray while he was in the VA hospital in Shreveport, Louisiana, in the summer of 1993. Both daughters testified to having tried to visit their father but were turned away by Mr. Gray's refusal to speak with them.

The trial court's reasons for judgment states that these "one or two visits" did not constitute communication within the meaning of Article 1621(12). On this point, we must disagree with the trial court. Actions taken to satisfy "communication" by the Louisiana courts could be characterized as trivial. The sending of two Christmas cards and a birthday card within a two year period has been accepted as a sufficient communication under Article 1621(12). *Succession of Steckler*, 665 So. 2d 561. In *Steckler*, the court went on to state "the only qualitative standard imposed on the communications ... is that it must be respectful and made known or conveyed to the parent." *Id*. at 565. In *Succession of Gruce*, 683 So. 2d at 366, the court found the "preparation and personal delivery of a casserole" by the party that the will disinherited to be a sufficient communication. In both *Steckler* and *Gruce*, it was noted that Article 1621(12) does not require the parent to respond to the communication.

Reviewing the testimony in light of the jurisprudence, we must conclude that actions by the daughters did constitute communications for the purposes of Article 1621(12). However, the parties must show by a preponderance of the evidence that two years had not elapsed between these communications. The evidence produced by Pamela Gray Williams and Michelle Gray as to the times of these encounters is sparse. The only dates offered since 1989 were when both of the daughter visited their father in the hospital in 1993 and by the testimony of decedent's sister,

Helen Sargent, stating she saw Pamela communicate with her father at the Belah grocery store and on White Sulphur Road in 1994. Therefore, we find that Pamela Gray Williams and Michelle Gray did not carry their burden of proof in rebutting the statement of fact as to why these parties were disinherited.

Opponents of the will contend that any failure to communicate with their father was due to just cause. Both daughters point to incidents in which they attempted visits at their father's home in Rogers, Louisiana, and Mr. Gray told them to leave. Pamela testified, which was corroborated by witnesses, that attempts to speak with her father at other locations than his home were similarly met.

Decedent's daughters point to *Succession of Bertaut*, 572 So. 2d 142 (La.App. 1 Cir.1990), *writ denied*, 573 So. 2d 1111 (La.1991), in support of their contention that their failure to communicate was with just cause. In *Bertaut*, the decedent left his family when one son was only two years old and the other was still in utero. He then moved to Baker, Louisiana, quickly remarried and started a new life. During the next fifty years Mr. Bertaut met with his children on very few occasions, and most of those meetings were not initiated by Mr. Bertaut. The court found that "Mr. Bertaut did not seek to establish any type of meaningful relationship with his sons." *Id.* at 147. The court felt that situation was not an ordinary one in which the aims of Article 1621, to encourage strong family ties, could not be achieved.

> This court is in accord with the trial court and legal scholars who feel that in ordinary situations La.C.C. art. 1621(12) places the burden of making the effort to communicate on the child. However, we do not think that a child must attempt to communicate with his parent when this attempt would be futile. If attempts by a child to communicate with his parent are futile, his failure thereafter to communicate with the parent is with just cause. A person should not be required by law to perform a vain and useless act.

Id.

The circumstances in the present case are not as extreme as in *Bertaut*. Though Mr. Gray did divorce Pamela and Michelle's mother and eventually moved to Rogers and later to Nebo, the decedent and his daughters once had good parent-child relationships. Mr. Gray had even lived with one daughter for a time in the last decade. The record reveals that a disagreement within the family concerning Mr. Gray's mother and the four attempts to prove her incompetent began the souring of this relationship. "[A]n argument that creates strained relations with the parent should not constitute 'just cause.' "*Bertaut*, 572 So. 2d at 146, (quoting K. Spaht, *Successions and Donations, Development in the Law*, 1984-1985, 46 La.L.Rev. 707 (1986)). Admittedly, since the decedent's move to Rogers, the parent-child relationship was indeed strained. However, the situation was not such that an effort to communicate was futile. Pamela testified that at times she did stop to talk with her father on the side of the road. Furthermore, they did visit their father while he was in the hospital in Shreveport. The evidence shows that some relationship between the decedent and his daughters did exist. Article 1621(12) places the burden on the children to maintain that relationship. After reviewing the evidence, we agree with the trial court that Pamela Gray Williams and Michelle Gray did not communicate with the decedent for a period of two years after their eighteenth birthday without just cause.

For these reasons, the judgment of the trial court is affirmed. Costs of this appeal are taxed against the appellants.

AFFIRMED.

NOTE

In *Succession of Steckler*, 665 So. 2d 561 (La. App. 5th Cir. 1995), a son had communicated with his mother by sending her three greeting cards over a period of about two years. He sent them by certified mail and a friend of the son's simultaneously executed an affidavit attesting to the mailing. The court found that the cards constituted communication even if they were sent as a formality to prevent disinheritance.

PROBLEM

Consider the following fact pattern:

In February, 2009, Howard discovered he had cancer. In March, he donated $225,000 to the American Cancer Society. In April, he donated $125,000 worth of Delta stock to Sally, his secretary of twenty years. Seven years ago, he had given Sally a beautiful bracelet in appreciation of her years of service. At the time, the bracelet was worth $8,000.

Howard died in May and left the following will, dated June 6, 1994, in proper form:

> I have taken care of my children all my life. They each received a good home, a good education, and much love. Therefore, it is my desire to leave them only the portion of my estate to which they are forced at the time of my death. I leave the rest of my estate to my beloved friend Margie.

Howard died possessed of a home worth $300,000 that he bought in 1990 for $200,000. He had a bank account with a balance of $100,000 in cash; certificates of deposit worth $10,000. He had medical bills of $110,000. Also, the Delta stock was valued at $50,000 at the time of Howard's death. Sally's bracelet was, at Howard's death, worth $12,000.

Consider the distribution of Howard's estate. Will Howard's children, Diane and Ben, who are healthy and over the age of twenty-four have any claim to his estate? What arguments could they present? How much of his estate would they be entitled to, if any? How could they enforce their right in the estate? Would your answer change if Diane was a paraplegic? What result if Ben had predeceased Howard, leaving two minor sons?

CHAPTER 12:
DONATIONS *OMNIUM BONORUM* AND DISPOSITIONS REPROBATED BY LAW
La. C.C. 1498, 1519-22, 1527, 1769

Introduction

While the general rules applied to the interpretation of donations, both *mortis causa* and *inter vivos*, are to honor the wishes of the donor or testator, in several instances the law imposes limitations on the donor in order to protect public policy interests of the state. The mechanism of forced heirship, as discussed in the previous chapter, places a limitation on the testator by preventing him from giving away his entire estate to the detriment of his young or disabled children. The state protects the testator's children from impoverishment and itself from the costs of caring for these children. Through the prohibition against donations *omnium bonorum*, the law protects the donor from himself, by declaring null those donations that divest the donor of all of his property to the extent that he fails to leave enough for his own subsistence. La. C.C. 1498. Thus, the state is spared the expense of providing for the overzealous donor.

In addition, the Code limits the ability of the testator or donor to impose immoral or impossible conditions. Such conditions imposed on a donation, are generally regarded as not written. La. C.C. 1519.

In the somewhat confusing area of prohibited substitutions, the law limits the ability of the testator to control the disposition of his property after death. The Civil Code provides that the testator cannot direct how his donee must dispose of the property during the donee's life or at his death. Thus, the testator is prevented from removing property from commerce for an indefinite period. Similar to the prohibited substitution is the *fidei commissum*–a donation which contains a request that the donee dispose of the property as the donor wishes, but does not impose on the donee a duty to preserve the property until such disposition.

Two other dispositions which resemble the prohibited substitution at first glance are specifically sanctioned by the Civil Code. One is the disposition of the usufruct to one and the naked ownership to another. La. C.C. 1522. The other is the vulgar substitution, a donation by which a third person is called to take a donation in case the donee does not take it. La. C.C. 1521. If the donee does not survive for the requisite time period specified in the Code, or is otherwise unable to take, the donation passes to the third party specified by the donor.

Donations *Omnium Bonorum* *Prohibits a person from donating all possessions & relying on the state.*

TRAHAN v. BERTRAND
952 So. 2d 809 (La. App. 3d Cir. 2007)

The plaintiff, Virgie Mae Bertrand Trahan, and the defendant, Alfred Louis Bertrand, Sr., both seek supervisory writs on the trial court's judgment granting in part and denying in part a peremptory exception of no right of action in favor of Alfred and the denial of his peremptory exception of prescription. For the foregoing reasons, we deny the writs.

FACTS

Ira Bertrand and Olivia Bellard Bertrand were the parents of Virgie and Alfred. On September 24, 1992 and September 30, 1992, Ira and Olivia executed inter vivos donations of immovable property in favor of Alfred. Ira passed away on October 25, 1992. Olivia passed away on September 2, 2000, after which Virgie was appointed administratrix of her estate. On July 11, 2005, Virgie filed a Petition to Declare Donations Null and Void seeking to have the 1992 donations to Alfred declared null and void as donations omnium bonorum, pursuant to LA.CIV.CODE art. 1489. She filed the petition individually as an heir and as administratrix of her mother's estate. In her petition, she alleged that the two donations divested her parents of all of their real estate and its accompanying income leaving them in necessitous circumstances. Thus, she alleged that the property or its value should be returned to her parents' estates and that Alfred was indebted to the estates for all proceeds generated from the property.

In response to the petition, Alfred filed an answer and peremptory exceptions of no right of action and prescription. Following a hearing on the exceptions, the trial court rendered judgment sustaining the exception of no right of action as to Virgie's standing to file the petition in her capacity as administratrix of her mother's estate and in her individual capacity as a forced heir to her mother. However, it denied the exception as to her capacity as a forced heir of her father. Finally, it denied the exception of prescription finding that a cause of action based on a donation omnium bonorum was imprescriptible. Virgie and Alfred both sought supervisory writs from this judgment.

ISSUES

In his writ application, Alfred questions whether Virgie has a right of action to challenge the donations made to him by his father, pursuant to LA.CIV.CODE art. 1498, and whether her claim has prescribed pursuant to the civil code articles pertaining to reduction of an excessive donation. Virgie, on the other hand, questions whether she has the right, as an heir of her mother, to seek the nullity of a donation omnium bonorum following the abolition of forced heirship pursuant to LA.CIV.CODE art. 1493. She further asks whether she has a right to seek the nullity of the donations in her capacity as administratrix of her mother's estate, and to sue for the loss of income to the estate occurring during the lifetime of the donor.

DONATION OMNIUM BONORUM

The cause of action known as a donation omnium bonorum is found in Article 1498 of the LOUISIANA CIVIL CODE, which provides:

> The donation *inter vivos* shall in no case divest the donor of all his property; he must reserve to himself enough for subsistence. If he does not do so, a donation of a movable is null for the whole, and a donation of an immovable is null for the whole unless the donee has alienated the immovable by onerous title, in which

case the donation of such immovable shall not be declared null on the ground that the donor did not reserve to himself enough for his subsistence, but the donee is bound to return the value that the immovable had at the time that the donee received it. If the donee has created a real right by onerous title in the immovable given to him, or such right has been created by operation of law since the donee received the immovable, the donation is null for the whole and the donor may claim the immovable in the hands of the donee, but the property remains subject to the real right that has been created. In such a case, the donee and his successors by gratuitous title are accountable for the resulting diminution of the value of the property.

Although there is not an abundance of jurisprudence, the following findings are evident from our review of the law pertaining to donations omnium bonorum. First, the right to attack such a donation may only be brought by the donor, during his/her lifetime, or by their forced heirs. *Maxwell v. Maxwell,* 180 La. 35, 156 So. 166 (La.1934); *Haynes v. Haynes,* 02-535 (La.App. 1 Cir. 5/9/03), 848 So. 2d 35; *Owen v. Owen,* 325 So. 2d 283 (La.App. 2 Cir.1975), *reversed on other grounds,* 336 So. 2d 782 (La.1976); *Succession of Moran v. Moran,* 25 So. 2d 302 (La.App. 1 Cir.1946).

Second, a donation omnium bonorum is absolutely null and, as such, is imprescriptible. *Broussard v. Doucet,* 236 La. 217, 107 So. 2d 448 (La.1958); *Abshire v. Levine,* 546 So. 2d 642 (La.App. 3 Cir.1989); *Owen,* 325 So. 2d 283; *Givens v. Givens,* 273 So. 2d 863 (La.App. 2 Cir.), *writ denied,* 275 So. 2d 868 (1973). LOUISIANA CIVIL CODE Article 7 provides, "Persons may not by their juridical acts derogate from laws enacted for the protection of the public interest. Any act in derogation of such laws is an absolute nullity." It is well settled that the public policy behind this statute is to prevent a donor from divesting him/herself of all of their property such that they become a ward of the state.

Based on the foregoing, we find that the trial court correctly granted the peremptory exception of no right of action with regard to Virgie's standing to bring this suit in her capacity as the administratrix of Olivia's estate. Further, based on the forced heirship laws in effect at the time of Olivia's death, the trial court correctly held that Virgie had no standing to bring this action as a forced heir of Olivia, but did have standing as a forced heir of Ira. The forced heirship laws, as amended in 1996, provided that only a child, twenty-three years old or younger at the time of his/her parent's death, qualified as a forced heir. The record suggests that Virgie was in her sixties in 1992; thus, she would have been well past the age limit for forced heirship when Olivia died in 2000.

Alfred argues that Virgie's claim in her capacity as a forced heir of Ira is prescribed as her claim is simply an action to reduce an excessive donation impinging on her legitime. He cites LA.CIV.CODE arts. 1503 and 1504. LOUISIANA CIVIL CODE Article 1503 states, "A donation, *inter vivos or mortis causa,* that impinges upon the legitime of a forced heir is not null but merely reducible to the extent necessary to eliminate the impingement." LOUISIANA CIVIL CODE Article 1504 provides:

An action to reduce excessive donations may be brought only after the death of the donor, and then only by a forced heir, the heirs or legatees of a forced heir, or an assignee of any of them who has an express conventional assignment, made after the death of the decedent, of the right to bring the action.

He further cites LA.CIV.CODE art. 3497, which allows an heir five years in which to bring an action to reduce an excessive donation.

Alfred cites several cases and the Louisiana Civil Law Treatise in support of his argument. The treatise states that "[f]orced heirs have been permitted to challenge such donations after the donor's death, yet only to the extent of their legitimes." Frederick William Swaim, Jr., and Kathryn Venturatos Lorio, 10 LOUISIANA CIVIL LAW TREATISE, SUCCESSION AND DONATIONS, § 11.11, p. 290 (1995) (citing *Succession of Turgeau,* 130 La. 650, 58 So. 497 (1912)). The authors then posed the following question:

> An interesting question remains as to the time forced heirs have to challenge such a donation. Is it five years as with any reduction, or is the action not subject to prescription because a donation *omnium bonorum* is absolutely null? If the action is to be treated as a reduction, limiting the forced heirs to their legitime, then perhaps the prescriptive period for reduction should control.

Id.

We disagree that the five-year liberative prescriptive period applies in this instance. Virgie's cause of action is based on alleged prohibited donations omnium bonorum, in which Olivia and Ira divested themselves of so much of their property that they could no longer support themselves. We agree with the trial court that once a donation is an absolutely nullity, it cannot somehow become legitimate again. As stated in *Pardon v. Moore,* 39,949, pp. 10-11 (La.App. 2 Cir. 8/17/05), 908 So. 2d 1253, 1259 (citing *Gram Realty Co. v. Northern Homes, Inc.,* 308 So. 2d 502 (La.App. 1 Cir.1975)), "The prescription of five years cannot cure a defect in a tax sale which is absolutely null and void as no peremptive or prescriptive period can breathe life into something that never existed." If the donations by Ira and Olivia are found to be donations omnium bonorum, then they are prohibitive donations which are absolutely null and void and considered as never having existed. Thus, we find no merit in Alfred's argument that just because the action is brought by Virgie, the donations are revived so that Article 3497 prevents her from pursing her cause of action. Rather, we agree with the second circuit that Article 3497 does not act in such a way that the five-year prescriptive period found therein cures the defective donations and then acts to deprive her of her cause of action. Accordingly, we find that the trial court correctly held that Virgie's right to bring this suit, in her capacity as a forced heir of Ira, is imprescriptible.

CONCLUSION

For the foregoing reasons, the writ filed by Alfred Louis Bertrand, Sr., on the peremptory exceptions of no right of action and prescription is denied. We further deny the writ filed by Virgie Mae Bertrand Trahan. The costs of these writs are assessed equally to the parties.

WRIT DENIED.

Simon, Note, *Donations Omnium Bonorum - Article 1497 [See La. C.C. 1498]**
Who May Object to Such Donations?
6 La. L. Rev. 98 (1944)
[Reprinted with permission]
(footnotes omitted)

Article 1497 provides that: "The donation inter vivos shall in no case divest the donor of all his property; he must reserve for himself enough for subsistence; if he does not do it, the donation is null for the whole." This article was adopted from the Spanish law. The Spanish commentator Febrero states that the raison d'etre was public consideration. The article did not appear in the LOUISIANA CIVIL CODE of 1808, but was adopted in 1825. In reflecting upon the significance of the article at the time of its adoption the redactors of the LOUISIANA CIVIL CODE of 1825 said: "We propose to re-establish this wise disposition which before existed and which the code had abolished, wherefore we have not learned," thus indicating that the article had been adopted for the protection of the public.

Louisiana jurisprudence instances a various application of this article. Insofar as the donor is concerned, his right to annul such a donation has repeatedly been recognized. Furthermore, the court decided that the donor was not estopped from annulling a donation of realty which had passed to a third person by sale, even though the purchaser had relied on the donor's assertion that the donee had good title. A donation will be considered void ab initio even if the donor had property left, provided that such residue is not enough for his subsistence. The right of the donor to annul is as forceful between spouses as against strangers. Hence a donation in consideration of marriage will be null and void, if the donor does not reserve enough for his subsistence. Furthermore, a donation, the object of which was community property, was held null for the whole and not for only half, where the action invoking Article 1497 was brought by the survivor of the spouses, the survivor having been the original donor.

Several times it has been said that it is the concern of the state that one shall not pauperize himself by his gratuities. Yet, however, inconsistent with this thought the right cannot be exercised by forced heirs of the donor while the donor is still living. But on the theory that such a donation is void ab initio and title has never left the donor, the forced heirs have been permitted to annul the donation after the death of the donor. Where, however, forced heirs rightfully exercise this right, it will be fatal to an annulment of the donation, if they fail to prove conclusively that the donation divested the donor of all of his property and that the value of the property exceeds by one-half the value of the services, for Article 1526 is a complete answer to Article 1497. Moreover, where there is a conveyance, purporting to be a sale, but which is proved by a preponderance of evidence to have been a donation, such conveyance will fall under the ban of Article 1497.

It is definitely settled that the collateral heirs have no right to annul a donation omnium bonorum, either during life of the donor or after his death.

It is difficult to reconcile the jurisprudence on Article 1497 and its public policy philosophy. The court apparently proceeds on the theory that it is to protect the public from the burden of supporting the donor, that a donation omnium bonorum is null ab initio; yet the right to annul the gift of all goods is denied to all but the donor while the latter lives, thus defeating what the article has been inaugurated to accomplish. The donor may become a burden upon the

---

* Bracketed material in italics added by author.

public, but the article is inoperative unless invoked by the donor. This seems repugnant to the spirit of this law.

The court has gone further and has permitted the forced heirs of the donor to annul such a donation after the death of the donor. This position is also difficult to reconcile. If Article 1497 is for the protection of the public against those who pauperize themselves by their gratuities, then those who are legally responsible for the support of the individual, including the state, should be allowed to bring the action during the lifetime of the donor if and only when they are called upon to support him. Certainly no action by anyone should be allowed after the death of the donor if the purpose of the article is to be carried out. If the forced heirs have been prejudiced by the donation, they have their remedy–reduction. Furthermore, if the case be that the donation was in compensation of such services then they still may reduce to the value of such services. By being allowed to annul the donation after the donor's death, forced heirs are permitted to circumvent positive laws delegating personal rights to the donor. In short, the effect is to deny the donor the right of freely allocating the disposable portion of his estate.

In this connection the jurisprudence grounds the annulment on the theory that since the donation is void ab initio, title has never left the donor; hence the forced heirs are merely asserting their rights to what is actually vested in them at the moment of the donor's death. The code article under discussion if adopted for the purpose stated does not support this theory. The article merely states that the donation shall be "null for the whole." Assuming for the moment, however, that the donation is void ab initio, it should then be an inevitable consequence that the legal heirs of the most remote degree would have a right to annul it. If title has never left the estate, and in consideration of the fact that they have a right to claim an intestate succession in the absence of closer heirs, they cannot be denied the right to assert their claim. The effect of this would be astounding. Suppose a widower who had lost his sons in this war donated all his property for the purpose of caring for the returning veterans. According to the ab initio theory, in such situations, the legal heirs would be able to annul the donation after the donor's death. This construction would seem contrary to the purpose of the article. It is submitted that the theory that the donation is void ab initio is an erroneous interpretation of the article.

The case of *Maxwell v. Maxwell* held that the right to invoke Article 1497 is personal to the donor and cannot be invoked by the forced heirs while the donor lives. If this right be personal, then presumably it perishes with its owner, the donor. As an analogy the treatment given to the right of the surviving spouse to the marital portion allowed under Article 2382 might be cited. The court has repeatedly held that this is a personal and optional right that the heirs do not and cannot receive this right by inheritance, because all personal rights die with the individual.

In *Succession of Turgeau*, where a donation was sought to be annulled the court said that the "attack after death of the decujus is of a personal character, and that only forced heirs can urge the ground to the *extent of their legitime.*" (Italics supplied.) The soundness of this notion should not be disparaged by the fact that it was presented by way of dicta. A close examination of Article 1497 in relation to the articles on reduction is convincing that the remedy of forced heirs is reduction.

Where public interest comes into conflict with personal rights, the latter should yield. Since, therefore, it is the concern of the public that an individual should not pauperize himself, he who has donated all his goods should forfeit his personal right of annulment to those who are immediately affected by his act. Under Article 229 of the REVISED CIVIL CODE, the children are bound to maintain their father and mother and other ascendants, who are in need. If it should be that a parent is in a state of destitution because of having donated his property, is it not equitable, sound and consistent with the public policy of this article such heirs should have the unquestionable right of annulling, then and there, such a donation? Article 1497 contemplates this situation. The article should not be emasculated by suspending its operation until after the donor is dead–after the commission of the damage against the public is completed.

The state should also have this right, if called upon to support the donor. Conceding that the purpose of the article is for the protection of the public, then the granting of this right to the state or to those legally responsible for support of the donor would be a complete fulfillment of this purpose, if granted during this lifetime and *only* if support is necessary.

If a person is allowed to annul a donation omnium bonorum during the life of the donor, certainly the benefits of the annulment should inure to the donor and not to anyone who should annul the donation.

In consideration of the fact that Louisiana does not recognize stare decisis and that the jurisprudence on this article is not too definitive nor multiple in nature, the court might shift its present position with regard to the rights of those concerned. Any of those who are legally bound and are called upon to support the donor, if the latter does not wish to exercise his right, should be able to annul any donation omnium bonorum, during the donor's lifetime, and the effect of the annulment should restore title in the donor. And conversely, no person whatsoever should be entitled to exercise the right provided in Article 1497 after the donor has died, since forced heirs are fully protected by their right to reduce any and all gifts.

NOTES

In *LeBourgeois v. Yeutter*, 550 So. 2d 314 (La. App. 3rd Cir., 1989), the Third Circuit court citing the Louisiana Supreme Court case of *Succession of Quaglino*, 95 So. 2d 481 (La. 1957), considered only the circumstances at the time of the donation in determining whether the donor left enough for her subsistence. Even though the donor no longer had enough for her subsistence at the time of suit, the court felt constrained to honor the donation because the donor had means to provide for herself at the time of the donation. *See also Manichia v. Mahoney,* 45 So. 3d 618 (La. App. 4th Cir. 2010), *writ denied*, 50 So. 3d 829 (La. 2010).

In *Pardue v. Turnage*, 383 So. 2d 804 (La. App. 1st Cir. 1980), the donor donated his prized stuffed bear to his sister and brother-in-law. The plaintiffs, donor's creditors, tried to seize the bear from the donees, claiming that the donation was *omnium bonorum*. In finding that the donation was not *omnium bonorum*, the court emphasized that the donor still had the ability to work.

Although a donation may be declared to be *omnium bonorum*, the donee may be able to substantiate a claim to the property on another legal theory. In *Givens v. Givens*, 273 So. 2d 863 (La. App. 2d Cir. 1973), the donee had initially been given land through a donation *omnium bonorum* over thirty years prior to the filing of suit by plaintiff to reclaim the land. The court, nonetheless, held that the donee was owner of the land as he had acquired it by possessing it openly and adversely to the donor who was the true owner, thus fulfilling the necessary time requirement to acquire by acquisitive prescription. In the earlier case of *Jenkins v. Svara*, 60 So. 232 (La. 1912), the donors, two brothers, donated their undivided interest in land to their sister in 1884. Their sister subsequently sold the land and then the land was transferred several more times by onerous title. The donation from the brothers was found to have divested them of all their property and was therefore null. When the brothers tried to reclaim the land from Svara, the last purchaser, in 1912, Svara claimed ten years acquisitive prescription. The court agreed with Svara and found that he had acquired ownership of the land through acquisitive prescription. Could the sister, the donee, have claimed ten year acquisitive prescription?

The law governing donations *omnium bonorum* was amended by Act 641, sec. 1 of 1982 to protect those who acquire an immovable by onerous title from the donee. The purchaser of the immovable or one who acquires a real right to the immovable will not be prejudiced should the donor or his heirs seek to annul the donation. The purchaser will be able to retain his acquisition. Thus, after the amendment, Svara would have been protected even if he had not possessed the property in good faith for ten years. However, the donee who sold the immovable would be required to return to the donor the value the immovable had at the time of the donation. If the donee had allowed a real right to be created against the immovable, the property once returned to the donor would remain subject to the real right created by onerous title or by operation of law and the donee would be obligated to account for the diminution in value caused by the recognition of this right. (La. C.C. 1498).

With the changes in forced heirship, limiting forced heirs to those under the age of twenty-four or disabled, how frequently do you suppose claims of *omnium bonorum* will be raised after the donor dies?

Immoral, Illegal and Impossible Conditions: La. C.C. 1519

SUCCESSION OF THOMPSON
132 La. 948, 49 So. 652 (1909)

MONROE, J.

[Edward Thompson died in 1908, leaving the forced portion of his estate to his three unmarried daughters and to his three minor grandchildren who were the children of his predeceased son. He left the residue of his estate to the Fink Asylum, a home for indigent widows and maidens, on the condition that the institution furnish room and support for his daughters should they ever be rendered homeless. The Fink Asylum was funded under a legacy in the will of John Fink, with the stipulation that the institution be used solely as a home for Protestant widows and orphans. Thompson's daughters did not qualify, as all were over the age of twenty-five and none had been married. Therefore, the City of New Orleans, as trustee of the funds donated to the Fink Asylum, contended that if the condition of supporting the daughters was impossible, it should be considered as not written, and the Thompson legacy should go unencumbered to the Fink Asylum].

Our reading of the will leads us to the conclusion that the main object of the testator was to make such provision for his three unprotected and unmarried daughters as would secure them a safe and comfortable place of refuge in the event of their losing the money which they were to inherit. The bequest to the "Home" (to use the language of the will) "is made upon the condition, to be made a matter of record at the institution, that a comfortable room and support will be furnished, at said Home, for either one, or all, of my three daughters, should misfortune render them homeless at any time." Not only is the bequest made upon the condition imposed by the testator, but, in order that there should be no misunderstanding in the matter, the fact that it was so made, together with the condition itself, are "to be made a matter of record at the institution."

The bequest cannot, therefore, be said to have been intended as a free gift to charity, any more than the donation of a right of way, on condition that a railroad be built on it, could be said to be a free gift to the railroad company, and the donee can no more take the property, unless it is able to comply with the condition, in the one case than in the other.

As the daughters of Edward Thompson are all past 25 years of age, and have never married, there is no contention that they are either orphans or widows, within the meaning of those words as used in the will of John D. Fink, and hence they can have no right to admission into an asylum erected with money left by Fink, and "to be used solely as an asylum for protestant widows and orphans."

It is said, however, that the city of New Orleans has accepted the bequest of Edward Thompson, in accordance with the terms and conditions thereof, that it is willing and able to comply with the condition imposed, and that the question of its right to do so is one which concerns the heirs of Fink, and not the executors or daughters of Thompson. We conceive that the violation of a trust, established by one who has departed this life, and therein the violation of the law which protects such trust, is a matter which concerns all who participate in such violation. But, assuming that the executors have no interest in seeing that the asylum or the city is in a position legally to comply with the condition upon which the city is to receive the legacy, and that the daughters of the testator have no interest in the question, whether they can be legally accommodated in the Fink Home, and assuming, also, that the heirs of Fink will be helpless, in the premises, we still have the "protestant widows and orphans of New Orleans," who will be entitled to be heard in resistance of the intrusion into the home, provided exclusively for them, of persons having neither moral nor legal right to enter there, and, above and beyond all, we have, as an obstacle to the course suggested, a principle of right which no court administering the law could ignore. John D. Fink, in departing this life, left the proceeds of the residue of his estate to "be applied to the creation and maintenance and support of a suitable asylum in this city, to be used solely as an asylum for protestant widows and orphans." This court, by its decree, withheld the money so bequeathed from the heirs at law of the testator, on the ground that the bequest inured to the benefit of the protestant widows and orphans designated; and further held that the city of New Orleans, alone, could administer it. The city accepted the trust and the money, and in doing so, bound itself to discharge the one and expend the other in accordance with the terms of the bequest. It has expended part of the money in the erection of an asylum "to be used solely as an asylum for protestant widows and orphans," since it could not legally have expended it for the erection of an asylum to be used for any other purpose, and so long as the asylum, thus erected, continues to be maintained by other of the money so received, it cannot be used by the city, without a violation of its trust, for any other purpose than that for which it was erected. Nor can the city be heard to say that it is willing and able to violate its trust.

In disposing of the remaining ground relied on by the city, our learned Brother of the district court says:

> But the testator added a condition to this legacy of such a nature that, if it be impossible or illegal, the bequest itself is null, notwithstanding article 1519 of the Civil Code. The French commentators agree, and the French Court of Cassation, interpreting a similar article, in the Code Napoleon, has repeatedly decided, that when the condition of a legacy is such that it is the prime, or moving, cause for

making the legacy, without which it would not have been made, in that case, the impossibility or illegality of the condition carries with it the nullity of the legacy itself. *See* Fuzier- Hermann on C. N. 900, Nos. 158, 159, 170, 171.

We have nothing to add to this, save that the rule stated is, and must needs be, the same in Louisiana as in France, since it is founded in the principle, recognized everywhere, that the first duty of a court, upon which is imposed the obligation of interpreting a will, is to ascertain the real intention of the testator.

* * *

Judgment affirmed.

LABARRE v. HOPKINS
10 La. Ann. 466 (1855)
[27 Loy. L. Rev. 260 (1981)]

Buchanan, J.

Mrs. Hopkins died on the 26th January, 1849, and her husband married again on the 15th May, 1851. The plaintiffs, heirs at law of the deceased Mrs. Hopkins, claim of the defendant to be put in possession of the estate of his deceased wife, in conformity to the dispositions of her will. The defendant excepts that the limitation of his usufruct under the will to the time of his second marriage is unlawful and void, as being in restraint of marriage, and is reputed in law not written. It is admitted that all the property left by Mrs. Hopkins was her separate estate.

* * *

Regarding it, then, as proved that James A. Hopkins has married again since the death of the testatrix, we find no text of the law of Louisiana which is violated by the term which she has thought fit to assign by her will to her husband's usufruct of her separate estate. The 603d Article of the Code declares that a usufruct, if limited by its title to determine in the event of a condition, terminates upon the happening of that condition.

By analogy, second marriages by no means appear to be recognized by, or, to say the least, do not appear to be special favorites of the law of Louisiana . . . And here we might conclude, for the plea of defendant has gone no farther than to assert the devise in question to be void, as being contrary to law. But the argument of his counsel has taken a much wider range. It is contended that the limitation of plaintiffs' usufruct by his wife's will is void, and to be taken as not written, because it is contrary to good morals. The Article 1506 of the Code, upon which this argument is based, is copied verbatim from Article 900 of the Code Napoleon. The application of this article to the case of a devise restrictive of marriage to particular classes and circumstances, or prohibitory of marriage absolutely or qualifiedly, of maids or widows, has afforded a fine field for the casuistical propensities of French commentators. . . The doctrine which may now be considered as established in France is, that the prohibition of marriage generally is contra bonos mores, but that the prohibition of a second marriage, whether there remain children of the first marriage or not, is not to be so considered.

Judgment affirmed, with costs.

SUCCESSION OF RUXTON
226 La. 1088, 78 So. 2d 183 (1955)
[30 Tul. L. Rev. 3338 (1956)]

FOURNET, Chief Justice.

Miss Virginia Brookshire, claiming to be entitled to recognition as special legatee under the provisions of the will of the late William Ruxton, deceased, prosecutes this appeal from a judgment of the District Court dismissing her opposition to the Second Provisional Account and plan of distribution filed by the executor.

William Ruxton died testate at his domicile in New Orleans on the 9th of March, 1951, leaving neither ascendants nor descendants. His last will and testament, executed December 4, 1947, contained the provision: ". . . Second: I give and bequeath unto Miss Virginia Brookshire, of Hendersonville, North Carolina, the sum of Ten Thousand Dollars ($10,000.000) cash, provided however, that she be still unmarried at the time of my death. In the event she not be unmarried at the time of my death, then I direct that the aforementioned bequest of Ten Thousand Dollars ($10,000.00) be added to the rest, residue and remainder of my estate to be disposed of as provided in paragraph Third hereof, and be considered as a part of my estate passing thereunder." At the time of the testator's death, the opponent was married to Joseph W. Appleyard; the executor, therefore, following the directive of the testator, added the $10,000 to the residue of the estate.

The opponent, relying on Article 1519 of the LSA-Civil Code, contends that a provision concerning her marital status at the time of the testator's death is a condition contra bonos mores and hence reputed not written.

Under the express provisions of the LSA-Civil Code, "The donor may impose on the donee any charges or conditions he pleases, provided they contain nothing contrary to law or good morals," Article 1527, "but those which are contrary to the laws or to morals, are reputed not written." Article 1519. In the instant case, it cannot be said that the provision in the will had a deterrent effect on the opponent, as she was not apprised of it until the decedent's death; but conceding, without deciding, that a legacy conditioned upon the legatee remaining unmarried is against the public policy of this State, it is apt to observe here that the provision under consideration is not one forbidding the donee to marry during her lifetime of even for a fixed period of time, nor one that directs the legacy shall lapse in case the legatee should marry in the future, but rather one that is conditioned upon her status at the time of the testator's death. Certainly, such a provision is not against good morals, and we know of no law prohibiting the same.

The argument that the testator had no motive impelling him to insert such a provision in his will, and that if there were such a motive it was one based upon his whim or caprice, has no basis in law, because under the clear provisions of Article 1527, supra, a donor may dispose of his property as he pleases and his motive cannot be inquired into except when the condition is considered to be morally or legally impossible.

For the reasons assigned, the judgment appealed from is affirmed.

SUCCESSION OF AUGUSTUS
361 So. 2d 474 (La. App. 4th Cir. 1978)

GULOTTA, Judge.

Decedent bequeathed to her husband the usufruct of her separate property under the following conditions, "…said usufruct to be for his lifetime and to terminate only upon his death or in the event he allows Thelma Poitant Augustus or Cecile Hill to enter this house."

By way of background, from 1937 to 1946, Leonard Augustus, the usufructuary, lived with decedent, Hattie Simon. In 1946, he married Thelma Poitant; however, shortly thereafter returned to live with decedent. In 1960, while Augustus was still married to Poitant, Simon executed the statutory will containing the conditions upon which the usufruct terminated. In 1968, Augustus divorced Poitant and married Simon, with whom he lived until her death in 1969. In 1971, Augustus remarried Poitant and they lived in the house upon which Augustus enjoyed a conditional usufruct.

The trial judge, pursuant to a rule brought by the executrix for termination of the usufruct, made the rule absolute and ordered Augustus to vacate the premises.

The legatee, Augustus, appeals. We affirm.

It is not disputed that Poitant lived in the premises with Augustus subsequent to the testator's death. Augustus seeks to set aside the condition terminating the usufruct on the ground that the condition is against public policy and Contra bonos mores. The testamentary usufructuary relies on LSA-C.C. art. 1527 which provides:

> Art. 1527. Charges or conditions imposed by donor
> The donor may impose on the donee any charges or conditions he pleases, provided they contain nothing contrary to law or good morals.

Citing dicta in *Succession of Ruxton*, 226 La. 1088, 78 So. 2d 183 (1955)[1] and French Commentators (Aubry and Rau) in CIVIL LAW TRANSLATIONS, Vol. 3, § 692, at page 290, Augustus claims that the condition for termination of the usufruct is a restriction of the legatee's right to remarry and is therefore contrary to law and against good morals.

In the first place, the condition places no restriction on the legatee's right to remarry. If, as contended by the legatee, the bequest does place such a restriction, we find no merit to his contention.

LSA-C.C. art. 542 provides:

> Art. 542. Absolute or conditional establishment of usufruct
> Usufruct may be established simply, or to take place at a certain day, or under condition; in a word, under all such modifications as the person who gives such a right may be pleased to annex to it.

Further, LSA-C.C. art. 1712 provides:

---

[1] The court, in dicta, said, "But conceding, without deciding, that a legacy conditioned upon the legatee remaining unmarried is against the public policy of this State."

Art. 1712. In the interpretation of acts of last will, the intention of the testator must principally be endeavored to be ascertained, without departing, however, from the proper signification of the terms of the testament.

In *Succession of Ruxton, supra*, the holding of the court was that a condition in a bequest based on the legatee's being unmarried at the time of testator's death is not contrary to good morals or public policy. Also, bequests in restraint of a second marriage are not opposed to the public policy of this state. *See Labarre v. Hopkins*, 10 La. Ann. 466 (1855). *See also* LSA-C.C. art. 916, the legal usufruct article, providing the usufruct shall cease upon remarriage.[2]

Although we conclude, in addressing legatee's argument, that a condition contained in the will terminating the usufruct upon the legatee's remarriage is not Contra bonos mores, we point out that we do not interpret the condition in the will in our case to restrict or prohibit the legatee's right to remarry. The condition merely prohibits Thelma Poitant from entering decedent's separate property. We fail to find this condition either violative of law or against good morals.

Accordingly, the judgment is affirmed.

SUCCESSION OF WAGNER
431 So. 2d 10 (La. App. 4th Cir. 1983)

BARRY, Judge.

Herbert U. Wagner died testate on August 26, 1975 at his domicile in Plaquemines Parish. He was married on October 4, 1917 to Byrtie A. Fisher and they had five children. Mr. Wagner's wife pre-deceased him and one of their children, Herbert G. Wagner, died on October 3, 1972 and was survived by a son. The dispositive portion of his will provides:

All of the property which I own is located in Louisiana and is community property, belonging to the community formerly existing between myself and my deceased wife.
I give and bequeath to Marie Amick:
A LOT OF GROUND, situated in Plaquemines Parish in Star Plantation, measuring 167′ feet front on the right descending side of Louisiana State Highway No. 23 by a depth of 200′ feet between equal and parallel lines. Said lot is to be taken from the upper portion of my property.
In the event that any of my children should object to the above and foregoing disposition of that particular lot to Marie Amick, then I will and bequeath to the said Marie Amick the disposable portion of my entire estate.

The will was probated on May 26, 1976. Marie Amick, the legatee, died January 6, 1979 and her brother-in-law, Willis Harrison Stanford, was placed in possession of her entire estate,

---

[2] Other persuasive Codal provisions are LSA-C.C. arts. 608 and 610.

including her interest in the Wagner succession. On November 12, 1979 Mr. Wagner's forced heirs filed a petition for possession urging that the decedent owned only an undivided one-half interest in the property and could not bequeath a particular portion to Amick. The heirs submit that the designated portion amounted to one-eightieth of the whole and Stanford (Amick's heir) is entitled to an undivided one-eightieth interest in the two plots. They further contend the alternate bequest of the disposable portion to Amick should be considered a penalty clause and is *contra bonos mores* under *Succession of Kern,* 252 So. 2d 507 (La.App. 4th Cir.) *writ denied* 259 La. 1050, 254 So. 2d 462 (1971).

Stanford filed an opposition to the petition for possession asserting he should receive the land bequest or, alternatively, the disposable portion of the decedent's estate. He concedes the testator could not bequeath full ownership of property in which he had an undivided one-half interest, however, Stanford contends the will afforded Wagner's children the option of conveying their one-half interest in the lot or receiving their legitimate with the disposable portion going to Mrs. Amick's heir.

The district court judgment granted an option to the forced heirs to either transfer their interest in the designated lot to Stanford or they would receive their forced portion and Stanford would receive the disposable portion.

The judgment allowed the forced heirs forty-five days to exercise their option and they now appeal suspensively. Stanford answered requesting that the decree be modified to set forth the exact boundaries of the designated lot or the manner for setting the boundaries.

LSA-C.C. Art. 1712 provides the basic principle to apply when interpreting testaments:

> In the interpretation of acts of last will, the intention of the testator must principally be endeavored to be ascertained, without departing, however, from the proper signification of the terms of the testament.

Our courts have stated the testator's "intention must be ascertained from the whole will, and effect must be given to every part of the will as far as the law will permit. No part of a will should be rejected, except what the law makes it necessary to reject. Where it is a question of the choice between two interpretations, one of which will effectuate, and the other will defeat, a testator's intention, the court should select that interpretation which will carry out the intention of the testator." *Succession of LaBarre,* 179 La. 45, 48, 153 So. 15, 16 (1934). See also *Carter v. Succession of Carter,* 332 So. 2d 439 (La.1976).

The entire will is dedicated to Marie Amick's receiving a portion of Wagner's estate. If the specific bequest was the only provision in the will Amick would be entitled to only an undivided one-half interest in the designated property because that was all Mr. Wagner owned. A testator cannot bequeath that which is not owned and any such legacy is void to that extent. LSA-C.C. Arts. 1519, 1639. *Succession of Marion,* 163 La. 734, 112 So. 667 (1927). However, the will convinces us that Mr. Wagner's intent was to give Amick full ownership of the lot, even though he knew he couldn't.

"The intention [of the testator] must be ascertained from the *whole* will and effect must be given ... as far as the law will permit." *Succession of LaBarre, supra.* (Our emphasis.) The testator acknowledged that all of his property was community which was the only reason for him to specify the alternate bequest. That leaves no doubt Mr. Wagner was fully aware he could not bequeath the particular lot in full ownership to Amick. He understood the concurrence of his children was necessary in order to effect his wishes.

The testator's intention was amplified by the testimony of Emile E. Martin, III, then an attorney who drafted the will. Judge Martin testified that Mr. Wagner's sole purpose for writing his will was to give Amick full ownership of the property where her trailer was located. Judge Martin advised Mr. Wagner that the "community" aspect of the property would be a problem unless his children agreed to transfer their interest to Mrs. Amick for her to acquire full ownership. Judge Martin said Mr. Wagner then became "adamant," reported that he and his children were not on good terms, and stated if they refused he wanted to leave Mrs. Amick his *entire* estate. Judge Martin then explained the laws on forced heirship and the subject will resulted containing the alternate legacy.

We are satisfied Mr. Wagner knew his bequest could not be accomplished without his children's cooperation. Foreseeing the possibility they would not comply, he saw fit to include the alternative provision.

Legitime imperanti parere necesse est-one lawfully commanding must be obeyed. We cannot require Mr. Wagner's children to transfer their interest in the lot to Amick's heir. They alone have the capability to comply with their father's request. Otherwise, the alternative disposition is effective which we view as a conditional donation and within the parameters of the law. LSA-C.C. Art. 1527.

The forced heirs argue that the alternate provision is a penalty clause and should not be given effect, citing LSA-C.C. Art. 1519 and *Succession of Kern, supra.* We disagree. *Kern* did not involve forced heirs. The provision in *Kern* was that a protest by *any* heir, not just a legatee under the will, would result in the entire estate going to a third party. This Court felt that provision "particularly vicious ... repugnant to law and morals" as it rendered the legatees "helpless and at the mercy of any heir not mentioned in the will. Such an heir need only to file suit in order to force a legatee to surrender a portion of his legacy to prevent the have-not heir from instituting legal proceedings."

That is not the case here. The option flows to the forced heirs, not to "any" heir. It puts no one in a position to defeat a legacy by merely objecting or contesting the will. It simply implements the alternative provision if the heirs do not comply with the testator's wishes. The alternative bequest will not deprive the forced heirs of anything they are legally entitled to, i.e., their legitime. The forced heirs have no "right" to the disposable portion; the testator has a right to bequeath the disposable portion in *any* manner. *Succession of Hyde,* 292 So. 2d 693 (La.1974). We find the optional bequest is not repugnant to law or good morals and is valid as a conditional legacy.

The testator died August 26, 1975, was survived by four children and one grandson from a pre-deceased son, and the disposable portion of his estate amounts to one-third.

Stanford's answer to this appeal requested we set forth or devise a manner to determine the exact boundaries of the designated lot. That request is premature until the forced heirs elect which option they choose, and then that matter must be resolved amicably or in the district court.

The judgment of the district court is affirmed at appellants' costs.

AFFIRMED.

NOTES

Compare *Succession of Kern,* 252 So. 2d 507 (La.App. 4th Cir.) *writ denied* 259 La. 1050, 254 So. 2d 462 (1971) which is mentioned in the *Wagner* case. How can these two cases be distinguished?

Also see La. R.S. 9:2119 of the LOUISIANA TRUST CODE which provides in part, "A settlor by the provisions of the trust instrument cannot forbid a sale of immovable property for a period beyond fifteen years from his death."

Ponder the following stipulation considered by the court in *Succession of Russell,* 590 So. 2d 606 (La. App. 3ʳᵈ Cir. 1991):

> It is my desire that the property I own at the time of my death be held together as long as possible. To this end, I make as a condition of ownership of the immovables which my two children and my grandson inherit from me that before any of them sell his or her interest in any such property to a third party he or she must offer to the other two the right to purchase the property jointly for not more than the price offered by such third party. The two to whom the offer to sell has been made shall have fourteen days from receipt of the offer to sell within which to accept or reject such offer to sell, and if the offer is accepted they shall have sixty days to complete the purchase of the property from the one desiring to sell. In the event one of the two to whom the offer to sell has been made desires not to purchase, the remaining one who wishes to purchase shall have the right to purchase the entire offering.

Is the condition imposed by the testator illegal? What arguments can be made for and against finding the condition illegal?

Prohibited Substitutions and *Fidei Commissa*: La. C.C. 1520

Substitutions remain one of the most confusing areas of Louisiana law. As described by Planiol, the substitution is a disposition by which the donor gives the property to another with the charge for him to keep it during his life, and to transfer it at death to a third person designated by the donor. It is a practical expression of a desire on the part of the donor or testator to order not only his own succession, but also the succession of the donee or legatee. Planiol points out that two aspects of substitutions arguably offend public policy: (1) giving to the first donee in less than full ownership by restricting his ability to dispose of the property at will; and (2) "tying up" the property for an extended period of time, keeping it effectively "out of commerce." *See* 3 Planiol, CIVIL LAW TREATISE No. 3265.

La. C.C. 1520 provides that a disposition not in trust, by which a donor gives full ownership of a thing to a "first donee" "with a charge to preserve the thing" and then deliver it to a "second donee" is null. Basically, three elements are necessary for the substitution to be prohibited. It must contain:

(1) a double disposition in full ownership;
(2) a charge on the donee to preserve and render the property to another;

(3) successive order.

~~If~~ all three elements are present and the donation is not in trust form, then the entire disposition is null. ✗

One must approach substitutions in trust with caution. Although a substitution which would otherwise be prohibited may be valid if it is in the form of a trust, not all prohibited substitutions in trust are sanctioned.

No reference to *fidei commissa* currently appears in the Civil Code. The term, *fidei commissa*, was deleted from the text of the code article in 1962, perhaps as an accommodation to the forthcoming adoption of the LOUISIANA TRUST CODE in 1964. *Fidei commissa* differ from prohibited substitutions in that there is no a duty on the part of the first donee to preserve the object. Prior to the deletion of the term *fidei commissa* from La. C.C. 1520, *fidei commissa* were treated by cases as dispositions with illegal conditions and only the condition to render the property was reputed as not written; but, as with the cases under La. C.C. 1519, the first donee was permitted to retain the gift free of the condition to later pass it on to another.

As one analyzes substitutions, one must remember that the vulgar substitution is permitted. A vulgar substitution calls a third person to take a gift in case the original donee is unable to take. La. C.C. 1521. In such a case, the object goes straight from the original donor to the third person. No middleman is given the gift first. Thus, this is a direct substitution and differs from the indirect prohibited substitution.

Indirect substitutions are often difficult to recognize. They frequently resemble dispositions in which one person is granted a usufruct, and another is granted a naked ownership. A donation of a usufruct and naked ownership is, of course specifically permitted. La. C.C. 1522. Again, however, the donation of the interests comes directly from the original donor, although the naked owner does not enjoy full ownership of the property until the termination of the usufruct.

SUCCESSION OF JOHNSON
223 La. 1058, 67 So. 2d 591 (1953)
[32 La. L. Rev. 208 (1972)]

LE BLANC, Justice.

This case presents the ever recurring problem before the Courts where there is a contest over a will which allegedly contains a disposition that is prohibited under our law and is therefore invalid...The law having reference to dispositions such as are reprobated is found in Article 1520 of the LSA-Civil Code, which reads in part as follows:

> Substitutions and *fidei commissa* are and remain prohibited.
> Every disposition by which the donee, the heir, or legatee is charged to preserve for or to return a thing to a third person is null, even with regard to the donee, the instituted heir or the legatee.

In order to better understand the issues that are presented in this case it is appropriate that we should state how they came to be presented to the Court.

Thomas Johnson, the testator, died at his domicile in the City of New Orleans on April 27, 1952. He had been married twice, his first marriage having been contracted with Mrs. Fern Wiggs who preceded him in death. Of this marriage there was born one child, a son, Robert T. Johnson. After his first wife's death he contracted a second marriage with Mrs. Sue Wiggs, her sister, and of this marriage there was born one child, a daughter, Martha Jane Johnson, married to Anton Erickson.

He left an estate at the time of his death consisting of stocks, bonds, and other securities and also a piece of real estate, with buildings, and improvements and certain household furniture and belongings.

* * *

On May 23d 1952, Robert T. Johnson again appeared in Court and filed a petition seeking to annul the will which had been ordered executed, averring that the whole of the said will is illegal null and void under the provisions of the CIVIL CODE OF LOUISIANA and according to the established jurisprudence of this Court. The will as quoted in full in his petition reads as follows:

New Orleans, La.

Nov. 2-51
To whom may consern
   I, Thomas Johnson do make this my Will and do here by leave evything to my wife Sue W. Johnson as long as she live and then she is to leave her step son Robert Thomas Johnson just 1/4 of the Share of what is left--and Martha Jane my only Daughter the rest. At my death Sue W. Johnson shall be the admistor of this will in my own writing at 3 P.M. Nov.--2-51
(s) Thomas Johnson

* * *

On May 28, 1952, Mrs. Sue Wiggs Johnson filed an exception of no cause or right of action to the petition of Robert T. Johnson to have the will annulled. She was joined in this exception by her daughter, Mrs. Martha Jane Johnson, wife of Anton Erickson... After trial in the District Court there was judgment in favor of Mrs. Sue Wiggs Johnson and Mrs. Martha Jane Johnson and against Robert T. Johnson maintaining the exception of no right or cause of action and dismissing the petition seeking to have the whole will of the decedent annulled. It was further ordered that letters testamentary issue to Mrs. Sue Wiggs Johnson, without bond and also it was ordered that the rights of Robert T. Johnson and Martha Jane Johnson, as children and heirs of the decedent be reserved to them to be asserted in the proceedings. From that Judgment Robert T. Johnson was granted and is prosecuting this appeal.

In approaching a decision of the first issue it becomes necessary to consider the language of the will in connection with the provisions of Article 1520 of the LSA-Civil Code quoted at the beginning of this opinion.

Whilst that article at first blush would seem to indicate that substitutions and *fidei commissa* are one and the same thing and affect the validity of the will in the same manner, it is undoubtedly settled by the jurisprudence of this State that there are differences between them and that it is very important to note the difference because in cases of prohibited substitutions the whole will is stricken with nullity whereas in cases of fidei commissa, it is only those dispositions which are tainted with that designation that are invalid. Under the provisions of Article 1519 of the LSA-Civil Code which provides that "In all dispositions inter vivos and mortis causa impossible conditions, those which are contrary to the laws or to morals, are reputed not written," they are considered as having no binding effect and may be legally regarded as not written.

In *Succession of Reilly*, 136 La. 347, 67 So. 27, one of the leading cases on the subject, the Court pointed out the distinction between substitutions and *fidei commissa* and the differences in their effect. On page 363 of 136 La., on page 32 of 67 So. We find the Court stating as follows:

> The essential elements of the prohibited substitution are that the immediate donee is obliged to keep the title of the legacy inalienable during his lifetime, to be transmitted at his death to a third person designated by the original donor or testator. Such a disposition is null even with regard to the original donee or legatee. In the *fidei commissa*, whereby the donee or legatee is invested with the title and charged or directed to convey it to another person or to make a particular disposition of it, only the charge of direction, as to the ultimate disposition of the donation or legacy, is null and is to be considered not written, leaving the donation or bequest valid as to the donee or legatee. A substitution is an attempt on the part of the donor or testator to make a testament for his donee or legatee along with his own will, and to substitute his own will for the legal order of succession from his donee or legatee. If permitted, the effect of a substitution would be to tie up the title and keep it out of commerce during the lifetime of the first donee, during which time neither he nor the person designated to receive the title at the donee's death could alienate it. A substitution is necessarily a *fidei commissum*, but a *fidei commissum* is not necessarily a substitution. In the *fidei commissum* the title is not tied up or kept out of commerce; the direction or charge, as to its disposition, is to be regarded only as a precatory suggestion addressed to the conscience of the donee or legatee, which, being illegal, but harmless, can have no binding effect, and may be legally regarded as not written.

It strikes us that the important words in Article 1520 of the LSA-Civil Code with regard to the nullity of the dispositions therein prohibited are those by which the donee or legatee "is charged to preserve for or to return a thing to a third person."[1] If the donee or the legatee is charged to preserve a thing for a third person, obviously he cannot dispose of it or dissipate it in any manner. The effect of such a disposition is, as was said in *Succession of Reilly, supra*, to tie up the title to property and keep it out of commerce during the life time of the first donee. That is principally the reason why such dispositions properly called "substitutions," are prohibited by the Article of the Code.

---

[1] According to the Editors of Louisiana Legal Archives, the word *or* as used in this phrase should have been translated *and*, the phrase should therefore read to "preserve for and to return a thing to a third person."

It becomes necessary therefore to interpret the language of the testator's will in this case to ascertain whether it constitutes that form of disposition.

The testator used the expression "I do hereby leave everything to my wife Sue W. Johnson as long as she live and then she is to leave her step son Robert Thomas Johnson just 1/4 of the Share of *what is left*." (Emphasis supplied.) Certainly there is no charge on the legatee to preserve anything for any one. Everything is left to her, as long as she lives; he bequeaths it to her and she can dispose of it, encumber it or dissipate it if she sees fit. It is only in the event that she does not so dispose of, encumber or dissipate the whole estate that she is to leave to Robert T. Johnson one-fourth of the share of *what is left*. The phrase *what is left* conveys the definite implication that title to all of the property was vested in the legatee and it was the intention of the testator to create such a title for her benefit to the exclusion of all other persons.

In *Dufour v. Deresheid*, 110 La. 344, 34 So. 469, the Court had before it for construction the disposition of a will written in French, the translation of the pertinent part of which reads as follows:

> I declare I have brought in marriage the sum of six thousand, five hundred dollars.
>
> I institute as my universal legatee my wife, Katharina Deresheid, to whom I give and bequeath the totality of the property which I shall leave on the day of my decease.
>
> At the death of my wife, I desire that, after deduction made of the above sum of six thousand, five hundred dollars which shall be paid to my natural heirs, the balance of what she will leave on the day of her decease shall be divided equally between my natural heirs and her own.

The disposition is one which we think bears a close resemblance to the one in the case now before us because the words "the balance of what she will leave on the day of her decease" have the same meaning as the words "she is to leave her step son Robert T. Johnson just 1/4 of the share of what is left," contained in the will in this case. In that case the Court stated:

> It is clear that this is not a disposition by which the legatee is charged to preserve for and return a thing to a third person or persons.
>
> The estate, under this will, is given outright, in full ownership, to the wife. She may do as she pleases with it. She may expend the funds on hand, sell the movables and immovables, reinvest their proceeds, or use the same as she otherwise may wish. No charge is imposed upon her to preserve any thing.
>
> If, however, at her death anything is left of the estate, the will expresses the wish that his natural heirs be given the sum of money he had brought into the marriage, and whatever else remained, after paying them such sum, that the same be given equally to his and her heirs.
>
> It is not a bequest to his and her heirs. The legatee is not charged to preserve $6,500.00 for his natural heirs which they are to take under the terms of the will at her death. Neither is she required to preserve any part of the estate for his and her natural heirs, th[at] which they should take under the will at her death.

As they (his natural heirs) take nothing under the will, they could take the estate left at her death only what she, following the expressed wish of her husband, might in her will bequeath to them. And if she made no will naming them as legatees, her heirs would take the estate under the law of inheritance.

That is a statement of the law as it may well be applied in the present case.

Another case which we think bears a similarity to the one at bar is that of *Succession of Heft*, 163 La. 467, 112 So. 301. The will in contestation there contained the following disposition:

I desire that all that I die possessed of, jewelry, clothing, investments, money in bank, or otherwise invested, to go to my only sister P. Barbara Heft to enjoy with interest thereof during her lifetime, after her death whatever may be left to be divided in three (3) equal parts (1/3) one third thereof to be equally divided between my then living brothers, ...

Whilst it is true that there was no contention that the will contained a prohibited substitution and the very question presented by one of the parties was that the language of the will was such as to convey only the usufruct of the estate to the legatee and the ownership of one-third of the estate to other parties named therein, the Court did go into a discussion of what constituted prohibited substitutions and *fidei commissa* and again pointed out the difference between them. It stated also that they are essentially different from the giving of the usufruct to one legatee and the ownership to another, which is expressly permitted by Article 1522 of the LSA-Civil Code. Continuing its discussion the Court stated further: "All that the court has to decide in cases like this is whether the testator expressed in his will the intention to give the property itself or only the usufruct to the first legatee. We agree with the judge of the civil district court that the intention expressed in this will was to give to the sister of the testatrix, not merely the usufruct of the estate, but the estate itself, with the wish--or bequest if you will--that whatever might be left of it in the possession of the legatee at the latter's death should go to the other persons and the two institutions named in the will. We construe the expression, 'After her death whatever may be left to be divided in three (3) equal parts,' etc., to mean that the sister might dispose of any or all of the property during her lifetime if she saw fit; which means that the property was given to her in full ownership with the request that she should distribute as directed whatever she might have of it at her death.'" The Court then went on to state why the expression in the will "to enjoy with interest thereof" did not express the intention to give only the usufruct of the estate, with which expression, of course, we are not concerned in this case as the will herein involved contains no statement or expression intimating that the property may have been left for the legatee's use or enjoyment. This, we believe also makes it unnecessary for us to discuss the idea suggested by counsel for appellant that certain language in the opinion in the case, *Succession of Hall*, 141 La. 860, 75 So. 802, may have created some confusion in construing Articles 1520 and 1522 of the Code.

There is a recent case decided by this Court which also bears on the subject of substitutions and *fidei commissa*. That is the case of *Girven v. Miller*, 219 La. 252, 52 So. 2d 843, 844 in which it was specifically held that a will which contained a disposition reading: "I leave all I die possessed of to Rev. William A. Miller, CSSR. to be disposed and administered according to my typed instructions," constituted a bequest that was absolute and constituted

Father Miller as universal legatee of the estate and was not rendered conditional, merely because of the language which followed it, namely, "to be disposed [of] and administered according to my typed instructions." The Court stated with regard to this language: "These words are not limitations upon the title of Father Miller; they are expressions of the testator's wish or request which, under familiar rules of interpretation of testaments, are to be viewed as a precatory suggestion addressed to the conscience of the legatee but which is "not binding in law and cannot affect the validity of the bequest of the estate to him." *See Succession of Hall*, 141 La. 860, 75 So. 802, 803, and authorities there cited.

Our conclusion on this issue in the present case is that the disposition made by the testator to the donee, Mrs. Sue W. Johnson, constituted a legal and valid bequest to her and conveyed a valid title to all the property bequeathed to her. The mere fact that the disposition reads that it was left to her "as long as she lived" does not affect the bequest or qualify it in any manner as is suggested by counsel for appellant; manifestly the testator could not leave her "everything" as he did for any longer period of time. The will does not contain a prohibited substitution which renders it totally null. The language to the effect that the legatee is to leave to other persons "what is left" constitutes a *fidei commissum* which, under the provisions of Article 1519 of the LSA-Civil Code are reputed as not written. That was the conclusion reached by the trial judge which we thoroughly approve.

*　　*　　*

We are of the opinion that the judgment appealed from is correct and for the reasons herein stated, it is affirmed at the costs of the appellant.

NOTE

The trial court in *Johnson* "ordered that the rights of Robert T. Johnson and Martha Jane Johnson, as children and heirs of the decedent be reserved to them to be asserted in the proceedings." To what rights is the court referring?

SUCCESSION OF MORGAN
260 So. 2d 1972 (La. App. 3rd Cir. 1972)

DOMENGEAUX, Judge.

This is a suit to have the olographic will of Woodrow P. Morgan declared null and invalid, brought by his widow, Evelyn Dunn Bryan, and his brother, Robert P. (L.) Morgan. Named defendants are Johnny C. Morgan, and Anna Mae Dunn as administratrix of the estate of her minor child, Randy P. Dunn.

The trial court rendered judgment in favor of petitioners, declaring the purported olographic testament of Woodrow P. Morgan to be null, void, and of no legal effect. Defendants appealed that judgment to this court, specifying as error the trial court's finding of invalidity of the will.

The testament in question deals with two tracts of land, one called the "home Land" and the second termed simply the "Ford." It was stipulated by counsel for both sides that the home Land referred to was the separate property of the testator, and that the "Ford" land was part of the community property of the testator and his wife. It was also stipulated that the form of the will was valid.

The will was obviously prepared by the testator without the assistance of an attorney, and is quoted as follows:

> Feb 14--1966
> I W P Morgan make my Last Will
> I will to Johny C Morgan my home Land at my W P Morgan and Evelyn Morgan Death this Land is not to Be Sold only By Johny C Morgan only after my and her Death
> The Ford I will to Randy P Dunn after W P Morgan and Evelyn Morgan Death and this Land is not to be sold only By Randy P Dunn at the age of 18 years
> By W P Morgan

Even the most cursory examination of the testament makes it clear that both of the dispositions therein made are tainted by prohibited substitutions. In the first the testator's "home Land" is willed to Johnny C. Morgan "at" his and his wife's death. In the second the "Ford" land is willed to Randy P. Dunn "after" the death of himself and his wife. In both cases the lands devised may be sold only by the ultimate legatees and they gain ownership thereof only when the testator's wife is also dead. This is an undisguised attempt on the testator's part to make a will for his widow, who presumably would hold the land until her death. Thus the widow is the immediate donee, but she is incapacitated from disposing of the property, either during her lifetime or by donation mortis causa. In the case of *In Re Succession of Abraham*, 136 So. 2d 471, this Court had occasion to consider LA.CIVIL CODE Article 1520, which prohibits substitutions in testaments, and wrote as follows:

> The essential elements of a Substitution are that the immediate donee is obliged to keep the title of the legacy inalienable during his lifetime, to be transmitted at his death to a third person designated by the original donor or testator. If permitted, the effect of a substitution would be to tie up the title and keep it out of commerce during the lifetime of the first donee, during which time neither he nor the person designated to receive the title at the donee's death could alienate it.

The wording of the testator's will makes it plain that the legatees, Morgan and Dunn, were not to obtain any interest in the property until the death of the testator's wife. Accordingly, we find no merit in appellants' contention that the will created a usufruct in favor of the widow and vested the naked ownership of the lands in Morgan and Dunn. It has long been held by our Supreme Court that in order to convey the usufruct of property to one legatee and the naked ownership of it to another, both interests must be transmitted directly from the testator and vested in the respective legatees immediately upon the testator's death. *Succession of Heft*, 163 La. 467, 112 So. 301.

Finally, we reject appellants' suggestion that the will created a trust under LSA R.S. 9:1753. That statute provides, in relevant part, that, "No particular language is required to create a trust, *but it must clearly appear that the creation of a trust is intended*." (Emphasis ours). We find no evidence of such an intention in the instrument before us, let alone a "clear" indication thereof.

We find it distasteful to thwart the intentions of the testator and frustrate his last wishes by declaring the nullity of his testament. No choice is given us, however, by the mandates and prohibitions of our law. La. Civil Code, Articles 7, 12, 13, 1520.

For the above and foregoing reasons the judgment of the district court is affirmed at appellants costs in both courts.

Affirmed.

BATEN v. TAYLOR
386 So. 2d 333 (La. 1979)
[42 La. L. Rev. (1982); 27 Loy. L. Rev. 259 (1981); 56 Tul. L. Rev. 350 (1981);
57 Tul. L. Rev. 145 (1982)]

DENNIS, Justice.

This case presents the question of whether a testator can make a valid will bequeathing his property to his wife, upon the condition that she survive him for thirty days, or, if the condition is not fulfilled, to his nephews.

The testator's sister unsuccessfully attacked the will in the district court and appealed. The court of appeal reversed, holding that the disposition is null because it conflicts with Civil Code Article 1520, which prohibits any disposition constituting a substitution as defined by that article, and Article 1609, which gives the universal legatee seizin of the succession immediately at the testator's death. Accordingly, the intermediate court decreed that the deceased's estate, which was his separate property, must be transferred as an intestate succession, effectively depriving the widow of her husband's property even though she had survived him for thirty days. We reverse, upholding the will, because the double conditional legacy is not a prohibited substitution as defined by the code and does not prevent seizin of the succession immediately at the testator's death.

Decedent, Gordon D. Baten, died testate on February 2, 1974 at his domicile in Beaumont, Texas, leaving separate immovable property situated in Louisiana. He was survived by his widow, Floy Taylor Baten, and his sister, Ruby Mae Baten Taylor. He left no ascendants or descendants.

The testament, valid in form, contains the following dispositive provisions:

2.

I give, devise and bequeath all of my property, real, personal or mixed, wheresoever located to my beloved wife, Floy Baten, should she be living at my death.

3.

In the event my said wife shall have predeceased me, or should my said wife and I die under circumstances that there is not sufficient evidence to determine the order of our deaths or if she shall die within a period of thirty (30) days after the date of my death, then all bequests, devises and provisions made herein to or for her benefit shall be void; and my estate shall be administered and distributed in all respects as though my said wife, Floy Taylor Baten, had predeceased me.

4.

In the event of any of the happenings set forth in paragraph numbered 3 of this my will, I then give, devise and bequeath all of my property, real, personal or mixed, as follows:

(a) An undivided one-fourth (1/4) thereof to Virgil Taylor, Box 3283, Radford, Virginia;

(b) An undivided one-fourth (1/4) thereof to Jon Taylor, who is the son of Virgil Taylor, and who teaches at the University of Jacksonville, Florida;

(c) An undivided one-fourth (1/4) to Dan Taylor, Radford, Virginia;

(d) An undivided one-fourth (1/4) to Bill Taylor, who resides in the State of Oregon.

Mrs. Baten survived her husband for thirty days, fulfilling the condition of survivorship. She instituted ancillary probate proceedings resulting in a judgment of possession on January 19, 1977, which recognized her as the surviving spouse of the decedent and, as legatee under his will, entitled to the ownership of all Louisiana property belonging to him.

On October 14, 1977, the decedent's sister, Ruby Mae Baten Taylor, filed a petition of intervention in the ancillary probate proceedings, seeking to annul the will and to have that portion of the judgment of possession recognizing Mrs. Baten's legacy set aside. Mrs. Taylor alleged that, as the decedent's sole intestate heir, she should be placed in possession of all of his Louisiana property, because the legacy to his widow contained a prohibited substitution and was therefore null.

The matter was tried on a joint stipulation of facts. The interpretation and validity of the testament were the only issues presented. After the trial, the district court rejected Mrs. Taylor's attack upon the will and upheld the universal legacy to the widow, Mrs. Baten. Mrs. Taylor appealed to the court of appeal.

*   *   *

Preliminarily, we must decide whether the condition attached to the wife's bequest is suspensive or resolutory. The condition of survivorship for thirty days is suspensive under a common sense interpretation, considering the nature and purpose of the clause. The brief period stipulated and the other provisions of the will indicate the testator's intention was to avoid multiple taxes and a transfer of the succession to his wife's heirs if she died closely following him. Thus, the survivorship clause is very similar to standard suspensive conditions employed for these purposes by practitioners in Louisiana and other states. *See*, Rubin & Rubin, LOUISIANA TRUST HANDBOOK, 164, 177 n. 16 (1968); Oppenheim, 10 LOUISIANA CIVIL LAW TREATISE,

SUCCESSIONS AND DONATIONS, § 128, p. 252; Atkinson, ATKINSON ON WILLS, 828 (2d ed. 1953); Murphy, 1 MURPHY'S WILL CLAUSES, 27 (1978). Although the testator's language is ambiguous, we do not think he intended to create the possibility of a vesting of full ownership in his wife for a period of less than thirty days and a subsequent transfer to his nephews.

The issues presented are: (1) whether a double conditional legacy, whereby the first legatee's bequest is subject to a suspensive condition that he survive the testator for thirty days and the second legatee's bequest is conditioned upon the lapse of the first legacy, is a substitution prohibited by Civil Code Article 1520 and (2) whether a universal legacy dependent upon a suspensive condition is in conflict with the rules of seizin.

1. Prohibited Substitution

The double conditional legacy is not a prohibited substitution because it does not: (1) constitute a double disposition, in full ownership, of the same thing to persons called to receive it one after another; (2) impose upon the first beneficiary a charge to preserve and transmit the succession property; and (3) establish a successive order that causes the property to leave the inheritance of the burdened beneficiary and enter into the patrimony of the substituted beneficiary. A prohibited substitution, as defined by Civil Code Article 1520, must have all of these characteristics.

LOUISIANA CIVIL CODE Article 1520, as amended in 1962, provides:

> Substitutions are and remain prohibited, except as permitted by the laws relating to trusts.
>
> Every disposition not in trust by which the donee, the heir, or legatee is charged to preserve for and to return a thing to a third person is null, even with regard to the donee, the instituted heir or the legatee.

The Louisiana State Law Institute, in its report to the Legislature accompanying the Trust Code, explained the essential elements of a prohibited substitution, defined by Civil Code Article 1520, as follows:

> The second paragraph of Article 1520 specifies and defines the disposition prohibited in the first paragraph, which is identical with its French counterpart, Article 896, C.N., except for the provisions relating to trusts. It is, for example, a disposition conceived in these terms: "I bequeath my farm Blackacre to Paul, and I charge him to preserve and transmit it at his death to LeDoux."
>
> The constituent characteristics of this prohibited substitution that are implicit in this definition are:
>
> (1) A double liberality, or a double disposition in full ownership, of the same thing to persons called to receive it, one after the other;
> (2) Charge to preserve and transmit, imposed on the first beneficiary for the benefit of the second beneficiary;
> (3) Establishment of a successive order that causes the substituted property to leave the inheritance of the burdened beneficiary and enter into the patrimony of the substituted beneficiary.

This is in accord with settled French doctrine and jurisprudence, and it is in this sense that the term "substitution" is used in the Civil Code, and by derivation from the Code in the Constitution. REPORT TRUST CODE 3A LSA.-R.S. p. XXXIII, XXXVIII (1965).

We are convinced that the Law Institute's interpretation of Article 1520 is correct. As its report indicates, the Article implies the foregoing definition of a prohibited substitution, and the term is used in this sense in French doctrine and jurisprudence. 3 CIVIL LAW TRANSLATIONS, Aubry & Rau § 694, pp. 307-23; 3 Planiol, CIVIL LAW TREATISE §§ 3278-83, pp. 593-95. Moreover, the report of the Law Institute is entitled to great weight as reflecting legislative intent in this instance. The Institute, to open the way for a new trust code which it had been instructed to draft by the Legislature, prepared amendments to Article 1520 to clarify the meaning of a prohibited substitution and to remove any obstacle to an effective trust device in Louisiana. *See* Oppenheim, *Trust Code Introductory Comment* 3A LSA.-R.S. XXVII p. XXIX (1965). The Legislature evidently endorsed the Law Institute's definition of a prohibited substitution by adopting the amendments and enacting the new trust code on the basis of its report.

The definition of a prohibited substitution which we infer from Article 1520, furthermore, is consonant with the original legislative motive for prohibiting substitutions. The reasons assigned for the prohibition are to prevent the making of gratuities to future generations; to prevent property left to an existing generation from being made inalienable, 3 Planiol, *supra*, § 3197; and to ward off all of the objectionable consequences from such dispositions. *See* Tucker, *Substitutions, Fideicommisa and Trusts in Louisiana Law: A Semantical Reappraisal*, 24 La.L.Rev. 439, 454 (1964).

The disposition at issue in the present case has none of the characteristics of a prohibited substitution, as defined by Article 1520. First, it does not make double disposition of the same thing, in full ownership, to persons called to receive it one after another. Since the widow's legacy was subject to a suspensive condition, she would not have received the succession in full ownership if she had failed to survive the testator for thirty days. The second legacy to the nephews was under condition of the failure of the condition of the widow's legacy. As a result of the retroactivity of the condition, the nephews could have received the property only in default of the widow's legacy, not after her.

Second, there was no charge to preserve resting on the first legatee. It is not necessary for the creation of a substitution that the disposer make use of the identical terms found in Article 1520. It suffices that the charge to preserve and to deliver necessarily result from the tenor of the disposition, or, what amounts to the same thing, that it is impossible to execute the disposition without preserving and making restitution of the property given or bequeathed. *See*, 3 Aubry & Rau, *supra*, § 694, p. 315. The disposition at issue in the present case, however, by its wording, purpose and tenor, does not imply a charge to preserve. If the suspensive period had been longer, it could be argued that the legacy would be impossible to execute without a charge to preserve. The brief thirty-day suspensive period, however, allows execution of the disposition without this effect.

Finally, for the same reasons that there was no double disposition, the will does not establish a successive order whereby the property could leave the inheritance of the first beneficiary and enter into the patrimony of the substituted beneficiary.

The type of double conditional legacy presented in this case has been approved repeatedly by the French Courts and commentators. French jurisprudence has held that there is no prohibited substitution "when a legacy, though made in full ownership, is made to depend on a suspensive condition, with the clause that in case the condition fails, the thing shall be given to a third person." 3 Aubry & Rau, *supra*, § 694, p. 309. An illustration of this double conditional legacy is the legacy made to Primus on the condition that he marries, or that he marries before a certain age, or that he lives to a certain age, with the stipulation that, if this condition is not accomplished, the property will be bequeathed to Secundus. Tucker, *supra*, at 481; 3 Aubry & Rau, *supra*, at 309; 3 Planiol, *supra*, § 3295, p. 601.

The underlying considerations upon which French jurisprudence has based its approval of such dispositions, according to John H. Tucker, Jr., are as follows:

> (1) It constitutes two legacies under a suspensive condition, the first legacy under the condition described in the illustration, the second legacy under the condition of the failure of the condition of the first legacy.
> (2) As a result of the retroactivity of the condition, the second legatee (Secundus) is considered as receiving the property not after the first legatee (Primus), but in default of him, and there is no successive order.
> (3) There is no real charge to preserve and render resting on the first legatee.
> (4) In such a case, the testator will be considered to have bequeathed the usufruct to Primus for the period intervening between his receipt of the legacy and the failure of the condition, even if he has not so specified.
> (5) In some instances, the courts have annulled a conditional legacy (e. g., "I bequeath my property to X if he attain 21 years; if he die before that this legacy will fail and be as not written."), as containing a resolutory condition. However, the jurisprudence generally has validated double conditional legacies of the type given in the illustration, where the testator intends to maintain the first legacy, only if the legatee attains a certain age, or accomplishes a fact before a certain age without being concerned with whether the condition is resolutory or suspensive.
> Tucker*, supra*, at 481-82.

The court of appeal reasoned that, because the disposition in the present case is indistinguishable from a classic substitution, its enforcement would render Article 1520 and the jurisprudence developed around it meaningless. The rationale is based on a faulty postulate, however, because a classic substitution is one which contains all of the characteristics stated or implied by the second paragraph of Article 1520 and listed in the Law Institute's Report. Thus, it is a disposition bequeathing property to A in full ownership, but requiring that he preserve the property and that, upon his death, it be delivered to B in full ownership. Since the disposition at issue in this case contains none of the three characteristics of a substitution, its enforcement does not conflict with Article 1520. Also, as the appellate court recognized, a review of the Louisiana cases reveals none in which a double suspensive conditional legacy was evaluated. The enforcement of the disposition here, therefore, does not conflict with the holdings in our previous opinions.

There is language in some of the cases which, if followed, would nullify conditional donations outside the ambit of Article 1520's strict definition of a prohibited substitution. Many of those decisions may be disregarded as obsolete because they were focused on prohibiting the common law trust in Louisiana, now adopted to some extent in our trust code. *See Succession of Walters*, 261 La. 59, 259 So. 2d 12, 16 (1972) (Barham, J., concurring); *Crichton v. Succession of Gredler*, 256 La. 156, 235 So. 2d 411, 421 (La.1970) (Sanders, J. dissenting). Fundamentally, however, all of the jurisprudence defining and applying the law of former Article 1520 must be reassessed in light of the amendments by which the Legislature has harmonized our definition of substitutions with French doctrine and the rule that penal and prohibitory laws should be strictly construed. Report Proposed Trust Code 3A LSA-R.S., p. XLI. *See State v. Executors of McDonogh*, 8 La.Ann. 171, 230 (1853); *Heirs of Cole v. Cole's Executors*, 7 Mart.N.S. 414 (1829).

We conclude, for these reasons, that the disposition in the present case is not a substitution prohibited by Article 1520.

*   *   *

Conclusions

The will in the present case contains a disposition made to depend on two suspensive conditional legacies. The disposition is not a prohibited substitution as defined by LOUISIANA CIVIL CODE Article 1520, and it does not have the effect of suspending seizin of the succession. Accordingly, the testator's will and the universal legacy to his wife are not contrary to law and should be enforced.

The judgment of the court of appeal is reversed and the judgment of the district court is reinstated at plaintiff-appellee's cost.

REVERSED; DISTRICT COURT JUDGMENT REINSTATED.

NOTE

The *Baten* court characterized the condition of survival of the wife for thirty days as a suspensive condition, thus eliminating the problems of a double disposition and successive ownership. What if the court had decided that the condition was resolutory?

La. C.C. 1521 was amended by Act 957 of 1984, which sanctioned a condition of survival not to exceed thirty days. The article was amended again by Act 680 of 1987 extending the sanctioned period to ninety days, and again by Act 825 of 2001, extending the period to six months. Should the duration of the suspensive condition affect the result in a case such as *Baten*? How do the amendments to La. C.C. 1521 affect your answer? *See* Jacobs, Comment, *A Reasoned Seizin and Prohibited Substitutions*, 56 Tul. L. Rev. 350, 364-366 (1981).

Despite some loose language used in early cases, it is now clearly settled that the effect of finding a prohibited substitution is that the entire substitution is deemed as not written, rather than the entire will. *Succession of Walters,* 261 La. 59, 259 So. 2d 12 (1972).

Disposition of Usufruct and Naked Ownership: La. C.C. 1522

SUCCESSION OF THILBORGER
234 La. 810, 101 So. 2d 678 (1958)

HAWTHORNE, Justice.

This is a suit instituted by the collateral heirs of Mrs. Louise Bartels Thilborger to have a provision of her last will and testament declared null as constituting a prohibited substitution. The provision of the will under attack reads:

(1) To Edward J. Thilborger my dear husband I give devise and bequeath the use of the Lodge and harbor, and cottages and the Louise Plantation as long as he lives and at his death to be given to the Charity Hospital to be used as a convalescent home to bring the sick for fresh air and regain their strength,

The lower court rendered judgment recognizing plaintiffs as being the sole heirs of the deceased, entitled as such to the ownership of the Louise Plantation on Bayou Barataria in Jefferson Parish, said to contain about 1,100 acres. From this judgment the Board of Administrators of the Charity Hospital of Louisiana at New Orleans has appealed.

Louise Bartels, wife of Edward J. Thilborger, died in New Orleans in 1936. Her will containing the provision here under attack was in due course admitted to probate, and a judgment was rendered decreeing Charity Hospital of Louisiana at New Orleans to be the owner of the plantation as a particular legatee, subject to the usufruct in favor of Thilborger. Thilborger died in 1939, and Charity Hospital took possession of the property.

Appellees take the position that the contested provision contains a prohibited substitution and is null and void under Article 1520 of the Civil Code, which provides:

Substitutions and *Fidei commissa* are and remain prohibited.

Every disposition by which the donee, the heir, or legatee is charged to preserve for or to return a thing to a third person is null, even with regard to the donee, the instituted heir or the legatee. . . .

In explaining the provisions of Article 1520 this court on numerous occasions has said that the simplest test of the substitution prohibited by our law is that it vests the property in one person at the death of the donor and at the death of such person vests the same property in another person, who takes the same directly from the testator but by a title which springs into existence only on the death of the first donee. Such a disposition destroys the power of alienation of the property by the first donee, because he is bound to hold it until his death in order that the person then called to the title may take it. At the same time no power of alienation exists in the second donee during the life of the first, because his title comes into being only at the death of the latter. *See Succession of Blossom*, 194 La. 635, 194 So. 572.

It is the position of appellant that the disputed provision of the will is the bequest of the usufruct to the husband and the naked ownership to Charity Hospital, and is therefore authorized by Article 1522 of the Code, which provides that the disposition inter vivos or mortis causa by which the usufruct is given to one and the naked ownership to another shall not be considered a substitution and is valid.

In the recent case of *Succession of Rougon*, 223 La. 103, 65 So. 2d 104, 107, the court said:

Citing the *Ledbetter* case (*Succession of Ledbetter*, 147 La. 771, 85 So. 908) (and other cases) the court in *Succession of Heft* said (163 La. 467, 112 So. (301) 302): It is well settled that a testamentary disposition containing the stipulation that at the death of the legatee the property shall go to another legatee named in the will is not the same thing as the giving of the usufruct to the one and the ownership of the property to the other legatee. . . . In order that a testament may convey the usufruct of property to one legatee and the ownership of it to another, the title to the property itself to the one legatee, as well as the usufruct to the other legatee, must be transmitted directly from the testator and invest the title in the one legatee and the usufruct in the other immediately at the death of the testator. . . .

In support of their position appellees cite and rely principally on *Succession of Williams*, 169 La. 696, 125 So. 858. In that case this court stated that under the language of the will under attack it was the intention of the testator to convey the title as well as the usufruct to his wife for the term of her natural life, and that it was only at the death of the wife that the ownership should vest in the second named legatee, the niece of the testator.

In 3 Loyola Law Review 185 ff., there appears an excellent comment written by James A. Bugea, then a member of the faculty of the Loyola School of Law, on the substitution-usufruct problem. He points out that the jurisprudence of this court is in a confused state, especially in that type of cases where the testator used qualifying words or phrases to designate the interest that the first party was to take, and that in such cases the decisions are conflicting, some where such qualifying words or phrases are used holding that the will is void as containing a prohibited substitution, and others where similar words or phrases are used holding that the will is valid as expressing a valid usufruct-naked ownership of disposition. *See also* dissenting opinion of Justice, now Chief Justice, Fournet, in *Succession of Fertel*, 208 La. 614, 23 So. 2d 234, where he takes cognizance of this conflict in the jurisprudence and discusses some of the cases.

The problem is indeed perplexing, and it is difficult to reconcile or distinguish *Succession of Williams, supra*, decided in 1930, cited and relied on by appellees, and *Succession of Fertel, supra*, decided in 1945, cited and relied on by appellant.

In *Succession of Williams* the testamentary disposition is as follows (169 La. 696, 125 So. 859):

I, D. F. Williams, do give and bequeath unto Mary A. Williams, my beloved wife, for her use and benefit all the property both personal and real to use for the period of her natural life and at her death everything shall belong to Lillian R. Williams, my niece...

The disposition in the *Fertel* case is (208 La. 614, 23 So. 2d 235):

Everything I possess. I leave (the use of it to my husband during his life time, at his death it goes as following.
To my 2 daughters Nettie and Annie and to my grandson Rodney Fertel Weinberg.

As stated previously, the court held that the will in the *Williams* case was null as containing a prohibited substitution. In the *Fertel* case it was held that the will contained a bequest of the usufruct to one and the naked ownership to others and hence was valid under Article 1522 of the Civil Code.

The majority opinion in *Succession of Fertel* did not mention or make any effort to distinguish the Williams case, but followed and relied on *Succession of Blossom, supra*, in which the bequest to the first legatee was of the "usufruct" of the property. In the *Fertel* case the court said that "An examination of these wills (the Blossom will and the Fertel will) reveals that while differing slightly in their wording, they are identical as to substance." In short, what the court held in the *Fertel* case was that the bequest of the Use of the property is tantamount to a bequest of the Usufruct of the property.

In *Succession of Blossom, supra*, (194 La. 635, 194 So. 575) the court found that the *Williams* case was without application because the court in the *Williams* case held that the language there used disclosed that "the clear intention of the testator was to convey the title of the property as well as the usufruct to his wife for the term of her natural life and that it was only at the death of the wife that the ownership should vest in the legatee."

The author of the opinion in the *Williams* case, after quoting the provisions of the will there involved, simply concluded that the words used disclosed a clear intent to convey to the wife both title and usufruct for the term of her natural life, but he gave no reasons as to how he reached this conclusion. However, under this conclusion the court must necessarily have recognized that the phrase "for her use and benefit" conveyed a usufruct to the wife, for it found that the disposition bequeathed both title and usufruct to her.

We see no real difference in a bequest of *Property for use and benefit* and a bequest of *the use of property*. However, *Succession of Fertel*, a more recent case and one of the latest cases in which the problem was discussed, is clearly authority for the proposition that a bequest of the *use* of property is a bequest of the *usufruct* of the property. That such is the holding in the *Fertel* case was recognized in the later case of *Succession of Rougon, supra*, wherein it was said: "In *Succession of Fertel*, 208 La. 614, 23 So. 2d 234, the court held that the immediate donee received a usufruct because in the will the bequest was for the *use of the property*."

We therefore conclude that the holding of this court in *Succession of Fertel* is decisive of the instant case, for it is apparent to the reader that the language of the bequest in the *Fertel* case is very similar to the language used in the bequest in the instant case. The testamentary disposition in the instant case more closely resembles the disposition in the *Fertel* case than that in the *Williams* case, because in the *Williams* case the testator gave his wife for her use and benefit all of his property, whereas in the *Fertel* case, as here, the testatrix gave her husband only the use of the property.

The bequest in the *Fertel* case, which we again quote, provides:

> Everything I possess. I leave (the use of it to my husband during his life time, at his death it goes as following.
> To my 2 daughters Nettie and Annie and to my grandson Rodney Fertel Weinberg.

In concluding that this bequest was not a prohibited substitution but was valid under the provisions of Article 1522 of the Civil Code, the court in the *Fertel* case said in a per curiam on application for rehearing:

…Here, the testatrix did not declare that she left her property to her husband, but declared that she left "the use of it" to her husband, and that at his death it should go to her two daughters and her grandson. By the term "the use of it" the testatrix must have meant the usufruct of the property, not the ownership of it. The expression that "at his death" it should go to the two daughters and the grandson of the testatrix meant merely that the possession of the property should be delivered to them at the death of the husband, who was to enjoy the use of it during his lifetime. The expression "at his death" did not mean that the title to the property should be vested in the husband of the testatrix, and at his death should pass from him to the two daughters and the grandson. It meant merely that the possession and use, or usufruct, of the property should be enjoyed by the husband until his death, and that during his lifetime only the naked ownership should be vested in the two daughters and the grandson of the testatrix.

Therefore, when the testatrix in the instant case said, "To Edward J. Thilborger my dear husband I give devise and bequeath the use of the Louise Plantation as long as he lives and at his death to be given to the Charity Hospital…," she was bequeathing to her husband the usufruct of the property and to Charity Hospital the naked ownership; and at the moment of her death the usufruct vested in the husband and title or naked ownership vested in Charity Hospital. Consequently the testamentary disposition here under consideration does not contain a prohibited substitution and is valid.

Appellees appear to value greatly, as supporting their position, a codicil which Mrs. Thilborger added to the will involved here, which codicil reads:

Should anything happen that my husband E. J. Thilborger and Myself die together in an accident or any other way I then appoint J. J. Cullinane and Mat A. Grace to take the place of E. J. Thilborger and give all that I have given to E. J. Thilborger to be given to Edith Pope my precious niece and may God bless her.

Appellees apparently feel that this codicil strengthens their argument that the disposition of the plantation is a prohibited substitution, but they are mistaken as this codicil in no way renders the legacy to Charity Hospital a prohibited substitution; all this appendix does is to make a vulgar substitution, permissible under Article 1521 of the Civil Code--that is, the niece would simply be substituted for the husband and would receive what it was intended for the husband to receive: the usufruct of the Louise Plantation.

For the reasons assigned the judgment appealed from is reversed, annulled, and set aside, and plaintiffs' suit is dismissed at their costs.

SUCCESSION OF FOURNET
195 So. 2d 333 (La. App. 3rd Cir. 1967)

CULPEPPER, Judge.

*　　　*　　　*

The sole issue on appeal is whether the provisions of the will creating successive usufructs must be considered a prohibited substitution.

The facts show that Mrs. Blanche Fleming Fournet died in 1956, leaving four surviving children: Reverend Lawrence M. Fournet; Fred G. Fournet; Beulah Fournet; and Maydell Fournet Theriot. She left a will dated November 28, 1952, which contained the following dispositions allegedly constituting a prohibited substitution:

> I will and bequeath unto my beloved daughter, Beulah Fournet, as an extra portion and advantage and besides the portion to which she will be entitled by law in my succession, the usufruct during her natural life of all my undivided rights, titles, interests, claims and pretentions in and to the following described property. (Then follows a description of a town lot with the drugstore, dwelling, furniture and fixtures located thereon.)
>
> I also will and bequeath my daughter, Maydell Fournet Theriot, the usufruct of all of the above specified property from and after the death of my daughter, Beulah Fournet, should the said Maydell Fournet survive said Beulah Fournet, said usufruct to be for her natural life from and after the death of said Beulah Fournet and up to the time of her death.
>
> The balance of my property I will and bequeath to all of my children, share and share alike.

The opponent to the probate of this will contends it contains a prohibited substitution in that the usufruct of the property was bequeathed to Beulah until her death, at which time the same usufruct devolves to the other daughter, Maydell, if she survives.

The contention is that such successive usufructs are invalid under Louisiana law.

We will first state some general principles of law. Substitutions are prohibited in this state by LSA-C.C. Article 1520 which reads as follows:

> Substitutions are and remain prohibited, except as permitted by the laws relating to trusts. Every disposition not in trust by which the donee, the heir, or legatee is charged to preserve for and to return a thing to a third person is null, even with regard to the donee, the instituted heir or the legatee. (As amended Acts 1962, No. 45, § 1.)

However, vulgar substitutions and donations of the usufruct to one, and the naked ownership to another, are excepted from this sweeping prohibition by the two following code articles:

> Art. 1521. The deposition (disposition), by which a third person is called to take the gift, the inheritance or the legacy, in case the donee, their heir or the legatee does not take it, shall not be considered a substitution and shall be valid.
> Art. 1522. The same shall be observed as to the disposition inter vivos or mortis causa, by which the usufruct is given to one, and the naked ownership to another.

Many cases state the essential elements of the prohibited substitution are that the immediate donee or legatee is charged with the duty to keep the title of the thing inalienable during his lifetime, to be transmitted at his death to a third person designated by the original donor or testator. The substitution-usufruct problem has been the source of much litigation, but we have found only three cases, discussed hereinafter, dealing with successive usufructs. The question is usually whether the bequest to the first legatee is a bona fide usufruct, permissible under LSA-C.C. Article 1522, or whether it is the naked ownership, passed from the first legatee to the second legatee, in which event it is a substitution.

Usufruct is defined in LSA-C.C. Article 533 as "the right of enjoying a thing, the property of which is vested in another, and to draw from the same all the profit, utility and advantages which it may produce, provided it be without altering the substance of the thing." Usufruct is a personal servitude, in the sense that it expires at the death of the usufructuary and does not pass to his heirs, LSA-C.C. Articles 606, 646.

We have concluded that successive usufructs are not prohibited substitutions in Louisiana. Although they are not expressly recognized (nor prohibited) in our Civil Code, there is sufficient basis to support their validity. This basis is as follows: Article 1522 expressly affirms a disposition of the usufruct to one legatee and the naked ownership to another. The divisibility of usufructs is recognized by Article 538, which can readily be construed to permit the creation of one usufruct divided between two persons. Article 542 provides that usufruct may be established to begin on a certain day or on the happening of a condition. And Articles 608 and 609 clearly imply that successive usufructs are permissible.

Despite the rule that usufructs expire on the death of the usufructuary, usufructs in favor of several persons jointly, and revertible from one person to the other, not terminating until the death of the last survivor, were recognized in French law, and have been affirmed in at least two Louisiana cases. It is logical that if such revertibility is permitted, successive usufructs should also be permitted.

Of course, successive usufructs, like other donations, are restricted by LSA-C.C. 1482 which provides:

Art. 1482. In order to be capable of receiving by donation inter vivos, it suffices to be conceived at the time of the donation. In order to be capable of receiving by last will, it suffices to be conceived at the time of the decease. But the donations or the last will can have effect only in case the child should be born alive.

Successive usufructs are recognized under the French and Spanish Civil Codes, despite the rule that usufructs terminate on the death of the usufructuary. The rationale is that the successive usufructuaries take directly from the original owner and hence there is no substitution.

As mentioned above, there are three Louisiana cases which involve successive usufructs. Although it can be argued that the holdings are dicta or inconclusive, all three cases approve successive usufructs. The first case is *McCalop v. Stewart*, 11 La.Ann. 106 (1856) in which the court said of the successive usufructs there at issue:

Again, the dispositions in favor of the testator's daughter and her husband, and in favor of his granddaughters, Mrs. Williams and Mrs. Dougherty, the mothers of the instituted heirs, cannot be viewed as substitutions. They are usufructs, and as such, are within the purview of Article 1509 of the Code. The duration of these usufructs is different, and it depends upon contingency whether that in favor of the testator's granddaughters shall have effect at all.

There is nothing in the dispositions of the will in this regard, which is contrary to law. Usufruct may, from its origin (des son origine), be conferred on several persons, in divided or undivided portions. C.C., 531. Usufruct may be established simply, or to take place at a certain day, or under condition; in a word, under all such modifications as the person who gives such a right, may be pleased to annex to it. C.C., 534. (This Article 1509 cited is from the Civil Code of 1925, the source of our present Article 538.)

The next case is *Succession of Buissiere*, 41 La.Ann. 217, 5 So. 668 (1889), in which the testator bequeathed the usufruct of part of his estate to his wife, with the provision that it continue in certain nephews and nieces after the death of the wife and end of the death of these latter usufructuaries. The testator's daughter was named as universal legatee, receiving the naked ownership of the property. Certain collateral heirs attacked the will on several grounds, one of which was that the provisions as to usufruct constituted a prohibited substitution. The court held:

> 2. We think that the charge that the will contains a prohibited substitution and *fidei commissum* is not tenable, for the reason that it does not appear that the legatee of the usufruct and the universal legatee where charged to preserve for, or to return a thing to, a third person. REV.CIVIL CODE, arts. 1520, 1522… The fact that the testator has expressed the desire that, after the death of his wife, certain nephews and nieces of his, or their descendants, should enjoy the like usufruct, is of no moment. If unwarranted by law, it must simply be reputed as unwritten. (*Id.* art. 1519,) and, in any event, it does not impair the validity of the disposition of usufruct in favor of the widow. *Succession of Law*, 31 La.Ann. 456.

The third case is *Fricke v. Stafford*, La.App., 159 So. 2d 52 (1st Cir. 1963). The will there provided:

> I give and bequeath to my daughter Wilhelmina Fricke a life usufruct of all property real, personal and mixed of which I may die possessed, subject only to the usufructuary claim of my wife should she survive me as fixed by law in her favor.

Although the successive usufruct in the *Fricke* case was not attacked as being a prohibited substitution, it was recognized as barring a suit for partition affecting the rights of the usufructuaries.

For the reasons assigned, the judgment appealed is affirmed. All costs of this appeal are assessed against the appellant.

Affirmed.

NOTES

Title III of Book II of the LOUISIANA CIVIL CODE (previously La. C.C. 533-645) was revised, amended, and reenacted by Act 103, Sec. 1 of 1976, effective January 1, 1977. Usufruct is now defined in La. C.C. 535, and is described as a personal servitude in La. C.C. 534. The possibility of dividing a usufruct is recognized in La. C.C. 541. Successive usufructuaries are specifically sanctioned in La. C.C. 546.

The *Succession of Goode*, 425 So. 2d 673 (La. 1982), dealing with mineral rights was decided under the revised property articles. Where the testator bequeathed "payments" rather than the "royalty interests" to a named legatee for life and then bestowed the payments after the death of the first legatee to be divided among other named legatees. Justice Dixon, on rehearing, noted that the testator was a "retired independent oil operator" who could be assumed to "understand the difference between a royalty payment and a royalty interest and deliberately donated the payments and not the interest." Thus, the Justice was able to characterize the disposition as one of usufruct, rather than ownership of the actual asset producing the payments. What result would follow if the testator had bequeathed the actual royalties?

If the first legatee of a prohibited substitution or a *fidei commissum* predeceased the testator, should the court enforce the donation in favor the second legatee? In *Succession of Kamlade*, 94 So. 2d 257 (La. 1957), and in the dissenting opinion of *Succession of Mydland*, 653 So. 2d 8 (La. App. 1st Cir. 1995), there is language indicating that the second named legatee should take where the first legatee predeceases.

Vulgar Substitutions: La. C.C. 1521

SWART v. LANE
160 La. 217, 106 So. 833 (La. 1926)

THOMPSON, J.

This is a suit by three brothers against the husband of their deceased sister.

The object of the suit is to annul an olographic will executed by the sister primarily in favor of her child and secondarily in favor of her husband.

The will is dated July 24, 1924, and reads as follows:

> In case of my death, I will and bequeath to my child all that I own, all my real estate and all my personal property. I appoint my husband, Carlyle Lane its guardian.
>
> In case of my child's death as well as my own, I will and bequeath to my husband, Carlyle A. Lane all my real estate, all my personal property, all that I own, with the exception of my two diamond rings one I will and bequeath to Mary Louise Swart, the other to Alice Hickman Swart, both being daughters of William Swart.

The nullity propounded against the will is that it contains a prohibited substitution; that is to say, that the entire estate is bequeathed first to the testatrix's child and then at the death of the child to the testatrix's husband.

It is the peculiar and unusual phraseology of the second clause of the will that gives rise to the contention that the will contains a prohibited substitution, and it must be admitted that there is some basis for two different interpretations.

It may be well to observe in this connection that one of the cardinal rules laid down by the Code, and uniformly recognized by jurisprudence in construing and interpreting a last will, is to ascertain the intention of the testator, if that can be done "without departing, from the proper signification of the terms of the testament." C. C. art. 1712.

And another rule is that a disposition must be understood in the sense in which it can have effect, rather than that in which it can have none. C. C. art. 1713.

In the case of *New Orleans v. Hardie*, 43 La. Ann. 251, 9 So. 12, it was said:

In the interpretation of wills the intention of the testator is the polar star by which the courts must be guided. It is their duty to realize such intention from quod voluit by ascertaining quod dixit.

And in *Succession of Meunier*, 52 La. Ann. 79, 26 So. 776, 48 L. R. A. 77, it was said:

Where a bequest in a will, in one view, is illegal, in another view, lawful, the latter will be adopted and the will sustained.

To fall, this legacy must come clearly within the scope of one or the other of these prohibitions, for the law and the courts lean to the upholding of the dispositions made by testators of their estates.

This well established rule has never been departed from so far as we are informed.

No will has ever been annulled on the ground that it contained a prohibited substitution, except when such substitution was clearly expressed, or where the language used by the testator was so much involved in doubt as to render it impossible for the court to maintain the will without departing from the true significance of the language of the will.

If the will in the instant case can be interpreted only as giving the estate to the child during its life and after its death, said death occurring after that of the testator, the estate is to go to the husband of the testatrix, then it is clear the will cannot be maintained.

On the other hand, if it can be reasonably construed as showing the intention of the testatrix to give the estate to the husband in the event that the death of the child preceded that of the testatrix, then there is obviously no prohibited substitution, but a vulgar substitution, which is permissible and does not invalidate the will under article 1521, C. C.

But if it can be said that the will is equally and easily susceptible of either of the two interpretations, the one making it valid and the other making it a prohibited substitution, we would under the law be compelled to adopt the one which would save the life of the will rather than the one which would strike it down. The scale hanging even between these two interpretations, it is made to preponderate in favor of the validity of the will. *Succession of May*, 109 La. 994, 34 So. 52.

It appears from the petition that at the time the will was written the testatrix was in an advanced state of pregnancy. She expected soon to become a mother. The child was born some 44 days after the date of the will, but lived only a few hours. The child's death was followed in a few hours by the death of the mother.

There is no doubt that this serious and important event in her life-- the birth of a child who was to become her heir--weighed upon the mind of the testatrix and furnished one if not the main motive for making the will. She was aware of the great danger attending such an event, and realized, no doubt, the possibility of not surviving the ordeal.

In the event of her own death and the survival of her child, she unquestionably wanted all of her property to go to the child. This intent is clearly expressed in the first clause of the will. In writing the second provision in the will we are strongly impressed with the fact that the testatrix realized the possibility of the death of her child occurring coincident with or preceding her own death, in which event she desired the property to go to her husband. This intent on the part of the testatrix we think, if not clearly expressed, is fairly deducible from the language used, supported as it is by the circumstances and conditions under which the will was made.

The language is, "in case of my child's death, as well as my own, I will and bequeath to my husband, etc."

From this verbiage it may be fairly assumed that the testatrix had in mind the death of her child before or contemporaneously with her own death, and it was this contingency that caused her to provide that the property should go to her husband. In making that disposition she did not anticipate that she would be survived by the child. She had already fully provided for that situation by giving the child all of her property. It is not to be presumed, and the will certainly does not indicate, any intention of the testatrix to give to the husband only in the event the child survived the mother.

Such a provision would have been a prohibited substitution pure and simple, and, moreover, would have been utterly useless, since the father would have succeeded to the estate of the child at its death without children of its own body.

Our conclusion is that the will is not null as containing a prohibited substitution, but, on the contrary, that the disposition in favor of the husband contemplated and intended to provide for the condition which actually happened--the death of the child before that of the mother.

The judgment appealed from rejected the plaintiff's demand on an exception of no cause of action. We think that judgment correct; and it is affirmed.

PROBLEMS

Consider the following wills, all valid as to form. Did the testator create a prohibited substitution, *fidei commissum*, usufruct, or something else?

1.   "Dec 7-1977,

If I should go before husband, John, I want the piece of land on other side of road to bayou about fifty acers [sic] more or less to be his until his death then it will return to Cleo. I am hoping everything will work out okay. Carry out as I wish.

    Signed
    Elma I.B. Moran"

See Succession of Moran, 479 So. 2d 350 (La. 1985).

2. "And the balance of whatever I may dies possessed of I give and bequeath unto Bishop Thomas Heslin, to be distributed as he sees fit among my people in Ireland and for the further education of Thomas Regan, hereby instituting Bishop Heslin my sole heir and universal legatee."

Bishop Heslin unfortunately died while the succession was still under administration and his brothers and sister claim through him.
See Succession of Reilly, 67 So. 27 (La. 1914).

3. "The house left like it is and the land and timber for Edward Earl Lawrence at this death it will come back to all brother Hulon and Sisters Children."
See Succession of Merritt, 581 So. 2d 728 (La. App. 1st Cir. 1991).

HYPOTHETICAL

Consider the following will left by the decedent, Herman Howard Harvey:

> To my nephew, Harry Harvey, I leave $20,000 provided that within one year of my death, he has a son and names him after me, Herman Howard Harvey. If my nephew should not fulfill the imposed condition, the money should be donated to the Louisiana Society for the Prevention of Cruelty to Animals (Louisiana SPCA) for the building of a new facility to be named after me.
>
> I leave the residue of my estate to my mother Henrietta Harvey, provided she survive me by three months. Anything left at my mother's death should be donated to the Louisiana SPCA.

1. How might Harry attack his uncle's will if he is unmarried? If he is married but he and his wife cannot have children? If he is married, but does not want any more children? Would his reasons for not wanting any more children matter? (i.e. financial, health, convenience) What could Harry hope to gain by attacking the condition imposed by his uncle?

2. How might the Louisiana SPCA oppose the will if a new facility had just been constructed? If a new facility is to be constructed, but it will be named after Philip Bates who donated $2,000,000? If the SPCA is in no position to presently build a new facility? What would the SPCA stand to gain by attacking the condition Herman imposed?

3. Could Henrietta attack the donations to Harry or the SPCA? What does she stand to gain by attacking these donations?

4. How might Herman's healthy thirty-year-old daughter attack her father's will?

CHAPTER 13:
DONATIONS *INTER VIVOS* AND
OTHER DONATIVE DEVICES
La. C.C. 1467-1469, 1526-1567.1

Introduction

The Louisiana Civil Code recognizes two methods of gratuitous disposition: (1) the donation *inter vivos* (during life) and (2) the donation *mortis causa* (in prospect of death). In general, to effectuate an *inter vivos* or *mortis causa* donation, one of the Code's prescribed forms must be used. La. C.C. 1467.

The donation *inter vivos* is one of the two methods of gratuitous dispositions recognized in the La. Civil Code. La. C.C. 1467. It is defined as "a contract by which a person, called the donor, gratuitously divests himself, at present and irrevocably, of the thing given in favor of another called the donee, who accepts it. La. C.C. 1468. The general rule is that a donation *inter vivos* must be made by authentic act. La. C.C. 1541. However, corporeal movables may be donated by manual gift accompanied by the actual delivery of the object. La.C.C. 1543.

As part of the overall revision of the Louisiana Civil Code conducted by the Louisiana Law Institute, Book III, Title II, Chapter 5, "Of Donations *Inter Vivos*" (Between Living Persons) formerly consisting of Articles 1523 through 1569.1 were revised, amended, and re-enacted by Act 204 of 2008, effective January 1, 2009. Many of the references in the following cases are to the previous code articles. In relevant places, the counterparts are referenced in brackets. It behooves the reader to cross-reference to the current articles. Note the similarities, any subtle differences, and occasionally substantive changes.

Donations *inter vivos* may either be gratuitous, onerous, or remunerative. A gratuitous donation is one made from a spirit of liberality. An onerous donation is burdened with a charge, La. C.C. 1526, and a remunerative donation is given as compensation for services previously rendered. La. C.C. 1527.

Understanding the kind of donation that the testator intended is crucial for determining the form requirements. The form requirements prescribed by the Code for donations need only be followed in the case of purely gratuitous donations and those remunerative and onerous donations where the value of the obligation imposed on the donee (onerous—La. C.C. art. 1526) or the value of services previously rendered (remunerative—La. C.C. art 1527) are less than two-thirds the value of the thing donated. These rules were based on former provisions of the LOUISIANA CIVIL CODE of 1870 (La. C.C. 1524-1526) and are significant when dealing with issues of forced heirship and other areas where distinctions are made between donations and other forms of contract.

The donor may places charges or conditions on a donation, "provided they contain nothing contrary to law or good morals. La. C.C. 1528. Only present property may be donated, La. C.C. 1529, and a donation *inter vivos* may not be subject to a condition whose fulfillment is solely in the hands of the donor. La. C.C. 1530. A donation may not be dependent on the payment of future debts or charges, unless those debts or charges are expressed in the act of donation. La. C.C. 1531.

A donor may make a donation subject to the right of return of the thing given, contingent on the survival of the donee or the donee and the donee's descendants. La. C.C. 1532. If returned, the thing donated is free of any "alienation, lease, or encumbrance made by the donee or his successors after the donation." La. C.C. 1533. A good faith transferee for value of the thing donated is protected from such return, although the donee and his successors by gratuitous title will be held accountable for any "loss sustained by the donor." La. C.C. 1533.

IN RE SUCCESSION OF VAN BROWN
134 So. 3d 186 (La. App. 3d Cir. 2014)

EZELL, Judge.

Pauletta Gedward, as administrator of the succession of her deceased husband, McKinley Van Brown, Jr., appeals a trial court judgment that ordered the return of $30,000.00 to his daughter, Daphne Brown. Ms. Gedward argues that the transfer of the $30,000.00 was a remunerative donation and the trial court erred in finding that an onerous contract existed between the deceased and his daughter.

FACTS
Daphne Brown was living with her parents when she gave birth to a son, Marcus, on October 9, 1996. Ms. Brown moved out of the home when Marcus was three or four years old. Marcus continued living with her parents, and then continued living with her father when her parents divorced in 2005. Mr. Brown provided all financial support for Marcus since his birth, including tuition for private school. Ms. Brown made no contributions for the financial support of Marcus. Marcus was living with his grandfather when Mr. Brown died on October 26, 2012. Marcus then moved in with his mother.

In 2009, Ms. Brown was involved in an accident resulting in a recovery of money in 2011. On August 31, 2012, Ms. Brown purchased a cashier's check in the amount of $30,000.00 payable to her father. Ms. Brown testified that she presented the check to her father to pay for the rest of her son's high school tuition in addition to college expenses.

After Mr. Brown's death, his wife, Pauletta Gedward, was appointed administrator. Ms. Brown and her sister, Jodi Lemon, filed a motion to traverse the detailed descriptive list filed by Ms. Gedward in addition to seeking revocation of the $30,000.00 donation. A hearing on the issue of the characterization of the $30,000.00 donation was held on April 26, 2013.

In its reasons for judgment, the trial court accepted the testimony of Ms. Brown that the funds were to be used to pay for her son's future education. The trial court ordered the return of the $30,000.00 since Mr. Brown was no longer in a position to carry out the conditions placed upon him. Ms. Gedward then filed the present appeal.

DISCUSSION
Ms. Gedward argues that the donation by Ms. Brown to her father was a remunerative donation for all the expenses he incurred in the past while raising Marcus. She claims that what Mr. Brown did for Marcus speaks louder than Ms. Brown's own self-serving testimony.

There are three types of inter vivos donations: (1) gratuitous; (2) onerous; and (3) remunerative. La. Civ. Code arts. 1468, 1526, and 1527. "The gratuitous donation is made purely from liberality; the onerous donation is burdened with charges upon the donee; and the remunerative donation is given to recompense the donee for services rendered in the past." 10 Kathryn Venturatos Lorio, *Louisiana Civil Law Treatise* § 8:13, p. (2d ed.2013). Rules that are applicable to donations inter vivos do not apply to onerous and remunerative donations when the value of the charge or service performed exceeds by two-thirds the value of the gift. La. Civ. Code arts. 1526 and 1527. The rules applicable to donations inter vivos do not apply because it is not a true donation. *Averette v. Jordan,* 457 So. 2d 691 (La. App. 2 Cir.1984). When it is not a true donation, the rules applicable to contracts apply. *Garcia v. Dulcich,* 237 La. 359, 111 So. 2d 309 (1959); *Maleig v. Maleig,* 435 So. 2d 496 (La.App. 4 Cir.), *writ denied,* 441 So. 2d 765 (La.1983).

In reasons for judgment, the trial court ruled that the donation of $30,000.00 was both a remunerative and an onerous donation. However, the trial court then discussed the donation as a completely onerous donation in which the donee's death prevented him from fulfilling the obligations imposed by the onerous donation. The trial court then applied La.Civ. Code art. 1876 and held that the contract was dissolved by the fortuitous event of Mr. Brown's death resulting in his inability to perform the obligation of paying for the education of Marcus.

It is clear that the parties differ on whether the donation was a reimbursement for Mr. Brown's payment of Marcus's educational expenses in the past or was compensation to help fund Marcus's future educational expenses. If the money was payment for past services, then the succession would keep the money because the contract was complete. However, if the money was for Marcus's future education, then Mr. Brown's death, just two short months after the presentation of the money, prevented him from carrying out the obligation imposed on him. Testimony was introduced by both sides as to the reason for Ms. Brown's presentation of the $30,000.00 cashier's check to her father.

Ms. Brown testified that she gave the money to her father because she wanted Marcus to go to college and to help pay for the remainder of his private high school education. Ms. Lemon's testimony confirmed her sister's version. Ms. Lemon knew nothing about the money until her father told her about it. She testified that her father told her that her sister had given him a check for $30,000.00 for Marcus for school expenses. Ms. Lemon stated that her father was happy about the money because Marcus was going to college in a few years.

On the other hand, Ms. Gedward testified that her husband told her that Ms. Brown gave him the money in appreciation for taking care of Marcus from the time he was born. She further testified that her husband had paid Ms. Brown's rent and utility bills for ten years after she moved out of the house and Ms. Brown gave him the money as a token of appreciation for what Mr. Brown did for her and Marcus.

Obviously, the trial court based its decision on the testimony of Ms. Brown and her sister in ruling that the money was given to Mr. Brown for the benefit of Marcus's future education. Under the manifest error/clearly wrong standard of review, findings by the trial court based on determinations regarding the credibility of witnesses are entitled to great deference because only the fact finder can be aware of the variations in demeanor and tone of voice that bear so heavily on the listener's understanding and belief in what is said. *Rosell v. ESCO,* 549 So. 2d 840 (La.1989).

The trial court obviously placed more credibility on Ms. Brown's testimony and that of her sister rather than Ms. Gedward's testimony. We find no manifest error in this ruling.

The judgment of the trial court is affirmed. Costs of this appeal are assessed to the Succession of McKinley Van Brown, Jr.

AFFIRMED.

SUCCESSION OF HENRY
104 So. 310 (La. 1925)

LAND, J.

*   *   *

The testatrix made the following declaration in said will:

> Having had poor health and a frail body for quite a long while, and in constant need of careful attention, and nursing and support, and that duty having fallen on my son, James M. Beckham, with whom I am now living, and have lived years, and expect to live the remaining years of my life, it is my desire that my said son should be compensated for his labor and affectionate attention to me, and that he should be repaid the cost and expense that my support has been to him, and, as evidence of my love and affection for him, I make this provision for him. I therefore will and bequeath to my said son, James M. Beckham, all my property of every kind and character, rights, credits and everything of value that I may die possessed of and own, he to have and possess in full ownership.
> While I consider this a poor reward to my said son for his faithful attention to me, and his care and support of me, for so long a time, and as evidencing my love and affection of his dutiful fidelity, it is all I can do, and I do this of my own volition. I have done for the rest of my children what I consider is an equivalent of what would be their portion of my estate as it now is, and I do not consider that I am depriving them of any just right in this disposition of my estate.

J. M. Beckham alleged in his petition for the probation of the will that the bequest made to him by the testatrix was a remunerative donation, and intended as such in express terms; that decedent had been living with petitioner and his family continuously for a period of nine years; that he had received no compensation for his services rendered for the support, maintenance, nursing, and waiting upon decedent during that time; that said services were well worth the sum of $360 per year, or $3,240; and that said will should stand and be sustained in its entirety, and petitioner should be recognized as heir and universal legatee of the decedent, and, as such, be sent into possession of the estate.

The probation of the will was opposed by the other heirs on the following grounds:

(1) That the will attached to the petition for probate was not the last will and testament of Mrs. Frances Caroline Henry.

(2) It was denied that the entire estate of deceased was left to petitioner for valuable services, or that any such services were rendered, or were worth $360 per year.

(3) It was denied that Beckham should receive any compensation for the services he did render, as decedent contributed to the support of Beckham and his family for more than would compensate for any services rendered by him to his mother.

(4) It was denied that the services rendered were worth more than the real estate.

(5) It was denied that said bequest was a remunerative donation or intended as such.

(6) It was alleged that if the will should be proven to be genuine, the donation mortis causa, under article 1493 of the Civil Code, should be reduced to the disposable portion.

*   *   *

The testatrix has recited in her will the constant need of careful attention during many years, on account of ill health and frail bodily condition. She has avowed the unfailing devotion to her of her son during all of these years in tenderly nursing her and in providing for her support. It is true that such language is eloquent of maternal love and gratitude; but, to our minds, it is also the clear expression of a mother's final wish that the unselfish services of her son should receive, in the end, a just reward and recompense at her hands. The intention of the testatrix that the bequest made to her son should be a remunerative donation is beyond all question or cavil.

*   *   *

Decedent was 70 years of age when she first made her home with her son and his family. She resided there 9 years, until her death, making occasional visits of short duration to the homes of several of her children.

The services rendered to her by her son and the members of his family were of the most devoted and unselfish character, as clearly shown by the testimony of the neighbors. Decedent was waited upon, nursed when ill, and furnished with board and room, which was occupied entirely by herself, except at brief intervals. She made no provision for her son's family, and, at her advanced age and in her frail condition, was incapacitated to render any services in keeping or caring for the home. Her income was meager, consisting of occasional rents from the house she owned and a small pension. Her property was mortgaged for a debt of $500. She used her small income in paying off the mortgage, while living with her son, and in supplying her simple needs as to clothing, medicine, etc.

A conservative estimate for room and board and attention received by decedent during the nine years she resided with her son cannot be fixed justly, in view of the testimony in the case, at less than $300 per annum. Should we deduct even twelve months during the period of her nine years' residence with her son and his family for occasional visits to the homes of her other children, he would be entitled to $2,400 as compensation for services rendered, or a sum in excess of the value of all the property bequeathed to him by his mother.

Opponents to the will attack the legacy made in this case upon numerous grounds among which is the contention that a remunerative donation cannot be legally made in a last will and testament.

This contention is predicated upon the argument that remunerative donations appear only under the head of "Donations Inter Vivos," in chapter 5 of the Civil Code, and are not mentioned under the heard of "Dispositions Mortis Causa," in chapter 6 of the Code.

The premise is false, and the conclusion drawn from same is wrong, for the reason that remunerative donations appear in the Civil Code also under the head of "Disposable Portion," and also under the head of "Donations Inter Vivos" (between living persons), and "Donations Mortis Causa" (in prospect of death).

Article 1570, par. 3, under the head of "Dispositions Mortis Causa," chapter 6, declares:

> Thus an act of last will, by which an individual disposes of his property or a part thereof, in any manner whatsoever, whether he has instituted an heir or only named legatees, whether he has or has not charged any one with the execution of his last will, is considered as a testament, if it be, in other respects, clothed with the formalities required by law.

It is clear, therefore, that this article authorizes a testator to make every disposition of his property by donations mortis causa which he could make by donations inter vivos.

The articles of the Civil Code carefully enumerate in chapter 4, under the head "Of Dispositions Reprobated by Law in Donations *Inter vivos* and Mortis Causa," all dispositions in donations *inter vivos* and donations mortis causa, which, as a general rule, are prohibited by law.

The redactors of the Civil Code embraced these reprobated dispositions in two articles of the Code, articles 1519 and 1520. Article 1519 declares that----In all dispositions *inter vivos* and mortis causa impossible conditions, those which are contrary to the laws or to morals, are reputed not written. Article 1520 provides that "substitutions and fidei commissa are and remain prohibited."

But we fail to find any prohibition against the inclusion of remunerative donations in last wills and testaments under chapter 4 of the Civil Code, "Of Dispositions Reprobated by Law in Donations *Inter vivos* and Mortis Causa."

Under title 2 of the Civil Code, "Of Donations *Inter vivos* (between living persons and Mortis Causa (in prospect of death")), and in chapter 2 of said title, under the head "Of the Capacity Necessary for Disposing and Receiving by Donation *Inter vivos* or Mortis Causa," article 1489 is found, and this article declares that:

> Doctors of physic or surgeons, who have professionally attended a person during the sickness of which he dies, cannot receive any benefit from donations *inter vivos* or mortis causa made in their favor by the sick person during that sickness.
>
> To this, however, there are the following exceptions:
> (1) Remunerative dispositions made on a particular account, regard being had to the means of the disposer and to the services rendered.
> (2) Universal dispositions in case of consanguinity. The same rules are observed with regard to ministers of religious worship.

This article, found under the head "Of Donations *Inter vivos* and Mortis Causa," specifically recognizes that remunerative donations may be made in dispositions mortis causa, as well as in dispositions inter vivos.

As an act of donation *inter vivos* is made by the Civil Code a legal mode for the making of a remunerative donation, what good reason can be assigned why a testator should not be permitted to discharge his obligations for services rendered through the vehicle of a last will and testament?

The testator is expressly authorized by article 1570 of the Civil Code to dispose of his estate "in any manner whatsoever," not prohibited by law, and there is no inhibition contained in the Civil Code against remunerative donations being made in dispositions mortis causa.

The right to make a remunerative donation in a last will and testament has passed hitherto unchallenged by both bench and bar in the legal history of this state, although there are numerous decisions recognizing and enforcing such donations in dispositions mortis causa. The clearness of such right under the provisions of the Civil Code is obviously the reason for the absence of attacks of this kind upon bequests of this character.

3. If the value of the services to be recompensed, appreciated in money, should be little inferior to that of the gift, the remunerative donation loses its legal status as a real donation, and, in consequence, the rules peculiar to donations *inter vivos* do not apply, as in such a case the remunerative donation becomes a dation en paiement. R. C. C. arts. 1525, 1526; Pothier Traite Du Vente, 607; *Semple v. Fletcher*, 3 Mart. (N. S.) 382; *McGuire v. Amelung*, 12 Mart. (O. S.) 649.

It is true that a remunerative donation may be reduced to the value of the services rendered, when the value of the object given exceeds by one-half that of the services. R. C. C. art. 1526.

But a remunerative donation cannot be reduced below the estimated value of the services rendered, if the value of such services should be little inferior to that of the gift, not even if such remunerative donation should trench upon the legitime of forced heirs. R. C. C. arts. 1525, 1513.

*   *   *

In the *Succession of Fox*, 2 Rob. 292, the children of the testator attacked as excessive a remunerative donation contained in the last will of their father to his brother, Bernard Fox, and prayed for the reduction of the bequest to the disposable portion.

The court said:

> If a remunerative donation exceed the disposable portion, the donee or legatee is bound to prove the value of his services, and the legacy will be reduced if he do not show that his services are worth the amount bequeathed to him. ... If the value of his services be equal to, or greater than the bequest, no reduction can be made.

Civ. Code, 1500 [R. C. C. art. 1513], 1512 [R. C. C. art. 1525].

*   *   *

It is therefore so patent from the language of the articles quoted that a remunerative donation is not subject to reduction below the value of the services, in determining the disposable portion, and, for this reason, may be carved out of the legitime of forced heirs, that we do not consider any extended discussion of this matter necessary, but, like our predecessors, will content ourselves with a mere citation of these plain and unmistakable provisions of the Civil Code, and the additional observation that the interest of a forced heir in a succession is purely residuary. If the debts and charges of the succession equal or exceed the value of the estate, there is no residuum to be left to forced heirs to be encroached upon as a legitime.

4. The rules relative to donations *inter vivos* are not applicable to the bequest in this case, as the value of the services rendered exceed the value of the property included in the universal legacy made by the testatrix to her son.

The bequest is not, therefore, a real donation, but a dation en paiement, the giving by the testatrix of her estate to the universal legatee in payment for his services.

The value of these services has been proven by satisfactory evidence to be in excess of the value of the gift which is not subject, therefore, to reduction, because of the legitimate portion claimed by the forced heirs.

*   *   *

The services rendered to the testatrix by her son have been detailed by her in the will, and her obligation to compensate him for these services has been acknowledged, and performed by the testatrix, in making the bequest to him of her estate.

The rights of the son as legatee of the property do not depend upon any contract of compensation with the decedent, or upon any intention on his part to have charged for his services, while his mother was alive and residing with him.

The legatee is not suing the succession in this case upon any contract, or upon a quantum meruit, for the recovery of the value of his services to the testatrix; but is claiming title to the property bequeathed to him, and which he has acquired by a dation en paiement from the testatrix, the services rendered having created the obligation, and the legal basis for the transfer of the property being the extinguishment of that obligation on the part of the testatrix. The law does not require in a donation, whether gratuitous, remunerative, or onerous, that the value of the thing given, of the services intended to be compensated, or the charges imposed, should be fixed and stated in the act. *Hearsey v. Craig*, 126 La. 824, 53 So. 17; *Bowlus v. Whatley*, 129 La. 509, 56 So. 423.

The last will and testament of the late Mrs. Frances Caroline Henry is therefore a legal and valid disposition mortis causa, and must be recognized and enforced as written and intended by the testatrix.

*   *   *

NOTES

The mere fact that the donee provided some services to the donor does not always render the donation onerous or remunerative, rather than gratuitous. It is largely a question of the intention of the donor gleaned from the wording of the donation. If the act indicates that the donation was made from gratitude and love, or the like, instead of a desire to remunerate, the donation will be viewed as gratuitous. *Placid Oil Co. Frazier*, 126 So. 2d 800 (La. App. 2d Cir. 1961). The courts also indulge something of a presumption that services in the nature of nursing or caring for a parent are insufficient to support a remunerative donation, but rather, are presumed to be gratuitous. *Placid Oil Co. v. Frazier, supra*; *Kinney v. Kinney* 150 So. 2d 671 (La. App. 3d Cir. 1963), at least in the case of an only child. *Kiper v. Kiper*, 214 La. 733, 38 So. 2d 507 (1948). Courts vary as to whether the presumption arises where there is more than one child. *Kiper v. Kiper, supra*. In any event, this is merely a presumption and not a hard and fast rule. The courts are fairly liberal in allowing evidence of valuable consideration and donative intent into evidence. *Succession of Danos*, 359 So. 2d 679 (La. App. 1st Cir. 1978). Services such as cooking and taking care of an elderly person, for example, may suffice as valid consideration to support a non-gratuitous donation. *Succession of Viola*, 138 So. 2d 613 (La. App. 4th Cir. 1962).

One thing the courts look to is whether the donor has compensated the donee for the services rendered either by other means after death (legacy) or by other means during life. For instance, if the donor has supported the donee during the time the services were being rendered, this fact might be found to constitute adequate compensation for him. *Placid Oil Co. v. Frazier, supra*.

If, however, a donor truly hoped to recompense his donee for future or past services, then the value of the donation must be compared to the value of the services in determining whether there has been a real donation subject to the rules of donation.

The donee bears the burden of proving the value of the services rendered. *Succession of Dickens v. Huey*, 217 So. 2d 228 (La. App. 2d Cir. 1968), and the opponent bears the burden of proving that the transaction was gratuitous by establishing that the value of the property given exceeds by one-half that of the charges or services. *Whitman v. Whitman*, 206 La. 1, 18 So. 2d 633 (1944); *Placid Oil Co. v. Frazier, supra*.

PROBLEMS

Consider the following gift. Has there been a remunerative, onerous, or gratuitous donation?

1. For two years every week, neighbor, Sam, while mowing his own lawn, mowed the lawn of Mr. Sanford, the older man who lived in the adjacent house. The value of his services was $600 per year. Mr. Sanford, on his death, bequeathed to Sam his bank account, which had a balance of $1850.

2. If Mr. Sanford had two forced heirs, and the $1850 bank account was all he owned, could the forced heirs attack the donation? If so, what portion of the donation could they claim? *Compare* La. C.C. 1510.

The Substance and Form of *Inter Vivos* Donations

In order for an act of transfer to constitute a donation, the donor must intend to make a donation, and the donee must intend to accept the donation. Generally, compliance with requirements of form indicates an intent to donate. However, this may not always be the case. If a grandmother hands her grandson $200 in cash, how are we to discern her intent without more information? Since cash is considered a corporeal movable, form requirements for donation by manual delivery have been met. But did grandmother have that intention, or was the transaction a loan, or something else?

The general rule is that donations *inter vivos* must be made by authentic act. La. C.C. 1541. An exception is made for corporeal movables that may be donated by real delivery. La. C.C. 1543. As new types of property have developed and become common, other acceptable forms of donating have been established to facilitate the transfer of these new types of property. Such incorporeal movables that are "evidenced by a certificate, document, instrument, or other writing," and that are "transferable by endorsement or delivery," may be made either by authentic act or by compliance with other requirements applicable to the transfer of such property. *See* La. C.C. 1550. For example, the form requirements for donation of stock and negotiable instruments are now contained in Louisiana's Commercial Laws in Title 10 of the Revised Statutes. One should be cautioned, however, that even if the forms requirements are met, the substantive requirement of intent to donate, mandated by the Civil Code, remains to be satisfied as well.

OTHER DONATIVE DEVICES

Shares of Stock

A share of stock is a fractional share in the ownership of a business. Ownership is determined by the number of shares a person owns in relation to the total number of shares available. Chapter 8 of Louisiana's Commercial Laws on Investment Securities contains the laws governing the acquisition and transfer of stock. Under Chapter 8, a stock is either classified as a "certificated security," which is evidenced by a stock certificate, or an "uncertificated security" which is not evidenced by an actual stock certificate. La. R.S. 10:8-102. The provisions governing transfer and indorsement of stocks are reproduced below.

PRIMEAUX v. LIBERSTAT
322 So. 2d 147 (La. 1975)

TATE, Justice.

The issue before us concerns whether certain shares of stock issued to a husband in 1961, 1962, and 1966, during a marriage, are his separate property or, instead, form part of the community which existed between himself and his divorced wife. The issue arises in a suit by the wife, Barbara, filed after the judicial separation, in order to partition the property acquired during the marriage. Gerald and Barbara Libersat were married in 1960 and judicially separated in 1973.

The trial court held that the stock shares were the separate property of the husband, Gerald, since the consideration for them was paid, not by community funds, but instead by Gerald's father, with the intention of donating to his son these shares in two family-held corporations. The court of appeal reversed this determination. 307 So. 2d 740 (La. App. 3d Cir. 1975). It held that none of the stock certificates had been validly transferred to the son, Gerald, for reasons to be noted. The intermediate court held that, since Gerald was not the legal owner of these stock certificates, they were neither his separate property nor the assets of the community formerly existing between him and his former wife, Barbara. We granted certiorari . . . .

*   *   *

Stock shares have been held to be incorporeal movables, Civil Code Articles 460, 474, and thus not susceptible to manual delivery without formality under Civil Code Article 1539. *Succession of McGuire*, 151 La. 514, 92 So. 40 (1922); *Succession of Sinnott v. Hibernia National Bank*, 105 La. 705, 30 So. 233 (1901) (stock certificate still in alleged donor's name). As incorporeal movables, stock shares themselves are of the species of property which fall within the terms of Article 1536, insofar as requiring a notarial act of donation.

Nevertheless, if a stock share is validly transferred by reason of the stock-transfer legislation, which inter alia permits shares to be transferred without consideration paid to the transferor, La. R.S. 12:624, 629(4), its transfer is valid as a donation without the necessity of the additional formality of a notarial act.

*   *   *

Accordingly, the present transfers are valid as donations of the stock shares to the son Gerald, despite the lack of a notarial act. Since the consideration furnished for them was intended to be a donation to him and his separate estate particularly, the shares issued thereafter are his separate property. Civil Code Article 2334, *Succession of Hemenway*, 228 La. 572, 83 So. 2d 377, 382 (1955).

In interpreting FRENCH CIVIL CODE Article 931, which is quite similar to our Article 1536, the French authorities have reached similar results. Despite the broad language of their article (similar to ours), the French have held that certain types of donations are dispensed from the requirement of form (i.e., an act passed before a notary and two witnesses or also, in France, before two notaries). Planiol, CIVIL LAW TREATISE, Volume 3, Sections 2533, 2543A--2554 (LSLI translation, 1959); Aubry & Rau, TESTAMENTARY SUCCESSIONS AND GRATUITOUS DISPOSITIONS, Section 659(2) (3 Civil Law Translations, 1969); Aubry & Rau, OBLIGATIONS, Section 343B, p. 324 (1 Civil Law Translations, 1965).

Planiol notes that "it is often possible to make a donation, that means to cause someone to acquire a property value gratuitously, without drafting such a special instrument." Section 2533, p. 236. As examples of the valid creation of a property right in a donee, without a special instrument to such effect, Planiol and Aubry & Rau list donations through a purchase in the name of another, by assignment or endorsement of credits or negotiable instruments, by transfer of securities valid under securities law, by stipulations for a third person (the donee), by gratuitous renunciations of a right, by release of obligations, and by other means.

Planiol points out that these various transactions are valid, since in a form authorized by general law, but that "Any transaction through which some right is assigned without the demand for a counter-performance is a donation. It is an intentional procurement of a gratuitous enrichment." Section 2543A, p. 244. He also notes, "In cases of purchase in the name of another person, the object of the donation is not the acquired property, but the cash paid for it. It is an equivalent of an indirect manual gift, relieving the nominal purchaser from the payment of the price. One could say this is a payment made Cum animo donandi (with the intention of giving)." Section 2545, p. 245. Planiol further suggests that the meaning of the code article is not that "all

13-11

donations must be made before a notary," but rather that the article "requires the notarial form only if a special instrument is drafted to declare the donation" and if such special instrument is required to effectuate the transaction itself. Planiol, Section 2533, p. 236.

For similar reasons, Louisiana interpretations hold the present transfers of shares of stock to the donee, valid under the stock-transfer act and effectively transferring irrevocable title to the shares to him, to be valid also as donations to him, because the consideration for their issuance was furnished by the donor with such donative intent.

We should note, however, that although this form of donation is exempted from the external formality of a notarial act otherwise required by Article 1536, it is subject to the substantive rules of donation, such as reduction and collation, etc...

NOTE

The Uniform Stock Transfer Act at La. R.S. 12:6221 et seq. was repealed by Section 6 of Acts 1978, No. 165. It has been replaced by Chapter 8 of Louisiana's Commercial Laws. (La. R.S. 10:8-101 et seq.)

La. R.S. 10:8-301. Delivery

(a) Delivery of a certificated security to a purchaser occurs when:
    (1) the purchaser acquires possession of the security certificate;
    (2) another person, other than a securities intermediary, either acquires possession of the security certificate on behalf of the purchaser or, having previously acquired possession of the certificate, acknowledges that it holds for the purchaser; or
    (3) a securities intermediary acting on behalf of the purchaser acquires possession of the security certificate, only if the certificate is (i) registered in the name of the purchaser, (ii) payable to the order of the purchaser, or (iii) specially indorsed to the purchaser by an effective endorsement or in blank.
(b) Delivery of an uncertificated security to a purchaser occurs when:
    (1) the issuer registers the purchaser as the registered owner, upon original issue or registration of transfer; or
    (2) another person, other than a securities intermediary, either becomes the registered owner of the uncertificated security on behalf of the purchaser or, having previously become the registered owner, acknowledges that it holds for the purchaser.

La. R.S. 10:8-302. Rights of purchaser

(a) Except as otherwise provided in subsections (b) and (c), purchaser of a certificated or uncertificated security acquires all rights in the security that the transferor had or had power to transfer.
(b) A purchaser of a limited interest acquires rights only to the extent of the interest purchased.
(c) A purchaser of a certificated security who as a previous holder had notice of an adverse claim does not improve its position by taking from a protected purchaser.

La. R.S. 10:8-304 Endorsement

(a) An indorsement may be in blank or special. An indorsement in blank includes an indorsement to bearer. A special indorsement specifies to whom a security is to be transferred or who has power to transfer it. A holder may convert a blank indorsement to a special indorsement.

(b) An indorsement purporting to be only of part of a security certificate representing units intended by the issuer to be separately transferable is effective to the extent of the indorsement.

(c) An indorsement, whether special or in blank, does not constitute a transfer until delivery of the certificate on which it appears or, if the indorsement is on a separate document, until delivery of both the document and the certificate.

(d) If a security certificate in registered form has been delivered to a purchaser without a necessary indorsement, the purchaser may become a protected purchaser only when the indorsement is supplied. However, against a transferor, a transfer is complete upon delivery and the purchaser has a specifically enforceable right to have any necessary indorsement supplied.

(e) An indorsement of a security certificate in bearer form may give notice of an adverse claim to the certificate, but it does not otherwise affect a right to registration that the holder possesses.

(f) Unless otherwise agreed, a person making an indorsement assumes only the obligations provided in R.S. 10:8-108 and not an obligation that the security will be honored by the issuer.

Checks and other Negotiable Instruments

Early cases dealing with the valid donation of checks focused on the question of whether the check was a corporeal or incorporeal movable. *See* Susan Molero Capone, Comment, *Donations Inter Vivos of Negotiable Instruments and Items of a Commercial Nature*, 33 Loy. L. Rev. 1053 (1988).

In *Succession of DePouilly*, 22 La. Ann. 97 (1870), the Louisiana Supreme Court held that a check given to and payable to the order of the donee by the donor was a valid manual gift of a corporeal movable under former La. C.C. 1526 (now La. C.C. 1543). The court maintained that the check, which was drawn and collected on the same day, was nothing more than a corporeal movable effect (money), and since the donation was accompanied by real delivery, it required no further formality. The check was the means or vehicle of delivery. It is significant to note that the check was collected before the donor's death.

In *Burke v. Bishop*, 27 La. Ann. 465 (La. 1875), the donor, Mr. Elliot, had received a check from another, Britton and Kountz, and had indorsed it over to the donee, Mrs. Risley. The donee failed to cash the check before the endorsor died. The court found that the manual transfer of the check, together with the indorsement, was a valid donation. It reasoned:

> If the thing given to Mrs. Risley had been a promissory note, her case would be covered by the cases of *Barriere v. Gladding*, 17 La. 144; *Morres v. Compton*, 12 R. 76; *Succession of DePouilly*, 22 An. 97; in all cases it was held that the donation of a promissory note must be preceded by the formalities required by article 1538 (1525) of the Code.
>
> If it had been a check drawn by Hampton Elliot, and he had died before the check was presented, and the check was a donation, the check would have

been worthless, because by the demise of the donor his mandate to his agent, the bank, was revoked.

But the check in question was not of Hampton Elliott's drawing. It was a check drawn to his order. The moment he indorsed it and handed it over to Mrs. Risley, his property in it ceased. It was not his money which the bank paid when it paid the check. It was Britton and Kountz's money. The bank paid under instructions from them and not under any mandate from Elliott.

The later case of *Succession of Leroy*, 163 La. 1087, 113 So. 544 (1927) involved a certified check which was issued to the donor shortly before his death as the balance due on certain real property previously sold by him. The donor indorsed the check in blank and delivered it to the donee as a donation *inter vivos* by manual gift. The court in *Leroy* decided that because the check was certified (where the bank had already charged the account of the drawer so the bank was primarily liable), and since the check was not drawn upon the decedent's own funds, that there was a valid manual gift and it did not matter that the check was not collected until after the death of the donor.

The *Succession of Schneider*, 199 So. 2d 564 (La. App. 3d Cir. 1967), involved the attempted donation of a check for $35,000 by an aunt to her nephew. The check was drawn by the aunt on her own account and made payable to the order of the nephew with the notation "donation" made in the corner of the check. Although the check was issued four months prior to the donor's death, the donee did not attempt to negotiate it until ten days after the donor's death. The bank returned the check unpaid. The donee claimed that the check was a valid donation. The defendant, however, claimed that the "mere issuance of the donor's own check prior to its acceptance by the drawee bank, is a gift of an incorporeal right and therefore, not subject to donation *inter vivos*," except by authentic act. The court adopted the defendant's position and also quoted the Louisiana Negotiable Instruments Law which was effective at the time of the decision. The Negotiable Instruments Law stated that a check represented an incorporeal right. The court held that a gift of a donor's own check is not equivalent to the gift of money on deposit in the bank. It is not an assignment of any rights to funds of the drawer until the check is accepted or certified by the drawee bank. The only thing which was given was an incorporeal right. The court recognized that to consider a gift of a donor's own check as equal to delivery of the funds does not take into consideration that a donor may revoke the gift by stopping payment. Therefore, there is not "real delivery" of "corporeal movables" under the manual gift theory until the actual funds have passed from the control of the donor to the donee.

The Louisiana law regarding negotiable instruments was revised after the *Schneider* case, removing the applicability of the form requirements of the Civil Code for donation of checks and other negotiable instruments. *See* La. R.S. 10:3-203(e). Today Louisiana's Negotiable Instrument Law is contained within Chapter 3 of Louisiana's Commercial Laws. Chapter 3 was revised again in 1992, by Acts 1992, No. 113, Sec. 3., effective January 1, 1994. Much remains the same; however, the numbering has changed since the cases that follow were decided.

Note that the transfer of a negotiable instrument is accomplished "when it is delivered by a person *other than its issuer* for the purpose of giving to the person receiving delivery the right to enforce the instrument. La. R.S. 10:3-203 (a). If the instrument has not been indorsed, the transferee can require the transferor's indorsement. As under the law prior to the adoption of Chapter 3, the donor's transfer of his own check (as an issuer) is not a valid donation until cashed by the donee, while the donor's indorsement of a check written to his order and delivered to a donee is a valid donation, enforceable before or after the donor's death.

The revision of 2008 enacted a new article dealing with the form required for donation of certain incorporeal movables. See La. C.C. 1550, as enacted by Act No. 204 § 1 of 2008, effective January 1, 2009.

La. R.S. 10:3-104. Negotiable instrument

(a) Except as provided in Subsections (c) and (d), "negotiable instrument" means an unconditional promise or order to pay a fixed amount of money, with or without interest or other charges described in the promise or order, if it:

(1) is payable to bearer or to order at the time it is issued or first comes into possession of a holder;

(2) is payable on demand or at a definite time; and

(3) does not state any other undertaking or instruction by the person promising or ordering payment to do any act in addition to the payment of money, but the promise or order may contain (i) an undertaking or power to give, maintain, or protect collateral to secure payment, (ii) an authorization or power to the holder to confess judgment or realize on or dispose of collateral, or (iii) a waiver of the benefit of any law intended for the advantage or protection of an obligor.

(b) "Instrument" means a negotiable instrument.

(c) An order that meets all of the requirements of Subsection (a), except Paragraph (1), and otherwise falls within the definition of "check" in Subsection (f) is a negotiable instrument and a check.

(d) A promise or order other than a check is not an instrument if, at the time it is issued or first comes into possession of a holder, it contains a conspicuous statement, however expressed, to the effect that the promise or order is not negotiable or is not an instrument governed by this Chapter.

(e) An instrument is a "note" if it is a promise and is a "draft" if it is an order. If an instrument falls within the definition of both "note" and "draft," a person entitled to enforce the instrument may treat it as either.

(f) "Check" means (i) a draft, other than a documentary draft, payable on demand and drawn on a bank or (ii) a cashier's check or teller's check. An instrument may be a check even though it is described on its face by another term, such as "money order."

(g) "Cashier's check" means a draft with respect to which the drawer and drawee are the same bank or branches of the same bank.

(h) "Teller's check" means a draft drawn by a bank (i) on another bank, or (ii) payable at or through a bank.

(i) "Traveler's check" means an instrument that (i) is payable on demand, (ii) is drawn on or payable at or through a bank, (iii) is designated by the term "traveler's check" or by a substantially similar term, and (iv) requires, as a condition to payment, a countersignature by a person whose specimen signature appears on the instrument.

(j) "Certificate of deposit" means an instrument containing an acknowledgment by a bank that a sum of money has been received by the bank and a promise by the bank to repay the sum of money. A certificate of deposit is a note of the bank.

La. R.S. 10:3-201. Negotiation

(a) "Negotiation" means a transfer of possession, whether voluntary or involuntary, of an instrument by a person other than the issuer to a person who thereby becomes its holder.

(b) Except for negotiation by a remitter, if an instrument is payable to an identified person, negotiation requires transfer of possession of the instrument and its indorsement by the holder. If an instrument is payable to bearer, it may be negotiated by transfer of possession alone.

La. R.S. 10:3-203. Transfer of instrument; rights acquired by transfer

(a) An instrument is transferred when it is delivered by a person other than its issuer for the purpose of giving to the person receiving delivery the right to enforce the instrument.

(b) Transfer of an instrument, whether or not the transfer is a negotiation, vests in the transferee any right of the transferor to enforce the instrument, including any right as a holder in due course, but the transferee cannot acquire rights of a holder in due course by a transfer, directly or indirectly, from a holder in due course if the transferee engaged in fraud or illegality affecting the instrument.

(c) Unless otherwise agreed, if an instrument is transferred for value and the transferee does not become a holder because of lack of indorsement by the transferor, the transferee has a specifically enforceable right to the unqualified indorsement of the transferor, but negotiation of the instrument does not occur until the indorsement is made.

(d) If a transferor purports to transfer less than the entire instrument, negotiation of the instrument does not occur. The transferee obtains no rights under this Chapter and has only the rights of a partial assignee.

(e) Donations *inter vivos* of instruments shall be governed by the provisions of this Chapter notwithstanding any other provision of the LOUISIANA CIVIL CODE or of any other law of this state, relative to the form of donations inter vivos, to the contrary.

SUCCESSION OF JONES
505 So. 2d 841 (La. App. 2nd Cir. 1987)
[Footnotes omitted]

JASPER E. JONES, Judge.

This is an appeal of a judgment rendered in a Rule to Show Cause why funds transferred by the decedent by check should not be returned to the estate. The plaintiff-appellant is the testamentary executor of the estate of Irene Belanger Barnes Jones. The defendant-appellee is the recipient of the funds, Wanda Poche.

FACTS

On or about March 22, 1985, Irene Belanger Barnes Jones was diagnosed as having terminal cancer. Mrs. Jones had incurred hospital bills and other medical bills in connection with this illness prior to this diagnosis. On April 5, 1985, she issued a check in the amount of $5,000 payable to Wanda Poche. The cancer diagnosis was confirmed on April 12, 1985. Ms.

Jones was admitted to the hospital on May 6, 1985, and remained there until her death on June 8, 1985. Her last will and testament directs the executor to pay all just debts and expenses of last illness.

By the Rule to Show Cause the plaintiff alleged, in relevant part, that Wanda Poche was the decedent's agent whose duties were to pay various bills associated with the decedent's illness and that said agency terminated upon the principal's death. The plaintiff asserted that Wanda Poche owed the estate an accounting on how the funds were expended as well as the balance remaining.

At the hearing on the rule Wanda Poche testified she was the decedent's landlady and close friend for eighteen years. She had not increased the decedent's rent of $70.00 per month during the length of their relationship. The amount of the rent was far below the market price. For two years before Mrs. Jones' death Mrs. Poche had taken the decedent shopping each week and otherwise generally looked after her needs. Mrs. Poche took days off from her job at a loss of compensation to do things for the decedent. Wanda Poche related that the decedent gave her the $5,000 check as a "gift" for her benevolence through the years. She also related that the decedent issued her two other checks at that time. One was for reimbursement for cost of cat food and for payment of accrued utility bills. The other was for two months rent that was due and owing. Wanda Poche added that the $5,000 check was accompanied by a "stipulation" that she: (1) file the decedent's Medicare and insurance papers; and (2) pay any balances due from the amount of the check after collecting Medicare benefits. Wanda Poche concluded by asserting she was a Medicare specialist with twelve years experience and had cashed the check. She added that the money was in a safe in her home and she was willing and ready to pay any Medicare deficit but related she did not know the amount of this deficit as the plaintiff had written a letter telling her not to pursue it.

The plaintiff testified and corroborated the long relationship between Wanda Poche and the decedent and acknowledged he did not handle any Medicare matters for the decedent. He related his aunt, the decedent, told him she had given Wanda Poche a sum of money to pay bills. He also related that he had received only one bill from the hospital, in the amount of $66.00, and had assumed there were no expenses outstanding as Wanda Poche was supposed to be paying them.

The plaintiff argued that as possession of the transferred funds had been established, the burden shifted to Wanda Poche to prove by clear and convincing evidence that it was a gift. The defendant responded by asserting that as the check was a negotiable instrument, then LSA-R.S. 10:3-201(4) superseded any other legal requirements. The plaintiff countered by asserting that the underlying validity of the donation is a "threshold" requirement that is not superseded by the Commercial Law. In particular, the plaintiff cited LSA-C.C. art. 1530 as a possible defect negating the existence of a valid donation as Wanda Poche was obligated to pay debts that were not ascertainable prior to the issuance of the check.

The trial court ruled that the Commercial Law was specific legislation that superseded the more general codal articles. The court also held that the record established by clear and convincing evidence that the $5,000 check was a "gratuitous thing" given because Wanda Poche's past acts of kindness. The court found the law and evidence in favor of defendant and rendered judgment dismissing the rule.

The plaintiff has appealed. The sole assignment of error presents the following issue for decision: Did the trial court err in ruling that LSA-R.S. 10:3-201(4) supersedes LSA-C.C. art. 1530 so that the donation is valid and the funds are not required to be returned to the estate?

We affirm the judgment on grounds other than those relied upon by the trial court and remand the matter so that the amount of any Medicare deficiency existing as of April 5, 1985, can be determined and paid to the decedent's estate.

Initially we note the trial court was wrong in holding that LSA-R.S. 10:3-201(4) supersedes the LOUISIANA CIVIL CODE in regard to any possible legal defect which may underlie an apparent donation of a negotiable instrument. It is evident that the Commercial Law is controlling only insofar as the form is concerned. Title of the legislative act creating the exception to the application of the code article to the Commercial Law reflects that the act provides for donations *inter vivos* to be construed by Chapter 3, Title 10, of LOUISIANA REVISED STATUTES of 1959 (law on commercial paper), rather than the civil code, "on the form of the donation." The same wording is found in the body of the statute. LSA-R.S. 10:3-201(4). The provisions of the statute do not expressly provide that all codal provisions on donations are to be replaced. Cf., LSA-R.S. 10:1-103. This act overruled the supreme court decision of *Succession of Miller*, 405 So. 2d 812 (La.1981), which held the donation of bearer bonds by delivery was invalid because the donation failed to comply with the provision of LSA-C.C. art. 1536 which required donations of incorporeal movables be in the form of an act before a notary public and two witnesses. *See also Succession of Payne v. Pigott*, 459 So. 2d 1231 (La.App. 1st Cir.1984). In this case the court held that the provisions of the Louisiana stock transfer legislation (LSA-R.S. 10:8-101 et seq.) controlled the form required for stock donations but the provisions of the civil code remained applicable to provide the substantive rules affecting the validity of the donation. We conclude the donation of the check in this case is controlled by the substantive rules on donations contained in the civil code.

The trial court was also incorrect in classifying the transfer as a gratuitous donation. The stipulations accompanying the $5,000 check, as well as the underlying benevolent motive, induced by rent far below market value supplied by Mrs. Poche to Mrs. Jones for 18 years and two years of errand running service supplied by Mrs. Poche for Mrs. Jones following the death of Mrs. Jones' husband, all compel the conclusion that it should have been construed as an onerous and a remunerative donation. *Victorian v. Victorian*, 411 So. 2d 473 (La.App. 3d Cir.1978).

The true issue in this appeal is to determine if the transaction is valid whether it be analyzed in accordance with the rules applicable to *inter vivos* donations or construed by the rules applicable to contracts in general. We conclude the transaction was legally valid, whichever method is used to interpret it.

LAW ON ONEROUS CONTRACTS AND ONEROUS AND REMUNERATIVE DONATIONS

A natural obligation arises from circumstances in which the law implies a particular moral duty to render a performance." LSA-C.C. art. 1760. "A natural obligation is not enforceable by judicial action. Nevertheless, whatever has been freely performed in compliance with a natural obligation may not be reclaimed. A contract made for the performance of a natural obligation is onerous." LSA-C.C. art. 1761. "A contract is onerous when each of the parties obtains an advantage in exchange for his obligation." LSA-C.C. art. 1909. The presence of a gratuitous intent to perform a service gives rise to a natural obligation. *Martin v. Bozeman*, 173 So. 2d 382 (La.App. 1st Cir.1965).

A gratuitous donation *inter vivos* is made without condition and merely from liberality. LSA-C.C. art. 1523. Donations are both onerous and remunerative when it is burdened with charges and is made to recompense for services rendered. *Victorian v. Victorian, supra*. The rules applicable to donations *inter vivos* do not apply to onerous and remunerative donations except when the value of the object given exceeds by one-half that of the charges or of the services. LSA-C.C. art. 1526. Conversely, where the value of the charge or service exceeds 2/3 of the value of the gift, the transfer is not a true donation. *Averette v. Jordan*, 457 So. 2d 691 (La.App. 2d Cir.1984).

Is the $5,000 transfer valid?

The appellant argues that the $5,000 transfer from the deceased to Wanda Poche was made on the condition that future Medicare debts and charges be paid out of the funds. As such, LSA-C.C. art. 1530 mandates the conclusion that the entire transfer, as an attempt at a donation *inter vivos*, is null. It is also asserted that LSA-R.S. 10:3-201(4) does not totally supersede the LOUISIANA CIVIL CODE Articles on donations and the possible existence of an underlying substantive legal defect in the donation is a valid "threshold test" to determine the validity of the donation before considering that the donation, by delivery of a check, complies with the commercial law requirements on form.

For the previously related reasons, we agree that such a "threshold test" is appropriate even where the form of the transfer is governed by the Commercial Law. However, appellant's position is premised upon the transfer being governed by the rules applicable to *inter vivos* donations. This position assumes: (1) that the value of the services rendered and charges imposed are not greater than 2/3 of the value of the gift; and (2) that the deceased intended Wanda Poche to pay Medicare bills as they accrued and became ascertainable in the future and the donee was to keep the remainder as a gift after present and future debts are paid. Whether the transaction is analyzed under the rules applicable to donations or under the rules concerning contracts in general, we conclude the transfer itself is valid and that the only issue is the amount of any Medicare deficit is due the decedent's estate as of the date of the transfer.

Assuming the analysis is to be made under the codal articles applicable to donations *inter vivos* for the reason that the value of the charges and services rendered are not greater than 2/3 the value of the gift, and for this reason does not trigger the exclusion of the application of the rules on *inter vivos* donations pursuant to LSA-C.C. art. 1526, we find, for the following reasons, that the legal impediment of the validity of the donation contained in LSA-C.C. art. 1530 is not applicable. The deceased issued two other checks to Wanda Poche at the time she gave her the $5,000 check. Both of these other checks reflect reimbursement or payment of accrued obligations. The deceased did not expressly specify that any future medical expenses were to be paid out of the "gift" as they accrued. We note it did not become necessary for her to be admitted into a hospital again until May 6, 1985, approximately one month later, and this circumstance makes it improbable that she was thinking about future medical expenses at the time she made the gift. We further note that the decedent executed her last will and testament [sic] April 16, 1985, eleven days after she gave the check gift to Mrs. Poche. In her will she specifically directed that her executor pay the expenses of her last illness. The provisions of the will reads as follows: "Upon my death, my executor shall pay all of my just debts, funeral expenses, expenses of last illness, and burial expenses, including a suitable marker for my grave...." The deceased's instructions to her executor in her last will and testament expressly specified that he pay her just debts and other expenses of her last illness from the assets of her estate. From the totality of the circumstances we conclude the deceased intended Wanda Poche to file the needed papers and pay any accrued expenses due as of April 5, 1985, not covered by Medicare, and that all subsequent expenses should be paid by her estate after her death.

The record does not directly provide evidence of the valuation of the rent donations and benevolent services provided by Wanda Poche to Mrs. Jones over the eighteen year period of her friendship with the deceased, nor of the valuation of the charges for the donee's efforts at filing the needed Medicare documentation. However, this determination is not critical because even if their value would be in excess of the entire value of the $5,000 check, causing the rules on donation *inter vivos* to be inapplicable, the rules applicable to contracts in general would support the transfer. This would be true because the very cheap rent and other services Mrs. Poche supplied to the decedent over the years of their friendship gave rise to a natural obligation owed by the decedent to Mrs. Poche which would support the $5,000 gift, as the transaction would be categorized as an onerous contract wherein both parties obtained an advantage for their respective obligation. LSA-C.C. arts. 1761, 1909; *Victorian v. Victorian, supra.*

Mrs. Poche owes the appellant, as a condition of the gift, the amount of Mrs. Jones' medical bills incurred through April 5, 1981, not covered by Medicare. This amount was not determined on the trial of the rule. We remand the case to the trial court and direct that evidence be produced to establish the amount of any deficit after applying to the bill sums collected from Medicare and direct that appellant be awarded a judgment against Mrs. Poche for the amount of such deficit.

CONCLUSION

The judgment is AFFIRMED subject to being amended to award appellant a judgment as per our directions on remand. All costs of this appeal are assessed against the appellant.

SUCCESSION OF TEBO
358 So. 2d 337 (La. App. 4th Cir. 1978)
[Footnotes omitted]

REDMANN, Judge.

By rule to traverse the descriptive list of the assets in this succession, a niece and a grandniece of decedent assert the effectiveness of *inter vivos* acts of decedent:

1. to donate checking account balances to the grandniece and a great-grandnephew by means of blank checks drawn by decedent to the niece's order, with written, dated and signed instructions to the niece, which the niece carried out prior to decedent's death, to close out the two checking accounts and to deliver the balances to the named grandniece and great-grandnephew; and
2. to donate certain bearer bonds located in decedent's bank box and specifically described in a note addressed to the grandniece, written by decedent but undated and unsigned and by decedent's order and in her presence delivered to the niece (who is that grandniece's mother) at the same time the blank checks and their instructions were delivered, when the niece had written standing authority from decedent to enter the bank box and "remove at will" its contents, but did not get the bonds from the box and deliver them to her daughter (the named grandniece) because the relatives (including the residuary legatee) who had keys to the box

would not give her a key to enable her to do so and, presumably, she and her daughter would not force the issue either by enlisting decedent's aid (decedent was then hospitalized but alert and lived two months longer) or by asserting her independent right to enter the bank box against the bank (through court proceedings if necessary).

The judgment appealed from held both acts ineffectual. We reverse as to the cashed checks and affirm as to the bonds.

The purely gratuitous donation *inter vivos* must be in the form of an act before notary public and two witnesses under penalty of nullity, La. C.C. 1536 and 1538, except that, as art. 1539 provides, "The manual gift, that is, the giving of corporeal movable effects, accompanied by a real delivery, is not subject to any formality."

Here there was no notarial donation. Thus no donation *inter vivos* was effected unless the described acts constituted manual gifts

The Checks

Because cash is considered a corporeal movable which may be donated by manual gift, the gift of an amount of money represented by the donor's check is a valid manual gift if "reduced to possession" by being cashed by the donee (prior to the donor's death), *Succession of De Pouilly*, 1870, 22 La.Ann. 97: "The check was the means or the vehicle of delivery." The principle which thus allowed De Pouilly to make a valid manual gift (upon fulfillment of his order), by ordering in writing his bank to deliver cash to a named donee, is equally applicable to allow our donor, Miss Tebo, to make a valid manual gift (upon fulfillment of her orders), by ordering in writing her bank to deliver cash to her named niece, whom she further ordered in writing to deliver the cash to the two intended donees. We are unable to distinguish the one-written-order situation in *De Pouilly* from the two-written-orders situation before us.

Prior to Miss Tebo's death the grandniece accepted this donation to herself by physically accepting the cash, thus completing the donation. The minor great-grandnephew's case is different although we reach the conclusion that an acceptance was made for him. Presumably because the written instructions were addressed to both the niece and a niece-in-law (enclosing two sets of blank checks, one payable to the order of the niece and the other to the niece-in-law), the niece delivered the money for the great-grandnephew to the niece-in-law, who is the grandmother of the great-grandnephew for whom the cash was intended. However, that niece-in-law and her husband (the grandparents) had reservations about the gift (in part because of an erroneous notion that gifts within three years prior to death were invalid) and therefore did not deliver the cash to the minor's father, as administrator of the minor's estate, C.C. 221. Nevertheless the grandfather did place the money in a savings account identified as for the benefit of the minor. We deem this an acceptance by an ascendant which is valid even though the ascendant not be the tutor of the minor, C.C. 1546.

Accordingly the cash actually transferred by both cashed checks was the subject of valid manual donations inter vivos, and the checking account balances are erroneously listed in the descriptive list of decedent's assets (as due from the niece).

The Bonds

Bearer bonds may also be transferred by manual gift, *Succession of McCrocklin*, 1962, 242 La. 404, 137 So. 2d 274, although as in any manual gift delivery must be had to make the gift effective, *Succession of Land*, 1947, 212 La. 103, 31 So. 2d 609. The delivery required by the law is delivery by the donor or (as in the case of the checks in *De Pouilly* and here) by another acting upon the donor's orders.

We hold the bonds not manually given because there was no showing of delivery by the donor, nor of any order by the donor for delivery by another. The absence of physical delivery may be ignored under the circumstances. The residuary legatee could not be allowed to increase his own legacy by preventing the testatrix from completing delivery, through the niece, of an *inter vivos* gift. Were that the case the residuary legatee (and other legatees who prevented delivery) should be estopped to assert non-delivery. But that is not the case. No delivery order by the testatrix to the niece is shown and therefore, had the niece gained entry to the bank box and physically delivered the bonds to her daughter, there would still have been no valid manual gift. The niece's understanding that she (or the niece-in-law) had orders to deliver the bonds arose from the facts that: (1) decedent's general note of instruction regarding the packet of several notes was "If I am very ill give this to (the niece-in-law and the niece) immediately", with the word immediately underscored thrice, indicating present urgency rather than testamentary intent; (2) the wording of the note to the grandniece included "these are to be used for down payment for house keep interest to add to principal", indicating donative intent; and (3) decedent had long previously given authority to niece and niece-in-law individually to enter the bank box and remove at will its contents, thus making it possible for either to obtain the bonds and to deliver them to the grandniece. (Decedent had also twice told the niece "there were some important envelopes in her desk that had to do with (the grandniece and great-grandnephew) . . . but what was in them I had no idea.") The niece's inference that decedent intended a present manual gift to be perfected by niece or niece-in-law's obtaining and delivering the bonds is a reasonable inference. But a reasonable inference is an insufficient foundation for an agent's power of attorney, or mandate, to make a donation: "to alienate . . . or do any other act of ownership, the power must be express", C.C. 2996; "the power must be express . . . where things to be done are not merely acts of administration," C.C. 2997. Because there is no testimony or other evidence of an express power authorizing the niece to give the bonds to the grandniece, we conclude that no manual gift has been established.

Accordingly the grandniece has no entitlement cognizable by law. At best there may exist the "natural obligation on those who inherit an estate . . . to execute the donations or other dispositions which the former owner had made, but which are defective for want of form only", C.C. 1758. "A natural obligation", however, "is one which can not be enforced by action, but which is binding on the party who makes it, in conscience and according to natural justice." C.C. 1757(2).

The bonds are correctly listed among the assets of decedent's succession.

*   *   *

13-22

Bank Accounts

Banks offer a wide variety of accounts, but they can be broadly divided into five types: savings accounts, basic checking accounts, interest-bearing checking accounts (sometimes referred to as NOW accounts), money market deposit accounts, and certificates of deposit. With certain monetary limitations, all of these accounts are generally insured by the Federal Deposit Insurance Corporation ("FDIC"). As will be seen in the cases below, Louisiana laws governing donations apply to bank accounts, and keep in mind that banking regulations may require additional documentation or information before funds are released to owners or successors.

IN RE SUCCESSION OF GASSIOTT
159 So. 3d 521 (La. App. 3d Cir. 2015), *writ denied,* 2015-0493 (La. 5/15/15)

GREMILLION, Judge.

The children of decedent, Cecil Vanderbilt Gassiott, appeal the trial court's judgment finding that his wife, Patricia Gassiott, did not have to reimburse decedent's estate for $77,768.83. For the following reasons, we affirm.

FACTUAL AND PROCEDURAL BACKGROUND

Cecil and Patricia were married at the time of Cecil's death on June 21, 2013. They executed a prenuptial agreement in May 2004, providing for a separate property regime. Cecil died testate, having executed a will on January 25, 2008. In April 2010, Cecil recovered funds from a medical malpractice lawsuit. Cecil deposited one-half of the proceeds into a separate checking account and the other half in a joint savings account shared by Cecil and Patricia. On June 17, 2013, Patricia withdrew the balance of the joint savings account, totaling $77,768.83.

Cecil's children, Jason Gassiott and Redena Droddy, filed a rule to show cause seeking the return of the $77,768.83 withdrawn by Patricia. Following an April 30, 2014 bench trial, the trial court found that the money in the savings account was for Patricia's benefit, and the estate was not due reimbursement of the $77, 768.83. The children now appeal.

ISSUES

1. Appellant contends that the Trial Judge erred or abused her discretion in finding that the decedent had capacity to effectuate a donation inter vivos at the time of the $77,768.83 withdrawal.
2. The Trial Judge erred or abused her discretion in finding that the subject withdrawal met the formal requirements to constitute a donation inter vivos.

DISCUSSION

We have reviewed the record and adopt the trial court's recitation of the facts as our own. The trial court issued extensive reasons for judgment, stating in part:

As to the separate settlement money, the court finds that the money in the savings account was placed there for the benefit of Patricia. Cecil Gassiott's donative intent was exhibited by the manner in which he opened the accounts at Capital One. The savings account had Patricia Gassiott's name on it but the checking account did not. Both he and his wife had to sign the savings account documents. Cecil Gassiott appeared to be a very meticulous man as evidenced by his pre-nuptial agreement, his will, and the insurance policies for his children. He took care of his children with the insurance policies and he took care of Patricia Gassiott with the savings account. This was confirmed by his statements to his preacher, Reverend Johnson, months before his death on June 21, 2013. He made it plain to Reverend Johnson that he put "some money in the bank for Pat and the kids don't know about it." The money was to take care of her because "she took care of him." He told his preacher that he did not want Pat to have any struggles. He, also, told the preacher that he had some money and the house for his children. This is further evidenced by the fact that the money in the savings account was never used or withdrawn by Cecil Gassiott after the initial deposit was made (as opposed to the money he put in the Capital one checking account.) The court finds that Cecil Gassiott made a donation inter vivos of money to his wife and placed same in a saving account opened by them for her benefit and containing her name Patricia Gassiott accepted that donation and signed bank documents evidencing said acceptance.

Donation Inter Vivos

The initial issue we must address is a legal one. "A donation inter vivos is a contract by which a person, called the donor, gratuitously divests himself, at present and irrevocably, of the thing given in favor of another, called the donee, who accepts it." La. Civ. Code art. 1468. Donations inter vivos must be by authentic act unless an exception applies. La. Civ. Code art. 1541. "The donation inter vivos of a corporeal movable may also be made by delivery of the thing to the donee without any other formality." La. Civ. Code art. 1543.

Louisiana Civil Code article 1550 (emphasis added), effective January 1, 2009, addresses certain exceptions to the requirement that the donation of incorporeal movables requires an authentic act:

> The donation or the acceptance of a donation of an incorporeal movable of the kind that is evidenced by a certificate, document, instrument, or other writing, and that is transferable by endorsement or delivery, may be made by authentic act *or by compliance with the requirements otherwise applicable to the transfer of that particular kind of incorporeal movable.*

In addition, an incorporeal movable that is investment property, as that term is defined in Chapter 9 of the Louisiana Commercial Laws, may also be donated by a writing signed by the donor that evidences donative intent and directs the transfer of the property to the donee or his account or for his benefit. Completion of the transfer to the donee or his account or for his benefit shall constitute acceptance of the donation.

Louisiana Revised Statute 10:3–203(e) provides that "Donations inter vivos of instruments shall be governed by the provisions of this Chapter notwithstanding any other provision of the Louisiana Civil Code or of any other law of this state, relative to the form of donations inter vivos, to the contrary." It appears that the trial court, closely tracking the language of La. Civ. Code art. 1550, found that when Patricia signed the documents creating the savings account, she "accepted" a donation of funds from Cecil.

Since the enactment of La. Civ. Code art. 1550, there has been little jurisprudence addressing this issue. It had long been held that savings accounts are incorporeal movables that required the formality of an authentic act for a donation inter vivos to be valid. *See Basco v. Central Bank & Trust Co.,* 231 So. 2d 425 (La. App. 3 Cir.1970). Appellants argue:

> A savings account is clearly an incorporeal movable. However, a savings account is not transferable by endorsement or delivery. As indicated above they can only be donated by executing an authentic act. There are no "special rules" applicable to this type of movable. Accordingly, the default rule, which requires two witnesses and notary, must be adhered to for a valid donation[.]

Appellants cite numerous cases decided prior to the enactment of La. Civ. Code art. 1550 and La. R.S. 10:3–201. It is clearly no longer the law that an authentic act is required pertaining to the transfer of negotiable instruments as defined under La. R.S. 10:3:201. However, appellants make a valid point that a savings account is not a negotiable instrument transferable by endorsement or delivery. Nevertheless, La. Civ. Code art. 1550 provides for other transfers evidenced by certificates or documents as long as the requirements applicable to that type of transfer have been met. There is no dispute that the joint savings account was validly created. A document issued by the bank listing the account information naming Cecil or Patricia as account holders was submitted into evidence. Once Cecil negotiated the settlement check and deposited the funds into the joint account, when coupled with his donative intent, the donation was effectively complete. Either could withdraw funds from the account at any time. *See* La. R.S. 6:312. Thus, for all practical purposes, a party divests himself of his control over an account when he names a joint co-owner who has identical rights to the funds.

Appellants cite *Broussard v. Broussard,* 340 So. 2d 1309 (La.1976), in which a husband purchased savings certificates in he and his wife's names with funds received from a settlement. The supreme court stated:

> There was no actual delivery of the cash to Mrs. Broussard. The purchases of certificates in the names of both spouses, without an actual withdrawal and delivery of funds to Mrs. Broussard, did not effect a manual gift or a donation to her. Rather, the purchases were analogous to a deposit in a joint savings account, which in and of itself, will not transfer ownership of the funds. Furthermore, an account on deposit is an incorporeal right, La.CC. arts. 460, 474, which may only be donated by a notarial act in compliance with Article 1536.

Id. at 1313 (citations omitted). Notably, however, unlike in this case, the supreme court found that the husband did not have the required donative intent.

Further, even prior to the enactment of La. Civ. Code art. 1550 and in contravention of its prior holdings, the supreme court has gone to great lengths to enforce the donative intent of the deceased pertaining to the withdrawal of cash from a joint savings account in the absence of a notarial act. *See Succession of Miller,* 405 So. 2d 812 (La.1981). In *Miller,* the deceased opened a joint savings account under the names of "Mildred M. Miller or Mrs. Albertha S. Meyer."

Meyer withdrew the $7,599.72 balance of the account the day before Miller died. The supreme court characterized the funds withdrawn from a jointly held savings account shortly before the death of the deceased as a corporeal movable, thus requiring no authentic act. The supreme court stated:

> A notarial act is required for the valid donation inter vivos of an incorporeal movable. C.C. art. 1536. However, the manual gift of a corporeal movable, accompanied by real delivery, is not subject to any formality. It is therefore evident that the savings account (an incorporeal movable) was not subject to manual gift, but the cash withdrawn from the account (a corporeal movable) could be subject to manual gift.
>
> ...
>
> The critical inquiry in the present case is whether the record establishes that decedent maintained an intention to donate the funds to Mrs. Meyer at a time when Mrs. Meyer possessed the funds in a form susceptible of manual gift.
>
> ....
>
> Accordingly, we hold that although decedent did not hand over the funds in cash to Mrs. Meyer and did not affirmatively demonstrate donative intent after the funds were converted to cash, Mrs. Meyer's possession of the cash, in accordance with decedent's express wishes, operated simultaneously with decedent's continuing will to accomplish a donation inter vivos.

Id. at 812–13.

The exact same situation occurred here. Patricia could have withdrawn the funds from the joint account at any time, making the cash a corporeal movable. Thus, there are potentially two means by which the donation inter vivos was effectuated: via donation at the time of creation of the joint savings account or via the conversion of the funds to a corporeal movable upon withdrawal thus requiring no formality. Regardless of the chosen method, there is no legal error in the trial court's finding that a valid donation inter vivos was completed.

Donative Intent

Donative intent is a question of fact which we will not reverse in the absence of manifest error. *Rose v. Johnson,* 06–518 (La. App. 3 Cir. 9/27/06), 940 So. 2d 181, *writ denied,* 05–2528 (La.12/15/06), 944 So. 2d 1273. We agree with the trial court that Cecil's intent was very clear, not only at the time he created the savings account, but from that point thereafter. At the time the joint account was created, Cecil and Patricia had a separate property regime. Cecil put half the funds in a separate account that was undoubtedly his separate property. He put the other half into the joint savings account. In the two weeks prior to his death, Cecil instructed Patricia to leave his bedside at the hospital and withdraw the funds. Patricia testified that she declined to do so staying by Cecil's side during his week-long hospital stay. Only after returning home, and at Cecil's insistence, did Patricia withdraw the funds. Further, it was clear that Cecil purposely kept the account from his children, neither of whom knew of its existence nor that the lawsuit had been settled, in an effort to be sure that Patricia would receive the funds he set aside for her. We find no manifest error in the trial court's credibility determinations and finding that Cecil intended for Patricia to have the money in the joint account. Accordingly, appellants' assignments of error are without merit.

CONCLUSION

The judgment of the trial court ordering that Patricia Gassiott did not owe reimbursement to the estate of Cecil Vanderbilt Gassiott is affirmed. All costs of this appeal are assessed to the appellants, Jason Gassiott and Redena Droddy.

AFFIRMED.

BASCO v. CENTRAL BANK & TRUST CO.
231 So. 2d 425 (La. App. 3rd Cir. 1970)

HOOD, Judge.

Plaintiff, Joseph Basco, instituted this suit against Central Bank & Trust Company primarily for judgment declaring him to be the owner of a savings deposit account in the defendant bank, and for attorney's fees. Judgment was rendered by the trial court dismissing the suit, and plaintiff has appealed.

The principal issue presented is whether the funds in the savings account are owned by plaintiff, individually, or by the estate of Louis Basco, deceased.

On September 3, 1968, Louis Basco opened a savings account in defendant bank, and on that day he deposited the sum of $880.00 in that account. The account was opened in the name of "Joseph Basco, by Louis Basco," and a Savings Department Deposit Book was issued by the bank showing that the account was in that name. This deposit book was given to Louis Basco. The signature card which was furnished to the bank when the account was opened showed that withdrawals from that account could be made only by Louis Basco. No funds have ever been withdrawn from that account.

Louis Basco died sometime during the year 1969. The day before he died he handed the Savings Department Deposit Book to plaintiff, Joseph Basco, who was a nephew of the decedent. After the death of Louis Basco, plaintiff presented the book to the bank with the request that the funds in that account be paid to him, but the bank refused to comply with that request...

The defendant bank gives two reasons for its refusal to comply with plaintiff's demands. One is that Louis Basco is the only person who is authorized to make withdrawals from that account, and the other is that a demand for the same funds has also been made on the bank by Person Otey Basco, or W. O. Basco, a brother of the decedent...

The trial judge concluded that the funds in the account belonged to Louis Basco, now deceased, and that the decedent had not made a valid donation *inter vivos* of those funds to plaintiff. Judgment thus was rendered rejecting plaintiff's demands.

We agree with the trial judge that the funds in the above-mentioned savings account were owned by the decedent, Louis Basco. He opened the account, he made the only deposit which was ever made to it, and he was the only person who was authorized to make withdrawals from it. The evidence shows that plaintiff did not make any deposits to the account, he was never authorized to make any withdrawals from it and there is nothing in the record which indicates that he had any proprietary interest in it, even though Louis Basco opened the account in plaintiff's name.

We also conclude that Louis Basco did not make a valid donation of the funds in that account to plaintiff. A donation *inter vivos* of an incorporeal thing, such as a credit, right or action, is not valid unless it is made by an act passed before a notary public and two witnesses. LSA-C.C. Art. 1536. Generally, an account on deposit in a bank is an incorporeal right, and a valid donation of such an account requires compliance with the provisions of Article 1536 of the Civil Code...

In *Bordelon v. Brown, supra,* a joint savings account was opened by plaintiff and his housekeeper, Edna Brown. The existence of the deposit was evidenced by a bank book, the possession of which was necessary to make withdrawals from the account. This bank book was delivered to plaintiff originally, but the parties later had an endorsement entered in the bank book to the effect that both parties had to sign to make withdrawals, and that in case of death the survivor "has complete account." Plaintiff then actually delivered the bank book to Mrs. Brown, and she still had it in her possession at the time of the trial. The Second Circuit Court of Appeal concluded that the savings account was an incorporeal thing, and that it could be validly donated to Mrs. Brown only be means of a notarial act, as provided in LSA-C.C. Art. 1536. The court held that the entering of the endorsement of the bank book and the manual transfer of possession of that book did not have the effect of transferring the account to Mrs. Brown.

In *Succession of Grubbs, supra,* the decedent had opened a savings account in the name of his wife, with the authorization that withdrawals could be made upon the signature of either Mr. or Mrs. Grubbs. All withdrawals had been made by Mrs. Grubbs, and she contended that she had become the owner of the account by donation inter vivos. Our brothers of the Second Circuit held that the account was an incorporeal thing, and that since a notarial act had not been executed pursuant to the provisions of the Civil Code, there had been no valid donation of the account to Mrs. Grubbs.

We think the cited decisions are applicable to the issues presented in the instant suit. The savings account was owned by the decedent, Louis Basco, and since there had been no compliance with the requirements of Article 1536 of the Civil Code, plaintiff never acquired the account, or the funds in it, by donation inter vivos. The defendant bank thus correctly refused to comply with plaintiff's demand that the funds be delivered to him.

*   *   *

NOTE

Do you think the court would have decided differently if Joseph had been Louis' son, rather than his nephew? Why or why not?

GRAFFEO v. GRAFFEO
576 So. 2d 596 (La. App. 4th Cir. 1991)
[Footnotes omitted]

WILLIAMS, Judge.

Defendant, Paul S. Graffeo, appeals a trial court judgment which held that a certain bank account was community property. The issue before us is whether the bank account is properly classified as community property or the husband's separate property, where it was comprised of funds acquired by the husband prior to the establishment of the community property regime, but where the account was carried in the name of the "husband or wife." We hold that, under the particular facts of this case, the trial court did not err in finding the account was community property. Accordingly, we affirm the judgment of the trial court.

The parties to this litigation were married on April 30, 1983. Prior to the marriage, Mr. Graffeo had an account with State-Investors Savings & Loan Association. The account was in the name of "Paul Graffeo or Deborah Graffeo" (defendant's daughter) and, after a $2,620.00 withdrawal on April 21, 1983, amounted to $20,370.18. On May 25, 1983, less than one month after the marriage, the name of defendant's daughter was removed from the account and replaced with the name of plaintiff/appellee, Gail Graffeo. The account number remained the same. According to the State-Investors records in evidence, interest accumulated and deposits were made on the account in the months following, so that the balance amounted to $24,881.83 on October 7, 1983. On that date, $22,381.83 were withdrawn from the account and transferred into a new account, a certificate listing Paul Graffeo as the sole account holder.

A petition for separation was filed March 7, 1984, a judgment of separation was rendered January 31, 1985, and the parties were divorced on February 1, 1985.

Following the divorce, Ms. Graffeo filed a petition for partition of the community property. Mr. Graffeo filed an answer to and traversal of the petition for judicial partition. The proceedings were referred to a Commissioner, who valued the account at $22,000.00 and recommended that it be classified as community property. The trial court initially signed a judgment affirming the recommendation of the Commissioner, then granted defendant's motion for a new trial as to two issues, one being the classification of the State-Investors account. After a hearing, the trial court adjudged the account community property. It is from this ruling that defendant appeals.

Things in possession of a spouse during the existence of the regime of community of acquets and gains are presumed to be community, but either spouse may prove that they are separate property. LSA-C.C. art. 2340. The separate property of a spouse is his exclusively and includes property acquired by a spouse prior to the establishment of a community property regime. LSA- C.C. art. 2341; *Longo v. Longo*, 474 So. 2d 500 (La.App. 4th Cir.1985), *writ denied*, 477 So. 2d 711 (La.1985).

The parties in the instant case do not dispute that the account was Mr. Graffeo's separate property at the time the community was established. Rather, Mr. Graffeo contends that the placing of his new wife's name on the account was insufficient under law to transfer his separate property to the community. Under the facts of this case, we disagree. The LOUISIANA CIVIL CODE sets forth special rules governing the transfer of separate property into the community. LSA-C.C. art. 2343.1 reads:

> The transfer by a spouse to the other spouse of a thing forming part of his separate property, with the stipulation that it shall be part of the community, transforms the thing into community property. As to both movables and immovables, a transfer by onerous title must be made in writing and a transfer by gratuitous title must be made by authentic act.

The record in the instant case contains the State-Investors form dated May 25, 1983, which names "Paul Graffeo or Gail Graffeo" on the account. It is clear from the record that Gail Graffeo's name was deliberately placed on the account in place of Deborah Graffeo so that Gail could have access to the account.

Further, the record in this case supports a finding that the transfer was by onerous donation. Gail Graffeo testified that Paul Graffeo placed her name on the account after she gave up her full time job at Mr. Graffeo's request and moved out of her house. She stated that, in placing her name on the account, Mr. Graffeo provided her with the security that she relinquished to marry him. Mr. Graffeo and his daughter testified that Ms. Graffeo's name was placed on the account only to provide for her needs in the event that Mr. Graffeo should become incapacitated.

In the area of domestic relations, the trial judge is vested with much discretion, particularly where the weight of the evidence is resolved primarily on the basis of the credibility of witnesses, and the trial court's factual findings are to be accorded substantial weight on review. *Teasdel v. Teasdel*, 454 So. 2d 886, 890 (La.App. 4th Cir.1984), *writ denied*, 458 So. 2d 925 (La.1984). Here, the findings of the trial court are not clearly wrong. We hold that, under the facts of this case, the substitution of Ms. Graffeo's name on the account constitutes sufficient writing and sufficient indication of intent to transfer the account into the community. *But see Young v. Young*, 549 So. 2d 437 (La.App. 3d Cir.1989).

For the foregoing reasons, we affirm the judgment of the trial court.

AFFIRMED.

Certificates of Deposit

Certificates of deposit (also known as CDs) are low-risk and relatively low-return investments provided by banks. CDs are one of the safest investments available. The purchaser of a CD deposits cash with the bank and is guaranteed a certain rate of return plus the money deposited with the bank after the investment period (known as the "term" or "duration") expires. Terms of CDs range from months to years. Because the money is left alone during the investment period, the bank pays an interest rate slightly higher than what would have been earned in a money market or checking account.

SUCCESSION OF LAWRENCE
650 So. 2d 398 (La. App. 3d Cir. 1995)

YELVERTON, Judge.

The issue in this case is the ownership of two certificates of deposit and a N.O.W. account. The accounts were in Jonesville Bank & Trust Company, and were payable to Julius C. Lawrence or Henry D. Jones, Jr. After Julius Lawrence died in January 1993, Jonesville Bank & Trust Company deposited the three bank accounts, totaling $175,061.64, into the registry of court, and provoked a concursus naming Jones as a defendant, as well as the deceased's legal heirs, consisting of his brother Jack, two sisters, and three children of a deceased sister...

The issue in the concursus was the ownership of the money that had been in the accounts in the bank. . . . In the concursus, the trial judge ruled that Henry D. Jones, Jr. had established his ownership of the funds by virtue of remunerative and onerous donations. Only the judgment declaring Jones the owner by virtue of remunerative and onerous donations is appealed. We affirm.

*   *   *

To begin with, Lawrence wanted his nephew Jones to have his money. That much is certain. He manifested that wish many times throughout his life. The first time that he overtly declared that intention was in 1978, fifteen years before his death, when he went to the bank and gave instructions to make his nephew an alternate payee on all three accounts. The accounts were never drawn on. The interest and the accounts were allowed to roll over regularly. In 1991 he manifested that wish again by going to a notary public and getting his signature notarized on a piece of paper that contained some typing and some blank spaces filled in with his handwriting. In this document he indicated simply and without elaboration that he wanted his nephew to have his property. This instrument was not a last will and testament. It sorely lacked the required formalities. Its testamentary language had been typed in by someone else. It demonstrated two things, that at that moment, in 1990, he wanted his nephew to have his money, and that he had no understanding of the legal requirements of how to go about doing it. So, two overt acts, one in 1978 and another in 1990, stand out as evidence that Lawrence wanted Jones to have his money.

It is just as certain, from the evidence, that the gift was not a pure gratuity. Lawrence lived on a small farm in Grant Parish. He never married or had any children or adopted anyone. He and his nephew Henry Jones were always close. Lawrence was a solitary individual. His closest companion was his nephew Jones. All his life Jones and his uncle lived in homes about 50 yards apart in Georgetown, Louisiana. From the time Jones was in his early teens until his uncle's death in 1993, he helped his uncle around the place. This service and assistance covered a period of 35 years. It was interrupted only once for a two year period while Jones was away in military service. When Jones was a young man Lawrence had one hundred head of cattle and Jones spent most of his time with his uncle helping with the cattle. After Lawrence sold his cattle in 1975, Jones continued to serve and assist his uncle by maintaining his land, his home, and his vehicles. It was in October 1978 that Lawrence made the changes in his bank accounts to name Jones as a payee. There was testimony that from then on, as his health worsened toward the end of his life, Lawrence depended on Jones increasingly for everything that required physical labor. By this time Jones was himself married and had children of his own. Jones went by the nickname of Dee. According to the testimony of L.M. Melton, a cousin to Lawrence and one of his closest friends, "Dee done it all."

In written reasons for judgment the trial court found that Jones had provided his uncle with assistance in managing and maintaining a cattle operation, yard maintenance, truck and equipment maintenance, carpentry work, plumbing and electrical work, and running errands. The trial court further found that these services were valuable and appreciable and had been rendered over a period from 1958 until the deceased's death in 1993. There was testimony regarding specific services down through the years, as much as could be remembered, and services that were rendered on a regular basis. The testimony assigned and explained values for each of these services. The trial judge found that Jones had proved a specific value of $172,205 for the services rendered. Concluding that his services were little inferior to the gift and that the value of the gift did not manifestly exceed the value of the owner's charges imposed upon Jones, the trial judge found that Jones was the recipient of remunerative and onerous donations during the lifetime of Lawrence and that Jones was accordingly the owner of the money.

On appeal the basic argument by appellants is that there was no donation *inter vivos* because there was no proof that ownership of the money passed to Jones while Lawrence was still living. Appellants characterize this case as an attempted donation mortis causa which failed because it did not comply with the required testamentary formalities. We reject this argument. We find that the gift of the money constituted *inter vivos* remunerative and onerous donations.

*   *   *

The next article tells us that onerous and remunerative donations are not subject to the rules peculiar to donations inter vivos, except when the value of the object given exceeds by one-half that of the charges or of the services. LA.CIV.CODE art. 1526. In the present case, the trial judge made a finding of fact, which we cannot say was clearly wrong, that the value of the bank accounts at the time of Lawrence's death did not exceed by one-half that of the services rendered by Jones and the charges imposed upon him during Lawrence's lifetime. Therefore, the mathematical proportion between the value of the gift and that of the services rendered and charges imposed satisfied the definitions of onerous and remunerative donations. In consequence, the rules peculiar to donations *inter vivos* do not apply in this case.

The applicable rules are those pertaining to conventional obligations or contracts. In *Victorian v. Victorian*, 411 So. 2d 473 (La.App. 3rd Cir.1982), this circuit found that there was a remunerative and onerous donation. There was a written conveyance of land reciting that no money was paid, but that the consideration was, "vendee agrees to take care of vendor's person and furnish him a place to stay until vendor's death." *Id.* at 474. Because the consideration was thus expressed only in onerous terms, a question arose as to whether the consideration might also have been intended as remunerative for services rendered prior to the conveyance. In finding that the true intent of the parties expressed in the instrument included the recompense to the donee for services rendered before the execution of the conveyance, this circuit applied the rules pertaining to contracts in general and to sales in particular. *Id.* at 476.

The court in *Succession of Jones*, 505 So. 2d 841 (La.App. 2d Cir.1987) held that the transfer of a $5,000 check as an onerous and a remunerative donation was valid under the rules applicable to contracts in general. The court construed the $5,000 gift as having been given in payment of an actual obligation owed by the donor for services rendered by the donee for many years. The court said that the gift could thus be construed as a valid onerous contract, under LA.CIV.CODE art. 1761, for the performance of a natural obligation. And it could be construed under LA.CIV.CODE art. 1909 as an onerous contract because each of the parties obtained an advantage in exchange for his obligation.

Finally, in affirming the trial judge in this case we rely on the *Succession of Theriot*, 532 So. 2d 260 (La.App. 3d Cir.1988). In that case Elma Theriot, while she was alive, caused certain certificates of deposit that had previously been in her name alone to be reissued naming her as a payee but naming as well Catherine Trahan as an alternate payee. When Theriot died the certificates were still in the bank and had never been cashed. Catherine Trahan sued the Succession of Theriot claiming ownership of the certificates as remunerative donations. The trial judge found as a fact that Catherine Trahan provided services and assistance to Elma Theriot sufficient to qualify the gifts as remunerative donations. The trial court held that Elma Theriot by placing Catherine Trahan's name on the certificates intended to transfer the certificates of deposit to Catherine Trahan. The trial court also concluded that by naming Catherine Trahan as an alternate payee, Theriot intended to make a remunerative donation. Finally, the trial court concluded that the donation was valid as a remunerative donation because remunerative donations do not require formal acts. This court affirmed.

The decision in *Succession of Miller*, 405 So. 2d 812 (La.1981), illustrates the extent to which courts will go to enforce the clear will of the parties. The case did not involve an onerous or remunerative donation, but rather, a gratuitous donation, and the rules applicable were accordingly those peculiar to donations *inter vivos*. A savings account stood in the name of "Mildred M. Miller or Mrs. Albertha S. Meyer (payable to either or survivor)." Ms. Meyer withdrew the funds from the account on May 24, 1976, and Ms. Miller died the next day, May 25. Before the court was the question of whether Ms. Meyer could keep the money as a valid donation inter vivos, it being clear that, because Ms. Miller's will had been declared invalid, Ms. Meyer could not get the money by virtue of a valid donation mortis causa. Since it was a gratuitous donation, it had to meet the strict formal requirements, one of which was the necessity for an act passed before a notary public and two witnesses. Manual gift is an exception to that formal requirement. The Supreme Court in this case upheld the donation of the savings account to Ms. Meyer as an *inter vivos* donation by construing it as a manual gift. The court recognized that the account itself was an incorporeal movable and as such not subject to a manual gift, but reasoned that the cash withdrawn from the savings account became a corporeal movable and was subject to a manual gift. Manual gift requires delivery, and the delivery took place in this case when Ms. Meyer withdrew the savings account, although she was the one who withdrew it. In reaching this ruling the Supreme Court went to some length to explain that the donor expressed her unqualified intent, on several occasions, that Ms. Meyer have the money.

LA.CIV.CODE art. 870 says that ownership of things or property can be acquired by the effect of obligations. An onerous contract is one where each of the parties obtains an advantage in exchange for his obligation. LA.CIV.CODE art. 1909. In this case we find that it was a pure onerous contract because the value of the gift was about equal to the services and the charges. Parties are free to contract for any object that is lawful. LA.CIV.CODE art. 1971. Contracts have the effect of law for the parties and may be dissolved only through the consent of the parties or on grounds provided by law. LA.CIV.CODE art. 1983. Interpreting the manifest intent of Lawrence that his nephew Jones should be the owner of his money in Lawrence's lifetime, we find that the transfer was inter vivos. Jones was the owner of the money. It was not part of the succession of Lawrence.

The judgment is affirmed at appellants' costs.

AFFIRMED.

* * *

Life Insurance

Life insurance is a versatile estate planning tool. In essence, a life insurance policy is a contract with an insurance company by which the company provides a lump-sum payment to named individuals (the beneficiaries) at the time of the death of the insured individual. In exchange, the owner of the policy pays premiums.

The owner is the person who has various rights outlined in the policy, such as the right to dividends, the right to surrender the policy for cash value, and the right to transfer ownership of the policy. The insured is the person whose death triggers payment to the beneficiaries of the policy. Often, the owner is the insured, but not always. The beneficiary, the one who gets paid at the death of the insured, may be a person, a company, a trust, or some other legal entity.

SIZELER v. SIZELER
170 La. 128, 127 So. 388 (La. 1930)

LAND, J.

Otto Sizeler married his niece, Miss Annie Fels, in Providence, R. I., on October 14, 1913, under a statute of that state which permits a marriage among the Jews, within the degrees of affinity or consanguinity allowed by their religion. Chapter 243, GENERAL LAWS OF RHODE ISLAND, 1909, §§ 1-4, and 9.

The contracting parties were of the orthodox Jewish faith. They were married in the city of Providence by Rabbi Bachrach, as under the Rabbinical law the marriage of uncle and niece is sanctioned. See testimony of Rabbi Mendel Silber, T. 135.

Otto Sizeler and his wife were residents of the city of New Orleans at the time of their marriage. They returned to that city after their marriage, and resided there until the death of Otto Sizeler, March 26, 1928.

The estate of decedent is insolvent. He left two policies of life insurance of $5,000 each, in which "Annie F. Sizeler, wife of insured" is named as beneficiary.

The plaintiffs, the three sons of Otto Sizeler by his first marriage, have instituted the present suit to enjoin the insurance company from paying, and the defendant, Mrs. Annie Fels Sizeler, from receiving payment of the amount of the policies in question.

The grounds for the injunction are: That the marriage in Providence, R. I. of Otto Sizeler to Miss Annie Fels, his niece, was in violation of a law of the state of Louisiana prohibiting marriage between uncle and niece; that the marriage was contracted to evade the laws of this state and was in bad faith; and that the marriage is null and void and without legal effect, since the contracting parties were residents of the state at the time of their marriage, and returned to the state to reside shortly thereafter. R. C. C. arts. 94, 95, 113.

It is therefore alleged by plaintiff that defendant was the mere concubine of Otto Sizeler, and, as such, was incapable of receiving the entire insurance of $10,000, for the reason that the policies of life insurance were donations *mortis causa*, and were made in violation of article 1481 of the Civil Code, which declares that those who have lived in open concubinage are incapable of making donations to each other of immovables, and that donations of movables are limited to one-tenth of the value of their estates.

Under our view of the case, we do not find it necessary to pass upon the validity of the marriage contracted between Otto Sizeler and his niece in the state of Rhode Island, nor to determine whether the same was entered into in good faith by either of the contracting parties.

We have arrived at this conclusion for the reason that the rules of our Civil Code relating to donations *inter vivos* and *mortis causa* have no application to life insurance policies, and there is no law of this state that prohibits any person from insuring his life in favor of any beneficiary that he may select.

In the case of *Mary Ticker v. Metropolitan Life Insurance Co.*, 11 Orleans App. 55 (1914), Mr. Justice St. Paul, then a judge of the Court of Appeals for the parish of Orleans, in reviewing our jurisprudence on the subject, said in part:

> As we appreciate the jurisprudence of this State, a life insurance policy is a contract sui generis, governed by rules peculiar to itself, the outgrowth of judicial precedent and not of legislation.
>
> For although it is quite certain that such a contract, when wholly gratuitous as to the beneficiary, can be assimilated only to a donation either *inter vivos* or *mortis causa* (C. C. 1773, 1467), *yet the Supreme Court of the State has uniformly refused to apply to life insurance policies the rules applicable to donations*, with the single exception to be found in *Ins. Co. v. Neal*, 114 La. 652, 38 So. 485. (Italics ours.)
>
> Thus the Court has repeatedly refused to apply to such policies the provisions of the Civil Code relative to donations *inter vivos*, to-wit, that they are revocable when made to one's husband or wife, and subject to collation when made to one's children or descendants. C. C. 1749, 1228; *Pilcher v. Ins. Co.*, 33 La. Ann. 322; *Putnam v. Ins. Co.*, 42 La. Ann. 739, 7 So. 602; *Lambert v. Ins. Co.*, 50 La. Ann. 1027, 24 So. 16; *Vinson v. Vinson*, 105 La. 31, 29 So. 701; *Succ. of Roder*, 121 La. 694, 46 So. 697, 15 Ann. Cas. 526.
>
> And a fortiori the Court has refused to apply to such policies the fundamental principle applicable to donations *mortis causa*, to-wit, that such donations are without avail until after payment of the debts of the deceased; the court holding in every instance that the proceeds of such policies form no part of the estate of the deceased, and inure to the beneficiary directly and by the sole terms of the policy itself. (*See* the authorities above quoted; also *Succ. Kugler*, 23 La. Ann. 455; *Succ. of Hearing*, 26 La. Ann. 326; *Succ. of Clark*, 27 La. Ann. 269; *Succ. of Bofenschen*, 29 La. Ann. 714; *Tutorship of Crane*, 47 La. Ann. 896, 17 So. 431; *Succ. of Emonot*, 109 La. 359, 33 So. 368).

As the proceeds of life insurance policies form no part of the estate of the deceased, and inure to the beneficiary "directly and by the sole terms of the policy itself," the right of the defendant to the avails of the policies in this case does not arise from legal coverture, nor from the civil effects of marriage contracted in good faith, but solely from the terms of the policies in which she has been named the beneficiary by the decedent. Whether the marriage of defendant to Otto Sizeler was valid or invalid has nothing to do with the case, and whether such marriage produced civil effects or not, as the result of the good faith of defendant in contracting it, is also beside the question.

Since the estate of the de cujus was insolvent, and as the proceeds of the policies in this case formed no part of his estate, it is difficult to conceive that there was anything in his succession to be disposed of by donation *mortis causa* unless, perchance, donations of this character may spring from such stuff as dreams are made of. As said in the *Succession of Hearing*, 26 La. Ann. 326: "A policy of insurance is not a piece of property; it is the evidence of a contract, the contract being that a certain sum of money will be paid upon the happening of a certain event, to a particular person, who is named in the policy, or who may be the legal holder thereof."

In *New York Life Insurance Co. v. Neal*, 114 La. 652, 38 So. 485, the Supreme Court of Louisiana applied for the first time to a life insurance policy the provisions of our Civil Code relative to donations, which limit a donation in favor of a concubine to one-tenth of the donor's estate. C. C., art. 1481. As this case cannot be reconciled with the long line of decisions which preceded and followed it, all holding that the policy or its proceeds never formed any part of the estate of the deceased, the decision in the *Neal* Case is clearly in conflict with the settled jurisprudence of the state and is overruled.

* * *

We do not find it legally possible to hold that a life insurance policy in which a concubine is named the beneficiary is a donation *mortis causa*, and is subject to the rules in our Civil Code applicable to such donations, but that this is not the rule as to any other beneficiary designated in such policies. In the absence of express legislation on the subject, we have no judicial authority or power to draw a distinction between the classes of beneficiaries named in life insurance policies.

Judgment in the lower court was rendered in favor of plaintiffs, declaring the marriage between Otto Sizeler and Miss Annie Fels null and void and contracted in bad faith, and decreeing defendant incapable of receiving the proceeds of the policies, except to the amount of one-tenth part thereof.

The judgment further decreed the payment to plaintiffs of nine-tenths of the proceeds of the policies.

For the reasons assigned, it is ordered that the judgment appealed from be annulled and reversed.

It is now ordered that the demands of plaintiffs be rejected, and that this suit be dismissed at plaintiffs' costs.

NOTES

Consider the following statutes which in essence codify the *Sizeler* rule.

La. Rev. Stat. 22:915
Donations *inter vivos* of life insurance policies; Laws respecting form inapplicable
A. Donations *inter vivos* of life insurance policies, and the naming of beneficiaries therein, whether revocably or irrevocably, are not governed by the provisions of the Revised Civil Code of 1870, or any other laws of this state relative to the form of donations *inter vivos*.

B. This section is remedial and retrospective. All donations *inter vivos* of life insurance policies made on or before July 31, 1968 are valid and effective, whether or not such donations were made in the form prescribed by the Civil Code or by any other laws of this state.

La. Rev. Stat. 22:912
Exemption of proceeds; life, endowment, annuity

A. (1) The lawful beneficiary, assignee, or payee, including the insured's estate, of a life insurance policy or endowment policy heretofore or hereafter effected shall be entitled to the proceeds and avails of the policy against the creditors and representatives of the insured and of the person effecting the policy or the estate of either, and against the heirs and legatees of either such person, and such proceeds and avails shall also be exempt from all liability for any debt of such beneficiary, payee, or assignee or estate, existing at the time the proceeds or avails are made available for his own use. For purposes of this Subsection, the proceeds and avails of the policy include the cash surrender value of the policy...

In the 1980's, as attention became focused on forced heirship, many legislative changes attempted to limit the effect of forced heirship. Among those was the amendment to La. C.C. 1505 in 1983, which was adopted verbatim as part of Act 77 of 1996.

La. C.C. 1505 (C)
Calculation of disposable portion on mass of succession

*   *   *

Neither the premiums paid for insurance on the life of the donor nor the proceeds paid pursuant to such coverage shall be included in the above calculation. Moreover, the value of such proceeds at the donor's death payable to a forced heir, or for his benefit, shall be deemed applied and credited in satisfaction of his forced share.

*   *   *

In analyzing the rights and obligations of parties with relation to insurance policies, consider the following excerpt from the *Succession of Jackson*, 402 So. 2d 753, 756-757 (La. App. 4th Cir. 1981):

> . . . the jurisprudence draws a clear distinction between ownership of a life insurance policy as opposed to the ownership of the proceeds of such a policy. The ownership of a policy of life insurance, whether it is separate or community property, is determined by the marital status of the owner at the time the policy is issued. Equally well known is the rule that death benefits or proceeds of a life insurance policy with a named beneficiary other than the estate of the insured owner, do not form part of the owner's estate either separate or community, but belong to the validly designated beneficiary. Consistent with these two different forms of ownership there are different benefits. The policy owner is entitled to the lifetime benefits payable under the insurance policy, that is, those exercisable by the owner pursuant to policy terms and provisions, during the lifetime of the owner. These benefits include: the right to cash surrender value, receive dividends, assign or pledge policy proceeds, borrow against the policy, name and change of beneficiary, and execute conversion rights. On the contrary, the owner of the death benefits or proceeds is entitled exclusively to the proceeds when the policy accrues at death. Another point to consider here is that the existence of the lifetime benefits for the policy owner differs when there is a term policy or a

whole life policy. In the case of the term policy the lifetime benefits are limited, whereas, the entire package of benefits is generally available for the whole life policy. No distinction as to the existence of benefits is made for the owner of the death benefits or proceeds as the proceeds for either a whole life or a term life policy are payable when the policy accrues.

What is the effect on Life Insurance Proceeds when there is an oral agreement for *mortis causa* distributions of the funds? While Life Insurance does not form part of the decedent's estate in Louisiana, courts have upheld agreements as to the distribution of proceeds received by a beneficiary of the policy. In *Succession of Gaston v. Koontz*, 49 So. 3d 1054 (La. App. 3 Cir. 11/3/2010), the decedent changed the beneficiary on his life insurance policy from his long-term partner, Christopher Robbins, to his sister, with an oral agreement that the sister would give $10,000 to each niece and nephew, pay off any estate debts, and then give the remaining amount to Robbins, in exchange for her receiving a piece of property in the testament. After receiving the proceeds, the sister refused to honor the agreement, arguing that the agreement altered the existing notarial testament, or that it created a trust. The court rejected both arguments, reciting that life insurance does not form part of the estate and that a testamentary trust must be created in one of the prescribed forms in the civil code. La. R.S. 9:1751.

PROBLEMS

1. (a) If the decedent named his eighteen year old daughter as the beneficiary of his life insurance policy, are the proceeds subject to claims of collation or reduction by other forced heirs?

   (b) If the decedent's daughter claims her forced portion from her father's estate, in addition to collecting the proceeds of the policy, what argument may be raised by the decedent's twenty-one year old son?

2. A husband and wife were both killed as a result of an automobile accident. The wife died instantly, whereas the husband died on the way to the hospital. The wife owned a life insurance policy, naming the husband as beneficiary. The husband's estate received the proceeds of the life insurance policy and these proceeds were the only assets of his estate. The wife's minor children from a previous marriage sued the husband's estate, claiming that his negligence caused the accident which killed their mother. If the children are successful in their suit, may they attach the life insurance proceeds in their step-father's estate? *See Succession of Romero*, 639 So. 2d 308 (La. App. 3rd Cir. 1994), *reh. den.* (1994). Would it make any difference if, due to procedural delays, the proceeds had not yet been paid to the step-father's estate?

3. Decedent had a life insurance policy with the proceeds payable to his estate and included a clause in his will expressing a desire that all "just debts" be paid. At the time of the decedent's death, if other assets in the decedent's estate are insufficient to satisfy the claims of creditors, may the creditors seize the proceeds from the life insurance policy? *See Succession of Sweeney*, 607 So. 2d 996 (La. App. 3rd Cir. 1992), *reh. den.* (1994). Would it make any difference if the decedent had been more specific as to how the debts should be paid? *See La. R.S. 22:912 (F)*.

Annuities

An annuity contract is an agreement by which a specified income is payable at intervals over a period of time, often a person's lifetime, in exchange for premiums paid over a period of time or in a single payment.

The Louisiana statutory provisions regarding annuities are similar, but not identical, to those regarding life insurance. Review the following statute, noting the similarities and differences.

La. R.S. 22: 912
Exemption of proceeds; Life, endowment, annuity

*   *   *

(B) The lawful beneficiary, assignee, or payee, including the annuitant's estate, of an annuity contract, heretofore or hereafter effected, shall be entitled to the proceeds and avails of the contract against the creditors and representatives of the annuitant or the person effecting the contract, or the estate of either, and against the heirs and legatees of either such person, **saving the rights of forced heirs**, and such proceeds and avails shall also be exempt from all liability for any debt of such beneficiary, payee, or assignee or estate, existing at the time the proceeds or avails are made available for his own use.

The term "annuity contract" shall include any contract which (1) is issued by a life insurance company licensed to provide the contract in the state in which it was issued at the time of issue; (2) states on its face or anywhere within the terms of the contract that it is an "annuity" including but not limited to an immediate, deferred, fixed, equity indexed, or variable annuity, irrespective of current pay status or any other definition of "annuity" in Louisiana law; (3) provides the contract owner the ability to defer United State income taxes on any interest earned and not distributed to the owner; (4) transfers some risk of financial loss to the insurance company for financial consideration; and (5) was approved as an annuity contract by the Department of Insurance of the state in which it was issued prior to issue.

SUCCESSION OF RABOUIN
201 La. 227 (La. 1942)

O'NIELL, Chief Justice.

The question in this case is whether the unpaid balance of the consideration for an annuity contract, at the time of the death of the annuitant, should be paid to the named beneficiary, without regard for the law of forced heirship, or must be considered as belonging to the estate of the annuitant for the purpose of computing the disposable portion of his estate.

There are two such annuity contracts in this case. The judge of the civil district court decided that the unpaid balance of the consideration for the annuities belonged to the estate of the annuitant. The beneficiary named in the contracts is appealing from the decision.

The facts are not disputed. Louis Henri Rabouin died leaving as his heirs four forced heirs, namely, two sons and two daughters, and leaving an estate consisting of stocks, bonds and cash in bank, amounting to $8,885.49. He left also two annuity contracts, one for $10,000 and the other for $5,000; in both of which contracts the annuitant's daughter, Marie Hilda Rabouin, was named as beneficiary. The cash value of the balance due under the two annuity contracts amounted to $8,854.60. If this cash value of the annuity contracts is to be considered a part of the estate of the annuitant the total value of the estate is $17,740.09; otherwise, the estate consists only of the stocks, bonds and cash in bank, amounting to $8,885.49.

The annuitant left a will in which he bequeathed to his daughter, Marie Hilda Rabouin, the disposable portion, being one-third, of his estate, and bequeathed to her and the other daughter and two sons the balance of his estate in equal portions. Miss Marie Hilda Rabouin therefore was bequeathed one-half of the estate, and each one of the three other heirs was bequeathed one-sixth of the estate. Miss Marie Hilda Rabouin claims the $8,854.60 due under the annuity contracts, as the beneficiary named in the contracts, and claims as legatee one-half of the stocks, bonds and cash in bank, amounting to $8,885.49. One of her brothers and her sister claim that the $8,854.60 due under the annuity contracts is a part of the estate and that each of them is entitled to one-sixth of the amount, and consequently that Miss Marie Hilda Rabouin is entitled to only one-half thereof. What is in contest, therefore, between Miss Marie Hilda Rabouin and the coheirs is half of the $8,854.60 due under the annuity contracts.

Miss Marie Hilda Rabouin relies upon the rule which is well established by the decisions of this court that the proceeds or avails of life insurance, if payable to a named beneficiary and not to the estate or to the heirs, executors or administrators of the insured, belong to the beneficiary named in the policy and should not be considered as a part of the estate of the insured for the purpose of computing the disposable portion of his estate under the law of forced heirship. Succession of Hearing, 26 La.Ann. 326; Succession of Bofenschen, 29 La.Ann. 711; Pilcher v. New York Life Ins. Co., 33 La.Ann. 322; Putnam v. New York Life Ins. Co., 42 La.Ann. 739, 7 So. 602; Stuart v. Sutcliffe, 46 La.Ann. 240, 14 So. 912; Bransford v. Bransford, 46 La.Ann. 1214, 15 So. 678; Tutorship of Crane, 47 La.Ann. 896, 17 So. 431; Lambert v. Penn Mut. Life Ins. Co., 50 La.Ann. 1027, 24 So. 16; Vinson v. Vinson, 105 La. 30, 29 So. 701; Succession of Emonot, 109 La. 359, 33 So. 368; Sherwood v. New York Life Ins. Co., 166 La. 829, 118 So. 35; Nulsen v. Herndon, 176 La. 1097, 147 So. 359. See, also, Kelly v. Kelly, 131 La. 1024, 60 So. 671; Succession of Desforges, 135 La. 49, 64 So. 978, 52 L.R.A.,N.S., 689; Toussant v. National L. & A. Ins. Co., 147 La. 978, 86 So. 415; Douglass v. Equitable Life Assur. Soc., 150 La. 519, 90 So. 834. On the same principle it has been held that a man may take out life insurance in favor of his concubine in defiance of article 1481 of the Civil Code, imposing certain limitations upon donations, either inter vivos or mortis causa, to the donor's concubine. Sizeler v. Sizeler, 170 La. 128, 127 So. 388.

The reason why life insurance, if made payable to a beneficiary other than the estate of the insured or his heirs, executors or administrators, is not considered as a part of the estate of the insured for the purpose of computing the disposable portion of his estate, under the law of forced heirship, is that the proceeds or avails of life insurance do not come into existence during the lifetime of the insured, and do not belong at any time to him, but pass by virtue of the contract directly from the insurer to the beneficiary named in the policy. That is not true of an annuity contract. In such a contract the payment to the beneficiary, if he or she survives the annuitant, is a payment of a fund which belonged to the annuitant during his lifetime.

By the terms of each annuity contract in this case the Equitable Life Assurance Society agreed to pay to the annuitant an annuity in monthly payments of a stipulated sum during the lifetime of the annuitant, with a refund provision set forth in the contract. One of the contracts was issued in consideration of the payment to the Society of $10,000 (called the consideration), for which the monthly payments were $78.50. The other contract was issued in consideration of the payment to the Society of $5,000 (called the consideration), for which the monthly payments were $40.65. The refund agreement was that, if, upon the death of the annuitant, the sum of the monthly payments made by the Society to him should be less than the consideration which he had paid to the Society, the Society would continue to make the monthly payments, by paying them to the named beneficiary, until the total amount of the annuity payments made by the Society would equal the consideration which the annuitant had paid originally. It was stipulated also in the refund agreement that, if both the annuitant and the beneficiary should die before the sum of the annuity payments made by the Society would equal the consideration paid originally by the annuitant, then, on the death of the one of them who survived the other, any annuity payments remaining unpaid should be commuted on the basis of 3% per annum compound interest and paid in a lump sum to the executors or administrators of such survivor. It was stipulated therefore that if, upon the death of the annuitant, the sum of the annuity payments made by the Society equaled or exceeded the amount of the consideration paid originally by the annuitant for the contract, the contract should terminate with the last payment made previous to the death of the annuitant.

It was stipulated also that, if and after the contract had been in force for two years,-but before the sum of the annuity payments made by the Society equaled the consideration which the annuitant had paid for the contract,-the contract might be surrendered for its cash surrender value, on or within thirty days after any date on which an annuity payment would be due; which surrender value should be the commuted value (discounted on the basis of 3 1/2% per annum compound interest) of the remaining annuity payments necessary to make the total amount of the annuity payments equal the consideration which the annuitant had paid originally for the contract.

This court has not had occasion heretofore to decide whether the right of a beneficiary named in an annuity contract, to claim the balance of the consideration remaining unpaid at the time of the death of the annuitant, is controlled by the law of forced heirship; but, by analogy, it seems that the prevailing opinion in other jurisdictions is that the right of a beneficiary in an annuity contract is subject to the laws of forced heirship.

In Rishel v. Pacific Mutual Life Ins. Co. of California, 10 Cir., 78 F.2d 881, 883, 131 A.L.R. 414, referring to a statute prohibiting delivery of any policy of insurance until its form was filed with the Commissioner of Insurance, the Circuit Court of Appeals for the Tenth Circuit declared: "It is very doubtful whether annuity contracts are insurance policies within the meaning of this section. Respectable courts have held they were not. Hall v. Metropolitan Life Ins. Co., 146 Or. 32, 28 P.2d 875, where the contention made here was denied; Carroll v. Equitable Life Assur. Soc., D.C., 9 F.Supp. 223; People v. Knapp, 193 App.Div. 413, 184 N.Y.S. 345, affirmed 231 N.Y. 630, 132 N.E. 916; Commonwealth v. Metropolitan Life Ins. Co., 254 Pa. 510, 98 A. 1072. Until the Colorado Supreme Court so rules, we are not prepared to hold that an annuity contract is an insurance policy as used in this statute. In many respects it is the exact converse, and in common parlance the word insurance does not embrace annuities."

In Carroll v. Equitable Life Assurance Society of United States, D.C., 9 F.Supp. 223, 224, it was said: "An examination of the authorities does not warrant the conclusion that an annuity contract is an insurance contract. * * * An annuity comprehends few of the elements of an insurance contract."

In Helvering v. Le Gierse, 312 U.S. 531, 61 S.Ct. 646, 649, 85 L.Ed. 996, in holding that an annuity was subject to an estate tax, and not exempted as "insurance." it was said: "Historically and commonly insurance involves risk-shifting and risk-distributing. * * * That these elements of risk-shifting and risk-distributing are essential to a life insurance contract is agreed by courts and commentators. * * * We cannot find such an insurance risk in the contracts between decedent and the insurance company."

In Commissioner of Internal Revenue v. Wilder's Estate, 118 F.2d 281, the Circuit Court of Appeals for the Fifth Circuit, in a Louisiana case, held that the annuity contract was not life insurance and hence not exempt from the estate tax.

In 3 C.J.S.Annuities, § 1, p. 1375, it is said:

> An annuity contract comprehends few of the elements of an insurance contract. The former is distinguished from the latter in that insurance, as generally understood, is an agreement to indemnify against loss in case of property damaged or destroyed or to pay a specified sum on the death of insured or on his reaching a certain age, while an annuity is generally understood as an agreement to pay a specified sum to the annuitant annually during life. The consideration for an insurance contract is generally termed a premium and is payable annually, semiannually, monthly, or weekly; the consideration for an annuity contract is not generally regarded as a premium and is usually covered by a single payment. The power to make insurance contracts and to grant annuities is generally regarded, therefore, as distinct.

It is argued for the appellant that the contract of annuity in this case is not such a contract of annuity as that which is described in the Civil Code, article 2793, thus: "The contract of annuity is that by which one party delivers to another a sum of money, and agrees not to reclaim it so long as the receiver pays the rent [interest] agreed upon."

In the next article it is said that the annuity referred to in article 2793 may be perpetual or for life. But there is nothing in these articles forbidding the making of a contract of annuity on terms different from those mentioned in the articles. In the Succession of Cotton, 172 La. 819, 135 So. 368, 370, it was said that the definition of an annuity, in article 2793 of the Civil Code, was "by no means all inclusive."

The judgment is affirmed.

PROBLEM

If annuities are subject to the rights of forced heirs, what did the court in *Succession of Fakier*, 541 So. 2d 1372, 1374 (La. 1988), *reh. den.* 1988, mean when it stated, "The annuities. . . are not subject to actual collation for the reason that they were not transferred by *inter vivos* donation."?

United States Savings Bonds

United States Savings Bonds have provided a method of saving for many years. Such bonds may be registered in the name of a single individual, in the name of more than one individual, or as "payable on death," in which case the government pays the named beneficiary at the death of the owner. The question of how they may be transferred or donated, whether they are subject to the Louisiana laws of donations, and if so, which laws, have presented controversy.

WINSBERG v. WINSBERG
56 So. 2d 730 (La. 1952)
[11 Loy. L. Rev. 315 (1962,63); 23 La. L. Rev. 272 (1963); 25 La. L. Rev. 110 (1964); 36 La. L. Rev. 370 (1976)]

McCALEB, Justice.

Plaintiff is appealing from the dismissal of her suit on an exception of no cause of action. The salient facts of the case, as alleged in the petition, are as follows:

Hermand Woodward Winsberg purchased three United States Government Series "G" Savings Bonds of a total face value of $2500 and designated his brother, Winfred J. Winsberg (the defendant), as payee on death. Subsequently, Hermand Winsberg married and a few months thereafter died leaving his widow who gave birth to a posthumous child, Kathleen Hilda Winsberg. In due course, his succession was opened in the Civil District Court for the Parish of Orleans and the bonds were inventoried as an asset of his separate estate. However, defendant had taken possession of the bonds on his brother's death and refused to deliver them or their proceeds to the succession. Plaintiff, as administratrix of the estate and also as natural tutrix of the child (sole heir of decedent), then instituted this suit demanding that defendant be ordered to deliver the bonds to her or, in the alternative, that a monied judgment be rendered against him for their cash value.

The cause of action is predicated on the contentions that:

1. A United States Government Savings Bond, which is payable on death to a named beneficiary, is a donation *mortis causa* under Article 1469 of the Civil Code,
2. That it is an invalid disposition as it is not in the form of a last will or testament, as required by the Civil Code, Article 1570, and that
3. Alternatively, should it be declared to be a lawful disposition *mortis causa*, it was rendered ineffective upon the birth of a child by virtue of Article 1705 of the Civil Code.

Contra, defendant maintains that it is immaterial that the gift of the bonds under the payable on death clause was a donation *mortis causa*, forasmuch as the bonds are valid Federal contracts, which are not subject to restraint in their enforcement by the Articles of the Civil Code pertaining to testamentary dispositions, and that the subsequent birth of the child could not affect either his ownership of the bonds or their proceeds as the gift is not a disposition by testament.

That the designation by the purchaser of Federal Savings Bonds (of the type presented in this suit) of a beneficiary, to whom the bonds become payable on the purchaser's death, constitutes a donation *mortis causa*, as defined by Article 1469 of the Civil Code, is no longer an open question in this State. It was held in *Succession of Raborn*, 210 La. 1033, 29 So. 2d 53, 54, that such bonds were gifts "made in contemplation of death" and were, therefore, subject to the State Inheritance Tax imposed by Act 127 of the Extra Session of 1921, LSA-R.S. 47:2401 et seq.

This being so, the question arises whether such a gift is unlawful in Louisiana since it is not in the form of a will. Article 1570 of the Civil Code provides that all dispositions *mortis causa* be made by testament and abrogates all other forms. And Article 1571 defines a testament to be the Act of last will by which the testator disposes of his property "either universally or by universal title, or by particular title."

Thus it is plain that, whereas the gift of the bonds was a disposition *mortis causa*, it has no standing under our law as it does not comply with any of the forms prescribed for testaments by the Articles of the Civil Code, Articles 1574 et seq. Accordingly, it would be absolutely null but for the vitality given it by the laws under which the bonds were issued. This Federal contract, which is a recognition by the Government of its obligation to the purchaser of the bond for a sum certain in money to be paid on his death to a designated person, is, of course, enforceable between the parties thereto in accordance with the conditions stated therein. And, obviously, we think, Louisiana is without right to change the beneficiary of the contract or to insist that the Federal Government recognize someone other than the payee as the owner of the bonds. Hence, in the nature of things, we are confronted with the fact that the U. S. Savings bond plan establishes an additional method of disposing of property *mortis causa*, which has been superimposed by Federal law and which is to be considered effective notwithstanding that it is not in the form prescribed by our Code.

But though these contracts are entitled to recognition as another way to dispose of property in prospect of death, it does not follow that they may be employed so as to nullify the laws applicable to the devolution of property or to confer upon the donees greater rights than they would have had if the devise had been in the form of a last will and testament. It is apt to observe that the Federal Government is neither concerned with nor interested in the application and enforcement of State laws respecting succession or inheritance of property. Indeed, it seems manifest that the regulations of the Treasury Department for the payment of savings bonds[1] (relied on by defendant in this case), were designed solely to facilitate the Government, by providing a simple method for the liquidation of these obligations, so that it would not be subjected to the inconvenience and delays attendant to the settlement of conflicting or disputed claims. There was not, in our opinion, any intention to interfere with the enforcement of the laws of descent and distribution of the various States. Therefore, forasmuch as the payment on death clause contained in such bonds must be considered as a valid appendage to our laws respecting the forms for dispositions *mortis causa*, it appears logical to apply all provisions pertaining to testamentary dispositions, except those dealing with forms, in determining rights and liabilities under such a devise.

---

[1] Section 315.36 of the Treasury Regulations provides: "If the registered owner dies without having presented and surrendered the bond for payment ... and is survived by the beneficiary, upon proof of such death and survivorship, the beneficiary will be recognized as the sole and absolute owner of the bond, and it will be paid only to him,...."

Article 1705 of the Civil Code declares: "The testament falls by the birth of legitimate children of the testator, posterior to its date."

This Article, which operates a revocation of all dispositions *mortis causa* made by a donor antedating the birth of a child, is founded, as stated by Chief Justice Slidell in *Lewis v. Hare*, 8 La.Ann. 378, "...upon the reasonable presumption that the testator would not have given his property to others had he foreseen that he would afterwards have offspring."

Counsel for defendant say that Article 1705 is inappropriate here because, by its very language, it pertains only to testaments and that the payment on death designations in the bonds are not testaments. True enough, they are not testaments, but are dispositions *mortis causa* and, as such, are substitutes for and have the same effect as testaments. The plain reason why Article 1705 deals solely with testaments is because that is the only method by which property may be devised in prospect of death under our law. Hence, as aforesaid, since dispositions *mortis causa* in the form of payment on death clauses are to be given the force and effect of testaments, a parity of deduction requires that they must be governed by all provisions relative to testaments, other than form. Adoption of this course is not novel; it is consonant with the views we have heretofore expressed in other cases when the right of a forced heir to his *legitime* was concerned, *Succession of Land*, 212 La. 103, 31 So. 2d 609, and the share of the wife to the community estate was at stake, *Succession of Geagan*, 212 La. 574, 33 So. 2d 118, 122. In the latter decision, it was well stated that, "... we will not permit William J. Geagan, Sr., to do by contract with the Federal government what he could not have done by donation *mortis causa* in this state, that is, dispose of his wife's share of the community property at his death in favor of a third person;...."

So we say in this case that the defendant cannot be accorded greater rights, merely because the donation is in the form of a Federal contract, than he would have had if it had been by last will and testament as prescribed by our law. And, while Louisiana may not require that the bonds be paid to anyone other than the named beneficiary, it undoubtedly has the power, which was reserved to it by the Tenth Amendment of the Federal Constitution, to decree that the beneficiary or payee is indebted to the estate of the former owner, or his heir, in an amount equal to the value of the gift.

The judgment appealed from is reversed; the exception of no cause of action is overruled and the case is remanded for further proceedings consistent with the views herein expressed. The costs of this appeal are to be borne by defendant.

SUCCESSION OF GUERRE
197 So. 2d 738 (La. App. 4th Cir. 1967)
[14 Loy. L. Rev. 274 (1967,68); 28 Loy. L. Rev. 630 (1982)]

BARNETTE, Judge.

This is a proceeding initiated on rules to show cause, directed to the testamentary executor of the decedent's succession, seeking a judgment ordering and directing him to strike certain United States Savings Bonds from the detailed descriptive list of property belonging to the succession. The rules further seek a judgment ordering the executor to deliver the bonds to the respective surviving alternate payees as unconditional owners thereof, free of all liens, claims or charges, on the authority of *Free v. Bland*, 369 U.S. 663, 82 S.Ct. 1089, 8 L.Ed.2d 180 (1962).

The trial court dismissed the rules on authority of *Yiatchos v. Yiatchos*, 376 U.S. 306, 84 S.Ct. 742, 11 L.Ed.2d 724 (1964), holding the principle of constructive fraud, as pronounced in that case, modified the rule of *Free v. Bland*, and that the forced heirs could not be deprived of their *legitime* by the device employed. From that judgment the movers have appealed.

The decedent Louis Francis Guerre died on August 21, 1966, leaving three children; namely, Mrs. Mabel Guerre Binnings, Mrs. Mildred Guerre Fabacher and Mrs. Hazel Guerre Gibson, all forced heirs. In his will he left to these named daughters "the *legitime* allowed them by law."

The remainder of his property he left to Mrs. Noemie Freret LeBlanc, Sr., Mrs. Marguerite Freret Hetzel and Mrs. Nell Heaphy Broders.

During the years 1961 and 1962, decedent acquired a total of 50 United States Savings Bonds of $1,000 denomination each, all of which were payable to Louis F. Guerre or the respective alternate co-owners as follows:

Mrs. Nell Heaphy Broders	14 Bonds
Mrs. Noemie Freret LeBlanc	10 Bonds
Mrs. Marguerite Freret Hetzel	10 Bonds
Mrs. Marguerite Heaphy	1 Bond
James D. Heaphy	3 Bonds
Alden J. Heaphy	5 Bonds
Russell L. Heaphy	5 Bonds
Gustav J. Freret	2 Bonds

All of the named co-owners except Gustav J. Freret are movers in the rules filed and are appellants before this court.

The bonds are appraised at $42,779.60. They are in possession of Lansing L. Mitchell, testamentary executor, and he has listed them as property belonging to the succession. The balance of the estate consists of $8,941.35 in bank deposits and a small amount of personal effects, making the total value of decedent's estate $52,507.95. Obviously, therefore, the exclusion of the $42,779.60, represented by the bonds from the assets of the succession, would greatly reduce the *legitime* due the forced heirs.

The three forced heirs were made respondents to the rules, along with Lansing L. Mitchell, testamentary executor. At the trial of the rules below, the only evidence submitted was a copy of United States Treasury Department Regulations governing United States Savings Bonds. There is no dispute of fact, and the issue presented below and on this appeal is entirely one of law. All parties in interest presented trial briefs and have briefed and argued the issues of law on this appeal.

The Supreme Court of Louisiana has clearly recognized the authority of Congress in the issuance of United States Savings Bonds to prescribe methods by which the ownership of such bonds can be transmitted or disposed of, in addition to the methods prescribed by the laws of Louisiana. The devices used are the co-owner bonds payable to A Or B and the beneficiary form bonds payable to A or Upon his death to B. While neither of these methods of transmission or disposition meets the requirements, as to form, of the laws of this State for donations *Inter vivos* or *Mortis causa*, they have been recognized as additional methods for transmitting or disposing of property superimposed on our law by federal law. *Winsberg v. Winsberg*, 220 La. 398, 56 So. 2d 730 (1952); *Succession of Weis*, 162 So. 2d 791 (La.App.4th Cir. 1964).

While recognizing the supremacy of federal law in this respect, our Supreme Court said in *Winsberg*:

> But though these contracts are entitled to recognition as another way to dispose of property in prospect of death, it does not follow that they may be employed so as to nullify the laws applicable to the devolution of property or to confer upon the donees greater rights than they would have had if the devise had been in the form of a last will and testament. It is apt to observe that the Federal Government is neither concerned with nor interested in the application and enforcement of State laws respecting succession of inheritance of property. Indeed, it seems manifest that the regulations of the Treasury Department for the payment of savings bonds (relied on by defendant in this case), were designed solely to facilitate the Government, by providing a simple method for the liquidation of these obligations, so that it would not be subjected to the inconvenience and delays attendant to the settlement of conflicting or disputed claims. There was not, in our opinion, any intention to interfere with the enforcement of the laws of descent and distribution of the various States....
>
> So we say in this case that the defendant cannot be accorded greater rights, merely because the donation is in the form of a Federal contract, than he would have had if it had been by last will and testament as prescribed by our law. And, while Louisiana may not require that the bonds be paid to anyone other than the named beneficiary, it undoubtedly has the power, which was reserved to it by the Tenth Amendment of the Federal Constitution, to decree that the beneficiary or payee is indebted to the estate of the former owner, or his heir, in an amount equal to the value of the gift. 56 So. 2d at 731--732.

In *Succession of Gladney*, 223 La. 949, 67 So. 2d 547 (1953), our Supreme Court quoted at length from *Winsberg* and reaffirmed its rationale there expressed. The Court also pointed out very aptly:

> There is no need of the federal government in its contractual regulations with its bondholders to encroach on the law of Louisiana, *when a reasonable construction can be given to both federal regulations and our State laws*. (Emphasis added.) 67 So. 2d at 549.

We think the present case is one in which effect can be given both to the federal regulations and the laws of Louisiana relative to the rights of forced heirs without the recognition or enforcement of either encroaching upon the other. In our opinion, *Free v. Bland*, upon which appellants principally rely, does not restrict us in the application of our State laws, provided we give primacy to the federal regulations in those respects only where they are in conflict. The Court in *Free* was careful to point out:

> While affording purchasers of bonds the opportunity to choose a survivorship provision which must be recognized by the States, the regulations neither insulate the purchasers from all claims regarding ownership nor immunize the bonds from execution in satisfaction of a judgment. 82 S.Ct. at 1094.

In *Free v. Bland*, the husband bought bonds with community funds issued to "Mr. or Mrs." Free. This was a Texas case where community property laws similar to those in Louisiana were involved. Under UNITED STATES TREASURY REGULATIONS, 31 C.F.R. § 315.62, the co-owner will be recognized as the sole and absolute owner upon the death of the other co-owner. Mrs. Free died, and Mr. Free claimed the bonds under the federal regulations as absolute owner. The trial court recognized his full ownership "but awarded reimbursement to the respondent (Mrs. Free's son by another marriage) by virtue of the state community property laws, making the bonds security for payment." (Emphasis added.) The Court of Civil Appeals sustained the judgment recognizing full ownership of the bonds in Mr. Free, but reversed the award of reimbursement. When this matter then came to the Texas Supreme Court, it reversed the Court of Civil Appeals and reinstated the judgment of the District Court. The Supreme Court of the United States granted writs.

The United States Supreme Court said:

> The relative importance to the State of its own law is not material when there is a conflict with a valid federal law, for the Framers of our Constitution provided that the federal law must prevail. Article VI, Clause 2. This principle was made clear by Chief Justice Marshall when he stated for the Court that any state law, however clearly within a State's acknowledged power, which interferes with or is contrary to federal law, must yield. *Gibbons v. Ogden*, 9 Wheat. 1, 210--211, 6 L.Ed. 23. *See Franklin National Bank of Franklin Square v. People of State of New York*, 347 U.S. 373, 74 S.Ct. 550, 98 L.Ed. 767; *Wissner v. Wissner*, 338 U.S. 655, 70 S.Ct. 398, 94 L.Ed. 424; *Sola Electric Co. v. Jefferson Electric Co.*, 317 U.S. 173, 63 S.Ct. 172, 87 L.Ed. 165. Thus our inquiry is directed toward whether there is a valid federal law, and if so, whether there is a conflict with state law. 82 S.Ct. at 1092.

The Court then held there was valid federal law and that the state court which awarded the co-owner title but "required him to account" (emphasis added) for half the value had in effect made the award of title meaningless. It then said:

> Making the bonds security for the payment confirms the accuracy of this view. If the State can frustrate the parties' attempt to use the bonds' survivorship provision through the simple expedient of requiring the survivor to reimburse the estate of the deceased co-owner as a matter of law, the State has interfered directly with a legitimate exercise of the power of the Federal Government to borrow money. 82 S.Ct. at 1093.

Apparently the Court did not mean to imply that it was the Making the bonds security for the payment but the Ordering of an accounting for half their value that was an interference with federal intent. The Court further said:

> We hold, therefore, that the state law which prohibits a married couple from taking advantage of the survivorship provisions of United States Savings Bonds

merely because the purchase price is paid out of community property must fall under the Supremacy Clause. 82 S.Ct. at 1094.

The Court did, however, foresee the possibility of an unintended federal sanction of the use of this device for transmission of property as a means to circumvent state laws enacted for the protection of property rights and said:

> The regulations are not intended to be a shield for fraud and relief would be available in a case where the circumstances manifest fraud or a breach of trust tantamount thereto on the part of a husband while acting in his capacity as manager of the general community property. However, the doctrine of fraud applicable under federal law in such a case must be determined on another day, for this issue is not presently here. 82 S.Ct. at 1094.

Then came the case of *Yiatchos v. Yiatchos* in which the Supreme Court, referring to the above reservation in *Free v. Bland*, said: "This is one of those cases." We think its holding in that case clearly modifies the effect of *Free v. Bland*.

In *Yiatchos*, the decedent purchased bonds with community funds registered in his name Payable on death to his brother. The brother brought suit in the Washington State Court to have his ownership of the bonds recognized under federal regulations.

The Supreme Court of Washington held the husband had done an act in fraud of the rights of his wife—"a void endeavor to divest the wife of any interest in her own property." It held that he breached his fiduciary duty to the wife in the management of community property, holding that the wife had a vested half interest in the bond proceeds. The Court held the brother was entitled to the bonds unless there was fraud or breach of trust. In determining if fraud was committed, the Court said it would look to state law to determine rights. It stated:

> But in applying the federal standard we shall be guided by state law insofar as the property interests of the widow created by state law are concerned. It would seem obvious that the bonds may not be used as a device to deprive the widow of property rights which she enjoys under Washington law and which would not be transferable by her husband but for the survivorship provisions of the federal bonds. 84 S.Ct. at 745.

The case was remanded to give the wife an opportunity to establish certain facts that might show constructive fraud and for an answer to certain questions about her community ownership rights saying:

> If under Washington law, the widow, after her husband's death, has no interest in specific assets owned by the community and her half of the community estate may be satisfied from property or money other than the bonds, petitioner is entitled to all of the bonds for then there is no fraud or breach of trust in derogation of the widow's property rights under state law. 84 S.Ct. at 746.

The Court held that a requirement that the bonds be disposed of by will or by state intestacy provisions is nothing more than an attempt by the state to prohibit the utilization of savings bonds to transmit property at death which is forbidden by *Free v. Bland*, but said:

> It would not contravene federal law as expressed in the applicable regulations to require the bonds to bear the same share of the debts that they would have borne if they had been passed to petitioner as a specific legacy under the will rather than by the survivorship provisions of the bonds. 84 S.Ct. at 747.

We think the application of this rationale is equally pertinent to the issue presented in this case relative to the rights of forced heirs. We conclude that its application here will enable us to give effect both to the federally designed method of transmitting the ownership of the bonds and the laws of Louisiana protecting the rights of forced heirs against excessive donations.

Appellants have made a pertinent distinction between the vested right which a wife has in Louisiana (as in *Yiatchos*) in community property and the right of a forced heir. It is argued that the wife has a vested right of ownership in one-half of the community property, whereas a forced heir has no vested right until the death of the parent from whom his inheritance flows. We concede that one cannot be defrauded of that in which he has no vested interest, but this is a distinction without a difference in the application of the Principle pronounced in *Yiatchos*.

We read that decision interpreting *Free v. Bland* to mean that co-ownership or survivor bonds are not intended under Federal Treasury Regulations to be used as a device to circumvent the established laws of the states enacted for the protection of the rights of its citizens and thus deprive them of property rights guaranteed by state laws. We think the Supreme Court did not intend to restrict the application of the principle of *Yiatchos* only to situations meeting the rigid test of fraud in its literal sense.

There is no right more sacred in our laws than the right of a forced heir to inherit no less than a fixed minimum, which we call the *legitime*. This right is so deeply ingrained in our civil law that it has been declared in the CONSTITUTION OF LOUISIANA in Article IV, Section 16, thus protecting it from the risk of legislative infringement. We must agree that a child has no vested right in his parent's property during the lifetime of the parent, but he has a constitutionally vested right of inheritance to no less than a fixed portion of his parent's property. This right his parent cannot divest him of by any device or means known to our law except for the causes of disinherison enumerated in LSA-C.C. art. 1621 and then only "by name and expressly." LSA-C.C. art. 1619. Therefore, we construe any attempt by a parent to breach this right by the means of converting his estate into United States Savings Bonds, payable to himself Or a stranger or to a stranger Upon his death, as a circumvention of the laws of Louisiana enacted for the protection of forced heirs from unwarranted disinherison. This is a wrong no less grievous than a breach of fiduciary trust in management of community property to the prejudice of his wife's vested property right. An act can be a wrong without meeting the rigid requirements of fraud.

A superimposition upon the laws of Louisiana of such a device as an additional method of disinherison of forced heirs could not conceivably serve any federal interest, such as we have conceded in respect to the superimposition upon our laws of that device as an additional method of transmitting or disposing of property. This point is also discussed by us in *Succession of Videau*, La.App., 197 So. 2d 655, this day decided.

Appellants have argued the analogy of the bonds in question to a life insurance policy, citing *Sizeler v. Sizeler*, 170 La. 128, 127 So. 388 (1930), through which means a person might effectively deprive a forced heir of his *legitime*. It is suggested that, upon the same rationale, the courts of Louisiana might recognize the device of co-owner or beneficiary bond purchase to accomplish the same end. While the analogy may appear relevant, except for dictum in *Succession of Tanner*, 24 So. 2d 642 (La.App.1st Cir.1946), our courts have not extended the analogy of life insurance contracts to other devices, and we know of no reason why it should be done in this case.

We therefore hold that the appellants named, as co-owners or alternate payees of the bonds respectively, are the owners of the bonds with the right of immediate possession as intended by 31 C.F.R . § 315.62. Thus, we give recognition and effect to the supremacy of the federal laws. The declared policy and expressed intent--that this be a means of transmission stripped of formality, delay, and expense incident to probate proceedings--will then have been honored.

We can make no distinction between the situation before us and one where the decedent elects to withdraw an equal amount of cash and make a donation to the named co-owner, or where he purchases and registers bonds in the name of the payee individually. Nor can we distinguish in principle the co-owner "or" bond from the beneficiary "payable on death" bond, in relationship to the point at issue.

As stated above, the courts of this State have recognized the method employed by decedent as a means of transmitting property (money) as additional to the methods provided by our laws for donations *Inter vivos* and *Mortis causa*. But our courts have consistently held that donations thus made are equally subject to the restrictions imposed by the laws of Louisiana, except as to form. *Succession of Mulqueeny*, 248 La. 659, 181 So. 2d 384 (1965); *Slater v. Culpepper*, 222 La. 962, 64 So. 2d 234, 37 A.L.R.2d 1216 (1953); *Winsberg v. Winsberg, supra; Succession of Geagan*, 212 La. 574, 33 So. 2d 118 (1948); *Succession of Land*, 212 La. 103, 31 So. 2d 609 (1947); *Succession of Raborn*, 210 La. 1033, 29 So. 2d 53 (1946); *Succession of Mulqueeny*, 172 So. 2d 326 (La.App.4th Cir. 1965); *Succession of Mulqueeny*, 156 So. 2d 317 (La.App.4th Cir. 1963).

We therefore hold that the forced heirs have a right to proceed according to law in an action for reduction of excessive donation against the surviving co-owner registrants of the bonds in question in the same manner as if an equal amount of money had been given to them through the medium of donation *Inter vivos*. But they have no right to interfere with the owners of the bonds taking immediate possession thereof and exercising all the rights of absolute ownership as intended by the Federal Treasury Regulations. Thus, effect will be given to the laws of Louisiana while at the same time recognizing the sole and absolute ownership of the surviving co-owners as required by 31 C.F.R. § 315.62.

Whatever doubt might seem to be cast upon the validity of this conclusion by a literal interpretation of *Free v. Bland*, as discussed in several excellent law review articles, we think has been removed by the later pronouncements in *Yiatchos v. Yiatchos*....

The judgment appealed from is reversed. Judgment is now rendered in favor of movers in rules against Lansing L. Mitchell, testamentary executor, ordering him to amend the descriptive list of assets belonging to the succession of Louis Francis Guerre by deleting and excluding therefrom the United States Savings Bonds described therein and to deliver same to the respective surviving co-owners named therein as sole and absolute owners thereof.

It is further ordered that this proceeding be remanded for further proceedings according to law consistent with the views herein expressed. Costs of this appeal are cast against the succession.

Reversed and remanded.

NOTES

The *Guerre* case discusses two important Supreme Court cases, *Free v. Bland*, 369 U.S. 663, 82 S. Ct. 1089 (1962) and *Yiatchos v. Yiatchos*, 376 U.S. 306, 84 S. Ct. 742 (1964), which dealt with the potential conflict between state laws and the Federal Savings Bond Regulations. Did *Free* overrule *Winsberg*? How can *Yiatchos* be used to argue that *Winsberg* can be distinguished from *Free*? Both Mr. Free and Mr. Yiatchos used community funds to purchase United States Bonds. Yet, in *Free*, the estate of Mrs. Free was not entitled to any reimbursement, whereas in *Yiatchos*, the Court entertained the possibility that Mrs. Yiatchos might be entitled to a one-half interest in the bonds. What facts distinguished these two cases? What legal principle? Which most closely resembles the *Winsberg* case?

Compare the *Guerre* case. Is it more like *Free* or *Yiatchos*? Would *Free* have been decided differently if Mrs. Free's son was a forced heir claiming an impingement on his *legitime*?

Consider the case of *Ridgway v. Ridgway*, 434 U.S. 46, 102 S. Ct. 49 (1981) in which Army Sergeant Ridgway, pursuant to a state divorce decree from his first wife, was to maintain life insurance under the Servicemen's Group Life Insurance Act with his three minor children of his first marriage named as beneficiaries. Upon remarriage, Sergeant Ridgway changed the beneficiary designation of the policy directing that the proceeds be paid as specified "by Law," resulting in the proceeds being paid to his spouse at the time of his death. Upon Ridgway's death, his widow claimed the proceeds, as did his first wife on behalf of the children. The Supreme Court held that according to the supremacy clause, the beneficiary and anti-attachment provisions of the Act prevail and the proceeds should be paid to the widow. The state divorce decree imposing a constructive trust over the proceeds in favor of the children should fail. The Court rejected an argument based on the fraud exception articulated in *Yiatchos*, reasoning that Ridgway had not committed a fraud or breach of trust by avoiding the state court created obligation. Rather, the Court noted that Ridgway had complete control of his life insurance policy, whereas Mr. Yiatchos did not enjoy unbridled control over the community funds he used to purchase the bonds in his case. Does a parent have complete control over his disposition of property during life, or does the potential claim of a forced heir limit that freedom? Is the interest as strong as that of a spouse in community? Should it be? *See Coffee, Ridgway v. Ridgway: Forced Heirship's Maine Connection*, 28 Loy. L. Rev. 629 (1982).

OSTERLAND v. GATES
400 So. 2d 653 (La. 1981)

MARCUS, Justice.

Mary Maude Greenlee Osterland died intestate on February 2, 1973, leaving two daughters, Alma Osterland Fey and Mary Osterland Gates. Her succession was opened and Alma Fey qualified as administratrix of the succession. Alma Fey, in her capacity as administratrix of the succession, filed an action in the succession proceeding against her sister and brother-in- law, Mary and Stanley Gates, seeking collation and repayment of debts owed to the succession. Defendants answered generally denying the allegations of the petition. The answer was subsequently amended to include a claim for collation of sums given by decedent to Alma Fey.

After trial, the judge ruled that Mary Gates was required to collate $49,890.91, and Alma Fey was required to collate $4,545.38. He further held that no collation was due from Stanley Gates. Although he did not address the issue of a $20,000 debt allegedly owed by Gates, Inc., a corporation owned by Stanley Gates, the judge observed that the debt seemed to have "long prescribed." U. S. Savings Bonds listing decedent and her daughters as co- owners were held not subject to collation. The administratrix appealed. Defendants answered the appeal.

The court of appeal affirmed the judgment of the district court except to rule that the claim to recover the $20,000 debt was properly before the court but had in fact prescribed and to order collation of the value of the U. S. Savings Bonds held by decedent's daughters. The administratrix as well as Mary and Stanley Gates applied for writs to this court. We granted both applications primarily to consider whether the court of appeal was correct in ordering that the U.S. Savings Bonds were subject to collation.

At trial, it was established that decedent purchased during her life a total of $56,000 in U.S. Savings Bonds listing her and Mary O. Gates as co-owners and a total of $25,000 of such bonds listing her and Mrs. Alma Osterland Fey as co-owners. The federal regulations governing bonds issued in the name of co-owners provide that when either co-owner dies, "the survivor will be recognized as the sole and absolute owner." 31 CFR § 315.62. Thus, when Mrs. Osterland died, her daughters became the sole and absolute owners of the bonds that each of them held in co-ownership with their deceased mother. The trial judge held that under the explicit holding in *Free v. Bland*, 369 U.S. 663, 82 S.Ct. 1089, 8 L.Ed.2d 180 (1962), these co-owner bonds were not subject to collation. The court of appeal recognized that under federal law the daughters were the sole owners of their bonds; however, it reversed the trial judge's denial of collation and held that "a parent cannot use survivor bonds to circumvent Louisiana's established law granting collation to their parent's succession." As this holding is contrary to *Free v. Bland*, *supra*, and *Yiatchos v. Yiatchos*, 376 U.S. 306, 84 S.Ct. 742, 11 L.Ed.2d 724 (1964), we must reverse that part of the judgment of the court of appeal.

In *Free v. Bland*, a husband used community funds to purchase U.S. Savings Bonds listing him and his wife as co-owners. Upon his wife's death, he claimed full ownership of the bonds by virtue of federal regulations. The Texas court recognized his sole ownership of the bonds but awarded reimbursement to his wife's estate by virtue of the state community property law. The Supreme Court reversed, holding that the survivorship provision under the federal regulations is a federal law that must prevail under the supremacy clause of the federal constitution if it conflicts with state law. If the state could frustrate the parties' attempt to use the bonds' survivorship provision through the simple equivalent of requiring the survivor to reimburse the estate of decedent co-owner as a matter of law, the state would have interfered directly with a legitimate exercise of the power of the federal government to borrow money. Therefore, the Court held that the state law that prohibits a married couple from taking advantage of the survivorship provisions of U. S. Savings Bonds merely because the purchase price was paid out of community property must fall under the supremacy clause. However, the Court added that federal regulations were not intended to be a shield for fraud and relief would be available in case of fraud or breach of trust tantamount to fraud.

Yiatchos v. Yiatchos, supra, decided two years later, was such a case. The decedent husband purchased U.S. Savings Bonds with community funds registered in his name and made payable on his death to his brother. The Supreme Court stated that under federal regulations decedent's brother was entitled to the bonds unless decedent committed fraud or breach of trust tantamount to fraud. Fraud would be determined as a matter of federal law; however, state law would be used to determine property interests. The Court stated that bonds may not be used as a device to deprive the widow of property rights which she enjoys under state law and which would not be transferable by her husband but for the survivorship provisions of the federal bonds. The case was remanded to give the wife an opportunity to establish facts that might show fraud and to determine her community property rights under state law.

Under the survivorship provisions of the federal regulations governing co-owner bonds and the decisions in *Free* and *Yiatchos,* we conclude that both daughters are entitled to their respective co-owner bonds in full ownership without any obligation to collate unless decedent committed fraud or breach of trust tantamount to fraud. Such fraud will have taken place if it can be shown that the bonds were used to deprive the daughters of property rights which they enjoy under Louisiana law and which would not have been transferable by decedent but for the survivorship provisions of the federal regulations.

In reaching its conclusion that a parent cannot use co-owner bonds as a device to circumvent Louisiana's collation law, the court of appeal relied on *Succession of Guerre,* 197 So. 2d 738 (La.App. 4th Cir.), *writ denied,* 250 La. 933, 199 So. 2d 926 (1967). In *Guerre,* the decedent was survived by three children who, under Louisiana law, were forced heirs. A donor cannot deprive forced heirs of the portion of his estate reserved for them by law (*legitime*), except in cases where he has a just cause to disinherit them. LA.CIV.CODE art. 1495. During his life, decedent had acquired a number of federal bonds listing himself and persons other than his children as co-owners. At death, these bonds were valued at $42,779.60, whereas his other assets totaled only $8,941.35. Failure to include the bonds in the assets of his succession would have greatly reduced the *legitime* due his forced heirs. The court concluded that any attempt by a parent to breach the right of a forced heir to his *legitime* by means of converting his estate to federal co- owner bonds was a circumvention of Louisiana law of forced heirship and a wrong equivalent to a breach of trust tantamount to fraud. The court held that the co-owners were the owners of the bonds by virtue of federal law but that the forced heirs were entitled to bring an action for reduction of excessive donations impinging upon the *legitime.*

The instant case is clearly distinguishable from *Guerre* as it does not involve an impingement of the *legitime*; it merely involves collation. The obligation of collation is founded on the equality between children in dividing among them the succession of their parents and on the presumption that what was given to children by their parents was an advance of what they might come to expect from their succession. LA.CIV.CODE art. 1229. Although our law contains a presumption in favor of collation and states that children coming to the succession of their parents must collate what they have received from their parents by donations *inter vivos,* directly or indirectly, it does allow a parent to make a gift exempt from collation by formally expressing his will that the donation was an advantage or extra portion. LA.CIV.CODE arts. 1228, 1231. Thus, under Louisiana law, Mrs. Osterland could have made the bonds exempt from collation by specifying that they were to be extra portions. Decedent's use of the co-owner bonds subject to right of survivorship on the surviving co-owner under federal regulations did not deprive either daughter of any property rights under Louisiana law which would not have been transferable by decedent but for the survivorship provisions of the federal regulations. Therefore, decedent did not commit fraud or a breach of trust tantamount to fraud by purchasing the co-owner bonds. Hence, neither daughter is obligated to collate her bonds or the value thereof.

*   *   *

For the reasons assigned, that part of the judgment of the court of appeal ordering collation of the co-owner bonds is reversed; otherwise, the judgment is affirmed. The case is remanded to the district court with instructions to the trial judge to render judgment recognizing plaintiff's undivided one-half interest in the cemetery lots described above and for further proceedings in accordance with law.

NOTE

How does the right to demand collation differ from reduction? Can a parent consciously decide to favor one forced heir over another? Can a parent deprive a child of her *legitime*? Have the changes in forced heirship diffused the distinction?

SUCCESSION OF WEIS
162 So. 2d 791 (La. App. 4th Cir. 1964)

McBRIDE, Judge.

Camille Weis died January 18, 1961, leaving an olographic will (which has been duly probated and registered), dated July 23, 1958, containing the following provisions relevant here:

> I, Camille Weis, of the Parish of Orleans, State of Louisiana, City of New Orleans, do hereby make and ordain this my last will and testament, revoking all others.
> 2. I give and bequeath the following, either in cash or securities of an equal value, undiminished by death taxes and other charges:
> $5000.00 (Five Thousand Dollars) to Howard Paul Beebe of Montz, La. (St. Charles Parish)
> 7. The entire remainder and residue of my estate, I give and bequeath to my niece, Mrs. Gertrude Weis Aron.

There were found in decedent's safety deposit box, among other securities, three United States Savings Bonds, Series "G" (interest thereon payable semi-annually), each having a face value of $1,000, registered in the joint names of "Camille Weis or Howard Paul Beebe" which had been purchased by the decedent in May 1949 before the execution of the will. The testator's own funds were used in making the purchase and only he had possession of said bonds and collected the periodic interest paid thereon.

Mrs. Gertrude Weis Aron was confirmed as decedent's testamentary executrix. In due course she tendered Howard Paul Beebe the three above-mentioned Series "G" bonds, together with an amount of cash sufficient to bring the total tender to $5,000. Beebe refused the tender.

Subsequently, Mrs. Aron, as residuary legatee, had herself placed into possession of decedent's estate; whereupon Beebe filed suit against her, individually and in her capacity of testamentary executrix, in which he prayed that he have judgment recognizing him as the owner of the three United States Savings Bonds, Series "G," standing in the names of Camille Weis or Howard Beebe, and ordering Mrs. Weis to deliver said bonds to him and in addition to pay him his legacy of $5,000, or, in the alternative, that he have judgment against Mrs. Weis for the aggregate sum of $8,000.

After a trial below, there was judgment in favor of Beebe recognizing him as the owner of the three bonds, together with all accrued interest thereon, and as decedent's special legatee of $5,000; the court further decreed that the judgment of possession of May 16, 1961, to the extent that it may be inconsistent with the judgment in favor of Beebe, be amended and modified to conform thereto. Mrs. Weis has appealed.

The sole question presented is whether a legatee who has been bequeathed $5,000 and is the registered co-owner with decedent of $3,000 of United States Bonds is entitled to both the $5,000 legacy and the bonds, or whether, as the defendant contends, he is entitled only to a legacy of $2,000 in cash and the $3,000 in bonds.

Appellant takes the position that whereas at the time of decedent's death the bonds were listed as part of his estate and both federal estate and Louisiana inheritance taxes were paid on their value, and whereas in *Winsberg v. Winsberg*, 220 La. 398, 56 So. 2d 730, the Supreme Court held that a United States Savings Bond, issued in the name of the purchaser, and in which the purchaser designated another person as payee on death, constituted a disposition *mortis causa*, that Beebe is not entitled both to $5,000 in cash and the $3,000 in bonds, in view of the revocation by the testator of all other wills and testaments made by him. The argument is made that such revocation effectively foreclosed Beebe's right to have the bonds as surviving co-owner thereof as such right arose from a disposition *mortis causa*.

True, in the *Winsberg* case it was held that the designation by the purchaser of Federal Savings Bonds (such as Series "G") of a beneficiary to whom the bonds become payable on the purchaser's death constitutes a donation *mortis causa* within the purview of LSA-C.C. art. 1469. The Supreme Court had previously held in *Succession of Raborn*, 210 La. 1033, 29 So. 2d 53, that such bonds were gifts "made in contemplation of death" and as such were subject to Louisiana inheritance taxes imposed by LSA-R.S. 47:2401 et seq.

Under the CODE OF FEDERAL REGULATIONS (Titles 30--31), when the decedent purchased the bonds and caused them to be registered to "Camille Weis or Howard Paul Beebe," he was designating himself and Beebe as conjoint owners of the bonds. No payee on death was provided for. Immediately upon their issuance, either the decedent or Beebe could have received payment of the bonds upon his separate request. If either co-owner died, the survivor is recognized as the owner.

Chapter II, Subpart L, of the regulations provides:

§ 315.60 During the lives of both co-owners. A savings bond registered in coownership form, for example, "John A. Jones or Mrs. Mary C. Jones," will be paid or reissued during the lives of both, as follows:
(a) Payment. The bond will be paid to either upon separate request, and upon payment to him the other shall cease to have any interest in the bond.

§ 315.61 After the death of one or both co-owners. If either coowner dies without the bond having been presented and surrendered for payment or authorized reissue, the survivor will be recognized as the sole and absolute owner.

The decedent left no ascendants or descendants and, hence, there are no forced heirs. In having himself and Beebe denominated as co-owners of the bonds, he was making no disposition *mortis causa* thereof, nor was it his intention to do so. Beebe became sole payee by virtue of the regulations of the Treasury Department and through no act of the decedent. The moment the bonds were issued Beebe's interest and ownership therein came into being, the only difference in Beebe's interest before and after decedent's death being that before death decedent and Beebe each had the right to make separate request for payment, while after death Beebe became the only person possessing that right. If as stated in the *Winsberg* case the United States Savings Bond Plan established and superimposed on the state law an additional method of disposing of property *mortis causa* (when a third person is designated on the bond as payee on death), by the same token we must say the United States Savings Bond Plan has established and superimposed on our law an additional method for disposing of property *inter vivos* which is to be considered effective notwithstanding that there was no authentic deed passed or manual delivery made. (*See* LSA-C.C. arts. 1536, 1538, 1539).

The United States Court of Appeals, Tenth Circuit, in *Brodrick v. Moore*, 226 F.2d 105, said:

The surviving co-owner of United States Treasury bonds becomes the sole owner upon the death of the other co-owner. Co-ownership creates "a present, vested, though defeasible, interest' in the bonds."

Had it been decedent's choice to accomplish a "defeasance," he could, at any time, have requested and received payment of the bonds, in which event Beebe's interest therein would have ceased. Camille Weis was an intelligent businessman (a Certified Public Accountant), and must be presumed to have intended the legal consequences of his own acts. Since May 1949 to his death in January 1961, he took no steps in the matter and permitted the bonds to remain in the names of the co-owners and was undoubtedly satisfied with that arrangement. Of course, Beebe did not have physical possession, but nevertheless he was recognized by the Treasury Department as a co-owner under the registration of the bonds as made by decedent. Under our law the possession by the decedent was not for himself exclusively, but was for himself and his co-owner, Beebe. *See Louisiana Land Co. v. Blakewood*, 131 La. 539, 59 So. 984. Our Supreme Court has in effect recognized that where a person purchases United States Bonds which are issued to him "or" another person, such constituted a gift thereof to that other person. In *Succession of Land*, 212 La. 103, 31 So. 2d 609 (*see* Syllabus 14), a testatrix purchased United States Bonds which were made out or issued to her "or" her daughter. The decedent had possession of the bonds at her death. The daughter was the sole legatee under the last will and testament although the testatrix also had a son. The son filed suit for a reduction of the will to the extent that his *legitime* would be preserved. The United States Bonds came into contest, and it was held that the daughter who became the sole owner thereof under the regulations of the Treasury Department was made to collate "because of these gifts." This clearly indicates that the Court was of the mind that the gifts had taken place prior to the decease of the testatrix; otherwise there could have been no collation due by the daughter. LSA-C.C. art. 1227 recites that the collation of goods is the supposed or real return to the mass of the succession which an heir makes of property which he Received in advance of his share or otherwise in order that such property may be divided together with the other effects of the succession.

We are not concerned with the question of disposable portion nor with a *legitime* or the doctrine of collation. United States Savings Bonds are governed strictly by the federal law and not by the state law. *Free v. Bland*, 369 U.S. 663, 82 S.Ct. 1089, 8 L.Ed.2d 180. It is to what extent these bonds figure in calculating the inheritance tax or a *legitime* or an interference with the rights of a child born subsequently to the naming of a payee on death that the state law governs. *Winsberg v. Winsberg, supra; Succession of Raborn, supra; Succession of Mulqueeny,* La.App., 156 So. 2d 317. The language used by the United States Supreme Court in *Free v. Bland, supra*, is apropos here:

> One of the inducements selected by the Treasury is the survivorship provision, a convenient method of avoiding complicated probate proceedings. Notwithstanding this provision, the State awarded full title to the co-owner but required him to account for half of the value of the bonds to the decedent's estate. Viewed realistically, the State has rendered the award of title meaningless. Making the bonds security for the payment confirms the accuracy of this view. If the State can frustrate the parties' attempt to use the bonds' survivorship provision through the simple expedient of requiring the survivor to reimburse the estate of the deceased co-owner as a matter of law, the State has interfered directly with a legitimate exercise of the power of the Federal Government to borrow money.

The fact that the will provides that Beebe was bequeathed $5,000 "either in cash or securities" (decedent's estate including some $19,000 of the latter) did not denote that the testator meant that he was leaving Beebe the $3,000 of Series "G" bonds involved herein plus $2,000. The right to the proceeds of the bonds was already Beebe's by virtue of his status of co-owner thereof. He is entitled to the bonds and his $5,000 legacy.

For the above and foregoing reasons, the judgment appealed from is affirmed.

NOTES

Are United States Savings Bonds considered part of a decedent's estate and thus subject to taxation? In the case of *U.S. v. Chandler*, 410 U.S. 257 (1973), the decedent owned several co-owner savings bonds which were registered in her name and in the name of her two granddaughters. The decedent attempted to give full ownership of the savings bonds simply by manually delivering them to the granddaughters, but because she failed to comply with federal regulations she remained the registered owner. Holding that the transfer to the granddaughters was unsuccessful, the United States Supreme Court clarified that savings bonds could only be transferred by strict compliance with federal regulations. Thus, the bonds were included in the grandmother's estate for purposes of federal estate tax.

In determining whether bonds were subject to Louisiana inheritance tax, a distinction was made between co-owner bonds and beneficiary bonds. In *Gaupp v. Tarver*, 691 So. 2d 107 (1997), (La. App. 1st Cir. 1997), the Louisiana First Circuit Court of Appeal, while noting that Louisiana co-owner bonds were not subject to Louisiana inheritance taxes, held that beneficiary bonds were subject to Louisiana inheritance tax because the rights of the beneficiary only arose upon the death of the registered owner, thus, rendering the bonds as made in "contemplation of death."

Note that Louisiana inheritance tax was phased out and no longer applies to inheritances from persons dying after June 30, 2004.

PROBLEMS

1. Herman and his wife Kayona died as a result of injuries sustained in a common car accident. Kayona died on the scene and Herman died five hours later in the hospital. Herman had a life insurance policy naming his brother Will as beneficiary. Kayona had a life insurance policy naming Herman as beneficiary. Will Herman's minor son have a claim to any of the life insurance proceeds? How? Why?

2. Assume the same facts as above, but rather than a life insurance policy, the property in question was an annuity.

3. Assume the same facts as above, but rather than being life insurance or an annuity, the property in question was an I.R.A.

4. Frank left a valid testament bequeathing all of the property which he possessed at his death to his dear friend Joe. Frank died possessed of a United States Savings Bond naming his wife as beneficiary. Does Joe have a valid claim to this bond? What if Joe, rather than being a friend of Frank's, was Frank's minor child?

5. Dimitri and Ana were married for five years. Dimitri had a son George from a previous relationship. During her marriage to Dimitri, Ana purchased a savings bond with community funds naming her mother Sophia as beneficiary. Dimitri and Ana died in a car accident. Sophia cashed in the savings bond. Does George have a claim to the proceeds of the savings bond? What other facts about George would help you make the decision?

Pensions

One of the most valuable assets one possesses may be his pension. In essence, a pension is a savings plan to provide income at the time of retirement. Pensions are of varied forms. They may be private pensions funded by an individual and often tax-deferred. One of the most popular types of pensions are employment-based where the employer makes all or some of the contributions, which is a form of deferred compensation.

The Employee Retirement Income Security Act of 1974, ERISA, is a federal law that is designed to offer protection for retirement plans by setting standards regarding participation, vesting, benefit accrual, and funding. Since ERISA is a federal law, it preempts any conflicting state laws regarding pensions.

T. L. JAMES & CO., INC. v. MONTGOMERY

On rehearing

TATE, Justice.

We granted rehearing primarily to reconsider what effect, if any, should be given to the contractual designation of a beneficiary to the profit-sharing and retirement fund proceeds. We held these proceeds by our opinion to be in the nature of deferred compensation (additional remuneration) to the employee for his labors during his working lifetime. (That last holding we reiterate and amplify by our present opinion on rehearing.)

* * *

The decedent, Thomas W. Montgomery, Jr., was married to Sybil Chauvin (former spouse) from 1935 to their divorce in 1958, and to Goldie Greig (surviving widow) from 1958 to his death in 1971. One son, Thomas III, was born during the first marriage and another, Monty George, during the second.

The decedent was employed by T. L. James from 1946 to his death. During his first marriage, he became a participant in the company's retirement and profit- sharing plans, which apply to all employees. At the time of dissolution by divorce of the first community, the wife's interest in the funds, if any, was not partitioned or settled between the spouses.

In 1970, his first son Thomas III was named the beneficiary of both plans. However, because a dispute arose as to who was entitled to the proceeds of the plan, T. L. James provoked a concursus proceeding and deposited the proceeds in the court registry.

Under the terms of the decedent's contracts with the respective group plans, the right of the decedent or his beneficiaries to receive any proceeds do not contractually vest until his death, retirement, or resignation from company employment. A separate account for each employee is maintained, to which annual increments are paid by the company based upon employment. At any given time, each employee's account is valued according to its share in the assets of the respective plans, based upon contractual formulae applicable to all employees.

The employee is given the right to designate a contractual beneficiary to whom the proceeds are to be paid. The plans further provide that no person shall have a right to the funds except as provided by the plan, which further prohibits anticipatory assignment, sale, or pledge.

* * *

Effect of contractual designation of a beneficiary to the decedent's interest in their funds of the plans

Having amplified and reaffirmed the essential holding of our original opinion, we now approach a supplementary issue (to reconsider which, was the primary purpose of granting rehearing): What is the effect, if any, of the decedent's contractual designation of a beneficiary to the now-payable proceeds attributable to his account in the funds?

This contractual agreement, as we have held, cannot (in the absence of legislation so authorizing) prejudice the rights of forced heirs or the community ownership of spouses of the wage earner, essentially, because rights of forced heirship and of spouses in community acquisitions are fundamental concepts of our legal system.

In our original opinion, however, we went further: We held that the contractual designation of a beneficiary was a complete nullity which transferred no property interest to the beneficiary, because it did not meet the requirements of the civil code for a valid testamentary disposition nor for a valid donation *inter vivos*.

Upon reconsideration, for reasons to be elaborated, we now conclude that, so long as the contractual devolution of the decedent's interest to the beneficiary does not infringe upon the *legitime* of a complaining forced heir nor upon the community ownership of a complaining spouse, no prohibition of law prevents the courts from recognizing the contractual rights of the beneficiary to the ownership of the proceeds (so acquired by reason of the contract between the deceased employee, his employer, and the respective plans). We are re-enforced in this conclusion by the legislative recognition of such a contractual right in two relatively recent legislative acts, La.R.S. 23:638 (as amended in 1966) and La.R.S. 47:2404 C (as amended in 1968 and 1972).

The first of these statutes, La.R.S. 23:638, was originally enacted in 1954. By amendments in 1960 and 1966, it was broadened. The effect of the statute is to permit a full discharge from any adverse claim to any employer or trustee who makes a payment or refund pursuant to a written retirement or employee benefit plan "unless, before such payment or refund is made, the employer (etc.) . . . has received . . . written notice by or on behalf of some other person that such other person claims to be entitled to such payment or refund...." (We note, however, that this legally protected right to pay the contractual beneficiary was not legislatively intended to permit the contractual beneficiary to receive the proceeds free and clear of adverse claims, such as by the forced heir or spouse in community. Contrast this with La.R.S. 22:912, which expressly recognizes the contractual right of the beneficiary or payee of a life insurance policy to receive the proceeds as even against the estate, heirs, and legatees of the insured.)

By the second of these enactments, La.R.S. 47:2404 C, the legislature specifically exempted from the state inheritance tax any proceeds payable to a beneficiary by reason of "any retirement or pension plan, trust, system or policy," which latter terms are broadly defined by the act. Implicit, if not explicit, by this provision is legislative recognition of the concept that the contractual beneficiary acquires an ownership right to the proceeds by virtue of the contract, not by virtue of inheritance or gift. (However, as in the case of the first cited statute the statutory recognition of the contractual right so legislatively recognized does not exclude any duty the beneficiary may have to account to forced heirs if their rights of inheritance are infringed by the contract, nor to spouses if their community ownership is violated by the contractual designation of a beneficiary.)

This legislative recognition of the contractual right of the beneficiary to receive the proceeds--without an equivalent legislative recognition of his right to do so free of his duty to account to forced heirs for invasion of their *legitime*, or to spouses in community for the share of the funds attributable to the latters' ownership interest in them--presents questions not expressly provided for by statute, insofar as the interests of forced heirs and of spouses for community ownerships. As in other unprovided-for situations, Civil Code Article 21 enjoins the judiciary: "In all civil matters, where there is no express law, the judge is bound to proceed and decide according to equity. To decide equitably, an appeal is to be made to natural law and reason, or received usages, where positive law is silent." *See* (concerning another area of law) *Minyard v. Curtis Products, Inc.*, 251 La. 624, 205 So. 2d 422 (1968).

We thus hold, consistent with the views expressed in the earlier part of this opinion (reaffirming the rationale of our original opinion as to these issues), that, although the contractual beneficiary may receive in full ownership the share of the funds passing to him by virtue of the decedent's contractual designation of him as beneficiary, he does so with the obligation to account to any complaining forced heir or spouse in community if his receipt of proceeds violates either the former's *legitime* or the latter's community ownership rights (as set forth more fully in the earlier part of this opinion). Where, before the disbursement to the beneficiary, the payors (as here) have received written notice of opposing claims of the estate or of a surviving spouse, they may provoke a concursus in which the claims of the beneficiary, of the estate (in which claims of forced heirs may be adjudicated), and of the surviving spouse to the proceeds may be apportioned in accordance with the views above set forth.

We thus adopt a judicial resolution of the competing legal interests analogous to that developed by our state courts in resolving the somewhat similar issues arising in federal savings bond cases--where likewise, by statute, a form of devolution of a property interest was recognized as valid, but was nevertheless subjected to the judicial requirement of an accounting, where requested, to the claims of any forced heir whose *legitime* was thereby prejudiced or of any spouse whose community ownership interests was thereby violated. *See: Winsberg v. Winsberg*, 220 La. 398, 56 So. 2d 730 (1952); *Succession of Guerre*, 197 So. 2d 738 (La.App.4th Cir. 1967); *Succession of Videau*, 197 So. 2d 655 (La.App.4th Cir. 1967); Comment, 25 La.L.Rev. 108, 108--19 (1964).

*   *   *

REVERSED AND REMANDED TO THE DISTRICT COURT.

NOTE

Following the *James* case, the Louisiana legislature passed legislation sanctioning the designation of beneficiaries to deferred compensation plans made in any form "permitted or required by the plan." (La. R.S. 23:652, as added by Acts 1976, No. 494, Section 1.) Thus, testamentary or authentic form is not necessarily required in order to name a beneficiary.

La. C.C. 1505 has been amended, differing from the *James* ruling in part.

La. C.C. 1505 (D)
Calculation of disposable portion on mass of succession

*   *   *

D. Employer and employee contributions under any plan of deferred compensation adopted by any public or governmental employer or any plan qualified under Sections 401 or 408 of the Internal Revenue Code, and any benefits payable by reason of death, disability, retirement, or termination of employment under any such plans, shall not be included in the above calculation, nor shall any of such contributions or benefits be subject to the claims of forced heirs. However, the value of such benefits paid or payable to a forced heir, or for the benefit of a forced heir, shall be deemed applied and credited in satisfaction of his forced share.

SUCCESSION OF DURABB
631 So. 2d 1324 (La. App. 4th Cir. 1994)

JONES, Judge.

Appellant, Sheridan Francis appeals the trial court's judgment ordering her to return funds which she removed from the estate of her mother and assessing legal costs to the estate. Appellee and succession administratrix, Carolyn Domingo, appeals the trial court's judgment finding that amounts Ms. Francis received in repayment of a loan and as proceeds on an IRA were not due the estate.

This appeal arises from the succession of Lillian Berggren Durabb. Mrs. Durabb suffered a stroke on February 7, 1982. Her husband, Walter Elmo Durabb, died on June 29, 1981. There are three heirs to the succession namely, appellant, Sheridan Francis, Lillian S. Haber and appellee, Carolyn D. Domingo, the succession administratrix.

Appellant was an agent under a Power of Attorney executed at the hospital after her mother suffered a stroke. She acted on her mother's behalf through that Power of Attorney until her mother's death. During her mother's illness, and up until the time of death, appellant managed her mother's affairs. She resided with her mother on St. Roch Street and cared for her during this time.

There was a dispute amongst the heirs to the estate regarding an IRA account, converted from a KEOGH account, left by Mr. Durabb to his wife. The trial court ruled that the Power of Attorney executed by appellant was valid and that she had the authority to execute an IRA application naming her as the beneficiary. The trial court's ruling was appealed and affirmed by this Court. 542 So. 2d 220 (La.App. 4th Cir.1989). Since that time, the trial court has conducted hearings on various legal issues involved in the administration and distribution of this estate. This appeal is pursuant to the trial court's September 25, 1992 judgment.

*   *   *

By her only other assignment of error, appellee argues that in the absence of a will, the alleged gift of $78,676.34 in IRA proceeds to Sheridan Francis is collatable and is deemed in satisfaction of her forced share. La.C.C. articles 888 and 1505(D). Appellant responds that La.C.C. article 1505(D) provides that IRA benefits are not subject to the claims of forced heirs.

LOUISIANA CIVIL CODE Article 1505(D) provides for the calculation of the disposable portion on the mass of a succession. Sub-paragraph "D" states:

> Employer and employee contributions under any plan of deferred compensation adopted by any public or governmental employer or any plan qualified under Sections 401 or 408 of the Internal Revenue Code, and any benefits payable by reason of death, disability, retirement, or termination of employment under any such plans, shall not be included in the above calculation, nor shall any of such contributions or benefits be subject to the claims of forced heirs. However, the value of such benefits paid or payable to a forced heir, or for the benefit of a

forced heir, shall be deemed applied and credited in satisfaction of his forced share.

Section 408 of the Internal Revenue Code deals specifically with Individual Retirement Accounts. A qualified IRA would fall under the exclusion above quoted. Therefore, we find that the trial court was correct in excluding the amount of the IRA proceeds from the mass of the succession, however the amount received by appellant in IRA proceeds will act as a credit towards her forced portion of her mother's estate.

For the foregoing reasons the trial court's judgment is affirmed.

AFFIRMED.

NOTES

The *James* case was the forerunner of a number of pension cases dealing with the rights of named beneficiaries of plans versus the interests of a spouse in community or descendant forced heirs. Protection for the account holder caught in the middle of such disputes was afforded by the following statute:

La. R.S. 9: 2449
Individual retirement accounts; payment of benefits
 A. Any benefits payable by reason of death from an individual retirement account established in accordance with the provisions of 26 U.S.C. 408, as amended, shall be paid as provided in the individual retirement account agreement to the designated beneficiary of the account. Such payment shall be a valid and sufficient release and discharge of the account holder for the payment or delivery so made and shall relieve the trustee, custodian, insurance company or other account fiduciary from all adverse claims thereto by a person claiming as a surviving or former spouse of a successor to such a spouse.
 B. No account holder paying a beneficiary in accordance with this Section shall be liable to the estate or any heir of the decedent nor shall the account holder be liable for any estate, inheritance, or succession taxes which may be due the state.
 C. The provisions of this Section shall apply notwithstanding the fact the decedent designates a beneficiary by last will and testament.

Following *James*, a number of Louisiana cases protected the interests of surviving spouses in community and of forced heirs. *See McVay v. McVay*, 476 So. 2d 1070 (La. App. 3rd Cir. 1985) and *Johnson v. Wetherspoon*, 669 So. 2d 589 (La. App. 1st cir. 1996), *aff'd*, 694 So. 2d 669 (La. 1997). Others recognized the potential need for such protection where the rights of spouses in community or forced heirs were shown to be impinged. *See Succession of Egan*, 543 So. 2d 940 (La. App. 5th Cir. 1989).

Today, much of pension plan law is federal, contained within the Employee Retirement Income Security Act of 1974 ("ERISA"). Questions regarding the preemption of state laws by ERISA had the federal circuits split in *Ablamis v. Roper*, 937 F.2d 1450 (9th Cir. 1991) and

Boggs v. Boggs, 82 F.3d 90 (5th Cir. 1996) until the United State Supreme Court in a 5-4 decision resolved the conflict in the following case.

BOGGS v. BOGGS
520 U. S. 833, 117 S. Ct. 1754 (1997)
[71 Tul. L. Rev. 1005 (1997) (discussing the 5th Cir. opinion); 58 La. L. Rev. 997 (1998)(discussing the history of ERISA preemption); 28 Golden Gate U. L. Rev. 571 (1998)]

Justice KENNEDY delivered the opinion of the Court.

We consider whether the Employee Retirement Income Security Act of 1974 (ERISA), 88 Stat. 832, as amended, 29 U.S.C. § 1001 et seq., pre-empts a state law allowing a nonparticipant spouse to transfer by testamentary instrument an interest in undistributed pension plan benefits. Given the pervasive significance of pension plans in the national economy, the congressional mandate for their uniform and comprehensive regulation, and the fundamental importance of community property law in defining the marital partnership in a number of States, the question is of undoubted importance. We hold that ERISA pre-empts the state law.

I.

Isaac Boggs worked for South Central Bell from 1949 until his retirement in 1985. Isaac and Dorothy, his first wife, were married when he began working for the company, and they remained husband and wife until Dorothy's death in 1979. They had three sons. Within a year of Dorothy's death, Isaac married Sandra, and they remained married until his death in 1989.

Upon retirement, Isaac received various benefits from his employer's retirement plans. One was a lump-sum distribution from the Bell System Savings Plan for Salaried Employees (Savings Plan) of $151,628.94, which he rolled over into an Individual Retirement Account (IRA). He made no withdrawals and the account was worth $180,778.05 when he died. He also received 96 shares of AT & T stock from the Bell South Employee Stock Ownership Plan (ESOP). In addition, Isaac enjoyed a monthly annuity payment during his retirement of $1,777.67 from the Bell South Service Retirement Program.

The instant dispute over ownership of the benefits is between Sandra (the surviving wife) and the sons of the first marriage. The sons' claim to a portion of the benefits is based on Dorothy's will. Dorothy bequeathed to Isaac one-third of her estate, and a lifetime usufruct in the remaining two- thirds. A lifetime usufruct is the rough equivalent of a common-law life estate. *See* LA. CIV.CODE ANN., Art. 535 (West 1980). She bequeathed to her sons the naked ownership in the remaining two-thirds, subject to Isaac's usufruct. All agree that, absent pre-emption, Louisiana law controls and that under it Dorothy's will would dispose of her community property interest in Isaac's undistributed pension plan benefits. A Louisiana state court, in a 1980 order entitled "Judgment of Possession," ascribed to Dorothy's estate a community property interest in Isaac's Savings Plan account valued at the time at $21,194.29.

Sandra contests the validity of Dorothy's 1980 testamentary transfer, basing her claim to those benefits on her interest under Isaac's will and 29 U.S.C. § 1055. Isaac bequeathed to Sandra outright certain real property including the family home. His will also gave Sandra a lifetime usufruct in the remainder of his estate, with the naked ownership interest being held by the sons. Sandra argues that the sons' competing claim, since it is based on Dorothy's 1980 purported testamentary transfer of her community property interest in undistributed pension plan benefits, is pre-empted by ERISA. The Bell South Service Retirement Program monthly annuity is now paid to Sandra as the surviving spouse.

After Isaac's death, two of the sons filed an action in state court requesting the appointment of an expert to compute the percentage of the retirement benefits they would be entitled to as a result of Dorothy's attempted testamentary transfer. They further sought a judgment awarding them a portion of: the IRA; the ESOP shares of AT & T stock; the monthly annuity payments received by Isaac during his retirement; and Sandra's survivor annuity payments, both received and payable.

In response, Sandra Boggs filed a complaint in the United States District Court for the Eastern District of Louisiana, seeking a declaratory judgment that ERISA pre-empts the application of Louisiana's community property and succession laws to the extent they recognize the sons' claim to an interest in the disputed retirement benefits. The District Court granted summary judgment against Sandra Boggs. 849 F.Supp. 462 (1994). It found that, under Louisiana community property law, Dorothy had an ownership interest in her husband's pension plan benefits built up during their marriage. The creation of this interest, the court explained, does not violate 29 U.S.C. § 1056(d)(1), which prohibits pension plan benefits from being "assigned" or "alienated," since Congress did not intend to alter traditional familial and support obligations. In the court's view, there was no assignment or alienation because Dorothy's rights in the benefits were acquired by operation of community property law and not by transfer from Isaac. Turning to Dorothy's testamentary transfer, the court found it effective because "[ERISA] does not display any particular interest in preserving maximum benefits to any particular beneficiary." 849 F.Supp., at 465.

A divided panel of the Fifth Circuit affirmed. 82 F.3d 90 (1996). The court stressed that Louisiana law affects only what a plan participant may do with his or her benefits after they are received and not the relationship between the pension plan administrator and the plan beneficiary. *Id.,* at 96. For the reasons given by the District Court, it found ERISA's pension plan anti-alienation provision, § 1056(d)(1), inapplicable to Louisiana's creation of Dorothy Boggs' community property interest in the pension plan benefits. It concluded that the transfer of the interest from Dorothy to her sons was not a prohibited assignment or alienation, as this transfer was "two steps removed from the disbursement of benefits." *Id.,* at 97.

Six members of the Court of Appeals dissented from the failure to grant rehearing en banc. 89 F.3d 1169 (1996). In their view, a testamentary transfer of an interest in undistributed retirement benefits frustrates ERISA's goals of securing national uniformity in pension plan administration and of ensuring that retirees, and their dependents, are the actual recipients of retirement income. They believed that Congress' creation of the qualified domestic relations order (QDRO) mechanism in § 1056(d)(3), whose requirements were not met by the 1980 judgment of possession, further supported their position. (A QDRO is a limited exception to the pension plan anti-alienation provision and allows courts to recognize a nonparticipant spouse's community property interest in pension plans under specific circumstances.)

The reasoning and holding of the Fifth Circuit's decision is in substantial conflict with the decision of the Court of Appeals for the Ninth Circuit in *Ablamis v. Roper*, 937 F.2d 1450 (1991), which held that ERISA pre-empts a testamentary transfer by a nonparticipant spouse of her community property interest in undistributed pension plan benefits. The division between the Circuits is significant, for the Fifth Circuit has jurisdiction over the community property States of Louisiana and Texas, while the Ninth Circuit includes the community property States of Arizona, California, Idaho, Nevada, and Washington. Having granted certiorari to resolve the issue, 519 U.S. 957, 117 S.Ct. 379, 136 L.Ed.2d 297 (1996), we now reverse.

II

ERISA pre-emption questions are recurrent, two other cases on the subject having come before the Court in the current Term alone, see *California Division of Labor Standards Enforcement v. Dillingham Construction*, 519 U.S. 316, 117 S.Ct. 832, 136 L.Ed.2d 791 (1997); *De Buono v. NYSA-ILA Medical and Clinical Services Fund*, --- U.S. ----, ----, 117 S.Ct. 1747, ----, --- L.Ed.2d ---- (1997). In large part the number of ERISA pre- emption cases reflects the comprehensive nature of the statute, the centrality of pension and welfare plans in the national economy, and their importance to the financial security of the Nation's work force. ERISA is designed to ensure the proper administration of pension and welfare plans, both during the years of the employee's active service and in his or her retirement years.

This case lies at the intersection of ERISA pension law and state community property law. None can dispute the central role community property laws play in the nine community property States. It is more than a property regime. It is a commitment to the equality of husband and wife and reflects the real partnership inherent in the marital relationship. State community property laws, many of ancient lineage, "must have continued to exist through such lengths of time because of their manifold excellences and are not lightly to be abrogated or tossed aside." 1 W. de Funiak, PRINCIPLES OF COMMUNITY PROPERTY 11 (1943). The community property regime in Louisiana dates from 1808 when the territorial legislature of Orleans drafted a civil code which adopted Spanish principles of community property. *Id.,* at 85-89. Louisiana's community property laws, and the community property regimes enacted in other States, implement policies and values lying within the traditional domain of the States. These considerations inform our pre-emption analysis. *See Hisquierdo v. Hisquierdo*, 439 U.S. 572, 581, 99 S.Ct. 802, 808, 59 L.Ed.2d 1 (1979).

The nine community property States have some 80 million residents, with perhaps $1 trillion in retirement plans. *See* Brief for Estate Planning, Trust and Probate Law Section of the State Bar of California as Amicus Curiae 1. This case involves a community property claim, but our ruling will affect as well the right to make claims or assert interests based on the law of any State, whether or not it recognizes community property. Our ruling must be consistent with the congressional scheme to assure the security of plan participants and their families in every State. In enacting ERISA, Congress noted the importance of pension plans in its findings and declaration of policy, explaining:

> [T]he growth in size, scope, and numbers of employee benefit plans in recent years has been rapid and substantial; ... the continued well-being and security of millions of employees and their dependents are directly affected by these plans; ... they are affected with a national public interest [and] they have become an important factor affecting the stability of employment and the successful development of industrial relations....

29 U.S.C. § 1001(a).

13-67

ERISA is an intricate, comprehensive statute. Its federal regulatory scheme governs employee benefit plans, which include both pension and welfare plans. All employee benefit plans must conform to various reporting, disclosure and fiduciary requirements, see §§ 1021-1031, 1101-1114, while pension plans must also comply with participation, vesting, and funding requirements, see §§ 1051- 1086. The surviving spouse annuity and QDRO provisions, central to the dispute here, are part of the statute's mandatory participation and vesting requirements. These provisions provide detailed protections to spouses of plan participants which, in some cases, exceed what their rights would be were community property law the sole measure.

ERISA's express pre-emption clause states that the Act "shall supersede any and all State laws insofar as they may now or hereafter relate to any employee benefit plan ...." § 1144(a). We can begin, and in this case end, the analysis by simply asking if state law conflicts with the provisions of ERISA or operates to frustrate its objects. We hold that there is a conflict, which suffices to resolve the case. We need not inquire whether the statutory phrase "relate to" provides further and additional support for the pre-emption claim. Nor need we consider the applicability of field pre- emption, *see Fidelity Fed. Sav. & Loan Assn. v. de la Cuesta*, 458 U.S. 141, 153, 102 S.Ct. 3014, 3022, 73 L.Ed.2d 664 (1982).

We first address the survivor's annuity and then turn to the other pension benefits.

III.

Sandra Boggs, as we have observed, asserts that federal law pre-empts and supersedes state law and requires the surviving spouse annuity to be paid to her as the sole beneficiary. We agree.

The annuity at issue is a qualified joint and survivor annuity mandated by ERISA. Section 1055(a) provides: "Each pension plan to which this section applies shall provide that--(1) in the case of a vested participant who does not die before the annuity starting date, the accrued benefit payable to such participant shall be provided in the form of a qualified joint and survivor annuity."

ERISA requires that every qualified joint and survivor annuity include an annuity payable to a nonparticipant surviving spouse. The survivor's annuity may not be less than 50% of the amount of the annuity which is payable during the joint lives of the participant and spouse. § 1055(d)(1). Provision of the survivor's annuity may not be waived by the participant, absent certain limited circumstances, unless the spouse consents in writing to the designation of another beneficiary, which designation also cannot be changed without further spousal consent, witnessed by a plan representative or notary public. § 1055(c)(2). Sandra Boggs, as the surviving spouse, is entitled to a survivor's annuity under these provisions. She has not waived her right to the survivor's annuity, let alone consented to having the sons designated as the beneficiaries.

Respondents say their state-law claims are consistent with these provisions. Their claims, they argue, affect only the disposition of plan proceeds after they have been disbursed by the Bell South Service Retirement Program, and thus nothing is required of the plan. ERISA's concern for securing national uniformity in the administration of employee benefit plans, in their view, is not implicated. They argue Sandra's community property obligations, after she receives the survivor annuity payments, "fai[l] to implicate the regulatory concerns of ERISA." *Fort Halifax Packing Co. v. Coyne*, 482 U.S. 1, 15, 107 S.Ct. 2211, 2219, 96 L.Ed.2d 1 (1987).

We disagree. The statutory object of the qualified joint and survivor annuity provisions, along with the rest of § 1055, is to ensure a stream of income to surviving spouses. Section 1055 mandates a survivor's annuity not only where a participant dies after the annuity starting date but also guarantees one if the participant dies before then. *See* §§ 1055(a) (2), (e). These provisions, enacted as part of the Retirement Equity Act of 1984 (REA), Pub.L. 98-397, 98 Stat. 1426, enlarged ERISA's protection of surviving spouses in significant respects. Before REA, ERISA only required that pension plans, if they provided for the payment of benefits in the form of an annuity, offer a qualified joint and survivor annuity as an option entirely within a participant's discretion. 29 U.S.C. §§ 1055(a), (e) (1982 ed.). REA modified ERISA to permit participants to designate a beneficiary for the survivor's annuity, other than the nonparticipant spouse, only when the spouse agrees. § 1055(c)(2). Congress' concern for surviving spouses is also evident from the expansive coverage of § 1055, as amended by REA. Section 1055's requirements, as a general matter, apply to all "individual account plans" and "defined benefit plans." § 1055(b)(1). The terms are defined, for § 1055 purposes, so that all pension plans fall within those two categories. *See* § 1002(35). While some individual account plans escape § 1055's surviving spouse annuity requirements under certain conditions, Congress still protects the interests of the surviving spouse by requiring those plans to pay the spouse the nonforfeitable accrued benefits, reduced by certain security interests, in a lump-sum payment. § 1055(b)(1)(C).

ERISA's solicitude for the economic security of surviving spouses would be undermined by allowing a predeceasing spouse's heirs and legatees to have a community property interest in the survivor's annuity. Even a plan participant cannot defeat a nonparticipant surviving spouse's statutory entitlement to an annuity. It would be odd, to say the least, if Congress permitted a predeceasing nonparticipant spouse to do so. Nothing in the language of ERISA supports concluding that Congress made such an inexplicable decision. Testamentary transfers could reduce a surviving spouse's guaranteed annuity below the minimum set by ERISA (defined as 50% of the annuity payable during the joint lives of the participant and spouse). In this case, Sandra's annuity would be reduced by approximately 20%, according to the calculations contained in the sons' state-court filings. There is no reason why testamentary transfers could not reduce a survivor's annuity by an even greater amount. Perhaps even more troubling, the recipient of the testamentary transfer need not be a family member. For instance, a surviving spouse's § 1055 annuity might be substantially reduced so that funds could be diverted to support an unrelated stranger.

In the face of this direct clash between state law and the provisions and objectives of ERISA, the state law cannot stand. Conventional conflict pre-emption principles require pre-emption "where compliance with both federal and state regulations is a physical impossibility, ... or where state law stands as an obstacle to the accomplishment and execution of the full purposes and objectives of Congress." *Gade v. National Solid Wastes Management Assn.*, 505 U.S. 88, 98, 112 S.Ct. 2374, 2383, 120 L.Ed.2d 73 (1992) (internal quotation marks and citation omitted). It would undermine the purpose of ERISA's mandated survivor's annuity to allow Dorothy, the predeceasing spouse, by her testamentary transfer to defeat in part Sandra's entitlement to the annuity § 1055 guarantees her as the surviving spouse. This cannot be. States are not free to change ERISA's structure and balance.

Louisiana law, to the extent it provides the sons with a right to a portion of Sandra Boggs' § 1055 survivor's annuity, is pre-empted.

IV.

Beyond seeking a portion of the survivor's annuity, respondents claim a percentage of: the monthly annuity payments made to Isaac Boggs during his retirement; the IRA; and the

ESOP shares of AT & T stock. As before, the claim is based on Dorothy Boggs' attempted testamentary transfer to the sons of her community interest in Isaac's undistributed pension plan benefits. Respondents argue further--and somewhat inconsistently--that their claim again concerns only what a plan participant or beneficiary may do once plan funds are distributed, without imposing any obligations on the plan itself. Both parties agree that the ERISA benefits at issue here were paid after Dorothy's death, and thus this case does not present the question whether ERISA would permit a nonparticipant spouse to obtain a devisable community property interest in benefits paid out during the existence of the community between the participant and that spouse.

A brief overview of ERISA's design is necessary to put respondents' contentions in the proper context. The principal object of the statute is to protect plan participants and beneficiaries. *See Shaw v. Delta Air Lines, Inc.*, 463 U.S. 85, 90, 103 S.Ct. 2890, 2896, 77 L.Ed.2d 490 (1983) ("ERISA is a comprehensive statute designed to promote the interests of employees and their beneficiaries in employee benefit plans"). Section 1001(b) states that the policy of ERISA is "to protect ... the interests of participants in employee benefit plans and their beneficiaries." Section 1001(c) explains that ERISA contains certain safeguards and protections which help guarantee the "equitable character and the soundness of [private pension] plans" in order to protect "the interests of participants in private pension plans and their beneficiaries." The general policy is implemented by ERISA's specific provisions. Apart from a few enumerated exceptions, a plan fiduciary must "discharge his duties with respect to a plan solely in the interest of the participants and beneficiaries." § 1104(a)(1). The assets of a plan, again with certain exceptions, are "held for the exclusive purposes of providing benefits to participants in the plan and their beneficiaries and defraying reasonable expenses of administering the plan." § 1103(c) (1). The Secretary of Labor has authority to create exemptions to ERISA's prohibition on certain plan holdings, acquisitions, and transactions, but only if doing so is in the interests of the plan's "participants and beneficiaries." § 1108(a)(2). Persons with an interest in a pension plan may bring a civil suit under ERISA's enforcement provisions only if they are either a participant or beneficiary. Section 1132(a)(1)(B), for instance, provides that a civil action may be brought "by a participant or beneficiary ... to recover benefits due to him under the terms of his plan, to enforce his rights under the terms of the plan, or to clarify his rights to future benefits under the terms of the plan."

ERISA confers beneficiary status on a nonparticipant spouse or dependent in only narrow circumstances delineated by its provisions. For example, as we have discussed, § 1055(a) requires provision of a surviving spouse annuity in covered pension plans, and, as a consequence the spouse is a beneficiary to this extent. Section 1056's QDRO provisions likewise recognize certain pension plan community property interests of nonparticipant spouses and dependents. A QDRO is a type of domestic relations order which creates or recognizes an alternate payee's right to, or assigns to an alternate payee the right to, a portion of the benefits payable with respect to a participant under a plan. § 1056(d)(3)(B)(i). A domestic relations order, in turn, is any judgment, decree, or order that concerns "the provision of child support, alimony payments, or marital property rights to a spouse, former spouse, child, or other dependent of a participant" and is "made pursuant to a State domestic relations law (including a community property law)." § 1056(d)(3)(B)(ii). A domestic relations order must meet certain requirements to qualify as a QDRO. *See* §§ 1056(d)(3)(C)-(E). QDRO's, unlike domestic relations orders in general, are exempt from both the pension plan anti-alienation provision, § 1056(d)(3)(A), and ERISA's general pre-emption clause, § 1144(b)(7). In creating the QDRO mechanism Congress was careful to provide that the alternate payee, the "spouse, former spouse, child, or other dependent of a participant," is to be considered a plan beneficiary. §§ 1056(d)(3)(K), (J). These provisions are essential to one of REA's central purposes, which is to give enhanced protection to the spouse and dependent children in the event of divorce or separation, and in the event of death of the surviving spouse. Apart from these detailed provisions, ERISA does not confer beneficiary status on nonparticipants by reason of their marital or dependent status.

Even outside the pension plan context and its anti-alienation restriction, Congress deemed it necessary to enact detailed provisions in order to protect a dependent's interest in a welfare benefit plan. Through a § 1169 "qualified medical child support order" a child's interest in his or her parent's group health care plan can be enforced. A "medical child support order" is defined as any judgment, decree, or order that concerns the provision of child support "made pursuant to a State domestic relations law (including a community property law) and relates to benefits under such plan." § 1169(a)(2)(B)(i). As with a QDRO, a "medical child support order" must satisfy certain criteria in order to qualify. See §§ 1169(a)(3)-(4). In accordance with ERISA's care in conforming entitlements to benefits with participant or beneficiary status, the statute treats a child subject to such a qualifying order as a participant for ERISA's reporting and disclosure requirements and as a beneficiary for other purposes. § 1169(a)(7).

The surviving spouse annuity and QDRO provisions, which acknowledge and protect specific pension plan community property interests, give rise to the strong implication that other community property claims are not consistent with the statutory scheme. ERISA's silence with respect to the right of a nonparticipant spouse to control pension plan benefits by testamentary transfer provides powerful support for the conclusion that the right does not exist. *Cf. Massachusetts Mut. Life Ins. Co. v. Russell*, 473 U.S. 134, 147-148, 105 S.Ct. 3085, 3092-3093, 87 L.Ed.2d 96 (1985). It should cause little surprise that Congress chose to protect the community property interests of separated and divorced spouses and their children, a traditional subject of domestic relations law, but not to accommodate testamentary transfers of pension plan benefits. As a general matter, "[t]he whole subject of the domestic relations of husband and wife, parent and child, belongs to the laws of the States and not to the laws of the United States." *In re Burrus*, 136 U.S. 586, 593-594, 10 S.Ct. 850, 853, 34 L.Ed. 500 (1890). Support obligations, in particular, are "deeply rooted moral responsibilities" that Congress is unlikely to have intended to intrude upon. *See Rose v. Rose*, 481 U.S. 619, 632, 107 S.Ct. 2029, 2037, 95 L.Ed.2d 599 (1987); *see also id.*, at 636-640, 107 S.Ct., at 2039-2041 (O'CONNOR, J., concurring). In accord with these principles, Congress ensured that state domestic relations orders, as long as they meet certain statutory requirements, are not pre-empted.

We conclude the sons have no claim under ERISA to a share of the retirement benefits. To begin with, the sons are neither participants nor beneficiaries. A "participant" is defined as an "employee or former employee of an employer, or any member or former member of an employee organization, who is or may become eligible to receive a benefit." § 1002(7). A "beneficiary" is a "person designated by a participant, or by the terms of an employee benefit plan, who is or may become entitled to a benefit thereunder." § 1002(8). Respondents' claims are based on Dorothy Boggs' attempted testamentary transfer, not on a designation by Isaac Boggs or under the terms of the retirement plans. They do not even attempt to argue that they are beneficiaries by virtue of the judgment of possession qualifying as a QDRO.

*   *   *

Reversed.

NOTE

Compare La. R.S. 9:2801.1: How is the statute reconcilable with *Boggs*?

PROBLEM

As illustrated by the various types of assets presented above, one has many options in using these tools to his benefit in planning his estate. Due to the differing natures of the devices with regard to payment, tax benefits, and other considerations, one instrument may preferable to another in achieving a desired result.

Consider the following:

George, a widower, has the following assets:
1) A house valued at $200,000
2) An auto, household contents, and personal effects valued at $50,000
3) A life insurance policy with a payable-on-death value of $100,000
4) A 401 K (ERISA) plan valued at $100,000
5) Savings bonds valued at $50,000 and a bank account with a balance of $100,000.

Assume George would like to leave as much as possible to his daughter Mary who is a forced heir and as little as possible to his other forced heir, his daughter Jane.

Determine which assets must be included in the fictitious collation to determine the amount of the forced portion. Suppose he wants to leave his house auto, household contents personal effects pension plan, savings bonds and bank account all to Mary? Is that possible? How?

Acceptance

A donation is not effective until it is accepted by the donee. Acceptance may be made in the act of donation, in a subsequent writing, or, in the case of corporeal movables, by mere possession by the donee. In any event, acceptance must be made during the lifetime of the donor, La. C.C. 1544, and the donee. La. C.C. 1546. The donee may accept personally or by a mandatary, La. C.C. 1545, but creditors of the donee may not accept on his behalf. In the case of an unemancipated minor, acceptance by a parent, other ascendant or tutor, is allowable, even if the person who accepts is also the donor. La. C.C. 1548. All charges that a donor has imposed on the thing donated remain and the donee acquires the thing subject to them, even those imposed between the time of the donation and the time of the acceptance. La.C.C. 1549.

WIEDEMANN v. WIEDEMANN
30 So. 3d 972 (La. App. 5th Cir. 2009), *writ denied*, 31 So. 3d 390 (La. 2010)

This is a suit to partition property. At issue here is the validity of an act of donation of immovable property in authentic form made by a then husband to his then wife. The trial judge found that the donee had not signed the act prior to the signing by the witnesses and notary, and entered partial summary judgment declaring the act a nullity, relying on *Zamjahn v. Zamjahn,* 02-871 (La.App. 5 Cir. 1/28/03), 839 So. 2d 309. For the following reasons we reverse that judgment.

*   *   *

We first note that donations inter vivos consist of two parts: the donation and the acceptance. Article 1541 (prior Art. 1536) of the LA. CIV.CODE provides that donations inter vivos "shall be made by authentic act under penalty of absolute nullity...." La. C.C. Art. 1544 (prior Art. 1540) now provides that the acceptance shall be made during the lifetime of the donor and "may be made in the act of donation or subsequently *in writing*" (emphasis added). La. C.C. Art. 1833 defines an authentic act as one executed in the presence of a notary and two witnesses and signed by the parties and the notary and witnesses. La. C.C. Art. 1835 states that an authentic act constitutes full proof as between the parties. Finally, La. C.C. Art. 1848 provides that testimonial or other evidence may not be admitted to negate or vary the contents of an authentic act except to show vices of consent, simulation or to prove modification by later agreement. The jurisprudence interpreting this article has also permitted such evidence to show error, fraud or duress. (See "Revision Comments-1984," to this article).

In the present case, the act of donation produced by the donee recites that it was executed in the presence of the notary and two witnesses and shows that it was signed by the parties and the notary and witnesses. It further recites that the donation was accepted by the donee. The donor attacked the validity of this act by offering the deposition testimony of the notary (given two years after the act was passed) to the effect that the donor, one witness, and she, the notary, signed the act at one time, but she had no recollection of when the second witness and the donee signed. The donor at first stated that he signed the document in the presence of both witnesses and the notary, but later said that he had no clear recollection of the events. He also introduced a purported copy of the last page of the act which shows the signatures of the donor, the two witnesses and the notary, but not that of the donee. This document was found in a file, but no one had any recollection of how or by whom it came to be made. The donee recalled that the parties, the witnesses and the notary were all together at a table when the document was signed, but could not recall specifically in what order the signatures were affixed. The two witnesses had no recollection of what transpired at the signing.

On the basis of the above evidence the trial judge found that the acceptance was invalid because the donee signed the act after the witnesses and the notary had done so. We hold that this was error for two reasons.

First, authentic acts are presumed to be valid and a party asserting otherwise must present strong and convincing proof of such magnitude as to overcome this presumption. *Meltzer v. Meltzer,* 95-0551, 95-0552 (La.App. 4 Cir. 9/2/95), 662 So. 2d 58, *writ denied* 95-2616 (La.1/5/96), 666 So. 2d 293. This is especially true when the passage of time has blurred memories. *Id.* Here the memories of the notary and the donee are in substantial disagreement, the witnesses are unable to recall anything, and the donor at first contradicted the notary in asserting that he signed in the presence of both witnesses. As to the purported copy of the document found in a file, there was no indication of how it came into existence. Considering all of the contradictions and uncertainties raised by the evidence presented, we hold that there was no showing by strong and convincing proof to overcome the presumption that the act is valid.

Second, effective January 1, 2009, prior Civil Code Art. 1540, which provided that acceptance had to be by authentic act, was amended and renumbered 1544, to provide that acceptance only need be in writing. Article 6 of the Civil Code provides that procedural laws apply both prospectively and retroactively, while substantive laws apply only prospectively. The issue here is thus whether that amendment is procedural or substantive. That section of the code relating to various acts is titled "Proof of Obligations." As such, these articles do not create obligations, but rather only define what level of proof is required to prove the existence of obligations. Similarly, the articles dealing with the forms required for gifts relate to proving that a gift has taken place. These are therefore procedural laws and are to be given retroactive effect. That being the case, we hold that the donee's signature on the act of donation is a sufficient writing to perfect the acceptance in accordance with present Art. 1544.

For the foregoing reasons, the judgment holding that the act of donation is a nullity is reversed and that act is hereby ruled to be valid. The matter is remanded to the district court for further proceedings consistent with this opinion.

JUDGMENT VACATED, REMANDED.

DUPRE v. FOGLEMAN
2015-47 (La. App. 3 Cir. 6/3/15)

PICKETT, Judge.

Sheryl Dupre Fogleman appeals the judgment of the trial court finding that two acts of donation from her parents to her are nullities.

STATEMENT OF THE CASE

In 1989, Mrs. Fogleman's father, John B. Dupre, had a debilitating stroke. His medical care was very expensive. On September 12, 1989, in an effort to prevent their creditors, including the Lafayette General Hospital, from seizing the land on which their home was situated, Mr. Dupre and his wife Dorothy executed an act of donation transferring a thirty-acre tract of land and an adjacent 13.06–acre tract of land to Mrs. Fogleman. In a separate act of donation, they transferred the mineral rights of those tracts to Mrs. Fogleman. Mrs. Fogleman filed the acts of donation in the St. Landry Parish public records. On the same date, Mr. and Mrs. Dupre allegedly also executed a counter letter indicating they wished the property subject to the donation to Mrs. Fogleman be divided equally between their four children, Mrs. Fogleman, John Barney Dupre, Jeff Bradley Dupre, and Benjamin Carol Dupre. On September 15, 1989, in a separate act of donation, Mrs. Dupre donated to Mrs. Fogleman her separate 1/6th interest in a twenty-seven-acre tract of land in Evangeline Parish.

Mr. Dupre died in 2002. Mrs. Fogleman purported to execute various transfers of title of the property to her husband, her mother, and her brother Jeff. Mrs. Fogleman paid the property taxes on the property. When Mrs. Dupre became ill, Jeff, who was living on the 13.06–acre tract of land, and Mrs. Fogleman had disagreements over her care. On December 5, 2013, Mrs. Dupre, her three sons, and the Estate of Mr. Dupre, represented by Jeff as administrator, filed a Petition for Declaratory Judgment seeking to nullify the donations to Mrs. Fogleman. They alleged that (1) the donations were invalid because they were simulations, as evidenced by the counter letter; (2) Mrs. Fogleman never accepted the donations by authentic act or by taking possession of the property; (3) Mrs. Fogleman acted in violation of the counter letter; (4) by donating the property, Mr. and Mrs. Dupre lacked sufficient resources to provide for their sustenance, making the donations null and void as they were donations omnium bonorum; or (5) Mr. and Mrs. Dupre lacked capacity to understand the legal effect of the donations. Mrs. Fogleman filed an exception of prescription.

Following a bench trial, the court ruled that Mrs. Fogleman never accepted the donations in the manner required by La. Civ. Code art. 1544, thus the donations were nullities and Mrs. Dupre and the Estate of Mr. Dupre were the true owners of the property. The trial court denied Mrs. Fogleman's exception of prescription. Mrs. Fogleman now appeals.

ASSIGNMENTS OF ERROR

Mrs. Fogleman alleges two assignments of error:

1. The trial court committed manifest error in finding that the two donations made by the parties were null and void because: (A) Sheryl Fogleman never accepted the donation, and (B) the counter agreements reflected the clear intent of the parties that all the children would inherit their parents' property in equal shares and therefore it was an absolute simulation and the donations had no effects between the parties.
2. The court erred in nullifying the donation from Mrs. Dupre to Sheryl Fogleman of her 1/6th interest in the twenty-seven acres in Evangeline Parish, as it never held that the donation was invalid in its reasons for judgment, yet gave it back to Mrs. Dupre in the judgment.

DISCUSSION

An appellate court may not set aside the trial court's findings of fact unless it finds manifest error. *Rosell v. ESCO*, 549 So. 2d 840 (La.1989). The only issue presented here is whether Mrs. Fogleman accepted the donations from Mr. and Mrs. Dupre. We must determine whether the trial court erred in finding that Mrs. Fogleman's actions did not constitute an acceptance as required by the Civil Code.

When the donations at issue were executed in 1989, La.Civ.Code art. 1540 stated:

A donation *inter vivos* shall be binding on the donor, and shall produce effect only from the day of its being accepted in precise terms.
The acceptance may be made during the lifetime of the donor by a posterior and authentic act, but in that case the donation shall have effect, with regard to the donor, only from the day of being notified of the act establishing that acceptance.

Civil Code Article 1541 provided for acceptance by possession: "Yet, if the donation has been executed, that is, if the donee has been put by the donor in corporeal possession of the effects given, the donation, though not accepted in precise terms, has full effect."

Civil Code Article 1554 required that the acceptance of a donation of immovable property be recorded: "When the donation comprehends immovable or rights thereto, the act of donation, as well as the act of acceptance, whether the acceptance be made by the same or a separate act, must be registered within the time prescribed for the registry of mortgages in the register of conveyances of the parish in which the immovable is situated."

The Civil Code articles regarding donations were revised in 2008 by 2008 La. Acts No. 204, effective January 1, 2009. The current relevant code article, cited by the trial court in its reasons for ruling, is La. Civ. Code art. 1544, which states:

> A donation inter vivos is without effect until it is accepted by the donee. The acceptance shall be made during the lifetime of the donor.
> The acceptance of a donation may be made in the act of donation or subsequently in writing.
> When the donee is put into corporeal possession of a movable by the donor, possession by the donee also constitutes acceptance of the donation.

The revisions did not change the law in any respect relevant to the case before us.

The three acts of donation transferring property from Mr. and Mrs. Dupre to Mrs. Fogleman, including the donation of Mrs. Dupre's separate property in Evangeline Parish, were placed in the record. They do not include language whereby Mrs. Fogleman accepts the donations. Mrs. Fogleman did not produce any authentic act whereby she, as donee, accepted the donations of the immovable property as required by the Civil Code. Her testimony that she filed the acts of donation at the clerk's office and paid taxes on the property is insufficient to meet the legal requirement for accepting a donation of immovable property. The trial court also specifically found that Mrs. Fogelman sent her brothers the counter letter evidencing her parents' intent to apportion the property equally among their four children. She did attempt to introduce documents evidencing her acceptance of the property executed the day of the trial, but the trial court properly ruled them inadmissible.

The trial court did not err in finding that the donations to Mrs. Fogleman never took effect and in declaring Mrs. Dupre and Mr. Dupre's heirs as the rightful owners of the property. We find of no consequence that the thorough reasons for ruling issued by the trial court do not mention the property in Evangeline Parish. It is axiomatic that where the judgment and the reasons for judgment differ, the judgment controls. *Moss v. Coury,* 97–640 (La.App. 3 Cir. 12/10/97), 704 So. 2d 1248, *writ denied,* 98–783 (La.5/29/98), 720 So. 2d 340. There is sufficient evidence in the record to support the trial court's ruling that the donation of property in Evangeline Parish had no legal effect because Mrs. Fogleman never accepted the donation.

CONCLUSION

The judgment of the trial court is affirmed. Costs of this appeal are assessed to Sheryl Dupre Fogleman.

AFFIRMED.

Revocation

Donations *inter vivos* may be:
1) Revoked due to ingratitude of the donee
2) Dissolved to due nonfulfillment of a suspensive condition or occurrence of a resolutory condition
3) Dissolved for nonperformance of other conditions or charges. La. C.C. 1556.

Causes for ingratitude include:
1) If the donee has attempted to take the life of the donor
2) If the donee has been guilty toward the donor of cruel treatment, crimes or grievous injuries. La. C.C. 1557.

An action for revocation for ingratitude prescribes one year from the time the donor knew, or should have known, of the act of ingratitude. If the donor dies within the one year period, his successors may bring the action for revocation, within the remaining time limit. If the donor died without having known of the act, then the successors have one year from the death of the donor to bring the act. Further, an action already brought by the donor may be pursued by his successors. If the donee is deceased, the donors may bring an action against his successors to revoke the donation. La. C.C. 1558.

Revocation for ingratitude does not affect any alienation, lease, or encumbrance made by the donee before the filing of the action to revoke. After the filing of the action for revocation, different rules apply as to movables and immovables. For movables, the alienation, lease, or encumbrance is still effective against the donor only when onerous and made in good faith by the transferee, lessee, or creditor. As to immovables, the laws of registry apply. La. C.C. 1559. When a donation is revoked for ingratitude, the donee must return the gift, or, if he cannot do so, he must restore its value as of the date the action for revocation was filed. La. C.C. 1560.

When a donation is dissolved due to the fact that a suspensive condition cannot be fulfilled, the dissolution takes place of right as soon as the condition cannot be fulfilled. However, in the case of dissolution due to the occurrence of a resolutory condition, dissolution takes place only by consent of the parties or by judicial decree. La. C.C. 1562. The latter rule also applies in the case of a condition that the donee has the power to perform or prevent. La. C.C. 1563. Dissolution for failure to fulfill conditions or perform charges prescribes in five years, starting on the day the donee fails to perform or fulfill the conditions. La. C.C. 1563. If the property donated was an immovable, it returns to the donor free from all alienation, lease, or encumbrance, subject to the law of registry. If it cannot be returned free of alienation, lease, or encumbrance, the donee is still accountable for diminution of value. Otherwise it must be restored at the value it was at the time of the filing of the action to dissolve. As to movables, an alienation, lease, or encumbrance is effective against the donee only when it is onerous and made in good faith by the transferee, lessee, or creditor. La. C.C. 1565.

Fruits and products of the donated items are due as of the date of written demand. In the case of dissolution for nonperformance, the court may order the donee to restore the value of fruits or products from the time the donee failed to perform if the failure was due to his fault. La. C.C. 1566.

In cases where a donee cannot restore the thing in the condition it was in at the time of donation, the donor may accept it as is and hold the donee accountable for the diminution in value at the time of delivery. La. C.C. 1567.

WHITMAN v. WHITMAN
730 So. 2d 1048 (La. App. 2nd Cir. 1999)

DREW, J.

William Newell Whitman appeals the judgment revoking two donations made to him by his former wife during their marriage. Arguing that the transactions were onerous donations and that he fulfilled the obligations imposed by the donations, Mr. Whitman contends that the trial court erred in finding that the property transfers were gratuitous donations and subject to revocation for ingratitude. The judgment of the trial court is hereby affirmed.

FACTS

On June 10, 1997, Marilyn Mann Whitman sued Mr. Whitman for divorce based upon his alleged adultery on June 7, 1997. The couple married in 1981 and had no children. In addition to the divorce, Mrs. Whitman requested that the court revoke for ingratitude a donation she made to Mr. Whitman on December 31, 1985 of her one-half interest in immovable property. On August 21, 1997, the trial court signed a divorce judgment in favor of Mrs. Whitman. In addition to prohibiting Mr. Whitman from physically or mentally threatening or harming Mrs. Whitman and enjoining both parties from disposing of community property, the judgment set remaining issues to be heard September 30, 1997. On August 26, 1997, Mrs. Whitman filed an amended petition which sought annulment of a second donation she made on August 28, 1981 to Mr. Whitman.

When the hearing on the donations commenced, Mr. Whitman had not answered the amended petition. The parties stipulated that Mr. Whitman made a general denial. The August 28, 1981 and the December 31, 1985 donations, along with the testimony and pleadings relative to the divorce, were placed into evidence without objection.

Shortly after their 1981 wedding, Mrs. Whitman donated to her husband a one- half interest in an acre tract on which their home was later built. On cross- examination, she acknowledged that her brother had transferred to her another acre of land adjacent to the property involved in the 1981 donation. In 1991, she also received another piece of contiguous property from her McKeithen cousins. Mrs. Whitman did not know if her husband was included on either the deed from her brother or the donation from the McKeithens. Mrs. Whitman testified she and Mr. Whitman had mortgaged the one-acre tract on two occasions and later paid off the loans.

Mrs. Whitman owned an undivided one-half interest of a 1/32 interest in a much larger tract, which fractional interest she had acquired from her mother. She owned an undivided 300-acre interest in the property in which a number of persons had ownership interests. In 1985, she donated to Mr. Whitman one-half of her undivided interest in that farm and timber land. She and her brother, George Allen Mann, had obtained the property from their mother in a transaction which Mrs. Whitman characterized as estate planning. Although Mrs. Whitman was unsure whether the transaction was a credit sale, whether they made yearly payments and whether the debt had been paid off, Mrs. Whitman acknowledged on cross-examination there was a credit sale deed from her mother and a note that was ultimately canceled. Although the note was canceled in 1990, she denied it had been paid off.

When asked whether yearly payments were made to her mother through rents and royalties, Mrs. Whitman responded "Not really. No." She explained that money given to her mother was always given back to them plus much more. In her view, payments were not made because they were given back to her and Mr. Whitman. She did not know if the payments were considered payments on the large tract and stated: "I mean, it was just a way to get around paying inheritance tax. There was never any actual exchange of money, because they simply gave it back to us. If you're alleging that my husband paid money to my mother, that's ludicrous."

She also acknowledged that the couple initially made payments with community funds to her mother pursuant to the credit sale arrangement. Concerning the 300-acre property interest, Mrs. Whitman did not recall discussing with Mr. Whitman the indebtedness related to the property and did not recall if the document specified the donation was to be irrevocable.

After the couple separated, she learned that Mr. Whitman was involved with another woman, news that was very embarrassing and which made her physically ill. Following Mrs. Whitman's testimony, plaintiff's attorney stated they had made a prima facie case for annulment of the donations and rested.

Mr. Whitman's first witness, Iley Evans, was accepted as an expert in abstracting, title examination and Caldwell Parish law practice. Evans testified that the August 28, 1981 donation from Mrs. Whitman to her husband of one acre contained only one condition; i.e., if Mr. Whitman predeceased Mrs. Whitman, the property returned to Mrs. Whitman, a resolutory condition.

In a related transaction, an April 10, 1984 cash sale deed (Caldwell Parish No. 155091, Con. Bk.148, p. 114) from George Allen Mann and Sonia Dugose Mann conveyed an adjacent one-acre tract to Mr. and Mrs. Whitman. Contiguous to the one-acre tract in the 1991 donation and the one acre conveyed to the Whitmans by the Manns in 1984 was a .7-acre tract donated (Caldwell Parish No. 172095, Con. Bk. 174, p. 427) to Mr. and Mrs. Whitman by the McKeithen trust on August 16, 1991. The acre donated in 1981 to Mr. Whitman and the two subsequent transfers of adjacent property to the couple comprised the tract on which the couple's home was located. Evans' search of the records revealed two mortgages executed by Mr. and Mrs. Whitman, one for $2,500, dated January 6, 1994, and the other for $25,000, dated June 6, 1984, on the tract where their home was located.

Concerning the December 31, 1985 donation (Caldwell Parish No. 160138, Con. Bk. 154, p. 449) from Mrs. Whitman to Mr. Whitman, Evans testified the instrument donated one-half of her one-half undivided interest in a large tract known at that time as the G.L. Shipp estate. The donation referred to a mortgage (Caldwell Parish No. 141123, Con. Bk. 130, p. 77; Mtg. Bk. 93, p. 380) and stated that Mrs. Whitman intended to donate to Mr. Whitman one-half of her undivided one-half of the 1/32 interest she acquired from her mother, Mary Alice Shipp Mann, on October 20, 1978 by credit deed. Evans described the October 20, 1978 transfer by credit deed from Mary Alice Shipp Mann to her two children, George Allen Mann and Mrs. Whitman (then Marilyn Shipp Dunn, a single woman). The purchase price was $360,000, at 6% interest, payable in 30 equal installments of $12,000. The note was canceled July 5, 1990 (Mtg. Bk. 93, p. 380).

Two subsequent partitions, both recorded May 31, 1988, dealt with that property. The Partition of the Patton Place (No. 165553 in Con. Bk. 163, p. 81) and the Partition of the G.L. Shipp Properties (No. 165554, Con. Bk. 163, p. 93) transferred property among the various owners in indivision. As a result, Mr. and Mrs. Whitman received three tracts which totaled approximately 300 acres in full ownership. Subsequently, Mr. and Mrs. Whitman and others and the Citizen's Progressive Bank made ratifications of the partition.

Mr. Whitman testified the couple constructed a home on the acre donated to him in 1981 by his wife. The two subsequent acquisitions of adjacent property were made in both their names. While they initially used savings and timber cut off the property to finance the construction, in 1984 or 1985, the couple borrowed $25,000 which they repaid to Caldwell Bank in 1987. They also borrowed and repaid a $2,500 loan.

* * *

In written reasons signed April 28, 1998, the trial court noted that the divorce was granted on grounds of adultery. The trial judge found that Mrs. Whitman had met her burden of proof in establishing that she was entitled to revoke the *inter vivos* donations based upon ingratitude. La. C.C. art. 1560(2). On May 12, 1998, Judge Joyce signed the judgment annulling the two donations from Mrs. Whitman to Mr. Whitman. Mr. Whitman suspensively appealed.

DISCUSSION

La. C.C. art. 1559(1) provides that a donation *inter vivos* may be revoked on account of ingratitude of the donee. Ingratitude can take place only in three cases: (1) if the donee has attempted to take the life of the donor, (2) the donee has been guilty of cruel treatment, crimes or grievous injuries against the donor, or (3) the donee has refused the donor food when the donor was in distress. La. C.C. art. 1560. [*See La. C.C. 1557 as enacted by Act No. 204, § 1 of 2008]*[*]. Only art. 1560(2) has any application to this dispute. A revocation for ingratitude must be brought within one year from the act of ingratitude or from the day the act was made known to the donor. La. C.C. art. 1561. Revocations based on ingratitude do not affect any alienation or mortgages made by the donee or any real encumbrances the donee placed upon the thing provided those transactions occurred before the filing of the suit for revocation. La. C.C. art. 1562. When a donation is revoked for ingratitude, the donee is obligated to restore to the donor the value of the thing given, estimating the value according to its worth at the time the action for revocation is brought and the fruits from the day it is brought. La. C.C. art. 1563. [*See La. C.C. 1557-1560, as enacted by Act No., 204, § 1 of 2008]*[*].

Onerous and remunerative donations are not real donations. The rules peculiar to donations *inter vivos* do not apply. Rules restricting the causes for revocations of a donation *inter vivos* apply only to purely gratuitous donations and not to onerous or remunerative donations. *Mobley v. Lee*, 318 So. 2d 631 (La.App. 3d Cir.1975).

First, Mr. Whitman asserts that the trial court erred in concluding that the donations were gratuitous and, therefore, subject to revocation for ingratitude. Appellant argues that the 1981 donation of one-half interest in a one-acre parcel plus a right of way was an onerous donation. Relying on his own testimony, Mr. Whitman asserts he agreed to build a home on the property in exchange for the donation and that he fulfilled the charge on the donation by building a 2,500 square foot home on the property. Except for the resolutory condition, the 1981 donation did not contain any kind of charge or obligation on Mr. Whitman. While Mr. Whitman's testimony was that the couple built a home on the property, there is no testimony that he was required to do so.

According to Mr. Whitman, the 1985 donation for the undivided interest in the large tract was subject to charges; i.e., his agreements to pay the installment notes on the mortgage on the property and to pay for the education costs for Mrs. Whitman's children from a previous marriage. Included in the education obligation was boarding school for Mrs. Whitman's daughter at $1,100 per month and college for both her son and daughter. According to appellant,

---

[*] Bracketed material in italics added by author.

[*] *Id.*

the credit deed introduced into evidence indicated the onerous nature of the 1985 donation which he contends he paid off in 1990. Notwithstanding Mr. Whitman's contention that his acceptance of the donation was subject to the terms in the document, the irrevocable donation states that "Said donee does hereby accept this donation with gratitude, and acknowledges delivery and possession of same." The donation simply identified the property donated by Mrs. Whitman as property "that she acquired from her mother, Mary Alice Shipp Mann, by act of credit deed sale dated October 20, 1978 and recorded November 2, 1978 and recorded in Mortgage Book 93, page 380, Conveyance Book 130, Page 77, Records of Caldwell Parish, Louisiana." The donation contains nothing indicating that Mr. Whitman personally assumed any obligation for the mortgage. His contention that he was obligated to pay the mortgage in the credit deed is belied by his testimony that he did not know if the mortgage was paid every year during the marriage. Further, the record is silent about Mr. Whitman being obligated to finance the education of Mrs. Whitman's children.

Mr. Whitman contends that the trial court erred in finding the presumption of community was rebutted through clear and convincing evidence, in finding the credit sale deed from her mother to Mrs. Whitman was a simulation, and in disregarding the doctrine of estoppel by deed. These complaints are without merit and have no application to this dispute. There is no indication that the trial court made any of those determinations. The trial court revoked the donation based upon cruel treatment of the donor by the donee who committed adultery during the marriage. The Civil Code provides that a revocation for ingratitude does not affect alienations, encumbrances or mortgages made by the donee prior to the time the suit for revocation is brought. La. C.C. art. 1563. Further, the donor's remedy when a donation is revoked for ingratitude is the restoration of the value of donation and the fruits thereof. La. C.C. art. 1563. The existence of the donations to Mr. Whitman and the subsequent transactions on the public records by the couple affecting the property are undisputed and do not hinder the donor's right to timely seek revocation for ingratitude.

Finally, Mr. Whitman contends that the trial court erred in interpreting the partition deed through aid of extrinsic evidence...

*　　*　　*

Even if evidence outside the donations were considered, the evidence presented does not support that these donations were onerous ones.

In *Mobley v. Lee, supra*, the court noted that if a donation is subject to a charge, it is not a true gratuitous donation. For an onerous or remunerative donation, the rules for interpretation of contracts would apply. If doubt arises from lack of a necessary explanation which one party should have given, then the contract is interpreted in the manner favorable to the other party. Under these circumstances, if the language of a donation was ambiguous, the ambiguity should be construed against the donor. The court found the donation made by an aunt in consideration for love and affection she had for her niece and "for her personal care" was purely gratuitous and unambiguous. The court further noted that, if "for her personal care" had been considered ambiguous, then the parol evidence at trial showed the donation was gratuitous. Because that donation was gratuitous, it could not be unilaterally revoked. Revocation required a showing of ingratitude. *Mobley v. Lee, supra*.

As purely gratuitous donations, Mrs. Whitman's gifts of land to Mr. Whitman during their marriage were subject to revocation for ingratitude. We find no palpable error in the trial court's conclusion that Mr. Whitman's adultery constituted cruel treatment and grievous injury to Mrs. Whitman. Therefore, the gratuitous donations made by her to him were revocable. Pursuant to her timely action based on his ingratitude, the donations were validly revoked. La. C.C. arts. 1559, 1560(2) and 1561.

DECREE

The judgment of the trial court is affirmed at appellant's costs.

AFFIRMED.

NOTE

In *Cotton v. Washburn*, 84 So. 2d 208 (La. 1955), just prior to his marriage, defendant purchased a home in the name of plaintiff, who was his fiancée, and himself. The vendors signed the act of sale; the vendees did not. Defendant used his own funds to pay for the home that was to become the home of his new wife and himself. After they married, the couple moved into the house, but within two years, they divorced. Defendant wanted the act of sale reformed to name only himself as owner. The court, however, found that defendant had intended to make a donation to his future wife of half the home, and she accepted through an act of corporeal possession as permitted pursuant to La. C.C. 1541. "Since the wife moved into the house, it constituted an act of corporeal possession."

PROBLEM

If donee signs an act of acceptance on December 29, but dates the act of acceptance "December 30," and donor signs on December 30 and so dates his act of donation, has there been a valid donation? *See Tweedle v. Brasseaux*, 433 So. 2d 133 (La. 1983) and La. C.C. 1544, Revision Comment – 2008, a.

NOTE

Conditional donations to religious institutions are now governed by the following:

La. R.S. 9:2321. Title quieted and perfected by lapse of time
There is hereby quieted and perfected title to real estate donated to church and religious representatives, religious associations or religious corporations, or their successors or religious assigns, where over ten years continuous and uninterrupted possession and use for the purposes intended by the donation have been had and elapsed since the date of the execution of the donation and where the real estate presently is being possessed and used for the purposes intended in the donation and where such donation is of record in the office of the clerk and recorder of the parish in which the donated property is situated.

La. R.S. 9:2322. Rights in property after perfection of title

In all cases the donees or their successors, assigns or representatives may effectively use, mortgage, hypothecate, encumber, alienate and/or dispose of the property donated or any part thereof without regard thereafter to the conditions or changes imposed in the donation, upon declaring the same to have been fully complied with to all intents and purposes by said lapse of time, possession and use in compliance with said conditions or changes, and upon declaring the public policy served thereby to be against restricting property from commerce.

PROBLEM

Decedent, Ivan, had been in an accident seven years before his death. During his convalescence, Brenda, his then girlfriend, now his wife, left her job to care for him. Ivan settled his personal injury claim for $75,000. The credit union where he did his banking did not allow accounts to exceed $30,000. When Ivan went to the credit union, he placed the funds in three separate accounts, one in the name of himself, the second in the name of himself and his wife Brenda, and the third in Brenda's name alone. Brenda took $3000 from the account in her name alone and got a facelift. Ivan knew about her surgery and where the funds were derived. Ivan and Brenda no longer live together, although they are not divorced.

Days before his death, Ivan, while in the hospital, wrote two checks. One was to his best friend Matthew for $5000. Ivan told Matthew that he was to use the funds to get Ivan an Armani suit as he wanted to leave the hospital in style. Anything left over, Matthew could keep. Matthew cashed the check, but did not have time to buy Ivan a suit because Ivan died the next day. Matthew has offered to use the funds to buy Ivan an Armani suit for his funeral.

Ivan wrote the second check to his girlfriend, Joan. When he gave Joan the check for $5000, he said that she could cash it if he died. Joan cashed the check the minute she heard that Ivan had died.

Anya, Ivan's daughter, argues that all three accounts as well as the $5000 Matthew and Joan each received, belong to her as the sole legatee in her father's will. She claims that Brenda must reimburse her father's estate for the $3000 spent on the face lift. Do you agree? What arguments can you make to demonstrate that Ivan successfully donated the funds to his wife and friends?

CHAPTER 14:
DISPOSITIONS *MORTIS CAUSA*
AND THE MARITAL PORTION
La. C.C. 1570-1616, 2432-2437

Introduction

A primary goal of the law dealing with donations *mortis causa* is to effectuate the wishes of the testator, by either: 1) promoting the intent of the testator as contained in his will; or 2) modifying his will in instances in which it is believed that the testator would have acted differently had he been aware, at the time of the execution of his will, of altered circumstances existing at the time of his death. The laws governing donations *mortis causa* were significantly modified by Act 1421 of 1997 which became effective July 1, 1999. As you read the cases to follow, consider how the result might be altered by the revised law. Do the changes "reform" the law?

Intent and Form

La. C.C. 1570 provides that "a disposition *mortis causa* may be made only in the form of a testament authorized by law." The substantive requirement that the testator possess an intent to dispose of property at death is suggested in the definition of donation *mortis causa* in La. C.C. 1469 which states that it is "an act to take effect, when the donor shall no longer exist, by which he disposes of the whole or a part of his property." If a will is in proper testamentary form and it is determined that the testator intended to make a disposition of his property, to take effect at death, "it is irrelevant that the testator may have intended it to be in a different form." La. C.C. 1570, comment b.

Testamentary Intent

Often the intent of the testator will be demonstrated by the formality of the act itself. However, where the form of the will is somewhat ambiguous as to the writer's intent, courts may look further for evidence of intent.

IN RE BILLIS' WILL
122 La. 539, 47 So. 884 (1908)

MONROE, J.

It is abundantly shown that this instrument is altogether in the handwriting of the decedent, so that the question of its sufficiency, in that respect, may be at once eliminated.

Counsel for opponents submits to this court (for the first time, there being nothing in the pleading on the subject) the proposition that, in order to establish a letter as a last will, it must appear that the writer so intended it, and he cites Demolombe, Baudry-Lacontinerie, and the Court of Cassation as supporting him. Conceding the soundness of the proposition, and taking the record as it is, we find nothing which suggests any doubt that the decedent intended the instrument here presented to take effect after his death and to operate as a final disposition, so far as he was concerned, of his property. That he did not intend it as a conveyance in praesenti is evident from the qualifying clause with which he begins the use of the dispositive language, to wit, "If anything happens to me, no matter what," or, as we find it in the record, "Any time something happens to me." In other words, the addressee was to take possession of the property and occupy the status accorded to him by the instrument only when, and if, something should happen to the writer, and the evidence offered by the opponents, in his handwriting, taken in connection with the facts subsequently developed, indicates clearly that the "something" which the writer had in contemplation was his own death. Then follow the words:

> Take possession of that which I have. I give you all that I have accumulated. That is my will.

It is true that the writer uses the word "volonte," and the learned counsel suggests that the French word "means simply volition, and not last will and testament." Nevertheless the records of our courts contain many testaments, written in the French language, in which "volonte" and "derniere volonte" are used as the equivalents of "will" and "last will," and the evidence shows that Joseph Billis had lived in this state, and in an English-speaking parish, for many years, so that, considering the context, it seems more than probable that he used the word "volonte" just as an American, similarly situated, would have used the word "will." He then proceeds to state his wish that his brothers should get nothing, and to give his reasons, which would have been altogether uncalled for--as, indeed, the whole instrument would have been--if he had not been making a disposition of his property, to take effect after his death, since, so long as he lived, his estate would have remained under his own control. He then writes:

> Settle my accounts. Do for my children as I said. I transfer [passe] to you all my rights. Take care of this letter.

The addressee, it will be remembered, was in a distant city, and there was no suggestion that he should go at that time to the parish of Grant, either to settle the accounts of the writer, to take possession of his property, to do for his children, or for any other purpose; his succession to the rights and obligations conferred and imposed upon him, and the action that he was expected to take, being dependent and contingent upon the happening of "something" to, or, in other words, the death of, the writer.

*   *   *

We therefore conclude that the *fidei commissum* alleged by opponents has not been proved, and the judgment appealed from is accordingly affirmed.

NOTE

Compare *Succession of Rhodes*, 899 So. 2d 658 (La. App. 2d Cir. 2005), in which the court held that a letter written by decedent to his attorney "attempt[ing] to explain" his "last desires" did not demonstrate testamentary intent. If a letter may be an acceptable will, what is the result for an instrument, purporting to be an adoption agreement, vesting the child with all rights of a forced heir? *See Succession of Brand*, 162 La. 111, So. 267 (1927). What about documents that were a part of a form for creating an *inter vivos* trust? *See Succession of Plummer*, 847 So. 2d 185 (La. App. 2d 2003).

SUCCESSION OF SHOWS
166 So. 2d 261 (La. 1964)

FOURNET, Chief Justice.

This case involves the validity of a document dated "Dec 3—61," purporting to be the last will and testament of Mrs. Mae Viola Cooper Shows, who died leaving no ascendants or descendants, in which is written the words "All to My Sister" and signed by the defendant,[1]

*   *   *

The undisputed facts reveal that the document offered for probate was entirely written, dated and signed in the handwriting of the decedent on December 3, 1961, the same day she went to Foundation Hospital where she was to be hospitalized for a serious physical condition; upon her arrival there, she gave an envelope to Mrs. Granier, who placed it in her purse in obedience to the instruction "to take good care of it." The envelope was opened a day or two after the death of Mrs. Shows, which occurred on December 18, 1961, in which the document offered for probate was found attached to a bundle of papers therein with a rubber band. The papers included certified copies of deeds to property, copies of the proceedings in the succession of Mrs. Shows' late husband, and various bills and receipts, as well as a savings account book showing a balance of $10,000.

*   *   *

A mere perusal of the instrument sought to be probated in the case at bar discloses it totally lacks any language to indicate the animus testandi of the decedent and the necessary

---

[1] Immediately underneath the statement All to My Sister:, the signature of Mrs. Shows appears in this manner:
Mrs. Mae V. C. Shows
Mrs. Mae V. C. Shows
Shows

words to constitute a valid will…. Furthermore, the instrument is void of any language connoting dispositions testamentary of the decedent's property.

*   *   *

SUCCESSION OF HAMMETT
183 So. 2d 416 (La. App. 4th Cir. 1966)

BARNETTE, Judge.

Appellant is an opponent of a document which was submitted for probate in the succession proceedings. He is appealing from the judgment of the district court ordering the document admitted to probate as an olographic will.

The document in its entirety reads as follows:

> Jan. 30, 1961
> To whom it may concern,
>   75% Of all my monetary, real estaste (sic) and stock holdings to Sam Zemurray III with James H. Atkinson as trustee to be held in trust at Sam's discretion until Sam is 35 years old.
>   25% Of all my monetary, real estaste (sic), and stock holding to James H. Atkinson.
>   Donald Albert Hammett is no longer my husband and I leave him nothing.
>
> Anne Zemurray Hammett

Evidence taken in the lower court established that the document was written entirely in the hand of the deceased. There is no question raised by appellant as to its authenticity or in regard to the formalities required of an olographic will. LSA-C.C. art. 1588.

Appellant's attack on the document is his argument that it does not indicate that the writer intended to make a testamentary disposition of her property. We think that his objection is not well founded, and that the document was properly probated.

*   *   *

The question before us is one of fact. Does the language of the document clearly indicate that the deceased intended to dispose of her property on her death by means of this instrument?

*   *   *

The last statement of the document indicates that the writer intended it to convey property on her death. The principal value of an olographic will is its simplicity; it can be confected by a layman without the assistance of legal counsel. *Succession of Gaudin*, 140 So. 2d 384

(La.App.1st Cir. 1962). This document contains the word "leave." One trained in the law might prefer the use of words such as "bequeath" or "devise," but we are dealing with a document written by a person not so trained, and certainly "leave," when used by a layman, indicates the necessary intent.

Appellant contends that even if the word "leave" does satisfy the requirement of clearly indicating an animus testandi in the statement in which it occurs, it should not be "interpolated" into the first two statements so at to qualify them as testamentary dispositions. The result of this approach would grant validity to the last statement while denying it to the first two statements. We believe that to perform such mechanistic surgery on this instrument would violate the purpose of an olographic will. The law does not require that it be phrased in precise legal language throughout. We have "interpolated" nothing. Rather we have carefully considered the document Taken as a whole and have found that it clearly indicates

(1) That the decedent intended to convey her property in the manner indicated,
(2) That she intended the conveyance to take place on her death, and
(3) That she intended to accomplish the conveyance by means of this document.
It is her olographic will and is entitled to probate.

Our conclusion is amply supported by the jurisprudence of our State under Civil Code Article 1713 to the effect that the interpretation of the purported will should be such as to support its validity where possible. The courts should seek to find in the instrument that which will support, rather than defeat, the apparent intention of the testator.

*   *   *

The judgment of the district court admitting the will to probate is affirmed. Appellant is to pay the cost of this appeal.

Affirmed.

HENDRY v. SUCCESSION OF HELMS
557 So. 2d 427 (La. App. 3d Cir. 1990)

GUIDRY, Judge.

Ms. Marguerite Ryan Helms executed a statutory will on July 1, 1985. On April 20, 1988, Ms. Helms met with her attorney, Charles Viccellio, and delivered to him a six page handwritten document (hereafter the document) which was written, dated and signed by her on April 13, 1988, which document we annex as appendix I. Ms. Helms died April 21, 1988 and thereafter, the July 1985 statutory will was probated.

Plaintiff-appellant, Joann Hendry, the only surviving relative of Ms. Helms, instituted this suit seeking to have the probate of the July 1985 will set aside and to have the document declared a valid olographic testament. The trial court dismissed plaintiff's petition concluding that, although written dated and signed by the decedent, the document did not, within its four corners, evidence testamentary intent on the part of the preparer. In making this determination, the trial judge, in oral reasons for judgment, stated:

> ...It is not clear to the Court that this is a document which was intended to be the last will and testament of the decedent.
>
> That is seen in the document itself when it appears that this document contains information which is intended to be furnished to someone else. There's all kinds of things in here, like how the telephone bill is paid, how the gas bill is paid, and where some insurance policies are, and where a gravesite is located and that its prepaid, and various other things, which is not usually found in wills or testaments. The Court concludes that this is merely a list, something that was being furnished to her attorney as information....

Plaintiff appealed.

*   *   *

Charles Viccellio, Ms. Helms' attorney, was the only witness to testify. Mr. Viccellio, as Notary Public, prepared the 1985 statutory will and officiated at its execution. He testified that on April 20, 1988, which was one week after preparation of the document, Ms. Helms appeared at his office to deliver the document and discuss with him the preparation of another statutory will. She was to return the following week to execute the new statutory will which Mr. Viccellio was to draft, pursuant to their discussion and the document which she left with Viccellio. Ms. Helms died the following day.

In brief to this court, appellant, in effect, concedes that the document was not intended by the decedent to be her last will but urges that since it is in valid form and expresses decedent's last wishes, it is entitled to probate. In argument, appellant states:

> There is no question that her last intentions were as found on the olographic will. There is probably not much question either that she wanted Mr. Viccellio to transform her wishes from that will to a statutory testament. She apparently died before that could be done. Are her last wishes to be frustrated because of the fact that she died before her lawyer could complete the simple task of typing up her demands into a statutory form?. . .Thus the trial court erred in finding that this particular paper had to be the paper intended by Mrs. Helms to be her last will.

We discern no error in the trial court's conclusion that the document dated April 13, 1988 is not the olographic last will and testament of Ms. Marguerite Ryan Helms.

*   *   *

There are two essential requirements for a valid will, i.e., the act must be in valid form and the clauses it contains, or the manner in which it is made must clearly establish that it is a disposition of last will. The document is in valid form, being entirely written, dated and signed by the decedent. However, in our view, the document fails as a valid will because it lacks the necessary animus testandi. Despite the fact that the document contains terms which arguably reflect an animus testandi (use of the words "bequest" and "bequests"; "to Mrs. Carl W. Hendry (Joann)"; "Trust Fund and divided among-equally"), the record makes crystal clear that the decedent did not intend the document to be her last will and testament. As found by the trial court, the document, considering the manner and the circumstances prompting its confection, was obviously intended as a listing of information to be used by Mr. Viccellio in the preparation of a statutory will for Ms. Helms. The testimony of Mr. Viccellio, introduced without objection, is unequivocal on this point. Further, there is no contrary evidence, i.e., supporting the conclusion that Ms. Helms intended the document as her olographic last will.

* * *

For these reasons, the judgment of the trial court is affirmed at appellant's cost.

AFFIRMED.

SUCCESSION OF CARROLL
988 So. 2d 778 (La. App. 5th Cir. 2008)
[Appendices and footnotes omitted.]

THOMAS F. DALEY, Judge.

Appellant, Susan Carroll, has appealed the trial court judgment annulling the probate of a letter written by the decedent, Kenneth Carroll and finding the last will and testament of decedent dated February 14, 1999 to be valid. For the reasons that follow, we affirm.

FACTS:
The decedent, Kenneth Carroll, was married to Leslie Carroll and they had four children. Leslie Carroll died in January 1999. Shortly thereafter, the decedent sought advice of Leslie's sister, Isabel Wingerter, an attorney, to assist in preparing a will. The decedent executed a statutory will on February 14, 1999, in front of Donald Wingerter, which established two testamentary trusts. One trust, known as the Carroll Trust, was for the benefit of the four children of his marriage to Leslie and the other was for the benefit of his granddaughter, Brittany Carroll. The will provided that everything of which he died possessed, other than the particular legacy for the Brittany Carroll Trust, go into the Carroll Trust in which his four children were the beneficiaries. The Carroll Trust was also the beneficiary of several life insurance policies. The will named Ms. Wingerter executrix of his estate and trustee of the testamentary trusts.

In October 2003, decedent traveled to Hawaii where he married Susan Carroll. Before leaving for this trip, on October 9, 2003, decedent hand wrote a letter addressed to Ms. Wingerter in which he instructed certain assets be provided to Susan Carroll if he died "before I am able to see you personally". The letter provided that certain assets were to be provided in the event Mr. Carroll died before the marriage and certain assets were to be provided to Susan Carroll if Mr. Carroll died after the marriage. This included the payment of health insurance premiums for Mrs. Carroll.

In December 2003, decedent gave Ms. Wingerter another writing, listing numerous life insurance policies, and allocating various assets to different heirs. This writing provides that Susan Carroll receive $100,000 in the event Mr. Carroll dies a natural death, $200,000 in the event he dies an accidental death and that Susan Carroll receive a share in the trust "equal to the kids".

Susan Carroll testified that she and decedent were married on October 15, 2003 in Hawaii. In October 2006, decedent was diagnosed with cancer. Decedent died on May 15, 2007. On June 13, 2007, Ms. Wingerter filed a petition to probate the February 14, 1999 will as well as the October 9, 2003 letter she termed a codicil. An affidavit was executed by two witnesses attesting that they knew the decedent and recognized his handwriting and signature on the October 9, 2003 document. On June 13, 2007, the trial court signed an order letting "the notarial testament along with the olographic codicil of Kenneth Eugene Carroll, deceased dated February 14, 2007 [1999] be filed and recorded and executed according to law." On September 18, 2007, Susan Carroll filed a rule to show cause why the executrix, Ms. Wingerter, should not turn over funds to her under the terms of the October 9, 2003 letter. This was in response to a letter Susan Carroll received from Ms. Wingerter stating the health insurance policy would terminate October 1, 2007. The trial court signed a judgment on October 29, 2007 ordering the health insurance premium continue to be paid and that the executrix file a petition for declaratory judgment to determine the validity of the codicil. On November 5, 2007, the Carroll children filed a petition to annul the probate of the October 9, 2003 letter, claiming it to be invalid and unenforceable. On November 13, 2007, Ms. Wingerter filed a petition for declaratory judgment requesting the court to determine whether the October 9, 2003 letter contains sufficient animus testandi as required by law to constitute a valid olographic codicil.

On November 16, 2007, following a hearing, judgment was rendered annulling the probating of the October 9, 2003 letter and ordering the executrix to carry out her duties pursuant to the February 14, 1999 will. Prior orders relative to disbursements to Susan Carroll were also annulled. This judgment was certified as a final appealable judgment and this timely appeal followed.

LAW AND DISCUSSION:

On appeal, Susan Carroll contends the trial court erred in excluding extrinsic evidence of decedent's intent. Mrs. Carroll argues that because the language of the October 9, 2003 letter, referred to by Mrs. Carroll as a codicil, is ambiguous, the trial court erred in not allowing the introduction of the December 2003 document to prove testamentary intent. Mrs. Carroll argues a reading of the transcript indicates the trial court based its holding on the phrase "before I can meet with you" in the bequest, concluding that since decedent took no action to follow up and meet with Ms. Wingerter upon return from Hawaii, he did not intend to implement the provisions of the October 9, 2003 letter. Mrs. Carroll contends that the court should consider the December 2003 writing together with the October 9, 2003 letter and the February 14, 1999 will to establish that the decedent had testamentary intent at the time he penned the October 9, 2003 letter. Mrs. Carroll goes on to argue that the trial court's interpretation of the October 9, 2003 letter is manifestly erroneous because the October 9, 2003 letter is in proper form for an olographic will and the December 2003 writing is a follow up to the October 9, 2003 letter which indicates testamentary intent to provide for Mrs. Carroll upon his death. Mrs. Carroll argues that it was not necessary for decedent to meet professionally with Ms. Wingerter to change the February 14, 1999 will because decedent had "taken his testamentary bequests into his own words and hand."

Mrs. Carroll argues that a disposition should be interpreted to give it effect rather than to deny its effect. Mrs. Carroll further argues that it does not make sense that decedent only intended for his surviving spouse to receive a portion of his estate until they returned from Hawaii and that his failure to meet with Ms. Wingerter renders this intention without effect.

In response, the Carroll children contend the trial court correctly excluded extrinsic evidence to prove intent. They contend the intent of the October 9, 2003 letter was that another document be prepared by Ms. Wingerter. The Carroll children point out that there is nothing in the October 2003 letter to show the decedent intended the letter to be his last will or codicil. They contend the October 9, 2003 letter imposes conditions before action was to be taken, i.e. he had to die before or after the marriage before returning to New Orleans for the conditions of this letter to take place. The Carroll children further argue that had the decedent intended to leave Mrs. Carroll the amounts included in the October letter, as a long time insurance agent, he could have simply made her a beneficiary on one of his numerous life insurance policies.

There is no question that the February 14, 1999 will is valid. The December 2003 writing is not before the court, as the petition for declaratory judgment only requests that the court determine whether the October 9, 2003 letter was a valid codicil and the judgment appealed from makes no determination relative to the December 2003 writing. Thus, the only question to be determined by this court is whether the trial court correctly annulled probate of the October 9, 2003 letter.

Civil Code article 1610 provides that any modification of a testament must be in one of the forms prescribed for testaments. There are two forms of testaments: olographic and notarial. LSA-C.C. art. 1574. An olographic testament is one entirely written, dated and signed in the handwriting of the testator. LSA-C.C. art. 1575. The only other requirement for an olographic testament to be valid is that the document itself evidence testamentary intent. Succession of Mott, 97-1419 (La.App. 3 Cir. 7/8/98), 715 So. 2d 1258. Extrinsic or parol evidence cannot be used to establish testamentary intent. Succession of Bernstine, 04-739 (La.App. 3 Cir. 12/22/04), 890 So. 2d 776, writ denied, 05-0182 (La.4/22/05), 899 So. 2d 555. In the absence of testamentary intent, there is no will. Succession of Faggard, 152 So. 2d 627 (La.App. 2 Cir.1963).

In Hendry v. Succession of Helms, 557 So. 2d 427 (La.App. 3 Cir.1990), writ denied, 560 So. 2d 8 (La.1990), the decedent executed a statutory will on July 1, 1985. On April 20, 1988 she met with her attorney and delivered a dated, signed, handwritten letter expressing her intention to draft a new will and instructions on the division of her assets in the new will. Decedent died the next day before the new will could be drafted. The court stated "a document presented for probate must reflect animus testandi." Id. at 429. The court found the letter to decedent's attorney could not be considered a valid olographic will because it lacked testamentary intent. It was determined by the court that the letter was intended as information to be used by decedent's attorney in drafting the new will.

In Succession of Rhodes, 39,364 (La.App. 2 Cir. 3/23/05), 899 So. 2d 658, writ denied, 05-0936 (La.6/3/05), 903 So. 2d 459, and writ denied, 05-1044 (La.6/3/05), 903 So. 2d 460, the decedent wrote a letter to his attorney instructing the attorney to remove his son from all inheritance privileges previously conferred upon him. In the letter, decedent asked his attorney to serve as administrator of his estate. The letter requested his attorney cancel all previous wills and instructed as to how he wanted his assets divided. The new will was never written and a proposed legatee under the letter sought to challenge the original will and to probate the letter. In affirming the trial court's denial to probate the letter, the Third Circuit noted the letter begins by stating "it is an 'attempt to explain' his 'last desire,' rather than saying the instrument is his last will or a disposition of his property." Id. at 661. The court further noted that in the letter decedent instructed the attorney to "take action" to remove his son and terminate the son's power of attorney. Id. The court concluded that these instructions were not consistent with a situation where the decedent intended to covey his property by means of this particular instrument. Rather, the court found, the statements demonstrate that the decedent expected the attorney to prepare additional documents to carry out his wishes. Id. Thus, the court concluded the decedent did not intend to dispose of his property upon his death by means of that particular letter and as such it did not constitute a valid olographic will. Id. at 662.

In Succession of White, 06-1002 (La.App. 1 Cir. 5/4/07), 961 So. 2d 439, the court found a three page dated, signed document which began with the location of various assets and how the assets are to be disposed to be a valid olographic will, even though the decedent did not use terms such as "bequest" or "bequeath". The court found that a reading of the documents as a whole "exemplifies more than mere hopes or an inventory of assets." Id. at 442. The court distinguished the facts from those in Hendry v. Succession of Helms, supra, noting there was no testimony that the document was given to an attorney as a guide for the drafting of a new will. The court concluded that on its face and by its own language, the intent of the document was to dispose of decedent's assets.

In the case at bar, the proposed olographic codicil contains the phrases "in the event of my death before I am able to see you personally please make arrangements to ..." and "if after the marriage and before I can meet with you, I die and she survives". We find this language indicates a conditional testamentary intent for a limited period of time. This letter contains clear instructions to decedent's attorney of how to proceed if something happens to him during his trip and before he returned and could meet with her. Ms. Wingerter testified that she saw decedent numerous times between October 2003 and the date of his death, some three and a half years later, and decedent never requested that she prepare a new will or make a formal modification to the 1999 will to include provisions for Mrs. Carroll. The evidence also indicates that decedent and Mrs. Carroll met with another attorney to execute a pre-nuptial agreement and that decedent employed other attorneys throughout his career as an insurance agent. Additionally, the decedent was diagnosed with a terminal illness some seven months before his death. Thus, the evidence presented indicates that decedent took no steps to formalize or make unconditional the instructions in the October 2003 letter. We reject Mrs. Carroll's position that it was not necessary for decedent to take any further steps to provide for Mrs. Carroll's well being after his death. The requisite testamentary intent contained in the October 9, 2003 was conditioned upon decedent not returning from Hawaii and having an opportunity to meet with Ms. Wingerter. As the evidence shows, decedent returned from Hawaii and saw Ms. Wingerter on numerous occasions, thus, the testament terminated by its own conditions. Additionally, the language in the October 9, 2003 letter is clear in its meaning and extrinsic evidence is not needed to interpret this language. Accordingly, the trial court correctly annulled the prior order admitting the October 9, 2003 letter to probate. This finding pretermits a discussion of the remainder of appellant's assignments of error.

CONCLUSION:

For the foregoing reasons, the judgment of the trial court is affirmed. Each party is to bear its own costs.

AFFIRMED.
Will Forms

Act 1421 of 1997, effective July 1, 1999, effected a deletion of a number of older will forms. Prior to the revision, the Code authorized four will forms specifically and legislation in La. R.S. 9:2442 added the statutory will form. The revision eliminated all but the olographic, La. C.C. 1575, and replaced the statutory form with the closely resembling notarial will. La. C.C. 1576.

Thus, while only the olographic and notarial testaments may be used for testaments written after July 1, 1999, wills written prior to the revision, in a form which was valid at the time, will be upheld as to form. For a description of the older will forms along with a sample of each, see Kathryn Venturatos Lorio, LOUISIANA CIVIL LAW TREATISE SUCCESSIONS AND DONATIONS, 2nd ed. (2009), § 12:2, pp. 395-420.

The Olographic Testament

An olographic will is one "entirely written, dated and signed in the handwriting of the testator." La. C.C. 1575. Although the testator's signature should appear at the end of the testament, La. C.C. 1575 states that, "[i]f anything is written by the testator after his signature, the testament shall not be invalid and such writing may be considered by this court, in its discretion, as part of the testament." A date must appear on the face of the will. La. C.C. 1575 describes the date as sufficient if, "the day, month and year are reasonable ascertainable from information in the testament, as clarified by extrinsic evidence, if necessary." Thus, "slash dates" (those in the form 2/8/15) and dates written as "Christmas 2014" are sufficient because extrinsic evidence may be introduced to establish with certainty the month and the day the testator dated the will. *See Succession of Boyd*, 306 So. 2d 687 (La. 1975).

HAMILTON v. KELLEY
641 So. 2d 981 (La. App. 2d Cir.1994)

BROWN, J.

Plaintiff, Tom R. Hamilton, was ten years old when his uncle, W.H. Hamilton, died. The five brothers and sisters of Hamilton, including plaintiff's father, claimed that he died intestate and obtained a judgment placing themselves in possession of decedent's property. Twenty-five years later, plaintiff's father, Boyce Hamilton, died. Plaintiff found among his father's effects an olographic testament written by his uncle, W.H. Hamilton, bequeathing all of his property to plaintiff. The testament was entirely written and dated by W.H. Hamilton; however, the signature was obviously and purposely cut off the document. Within one year of discovering the testament, plaintiff filed this action to annul the judgment of possession because of fraud and ill practices and to probate the olographic testament. See LSA-C.C.P. Art. 2004. Although finding that the testament was entirely written and dated by W.H. Hamilton and that it had been signed, the trial court "reluctantly" found that plaintiff did not prove the authenticity of the missing signature and dismissed plaintiff's action "based on a strict and narrow interpretation of the law." For the following reasons, we reverse and render judgment in plaintiff's favor.

FACTS/PROCEDURAL HISTORY

W.H. Hamilton was never married and died without ascendants or descendants on November 15, 1963. His brothers and sisters, asserting that W.H. Hamilton died intestate, obtained a judgment giving them possession of his estate on September 11, 1964. His estate consisted primarily of land inherited from his parents, including an undivided 1/6th interest in 640 acres in Union Parish, a 20 acre tract in Union Parish (his parents' homeplace) and an undivided 1/12th interest in a lot in Dubach, Louisiana.

After the death of Boyce Hamilton (plaintiff's father) in December 1990, plaintiff found in his father's belongings the olographic testament of his uncle, W.H. Hamilton. The will was entirely handwritten and dated by testator on a small blue piece of paper. The right bottom corner containing the signature had been cut off the testament. The will made plaintiff, who at the time of his uncle's death was 10 years old, the sole beneficiary. The intact portion of the testament read as follows:

To: Whom it may concern;

I, William Henry Hamilton, being of sound mind, declares this as my last and only will. In the event and at the time of my death, I bequest and will everything I own to my brother's son, Tom Hamilton.

Signed this 4th day of March 1962.

On May 3, 1991, Tom R. Hamilton filed this action to annul the 1964 judgment of possession and to probate the olographic will. Named as defendants were W.H. Hamilton's living sisters and the heirs of his deceased siblings. Plaintiff's petition alleged that W.H. Hamilton's brothers and sisters cut off the signature of the instrument to defraud plaintiff of his inheritance.

*   *   *

W.H. Hamilton had five brothers and sisters. At the time of trial, two brothers, Boyce and Alton Hamilton, and one sister, Gordie Mosely, were deceased. Another sister, Opal Murray, was living in New York, but was physically unable to attend the trial. Viola Hamilton, the widow of Alton, testified on plaintiff's behalf. Hazel Kelley, the remaining sister, testified on behalf of the defense.

Plaintiff testified that his parents were Boyce Henry Hamilton and Rita Tabor Hamilton. He stated that his uncle, William Henry Hamilton, was his father's youngest brother. His uncle was never married nor did he have any children. Plaintiff's testimony was supported by documents filed in the record of W.H. Hamilton's succession. Plaintiff's father died on December 30, 1990, and in early 1991, plaintiff discovered the testament of his uncle while sorting through his father's papers. Plaintiff had no knowledge of the document prior to this time.

Viola Hamilton testified that when W.H. Hamilton died, her husband, Alton, who was in bad health, was concerned about dissension among his siblings caused by the will. Viola testified that she was present during a conversation between Boyce and Alton concerning the testament and heard Boyce's statement to Alton that he would invalidate the will by cutting off the signature. She witnessed Boyce cut the signature off the will and give it to Alton. She saw Boyce fold the remaining testament and put it in his pocket. She observed Alton place the signature part in his "business drawer" and state that he "didn't have the heart to destroy it." Viola further testified that Hazel Kelley came over the next day and got the signature part out of the drawer. She told Hazel to put it back, but she would not. She never told her husband, who died eight months later, that Hazel took the signature. Viola testified that she saw the document and that it was entirely written, dated and signed by W.H. Hamilton.

Hazel Kelley testified that W.H. Hamilton, her youngest brother, died in 1963. Hazel Kelley testified that she was much older than W.H. Hamilton and that she took care of him like her own child. Hazel Kelley testified that after W.H. Hamilton died, she and her sister, Gordie, went through his billfold. She saw Boyce later that same day and he requested the billfold for a keepsake. She testified that Boyce left with the billfold but returned about two hours later. Boyce stated to her that he had found W.H. Hamilton's will in the billfold. Boyce then showed it to Hazel Kelley and several others who viewed the will for the first time. Hazel Kelley stated that she saw the will and the signature. At trial, she testified that the handwriting on the exhibit was "too neat" to be that of W.H. Hamilton, "but it looks like his---." Hazel Kelley testified that she thought the writing on the will was that of W.H. Hamilton's, but that the signature she saw was not. She admitted that the document had a signature purporting to be W.H. Hamilton's, but that she knew his writing as well as her own and that it was not his signature. She denied seeing the document again after it was first shown to her by Boyce. Hazel Kelley testified that she signed the affidavit of heirship stating that W.H. Hamilton died intestate **because their lawyer stated that the signature was not W.H. Hamilton's**. (Emphasis added).

Aubrey Ray, a good friend and lifelong neighbor of W.H. Hamilton, testified that one day at W.H. Hamilton's home, he observed W.H. Hamilton writing on a blue piece of paper and was told that it was his will. Hamilton further told Ray that he was leaving everything to Boyce's boy, Tom, because Tom was the only grandchild with the Hamilton surname.

James Marvin Simpson testified that he and W.H. Hamilton were like brothers and that Hamilton told him that he wrote a will leaving everything to his nephew, Tom, because Tom was the only grandchild with the Hamilton surname. Simpson admitted that he never saw the will.

Robert Foley, a forensic document examiner, did not testify because the parties stipulated that he would testify in accordance with his written report and addendum. Foley, who holds master's degrees in chemistry and criminal justice, as well as a juris doctor degree in law, is widely recognized as a questioned document examiner. Foley concluded, from known samples, that W.H. Hamilton was the writer of the testament (minus the signature) at issue. After considering all the testimony, the trial court found: "In this case, there is not a question of the testator's intent. Most significant is that the will which reflects the intent of the testator was written by him. This fact was uncontradicted."

The trial court's determination was clearly correct. No one seriously contested the intent of W.H. Hamilton to leave his property to his nephew, Tom. Further, the trial court determined that the testament was entirely written and dated by W.H. Hamilton. A letter from Opal Murray to Boyce Hamilton, also found among Boyce's papers, was placed into evidence. This letter, with its envelope postmarked December 22, 1963, confirmed the existence of the will as well as the dissension among the siblings over the contents of the will. The letter stated as follows:

As far [sic] the slip of blue paper -- Boyce I can't believe W.H. meant it that way and I don't think he remembered he had it in his billfold . . . as far [sic] that will Boyce, you were the only one who knew anything about it and you yourself said you had told him you would not accept it because you did not think it was right. You also said that if everyone was not happy with it you would burn it. I can't understand how you could expect anyone to be happy about it. What if it had been someone else? How would you feel?

Hazel Kelley testified that she saw the will and that it contained a signature. The trial court stated that:

> . . . . [T]he court is firmly convinced that the testator's intent was to give his property to his nephew, Tom Hamilton. The court is further convinced that a testament was written and dated in the testator's hand, directed toward that end. The only question which remains then, is whether the testament was signed by the hand of the testator.

The trial court then determined that:

> In this case, there was no disagreement that the testament was originally intact and was signed with a handwritten signature. Viola testified that she saw the document in its original form and that it was entirely written, dated and signed in the handwriting of W.H. Hamilton. However, no testimony was elicited in regard to her familiarity with the handwriting of W.H. Hamilton. Hazel testified that she, too, had seen the document in its original form. She said that there was a handwritten signature but that it was not the signature of W.H. Hamilton. She stated that she cared for her younger brother for many years and was very familiar with his handwriting. There was no other evidence or testimony regarding the authenticity of the signature.

As is evident from the above excerpts, the trial court found the testament to be authentic, that the handwriting was that of W.H. Hamilton and that it contained a signature purporting to be W.H. Hamilton's. It found, however, that the missing signature had not been proven to be that of W.H. Hamilton.

DISCUSSION

In *Succession of Nunley,* 224 La. 251, 69 So. 2d 33 (La. 1953)*,* a lost will was allowed to be probated. *Nunley* recognized the rule that a testator is presumed to have destroyed a will which had been lost before his death. This presumption can be overcome by proof (1) that the testator made a valid will, (2) of the contents of the will, and (3) that the will was never revoked by any act of the testator.

The trial court found and the record clearly supports that W.H. Hamilton intended to leave his entire estate to plaintiff. This intent is stated in the document itself and confirmed by Hamilton's two close friends. Further, all the testimony demonstrates that Hamilton did not revoke the olographic testament. Viola Hamilton and Hazel Kelley testified that the destruction of the will, by excising the signature, occurred after W.H. Hamilton's death. Thus, the remaining issue concerns the sufficiency of proof that a will in valid form existed. The trial court's ruling concerning the existence of a valid testament focused on the excised signature.

In order to be a valid olographic testament, it must be entirely written, dated and signed by the hand of the testator. It is subject to no other form and may be made anywhere, even out of the state. LSA-C.C. art. 1588. Erasures not approved by the testator are considered as not made, and words added by the hand of another as not written. LSA-C.C. art. 1589. The proponent of an alleged olographic will has the burden of proving that it was entirely written, dated and signed by the testator. LSA-C.C.P. art. 2903.

Tom R. Hamilton produced three witnesses and offered the report of Robert Foley, a handwriting expert, to prove the validity of W.H. Hamilton's olographic testament. Viola Hamilton testified that the handwriting which appeared on the testament was that of W.H. Hamilton. She also testified that the signature which, before it was cut off the paper, appeared at the end of the testament, was that of W.H. Hamilton. Furthermore, Viola Hamilton testified that she overheard Alton and Boyce Hamilton talking about the will and discussing W.H. Hamilton's signature. In her testimony, the following was revealed:

Q. What do you remember they said?
A. ...What was said was that Boyce talked to Alton about that he had talked to a lawyer and the lawyer had told him if he cut the name off -- the signature off of that will it would be invalid.

Plaintiff argues that although Boyce was not alive to testify at trial, his actions, specifically his wanting to remove the signature, apparently believing it to be authentic, prove the authenticity of W.H. Hamilton's signature. Plaintiff argues that the conversation between Alton and Boyce Hamilton should have been considered as recognition that the will had been signed by W.H. Hamilton. Plaintiff argues that the testimony of Viola Hamilton as to what Alton and Boyce said and did are exceptions to the hearsay exclusions. *See* LSA-C.E. art. 894(B)(3) & (6). Plaintiff concludes that the testimony of Viola, Alton and Boyce establishes that W.H. Hamilton did indeed sign the will.

Aubrey Ray testified that he observed W.H. Hamilton writing on a blue piece of paper. He inquired as to what W.H. Hamilton was writing and Hamilton replied "a will" leaving his property to plaintiff. James Marvin Simpson testified that Hamilton told him that he wrote a will leaving everything to Tom R. Hamilton because he was the only grandchild with the Hamilton surname. However, Simpson admitted that he never saw the will.

We find that the testimony of Viola Hamilton, Aubrey Ray and James Marvin Simpson, coupled with the report of Mr. Foley, the handwriting expert, and all the other evidence presented, specifically the letter sent to Boyce Hamilton from Opal Murray postmarked December 22, 1963, sufficiently establishes the authenticity of the will. This is in agreement with the trial court's finding that the writing on the will was that of W.H. Hamilton.

The fact that a third party removed the testator's signature does not, ipso facto, render the will invalid. In the absence of a showing that the signature was removed pursuant to the testator's request to revoke the will, the removal of the signature is ineffective in law. The removal of a testator's signature by a third party cannot operate to invalidate the olographic testament. *See Rivette v. Moreau,* 341 So. 2d at 459 (La. App. 3d Cir. 1976).

At trial, Hazel Kelley testified that she knew W.H. Hamilton's writing like her own and that while the document shown to her in 1963 contained a signature purporting to be W.H. Hamilton's, she knew it was not his. In a motion for new trial, plaintiff argued that the trial court erred in finding credible the testimony of Hazel Kelley. In support of the motion for new trial, the pre-trial deposition of Hazel Kelly was submitted, which in part contradicted her trial testimony.

The trial court ruled that, "assuming that Mrs. Kelley's testimony at trial was untrue, the court cannot state that its inability to find Mrs. Kelley a credible witness will affirmatively establish the signature of W.H. Hamilton at the end of the olographic testament in accordance Louisiana Code of Civil Procedure article 2883." Whether Hazel Kelly's pre-trial deposition was allowed into evidence is unclear; however, its consideration is unnecessary.

Code of Civil Procedure article 2883 dictates that an olographic testament be proven by the testimony of two credible witnesses. In the instant case, the testimony of Viola Hamilton, Robert Foley, Aubrey Ray, James Simpson, and Hazel Kelley and the submitted documents adequately established that an olographic testament in valid form was made by W.H. Hamilton. Only Hazel Kelley's testimony questioned whether W.H. Hamilton actually signed the document and that testimony was discredited by her complicity in the removal of the signature at the bottom of the document and the concealment of the testament. Further, defendant, Opal Murray, did not testify. Although evidence indicated that she was unable to attend the trial due to a broken hip, her testimony could have been taken by deposition. Thus, the circumstantial evidence convincingly showed that W.H. Hamilton wrote, dated and signed the olographic testament.

Further, the law clearly imposed on the brothers and sisters of W.H. Hamilton the duty to present the olographic testament to the court. LSA-C.C. Art. 2853. If it was in fact invalid, the court could have so found. Rather than presenting the testament to the court, they concealed it and excised the signature from the document. Their obvious intent was to deny plaintiff the ability to prove the testator's signature.

Thus, by their acts, the brothers and sisters of W.H. Hamilton attempted to circumvent his clear intent and deprive plaintiff of the inheritance. Their actions speak louder than words that the testament was entirely written, dated and signed by W.H. Hamilton. We should not allow these siblings to profit by their wrongful deeds. *See Standard Life & Accident Insurance Co. v. Pylant,* 424 So. 2d 377 (La. App. 2d Cir. 1982), *writ denied,* 427 So. 2d 1212 (La. 1983). Because plaintiff clearly proved the testator's intent and the execution of a will to achieve that desire, it should fall upon those who acted to remove the signature for their personal gain to prove that the excised signature was not the testator's. Hazel Kelly's testimony at trial, in light of her participation in the scheme to destroy and hide the will, is insufficient to carry that burden of proof.

Defendants have reurged their exception of prescription under LSA-C.C.P. Art. 2893. The trial court correctly denied this exception. Under the doctrine of contra non valentem, as well as, LSA-C.C.P. Art. 2004, plaintiff had one year from discovery of the testament to institute this action. It was not the legislative intent in adopting Art. 2893 to place it within the power of heirs *ab intestato*, who have obtained possession of a testament, to deprive a legatee of his rights by fraudulently concealing the existence of the testament. *See Fuller v. Qualls,* 241 Ala. 673, 4 So. 2d 418 (Ala. 1941).

Under the facts of this case, the evidence precludes any other reasonable inference except that the will was signed by the testator. Accordingly we reverse the trial court ruling, annul the judgment of possession and order the testament in olographic form to be probated. Costs are assessed to defendants.

REVERSED and REMANDED.

PROBLEM

Consider the following facts taken from the *Succession of Raiford*, 404 So. 2d 251 (La. 1981). Has the date been established with sufficient certainty?

A booklet was found between mattresses of decedent's bed. On a page of the booklet the deceased had written the following notation:

> Monday. 8 1968
> I wont gwen cooper
> to have what I got when I died
> My land and all
> Melisa Raiford

The eighth day of the month occurred on a Monday in 1968 in the months of February, April and July. A note in the booklet immediately following the purported will was dated July 8. A witness testified to seeing the notebook in decedent's hands one summer day in 1968.

SUCCESSION OF BURKE
365 So. 2d 858 (La. App. 4th Cir. 1978)
[footnotes omitted]

GARRISON, Judge.

*   *   *

Emmett Joseph Burke died on August 14, 1974, and after a search, the disputed testament, dated January 15, 1961, was found. In it he attempted to bequeath his interest in the property at 6315 West End Boulevard to his sister Delia Burke Derbes, as well as the balance in his Whitney Bank account. His life insurance was to be divided equally between his sisters, Mrs. Derbes and Mrs. Schreiner.

Burke left a host of collateral relations, but no forced heirs....

The only issue presented on appeal is whether the document purporting to be the will of Emmett Joseph Burke which was offered for probate is a valid olographic will under the requirements of Civil Code Article 1588. The trial court held the questioned document to be valid after a contradictory hearing pursuant to Article 2881 of the Code of Civil Procedure.

The questioned will was written by the decedent, Emmett Joseph Burke, on printed will paper designed for a statutory will. The following portions were printed on the face of the document:

I, _____, being of sound and disposing mind and memory, and considering the uncertainty of this life, do make, publish and declare this to be my last WILL and TESTAMENT as follows, hereby revoking all other former Wills by me at any time made.

First, after my lawful debts are paid, I give. . .

In his own handwriting, Burke had written the date, "Jan. 15, 1961," and his own name in the blank following the printed "I." After the printed "I give," he wrote the following:

. . . to my sister Delia (Mrs. M. J. Derbes); my interest in property at 6315 West End Blvd Also whatever Bank Balance I have in the Whitney National Bank, City Branch Bank and Insurance as covered by Policy of F. F. Hansell & Bro. Ltd. To be shared equally with my other sister Mrs. C. A. Schreiner

The second page of this document had printed provisions for the naming of executors, which Burke began, but did not complete. Below this Burke signed the document and marked through the superscription.

Article 1588 of the Civil Code prescribes that an olographic will must be entirely written, dated and signed by the testator in his own hand. However, the fact that there is other writing or printing, not in the hand of the testator, such as the printed portions here, will not necessarily invalidate the testament. Those words will simply be considered as not written. C.C. Art. 1589; *Jones v. Kyle*, 168 La. 728, 123 So. 306 (1929); *Succession of Robertson*, 49 La.Ann. 868, 21 So. 586 (La.1897). Specifically, "an instrument written on a stationer's printed form with the blanks filled in by the testator in his own handwriting is valid when the will contains, exclusive of the printed matter, all of the essential formalities of an olographic will." 2 Loyola L.Rev. 164, 168 (1944).

The trial court admitted Burke's will to probate. We agree. From the words written by decedent, his testamentary intent is unmistakable. Although the printed form contains many words which must be disregarded, there remain sufficient words in the testator's own handwriting to provide the essential formalities of an olographic will.

It is true that in *Succession of Shows*, 246 La. 652, 166 So. 2d 261 (La.1964) the language was very similar, with the sole phrase "All to my sister" having been held to lack testamentary intent. However, a distinction is apparent. In that case, Show's words "All to my sister" could have been, e.g., a reply to a question such as: "To whom shall we send the bills?"

The text which Burke wrote, on the contrary, seems inexplicable other than as a testament:

to my sister Delia . . . my interest in property at 6315 West End Blvd . . . Bank Balance . . . and insurance. To be shared equally with my other sister Mrs. C. A. Shreiner.

That writing speaks of decedent's immovable property, money (in the bank) and insurance and says it is "to be shared" by two sisters. Thus that writing (like "Pay to" in *Succession of Gafford, supra*) does contain, in a context referable to the testator's intent, a verb.

For the reasons assigned we find that the trial judge did not err in finding the will valid and admitting it to probate. Therefore the judgment is affirmed.

AFFIRMED.

NOTE

Should a document written and dated by a decedent and signed as "Auntie" be probated as a valid olographic will? Why or why or why not? *See Succession of Caillouet*, 935 So. 2d 713 (La. App. 4th Cir. 2006).

The Notarial Testament

The notarial testament (similar to the pre-revision "statutory" will) consists of two parts, the substantive section containing the testator's disposition of all or part of his property and an attestation clause. A notary and two witnesses must be present at the execution. Variations as to the manner of execution depend on the testator's knowledge and ability to sign his name and read. La. C.C. 1577-1579. Additionally, special forms are provided for a testator who knows how and is physically able to read Braille, La. C.C. 1580, and for the deaf or deaf and blind. La. C.C. 1580.1. In all cases, the testator is required to declare or signify to a notary and two witnesses that the document is his last will and testament. The testator, or someone else, if the testator is unable to sign his name, will be required to sign or affix the testator's mark at the end of the last page of the testament and on every additional page. Following the declaration and signing of the document, the notary and witnesses are required in the presence of the testator to sign an attestation clause, testifying to the fact of proper execution and to the date of the testament's execution.

SUCCESSION OF HENDRICKS
28 So. 3d 1057 (La. App. 1st Cir. 2009)
[footnotes omitted]

The testator's surviving spouse appeals a judgment pertaining to findings of the invalidity of a testament and the revocation of another testament, both of which had been executed by her husband. The testator's children answered the appeal, seeking reversal of the portion of the judgment that voided and recalled letters of independent administration which been issued to them. For the following reasons, we affirm.

Facts and Procedural Background

On November 27, 2007, Gerald Hendricks (Gerald) died, leaving a notarial testament dated July 31, 2006. At the time of his death, Gerald was married to Melinda Hendricks (Melinda), and, in addition to Melinda, his three sisters were named as legatees in the 2006 testament. In January 2008, Melinda filed a petition to probate Gerald's testament and for appointment as the testamentary executrix. Melinda was appointed as executrix, and letters testamentary were issued to her on January 29, 2008. Shortly thereafter, Gerald's three surviving children from a former relationship-Donnie Franklin, Jamie Franklin, and Sherall Franklin (collectively, the Franklins)-filed a rule to show cause why Gerald's notarial testament should not be declared null and void pursuant to LSA-C.C. art. 1573, because one of the pages of the testament had not been signed by Gerald as required by LSA-C.C. art. 1577. Following a March 14, 2008 hearing, the court orally ruled that Gerald's 2006 testament was null and void *ab initio,* and Melinda was removed as executrix.

On March 18, 2008, the Franklins filed a pleading to have Gerald's succession declared to be intestate and for the appointment of themselves as independent administrators. The next day, Melinda filed an opposition to the appointment of independent administrators, as well as a petition to file a testament by Gerald dated August 27, 1993, and for the appointment as testamentary executrix. The Franklins opposed Melinda's petition, seeking to have the 1993 testament invalidated pursuant to LSA-C.C. art. 1607. Additionally, upon discovery that two of the legatees named in the 2006 testament had not been properly served, the Franklins requested that those legatees be ordered to show cause why the 2006 testament should not be declared null and void due to Gerald's failure to follow certain codal requirements. A hearing was held on all of those matters on May 15, 2008.

In a May 27, 2008 judgment, the trial court (1) declared Gerald's 2006 testament to be null and void *ab initio;* (2) voided and recalled the letters testamentary issued to Melinda on January 29, 2008; (3) declared Gerald's 1993 testament to have been revoked by an authentic act, *i.e.,* the annulled 2006 testament; (4) recalled the letters testamentary issued to Melinda on April 25, 2008; (5) recalled the letters of independent administration issued on April 3, 2008, in favor of the Franklins; and (6) declared that Gerald's succession was intestate. The judgment further provided that any future appointment of an administrator be made by a rule to show cause. Melinda appealed, challenging the trial court's determination of the invalidity of the 2006 testament and the revocation of the 1993 testament. In an answer to the appeal, the Franklins sought the reversal of that portion of the judgment that voided and recalled the letters of independent administration issued to them.

Validity of the 2006 Testament

Melinda urges that the trial court improperly declared the 2006 notarial testament to be null and void. A disposition mortis causa may be made only in the form of a testament authorized by law. LSA-C.C. art. 1570. The formalities prescribed for the execution of a testament must be observed or the testament is absolutely null. LSA-C.C. art. 1573. A notarial testament is one that is executed in accordance with the formalities of Articles 1577 through 1580.1. LSA-C.C. art. 1576. A notarial testament may be made in one of several ways, but the 2006 notarial testament was subject to the formalities of Article 1577, which provides:

> The notarial testament shall be prepared in writing and dated and shall be executed in the following manner. If the testator knows how to sign his name and to read and is physically able to do both, then:

> (1) In the presence of a notary and two competent witnesses, the testator shall declare or signify to them that the instrument is his testament and shall sign his name at the end of the testament and **on each other separate page.**

(2) In the presence of the testator and each other, the notary and the witnesses shall sign the following declaration, or one substantially similar: "In our presence the testator has declared or signified that this instrument is his testament and has signed it at the end and on each other separate page, and in the presence of the testator and each other we have hereunto subscribed our names this _____ day of _____, _____." [Emphasis added.]

Article 1577 provides that this form of a notarial testament "shall be executed" in a certain manner. The word "shall" is mandatory. LSA-R.S. 1:3; *Succession of Brown,* 458 So. 2d 140, 142 (La.App. 1st Cir.1984). To properly execute this form of a notarial testament, the following actions must be taken: (1) in the presence of a notary and two competent witnesses, the testator shall declare that the instrument is his testament; (2) in the presence of a notary and two competent witnesses, the testator shall sign his name at the end of the testament and on each other separate page of the testament; and (3) in the presence of the testator and each other, the notary and the witnesses shall sign the declaration set forth in Article 1577, or one substantially similar. *See* LSA-C.C. art. 1577. Comment (b) of the 1997 revision comments to LSA-C.C. art. 1577 clarifies that the testator need not sign after both the dispositive or appointive provisions of the notarial testament and the declaration. If the testator is disposing of property, appointing an executor, or making other directions in the body of the testament itself, he need only sign at the end of the dispositive, appointive, or directive provisions. LSA-C.C. art. 1577, Revision Comments-1997, comment (b).

The intention of the testator as expressed in the testament must govern. However, the intent to make a testament, although clearly stated or proved, will be ineffectual unless the execution thereof complies with codal requirements. *See Succession of Roussel,* 373 So. 2d 155, 157 (La.1979). A material deviation from the manner of execution prescribed by the code will be fatal to the validity of the testament. *Id.*; *see* LSA-C.C. art. 1573. The fact that there is no fraud, or even suggestion or intimation of it, will not justify the courts in departing from the codal requirements, even to bring about justice in the particular instance, since any material relaxation of the codal rule will open up a fruitful field for fraud, substitution, and imposition. *Succession of Roussel,* 373 So. 2d at 157. The purpose of the codal article in prescribing formalities for the execution of testaments is to guard against and prevent mistake, imposition, undue influence, fraud, or deception, to afford means of determining their authenticity, and to prevent the substitution of some other writing. *Id.* at 158. Thus, the law precludes additional evidence on the issue of intent when the testament was not confected in accordance with LSA-C.C. art. 1577. *Succession of Richardson,* 05-0552 (La.App. 1st Cir.3/24/06), 934 So. 2d 749, 752, *writ denied,* 06-0896 (La.6/2/06), 929 So. 2d 1265. If there is any area of our civil law in which the goal of certainty of result has particular significance, it is that of successions. *Id.* at 752 (Gaidry, J., concurring).

It is undisputed that Gerald did not sign one of the pages of the 2006 testament that contained dispositive provisions in favor of his three sisters. Thus, Gerald did not comply with one of the formalities of LSA-C.C. art. 1577(1) in that he did not sign on each other separate page of the testament. If the formalities prescribed for the execution of a testament are not observed, the testament is absolutely null. *See* LSA-C.C. art. 1573. In light of Gerald's failure to comply with one of the formalities of LSA-C.C. art. 1577(1), we are unable to find legal error in the trial court's determination that the 2006 testament is absolutely null in its entirety. Although we (like the trial court) find this to be a harsh result under the circumstances of this case, we are bound to follow the law. We were unable to find any codal or jurisprudential authority to support a finding that only the unsigned page containing dispositive provisions should be declared null as suggested by Melinda. *See Evans v. Evans,* 410 So. 2d 729 (La.1982); *Succession of Roussel,* 373 So. 2d 155; *Succession of Hoyt,* 303 So. 2d 189 (La.App. 1st Cir.1974); *Land v. Succession of Newsom,* 193 So. 2d 411 (La.App. 2nd Cir.1967), *writ denied,* 250 La. 262, 195 So. 2d 145 (1967). *Cf. In re Succession of Simonson,* 07-742 (La.App. 5th Cir.3/11/08), 982 So. 2d 143.

The fact that the testator in this case failed to sign a page of the testament containing dispositive provisions makes this case distinguishable from *Succession of Guezuraga,* 512 So. 2d 366, 368 (La.1987), in which the supreme court discussed the formal requirements of a statutory will. *See* former LSA-R.S. 9:2442 to 2445. The issue in *Succession of Guezuraga* was whether a statutory will was valid if the testatrix signed the page containing all dispositive portions and the beginning of the attestation clause, but failed to sign the page containing only the conclusion of the attestation clause. *Succession of Guezuraga,* 512 So. 2d at 366. In the will, the testatrix left the forced portion of her estate to her two adoptive children and the disposable portion to her four sisters. Over the objection of the testatrix's adoptive children, the trial court ordered the will probated. Relying on *Succession of Hoyt,* 303 So. 2d 189, and *Land,* 193 So. 2d 411, the fourth circuit reversed, holding that the failure of the testatrix to sign each sheet was fatal to the validity of the will. *Succession of Guezuraga,* 503 So. 2d 187, 188 (La.App. 4th Cir.1987).

Based on the fact that the testatrix in *Succession of Guezuraga* had signed on the page containing all of the dispositive portions, the supreme court found that *Hoyt* and *Land* were distinguishable and reversed the appellate court's holding that the will was not valid. *Succession of Guezuraga,* 512 So. 2d at 367. The supreme court observed that former LSA-R.S. 9:2442(B)(1) required that the testator declare to the notary and witnesses that the "instrument" was his last "will" and to sign his name at the end of the "will" and on each separate page of the "instrument." After finding that the legislature intended to use the terms "will" and "instrument" interchangeably and that the reference in each instance was only to the entirety of the testator's dispositions or recitations, the supreme court concluded that the testatrix had fulfilled the statutory requirement to sign her name at the end of the "will" and on each separate page of the "instrument" by signing the page that contained all of the dispositive provisions. *Succession of Guezuraga,* 512 So. 2d at 367-68.

In *Succession of Guezuraga,* the supreme court declined to interpret the terms "will" and "instrument" as strictly as the forced heirs requested, stating:

> But we are not required to give the statutory will a strict interpretation. The Legislature adopted the statutory will from the common law in order to avoid the rigid formal requirements of the Louisiana Civil Code. "The minimal formal requirements of the statutory will are only designed to provide a simplified means for a testator to express his testamentary intent and to assure, through his signification and his signing in the presence of a notary and two witnesses, that the instrument was intended to be his last will." In accordance with this legislative intent, courts liberally construe and apply the statute, maintaining the validity of the will if at all possible, as long as it is in substantial compliance with the statute. In deciding what constitutes substantial compliance, the courts look to the purpose of the formal requirements-to guard against fraud.
>
> Where the departure from form has nothing whatsoever to do with fraud, ordinary common sense dictates that such departure should not produce nullity. It

was the intent of the legislature to reduce form to the minimum necessary to prevent fraud. It is submitted that in keeping with this intent, slight departures from form should be viewed in the light of their probable cause. If they indicate an increased likelihood that fraud may have been perpetrated they would be considered substantial and thus a cause to nullify the will. If not, they should be disregarded. Thus testators and estate planners will have the security that the legislature intended to give them.

Succession of Guezuraga, 512 So. 2d at 368 (citations omitted). On rehearing, the supreme court observed that the attestation clause is a certificate to a will and not part of the will itself. Therefore, the supreme court reaffirmed its holding that the testatrix's failure to sign the page containing only the conclusion of the attestation clause was not fatal to the validity of the statutory will. *Succession of Guezuraga,* 512 So. 2d at 370 on reh'g).

With respect to the dispositive provisions, the court in its original opinion in *Succession of Guezuraga* set forth the following, in pertinent part:

The dispositive provisions of the testament are what primarily concern the testator, and as to which we require the testator's affirmance by a signature.... This is our assurance that the testament is an accurate reflection of the testator's wishes. So long as the signature is located beneath the dispositive provisions and affixed in time after they are written, we are permitted to infer the testator's approval.... [B]arring other problems with a disposition, it is valid if it appears above the signature of the testator....

Succession of Guezuraga, 512 So. 2d at 369, *quoting* H. Alston Johnson, Successions and Donations, 43 La.L.Rev. 585, 595-96 (1982). Although *Evans* was not mentioned in *Succession of Guezuraga,* the court's reference to dispositive provisions seems to be consistent with, and does not reflect an intent to stray from, the holding in *Evans.*

* * *

Decree

For the foregoing reasons, the judgment of the trial court is affirmed. Each party is to bear their own costs related to this appeal.

AFFIRMED.

SUCCESSION OF DUSKIN
153 So. 3d 567 (La. App. 4th Cir. 2014), *reh'g denied,* (Dec. 17, 2014),
writ not considered, 163 So. 3d 800 (La. 2015)

SANDRA CABRINA JENKINS, Judge.

This appeal arises from prolonged litigation pertaining to the succession of Manuel Duskin. Appellant appeals the trial court's judgment granting appellees' motion to annul a previously signed order, sustaining appellees' exceptions, and overruling appellant's exceptions. For the reasons set forth below, we affirm.

FACTUAL AND PROCEDURAL BACKGROUND

Manuel Duskin ("Mr. Duskin") died testate on March 19, 2004. On June 23, 2004, his daughters, Lawanda Otis and Rose Duskin Champagne ("daughters"), filed a petition to probate their father's March 12, 2004 testament and place them into possession of his estate. At the time of his death, Mr. Duskin owned twenty percent (equal to one hundred shares) of the Mahalia Jackson Family Corporation ("the Corporation"). Mr. Duskin's March 12, 2004 testament granted his ownership interest in the Corporation to his daughters. A judgment of possession was signed on June 24, 2004, and amended for a typographical error on September 27, 2004, awarding each daughter ten percent interest in the Corporation.

On May 9, 2007 appellant, Bishop Frank E. Lott, initiated a new action involving Mr. Duskin's succession by filing a petition to probate, which was later denied for failure to "follow form required by law." Appellant filed numerous other petitions over the next several months which were likewise denied for failure to follow form. On August 7, 2007, appellant filed an amended petition to probate a document from 1994 ("the 1994 Document") allegedly executed by Mr. Duskin. An order granting this petition was signed and entered into the record on September 7, 2007. Appellant then filed a petition for nullification on September 13, 2007 seeking to invalidate the last will and testament the daughters probated. The petition for nullification was denied for its nonconformity with the mandates of La. C.C.P. art. 2931. Appellant filed an additional pleading attempting to remedy the deficiency along with a written request asking the court to view a videotape which he contends automatically validates the 1994 Document because the video shows Mr. Duskin signing the instrument. The court did not act on this request.

The court consolidated the two actions on its own motion on July 14, 2009. A contradictory hearing on appellant's motion to nullify the testament was scheduled for July 17, 2009, but was continued without date at the appellant's request. Appellant filed another petition to nullify the testament on May 3, 2011, to which appellees filed an exception of prescription. The exception was initially sustained, but the court granted a new trial on its own motion and ultimately overruled appellees' exception.

On February 14, 2012, appellant instituted a new action by filing a petition for damages against appellees, alleging that the testament offered for probate by the daughters was forged and that he is a rightful legatee under the 1994 Document. In response to this petition, appellees filed exceptions of prescription, no right of action, and no cause of action. Appellees also filed a Motion to Vacate or in the Alternative, Annul an Order Previously Signed ("motion to annul"), in reference to the September 7, 2007 order probating the 1994 Document. Appellant filed exceptions to appellees' motion to annul on the grounds of no cause of action, no right of action, and prescription.

Appellant's exceptions and appellees' exceptions and motion were heard on September 6, 2013. On September 10, 2013, the trial court rendered judgment: (1) overruling appellant's exceptions of prescription, no right of action, and no cause of action; (2) granting appellees' motion to annul; (3) sustaining appellees' exception of no right of action; and (4) sustaining appellees' exception of no cause of action concerning the contractual action. Appellant timely filed a motion for new trial, which was subsequently denied, and this appeal followed.

DISCUSSION
No Right of Action
This Court recently discussed the concept of a peremptory exception of no right of action and stated that this exception assumes that the petition offers a valid cause of action and considers whether the instant plaintiff is a member of the class that has a legal interest in the underlying case. *Weber v. Metro. Cmty. Hospice Found., Inc.*, 13–0182, p. 4 (La.App. 4 Cir. 12/18/13), 131 So. 3d 371, 374 (citing *Indus. Companies, Inc. v. Durbin*, 02–0665, p. 12 (La.1/28/03), 837 So. 2d 1207, 1216). La. C.C.P. art. 681 states "[e]xcept as otherwise provided by law, an action can be brought only by a person having a real and actual interest which he asserts." Thus, one must have a justiciable interest in the succession proceeding in order to have standing to maintain an action to annul the testator's testament. *In re Succession of Vickers*, 04–0887, p. 12 (La.App. 4 Cir. 12/22/04), 891 So. 2d 98, 106 (Love, J., concurring).

Here, appellant is not an heir or related to the decedent in any way. Appellant's only avenue of establishing an interest in Mr. Duskin's succession is through the 1994 Document. Appellant contends the 1994 Document is either a valid testament or, in the alternative and at the very least, an enforceable contract. Accordingly, in relation to the exception of no right of action, our consideration begins with determining whether the 1994 Document meets the requirements of a testament, and if not, turns to whether it can stand as a contract.

Before we determine whether the 1994 Document is a testament or perhaps a contract, a depiction of the document is warranted. The 1994 Document is a two-page, handwritten document titled "Irrevocable and Last Will and Testament." The "testators" to the 1994 Document are Mr. Duskin and Mr. Edison Lazard, president and vice-president, respectively, of the Mahalia Jackson Family Resial [sic] Corporation. The 1994 Document attempts to bequeath appellant the rights relative to the Mahalia Jackson name, proceeds, and book belonging to Mr. Duskin and Mr. Lazard. The 1994 Document is not dated, but is notarized, and also signed by Mr. Duskin, Mr. Lazard, and one witness.

A. Testament
There are two forms of testaments in Louisiana, olographic and notarial. La. C.C. art. 1574. A valid testament can only be executed by one testator, regardless of whether it is olographic or notarial. La. C.C. art. 1571 ("Nor may more than one person execute a testament in the same instrument."). Thus, the fact that the 1994 Document grants Mr. Duskin and Mr. Lazard's property together is fatal to it prevailing as a valid testament. Nevertheless, in the interest of completeness for appellant's sake, we will examine the formality requirements of an olographic and notarial testament.

1. Olographic Testament
An olographic testament must be entirely written, dated, and signed in the handwriting of the testator. La. C.C. art. 1575. If an olographic testament is probated, at least two credible witnesses must testify that the handwriting on the instrument is that of the testator. La. C.C.P. art. 2883.

Although the 1994 Document is handwritten and bears the testators' signatures, the only date present is from the notary stamp. This precise issue has been addressed by the Louisiana

Supreme Court which reversed a ruling that upheld an olographic testament written entirely in the hand of the testator, but the only date appearing on the document was filled in by the notary. See *In re Succession of Aycock*, 02–0701 (La.05/24/02), 819 So. 2d 290. Finding that the testament was invalid as to form, the Court went on to state that while extrinsic evidence can be admitted to clarify an ambiguous date, "when the testament contains no date at all in the handwriting of the testator, a date cannot be inferred." Id. (citing Succession of Boyd, 306 So. 2d 687, 692 (La.1975)) ("An absent date cannot be supplied, for it must come from the hand of the testator."). For this reason, we find the 1994 Document fails to satisfy the formality requirements of an olographic testament.

2. Notarial Testament

A notarial testament must be in writing, dated, and if the testator knows how to and is physically able to sign his name and read, the testator must declare or signify in the presence of a notary and two witnesses that the instrument is his last will and testament. La. C.C. art. 1577. Additionally, the testator must sign his name at the end of the testament and on each separate page and the notary and two witnesses must sign a declaration in the presence of each other and the testator attesting that these formalities have been followed. Id. While a material deviation from the manner of execution prescribed by La. C.C. art. 1577 will be fatal to the validity of the testament, the form of the attestation clause is not absolute. In re Succession of Holbrook, 13–1181, p. 9 (La.1/28/14), 144 So. 3d 845, 851 (quoting Succession of Morgan, 257 La. 380, 242 So. 2d 551, 552 (1970)). Thus, as long as the testament contains a clause signed by the witnesses and the notary that encompasses the requisites mentioned in La. C.C. art. 1577, the attestation clause will be sufficient. Id. (quoting *Succession of Morgan*, 242 So. 2d at 552–53).

The 1994 Document was only signed by one witness and, as previously acknowledged, is not dated. Appellant argues that despite the 1994 Document only bearing one witness's signature, two witnesses actually observed Mr. Duskin sign the document and the two affidavits he submitted from these witnesses remedies any potential defect. Although the record contains the affidavits, this does not cure the deficiency because it remains that the witnesses never signed the declaration in the presence of each other, the notary, and the testator. Accordingly, we find that the 1994 Document falls short of complying with the formalities prescribed for a notarial testament. See *In re Succession of Carlton*, 09–1339, p. 4 (La.App. 3 Cir. 4/7/10), 34 So. 3d 1015, 1018 (holding that an invalid notarial testament could not be cured by submitting affidavits by witnesses and the notary). Having determined that the 1994 Document is not a valid testament, we now turn our attention to appellant's argument that the 1994 Document stands as a contract.

B. Contract

In Louisiana, the four elements that are required for formation of a contract are: the capacity to contract, mutual consent, a certain object, and a lawful cause. *In re Succession of Flanigan*, 06–1402, p. 6 (La.App. 4 Cir. 6/13/07), 961 So. 2d 541, 544 (citing *Fairbanks v. Tulane University*, 98–1228, p. 4 (La.App. 4 Cir. 3/31/99), 731 So. 2d 983, 986; La. C.C. arts. 1918, 1927, 1966, and 1971). Contracts are either unilateral or bilateral and onerous or gratuitous. A contract is unilateral when the accepting party does not assume a reciprocal obligation, and bilateral when the parties obligate themselves reciprocally. La. C.C. arts. 1907–08. Likewise, a contract is onerous when both parties obtain an advantage in return for their obligation, and gratuitous when only one party obligates himself for the benefit of the other without obtaining any advantage. La. C.C. arts. 1909–10.

Considering these principles, we first find the 1994 Document is unilateral in that the accepting party (appellant) did not assume any reciprocal obligation; and second find it is gratuitous as the decedent obligated himself for appellant's benefit without obtaining an advantage in return. When, as here, a contract is gratuitous, property can only be acquired or disposed of by donations inter vivos or mortis causa. La. C.C. art. 1467. A donation mortis causa can only be made in the form of an olographic or notarial testament. See La. C.C. arts. 1570 and 1574. Thus, the 1994 Document does not purport to be a donation mortis causa as it fails to meet the formality requirements for both forms of testaments.

Because we find the 1994 Document is gratuitous and not a donation mortis causa, the document must satisfy the requirements of a donation inter vivos in order for it to prevail as a contract. A donation inter vivos is a "contract by which a person, called the donor, gratuitously divests himself, at present and irrevocably, of the thing given in favor of another, called the donee, who accepts it." La. C.C. art. 1468. Pursuant to La. C.C. art. 1541, "[a] donation inter vivos shall be made by authentic act under the penalty of absolute nullity." The requirements for an authentic act are specified in La. C.C. art. 1833, which states in pertinent part:

> A. An authentic act is a writing executed before a notary public or other officer authorized to perform that function, in the presence of two witnesses, and signed by each party who executed it, by each witness, and by each notary public before whom it was executed. The typed or hand-printed name of each person shall be placed in a legible form immediately beneath the signature of each person signing the act.
>
> B. To be an authentic act, the writing need not be executed at one time or place, or before the same notary public or in the presence of the same witnesses, provided that each party who executes it does so before a notary public or other officer authorized to perform that function, and in the presence of two witnesses and each party, each witness, and each notary public signs it. The failure to include the typed or hand-printed name of each person signing the act shall not affect the validity or authenticity of the act.

Despite the foregoing rules, appellant contends an authentic act is not necessary because only "an express and unconditional acceptance" is required. While appellant is correct in that not all donations inter vivos must be executed by authentic act, the rights that are attempting to be donated in the 1994 Document are incorporeal in nature, which are not susceptible to the manual delivery exception. See La. C.C. art. 1543. Thus, contrary to appellant's suggestion, the 1994 Document must be executed by authentic act.

Nevertheless, appellant further asserts that if an authentic act is necessary, the 1994 Document satisfies the requirements because of the two affidavits he submitted. An authentic act is valid, even if signed at different times, as long as all parties sign the document. *Meltzer v. Meltzer*, 95–0551, p. 5 (La.App. 4 Cir. 9/28/95), 662 So. 2d 58, 61 (holding that an authentic act will be valid provided that the "notary and witnesses themselves also sign the act, although not necessarily at the time that any party signs it.") (quoting *Rittiner v. Sinclair*, 374 So. 2d 680, 685 (La.App. 4 Cir.1978)). The instant case does not comport with the rule expressed in Meltzer because here, neither of the alleged "witnesses" actually signed the 1994 Document and instead only signed affidavits. For that reason, the 1994 Document is not a properly executed authentic act and thus cannot serve as a donation inter vivos.

Therefore, having found the 1994 Document does not meet the formality requirements of a contract or testament, it follows that appellant does not belong to "the class of persons that has a legal interest in the subject matter of the litigation." *J–W Power Co. v. State ex rel. Dep't of Revenue & Taxation*, 10–1598, pp. 7–8 (La.3/15/11), 59 So. 3d 1234, 1239 (citing *Reese v. State, Dept. of Public Safety & Corrections*, 03–1615, p. 3 (La.2/20/04), 866 So. 2d 244, 246). Accordingly, sustaining appellees' exception of no right of action was not error as appellant has no interest in the succession proceeding.

No Cause of Action

The trial court sustained appellees' exception of no cause of action as it relates to plaintiff's contractual action only. Thus, our review of this exception is limited to determining whether the 1994 Document can stand as a contract.

Having determined the 1994 Document fails to meet the formality requirements of a contract pretermits any discussion of appellant's claim that the trial court erroneously sustained appellees' exception of no cause of action. Accordingly, this assignment is without merit.

Motion to Vacate and/or Annul Order

The final ruling appellant is challenging is the trial court's ruling granting appellees' motion to annul the September 7, 2007 order probating the 1994 Document. When reviewing the trial court's finding on an action in nullity, the appellate court should determine whether the trial court's finding was reasonable, not whether the finding is right or wrong. *West v. Melancon*, 05–1183, p. 3 (La.App. 4 Cir. 4/26/06), 929 So. 2d 809, 811 (citing Belle Pass Terminal, Inc. v. Jolin, Inc., 01–0149, p. 6 (La.10/16/01), 800 So. 2d 762, 766).

Appellant argues granting the motion to annul was error because it runs afoul to Mr. Duskin's intent as evidenced in the 1994 Document. This contention is misguided as it is well established that a testator's intent is not reached unless the testament is in proper form. See La. C.C. art. 1573; *In re Succession of Dunaway*, 11–1747, pp. 4–5 (La.App. 1 Cir. 5/2/12), 92 So. 3d 555, 557 (citing *Succession of Hendricks*, 08–1914, p. 5 (La.App. 1 Cir. 9/23/09), 28 So. 3d 1057, 1060). Having determined that the 1994 Document is absolutely null for failure to satisfy the form requirements for either testament, Mr. Duskin's intent is of no moment.

Appellant also asserts that not admitting the videotape which portrays Mr. Duskin signing the 1994 Document was error. It is important to note that La. C.C.P. art. 2904, the article relating to the admissibility of videotapes to prove the validity of a testament, was not enacted until 2005. The document that appellant is attempting to probate was executed in 1994, at which time no means existed to prove a testament through a videotape. Therefore, this article is inconsequential to the instant document and, despite appellant's argument otherwise, the trial court's failure to admit the videotape was not error.

After reviewing the record before us, we find the trial court's judgment granting appellees' motion to annul the September 7, 2007 order probating the 1994 Document was reasonable as an order cannot give legal effect to a testament that is absolutely null. This final assignment of error is without merit.

DECREE

For the foregoing reasons, we find the trial court did not err in overruling appellant's exceptions, granting appellees' motion to annul, and sustaining appellees' exceptions. The trial court judgment is affirmed.

AFFIRMED.

SUCCESSION OF HOLBROOK
144 So. 3d 845 (La. 2014)

GUIDRY, Justice.

The issue in this case is whether an incomplete date in an attestation clause invalidates a testament when the full date appears in the first paragraph of the testament and on every page of the testament, including the page of the attestation clause. The district court granted the testator's daughter's motion for summary judgment seeking to set aside the will as invalid because the attestation clause was not fully dated and, thus, failed to meet the requirements of La. Civ. Code art. 1577. The court of appeal affirmed that judgment. Because we conclude the attestation clause in the notarial testament substantially complies with the requirements of Art. 1577, we reverse the district court's judgment and remand the matter for further proceedings.

FACT AND PROCEDURAL HISTORY
The facts in this case are not disputed. James Jason Holbrook, Sr., died testate on July 4, 2010. In his last will and testament, allegedly executed on April 8, 2009, Mr. Holbrook named his wife, Llevonne H. Holbrook, as executrix of his estate. Following Mr. Holbrook's death, Mrs. Holbrook filed a petition on July 10, 2010, to have the will probated, to be appointed executrix, and to be put in possession of Mr. Holbrook's estate. The will was probated, and a judgment of possession was signed by the district court on July 14, 2010. Subsequently, on in November 2010, Mr. Holbrook's daughter, Dianne Carlucci, filed a petition seeking to set aside the judgment of possession and the will, for violations of the requirements for a notarial will and for undue influence. In response to this petition, Mrs. Holbrook filed a general denial and reconventional demand. Mrs. Carlucci answered the reconventional demand, generally denying the allegations therein. In July 2011, Mrs. Carlucci filed a second petition seeking to set aside her father's will.

Thereafter, in February 2012, Mrs. Carlucci filed a motion for summary judgment, asserting the will was invalid due to the fact that the attestation clause was not dated, and, therefore, the will did not meet the statutory requirements of La. Civ. Code art. 1577. Mrs. Carlucci maintained there was no genuine issue as to any material fact and that she was entitled to summary judgment as a matter of law. In her opposition, Mrs. Holbrook acknowledged that the notary who handled her husband's will had inadvertently failed to put the day in the date section of the attestation clause. Mrs. Holbrook noted, however, that every page of the will was dated April 8, 2009, including the last page of the will that included the attestation clause itself. Mrs. Holbrook submitted the affidavits of the notary and one of the witnesses who both stated that Mr. Holbrook had executed his will before them on April 8, 2009.

Following a hearing, the district court granted Mrs. Carlucci's motion for summary judgment. Finding that the testament was prepared in accordance with Civil Code articles 1576 et seq. governing as to form, the district court held that the attestation clause must be dated as provided in La. Civ. Code art. 1577 and that this testament was invalid due to the omission of the date in the attestation clause.

Mrs. Holbrook appealed, asserting the district court erred in holding the will was invalid because the attestation clause was not dated. The court of appeal affirmed. *Succession of Holbrook*, 2012–1655 (La. App. 1 Cir. 4/26/13), 115 So. 3d 1184. We granted Mrs. Holbrook's writ application to determine the correctness of the lower courts' rulings. *Succession of Holbrook*, 2013–1181 (La.9/13/13), 120 So. 3d 275.

LAW AND ANALYSIS

Currently, there are two forms of testaments in Louisiana. La. Civ. Code art. 1574. The olographic testament is handwritten, dated, and signed by the testator. La. Civ. Code art. 1575. The notarial testament must be executed in accordance with the formalities of La. Civ. Code arts. 1577—1580.1. La. Civ. Code art. 1576. This matter concerns a notarial testament, which must be written and notarized. La. Civ. Code art. 1577 provides:

The notarial testament shall be prepared in writing and dated and shall be executed in the following manner. If the testator knows how to sign his name and to read and is physically able to do both, then:

(1) In the presence of a notary and two competent witnesses, the testator shall declare or signify to them that the instrument is his testament and shall sign his name at the end of the testament and on each other separate page.

(2) In the presence of the testator and each other, the notary and the witnesses shall sign the following declaration, or one substantially similar: "In our presence the testator has declared or signified that this instrument is his testament and has signed it at the end and on each other separate page, and in the presence of the testator and each other we have hereunto subscribed our names this __ day of ____, __."

The attestation clause in Mr. Holbrook's will omitted the "day" in the date:

IN OUR PRESENCE THE TESTATOR has declared or signified that the instrument is his testament and has signed it at the end and on each other separate page, and in the presence of the TESTATOR and each other we have hereunto subscribed our names on this ..... day of April, 2009, in Covington, Louisiana.

WITNESSES:

/S/ Vicki M. Wilson   /S/Peggy G. Vallejo, Bar No. 26539
                                                                              Notary Public
/S/ Carolyn Garlick   428 West 21st Avenue
Covington, LA 70433   My Commission Expires at Death

The executrix, Mrs. Holbrook, asserts the testament substantially conforms to the statutory formalities and that any ambiguity as to the omitted "day" may be resolved by the date set forth on each page of the will and the affidavits of the notary and the witness. Citing *Succession of Songne*, 94–1198 (La. App. 3 Cir. 11/2/95), 664 So. 2d 556, writ denied, 95–2877 (La.2/2/96), 666 So. 2d 1101, Mrs. Holbrook further asserts that, because the date is set forth on each page of the will, the affidavits submitted in opposition to the motion for summary judgment are sufficient to resolve any ambiguity in the date.

As the court of appeal noted, La. Civ. Code art. 1577 provides that a notarial testament "shall" be executed in a certain manner. The word "shall" is mandatory. La. Rev. Stat. 1:3. When a law is clear and free from all ambiguity, the letter of it is not to be disregarded under the pretext of pursuing its spirit. La. Rev. Stat. 1:4. La. Civ. Code art. 1577 states that the notarial testament shall be prepared in writing and be dated.

In *Succession of Holloway*, the court reiterated that "the month, without the day, is no date." 531 So. 2d 431, 433 (La.1988) (quoting Heffner v. Heffner, 48 La. Ann. 1089, 20 So. 281 (1896)). In that case, the question was whether "the ___ day of February, 1984" was a sufficient date within the meaning of former La. Rev. Stat. 9:2442 (as amended in 1974 by Act No. 246), the predecessor to Art. 1577, enacted in 1997 by Act No. 1421, § 1, eff. July 1, 1999. La. Rev. Stat. 9:2442, similar to what Art. 1577 does today, provided that "[t]he statutory will shall be in writing ... shall be dated, and shall be made in the following manner: ...." La. Rev. Stat. 9:2442 then set forth an attestation clause that included the verbiage "this ___ day of ___, 19__." This court explained that La. Rev. Stat. 9:2442 as amended in 1974 thus required the will to be dated, explaining that the previous version of the statute did not so require. The court then went on to invalidate the will because it contained no complete date anywhere within the testament.

Although Art. 1577, like former La. Rev. Stat. 9:2442, mandates the will be dated, it does not specify the location in the testament where the date must appear. Indeed, Comment (g) to La. Civ. Code art. 1577 specifically addresses the issue of the date and its location:

> This Article requires that the testament be dated but intentionally does not specify where the date must appear, nor does it require that the dating be executed in the presence of the notary and witnesses or that the dating be made by the testator. It is common practice to have a typewritten testament that is already dated, and that testament should be upheld if it is valid in all other respects. The first paragraph of the Article states that "the ... testament shall be prepared in writing and shall be dated", and the subsequent language (with reference to execution) intentionally contains no language that refers to the dating having been executed in the presence of the witnesses or the notary. Nor is there any requirement that the testator be the one to date the testament. The critical function of the date is to establish a time frame so that, among other things, in the event of a conflict between two presumptively valid testaments, the later one prevails.

La. Civ. Code art. 1577, Official Revision Comments (g).

In the instant case, there can be no doubt the testament itself is dated, as it is dated numerous times. A complete date, April 8, 2009, is printed on each page of the testament. The first paragraph of the dispositive portion of the testament also recites the full date: "James Jason Holbrook, SR, Testator, being of sound mind and knowing how to and being physically able to read and write, makes and declares this Last Will and Testament, on the 8th day of April, 2009." The penultimate paragraph, in which Mr. Holbrook attests that he has executed the testament in accordance with Article 1577's formalities, references this date once again:

> IN WITNESS WHEREOF, I have signed on each page and declared this to be my
> Last Will and Testament in the presence of the Notary Public and the witnesses

hereafter named and undersigned, at the date and place first above written. (emphasis added).

The testator thereafter signed his full name. The undated attestation clause, which comprises the last paragraph of the will, is thus located between two unambiguous references to the full date on which the testament was executed: the penultimate paragraph referencing the date in the first paragraph and the printed date at the bottom of the page on which the attestation clause was placed. Article 1577 merely requires the testament to be "dated," and, as clarified by the article's comments, the date can appear anywhere on the testament and does not have to be written in the presence of the notary and two witnesses. La. Civ. Code art. 1577, Official Revision Comments (g). Accordingly, the testament itself has been properly dated.

The question presented, however, is whether the attestation clause signed by the witnesses and the notary is "substantially similar" to the form found in Art. 1577(2) and must itself be dated as provided for in the article. The lower courts, relying on Succession of Holloway, concluded the attestation clause must itself contain a date, and the date without the day is no date.

We disagree with that conclusion under the facts of this case. *Succession of Holloway* is distinguishable on its facts, as there was no complete date found anywhere in the testament. Furthermore, the court there was called upon to determine whether the 1974 amendments to La. Rev. Stat. 9:2442 added a mandatory requirement that the will be dated to be valid, because the prior version did not necessarily mandate the will be dated, and under that prior version, "if the will is undated, the date 'may be established for the statutory will by ordinary proof when and if proof of it is needed.' "See *Succession of Holloway*, 531 So. 2d at 431–32 (discussing and quoting *Succession of Gordon*, 257 La. 1086, 245 So. 2d 319 (1971)(the will in Gordon contained no date whatsoever)). The court in *Succession of Holloway* merely held that the statutory will, now called a notarial testament, must be dated and that an incomplete date will not suffice.

Nevertheless, courts need not strictly adhere to the formal requirements of the statutory will, to the extent of elevating form over function. As we explained in Succession of Guezuraga, 512 So. 2d 366 (La.1987):

> But we are not required to give the statutory will a strict interpretation. The Legislature adopted the statutory will from the common law in order to avoid the rigid formal requirements of the Louisiana Civil Code. "The minimal formal requirements of the statutory will are only designed to provide a simplified means for a testator to express his testamentary intent and to assure, through his signification and his signing in the presence of a notary and two witnesses, that the instrument was intended to be his last will." *Succession of Porche v. Mouch* [*Succession of Porche*], 288 So. 2d 27, 30 (La.1973). In accordance with this legislative intent, courts liberally construe and apply the statute, maintaining the validity of the will if at all possible, as long as it is in substantial compliance with the statute.... In deciding what constitutes substantial compliance, the courts look to the purpose of the formal requirements—to guard against fraud.

> Where the departure from form has nothing whatsoever to do with fraud, ordinary common sense dictates that such departure should not produce nullity. It was the

intent of the legislature to reduce form to the minimum necessary to prevent fraud. It is submitted that in keeping with this intent, slight departures from form should be viewed in the light of their probable cause. If they indicate an increased likelihood that fraud may have been perpetrated they would be considered substantial and thus a cause to nullify the will. If not, they should be disregarded. Thus testators and estate planners will have the security that the legislature intended to give them.

Succession of Guezuraga, 512 So. 2d at 368 (citations omitted).

With regard to the attestation clause itself, this court explained:

All of the formal requisites for the composition of our statutory will must be observed; otherwise the instrument is null and void. There must be an attestation clause, or clause of declaration. However, its form is not sacrosanct: It may follow the form suggested in the statute or use a form substantially similar thereto. The attestation clause is designed to evince that the facts and circumstances of the confection and execution of the instrument conform to the statutory requirements. In construing the attestation clause of this type of will, this court has been most liberal in its determination of whether the clause complies in form and whether it evidences the requisites to supply validity to the instrument. See Succession of Eck, 233 La. 764, 98 So. 2d 181 [(1957)]; *Succession of Nourse*, 234 La. 691, 101 So. 2d   204 [(1958)]. In *Succession of Thibodeaux*, 238 La. 791, 116 So. 2d 525 [(1959)],   we reiterated a basic principle of construction of wills, that the validity of a will is to be maintained if possible. In construing an attestation clause we will not require strict, technical, and pedantic compliance in form or in language. Rather, we will   examine the clause to see whether there is substantial adherence to form and   whether it shows facts and circumstances which evidence compliance with the formal   requirements   for   testamentary validity.

Succession of Morgan, 257 La. 380, 386, 242 So. 2d 551, 552–53 (1970). See also Kathryn Venturatos Lorio, *La. Civ. L. Treatise, Successions and Donations* § 12:2 (2nd ed.) ("The statutes [former La. Rev. Stat. 9:2442] provided a sample attestation clause, but the form was not 'sacrosanct.'").

Louisiana courts have held that the complete absence of an attestation clause will be fatal to the validity of a notarial will. See *In re Succession of Richardson*, 05–0552 (La. App. 1 Cir. 3/24/06), 934 So. 2d 749, writ denied, 06–0896 (La.6/2/06), 929 So. 2d 1265; *Succession of English*, 508 So. 2d 631, 633 (La. App. 2 Cir.1987). However, courts have also held the attestation clause itself must only be "substantially similar" to the attestation clause in Art. 1577, such that minor deviations in form with regard to the date in the attestation clause do not render the testament invalid in the absence of any indication of fraud. See *In re Succession of Hebert*, 12–281 (La. App. 3 Cir. 10/3/12), 101 So. 3d 131; *Succession of Armstrong*, 93–2385 (La. App. 4 Cir. 4/28/94), 636 So. 2d 1109, writ denied, 94–1370 (La.9/16/94), 642 So. 2d 196; cf. *Succession of Bel*, 377 So. 2d 1380 (La. App. 4th Cir.1979)(statutory will that contained a date in the attestation clause but not in the will itself was nevertheless valid).

In *Succession of Hebert*, the court upheld the validity of a statutory will under La. Rev. Stat. 9:2442, wherein the attestation clause was split between the witnesses and the notary, with only the attestation of the notary dated. The court rejected the argument that there should have been one, single witness/notary attestation clause, that it should have been dated, and that the notary should not have used a separate notarial certification. The court reasoned that split attestations between the testator, the witnesses, and the notary do not invalidate the will. As to the omission of the date, the court reasoned that the date of March 24, 1999, appeared twice, both above and below the witnesses' attestation clause: in the testator's attestation of signing and in the notary's attestation clause. *Succession of Hebert*, 12–281, p. 11, 101 So. 3d at 139. Further, the court noted, the date was incorporated by reference as "the date hereof" in the witnesses' attestation clause, which was sandwiched between the two dated clauses. Id., pp. 11–12, 101 So. 3d at 139. Accordingly, the court found that, while the attestation clauses did not contain the exact language or be in the exact form traditionally used, their content clearly showed compliance with the law for a valid will. Id., p. 12, 101 So. 3d at 140.

In *Succession of Armstrong*, the attestation clause was not dated, having no "day" similar to the instant case, but the will was nevertheless upheld. The court reasoned that, while the failure to date the attestation clause is a serious defect, the date was placed at the end of the disposition portion of the will and again at the end of the attestation portion below the witnesses' signatures and immediately above the notary's signature. 636 So. 2d at 1112.

In *Succession of Bel*, the court upheld the validity of a will that contained a date in the attestation clause but no date in the body of the will; thus, the issue presented was whether the 1974 amendments to La. Rev. Stat. 9:2442 required both the will and the attestation clause be dated. 377 So. 2d at 1382. The court relied on the language of La. Rev. Stat. 9:2442, see Note 2, supra, pointing out that the statute required the dispositive portion of the will be signed in the presence of the notary and two witnesses, and that the notary and witnesses must execute a dated attestation clause signifying the fact of the execution of the will in their presence. Id. Because the statutory form for the attestation clause provided for a date, the court concluded that "so long as the attestation clause is dated, it is not sacramental that the dispositive portion was not dated." Id.

"Under Louisiana law, there is a presumption in favor of the validity of testaments in general and proof of the nonobservance of formalities must be exceptionally compelling to rebut that presumption." *Succession of Armstrong*, 636 So. 2d at 1111. Although Mr. Holbrook's will does not contain a complete date, we find the "facts and circumstances ... evidence compliance with the formal requirements for testamentary validity." *Succession of Morgan*, 257 La. at 386, 242 So. 2d at 553. Here, the incompletely-dated attestation clause falls clearly between two unambiguous references to the full date on which the testament was executed: the testator's attestation clause referencing the date of April 8, 2009, and the printed date of April 8, 2009, on the bottom of the page on which the attestation clause of the witnesses and notary is located. There is no indication of fraud in the record before us, and in all other respects, Mr. Holbrook's testament and the attestation clause comply with La. Civ. Code art. 1577. Accordingly, we find the attestation clause in the will is substantially similar to the form found in La. Civ. Code art. 1577(2), such that the district court erred in granting summary judgment in favor of Mrs. Carlucci and invalidating the will on that basis.

CONCLUSION

Having conducted a de novo review of the district court's grant of the motion for summary judgment, we conclude the attestation clause in Mr. Holbrook's testament substantially complies with Art. 1577, and thus summary judgment was not warranted in favor of Mrs. Carlucci. Accordingly, we reverse the district court's summary judgment and remand the matter for further proceedings.

DECREE

REVERSED AND REMANDED.

NOTES

In *Succession of Holloway*, 531 So. 2d 431, (La. 1988), the testament contained only the month and year of execution. The testament stated that it was executed "the _____ day of February 1984." The court held that the statute (*Former La. R.S. 9:2442*) expressly required a date, and a date consists of a month, day, and year. Therefore, the will was invalid. However, as was mentioned above (in the case of olographic wills), and as the court noted in *Holloway*, when an incomplete date is given, extrinsic evidence may be introduced to remove any ambiguity. In *Succession of Roniger*, 706 So. 2d 1025 (La. App. 4th Cir. 1998), the Louisiana Fourth Circuit introduced extrinsic evidence to determine the date of the statutory will's execution when the date recited in the document was after the testator's death. Do these two decisions seem fair or consistent with the state's policy of promoting the testator's intent?

PROBLEMS

1. If both witnesses are not present at the same time, but the testator declares separately to each that the document is his will, has there been substantial compliance?

2. Look over the four methods of executing a notarial testament in articles 1577-1580. Consider which form should be used in the following situations.

   a. Testatrix is deaf, but can read and write.

   b. Testator is deaf and blind, unable to read Braille well, but can speak some and can interpret sign language.

   c. Testator is not in any way physically disabled, but is illiterate and hesitant about signing his name.

   d. Testatrix is competent, literate, and knows how to sign her name. Due to a stroke, she is paralyzed and physically unable to sign her name.

3. Is a one-page signed and dated document in valid form of a notarial testament where the final paragraph states, "I hereby sign my name in the presence of the two undersigned competent witnesses and notary public affirming this is my last will and testament on the date aforementioned above" a valid will? Why or why not? *See Succession of Simno*, 948 So. 2d 315 (La. App. 4th Cir. 2006).

NOTES

A will must be executed by the testatrix, herself, and not by a mandatary for the testatrix. La. C.C. 1571. A single instrument may not contain the testament of more than one person. La. C.C. 1571.

No witness to a notarial testament may be insane, blind, under the age of sixteen, or unable to sign his name. La. C.C. 1581. In addition, a witness to the will of a testator who does not know how to read or is physically unable to read, La. C.C. 1579, may not be deaf or be unable to read. La C.C. 1581.

Generally, a witness or a notary to a will may not take under the will. If a legatee serves as a notary or witness, the entire testament will not be invalid, but only the affected legacy. La. C.C. 1582. However, a witness (not a notary) to a will, who would be an intestate heir of the testator, "may receive the lesser of his intestate share or the legacy in the testament." La. C.C. 1582. Note that this is a change from pre-revision law, under which a legacy to any witness was invalid. *See* La. C.C. 1592 (repealed).

Designation of Executor and Attorney

For many years, it had been the custom in Louisiana to name an attorney in a will who would serve the executor after the decedent's death. In 1929, the designation of such an attorney was held "valid and binding" on the executor and those taking under the will. *Rivet v. Battisella,* 167 La. 766, 120 So. 289 (1929). At the time, there existed a jurisprudentially established rule that the client may discharge his attorney at any time and without cause, but the *Rivet* case did not consider whether its holding was in conflict with this rule. *Rivet* was overruled in *Succession of Jenkins,* 481 So. 2d 607 (La. 1986). In its next regular session the Louisiana legislature enacted La. R.S. 9:2448 that essentially provided that an attorney designated by a testator in his will could only be removed for "just cause." The Louisiana Supreme Court found the statute to be "in direct, irreconcilable conflict" with Rule 1.16 (a)(3) of the Rules of Professional Conduct and thus, "unconstitutional, null void, and of no effect." *Succession of Wallace*, 574 So. 2d 348 (La. 1991).

NOTE

Who does the attorney for the estate truly represent, the decedent or the executor?

La. C.C. 1583 further provides that the designation of a succession representative, trustee or attorney is not a legacy.

Types of Legacies, Lapsed Legacies, and Accretion

Introduction

Under prior and current law, the Code defines three types of legacies. The present Code recognizes universal, general, and particular legacies which have replaced the three types of legacies that existed under prior law, that is, universal legacies, legacies under universal title and particular legacies. *Compare* La. C.C. art. 1584 and former La. C.C. art. 1605. When a legacy of any of the three types is made to two or more persons, it must be further classified as either separate (when the testator assigns shares) or joint (when he does not). La. C.C. 1588. As you read the cases decided under pre-revision law, determine how the legacies discussed would be classified today.

Traditionally, a legacy's classification was important in that it determined how the debts of the estate would be apportioned among the legatees and it also determined which legatee would benefit from lapsed legacies, legacies that a named legatee does not, or cannot, take. The revision altered the relationship between classification of a legacy and determination of both apportionment and accretion of lapsed legacies.

Types of Legacies: Universal, General, and Particular

A universal legacy is a disposition of all the donor's property, or the balance remaining after the payment of particular legacies in favor of one or more persons. La. C.C. 1585. The universal legatee will benefit from most lapsed legacies. La. C.C. 1595. A general legacy is defined as the disposition of a fraction or proportion of the estate, or a fraction or proportion of the balance of the estate that remains after particular legacies, (such as 2/3 of all property or 2/3 of the balance after paying particular legacies), or a disposition of all or a portion of a category of the donor's property, (such as all movables, or 1/3 of all immovable property). The categories of property that may be donated in the form of a general legacy are provided in article 1586: "separate or community property, movable and immovable property, or corporeal and incorporeal property." This list is exclusive. La. C.C. 1586. A particular legacy is defined as any legacy that is neither universal nor general. La. C.C. 1587. "All my bank accounts to A" or "my car to B" would both qualify as particular legacies. While a donation of all or a portion of the testator's *corporeal* property would be a general legacy, the donation of all or a portion of the testator's *corporeal movables* would be a particular legacy. La. C.C. 1586, comment f.

Under the prior law, the Code contained little guidance on how the legacy of the residuum of the decedent's estate should be classified. For example, if the testator left his house to A and the balance of his estate to B, was the legacy to B universal? The courts concluded that the legacy to B was a universal legacy because the intention of the testator was construed such that he wanted to give B a vocation to the entire estate, the universality, to everything not otherwise disposed of. An important consequence of finding B a universal legatee was that, if the legacy to A failed (or lapsed) for some reason, such as his predecease, then B kept the house as a residuary universal legacy. The revision has followed the jurisprudential solution. A donation of the balance of the donor's estate, following one or more particular legacies, is under current law a universal legacy. La. C.C. 1585.

If the donation of a residuum follows a general legacy, how should the residuum be classified? If the testator leaves 1/3 of his property to A, 1/3 to B, and the remainder to C, how should the remainder be classified? Under both prior case law and the current codal definitions of the three types of legacies, the legacy to C cannot be classified as a universal legacy. The legacy to C is a general legacy, as the testator has left C the remaining 1/3 of his estate. However, has the testator granted C a vocation to the whole, such that, should B predecease the testator, C should take B's lapsed legacy? Where would the testator want B's legacy to pass - to C? Or to the testator's intestate heirs? La. C.C. 1595, after the revision, provides "[w]hen a general legacy is phrased as a residue or balance of the estate without specifying that the residue or balance is the remaining fraction or a certain portion of the estate ... it shall be treated as a universal legacy for purposes of accretion." Because a universal legatee would benefit by the lapse of B's legacy under current law, C will as well.

SUCCESSION OF BURNSIDE
35 La. Ann. 708 (1883)

*   *   *

Manning, J.

John Burnside died on June 29, 1881. Shortly thereafter his will was admitted to probate and was ordered to be executed. It begins thus:

New Orleans, April 28th, 1857.

I, John Burnside, being of sound mind and body, but mindful of the uncertainty of life, do by this my last Will and Testament, dispose of all my worldly estate, as follows:

Eighteen numbered clauses then follow, the first fifteen of which contain legacies to several persons and charitable institutions. The last three are in these words:

16. I do nominate and appoint Oliver Beirne, my late partner in trade, my sole executor to carry this, my last will, into full execution; no security shall be exacted from said executor, Oliver Beirne, for the faithful discharge of the duties imposed on him by this, my last will and testament.
17. The residue of my property of every description-say stock in trade, promissory notes, accounts, my interest in the firm of J. Burnside & Co., stocks, etc., etc., etc., I bequeath to my executor, Oliver Beirne, subject to the payment of all my just and lawful debts, and the expenses incidental to my succession, as a token of my sincere regard for his uniform kindness and services rendered to me in early life.
18. At the end of twelve months after my demise, my executor, Oliver Beirne, will pay the bequests herein made, or as soon thereafter as possible.

John Burnside.
New Orleans, April 28, 1857.

*   *   *

Legacies amounting to $138,000 have lapsed by the death of the legatees before the death of the testator, and it is contended on the one hand that these legacies enure to the benefit of the universal legatee, and on the other, to the heirs and in default of heirs, the State.

*   *   *

There can be no doubt that John Burnside, when he wrote his will, intended to leave the residue of all property he then had to Oliver Beirne-in other words, he intended that Beirne should take his whole estate, subject only to the charges in the form of legacies. The will was made to avoid intestacy as to any part of his property, and had he died then, there could have been no question about the effect of the will.

Let us in the outset recognize the fact that the Code does not designate any words which must be employed to institute an heir, or to bequeath an universal legacy. It defines the latter simply as a testamentary disposition by which a testator gives to a person the whole of the property which he leaves at his decease. REV. CIV. CODE Art. 1606. It gives the name of legacy under a universal title to that disposition by which a testator bequeaths a fixed proportion of his estate or all of a particular kind of property, or a fixed proportion of a particular kind, *Ibid*, Art. 1612, and then groups all others under one head in the class of legacies under a particular title. *Ibid*, Art. 1625.

It is not claimed that the bequest to Beirne is a legacy under an universal title. It certainly is not a legacy of specific property like the square of ground to McStea, or of a fixed sum of money like those to Andrew Beirne and others-"a thing bequeathed," in the language of the next article of the Code; and it is argued as evident that it is not a universal legacy because it is not a disposition of his whole property.

The words of the Code are not sacramental. It is not needful that a testamentary bequest shall be couched in the identical language of the Code, and if it is essential to constitute a universal legatee that all shall be given him without diminution, the only will by which such legatee could be named would be one which contained that disposition and no other.

Demolombe considers the question in two aspects, whether the legacies which precede the disposition of the residue are under a particular or universal title, (and we are concerned here only with the former) and after stating the arguments of preceding commentators says, the particular legacies which have been first made, not being of fractional parts of the whole-n'ayant pas fractione l'universalite-the legacy which follows will naturally embrace the entirety. 4 DONATIONS ET TESTAMENTS, Nos. 541-2. 3 Troplong DONATIONS ET TESTAMENTS, No. 1783.

The whole discussion of the French commentators upon this subject was before this Court in *Compton v. Prescott*, 12 Rob. 56, and it was admitted there may be cases in which the legatee of the residue, or of the remainder of an estate, may claim as universal legatee, p. 66, and it was later expressly adjudicated in *Suc. of Fisk*, 3 Ann. 705, wherein the Court, quoting Toullier-if a testator first give a particular legacy, and then bequeath the surplus or residue of his estate to another, the latter will be an universal legatee-applies it as a rule of construction which controlled that case. It therefore follows that this is either an universal legacy, or it is a nondescript. When the Code divides all legacies into three classes, and a legacy is of such kind as to exclude it from two of them, it must be in the remaining class or not exist. But it would exist without classification. The testator's disposition is there, and effect must be given to it. It can be included in no other class but that of universal legacies.

*   *   *

One other question remains. To whom do the lapsed legacies fall?

*   *   *

The identical question in the case at bar was presented to this Court in *Prevost v. Martel*, 10 Rob. 512, where quoting the last Article at length and others pertinent to the matter in hand, the Court say: "it is clear therefore that there being no forced heir, the universal legatee is bound to discharge all the legacies, and that in case of their failure, he should be entitled to take them as a part of the succession," p. 518.

*   *   *

In *Suc. of Foucher*, 18 Ann. 409, it was said it was optional with the testatrix, having no forced heirs, to bequeath to or withhold from her relatives, and the construction must prevail that she desired the property to be distributed among her instituted heirs, and that the will should be read as if the name of the legatee of the lapsed legacy had never been in it.

These were followed by *Hoover v. York*, 24 Ann. 375, where the Court say, the lapse of a particular legacy, by reason of the incapacity of the legatee, enured to the benefit of the universal legatees, and not to the collateral heirs, p. 380. In the *Suc. of Dougart*, 30 Ann. 268, the Court cited *Hoover v. York*, and said, if these parties are universal legatees, they profit by the caducity of legacies to the exclusion of the heirs at law, p. 273, and this long line of uninterrupted and consistent ruling culminates in *Suc. of Dupuy*, 33 Ann. 277, where it was held that a legacy lapsing by the death of the legatee before the testator, enured to the benefit of the universal legatees, p. 282, thus exhibiting a remarkable consensus of opinion upon this particular question, this Court having seven times affirmed the principle, and on each occasion with a different personnel of this Bench-seven courts, each differently constituted from the others.

And why should it not be so? The testator had formally and expressly disposed of all his estate, selecting a stranger in blood as the object of his bounty, and thereby evincing his intention to put him in his own stead and place, to the exclusion of kindred. It is he that ought to take adempted legacies, they being a part, when caducity occurs, of the universality of the property.

*   *   *

NOTES

The revision law follows *Burnside* and defines a universal legacy as both "a disposition of all of the estate or the balance of the estate that remains after particular legacies." La. C.C. 1585. The general rule is that lapsed legacies accrete in favor of the universal legatee. La. C.C. 1595. However, there are instances in which a lapsed legacy may accrete in favor of a particular or general legatee. Under prior law, a lapsed legacy would accrete in favor of a particular or general legatee if the lapsed legacy was a charge on the lapsed legacy. La. C.C. 1704 (repealed). For instance, if testator provided "all of my immovables to A, except my house to B" and "all of

14-40

my books to C, except my law books to D," the legacies to B and D are charges on the legacies to A and C respectively. If the legacies to B and D lapse, A and C benefit. The revised La. C.C. art. 1591 provides the same result.

PROBLEMS

Consider the following fact situations and then answer the questions, using the provisions of La. C.C. 1584-1596, as amended by Act 1421 of 1997, effective July 1, 1999.

1. Baptiste died in 1868. At the time Baptiste lived, if a person died without descendants but with at least one surviving parent, the parent was a forced heir. Cognizant of this, and without any children, Baptiste wrote a will, leaving 1/3 of his property to his mother. He bequeathed the usufruct of the balance of his property to his wife, and the naked ownership of that balance to his niece and nephew, the children of his sister. Baptiste died survived by his wife and his niece and nephew. His mother predeceased him. (*See Succession of Dougart,* 30 La. Ann. 268 (La. 1878).)

      (a) Classify the legacies to Baptiste's mother, wife and niece and nephew. (*See* La. C.C. 1586, comment c.)
      (b) Has the legacy to Baptiste's mother lapsed? (*See* La. C.C. 1589.) If so, who would benefit from the lapse? (*Consider* La. C.C. 1591, 1595.)

2. Myrtle left a will containing several particular legacies and "the remainder of her movables to Dr. Hymel." The only property Myrtle died possessed of, other than the itemized items left to particular legatees, was movable property. (*See Succession of Moffat,* 577 So. 2d 1210 (La. App. 4th Cir. 1991.)

      (a) How should the legacy to Dr. Hymel be classified?
      (b) If one of the particular legacies to a named legatee lapsed, could Dr. Hymel benefit from the lapse?

Joint or Separate Legacies

A legacy made in favor of two or more persons is either joint or separate. La. C.C. art. 1588. According to article 1588, a legacy is "separate when the testator assigns shares and joint when he does not." The testator, however, may expressly provide that the legacy is to be joint or separate. Whether a legacy is joint or separate has consequences, if the legacy to one of the legatees lapses. If the legacy to the legatees is joint, the lapsed portion *may* accrete to the remaining joint legatee or legatees. If the legacy is separate, no accretion will occur in favor of the joint legatee.

A recurring problem in the jurisprudence, illustrated by the cases to follow, is whether there has been an assignment of shares. In cases where the testator does not say "one-half to A and one-half to B," but rather "to A and B, share and share alike" or perhaps, "to A and B, to be divided between them" has there been an assignment of shares to A and B?

SUCCESSION OF LAMBERT
28 So. 2d 1 (La. 1946)

HAMITER, Justice.

Frederick Lambert, who was never married, died in the City of New Orleans on June 25, 1942, leaving a nun-cupative will by public act of date July 18, 1927. His estate, consisting principally of cash and real estate, was inventoried and valued at $186,765.11.

In the testament the testator made numerous specific bequests to relatives (principally nephews and nieces, but also his brother William Lambert to whom he bequeathed $10,000) and to friends; and he appointed his other brothers Robert Lambert and Albert Lambert executors without bond. The instrument further provided: "After all my debts and obligations are paid I leave the residue of my estate to my brothers Robert Vincent Lambert and Albert Lambert share and share alike." Albert Lambert predeceased the testator.

After the will was probated, the executor confirmed, and the specific cash legacies and debts paid, Robert V. Lambert, the surviving residuary legatee, was sent and put into possession, by an ex parte judgment, of the residue of the estate, it having a value of $142,293.71.

Subsequently, William L. Lambert and Albert E. Lambert, brother and nephew respectively of the testator, instituted this suit attacking the judgment that placed Robert Vincent Lambert in possession of the residuum. In the petition they alleged:

> That by the terms of the nuncupative will by public act the decedent Fred Lambert disposed of the residue of his property, in the proportion of one-half to each of his two brothers, namely, Robert Vincent Lambert and Albert Lambert.
>
> That Albert Lambert having died before the death of the testator, that that portion of the testator's estate bequeathed to Albert Lambert, was therefore not disposed of by last will and testament, and should devolve upon the legal heirs in accordance with the provisions of Article 1709 of the REVISED CIVIL CODE.
>
> "Petitioners further aver that they together with Robert V. Lambert, and the children of Christopher Lambert, are the sole and only heirs at law of said decedent, and, as such, they are entitled to inherit all of the property of the decedent which had not been disposed of by last will and testament."

To this petition the defendant, Robert V. Lambert, tendered exceptions of no cause and no right of action. The district court, accepting the allegations of the petition as being true and correct (a copy of the will was not attached), overruled the exceptions.

*　　*　　*

It is a cardinal rule of testamentary construction that each and every part of the will shall be given effect; no word, phrase or clause shall be declared surplusage if it can be afforded a reasonable and legal interpretation. On this subject we said in *Succession of Price*, 202 La. 842, 13 So. 2d 240, 244, that:

To determine the intention of the testator the whole will is to be taken into consideration. Every word must be given effect if that can be done without defeating the general purpose of the will which is to be made effective in every reasonable method.

* * *

In the popular and ordinary sense, the phrase "share and share alike" means in equal shares or proportions. Such is the definition given it in Webster's New International Dictionary, Second Edition, as well as in both Black's and Bouvier's Law Dictionaries. If then the expression signifies an equal division the using of it in a conversation or in a writing is to apportion one-half to each where two persons are concerned, one-third to each if there are three, one-fourth to each if there are four, and so on. Thus, if a mother says to her three children, "I give to all of you this pie share and share alike," certainly each child is entitled to receive a definite one-third of it.

By giving effect, therefore, to all of the words of the will in question as must be done, especially those in the controversial clause, and by interpreting them reasonably using their popular and ordinary meaning, the conclusion is inescapable that the testator when employing the phrase "share and share alike" deliberately and definitely divided the residue of the estate between his brothers, Albert and Robert Lambert, leaving it to them in the proportion of one-half to each; he, in other words, assigned the part of each co-legatee in the thing bequeathed. It follows logically that the legacy is not governed by the above discussed exception (R.C.C. Art. 1707) to the general rule respecting testamentary accretion (R.C.C. Art. 1706), and that the lapsed portion bequeathed to Albert Lambert devolves upon the legitimate heirs of the testator (R.C.C. Art. 1709).

To reach a contrary conclusion, that is that the testator did not assign the part of each co-legatee, is to disregard or to delete from the will the "share and share alike" phrase in contravention of the above mentioned cardinal rule of testamentary interpretation.

* * *

For the reasons assigned the judgment appealed from is reversed and set aside, the exceptions of no right and no cause of action are overruled, and the case is remanded to the district court for further proceedings according to law and consistent with the views herein expressed. Costs of this appeal shall be paid by defendant; all other costs shall await the final determination of the litigation.

NOTE

After the revision of 1997, if a testator leaves a legacy to A and B "share and share alike" and also says he wants that legacy to be treated as a joint legacy, what result? What if the testator leaves the legacy to A and B "share and share alike" and says no more?

HOPSON v. RATCLIFF

DOUCET, Judge.

Petitioners herein appeal the district judge's interpretation of an olographic will whereby lapsed particular and residual legacies were granted to respondents, legal heirs of legatee who predeceased the testatrix, rather than the named surviving legatees. We affirm.

The issues presented on appeal are: (1) whether the residuary clause of decedent's will was distributive rather than conjoint, thereby precluding accretion in favor of the surviving legatees; and (2) whether property subject to a particular legacy should devolve upon the heirs at law rather than fall into the residuum of the estate for distribution to the surviving residuary legatee.

We have carefully scrutinized the record in this case and have concluded that it contains no grounds for reversal or modification. That the learned trial judge accurately assessed the facts is undisputed and we concur in his legal analysis thereof. Inasmuch as excellent written reasons for judgment were assigned by the trial court, we hereby adopt the following as our own:

> This is a suit for a declaratory judgment to interpret the olographic will of Clara F. Heins.
>
> The contest is between the testamentary heirs and the legal heirs.
>
> The deceased had no forced heirs. At the time she made her will, her kin consisted of a sister, Katherine F. Maxfield, four nieces, Helen F. Ratliff, Lucille F. Kincannon, Elaine F. Valentine and Wilma Lee Hopson, and one grand- niece, Marianne Bell Tweel. At the time of her death her sister, Katherine F. Maxfield, was predeceased.
>
> In her will, deceased provided for her sister and three of her nieces. She made no mention of her fourth niece, Helen F. Ratliff, or her grand- niece, Marianne Bell Tweel.
>
> The dispute is over what happens to the lapsed bequests to the testatrix' sister. Does this property go to the surviving legatees, exclusively, or do the two legal heirs unnamed in the will get a share?
>
> The will itself made a specific bequest to each of the four legatees, and then left the remainder to the same four, "To be divided equally among them." The legacies which created this dispute, caused by the lapse of legacies to the predeceased sister, are here recited:
>
>> To my sister Katherine F. Maxfield, I bequeath the lot adjoining her house and all of my interest in Katherine Heights # 1 and # 2 including the duplex and all of my government bonds.
>> To my sister Katherine F. Maxfield, and to my three nieces, Wilma Lee Hopson, Lucille Kincannon, and Elaine Valentine--I give, devise and bequeath all of my property--real, personal (jewelry) and mixed, of which I possess or to which I am entitled at the time of my death; including such stocks, bonds, mortgages, bank deposits, building loan savings, cash and bank savings (with the exception of separate bequeaths which I have listed). And all of

my interest in my inherited properties (with the exception of separate bequeaths.) To be divided equally among them.

The legacy to Katherine F. Maxfield of the lot adjoining her house and all of my interest in Katherine Heights # 1 and # 2 including the duplex and "all of my government bonds" is a particular legacy. LA.CIV.CODE Art. 1625.

The other legacy which is a legacy of the residuum, "To my sister Katherine F. Maxfield and to my three nieces ... I give ... all ... (with the exception of separate bequeaths). To be divided equally among them," is either a universal legacy or a legacy under a universal title. Arts. 1606 and 1612. What it is depends on whether this was a conjoint or a distributive legacy.

Whether the legacy of the residuum is conjoint or distributive determines whether or not the right of accretion subsists, as provided by Arts. 1706 and 1707.

Of these issues, we will first determine whether the residuum was conjoint or distributive.

Art. 1707 defines a conjoint legacy:

The legacy shall be reputed to be made conjointly when it is made by one and the same disposition without the testator's having assigned the part of such co-legatee in the thing bequeathed.

The testatrix here used the language "To be equally divided among them." These were the identical words of the will in the case of *Parkinson v. McDonough*, 4 Mart., N.S. 246 (La.1826). The court in that case said that was a conjoint legacy. In *LeBeau v. Trudeau*, 1855, 10 La.Ann. 164, similar language: "Shall be divided, in equal portions, among the persons hereinafter named," was held to constitute the beneficiaries conjoint universal legatees. *Succession of Wilcox*, 165 La. 803, 116 So. 192 (1928), and *Succession of Maus*, 177 La. 822, 149 So. 466 (1933) picked up on *Parkinson* and *LeBeau* and held that the words "share and share alike" imported conjointness.

Then things changed. *Succession of Lambert*, 210 La. 636, 28 So. 2d 1 (1946), dealing with language "share and share alike" overruled *Wilcox* and *Maus*, saying that the phrase "share and share alike" is distributive, not conjoint, pretty much as a matter of law. Lambert emphasized that its result comported with the testator's clear intent. Lambert quietly apologized for the earlier cases by explaining that all of them were simply striving to carry out the clear intent of the testator.

Next came *Succession of McCarron*, 247 La. 419, 172 So. 2d 63 (1965).

*   *   *

But if the discussed early decisions mean that, in the absence of any showing of intent, the phrase "to be divided equally" does not constitute an assignment of parts, and differs from the phrases "in equal portions" and "share and share alike", then we do not choose to follow them. We consider a distinction of that kind, as a hard and fast rule of testamentary construction, is entirely too "subtle and refined" to stand as the basis for the interpretation of wills which in many, if not most, cases are composed by persons of ordinary understanding and not by judicial writers.

Thus, the state of the law appears to be that the phrase "share and share alike" is incapable of creating a conjoint legacy, while the phrase "to be equally divided among them" may, under some circumstances, be conjoint, but only if such interpretation will effectuate the obvious intention of the testator.

On the question of intent, counsel have presented the court with excellent arguments. Counsel for the heirs say the intent sought is the narrow one of whether the testatrix wanted to distribute the residuum of her estate conjointly among the named legatees, or distribute it equally among the named legatees. The argument of the legatees, on the other hand, is that the intent element we are trying to determine is the underlying question of where the testatrix wanted her property to go. I have concluded that the latter is the intent we are trying to determine.

The Code article which instructs us on this subject is Art. 1712:

> In the interpretation of acts of last will, the intention of the testator must principally be endeavored to be ascertained, without departing, however, from the proper signification of the terms of the testament.

Helen Farquhar Ratliff and Marianne Bell Tweel were the only two of deceased's kin that she did not provide for in her will. These two were descendants of one of the testatrix' brothers, Benjamin H. Farquhar. Their absence from the will surely was not an oversight. Deceased made particular legacies to her sister and three nieces and then named the same four as her residuary legatees. Since she named each of those four legatees twice, and failed to make any provision for the other two persons, it is arguable that she wanted to exclude Helen Farquhar Ratliff and Marianne Bell Tweel from sharing in her estate. Viewed this way, one may be inclined to interpret her language as creating a conjoint legacy, because only by such an interpretation can the intent of the testatrix to exclude the (arguably) unfavored heirs be carried out.

But was it her intent to exclude the two unnamed heirs absolutely? She does not say so in the will. Also, we can only guess what she would have done had she known at the time of the making of the will that her sister would predecease her. All we know for certain, based on the will itself, is that her intent when her sister Katherine was alive was to leave everything to her sister Katherine and her then three favored nieces. It is quite possible that had she anticipated her sister's predecease, she might have provided for her other niece and her grandniece.

For these reasons, I cannot say that it was the "obvious intention" of the testatrix to exclude the other two nieces from sharing in her estate. Only by finding that it was her obvious intention can the court be justified in interpreting the words "to be shared equally among them" to be a conjoint legacy. To paraphrase from an ancient case, quod voluit must depend ultimately on quod dixit. I conclude that the legacy was distributive, and the remaining legatees do not benefit from the lapse of Katherine's share of the residuary legacy.

This disposes of how the residuum will devolve. There remains, however, the question of what happens to the lapsed particular legacy to Katherine Maxfield. The legatees argue that if they do not hold the residuum conjointly, they are legatees under universal title and should therefore get the lapsed particular legacy. They base this contention on La.Civil Code Art. 1704:

> Legatees under a universal title, and legatees under a particular title, benefit by the failure of those particular legacies which they are bound to discharge.

The universal legatee always benefits by the failure of particular legacies. Article 1704 makes provision for legatees under a universal title and legatees under a particular title to benefit also, but only under the limited circumstance where there is a failed particular legacy which they are bound to discharge. Therefore the critical language to this article's application is the phrase "bound to discharge."

On this subject, *Compton v. Prescott*, 12 Rob. 56 (La.1845), says the residuary legatees under a universal title have no right to the whole succession and are not seized, of right, to its effects;

> …they are bound to demand the delivery of their portion from the heirs . . . or from the executors . . .
> They are not bound by the will to discharge any particular legacies; art. 1697; they are to take what may remain; the execution of the will is devolved upon the testamentary executors therein named . . . .

See also Succession of Dougart, 30 La.Ann. 268 (1878), by which we are taught that for one legacy to be a charge upon another, it arises either because the testament says so, or a rule of law says so.

In the instant will the testatrix did not bind the residuary legatees to discharge the particular legacy to Katherine Maxfield. Not being universal legatees they were not bound to do so. Instead, executors were appointed by the testatrix to discharge the particular legacies. Therefore, this legacy was not one the residuary legatees were bound to discharge, and it does not accrete to them.

The same arguments are advanced by petitioners on appeal. Appellants seek to distinguish *Succession of McCarron, supra*, relied upon in part by the trial judge, in that there appeared to be no intent on the part of the testatrix *McCarron* to preclude the children of either of her brothers in the event that one predeceased her whereas, in the instant case, only one of the testatrix's siblings (Katherine Maxfield) was living at the time the will was written and only the descendants of Benjamin H. Farquhar were not mentioned in the will. Such a distinction, appellants contend, should be made so as to lead to the legally favored interpretation effecting testacy, not intestacy. We disagree, finding *McCarron* to be controlling. Although decedent made no mention of respondents, she made no express provision for allocation of her wealth should any of the named legatees predecease her. There is no provision that a co-legatee should benefit by any lapse as to the part of one. In the absence of clear intent, how the decedent would have wanted her estate distributed under the circumstances is merely speculation. Inasmuch as the bequest was not made conjointly, no accretion takes place in favor of the surviving legatees. LSA-C.C. Art. 1706.

Furthermore, we agree with the trial judge that the residuary legacy is not a universal legacy, therefore the lapsed particular legacy devolves upon the decedent's legal heirs according to the rules of intestate successions. We consider *In the Matter of the Succession of Moore*, 353 So. 2d 353 (La.App. 1st Cir.1977) *writ denied*, 354 So. 2d 1382 (La.1978), to be inapposite inasmuch as the opinion does not disclose whether there were universal legatees.

In conclusion, appellants obviously would prefer a construction of the will granting them the whole of decedent's estate, thereby precluding respondents from sharing in her wealth. However, the testatrix's intention with regard to lapsed legacies is not clear, thus the trial judge properly declared such property distributed according to the rules of intestate successions. ...

* * *

NOTE

If the *Hopson* case were to be decided under post-revision law, what other information would be relevant to determine how the legacies to the predeceased sister would pass? Under any scenario, might the particular legacy still pass intestate? Would it matter whether the predeceased sister had children or not? What about the other legacy?

Act 1421 of 1997 provided new accretion articles which would alter the result in the cases above by providing "anti-lapse" resolutions, preventing the legacy from falling intestate. These are discussed in more detail in the materials that follow.

Lapsed Legacies and Accretion

La. C.C. 1589 lists seven ways in which a legacy may lapse. La. C.C. 1590 provides that if a legacy lapses, the lapsed legacy will accrete as provided for in the testament or if nothing is there provided, according to the rules La. C.C. 1591-1596.

The first place to look to see how this is done is in the testament itself to see if any provision provides what to do in the case of a lapse. If there is such a provision, it must be followed. La. C.C. 1590. If not, then the next step is to determine if the lapsed legacy is either particular or general. If so, then "accretion takes place in favor of the successor, who, under the testament, would have received the thing if the legacy had not lapsed." La. C.C. 1591. If the lapsed legacy is a joint one, then accretion would take place ratably in favor of the joint legatee, in most cases. La. C.C 1592.

There is an exception to these rules if the legatee, whether joint or otherwise, is a child or sibling of the testator, or a descendant of a child or sibling of the testator. In such cases, accretion takes place in favor of the descendants of the testator by roots who were in existence at the time of the decedent's death. La. C.C. 1593. If lapsed legacies do not fall under the preceding rules, they accrete ratably to the universal legatees. Although the general rule is that a legacy that follows a general legacy cannot be universal and thus, presumably would not be able to pick up lapsed legacies, a special rule alters the effect of that result. In cases, where a general legacy is phrased as a residue or balance of the estate and not as a fraction or portion of the estate, that general legacy is treated as a universal legacy for purposes of accretion, allowing the general legatee to pick up lapsed legacies. La. C.C. 1595.

Any parts of the estate not covered by these rules devolved under the rules of intestacy. La .C.C. 1596.

PROBLEMS

Look over the following testamentary dispositions. Answer the questions presented as you believe the testator would have wanted them answered. Then answer them under the new rules of accretion. Do the new rules more closely coincide with testators" wishes?

1. "To my friend, Mark, I leave my home on Maple Street. The rest of my estate, I leave to my two children." Mark, who has two children, predeceases the testator. To whom should the house pass?

2. "To my friend Carol, who has cared for me during my last years, I leave my house and car. The rest of my estate, I leave to my two children." Carol has two children of her own. Carol is financially secure and not in need. She renounces the legacies in the testament. To whom should the house and car pass?

3. "I leave ¼ of my estate to my niece, Rebecca and thank her for the care she has provided me in my final years. I leave ¾ of my estate to my best friend, Dimitra, in gratitude for the thirty years of companionship with which she graced my life." Testatrix has two healthy adult children over the age of twenty-four, to whom she has not spoken for years. If Rebecca predeceased testatrix, who should take the legacy left to her? If Dimitra predeceased testatrix, who should take her legacy?

4. "To my daughter, I leave my jewels. The rest of my estate, I leave to my two sons and daughter to be divided equally." The daughter predeceases her mother, leaving a son and a daughter. Besides these two grandchildren, the testator has four other grandchildren. To whom should the jewels and the remainder of the estate pass?

5. "I leave my car and stocks to my daughter and her husband. The remainder of my estate I leave to the Red Cross. Testatrix's daughter predeceases the testatrix and has no children. Who gets the car and stocks? If testatrix had a daughter, would it make a difference?

6. Consider the following legacy made in the *Succession of Willis v. McKeithen*, 184 So. 2d 748 (La. App. 2d Cir., 1966):

I leave unto the following persons the respective fractional portions set opposite the name of each of my oil and gas royalties in Richland Parish properties which are on the date of this will included in the Delhi Field-Wide Unit:

To Berry Drew Willis, Sr., my brother 1/7
To Mrs. Rosa Lee Rose, my sister 1/7
To Mrs. Laconia E. Schucker, my sister 1/7
To Mrs. Susie W. Wilkins 1/21

. . . .All the rest and remainder of all the property, real, personal, mixed, rights and credits of which I shall die possessed I leave unto Mrs. Lucille Thompson McKeithen. . . .

a. Under current law how would the legacies of the mineral royalties be classified? What about the legacy to Mrs. McKeithen?

b. If Mrs. Schucker predeceased testator and left a daughter, to whom would her legacy pass?

c. If Mrs. Schucker was convicted of killing the testator, but had a daughter, to whom would her legacy pass?

d. If Mrs. Schucker predeceased testator and left no children or grandchildren, to whom would her legacy pass?

e. If Mrs. Wilkins predeceased, to whom would the legacy pass? Suppose testator had written after the disposition of the mineral royalties, "the legacies of the above mineral royalties are joint"?

f. If Mrs. McKeithen renounced her legacy, and had two children, to whom would her legacy pass? If she had no children, but had a sister, to whom would the legacy pass?

Payment of Debts

La. C.C. 1416-1419 governs the rights of creditors of the decedents. La. C.C. 1416 provides that the universal successor is liable to the decedent's creditors "only to the extent of the value of the property received by him, valued as of the time of receipt." La. C.C. 1420-1428 determines the obligations of the successors among themselves. Generally, debts of the decedent are charged first to the property that is the object of a universal or general legacy. La. C.C. 1423-1424. However, if a debt is "attributable to identifiable property" then the debt is charged to that property. La. C.C. art. 1422.

For a thorough discussion of the payment of estate debts, see Kerry J. Miller, *The New Forced Heirship, its Implementing Legislation, and Major Substantive Policy Changes of the Louisiana State Law Institute's Proposed Comprehensive Revision of the Successions and Donations Laws*, 71 Tul. L. Rev. 223, 260-268 (1996).

SUCCESSION OF FARWELL
4 So. 3d 124 (La. 4th Cir. 2009)

Marie Dennette Farwell Collins ("Collins"), the appellant, appeals a ruling of the trial court placing the appellee, James P. Farwell ("Farwell"), in possession of a legacy of his mother's succession without requiring him to share in the expenses of administering the Succession. After reviewing the record and applicable law, we affirm the judgment.

The decedent, Marie Panfield Farwell, died on 20 October 2005, and was survived by two children: Farwell and Collins. The decedent's last will and testament in notarial form, dated 17 June 2003, provided five particular bequests to Collins, to-wit: the decedent's home and all of its contents, the decedent's one-half interest in a condominium, and three investment accounts. The will also provided for one particular legacy to Farwell, consisting of all the decedent's interest in the equity account number 495-07272-1-6, and any successor account, held with Edward Jones, a securities brokerage firm. While the decedent's will provided that the remainder of her estate was to be divided equally between Collins and Farwell, the particular bequests to her children comprised the entirety of the estate, leaving no residual. The decedent appointed Farwell as the executor of her estate; however, Farwell declined the appointment and, on 16 November 2005, Collins was appointed dative testamentary executrix of the decedent's succession.

On 13 November 2007, Farwell filed a Petition for Possession seeking to be placed in possession of the particular legacy. While Collins did not object to Farwell being placed in possession, Collins opposed the rule arguing that she had incurred substantial legal fees and other administrative expenses as Executrix, some of which she claimed Farwell was obligated to pay. Farwell refused to pay the claimed expenses on the basis that, as a particular legatee, and by virtue of La. C.C. arts. 1423 and 1424, he was not responsible for paying estate debts of the decedent or administration expenses.

The matter came for hearing on 22 February 2008, and on 5 March 2008, the trial court rendered a judgment that ordered that Farwell be placed into possession of the particular legacy account number 2280-0101 with Linsco/Private Ledger (formerly, equity account number 495-07272-1-6), and ordered that he not be taxed with succession expenses. In its reasons for judgment, the trial court determined that Collins was, in fact, the universal legatee of the succession of the decedent and, as such, there was no requirement under La. C.C. arts. 1423 and 1424 for Farwell, as a particular legatee, to pay any of the succession expenses.

La. C.C. art. 1423 states:
> Debts of the decedent are charged ratably to property that is the object of general or universal legacies and to property that devolves by intestacy, valued as of the date of death. When such property does not suffice, the debts remaining are charged in the following order:
>> (1) Ratably to the fruits and products of property that is the object of general or universal legacies and of property that devolves by intestacy; and
>> (2) Ratably to the fruits and products of property that is the object of particular legacies, and then ratably to such property.

La. C.C. art. 1424 states:

> Administration expenses are charged ratably to the fruits and products of property that is the object of the general or universal legacies and property that devolves by intestacy. When the fruits and products do not suffice to discharge the administration expenses, the remaining expenses are charged first to the property itself, next to the fruits and products of property that is the object of particular legacies, and then to the property itself.

We note that in pertinent part, the Official Revision Comment to article 1424 states:

> (a) Consistent with the provisions of Article 1423, which refers to debts of the decedent, this article sets forth the identical principle for administration expenses, namely that they are not charged to particular legacies but ratably to the fruits and products of general or universal legacies and the property that passes by intestacy. The basic distinction between Articles 1423 and 1424 is that Article 1423 refers to "debts of the decedent" and Article 1424 refers to "administration expenses." Debts of the decedent are charged to the property of the estate, but administration expenses are charged to the fruits and products of the property. If the fruits and products are insufficient, then the administration expenses are charged to the property itself. The creditors are entitled, of course, to be paid out of either source, and if the property that is the object of general or universal legacies is not sufficient, either by virtue of its fruits and products or of the property itself, then the administration expenses are charged to the fruits and products of the particular legacies, and if that resource, too, is not sufficient, then they are charged to the property that is the object of the particular legacy itself. In all instances, where there are several items of property among which the charge may be allocated, the charge is made ratably.
>
> (b) This article, in conjunction with Article 1423, attempts to set forth a priority, allocating the decedent's debts to property of the estate and administration expenses to revenues of the estate, then further breaking down those categories so that particular legacies do not bear any responsibility for these expenses unless they fall within one of the recognized exceptions, such as being encumbered to secure a debt or having a debt attributable to the object of the particular legacy as identifiable property.
>
> (c) In most instances professional fees such as the fees of the attorney who handles the estate, or accounting fees, or the compensation paid to the executor are incurred in part for administration purposes and in part as a result of the death of the decedent, so that they should be allocated partially to principal and partially to income.

Collins filed a motion for new trial, which was denied, and the instant appeal ensued. The sole issue presented herein is whether the trial court erred in placing Farwell into possession of his particular legacy without requiring him to share in the expenses of the administration of the estate.

We first determine the legal status of each party. It is undisputed that the five particular bequests to Collins comprised the decedent's entire estate with the exception of the one particular legacy to Farwell. The parties also agree that no residual estate exists once the bequests are made.

Pursuant to La. C.C. art. 1585 which states in pertinent part:

> A universal legacy is a disposition of all of the estate, or the balance of the estate that remains after particular legacies.

Comment (a) of the 1997 Revision Comments to article 1585 states that:

> This Article retains the name of the "universal" legacy and codifies the principle that such a legacy need not be of the entire estate, so long as it is a legacy of the residuum of the estate remaining after particular dispositions.

In addition, La. C.C. art. 1587 states:

> A legacy that is neither general nor universal is a particular legacy.

Comment (a) of the 1997 Revision Comments to article 1587 states that: "[i]n one sense, however, it defines the particular legacy in the negative by providing that it is any disposition that is not either of the other two types of legacies."

While the will indicates that Collins is a particular legatee, she received the remainder of the estate after the particular legacy to Farwell. Thus, under the law, we find, as did the trial court, that Collins is the universal legatee and Farwell is a particular legatee.

As a particular legatee, Farwell is not responsible for any debts or administrative expenses of the succession in accordance with La. C.C. arts. 1423 and 1424.

Based on the foregoing, we affirm the judgment of the trial court, each party to bear his or her own costs.

AFFIRMED.

Revocation

Revocability is an inherent element of a donation *mortis causa*. La. C.C. 1469 defining donations *mortis causa* describes them as revocable and La. C.C. 1606 provides that the right of revocation may not be renounced. An entire testament or any provision of a testament may be specifically revoked. Under earlier law, the Code defined two methods of revocation, express and tacit. La. C.C. 1691 (repealed). Express revocations were those accomplished in a written act in the form prescribed for testaments, whereas, tacit revocations "result[ed] from some act which supposes a change of will." *Id.* The Code specifically described some forms of tacit revocation. *Compare* La. C.C. 1607. For example, former article 1693 provided that a later inconsistent testamentary disposition of the thing would revoke an earlier testamentary disposition even without an express revocation, and former article 1694 provided that a revocation would be assumed if the testator had made an alienation *inter vivos* of the thing bequeathed. Relying on the definition of tacit revocation as any "act which supposes a change of will," the courts recognized other forms of tacit revocation, including the destruction or mutilation of the testament. *See, e.g., Succession of Muh,* 35 La. Ann. 394 (La. 1883).

The revision does not divide revocations into express and tacit. Rather, the new articles have categorized revocations as those that revoke an entire testament, La. C.C. 1607, and those that revoke only a testamentary provision. La. C.C. 1608. The comments however note that there have been few substantive changes except for the creation of new methods of express revocation. La. C.C. 1607, comment. However, the revision does not contain a general definition of tacit revocation, but lists several examples of tacit revocation. *See* Cynthia Samuel, *The 1997 Successions and Donations Revision–A Critique in Honor of A.N. Yiannopoulos,* 73 Tul. L. Rev. 1041 (1999).

A testator may revoke his testament at any time and that right cannot be renounced. La. C.C. 1606. There are separate rules for the revocation of an entire testament, as opposed to a legacy or other testamentary provision. The revocation of an entire testament takes place where the testator:

(1) Physically destroys the testament has it destroyed at his direction.
(2) So declares in one of the forms prescribed for testaments or in an authentic act.
(3) Identifies and clearly revokes the testament by a writing that is entirely written and signed by the testator in his own handwriting. (Note that a date is **not** required.)

La. C.C. 1607.

A legacy or other testamentary disposition may be revoked when the testator:

(1) So declares in one of the forms prescribed for testaments.
(2) Makes a subsequent incompatible testamentary disposition or provision.
(3) Makes a subsequent *inter vivos* disposition of the thing that is the object of the legacy and does not reacquire it.
(4) Clearly revoke the provision or legacy by a signed writing on the testament itself.
(5) Is divorced from the legatee **after** the testament is executed **and** at the time of his death, unless the testator provides to the contrary." The same applies to testamentary designation or appointments of a spouse.

La. C.C. 1608.

If the revocation is revoked before the testator's death, these rules do not apply except with regard to physical destruction of the testament, subsequent *inter vivos* disposition, or divorce. La. C.C. 1609. Any other changes to the will must be in one of forms prescribed for testaments. La. C.C. 1610. Revocation of testamentary dispositions may be made for the same causes for which revocation of a donation *inter vivos*. La. C.C. 1610.1.

Consider the following cases that were decided under prior law. Would the results be the same under the revision?

SUCCESSION OF MUH
35 La. Ann. 394 (La. 1883)

Manning, J.

On May 4, 1875, Louis Muh made his olographic will in due form, and died November 13, 1882. A notary placed seals upon his effects on the day of his death, and put a guardian over them. A few days after, this officer in the presence of witnesses removed the seals, and made search for a will. A bureau, secretary, and some trunks were searched without success. A table stood in the bedchamber of the deceased, the drawer of which was locked. This drawer had also been sealed by the notary. The key broke in the effort to unlock it, and it was opened by a locksmith. In the drawer was found an envelope, superscribed -"Ceci est mon Testament Olograph Pour etre ouvert apres mon Dec2es, 'D'"" underneath which was his signature with a paraph. This envelope had once been sealed with three wax seals. They had been broken.

The paper within was presented for probate as the will of the deceased.

*　　*　　*

All of these legacies, except four, had been erased by drawing a line of ink through them, but the words can be read. The clause in which his executors are named is erased in like manner, and their names are more obliterated than the other parts of that clause, the pen evidently being pressed harder and with a more copious flow of ink. The paper had been signed, and the signature is covered with ink, the erasing pen having been moved in several ways, and with various and different strokes, which extend over the paraph. A minute inspection reveals the name to those who know what it was already. Experts state on the trial they can see both the signature and the paraph through the superimposed ink. It would be difficult to blotch it more, but portions of the capital letters of the name appear when the eye has rested some time upon them. The ink of the erasures is blacker than the writing.

…On the margin, outside the colored line on legal cap, and abreast each legacy to the nieces, is written with a paler ink, "fille de ma soeur Elisabeth," manifestly written at a different time from the will, and as additionally descriptive of the person intended. A like marginal description is abreast the partially erased legacy to Eugenie Ducayet, the name "Jenny" being there written, and the unerased part of her legacy is his book case, "ma Bibliotheque sans le contenu." These indicate unmistakably that when he was reading the will over with a view to make another, he revised it, and added these descriptive words to be put in the new will.

There is other and stronger internal evidence that his own hand made these erasures and blottings.

*　　*　　*

That his intention was to annul the will, make it void and of no effect, cannot reasonably be doubted. The painstaking and elaborate defacing and blotting out the signature was the act which, to his apprehension, destroyed it as a will. The obliteration of the names of the executors was almost as complete, but the legacies that were not intended to be repeated had simply an ink line drawn through them, and the sentences that were untouched received marginal additions as memoranda, or were left entire for use in copying.

*　　*　　*

It is contended that, whatever may have been the intention of the testator in making these erasures and obliterations, conceding they were made by himself, yet they do not revoke the will because the Code has provided the several modes of revocation, of which this is not one, and the erasures must be considered as not made, because they were not approved by the testator. And the argument is elaborated and extended until it culminates in this extraordinary proposition, that the destruction of a will by the hands of the testator animo revocandi is not a legal revocation. Says the brief on behalf of Epps:

> It is simply making it impossible to produce and probate the destroyed or suppressed instrument, unless perchance parties in interest should procure secondary proof, sufficient for the purpose. Hence, testators usually resort to this mode of getting rid of-not of legally revoking their will.

*　　*　　*

The meaning [of the codal article on revocation] is plain. If the testator has made another disposition, repugnant to and inconsistent with the previous one, although nothing is said about revoking the former, a tacit revocation will thereby be made. So also if he has done any act which supposes a change of will, let that act be what it may, provided always the intention to revoke is fairly and legally deducible from it, a tacit revocation will result from the act.

With language so unambiguous as the text of the Code before us, the argument upon it is startling. It can be epitomized thus: "The word act does not mean act in the sense of something done, a deed, or such like, but an act, that is to say, a testamentary instrument. It is defined in the next Article which reads, the act, by which a testamentary disposition is revoked, must be made in one of the forms prescribed for testaments and clothed with the same formalities. In the words of the brief: that is the general rule both as regards express and tacit revocation. There must be a writing, and the instrument must have all the elements of a valid will."

By this reasoning it follows,-when the Code enacts that a revocation of a will may be express or tacit, it means by express, a formal declaration in writing to that effect; and by tacit, a declaration still more formal, viz., a testamentary act.

A similar perversion of Art. 1589 (1582) is urged. By that Article erasures not approved by the testator are considered as not made, and it is insisted that this applies to the erased signature equally as to erased legacies. No particular method of approval is specified, nor does it seem essential that approval shall be indicated by writing, in which respect our Code differs from the English statute of Wills. There is no indication of the testator's approval of the erasures other than the approval which erasure by his own hand manifests. But it is apparent the Article is not treating of the erasure of a signature to a will. The erasures, which are considered not made if not approved, are those which change or strike out parts or clauses of a paper recognized as an existing will, not that part, the erasure of which would destroy it as a will. Erasures of clauses in the body of the will affect only the dispositions erased. Erasure of the signature strikes at the existence of the instrument as a will.

The same Article further provides: if the erasures are so made as to render it impossible to distinguish the words covered by them, it shall be left to the discretion of the judge to declare if he considers them important, and in this case only to decree the nullity of the testament.

All the numerous counsel treat the adjective "important" as qualifying "words." On one side it is urged that the signature is a word, and since the judge has discretion to declare if he considers that word important, the erasure of the signature is not more significant than the erasure of an ordinary word. It would be remarkable indeed if the Code in any place had treated the signature to a will, even by implication, as a thing the importance of which varied with the discretion of judges, since it emphatically attaches so much importance to it that signing an olographic will cannot be dispensed with.

It is not the words that the judge must consider important, but the erasures, as is evident when we observe that only in the case of their being important can he decree the nullity of the will. The Article can be paraphrased thus: if the erasures so obliterate the words that it is impossible to distinguish them, and the judge considers the erasures important, that is to say, of material words, he shall pronounce the nullity of the will, but if he considers these erasures unimportant, he cannot decree nullity.

And thus erasures are recognized as one of the acts which will operate a revocation of a will. This might have been expected, since it is the law both in England and France, the two countries whose legislation and jurisprudence have molded our own.

*　　*　　*

…The Code has provided for the tacit revocation of wills, and that provision is of the most enlarged and comprehensive kind, viz., by any act that denotes a change of intention. Of course, the acts are not specified. They could not be. They are as numerous and as varying as the different circumstances under which men act on such occasions. The compilers of our Code were careful to omit even the classification of these kinds of acts into erasure, laceration, suppression, destruction, etc. Those clashing commentaries, in which jurisconsults had invented the most subtle distinctions, were before them, and they therefore formulated a general rule, leaving to courts, of necessity, to apply it to each particular case that fell within its scope.

How could it be otherwise? How could any community or people get on with a law that declared the perpetuity of a will, unless revoked by an act as solemn as that by which it was made?...

*　　*　　*

This effacement and obliteration as we see it in the original brought up with the record, was in our opinion done with the intent to revoke the will, and this intent should be given effect to by the Court. The lower court so held.

Judgment affirmed.

NOTE

Has Mr. Muh committed an act of physical destruction under the present law? *See* La. C.C. 1607(1).

SMITH v. SHAW
60 So. 2d 865 (La. 1952)

FOURNET, Chief Justice.

*   *   *

...The defendants, Mrs. Ethel Galvin and Mrs. Allen Shaw (legal heirs of Mrs. Jones' deceased husband), in answer, admitted that they claim an interest in the property, and assuming the position of plaintiffs in reconvention, alleged that they became owners of a one-fourth interest each as testamentary legatees under a valid olographic will executed by the deceased in January, 1947, which they assert should be given legal effect and secondary proof thereof allowed in view of the fact that said will was destroyed on October 10, 1948, when the testatrix executed a nuncupative will by public act, the latter will in turn having been destroyed some ten days later (October 20, 1948) upon execution of another nuncupative will by public act, and this last will having been declared null and void upon being presented for probate in the Succession proceedings. The defendants, plaintiffs in reconvention, claim that the three wills contained the same testamentary disposition, namely, that the property was to be sold and the proceeds divided equally between the plaintiffs in suit and the plaintiffs in reconvention.

*   *   *

There is no dispute as to the execution of the olographic will, its formal validity, and its actual destruction through mutilation, the document having been torn in pieces and discarded by decedent's attorney, Mr. Lincove, at her suggestion and in her presence, after he had completed the first nuncupative will by public act. The defendants (appellants) contend, however, that the olographic will was destroyed through error of both fact and law, induced by belief in Mr. Lincove's representation that the document prepared by him was a valid instrument; but, because it was defective, a second nuncupative will by public act was drawn (by another attorney, Mr. Woodley) to replace it, and since the latter was subsequently declared null for want of proper form, the olographic will was not revoked and should be admitted to probate. Relying on a so-called "Doctrine of Dependent Relative Revocation," said to be supported by decisions from numerous states and widely recognized in England and Canada, the defendants argue that the revocation of the olographic will was conditioned on the validity of the new testament; and with the intention of the testatrix so clearly manifested in three wills executed within a short time of her death, each containing the same provision relative to disposition of the residue of her estate, it would be wholly unreasonable to assume that she wished to die intestate rather than to have her property distributed according to the provisions of her olographic will.

Under our system of law there is no such doctrine as "Dependent Relative Revocation," Article 1691 of the LSA-Civil Code providing that "The revocation of testaments by the act of the testator is express or tacit"-- express when the testator has formally declared in writing that he revokes the testament, tacit "when it results from some act which supposes a change of will;" and while the Code does not specify that the destruction of a testament constitutes a revocation thereof, the fact of intentional destruction by the testator as constituting the most effective method of invalidation has been recognized by this Court on many occasions. . . .[*See La. C.C. art. 1607*][*]

In the landmark case on the subject matter, *Succession of Hill, supra*, this Court, after noting the two modes of revoking a testament provided in Article 1691, and the fact that the Code nowhere speaks of the destruction of a testament as a means of revocation, reasoned. . . . . if the testament was destroyed, there was an end of all testamentary disposition, so far as that testament was concerned, and the testator was in a situation as though he had never disposed by last will, and there was no necessity for an express or a tacit revocation. If the testator burns or tears up the will, there is no will in existence; no testament that can be probated. 47 La.Ann. at page 334, 16 So. at page 821.

We think, therefore, paraphrasing the language used in the *Succession of Dambly, supra*, that the first will made by Mrs. Myra D. Jones did not, and could not, go into effect for the reason that she caused it to be destroyed by mutilation.

For the reasons assigned, the judgment of the district court is affirmed.

NOTE

Has the testator's intent been honored? She wrote three wills, but died intestate. The case discussed the concept of dependent relative revocation followed in some common law states. Under the doctrine, if the testator revoked a will through some mistake of law or fact, the revoked testament may be reinstated if that is what the court believes would have been the testator's intent. *Murchinson v. Smith*, 508 S.E.2d 641, 644 (Ga. 1998). Might the legislature consider adopting a form of dependent relative revocation?

SUCCESSION OF BAGWELL
415 So. 2d 238 (La. App. 2d Cir. 1982)

HALL, Judge.

Alleging that the decedent left a will which could not be located because it was destroyed, misplaced, or suppressed by a nephew of the decedent, plaintiff Martin petitioned to probate the alleged will which named him and his wife as legatees. An unsigned copy of the will was attached to plaintiff's petition. ... After trial, the district court found that plaintiff failed to prove the will was destroyed by the nephew and further found that the will was destroyed by the decedent himself prior to his death. From a judgment rejecting plaintiff's demands, he appealed. We affirm.

A lost or accidentally destroyed will may be probated if it can be established that the testator made a valid will, what the content or substance of the will was, and that after a diligent search the will could not be found and was never revoked. *Airey v. Airey*, 262 La. 383, 263 So. 2d 330 (1972). The fact that a will shown to have been in the possession of the testator cannot be found after the testator's death gives rise to a presumption that the testator revoked the will by

---

[*] Bracketed material in italics added by author.

destroying it. This presumption may be rebutted by proof that the testator did not revoke the will.

*　　　*　　　*

These rules apply to an action to probate a will where it is alleged that the will cannot be located because it has been destroyed by someone other than the testator. Clear and convincing proof that a person other than the testator destroyed the will without the direction, consent, or permission of the testator would be sufficient to overcome the presumption that the testator revoked the will by destroying it.

Decedent died July 18, 1979, survived by a number of collateral relations-- brothers, sisters, nieces, and nephews. It was established that in October 1978 decedent executed a statutory will at the office of his attorney, bequeathing all of his property to Mr. and Mrs. Martin who were decedent's close friends and who had provided attention to him for many years. It was further established that on May 29, 1979, decedent went to the attorney's office, expressed dissatisfaction with the Martins and an intent to change his will, and obtained either the original or an executed duplicate copy of the will from the attorney. The evidence shows that decedent had a falling out with plaintiff about that time, probably relating to the fact that plaintiff and his wife had separated.

Four witnesses testified decedent told them shortly before his death that he had torn up the will. One witness was the nephew accused of destroying the will who would inherit a small fractional interest in decedent's modest estate if decedent died intestate. The other witnesses were a neighboring couple without any interest in the matter, and plaintiff's son, whose interest would seem to lie with the plaintiff.

Plaintiff's wife testified that decedent obtained from her a copy of the will, stating that he intended to eliminate plaintiff from the will, but that decedent later told her he had not changed the will. Decedent's brother and his wife testified that decedent told them shortly before his death he still had the will and had "something" to take care of Mrs. Martin.

It was established that the nephew had possession of decedent's metal strongbox where he kept his papers and records, and that it was given to the nephew by the decedent when the nephew, at decedent's request, took him to the hospital during his last illness. There was some evidence that a window in the house had been broken during decedent's illness and that a piece of furniture had been tampered with at some unestablished time, but the evidence did not establish that the house had been ransacked as contended by plaintiff.

Plaintiff's evidence was insufficient to rebut the presumption that the decedent destroyed the will. Plaintiff proved that the decedent made a valid will and proved the content of the will, but he failed to prove the will was not revoked by the decedent. In fact, as found by the trial court, the preponderance of the evidence is that the decedent, because of the falling out with plaintiff, obtained the will or a signed copy from the attorney and destroyed it. The nephew had the opportunity to destroy the will if it existed at the time plaintiff went to the hospital, but there is no evidence that he did so or that he had any significant reason to do so.

*　　　*　　　*

SUCCESSION OF JUSTICE
679 So. 2d 597 (La. App. 2d Cir. 1996)

STEWART, Judge.

Appellant, James Walter Justice ("Jamie") appeals the judgment of the trial court declaring his grandmother's 1978 will invalid and dismissing his petition to probate a copy of that will. We affirm the decision of the trial court.

FACTS

On November 16, 1978, James Winfred Justice, Sr. ("Mr. Justice") and Bessie Louise Manning Justice ("Mrs. Justice") each executed a statutory will drafted by their attorney, Mike Coyle. In her testament, Mrs. Justice left her community property to her husband, divided her separate property equally between her son, James Winfred Justice, Jr. ("James") and her grandson, Jamie, with Jamie's interest subject to a testamentary trust set forth in the will, and made specific bequests of jewelry to Jamie. Mr. Coyle gave the originals to Mrs. Justice and kept copies in his office.

On September 21, 1990, Mrs. Justice executed a second instrument before a notary on a printed form prepared for execution in other states and which contained printed language providing for revocation of "any and all other Wills and Codicils heretofore made" by the testator. The 1990 instrument purporting to be Mrs. Justice's will increased the legacy to Jamie to include all of her separate property thereby excluding James, altogether. In a prior judgment, the trial court found the 1990 instrument to be invalid as to form and, therefore, a nullity.

Jamie obtained a copy of the 1978 will, which Mr. Coyle had retained in his files, and filed a petition to probate the copy of the 1978 will. The evidence and testimony adduced at trial established that the original of Mrs. Justice's 1978 will was missing from the family safe and that the 1990 instrument had been placed in the safe in the same envelope with Mr. Justice's 1978 will. Mr. Justice testified that he did not remove Mrs. Justice's 1978 will from the safe and that, other than himself, only Mrs. Justice had access to the safe. Her 1978 will was not found in any of Mrs. Justice's other possessions.

The testimony of several witnesses at trial revealed that Mrs. Justice continued until the time of her death to believe that she would not die intestate and that through the dispositions in her will she had provided for Jamie. Mr. Justice also confirmed this testimony.

Following the trial, the court ruled the 1978 will invalid and dismissed the probate of that instrument. The court concluded that the revoking language in Mrs. Justice's invalid 1990 will coupled with the disappearance of the original 1978 will operated to revoke the 1978 will.

Jamie now appeals that ruling of the trial court contending that the court erred in finding that his grandmother revoked her 1978 will.

LAW

*   *   *

When a will, shown to have been in the possession of or accessible to the deceased, cannot be found at the testator's death a presumption arises that the testator has destroyed the will with intent to revoke the prior testament. The party seeking to establish the will may rebut the presumption by clear proof of the following: (1) the testator made a valid will; (2) proof of the contents or substance of the will; (3) the will, though not found at testator's death, was never revoked by the testator. *Succession of Talbot*, 530 So. 2d 1132 (La.1988); *Succession of Nunley*, 69 So. 2d 33 (La.1953); *Hamilton v. Kelley*, 641 So. 2d 981 (La.App. 2d Cir.1994).

The copy of the 1978 will obtained from Mr. Coyle's files provided proof of the only valid will executed by Mrs. Justice and the contents of that will. The issue presented to this court is whether, at trial, sufficient evidence demonstrated that no revocation of the 1978 will as permitted under Louisiana law was executed by Mrs. Justice prior to her death.

The proponent of a will bears the burden of establishing that the testator, "who intentionally destroyed a copy of his will under circumstances consistent with his having an aim to revoke" either did not authorize or commit the destruction of the testament or did not intend to revoke the will by destroying it. *Succession of Talbot, supra*, at 1135.

La.C.C. article 1691 provides methods of revoking a testament. When the testator formally declares an intent to revoke in a writing which would be valid as a testament pursuant to Louisiana law, the testator has expressly revoked his will. La.C.C. article 1692. A testator may tacitly revoke by "some other disposition of the testator," (such as a subsequent incompatible testamentary disposition or the sale or donation of the object of a particular legacy) or "from some act which supposes a change of will." La.C.C. article 1691. Although no specific reference to destruction of a will is made by that article, the general language of the phrase "from some act which supposes a change of will" would encompass the testator's destruction of the will as a tacit revocation. [*Compare La. C.C. 1607*][*]

Any act of the testator which indicates a change of will would be a tacit revocation provided the intent to revoke is "fairly and legally" evident from such act. *Succession of Nunley, supra*. While the act of destruction is the first fact essential to prove a tacit revocation by destruction, the court, in that case, emphasized the importance of reviewing additional evidence, if available, of the testator's withdrawal of the testamentary intent memorialized in the prior formal act.

DISCUSSION

After thorough review and careful consideration of the record, we cannot say that the trial court was clearly wrong in finding a tacit revocation of the 1978 will.

The presumption of revocation raised by the missing will was further supported by evidence that Mrs. Justice had access to the family safe and that the 1990 instrument was placed in the safe in the envelope with Mr. Justice's 1978 will. Those facts strongly suggest that Mrs. Justice removed her 1978 will from the safe and destroyed it. Although the trial court properly found the 1990 testament was not an express revocation pursuant to La.C.C. article 1962 because that instrument did not meet the formalities required by Louisiana law, the revocation language in that document was additional evidence that Mrs. Justice tacitly revoked her 1978 will. Under *Succession of Talbot*, these circumstances seem consistent with Mrs. Justice "having an aim to revoke" and support a finding that she did in fact destroy the 1978 will. [*Compare La. C.C. 1607*][*]

---

[*] Bracketed material in italics added by author.

[*] Bracketed material in italics added by author.

We do not find that Jamie has met his burden of clearly proving that the 1978 will was never revoked by Mrs. Justice. Although the testimony, particularly that of Mrs. Gillum, indicated that Mrs. Justice continued to believe that she had provided for Jamie, and although the evidence indicated that the testamentary intent expressed in the 1978 will was not changed by the invalid 1990 instrument, the totality of record establishes that Mrs. Justice tacitly revoked her 1978 testament by destroying it and replacing it with another instrument, albeit an invalid one.

Based on the evidence presented, we find that this case is distinguishable from *Armorer v. Case*, 9 La.Ann. 288 (1854), and do not conclude that Mrs. Justice's intent to revoke her 1978 will arose through any mistake or error because her testamentary intent apparently did change in that Mrs. Justice left no legacy to her son in the 1990 instrument.

CONCLUSION

For the reasons assigned above, the judgment of the trial court is affirmed. Costs of this proceeding are assessed to appellant.

AFFIRMED.

SUCCESSION OF ROLLING
86 So. 2d 687 (La. 1956)

HAMITER, Justice

Shortly after her death an olographic last will and testament made by the decedent on May 4, 1946 was located, following a search by a commissioned Notary Public, in her safety deposit box in the Whitney National Bank of New Orleans. On the petition of all of the children the court probated it and ordered the taking of an inventory of decedent's estate.

Some months later, while the inventory was being made, Miss Bonnie W. Rolling unexpectedly discovered among the effects of the decedent in the premises where she resided another olographic will and an attached codicil, these having been dated June 14, 1941 and July 29, 1941, respectively. They, on the petition of the daughter, were also probated.

*   *   *

It is the contention of the appellants (the four sons) that the document of May 4, 1946 constituted decedent's last will and testament, and that by it she tacitly revoked the prior will (together with the attached codicil) in its entirety.

On the other hand appellee, the daughter, urges (as the trial court held) that the posterior document effected only a particular revocation of specific dispositions of the prior one; and that the provisions of both wills, except where conflicting, must be carried out. In their brief her counsel state:

> ...In her will of 1946, she repeated two particular legacies given to her daughter in her 1941 will and disposed of the $10,000.00 in bonds previously left to her husband, and gave the jewelry, household effects, and so forth, to her

daughter, but not as an extra portion as she did in the 1941 will, thereby making a change of this particular legacy.

* * *

A subsequent will, showing by its whole tenor that it was intended to contain all the testamentary dispositions of the deceased, revokes a prior will, in so far as it contains dispositions incompatible with those contained in the will last made.

Succession of Bobb, 42 La. Ann. 40, 7 So. 60...

Viewing the documents presently under consideration in the light of the above announced principles we find that the one dated May 4, 1946 disposed of the entire estate of decedent and contained dispositions which for the most part were incompatible with those previously made; and we therefore conclude that it was intended as her last and only will and testament.

Thus, in the posterior instrument the testatrix bequeathed to the daughter her personal effects without reciting that they were to be an extra portion as she had stated in the former one. Again, the testatrix initially made particular bequests of all of the real estate that she owned (two separate parcels, as revealed by the inventory) and of certain bonds, and she directed that the remainder of her stock and bonds were to be equally divided among her four sons; whereas, subsequently, she made no particular bequests of her mentioned real estate and bonds but, on the contrary, included them in a residual clause reciting that "The remainder of my estate consisting of stock, bonds, and real estate, to share and share alike." Also, incompatibility is noticed between the provisions of the two instruments respecting the appointment of executors, John Rau formerly having been named along with Miss Bonnie W. Rolling, and Reverend Felix Miller later having been selected to serve.

Moreover, had the testatrix not intended the document of May 4, 1946 to be her last and only will it seems that she would have omitted therefrom the description of herself and the bequest respecting the tomb in Metairie Cemetery, both of which were substantially identical with those contained in the first document. Particularly appropriate in this connection is the following observation contained in *Succession of Pizzati, supra* [141 La. 645, 75 So. 504]:

...[E]ach of the wills carries a complete disposition of the entire estate, and contains recitals which would have been entirely superfluous in a will intended to be merely additional, supplementary to, or designed to be read in connection with, another, and not to stand independently by itself as the sole and only will. We refer to the clause wherein the testator gives information about himself.

Additionally, we are impressed by the fact that this testatrix had amended her first will by a codicil. She, therefore, was apparently aware of that method of changing particular portions of a testament without affecting the remainder of the bequests. However, in 1946, rather than "amending" by a codicil as she had formerly done, the testatrix made a new will declaring that "I...do make and constitute this my last will and testament." Having said this she then proceeded to dispose of her whole estate, through bequests entirely different from those previously made, thereby indicating that she intended to and did tacitly revoke the prior testament.

SUCCESSION OF BERDON
12 So. 2d 654 (La. 1943)

HIGGINS, Justice.

[In a will and codicil the testator bequeathed 1200 shares of Whitney National Bank stock to several legatees. At all times the testator owned no more than 775 shares of such stock.]

*   *   *

The trial judge held that the bequests in the will and the codicil thereto of more of a particular kind of shares of stock than the testator owned causes a contradiction and, therefore, what the testator ordered to be done in the codicil prevails over what he ordered to be done in his will, citing Article 1723 of the Revised Civil Code. He further decreed that the 425 shares of bank stock that the estate was lacking be taken from the particular bequest of 500 shares in favor of the widow, on the theory that that was the first particular bequest of stock and each of the later particular legacies prevailed over it. The result was that there was sufficient stock to carry out all of the particular legacies for Whitney National Bank stock, except the widow's legacy of 500 shares, the trial judge only awarding her 75 shares.

*   *   *

A testator may likewise tacitly revoke a previous will, codicil, or bequest, provided he conforms with the law in doing so. In order to have the effect of a tacit revocation, the subsequent disposition or act of the testator must show a change of will or intention by the last disposition or act being incompatible with, contrary to, entirely different from, or contradictory with the former. For instance, if the bequest is of a particular object and the testator during his lifetime sells, or destroys, or gives it away, there is a tacit revocation of this particular legacy of a particular object. If, in the codicil, the testator gives a particular object to a different person than he bequeathed it to in his will or previous codicil, the legacy is tacitly revoked.

In the case at bar, while we are dealing with particular legacies they are not particular legacies of a particular object, consequently, the bequests of 500 shares of the Whitney National Bank stock to the Hermann minors in itself does not show that the testator changed his intention by doing something incompatible with, contrary to, entirely different from or contradictory with his previous express intention and thereby tacitly revoked any one of the previous bequests of Whitney National Bank stock to the other particular legatees.

*   *   *

In the case of the *Succession of Lizzie Lee Homan*, La.Sup., 12 So. 2d 649, this day decided, we held that where the testator in the will and the codicil gave to the same parties identical numbers of shares of homestead stock without describing the certificates of stock and did not expressly revoke the former bequests or limit the latter ones, the legacies were not repetitious but cumulative, because they were not contradictory to, incompatible with, contrary to, or entirely different from each other and, therefore, there was no tacit revocation of the first bequests by the second ones.

In the *Succession of Stallings*, 197 La. 449, 1 So. 2d 690, the testatrix gave particular legatees $5,000 and $10,000, respectively, and in codicils, gave the same parties identical amounts, without expressly revoking the previous bequests or limiting the bequests to the latter ones only. We held that each legatee was entitled to double legacies because there was nothing to indicate that the testatrix intended the legacies to be in the disjunctive since the second bequests were not incompatible with, contrary to, entirely different from, or contradictory with the first bequests, and therefore there were double valid legacies, as the first ones were not tacitly revoked by the later bequests.

While the facts in the two cited cases are not like those of the instant one, those authorities are in point on the question of tacit revocation, because they follow the doctrine announced in the Articles of the Code that in order for the testator to show a change of intention, his subsequent acts or dispositions must be contradictory with, contrary to, incompatible with, or different from his previous ones.

In the case under consideration, it is clear that if the testator had owned 1,200 shares of stock of the Whitney National Bank at the time of his death, each of the legacies would have been fully carried out or discharged. This demonstrates that there is nothing contrary, contradictory, or incompatible between the bequests in the will and the codicil. It is obvious that there is merely a shortage in the stock devised by the testator and not a contradiction in the legacies of the stock.

*   *   *

With reference to the second alternative plea of the widow that the legacies should be proportionately reduced because they are all valid and there is insufficient stock to satisfy them fully, Article 1635 is pertinent:

1635. If the effects do not suffice to discharge the particular legacies, the legatees [legacies] of a certain object must be first taken out. The surplus [balance] of the effects must then be proportionately divided among the legatees of sums of money, unless the testator has expressly declared that such a legacy shall be paid in preference to the rest, or that the legacy is given as a recompense for services. (Brackets ours.)

*   *   *

It is our opinion, since the testator has restricted and limited the particular legacies in question to shares of stock of the Whitney National Bank and there were insufficient shares of stock to pay them in full, and as there is no express or tacit revocation of any of the legacies or a preference granted one over the other, the 775 shares of stock must be "proportionately divided," among the particular legatees of Whitney National Bank Stock.

SUCCESSION OF HUGUET
708 So. 2d 1302 (La. App. 1st Cir. 1998)
[footnotes omitted]

SHORTESS, Judge.

Does the exchange of immovable property for interest in a partnership revoke a testamentary legacy of the testator's "right, title and interest" in the immovable property? The executor of the succession of Thelma S. Prescott Huguet brought this declaratory judgment action seeking an answer to this question. The trial court answered this question affirmatively, using the following syllogism:

A sale equals a revocation.
An exchange equals a sale.
Therefore, an exchange equals a revocation.

The executor appeals, contending the trial court's logic is flawed because the minor premise, i.e., that an exchange equals a sale, is legally incorrect.

FACTUAL BACKGROUND

Thelma S. Prescott Huguet died August 20, 1994, leaving as her only descendants two daughters, Grace Garner and Ann Garner McCulloch, and a grandson, Wayne Brogdon, who is Grace Garner's son. On May 14, 1992, Huguet executed a last will and testament that contained certain specific bequests to her three descendants and left the remainder of her estate to Garner and McCulloch. The specific bequest at issue herein was to Brogdon of "all of my right, title and interest in and to ... [m]y undivided interest in that certain one hundred eighty (180) acre tract of land located in West Baton Rouge Parish, Louisiana...."

On December 23, 1993, Brogdon and Huguet formed a limited partnership named Brogdon Development, A Louisiana Partnership in Commendam. Brogdon was the general partner; Huguet was the limited partner. Brogdon contributed $5,000.00 to the partnership and owned 1.64% thereof. Huguet exchanged her interest in the West Baton Rouge Parish property for a 98.36% interest in the partnership. On the same date, Huguet donated to Brogdon a 6.55% interest in the partnership, valued at $20,000.00. She made an identical donation on January 3, 1994. Thus, at the time of Huguet's death, she owned 85.26% of the partnership, and Brogdon owned 14.74%.

*   *   *

Brogdon is the testamentary executor of Huguet's will. Brogdon contends that his duty as executor is to fulfill the testatrix's intent, and that her intent was to give all her interest in the West Baton Rouge Parish property to Brogdon, "regardless of in what form that interest was held." McCulloch disagreed, contending the bequest was a lapsed legacy because Huguet owned no interest in the property when she died. Because of these conflicting interpretations, Brogdon filed this declaratory judgment action.

LEGAL ANALYSIS

Brogdon contends the trial court erred in two respects: (1) in finding an exchange equals a sale and thus revokes a legacy under Louisiana Civil Code article 1695; and (2) in failing to consider Huguet's intent.

Does an exchange equal a sale?

An exchange and a sale are clearly two different types of contracts. The articles on sale are found in Title VII of the Civil Code, while the rules for exchanges are found in Book III, Title VIII. Exchange is defined in article 2660 as "a contract, by which the parties to the contract give to one another, one thing for another, whatever it be, except money; for in that case it would be a sale." (Emphasis added.) The Code provides in article 2667, however, that the general rules of sale apply to the contract of exchange.

McCulloch relies on article 2667 to support the minor premise in the trial court's syllogism, i.e., that an exchange equals a sale. We agree with Brogdon's contention, however, that this case cannot be resolved so simplistically. An exchange is not equal to a sale. The Code makes them separate and distinct legal concepts, so the trial court's syllogism must fall.

The failure of the trial court's syllogism, however, does not resolve whether Huguet's legacy to Brogdon lapsed when she exchanged the property for a partnership interest. To answer this question, we must examine the codal and jurisprudential guidelines for interpretation of wills and partnership law regarding ownership of real property.

Interpretation of wills

Our Civil Code provides generally that in interpreting a will, the court must first try to ascertain the testator's intent, without departing from the proper signification of the will's terms. The disposition should be understood in the sense in which it can have effect; and when the intent cannot be ascertained from the terms used by the testator, the court may look to all circumstances that may aid in discovering his intent. In *Succession of Blakemore*, the supreme court explained: "The testator's intention is his will. This is the first rule of interpretation, to which all others are reduced. The intention must be enforced as far as it can be done legally." If the will contains no ambiguity, however, the will must be enforced as written without reference to outside information regarding the testator's intent.

Brogdon contends the trial court ignored Huguet's intent. McCulloch argues, on the other hand, that the will is unambiguous and thus the court did not need to determine Huguet's intent. The answer to this question turns on whether Huguet owned any right, title, or interest in the West Baton Rouge Parish property when she died.

Partnership law

A partnership is a juridical person, distinct from its partners. It has its own domicile, its own patrimony, the right to sue and be sued in its own behalf, and the capacity to make donations and to receive legacies and donations. The entity theory, i.e., the idea that a partnership is a distinct legal entity from the individuals composing it, has been recognized in our jurisprudence since 1848. Our supreme court explained how this concept affects the ownership of property in *Smith v. McMicken*:

> The partnership once formed and put into action, becomes, in contemplation of law, a moral being, distinct from the persons who compose it. It is a civil person which has its peculiar rights and attributes.... Hence, therefore, the partners are

not the owners of the partnership property. The ideal being thus recognized by a fiction of law, is the owner; it has a right to control and administer the property, to enable it to fulfil[l] its legal duties and obligations; and the respective parties, who associated themselves for the purposes of participating in the profits which may accrue, are not the owners of the property itself....

Brogdon contends the exchange herein was a "mere formal change" in the legacy and thus did not revoke the legacy. He cites two common law cases, *In Re Estate of Creed* and *Pepka v. Branch*, to support this contention. In each of those cases, the testator donated real property to a corporation, and the court found the donation was a mere change in the form of the property that did not revoke a legacy. While this may be true in common law jurisdictions that have not adopted the entity theory, the entity theory applies to both partnerships and corporations in Louisiana. In Louisiana, when the title to real property is transferred to a partnership or corporation, a real change in ownership, not a mere change in form, occurs, and the partners or shareholders no longer have any direct ownership interest in the property. Thus, when the exchange was made, the West Baton Rouge property left Huguet's hands, and she no longer had any ownership interest in it.

Should the trial court have determined Huguet's intent?

The proposition is so clear as to require no citation of authority that one cannot donate or give away what one does not own. A testamentary bequest is a donation. At the time of her death, Huguet did not own any right, title, or interest in the West Baton Rouge Parish property, and thus she could not donate it to Brogdon or to anyone else. There is no obvious ambiguity in the testamentary bequest to Brogdon of all Huguet's right, title, and interest, and thus the trial court did not need to resort to extrinsic evidence to determine Huguet's intent. This legacy fell when the partnership became the owner of the property, and thus the trial court reached the correct result, albeit for the wrong reasons.

Application of Civil Code article 1695

The parties have gone to great lengths to argue whether Civil Code article 1695 is applicable herein. The differences in the FRENCH CIVIL CODE and the LOUISIANA CIVIL CODE are interesting, and it is most curious that the Code Napoleon of 1804 specifically listed exchange as an act that revoked a testamentary legacy, while the Projet de Government of 1800 and the 1808, 1825, and 1870 Civil Codes listed only donations inter vivos and sales. We need not reach this issue, however, in light of our previous conclusion that the legacy lapsed.

CONCLUSION

For the foregoing reasons, we affirm the judgment of the trial court declaring that the bequest by Huguet to Brogdon of all her right, title and interest in that certain 180-acre tract of land located in West Baton Rouge Parish, Louisiana, lapsed as a result of the exchange of the property for interest in Brogdon Development, a Louisiana Partnership in Commendam. Brogdon, as executor of the estate of Thelma S. Prescott Huguet, is cast for all costs of appeal.

AFFIRMED.

NOTES

Succession of Melancon, 330 So. 2d. 679 (La. App. 3d Cir. 1976), decided under pre-revision law, was a case that elicited much controversy. Dr. Melancon executed a three-page statutory will, including some specific legacies. When he died, two of the legacies were lined out with notations "I revoke" and "This item revoked" followed by the signature, "Dr. C.T. Melancon." The markings, notes, and signatures were clearly those of the testator. However, the notations were not dated. Since the attempted revocations were not in the form of a testament, the revocations were held to be without effect.

As you read over the comments to present La. C.C. 1608, you will note that the new legislation is designed, in particular, to change the result reached in *Melancon*. If Dr. Melancon had not signed, but only initialed the revocation, would it pass muster under current law? Under new La. C.C. 1607, an entire testament may also be revoked by a signed writing in the testatrix's own hands that identifies and clearly revokes the testament. The writing need not be on the testament itself (as is the case for the revocation of a legacy). What constitutes a writing? If the testatrix crosses out her signature on the last page of the testament, writes void and signs her name under the word "void" is there a revocation? If the testatrix is weak, and only crosses out her signature, could it be argued that this cross mark is both her writing and a mark that substitutes as her signature? Under prior law the First Circuit found that a will, upon which the testatrix had crossed out her signature, was not a valid revocation. *See Succession of Parham*, 755 So. 2d 265 (La. App. 1st Cir. 1999).

SUCCESSION OF DAMBLY
186 So. 7 (La. 1938)

ODOM, Justice.

[The testator executed one will and then later executed another one expressly revoking the first will. Later she tore up the second will.]

* * *

The pleadings in this case are numerous and lengthy. But, as revealed by them, it is clear that, in the last analysis, the only pertinent question involved in this litigation is whether the first will made by Mrs. Dambly on August 27, 1927, was revoked by the second will made on April 5, 1928. If it was, then Mrs. Dambly died intestate and her only child, Mrs. Pearl Riley Hogan, is her sole heir and should be appointed administratrix.

The first will is olographic in form. It is testamentary in terms, and it is admitted by all parties that it was entirely written, dated and signed by the testatrix. ...

* * *

The second will was dated April 5, 1928. Like the first one, it was olographic in form, testamentary in terms, and it is admitted that it was entirely written, dated and signed by Mrs. Dambly. ...

The opening statement of this will reads as follows:

I Leontine A. Dambly born Grigsby being of sound mind and aware of the uncertainty of life do make this last will, revoking all others.

* * *

It is conceded by all parties that this second will was thus mutilated by Mrs. Dambly, the testatrix, with her own hands, and that after it was mutilated she put the large fragment in an envelope, and that the unsealed envelope was by her deposited in a bureau drawer; and further conceded that she put the other two fragments in her work basket along with a lot of old rags and other cast off articles and hung the basket up in a closet. In fact, it was specifically alleged by Mrs. Hogan and others who opposed the probate of the first will that the second will was torn up, or mutilated, by the testatrix herself.

It was alleged by Mrs. Hogan and others, and it is now argued by their counsel, that by mutilating the second will in the manner above stated the testatrix intended to, and did as a matter of law, tacitly revoke it, and they cite the *Succession of Muh*, 35 La.Ann. 394, 48 Am.Rep. 242, in support of their argument. The trial judge held that the second will was revoked by mutilation.

The trial judge held also that the second will, having been thus mutilated by the testatrix, could not be admitted to probate. The ruling on this point was based upon the decision of this court in the *Succession of Hill*, 47 La.Ann. 329, 16 So. 819, where it was said [page 821]: "If the testator burns or tears up the will, there is no will in existence; no testament that can be probated."

This was the theory originally advanced by counsel for Mrs. Hogan and others. They alleged that Mrs. Dambly had torn the second will up and that at the date of her death it could have no effect. In fact, they prayed that "it be adjudged and decreed that the said will dated the 5th day of April, 1928 has been revoked and neither any of the legacies therein contained nor the appointment of the said Albert Ligon as executor thereof has any effect whatsoever."

Counsel's argument was from the beginning, and now is, that Mrs. Dambly died intestate, and it was so held by the trial judge. This argument and ruling are based upon the theory that the second will by express terms revoked the first one, and that the revocation took effect the moment the second will was written and signed by Mrs. Dambly; that thereafter the first will had no vitality, was a dead thing, a mere scrap of paper; and that, when Mrs. Dambly mutilated, tore up, the second will, it likewise had no vitality, could not be probated, and could not be made effective as a last will--hence that Mrs. Dambly died intestate.

The theory of counsel and the ruling of the trial judge that the second will, because of its mutilation by the testatrix, could not be probated and could have no effect as a last will, are unquestionably correct. ...

In *Succession of Hill, supra*, the court said:

If the testator burns or tears up the will, there is no will in existence; no testament that can be probated. And the same may be said by obliteration, defacement, the erasure of names of legatees, and the erasure of the testator's signature. In either case there is no will in existence, and no question of revocation can be presented. But no more complete revocation could be made than by the destruction of the testament. Article 1691 of the Code does not mention it as a mode of revocation.

Mrs. Dambly's second will expressly revoked all others. But the second will had no legal existence at the time of her death. Conceding this to be true, counsel for Mrs. Hogan and others, the appellees, argue that the first will was nevertheless revoked by the second one, and that the revocation of the second will did not revive the first one.

Speaking of the second will, the one dated April 5, 1928, counsel for the appellees say in their brief at Page 32:

> That will was an olographic will in due form as we have proved. It was in full force on April 5th, 1928 when it was made and remained in full force thereafter until it was mutilated sometime subsequent to the time Mr. Kizer saw it intact shortly before Mrs. Dambly's death.
>
> The will of August 27th, 1927 was certainly revoked on April 5th, 1928, by the will of that date and certainly remained revoked as long as the will of April 5th, 1928 remained intact.

Reference to certain articles of the REVISED CIVIL CODE of 1870 reveals the error into which counsel have fallen. Article 1692 of the REV.CIV.CODE says that:

> The act by which a testamentary disposition is revoked, must be made in one of the forms prescribed for testaments, and clothed with the same formalities. [*Compare La. C.C. 1607(3)*][*]

This is not the only kind of revocation recognized by the REV.CIV.CODE, for Article 1691, as amended by Act No. 114 of 1928, provides that the revocation of testaments "by the act of the testator is express or tacit," and "It is express when the testator has formally declared in writing that he revokes his testament," and "It is tacit when it results from some other disposition of the testator, or from some act which supposes a change of will."

The contention in this case is that the revocation of the first will was "express," by an "act" of the testatrix in which she formally declared in writing that she revoked it. The revocatory act referred to is the second will. The form of that revocatory act met the requirements of Article 1692 of the Code. It was "made in one of the forms prescribed for testaments, and clothed with the same formalities." In fact, it was an instrument intended to be, and was, a testament mortis causa, in which was written a clause expressly revoking all prior wills.

But that testament never went into effect. Mrs. Dambly destroyed it. Dispositions mortis cause (in prospect of death) do not take effect during the life of the testator. ...

*   *   *

---

[*] Bracketed material in italics added by author.

These articles make it clear: (1) That a testament mortis causa--such was the second will of Mrs. Dambly by which it is argued that the first will was revoked--is an act which takes effect "when the donor shall no longer exist;" (2) that such an act has no effect until it is probated, and (3) that it cannot be probated "until the decease of the testator has been sufficiently proved to the judge to whom the testament is presented."

It has been repeatedly held by this court that a will has no effect until probated and ordered to be executed by a competent court. ...

The reason why a disposition mortis causa has no effect until the death of the testator is that it is revocable. The first paragraph of Article 1690 of the Revised Civil Code provides that "Testaments are revocable at the will of the testator until his decease," and the second paragraph of that article provides that: "The testator cannot renounce this right of revocation nor obligate himself to exercise it only under certain words and restrictions, and if he does so, such declaration shall be considered as not written." In *Succession of Gilmore*, 157 La. 130, 102 So. 94, this court said [page 95]: "As testaments cannot take effect until the death of the testator, it is elementary that the testator is at liberty to revoke all former testaments at will. This right of revocation cannot be renounced or restricted by the testator. R.C.C. art. 1690." *See, also, Succession of Nelson*, 163 La. 458, 112 So. 298.

A written instrument intended to be a last will is a statement of the purpose, the desire or wish, of a person as it exists at the time of making the instrument. If his purpose or wish changes, and as often as it changes, he may change the expression of his wish or purpose. The rule here and elsewhere is that a will is ambulatory until the death of the maker. It is only at his death that it ceases to be ambulatory or that it acquires a fixed status.

The second will made by Mrs. Dambly did not, and could not, go into effect, for the reason that she destroyed it by mutilation. It follows that her first will, dated August 27, 1927, was never revoked and must stand as her last will.

Counsel for appellees have devoted a considerable portion of their brief to a discussion of the question whether a will which is revoked by a subsequent will is revived when the second, or revoking, will is itself revoked. Their theory is that the first will is not revived, and they cite, in support of their argument, French authorities and English cases which follow the Ecclesiastical Law of England. They say that the French authorities are divided on the question. Naturally, counsel approve those which support their theory. But these authorities cannot be considered as even persuasive in determining the question here involved. The reason is that in this state the method of revoking wills and the question as to when a will takes effect are purely statutory. It seems that under the French law a testator may revoke a former will by making a notarial declaration declaring that it is his intention to revoke it. But that is not the law in this state. Rev.Civ.Code, art. 1692.

Much is said by counsel regarding the "revival" of a will in case the revoking will is itself revoked. They not only concede, but argue, that in the case at bar the revoking will was revoked.

The question in this case is not whether the first will was revived when the revoking will was revoked, but whether the first will was ever revoked. Our opinion is, and we hold, that the first will was never revoked.

In the recent case of *Succession of Feitel*, 187 La. 596, 175 So. 72, on rehearing, this court discussed at length four wills made by the testator on different dates, and in the course of our opinion we said, at page 618, 175 So. at page 80:

During the trial of the case the attorney representing the plaintiff put great stress upon the fact that each one of the four wills was prefaced with a clause revoking all previous wills, thus: "This is my last will and testament and I hereby revoke all previous wills made by me." The law on the subject, however, is that, if a will containing a clause revoking a previous will, or revoking all previous wills of the testator, is annulled, the revoking clause loses its effect, and the last preceding will stands unrevoked. REV.CIV.CODE, art. 1692; *Hollingshead v. Sturgis*, 21 La.Ann. 450; *Succession of Hill*, 47 La.Ann. 329, 16 So. 819. The reason for this is that the Civil Code requires, in article 1692, that an express revocation of a testament or testamentary disposition, to have effect, must be made in one of the forms prescribed for testaments, and (be) clothed with the same formalities.

*   *   *

SUCCESSION OF CANNON
2015 WL 1361132, 2014-0826 (La. App. 1 Cir. 3/25/15),
writ denied, 2015-0816 (La. 6/5/15)

CRAIN, J.

In this succession proceeding, the executrix appeals a judgment denying and dismissing a petition to probate an alleged olographic codicil to the decedent's last will and testament. We affirm.

FACTS

Edward A. Cannon, Jr. (Edward) died testate on June 29, 2012. He was survived by his spouse and four children from a prior marriage, namely Edward A. Cannon, III, Wayne A. Cannon, Deanna L. Cannon, and Brenda A. Cannon (Brenda). Edward executed a statutory will on November 20, 1981, that bequeathed all of his property to his four children, in equal parts, through a testamentary trust and appointed Brenda to serve as executrix of his estate. Shortly after her father's death, Brenda commenced this succession proceeding and obtained an order probating the 1981 statutory will and appointing her as executrix of Edward's estate. The principal assets in the succession are the shares of EACCO, Inc., a privately held business that was wholly owned by Edward, and a building that housed EACCO's operations. The control of EACCO after Edward's death has caused considerable discord between Brenda and her siblings during the administration of the succession.

Approximately 13 months after probating the 1981 statutory will, Brenda filed a petition seeking to probate an alleged olographic codicil that consists of the following two pages (sometimes referred to hereinafter as the "1998 document"):

Edw A Cannon   5-23-98

— Will —
(change from existing)

Current or existing terms:
  Split between 4 children
  Brenda, Dee, Wayne & Bud III

Current worth (net)
Current debt

A. Bldg. 1015-1017 Jefferson Hwy (100%)
  50% to Brenda (controller + mgr.)
% of revenue
  16% to Dee   16% Jo Ann
  16% to Wayne   16% Marg
  16% to Bud III

9-7-99
Sell B. Home in Jolson ~~same as above~~
   ~~4 children Brenda, Dee, Wayne, Bud~~
C. Business: EACCO, Inc. (current lia. $96,170)
  100% to Brenda
  ? % to Dee
  ? % to Wayne
  ? % to Bud III

— next page —

D. Life Insurance
  Largest pay off bldg. note $309,000.00
  $100,000.00 to Marge (own policy) (Marg)
  $300,000.00 to EACCO

E. Social Security to Margi
  can't leave anything to Jo Ann, but,
  children could help her!

F. Sell bldg. to EACCO (create cash?)

Questions:
  Is there any way that I could get some of my money out of EACCO tax free?
  If not, what would the tax rate be?
  Would creating a Trust protect my Estate from liability suits?
  Can I sell the Bldg. to EACCO?
  What are the problems w/this?

Social Security $1,000 ± mo'ly

Brenda submitted affidavits from two individuals who attested that they were familiar with Edward's handwriting and that the writing on the document is entirely Edward's handwriting. According to Brenda, the 1998 document is an olographic codicil that amends the 1981 statutory will and, among other changes, bequeaths full ownership of EACCO to her. Brenda's siblings objected and asserted that the document, which they characterized as a set of notes written by their father in an attempt to organize his thoughts, did not comply with the requirements for an olographic codicil, because it was not signed at the end and did not reflect testamentary intent.

At the conclusion of a contradictory hearing on the matter, the trial court agreed with the siblings and denied the request to probate the document. The trial court signed a judgment on September 17, 2013, denying and dismissing the petition to probate the alleged codicil, and Brenda appealed.

DISCUSSION

Brenda assigns as error the trial court's failure to probate the 1998 document, specifically asserting that the trial court erred in finding a lack of both form and testamentary intent. Brenda also asserts that the trial court erred in refusing to allow her to present evidence in support of her petition to probate.

A codicil is an addition or qualification to a will and is considered part of the will. *See Succession of Ledet,* 170 La. 449, 452, 128 So. 273, 274 (1930); *Succession of Manion,* 143 La. 799, 808, 79 So. 409, 412 (1918); *Succession of Hinds,* 06–846 (La. App. 3 Cir. 2/28/07), 952 So. 2d 842, 846. To be valid, a codicil must be made in one of the forms prescribed for a valid testament and clothed with the same formalities. *See* La. Civ. Code arts. 1570, 1610; *Succession of Mydland,* 94–0501 (La.App. 1 Cir. 3/3/95), 653 So. 2d 8, 12 n. 3. There are two forms of testaments: olographic and notarial. La. Civ, Code art. 1574. An olographic testament is one entirely written, dated, and signed in the handwriting of the testator. *See* La. Civ. Code art. 1575; *In re Succession of Aycock,* 02–0701 (La.5/24/02), 819 So. 2d 290 (*per curiam*).

In addition to the form requirements, an olographic testament must contain testamentary intent, which is to say, "it must, by its own language, show on its face that it purports to dispose of the property of the testator on his death." *In re Succession of White,* 06–1002 (La. App. 1 Cir. 5/4/07), 961 So. 2d 439, 441 (quoting *Succession of Shows,* 158 So. 2d 293, 295 (La. App. 1 Cir.1963), *affirmed,* 246 La. 652, 166 So. 2d 261 (1964)). A valid olographic testament must do more than express or explain the wishes or desires of a decedent; the document must show intent to convey the decedent's property by the instrument itself. *In re Succession of Carroll,* 09–219 (La. App. 5 Cir. 12/8/09), 30 So. 3d 11, 17–18. A paper is not established as a person's will merely by proving that he intended to make a disposition of his property similar to or even identically the same as that contained in the paper. It must satisfactorily appear that he intended the very paper to be his will. *Succession of Patterson,* 188 La. 635, 641–42, 177 So. 692, 694 (1937); *In re Successions of Lain,* 49,261 (La. App. 2 Cir. 8/20/14), 147 So. 3d 1204, 1209–10. Simply stated, not every instrument that one writes, signs, and dates is a last will and testament; the author must; intend for the instrument to serve that purpose, and that intent must be evident on the face of the document.

We first consider Brenda's assertion that the trial court erred in refusing to allow certain evidence in support, of the petition to probate the 1998 document. Specifically, Brenda attempted to introduce an audio recording that, according to Brenda, was made in 2011 while Edward was a hospital patient. Brenda evidently made the recording surreptitiously, as there is no indication that Edward was aware that his communications with his healthcare providers and Brenda were being recorded. Most of the recording consists of exchanges between Edward and his healthcare providers, but at some point, Edward apparently tells an attending healthcare provider, with Brenda still present in the room, "My daughter has been with [inaudible] for 12 years, and I've already put her in my will. She gets the business, not her siblings, when I die." Brenda also proffered her affidavit attesting that her father told her numerous times that he put arrangements in place to pass ownership of his, EACCO shares to her upon his death. One of those occasions, according to the affidavit, was at a family meeting attended by several other family members. Brenda also offered an affidavit from Edward's widow, Marjorie Cannon, who attested that Edward told her on numerous occasions, and told others in her presence, that he had put estate planning arrangements in place to pass ownership of EACCO to Brenda upon his death. The siblings objected to these items as irrelevant, hearsay, and improper parol evidence of a testament or purported codicil. The trial court sustained the objections.

The standard of review for a trial court's evidentiary rulings is abuse of discretion; the trial court's ruling will not be disturbed unless it is clearly erroneous. *Gorman v. Miller,* 12–0412 (La.App. 1 Cir. 11/13/13), 136 So. 3d 834, 840 (*en banc*), *writ denied,* 13–2909 (La.3/21/14), 135 So. 3d 620. Extrinsic or parol evidence cannot be used to establish testamentary intent. *See Succession of Shows,* 246 La. 652, 657, 166 So. 2d 261, 263 (1964); *Successions of Lain,* 147 So. 3d at 1210; *In re Succession of Bernstine,* 04–739 (La.App. 3 Cir. 12/22/04), 890 So. 2d 776, 779, *writ denied,* 05–0182 (La.4/22/05), 899 So. 2d 555; *Succession of Carroll,* 30 So. 3d at 17. To be a valid testament, the instrument "must, *by its own language, show on its face* that it purports to dispose of the property of the testator on his death." *Succession of White,* 961 So. 2d at 441 (emphasis added; quoting *Succession of Shows,* 158 So. 2d at 295).

Brenda argues that extrinsic evidence is admissible to prove that a decedent revoked a legacy or will, and, therefore, such evidence should be admissible to prove that a testator intended to modify his will. Brenda cites *Succession of Justice,* 28,363 (La. App. 2 Cir. 8/23/96), 679 So. 2d 597, 600, which addressed whether a testator destroyed the original of a testament that could not be found, and *Succession of Dauzat,* 212 So. 2d 523, 526 (La. App. 3 Cir.1968), wherein the court held that a will dictated by the testator to the notary in French was invalid because it was written and read back to the testator in English, which the testator did not understand. *Succession of Dauzat* addressed the testator's capacity to understand the document that purported to be her testament, and the holding has no application to the present proceeding.

Succession of Justice involved the presumption that a testament was revoked by the destruction of the instrument, a presumption that arises when the original testament cannot be located after the testator's death. *See* La. Civ. Code art. 1607; *Succession of Talbot,* 530 So. 2d 1132, 1134–35 (La.1988). Under those circumstances, the presumption may be supported or rebutted by evidence of whether the testator was the author of the will's destruction, whether he expressed an intention to revoke the will, whether he had access to other originals of the will prior to his death, whether he treated any extant copy of the will as not having been revoked, and as to any other issue bearing upon the testator's intention with respect to the destruction and revocation of the will. *See Succession of Talbot,* 530 So. 2d at 1135. Because the original will cannot be located in those instances, extrinsic evidence of the testator's intent is relevant and necessary to determine whether he destroyed the testament and thereby revoked it. However, such evidence is not necessary when the original instrument has been located and presented to the court for probate, as was done in the present case. Under these circumstances, a court looks no further than the face of the document to determine whether testamentary intent was present when it was executed. *See Succession of Shows,* 246 La. at 657, 166 So. 2d at 263; *Succession of White,* 961 So. 2d at 441; *Successions of Lain,* 147 So. 3d at 1210; *Succession of Bernstine,* 890 So. 2d at 779; *Succession of Carroll,* 30 So. 3d at 17. The trial court correctly refused to allow the proffered evidence. This assignment of error has no merit.

Brenda next contends that testamentary intent is not necessary for a valid codicil and that the 1998 document satisfies the form requirements for an olographic will because it was written, signed, and dated in Edward's handwriting. Alternatively, she maintains that testamentary intent, if required, is established on the face of the document. The siblings counter that while the document was written and dated by Edward, it was not properly signed, because Edward's name, if intended to be a signature, appears at the very top of the instrument rather than at the end. The siblings further contend that the document lacks testamentary intent, because it does not show an "intent to convey decedent's property by the instrument itself." Finding merit in this second argument, we address that basis for the trial court's judgment and pretermit consideration of whether Edward's signature at the top of the document satisfies the form requirements for an olographic will under Louisiana Civil Code article 1575.

Brenda initially argues that testamentary intent is not required for a valid codicil to a will. The modification of a testament by a codicil is governed by Louisiana Civil Code article 1610, which requires that the modification be in "one of the forms prescribed for testaments." Similarly, Louisiana Civil Code article 1608 provides that a legacy is revoked when the testator "[s]o declares in one of the forms prescribed for testaments" or "[m]akes a subsequent incompatible testamentary disposition or provision." Brenda contends that this codal language only requires proper testamentary "form" for a valid codicil and does not require testamentary intent.

The references to "form" in Articles 1610 and 1608 are not materially different from similar references in Article 1575, which governs the form for an olographic testament, and Articles 1576 and 1577, which govern the form for a notarial testament. While all of these articles address "form" requirements, those requirements expressly apply to the creation or modification of a "testament," meaning an instrument that is intended by its author to dispose of his property by a *mortis causa* disposition upon his death. *See* La. Civ. Code art. 1570; *Succession of Patterson,* 188 La. at 641–42, 177 So. at 694; *Succession of White,* 961 So. 2d at 441. Our courts have consistently held that a valid testament requires testamentary intent, and we see no basis to require anything less for the *modification* of a valid testament by a codicil. *See Succession of Carroll,* 30 So. 3d at 17–18 (document that lacked testamentary intent was not a valid codicil). Brenda's argument to the contrary is without merit.

Brenda alternatively asserts that the 1998 document adequately reflects testamentary intent. The document must be read as a whole to determine whether the necessary testamentary intent was present when it was executed. *See In re Succession of White,* 961 So. 2d at 442. Although the caption of the 1998 document—"Will (change from existing)"—is suggestive of testamentary intent, the body of the document repeatedly reflects Edward's uncertainty and indecision as to how his estate should be divided and managed.

The first lettered paragraph identifies a building followed by a list of six people, identified only by first name, with corresponding percentages for each person that cumulatively total 130%. A provision indicating a possible distribution of percentage to Edward's "grand children" has been struck through, and the phrase "% of revenue" appears in the margin. The uncertainty concerning the disposition of this building is compounded by the last lettered paragraph in which Edward questions whether he should sell the building to EACCO to "create cash." At the end of the document, he inquires, "Can I sell the Bldg. to EACCO? What are the problems w/this?"

The next paragraph identifies the "Home in Folsom" and contains some redacted text that referred to the previous paragraph. A note in the margin provides "4–7–99 Sell," indicating an apparent conveyance of the house, which does not appear as an asset of the succession in the detailed descriptive list filed in the record.

The next paragraph addresses EACCO and is the focal point of Brenda's appeal, as she asserts that this paragraph bequeaths all of the company's shares to her. While that paragraph does include the notation "100% to Brenda," the same paragraph also identifies the three remaining children with "? %" preceding each name, as well as a reference to "current employees" that has been struck through. The presence of multiple question marks in this paragraph undermines Brenda's assertion that the provision was intended by Edward to be a final, complete codicil to his will. To the contrary, it demonstrates a continuing uncertainty about the distribution of the company and any modification to the will in that regard. The remaining information in the document includes references to life insurance and social security benefits, followed by a series of questions that further illustrate the unresolved nature of Edward's estate planning.

Further adding to the uncertainty of the document is the lack of a signature after any of the purportedly dispositive provisions. While we express no opinion as to whether a signature at the top of the document satisfies the form requirement for an olographic will, the location of the signature may nevertheless be relevant for ascertaining testamentary intent. The purpose in requiring the testator to sign his testamentary dispositions is to make certain that they constitute his last will. *Succession of Fitzhugh,* 170 La. 122, 126, 127 So. 386, 387 (1930). Where, as in the present case, the document reflects uncertainty concerning the purported bequests, the absence of any signature after those provisions further suggests a lack of testamentary intent. In *Succession of Fitzhugh,* a party attempted to probate an alleged olographic will, although the testator's signature appeared only on the envelope containing the document. In affirming the trial court's refusal to probate the document, the supreme court stated:

> It is not beyond the bounds of reason that the testatrix, after writing down the testamentary dispositions and dating them, was undecided as to whether to complete the dispositions by affixing her signature at the end of them, and therefore placed them in an envelope, sealed the envelope for security, and placed the superscription thereon for her own convenience, so as to identify the envelope readily, intending, if she later concluded that the dispositions met with her wishes, to do the ordinary, usual, and naturally suggestive act of signing them at their close, so as to show what was written above was her last will, just as she would in completing any other solemn document.

Succession of Fitzhugh, 170 La. at 127, 127 So. at 387.

Similarly, in the present case, the absence of a signature after the allegedly dispositive provisions suggests that Edward may have been "undecided as to whether to complete the dispositions by affixing [his] signature at the end of them." *See Succession of Fitzhugh,* 170 La. at 127, 127 So. at 387.

In arguing that the document does reflect testamentary intent, Brenda relies primarily on *Succession of White,* but the document before the court in that case differs significantly from the 1998 document. In *Succession of White,* the three-page document contained a list of assets followed by the testator's specific wishes for the distribution of her property to several legatees. The testator signed and dated the instrument at the top of the first page and at the bottom of the third page. Nothing on the face of the instrument suggested that it was incomplete or that the testator was undecided about the distributions. In an attempt to invalidate the will, the intestate heirs argued that testamentary intent was lacking because of a notation on the reverse side of the third page, which stated "Listing assets—Temporary only in case of emergency" and noted that "[v]ery little" was in an identified bank box. The court reasoned that this notation, which was not contained within the dated and signed pages, could reasonably be interpreted as a note to the decedent's family directing them to look for a "temporary" listing of assets in her bank box, or as a note to herself to update her list of assets if her savings were substantially depleted by medical costs. *Succession of White,* 961 So. 2d at 443. Therefore, the court found that the trial court did not err in finding that the document was a valid last will and testament. *Succession of White,* 961 So. 2d at 443.

In contrast to the definitive nature of the document presented to the court in *Succession of White,* the 1998 document, through numerous question marks and unanswered questions, demonstrates Edward's uncertainty as to how his estate should be distributed. We also note that the court in *Succession of White* relied on the premise that "[g]iven multiple interpretations of writings, a court must opt for the one that grants testacy and turns away intestacy." *Succession of White,* 961 So. 2d at 443. In the present case, we are not confronted with an estate that will be subject to intestacy if the codicil is not probated. Nor are we attempting to construe an ambiguous legacy or other provision in a valid testament, in which case every endeavor should be made to give effect to the disposition, and the law is indulgent if the testament is written without aid of counsel. *See* La. Civ. Code art. 1612; *Carter v. Succession of Carter,* 332 So. 2d 439, 442 (La.1976). To the contrary, Brenda is seeking to modify the terms of a valid statutory will that, without contest, was probated in this proceeding and contains an unambiguous declaration by Edward of how his estate should be distributed upon his death. That unequivocal expression of intent should not be lightly disregarded or modified without sufficient proof that Edward subsequently executed a valid codicil to change his will.

Considering the entirety of the 1998 document, we do not find that Edward intended this very instrument, which contains more questions than purported bequests, to be a final codicil to his will. Although Edward may have been contemplating a modification of his will, the 1998 document, at best, is a work-in-progress that Edward never completed prior to his death. Accordingly, the trial court did not err in denying and dismissing the petition to probate the alleged olographic codicil, and these assignments of error have no merit. *See In re Succession of Rhodes,* 39,364 (La.App. 2 Cir. 3/23/05), 899 So. 2d 658, 662, *writs denied,* 05–0936, 05–1044 (La.6/3/05), 903 So. 2d 459, 460 (letter instructing attorney as to how individual wished his estate to be distributed and requesting cancellation of prior wills lacked sufficient testamentary intent to establish that he intended to dispose of his property by means of that particular instrument); *Succession of Carroll,* 30 So. 3d at 17–18 (document setting forth inventory of assets and desired bequests that was given to an attorney was never finalized and lacked testamentary intent).

CONCLUSION

The trial court's September 17, 2013 judgment, as amended by the February 6, 2015 judgment, is affirmed. All costs of this appeal are assessed to Brenda A. Cannon, individually and as executrix of the Succession of Edward A. Cannon, Jr.

MOTION TO DISMISS APPEAL DENIED; SEPTEMBER 17, 2013 JUDGMENT, AS AMENDED BY THE FEBRUARY 6, 2015 JUDGMENT, AFFIRMED.

NOTES

Former La. C.C. 1705 provided for revocation of a testament by the subsequent birth, adoption, or legitimation of a child, unless the testator provided otherwise. Under the present Code, the subsequent birth of a child does not affect a legal revocation. The law of forced heirship was deemed sufficient to protect children. However, under the revised law, if the testator is divorced from a legatee, subsequent to the writing of a testament and at the time of his death, the legacy to that former spouse will be revoked, unless the testator had provided to the contrary in the testament. La. C.C. 1608 (5).

May a testament be revived by reference? If, for example, a testator wrote a statutory will in 1983, and another olographic will in 1985, revoking the earlier will, followed by a codicil declaring that the codicil is meant to supplement the 1983 will, which will is valid? *See Succession of Vicaro*, 612 So. 2d 839 (La. App. 1st Cir. 1992).

Interpretation of Legacies

La. C.C. 1611 is the prime directive on interpretation of legacies. The testator's intent "controls the interpretation of his testament." However, where the language of the document is clear and unambiguous the court may not depart from the proper signification of the terms "under the pretext of pursuing its spirit." La. C.C. 1611. By Act No. 560, § 1 of 2001, the legislature added paragraph B to La. C.C. 1611, giving direction for interpretation of will written prior to the changes in forced heirship law.

La. C.C. 1612 dictates that a disposition should be understood in a way to make it effective, since it is obvious that the testator intended that it have effect. The rest of the interpretation articles are designed to assist the courts in finding the testator's intention and giving it effect. La. C.C. 1614 provides that all dispositions shall be interpreted as referring to the "property the testator owned at death" unless the testament states otherwise. Prior to the 1997 revision, dispositions were presumed to refer to the property the testator owned at the time of the will's execution.

If a will contains contradictory provision, the one written last is followed. Also, when a testament leaves a collection or group of things and also leaves some of all of the same objects the legacy of some or all prevails. La. C.C. 1615. Unless the testator clearly so provides, a legacy to a creditor is not applied in satisfaction of the debt. La. C.C. 1616.

SUCCESSION OF McAULEY
29 La. Ann. 33 (1877)

Manning, C. J.

On the twenty-third of November, 1874, Margaret McAuley, wife of John A. O'Brien, made her olographic will in form as follows:

New Orleans, November 23, 1874.

I, Margaret O'Brien, of the city of New Orleans, and State of Louisiana, being of sound mind leave this my last will and testament.

I name my husband executor of my last will. All my debts must be paid out of estate. Rent for store my husband must not be held responsible as he has signed notes for same for me. All bills for goods bought by me a note of Washington Smith of New York, for the sum of four hundred dollars said is mine but is signed by my husband John A. O'Brien. All my funeral expenses, I desire to be buried as plain as possible a plain stone to mark my last resting place. The sum of three thousand dollars to be paid to my husband with 8 per cent interest, from 16 August 1872. All my furniture is his. All my jewelry that is a diamond set breast-pin earrings and bracelets a diamond ring, my wedding ring I desire to be buried with. My diamond watch and chain I leave to my sister Frances Dowling.

After all my funeral expenses are paid Dr. bill and all sundries expenses are paid if there is any money left I wish it settled on my sister Frances Dowling children for their use and benefit. If I should leave a child all this will to be null as all I have belongs by right to my child, either male or female. I want my child put under the care of Sister Chantreral as I know she will take good care of it my husband to pay her out of the revenues of my estate.

MARGARET O'BRIEN."D"

The writing covers the first and part of the second page of the paper. The signature made at that time is at the bottom of the second page, leaving a space of several lines between it and the concluding words of the will. In January, 1875, the testatrix was delivered of a child, which survived its birth but a short time. On the nineteenth of August, 1875, after the death of her child, the testatrix affixed her signature to the writing of the previous November immediately under the last line and added the following words between that signature and the first signature, at or near the bottom of the page:

New Orleans, August 19, 1875.

If I and my husband should die during my trip from home, after all my debts are paid whatever I die possessed I leave to St. Mary's Orphan Boys' Asylum less six hundred dollars   MARGARET O'BRIEN. for my mother.   MARGARET O'BRIEN.

ADELINE SHELSTONE.

* * *

On the fourth of October of the same year, the mother and sisters of the deceased, who are her heirs-at-law, instituted an action to annul the probate and set aside the wills upon the grounds that the first writing, which they call the first will, was revoked by the birth of a child posterior to its date, and the second falls because the event upon the happening of which the institution of the universal legatee was made to depend has not happened and cannot now happen; i.e., the death of both husband and wife during their trip north.

The executor answers by a general denial. The St. Mary's Orphan Boys' Asylum pleads the general issue and specially avers that the two instruments constitute but one will, and that both comply with the requisites of an olographic will, and that the dispositions made are "in conformity to law and can be easily executed, being intelligible and comprehensible in its extent and designs," and last, that the document was signed and dated by the deceased subsequent to the birth and death of her child.

Much stress has been laid in the arguments, both oral and written, on the fact that the two writings are of different dates, were written with two shades of ink, the signature first spoken of being of the same shade as the body of the writing of November, 1874, and the others of the same shade as the body of what is termed by some the second will and by others the codicil. The different shades of ink are worthy of observation only because they assist us in ascertaining the circumstances under which the two writings were made. We find no difficulty in the different dates.

*   *   *

We consider the writings before us as one will. The testatrix knew at the time of the first signature that she bore in her bosom a child whose birth would annul her testament. The child was born less than two months from the date of the instrument, and she writes "if I should leave a child, all this will to be null." After the death of the child, and when about to make her will in view of a projected trip north, she mentally reverts to her former disposition of her property, draws the paper containing it from its place of deposit, and signs it anew immediately after its concluding words. Manifestly this was intended by her as a republication of that writing as a part of her will. The death of the child had destroyed the vitality of the will as then written. The republication revivified it. The testatrix then added another clause providing a disposition of her property upon a contingency expressed therein, and signed the whole instrument, and dated it, and this last date is the date of the will.

We have now to consider the effect of this last clause.

The counsel for the defendants, in a brief which has been very serviceable to us, have argued with equal ingenuity and subtlety that the language used by the testatrix does not express her meaning. Undoubtedly a fundamental rule in the interpretation of wills is that the intention of the testator must be ascertained, and when ascertained, effect given to it; and in order to ascertain the intention courts look outside and behind the ipsissima verba of the instrument, and resort to the evidence of circumstances when the literal meaning leads to absurd or impossible consequences. This is when the words are ambiguous or contradictory, or the meaning latent. Pothier in his fourth rule for the interpretation of testaments teaches that the law prefers the sense which saves from intestacy, and that reference may be had to surrounding circumstances to ascertain the sense; and in his eighteenth rule, that "a will should be interpreted by means of surrounding circumstances." Traite des Testaments, chap. vii. These rules are embodied in our Civil Code in articles 1705, 1706, 1708, new numbers 1712, 1713, 1715.

The circumstances surrounding the confection of these two writings are developed in the evidence, and have already been adverted to. In November, 1874, she made her will, giving specific instructions concerning certain debts, and explaining other matters which might not have been understood without that explanation, and appointing her husband executor. She either intended to add something later, or she thought, as many illiterate persons do, that she must sign at the bottom of the page, and accordingly her signature in the same shade of ink is found there. That will was intended to provide a disposition of her property in case her death should precede the birth of her child. In August, 1875, when she knew that the will already written was null, since the event which caused its invalidation had occurred meanwhile, and being about to commence a journey-troubled, too, by a presentiment that she would never return-and perceiving that the paper contained what she wished, so far as it went, but apprehensive that the addition of another clause with a new date might not sufficiently evince her desire to continue the dispositions contained in it in force, she signs it again, and writes the clause relative to the asylum.

We are not embarrassed, as are the counsel for the asylum, by the seeming inconsistency of naming her husband executor in the first part of her will and providing for the contingency of his death in the concluding part. The thought present to her mind evidently was to provide for the two contingencies of her own death, her husband surviving, and the death of both of them. In the writing of November, 1874, she also contemplates the survival of her child, and directs that it be placed under the care of a particular person, and in that of August, 1875, when her child was dead, she provides what shall be done if her husband and herself shall both die during their trip.

The counsel for the asylum, pursuant to their theory that the intention of the testatrix has not been accurately expressed, propose a new reading of the last clause of the will, effected by a transposition of words, thus:

THE TEXT.	THE INTENTION.
If I and my husband should die during my trip from home after all my debts are paid whatever I die possessed I leave to St. Mary's Orphan Boys' Asylum less six hundred dollars for my mother.	If I should die during my and my husband's trip from home after all my debts are paid whatever I die possessed I leave to St. Mary's Orphan Boys' Asylum, less six hundred dollars for my mother.

*   *   *

The transposition is then permissible when the words used by a testator do not convey any meaning, or where the expression is senseless or contradictory, or when such transposition is warranted by the context and like cases; but a conjectural hypothesis is not permitted in opposition to the plain and obvious sense of the language. ...

The words used by the testatrix in the will now before us are intelligible in the order in which they stand: "If I and my husband should die during my trip from home." The objection to the new collocation proposed by the counsel for the asylum is that it is not our province to make a will for the deceased, but to interpret and give effect to the one she made. If she chose to make her institution of the asylum as her universal legatee contingent upon the death of her husband and herself, it is not for us to say that she meant otherwise, or that it would have been more reasonable and proper to have made that contingency her own death only.

*   *   *

It is therefore ordered, adjudged, and decreed that the judgment of the lower court be and it is hereby affirmed with costs.

SUCCESSION OF SOILEAU
918 So. 2d 563 (La. App. 3d Cir. 2005)

GENOVESE, Judge.

This matter involves a dispute over the interpretation of a will. The decedent's only child, Sandra Kay Soileau Leake ("Leake"), is appealing the grant of summary judgment in favor of the decedent's first cousin, Sadie Veillon ("Veillon"). The trial court named Veillon as the succession representative and also found her to be the sole legatee of the decedent, Attward Joseph Soileau ("Soileau"). For the following reasons, the judgment of the trial court is reversed and the case is remanded to the trial court for further proceedings.

FACTUAL AND PROCEDURAL BACKGROUND

Soileau executed the will in question on May 15, 1990, and died on July 13, 2003. The testament provides, in pertinent part:

> I, Attward J. Soileau, a citizen and resident of Rapides Parish, Louisiana, make this my last and testament, revoking all others.
> I desire that all of my just debts be paid.
> After all of my just debts have been paid, I will, give and bequeath the disposable portion of all of the property of which I die possessed, whether movable or immovable, choate or inchoate, corporeal or incorporeal, both separate and community, to my first cousin, Sadie L. Veillon.
> It is my wish that the ownership of all of the remainder of the property of which I die possessed, whether movable or immovable, choate or inchoate, corporeal or incorporeal, both separate and community, pass to my child, namely Sandra K. Soileau Leake, in accordance with the intestate laws of the State of Louisiana.
> I hereby expressly provide that in no event will my former wife, Lucille D. Soileau, have any usufruct, provided under the laws of the State of Louisiana, over any of the property.
> I appoint George Veillon, as the executor of my estate with full seizin and to serve without bond.
> I appoint Ralph W. Kennedy, Attorney at Law, Alexandria, Rapides Parish, Louisiana, as attorney for the executor.
> In witness whereof, I have signed this my last will and testament in the presence of the witnesses and Notary Public hereinafter named and undersigned.
>
> /s/ Attward J. Soileau
> ATTWARD J. SOILEAU (Testator)
> SIGNED AND DECLARED by Attward J. Soileau, testator above named, in our presence to be his last will and testament, and in the presence of the testator and each other we have hereunto subscribed our names on this Fifteenth day of May, One Thousand Nine Hundred Ninety.
> /s/ Attward J. Soileau
> ATTWARD J. SOILEAU (Testator)
>
> /s/ Martha P. Kennedy
> MARTHA P. KENNEDY (Witness)
>
> /s/ Janey L. Safford

JANEY L. SAFFORD (Witness)

/s/ Ralph W. Kennedy
RALPH W. KENNEDY
(Notary Public)

On August 6, 2003, Leake filed a request for notice with the Rapides Parish Clerk of Court's office asking to be notified of the opening of her father's succession. On September 23, 2003, Veillon petitioned the court to appoint a notary to inventory Soileau's safe deposit box. The court appointed Ralph W. Kennedy to perform said inventory.

On December 17, 2003, Leake petitioned the court for appointment as the provisional administratrix of her father's succession. In his will, Soileau had designated George Veillon as his executor, but George Veillon predeceased Soileau. Sandra Veillon opposed the appointment of Leake as the succession representative.

On April 20, 2004, Veillon filed a motion for summary judgment alleging that she was entitled to a judgment as a matter of law declaring: (1) that Leake is not qualified for the position of succession representative of the Soileau estate; (2) that Veillon should be appointed dative executrix of the succession; and (3) that Veillon is the only legatee under Soileau's will.

Leake filed a motion in limine on September 17, 2004, requesting the exclusion of certain verbal testimony and the striking from evidence of an affidavit submitted by Veillon in support of her motion for summary judgment. Leake also filed a cross-motion for summary judgment on October 8, 2004, asserting that she was entitled to a judgment declaring "that the provision in the testament, submitted by Veillon for probate, purportedly making a disposition to Veillon, is both superceded and revoked by the subsequent and last written disposition to Leake."

Prior to the hearing on the motion for summary judgment, the trial court heard arguments on Leake's motion in limine. By this motion, Leake attempted to prevent the introduction of live testimony from Appellee Sadie Veillon, Jerome Veillon, Martha Louise Kennedy and Ralph Kennedy. Further, Leake also wanted stricken from the summary judgment evidence the affidavit of Ralph Kennedy, which was submitted by Veillon attached to and in support of her motion for summary judgment, on the basis that Mr. Kennedy's affidavit did not contain personal knowledge as to Soileau's testamentary intent. After taking the matter under advisement, the trial court rendered judgment on October 27, 2004, immediately prior to the contradictory hearing on the cross-motions for summary judgment, granting Leake's motion in limine. The trial court declared it would "prohibit the use of witnesses and/or affidavits from those witnesses" in the summary judgment proceeding.

Immediately thereafter, the parties proceeded to present their arguments on the issue of the application of the civil code rules and the jurisprudential interpretations of the dispositions in Soileau's will to Veillon and Leake. Veillon argued that the testament limits Leake to the forced portion; therefore, because Leake is not a forced heir by the law in effect on the date of Soileau's death (July 13, 2003), the disposable portion bequeathed to Veillon is the entire estate. Relying on La.Civ.Code art. 1615, Leake argued that Soileau revoked his testament to Veillon in the very next paragraph when he wrote a "contradictory provision" which disposed of the remainder of his property bequeathed to Leake "in accordance with the intestate laws of the State of Louisiana." Leake asserted that this provision, the one written last, entitles her to receive the entirety of Soileau's estate.

The trial court issued its written reasons for judgment on December 1, 2004 as follows: (1) denying Leake's application to be appointed the provisional administrator of the succession; (2) granting Veillon's motion for summary judgment and decreeing her to be the sole legatee under Soileau's will declaring "that she is entitled to the disposable portion of the Succession, which the Court finds to be 100%;" (3) denying Leake's cross-motion for summary judgment; and (4) appointing Veillon as dative executrix of this succession proceeding with no security required. The trial court reasoned that Leake is neither an heir nor a legatee of the estate, that Soileau left the disposable portion of his estate to Veillon, and that Leake receives nothing under Soileau's will since "the disposable portion, where a decedent leaves no forced heirs, is 100%." The trial court, however, specifically stated in its reasons that "the affidavit of Mr. Kennedy (the attorney that originally prepared the will) expressly shows that the intent of the testator was to leave his daughter nothing." Leake appeals the grant of summary judgment in favor of Veillon.

LAW AND ANALYSIS
ASSIGNMENTS OF ERROR
On appeal, Leake asserts the following assignments of error:

(1) The trial court committed reversible error by granting Leake's motion in limine excluding all evidence but then without notice to Leake and giving her a hearing at which to present her evidence ignored its ruling and considered evidence only from Veillon that informed the court's decision.
(2) The trial court committed reversible error by relying in part on incompetent and extrinsic evidence in interpreting a will that both parties agreed was clear.
(3) The trial court committed reversible error by not considering the entirety of the language of the will in interpreting it.
(4) The trial court committed reversible error by not applying specific controlling codal articles directing how the court must resolve contradictory and incompatible provisions in the will.

DISCUSSION
Though Leake alleges four (4) specifications of error for review, the crux of her appeal is the trial court's ruling on the cross-motions for summary judgment. The trial court granted Veillon's motion for summary judgment and denied Leake's motion for summary judgment.

On October 27, 2004, the trial court granted the motion in limine excluding testimony and affidavits and also heard the arguments on the cross-motions for summary judgment and took evidence on the parties' applications for succession representative. On December 1, 2004, the trial court issued written reasons for judgment granting Veillon's motion for summary judgment, declaring her to be the sole legatee under Soileau's will, and then appointed her as the succession representative.

Appellate courts review summary judgments de novo using the same criteria that govern the trial court's consideration of whether summary judgment is appropriate. Richard v. Hall, 03–1488 (La.4/23/04), 874 So. 2d 131; Goins v. Wal–Mart Stores, Inc., 01–1136 (La.11/28/01), 800 So. 2d 783. The appellate court must determine whether "the pleadings, depositions, answers to interrogatories, and admissions on file, together with the affidavits, if any, show that there is no genuine issue as to material fact, and that mover is entitled to judgment as a matter of law." La.Code Civ.P. art. 966(B).

We will address the trial court's grant of summary judgment in favor of Veillon first. The trial court erred in relying in part on the affidavit of Kennedy in deciding the motions for summary judgment when the trial court had previously granted the motion in limine precluding same. The trial court's ruling on the motion in limine was not appealed. The trial court's written reasons clearly establish that the affidavit of Ralph Kennedy was considered to support its conclusion that Soileau's intent was to "leave his daughter nothing." We find that the trial court's grant of summary judgment in favor of Veillon was legal error due to the trial court's obvious use of this evidence in deciding the motion for summary judgment. This court does not pass on the merits of the case involving Soileau's intent, but simply reverses the summary judgment finding that the trial court erred in its rendition of a judgment which purports to determine said intent. Though summary judgments are favored under our law as set forth in La.Code Civ.P. art. 966(A)(2), "factual inferences reasonably drawn from the evidence must be construed in favor of the party opposing the motion, and all doubt must be resolved in the opponent's favor." *Willis v. Medders*, 00–2507, p. 2 (La.12/8/00), 775 So. 2d 1049, 1050; *Indep. Fire Ins. Co. v. Sunbeam Corp.*, 99–2181, 99–2257 (La.2/29/00), 755 So. 2d 226. Issues pertaining to subjective facts such as intent are usually not appropriate to a summary judgment determination. *Murphy's Lease & Welding Serv., Inc. v. Bayou Concessions Salvage, Inc.*, 00–978 (La.App. 3 Cir. 3/8/01), 780 So. 2d 1284, *writ denied*, 01–1005 (La.6/1/01), 793 So. 2d 195; *Belgard v. American Freightways, Inc.*, 99–1067 (La.App. 3 Cir. 12/29/99); 755 So. 2d 982, *writ denied*, 00–293 (La.3/31/00); 756 So. 2d 1147.

Due to its evidentiary limitations, summary judgment is not the proper procedural device for the resolution of all legal matters, particularly the resolution of succession matters dealing with disparity in testamentary dispositions and intent of the testator. Though counsel agree on the record that the testator's will was "clear," in truth and in fact, such is not the case herein. For if the will was clear, there would be no appeal regarding interpretation thereof. Considering the facts presented in this case and decedent's will, the legal issue of Soileau's testamentary intent cannot be resolved by the use of summary proceedings and must be resolved at trial on the merits. Further, we find the record reflects the existence of a genuine issue of material fact regarding Soileau's intent which should be the subject of a determination on the merits. This suit is simply not ripe for disposition by summary judgment.

Leake asserts the will is clear, but contains a contradictory provision, and argues that only the application of La.Civ.Code art. 1615 is necessary. Louisiana Civil Code Article 1615 provides:

When a testament contains contradictory provisions, the one written last prevails. Nonetheless, when the testament contains a legacy of a collection or a group of objects and also a legacy of some or all of the same objects, the legacy of some or all of the objects prevails.

Louisiana Civil Code articles 1611 through 1616 govern interpretation of testaments. When Soileau's succession was opened, Article 1611 provided:

A. The intent of the testator controls the interpretation of his testament. If the language of the testament is clear, its letter is not to be disregarded under the pretext of pursuing its spirit. The following rules for interpretation apply only when the testator's intent cannot be ascertained from the language of the testament. In applying these rules, the court may be aided by any competent evidence.

B. When a testament uses a term the legal effect of which has been changed after the date of execution of the testament, the court may consider the law in effect at the time the testament was executed to ascertain the testator's intent in the interpretation of a legacy or other testamentary provision.

The case of *In re Succession of Helms,* 01–1357 (La.App. 3 Cir. 3/6/02), 810 So. 2d 1265, involved similar facts to the case sub judice. In Helms, the testator bequeathed "the minimum portion allowed by Louisiana law at the time of my death" to be held in trust for his second daughter. The testator's second daughter argued that the bequest, together with the creation of a testamentary trust, should compel the interpretation of the will as leaving her "something" as opposed to "nothing." We affirmed the trial court's judgment which interpreted testator's bequest as providing nothing to the testator's second daughter.

Though Helms was an appeal from a trial on the merits as opposed to a summary judgment, this court's pronouncement of relevant case law provides pertinent guidance in the instant case.

"Courts must interpret a will according to its plain language since 'the intent of the testator is the paramount consideration in determining the provisions of a will.'" *Succession of Hackney,* 97–859, p. 5 (La.App. 3 Cir. 2/4/98); 707 So. 2d 1302, 1306, *writ denied,* 98–596 (La.4/24/98); 717 So. 2d 1172 (quoting *Succession of Schiro,* 96–1567, p. 6 (La.App. 4 Cir. 4/9/97); 691 So. 2d 1374, 1377, *writs denied,* 97–1400, 700 So. 2d 518 (La. 9/5/97), 97–1423 (La.9/5/97); 700 So. 2d 518). The intention of the deceased must be ascertained from the whole will, and effect must be given to every part of the will as far as the law will permit. "Where it is a question of the choice between two interpretations, one of which will effectuate, and the other will defeat, a testator's intention, the court will carry out the intention of the testator." *Carter v. Succession of Carter,* 332 So. 2d 439, 441 (La.1976) (quoting *Succession of LaBarre,* 179 La. 45, 48, 153 So. 15, 16 (1934)). Additionally, Louisiana case law has recognized that in the interpretation of wills, the first and natural impression conveyed to the mind on reading the will as a whole is entitled to great weight. "The testatrix is not supposed to be propounding riddles but rather to be conveying her ideas to the best of her ability so as to be correctly understood at first view." *Succession of Meeks,* (La.App. 2 Cir.1992); 609 So. 2d 1035, 1038, *writ denied,* 612 So. 2d 86 (La.1993).

Leake contends the trial court erred by relying in part on incompetent and extrinsic evidence in interpreting a will that both parties agreed was clear. The record indicates that the trial court attempted to approach this issue from the standpoint of the will being clear and unambiguous. The trial court even ruled it would not consider the extrinsic evidence offered by Veillon, specifically, Ralph Kennedy's affidavit. However, the trial court's ultimate use of said extrinsic evidence is confirmation to this court that the trial court did deem the terms of the will as unclear and ambiguous. When a bequest is clear and unambiguous, the need for extrinsic evidence is precluded since, according to Louisiana Civil Code Article 1611, evidence is only to be a reference in the event that a testament's language is not clear. *In re Succession of Delcambre,* 04–1227 (La.App. 3 Cir. 2/2/05), 893 So. 2d 167, *writ denied,* 05–527 (La.4/29/05), 901 So. 2d 1069. After thorough review and consideration, we find the trial court's judgment to be an error of law, and we remand this matter to the trial court for proper evidentiary consideration.

Because Leake's appeal to this court does not include an opposition to the trial court's appointment of Veillon as dative executrix of this succession proceeding, that issue is not before this court, and therefore, is not considered.

We reverse the trial court's ruling on the cross-motions for summary judgment and find that there are material questions of fact which exist as to testamentary intent. We remand this matter to the trial court for trial on the merits to determine the testamentary intent and legal interpretation of Soileau's will. Costs of this appeal are assessed equally against Appellant and Appellee.

REVERSED AND REMANDED.

NOTES

In *Succession of Montero*, 365 So. 2d 929 (La. App. 4th Cir. 1978), the testator wrote a will stating "in the event I do not come out of this surgery," yet survived the surgery. The court upheld the will as operative at the time of the testator's death months later. The court interpreted the quoted phrase to mean "in the event of my death."

In *Succession of Johnson*, 387 So. 2d 1378 (La. App. 2d Cir. 1980) the testatrix apparently believing that she owned 20 acres of land, bequeathed, certain portions to five legatees. In actuality, the testatrix owned an undivided one-half interest in forty acres that she had inherited from her parents. The testament did provide, however, that if the testatrix owned more or less than twenty acres, the legatees should receive the same proportion of the total acreage as willed to them. The court upheld the will noting that Louisiana is in favor of upholding a will if at all possible," therefore the legatees should be given the same proportionate amount with respect to the decedent's actual interest in the property.

Does the result reached in *Huguet* (*supra*, p. 14-67) seem fair after reading *Johnson*?

The Marital Portion: La. C.C. 2432-2437

The Civil Code, in Title VI, dealing with Matrimonial Regimes, affords a protection to a surviving spouse of a decedent who dies relatively rich in comparison with the survivor. This "marital portion" is not an incident of the community property regime, but of the matrimonial regime itself and may be claimed even by a spouse who is separated from the decedent, provided the separation was not the fault of the survivor. La. C.C. 2432-2433. "Rich in comparison" or relatively rich is not defined by the Code, although cases have used a rough estimate of a differential of five-to-one. La. C.C. 2432, comment (c).

Once the determination is made that the decedent died "rich in comparison" to the survivor, a quantum of one-fourth of the succession is applied if the decedent died without children, one-fourth in usufruct if the decedent is survived by three or fewer children, and a child's share of such usufruct if the decedent is survived by more than three children however, the amount may not exceed one million dollars. La. C.C. 2434. Legacies and payments due to the survivor are deducted from this portion. La. C.C. 2435. The right to claim the marital portion is personal and nonheritable. La. C.C. 2436. In the course of administration of a succession where it appears a marital portion would be appropriate, the survivor may demand a periodic allowance, which would be fixed by the court where the succession is pending. La. C.C. 2437.

SUCCESSION OF ALVIN LICHTENTAG
363 So. 2d 706 (La. 1978).
[footnotes omitted]

MARCUS, Justice.

Alvin P. Lichtentag died testate on December 14, 1975, leaving neither descendants nor ascendants and was survived by his wife, Nolia E. Langenbecker. Prior to marriage, decedent and his wife entered into a marriage contract (duly recorded) in which they agreed that there would be no community of acquets and gains existing between them. Succession proceedings were opened in the district court. Decedent's olographic will dated August 1, 1968, and codicils dated November 9, 1968, and April 6, 1975, were duly probated, and Robert A. Katz was confirmed as testamentary executor. According to sworn descriptive list filed in succession proceedings, the net value of decedent's estate is approximately $1,400,000.

Under the terms of his testament, decedent left his wife the usufruct of the family home for the remainder of her life, or until remarriage, or failure to occupy the property as her home. In addition, decedent left his wife all of the contents, appurtenances, and personal property located in the home, together with his automobile and jewelry. The balance of his estate was placed in a usufructuary trust and the usufruct of the income of the trust was bequeathed to his wife. The testamentary executor, Katz, was named trustee and directed to distribute funds out of the usufructuary trust account to Mrs. Lichtentag in a sum not to exceed $1,300 per month, unless an emergency arises or as the trustee in his discretion deems necessary.

Mrs. Lichtentag filed a petition in the succession proceedings alleging that her husband died "rich" and that she, as surviving spouse, was entitled to the marital portion authorized by LA. CIVIL CODE art. 2382. As decedent left no children, Mrs. Lichtentag contended that she was entitled to a fourth of the succession in full property. ...

*   *   *

Two issues are presented for our resolution: (1) whether a surviving spouse can renounce the legacy of the decedent spouse and retain the right to the marital portion under article 2382 of the civil code; and (2) if so, whether the value of the renounced legacy must be included in determining the value of the marital portion.

We first address the issue as to whether the surviving spouse can renounce the legacy and still retain the right to claim the marital portion.

The position of an article in the civil code is an important consideration in its interpretation and application. Article 2382, the codal source of the surviving spouse's right to claim the marital portion, is located in the civil code in Title VI of Book III under the heading, "Of the Marriage Contract, and of the Respective Rights of the Parties in Relation to their Property." Title I of Book III is that section of our code which relates to successions: testamentary, legal, and irregular. We consider that the placement of article 2382 in the section of our code dealing with the marital relationship to be persuasive evidence of the fact that the redactors of the code did not consider the marital portion as an inheritance devolving upon the surviving spouse. Our jurisprudence reinforces this view.

The right to claim the marital portion derives from the mutual marital obligations enunciated in LA. CIVIL CODE arts. 119 and 120, and particularly those of fidelity, support, and assistance. Our courts have referred to the marital portion as a bounty bestowed by law and as one of the civil effects flowing from the marriage.

* * *

[T]he marital portion is not an inheritance which must be accepted or renounced with the succession. Hence, articles 986 and 1016, prohibiting conditional renunciation or partial acceptance of successions, have no application here. Accordingly, we conclude that Mrs. Lichtentag can renounce her legacy and still claim her right, if any, to the marital portion.

We must next determine whether the value of the renounced legacy must be included in the marital portion claimed by the surviving spouse.

Article 2382 provides that the surviving spouse who claims the marital portion "is bound to include in this portion what has been left to him as a legacy by the husband or wife, who died first." The jurisprudence interpreting this article has held that the surviving spouse who accepts a legacy must include the value of that legacy in the determination of the value of the marital portion. *Succession of Piffet, supra; Melancon's Widow v. His Executor*, 6 La. 105 (1833). However, the issue as to whether the value of a renounced legacy must be included in the marital portion is Res novo in Louisiana.

In *Succession of Guillon*, 150 La. 587, 91 So. 53 (1922) (on rehearing), this court held that the language of article 2382 is plain and free from ambiguity, and cannot be disregarded under the pretext of pursuing its spirit, citing LA. CIVIL CODE art. 13. We also note that the words of a code article are to be understood in their most usual signification and terms of art or technical terms and phrases are to be interpreted according to their received meaning and acceptation with the learned in the art, trade, or profession to which they refer. LA. CIVIL CODE arts. 14 and 15.

Applying these rules of interpretation to the language of article 2382, we consider that the word "legacy" as used in the article connotes a direct disposition which the testator makes for the benefit of one or more persons, either of the whole or a portion of his estate, or of some particular thing. See LA. CIVIL CODE arts. 1605, 1606, 1612 and 1625. To include within the meaning the word "legacy" an acceptance of such legacy would be to disregard the letter of the law as it appears before us. If the redactors of the code had intended that the legacy must be accepted by the surviving spouse before its value was to be included in the marital portion, we believe they would have used express language to that effect.

We are strengthened in our interpretation of the word "legacy" as it appears in article 2382 by the policy of the law that underlies the marital portion doctrine. As stated earlier in this opinion, the marital portion doctrine derives from the mutual marital obligations of fidelity, support and assistance. *Malone v. Cannon, supra*. It is apparent that whatever legacy a deceased spouse leaves the surviving spouse is, whether eventually accepted or renounced, at least a partial compliance with the obligation to provide created by the pre-existing marital relationship. Article 2382, on the other hand, contemplates that the decedent spouse has to some degree left unfulfilled his marital obligation to provide. In the instant case, the terms of the testament indicate that decedent intended to provide some financial support for his surviving wife. Hence, to hold that the value of the legacy renounced by Mrs. Lichtentag is not to be included in the marital portion claimed by her would be to disregard the spirit as well as the letter of article 2382.

In sum, we consider that, even though a surviving spouse renounces a legacy left to her by the decedent spouse, the value of that renounced legacy must be included in the calculation of the marital portion. ...

* * *

NOTES

In *Francois v. Tufts*, 571 So. 2d 813 (La. App. 1990), the surviving spouse argued that donations prior to the decedent's death should have been fictitiously added for the purpose of calculating the marital portion. The court noted that the Code "limits collation and reduction of donations to forced heirs." While the court could envision extreme situations that may require the reduction of a donation for the purpose of determining the marital portion, it found that the surviving spouse was not entitled to the marital portion.

In *Succession of LaBorde*, 540 So. 2d 966 (La. App. 1st Cir. 1998), the decedent died while separated in fact from his wife. (They were living separate and apart.) The surviving wife claimed entitlement to the marital portion. Interpreting La. C.C. 2433, the court explained that the requirement that the surviving spouse be "free from fault" requires *only* that she be "free from fault which may be of a serious nature and would constitute an independent contributory cause of the breakup of the marriage, and would have entitled the decedent to a separation or divorce." *Id.* (citing *Jergins v. Jergins*, 451 So. 2d 1336 (La. App. 1st Cir. 1984)). Since the couple was separated in fact at the time of the decedent's death, the court held that the surviving spouse had the burden of proving that the separation occurred without her fault. As she failed to do so by a preponderance of the evidence, she was not deemed entitled to the marital portion.

In *Succession of Monroe*, 494 So. 2d 336 (La. App. 4th Cir. 1986), although the assets of the surviving spouse at the time of her husband's death were mostly gifts from her deceased husband, these assets were not deducted from the marital portion.

HYPOTHETICAL

During her life decedent had written two testaments in valid form. Both were notarial testaments and both were found among decedent's things after her death. Both the first and second will contained the following dispositions:

To my daughters Kenya and Ivory, I leave my Rolls Royce to be shared by them. This gift is more than that of an automobile. In this my final offering to them, I hope to teach them how to cooperate and share with one another, something that I was unable to do while living.

To my son, Ricky, I leave one-half of the remainder of my estate.

The balance of my estate I leave to my friend and lover of 25 years Carlos.

In the second will the testatrix also left her home to her friend Linda. She had scratched this provision out such that it was no longer legible, however a Xerox copy of it was found in testatrix's safe-deposit box. On top of the other legacies, she had written in pencil in big letters "OK."

Ivory predeceased her mother and left no children.

Consider the following questions:

1. Has the second will or any part of it been validly revoked? What may Linda argue? What may Ricky and Carlos argue?

2. Assume Carlos renounces his share of the testatrix's succession, because he believes that her estate should all fall to testatrix's children. Will the estate fall to Kenya and Ricky? Might Ricky argue that Carlos' lapsed legacy should fall to him?

3. What result if Ricky renounces his share of the succession because he wishes to share it with Kenya?

CHAPTER 15:
TRUSTS IN LOUISIANA
La. R.S. 9:1721 -2252, La. C.C. 1520

Introduction

The Revised Statutes define a trust as "the relationship resulting from the transfer of title to property to a person to be administered by him as a fiduciary for the benefit of another." La. R.S. § 9:1731. While the definition is correct, it is not very illuminating for those not acquainted with trusts. The trust is a relationship created or "set up" by a "settlor" for the benefit of himself or another. The relationship is created when the settlor turns over his property to a trustee with the stipulation that the trustee manage it and distribute it for the benefit of others called the beneficiaries. The trustee and beneficiaries both have interests in the property, the former as a fiduciary for the latter. Moreover, there may be more than one type of beneficiary. The beneficiaries may be either income or principal beneficiaries. Income beneficiaries enjoy the income produced by the property held in trust, while the principal beneficiaries will enjoy the corpus when the trust is terminated.

The trust provides various benefits which serve to protect a beneficiary who may be young or incompetent, by providing competent management of the property, until a time when the beneficiary may be able to administer the property on his own. As enumerated in the informative article by Edward F. Martin, *Louisiana's Law of Trusts 25 Years After Adoption of the Trust Code,* 50 La. L. Rev. 26 (1990), benefits afforded by trusts include central management of property for the benefit of a number of beneficiaries, preservation of property for later recipients, avoidance of some aspects of probate and possible tax savings.

History

Time and again trusts were found to be incompatible with Louisiana's system of laws. *See, e.g. Succession of Franklin*, 7 La. Ann. 395 (1852). In the *Franklin* case, the testator tried to pass his Louisiana immovable property into a Tennessee trust. The Louisiana Supreme Court found the attempted transfer invalid, noting:

> The title which the testator has attempted to create, belongs to a class of tenures familiar in the other States of this Union, where the common law prevails, but unknown to the laws of Louisiana. And the jurisprudence regulating and defining the almost infinite variety of those tenures, and the rights of obligations arising under each, forms one of the most important and intricate portions of that artificial system of laws. I do not see the possibility of recognizing trust estates here, without letting in all the law which regulates that particular tenure of property. *Id.* at 412-13.

The following article describes the difficulties which Louisiana experienced in the adoption of the trust concept and the manner in which the state accommodated the foreign doctrine into its predominantly civil law system.

DISPUTES INVOLVING TRUSTS: THE LOUISIANA EXPERIENCE*
Kathryn Venturatos Lorio**
[Reprinted with permission]

*   *   *

If in the field of trusts, Louisiana capitulated to the common law, it was an honorable surrender.[1]

Incorporating a common law concept into a jurisdiction of the civil law tradition presents many difficulties, not only in terminology, but in basic underlying legal concepts. Not only do answers to questions vary in the two traditions, but the questions themselves are entirely different in many instances.[2] Such was the dilemma faced by Louisiana, a civil law island in a sea of common law jurisdictions, as it debated the acceptance of the trust concept. The trust was a flexible economic and social institution that had proven its usefulness in the surrounding states and offered participants various functional and tax advantages. Yet, coordinating a common law concept into the Louisiana mold was no easy task.

OBSTACLES TO THE TRUST

Perhaps the greatest obstacle to the adoption of the trust by any jurisdiction with a civilian legal tradition is the duality of ownership inherent in the common law trust. Initially created as a vehicle for avoiding some of the feudal incidents of ownership,[3] the trust divides it interests into the legal title held by the trustee on behalf of the beneficiary, or *cestui que* trust, and the equitable title held by the latter.[4]

This duality of ownership appears to be in direct conflict with the civilian concept of autonomous and indivisible ownership which first appeared in Justinian's Code and, after a

---

* This is a revision of the article "Louisiana Trusts: The Experience of a Civil Law Jurisdiction with the Trust", which was originally published in 42 Louisiana Law Review 1721. Copyright 1982, The Louisiana Law Review. All rights reserved. The author thanks the editors of the Louisiana Law Review for permission to reproduce this article in its revised state. This paper was delivered at the International Bar Association 26th Biennial Conference in Berlin, Germany in 1996 and appears as the last chapter of Disputes Involving Trusts, published in 1999 by Helbing & Lichtenhahn Verlag AG, and is reprinted with permission. [Additional updates are included in bold.]

** Member Louisiana State Bar; Associate Dean for Academic Affairs and Leon Sarpy Professor, Loyola University School of Law, New Orleans. The author appreciates the research assistance of Linda Rose Gallagher in the preparation of the original article and of Laura Anne Mauffray in its revision, which were made possible by the support afforded by the Alfred J. Bonomo Sr. Family and the Rosaria Sarah LaNasa Family.

[1] Wisdom, *Civil vs. Common Law Trusts*, 96 Trusts and Estates 1194, 1196 (1957) [hereinafter cited as Wisdom].

[2] *See* Merryman, *Ownership and Estate*, 48 Tul. L. Rev, 916, 941 (1974).

[3] H. Hanbury & R. Maudsley, *Modern Equity* 8 (10th ed. 1976).

[4] Wright, *Trusts and the Civil Law--A Comparative Study*, 6 West Ont. L. Rev. 114, 115 (1967) [hereinafter cited as Wright].

period of dormancy, was revived in Article 544 of the Code Napoleon,[5] which defined ownership as "the right to enjoy and dispose of things in the most unlimited manner provided one does not use the same in a way prohibited by the laws or ordinances."[6]

This endeavor to discard remnants of feudal burdens which restricted ownership was characteristic of post-Revolutionary France[7] and surfaced in the Louisiana Digest of 1808, which defined absolute ownership in corresponding terms.[8] That article was essentially retained in the subsequent Louisiana Codes of 1825[9] and 1870.[10]

Yet, despite the enunciation of autonomous ownership as a primary precept of the civil law, history reveals that split ownership was not foreign to the Roman classical period. One writer observes that double ownership existed in Rome in the *dos*, or wife's separate property, with interests quite similar to the legal and equitable interests in trusts.[11] Additionally, the institution of the *peculium castrense* allowed a son powers of administration over his separate property, subject to the rights of inheritance in the *paterfamilias*.[12] Thus, it is suggested that the dichotomous nature of ownership is not an utterly alien concept to the civil law tradition.

Another proposed obstacle to the adoption of the trust concept is the doctrine of apparent ownership or publicity, which is basically designed to alleviate hidden rights in property [13] by requiring public registration of transactions creating rights *in rem* in order for them to be enforceable.[14] Yet, only those transactions specifically enumerated in a code's list of rights or its *numerus clausus* would be eligible for such registration.[15] It is contended by those who view this as an obstacle to the introduction of trusts that the registry of the trustee as owner in the official record would deprive the beneficiary of an enforceable right should the trustee breach his duty.

Yet, proponents of the trust suggest that the official register could merely be expanded to protect the interests of beneficiaries.[16] To many civilians the Anglo-American trust is considered functionally unnecessary in light of the many existing civilian mechanisms which may be used to accomplish the same ultimate results.[17] Pierre LePaulle in his article "Civil Law Substitutes for Trusts" suggests that the real substitute for the trust is the Romanistic concept of *fiduciae*,[18] composed of two elements--(1) the real portion, consisting of the conveyance of *dominium* of the *res* to the fiduciary and (2) the personal or contractual portion, consisting of the agreement by which the fiduciary assumes duties toward the beneficiary, or *fideicomitente*, to use the property

---

[5] Comment, *Why No Trusts in the Civil Law?*, 2 Am. J. Comp. L. 204, 210 (1953) [hereinafter cited as Why No Trusts].

[6] Code Napoleon art. 544 (1804).

[7] Why No Trusts, *supra* n. 5, at 210.

[8] La. Digest of 1808, art. 1, at 102.

[9] LA. CIV. CODE art. 483 (1825).

[10] LA. CIV. CODE art. 491 (1870).

[11] Why No Trusts, *supra* n. 5, at 206.

[12] *Id.*

[13] Newman, Trusts, *Civil Law Concepts and Legal Realism*, 3 Inter-Am. L. Rev. 379, 387-88 (1961).

[14] Mayda, *"Trusts" and "Living Law" in Europe*, 103 U. Pa. L. Rev. 1041, 1042 (1955).

[15] Wright, *supra* n. 4, at 116; Why No Trusts, *supra* n. 5, at 212.

[16] Why No Trusts, *supra* n. 5, at 214.

[17] K. W. Ryan, *An Introduction To The Civil Law* 219-20 (1962) [hereinafter cited as Ryan]; P. LePaulle, *Civil Law Substitutes for Trusts*, 35 Yale L. J. 1126 (1927) [hereinafter cited as LePaulle].

[18] LePaulle, *supra* n. 17, at 1138.

for the latter's benefit under specified conditions imposed and then to return the property when the purpose is fulfilled, either to the original transferor or to a third party nominated by him.[19] Although this concept appears quite similar to the common law trust, the beneficiary in the *fiducia* has no enforceable action at strict law, but only an action *in personam*,[20] the enforcement of which is left to the equitable discretion of the judge.[21] Thus, the property is not segregated from that of the fiduciary and, should the latter declare bankruptcy, the settlor would be treated as a general creditor.[22]

Frequently, the trust is compared to the German concept of *Treuhand*, a fiduciary relationship which offers more protection for the settlor than does the *fiduciae*. Under this arrangement, the settlor transfers property to the fiduciary, or *Treuhander*, subject to a resolutory condition.[23] If the *Treuhander* breaches his duty, the property will be reconveyed to the settlor.

Additionally, the property remains separate from that of the *Treuhander*, thus protecting it from the fiduciary's creditors.[24] Even the *Treuhand*, however, does not provide the same benefits as the trust, since protection from the creditors of the *Treuhander* only applies where the settlor is the beneficiary. Otherwise, the beneficiary has only a personal right. Also, the protection against creditors generally extends only to the specific property conveyed and not to any substituted forms it may take.[25] Finally, if the *Treuhander* breaches his duty, the entire trust fails[26] thus defeating its original purpose.

The Roman *fidei commissium* also performed a function similar to the trust. Under this concept, property is given to a fiduciary who is to later turn the property over to another, the *fidei commissarius*. Although this resembles the trust in that the property may be real or personal and the second person need not be alive at the creation of the *fidei commissum*,[27] it differs significantly from a trust in that the first grantee or beneficiary manages the property for his own interests and under no specific instructions from the transferor.[28] The interests of the grantees are thus successive, rather than concurrent, as in a trust.[29] Finally, the *fidei commissum* may only be created by testament[30] and even then, only under certain conditions varying from country to country.[31]

In addition to these concepts that are frequently compared to the trust, other civilian concepts may fulfill some of the same objectives as a trust. LePaulle points out that many of these serve the function of providing management for an incapable person's property.[32] The

---

[19] Ryan, *supra* n. 17, at 224; Garrigues, *Law of Trusts*, 2 Am. J. Comp. L. 25 (1953) [hereinafter cited as Garrigues]; Wright, *supra* n. 4, at 118.

[20] Ryan, *supra* n. 17, at 225.

[21] Garrigues, *supra* n. 19, at 26-27.

[22] Wright, *supra* n. 4, at 119.

[23] Ryan, *supra* n. 17, at 226.

[26] Ryan, *supra* n. 17, at 229.

[27] LePaulle, *supra* n. 17, at 1143.

[28] *Id.*

[29] Wright, *supra* n. 4, at 118.

[30] LePaulle, *supra* n. 17, at 1143; Vilella, *The Problems of Trust Legislation in Civil Law Jurisdictions: The Law of Trusts in Puerto Rico*, 19 Tul. L. Rev. 374, 383 (1945) [hereinafter cited as Vilella]; Wright, *supra* n. 4, at 118.

[31] LePaulle, *supra* n. 17, at 1143.

[32] *Id.* at 1134-35.

concepts of tutorship and curatorship perform such a function.[33] Yet, neither of these is quite as flexible as the trust, since each involves the management of all the property belonging to the incapable person, rather than just particular portions, and since the tutor and curator have less autonomy of operation due to the necessary court supervision.[34] Other examples, suggested by LePaulle, of civilian concepts offering third-party management include a donation or legacy with a charge, a contract for the benefit of third persons, and a deposit or mandate coupled with a contract for the benefit of a third person.[35] If the objective is to provide a donee with temporary enjoyment of property, while retaining an interest for oneself or one's heirs, LePaulle notes that the granting of some combination of the three elements of *usus*, *abusus*, and *fructus* is available in the civil law[36] without resort to foreign concepts of income and principal beneficiaries.

VARIOUS CIVILIAN APPROACHES

Yet, despite all the possible substitutes for the trust, none seems to provide all the benefits of the trust which was deemed by Maitland as "the most distinctive achievement of English lawyers."[37] Thus, countries of the civilian tradition began to adopt the trust concept in their own individual ways.

One approach was to enact a trust statute using familiar civilian terms. Such was the method employed by Ricardo J. Alfaro, "the father of the Latin-American legislation on trust."[38] His book *El Fidei Comiso*[39] became the basis for the Panamanian trust, which is defined as "an irrevocable mandate by virtue of which property is conveyed to a person, the trustee (*fiduciario*), to be disposed of as ordered by the one who conveys it, the creator of a trust (*fideicomitente*), for the benefit of a third party, the beneficiary (*fideicomisario*)."[40] The problem with that approach is that although civilians are familiar with the concept of mandate, the idea of an irrevocable mandate is itself foreign to them.[41] Another approach was that proposed by the Institutionalists, most notably represented by Pierre LePaulle of France and Marcel Faribault of Quebec.[42] Under this theory, the trust itself is an institution recognized by law and given the right to hold property. It is in essence viewed as a juristic person, or as LePaulle phrased it, *a patrimonie affecte*.[43] The trustee is a mere administrator and any claim of the beneficiary lies against the property itself.[44]

---

[33] *See* Pascal, *The Trust Concept and Substitution*, 19 La. L. Rev. 273, 274 (1959) [hereinafter cited as Pascal].

[34] LePaulle, *supra* n. 17, at 1134-35.

[35] *Id.* at 1136-39.

[36] *Id.* at 1140-41.

[37] Frederic W. Maitland, *Equity* 23 (1936).

[38] Goldschmidt, *The Trust in the Countries of Latin America*, 3 Inter-Am. L. Rev. 29, 31 (1961).

[39] R. Alfaro, *El Fidel Comiso* (1920).

[40] Law 17 of 1941 of Panama, art. 1. The same definition appeared in Article 834 of the Civil Code of Puerto Rico and is retained in the laws of Puerto Rico under Section 2541 of Title 31, as enacted in 1952.

[41] Vilella, *supra* n. 30, at 384.

[42] *See* Mettarlin, *The Quebec Trust and the Civil Law*, 21 McGill L. J. 175, 211 (1975) (wherein the author refers to P. LePaulle, *Traité Théoretique et Pratique des Trusts* (1932) [hereinafter cited as LePaulle] and M. Faribault, *La Fiducie Dans la Province de Quebec* (1936)).

[43] LePaulle, *supra* n. 42, at 31.

[44] *Id.* at 26-27. *See also* Wisdom, *supra* n. 1, at 1195 (wherein the author points out that Mexico abandoned Alfaro's mandate in favor of LePaulle's institucion fiduciaria in 1932 and 1941).

Louisiana has taken a third approach. It decided to adopt "the traditional Anglo-American trust concept . . . but to define with precision the uses of the word 'trust' within a civil law framework so far as practicable and desirable."[45] Yet, this adoption was not easy or swift, nor was it unanimously welcomed.[46]

SUBSTITUTIONS AND *FIDEI COMMISSA*

One of the major stumbling blocks to the acceptance of the trust in Louisiana was Louisiana's prohibition of substitutions and *fidei commissa* which appeared in the Digest of 1808[47] and was also included in the Civil Codes of 1825[48] and 1870.[49] Whether or not this prohibition was meant to include the trust is a question which has not been consistently answered by the courts or the commentators.

In the Roman law, the term substitution included the vulgar and the pupillary substitutions.[50] The vulgar substitution provided for a substitute to receive a legacy if the named legatee was incapable or failed to accept.[51] This type of substitution was particularly sanctioned in Louisiana by Article 1521 of the Civil Code of 1870.[52] The pupillary substitution was a means by which a father named an heir to substitute for his minor child in the event the child died after the father but before attaining testamentary capacity.[53] Another substitution, the exemplary, was an outgrowth of the pupillary and allowed for a parent to name a substitute for an insane child that died without ever regaining his sanity.[54] The pupillary and exemplary substitutions were effective in Louisiana during the Spanish regime[55] and may have been effective during the French colonial period as well.[56]

The *fidei commissa*, first appeared at the end of the Roman Republic.[57] During the Republic, however, the charge, imposed by the donor on the original donee, to transfer the property at a stated time to a third person designated by the donor was not enforceable but its execution rested on the good faith of the first donee, or *heres*.[58] During the reign of Augustus, the

---

[45] L. Oppenheim, *Trusts* § 11 in 11 Louisiana Civil Law Treatise (1977) [hereinafter cited as Oppenheim].

[46] Professor Joseph Dainow points out that "one of the strongest positions of antagonism to the common law trust was taken by the American State of Louisiana." Joseph Dainow, *The Introduction of the Trust in Louisiana*, 39 Canadian B. Rev. 396, 397 (1961).

[47] La. Digest of 1808, art. 40, at 216.

[48] LA. CIV. CODE art. 1507 (1825).

[49] LA. CIV. CODE art. 1520 (1870).

[50] 2 Jean Domat, *The Civil Law in Its Natural Order* §§ 3764-65 (L. Cushing ed., W. Strahan trans. 1850) [hereinafter cited as DOMAT]; Pascal, *supra* n. 33, at 277; John H. Tucker, Jr., *Substitutions, Fideicommissa and Trusts in Louisiana Law: A Semantical Reappraisal*, 24 La. L. Rev. 439, 443-44 (1964) [hereinafter cited as Tucker].

[51] Domat, *supra* n. 50, § 3771; Las Siete Partidas bk. VI, tit. V, L. IV (S. Scott trans. 1931).

[52] *See also* LA. CIV. CODE art. 1508 (1825); La. Digest of 1808, art. 41, at 218; Code Napoleon art. 898 (1804).

[53] Domat, *supra* n. 50, § 3787; Las Siete Partidas bk. VI, tit. V, Ls. V-X (S. Scott trans. 1931).

[54] Domat, *supra* n. 50, § 3797; Las Siete Partidas bk. VI, tit. V, L. XI (S. Scott trans. 1931).

[55] Colonel Tucker notes that Las Siete Partidas includes these under the substitutions in Title V of Book VI. Tucker, *supra* n. 50, at 444.

[56] *Id.*

[57] *Id.* at 444-45.

[58] W. Buckland, *A Text-Book of Roman Law From Augustus to Justinian* 353 (1932).

duty to deliver the property to the second donee was enforced by the administrative authority of the counsuls. Eventually a special praetor, the *praetor fidei commissarius*, was appointed to regulate the relations between the heres and the fidei commissarius.[59] Under Vespasian, it was provided that the first donee could retain one-quarter of the whole, the remainder of which he was required to deliver to the third person.[60] During the reign of Justinian, the part retained by the first donee became known as the Trebellianic portion.[61]

In the twelfth century, the *fidei commissum* was introduced in France with the revival of the Roman law and was freely used until the mid-sixteenth century in order to keep land within the family.[62] Restrictions were later imposed, culminating in the abolition of *fidei commissa* in Article 896 of the Code Napoleon.[63] Las Siete Partidas, which derived much from Justinian's Corpus Juris Civilis, included a section on the *fidei commissaria* and specifically provided for the Trebellianic portion.[64]

An analysis of Article 40 of the Louisiana Digest of 1808[65] demonstrates that the first two paragraphs of that article basically correspond to Article 896 of the Code Napoleon, except that Article 40 prohibits substitutions and *fidei commissa* whereas Article 896 speaks only of substitutions. The last paragraph of Article 40, dealing with the Trebellianic portion, corresponds to Law 14, Title V of the Sixth Partidas.[66] Thus, it has been suggested that the prohibition contained in Article 40 of the Digest, which also appears in Article 1520 of the LOUISIANA CIVIL CODE of 1870, was a prohibition against the Roman *fidei commissum*.[67]

The major difficulty in the interpretation of the Louisiana prohibition is that the prohibition appearing in the Digest of 1808 and in the Codes of 1825 and 1870 is of substitutions and *fidei commissa*. One explanation is that the redactors used both terms out of an "abundance of caution," but really meant to prohibit the concept known in France as a substitution, which was prohibited there in 1792 and was the very same concept referred to as a "*fidei commissaria*" that was permitted in Spain at the time of the drafting of the LOUISIANA CIVIL CODE.[68]

This theory, however, is not reflected in the Louisiana cases, which appear to find a distinction between substitutions and *fidei commissa*. One theory distinguishes the two concepts based on the first donee's charge to preserve the property and then to transmit it to the third person. The duty to preserve is deemed the characterizing element of the prohibited substitution, rendering the entire disposition null. The *fidei commissum*, however, merely directs the first donee to later convey the property to the third person with no duty to preserve the property. Thus, the disposition to the first donee is upheld, but the charge to convey is deemed as not having been written.[69]

---

[59] *Id.*

[60] Tucker, *supra* n. 50, at 444.

[61] *Id.*

[62] *Id.*

[63] *Id.*

[64] Las Siete Partidas bk. VI, tit. V, L. XIV (S. Scott trans. 1931). *See also* Spanish Civ. Code art. 781 (1889).

[65] La. Digest of 1808, art. 40, at 216.

[66] Tucker, *supra* n. 50, at 463.

[67] *Id.* at 461-62.

[68] *Id.* at 465-66.

[69] Succession of Reilly, 136 La. 347, 67 So. 27 (La. 1914).

Another view, which perhaps did the most to discourage adoption of the trust in Louisiana, is that the prohibition against *fidei commissa* was nothing more than a prohibition of the Anglo-American trust.[70] There is some indication that *fidei commissa* and substitutions were permitted in Louisiana to some extent prior to the Digest of 1808.[71] However, with the prohibition of substitutions appearing in the Digest of 1808 and its reiteration in the later Codes, coupled with the opinion that trusts were a form of substitution, courts refused to recognize trusts in Louisiana without an enabling act. The first such act came, perhaps more than coincidentally, in 1882 when Paul Tulane wished to make a sizable donation for the establishment of an educational institution.[72] In that year the legislature exempted from the laws against substitutions and *fidei commissa* all donations for educational, charitable, or literary purposes.[73] In 1902 the legislature authorized banks to act as trustees,[74] and in 1914 trustees were authorized to accept mortgages in their capacity as trust representatives.[75]

Finally, in 1920, private trusts of a limited duration were permitted.[76] Yet, the duties of the trustee, settlor, and beneficiary were not well defined. The 1920 legislation was repealed in 1935[77] and was followed in 1938 by the Trust Estates Act[78] the first complete code of trust law adopted by a North American state.[79] Its sources included the American Law Institute's *Restatement of the Law of Trusts*, the Uniform Trusts Act, the Uniform Principal and Income Act, the Uniform Trustees' Accounting Act, Dean Griswold's Model Spendthrift Trust Act, and common trust fund provisions from a tentative draft of the Uniform Trusts Act.[80]

The Trust Estates Act, however, was not satisfactory as it was not well integrated with the LOUISIANA CIVIL CODE, leaving problems concerning such concepts as forced heirship and the rule against substitutions and *fidei commissa*.[81] In 1952, the Louisiana Trust Estates Act was amended, extending the possible duration of the trust from the previous limit of ten years from the settlor's death or ten years from the beneficiary's majority, to a limit of ten years from the settlor's death or until the beneficiary's death, whichever was longer.[82]

In 1959, Professor Leonard Oppenheim was appointed by the Louisiana Law Institute as Reporter to study the Trust Estates Act and to propose possible revision.[83] The study culminated

[70] *See* Nabors, *Restrictions Upon the Ownership of Property in Louisiana-- Trusts, Fidei Commissa and Substitutions*, 4 Tul. L. Rev. 1, 4 (1929) (wherein the author cites E. Saunders, *Lectures on the Civil Code of Louisiana* 305 (A. Bonomo ed. 1925)).

[71] *Ducloslange v. Ross*, 3 La. Ann. 432, 432 (La. 1848).

[72] Stone, *Trusts in Louisiana*, 1 Int'l & Comp. L. Q. 368, 370 (1952).

[73] 1882 La. Act 124.

[74] 1902 La. Act 45.

[75] 1914 La. Acts, No. 72.

[76] 1920 La. Act 107.

[77] 1935 La. Act, 3d Ex. Sess., No. 7.

[78] 1938 La. Act 81.

[79] Patton, *Trust System in the Western Hemisphere*, 19 Tul. L. Rev. 398, 412 (1945).

[80] Wisdom, *supra* n. 1, at 1196.

[81] Oppenheim, *supra* n. 45 § 1, at 2.

[82] LA. REV. STAT. 9:1794 (1950), as amended by 1952 La. Acts, No. 209, § 1 (repealed 1964).

[83] Oppenheimer, *supra* n. 45 § 1, at 3.

in the Louisiana Trust Code of 1964. Prior to the adoption of that Code, remedial legislation was proposed in 1962, partially because of the substitution questions which arose in the cases of *Succession of Guillory*[84] in 1957 and *Succession of Meadors*[85] in 1961.

Succession of Guillory arose as a result of the death of a Texas domiciliary possessed of Louisiana real estate which he bequeathed to a Texas bank to hold in trust "during the lifetime of Terrell Guillory." At the time of Terrell's death, the naked ownership and possession of the property was to go "to the Baptist General Convention of the State of Louisiana" and was to be retained by it, so that revenues could be used for the benefit of the Louisiana Baptist denomination.[86] Without explaining the reasoning for its decision, the Louisiana Supreme Court deemed the bequest a clear prohibited substitution.

Deeming *Guillory* "decisive," the Second Circuit found a prohibited substitution in the *Meadors* case. This case also involved the death of an out-of-state domiciliary who owned real property in Louisiana. The will of the decedent contained a bequest that the residue of his property, after making certain particular legacies, was to go to a Tennessee bank in trust, with instructions to pay the decedent's sister $100 per month for her life and to pay the remaining income to decedent's wife for life. On the death of either the wife or sister, all income was to be paid to the survivor until her death, at which time the trust was to terminate with the property to be distributed to decedent's heirs according to the intestate succession laws of Tennessee. By finding that title to the decedent's property did not vest in the legal heirs until the trust terminated, the court found that a double disposition prohibited by Article 1520 of the Civil Code and Article 4, Section 16 of the Louisiana Constitution of 1921 had been created. Appellee asserted that, because the wife and sister merely held a beneficial interest in income, the heirs held a beneficial interest in principal which vested at the time of the creation of the trust. This theory was rejected by the court, creating much anxiety among attorneys as to whether any trust containing separate income and principal beneficiaries would be upheld in Louisiana.[87]

One of the remedial actions taken in 1962 was the enactment of Act No. 521 which amended Article 4, Section 16 of the Louisiana Constitution and provided in part: "Substitutions, not in trust are and remain prohibited, but trusts may contain substitutions to the extent authorized by the Legislature." Similarly, Act 45 of 1962 amended Civil Code Article 1520, indicating that substitutions in trust were permitted, and deleted any prohibition of *fidei commissa*. Both provisions were designed to encourage trust legislation and pave the way for the new Trust Code.[88] In 1962, other changes in the Trust Estates Act were made, including clarifying the duration of the trust,[89] confirming the propriety of mixed private and charitable trusts,[90] and affirming the possibility of separate beneficiaries of income and principal.[91] Finally in 1964 the present Louisiana Trust Code was adopted.[92]

---

[84] 232 La. 213, 94 So. 2d 38 (La. 1957).

[85] 35 So. 2d 679 (La. App. 2d Cir. 1961).

[86] 232 La. at 215, 94 So. 2d at 38-39. [82]LA. REV. STAT. 9:1794 (1950), as amended by 1952 La. Acts, No. 209, § 1 (repealed 1964).

[87] *See also* Succession of Simms, 250 La. 177, 195 So. 2d 114 (La. 1965), *cert. and rehearing denied sub nom.,* Kitchen v. Reese, 389 U.S. 850, 88 S.Ct. 47, 19 L.Ed. 2d 120 (1967) (which was decided on the basis of the law in effect prior to the 1964 Trust Code).

[88] Oppenheimer, *supra* n. 45 § 10, at 19.

[89] 1962 La. Act 74, amending LA. REV. STAT. 9:1794 (1950) (repealed 1964).

[90] 1962 La. Act 44, adding LA. REV. STAT. 9:1844 (repealed 1964).

The Code itself set up the mode for its interpretation. Its provisions were to be liberally construed in favor of freedom of disposition, with resort being had to the Civil Code only when the Trust Code was silent on an issue.[93]

THE NEW TRUST CODE AND SUBSTITUTIONS

The adoption of the Trust Code did not automatically usher in total acceptance of the trust concept. Even after its adoption, trusts were closely scrutinized and some were invalidated on the grounds that they contained prohibited substitutions, as in the Louisiana Supreme Court's decision in *Crichton v. Succession of Gredler*.[94] Mrs. Gredler's will created trusts in favor of her two nephews, as beneficiaries, and stated that if either nephew died before the termination of the trusts, the income and principal should be paid to his children. If the deceased nephew was not survived by children, that interest would go to the surviving beneficiary, or if the other beneficiary were also deceased, to his children. If neither the nephews nor their children were living at the termination of each trust, the income and principal were to be paid to the children of a predeceased brother of the decedent. The Court deemed the trusts null as containing prohibited substitutions, reasoning that the substitutions took effect after the trusts terminated. As they were thus not "in trust," even the Trust Code could not save them. If the Court had interpreted the trusts liberally, it could have viewed the provisions as merely unnecessary contingent alternate provisions due to the nephews' having survived the decedent, or it could have merely invalidated the illegal portions while upholding the remaining provisions of the trusts.[95] Instead, many of the pre-1964 attitudes toward trusts seemed to permeate the majority's opinion.

A more liberal view toward substitutions arose in the 1970s. One striking example is the First Circuit case of *Succession of Materiste*,[96] in which the decedent established a testamentary trust naming as income beneficiaries her mother as to one-half and her brothers and sisters as to the other half. The testatrix provided that on her mother's death certain nieces and nephews were to succeed to the mother's half interest. Should any of the nieces and nephews die, his or her share was to be divided among the survivors. On the death of the last sibling of the testatrix, the trust was to terminate, with 45% of the corpus to be divided by roots among the siblings' descendants, or should any sibling die without descendants, his or her portion would be divided by roots among the brothers and sisters leaving descendants. Another 45% was to go to certain nieces and nephews who had been named as alternate income beneficiaries at the time of the testatrix's mother's death, and 10% was to go to a particular church. The court viewed those who were to take at the termination of the trust, not as substitutes, but as principal beneficiaries. The creation of successive income beneficiaries was sanctioned, and the provision for a substitute as to the 45% of the principal for the descendants of the brothers and sisters of the decedent was viewed as an allowable vulgar substitution.

---

[91] 1962 La. Act 44, amending LA. REV. STAT. 9:1903 (1950) (repealed 1964); 1962 La. Act 74, § 2, amending LA. REV. STAT. 9:1921 (1950) (repealed 1964).

[92] 1964 La. Act 338.

[93] LA. REV. STAT. 9:1724 (Supp. 1965).

[94] 256 La. 156, 235 So. 2d 411 (La. 1970).

[95] Oppenheim, *supra* n. 45 § 25, at 68.

[96] 273 So. 2d 617 (La. App. 1st Cir. 1973).

Similarly in *Succession of Stewart*,[97] the Louisiana Supreme Court, in interpreting a trust which went into effect prior to the Trust Code of 1964, upheld the trust against a challenge that it contained a prohibited substitution, stating that "the bequest to the trustees was not made to them as owners or as beneficiaries but rather 'in trust' subject to the terms and conditions as therein set forth."[98]

Again, in *Succession of Burgess*,[99] the Fourth Circuit upheld a trust in which the settlor provided that, should a grandchild beneficiary die, intestate and without descendants, during the trust, his interest would vest in the settlor's surviving grandchild or grandchildren or their descendants "per stirpes." Although the court held that the trust did not meet the requirements of a class trust which would have permitted such a substitution,[100] it still upheld the trust since the grandsons were free to leave the property to others by testament and were not controlled by the will of the original testatrix.

The more liberal view toward trusts is further illustrated in the later case of *Succession of Payne*.[101] In that case, the testator left an olographic will in which he left "1/2 of the community to Henry K. Payne to be divided equally Between My Twin Granddaughters when they Become 21 years of age."[102] The trial court annulled the will, holding that it contained a prohibited substitution.[103] The appellate court reversed and remanded the case, interpreting the will as creating a valid trust.[104] Reasoning that "when the terms of a disposition attacked as a prohibited substitution are susceptible to interpretation in two ways--one that the disposition contains the elements of a prohibited substitution, and the other that it does not contain them--it is preferable to uphold the interpretation that maintains the disposition."[105] Noting that no particular language is required to create a trust, the court analyzed the disposition with regard to the necessary elements of a trust, finding that Henry K. Payne was the intended trustee of the property identified in the will and the granddaughters were the beneficiaries.[106]

Currently, the Trust Code itself sanctions provisions which would previously have been viewed as substitutions. One example is the possibility within class trusts of a shifting in principal to other members of a class when a member of the class dies intestate and without descendants during the term of the trust,[107] Additionally, Section 1 of Act 160 of 1974[108]

---

[97] 301 So. 2d 872 (La. 1974).

[98] *Id.* at 883.

[99] 359 So. 2d 1006 (La. App. 4th Cir. 1978), *writ denied*, 360 So. 2d 1178 (La. 1978).

[100] LA. REV. STAT. 9:1891 (Supp. 1965).

[101] 524 So. 2d 803 (La. App. 3d Cir. 1988), *writ denied*, 525 So. 2d 1044 (La. 1988).

[102] *Id.* at 804.

[103] *Id.* at 803.

[104] *Id.* at 806.

[105] *Id.*

[106] *Id.*

[107] LA. REV. STAT. 9:1895 (West 1991). [**LA. REV. STAT. 9:1895 was amended after the publication of this paper to also state that the trust instrument, except as to the legitime in trust, may provide that "the interest of a member of the class who dies without descendants during the term of the trust or at its termination vests in the other members of the class."**] Note that a class may consist of "some or all" of the settlor's "children, grandchildren, nieces, nephews, grandnieces, or grandnephews, or any combination thereof, although some members of the class are not yet in being at the time of the creation of the trust, provided at least one member of the class is then in being." LA. REV. STAT. 9:1891 (West 1991). [**LA. REV. STAT. 9:1891 was amended in 1997, after the publication of this paper , expanding the potential members of the class, allowing a class to consist of "some or all of his {the settlor's}**

contained a general provision governing the shifting of interests in principal and allowed the settlor to name substitute principal beneficiaries to take in the event that the original beneficiary died intestate and without descendants during the term of the trust or at the time of its termination.[109] The settlor's right in the latter instance was originally made subject to the requirement that the substitute be in being and ascertainable at the creation of the trust. In 1982, by Act 455, the legislature altered the requirement, allowing for the possibility of the interest shifting to a substitute who may not have been in being at the creation of the trust. The amended article allows for the trust instrument to provide that the interest of the principal beneficiary who was a descendant of the settlor and who died intestate and without descendants during the term of the trust or at its termination could vest in one or more of the settlor's descendants who were in being and ascertainable, not necessarily at the time of the creation of the trust but rather *at the time of the death of the principal beneficiary*.[110]

TITLE AND THE TRUSTEE

One of the first questions addressed by the Reporter and Advisory Committee preparing the Trust Code of 1964 was whether the trustee was to have title of the trust property. The decision to retain the Anglo-American concept of trust, with the trustee as legal title holder was unanimously adopted by the Reporter and the Committee and subsequently sanctioned by the Council of the Louisiana Law Institute.[111] Accordingly, Article 1781 of the Trust Code states that "a trustee is a person to whom title to the trust property is transferred to be administered by him as a fiduciary."

---

descendants in the direct line, regardless of degrees, or any of his descendants in any collateral line, regardless of degrees, or any combination thereof, although some members of the class are not yet in being at the creation of the trust, provided at least one member of the class is then in being." This extension permitting class trusts for unlimited generations has been criticized as inconsistent with the vesting requirements of the Trust Code. Accordingly, in 2001 the Louisiana legislature amended La. R.S. § 9:1891 once again, but this time restricting the potential class to "children, grandchildren, great grandchildren, nieces, nephews, grandnieces, grandnephews, and great grandnieces and great grandnephews, or any combination thereof." La. R.S. §9:1891 was amended again by Act 219 of 2015, effective August 1, 2015, to provide that a testator can create a trust in favor of a class consisting of some or all of his children, grandchildren, great-grandchildren, nieces nephews, grandnieces, grandnephews and great-grandnieces and great-grandnephews of the settlor *or of the settlor's current, former, or predeceased spouse,* or any combination thereof, although some members of the class are not yet in being at the time of the creation of the trust, provided at least one member of the class is then in being.

[108] LA. REV. STAT. 9:1972 et seq. (West 1991) (amended 1996).

[109] Not only is this shifting a form of substitution but, when Louisiana provided for ascendant forced heirship, it also allowed for the possibility of depriving an ascendant forced heir of his legitime. *See* LA. CIV. CODE art. 1494, prior to its repeal by 1981 La. Acts, No. 442. For an interpretation of the shifting provision in general, *see* Lewis v. Williams, 622 S. 2d 281 (La. App. 1st Cir. 1993), *writ denied*, 629 So. 2d 1170 (La. 1993). [LA. REV. STAT. 9:1973 was amended after the publication of this paper to allow for successive substitutions and to state that, except as to the legitime in trust, "the trust instrument may provide that the interest of either an original or a substitute principal beneficiary who dies without descendants during the term of the trust or at its termination vests in some other person or persons, each of whom shall be a principal beneficiary.]

[110] LA. REV. STAT. 9:1978 (West 1991). [LA. REV. STAT. 9:1978 was amended after the publication of this paper to conform to the amendment in LA. REV. STAT. 9:1973 and to remove the requirement that the original principal beneficiary be a descendant of the settlor.]

[111] Oppenheim, *supra* n. 45 § 11, at 20.

Prior to the Trust Estates Act, vesting of legal title in the trustee was viewed by the courts as a common law concept prohibited by Louisiana law.[112] Later cases, however, repeatedly recognized the trustee as the legal title holder for the benefit of himself or another.[113] With that recognition came the right of the trustee, to whom succession property had been left in trust, to be placed in possession without an administration [114] and the right of a trustee-executor to be recognized as the particular legatee of property left in trust by the settlor, thus alleviating any need for the trustee to make a demand on himself as executor in order to claim the interest on any stocks held in trust.[115] Even where a beneficiary of a usufruct in trust had the naked ownership of part of the burdened property, no confusion of interests was found to exist, since the trustee was deemed to be the holder of "title" of the usufruct.[116]

Yet, is the trustee as title holder also the owner of the property? If so, is that ownership absolute and indivisible as required by civilian tradition? These questions were posed in the case of *Reynolds v. Reynolds*.[117] Mrs. Reynolds had been designated as one of four beneficiaries of a testamentary trust created on the death of her grandmother, which occurred prior to Mrs. Reynolds's marriage. During the Reynolds' marriage, part of the trust income had been distributed to the wife and kept in a bank account under her exclusive control, while another portion remained undistributed and was retained by the trustee pursuant to the discretionary powers outlined in the trust. Because Mrs. Reynolds had not recorded a declaration of paraphernality indicating that she would administer her separate property,[118] any income from her separate property would be deemed community property.

Upon divorce, Mr. Reynolds therefore sought to characterize all the trust income accruing during the marriage as community property. This assertion was supported by a case decided by the United States Fifth Circuit Court of Appeals in 1949, *United States v. Burglass*,[119] which was decided under the Louisiana Trust Estates Act of 1938. In *Burglass*, the Fifth Circuit found the beneficiary's interest in trust income to be community property and recognized the trustee as legal title holder and the beneficiaries as "owners in indivision" of the property.[120] In contrast, Mrs. Reynolds claimed that the trust income was all separate property, relying on the case of *Dunham v. Dunham*,[121] which held as separate property the income from a trust of which one of

---

[112] *Buck v. Larcade*, 183 La. 570, 578, 164 So. 593, 595 (La. 1936).

[113] Succession of Carriere, 216 So. 2d 616 (La. App. 4th Cir. 1968), *writ denied*, 253 La. 639, 219 So. 2d 175 (La. 1969); Succession of Hines, 341 So. 2d 42 (La. App. 3d Cir. 1976).

[114] Succession of Carriere, 216 So. 2d 616 (La. App. 4th Cir. 1968), *writ denied*, 253 La. 639, 219 So. 2d 175 (1969).

[115] 341 So. 2d 42.

[116] Succession of Harper, 147 So. 2d 425 (La. App. 2d Cir. 1962), *application not considered*, 243 La. 1012, 149 So. 2d 766 (La. 1963).

[117] 388 So. 2d 1135 (La. 1979).

[118] LA. CIV. CODE art. 2386 (as amended by 1944 La. Act 286). At the time of the *Reynolds* case, only the wife could execute an instrument reserving the fruits of her paraphernal property and her intention to administer that property separately. Since the husband was the "head and master" of community with power of administration, no such protection was necessary for him. (LA. CIV. CODE art. 2404, as amended by 1926 La. Act 96). With the adoption of a system of equal management (LA. CIV. CODE art. 2346, as adopted by 1979 La. Act 709, § 1), the opportunity to reserve the fruits of separate property is now afforded to each spouse. (LA. CIV. CODE art. 2339, as amended by 1980 La. Act 565, § 2).

[119] 172 F. 2d 960 (5th Cir. 1949).

[120] *Id.* at 963.

[121] 174 So. 2d 898 (La. App. 1st Cir. 1968).

the spouses was a beneficiary. The income had accrued during the marriage of the parties. Under the terms of the *Dunham* trust, none of the trust income was actually distributed to the beneficiary spouse during the term of the trust. Yet, the court used the opportunity to repudiate the *Burglass* conclusion that ownership of the corpus rested in the beneficiary and title vested in the trustee. The *Dunham* court stated that "the intent of our trust laws as expressed in the language employed therein by the legislature is to clearly and unmistakably vest both title and ownership of the trust corpus in the trustee."[122]

In *Reynolds*, the Louisiana Supreme Court on original hearing held that all the income, both distributed and undistributed, was the separate property of the beneficiary spouse. Approving of *Dunham*, the Court equated the trustee's title with ownership. However, on rehearing, a plurality of the Louisiana Supreme Court held that the distributed income was community property and that the undistributed income remained the separate property of the beneficiary spouse. The Court, citing LOUISIANA CIVIL CODE Article 477 and former Article 489, stated that the beneficiary's interest was clearly less than full ownership[123] and that title to the property vested in the trustee.[124] The Court characterized the beneficial interest as an incorporeal right and the distributed revenues from that incorporeal right were deemed civil fruits.[125]

Chief Justice Dixon dissented to the characterization of the distributed income as community property, pointing to the distinction between a beneficiary's right to receive the corpus itself and a beneficiary's right to receive the income produced by that corpus. Justice Dixon viewed Mrs. Reynolds's income interest, which was subject to spendthrift provisions, as an annuity or alimentary pension, rather than a usufruct, or right to fruits.[126] Additionally, since Mrs. Reynolds's interest in the corpus was less than full "ownership" of separate property, the income from it could not be deemed fruits from separate property and therefore was not subject to community property designation. Thus, "the trust agreement conferred upon her, as a donation *mortis causa*, an independent interest in receiving those funds," and therefore the funds were her separate property.[127] *Reynolds* thus illustrates some of the fundamental problems that exist in determining the ownership interests in trust. The Supreme Court itself rendered only a plurality decision, leaving the characterization of interests rather tenuously defined.[128]

THE *LEGITIME* IN TRUST

Since a settlor may wish to establish a trust naming his children as beneficiaries, and since the latter are descendant forced heirs, some accommodation of these two concepts was

---

[122] *Id.* at 907.

[123] 388 So. 2d at 1141.

[124] *Id.* at 1142.

[125] *Id. Cf.* St. Charles Land Trust v. St. Amant, 253 La. 243, 217 So. 2d 385 (La. 1968), in which a beneficiary's interest in a trust corpus comprised of a mineral interest was characterized as an incorporeal immovable for inheritance tax purposes.

[126] 388 So. 2d at 1146.

[127] Id. at 1148.

[128] *See* Gerald Le Van, *Forum Juridicum-Louisiana Counterparts to Legal and Equitable Title*, 41 La. L. Rev. 1177, 1185 (1981) (wherein the author notes the "air of instability" of *Reynolds*); also see David William Gruning, Comment, *Reception of the Trust in Louisiana: The Case of Reynolds v. Reynolds*, 57 Tul. L. Rev. 89, 116 (1982) (wherein the author labels the holding "fragile").

necessary in Louisiana. The Louisiana Trust Estates Act of 1938 specifically permitted the placing of the *legitime* in trust.[129] In *Succession of Earhart*,[130] the Louisiana Supreme Court upheld the placing of the *legitime* in trust over the appellant's challenge that this conflicted with Article 4, Section 16 of the LOUISIANA CONSTITUTION of 1921, which prohibited the abolition of forced heirship. The Court noted that, although the legislature could not abolish forced heirship, it could regulate it.[131]

Article 1841 of the Louisiana Trust Code of 1964 specified that the *legitime* may be placed in trust, provided: (1) the income accruing to the forced heir be paid to him at least once a year; (2) there be no charges or conditions on the forced heir's interest other than those dealing with spendthrift provisions, with a legally sanctioned usufruct burdening the *legitime*, and with conditions imposed in the class trust;[132] (3) the term of the trust as it affects the *legitime* not exceed the life of the forced heir, except where the *legitime* is burdened with a legal usufruct held by the settlor's surviving spouse; and (4) the principal be delivered to the forced heir, his heirs, legatees or assignees at the termination of the part of the trust affecting the *legitime*. Article 12, Section 5 of the LOUISIANA CONSTITUTION of 1974 also expressly permitted the *legitime* to be placed in trust, and subsequent cases have sanctioned the placing of the entire *legitime*[133] or any heir's individual forced portion[134] in trust. Additionally, the recent amendment to Article 12, Section 5, which so severely altered the concept of forced heirship in Louisiana,[135] continues to emphatically authorize the possibility of placing the forced portion in trust.

Article 1844 of the Trust Code, as amended in 1974,[136] allows a *legitime* in trust to be burdened with an income interest or usufruct in favor of the settlor's surviving spouse to the same extent as such is possible out of trust. Recent amendments to the LOUISIANA CIVIL CODE have expanded the possible limits of the spousal usufruct.[137]

---

[129] LA. REV. STAT. 9:1793 (1950) (repealed 1964).

[130] 220 La. 817, 57 So. 2d 695 (La. 1952).

[131] Id. at 697. *See also* Succession of Singlust, 169 So. 2d 10 (La. App. 2d Cir. 1964), *writ refused*, 247 La. 262, 170 So. 2d 512 (La. 1965).

[132] The amendment of Section 1841 of the 1964 Trust Code (LA. REV. STAT. 9:1941) by Act 160 in 1979 resulted in the possibility that an ascendant forced heir might be deprived of *his* legitime if the person from whom he would inherit was a principal beneficiary of a trust and had died intestate without descendants. In such a case, the settlor of the trust could name a substitute principal beneficiary, completely bypassing any ascendant forced heirs of the initial beneficiary. *See* 1981 La. Acts, No. 442 (abolishing ascendant forced heirship). Note also that the amended version of LA. REV. STAT. 9:1841 accommodates for the possibility of shifting of principal as provided for in LA. REV. STAT. 9:1973 et. seq. **[LA. REV. STAT. 9:1841(1) was amended after the publication of this paper by Act No. 967 , § 1 of 1999 to provide that "[T]he trustee after taking into account all of the other income and support to be received by the forced heir during the year shall distribute to the forced heir, or to the legal guardian of the forced heir, funds from the net income in trust sufficient for the health, maintenance, support, and education of the forced heir." The amendment was meant to allow disabled forced heirs to remain eligible for government assistance and to allow the income interest of the legitime in trust to supplement state aid.]**

[133] Succession of Tatum, 347 So. 2d 79 (La. App. 2d Cir. 1977), *writ refused*, 350 So. 2d 896 (La. 1977); Succession of Steckler, 665 So. 561 (La. App. 5th Cir. 1995).

[134] Succession of Mohana, 351 So. 2d 1287 (La. App. 1st Cir. 1977), *writ denied*, 354 So. 2d 200 (La. 1978).

[135] 1995 La. Act 1321.

[136] 1974 La. Act 126, § 1.

[137] LA. CIV. CODE art. 890, as amended by 1996 La. Act 77 provides:

However, the forced heir's interest may not be satisfied by an income interest in trust,[138] anymore than a usufruct could satisfy that interest out of trust.[139] An interesting question thus arises when a settlor places the *legitime* in trust and when the corpus consists only of non-income producing property. In *Succession of Burgess*[140] the Fourth Circuit held that, absent a situation where the *legitime* was subject to a sanctioned legal usufruct of the surviving spouse, a *legitime* could not be satisfied by an interest in a trust when insufficient income was generated. The income, to be adequate, would have to correspond to the present value of the future income which the forced heir could expect on the basis of his present life expectancy. Without that necessary income, the trust would have to be reformed, allowing for the sale of enough of the corpus and its conversion into income-producing property sufficient to satisfy the *legitime*.[141]

DISTINGUISHING FEATURES OF THE LOUISIANA TRUST

In addition to the policy decisions concerning title, substitutions, and *legitime*, other provisions of the Trust Code render it uniquely a product of Louisiana. For example, rejecting any duration period based on the common law Rule Against Perpetuities,[142] the Committee adopted a time period for the trust based on the lifetime of an income beneficiary.[143] By affirmative stipulation in the trust, the settlor could provide for a duration of fifteen years, now amended to twenty years,[144] from the death of the settlor when he is a natural person or from the

---

> If the deceased spouse is survived by descendants, the surviving spouse shall have a usufruct over the decedent's share of the community property to the extent that the decedent has not disposed of it by testament. This usufruct terminates when the surviving spouse dies or remarries, whichever occurs first.

LA. CIV. CODE art. 1499, as amended by 1996 La. Act 77 provides:

> The decedent may grant a usufruct to the surviving spouse over all or part of his property, including the forced portion, and may grant the usufructuary the power to dispose of nonconsumables as provided in the law of usufruct. The usufruct shall be for life unless expressly designated for a shorter period. A usufruct over the legitime in favor of the surviving spouse is a permissible burden that does not impinge upon the legitime, whether it affects community property or separate property, whether it is for life or a shorter period, whether or not the forced heir is a descendant of the surviving spouse, and whether or not the usufructuary has the power to dispose of nonconsumables.

[138] Sachnowitz v. Nelson, 357 So. 2d 894 (La. App. 1st Cir. 1978), *writ denied*, 359 So. 2d 627 (La. 1978).

[139] *See* LA. REV. STAT. 9:1845 (Supp. 1965) **[See revised LA. REV. STAT 9:1844]**; Succession of Williams, 184 So. 2d 70 (La. App. 4th Cir. 1966), *cert. denied sub nom.*, State in Interest of Bolds, 250 La. 748, 199 So. 2d 183 (La. 1967). After Williams, Section 1845 was deemed obsolete and was repealed by 1979 La. Acts, No. 160.

[140] 359 So. 2d 1006 (La. App. 4th Cir. 1978), *writ denied*, 360 So. 2d 1178 (La. 1978).

[141] *Id.* at 1020.

[142] Oppenheim, *supra* n. 45 § 11, at 21.

[143] Specifically excluded from the definition of beneficiary for purposes of fixing the maximum allowable term of a trust are the heirs, legatees, or assignees of a designated beneficiary, as well as substituted beneficiaries provided for in LA. REV. STAT. 9:1973-1978.

[144] LA. REV. STAT. 9:1831, as amended by 1968 La. Act 132, § 1. The possibility of a trust surviving beyond the lives of the income beneficiaries has been criticized on the grounds that such could result in the continuation of a trust only for the benefit of the trustee. Robertson, *Some Interesting Features of the Proposed Trust Code*, 24 La. L. Rev. 712, 713 (1964).

creation of the trust if the settlor is not. In the case where neither the settlors nor any income beneficiaries are natural persons, the term of the trust could be up to fifty years.[145]

Related to the question of duration was that of termination of the trust. Following the American rule first established by the 1889 case of *Claflin v. Claflin*,[146] the Committee adopted a policy of indestructibility of trusts even if all parties consented to terminating the trust and even if a *legitime* were involved.[147] In the case of *Albritton v. Albritton*,[148] the Louisiana Supreme Court guarded a trust from termination contrary to the settlor's clearly expressed intent. The settlor left a will bequeathing to his grandson an undivided one-fourth interest in the naked ownership of his residuary estate. The testator made the interest subject to a life usufruct in favor of his son and also subject to an irrevocable testamentary spendthrift trust. One-half of the trust was to terminate when the grandson became twenty-one and the other half, when the grandson became twenty-six. Four months before his twenty-first birthday, the grandson, at his father's request, signed a document, purporting to extend the trust for his lifetime. Sixteen years later, when the grandson sought to have the extension annulled, the trial judge ruled that the action prescribed reasoning that even if the extension violated the Trust Code, the violation was merely a relative nullity which prescribed in five years. After affirmation by the appellate court, the decision was reversed by the Louisiana Supreme Court. Finding a "public policy of protecting the trust instrument from any modification or termination contrary to the settlor's clearly expressed intent,"[149] the Supreme Court held the agreement to extend the trust to be an absolute nullity and therefore imprescribable.

A few other policy determinations give the Louisiana trust a civilian perspective. Rejecting the notion of common law contingent remainders, the Louisiana Trust Code requires that all beneficiaries be in being and definitely ascertainable at the time of the creation of the trust,[150] or, in the case of revocable trusts, by the time the trust becomes irrevocable.[151] Exceptions to this rule include class trusts in which only one member of the class need be in being at the creation of the trust,[152] trusts for employees,[153] and trusts for mixed private and charitable purposes.[154]

Another concept that is foreign to civilian theory, and basically rejected in Louisiana, is recognizing powers of appointment. However, the Trust Code does allow for the invasion of principal by the trustee for the benefit of the income beneficiary even when income and principal

---

[145] LA. REV. STAT. 9:1831 (West 1991). One commentator notes that this is shorter than the maximum period provided in any other state. Joachim Zekoll, *The Louisiana Private-Law System: The Best of Both Worlds*, 10 Tul. Eur. & Civ. L.F. 1 (1995).

[146] 149 Mass. 19, 20 N.E. 454 (Mass. 1889).

[147] *See* McLendon v. First National Bank of Shreveport, 299 So. 2d 407, 410 (La. App. 2d Cir. 1974) (which was decided under the terms of the Trust Estates Act, but which noted that "the concept of indestructibility has been carried over in the new trust code").

[148] 600 So. 2d 1328 (La. 1992), *rev'd on other grounds after remand*, 622 So. 2d 709 (La. 1993).

[149] *Id.* at 1332.

[150] LA. REV. STAT. 9:1803 (West 1991).

[151] LA. REV. STAT. 9:2011 (West Supp. 1996).

[152] LA. REV. STAT. 9:1891 (West 1991).

[153] LA. REV. STAT. 9:1921 (West 1991).

[154] *See* LA. REV. STAT. 9:1951 (West 1991), as amended by 1972 La. Act 659, § 1.

beneficiaries are not identical.[155] By requiring "objective standards" for such invasion, the drafters attempted to gain favorable federal tax treatment[156] and to maintain a consistency with the LOUISIANA CIVIL CODE which prohibits powers of appointment.[157]

The spendthrift provisions of the Louisiana Trust Code provide an example of trust provisions which are alien to the civilian concept of control over one's own property. Although most creditors are restricted from seizing the beneficiary's interest in the trust, specific exceptions are provided for those owed alimony, those who have provided necessary services or supplies, and to tort victims.[158]

CONCLUSION

Louisiana, with its civilian tradition, has adopted the Anglo-American trust. As a corollary, however, it has experienced difficulties in integrating some of the trust characteristics with the civilian tradition.

Questions of title still exist, as illustrated in the *Reynolds* case. Although the Louisiana courts have been more liberal recently in their interpretation of trusts, drafters should still use caution in order to avoid the possibility of including substitutions that are not sanctioned by the Trust Code. Additionally, when placing the *legitime* in trust, care must be taken to assure the production of adequate annual income for payment to the forced heirs. Despite its limitations, the trust does indeed function in Louisiana. If used with caution, it offers a valuable tool for tax and estate planning to the Louisiana domiciliary. As stated by an astute scholar observing the Louisiana experience with the trust:

> As private law evolves and the limitation on "pure" common-law or civil-law approaches encounter limits, Louisiana stands as an example of a jurisdiction which has successfully chosen the best of both worlds, by adopting commercially sound rules without compromising its civilian heritage.[159]

Creation of a Trust and Its Component Parts: La. R.S. 9:1731-1755; 1821-1824

As opposed to other states, *all* Louisiana trusts must be in writing. A testamentary trust must be "created in one of the forms prescribed by the laws regulating donations mortis causa." La. R.S. § 9:1751. An *inter vivos* trust may be created by authentic act or act under private signature in the presence of two witnesses and duly acknowledged by the settlor or by the affidavit of one of the attesting witnesses. La. R.S. § 9:1752. La. R.S. § 9:1753 requires no

---

[155] *See* LA. REV. STAT. 9:2068 (West 1991), as amended by 1968 La. Act 133, § 1; 1972 La. Act 661, § 1; 1974 La. Act 158, § 1; 1989 La. Act 113, § 1; 1995 La. Act 220, § 1. The amendments clarify that "objective standards" are not limited to support, maintenance, education or medical expenses of the income beneficiary. Additionally, the trust instrument may direct the trustee to pay accumulated income or principal to an income beneficiary upon the request of the beneficiary.

[156] Thomas B. Lemann, *Invasion of Principal in Louisiana*, 42 Tul. L. Rev. 829, 834 (1968).

[157] LA. CIV. CODE art. 1573 (1870).

[158] LA. REV. STAT. 9:2001-2007 (West 1991 & Supp. 1996).

[159] Zekoll, *supra* n. 145, at 30.

particular language be used in the instrument creating the trust. However, "it must clearly appear that the creation of a trust is intended." La. R.S. § 9:1754.

The settlor is the "person who creates a trust." La. R.S. § 9:1761. More than one person may be a settlor. La. R.S. § 9:1762. Others may transfer property to the trust after its creation; however, such persons are not deemed "settlors." La. R.S. § 9:1761. For example, grandparents may create a trust for the benefit of their granddaughter and later the granddaughter's parents may transfer funds into the trust. The grandmother and grandfather are the trust settlors; the parents are not.

In order for the trust to come into existence, property must be transferred into it. Any "property susceptible of private ownership and any interest in such property may be transferred in trust." La. R.S. § 9:1771. The Trust Code specifies that life insurance may be placed in trust, La. R.S. § 9:9:1981, and that the marital portion may be placed in trust. La. R.S. § 9:1851. Even the "*legitime* or any portion thereof may be placed in trust" subject to certain provisions which will be discussed later. La. R.S. § 9:1841.

One or more persons or entities must be designated as trustee to receive and manage the property that has been transferred into the trust. La. R.S. § 9:1781-1782. All capable citizens and residents of the United States as well as federally insured depositary institutions may serve as trustees. La. R.S. § 9:1783. Generally the settlor will name a trustee in the trust instrument; however, the failure to do so will not invalidate the trust. If a trustee is not named or if the named trustee declines to accept the position, a proper court may appoint one. La. R.S. § 9:1785.

The beneficiary is the "person for whose benefit the trust is created and may be a natural person, corporation, partnership, or other legal entity having the capacity to receive property." La. R.S. § 9:1801. The beneficiary should be in being when the trust is created and objectively ascertainable "solely from standards stated in the trust instrument." La. R.S. § 9:1802-1803. The only exception to this rule is in the case of class trusts and shifting interests in principal, both to be discussed later. La. R.S. §§ 9:1891 and 9:1973. One person may serve as both the income and principal beneficiary, or the settlor may name different persons as income and principal beneficiary or he may name several income and principal beneficiaries. La. R.S. § 9: 1806. Further, income beneficiaries "may be designated to enjoy income successively." La. R.S. § 9:1807.

SUCCESSION OF PAYNE
524 So. 2d 803 (La. App. 3rd Cir. 1988) *writ. den.* 525 So. 2d 1044 (La. 1988)

WILLIAM A. CULPEPPER, Retired, Judge Pro Tem.

This case concerns the validity of a will. The testator prepared an Oklahoma "statutory" will on January 7, 1969. On June 15, 1986 he prepared an olographic will in Louisiana. See Appendix 1. On July 12, 1986 the testator took the life of his wife and then his own. His three children subsequently came forward, as heirs, with a petition for probate of the statutory will and with a rule to show why the olographic will should not be declared invalid, both in form and because it contains a prohibited substitution. Since the olographic will named three nonresident beneficiaries, an attorney was appointed to represent them. Through their court-appointed attorney the beneficiaries of the olographic will have opposed the annulment of the will, asserting it to be valid both in form and in creation of a valid testamentary trust. The position of the nonresident beneficiaries is that the trust makes Henry K. Payne (testator's brother) the trustee for the testator's twin granddaughters until they attain the age of 21 years.

At the rule to show cause the trial court annulled the olographic will on the ground that, although it was valid in form, it contained a prohibited substitution. The court, in its reasons for judgment, found the disposition did not comply with LSA-R.S. 9:1731, *et seq.* of the trust code. The statutory will was proved and admitted to probate. The beneficiaries under the trust (allegedly created by the olographic will) appeal this judgment.

ASSIGNMENT OF ERROR

The appellants allege the court erred in invalidating a bequest which was intended to be, and qualifies as, a disposition in trust.

APPLICABLE LAW

The trial court found the olographic will to be valid in form. Since the will contains the necessary animus testandi, date, and signature of the testator and was proved to be written entirely by the testator himself, we affirm the trial court's finding that it is valid in form. *See* LSA-C.C. art. 1588.

The appellees assert that the olographic will is null under LSA-C.C. art. 1520 because it contains a prohibited substitution. LSA-C.C. art. 1520 states:

> Art. 1520. Substitutions and fidei commissa
> Substitutions are and remain prohibited, except as permitted by the laws relating to trusts.
> Every disposition not in trust by which the donee, the heirs, or legatee is charged to preserve for and to return a thing to a third person is null, even with regard to the donee, the instituted heir or the legatee.

A prohibited substitution is defined in *Baten v. Taylor*, 386 So.2d 333 (La.1979), as having three elements:

> (1) A double liberality, or a double disposition in full ownership, of the same thing to persons called to receive it, one after the other;
> (2) Charge to preserve and transmit, imposed on the first beneficiary for the benefit of the second beneficiary;
> (3) Establishment of a successive order that causes the substituted property to leave the inheritance of the burdened beneficiary and enter into the patrimony of the substituted beneficiary.

A trust is defined in LSA-R.S. 9:1731:

> § 1731. Trust defined

A trust, as the term is used in this Code, is the relationship resulting from the transfer of title to property to a person to be administered by him as a fiduciary for the benefit of another.

The pertinent language of the olographic will is:

Scense [sic] this is a divorce involed [sic] I leave 1/2 of the community to Henry K. Payne to be divided equally Between My Twin Granddaughters when they become 21 years of age.

The language of the olographic will appears to fit within either of the definitions mentioned above, LSA-C.C. art. 1520 or LSA-R.S. 9:1731. However, when the terms of a disposition attacked as a prohibited substitution are susceptible to interpretation in two ways-- one that the disposition contains the elements of a prohibited substitution, and the other that it does not contain them--it is preferable to uphold the interpretation that maintains the disposition. *Succession of Moran*, 479 So.2d 350 (La.1985). Also, when a will has been written in laymen's terms and without the aid of counsel, the courts must exempt the language from technical interpretation and seek the clear intent of the testator in a purpose consistent with upholding the testament. *Succession of Moran, supra*; LSA-C.C. art. 1712. A disposition must be understood in the sense in which it can have effect, rather than that in which it can have none. LSA-C.C. art. 1713. The court must presume the testator did not intend to make an invalid disposition. *Succession of Moran, supra*. These principles mandate an interpretation of the will as creating a trust instead of as creating a prohibited substitution.

Moreover, while the first element of a prohibited substitution mentioned in *Baten v. Taylor, supra,* is arguably lacking from the will, the third element is definitely missing. The testator has not established an order of succession, since he did not arrange for the property to leave Henry K. Payne's patrimony at his death and enter the patrimony of his granddaughters. Rather, he left the property to Henry K. Payne only until his granddaughters reach 21 years of age. Therefore, the will does not contain a prohibited substitution, since every requirement must be met for the disposition to be construed as such. *Succession of Moran, supra.*

We find, instead, that a trust has been created. The fact that the testator did not call it a trust is not dispositive of the issue since he wrote his will as a layman without the benefit of legal counsel. No particular language is required to create a trust. LSA-R.S. 9:1753; *St. Charles Land Trust, Achille Guibet v. St. Amant*, 253 La. 243, 217 So.2d 385 (1968). In *Wilbert v. Wilbert*, 155 La. 197, 99 So. 36 (1923), the court held that a mystic will which made the testator's two sons universal legatees, subject to the condition that the effects bequeathed by him were not to be divided for five years and were to be managed by his executors for that time or until the happening of a certain condition, created a five-year trust estate, although the word "trust" was not included in the will. *See* Appendix 2. *See also In re Succession of Abraham*, 136 So.2d 471 (La.App. 3d Cir.1962). In *Wilbert*, the court summed up the State's policy as to trust estates as:

In other words, a testator, looking to the welfare of his children, after his death, is no longer limited by the provision of article 1710 of the Civil Code, prohibiting charges or conditions from being imposed by him on the legitimate portion of forced heirs, if he should see fit to designate "trustees" in his last will and testament for the protection of his heirs, and, to that end, should direct a prudent administration, in safe hands, of his estate for their benefit.

The court found that an interpretation of the will as merely preventing a partition of the testator's estate for five years, thus nullifying the provision, would be a "complete repudiation of all that the testator clearly intended, and the sole purpose of his last will and testament would be defeated." Therefore, since the intention of the testator to create a trust clearly appeared from the language of the will and the trust was a legal and valid disposition, the will was given full effect as written.

Having disposed of the issue of the language necessary to create a trust, we now turn to the requisite elements of a trust. Certain elements must be contained in the trust instrument if the validity of the trust is to be sustained. L. Oppenheimer & S.P. Ingram, *Trusts*, 11 LA. CIVIL LAW TREATISE § 102, p. 124 (1977):

> The trust instrument technically is not required to contain specific language of conveyance provided it is clear that title is being transferred to the trustee, because the creation of a trust automatically and by definition effects a transfer of title to the trust property.
>
> Also, although it is not necessary that the settlor use the word 'trust' in the trust instrument, if the settlor clearly indicates in other language of the instrument that he intends to create a trust, still the settlor should state in the trust instrument that he is creating a "trust," to insure that his true intentions are carried out.
>
> The trust instrument must identify the property that is being transferred in trust, either specially (as in a description of land) or generally (as under a universal legacy).
>
> The trust instrument is not required either to name the trustee or to provide a method for the selection of the trustee. If the trust instrument is silent, a trustee will be appointed by the court. It is advisable, however, to name the trustee in the trust instrument so that the intentions of the settlor will be carried out more closely and so that there will be less delay in setting the trust in operation.
>
> Except with regard to certain particularized types of trusts discussed below, a beneficiary must be designated by the trust instrument. The trust fails only if neither an income nor a principal beneficiary is named in the trust instrument. The trust instrument is not required to provide for the modification, termination or rescission of the trust, to state the terms of the trust, or to regulate the duties and powers of the trustee, the compensation and indemnity of the trustee, or the liabilities of the trustee.

See LSA-R.S. 9:1731, 9:1753, 9:1785, 9:1802. The will before us transfers the property to Henry K. Payne, who is the intended trustee, the property is identified in the will, the trustee and the beneficiaries are named and the nature of the relationship created in the will is that of a trust relationship. A trust instrument shall be given an interpretation that will sustain the effectiveness of its provisions, if the trust instrument is susceptible of such an interpretation. LSA-R.S. 9:1753; *St. Charles Land Trust, Achille Guibet v. St. Amant, supra.* Since all the requirements for a trust are met, and upholding the interpretation of the will as creating a trust effectuates the clear intent of the testator, we find that a valid testamentary trust has been created.

The appellees also assert that, even if the disposition is construed as a trust, the trust is invalid because it is not in the proper form for a trust under LSA-R.S. 9:1752. However, the appellees err in citing R.S. 9:1752, since it is applicable to inter vivos trusts only. This case involves a testamentary trust, under LSA-R.S. 9:1733.

§ 1733. Testamentary trust defined
A trust is testamentary when it is created by donation mortis causa.
§ 1751. Form of testamentary trust
A testamentary trust may be created in one of the forms prescribed by the laws regulating donations mortis causa.

The testamentary trust herein clearly meets the requirements under LSA- 9:1751. The olographic will creating the trust is valid in form. Therefore, the testamentary trust is valid in form.

Finally, the appellees contend that the language of the will indicates the testator was having "difficulty in his reasoning facilities." No contention or evidence of lack of capacity of the testator was introduced into the pleadings or record. Therefore the argument cannot be considered in this appeal.

CONCLUSION

Accordingly, for the reasons assigned above, the judgment of the trial court is reversed and the case is remanded for further proceedings consistent with this opinion. Costs of this appeal are assessed to the appellees.

REVERSED AND REMANDED.

PONZELINO v. PONZELINO
26 N.W.2d 330 (Iowa 1947)

GARFIELD, Justice.

Plaintiff and defendant were married in 1921. In October 1944, defendant (wife) was granted a divorce. The decree awarded her four lots near the city of Des Moines, title to which plaintiff now seeks to have quieted in himself as trustee. Prior to September 5, 1939, plaintiff owned the four lots and 10 others. On that date he executed a purported trust deed of the 14 lots to himself as trustee at least nominally for the benefit of his wife (defendant) and their four children. Defendant signed the instrument apparently to release her dower right in the property.

In this action plaintiff contends in effect the court was without jurisdiction in the divorce suit to award defendant any part of the so-called trust property because, it is said the trustee was not a party to the divorce suit and for other reasons. The trial court rejected such contention and confirmed defendant's title to the four lots in controversy.

Upon this appeal defendant seeks an affirmance upon two grounds: First, it is said the trust deed is void because it imposes no enforceable duties upon the trustee and attempts to clothe him with absolute and unlimited discretion and for other reasons. Second, it is argued plaintiff as trustee was properly a party to the divorce suit and is bound by the decree therein. Defendant urged both these contentions in the court below.

Unquestionably the attack plaintiff now makes on the divorce decree cannot be sustained if, as defendant contends, the so-called trust deed did not create a valid trust. In that event, plaintiff owned not only the legal title but also the beneficial interest to the property in question. Clearly the court in the divorce suit had jurisdiction to award defendant (wife) for the support of herself and minor children, whose custody was awarded her, any property owned by plaintiff individually.

*   *   *

A trust is not created unless the settlor manifests an intention to impose upon the transferee duties which are enforceable in the courts. RESTATEMENT, TRUSTS, section 25, section 125, comment a; *Hodgson v. Dorsey*, 230 Iowa 730, 736, 298 N.W. 895, 897, 137 A.L.R. 456, 460. *See also* 54 Am.Jur. 47, section 35; *Morsman v. Commissioner of Internal Revenue*, 8 Cir., 90 F.2d 18, 113; A.L.R. 441, 444. Indeed a trust is defined as a fiduciary relationship with respect to property, subjecting the person by whom the property is held to equitable duties to deal with it for the benefit of another. RESTATEMENT, TRUSTS, section 2. *See also* 54 Am.Jur. 21, section 4; 65 C.J. 212, 213, section 1; *Maxwell v. Wood*, 133 Iowa 721, 111 N.W. 203; *Andrew v. State Bank of New Hampton*, 205 Iowa 1064, 1069, 217 N.W. 250.

A corollary to the rule that a trust involves the imposition of enforceable duties upon the transferee is that there is no property which can be the subject of a trust where its application to the purposes of the trust depends upon the absolute and unconditional discretion of the person in control of the property. Obviously a court of equity cannot direct what disposition one shall make of property which is given to him to dispose of as he chooses. Unbridled discretion in a trustee not only negatives the necessary separation of legal and equitable ownerships, but is also objectionable, so far as the existence of a trust is concerned, by reason of the uncertainty it involves. 54 Am.Jur. 47, section 36; *Burke v. Burke*, 259 Ill. 262, 102 N.E. 293, 295; *Booth v. Krug*, 368 Ill. 487, 14 N.Ed.2d 645, 117 A.L.R. 1193, 1197. *See also* RESTATEMENT, TRUSTS, section 125.

> While a trust is valid where it is imperative as to the amount to be used for the beneficiary, where the amounts, if any, which the beneficiaries are to receive are wholly discretionary with the alleged trustee, the trust is too uncertain to be enforceable.

65 C.J. 273, section 53.

We think the alleged trust deed now before us is invalid because no enforceable obligation is imposed upon plaintiff as trustee and he is given absolute and unconditional discretion with respect to the property transferred. The instrument fills 13 pages of the printed record and is too long to set out here in full. However, we refer to various provisions we believe justify our holding.

The instrument provides; the beneficiaries shall not be entitled to receive any benefits during the continuance of the trust except such as the trustee may confer upon them; the trustee shall have the right, without compensation, to maintain his home upon the property and to keep his family thereon, and either individually or together with any or all of his family, to occupy any improvements thereon; the trustee may, but shall not be compelled to, pay the living expenses of the beneficiaries (his wife and four children); the trustee may in his discretion, but without liability to do so, during the continuance of the trust, give to any beneficiary who reaches majority or marries such part of the property as in the judgment of the trustee may seem desirable--such gift to be accepted as full and complete satisfaction of such beneficiary's interest in the trust and there shall be no liability to any beneficiary because of such donation or distribution; at any time the trustee may see fit he may make any property settlement with his wife (defendant), one of the beneficiaries, which shall be in full settlement of her interest in the trust estate and the trustee may use for such purpose any of the trust estate—"But nothing herein shall be construed as compelling the trustee to make any such settlement;" the trustee shall be the sole judge of the propriety of the expenses or liabilities against the trust estate hereby authorized; the trustee shall not be liable for the use of any trust property although such use may be partially or wholly for the benefit of either Ponzelino or his wife; the trustee shall not be liable for any damages to the property of the trust estate, or in any manner sustained by any beneficiary, nor shall the trustee be answerable for any negligence, waste or dissipation of the trust property; the exercise of any right or authority granted the trustee, including the authority to sell, mortgage or exchange trust property, shall rest exclusively within the judgment and discretion of the trustee.

The trust instrument further provides that unless the trust property is sooner disposed of or exhausted or, because of unforeseen or unavoidable circumstances, wasted or dissipated, the trust shall continue until the youngest child-beneficiary becomes 21 (at the time of trial he was about 13). Within one year thereafter the trustee may terminate the trust: (1) by conveying the entire trust estate to plaintiff, individually, which conveyance shall vest in him the entire interest of the trust in the property and completely bar any right of the beneficiaries thereto; (2) by dividing the property among the beneficiaries in such proportions as the trustee may elect-- he to be the sole judge of the kind and amount of trust property each beneficiary shall receive, and no beneficiary shall have any claim or cause of action against the trustee because of his distribution of the property or because the trustee shall have entirely excluded one or more of the beneficiaries from the receipt of any part of the trust estate; (3) by the conveyance of such part of the trust property as the trustee may see fit to plaintiff individually so as to bar all rights of the beneficiaries therein; the trustee may then distribute among the beneficiaries, or such of them as he may elect, and in such proportions as he may determine, the remainder of the trust property, and the beneficiaries shall have no claim or cause of action against the trustee or plaintiff individually because of such distribution or his refusal to convey trust property to one or more of the beneficiaries.

The deed further provides the trust shall also terminate upon the death of the trustee, Harry Ponzelino, in which event the trust property shall be divided among the beneficiaries according to the laws of descent just as if Harry Ponzelino had died seized of the title to said property.

We are not to be understood as holding any one of the above provisions invalidates the so-called trust. Of course broad discretion may be given the trustee. 54 Am.Jur. 48, section 36. Also there can be a trust of which the beneficiaries are members of a definite class among whom the trustee is authorized to select who shall take and in what proportions. RESTATEMENT, TRUSTS, sections 120, 121, 127, comment e; 65 C.J. 274, section 54; *Moskowitz v. Federman*, 72 Ohio App. 149, 51 N.E.2d 48, 53; *In re Dewey's Estate*, 45 Utah 98, 143 P. 124, Ann.Cas. 1918A, 475, 479. The above provision designated "(2)," for dividing the property among the beneficiaries in such proportion as the trustee may elect, seems, under the rule just stated, to be valid. But it will be noticed the instrument also authorizes the trustee to convey any or all of the trust property to himself individually and thereby entirely deprive the so-called beneficiaries thereof.

This is not a case where the invalid portions of a trust can be rejected without invalidating the entire instrument. *See* 54 Am.Jur. 39, section 24; 65 C.J. 333, section 96; RESTATEMENT, TRUSTS, section 65. Here the entire scheme which the instrument attempts to establish is ineffectual as a trust.

There is no attempt in the entire trust instrument to impose any enforceable obligation upon the trustee. No trust is created which any beneficiary is capable of enforcing. At least until plaintiff's death, the claims of the wife and children against the trust are not more than mere hopes or chances. The obvious purpose of plaintiff as settlor seems to have been to vest unlimited discretion in himself as trustee whether to apply the so-called trust estate for the benefit of those named as beneficiaries or withdraw it from such purpose and apply it, as he might see fit, to his own use. For all practical purposes plaintiff remained the owner of the property. Consequently under the authorities heretofore cited no valid trust was created. The court thus had jurisdiction in the divorce suit to award defendant the four lots in controversy here.

* * *

Affirmed.

All Justices concur.

Prohibited Substitutions and Trusts

One of the difficult questions posed by trusts was their resemblance to prohibited substitutions. Courts struggled with accommodating these two concepts that, at first glance, appear so similar. As you read the following case, consider a theory which would have served to uphold the attempted trust.

CRICHTON v. GREDLER
256 La. 156, 235 So. 2d 411 (1970)
[footnotes omitted]

* * *

SUMMERS, Justice.

The contested will is in olographic form and is dated March 6, 1963. After provisions revoking all prior wills, appointing Thomas Crichton, Jr., her brother, as executor and directing the payment of her debts, the will provides:

...[A]nd I do hereby give and bequeath to the said Thomas Crichton jr. as trustee for the benefit of his two sons, my nephews, Thomas Crichton Third, and John H. Crichton, all the rest, residue and remainder of my property, both real and personal, except my residence with contents therein, located at Creton Lake Road in the town of Bedford, County of Westchester, State of New York, and except also all moneys now to the credit of my account in the First National City Bank of New York (Mt. Kisco branch); shall thereafter be held in an undivided one-half interest in each of the aforementioned two trusts, each trust created and named for its above named beneficiary, and both trusts shall be Louisiana trusts, administered in the State of Louisiana, in accordance with the laws of Louisiana-- I appoint Thomas Crichton, jr., my brother, Trustee of each of above named trusts. In the event that Thomas Crichton, jr. should die, become incapacitated or refuse to act, prior to the termination of these trusts, then the First National Bank of Shreveport, Louisiana, shall become Trustee. The trustee, Thomas Crichton, jr., shall have full power to sell, mortgage, or lease all property, and otherwise manage all trust property with the same control and freedom as though trustee owned said property personally.

In the event that either beneficiary, Thomas Crichton third or John Hayes Crichton be not living when this trust is terminated, both income and corpus of such said trust shall be paid over or conveyed by Trustee to the child or children of said deceased beneficiary in equal, undivided portions. In event that neither a beneficiary nor his child or children are living upon the termination of this trust, then said income and corpus shall be paid over or conveyed by the Trustee to the other trust beneficiary or, if he be not living, then to his child or children equal or undivided portions. In the event that neither beneficiary, no (sic) any of their children be living upon termination of these trusts, as above herein set forth, then the income and corpus of these trusts shall be paid over or conveyed to the children of my deceased brother, Powell Crichton; namely, Powell Crichton, jr., Kate Crichton, Edward B. Crichton and Gloria Crichton McGehee in equal or undivided portions.

The Trust Estates Law of 1938, as amended, Section 16 of Article IV of the Constitution, as amended in 1962 to provide that a trust may contain substitutions to the extent authorized by the Legislature, and Article 1520 of the Civil Code, as amended in 1962 to make substitutions in trust an exception to the prohibitions of that article, were all in effect when Mrs. Gredler drew her will on March 6, 1963. Thereafter the Trust Estates Law of 1938 was superseded by the Louisiana Trust Code (La.R.S. 9:1721--2252) enacted in 1964.

At the time of Mrs. Gredler's death in 1965, therefore, the law applicable to trusts was contained in Section 16 of Article IV of the Constitution as amended in 1962, Article 1520 of the Civil Code as amended in 1962 and the LOUISIANA TRUST CODE of 1964. All parties concede that the Trust Code applies to the trusts in this case.

The suit to annul Mrs. Gredler's will was instituted in 1967. Aside from the primary contention that the will was a nullity because it contained a prohibited substitution, the attack also asserts that the will is defective because it suspends until a future indeterminate time the ultimate vesting of the decedent's estate in her legatees, and because it dictates that persons succeed to the estate who were neither ascertainable nor necessarily in being at the decedent's death.

Proponents of the will defend its validity on the ground that the condition under which the trust property devolves upon the successor legatees is impossible of fulfillment and should be considered as not written; if the language of the trust provision dictating the transfer of principal after the termination of the trusts creates a prohibited substitution, Sections 2026 and 2027 of the Trust Code permit the deletion of these transfer provisions without defeating the purposes of the trusts, and the broad powers granted to the trustee constituted the contested disposition nothing more than a *Fidei commissum*.

Does the will contain a substitution? The answer is yes.

* * *

The law forbidding substitutions was considered to be of such importance that the Constitution adopted in 1921 incorporated the prohibition in Section 16 of Article IV. . . .

* * *

In construing Article 1520, our cases have formulated a distinction between the substitution and the *fidei commissum* and clarified the definitions applicable to each. Most often quoted to illustrate this development is the case of *Succession of Reilly*, 136 La. 347, 67 So. 27 (1915), in which the will under attack contained the following language:

> And the balance of whatever I may die possessed of I give and bequeath unto Bishop Thomas Heslin, to be distributed as he sees fit among my people in Ireland and for the further education of Thomas Regan, hereby instituting Bishop Heslin my sole heir and universal legatee.

As organ of the court, Chief Justice O'Niell declared that the bequest amounted to a *fidei commissum* in which the directions to Bishop Heslin were merely precatory and would be considered not written. This is what he wrote:

> In more than a century of jurisprudence on the subject of substitutions and *fidei commissa,* prohibited by Article 1520 of the Civil Code, the distinction between them and the difference in their effect has been consistently observed. The essential elements of the prohibited substitution are that the immediate donee is obliged to keep the title of the legacy inalienable during his lifetime, to be transmitted at his death to a third person designated by the original donor or testator. Such a disposition is null even with regard to the original donee or legatee. In the *fidei commissum*, whereby the donee or legatee is invested with the title and charged or directed to convey it to another person or to make a particular disposition of it, only the charge or direction, as to the ultimate disposition of the donation or legacy, is null and is to be considered not written, leaving the donation or bequest valid as to the donee or legatee. A substitution is an attempt on the part of the donor or testator to make a testament for his donee or legatee

along with his own will, and to substitute his own will for the legal order of succession from his donee or legatee.

In *Succession of Heft*, 163 La. 467, 112 So. 301 (1927), a prohibited substitution was defined as, "A bequest of property to one legatee with the stipulation and on the condition that at his death and without an act of conveyance from him it shall belong to another legatee named in the will." Other cases not involving trusts are to the same effect. *See Succession of Ryan*, 228 La. 447, 82 So.2d 759 (1955); *Girven v. Miller*, 219 La. 252, 52 So.2d 843 (1951); *Maddox v. Butchee*, 203 La. 299, 14 So.2d 4 (1943); *Succession of McCan*, 48 La.Ann. 145, 19 So. 220 (1896); *Anderson v. Pike*, 29 La.Ann. 120 (1877); *Provost's Heirs v. Provost*, 13 La.Ann. 574 (1858); *Farrar v. McCutcheon*, 4 Mart. (N.S.) 45 (La.1825); *Cloutier v. Lecomte*, 3 Mart. (O.S.) 481 (La.1814).

Cases involving trusts created after the Trust Estates Law of 1938 but prior to the Trust Code of 1964 have also recognized that wills which attempt to create prohibited substitutions must be nullified. *Succession of Simms*, 250 La. 177, 195 So.2d 114 (1967); *Succession of Guillory*, 232 La. 213, 94 So.2d 38 (1957); *Succession of Meadors*, 135 So.2d 679 (La.App.1961).

In *Succession of Simms* the principles involved in prohibited substitutions were reviewed and restated:

It is obvious, therefore, that a prohibited substitution exists when a testator places the title of the property bequeathed in a first named legatee (referred to as the instituted heir) at his death, and directs that, at the end of a specified period, usually but not necessarily at the death of the instituted legatee, this title is to be turned over, transmitted, or passed to a second legatee (referred to as the substitute heir), with the result that both parties take their title directly from the testator, the title of the institute being one that he cannot alienate because of the charge that he is to transmit it to the substitute at some time in the future and the title of the substitute being one that the substitute cannot alienate because it does not exist until some date in the future when the property is to eventually "vest" in him. *Marshall v. Pearce,* 34 La.Ann. 557. In thus indicating a desire to give the property away "twice" to two named legatees, the testator, as pointed out in *Succession of Reilly, supra*, not only makes his own will, but attempts also to make the will of the instituted legatee, thus endeavoring to determine the law of successions by substituting "his own will for the legal order of succession from his donee or legatee."

It is to check the power of a testator to thus control the descent and distribution of his property after title has vested in the first legatee upon his death, in contravention of the laws establishing the order of inheritance, as well as to present restraints upon the alienation of property, that the law, as a penalty, strikes down the entire disposition, the second paragraph of Article 1520 clearly providing that "Every disposition by which the donee, the heir, or the legatee is charged to preserve for or return a thing to a third person is null even with regard to the donee, the instituted heir, or the legatee." As pointed out in *Succession of Johnson*, 223 La. 1058, 67 So.2d 591, "in cases of prohibited substitutions the whole will is stricken with nullity whereas in cases of *fidei commissa*, it is only those dispositions which are tainted with that designation that are invalid," the vital distinction being whether the instituted legatee has under the bequest the authority to alienate the title placed in him.

Our first problem is to examine the contested Gredler will in the light of these definitions of prohibited substitutions and determine whether such a substitution is present. Section 1821 of the Trust Code stipulates that "A testamentary trust is created at the moment of the settlor's death." The interest in the bequest of the universal legatees or principal beneficiaries of the trust also vests at the moment of the testatrix's or settlor's death.

As the will provides no term for the trusts, each of them will terminate upon the death of its respective beneficiary in accordance with Section 1833(1) of the Trust Code, providing that "If the trust instrument stipulates no term, the trust shall terminate: (1) Upon the death of the last income beneficiary who is a natural person." LA. TRUST CODE § 1833(1). And at the death of the beneficiaries the principal devolves upon their heirs. LA. CIVIL CODE art. 940; LA. TRUST CODE § 1972.

Thus, the two principal beneficiaries cannot be living at the time the trusts terminate, since their respective deaths, by operation of law, will be the terminating events. Nevertheless, the testatrix named Thomas Crichton III and John H. Crichton as beneficiaries of the trusts created by her will, and she provided that at their death the trust properties should be paid over and conveyed to their respective children. Therefore, inasmuch as a substitution consists of successive principal interests, and of the making of a will for the first named legatee by the decedent, the present will provides for the successive interests to vest after the termination of the trust. The substitution is therefore not "in trust" as the Trust Code could permit. It is, instead, out of trust. Moreover, in so providing the testatrix makes the will of the first legatees. In so doing she creates a substitution prohibited by law.

What, then, is the effect of the 1962 amendment to Section 16 of Article IV of the Constitution, the 1962 amendment to Article 1520 of the Civil Code and the LOUISIANA TRUST CODE on the substitution determined to exist in this will under prior law?

The 1962 amendment to Section 16 of Article IV of the Constitution abolished many of the restraints theretofore imposed upon trusts, but it retained the traditional prohibition against substitutions except as they might be authorized by the Legislature. Insofar as it is pertinent here, the amendment provides: "Substitutions not in trust are and remain prohibited; but trusts may contain substitutions to the extent authorized by the Legislature."

In like manner, the amendment to Article 1520 of the Civil Code retained the prohibition against substitutions except insofar as substitutions might be permitted in the laws relating to trust. As Amended in 1962 the Article now reads:

> Substitutions are and remain prohibited, except as permitted by the laws relating to trusts.
> Every disposition not in trust by which the donee, the heir, or legatee is charged to preserve for and to return a thing to a third person is null, even with regard to the donee, the instituted heir or the legatee.

The amendments of 1962, therefore, do nothing to legitimate substitutions, except insofar as they authorize the Legislature to permit substitutions in trust, that is, the Trust Code of 1964 or other legislative acts must implement the authorizations contained in the amended Constitution and Civil Code.

Despite Section 1723 declaring that "A disposition Authorized by this Code may be made in trust although it would contain a prohibited substitution if it were made free of trust," study of the Trust Code discloses no provision permitting a substitution in trust. To the contrary, Sections 1971 and 1972 of the Trust Code embody prohibitions which effectively prevent the creation of substitutions in trust: § 1971. The interest of a principal beneficiary is acquired immediately upon the creation of a trust, subject to the exceptions provided in this Code. § 1972. Upon a principal beneficiary's death, his interest vests in his heirs or legatees, subject to the trust, except as to class trusts. Class trusts mentioned as an exception in Section 1972, which contemplate shifting of principal, are not involved here, for they apply exclusively to children or grandchildren of the settlor. *See* LA. TRUST CODE § 1891 et seq.

By the terms of Section 1971 the interest of a principal beneficiary "is acquired immediately upon the creation of a trust." The implications of the language of Section 1971 is explained in Comment (c) to that section: "Although under this Code interests that are the approximate equivalent of the Anglo-American shifting interest are permitted in income, such interests are not permitted in principal except as to class trusts and invasion of principal."

When the trust is created in the ordinary situation, therefore, the interest of a principal beneficiary must be acquired immediately upon the creation of that trust. (LA. TRUST CODE § 1971). The provisions of the will of Mrs. Gredler violated this rule. By providing that upon termination of each trust, if the named beneficiary thereof is not living, the trust property is to be delivered to the child or children of the deceased beneficiary, and in the absence of a living child or children to successively named alternate beneficiaries, Section 1972 is also violated. At the same time the will created a prohibited substitution and as a consequence the entire will is null. LA. CIVIL CODE art. 1520; *Succession of Simms*, 250 La. 177, 195 So.2d 114 (1967); *Succession of Johnson*, 223 La. 1058, 67 So.2d 591 (1953).

It has been suggested in brief by amicus curiae that the decision in this case should rest upon Sections 1971 and 1972 alone, reference to substitutions being unnecessary. In addition to the fact that the primary issue posed by plaintiff's pleadings and briefs is whether the will contains a substitution, the suggestion overlooks the very significant and all important difference which results from a finding that a prohibited substitution is contained in the will and a finding that Sections 1971 and 1972 are violated by certain provisions of the will. In the case of the prohibited substitution the entire will is rendered null, whereas if we should confine our decision to a holding that Sections 1971 and 1972 were violated, the invalid provisions of the will could be excised without declaring the entire will null. LA. TRUST CODE § 2251.

Our finding that a substitution exists in Mrs. Gredler's will amounts to a rejection of all other contentions or makes an answer to those contentions unnecessary.

For the reasons assigned, the judgment of the Court of Appeal is affirmed.

*   *   *

NOTES

Today, courts recognize that trusts are not the same as prohibited substitutions and indeed, the Civil Code sanctions some provisions which might otherwise be prohibited substitutions if those provisions are "permitted by the laws relating to trusts." La. C.C. 1520.

Under certain limited circumstances, the interest of a principal beneficiary may not be acquired at the trust's creation. If the right to principal is subject to the condition that the principal beneficiary survive the testator-settlor for a period of time as allowed under La. C.C. art. 1521 (A), the beneficiary's interest may be lost should he not survive for the stipulated time. Further, La. R.S. § 9:1973 allows a substitute principal beneficiary to take the principal if the original principal beneficiary or a substitute principal beneficiary dies during the term of the trust without descendants. If the principal beneficiary is a forced heir, a substitute will be allowed to step into the forced heir's place only if he dies without descendants *and* intestate. La. R.S. § 9:1973 (A). As a special exception to the "in being and ascertainable" rule as applied to beneficiaries, La. R.S. § 9:1978 allows for the trust instrument to provide that a beneficiary who was *not in being* at the time of the trust creation, but who was in being and ascertainable on the date of death of the original beneficiary may be a substitute principal beneficiary if the original dies during the term of the trust. The substitute beneficiary in this case *must* be a descendant of the settlor. La. R.S. § 9:1978.

Nature of the Beneficiary's Interest

As you read the following cases, ask yourself what exactly is the beneficiary's interest in the trust? Is he the owner? If so, of what? How is his ownership interest different from title?

REYNOLDS v. REYNOLDS
388 So. 2d 1135 (La. 1979)
[footnotes omitted]

SUMMERS, Chief Justice.

Minnie Smith, widow of W. H. Sledge, executed her last will and testament on January 8, 1957. Her will created a spendthrift trust in which she bequeathed her farm consisting of 640 acres in Vermilion Parish, together with its improvements, to C. H. Brookshire as trustee. The will stipulated the trustee was to hold the property in trust for her grandchildren who survived her and until her youngest grandchild attained the age of twenty-one. The trustee was directed to hold, process, manage and control the trust estate with full power to alienate and encumber the trust estate.

At her death in 1959, Minnie Smith's will was probated and by a judgment in her succession on January 9, 1962 Brookshire was recognized as trustee under her will and, as legatee and trustee, recognized as "owner" and placed in possession of decedent's interest in the farm in Vermilion Parish. The judgment further decreed that the property be vested in the trustee and to continue until such time as the youngest of decedent's grandchildren shall attain the age of twenty-one years. The trustee was then to deliver the entire estate to the beneficiaries in equal proportions and in full ownership.

Thereafter, while the property was still held in trust, one of the grandchildren Margaret Susan Romero married Glynn W. Reynolds on July 9, 1966. During the existence of the marriage the wife received as distributed trust income the sum of $11,913.85. These funds were deposited in a checking account in the Kaplan State Bank under her exclusive control. At trial the parties stipulated that from this account the wife expended the sum of $9,660.26 on items of clothing for herself and the children and for household expenses. On February 6, 1970 Margaret and Glynn were judicially separated. Upon dissolution of the community a balance of $555.18 remained of this distributed trust income. And on February 6, 1970 when the community was dissolved there existed the sum of $11,434.80 in the account of the trustee, representing undistributed earnings of the trust estate in which Margaret owned an interest.

The wife did not execute and record an affidavit of paraphernality pursuant to Article 2386 of the Civil Code which provides:

> The fruits of the paraphernal property of the wife, wherever the property be located and however administered, whether natural, civil, including interest, dividends and rents, or from the result of labor, fall into the conjugal partnership, if there exists a community of acquets and gains; unless the wife, by written instrument, shall declare that she reserves all of such fruits for her own separate use and benefit and her intention to administer such property separately and alone. The said instrument shall be executed before a Notary Public and two witnesses and duly recorded in the Conveyance Records of the Parish where the community is domiciled.

> If there is no community of gains, each party enjoys, as he chooses, that which comes to his hand; but the fruits and revenues which are existing at the dissolution of the marriage, belong to the owner of the things which produce them.

On July 5, 1971 the trust was terminated and the share of the trust property to which she was entitled was transferred by the trustee to Margaret Susan Romero. On August 21, 1972 the parties were divorced.

An agreement was entered into between the husband and wife on December 6, 1977 in which they settled the bulk of the community property. The only property, the status of which remained in dispute, was the $555.18 distributed to the wife by the trustee and the $11,434.80 in the account of the trustee representing undistributed earnings of the trust estate.

The wife contends that the distributed trust income and her proportionate share of the undistributed trust income constitutes her separate property. She asserts also that she is entitled to restitution of the $9,660.26 expended from those separate funds for the benefit of the community. It is the husband's position that the distributed and undistributed income constitute "fruits" of the paraphernal property of his former wife, which, because she did not execute and record the affidavit of paraphernality required by Article 2386 of the Civil Code, formed part of the community of acquets and gains which existed between them. Therefore, the husband contends that the wife's demand for restitution of the $9,660.26 should be rejected. He should be awarded, he asserts, judgment against his former wife for half of the distributed trust income on deposit at the time of the dissolution of the community, the sum of $277.59; and half of his former wife's proportionate share of the undistributed income amounting to $1,429.25 which he contended is also part of the community which existed between them.

The trial court decided that both the *distributed and undistributed* trust income belonged to the separate estate of the wife. The decision was based upon the theory that the fruits of the trust estate did not belong to the wife's separate estate because she was not the owner of the property which produced them. Instead, the court held, during the existence of the trust the corpus of the trust belonged to the trustee. The decision was based upon Section 1781 of Title 9 of the Revised Statutes to the effect that "(a) trustee is a person to whom title to the trust property is transferred to be administered by him as a fiduciary." (emphasis added).

Although concluding that the distributed income was the separate property of the wife, the trial judge denied her claim for restitution. He was of the opinion that that expenditure was free and voluntary and that money was apparently spent for gifts and contributions without any expectation of anything in return. There was no proof, he held, that those expenditures enhanced the community.

On appeal to the Third Circuit the wife complained that she was improperly denied restitution of the funds she alleged she expended for the community. The husband answered contending that the trial court erroneously denied his claim that the funds at issue were community property.

The Third Circuit reasoned that "on the date of their marriage the wife, as a beneficiary under the trust, was vested with an interest in the corpus of the trust, which interest formed part of her separate estate. Therefore, not having executed and recorded the declaration of paraphernality required by Article 2386, the fruits of her separate estate fell into the community of acquets and gains. These fruits were the distributed income."

The Court of Appeal also decided that the undistributed income as well was "fruits" of her separate property and for the same reason fell into the community. In arriving at this result the Court of Appeal rejected the trial court's holding that the trustee was the owner of the trust corpus during the existence of the community between the parties and therefore the fruits of the property held in trust did not fall into the community. The appellate court was of the opinion that the wife as beneficiary of the trust was the owner of the corpus of the trust, compelling the conclusion that the fruits of that separate property inherited from her grandmother fell into the community because of the wife's failure to execute the affidavit of paraphernality.

It was primarily to settle these issues and reconcile the decision of *United States v. Burglass*, 172 F.2d 960 (5th Cir. 1949) with the decision in *Dunham v. Dunham*, 174 So.2d 898 (La.App.1965) that we granted this writ on the wife's application. 365 So.2d 530 (La.App.).

> A trustee is a person to whom *title* to the trust property is transferred to be administered by him as fiduciary." (emphasis added). La.Rev.Stat. 9:1781.

That the title transferred to the trustee in the case at bar was intended to vest ownership in the trustee is made manifest by the meaning of the word "title". Perhaps the most common use of the word in the law is in the sense of ownership of property. 86 C.J.S., Title p. 907. It is therefore contrary to well accepted principles of statutory construction to disregard the clear meaning and letter of the statute under the pretext of pursuing its spirit. LA.CIVIL CODE art. 13. Words of a law are generally to be understood in their most usual signification. LA.CIVIL CODE art. 14. When ownership is vested in the trustee with full powers as such it cannot be said that the beneficiary of the trust then has rights in the property which entitle her to its fruits unless, as in this case, the trustee willed it so. "The ownership of a thing is vested in him who has the immediate dominion over it, and not in him who has a mere beneficiary right in it." LA.CIVIL CODE art. 489.

Act 180 of 1979 to become effective January 1, 1980, enacts Article 477 of the Civil Code to explicitly embody in its provisions principles which have heretofore been part of our Civil Code by implication. *See* Articles 488 and 491. The new article provides:

15-34

Ownership is the right that confers on a person direct, immediate and exclusive authority over a thing. The owner of a thing may use, enjoy, and dispose of it within the limits and under the conditions established by law." *See also* 3 Planiol Ripert, Traité pratique de droit Civil Français 220 (2d ed. Picard, 1972).

No statute in Louisiana confers upon a trust beneficiary the ownership of the corpus of the trust; the interest of the beneficiary referred to in Sections 1971 and 1972 of Title 9 of the Revised Statutes is an interest in the trust, not in the corpus. Likewise, no Louisiana case (*Succession of Stewart*, 301 So.2d 872 (La.1974) and *St. Charles Land Trust v. St. Amant*, 217 So.2d 385 (La.1969), in particular) confers upon the beneficiary a right of ownership in the corpus of the trust.

There are other factors which persuade us to conclude that the trustee acquired and exercised ownership of the corpus of the trust during the tenure of the trust. The very language of the trust instrument is explicit in this respect. When the testator gave the property to the trustee "to have and to hold" she transferred ownership to the trustee "(t)o hold, possess, manage, (and) control the said trust estate and every part thereof, with full power to lease for a period which may extend beyond the terms of the trust, and to sell, transfer, convey, and dispose of the said property, upon such terms and in such manner and for such prices as the trustee shall deem reasonable and proper." While this ownership remained in the trustee the fruits of the property could not fall into the community between the beneficiary wife and her husband. *Dunham v. Dunham*, 174 So.2d 898 (La.App.1965).

The beneficiary of this trust had no right to administer the trust property; the full authority in that respect was vested in the trustee. As beneficiary she could not sell, mortgage, lease or otherwise alienate or encumber the trust property. She was without even the slightest indicia of ownership so long as the trust endured. She could not demand any action on the part of the trustee, not even the trust income or the monies which the trustee chose to deposit in her bank account. The discretion granted the trustee in this regard was "absolute and not subject to be questioned by any of the beneficiaries of the trust."

Thus the funds transferred to the wife as beneficiary of the trust prior to the dissolution of her marriage were not the fruits of her property. The funds were, instead, "property" which she received from the income of the trust corpus owned by the trustee. If however, these funds, once transferred to the wife's account, had produced revenues in the form of interest or otherwise, that interest would have become "fruit" of her separate property and as such would fall into the community existing between the parties. But there is no evidence that these funds produced interest or other income subject to classification as community property. Therefore the failure of the wife to execute the affidavit of paraphernality had no effect on this property for it had produced no fruits. To the contrary she utilized these funds to purchase gifts for her family and for herself.

For the reasons assigned by the trial judge we are also of the opinion that the wife is not entitled to be reimbursed for the funds she claims she spent for the benefit of the community from the distributed trust revenues.

This same result, although somewhat differently postured factually, pertains to the undistributed trust revenues. Only the trustee had the right to order these revenues paid to the grandchildren beneficiaries and then for the purpose of their maintenance and education in his discretion during the existence of the trust. So long as the trustee retained them, they remained the property of the trust. *Dunham v. Dunham, supra.*

The settlor of the trust plainly did not intend that the beneficiaries of the trust acquire administration or control of the corpus or undistributed revenues of the trust until the trust was terminated. At that time the corpus of the trust and its remaining revenues were to be delivered to her grandchildren, the beneficiaries. Until that time the beneficiaries could not invoke Article 2386 with respect to property and its revenues owned by the trustee.

These reasons result in this Court's approval of *Dunham v. Dunham, supra,* and our decision not to consider *United States v. Burglass,* 172 F.2d 960 (5th Cir. 1939) authoritative in Louisiana State courts.

The other issues resolved by the trial judge are approved.

For the reasons assigned, the judgment of the Court of Appeal is reversed and set aside, and the judgment of the trial court is reinstated and made the judgment of the court.

MARCUS, J., dissents, being of the opinion that the judgment of the court of appeal is correct.

DENNIS, J., dissents and assigns reasons.

BLANCHE, J., dissents, being of the opinion that the judgment of the court of appeal is correct.

DENNIS, Justice, dissenting.

I respectfully dissent.

After reviewing the record and the law in this case, I conclude that the court of appeal was correct in its judgment: both the distributed and undistributed funds from the trust income represent fruits of Mrs. Reynolds' separate property interest in the Minnie Smith Sledge Trust. Since Mrs. Reynolds failed to file an affidavit pursuant to Civil Code article 2386, this income fell into the community of gains.

Title to trust property is vested in the trustee so that he may administer the property as a fiduciary for the benefit of the principal and income beneficiaries. La.R.S. 9:1731, 1781; *St. Charles Land Trust v. St. Amant,* 253 La. 243, 217 So.2d 385 (1969). Under the Louisiana trust law in effect at the time the Sledge trust was created, the same principle existed. *See* former La.R.S. 9:1792(16) and 9:1811. The trustee's position as a title holder differs significantly from that of an ordinary owner of property, because the trustee holds title solely for the benefit of the beneficiaries under the terms of the trust. La.R.S. 9:2082; *see* former La. 9:1962(2); L. Oppenheim, 2 Civil Law Treatise-Trusts § 131. In fact, a trustee does not receive title to trust property as "owner" but rather as a fiduciary with exclusive powers of management and control over the property. *Succession of Stewart,* 301 So.2d 872 (La.1974).

Although the trustee has legal title to the trust corpus in his capacity as trustee, the principal beneficiary also has an interest in the corpus sufficient to constitute a form of ownership. This variety of ownership is peculiar to the law of trusts, a creation of the common law adopted by Louisiana in its Trusts Estates Law and its Trust Code. Such ownership does not mix easily with the Louisiana Civil Code concepts of ownership. Under the Civil Code article 488 ownership is the right by which a thing belongs to someone in particular, to the exclusion of all other persons. The ownership of a thing is vested in him who has the immediate dominion of it and not in him who has only a beneficial interest in the thing. However, the law of trusts recognizes a vesting of a beneficial interest in the principal beneficiary at the creation of a trust and a further vesting of this interest in the heirs of the principal beneficiary at his death. La.R.S.

9:1971, 1972; former 9:1921. In *St. Charles Land Trust* and *Succession of Stewart, supra,* this Court recognized that a principal beneficiary has a property interest in the trust corpus in the nature of a beneficial right to the trust property, and this interest is taxable and heritable. Furthermore, a beneficiary may transfer his interest unless the trust instrument precludes or limits alienation. La.R.S. 9:2001, 2002.

Mrs. Reynolds, as the principal beneficiary of the Sledge trust, had a property interest in the corpus, the rice farm, and this interest constituted her separate property. Civil Code article 2334. The income arising out of farming operations and oil and gas leases on the farm represents fruits of her separate property. La.C.C. art. 2386. As such, under the literal wording of article 2386, these fruits are community property, because Mrs. Reynolds failed to file an affidavit declaring her intention to administer for her separate use and benefit the trust property.

Counsel for the defendant argues in his brief that if the trust income is considered fruits under article 2386, the wife need not have executed the affidavit because the trustee had exclusive administration of the property and thus it would be absurd to require Mrs. Reynolds to execute a declaration that she intended to administer her separate property. While it is correct that article 2386 requires an affidavit declaring a wife's "intention to administer such property separately and alone," I do not consider the article to be concerned with who in fact administers the property. I conclude that the article provides a substantive and exclusive means by which a wife may preserve the fruits of her separate property for her own benefit and that under the article the administration of the property in fact is irrelevant.

Prior to 1944 the Civil Code in article 2386 provided that the fruits of the wife's paraphernal property fell into the community of gains when the property was managed by the husband or by the wife and him "indifferently." If neither was the situation, then the fruits remained the wife's separate estate. There developed cases in which the wife proved that the husband who had administration in fact was merely an "agent" of the wife. *See Miller v. Handy,* 33 La.Ann. 160 (1881); *Paul v. Arnoult,* 164 La. 841, 114 So. 706 (1927). Apparently in response to this line of jurisprudence which was beset with problems of proof in relation to the administration of the wife's separate property, the legislature in 1944 amended Civil Code article 2386. As amended and as it now stands, article 2386 provides that the fruits of the wife's paraphernal property, however administered, fall into the community unless the wife executes a notarial act declaring her intention to administer the property for her separate use. C. Morrow, *Matrimonial Property Law in Louisiana,* 34 Tul.L.Rev. 1, 13 (1960).

The situation of a trust in which the trustee has sole power of administration was not contemplated by the legislature in 1944. However, I conclude that article 2386 admits of no proof on the issue of administration, for to conclude otherwise would be to ignore the plain wording of the first clause of article 2386 which states that the fruits are community regardless of administration.

The court of appeal below determined that without the affidavit the husband is considered to have the administration and enjoyment of the wife's separate property. *Reynolds v. Reynolds,* 365 So.2d 530, 537 (La.App. 3d Cir. 1978); following *Guillot v. Guillot,* 361 So.2d 1271 (La.App. 3d Cir. 1978); *see also* La.C.C. art. 2385. I do not think it necessary to engage this conclusive presumption in order to reach the same result. I would hold that article 2386 is dispositive of the status of the fruits of the wife's separate property, and such fruits fall into the community of gains however administered unless the wife executes the affidavit.

For the foregoing reasons I respectfully dissent from the majority opinion.

ON REHEARING

WATSON, Justice.

This is a dispute between two former spouses over income from a trust. This court originally held that the trustee owned the corpus of the trust; that the wife's beneficial interest did not have the indicia of ownership; therefore, that the income from the trust was not a fruit of the wife's separate property and did not fall into the community; that both the distributed and undistributed trust income was the wife's separate property; and that the wife was not entitled to reimbursement of the funds expended from the distributed trust income because there was no enhancement of the community.

A rehearing was granted to reconsider the status of the trust income and the wife's right to reimbursement.

The beneficiary wife is Margaret Susan Romero Reynolds. The trust was established in the will of her grandmother, Minnie Smith Sledge. A farm was placed in trust for the benefit of Ms. Sledge's grandchildren, present and future. Ownership of the property was transferred to the trustee, who had authority to sell or otherwise dispose of the property as he saw fit. The time and amount of disbursements to the beneficiaries for their support were at his discretion.

The beneficial interest of Ms. Reynolds in the trust is clearly less than full ownership. LSA-C.C. art. 477 and former art. 489. Title to the property vested in the trustee. LSA-R.S. 9:1731. The undistributed income from the trust was under the control and dominion of the trustee. It accrued to the trustee during the term of the trust, as a civil fruit unseparated from the corpus of the trust. LSA-C.C. art. 489 and former art. 499. Ms. Reynolds had no right to this money until the trustee decided to distribute it. The undistributed income did not fall into the community.

Although Margaret Susan Romero Reynolds did not own the corpus of the trust, her paraphernal estate included a beneficial interest, an incorporeal right. LSA-C.C. art. 461 and former art. 460. The distributed revenues from that incorporeal right were civil fruits. LSA- C.C. art. 551 and former art. 545. *See* the definitive discussion by Professor A. N. Yiannopoulos, 2 La.Civ.Law Treat.2d, § 25 and § 26. Once distributed, the wife had full ownership of this income. These fruits of the wife's paraphernal property fell into the community because no instrument was filed to reserve them for the wife. LSA-C.C. art. 2386 and the successor article, LSA-C.C. art. 2339.

Since the wife kept the distributed fruits under her control in a separate checking account, they were not delivered to the community for its use. She has no right to restitution of the income from the trust which she spent during the marriage. The funds were expended prior to the effective date of the new Matrimonial Regimes legislation, January 1, 1980, and the matter is governed by former Civil Code articles, 2388, 2390, and 2391. *Slater v. Culpepper*, 233 La. 1071, 99 So.2d 348 (1957). The test is not enhancement or benefit to the community. Under the prior law, only the husband, who manages the community assets, is required to show an enhancement of the community to obtain restitution of his separate funds. The wife must only show delivery to the community for its use. The wife did not meet that burden here, and her claim must be denied.

Therefore, the original opinion correctly held that: (1) the undistributed trust income of $11,434.80 did not fall into the community; and (2) the wife had no right to reimbursement of the funds she expended. However, the opinion erred in holding that the balance of the distributed

15-38

income was not a civil fruit of the wife's paraphernal property. The $555.18 balance of the distributed trust income is a community asset.

Therefore, the original opinion is amended as to the trust income distributed during the existence of the community, to declare the sum of $555.18 to be a community asset.

DIXON, C. J., dissents in part and concurs in part with reasons.

CALOGERO, J., dissents in part and concurs in part for reasons assigned by DIXON, C.J.

MARCUS, J., concurs in part and dissents in part and assigns reasons.

DENNIS, J., concurs in part and dissents in part for reasons.

BLANCHE, J., dissents, being of the opinion that the judgment of the Court of Appeal is correct.

DIXON, Chief Justice (dissenting in part and concurring in part).

Rehearing was granted in this case in order to clarify the issue which is crucial to our determination of whether the funds disbursed to Mrs. Reynolds in accordance with her grandmother's testamentary trust were separate property or community property: the nature of her interests in the trust.

Our original opinion held that because ownership of the trust corpus was vested in the trustee, income derived from that corpus could not be considered a fruit of the beneficiary's separate property. The dissent concluded, on the other hand, that Mrs. Reynolds' beneficial interest in the trust corpus constituted a property interest sufficient to make the corpus her separate property, so that income produced by the corpus was a fruit of her separate property. An amicus brief submitted in support of the application for rehearing buttresses the dissent's viewpoint by interpreting the trustee's title to trust property as a mere "fiduciary title," similar to the power to manage property for the benefit of others vested in curators, tutors and administrators of successions, and insufficient to deprive the beneficiary of actual ownership of the trust corpus.

These analyses are less than satisfactory because they fail to recognize that the formation of a trust may create two separate and independent beneficial interests, not merely one single interest which produces "fruits." All of the interpretations advanced thus far have assumed that a beneficiary has only one interest, an interest in the corpus, and that the income produced by the corpus is distributed to the beneficiary as the fruit of that interest or of the trust corpus. The sole point of disagreement has been whether that beneficial interest can be characterized as ownership of the trust corpus.

Actually, however, the LOUISIANA TRUST CODE makes it clear that two separate interests are involved: a right to receive some or all of the income produced by the corpus, in accordance with conditions provided by the trust instrument, and a right to receive the corpus itself, as owner, at a future time, also as provided by the terms of the trust. The Trust Code defines these interests by characterizing the holder of one type as an income beneficiary, the holder of the other type as a principal beneficiary. The code also provides that these interests may be held concurrently by a single beneficiary or allocated separately to different beneficiaries. The independent nature of the two interests is most apparent when they are held by different beneficiaries, as is the case under many trust agreements. Bogert and Bogert, LAW OF TRUSTS, Fifth Edition, 405 (1973). Because the interests may be in conflict, especially in this situation, the LOUISIANA TRUST CODE (R.S. 9:2141-2156) and the RESTATEMENT SECOND OF TRUSTS (§§ 232-241) provide specific rules for the allocation by the trustee of receipts and expenses to principal or income, in conformity with his duty to act impartially.

That these interests retain their independent and separate nature even when both are held by one beneficiary is seen most clearly when the law requires or permits the interests to be treated differently. In many jurisdictions, for instance, a beneficiary's interest in the corpus of a trust is treated differently from his interest in income, with regard to creditors' rights to seizure. *See* R.S. 9:2004, 9:2005; Annotation, *Trust Income or Assets as Subject to Claim Against Beneficiary for Alimony, Maintenance, or Child Support*, 91 A.L.R.2d 262 (1963); *Shelley v. Shelley*, 223 Or. 328, 354 P.2d 282 (1960). Similarly, these interests are distinguished under provisions of the federal gift tax, 26 U.S.C. § 2501 et seq., which excludes future interests in property from the definition of taxable gifts, but not present interests which may be diminished by the exercise of a power of another. In *Herrmann's Estate v. Commissioner of Internal Revenue*, 235 F.2d 440, 443 (5th Cir.1956), the United States Fifth Circuit Court of Appeals stated:

> The disposal of property in trust under an agreement deferring distribution of principal may be regarded for Federal gift tax purposes as a two-fold transfer creating one interest in the income and another in the principal. . .

See also Commissioner of Internal Revenue v. Thebaut, 361 F.2d 428 (Fifth Cir.1966); *Commissioner of Internal Revenue v. Herr*, 303 F.2d 780 (Third Cir.1962).

In order adequately to determine the nature of the funds received by Mrs. Reynolds from the trustee, it is therefore necessary that we examine both of the interests conferred upon her by the terms of her grandmother's will. It is significant that the will does not explicitly invest her, as a trust beneficiary, with any rights. Instead, her rights, or interests, exist only as implied correlatives to the duties imposed upon the trustee, to whom title to the trust property was conveyed.

The nature of Mrs. Reynolds' interest in income may be inferred from the following provisions:

> (a) During the duration of the trust hereinabove created, the Trustee shall pay to the beneficiaries, who are my grandchildren, those presently living being Margaret Susan Romero, Alton Romero, Jr. and Ignance Joseph Romero, monthly, or at such periodic intervals as the Trustee may determine best in his discretion, such sums as may be necessary to permit the beneficiaries to properly maintain themselves and care for all of their needs, including those ordinary and usual luxuries which the Trustee, in his discretion, may deem reasonable and proper, and in order to provide for their proper education, and in order to insure the maintenance of their customary and usual standard of living. The amount to be paid to the beneficiaries shall, as far as possible, be paid from the income derived from the property placed in trust, provided, however, that in the event the net income is at any time insufficient, in the opinion of the Trustee, to provide for the support, comfort, maintenance and general welfare of the beneficiaries, then the

Trustee shall pay to or spend, for the benefit of such beneficiary or beneficiaries, such sum from the principal of the property held in trust, as, in the sole discretion of the Trustee, may be necessary or desirable for such purpose, and the discretion given to the Trustee shall be absolute and not subject to be questioned by any of the beneficiaries of the trust. The Trustee shall have full authority to sell and dispose of any and all property, real and personal, by any title whatsoever and for such consideration as he deems proper in his sole discretion.

> (1) The interest of the beneficiary hereunder, either as to income or principal shall not be anticipated or alienated (either voluntarily or involuntarily), nor in any other manner be assigned by the beneficiary, and shall not be subject to execution or seizure or any other legal process or bankruptcy proceedings or interference or control by creditors or others, except as is provided under R.S. 9:1923 and the laws of the State of Louisiana.

Mrs. Reynolds' interest thus consisted of the right to receive such amounts as the trustee determined to be necessary for her proper maintenance, at intervals to be determined by the trustee. These disbursements were to be made by the trustee from funds accruing to the trust as income and, if judged necessary by the trustee, from the trust corpus itself. It is important to note that the income derived from the trust property, or its fruits, was received and entirely controlled by the trustee, subject only to his duty to provide for each beneficiary's support. Mrs. Reynolds, on the other hand, had no right to these funds, only a right to sums necessary for her support. This kind of interest may be viewed as an annuity or an alimentary pension rather than as a usufruct or a right to fruits. Oppenheim, *A New Trust Code for Louisiana*, 23 La.L.Rev. 621, 627 (1963). It is also significant that Mrs. Reynolds had no power to anticipate or alienate this interest except to the extent that it was made available to her creditors by statute.

Mrs. Reynolds' interest in the corpus of the trust is derived from the following rights conveyed to the trustee and duties imposed upon him:

> 1. I give and bequeath my farm property comprising six hundred and forty (640) acres, more or less, situated in the Parish of Vermilion, Louisiana, together with all improvements, equipment, farm implements and movable property situated thereon, unto C. H. Brookshire, a resident of the Parish of Vermilion, Louisiana, Trustee, to have and to hold all of the said property in trust for my grandchildren, the children of Willie Mamye Sledge Romero, who may be living at the time of my death, the beneficiaries, said beneficiaries to share and participate in the said property pursuant to this trust in equal proportions. The said trust shall continue until such time as the youngest of the said grandchildren living at the time of my death shall attain the age of twenty-one (21) years, at which time the trustee shall render a final accounting to the said grandchildren and deliver the entire trust estate unto the said beneficiaries in equal proportions and in full ownership. In the event any one of the grandchildren living at the time of my death dies before attaining the age of twenty-one (21) years, the interest in the said property inherited by the said child pursuant to this will, shall be inherited by the heirs and legal representatives of the said grandchild, and this trust shall

terminate at such time as the youngest living grandchild reaches the age of twenty-one (21) years.

2. The Trustee shall hold and manage the property herein conveyed, together with such other property as may be acquired during the existence of this trust, all of which said property will hereafter be referred to as the "Trust Estate" upon the terms and conditions and for the uses and purposes and with the duties and powers vested in him, which said powers are specifically referred to as follows:

(a) To hold, possess, manage, control the said trust estate and every part thereof, with full power to lease for a period which may extend beyond the terms of the trust, and to sell, transfer, convey and dispose of the said property, upon such terms and in such manner and for such prices as the Trustee shall deem reasonable and proper.

(b) The Trustee, in addition to and not in limitation of the statutory authority, is hereby given full power and authority to invest and reinvest all or any part of the said trust estate which may come into his hands in such a manner and in such securities or other property, personal or real, and upon such terms and for such length of time, as the Trustee shall deem reasonable and proper, it being intended hereby to give unto the Trustee full and complete authority to hold, possess, manage, control, sell, convey, encumber, lease, invest and reinvest, the whole and every part of the said trust estate according to his sole judgment and discretion.

It is apparent that the only interest bequeathed to Mrs. Reynolds was the right to receive a portion of the trust corpus at some time in the future. It should be noted that not only was the time at which this right could be exercised made indefinite by the terms of the will (dependent upon the possible birth of additional grandchildren before the testator's death and the possible deaths of the grandchildren before the age of twenty-one) but that the amount of the property to be received was also indefinite. That is, the percentage of the total corpus she could ultimately receive was dependent upon the number of grandchildren living at the time of the testator's death, while the nature and value of the corpus itself were dependent upon the manner in which the trustee exercised his powers to manage, lease, sell and encumber the trust property, to invest and reinvest, and to make payments of principal to the various beneficiaries in accordance with their needs. It is conceivable that there might be no trust property upon which Mrs. Reynolds could exercise her right to delivery at the termination of the trust. It is because of the indeterminate nature of the interest in principal (and also in income, under the terms of this trust agreement) that "eventual interests in trusts usually are not readily assignable." Pascal, *Of Trusts, Human Dignity, Legal Science, and Taxes*, 23 La.L.Rev. 639, 649-650 (1963). It should be noted that under this agreement Mrs. Reynolds had no right to assign, alienate or anticipate her interest in the corpus, as she also had no right to do with her interest in income.

It is unreasonable to characterize Mrs. Reynolds' right to receive an indefinite amount of property at an undetermined future date as an interest which constitutes ownership of property under the principles of this state's property law, as embodied in C.C. 477, 1979 revision, and former C.C. 489. Article 489 provided:

The ownership of a thing is vested in him who has the immediate dominion of it, and not in him who has a mere beneficiary right in it.

Article 477 now provides:

Ownership is the right that confers on a person direct, immediate, and exclusive authority over a thing. The owner of a thing may use, enjoy, and dispose of it within the limits and under the conditions established by law.

It is obvious that Mrs. Reynolds' future and indefinite right is devoid of the indispensable elements of ownership: immediacy, dominion, and authority. It is argued that these elements are also absent in situations of curatorship, tutorship and the administration of successions, but that interdicts, minors and heirs are nonetheless "owners" of their property. In common law jurisdictions, the relationship established by a trust is distinguished from the relationship involved in situations like curatorship through the concept of title: a curator has possession and powers of disposition, but the title to the property remains in the ward, so that the curator may be likened to the ward's court appointed agent. Bogert and Bogert, LAW OF TRUSTS, 37 (1973); RESTATEMENT SECOND OF TRUSTS, 22-23 (1959). The concept of title also forms an integral part of Louisiana trust law. R.S. 9:1811 of the Trust Estates Act stated that a trust was created when legal title was transferred to a trustee; R.S. 9:1731 now provides that a trust is the relationship resulting from the transfer of title to property to a trustee. One writer has indicated that "Louisiana has gone the full way and adopted the common law trust with no local trappings, no subterfuges, or restrictions that cut the ground from under the trustee as holder of the legal title." Wisdom, *A Trust Code in the Civil Law*, 13 Tul.L.Rev. 70, 83 (1938). The answer is not found in analogy; it is found in the Louisiana concept of ownership.

The rights granted to the trustee by the settlor constitute ownership under our law. Under prior article 490 the trustee's ownership would be characterized as an imperfect ownership, because it was to terminate on a condition (the youngest beneficiary's attainment of the age of twenty-one). The 1979 revision abandoned the distinction between perfect and imperfect ownership. Instead, article 478 now provides that "(t)he right of ownership may be subject to a resolutory condition," and the Comment to that article states that the new provision does not change the law. Regarding imperfect ownership, prior article 492 provided:

Imperfect ownership only gives the right of enjoying and disposing of property, when it can be done without injuring the rights of others; that is, of those who may have real or other rights to exercise upon the same property.

Present Article 477, *supra*, similarly authorizes the restriction of an owner's rights "within the limits and under the conditions established by law"--here the duties imposed upon a trustee by the LOUISIANA TRUST CODE.

We therefore should find that Mrs. Reynolds' interest in the corpus of the trust did not constitute an "ownership" of separate property which could produce either income payments or undistributed income as "fruits." Instead, the trust agreement conferred upon her, as a donation mortis causa, an independent interest in receiving those funds; the income is hers by virtue of the donation mortis causa, and therefore her separate property. Her husband's claim to these funds was properly denied.

In his dissent to our original opinion in this case, Justice Dennis concluded that the trust dividends distributed to the income beneficiary were fruits of her paraphernal property, because she had an "interest in the corpus sufficient to constitute a form of ownership." Recognizing that such "ownership" is incompatible with the concepts of ownership in the LOUISIANA CIVIL CODE, the dissent finds an intent to create a different kind of ownership in the trust code.

Principles established in the Civil Code are designed to function in an entire system of laws in this state. When the principle is clear, concise, broad and universally understood and accepted, it should not be deemed changed or abandoned by inference. If subsequent legislation clearly indicates that our former concept of ownership is hereafter changed or modified in some respect, the change should be accepted. Further, if the legislature establishes a relationship between persons and property that cannot function, or will be hampered and impeded in its operation by adhering to the established concept of ownership, then, and only then, would we be justified in finding an inference that the legislature intended to change the law of ownership.

Here there is neither statutory provision changing the meaning of ownership, nor conceptual hiatus requiring us to find an inference of intent to change it, in order to permit the legislative scheme to function. The trust is permitted by the Constitution (Article 12, § 5) and the statutory scheme is as complete as it need be. Absolutely no impediment to the function of the trust will occur by the application of the accepted Civil Code concept of ownership. The unknown factor in this case would be the effect of holding that the income beneficiary and the trustee both have ownership interests in the property constituting the corpus.

The statutes do not say whether the trustee or the beneficiary is the owner of the corpus. The trustee has title. R.S. 9:1731 contains no inference that the beneficiary is the owner:

> A trust, as the term is used in this Code, is the relationship resulting from the transfer of title to property to a person to be administered by him as a fiduciary for the benefit of another.

Section 1731 fixes the relationship of the trustee as a fiduciary to administer the corpus for the benefit of another. The will gave him all the powers of ownership. Ownership powers in the trustee are not essential for the validity or utility of a trust, but this trustee is the owner. R.S. 9:1781 repeats:

> A trustee is a person to whom title to the trust property is transferred to be administered by him as a fiduciary.

Section 1781 does not say or imply that the trustee does not or cannot be the owner, subject to a resolutory condition, or otherwise.

The *Succession of Stewart*, 301 So.2d 872 (La. 1974), mentioned in the dissent referred to, did not decide, because it was not an issue, whether the income beneficiaries had an ownership interest in the corpus. The trust instrument was different. It did not, by its terms, convey the powers of ownership to the trustees, and, to the contrary, required that the trustees "retain the real estate intact" insofar as possible. 301 So.2d at 874. The trustees were to administer the property for the benefit of the settlor's nieces and nephews. The settlor intended that the bulk of his estate be distributed before the termination of the trust, the object of which was thus stated: "... my intention in creating it is to provide for my family, subject to the discretion of said Trustees, as I am confident the Trustees can increase said estate." 301 So.2d at

875. If the trust was valid, as the majority held, then "(T)he trust was created with the immediate vesting of interest in the beneficiaries at the moment of the settlor's death." 301 So.2d at 883. Of course the beneficiaries had an interest, which arose at the time of the death of the settlor; but they did not own, and we did not hold that they owned, the corpus or the property composing the corpus.

It is clear, therefore, that the undistributed trust income, not yet the property of the beneficiary, did not fall in the community.

The distributed income, in my view, was not the "fruit" of the beneficiary's separate property, but was the materialization of the gift of a future interest in property. It was, itself, a gift from the settlor, and not the produce of the beneficiary's separate property.

With regard to Mrs. Reynolds' claim for reimbursement of the amounts of this separate property she expended for herself, the children, and household expenses, the trial court found that these were gifts freely made without any expectation of return, and that she had failed to prove a resulting enhancement of the community. The conditions under which a wife may be reimbursed for the expenditure of her separate property have often been described in this state's jurisprudence. In *Slater v. Culpepper*, on rehearing, 233 La. 1071, 1102- 1103, 99 So.2d 348, 360 (1957), this court stated:

> … Under our law the wife, unlike the husband, has the absolute right to restitution for her paraphernal effects and their fruits, *either delivered* to her husband *or delivered* for use to the community, save in instances governed by Article 2389 of the Civil Code, which is not applicable here. In the case of the husband, it is incumbent upon him to establish that his separate property has been employed to enhance the community at its dissolution. *Munchow v. Munchow*, 136 La. 753, 67 So. 819; *Vicknair v. Terracina*, 168 La. 417, 122 So. 276; *Succession of Provost*, 190 La. 30, 181 So. 802 and *Abunza v. Olivier*, 230 La. 445, 88 So.2d 815....

(Emphasis added).

In all subsequent cases, the courts have agreed that enhancement of the community must be shown only by a husband who seeks restitution of his separate property, because of his exclusive authority to manage the community, and not by a wife. The trial court erred, therefore, in imposing this requirement upon Mrs. Reynolds. The courts have disagreed, however, as to whether or not a wife must show delivery of her separate funds to her husband or (delivery) for use to the community, a requirement specified in *Slater*. A showing of delivery was required in *Foster v. Foster*, 330 So.2d 638 (La.App. 4th Cir. 1976); *Guilott v. Guilott*, 326 So.2d 551 (La.App. 3rd Cir. 1976), stating explicitly that delivery is a prerequisite to restitution; *Emerson v. Emerson*, 322 So.2d 347 (La.App. 2d Cir. 1975); *Troxler v. Cubbage*, 235 So.2d 170 (La.App. 4th Cir. 1970); *Succession of Smith*, 232 So.2d 569 (La.App. 4th Cir. 1970), also requiring that a wife abandon control of her separate property; and *Broyles v. Broyles*, 215 So.2d 526 (La.App. 1st Cir. 1968). On the other hand, in two cases, *Succession of Slavich*, 232 So.2d 846 (La.App. 4th Cir. 1970) and *Gouaux v. Gouaux*, 211 So.2d 97 (La.App. 1st Cir. 1968), the appellate courts found that a wife must show either that the funds were delivered to her husband or that they were expended for the benefit of the community. These two cases make a showing of benefit to the community an alternative to a showing of delivery, perhaps on the basis of a misreading of the language of *Slater*. Whatever its genesis, this interpretation should be abandoned as inconsistent with the principles of community property law and in conflict with the line of cases following *Slater*.

The expenditures voluntarily made by Mrs. Reynolds from her separate checking account for family and household expenses do not contain the element of delivery to the community, for its use, which is a prerequisite to a wife's claim for reimbursement of her separate property. I agree with the conclusion of the majority that this claim should be denied.

I therefore concur in the conclusion of the majority that the undistributed trust income did not fall into the community, and dissent from the holding that the distributed trust income was a community asset.

MARCUS, Justice (concurring in part and dissenting in part).

In my view, both the distributed and undistributed revenues from the trust fall into the community in absence of the wife complying with LA. CIV. CODE art. 2386. I agree with the judgment of the court of appeal. Accordingly, I respectfully concur in part and dissent in part.

DENNIS, Justice, concurring in part and dissenting in part.

For the reasons I assigned in my dissent on original hearing, I believe both the distributed and undistributed revenues from the trust fell into the community in the absence of a reservation pursuant to Article 2386. Accordingly, I respectfully concur in part and dissent in part.

ST. CHARLES LAND TRUST, ACHILLE GUIBET v. ST. AMANT
217 So. 2d 385 (La. 1968)
(15 Loy. L. Rev. 382 (1968,69); 43 Tul. L. Rev. 915 (1969))
[footnotes omitted]

SANDERS, Justice.

The trustees of the St. Charles Land Trust, holders of mineral interests in St. Charles Parish, applied to the Court for instructions pursuant to LSA- R.S. 9:2233. They seek authority to transfer a deceased beneficiary's interest in the trust under the order of a court of California, where the beneficiary was domiciled, without ancillary succession proceedings or the payment of inheritance taxes in Louisiana.

The district court instructed the trustees that the decedent's beneficial interest was incorporeal, immovable property, subject to Louisiana inheritance taxes and transferable only pursuant to ancillary succession proceedings in this state.

The Court of Appeal reversed and instructed the trustees that the decedent's beneficial interest was incorporeal, movable property, exempt from Louisiana inheritance taxes and transferable upon the order of the California Court. Judge Chasez dissented from these instructions. La.App., 206 So.2d 128.

On application of the Inheritance Tax Collector, we granted certiorari to review the judgment of the Court of Appeal. 251 La. 1058, 208 So.2d 327. In this Court, the State of Louisiana through the Attorney General appeared as Amicus curiae to support the position of the Inheritance Tax Collector.

The St. Charles Land Company, a Maryland corporation, owned mineral leases and servitudes on lands located in St. Charles Parish, Louisiana. An amendment to its Articles of Incorporation adopted by its shareholders provided that in the event of liquidation the directors could transfer the corporate property to a trust for the benefit of the shareholders. Acting under this authority, the liquidator transferred the mineral leases and servitudes to the trustees of the St. Charles Land Trust for the benefit of the former shareholders. The transfer in trust was made by an authentic act entitled "Transfer and Trust Instrument" dated April 2, 1962. The instrument designated the shareholders as beneficiaries for both principal and income in the same proportion as their former stock ownership.

Under the terms of the trust instrument, the sole purpose of the trust is to conserve the trust estate and distribute the income to the beneficiaries after the payment of expenses. The trustees are prohibited from engaging in the development of mineral property or other business activities. They are also prohibited from acquiring new properties. The trustees can sell or dispose of trust property with the approval of 75% in interest of the beneficiaries. They can cancel an existing lease and grant a new lease with the approval of 66 2/3% in interest of the beneficiaries. The term of the trust is fixed as "the maximum period permitted by present or future laws of Louisiana" subject to the right of the trustees to terminate the trust at an earlier time.

The instrument further provides:

The interests of the beneficiaries are classified as movable property, notwithstanding that the trust estate consists in whole or in part of immovable property; provided that the trustees shall have the right, but shall not be bound, to require, as a condition precedent to recognition of the validity or effectiveness of any transfer of the interest of a beneficiary, compliance in respect thereof with the formalities attendant on like transfers of immovable property.

Mrs. Ella E. Watkins, a beneficiary, died in California where she was domiciled on October 28, 1965. She left no forced heirs. In due course, a California court granted an order as to the Louisiana trust interest.

Louisiana levies a tax on inheritances. As to the scope of the tax, LSA- R.S. 47:2404 provides:

Except to the extent of the exemptions provided in R.S. 47:2402 the tax shall be imposed with respect to all property of every nature and kind included or embraced in any inheritance legacy or donation or gift made in contemplation of death, including all immovable property and all tangible movable property physically in the State of Louisiana, whether owned or inherited by, or bequeathed, given, or donated to a resident or nonresident, and whether inherited, bequeathed, given or donated under the laws of this state or of any other state or country. The tax shall also be imposed with respect to all movable property, tangible or intangible, owned by residents of the State of Louisiana, wherever situated; provided that the tax shall not be imposed upon any transfer of intangible movable property owned by a person not domiciled in this state at the time of his death.

Under the above provision, the inheritance of a non-resident's immovable property, tangible or intangible, situated in this state is taxable. The inheritance of intangible movable property owned by a nonresident is immune from the tax. The trustees assert that the beneficiary's interest in the trust, like that of a corporate stockholder, is an incorporeal movable, both under the terms of the trust instrument and Louisiana law. Hence, they reason, the interest is free from Louisiana inheritance taxes.

The opponents first assert the instrument relied on created no trust, but rather a partnership or agency. Alternatively, they contend the beneficiary's interest in the trust is an immovable under Louisiana law. Hence, they submit, the Louisiana inheritance tax law applies.

A trust is a relationship resulting from the transfer of title to property to a person to be administered by him as a fiduciary for the benefit of another. Former LSA-R.S. 9:1792(16); 1 Bogert, TRUSTS AND TRUSTEES, § 1, p. 1 (1951); 1 SCOTT ON TRUSTS, § 2.3, pp. 37--38 (1967); Oppenheim, *A New Trust Code for Louisiana*, 39 Tul.L.Rev. 187, 197--198.

At the time of the execution of the instrument in contest, the applicable statute was the Trust Estates Act of 1938, as amended (former LSA-R.S. 9:1791-- 2212). In LSA-R.S. 9:1811, the statute provided:

> A trust shall be created when a person in compliance with the provisions of this Chapter transfers the legal title to property to a trustee in trust for the benefit of himself or a third person.

No particular language is required to create a trust. Former LSA-R.S. 9:1815. It suffices if the instrument as a whole reflects the intent to establish a trust relationship. When it can reasonably do so, the Court will construe the trust instrument to sustain the validity of the trust. *See Lelong v. Succession of Lelong*, La.App., 164 So.2d 671 and 90 C.J.S. Trusts § 161h, p. 24.

Our examination of the instrument in contest here discloses that it transfers legal title of the property to the trustees, defines their duties and powers as fiduciaries, designates the shareholders as income and principal beneficiaries, and fixes the term of the trust as the maximum period permitted by law. The trustees appeared in the instrument to accept the trust.

The trust opponents contend the limitations on the trustees' powers thwarted the creation of a trust and converted the relationship to a partnership or agency. They refer to the limitations on the sale of trust property, cancellation of leases, and other business transactions. The sale of trust property and cancellation of leases, as we have noted, requires the approval of a designated percentage of the beneficiaries. Although the power limitations are substantial, we find nothing in the Trust Estates Law of 1938 to prohibit them. Specifically, LSA-R.S. 9:1941 provided that the duties and powers of the trustees could be fixed by the terms of the trust. The settlor, under LSA-R.S. 9:1841, could stipulate any conditions not prohibited by law.

The relationship has all the features of a trust and lacks certain essential features of both partnership and agency. A partnership is created by contract among the partners. LSA-C.C. Art. 2801. The beneficiaries were not parties to the trust instrument. Clearly, therefore, there can be no contract of partnership among them.

The contention that the relationship is a mandate, or agency, rather than a trust, is equally weak. Without attempting to enumerate all the distinctions between a trust and agency, we note that the trust instrument vests title to the property in the trustees in a relationship that is neither terminable at the will of the beneficiaries not upon the death of any of them. In an agency, on the other hand, title to the property normally remains in the principal and the mandatary has the power to bind the principal by contract. LSA-C.C. Art. 3021. An agency terminates upon the death or at the will of the principal. LSA-C.C. Art. 3027.

We conclude, as did the Court of Appeal, that the instrument creates a trust.

The classification of the beneficiary's interest in the trust in terms of recognized property concepts raises difficult questions. This classification has been the subject of much controversy in the common law. See 1A Bogert, TRUSTS AND TRUSTEES, § 183, pp. 174--179 (1951) and 2 SCOTT ON TRUSTS, § 130, pp. 1050--1062 (1967). To remove uncertainty, a number of states have enacted statutory provisions classifying the interest. See 1A Bogert, *supra*, § 184, pp. 179-- 182.

Louisiana trust laws contain no provision classifying the principal beneficiary's interest as movable or immovable. It is quite clear, however, that the trustees hold title to the property for the benefit of the income and principal beneficiaries. Furthermore, upon the death of a principal beneficiary, his interest vests in his heirs, subject to the trust. Former LSA-R.S. 9:1921. Hence, it may be said that the principal beneficiary's interest is an incorporeal right enforceable at law. But fixing title in the trustees does not resolve the question of whether the beneficiary's incorporeal right is movable or immovable. Since the trust laws are silent, a resolution of the question depends upon basic property concepts of the LOUISIANA CIVIL CODE and related statutes.

Article 470 of the LOUISIANA CIVIL CODE provides:

> Incorporeal things, consisting only in a right, are not of themselves strictly susceptible of the quality of movables or immovables; nevertheless they are placed in one or the other of these classes, according to the object to which they apply and the rules hereinafter established.

Under Louisiana law, the mineral leases and servitudes held by the trustees are immovable property. LSA-C.C. Art. 471; LSA-R.S. 9:1105; *Succession of Simms*, 250 La. 177, 195 So.2d 114. Since the trust is upon such property, the object to which the beneficial interest applies is immovable property. Hence, under the above code article, the right itself is immovable, unless the right is excepted from this classification by other code articles. LSA-C.C. Art. 470; Yiannopoulos, CIVIL LAW OF PROPERTY, §§ 60, 61, pp. 178--182 (1966); 2 Aubry & Rau, PROPERTY, § 165(29), p. 35 (English translation by the Louisiana State Law Institute).

LOUISIANA CIVIL CODE Article 471 provides that a usufruct of immovable things, a servitude on an immovable estate, and an action for the recovery of an immovable estate or an entire succession "are considered as immovable from the object to which they apply." The language of this article and its history leave no doubt that the immovable rights mentioned are illustrative and not exclusive. *See* Yiannopoulos, *supra*, § 61, pp. 180--181 and the authorities cited. For this reason, other rights may be classified as immovable when they apply to an object that is immovable.

The trustees contend, however, that the trust interest is classified as a movable by Article 474 of the LOUISIANA CIVIL CODE. That article declares movable "shares or interests in banks or companies of commerce, or industry or other speculations, although such companies be possessed of immovables."

The provision creates a special exception to the general rule of Article 470. The exception originated in Article 529 of the Code Napoleon. The codal language refers to shares or interests in business organizations, such as corporations or partnerships. Yiannopoulos, *supra*, § 66, pp. 194--195; 2 Aubry & Rau, *supra*, § 165(31), pp. 39--40; 1 Planiol, TRAITÉ ÉLEMENTAIRE

DE DROIT CIVIL No. 2260, pp. 335--336 (English Translation by the Louisiana State Law Institute). The trust is a unique institution of Anglo-American origin. It has a wide variety of uses in making dispositions of property, especially in estate planning. It may contain any conditions not forbidden by law or public policy. See, generally, Rubin and Rubin, LOUISIANA TRUST HANDBOOK (1968) and 1 Scott, *supra*, § 1, pp. 3--5. Based upon any type of property susceptible of private ownership, a trust can be created either by testament or Inter vivos transfer. Although we respect analogy in codal application, we are of the opinion the beneficial interest in the trust does not fall within the exception of Article 474.

Finally, the trustees rely on the clause of the trust instrument itself which classifies the beneficiary's interest as movable. It is true, as contended by the trustees, that such clauses are recognized and enforced in some common law jurisdictions. In essence, these clauses are applications of the doctrine of equitable conversion. *See* 1A Bogert, *supra*, § 185, pp. 182--184. We find no sound basis in Louisiana law for enforcing such a clause against the State of Louisiana. To give it effect here, moreover, would permit the parties to a trust instrument to upset long-established, legislative property classifications to the prejudice of state tax agencies, though the State is a stranger to the instrument.

We hold that the principal beneficiary's interest in the trust is an incorporeal immovable for Louisiana inheritance tax purposes.

Recognizing its interest in protecting the rights of local creditors and in assuring proper administration of its tax laws, Louisiana has for many years required ancillary probate proceedings when a non-resident dies leaving property situated in the state. *See* LSA-C.C.P. Book VI, Title IV: Ancillary Probate Procedure (Introduction); *Bender v. Bailey*, 130 La. 341, 57 So. 998; *Succession of De Roffignac*, 21 La.Ann. 364; and *Heirs of Henderson v. Rost*, 15 La.Ann. 405.

Since we have determined that the decedent owns immovable property situated in Louisiana, it follows that the codal provisions relating to ancillary probate procedure apply. LSA-C.C.P. Arts. 2811, 3401.

For the reasons assigned, the judgment of the Court of Appeal is reversed, and the judgment of the district court is reinstated and made the judgment of this Court.

*   *   *

Rights of Beneficiaries to Income and Principal

The income beneficiary is entitled to the income produced by the trust property. The income "may be given for the life of a beneficiary or for a term, certain, or uncertain, not exceeding the life of a beneficiary." La. R.S. § 9:1961. The settlor may designate that an income beneficiary is entitled to a portion or all of the income. Any income not allocated to an income beneficiary will be allocated to principal. La. R.S. § 9:1961(B). The settlor may stipulate when income is to be paid or may leave the payment schedule up to the trustee. La. R.S. 9:1963. If no provision is made for the frequency of payment, income should be distributed "at least every six months." La. R.S. § 9:1962. In addition, except as otherwise provided with respect to the *legitime* in trust, the settlor may grant a trustee who is not a beneficiary of the trust discretion to allocate income in different amounts among the income beneficiaries or to allocate some or all of the income to principal. La. R.S. § 9: 1961(c)). This particular provision granting the trustee sole discretion to distribute income was enacted in 1997 by Acts 1997, No. 767, §1 for a discussion of this addition to Louisiana's trust law and its tax implication, *see* Kenneth A. Weiss, *Drafting Louisiana's Income "Spray" Trusts: After the 1997 Trust Code Amendments*, 72 Tul. L. Rev. 1329 (1998).

As a general rule, the principal beneficiary's right to the trust corpus is acquired at the trust's creation. The settlor determines the portion due to each principal beneficiary. A trustee may not be given discretion to determine how principal should be allocated among principal beneficiaries. However, the trustee may be given discretion to "invade" trust principal for the benefit of *income* beneficiaries. If the settlor grants the trustee this authority, the instrument must provide that the trustee's exercise of this power is made for the support, maintenance, education or medical expenses of the income beneficiary or, pursuant to another objective standard, for any purpose. La. R.S. § 9:2068.

Under certain limited circumstances, the interest of a principal beneficiary may not be acquired at the trust's creation. If the right to principal is subject to the condition that the principal beneficiary survive the testator-settlor for a period of time as allowed under La. C.C. art. 1521(A), the beneficiary's interest may be lost should he not survive for the stipulated time. Further, La. R.S. § 9:1973 allows a substitute principal beneficiary to take the principal if the original principal beneficiary or a substitute principal beneficiary dies during the term of the trust without descendants. If the principal beneficiary is a forced heir, a substitute will be allowed to step into the forced heir's place only if he dies without descendants *and* intestate. La. R.S. § 9:1973(A). As a special exception to the "in being and ascertainable" rule as applied to beneficiaries, La. R.S. § 9:1978 allows for the trust instrument to provide that a beneficiary who was *not in being* at the time of the trust creation, but who was in being and ascertainable on the date of death of the original beneficiary may be a substitute principal beneficiary if the original dies during the term of the trust. The substitute beneficiary in this case *must* be a descendant of the settlor. La. R.S. § 9:1978.

NORTON FAMILY TRUST FIRST NATIONAL BANK OF COMMERCE v. SCHMITT
655 So. 2d 398 (La. App. 5th Cir. 1995)
[footnotes omitted]

CANNELLA, Judge.

First National Bank of Commerce, Trustee of the Norton Family Trust, filed a Petition for Instructions and ordered the trust beneficiaries to show cause why the principal invasion requested by the income beneficiary should not be paid by the trustee. The trial court, by judgment dated October 14, 1994, ordered the trustee to invade the corpus of the trust in the amount of $6,500 per month in favor of Eileen Jackson Norton commencing from June 21, 1994. We affirm.

On November 23, 1988, after twenty years of marriage, Dr. John M. Norton and Eileen Jackson Norton created "The Norton Family Trust." They funded the trust with $120,000 cash, all of which was community property. Accordingly, they were the Settlors of the trust. They designated themselves as the Trustees and the income beneficiaries. Upon the death of either, his or her interest vested in the surviving income beneficiary spouse. Dr. Norton's seven children from a previous marriage were designated as the principal beneficiaries. The trust also contained a paragraph permitting the Trustees, in their discretion, to invade principal in certain specified circumstances, for the benefit of the income beneficiaries, even though such a distribution might impair the interests of the principal beneficiaries. The term of the trust was through the life of the last income beneficiary.

On September 27, 1990, Dr. Norton died. Under the terms of the trust, Eileen Jackson Norton thereupon became the sole income beneficiary of the trust for the remainder of her life. In addition, as legatee under the Last Will and Testament of Dr. Norton, Eileen Jackson Norton inherited a lifetime usufruct over his half of the community and over all of his separate property. Also, in accord with Dr. Norton's will, his son Daniel Terrance Norton became the Executor of his estate. And under the terms of the trust, Daniel Terrance Norton became the Successor Co-Trustee of the trust along with Eileen Jackson Norton. From the moment that Daniel Terrance Norton became Co-Trustee, all income disbursements to Eileen Jackson Norton ceased.

Within the year following her husband's death, Eileen Jackson Norton was diagnosed with inoperable terminal lung cancer. She began to incur substantial medical and other related bills due to her condition. Daniel Terrance Norton still refused to authorize any income distributions from the trust to Eileen Jackson Norton. No income distributions were made for more than three years. On February 11, 1994, Eileen Jackson Norton filed suit against Daniel Terrance Norton, seeking: (1) that all accumulated income be distributed to her immediately; (2) that income be distributed to her in the future on a current basis; (3) that principal be distributed to her as necessary to provide for her medical care throughout the term of her illness to the extent that the income was insufficient to do so.

* * *

A hearing was held on the matter on March 14, 1994. The trial court permitted post trial memoranda. Thereafter, on April 1, 1994 the trial court rendered judgment ordering Daniel Terrance Norton to distribute all accumulated income in the trust to Eileen Norton, removing Daniel Terrance Norton and Eileen Jackson Norton as Co-Trustees, appointing First National Bank of Commerce as sole trustee, ordering First National Bank of Commerce to distribute net income to Eileen Jackson Norton on a regular monthly basis and to distribute to Eileen Jackson Norton "so much of the principal of the Trust during the term of her interest as income beneficiary as is appropriate in accordance with the terms and conditions of the Trust." Neither party sought a new trial from this ruling nor did they appeal. Accordingly, the judgment of April 1, 1994 is final.

On June 21, 1994, Eileen Jackson Norton, through counsel, submitted a request to the Trustee, First National Bank of Commerce, that it distribute to her $6,000 per month from the principal of the Trust because her medical expenses exceeded her income, less other expenses, by that amount. Eileen Jackson Norton's attorney provided a copy of the request to Daniel Terrance Norton, who advised the Trustee that he thought such a disbursement was inappropriate and that he opposed such a distribution. He considered such a distribution by the Trustee to be a breach of the Trustee's fiduciary duty to the principal beneficiaries.

Faced with this conflict, on July 13, 1994, the Trustee filed a Petition for Instructions in district court. The petition named Eileen Jackson Norton and all of the principal beneficiaries as parties to the suit. Eileen Jackson Norton and one principal beneficiary, Jean Adair Norton, filed an answer to the petition. She asserted that Eileen Jackson Norton was not due distributions of principal under the trust provisions while she possessed over $100,000 in cash type assets.

Eileen Jackson Norton asserted that the intent of the trust, as established by herself and her husband, was to allow themselves access to their funds during their lifetime when necessary for medical expenses, among other things. She requested that the Trustee be ordered to distribute from principal the amount of $6,900 per month for medical expenses that exceeded her income less her expenses. She also requested invasion of principal and disbursement to her of approximately $30,000 representing past medical expenses that had exceeded her income over the previous three years. Also, she requested invasion of principal for attorney's fees and costs expended in the previous lawsuit to obtain disbursement of income and removal of Daniel Terrance Norton as Co-Trustee.

On August 22, 1994, a hearing was held in the matter. The trial court requested post-trial memoranda. Thereafter, on October 14, 1994, the trial court rendered judgment ordering the Trustee to "invade the corpus of the trust in the amount of Six Thousand Five Hundred and no/100 ($6,500.00) Dollars per month and pay such amount over to the income beneficiary, Eileen Jackson Norton, payments retroactive to June 21, 1994, in addition to any other payments she receives under said trust." The judgment was silent as to all other claims.

On November 3, 1994, Jean Adair Norton filed a Motion and Order for Suspensive Appeal, which was signed on November 8, 1994. She argues that the trial court erred in ordering the Trustee to invade the principal of the trust in favor of the income beneficiary, Eileen Jackson Norton.

Eileen Jackson Norton died on December 25, 1994. On January 20, 1995, the Testamentary Executrix of Eileen Jackson Norton's Succession, her daughter by a previous marriage, Kathleen Chopp Schmitt, was substituted for Eileen Jackson Norton and filed an answer to the appeal. She argues in favor of the judgment insofar as it ordered the invasion of principal to pay her mother's medical expenses, but argues that the trial court erred in not addressing Eileen Jackson Norton's other claims and in not making the appropriate awards.

The substance of this appeal involves an interpretation of the trust instrument signed by Eileen Jackson Norton and her husband, as Settlors, Trustees and Beneficiaries. There are several provisions of that trust instrument which are pertinent to the questions before the court.

VII. POWERS OF THE TRUSTEE

7.1 The Trustees shall have all of the powers that are conferred upon trustees under applicable law. If a question should arise as to whether Trustees have a particular power, this Trust Instrument shall be liberally construed as granting such power. Should future changes in the law expand the powers of trustees, the Trustees shall have those expanded powers.

VII.(sic) SPECIAL POWERS OF THE TRUSTEE ACCUMULATION AND DISTRIBUTION OF INCOME

8.1 Accumulation and Distribution of Income. Pursuant to LSA-R.S. 9:1721 et seq., trustees shall have the discretion to determine the time or frequency of distribution of income. Unless so distributed, trust income shall be allocated to principal.

8.2 Invasion. Should Trustees determine that an income beneficiary needs resources for health, education, maintenance or support in addition to his interest in the trust and in addition to and taking into account funds available from other sources known to the Trustees, Trustees are authorized to make one or more distribution to that income beneficiary from accumulated income or principal, even though such distribution thereby impairs the interest of another beneficiary. In making such distributions, the Trustees shall be guided by immediate needs of the income beneficiary, without regard to the future needs of that beneficiary or of the future needs of other beneficiaries.

8.3 Facility of Payment. If a beneficiary is under legal disability or, if in the Trustees' opinion, is incapable of properly managing his affairs due to illness, age or other cause, the Trustees may use or apply trust income or principal for his benefit.

These provisions must be considered in the context that the trust was created. First, the Settlors of the trust were husband and wife for twenty years, who took a large portion of their liquid assets, which were community property, and placed them in the trust that they thereby created. They named themselves as Trustees and income beneficiaries. Under the provisions of the trust, they gave themselves, as Trustees, the discretion to distribute income and, under certain circumstances, principal. They gave themselves all powers conferred by existing law and any powers expanded by future changes in the law. It was expressly provided that if any question arose concerning the powers of the Trustees, the trust instrument was to be "liberally construed as granting such power."

Upon review, it is clear, as stated in the original petition filed by Eileen Jackson Norton, and not contradicted, that the settlors intended that these funds, income and principal, would be available to them during their lifetime to care for their needs regarding "health, education, maintenance or support." They placed their liquid assets in trust, to avoid probate, and granted themselves the broadest powers to distribute the funds in their discretion.

Within this context, we must consider whether the trial court judgment, permitting the invasion of the trust principal in favor of the income beneficiary/settlor/Trustee for her medical expenses in excess of her overall income less her personal expenses, without first dissipating her personal estate, was erroneous. We find no error in this judgment.

As stated above, the trust instrument itself places in the Trustees the broadest powers and discretion. While First National Bank of Commerce is presently the Trustee, the intent of the Trust Instrument must be considered as originally created, with the Settlors naming themselves as Trustees and granting to themselves the discretion to distribute income and principal.

The principal beneficiary, Jean Adair Norton, argues that under the provisions of the trust, Eileen Jackson Norton should first deplete her personal assets before the trust principal can be invaded for her medical needs. We find no such requirement either expressed or implied in the trust instrument. To the contrary, the trust provides very few particulars or specifics, leaving distributions largely to the discretion of the trustee. While the trust instrument does provide that the Trustee should "tak[e] into account funds available from other sources known to the Trustee" in determining that an income beneficiary needs additional resources which may be taken from principal, it does not state that the income beneficiary must first deplete all of his/her assets before such a distribution from principal can be made. The trust instrument, in expressly addressing disbursements of principal to income beneficiaries, authorizes such distributions to income beneficiaries even though it impairs the rights of the principal beneficiaries.

The trial judge heard the testimony and observed the witnesses. We note that the trial judge seemed particularly concerned with Daniel Terrance Norton's possible bad faith in keeping Dr. Norton's Succession under administration for an unduly long time and simultaneously denying Eileen Jackson Norton any income distributions from the trust, all while she was seeking medical care for her diagnosed, inoperable, terminal cancer. In rendering judgment, the trial court found that denying Eileen Jackson Norton access to her own money in her time of medical need was not what was intended by the trust. Under the circumstances of this case, we find no error in the trial court ruling, ordering the trustee to invade principal of $6,500 per month to cover Eileen Jackson Norton's medical and related expenses that exceeded her income less her other expenses without requiring her to first dissipate her personal estate. And, we do not find any error in the trial court's determination that the judgment should be retroactive to June 21, 1994, the date of demand.

* * *

Accordingly, for the reasons stated above, we affirm the trial court judgment, ordering the Trustee to distribute $6,500 per month in principal from the trust to Eileen Jackson Norton, retroactive to June 21, 1994. Costs of this appeal are to be paid by appellant.

AFFIRMED.

Legitime in Trust: La. R.S. 9:1841-47

One of the areas of concern when Louisiana was contemplating the adoption of the trust concept was how to accommodate forced heirship to trusts. It was ultimately decided that "the *legitime* or any portion thereof" could be placed in trust. However, certain conditions had to be met. Initially, it was decided that the net income accruing to the forced heir would have to be paid to him no less than once a year. (This was later amended to allow the trustee to take into account all other income and support to be received by the forced heir during the year, and distribute funds for the health, maintenance, support, and education of the forced heir, thus not requiring a yearly payment of net income). Also, the forced heir's interest would be subject to no charges or conditions except those relating to spendthrift restrictions, the allowance of an income interest or usufruct in favor of the settlor's surviving spouse, and provisions relating to class trusts. Except as relating to the income interest or usufruct in favor of the settlor's surviving spouse, the trust, as it affected the *legitime*, could not exceed the life of the forced heir. Finally, the principal had to be delivered to the forced heir, his legatees or assignees free of trust at the termination of the portion of the trust that affected the *legitime*. La. R.S. § 9:1841.

SUCCESSION OF BURGESS
359 So. 2d 1006 (La. App. 4th Cir. 1978)

SCHOTT, Judge

* * *

THE *LEGITIME*

The following provisions of the will and codicil are here pertinent:

Will 5 "(a) I direct that all my just debts, funeral expenses and costs and expenses of the administration of my estate, be paid out of my one-half interest in the community property belonging to my husband and myself, and that one-half of the indebtedness of the community estate to my separate estate be paid out of my one-half interest in said community property.

(b) I direct that my executor pay all death, succession, transfer, estate and inheritance taxes, Federal and State, levied or assessed upon or with respect to any property which is included in my estate for purposes of computing any such taxes, out of my residuary estate, to-wit: If my husband survives me, out of the one-half of my separate property not devised to my husband, and if the same is insufficient, out of my one-half interest in the community property, or, if my husband predeceases me, out of my residuary estate, I further direct that neither my executor nor my estate shall have right or claim to reimbursement for such taxes from any person who is a beneficiary, transferee, legatee or devisee of any property upon or with respect to which any such tax is assessed or levied, it being my intention that said persons receive their legacies in full."

Codicil 2 "I desire to, and herewith do, add the following provision to subparagraph (b) of the Fifth Article of my last will and testament dated May 9, 1966, to-wit: The *legitime* of my son, GEORGE EVANS BURGESS, JR., which I am bequeathing to him, but in trust only, as more fully set forth in the Eleventh Article of my last will and testament of May 9, 1966, shall be charged with the proportionate amount of Federal Estate Taxes applicable to the property constituting said *legitime*, and with the State of Louisiana Inheritance Taxes assessed and levied upon his said inheritance (*legitime*), and such amounts of Federal Estate Taxes and State of Louisiana Inheritance Taxes shall be deducted from his *legitime*."

Will 6 "I confirm the usufruct which my husband, George Evans Burgess enjoys under the law, to my interest in the community property which we own at the time of my death, which usufruct shall cease at the time of his death or remarriage."

Will 7 "I give and bequeath to my husband, George Evans Burgess, one-half (1/2) of my separate estate." Codicil 4 "I give and bequeath to the following named persons the following special legacies in the amounts hereinafter set forth, all subject to the legal usufruct of my husband, George Evans Burgess, which is hereby confirmed and which legacies shall be payable upon my said husband's death or remarriage without interest, to-wit:

To my niece, Mrs. Gene Kenny Rodgers, Thirty thousand dollars ($30,000.00); to my nephew, James Preston Kenny, Jr., Thirty thousand dollars ($30,000.00); to my brother, Jonte Victor Leland, Thirty thousand dollars ($30,000.00); to my daughter-in-law, Mrs. Lenore Williamson Burgess, Ten thousand dollars ($10,000.00).

I relieve and release my said husband from the necessity of furnishing security or bond or separate inventory of the property subject to the usufruct herein confirmed and granted in his favor. In the event any of the legatees herein named should predecease me, the bequest made to such predeceased legatee shall be come null and void and shall be considered as not having been made."

Will 11 "To provide for the *legitime* to which my son, George Evans Burgess, Jr., is entitled and to which I herewith restrict his interest in my estate, I make the following provision, to-wit:"

Codicil 6 (Amending will 11) "I desire to, and do herewith, amend the provision of paragraph (a) of the Eleventh Article of my last will and testament of May 9, 1966, to read as follows: 'I give and bequeath to The Whitney National Bank of New Orleans, Louisiana, a Louisiana corporation, and William A. West, as Trustees, to hold in trust as set forth below, one-third of my net estate as hereinafter defined for the benefit of my husband, George Evans Burgess, as income beneficiary, hereby recognizing and confirming his usufruct thereon, and for the benefit of my son, George Evans Burgess, Jr., as principal beneficiary.'"

Will 11(b) "I appoint the Whitney National Bank of New Orleans, Louisiana, as trustee, and grant unto said trustee all powers which are conferred upon a corporate trustee by the Louisiana Trust Code, including power to manage, hold and deal with real estate and other property, to sell and lease such real estate or other property, to borrow money and to pledge or hypothecate assets of this trust, if necessary, and make mineral leases on such terms and conditions as said trustee sees fit, and said trustee shall have and is specifically herein given the right to execute any and all contracts or leases, either for the surface rights or for the purpose of exploring, seeking, searching for, developing, producing and removing any oil, gas or other minerals including sulphur, from all or any part or portions of the lands, or with respect to the mineral rights, constituting part of the trust estate on such terms and conditions, and for such considerations as said trustee may deem advisable, including the right to make leases and mineral leases extending beyond the term of this trust when necessary, provided, however, that I specifically instruct the trustee not to sell any stock of St. Charles Air Line Lands, Inc. or Ranger Land Company, or any lands which form part of that trust, except if so instructed in writing by the investment advisors; all cash shall be invested and reinvested.

(c) My son, George Evans Burgess, Jr., shall be the beneficiary of the principal of this trust.

(d) The trustee shall pay the net income of this trust in monthly installments to my husband, George Evans Burgess, usufructuary of the property of this trust, until his death or remarriage.

(e) Upon the death or remarriage of my said husband, the trustee shall pay the net income of this trust in monthly installments to my son, George Evans Burgess, Jr.

(f) This trust shall terminate at the death of my son, George Evans Burgess, Jr.

(g) The value of my net estate is to be computed as follows for the purpose of determining the *legitime* of my son, George Evans Burgess, Jr.:

> My entire gross estate consists of a one-half interest in and to all the property belonging to the community existing between myself and my husband, George Evans Burgess, at the time of my passing, and my entire separate estate. All my just debts, funeral expenses and costs, and expenses of the administration of my estate, and all death, succession, transfer, estate and inheritance taxes, Federal and State, shall be deducted from my said gross estate. The balance remaining thereafter shall constitute my net estate.

(h) In the event my trustee shall require the services of an attorney at law, the selection of such attorney shall be made by the investment advisors of this trust.

(i) The purpose and intent of establishing the herein trust, is to give my son, George Evans Burgess, Jr., the *legitime* to which he is entitled under the laws of the State of Louisiana and in accordance with the provision of the Louisiana Trust Code, and particularly these provisions of the Trust Code authorizing the placing of the *legitime* in trust, and any provision of this instrument that is incompatible with such provisions of the Louisiana Trust Code, shall be reformed to comply therewith."

Appellant contends that these provisions are illegal because they 1) mandate a method of computing his *legitime* which is inconsistent with the law; 2) burden his forced portion of decedent's separate property with an income interest in favor of his father; 3) load charges on his *legitime* in violation of the Trust Code, LSA-R.S. 9:1721, et seq.; and 4) necessarily result in a deprivation of his *legitime*.

On the first contention, C.C. Art. 1493 provides that decedent's donations *inter vivos* or *mortis causa* cannot exceed two-thirds of her property since appellant is her only child. Art. 1502 provides:

Any disposal of property, whether inter vivos or mortis causa, exceeding the quantum of which a person may legally dispose to the prejudice of the forced heir, is not null, but only reducible to that quantum.

Art. 1505, which provides:

To determine the reduction to which the donations, either inter vivos or mortis causa are liable, an aggregate is formed of all the property belonging to the donor or testator at the time of his decease; to that is fictitiously added the property disposed of by donation inter vivos, according to its value at the time of the donor's decease, in the state in which it was at the period of the donation.

The sums due by the estate are deducted from this aggregate amount, and the disposable quantum is calculated on the balance, taking into consideration the number of heirs and their qualities of ascendant or descendant, so as to regulate their legitimate portion by the rules above established.

Appellant is correct in that decedent cannot direct the manner in which his *legitime* is to be computed inconsistent with the law. Her definition of "net estate" in W 11(g) on which appellant's *legitime* is to be computed is not enforceable as written because it ignores the fictitious addition of donations prescribed by Art. 1505. Furthermore, her directions in W 5(b) that all legacies other than appellant's be delivered tax free could result in an impingement on the *legitime*.

Apparently the executors agreed with appellant on this point because in their rule against appellant for summary judgment they prayed that these provisions be interpreted to the effect that appellant's *legitime* in trust be computed according to law.

Appellant is not satisfied with that relief, contending that he is entitled to have the entire will annulled. As we have already indicated, we do not subscribe to that position.

It was decedent's intention to place the *legitime* in trust as authorized by § 1841 of the Trust Code. If the amount placed in trust for him under her method of computation is insufficient his remedy of reduction is available to him regardless of the terms of W 5(b) and W 11(g).

Appellant's next contention is against the will's provision which would burden his forced portion of decedent's separate property with the usufruct in favor of his father. As can be seen from the quoted provisions of her will and codicil, decedent placed one-third of all of her property, both separate and community, in trust and designated her husband as the lifetime income beneficiary of the trust.

Section 1844 of the Trust Code equates usufruct and income interest. C.C. Art. 916 confers on a surviving spouse the usufruct over the decedent's share of community property and the testatrix may confirm this usufruct in her will *Succession of Waldron*, 323 So.2d 434 (La.1975). But the law does not permit separate property making up the *legitime* to be burdened with the usufruct and to that extent the usufruct is excessive.

Here again, the executors agreed in their rule against appellant to consider the usufruct or income interest in favor of the surviving spouse as limited to the community property, and with this limitation appellant is granted the relief to which he is entitled. This solution is sanctioned by § 2251 of the Trust Code.

Appellant's third complaint stems from the will's provision for appointment of investment advisors for the trustees which will be discussed in detail hereafter. A reference to these advisors is made in W 11(b) quoted above. Appellant contends that these provisions will necessarily violate the Trust Code's § 1841(2) which provides that the forced heir's interest is subject to no charges, but appellant has no present basis for his complaint. If the trustees attempt to charge his interest in violation of the Code he may avail himself of the provision of § 2088.

Appellant's fourth contention with respect to the impingement on his *legitime* has considerable merit and is one of the two most difficult problems presented by this case. His argument can be summarized as follows: The major portion of decedent's estate consists of thousands of acres of swamp lands. The liquid assets of the estate will be and in large measure have already been used for the payment of taxes said to be $782,000, expenses of administration and legacies. Thus, what is left to be placed in trust is for the most part a one- third interest in decedent's undivided interest in the swamp lands which do not provide any income. Under the terms of W 11(b) these lands may not be sold absent instructions from the investment advisors. The trust is not to terminate until appellant's death so that the *legitime* conferred on appellant will never have any value during his lifetime.

We must recall at this point that this case is before us on an appeal from a summary judgment. In the affidavit appellant attached to his summary judgment some of the facts discussed above are alluded to, but he has yet to try his case. Since we are not concerned with the dismissal of his motion for summary judgment we will consider his argument with respect to the summary judgment declaring this will valid. In other words, if we assume that appellant can prove what he alleges, does that necessarily require the nullification of the will or at least of the *legitime* trust?

An answer to the last question requires us first to answer the threshold question posited by appellant. Assuming that what goes into the trust has a theoretical market value which is sufficient to satisfy the *legitime* but will produce little income for the lifetime of appellant, does this meet the requirements of our law? Art. 4, § 16 of the Constitution of 1921, provides:

> The Legislature may authorize the creation of express trusts for any purpose, including but not limited to private trusts, trusts for the benefit of employees, trusts for educational, charitable, or religious purposes, and mixed trusts for any combination of purposes. Substitutions not in trust are and remain prohibited; but trusts may contain substitutions to the extent authorized by the Legislature. *No law shall be passed abolishing forced heirship; but the legitime may be placed in trust to the extent authorized by the Legislature.* Children lawfully adopted shall become forced heirs to the same extent as if born to the adopter and shall retain their rights as heirs of their blood relatives, but their blood relatives shall have their rights of inheritance from these children terminated.

(Emphasis supplied).

In the implementation of this provision the legislature adopted §§ 1841-1847 of the Trust Code. The following sections are pertinent:

> § 1841. General rule
> "The *legitime* or any portion thereof may be placed in trust provided:
>> (1) The net income accruing to the forced heir therefrom is payable to him not less than once each year; and
>> (2) The forced heir's interest is subject to no charges or conditions except as provided in R.S. 9:1843 and 9:1844; and
>> (3) The term of the trust, as it affects the *legitime*, does not exceed the life of the forced heir; and

(4) The principal shall be delivered to the forced heir or his heirs, legatees, or assignees free of trust, upon the termination of the portion of the trust that affects the *legitime*.

§ 1845. *Legitime* satisfied by income interest

An unconditional income interest in trust, without an interest in principal, payable not less than annually for a term or for the life of a beneficiary satisfies the *legitime* to the same extent as would a usufruct of the same property for the same term.

§ 1846. *Legitime* satisfied by principal interest

An interest in the principal of the trust, without an interest in income, satisfies the *legitime* to the same extent as would the naked ownership of the same property.

On the surface decedent's will and codicil seem to comply with these provisions of the Code in that they speak of income from the trust which would go to appellant except for the usufruct in favor of his father and the term of the trust does not exceed his lifetime. Section 1843 permits restraints on the alienation of the *legitime* in trust. But if appellant can prove his case and there is no income the terms of the will establishing the trust become meaningless.

From the wording of § 1841 it is clear that the legislature contemplated income from the trust in authorizing the placing of the *legitime* in trust. If there is sufficient income from the trust this will satisfy the *legitime* and the forced heir need not be given a principal interest under § 1845. Only § 1846 provides that the *legitime* may be satisfied without an income interest, but that is only where the usufruct on community property has been conferred on the surviving spouse pursuant to C.C. Art. 916. From this analysis we have concluded that appellant's *legitime* will not be satisfied if the income generated from the corpus is insufficient. The next question is then, does this mean the trust is invalid?

The last question is answered by § 1842 which provides:

A provision of a trust instrument that is incompatible with the provisions of this Sub-part shall be reformed to comply herewith.

The intent of the testatrix was to provide appellant with no more than his *legitime*, place it in trust for the duration of his life, pay the income from the trust property to her surviving spouse until his death and then commence income payments to appellant. If the provision in her will preventing sale of the land or other property in trust prevents appellant from getting his *legitime* in the form of an income interest which she intended the trust provision may be reformed in accordance with § 1842, so as to permit a sale of the land and/or other property with corresponding conversion to assets which do produce sufficient income.

That issue is beyond the scope of the summary judgment inquiry before us and can be litigated on the merits. Thus, appellant's rights are reserved to show that the income from the trust property is insufficient to satisfy his *legitime* as required by § 1845 and to require that the trustees take whatever action is necessary including sale of the property in trust in order to generate sufficient income to satisfy the *legitime*. The amount of income necessary for this purpose would be the present value of future income appellant can expect based on his present life expectancy with these computations made without regard to the surviving spouse's taking all income from the trust (originating from community property only) until his death or remarriage. In the event that a sufficient amount of income cannot be generated from the trust property in order to satisfy appellant's *legitime* with an income interest the principal may be invaded by the trustees in order to accomplish this purpose.

AMENDED AND AFFIRMED

REMANDED

NOTE

By Act No. 967, § 1 of 1999, La. R.S. § 9:1841 (1) was amended to provide that:

The trustee after taking into account all of the other income and support to be received by the forced heir during the year shall distribute to the forced heir, or to the legal guardian of the forced heir, funds from the net income in trust sufficient for the health, maintenance, support, and education of the forced heir.

This amendment was intended to afford the parents of disabled forced heirs the opportunity of placing the child's *legitime* in trust without jeopardizing the child's right to receive governmental aid. The trust income would merely "supplement" the benefits afforded by the state.

Where does the excess income go? Can it be diverted to someone other than the forced heir? What if the forced heir is not disabled but has other resources to provide for his health, maintenance, support, and education?

Duties of the Trustee

It is the trustee's duty to "administer the trust solely in the interest of the beneficiary." La. R.S.§ 9:2082. Failure to do so is a breach of trust. La. R.S. § 9:2081. The Trust Code has specific provisions delineating the boundaries for the trustee with regard to dealing on his own account, La. R.S.§ 9:2083, loans to himself, La. R.S. § 9:9:2084, sales to the trustee, La. R.S. 9:2085, and purchases from the trustee. La. R.S. 9: 2086.

La. R.S. § 9:2090 provides that the "trustee shall administer the trust as a prudent person would administrate it." In so doing, the trustee shall exercise "reasonable care and skill." A trustee who has "special skills or expertise" or has held out as having them, has a duty to use those special skills or expertise.

To ensure that an individual acting as trustee faithfully performs his duty, the Trust Code requires that he furnish security. La. R.S. § 9:2171. The trust instrument may relieve the trustee of the necessity of providing security. La. R.S. § 9:2171. A corporate trustee need not provide security unless required by the trust instrument. La. R.S. § 9:2171. Upon application of an interested party, a proper court, however, may require security be furnished "even if the trustee is not otherwise required to furnish security. La. R.S. § 9:2172.

A trust instrument may relieve a trustee of his liability. La. R.S. § 9:2206(A). Such a provision in a trust instrument may be necessary so as to entice a trustee to take on the responsibility of managing the trust. However, in no case may the trust instrument relieve the trustee of his duty of loyalty to the beneficiaries or for acts of bad faith in performing his duties. La. R.S. § 9:2206(B). The trustee's duty of loyalty encompasses the trustee's duty to act in the beneficiary's best interest. Further, if the trustee obtained the provision relieving him from liability by breaching his fiduciary relationship with the settlor, the provision is ineffective. La. R.S. § 9:2206(C). For example, if the settlor's attorney, named as trustee, extracted the provision granting him relief from liability by exercising undue influence upon the settlor, the provision should be found ineffective.

In addition, a beneficiary can relieve a trustee from liability. La. R.S. § 9:2207. However, the trustee may in no cases be relieved of responsibility for "improperly advancing money or conveying property to a beneficiary of a spendthrift trust." La. R.S. § 9:2207. Nor may the beneficiary prospectively relieve the trustee of his duty of loyalty or for acts committed in bad faith. La. R.S. § 9:2207.

IN RE SUCCESSION OF DUNHAM
408 So. 2d 888 (La. 1981)

CALOGERO, Justice

*   *   *

REMOVAL OF MRS. DUNHAM AND BILLY ALEXANDER AS TRUSTEES

Ted F. Dunham, Sr., created eight testamentary trusts. He provided that Katherine, Billy Alexander and Fidelity National Bank of Baton Rouge would be the co-trustees of these trusts. Fidelity declined acceptance of the trusts and Louisiana National Bank of Baton Rouge was appointed as replacement co-trustee. All the beneficiaries of the trusts have joined in the petition to have Katherine and Billy Alexander removed as trustees.

The trial court granted their request in part and ordered Katherine and Billy Alexander removed as trustees for the two trusts of which the sons, Ted, Jr., and Richard, were the beneficiaries. The Court of Appeal affirmed that ruling but amended it to provide that Katherine and Billy Alexander should also be removed as trustees to the six grandchildren's trusts also. We affirm that ruling.

As stated by the trial court there are only two cases in Louisiana dealing with the removal of trustees. *Succession of Supple*, 274 So.2d 790 (La.App. 4th Cir. 1973) and *Holladay v. Fidelity National Bank*, 312 So.2d 883 (La.App. 1st Cir. 1975). Both of these cases generally provided that mere animosity between the trustees and beneficiaries was insufficient ground for removal of the trustee.

However, while mere animosity is not sufficient ground for removal of the trustee, the statutory provisions relative to the responsibilities of a trustee are very rigid and hold the trustee to an even higher fiduciary responsibility to his beneficiary than that owed by a succession representative to heirs. The very word "trustee" implies the strongest obligation on the part of the trustee to be chaste in all dealings with the beneficiary.

Several provisions in the Trust Code indicate the high standard to which a trustee is held. R.S. 9:2082 provides that "a trustee shall administer the trust solely in the interest of the beneficiary." R.S. 9:2090 provides that "a trustee in administering a trust shall exercise such skill and care as a man of ordinary prudence would exercise in dealing with his own property." R.S. 9:2085 prohibits the trustee from buying or selling trust property directly or indirectly from or to himself, his relative, his employer, employee, partner or other business associate. R.S. 9:2091 provides that "a trustee is under a duty to a beneficiary to take reasonable steps to take, keep control of, and preserve the trust property." These provisions of the Trust Code evidence the intention by the Legislature to place the very highest possible fiduciary responsibility on the trustee towards the beneficiaries.

Under R.S. 9:1789, "(a) trustee may be removed in accordance with the provisions of the trust instrument or by the proper court for sufficient cause shown." As held by the Court of Appeal, sufficient cause was shown here to require the removal of Katherine and Billy Alexander as trustees of all eight of the trusts.

As succinctly stated by the Court of Appeal:

It is shown that Mrs. Dunham and Mr. Alexander conveniently delayed their acceptances of the trusts for the two sons until such time as the stock redemption had taken place. The sale took place February 27, 1978, and the pleadings and briefs show that Mrs. Dunham and Mr. Alexander did not accept the trusts until shortly after the sale had taken place. It was their duty either to have recused themselves as trustees as it is obvious that they intended to accept the trusts as soon as the redemption had taken place, or to have accepted the trusts and actively opposed the sale in their capacities as trustees. They did neither. Rather than opposing the sale or recusing themselves, as would appear to have been the more proper course, they did nothing, thereby permitting the succession and the trusts to sustain a substantial injury. This was a breach of their fiduciary duties as trustees, having been both a breach of the duty to act prudently in selling investments (LSA-R.S. 9:2127), and their duty to administer the trust solely in the interest of the beneficiaries (LSA-R.S. 9:2082), as the sale benefited Mrs. Dunham as shareholder and strengthened Mr. Alexander's position as corporate president. Also, as trustees it was their duty to have caused the principal trust property, stock in Anderson-Dunham, to be productive of the income. Income from the stock to the trusts would necessarily have had to have been in the form of dividends distributed by Anderson-Dunham. Trustees are under a duty to take reasonable steps to obtain possession of legacies. Comment (c) under LSA-R.S. 9:2091. It was the trustees' duty to have exerted pressure by threatening to demand delivery of the legacy, viz, corporate stock in trust, thereby influencing the corporation to distribute dividends, or to demand delivery of the stock from Mrs. Dunham in her capacity as executrix, so that the trustees could vote the stock in such a manner that the corporation would declare dividends. They did neither. Thus, they again breached their fiduciary duty. We, therefore, hold that the trial court was correct in removing Mrs. Dunham and Mr. Alexander as trustees of the trusts for the two children. Likewise, we find that they should have been removed as trustees of the trusts for the six grandchildren. The same injury that occurred to the children also occurred to the grandchildren. The grandchildren also suffered from Mrs. Dunham's and Mr. Alexander's failure as trustees to oppose the sale of the stock as the stock redemption, or to recuse themselves. The grandchildren also suffered from the failure of the corporation to declare dividends. It is, therefore, apparent that Mrs. Dunham and Mr. Alexander should be removed as trustees of the grandchildren's trusts as well.

Types of Trusts

Spendthrift Trusts

The spendthrift trust is one that prevents the beneficiary from alienating his interest in the trust voluntarily, for example, by selling this interest, or involuntarily, by having a lien placed upon it. La. R.S. § 9:2002. The spendthrift provision, when contained in a trust, provides the settlor with a further means of protecting his beneficiary since a declaration in the trust instrument that the interest is subject to a "spendthrift trust" is "sufficient to restrain alienation by a beneficiary of the interest to the maximum extent permitted." La. R.S. § 9:2007.

La. R.S. § 9:2004 prohibits a settlor from forming a trust, naming himself as beneficiary, and then "spendthrifting" his interest in the trust so as to evade his creditors. Also, La. R.S. § 9:2004 would prevent the beneficiary of a trust from adding his property to a spendthrift trust created by another so as to evade the beneficiary's creditors. Additionally, certain creditors may seize property within a trust notwithstanding a spendthrift provision. Those creditors include those due alimony or maintenance payments from the beneficiary, and those who are owed payment for necessary service, either to the beneficiary or to one whom the beneficiary is obligated to support.

READ v. UNITED STATES
169 F.3d 243 (5th Cir. 1999)
[Footnotes selectively omitted]

Settlor was survived by his wife, Nathalie Owings Read, and their four children, all majors, one of whom is Stephen, and another of whom-- Michael O. Read--succeeded his mother as co-Trustee and in that capacity is an appellant herein. In his validly executed and duly probated testament Settlor created the Trust, designating his wife and their four children as beneficiaries, and appointing his wife and Henry J. Read as co-Trustees. With the exception of certain automobiles, stock in Subchapter S corporations, and policies of insurance on the widow's life, Settlor's entire estate was put in trust.

Settlor's testamentary plan, as embodied in the Trust, reflects his manifest determination to minimize the amounts and postpone the payment of federal estate taxes, and to control Stephen's *legitime* and his rights to deal with and enjoy it.[1]

---

[1] Although significant only by way of background and understanding of the Settlor's motivation and the scheme of his testament, Stephen's profligacy is more than amply demonstrated in the record on appeal and in the appellate briefs, removing any doubt as to the Settlor's determination to leave Stephen no more than the absolute minimum share as dictated by the Constitution and Civil Code of Louisiana at the times of the confection of the will and

Several testamentary provisions confirm Settlor's intention to leave Stephen only his bare *legitime* and to subject that legacy to the maximum restraints, restrictions, and burdens that the law would permit. In the particular legacy of the insurance policies on Nathalie's life, for example, Settlor left Stephen only an undivided 13% interest (rounded up from his 12.5% share of the forced portion of Settlor's estate) but left the remaining 87% equally to Stephen's three siblings, 29% each. In like manner, Stephen was bequeathed only his one-eighth *legitime* share of the residue of Settlor's estate, and even that was left in trust for Stephen's lifetime (the maximum allowed term), burdened by Nathalie's life income interest, and as a spendthrift trust, i.e. subject to the maximum restraints on alienation, both voluntary and involuntary, that the Trust Code allows. In contrast, Stephen's siblings were designated as the equal beneficiaries of the remaining seven- eighths interest in the Trust, likewise subject to their mother's income interest for life; but--unlike Stephen's--their interests are to be delivered to them, free of trust, at their mother's death.

In addition to specifying that "[t]his Trust shall continue as to the interest of Stephen ... for his lifetime," the Settlor continued with this directive on the distribution of trust assets to Stephen:

> *Distributions to Stephen....* After the termination of my wife's income interest, the remaining Trustee shall pay, or apply the net income of the trust attributable to Stephen's *legitime* to or for his benefit *at least annually* or at such more frequent intervals as the Trustee deems fit. Income not attributable to his *legitime* may be distributed or accumulated in such amounts and at such times as the Trustee determines in the Trustee's sole discretion. *After the termination of my wife's income interest*, the Trustee may invade and distribute to or apply for the benefit of Stephen such portion or portions of his share of the accumulated income, if any, principal or both, *at such time and in such amounts as the Trustee deems necessary, advisable or proper*. After the termination of my wife's income interest, the Trustee may terminate the trust or may distribute any part of the property held in trust if the Trustee considers such action to be in the best interest of Stephen, considering his demonstrated ability to handle money wisely, his judgment, prudence and discretion, and any other factors the Trustee may consider relevant. A partial termination of Stephen's interest in the trust shall not affect his right to receive distributions of income from the trust attributable to his share of the principal remaining in trust.

[Emphasis added.]

Consistent with Settlor's approach to the minimization of Stephen's legacy, the Trust specifies that if Settlor is predeceased by Nathalie, seven-eighths of his estate would pass to Stephen's three siblings free of trust, but Stephen would receive only "his *legitime*, to be held in trust for his lifetime."

In sum, the clearly demonstrated intent of Settlor as to Stephen was to comply with Louisiana's law of forced heirship but, in essence, to restrict Stephen's access to that mandatory

---

Settlor's death, and to deny him enjoyment and control over that forced legacy to the fullest extent and for the longest time permitted by law.

legacy for the rest of his life. The only exceptions permitted by the trust instrument--distributions of income more frequently than once a year and invasion and distribution of principal prior to Stephen's death--were conditioned on the exercise of discretion by the Trustees.

*   *   *

After her divorce from Stephen, Patricia obtained two Florida judgments against him which subsequently were made executory by the Louisiana court.

*   *   *

Given the nature of the case at bar, implicating as it does the efforts of Patricia, as an alimony judgment creditor, and the government, as the holder of a tax lien, to force the involuntary alienation of, indeed seize, Stephen's interests in the Trust, a thorough review of the structure of the Trust Code and the framework that it provides for analyzing the issues presented by this appeal is imperative. Judicial review of issues of Louisiana trust law, like such review of all issues of Civil Law, begins not with an examination of jurisprudence but with the plain wording of the Trust Code, read as a whole and interpreted according to its own rules of construction. Section 1724 provides:

> Construction of Code
> The provisions of this Code shall be accorded a liberal construction in favor of freedom of disposition. Whenever this Code is silent, resort shall be had to the Civil Code or other laws, but neither the Civil Code nor any other law shall be invoked to defeat a disposition sanctioned expressly or impliedly by this Code.

In Part II, Creation of the Trust, the initial section contains a definition of a trust unique to Louisiana: "A trust ... is the relationship resulting from the transfer of title to property to a person [the trustee] to be administered by him as a fiduciary for the benefit of another." In thus defining a trust, Louisiana stands apart from common law jurisdictions. With title to trust property vested in the trustee alone, only the trustee has a civilian "real right" in trust property. Conversely, the beneficiary has no title to or ownership interest in trust property, but only a civilian "personal right," vis-a-vis the trustee, to claim whatever interest in the trust relationship the Settlor has chosen to bestow. This personal right, as confected by the Settlor, is further tempered by mandatory provisions of law. Among those provisions most central to the instant appeal are the rules governing the *legitime* in trust and those governing the beneficiary's right to alienate his interest in the trusts. Of particular note is the section listing the only three exceptions to the power of a settlor to restrict involuntary alienation of the beneficiary's interest.

Section 1736 of the Trust Code states that "[a] trust or a disposition in trust may be made subject to any condition not forbidden in this Code and not against public order or good morals." Emphasizing and supplementing this authorization for a settlor to make conditional dispositions, section 1737 notes that "[a] settlor may dispose of property in trust to the same extent that he may dispose of that property free of trust and to any other extent authorized by this Code." Continuing, section 1753 augments the liberal construction mandate of section 1724 by acknowledging that no particular magic words are necessary to create a trust and that "[a] trust instrument shall be given an interpretation that will sustain the effectiveness of its provisions if the trust instrument is susceptible of such an interpretation."

Section 1781's definition of the trustee as the "person to whom title to the trust property is transferred to be administered by him as a fiduciary" confirms that title to all trust property is vested in the trustee alone. Juxtaposed to this definition of the trustee is section 1801's definition of the beneficiary as "a person for whose benefit the trust is created." Notably, no mention of title or ownership of trust assets, either legal or beneficial, appears in the definition of the beneficiary.

Section 1805 provides that "[t]here may be one beneficiary or two or more beneficiaries as to income or principal or both. There may be separate beneficiaries of income and principal, or the same person may be a beneficiary of both income and principal, or the same person may be a beneficiary of both income and principal, in whole or in part." The two succeeding sections--1806 and 1807--amplify those possibilities by specifying that there may be several concurrent beneficiaries of income or principal or both, and that several beneficiaries may be designated to enjoy income successively. Part II, Subpart I contains the rules governing the *legitime* in trust and specifies those provisions that such a trust may contain to qualify.

*   *   *

Central to the disposition of this appeal is an understanding of the nature and extent of Stephen's interest in the trust, for that is what Patricia and the government seek to alienate involuntarily, and obviously that is the most that either can cause to be alienated. Part III of the Trust Code addresses the interest of the beneficiary. As Stephen is both an income and principal beneficiary, we must perforce examine the Trust Code's treatment of each of these interests.

In Subpart A of Part III, section 1961 speaks to the nature of the interest of an income beneficiary. The first paragraph acknowledges that an income interest in trust may be absolute or conditional and may be for the life of a beneficiary or for a lesser term, certain or uncertain. The second paragraph acknowledges the authority of the settlor to allocate a portion of trust income to an income beneficiary. Section 1964 specifies that an interest in trust income terminates at the death of the income beneficiary unless the trust instrument calls for an earlier termination. In Subpart B of Part III, addressing the interest of the principal beneficiary, section 1972 provides that such a beneficiary's interest vests in his heirs or legatees at his death.

c. Alienation of the interest of the beneficiary

Subpart D of Part III is composed of seven sections and addresses another matter central to the instant appeal: alienation of the beneficiary's interest. In keeping with the structural recognition that a Louisiana trust is a relationship, and that the trustee, and not the beneficiary, is the sole owner of trust property, section 2001 speaks to alienation of the beneficiary's interest in the trust, not alienation of trust property. It states the general rule of voluntary alienation: the beneficiary may "transfer or encumber" all or part of his interest in the trust "unless the trust instrument provides to the contrary." Section 2002 follows with the express identification of that which is implicit in the "unless" clause of section 2001, i.e., a stipulation "to the contrary." Section 2002 authorizes a settlor to prohibit both voluntary and involuntary alienation of the beneficiary's interest in the trust. Under this section, the settlor is free to impose restraints on voluntary alienation, but his ability to restrict involuntary alienation is subject to limitations as specified in the remaining sections of Subpart D. Section 2004 limits the settlor's authority to prohibit involuntary alienation, that is, seizure of the beneficiary's interest by his creditors, to those instances in which the settlor also prohibits voluntary alienation.

Subpart D clearly reflects the overall public policy of the Trust Code favoring freedom of disposition by the settlor. Together, the seven sections of Subpart D give the settlor the option either to remain silent and thereby allow unfettered alienation by the beneficiary, thus exposing the interest of the beneficiary to transfer, encumbrance, or seizure; or specify that the beneficiary's interest shall not be transferred or encumbered or seized by creditors, that is, neither voluntarily nor involuntarily alienated. To proscribe all alienation the settlor may either spell out such restraints in the trust instrument or employ the shorthand method authorized in section 2007 and simply declare that the interest of the beneficiary shall be held subject to a "spendthrift trust." For purposes of the Trust Code, either method is sufficient to restrain alienation to the maximum extent permitted by Subpart D.

As made manifestly clear by section 2005, however, maximum extent is not synonymous with unlimited. This section provides, in pertinent part:

> Notwithstanding any stipulation in the trust instrument to the contrary, the proper court, in summary proceedings to which the trustee, the beneficiary, and the beneficiary's creditor shall be parties, may permit seizure of a portion of the beneficiary's interest in trust income and principal in its discretion and as may be just under the circumstances if the claim is based upon a judgment for: (1) alimony, or maintenance of a person whom the beneficiary is obligated to support.

*   *   *

Within the structure of the Trust Code, section 2005 specifies three exceptions to the settlor's broad freedom to innoculate the interest of the beneficiary against both voluntary and involuntary alienation. Section 2005 must be narrowly construed. Thus, in parsing its language to determine what appropriately may be seized by, inter alia, an alimony judgment creditor--notwithstanding any "contrary" "stipulation in the trust instrument"--two determinations are key: (1) just what is it that may be seized and (2) just what is it that the stipulation in the trust instrument is contrary to?

The answer to the first inquiry is clear from the plain and unambiguous wording of section 2005: that which may be seized is "the beneficiary's interest in trust income and principal." The court may not permit direct seizure of trust property, of which, as noted, the trustee is the sole owner. The only thing the court may authorize one of the specially favored creditors to seize is the beneficiary's personal right--his interest in the trust relationship. When that is done, the creditor steps into the shoes of the beneficiary--whatever size and shape they may be, as dictated by the trust instrument.

The answer to the second question (what is it that the "stipulation in the trust instrument" is contrary to?) can be nothing other than "a restraint upon involuntary alienation by a beneficiary," i.e., a section 2002 stipulation prohibiting involuntary alienation--seizure--of "the beneficiary's interest in trust income and principal." Clearly then, the court is not authorized by section 2005 to disregard any other provision or stipulation, whether in the trust instrument or in law, to permit seizure of the interest of the beneficiary.

*   *   *

With this construction of Subpart D on antialienation firmly in mind, we now address PART V. DUTIES AND POWERS OF THE TRUSTEE. In keeping with section 1724's fundamental policy favoring freedom of disposition, section 2061 prescribes:

> The nature and extent of the duties and powers of a trustee are determined from the provisions of the trust instrument, except as otherwise expressly provided in this Code [mandatory provisions], and, in the absence of any provisions of the trust instrument, by the provisions of this Part and by law.

[suppletive provisions].

As with the interest of the beneficiary, and the rights and limitations on the beneficiary's use and enjoyment of his interest in the trust, the powers and duties of the trustee are determined by the settlor. With the sole exception of a provision that would dispense with the duty of loyalty to the beneficiary, the latitude of the settlor in vesting the trustee with powers and duties is virtually boundless. Indeed, to deviate from duties imposed by the settlor, the trustee must obtain consent from the beneficiary, which cannot be prospective and cannot limit the duty of loyalty. To deviate from administrative and investment provisions of the trust instrument or from the administrative provisions of the Trust Code, the trustee must obtain judicial authority.

In contrast to the Trust Code's admittedly scant provision controlling deviation from the duties of the trustee, it contains no parallel provisions regarding powers. Lawful powers given to the trustee by the settlor are immutable; indeed, not even a court can control the trustee's exercise of discretionary powers or force their exercise.

*   *   *

Pertinent to this appeal are the two sections of Subpart A of Part V of the Trust Code that address invasion of principal. The first of these, section 2067, contains the limited list of occasions when the court may direct or permit a trustee to pay income or principal from the trust property. This list allows for court directed invasion of principal for the necessary support, maintenance, education, medical expenses, or the welfare of a beneficiary before the time he is entitled to such distributions. We must note two important observations. First, the finite list warranting invasion of principal is limited to those instances involving the objective needs of the beneficiary only, not the needs of any creditors, even a former spouse or other dependent, and then only if such invasion will not impair the interest of any other beneficiary. A comparison of section 2067 and section 2005 reveals that, whereas the court may authorize seizure of the beneficiary's interest by an alimony judgment creditor, the court is not authorized to direct the trustee to invade principal and distribute trust property to such a judgment creditor unless the beneficiary himself would be entitled to enjoy such trust property. It appears indisputable that the authority of the court to disregard restrictions on alienation, and to permit seizure of the interest of the beneficiary by an alimony judgment creditor, does not include the authority to order a trustee to invade and distribute principal to a judgment creditor when, as here, the trust instrument leaves invasion of principal to the unfettered discretion of the trustee. Second, invasion cannot be ordered by the court for any reason, even those on section 2067's permitted list, before such time as the beneficiary would be entitled to demand distribution of trust property--and never if invasion would impair the interest of another beneficiary.

$$* \qquad * \qquad *$$

At the heart of this issue, then, is the critical inquiry whether any court can substitute its discretion for that which a settlor has vested exclusively in the trustee, and thereby force the premature distribution of trust property by distributing same not to the beneficiary but to his seizing creditors. We are persuaded that question must be answered in the negative.

We conclude that the district court abused its discretion when it ordered the Trustees to make distributions, whether of income or principal, "immediately upon being authorized" under the terms of the Trust to do so. This aspect of the judgment must therefore be modified to command the making of distributions directly to Patricia--and subsequently to the government-- only at times when, under the terms of the Trust, Stephen becomes "entitled to the enjoyment of that income or principal, if the interest of no other beneficiary of the trust is impaired thereby."

$$* \qquad * \qquad *$$

Revocable Trusts

The Trust Code permits the settlor to create a trust, reserving the right to revoke or modify it. (La. R.S. § 9:2041) When a revocable trust is created, the beneficiaries need not be named upon the trust's creation, but may be determined later by a method provided in the trust, at a time no later than the time the trust become irrevocable.(La. R.S. § 9:2011)

Class Trusts

La. R.S. §§ 9:1891-1906 regulate class trusts. Class trusts are created to benefit members of a class defined by the settlor. Amendments to the Trust Code in 1997 permitted the settlor to include within a class any descendants of the settlor in the direct line and any descendants in the collateral line. This amendment expanded the potential members to such an extent that a trust could virtually go on forever. Criticisms of that extension have prompted the introduction of legislation, recommended by the Louisiana State Law Institute, to limit the class to "children, grandchildren, great grandchildren, nieces, nephews, grandnieces, grandnephews, and great grandnieces and great grandnephews, or any combination thereof." Act No. 594, § 3 of 2001. Another significant amendment was passed by Act 219 of 2015, effective August 1, 2015, allowing the class to consist of "some or all of the children, grandchildren, great grandchildren, nieces, nephews, grandnieces grandnephews, and great grandnieces and great grandnephews of the settlor **or of the settlor's current, former, or predeceased spouse** or any combination thereof, provided at least one member of the class is then in being."

The class trust is unique because only one member of the class need be in being at the time the class trust is created. La. R.S. § 9:1981. The number of beneficiaries may fluctuate until the class closes. By employing a class trust, a settlor may provide for his grandchildren, then living and those yet to be conceived or adopted. Class members must be the sole beneficiaries of an interest in trust. La. R.S. § 9:1893. The settlor cannot create a trust naming as both income and principal beneficiaries his present and future grandchildren, as well as his friend, John. The settlor may name his friend, John, as income beneficiary and his present and future grandchildren as principal beneficiaries. Also, the settlor may give the trustee authority to act as in any other trust, that is to invade principal for the benefit of income beneficiaries as provided in La. R.S. § 9:2608 or to determine when and how often income is to be distributed, except as to the *legitime*. La. R.S. §§ 9:1893 and 9:1899.

La. R.S. §9:1894 provides that if a person dies before the creation of trust in which he would have been a member of a class if he had not died, his descendants shall be considered members of the class by representation, unless the trust instrument provides otherwise .The provision was amended by Act 219 of 2015, effective August 1, 2015 to provide that in such cases of representation, the division is made by roots. If a class member dies during the term of the trust or at its termination, the trust instrument may provide that the deceased member's share vest in the other members of the trust should the deceased die without descendants. La. R.S. § 9:1895. If the deceased beneficiary is a forced heir and his *legitime* is in trust, he must die without descendants *and* intestate for this provision to apply. La. R.S. § 9:1895.

A class closes at a time stated in the trust instrument or, if nothing is stipulated, when "because of the definition of the class, members may no longer be added." La. R.S. § 9:1896.

Charitable Trusts

In addition to the Louisiana Trust Code which essentially governs trusts for the benefit of private persons and entities, the ancillaries to the Civil Code also provide for the regulation of trust created for the benefit of charitable institutions. La. R.S. §§ 9:2271-2291. Several important differences exist between private and charitable trusts. First, a charitable trust may exist forever as long as there is a competent person or institution to administer it, although a settlor may provide for a shorter term. La. R.S. § 9:2291. Second, under the *cy pres* doctrine, if, due to a change in circumstances, the terms of the charitable trust cannot be fulfilled because they have become illegal or impractical, the court may modify the trust to accomplish the purposes of the trust "as nearly as practicable under existing conditions." La. R.S. § 9:2331.

Act 219 of 2015, effective August 1, 2015 provides for the creation of a trust for the care of an animal.

Duration, Modification and Termination

Duration

The Trust Code provides that, if at least one settlor and one income beneficiary are natural persons, then the trust must terminate on the death of the last income beneficiary or twenty years from the death of the settlor, whichever occurs last. La. R.S. § 9:1831(1). Additional provisions govern those instances where either the settlor or the income beneficiaries are not natural persons. La. R.S. § 9: 1831(2)-(4). Of course, as mentioned above, special duration rules apply to class trusts.

Modification and Termination

Under limited circumstances, the court may order the modification or termination of a trust at a time not otherwise provided for in the trust instrument. La. R.S. § 9:2026. A modification or termination of a trust may be allowed where the failure to terminate or modify would impair the purposes of the trust or where, because the trust has so few assets (under $100,000), the administration costs would defeat the purposes of the trust. La. R.S. § 9:2026.

ALBRITTON v. ALBRITTON
600 So. 2d 1328 (La. 1992), *reh den.* 1992
(38 Loy.L.Rev. 1159 (1993))
[footnotes omitted]

MARCUS, Justice.

Plaintiff, Alvin H. Albritton, is the son of Dr. A. Stirling Albritton and the grandson of Alvin R. Albritton, and was born on January 23, 1952. On December 3, 1957, plaintiff's grandfather died, leaving a will that bequeathed to plaintiff an undivided one-fourth interest in the naked ownership of his residuary estate. This interest was subject to a life usufruct in favor of his father and was further subject to an irrevocable testamentary spendthrift trust, with plaintiff's father and uncle (William Louis Albritton) acting as trustees. The trust was set to terminate in two stages: one-half of the trust would terminate on plaintiff's twenty-first birthday (January 23, 1973); the other half would terminate on plaintiff's twenty-sixth birthday (January 23, 1978). On September 21, 1972, approximately four months prior to the termination of the first part of the trust, plaintiff, at the request of his father, signed as settlor and beneficiary a document entitled "Extension of Trust." That document provided in pertinent part:

> 3. Settlor does hereby, and acting as Settlor, extend the term of the Trust described above [the Alvin R. Albritton Testamentary Trust] insofar as Settlor is beneficiary thereunder to provide that the term is for the lifetime of the Settlor.
> 4. If it should be determined that the Trust described above cannot be extended in this manner, then Settlor declares that Settlor's interest in the Trust described above shall be held and is hereby placed irrevocably in trust and shall be managed and invested and reinvested and held with and distributed in exactly the same manner as set forth in the Trust described above, but for Settlor's lifetime, by the same Trustees and successors as provided therein, and, in that event, Settlor incorporates the trust agreement described above into this act by reference as a new trust.

In addition to plaintiff's signature, the document was signed by plaintiff's father and uncle as co-trustees and by a notary and two witnesses. On January 29, 1973, the trial judge signed an ex parte order upon petition of the trustees, which purported to validate the extension.

On January 12, 1988, sixteen years after the 1972 document was executed, plaintiff filed suit against the trustees, seeking a declaration that the agreement executed by him on September 21, 1972 was of no force and effect, or alternatively, that any trust created in connection therewith be terminated and annulled. The essence of plaintiff's petition was that he was misled by the trustees and that he signed the agreement in error, believing it applied only to a part of the trust property known as Stoney Point. Subsequently, the trustees filed a peremptory exception of prescription. After a hearing, the trial judge sustained the exception of prescription and dismissed plaintiff's claims. In his oral reasons, the trial judge stated that even if the extension of trust agreement violated the trust code, such a violation only gave rise to a relative nullity, which prescribed in five years. He reasoned that plaintiff had five years to bring suit after learning he signed the agreement in error. The trial judge found plaintiff learned at least by 1980, if not sooner, that more property than Stoney Point was involved in the agreement; therefore, his 1988 suit was outside of the five year prescriptive period. Plaintiff appealed. The court of appeal affirmed. Upon plaintiff's application, we granted certiorari to consider the correctness of that decision.

The sole issue before us is whether plaintiff's right to raise the nullity of the 1972 extension of trust agreement has prescribed.

*   *   *

The trial judge assumed that any modification of the existing trust would be null, since it would violate the provisions of the trust code. Nonetheless, he went on to find that if plaintiff entered into such an agreement in error, the agreement would be a relative, rather than absolute, nullity, reasoning that the trust code set forth rules intended for the protection of private parties and did not set forth rules of public order. We disagree.

We believe there is a strong public policy in effectuating and protecting the settlor's intent as set forth in the trust document. In *Richards v. Richards*, 408 So.2d 1209 (La.1981), we stated:

> In construing a trust, the settlor's intention controls and is to be ascertained and given effect, unless opposed to law or public policy.

The trial judge mistakenly focused on plaintiff's intent in entering into the agreement, rather than on the settlor's intent. In doing so, he implicitly held that in the absence of any vices of consent, plaintiff could enter into an agreement affecting the trust, even if the agreement was contrary to the settlor's intent. This cannot be so. The trust would hardly be a stable device for the transmission of property if the beneficiaries and trustees could make agreements that could modify the settlor's fundamental intent in setting up the trust. We believe such modifications are contrary to the rules expressed in the trust code in La.R.S. 9:2021 and 9:2025:

§ 2021. General rule; modification
The settlor may modify the terms of the trust after its creation *only to the extent he expressly reserves the right to do so*. (emphasis added).

§ 2025. Delegation of right to terminate or to modify administrative provisions
A settlor may delegate to another person the right to terminate a trust, or to modify the administrative provisions of a trust, *but the right to modify other provisions of a trust may not be delegated*. (emphasis added).

Thus, under the scheme of the trust code, even the settlor has no power to modify the trust he has created unless he expressly reserves the power to do so. More importantly for our purposes, the trust code prohibits the delegation of the power to modify provisions of the trust other than the administrative provisions. Oppenheim & Ingram, 11 LOUISIANA CIVIL LAW TREATISE--TRUSTS § 294 (1977). Likewise, La.R.S. 9:2028 sets forth a concept of trust indestructibility:

> The consent of all settlors, trustees and beneficiaries shall not be effective to terminate the trust or any disposition in trust, unless the trust instrument provides otherwise.

We have held this concept of trust indestructibility is "inherent in our Louisiana trust law." *Richards,* 408 So.2d at 1210. Taken as a whole, we believe these rules set forth a public policy of protecting the trust instrument from any modification or termination contrary to the settlor's clearly expressed intent. These are imperative rules of public order, and any violation of these rules is an absolute nullity. *See Badon's Employment, Inc. v. Smith*, 359 So.2d 1284 (La.1978); *E.L. Burns Co. v. Cashio*, 302 So.2d 297 (La.1974).

Turning to the facts of the present case, we find the settlor's intent was that the trust should terminate as to plaintiff upon his twenty-first and twenty-sixth birthdays. The extension of trust purports to extend the trust for plaintiff's lifetime. Clearly, this extension is contrary to the settlor's intent and acts to modify the trust. Accordingly, the extension of trust agreement is an absolute nullity, which is imprescriptible, and we find the trial judge erred in sustaining the exception of prescription.

Nonetheless, a finding that the extension of trust is an absolute nullity will not end the case. In the event that the extension is invalid, the agreement alternatively purports to create a new trust with plaintiff as settlor. The trustees in brief to this court have argued that the agreement created a valid irrevocable inter vivos trust, which was funded when plaintiff obtained the right to the distribution of the corpus of his grandfather's trust in 1973 and in 1978. By contrast, plaintiff argues that at the time the alleged new trust agreement was executed in 1972, he had not yet reached the age of twenty-one and therefore had no property to place in trust. He further argues there is no evidence that he ever placed property in the alleged new trust.

We believe that the alleged new trust, like the extension of trust, must be considered an absolute nullity. The clear language of the agreement leads to the inescapable conclusion that it attempted to create a new trust on the date it was executed (September 21, 1972), which was during the existence of the prior trust: "Settlor declares that Settlor's interest in the Trust described above *shall be held* and *is hereby placed* irrevocably in trust...." (emphasis added). Since we have found the settlor of the prior trust did not intend for that trust to be extended beyond the termination dates expressed in the trust, it follows that the settlor would not have intended for the same result to be achieved by a different means. Whether the agreement attempts to extend the existing trust, or whether it attempts to create a new trust prior to the termination of the existing trust, the effect is the same: the settlor's intent that the trust be terminated at age twenty-one and age twenty-six is frustrated. Further, the settlor also intended that this trust be a spendthrift trust. La.R.S. 9:2007 provides:

A declaration in a trust instrument that the interest of a beneficiary shall be held subject to a "spendthrift trust" is sufficient to restrain alienation by a beneficiary of the interest to the maximum extent permitted by this Subpart.

Restraining alienation means the beneficiary cannot transfer, assign or encumber his interest in the trust. Comment, *Spendthrift Trusts In Louisiana*, 33 La.L.Rev. 391 (1973). We believe that by attempting to create a new trust during the existence of the prior trust, the beneficiary was attempting to alienate his interest in violation of the concept of the spendthrift trust and in violation of the settlor's intent that the interest in trust not be alienated while in trust. Therefore, under the facts of this case, we find the attempt to create the new trust is an absolute nullity.

In sum, we find the trial judge erred in sustaining the exception of prescription. We hold that the agreement which purports to extend the existing trust or alternatively create a new trust is an absolute nullity and is imprescriptible. We remand the case to the trial court to grant the relief to which plaintiff is entitled.

DECREE

For the reasons assigned, the judgment of the court of appeal is reversed. The exception of prescription is overruled. The case is remanded to the district court for further proceedings. All costs are assessed to defendants.

DENNIS, J., concurs with reasons.

DENNIS, Justice, concurring.

I respectfully concur.

I disagree, however, with the majority's view that La.R.S. 9:2028 is a "law [ ] enacted for the protection of the public interest [or that] [a]ny act in derogation of [La.R.S. 9:2028] is an absolute nullity." La.C.C. art. 7 (1988). As eminent scholars have observed, La.R.S. 9:2028 was probably enacted to protect the interests of trust companies and not the public.

La.R.S. 9:2028 provides that a trust is not terminable at the will of all the parties at interest--settlors, beneficiaries, and trustees--unless the trust instrument reserved a power of revocation. This stringent provision against terminability is contrary to the laws of most other states, which permit the settlor and all the beneficiaries to terminate the trust, even in the face of active opposition by the trustee, proceeding on the theory that a trustee has no such interest in the trust as to entitle him to oppose termination. It has been strongly urged that, as a general rule, a trust should be terminable by the will of all the beneficiaries. If prohibiting termination by the beneficiaries is undesirable, then by definition a provision prohibiting termination by all the parties at interest is entitled to strenuous criticism. D. Robertson, *Some Interesting Features of the Proposed Trust Code,* 24 La.L.Rev. 712 (1964).

As stated by Professor Nabors:

> Where alienability, voluntary and involuntary, exists, as for the non-spendthrift trust in Louisiana, a restraint on the beneficiary's right to terminate the trust will make the beneficiary who does dispose of his interest sell at a discount, and,

therefore, the rule is of questionable validity. *The motivating force back of the rule ... against termination probably was the desire of trust companies to have a rule which would tend to continue the trust in their hands.*

Nabors, *The Shortcomings of the Louisiana Trust Act and Some Problems of Drafting Trust Instruments Thereunder*, 13 Tul.L.Rev. 179, 199 (1939) (Emphasis added).

Professor Pascal observed:

Such rules, the writer submits, are abusive because they violate the dignity of the human person. Men have reason and free will. It is proper to the nature of the human person, therefore, that he should be allowed to decide for himself how he should live, and this living includes the use of wealth properly appropriated by or transferred to him for his use and benefit.

Pascal, *Of Trusts, Human Dignity, Legal Science, and Taxes*, 23 La.L.Rev. 639, 645 (1963) (Footnote omitted).

Consequently, I cannot agree that La.R.S. 9:2028 was enacted to preserve good morals or to protect the public interest. Therefore, I do not believe that a juridical act in derogation of that law should be declared absolutely null.

Nevertheless, I concur in the conclusion that the juridical act is absolutely null because it derogated from other laws that were enacted for the protection of the public interest. In fact, the act sought to accomplish an end far less innocuous than to terminate a non-spendthrift trust by the will of all interested persons for the immediate advantage of the beneficiary. Indeed, because the trust which the trustee sought to either extend or to convert into a new trust to the disadvantage of the beneficiary was a spendthrift trust, the juridical act was in derogation of laws providing that the interest of a beneficiary of such a trust shall not be subject to voluntary alienation by a beneficiary. La.R.S. 9:2002, 9:2007. By inducing the beneficiary to alienate his interest so as to put it beyond his reach for the rest of his life, the trustee entered a juridical act also in derogation of laws imposing a duty upon the trustee to uphold the provisions of the trust unless permitted to deviate therefrom by court order. La.R.S. 9:2061, et seq.

"Spendthrift trust" is the term commonly applied to those trusts that are created with a view to providing a fund for the maintenance of another, and at the same time securing it against his own improvidence or incapacity for self- protection. G. Bogert, *Trusts* § 40, at 149 (6th ed. 1987). Although there has been much debate as to whether spendthrift clauses should be enforceable, *Id.*, at 150, when the legislature has sanctioned them because it deems them necessary to the protection of inexperienced and incompetent persons, an act by which a trustee violates his legal duty to uphold the trust provisions and causes a beneficiary to alienate his interest contrary to the trust and the trust code plainly derogates from laws enacted for the protection of the public interest.

NOTE

In *In re Guidry*, 713 So.2d 631 (La. App. 3rd Cir. 1998), a settlor had placed in an irrevocable trust, settlement funds which she received for the wrongful death of her husband, and named herself as sole beneficiary. She named her attorney as trustee, with a provision in the trust for termination when the trustee in his "sole discretion" deemed it in the best interest of the beneficiary, considering the beneficiary's ability to handle the money wisely. The settlor-beneficiary wished to terminate the trust before the trustee deemed it appropriate. The court denied the request for termination.

HYPOTHETICAL

Mark died leaving two daughters, Julia who was twenty-four and Allyson who was seventeen at the time of Mark's death. He had been an attorney and left behind the fairly thorough olographic will parts of which were as follows:

> I leave one-half of my estate in trust subject to the spendthrift provisions of the Louisiana Trust Code for the benefit of my darling daughters, Julia and Allyson. My daughters shall be income and principal beneficiaries. I name as trustee, my wife, Jacquelyn.
> The trustee shall distribute the income to my daughters for life in the amounts and at the times she deems necessary so as to provide for their education, health, maintenance and support. Any income not apportioned to them in a given year shall be allocated to principal.
> On the death of either daughter without descendants, her share of the trust corpus shall be allocated to her sister.
> I hereby relieve the trustee of all liability to the beneficiary and of any duty to furnish security.

1. May Julia or Allyson complain about the provisions regarding the distribution of income? What about the provision regarding principal?

2. If three years after the formation of the trust, Allyson believes that her mother has sold a house owned by the trust to the mother's new boyfriend for less than its fair market value, will her mother be shielded from liability by the provision in the trust relieving her of liability?

3. Julia believes that her mother sold trust stock in a closely held corporation for less than its fair market value. Julia does not believe the mistake was intentional; however, she does believe that her mother was careless in not hiring someone to appraise the value of the stock. Will her mother be shielded from liability in this instance?

4. Julia wants to buy a new car and attempts to sell her interest in the trust to Tony. Will she be permitted to do so?

APPENDIX A

SUCCESSIONS
HYPOTHETICALS

How should the property of the decedent be divided in each of the following situations:

1. A dies survived by his daughter, D; his wife, W; his parent's, M and F; and his sister, S. A has both separate and community property.

2. A dies survived by his father, F; his mother, M; his siblings B & C; and by E, the child of his predeceased brother D.

3. Same as "2," except M and F have predeceased A, and A is survived by MGM, his maternal grandmother; Q, his paternal aunt; and X, his cousin, a child of a predeceased uncle, U, on his mother's side.

4. A marries B, and they have three children C, D, and E. C, although now deceased, had a child of his own, O. Before marrying A, B had been married to Z, and B and Z had two children, U and V. B and Z's marriage ended in divorce. B is now deceased, and A has remarried T. A and T adopted one son, Q. D dies. Distribute D's property and indicate in what way each heir takes.

5. Same facts as "4," except D does not die. Instead, A dies.

6. X dies survived by her maternal grandmother, MGM; her maternal grandfather's mother, MGGM; both grandparents on her father's side, PGM and PGF; and by his mother's sister, A.

7. A dies survived by his wife, W; his nephew, X, son of his predeceased brother, B; by his mother, M; and by his paternal grandmother, PGM. A has both separate and community property.

8. Same facts as "7," except M and X also predecease A.

9. A dies survived by his paternal grandmother, PGM; his maternal grandfather, MGF; and his half-brother, H, the product of the marriage between his mother and her first husband, X.

10. X dies survived by his paternal great aunt, PGA; and C, his cousin, the son of his mother's brother.

11. Same facts as "10," except X is also survived by A, his father's sister.

12. X is survived by his father, F; his mother, M; his siblings B & S; and by O & P, the children of his predeceased brother T. Who inherits and in what proportions?

13. X dies survived by his sister, S; his mother, M; and her new husband, H2 (X's stepfather); and N, the child of his predeceased half-brother, B, a product of the marriage between M and H2.

14. Same facts as "2," except H2 dies rather than X.

15. X dies survived by his uncle, U; and his cousin, C, the son of a predeceased aunt, A.

16. Same facts as "4," except U predeceases X. X is also survived GM, his grandmother; by PGGM, his great grandmother, the mother of his predeceased grandfather, GF.

17. X has three children, A, B, C. X dies. A predeceases X, but has a son, Q. B also predeceases x, but has two children, Y and Z. Finally, C too predeceased X, but has three children, M, N, and O. Who inherits, in what proportions, how, and why?

APPENDIX B

Experiential Module 1: Client Interview

Course: Donations & Trusts

Contents:　　This "Experience 1" contains the following:

1. Phone message in file
2. Quick Notes: "How to Prepare for a Client Interview"
3. Quick Notes: "How to Conduct a Client Interview"
4. Effective note taking during the client interview examples

Your Task

During Experience 1, our class time will be dedicated to meeting a client, Mr. Giovanni A. Tempesta, a retired successful businessman.[1] He has come to your office seeking legal advice on estate planning. During the interview it is up to you to gather enough facts to adequately prepare a draft of estate planning documents to satisfy his wishes. To do so, you may need to research the law before conducting the interview. This exercise is dedicated to learning the skill of gathering information through the interview process. Local attorneys will play the client and show you how to conduct an effective interview.

Your task is to bring a list of questions relevant to an interview on estate planning. Please bring two copies of the questions, one to turn in and another to use for your own purposes during class. Although this may sound like an easy task, we encourage you to prepare for the interview by researching practice guides and the law to understand the importance of relevant questions. Remember, the facts gathered during the interview are necessary to draft the legal documents for Experience 2.

During the interview, you should take notes from which you will draft the client's Last Will and Testament, Power of Attorney, and Living Will, based on his wishes.

This packet is designed to help you understand how to prepare and conduct an initial client interview.

Assignment:

Bring a typed list of questions with your name in the upper right hand corner. Make sure to bring two copies: one to turn in to the professor who will assess the questions and a second to use during class.

Skill competencies developed during this experiential module include:

- Effectively prepare for the interview by arranging topical discussions with specifically designed questions
- Professional preparation using template note taking method and strategic questioning
- Build upon knowledge of professional rules of conduct in the context of

---

[1] This exercise is a simulation of a client interview. We will not have a real client in class due to ethics rules; however, we will try to achieve a real life experience to help you prepare for practice.

establishing an attorney client relationship
- Identify ethical considerations regarding attorney client relationship
- Research legal issues preconceived as relevant to client's factual issue
- Research legal issues after the facts developed from interview
- Observe the building of a client relationship through opening remarks
- Observe how attorneys explain procedures of the interview to client thereby showing authority over the subject and control in the procedure
- Observe how attorneys organize factual questioning arranged by topic
- Observe how attorneys elicit facts necessary to determine legal issues
- Accurately identify legal problems/issues of client
- Recognize difference between legal and non-legal issues
- Recognize need for further information in determining legal issues
- Develop sufficient questions to understand facts and identify all appropriate legal theories
- Identify factual inconsistencies in order to discard inappropriate theories
- Anticipate legal and factual arguments from adversaries and others
- Develop sufficient facts to establish emotionally sensitive theories
- Observe how attorneys treat client with respect and build trust
- Listen to concerns /issues voiced by client
- Observe how attorneys respond in an empathetic manner to client
- Observe how attorneys foster confidence by client in representation
- Observe how attorneys advise client on next course of action specifically significant dates and procedures
- Observe how attorneys educate client to better protect their own interest
- Observe how attorneys confidently ended the interview in a manner effective in building the client relationship

Evaluation
This assignment is evaluated and is calculated into your final grade. Students should put forth a good faith effort in preparing questions for the interview. The questions will assist in a better work product submitted in Experience 2.

Collaboration Rules
For Experiential Module 1, you are encouraged to collaborate with classmates prior to the interview to effectively prepare similar to that in real practice.

The following phone message is in the file:

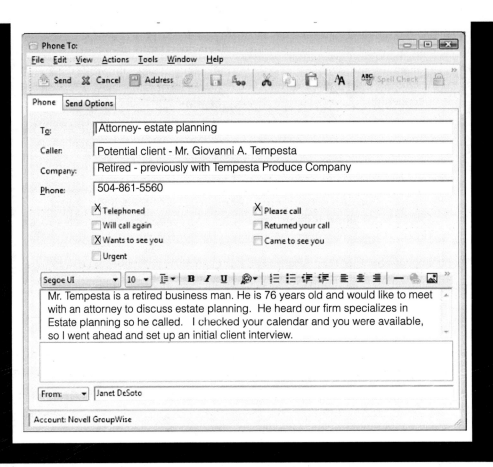

Phone To:

File   Edit   View   Actions   Tools   Window   Help

Send   Cancel   Address | | | | | AA   ABC Spell Check

Phone | Send Options

To: Attorney- estate planning

Caller: Potential client - Mr. Giovanni A. Tempesta

Company: Retired - previously with Tempesta Produce Company

Phone: 504-861-5560

X Telephoned   X Please call
☐ Will call again   ☐ Returned your call
X Wants to see you   ☐ Came to see you
☐ Urgent

Segoe UI   10 | B I U | | | | | | | | | | | — |

Mr. Tempesta is a retired business man. He is 76 years old and would like to meet with an attorney to discuss estate planning. He heard our firm specializes in Estate planning so he called.   I checked your calendar and you were available, so I went ahead and set up an initial client interview.

From: ▼   Janet DeSoto

Account: Novell GroupWise

Quick Notes: "How To Prepare for the Client Interview"

- <u>Attorney-client relationship rules</u>: Remember, the initial client interview is one of the most critical meetings especially if you are first establishing the attorney-client relationship. This first meeting is the foundation for the relationship and first impressions may be long lasting. Is the attorney-client relationship established? If not, review the professional rules of responsibility to ensure your interview is structured accordingly.

- <u>Documents</u>: Do you need the client to bring documents? If so, make sure you are familiar with the format of the documents. Do you need to bring blank documents for client's signature, such as medical or employment record release or legal service agreement?

- <u>Consult Practice Guides</u>: For example, See Louisiana Civil Practice Forms (West) (on reserve and at the reference desk).

- <u>Prepare Questions</u>: Make sure you review any files you have on the case including notes from paralegal or secretary. What do you know about the client? What do you know about the case? Does the client have special needs? Have you thought about possible topics to guide the interview? Have you arranged the questions according to a topic? Have you thought about the best type of question to solicit the information while building the relationship? Has someone else in your office reviewed your questions?

- <u>Prepare Interview Room:</u> Remember, the setting will help foster the type of relationship you want to build with the client. How will the room provide the proper amount of comfort and authority to build the relationship?

Quick Notes: "How To Conduct the Client Interview"

- The Greeting: How will you make the client feel welcomed and comfortable? What type of first impression will you make?

- The Beginning: How will you open the conversation by not immediately discussing the client's legal issue?

- The Substance: How will you allow the questioning to flow arranged by topics? Who will take notes without impeding on the ability to build a relationship with the client?

  - The legal theory: Have you researched areas of law involving client's factual issue to ensure your questions align with the legal theory? Are there other areas of law you need to research? What facts would change the application of the legal theory?

  - The facts: Did you review documents the client brought to the interview? Do you have a clear picture of what happened, who was involved, specifically the names and contact information for witnesses? Are there any inconsistencies in the client's story? Have you mapped out the chronology of events relevant to the legal theory?

- The Conclusion: Have you covered everything? Are all documents signed?

  - The next plan of action: What will you do next in the client's case? When will you contact the client? How will you contact the client? Have you let the client know? Is there any advice or counseling you want to provide? Does the client have your contact information? How will the client know the interview is complete?

Effective Note Taking Examples

Example 1: Questions and Notes

Questions	Notes
Topic: Background	
What is your full name?	

Example 2: Checklist

1. CLIENT BACKGROUND INFORMATION
Full name
Nickname/former name
Current address
Address last ten years
Phone no. (home/work/cell/pda)
Fax
Email
Soc. Sec. no.
DOB
Marital Status
Spouse's name
Children
Current employer
Address
Phone
Employment duties/title
Supervisors
Salary
Other annual earnings/income
Former employment last ten years

> The example is a checklist for a personal injury case, but you can create your own checklist specific to the relevant area of law.

2. INCIDENT INFORMATION
Date
Place
Summary of incident
Known witness
Other parties involved in incident
Third parties who may be responsible
Incident job related (Y/N)
Investigating authority
Investigating officer
Accident report (copy Y/N)

Other physical evidence.

3. PROPERTY DAMAGE ...

End of excerpt – this list could go on for several more pages depending upon what information the attorney deems necessary.

Example 3: Time line (drawn by either client or attorney or both)

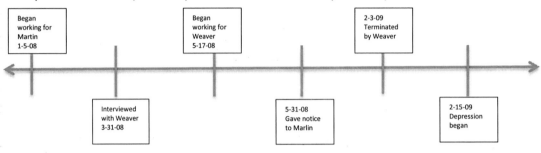

APPENDIX C

Experiential Module 2:
After the client interview:
Drafting the Will, Power of Attorney and Living Will

Course: Donations & Trusts

Contents: This "Experience 2" contains the following:

1. Memo from the Senior Partner
2. Example Will

Your Task
Based on the facts gathered from the client interview, your assignment is to draft the following:
1) Will for Mr. Tempesta
2) Power of Attorney for Mr. Tempesta
3) Living Will for Mr. Tempesta

Essentially, your firm represents Mr. Tempesta who is seeking advice on estate planning. You must ensure all of the above documents meet the needs as expressed in the client interview.

Objectives
- To learn how to draft a Will, Power of Attorney and Living Will.
- To understand how client facts impact the strategy in estate planning
- To identify and address potential issues in the drafting process based on client needs.
- To conduct legal research sufficient to identify possible issues and theories of law.
- To acquire sufficient substantive legal knowledge relevant to estate planning.
- To gain experience in the practical aspects of drafting techniques and thought process of experienced attorneys in the related area of law.

Evaluation
This experience will be evaluated on the form and content of your documents and calculated into your final grade. You will be expected to use the Resource cited in the memo and also relevant Code provisions. On the date the documents are due, you must bring two copies of each; one set will be turned in to the professor and you will use the other to conduct your own edit guided by the practitioners.

Collaboration Rules
Students must work on their own assignment and the work product should solely a student's individual effort. Do not consult with an outside practitioner (i.e. lawyers, judges, family members who are attorneys). A violation of the rules on collaboration equate to a breach in the honor code policy. Please exercise diligence in maintaining strict adherence to the policy.

To: Associate Attorney
From: Senior Partner Chip LoCoco
Re: In re: Tempesta

As you are aware, we recently interviewed Mr. Tempesta, a client seeking advice on estate planning and assistance with necessary documents to protect his long term interest. Based on the interview and certain facts provided by Mr. Tempesta, I think we need to proceed with drafting a Will, Power of Attorney and Living Will for him. I thought I would give you the assignment to first draft and then I will take a look at your work. I know this is your first experience drafting, so I have attached a list of resources I would highly recommend you consult before you begin drafting.

Although there are several examples and templates out there on the internet, I highly recommend you consult the below resources. I'm always amazed at how people will use standard templates found online on such personal and individual interest like estate planning. Remember, we are attorneys who craft our legal documents much like an artist crafts a painting. At all times, remember the client interview and the facts provided by Mr. Tempesta. Try to craft the documents with our client in mind. What are his concerns? What language will you use to help protect his interests? What provisions would help him and his family?

Once you begin your work on these documents, I suspect you might have additional questions for Mr. Tempesta. I will be able to contact Mr. Tempesta, so please let me know and I will relay those questions to him.

Thank you for your help with this matter and good luck!

Resources:
Example Will, attached to this memo

Louisiana Civil Practice Forms (West)

Secretary of State's website:
http://www.sos.la.gov/OurOffice/PublishedDocuments/LivingWillDeclarationForm.pdf

Max Nathan, Jr. & Carole Cukell Neff, Louisiana Estate Planning, Will Drafting, and Estate Administration (Lexis)

LAST WILL AND TESTAMENT

New Orleans, Louisiana
Month, date, year

I, JOHN A. EXAMPLE, being of sound mind, make this my last will and testament, hereby revoking any and all prior wills and codicils that I have or may have made.

ARTICLE 1

1.1   I have been married but once and then to MARY H. EXAMPLE. Of this union, two children were born, namely VINCENT EXAMPLE, born on July 5, 2000, and MARIE EXAMPLE, born on Month, date, year.

1.2   I hereby provide that any gifts that I have made during my lifetime to any of my children or grandchildren shall be extra portions and shall be exempt from collation.

ARTICLE 2

2.1   I leave the lifetime usufruct of my entire estate of which I die possessed to my wife, MARY H. EXAMPLE.

2.2   MARY H. EXAMPLE shall not be required to furnish bond or security as usufructuary and I relieve her from any separate inventory.

2.3   I further specifically provide that MARY H. EXAMPLE shall have the full complete right, power and authority to dispose of non-consumables as that term is defined in the Louisiana Civil Code or other applicable Louisiana law. I further specifically provide that if any property subject to the usufruct, including non-consumables, should be sold or otherwise disposed of during the existence of the usufruct, then the usufruct shall not terminate but shall attach to the proceeds of such sale or other disposition and the reinvestment thereof. This right to dispose does include the authority to donate property subject to the usufruct.

2.4   MARY H. EXAMPLE may sell or exchange property subject to her usufruct without consent or concurrence of the naked owner(s) or of any fiduciary acting on behalf of any naked owner(s). Her usufruct shall continue to apply to all property received in the sale or exchange and to the property acquired by the reinvestment of proceeds. She shall be responsible for all taxes resulting from the sale or exchange of property subject to her usufruct.

2.5   The usufruct shall be eligible for the marital deduction in computing my federal estate taxes, if any, but only to the extent that my Executor elects to treat it as such, in whole or in part.

_____
JOHN A. EXAMPLE, TESTATOR

ARTICLE 3

1.

1.1   Subject to the foregoing usufruct, I leave my entire estate of which I die possessed to my two children, namely VINCENT EXAMPLE and MARIE EXAMPLE, but in Trust as set forth hereafter. Said Trust shall be named the Example Children's Testamentary Trust.

1.2   If any other child or children are born to or adopted by me subsequent to the execution of this Will, then this Will shall not be revoked, but the legacy contained herein to my children shall be to all of my children who survive me, in equal portions, subject to the usufruct to my spouse, if she survives me and the Trust established herein.

1.3   Except with regard to the usufruct to my wife, pursuant to Article 1521 of the Louisiana Civil Code, I specifically provide that if any heir or legatee provided for herein does not survive me for a period of 180 days, then any such heir or legatee shall be considered as having predeceased me.

1.4   The Trust is established pursuant to the provisions of the Louisiana Trust Code, particularly La. Rev. Stat. 9:1721 et seq., as now written or hereafter amended, for the benefit of all my children as both income and principal beneficiaries, and their interests shall be equal.

2.

2.1   I name my wife, MARY H. EXAMPLE, as the first and sole Trustee. If for any reason, she is unwilling or unable to serve or to continue to serve as such, then I name as her successor, JANET LAMBERT, as substitute Trustee. If for any reason, she is unwilling or unable to serve or to continue to serve as such, then I name as her successor, PAMELA MOON, as substitute Trustee. If for any reason, she is unwilling or unable to serve or to continue to serve as such, then I name as her successor, the person designated in writing by PAMELA MOON to act as substitute Trustee.

2.2   In the event of any vacancy in the office of Trustee, the proper court shall appoint a Trustee from federally insured depository institutions organized under the laws of Louisiana, another State, or of the United States, or financial institutions or trust companies authorized to exercise trust or fiduciary powers under the laws of Louisiana or of the United States.

2.3   No Trustee shall be required to post bond or security of any kind as Trustee.

3.

3.1   After the termination of the usufruct in favor of my wife, MARY EXAMPLE, the Trustee may distribute income from the Trust, and if necessary may invade and distribute principal of the Trust for any reasonable need for the benefit of the beneficiary(ies). This power to invade the principal shall be without restriction and the Trustee shall have the sole authority and discretion to determine the reasonableness of the needs of the beneficiary(ies).

_____
JOHN A. EXAMPLE, TESTATOR

4.1   As to each beneficiary, the Trust as to such beneficiary's interest shall terminate when he/she attains the age of twenty-five (25) years, but in no event shall the Trust terminate prior to the termination of the usufruct in favor of my wife, MARY EXAMPLE.

4.2   If any beneficiary should die while the Trust for that beneficiary is in existence, then to the maximum extent permitted under La. Rev. Stat. 9:1973 et seq, as now written or hereafter amended, if such beneficiary dies without descendants (or to the extent that the beneficiary's interest in the trust constitutes that beneficiary's legitime, if such beneficiary dies both intestate and without descendants), that beneficiary's interest shall vest in my surviving children equally, as substitute beneficiaries, or, if any of my other children are then deceased, in their children by representation equally, as substitute beneficiaries, and the Trust as to their interests shall terminate in accordance with the termination provisions set forth in Section 4.1, above.

4.3   If any beneficiary should die survived by descendants while the Trust for that beneficiary is in existence, or if the beneficiary dies testate, to the extent that his interest in the Trust comprises his legitime, in whole or in part, then the Trust as to the deceased beneficiary's interest shall not terminate, but his interest shall vest in his heirs and legatees, as the case may be, and the Trust shall continue for the longest period of time permitted by Louisiana law.

4.4   Notwithstanding any of the provisions in Section 4.1, 4.2, and 4.3, above, the Trustee may terminate this Trust, in whole or in part, and/or for any beneficiary(ies), at any time prior to the stipulated termination date, whenever, in the Trustee's sole discretion, deems it appropriate or desirable to do so; provided, however, that in no event shall the Trust terminate, in whole or in part, prior to the termination of the usufruct in favor of my wife, MARY EXAMPLE.

5.

5.1   The Trustee shall be responsible only for reasonable care, diligence, and business prudence in the administration of the Trust, and is relieved from all liability in connection with the administration of this Trust, except any such liability as may result from the Trustee's bad faith in the administration of the Trust, or from the Trustee's gross negligence or gross misconduct, provided however that nothing contained herein shall relieve the Trustee of his or her duty of loyalty to the beneficiary(ies).

6.

6.1   To the maximum extent permitted by Louisiana law, and particularly the spendthrift provisions of La. Rev. Stat. of 1950, 9:2001, et seq., and any and all future amendments thereto, which are expressly made applicable to this Trust, the beneficiaries are prohibited from alienating or encumbering any interest in the Trust, voluntarily or involuntarily. The restraints in no way, however, prohibit the termination of the Trust, in whole or in part, as provided in Section 4.4, above.

_____
JOHN A. EXAMPLE, TESTATOR

7.1   The Trustee shall have and possess and may exercise all the rights, powers and authorities incident to the office of Trustee or required in and convenient for the discharge of the Trust or impliedly conferred or vested in Trustees under the Louisiana Trust Code or any law of the State of Louisiana hereafter enacted.

7.2   The Trustee shall have, in the investment and reinvestment and administration of the securities and property forming the subject of this Trust, the widest latitude and authority permitted by Louisiana law.

7.3   The compensation of the Trustee, as well as any taxes due by the Trust and any and all expenses incurred in connection with the administration thereof, such as fees for the preparation of income tax returns, legal fees, periodic accountings, investment counseling or any other expenses shall be charged entirely against the income of the Trust to the extent that income is available and any excess charged against the principal. The fees of the Trustee and other professionals shall be commensurate with the custom and practice of this area at the time of the administration of the Trust.

7.4   The Trustee is authorized to select an investment advisor, an attorney, and an accountant for the Trusts created herein.

7.5   The allocation to income and principal in this Trust shall not be governed by Sections 2141-2157 of the Louisiana Trust Code, but shall be in accordance with generally accepted accounting principles.

7.6   The Trustee may receive additional property into the Trust from third persons, provided, however, that any such additions shall be subject to all the terms and conditions of the Trust as provided herein. Unless it is specified in such addition that the same shall be specially allocated, in whole or in part, to the share(s) of one or more beneficiary(ies), then any such additions shall be allocated pro rata among all the beneficiaries' shares.

8.

8.1   With respect to each beneficiary, this instrument shall be deemed to create separate Trusts, but for the purposes of administration and investment, the Trustee may hold, invest and administer as one Trust.

8.2   Whenever the term "Trust" has been used herein, the singular shall mean the plural, and the plural the singular, unless the context clearly requires only the singular or the plural.

ARTICLE 4

In the event my wife, MARY EXAMPLE, predeceases me, or if we die as a result of a common occurrence, or if she does not survive me for a period of 180 days, I leave my entire estate of which I die possessed to my children, VINCENT EXAMPLE and MARIE EXAMPLE, but in Trust, as provided in Article 3, above.

_____
JOHN A. EXAMPLE, TESTATOR

ARTICLE 5

In the event that any of my children predecease me, or if we die as a result of a common occurrence, or if he/she does not survive me for a period of 180 days, and that deceased child leaves a child or children who survive me, then I leave the share of such predeceased child to that child's child or children, equally, but in Trust, subject to the usufruct granted to my wife, MARY EXAMPLE, above, and further subject to the terms and conditions of the Trust provided in Article 3 above, but in no event shall the Trust terminate prior to the termination of the usufruct in favor of my wife, MARY EXAMPLE.

ARTICLE 6

In the event that none of my children survive me, or do not survive me for a period of 180 days, and they leave no descendants who survive me or do not survive me for a period of 180 days, I then leave all of my property of which I die possessed to my wife, MARY EXAMPLE, in full ownership.

ARTICLE 7

In the event that my children do not have descendants at the time of my death, and my wife, MARY EXAMPLE, predeceases me, or if we die as a result of a common occurrence, or if she does not survive me for a period of 180 days and all of my children predecease me, or if we all die as a result of a common occurrence, or if they all do not survive me for a period of 180 days, I then leave my entire estate, that I die possessed of conjointly to PAMELA MOON, TWEEDLE DEE and TWEEDLE DUM, except that if any of them predecease me, then I direct that their share shall go to their direct descendants, if any, per stirpes.

ARTICLE 8

Should my wife, MARY EXAMPLE, predeceases me, or if we die as a result of a common occurrence, and if any of my children are minors, then I name and appoint JANET LAMBERT as Tutor of my children and PAMELA MOON as Undertutor, without the necessity of them furnishing bond or giving separate inventory. Should security be required, then I direct that the security furnished shall be the minimum required by law.

ARTICLE 9

9.1   I name my wife, MARY EXAMPLE as the Executrix of my estate and relieve her of any bond or separate inventory. Should she be unable or unwilling to serve, I then name JANET LAMBERT as substitute executrix and relieve her also of any bond or separate inventory. If for any reason, she is unwilling or unable to serve or to continue to serve as such, then I name as her

_____

JOHN A. EXAMPLE, TESTATOR

successor, PAMELA MOON, as substitute Executrix, and relieve her also of any bond or separate inventory. If for any reason, she is unwilling or unable to serve or to continue to serve as such, then I name as her successor, the person designated in writing by PAMELA MOON to act as substitute Executrix, and relieve him/her also of any bond or separate inventory.

9.2   In accordance with the provisions of Article 3396.2 of the Louisiana Code of Civil Procedure, I hereby provide that my succession representative shall serve as Independent Executrix with all the rights, powers, and authority of an independent succession representative permitted by the law of Louisiana at the time of my death.

9.3   In accordance with the provisions of Article 1572 of the Louisiana Civil Code, I expressly delegate to my Executrix the authority to allocate specific assets to satisfy any legacy.

9.4   My Executrix shall have authority to elect what portion of my gross estate shall qualify for the Unified Credit then in existence at the time of my death as provided in the Internal Revenue Code, Section 2010 and shall further have the authority to elect what portion of my estate shall qualify for the marital deduction as defined by the Internal Revenue Code. My Executrix shall incur no liability as a result of such decision.

IN WITNESS WHEREOF, I have signed this my last will and testament in the presence of the Notary Public and witnesses hereinafter named and undersigned.

_____
JOHN A. EXAMPLE, TESTATOR

In our presence the testator has declared or signified that this instrument is his testament and he has signed it at the end and on each other separate page, there being six (6) pages in all, and in the presence of the testator and each other we have hereunto subscribed our names this __ day of _____, ___.

WITNESSES:

_____

_____

_____
YOUR NAME, La. Bar # 12345
NOTARY PUBLIC

_____
JOHN A. EXAMPLE, TESTATOR

Kathryn Venturatos Lorio is the Leon Sarpy Professor of Law at Loyola University College of Law in New Orleans, where she has served as Associate Dean for Academic Affairs, as well as Interim Dean. She received her B.A. Degree from Newcomb College of Tulane University where she was a member of Phi Beta Kappa. After receiving her J.D. from Loyola Law School where she was the Case note Editor of the Loyola Law Review, she practiced with the law firm of Deutsch, Kerrigan, and Stiles in New Orleans, prior to joining Loyola's law faculty where she has been teaching Successions and Donations for over thirty years. She was named an Academic Fellow of the American College of Trust and Estate Counsel in 1992. She is a member of the American Law Institute since 1994, as well as a member of the Louisiana State Law Institute where she serves as a member of its Council and on the Committees revising Family Law and Successions and Donations. She is author of numerous articles and book chapters, and also the author of the LOUISIANA CIVIL LAW TREATISE ON SUCCESSIONS AND DONATIONS published by West Publishing Company.

Monica Hof Wallace is the Dean Marcel Garsaud, Jr. Professor of Law at Loyola University College of Law in New Orleans. She received her B.S. Degree from Louisiana State University in Baton Rouge where she graduated *cum laude*. After receiving her J.D. *summa cum laude* from Loyola Law School where she was the Chairman of the Moot Court Board, a member of the Loyola Law Review and graduated first in her class, she clerked for the Honorable Jacques L. Wiener, Jr. of the United States Court of Appeals for the Fifth Circuit and then for the Honorable Barry Ted Moskowitz of the United States District Court for the Southern District of California. She then practiced with the law firm of Correro Fishman Haygood Phelps Walmsey and Casteix in New Orleans, prior to joining Loyola's law faculty where she has been teaching Successions, Donations, and Trusts, Persons, and Community Property. She is an active member of the Louisiana State Law Institute, the St. Thomas More Inn of Court, and she was named a Fellow for the IAALS Educating Tomorrow's Lawyers. She has written several articles and given numerous presentations on issues of family law, successions, donations, and trusts.